NTA UGC NET/JRF/SET

PAPER - 2

Psychology

Author

Monika Majumdar, Gargi Bansal
Pradyuman Tripathi, Tushar Shukla

ARIHANT PUBLICATION (INDIA) LIMITED

卐 **Administrative & Production Offices**

Regd. Office

'Ramchhaya' 4577/15, Agarwal Road, Darya Ganj, New Delhi -110002
Tele: 011- 47630600, 43518550

卐 **Head Office**

Kalindi, TP Nagar, Meerut (UP) - 250002
Tel: 0121-7156203, 7156204

卐 **Sales & Support Offices**

Agra, Ahmedabad, Bengaluru, Bareilly, Chennai, Delhi, Guwahati, Hyderabad, Jaipur, Jhansi, Kolkata, Lucknow, Nagpur & Pune.

卐 **PRICE** ₹745.00

卐 PO No. : TXT-59-T069946-3-26

Published by Arihant Publications (India) Ltd.

For further information about the books published by Arihant, log on to www.arihantbooks.com or e-mail at info@arihantbooks.com

PREFACE

The National Eligibility Test also known as UGC NET or NTA-UGC-NET, is a test to determine the eligibility for College and University level lectureship and for the award of Junior Research Fellowship (JRF) for Indian Nationals. From December, 2018 onwards, National Testing Agency (NTA) is conducting this exam.

The key idea behind writing this book is to provide such a book that will be a complete package for the aspiring candidates of UGC NET in Psychology. The focus of this book is to provide exhaustive, crisp text resource and an enormous question bank with answers to help aspiring students of UGC NET to reach goal of passing this prestigious exam in the first attempt. The book has been prepared as per the latest syllabus applicable from June, 2019 onwards. The level of difficulty for this exam is kept in mind, while composing the text and questions.

Salient Features of the Book

- Theoretical aspect of the subject has been written in a very simple language.
- Main contents of the chapter are highlighted, so that brush-up can be done quickly before the exam.
- Units are divided in different number of chapters, according to the topic so as to synchronise the entire syllabus and helps student to correlate the topics.
- Question Bank of approx 4000 multiple choice questions are provided, which covers conceptual issues that enables the student to pierce the topic and understand its depth.

We hope and believe that the book will cater to the requirements of the students and wish the readers a happy and enriching experience, while reading this book. However, in order to make the book more useful, suggestions from teaching fraternity and students are always welcome.

Authors

SYLLABUS

1. Emergence of Psychology

Psychological thought in some major Eastern Systems: Bhagavad Gita, Buddhism, Sufism and Integral Yoga. Academic psychology in India: Pre-independence era; Post-independence era; 1970s: The move to addressing social issues; 1980s: Indigenisation; 1990s: Paradigmatic concerns, disciplinary identity crisis; 2000s: Emergence of Indian psychology in academia. Issues: The colonial encounter; Post colonialism and psychology; Lack of distinct disciplinary identity.

Western: Greek heritage, medieval period and modern period. Structuralism, Functionalism, Psychoanalytical, Gestalt, Behaviourism, Humanistic-Existential, Transpersonal, Cognitive revolution, Multiculturalism. Four founding paths of academic psychology - Wundt, Freud, James, Dilthey. Issues: Crisis in psychology due to strict adherence to experimental-analytical paradigm (logical empiricism). Indic influences on modern psychology.

Essential aspects of knowledge paradigms: Ontology, epistemology and methodology. Paradigms of Western Psychology: Positivism, Post-Positivism, Critical perspective, Social Constructionism, Existential Phenomenology and Cooperative Enquiry. Paradigmatic Controversies. Significant Indian paradigms on psychological knowledge: Yoga, Bhagavad Gita, Buddhism, Sufism and Integral Yoga. Science and spirituality (avidya and vidya). The primacy of self-knowledge in Indian psychology.

2. Research Methodology and Statistics

Research: Meaning, Purpose and Dimensions. Research problems, Variables and Operational Definitions, Hypothesis, Sampling. Ethics in conducting and reporting research.

Paradigms of research: Quantitative, Qualitative, Mixed methods approach. Methods of research: Observation, Survey [Interview, Questionnaires], Experimental, Quasi-experimental, Field studies, Cross-Cultural Studies, Phenomenology, Grounded theory, Focus groups, Narratives, Case studies, Ethnography.

Statistics in Psychology: Measures of Central Tendency and Dispersion. Normal Probability Curve. Parametric [t-test] and Non-parametric tests [Sign Test, Wilcoxon Signed rank test, Mann-Whitney test, Kruskal-Wallis test, Friedman]. Power analysis. Effect size.

Correlational Analysis: Correlation [Product Moment, Rank Order], Partial correlation, Multiple correlation.

Special Correlation Methods: Biserial, Point biserial, tetrachoric, phi coefficient. Regression: Simple linear regression, Multiple regression. Factor analysis: Assumptions, Methods, Rotation and Interpretation.

Experimental Designs: ANOVA [One-way, Factorial], Randomised Block designs, Repeated Measures design, Latin Square, Cohort studies, Time series, MANOVA, ANCOVA. Single-subject designs.

3. Psychological Testing

Types of tests, Test construction: Item writing, item analysis, Test standardisation: Reliability, validity and norms.

Areas of testing: Intelligence, Creativity, Neuropsychological tests, Aptitude, Personality assessment, Interest inventories, Attitude scales – Semantic differential, Staples, Likert scale. Computer-based psychological testing.

Applications of psychological testing in various settings: Clinical, Organisational and business, Education, Counselling, Military. Career guidance.

4. Biological Basis of Behaviour

Sensory systems: General and specific sensations, Receptors and processes. Neurons: Structure, Functions, Types, Neural impulse, Synaptic transmission. Neurotransmitters. The Central and Peripheral Nervous Systems – Structure and functions. Neuroplasticity.

Methods of Physiological Psychology: Invasive methods – Anatomical methods, Degeneration techniques, Lesion techniques, Chemical methods, Microelectrode studies. Non-invasive methods – EEG, Scanning methods.

Muscular and Glandular system: Types and functions Biological basis of Motivation: Hunger, Thirst, Sleep and Sex. Biological basis of emotion: The Limbic system, Hormonal regulation of behaviour. Genetics and behaviour: Chromosomal anomalies; Nature-Nurture controversy [Twin studies and adoption studies].

5. Attention, Perception, Learning, Memory and Forgetting

Attention: Forms of attention, Models of attention, Perception: Approaches to the Study of Perception: Gestalt and physiological approaches, Perceptual Organisation: Gestalt, Figure and Ground, Law of Organisation

Perceptual Constancy: Size, Shape and Color; Illusions, Perception of Form, Depth and Movement Role of motivation and learning in perception.

Signal detection theory: Assumptions and applications, Subliminal perception and related factors, information processing approach to perception, culture and perception, perceptual styles, Pattern recognition, Ecological perspective on perception.

Learning Process: Fundamental theories: Thorndike, Guthrie, Hull, Classical conditioning: Procedure, phenomena

and related issues, Instrumental learning: Phenomena, paradigms and theoretical issues; Reinforcement: Basic variables and schedules; Behaviour modification and its applications, Cognitive approaches in learning: Latent learning, observational learning. Verbal learning and Discrimination learning, Recent trends in learning: Neurophysiology of learning.

Memory and Forgetting, Memory processes: Encoding, Storage, Retrieval, Stages of memory: Sensory memory, Short-term memory (Working memory), Long-term memory (Declarative – Episodic and Semantic; Procedural). Theories of Forgetting: Interference, Retrieval Failure, Decay, Motivated forgetting.

6. Thinking, Intelligence and Creativity

Theoretical perspectives on thought processes: Associationism, Gestalt, Information processing, Feature integration model, Concept formation: Rules, Types and Strategies; Role of concepts in thinking; Types of Reasoning ,Language and thought.

Problem solving: Type, Strategies and Obstacles, Decision-making: Types and models.

Metacognition: Metacognitive knowledge and Metacognitive regulation, Intelligence: Spearman; Thurstone; Jensen; Cattell; Gardner; Stenberg; Goleman; Das, Kar and Parrila; Creativity: Torrance, Getzels and Jackson, Guilford, Wallach and Kogan, Relationship between Intelligence and Creativity.

7. Personality, Motivation, Emotion, Stress and Coping

Determinants of personality: Biological and socio-cultural Approaches to the study of personality: Psychoanalytical, Neo-Freudian, Social learning, Trait and Type, Cognitive, Humanistic, Existential, Transpersonal psychology.

Other theories: Rotter's Locus of Control, Seligman's Explanatory styles, Kohlberg's theory of Moral development.

Basic motivational concepts: Instincts, Needs, Drives, Arousal, Incentives, Motivational Cycle. Approaches to the study of motivation: Psychoanalytical, Ethological, S-R Cognitive, Humanistic; Exploratory behaviour and curiosity, Zuckerman's Sensation seeking, Achievement, Affiliation and Power, Motivational Competence, Self-regulation , Flow Emotions: Physiological correlates Theories of emotions: James-Lange, Canon-Bard, Schachter and Singer, Lazarus, Lindsley. Emotion regulation, Conflicts: Sources and types

Stress and Coping: Concept, Models, Type A, B, C, D behaviours, Stress management strategies [Biofeedback, Music therapy, Breathing exercises, Progressive Muscular Relaxation, Guided Imagery, Mindfulness, Meditation, Yogasana, Stress Inoculation Training].

8. Social Psychology

Nature, scope and history of social psychology, Traditional theoretical perspectives: Field theory, Cognitive Dissonance, Sociobiology, Psychodynamic Approaches, Social Cognition.

Social perception [Communication, Attributions]; Attitude and its change within cultural context; Prosocial behaviour.

Group and social influence [Social facilitation; Social loafing]; Social influence [Conformity, Peer Pressure, Persuasion, Compliance, Obedience, Social Power, Reactance]. Aggression. Group dynamics, Leadership style and effectiveness. Theories of intergroup relations [Minimal Group Experiment and Social Identity Theory, Relative Deprivation Theory, Realistic Conflict Theory, Balance Theories, Equity Theory, Social Exchange Theory].

Applied social psychology: Health, Environment and Law; Personal space, crowding and territoriality.

9. Human Development and Interventions

Developmental processes: Nature, Principles, Factors in development, Stages of Development. Successful aging. Theories of development: Psychoanalytical, Behaviouristic and Cognitive various aspects of development: Sensory-motor, cognitive, language, emotional, social and moral.

Psychopathology: Concept, Mental Status Examination, Classification, Causes.

Psychotherapies: Psychoanalysis, Person-centered, Gestalt, Existential, Acceptance Commitment Therapy, Behaviour therapy, REBT, CBT, MBCT, Play therapy, Positive psychotherapy, Transactional Analysis, Dialectic behaviour therapy, Art therapy, Performing art therapy, Family therapy.

Applications of theories of motivation and learning in school, Factors in educational achievement Teacher effectiveness, Guidance in schools: Needs, organisational set up and techniquesm, Counselling: Process, skills and techniques.

10. Emerging Areas

Issues of Gender, Poverty, Disability and Migration: Cultural bias and discrimination. Stigma, Marginalisation and Social Suffering; Child Abuse and Domestic violence.

Peace psychology: Violence, non-violence, conflict resolution at macro level, role of media in conflict resolution.

Well-being and self-growth: Types of well-being [Hedonic and Eudemonic], Character strengths, Resilience and Post-Traumatic Growth.

Health: Health promoting and health compromising behaviours, Life style and Chronic diseases [Diabetes, Hypertension, Coronary Heart Disease], Psychoneuroimmunology [Cancer, HIV/AIDS].

Psychology and technology interface: Digital learning; Digital etiquette: Cyber bullying; Cyber pornography: Consumption, Implications; Parental mediation of digital usage.

CONTENTS

Unit VII Personality, Motivation, Emotion, Stress and Coping

Unit VIII Social Psychology

Unit IX Human Development and Interventions

Unit X Emerging Areas

Psychology (Paper-2) Solved Paper, August 2024

General Instructions

1. There are total one hundred questions in this paper. Each question carries 2 marks.
2. All questions are compulsory.

---

1. Hull's approach to theory construction is called
(1) Hypothetical deductive
(2) Hypothetical inductive
(3) Hypothetical intuitive
(4) Hypothetical tautology

2. Place the components of 'Broaden-and-Build Model of Positive Emotion' in correct sequence
A. Building Enduring Personal Resources
B. Positive Emotions
C. Enhanced Health Fulfillments
D. Novel Thoughts, Activities, Relationships
Choose the correct answer from the options given below.
(1) B, D, A, C (2) B, A, D, C
(3) D, B, A, C (4) D, A, B, C

3. Cognitive psychologists and survey researchers have acknowledged that answering survey questions can be a complex cognitive task. Research suggests that when people answer survey questions, they go through four stages. Arrange the stages in order.
A. Comprehension
B. Judgement
C. Response communication
D. Retrieval
Choose the correct answer from the options given below.
(1) A, D, B, C (2) A, B, D, C
(3) B, A, D, C (4) B, C, A, D

4. Who is the Personality Theorist who believed that individuals are in the process of 'becoming' and nothing is predetermined?
(1) Sigmund Freud (2) Alfred Adler
(3) Carl Jung (4) BF Skinner

5. Read the following situations. Then order them in the sequence of nominal, ordinal, equal interval and ratio.
A. Eggs in the supermarket are graded as small, medium, large and jumbo
B. Employees are assigned identification numbers
C. Achievement motivation of hockey players
D. Players' height
Choose the correct answer from the options given below.
(1) B, C, D, A (2) B, A, C, D
(3) A, B, D, C (4) A, C, B, D

6. Advaita Vedanta asserts that sensory knowledge is
A. Illusionary
B. Absolutely false
C. Possible in a transcendental state
D. Relatively true, but not absolutely true

Choose the correct answer from the options given below.
(1) C, D only
(2) A, B only
(3) A, D only
(4) B, C only

7. Following are the steps that should be followed to enhance critical thinking. Arrange them in sequential order.
A. Adopt the attitude of a critical thinker
B. Evaluate information sources
C. Recognise and avoid critical thinking hindrances
D. Identify and characterise arguments
E. Evaluate arguments
Choose the correct answer from the options given below.
(1) A, C, D, B, E (2) A, B, C, E, D
(3) B, A, C, E, D (4) C, A, B, E, D

8. The distribution, which is skewed to the left, has one high point and has many high scores is called
(1) Evenly distributed distribution
(2) Platykurtic distribution
(3) Negatively skewed distribution
(4) Positively skewed distribution

9. Match List- I with List-II.

List I		List II
A. Synthetic skill	I.	Decisions about how to deploy the skills available to a person
B. Analytic skill	II.	To see problem with new points of view and get rid of conventional thinking
C. Practical contexual skill	III.	To recognise which idea are worth pursuing and which are not
D. Thinking styles	IV.	To know how to persuade others regarding one's ideas

Choose the correct answer from the options given below.

	A	B	C	D
(1)	II	IV	III	I
(2)	II	III	IV	I
(3)	I	II	IV	III
(4)	IV	III	I	II

10. The functions of Gamma-Aminobutyric Acid (GABA) can be described in terms of.
(1) Excitatory or inhibitory, involved in arousal, attention, memory
(2) Mainly excitatory, involved in arousal and mood
(3) Majorly inhibitory involved in sleep and inhibitory movement
(4) Inhibitory neural regulation, involved in pain relief

11. Match List-I with List-II

List-I	List-II
A. Krodha	I. Disgust
B. Bhaya	II. Wonder /Astonishment
C. Jugupsa	III. Anger
D. Vismaya	IV. Fear

Choose the dorrect answer from the options given below.

	A	B	C	D		A	B	C	D
(1)	III	IV	I	II	(2)	I	IV	II	III
(3)	II	IV	I	III	(4)	IV	III	II	I

12. Peterson and Seligman carried out their famous work on strengths, virtues and character. This work is referred as
(1) Characters in Action Pproject
(2) Strength in Action Project
(3) Virtues in Action Poject
(4) Values in Action P

13. Arrange the following behaviours of a University professor in a hierarchical order as per Maslow's theory of motivation.
A. Buys a two-bedroom flat
B. Attends at least one refresher course in his discipline every year
C. Applies regularly for various awards
D. Tries to maintain close relationship with the students
Choose the correct answer from the options given below.
(1) A, D, C, B (2) D, A, B, C
(3) D, C, B, A (4) A, B, D, C

14. Richardson's Resilience model refers to which of the following?
A. Reintegration with a loss
B. Resistance index
C. Biopsychospiritual homeostasis
D. Disruption
E. Outcome index
Choose the correct answer from the options given below.
(1) B, C, E only (2) C, D, E only
(3) A, C, D only (4) B, C, D only

15. Which of the following are not true about the differences between simple regression and multiple regression?
A. The number of predictors
B. The number of criteria
C. Coefficient of determination
D. Sample size

Choose the correct answer from the options given below.
(1) A, C, D only (2) A, B, D only
(3) B, C, D only (4) A, B, C only

16. Some casual factors occurring relatively early in life may not show their effects for many years. that may contribute to a predisposition to develop a disorder. These would be considered as
(1) Proximal risk factors
(2) Distal risk factors
(3) Fixed risk factors
(4) Concomitant risk factors

17. The leading neuroscience theories of intelligence is called
(1) Parieto-Frontal interpolated theory
(2) Frontal-Occipital integration theory
(3) Parieto-Frontal integration theory
(4) Frontal-Parietal symbolic theory

18. Which of the following softwares can be more helpful for analysis in qualitative research by a psychologist?
A. SPSS B. AMOS
C. NVIVO D. ATLAS
E. R
Choose the correct answer from the options given below.
(1) A, B only (2) B, D only
(3) C, D only (4) B, D, E only

19. Which of the following methods can be used to determine the number of factors to be extracted in Exploratory Factor Analysis?
A. Liserel analysis
B. Scree test
C. Eigen value criteria
D. Rotation
Choose the correct answer from the options given below.
(1) A, B only (2) B, C only
(3) C, D only (4) A, D only

20. Arrange the following literary works on different facets of "Yoga" in chronological order.
A. 'Anashshakti Yoga' by Mahatma Gandhi
B. 'Gitarahasya' by BG Tilak
C. 'Gatha' by Tukaram
D. 'Upadesha' by Raman Maharishi
Choose the correct answer from the options given below.
(1) C, D, B, A
(2) C, B, D, A
(3) B, C, D, A
(4) B ,C, A, D

21. According to which theory of emotion the physiological reaction and the emotion are assumed to occur simultaneously?
(1) James-Lange Theory
(2) Cannon-Bard Theory
(3) Cognitive-Arousal Theory
(4) Cognitive-Mediational Theory

22. One behavioural scientist is developing a questionnaire to assess the attitude towards workplace support. Which of the following will be the best way to establish construct validity of the questionnaire?
(1) Croanbach Alpha
(2) Inter-item Correlation
(3) Factor Analysis
(4) Kuder-Richardson Formula

23. Which of the following are community based protective factors for resilience among children?
A. Ties to pro-social organisations
B. Authoritative parenting
C. Organised home environment
D. Neighbourhood with high collective efficacy
E. Effective schools
Choose the correct answer from the options given below.
(1) A, C, D only (2) A, D, E only
(3) C, D, E only (4) B, C, D only

24. One organisational psychologist wanted to verify the efficacy of a group based development intervention. For this purpose he undertook an Action Research. Suggest the correct sequence of the following components of his research.
A. Acting through the intervention
B. Observation
C. Planning about the intervention
D. Reflection
Choose the correct answer from the options given below.
(1) B, C, D, A (2) C, B, A, D
(3) C, A, B, D (4) B, C, A, D

25. Spreading rumours behind someone's back can most appropriately be referred as
(1) Social aggression (2) Relation aggression
(3) Indirect aggression (4) Physical aggression

26. Which of the following refer to the theories of Health Behaviour?
A. Reflection-Action Theory
B. Protective Motivation Theory
C. Dialectical Behavioural Theory
D. Precaution Adoption Process Model
E. Organismic Integration Theory

Choose the correct answer from the options given below:
(1) A, C, D only
(2) B, C, D only
(3) A, C, E only
(4) B, D, E only

27. Which of the following statements are correct?
A. Internal locus of control enhances the perception of stress
B. Stress functions as a motivator
C. The behavioural indicators of stress in children are seen in cognitive abilities, social competence and academic performance
D. In resistance stage of General Adaptation Syndrome (GAS), the physiological arousal peaks upto the all time high
E. Neglect, victimisation, physical assault constitute toxic stress for children

Choose the correct answer from the options given below.
(1) A, C, E only (2) B, C, E only
(3) A, C, D only (4) C, D, E only

28. Match List-I with List-II.

List-I	List-II
A. Premek Principle	I. The rapid change in performance level as the size of reinforcement is varied
B. Zeigamik Effect	II. Reinforcement strengthens the neighbouring response in addition to the response that it produced
C. Crespi Effect	III. The opportunity to engage in frequently occurring activity can be used to reinforce a less frequently occurring activity
D. Spread of Effect	IV. The tendency to remember incomplete tasks longer than complete ones

Choose the correct answer from the options given below.

	A	B	C	D
(1)	II	I	IV	III
(2)	I	III	II	IV
(3)	IV	III	I	II
(4)	III	IV	I	II

29. In the equation for linear regression $Y = a + bX$, b stands for
(1) Y intercept on X
(2) Regression coefficient
(3) X intercept on Y
(4) Constant

30. Match List-I with List-II

List-I	List-II
A. Dukha	I. Suffering is a part of Life
B. Dukha-Samudaya	II. Suffering has an end
C. Dukha-Nirodha	III. Suffering has a cause
D. Dukh-nirodha Marga	IV. There is a way to end suffering

Choose the correct answer from the options given below.

	A	B	C	D
(1)	I	II	IV	III
(2)	II	I	III	IV
(3)	III	I	II	IV
(4)	I	III	II	IV

31. Five ways to be proactive includes the following
A. Predict B. Prevent
C. Program D. Plan
E. Participate

Choose the correct answer from the options given below.
(1) A, B, C, E only
(2) B, C, D, E only
(3) A, B, D, E only
(4) A, B, C, D only

32. Which of the following are included in Bruner's theory of cognitive development?
A. Enactive B. Echoic
C. Iconic D. Symbolic
E. Deontic

Choose the correct answer from the options given below:
(1) A, B, C only (2) A, C, D only
(3) A, C, E only (4) A, B, E only

33. Match List-I with List-II.

List-I	List-II
A. Taysach disorder	I. The 23rd Pair is actually missing an X
B. Down's syndrome	II. Fatal neurological disorder
C. Klinefelter's syndrome	III. An extra chromosome in What normally be the 21st Pair
D. Turner's syndrome	IV. The 23rd set of sex chromosomes is XXY

Choose the Correct answer from the options given below

	A	B	C	D
(1)	III	IV	II	I
(2)	II	III	IV	I
(3)	IV	I	III	II
(4)	I	III	II	IV

34. Pineal Gland

A. helps increase the blood calcium level

B. secretes a hormone called 'melatonin'

C. is located in epithalamus

D. Secretes hormones called 'parathormone' and 'calcitonin'

E. Is used to be known as the 'Third eye'

Choose the correct answer from the options given below:

(1) A, D, E only (2) B, C, E only

(3) C, D only (4) A, B, C, E only

35. A psychologist was interested to conduct a study on gamblers. Identifying the gamblers, even with the help of police, is a challenging task. Which of the following sampling technique will be more appropriate to take up the study?

(1) Quota sampling

(2) Cluster sampling

(3) Snowball sampling

(4) Stratified sampling

36. Which of the following is one of the non-parametric counterpart of ANOVA?

(1) Kruskal-wallis Test

(2) Mann-Whitney Test

(3) Kendell's Test

(4) Wilcox"s Test

37. In the disease called Multiple Sclerosis (MS)

(1) The myelin Sheath is destroyed.

(2) The myelin Sheath is thick.

(3) The myelin shows bumps in some places.

(4) The electrical signals jump.

38. The multitrait-multimethod design does not provide which one of the following?

(1) Predictive evidence validity

(2) Discriminant evidence validity

(3) Convergent evidence validity

(4) Reliability

39. Arrange the following cognitive points sequentially to explain helping behaviour as suggested by Darley and Latane.

A. Taking responsibility

B. Defining an emergency

C. Taking action

D. Noticing

E. Planning a course of action

Choose the correct answer from the options given below.

(1) B, D, E, A, C

(2) B, E, D, A. C

(3) D, A, B, E, C

(4) D, B, A, E, C

40. While Carkhuff's Model describes communication skills as pre-processing skills, Ivey and Ivey call it a ....

(1) Basic communication skills

(2) Life skill model

(3) Micro skill approach

(4) DASIE model

41. Reality Therapy in counselling

A. is based on principles of choice

B. emphasises self-evaluation

C. focuses on the way we live and exist

D. views empowerment from a strength-based perspective

E. Follows the stages of Wants, Direction, Evaluation and Planning (WDEP)

Choose the correct answer from the options given below.

(1) A, B, E only

(2) A, C, E only

(3) A, B, D only

(4) C, D, E only

42. Match List-I with List-II.

List-I	List-II
A. Eros Love	I. Treating love as a game
B. Ludos Love	II. Treating love as a friendship
C. Storge Love	III. Loving an ideal person
D. Agape Love	IV. Selfless love

Choose the correct answer from the options given below.

	A	B	C	D
(1)	II	III	I	IV
(2)	I	II	IV	III
(3)	III	I	II	IV
(4)	IV	I	III	II

43. Match List-I with List-II.

List-I	List-II
A. Phenomenology	I. Indepth detailed examination of an entity in real world context
B. Case study	II. Application of inductive reasoning
C. Ethnography	III. Lived experiences
D. Grounded theory	IV. Description of peoples and culture

Choose the correct answer from the options given below.

	A	B	C	D
(1)	III	II	I	IV
(2)	II	I	III	IV
(3)	III	I	IV	II
(4)	I	III	IV	II

44. The area responsible for interaction between frontal, temporal and motor areas in order to produce speech is called
(1) Primary Auditory Cortex
(2) Broca's Area
(3) Spery's Area
(4) Wernicke's Area

45. Arrange the early schools of psychology in order
A. Structuralism B. Functionalism
C. Behaviourism D. Humanistic
Choose the correct answer from the options given below.
(1) B, A, C, D (2) B, C, A, D
(3) A, B, C, D (4) A,C, B, D

46. Asking for a small commitment and after gaining compliance, asking for a bigger commitment is known as
(1) Foot-in-the-door technique
(2) Low-ball technique
(3) Progressive ball technique
(4) Door-in-the-face technique

47. Match List-I with List-II.

List-I	List-II
A. Principle of Closure	I. Tendency to complete incomplete experiences to make them more meaningful
B. Principle of Polarity	II. Learned material is most performed in the same direction in which it was originally learned
C. Principle of Parsimony	III. Choosing the simple one out of two equally effective theories
D. Principle of Falsification	IV. In order for theory to be scientific, it must make risky prediction if not confirmed would refute the theory

Choose the correct answer from the options given below.
A B C D
(1) I II III IV
(2) II I IV III
(3) III I II IV
(4) II III I IV

48. Which of the following terms are associated with Gestalt approach
A. Molar
B. Nativistic
C. Atomistic, elementistic
D. Cognitive, phenomenological
E. Objective

Choose the most appropriate answer from the options given below.
(1) A, C, D only
(2) A, B, D, E only
(3) B, C, D, E only
(4) A, B, D only

49. The situation of conflict arising upon allocation of funding to different groups is an example of conflict arising over issues of
(1) interest
(2) values
(3) growth
(4) demand characteristics

50. The disorder where an extra sex chromosome in the 23rd pair resulting in XXY producing a male with reduced masculine characteristics resulting in enlarged breasts, obesity and excessive height is called
(1) Phenylketonuria (PKU)
(2) Turner's syndrome
(3) Tay-sachs disorder
(4) Klinefelter's syndrome

51. Which of the following attribute, according to Mahatma Gandhi as well as Patanjali, is an essential condition for practicing non-violence?
(1) Dukha (2) Vairagya
(3) Krodha (4) Utsaha

52. People living on railway platforms, crowded market area on the main roads with heavy traffic are likely to experience
(1) Energetic stress (2) Ergonomic stress
(3) Anthropogenic stress (4) Tropical stress

53. A key element in all therapeutic process is the development of an effective
(1) challenging
(2) rersonal integration
(3) advanced empathy
(4) working alliance

54. Match List-I with List-II.

List-I	List-II
A. Material form	I. Vedana
B. Feeling of sensation	II. Vinnana
C. Perception	III. Rupa
D. Reason or intelligence	IV. Sana

Choose the correct answer from the options given below.
A B C D
(1) III I IV II
(2) II I III IV
(3) I IV II III
(4) III II I IV

55. Which of the following are components of hardiness?
(1) Control, coherence, challenge
(2) Challenge, constructivity, confidence
(3) Control, commitment, challenge
(4) Commitment, collaboration, control

56. Which of the following statements are correct?
A. Emotionally arousing stimuli have also been seen to lead to amnesia.
B. Some cognitive processing must occur before an individual can experience an emotional response to an event.
C. Repression is a form of motivated forgetting.
D. Functional Magnetic Resonance Imaging (FMRI) and Position Emission Topography (PET) are invasive scanning techniques of studying the brain functioning.
E. Theories of emotions have not changed much over the years.
Choose the correct answer from the options given below.
(1) A, B, C only (2) A, B, D only
(3) B, C, D, E only (4) A, B, D, E only

57. Match List-I with List-II.

List-I	List-II
A. Drive-Reduction Theory	I. Yerkes and Dodson
B. Personality and Nach	II. Richard Ryan and Edward Deci
C. Arousal Theory	III. Carol Dweck
D. Self-Determination Theory	IV. Hull

Choose the correct answer from the options given below.

	A	B	C	D
(1)	IV	I	II	III
(2)	IV	III	I	II
(3)	II	III	IV	I
(4)	I	IV	II	III

58. Match List-I with List-II.

List-I	List-II
A. Standard scores always has a mean of 50 and SD of 10	I. Percentile
B. Standard scores change the unit of measurement	II. Z-score
C. Standard with a mean of zero and SD of 1	III. T-score
D. Units in testing that help to evaluate a person's performance in comparison with others who took the same test	IV. Standard score

Choose the correct answer from the options given below.

	A	B	C	D
(1)	III	II	I	IV
(2)	II	III	I	IV
(3)	III	I	II	IV
(4)	IV	III	I	II

59. Which of the following is not included in Sullivan basic modes theory
(1) Prototaxic mode (2) Pretaxic mode
(3) Parataxic mode (4) Syntaxic mode

60. The first psychology department in India was formally started in 1916 by
(1) Girindra Shekhar Bose
(2) NN Sengupta
(3) MV Gopalaswami
(4) SM Mohsin

61. The four phases of forgiveness according to Enright, Freedman and Rique includes
(1) Undercovering, Contemplation, Work and Recovering
(2) Uncovering, Decision, Work and Deepening
(3) Uncovering, Covering, Contemplating, Recovering
(4) Understanding, Balming, Generosity, Recovering

62. The process by which one person tries to change the belief, opinion, position or course of action of another person through argument, pleading or explanation is an example of
(1) Social influence
(2) Deindividuation
(3) Persuasion
(4) Prosocial behaviour

63. Who among the following is not considered as a reinforcement theorist?
(1) Thorndike
(2) Gutherie
(3) Hull
(4) Skinner

64. Which of the following are methods used in challenging in counselling as per the Developmental model of Egan?
A. Reviewing better times
B. Asocial response
C. Identification of models
D. Immediacy
E. Self-disclosure
Choose the correct answer from the options given below.
(1) B, D, E only (2) A, C, D only
(3) A, D, E only (4) C, D, E only

65. Which of the following are included in the steps of Eye Movement Desensitisation Reprocessing (EMDR) therapy?

A. Assessment
B. Cognitive restructuring
C. Installation
D. Skill acquisition
E. Body scan

Choose the correct answer from the options given below.

(1) A, C, D only (2) A, C, E only
(3) B, D, E only (4) B, C, D only

66. Arrange the following in a sequence as per the health belief model where an individual.

A. Reads about the various factors related to cancer
B. Stops smoking
C. Feels that since his father died of cancer he is likely to be genetically disposed
D. Understands that if he continues to smoke there is higher possibility of his suffering from cancer

Choose the correct answer from the options given below.

(1) C, D, A, B (2) D, A, C, B
(3) A ,C, D, B (4) D ,C, A, B

67. Which of the following are measures of dispersion?

A. Standard deviation
B. Quartile deviation
C. Mode
D. Variance
E. Range

Choose the correct answer from the options given below:

(1) A, B, E only
(2) B, C, D only
(3) A, B, D, E only
(4) A, B, C, D only

68. Match List-I with List-II.

List-I (Parts of Nervous System)	List-II (Function)
A. Hypothalamus	I. Fear responses and memory of fear
B. Hippocampus	II. Regulates body Temperature, thirst, hunger
C. Amygdala	III. Forms long-term declarative memories
D. Cingulate cortex	IV. Selective attention, working memory

Choose the correct answer from the options given below.

	A	B	C	D
(1)	III	IV	I	II
(2)	II	I	III	IV
(3)	II	III	I	IV
(4)	I	III	IV	II

69. Which one of the following is correct with regard to PASS model developed by JP Das and his associates?

(1) Planning, Arousal, Successive and Simultaneous processing
(2) Programing, Attentive, Sequencing and Simultaneous processing
(3) Processing, Awakening. Simultaneous and Successive processing
(4) Planning, Attention, Arousal, Simultaneous and Successive processing

70. Which of the following are characteristics of a good hypothesis?

A. Affirmative statement
B. Interrogative statement
C. Falsifiability
D. Conjectural
E. Concludes relationship between variables

Choose the correct answer from the options given below:

(1) B, D, E only
(2) A, C, D only
(3) B, C, D only
(4) A, C, E only

71. In order to interpret individual test scores and to calculate confidence interval, which of the following is important and necessary?

(1) Pearson product moment correlation
(2) Test variance
(3) Spearman-Brown formula
(4) Standard error of measurement

72. Match List-I with List-II.

List-I	List-II
A. Entropy	I. Comparative assessment of facilitating and restraining forces in the environment
B. Decay Curve	II. A sudden downward drop in the curve of health behaviour
C. Force Field Analysis	III. Ginzberg's theory of career development
D. Fantasy, Tentative, Realistic	IV. A gradual progressive decline in the health behaviour curve

Choose the correct answer from the options given below

	A	B	C	D
(1)	II	IV	I	III
(2)	IV	III	II	I
(3)	III	II	I	IV
(4)	I	III	IV	II

73. The different states of consciousness like wakefulness, dream, deep sleep as well as extraordinary state (turiya avastha) are described in

(1) Mandukya Upanisad
(2) Katha Upanisad
(3) Svetasvatara Upanisad
(4) Mimamsa

74. Match List-I with List-II.

List-I	List-II
A. Gestalt Therapy	I. Five universal human needs
B. Reality Therapy	II. You are the architect of your life
C. Existentialism	III. Empty hair technique
D. Solution Focused Therapy	IV. Steve de Shazer and Insoo Kim Berg

Choose the correct answer from the options given below.

	A	B	C	D
(1)	II	I	IV	III
(2)	I	II	III	IV
(3)	IV	I	II	III
(4)	III	I	II	IV

75. Which one of the following are the reasons for forgetting?

A. The information is not attended to and fails to be encoded.
B. Information accessed repeatedly decays.
C. Older information in memory interfers with the learning of new information.
D. Never information interfers with the retrieval of older information.
E. Information attended and perception is poor.

Choose the correct answer from the options given below:

(1) A, C, D only (2) A, B, C, D only
(3) A, B, D only (4) B, C, D, E only

76. Kohlberg's stages of moral development follows

A. being a moral person in the eyes of others
B. makes moral choices based on beliefs
C. behaves appropriately to avoid punishment
D. conflicts with moral principles and individual rights
E. Makes choices based on what is right-behaviour

Choose the correct answer from the options given below.

(1) C, E, A, B, D
(2) D, E, B, A, C
(3) A, D, C, E, B
(4) B, E, C, D, A

77. Arrange the following behaviours of the child as per Piaget's stages of cognitive development.

A. The child says the volume of water in a long glass is same even when it is poured into flat bowl.
B. The child looks for an object in the same place where it was hidden earlier.
C. The child says that the clay ball in round shape is smaller than that the one flattened right in front of her.
D. The child argues that cycling gives a better exercise to hip muscles than bending exercises by citing reasons.

Choose the correct answer from the options given below.

(1) B, C, A, D
(2) B, A, C, D
(3) A, C, B, D
(4) C, A, B, D

78. The theory which is used to compare judgements or the decisions we make under uncertain conditions is called

(1) Subliminal perception theory
(2) Signal detection theory
(3) Judgemental process theory
(4) Decision processing theory

79. One psychologist has developed a tool on nature connectedness. What would be correct sequence of the following psychometric activities.

A. Carrying out Exploratory Factor Analysis
B. Establishing Percentile Norm
C. Examining Croanbach Alfa
D. Verifying Predictive Validity
E. Establishing Content Validity

Choose the correct answer from the options given below.

(1) E, C, A, D, B
(2) E, C, A, B, D
(3) C, A, E, B, D
(4) C, E, A, D, B

80. The five sheaths (panchakosas) theory is explained in

(1) Katha Upanisad
(2) MandukyaUpanisad
(3) PrasnaUpanisad
(4) TaittiriyaUpanisad

81. In addition to tripartite system of working memory, Baddeley, Allen and Hitch (2011) added a fourth component which is called
(1) Iconic Sketchpad
(2) Storage Rehearsal
(3) Phonological loop
(4) Episodic buffer

82. Which of the following refer to Advanced Empathy as per the Developmental Model of Counselling?
A. Confrontive challenging
B. Theme identification
C. Connecting islands
D. Making the implicit explicit
E. Fortune telling
Choose the correct answer from the options given below.
(1) A, B, E only (2) C, D, E only
(3) B, C, D only (4) B, D, E only

83. A famous study called the 'Robber's Cave' conducted by Sherif et all in 1961 demonstrated the social behaviour known as
(1) Social comparison
(2) Equal status contact
(3) Self-fulfilling prophecy
(4) Recipracity of liking

84. Arrange the following stages of therapy advocated by Adler.
A. Building therapeutic relationship
B. Gathering information
C. Developing new skill
D. Gaining insight
Choose the correct answer from the options given below.
(1) B, A, D, C (2) A, B, D, C
(3) B, A, C, D (4) A, C, B, D

85. Which one of the following is not a component of creativity according to Torrance?
(1) Flexibility (2) Elaboration
(3) Abstractness of titles (4) Verification

86. Match List-I with List-II.

List-I		List-II
A. Non-maleficence	I.	Response to stress
B. HPA Axis	II.	Encountering paradoxes of life
C. Art Therapy	III.	Counselling ethics
D. Existentialism	IV.	Intervention for emotional release

Choose the correct answer from the options given below.

	A	B	C	D		A	B	C	D
(1)	II	III	I	IV	(2)	IV	II	III	I
(3)	III	I	II	IV	(4)	III	I	IV	II

87. Which one of the following is the preferred method for determining item bias?
(1) Item difficulty level
(2) Item discrimination index
(3) Item characteristic curve
(4) Inter item correlation matrix

88. According to social identity theory, formation of a person's identity within a particular social group is explained by the sequential process of ......
(1) Social categorisation, social identity and social comparision
(2) Social identity, social categorisation and social comparision
(3) Social comparision, social identity and social categorisation
(4) Social comparision, social categorisation and social identity

89. In case of normal probability curve, the graph/curve is plotted for
(1) scores and respective frequencies
(2) scores and respective deviations
(3) 'z' scores and respective relative frequencies
(4) 'z' scores and respective standard deviations

90. Arrange the following in the sequence of personality development propounded by psychoanalitic theory.
A. Children refuse to defecate in the toilet, while some hold back the feces
B. Children enjoy breast feeding by mother and put everything in mouth
C. Children develop interest in opposite sex
D. Children are found to play with their genital organs
Choose the correct answer from the options given below.
(1) A, C, D, B (2) B, C, D, A
(3) B, A, D, C (4) D, A, B, C

Directions (Q. Nos. 91-95) *Read the passage carefully and answer the following questions given below.*

The researchers assumed that older adults are different from younger adults in their suicidal ideation and in their reasons for thinking about committing suicide because of differences in life experiences and coping competence. Hence, they used cross sectional research and recruited 150 older adults (60-95 years) who were matched with 150 younger adult (17-34 years) on gender ethnicity, religion and self-reported health status. Beck's scale for suicidal ideation was used to measure suicidal ideation. They used 't' test for comparison of variables and found no significant difference. According to Siegler, neither cross sectional nor longitudinal study provide much information about how those changes occur over time. He discussed a method that involves carefully observing behaviour during periods when rapid change is occurring and collecting both quantitative and qualitative information.

91. What is the method Siegler discussed for studying the process of change?
(1) Macrogenetic method
(2) Exogenetic method
(3) Chromogenetic method
(4) Microgenetic method

92. What is the df for the 't' test used here
(1) 297 (2) 296
(3) 294 (4) 298

93. The combination of cross sectional and longitudinal research is called
(1) Time series research
(2) Correlational research
(3) Sequential research
(4) Thematic research

94. A potential problem with cross sectional research is that there may be other variables that are confounded with age. This problem is called
(1) Habitat effect (2) Cohort effect
(3) Interrupted effcect (4) Protective effect

95. When null hypothesis is false and we are accepting it then we make
(1) Type I error
(2) Type II error
(3) Error of falsifiability
(4) Acceptance error

Directions (Q. Nos. 96-100) *Read the passage carefully and answer the questions given below.*

Motivation is the driving force behind human activities. Researchers identified three components of motivation. Motivation originates externally or internally, are defined action or non-action and can be categorized as extrinsic, identified, intrinsic or introjected. One of the causes of flow motivation is "just because an approach or method worked for someone else does not mean that it will work for you". Self-determination theory is built on the idea that people are actively motivated to persue their goals.

96. Self-determination theory is developed by
(1) Shelley E. Taylor
(2) Deci and Ryan
(3) Barbara Frederick
(4) Seligman and Lubomirsky

97. What are the three components of motivation ?
(1) Need, persistence, goal
(2) Activation, persistence and intensity
(3) Intensity, identification, drive
(4) Activation, intensity and goal

98. What are the components of intrinsic motivation?
(1) Autonomy, competence, tendency
(2) Competence, mastery, purpose
(3) Mastery, tendency, competence
(4) Autonomy, mastery and purpose

99. Introjected motivation is
(1) a negative internalised motivation.
(2) a positive externalised motivation.
(3) a negative externalised motivation.
(4) a positive internalised motivation.

100. "Just because an approach or method worked for someone else does not mean that it will work for you" refers to
(1) one size fits all
(2) Absurd function approach
(3) there is no common approach for all
(4) the approach will work for me

ANSWERS

1 (1)	2 (1)	3 (1)	4 (1)	5 (2)	6 (1)	7 (1)	8 (3)	9 (2)	10 (3)
11 (1)	12 (4)	13 (1)	14 (1)	15 (3)	16 (2)	17 (3)	18 (3)	19 (2)	20 (2)
21 (2)	22 (2)	23 (2)	24 (2)	25 (3)	26 (4)	27 (2)	28 (4)	29 (2)	30 (4)
31 (3)	32 (3)	33 (2)	34 (2)	35 (3)	36 (1)	37 (1)	38 (1)	39 (4)	40 (3)
41 (1)	42 (3)	43 (3)	44 (3)	45 (3)	46 (1)	47 (1)	48 (4)	49 (1)	50 (4)
51 (2)	52 (3)	53 (4)	54 (4)	55 (3)	56 (1)	57 (2)	58 (3)	59 (2)	60 (2)
61 (2)	62 (3)	63 (2)	64 (2)	65 (2)	66 (3)	67 (3)	68 (3)	69 (4)	70 (2)
71 (4)	72 (1)	73 (1)	74 (1)	75 (1)	76 (1)	77 (1)	78 (2)	79 (4)	80 (4)
81 (4)	82 (3)	83 (2)	84 (2)	85 (4)	86 (4)	87 (3)	88 (1)	89 (3)	90 (3)
91 (4)	92 (4)	93 (3)	94 (3)	95 (2)	96 (2)	97 (2)	98 (4)	99 (1)	100 (3)

Psychology (Paper-2)

Solved Paper, June 2023

General Instructions

1. There are total one hundred questions in this paper. Each question carries 2 marks.
2. All questions are compulsory.

---

1. .... Vidya is the disciplined and systematic knowledge of the self and the environment attained through precise observation and critical reasoning.

(1) Adhibhoulika (2) Adhyatmika
(3) Bhoutika (4) Atmika

2. The Bhagavad Gita has 18 Chapters (Adhyaya) named after some form of Yoga. Which is not the correct Adhyaya out of the following?

(1) Dhyana Yoga (2) Aksara-Brahma Yoga
(3) Purusottama Yoga (4) Jagrata Yoga

3. Paedocentrecism is

(1) Show the path of knowledge and guide the child to get knowledge
(2) Centre on child's skill and behaviour
(3) Involve child's behaviour with parents and teachers
(4) Focus how the child works and the progress he/she makes

4. There are three types of post-modern therapies, which out of the following is not a part of post-modern therapy?

(1) Solution focused therapy
(2) Field based therapy
(3) Narrative therapy
(4) Collaborative therapy

5. To conduct a study on Anganwadi workers, the researcher randomly selected five districts out of 30 districts of a state and collected data from each and every Anganwadi worker from these five districts. This is an example of....

(1) Stratified sampling (2) Cluster sampling
(3) Quota sampling (4) Convenient sampling

6. One sports psychologist wanted to carry out a biographical study by writing and recording the experiences of a hockey legend. This is an example of ...... approach.

(1) Phenomenology (2) Ethnography
(3) Narrative study
(4) Grounded theory approach

7. "The present article describes a qualitative study of the career development of 16 prominent, highly achieving Indian women across six occupational fields. Our overall aim was to explore critical influences on the career development of these women particularly those related to their attainment of professional success".

The above mentioned purpose statement indicates a ....

(1) Phenomenological study
(2) Grounded theory study
(3) Ethnographic study
(4) Case study

8. Standard deviation of sampling distribution is known as ....
(1) Effect size (2) Sampling error
(3) Parameter (4) Transitivity

9. The test requires someone to demonstrate his/her tailoring ability is best classified as
(1) Self-report test
(2) Standardised test
(3) Test of maximal performance
(4) Objective test

10. A basic set of beliefs that guide action is called
(1) Axiology (2) Paradigm
(3) Rhetorical (4) Ontology

11. A researcher carried out an analysis in which he looked for underlying theoretical structures in his construct.
Which one of the following design he used?
(1) Linear regression
(2) Analysis of variance
(3) Exploratory factor analysis
(4) Confirmatory factor analysis

12. The formula used to estimate how many homogeneous test questions should be added to a test to raise its reliability to the described level is
(1) Coefficient alpha
(2) Spearman Brown formula
(3) Pearson product moment correlation
(4) KR-20

13. Which parts of the brain are connected by the cerebral aqueduct?
(1) Third and fourth ventricles of the brain
(2) Lateral ventricles of the brain
(3) Left and right frontal lobe
(4) Frontal and parietal lobe

14. A unipolar neuron found in the soma to sensory system are sensitive to
(1) Visual sensations (2) Auditory sensations
(3) Tactile sensations (4) Olfactory sensations

15. Amygdala, part of the Limbic system, is specifically responsible for one of the following functions
(1) Thinking (2) Leaming
(3) Memory (4) Emotion

16. Which one of the following areas is not located in the Temperal Lobe?
(1) Area for perception of body sensations such as, heat, cold, touch, pressure and pain
(2) Area for perception of movements and recognition of faces
(3) Broca's speech area
(4) Primary auditory area

17. What is meant by stroboscopic motion?
(1) We perceive an object is in motion whenever its image moves across our retina
(2) Loss in sensitivity to motion
(3) Tracking objects only in darkness
(4) Tracking only the upward motion of objects

18. What is Thorndike's law of effect?
(1) Behaviour that operates on the environment producing consequences
(2) Behaviours followed by favourable consequences become more likely and that behaviours followed by unfavourable consequences become less likely to occur
(3) Learning that certain events occur together
(4) Behaviour that occurs as an automatic response to some stimulus.

19. When a lighting flashes nearby, we wince and start to prepare ourselves for the thunder to follow. This response to impending thunder is known as
(1) Unconditioned stimulus
(2) Unconditioned response
(3) Conditioned stimulus
(4) Conditioned response

20. Which among the following is true about process of extinction of behaviour in classical conditioning?
(1) Increase in magnitude of CR
(2) Gradual diminishing of CR
(3) CS and UCS develop strong association
(4) UCS follows CS

21. What is meant by Stroop Effect?
(1) The tendency to focus on a superficial feature of the problem at hand
(2) Automaticity of the reading process
(3) Planning before acting
(4) Role of silence in language

22. Which of the following is not a meta cognitive activity?
(1) Wondering how one could have been mistaken
(2) Reflecting on our own thinking process
(3) Theory of mind
(4) Communicating one's present postal address

23. Which of the following is true about the concept of heritability?
(1) The heritability of a trait refers to differences in percentages of a trait within an individual
(2) Heritability refers to a population, not to individual
(3) The heritability of a trait is a single and fixed number
(4) Heritability tells us about the source of mean differences between groups

24. Which of the following is not a chromosomal disorder characterised by subaverage intellectual functioning?
(1) Down syndrome (2) Fragile X syndrome
(3) Cerebral palsy (4) Trisomy 13

25. As per Values in Action (VIA), classification of character strengths and virtues are as under
(1) Character strengths - 20; Virtues - 06
(2) Character strengths - 24; Virtues - 06
(3) Character strengths - 18; Virtues - 06
(4) Character strengths - 24; Virtues - 04

26. Three stage model of chronic stress formulated by Hans Selye is called
(1) GAS - General Adjustment Syndrome
(2) GAS - General Adjustment System
(3) GAS - General Adaptation System
(4) GAS - General Adaptation Syndrome

27. The emergence of the Oedipus and Castration complexes are the chief events of which stage of development in the Freudian theory?
(1) Oral stage (2) Anal stage
(3) Phallic stage (4) Genital stage

28. Who is the author of the book "Escape from Freedom"?
(1) Fromm (2) Sullivan
(3) Adler (4) Horney

29. Women are likely to gain more number of valued positions during the time of crisis. This is referred as ....
(1) Glass ceiling effect (2) Glass-cliff effect
(3) Tokenism (4) Singlism

30. Efforts to cope with the knowledge that we will die is known as ......
(1) Magical Thinking
(2) Terror Management
(3) Planning Fallacy
(4) Availability Heuristics

31. Which therapeutic approach to counselling is based on the premise 'You are the architect of your life'?
(1) Gestalt
(2) Existential
(3) Adlerian
(4) Reality

32. Late adulthood often involves a gradual withdrawal from the world on physical, psychological and social levels. Which theory supports this?
(1) Disengagement theory
(2) Activity theory
(3) Continuity theory
(4) Selective isolation theory

33. Simple skills develop in infants separately and independently and later develop into more complex skills.
Which governing principle of growth is applied here?
(1) Proximodistal principle
(2) Cephalocaudal principle
(3) Principle of hierarchical integration
(4) Principle of independence of the systems

34. Which of the following is not correct about REBT?
(1) REBT aims to help individuals think clearly, feel appropriately and act effectively.
(2) REBT uses the A-B-C theory of personality to identify client's problems.
(3) The focus of the therapist is on the feelings and behaviour of the individual rather than on the incident that induced the negative feelings
(4) REBT aims at a combination of philosophical change with cognitive emòtional and behavioural strategies.

35. Which of the following is correct about the impact of stress on immune system of an individual?
(1) The immune system is weakened because of an increase in the blood pressure in the face of stress.
(2) Increased release of glucose from the liver during stress neutralises the immune functioning of the WBC.
(3) Increased level of ACTH in blood destroys the T cells.
(4) Increased level of cortisol ill blood destroys the T cells.

36. Which of the following contributes to maintaining a health risk behaviour?
(1) Lack of knowledge and the health risk behaviour helping the individual in avoidance of pain
(2) The incentive ingrained in health risk behaviour and availability of leisure time
(3) Avoidance of pain and need to spend money
(4) Avoidance of pain and high self-efficacy

37. Which of the following describes resilience?
(1) Individuals at risk whose performance is better than expected
(2) Individuals in enriched environment excelling in performance
(3) Individuals with very good performance sliding down following a traumatic experience
(4) Individuals who avoid risks and are happy with their average performance

38. Which of the following does not come under Cardiovascular Disease (CVD)?
(1) Myocardial infarction (2) Crohn's disease
(3) Angina pectoris (4) Cardiomyopathy

39. Which one of the following is not a principal characteristic of the REM sleep?
(1) EEG desynchrony (Rapid Irregular Waves)
(2) Lack of muscle tonus
(3) Lack of genital activity
(4) Dreams

40. Which of the following behaviours is not a stage of observational learning?
(1) Be motivated to reproduce the behaviour
(2) Remember what was observed
(3) Exploring the environment
(4) Pay attention to the model's behaviour

41. The basic aspects of the philosophy of early Buddhism fall into
I. Theory of Knowledge
II. Theory of Society
III. Theory of Reality
IV. Theory of Perception
Choose the most appropriate answer from the options given below.
(1) I and IV (2) I, II and III
(3) I, III and IV (4) II and IV

42. Existentialism is associated with which of the following names?
I. Soren Kierkegaard II. Vlademier
III. Friedrich Nietzsche IV. Husserl
Choose the most appropriate answer from the options given below.
(1) I and II (2) I, II and III
(3) I, III and IV (4) I, II and IV

43. Which of the following should be assured before going for parametric Analysis of Variance?
I. Independence of scores of the subjects
II. Categorical dependent variable
III. Random assignment of subjects to the treatments
IV. Homogeneity of variance of the subjects' scores
Choose the most appropriate answer from the options given below.
(1) I, II, III and IV (2) I, II and III
(3) I, III and IV (4) II, III and IV

44. Which of the following are true about multiple regression?
I. It is linear regression.
II. There are more than one criterion.
III. There are more than one predictor.
IV. It doesn't have intercept constant.
Choose the most appropriate answer from the options given below:
(1) II and III (2) I and III
(3) I, II and IV (4) II, III and IV

45. Which of correct about Multitrait - Multimethod design?
I. Investigates construct validity
II. Associates with Coombs and Holladay
III. Associates with Campbell and Fiske
IV. Investigates composite reliability
Choose the most appropriate answer from the options given below.
(1) I and II (2) I and III
(3) II and III (4) II and IV

46. In the context of formula for Cohen's Kappa
I. $K = \dfrac{f_0 - f_c}{N - f_c}$ II. f_0 = observed frequency
III. f_c = expected frequency
IV. N = Overall total of data points in the frequency matrix
Choose the most appropriate answer from the options given below.
(1) I and II (2) I and III
(3) I, II and III (4) I, II, III and IV

47. A specific brain region can be destroyed by some of the following methods. Choose the correct answers.
I. Immunocytochemical method
II. Radio frequency lesion method
III. Excitotoxic lesion method
IV. Fluorogold method
V. Experimental ablation method
Choose the most appropriate answer from the options given below.
(1) II, III and V (2) I, II and III
(3) III, IV and V (4) I, IV and V

48. Which of the following is true about negative reinforcement?
I. It strengthens a response.
II. It works by reducing or removing something undesirable or unpleasant.
III. Fastening a seat belt in car to turn off beeping sound is an example of negative reinforcement.
IV. It weakens a response.
V. It works by increasing desirability and pleasantness of a stimulus.
Choose a most appropriate answer from the options given below:
(1) IV and II (2) I, II and III
(3) I and V (4) IV, II and III

49. Which of the following are true about perceptual constancy?
I. It applies to perception of size and colour only.
II. Many visual illusions may be explained by the various constancies.

III. Constancies occur in all sensory modalities.
IV. It keeps the appearance of objects the same in spite of large variations in the initial representation of the stimuli received by the sense organs that are engendered by various environmental factors.

Choose the most appropriate answer from the options given below.
(1) I, II and IV (2) II, III and IV
(3) I and II (4) Only IV

50. What is meant by theory of mind?
I. People's idea about feelings perceptions and thoughts of self and others and the behaviour these might predict.
II. A term first coined by Daniel Goleman.
III. People's ideas about their own and other's mental states.
IV. By the age of six months, children worldwide display an advanced level of theory of mind acquisition.
V. People with autism are said to have an impaired theory of mind.

Choose the most appropriate answer from the options given below.
(1) I and III (2) I, III and V
(3) I and II (4) III and V

51. Which of the following is true about a Phoneme?
I. It refers to the disrupted language of a patient with aphasia.
II. Every language has its own set of phonemes.
III. A phonema is a category of speech sounds.
IV. It is the smallest twit of language that carries meaning.

Choose the most appropriate answer from the options given below:
(1) Only I (2) II and IV
(3) II and III (4) Only IV

52. Self-determination theory of Deci and Ryan focused on following basic needs to explain well-being.
I. Creativity II. Engagement
III. Competence IV. Relatedness
V. Autonomy

Choose the most appropriate answer from the options given below:
(1) I, II and III (2) III, IVand V
(3) II, IV and V (4) I, III and IV

53. The structural components of the collective unconscious (lung) are called by different names.
I. Archetypes II. Imagoes
III. Creative ego IV. Libido
V. Dominants

Choose the most appropriate answer from the options given below.
(1) I, V and III (2) II, III and IV
(3) I, II, III and V (4) I, II and V

54. In late adulthood, retirement from job follows specific stages, as per Atchley (1982).
I. Honeymoon
II. Disenchantment
III. Craving for money
IV. Reorientation
V. Social withdrawal

Choose the most appropriate answer from the options given below.
(1) I, II and V (2) II, III and IV
(3) III, IV and V (4) I, II and IV

55. As indicated by reflexes, a new born baby responds to touch around the area of
I. Head, neck and mouth
II. Belly, foot and neck
III. Mouth, calf and head
IV. Mouth and foot
V. Palm

Choose the most appropriate answer from the options given below:
(1) I and II (2) II and III
(3) III and II (4) IV and V

56. Etiological models of psychopathology includes
I. Nervous system going awry
II. Social conflicts
III. Intrapsychic conflicts
IV. Learning dysfunctional behaviour
V. Indulgence in religion

Choose the most appropriate answer from the options given below.
(1) I, II and III (2) II, III, IV, II
(3) I, III and IV (4) I, III, IV, V

57. Conflicts are readily kindled and fueled by
I. Competition II. Conciliation
III. Cooperation IV. Misperception
V. Social dilemma

Choose the most appropriate answer from the options given below.
(1) I, II and III (2) II, III and IV
(3) III, IV and V (4) I, IV and V

58. What is meant by bottom-up processing?
I. It always distorts our observations.
II. Sensory analysis that starts at the entry level.
III. When our experience and expectations guide our perception.

IV. Higher level mental processes are involved.
V. Helps to detect the lines, angles and colours.

Choose the most appropriate answer from the options given below.

(1) I and II (2) I, III and IV
(3) II and V (4) III and V

59. Robert Sternberg proposed a triarchic theory of following intelligence types

I. Creative II. Analogical
III. Analytical IV. Emotional
V. Practical

Choose the most appropriate answer from the options given below.

(1) I, III and V (2) I, II and IV
(3) I, II and III (4) I, III and IV

60. Which of the following is/are related to developmental screening tests?

I. Gesell Developmental Schedule
II. Denver Developmental Screening Test
III. Holland Developmental Schedule
IV. Bruner Developmental Screening Test

Choose the most appropriate answer from the options given below.

(1) I and III (2) II and IV
(3) I and II (4) III and IV

61. Human personality is analysed into five factors as viewed by Buddhism. Choose the correct factors included in personality.

I. Material, Perception, Feeling
II. Disposition, Consciousness
III. Thinking, Belief, Intelligence
IV. Memory, Attention

Choose the most appropriate answer from the options given below.

(1) I and II (2) II and III
(3) III and IV (4) I and IV

62. Which of the following is true about stimulus generalisation?

I. People's emotional reactions to one stimulus generalise to similar stimuli.
II. With repeated exposure and reinforcement dogs can differentiate between types of sounds.
III. Normally desirable foods such as cakes and pastries are unappealing when shaped to resemble dog's feces.
IV. Sudden appearance of forgotten response.

Choose the most appropriate answer from the options given below.

(1) I and IV (2) I and III
(3) I and II (4) II and IV

63. Which of the following does not come under the matrix reasoning subtest of WAIS IV?

I. Visuospatial reasoning
II. Psychomotor speed
III. Abstract reasoning
IV. Visual organisation
V. Ability to follow directions

Choose the most appropriate answer from the options given below

(1) I, II and III (2) I, III and IV
(3) II, III and IV (4) I, II, III and IV

64. Identify the components of the 'Ethical Decision Making

I. Moral awareness II. Moral anxiety
III. Moral intent IV. Moral judgement
V. Moral context

Choose the most appropriate answer from the options given below.

(1) I, II and III (2) II, III and IV
(3) III, IV and V (4) I, III and IV

65. Informed consent, as suggested by Diener and Crandall includes the components.

I. Voluntarism
II. Researcher's competence
III. Information
IV. Comprehension

Choose the most appropriate answer from the options given below.

(1) I and III (2) I, II and III
(3) I, III and IV (4) II, III and IV

66. Match List-I with List-II.

List-I	List-II
A. Samacariya	I. Transformation wholeness
B. Tanha	II. Desire
C. Satori	III. Healthy virtuous
D. Sammadithhi	IV. Thinking

Choose the correct answer from the options given below.

	A	B	C	D		A	B	C	D
(1)	III	I	II	III	(2)	IV	I	II	III
(3)	III	II	I	IV	(4)	II	III	I	IV

67. Match List-I with List-II.

List-I	List-II
A. Grounded Theory	I. Lives of individual studied and retold to develop a chronology
B. Phenomoenological Research	II. Studying intact cultural group in national setting.
C. Narrative Research	III. Deriving a general abstract theory through views of participants
D. Ethnography	IV. Understanding lived experiences of a small member of participants

Choose the correct answer from the options given below

	A	B	C	D		A	B	C	D
(1)	III	I	IV	II	(2)	II	IV	I	III
(3)	II	I	IV	III	(4)	III	IV	I	II

68. Match List-I with List II.

List-I	List-II
A. Preferred method for determining item bias	I. Slope
B. Coefficient for correlating two absolutely dichotomous variables	II. Intercept
C. The place where the regression line crosses the y-axis	III. Phi coefficient
D. The expected change in Y for every one unit change in X on the regression line	IV. Item characteristic curve

Choose the correct answer from the options given below.

	A	B	C	D		A	B	C	D
(1)	IV	III	II	I	(2)	III	IV	II	I
(3)	I	III	II	IV	(4)	I	II	IV	III

69. Match List-I with List-II.

List-I	List-II
A. Effortful processing	I. Associates new and old information and solves problem
B. Spacing Effect	II. Encoding of space, time and word meanings
C. Working Memory	III. Remembering the concepts of psychology
D. Automatic Processing	IV. Better-long term retention through distributed practice

Choose the correct answer from the options given below.

	A	B	C	D		A	B	C	D
(1)	I	II	III	IV	(2)	II	III	I	IV
(3)	III	IV	I	II	(4)	IV	II	III	I

70. Match List-I with List-II.

List-I	List-II
A. Young-Helmholtz theory	I. Colour perception
B. Place theory	II. High pitches
C. Touch sensations	III. Rubber-hand illusion
D. Gate control theory	IV. Pain

Choose the correct answer from the options given below.

	A	B	C	D		A	B	C	D
(1)	IV	III	II	I	(2)	I	II	III	IV
(3)	II	I	III	IV	(4)	III	IV	I	II

71. Match List-I with List-II.

List-I	List-II
A. Sigmund Freud	I. Genetic view
B. B.F. Skinner	II. Psychoanalytic view
C. Carl Rogers	III. Behavioural view
D. Hans Eysenck	IV. Humanistic view

Choose the correct answer from the options given below.

	A	B	C	D		A	B	C	D
(1)	IV	I	II	III	(2)	II	III	I	IV
(3)	II	III	IV	I	(4)	I	II	IV	III

72. Match List-I with List-II.

List-I	List-II
A. Manic Disorder	I. Frontal-striatal region of the brain implicated
B. Panic Disorder	II. Elevated expansive mood and increased energy
C. Schizophrenia	III. Heightened awareness of emotion specific stimulus
D. ADHD	IV. Delusion, hallucination, incoherent speech

Choose the correct answer from the options given below.

	A	B	C	D		A	B	C	D
(1)	II	III	IV	I	(2)	I	IV	II	III
(3)	III	II	I	IV	(4)	IV	III	II	I

73. Match List-I with List-II.

List-I	List-II
A. Object Permanence	I. Pre operation
B. Abstract thinking	II. Sensory motor
C. Ego centrism	III. Concrete operation
D. Conservation	IV. Formal operation

Choose the correct answer from the options given below.

	A	B	C	D		A	B	C	D
(1)	II	IV	III	I	(2)	II	IV	I	III
(3)	II	I	IV	III	(4)	IV	III	II	I

74. Match List-I with List-II.

List-I	List-II
A. Rosenstock	I. Protective Motivation Theory
B. Rogers	II. Health Belief Model
C. Fishbein	III. Self-Regulation Model
D. Leventhal	IV. Theory of Reasoned Action

Choose the correct answer from the options given below.

	A	B	C	D		A	B	C	D
(1)	II	I	IV	III	(2)	II	III	I	IV
(3)	II	IV	I	III	(4)	II	I	III	IV

75. Match List-I with List-II.

List-I	List-II
A. Pratyahara	I. Concentration
B. Dharana	II. Attaining Oneness or Integration
C. Dhyana	III. Control over thoughts
D. Samadhi	IV. Meditation

Choose the correct answer from the options given below.

	A	B	C	D		A	B	C	D
(1)	II	I	IV	III	(2)	III	II	I	IV
(3)	III	I	IV	II	(4)	II	I	III	IV

76. Arrange Erik Eriksons stages of psychosocial development and basic strengths.

I. Trust *vs* mistrust
II. Initiative *vs* guilt
III. Industriousness *vs* inferiority
IV. Autonomy *vs* doubt and shame

Choose the correct answer from the options given below.

(1) I, IV, II, III (2) I, III, II, IV
(3) I, II, IV, III (4) II, III, I, IV

77. Prepare the steps involved in Action Research in correct sequence with reference to behavioural science.

I. Action II. Observation
III. Plan IV. Reflection

Choose the correct answer from the options given below

(1) I, II, III, IV (2) II, III, I, IV
(3) III, I, II, IV (4) III, II, IV, I

78. Arrange the following statements in the correct sequence of the movement of ions during the action potential.

I. Na^+ channels open, Na^+ begins to enter cell.
II. K^+ continues to leave cell, causes membrane potential to return to resting level.
III. K^+ channels open, K^+ begins to leave cell.
IV. K^+ channels close, Na^+ channels reset.
V. Na^+ channels become refractory, no more Na^+ enters the cell.

Choose the correct answer from the options given below.

(1) I, II, III, IV, V (2) I, III, V, II, IV
(3) I, V, III, IV, II (4) IV, V, I, III, II

79. Correctly arrange the components of emotion as explained in the two-factor theory of Schachter and Singer, 1962.

I. Stimulus
II. Cognitive appraisal of arousal
III. General physiological arousal
IV. Subjective experience of emotion

Choose the correct answer from the options given below.

(1) I, II, III, IV
(2) I, III, II, IV
(3) IV, I, III, II
(4) III, II, IV, I

80. What would be the correct order of the steps involved in prosocial behaviour?

I. Accept the responsibility for helping
II. Noticing something unusual
III. Decision about possession of required knowledge or skills
IV. Interpreting the event as emergency
V. Deciding to actually help

Choose the correct answer from the options given below.

(1) I, III, II, IV, V (2) II, IV, I, III, V
(3) II, IV, III, I, V (4) V, II, IV, III, I

81. Arrange the following in sequence as per development model of counselling.

I. Identification of blind spots
II. Brain storming
III. Developing possibilities
IV. Force-field analysis

Choose the correct answer from the options given below.

(1) I, III, II, IV (2) II, III, I, IV
(3) I, III, IV, II (4) I, II, IV, III

82. Arrange the following physiological response to stress sequentially.

I. Release of Adrenocorticotropin hormone from pituitary gland
II. Release of CRF from hypothalamus
III. Perception of stress
IV. Suppression of immune system functioning
V. Glurcorticoid release from Adrenal gland

Choose the correct answer from the options given below.

(1) II, III, V, I, IV (2) III, II, I, V, IV
(3) I, III, IV, II, V (4) V, IV, III, I, II

83. Arrange 'Pancha Kosha' in order.

I. Annamaya Kosha
II. Manomaya Kosha
III. Vijnanamaya Kosha
IV. Pranamaya Kosha
V. Anandamaya Kosha

Choose the correct answer from the options given below.

(1) I, V, II, IV, III (2) I, IV, II, III, V
(3) I, II, IV, III, V (4) I, III, II, V, IV

84. Arrange the emergence of following leadership approaches in a chronological order.

I. Behavioural approach
II. Transformational approach
III. Trait approach
IV. Contingency Approach

Choose the correct answer from the options given below.
(1) I, III, II, IV (2) I, III, IV, II
(3) III, I, II, IV (4) III, I, IV, II

85. Sequentially arrange the sections of the vertebrae of the spinal column from top to bottom.
I. Thoracic vertebrae
II. Sacral vertebrae
III. Cervical vertebrae
IV. Lumbar vertebrae
Choose the correct answer from the options given below.
(1) I, IV, II, III (2) III, I, IV, II
(3) I, III, II, IV (4) II, I, IV, III

86. Given below are two statements, one is labelled as Assertion (A) and the other is labelled as Reason (R).
Assertion (A) There are five universal human needs according to reality therapy.
Reason (R) These needs are-survival, love and belonging, power, freedom and fun.
In the light of the above statements, choose the most appropriate answer from the options given below.
(1) Both A and R are true and R is the correct explanation of A.
(2) Both A and R are true, but R is not the correct explanation of A.
(3) A is true, but R is false.
(4) A is false, but R is true.

87. Given below are two statements, one is labelled as Assertion (A) and the other is labelled as Reason (R).
Assertion (A) To eliminate the impact of an extraneous independent variable, the researcher can choose participants who are homogeneous on that independent variable.
Reason (R) Matching is one of the method to control extraneous variance.
In the light of the above statements, choose the most appropriate answer from the options given below.
(1) Both A and R are true and R is the correct explanation of A.
(2) Both A and R are true, but R is not the correct explanation of A.
(3) A is true, but R is false.
(4) A is false, but R is true.

88. Given below are two statements, one is labelled as Assertion (A) and the other is labelled as Reason (R).
Assertion (A) Monozygotic twins are called fraternal twins, who share half of their genes. Both members of the twins may be males or females.
Reason (R) Dizygotic twins develop from two different eggs and share the genes like a brother and sister. One of the twins may be a male and the other one may be a female.
In the light of the above statements, choose the most appropriate answer from the options given below.
(1) Both A and R are true and R is the correct explanation of A.
(2) Both A and R are true, but R is not the correct explanation of A.
(3) A is true, but R is false.
(4) A is false, but R is true.

89. Given below are two statements, one is labelled as Assertion (A) and the other is labelled as Reason (R).
Assertion (A) Project Head Start and other preschool quality programme boost children's chances of success in future by increasing their school readiness.
Reason (R) Genes and experience together determine cognitive and social skills.
In the light of the above statements choose the most appropriate answer from the options given below.
(1) Both A and R are true and R is the correct explanation of A.
(2) Both A and R are true, but R is not the correct explanation of A.
(3) A is true, but R is false.
(4) A is false, but R is true.

90. Given below are two statements.
Statement (I) Motivation is a condition that energizes behaviour but gives no direction.
Statement (II) Motivational States arise only from external incentive factors.
In the light of the above statements, choose the most appropriate answer from the options given below.
(1) Both statement I and Statement II are correct.
(2) Both statement I and Statement II are incorrect.
(3) Statement I is correct, but Statement II is incorrect.
(4) Statement I is incorrect, but Statement II is correct.

91. What is the degrees of freedom for the test?
(1) 10 (2) 11 (3) 6 (4) 5

92. What statistical test should be used to analyse the data?
(1) Mann-Whitney U test
(2) Wilcoxon signed Rank test
(3) Correlated 't' test
(4) Independent 't' test

93. Rejection of null hypothesis indicates
(1) Participation in meditation leads to significant difference in well-being scores
(2) Participation in meditation leads to just above the well-being score after meditation
(3) Participation in meditation leads to lower well-being scores
(4) Participation in meditation has no significant effect

94. Which of the following is correct about directional hypothesis?
(1) Meditation has effect on well-being
(2) Meditation has positive effect on well-being
(3) Meditation has both positive and negative effect on well-being
(4) Meditation has direction for well-being

95. Which of the following is correct about interval scale?
(1) Identity, magnitude equal unit size and absolute zero are the properties of this scale.
(2) Identity and equal unit size are its properties
(3) Identity, magnitude and equal unit size are its properties
(4) Identity and magnitude are the properties of this scale

96. The theory of Vygotsky is called
(1) Cultural theory of cognitive development
(2) Social theory of cognitive development
(3) Social cultural theory of cognitive development
(4) Bio social cultural theory of cognitive development

97. The ZPD stands for
(1) Zone of Postnatal Development
(2) Zone of Proximal Development
(3) Zone of Proximodistal Development
(4) Zone of Proximal Distance

98. ZPD is defined by Vygotsky as
(1) the region of sensitivity for learning characterised by the difference between the developmental level when the child is working alone and the level he/she is capable of reaching with the aid of an adult.
(2) the region of difference between inability to use a known dung and benefit from the use of such a strategy.
(3) the region of learning what a child has learnt from experience and knows about the world in general.
(4) the region of ability to fit into change and choose environments that best fulfill the child's needs and desires to learn from society and culture.

99. The instructional process in which the more knowledgeable partner adjusts the amount and type of support he offers to fit with the child's learning needs over the course of interaction is called
(1) Tacit knowledge (2) Social referencing
(3) Pragmatics (4) Scaffolding

100. The psychological tools and signs such as language, counting, mnemonics, algebric symbols, art and writing that facilitate and direct thinking process is called by Vygotsky as
(1) Moderators (2) Mediators
(3) Confounders (4) Facilitators

ANSWERS

1	(2)	2	(4)	3	(1)	4	(2)	5	(2)	6	(3)	7	(2)	8	(2)	9	(3)	10	(2)
11	(3)	12	(4)	13	(1)	14	(3)	15	(4)	16	(1, 3)	17	(1)	18	(2)	19	(4)	20	(2)
21	(2)	22	(4)	23	(2)	24	(3)	25	(2)	26	(4)	27	(3)	28	(1)	29	(2)	30	(2)
31	(2)	32	(1)	33	(3)	34	(3)	35	(4)	36	(1)	37	(1)	38	(2)	39	(3)	40	(3)
41	(2)	42	(3)	43	(3)	44	(2)	45	(2)	46	(4)	47	(1)	48	(2)	49	(2)	50	(2)
51	(3)	52	(2)	53	(4)	54	(4)	55	(4)	56	(3)	57	(4)	58	(3)	59	(1)	60	(3)
61	(1)	62	(2)	63	(*)	64	(4)	65	(3)	66	(3)	67	(4)	68	(1)	69	(3)	70	(2)
71	(3)	72	(1)	73	(2)	74	(1)	75	(3)	76	(1)	77	(3)	78	(2)	79	(2)	80	(2)
81	(1)	82	(2)	83	(2)	84	(4)	85	(2)	86	(1)	87	(2)	88	(4)	89	(1)	90	(2)
91	(3)	92	(3)	93	(1)	94	(2)	95	(3)	96	(3)	97	(2)	98	(1)	99	(4)	100	(2)

** Dropped by UCG/NTA*

Solved Paper

2022

Psychology (Paper-2)
Solved Paper, October 2022

General Instructions

1. There are total one hundred questions in this paper. Each question carries 2 marks.
2. All questions are compulsory.

---

1. In Weber's Law, $\frac{\Delta I}{I} = K$, ΔI stands for?

(1) Noticeable difference
(2) Point of subjective equality
(3) Constant proportion
(4) Differential threshold

2. Rational concept is that which involves

(1) a combination of several attributes
(2) relationship among elements in a situation
(3) at least one element from a number of elements
(4) All the above

3. What will happen with the continuous stress?

(1) Stage of exhaustion
(2) Body resources drained
(3) Stress hormones depleted
(4) All of the above

4. What percentage of participants fully obeyed the experimenter's command to deliver a 450-volt shock to the learner in the experiment detailed in the text?

(1) 5% (2) 20%
(3) 35% (4) 65%

5. Which of the following neurous of cortex produce most EEG?

(1) Pyramidal (2) Cuboidal
(3) Tubular (4) Cylindrical

6. According to Kohlberg .... and ..... are the major reasons of moral behaviour during the stage of conventional morality.

(1) gaining acceptance; getting rewards
(2) avoiding censure by others; achieving justice
(3) gaining acceptance; avoiding censure by others
(4) avoiding censure by others; achieving justice

7. Who is known for the development of the drive theory?

(1) Clark Hull (2) Dweck
(3) Susan Harter (4) Piaget

8. Implicit thinking involves mainly

(1) motor activity
(2) sensory activity
(3) reflex activity
(4) glandular activity

9. Working memory involves which of the following?

(1) Storage capacity and Biographical information
(2) Semantic information and Processing capacity
(3) Storage capacity and Processing capacity
(4) Biographical information and Semantic information

10. Which famous psychologist applied gestalt principles to explain his theory of personality?

(1) Kurt Lewin (2) Abraham Maslow
(3) Freud (4) Guildford

11. What is 'Supra mentalisation' in integral Yoga?
(1) Realisation of enlightenment
(2) Realisation of the supermind
(3) Realisation of illumination
(4) All of the above

12. In instrumental conditioning
(1) reinforcement is given irrespective of the production of an appropriate response.
(2) reinforcement is given before the on set of the response.
(3) appropriate response is immediately followed by reinforcement.
(4) reinforcement is not given.

13. Mental images
(1) represent abstract ideas
(2) consist entirely of unconscious information
(3) have a picture like quality
(4) always prototype

14. Who said, "psychology has a long past but only a short history"?
(1) Hermann Ebbinghaus
(2) Skinner
(3) Aristotle
(4) Watson

15. Which of the following factors influence developmental process?
(1) Normative influences
(2) Education and Training
(3) Hereditary factors
(4) All of the above

16. With the help of classical conditioning, emotional responses
(1) are learned best
(2) are equal to other responses
(3) are learned very slowly
(4) are learned only when US (unconditioned sitmulus) is powerful

17. Who discovered a new device pupilometrics?
(1) Wundt
(2) Eckhard Hess
(3) Friensen
(4) Engen

18. According to George Polya problem solving means
(1) finding way around an obstacle.
(2) it is specific achievement of intelligence.
(3) attaining an aim that was not immediately understandable.
(4) All of the above

19. We are more likely to experience which of the following during adolescence than at any other time in our lives?
(1) Moodiness
(2) Parent-child conflicts
(3) Risky behaviour
(4) All of the above

20. A network of associated facts and concepts that make out general knowledge of the world is referred to as
(1) episodic memory
(2) explicit memory
(3) implicit memory
(4) semantic memory

21. Which ligand is introduced in body during PET scan?
(1) Chlorine-4 (2) Helium-20
(3) Fluorine-18 (4) All of these

22. Social psychology focuses on .... and their ....
(1) individuals; feelings
(2) groups; experiences
(3) people, feelings
(4) people; thoughts

23. Which of the following is an application of operant conditioning?
(1) Aversive conditioning
(2) Behaviour modification
(3) Systematic desensitisation
(4) Transfer of learning

24. Match List I with List II.

List I (Psychologist)	**List II** (Contributions)
A. Viktor Frankl	I. Shadow
B. Rollo May	II. Logotherapy
C. Fritz Pearls	III. Paradoxical intentions
D. Carl Rogers	IV. Gestalt therpy

Codes

	A	B	C	D		A	B	C	D
(1)	I	II	III	IV	(2)	IV	III	I	II
(3)	III	II	IV	I	(4)	III	I	II	IV

25. Consider the following statements.
I. The semi-interquartile range measures the spread of the middle 50% of scores.
II. Standard deviation is the measure of dispersion of results from the mean result.

Codes
(1) Only I (2) Only II
(3) Both I and II (4) None of these

26. Arrange in order the scientific thoughts according to their emergence.

I. Rationalism II. Positivism
III. Critical research IV. Post-positivism

Codes

(1) I, II, III, IV (2) IV, I II, III
(3) I, II, IV, III (4) II, I, IV, III

27. Abstract, idealised representation that captures an average or typical member of a category of things is referred to as

(1) Exemplar (2) Prototype
(3) Concept (4) Schemes

28. Who among the following presented decisive experimental evidence for exploration and curiosity to be motivational concepts?

(1) Fantz (2) Lorenz
(3) Gibson (4) Harlow

29. In the present era of competitive marketing some of the companies are offering door-to-door sales services. In such case which kind of reinforcement schedule is practiced by the company for their sales executives?

(1) Fixed-ratio schedule
(2) Fixed-interval schedule
(3) Variable-ratio schedule
(4) Variable-interval schedule

30. Which of the following is most effective in conditioning?

(1) Backward Conditioning
(2) Delayed Conditioning
(3) Simultaneous Conditioning
(4) Trace Conditioning

31. Out of the following, which approach used in assessment of intelligence, is oldest one?

(1) Psychometric Approach
(2) Biological Approach
(3) Culture Fair
(4) Chronometric Analysis

32. Ruby was listening to a tape recording of a famous speech that was played backward. She just heard gibberish until a classmate said the phrase 'meet me in St Louis' was clearly spoken. The tape was rewound and as Ashlynn listened this time, she also clearly heard the same phase. Ruby's ability to detect the phrase the second time through the tape illustrates

(1) the opponent-process model of perception
(2) the top-down processing model of perception
(3) the bottom-up processing model of perception
(4) the electric model of perception

33. The DSM-IV-TR definition of mental disorder is perhaps the best current definition because

(1) it includes information about both violation of social norms and dysfunction.
(2) it includes many components none of which can alone account for mental disorder.
(3) it is part of the current diagnostic system.
(4) it recognises the limits of our current understanding.

34. Milly generally likes to go home to visit her family during vacation. How, after her father tells her she must be home during spring vacation, Milly decides to remain at college. We can probably best understand Milly's behaviour in terms' of

(1) reaction formation
(2) regression
(3) psychological reactance
(4) self-serving bias

35. Arrange the following steps involved in test construction in chronological order

I. specifying construct of interest
II. evaluating reliability and validity of test
III. choosing a method
IV. deciding test's function
V. designing item content

Codes

(1) I, IV III, V, II
(2) I, III, IV, V, II
(3) I, IV, III, II, V
(4) I, III, IV, II, V

36. Which of the following statements is/are correct?

I. Women are easier to convince.
II. Referent informational influence is a concept derived of social identity theory.
III. Social identity theory does not give rise to inter-group discrimination.
IV. Henri Tajfel proposed social identify theory.

Select the correct answer using the codes given below.

(1) I and II (2) II and III
(3) III and IV (4) II and IV

37. Arrange the phases of Cooperative Inquiry in sequence of their occurrence.

I. Experiences leading to new fields
II. Reframe
III. Reflection
IV. Action

Codes

(1) I, II, III, IV (2) IV, III, II, I
(3) III, IV, I, II (4) I, III, II, IV

38. Match List I with List II.

List I (Concept)	List II (Researchers)
A. Flashbulb memory	I. Broadbent
B. Organisation as in library	II. Brown and Kulik
C. VLTM	III. Bahrick and Bahrick
D. STM	IV. Wickens

Codes

	A	B	C	D		A	B	C	D
(1)	II	I	IV	III	(2)	II	I	III	IV
(3)	I	II	III	IV	(4)	IV	I	III	II

39. Depending upon the task characteristics, there is a gradual transition from simpler forms of learning to the level of higher complex ones. These different forms are

I. Establishment of simple S-R relationships

II. Acquiring motor and verbal skills

III. Concept formation

IV. Problem-solving

The correct order of learning sequence is

(1) I, IV, II, III (2) I, II, III, IV

(3) II, IV, I, III (4) II, III, IV, I

40. "The most important thing a psychologist can study is how a behaviour or thought helps a person navigate the world, rather than how that thought comes to be or what it is made of." This viewpoint probably comes from somebody who believes in what historical theoretical approach?

(1) Structuralism (2) Functionalism

(3) Gestalt (4) Psychoanalysis

41. Consider the following statements.

I. Guilford classify mental abilities the same way chemical element classified in periodic table.

II. Mednick said that true creativity is the ability to think a remote idea.

Which of the statements given above is/are correct?

(1) Only I (2) Only II

(3) I and II (4) None of these

42. Match List I with List II and select the correct answer by choosing from the codes given below.

List I (Books)	List II (Authors)
A. Toward a Psychology of Being	I. May
B. A Way of Being	II. Maslow
C. Man's Search for Meaning	III. Rogers
D. Love and Will	IV. Frankl

Codes

	A	B	C	D
(1)	I	II	III	IV
(2)	II	III	IV	I
(3)	III	II	I	IV
(4)	IV	I	II	III

43. Sanam has just finished a long exhausting 6 mile run. She and her friend Jamal are gasing at a hill they need a climb to get back to their car Jamal asks Sanam, "Gee how steep do you think that hill is"? Based on research by Proffitt and his colleagues Sanam is likely to

(1) make a reasonably accurate estimate of the hill's slant, as most people do.

(2) underestimate the hill's slant, as most people do.

(3) coverestimate the hill's slant, but to a lesser degree than she would have before her exhausting run.

(4) overestimate the hill's slant to an even greater degree than she would have before her exhausting run.

44. Read each of the following two statements labelled as Assertion (A) and Reason (R) and indicate your answer using the codes given below.

Assertion (A) Both, context dependent memory and state dependent retrieval refer to the ease with which one can recall information in a similar context or state as when it was acquired.

Reason (R) According to encoding specificity principle retrieval of information is successful to the extent that the retrieval cues match the cues the learner used during the learning phase.

Codes

(1) Both A and R are true and R is the correct explanation of A.

(2) Both A and R are true, but R is not the correct explanation of A.

(3) A is true, but R is false.

(4) A is false, but R is true.

45. Consider the following statements.

I. Median is preferred method for highly systematic distributions.

II. The mode is most used measure of central tendency.

Which among the above is/are correct?

(1) Only I

(2) Only II

(3) Both I and II

(4) None of the above

46. Which of the following is not consequence of Spreadman's Theory?

(1) The correlation between different measures of intelligence will be positive.

(2) The correlation between measures of intelligence will be equal to $r_{1g} \times r_{2g}$, where 1 and 2 represent the two different measures and g represents general factor.

(3) The correlation between to measures of intelligence will be equal to $r_{1g} + r_{2g}$, where 1 and 2 represent the two different measures and g represents general factor.

(4) The law of tetred difference will mold for four measures of intelligence.

47. Arrange the steps in order in Pavlov's experiment

I. Selecting stimulus and response

II. Establishing classical conditioning

III. Testing for Conditioning

Codes

(1) I, II, III (2) III, I, II

(3) II, I, III (4) I, III, II

48. Match List I with List II.

List I	List II
A. Preparation	I. Ideas are ascertained, checked and reassured by themselves and by other confirming the validity of their hypothesis.
B. Incubation	II. 'Happy thoughts' do not occur to lazy persons; they arise in well prepared and well stocked minds.
C. Illumination	III. The climax of the process of creative thinking dawns the saving-guiding idea, which is the forerunner of the final solution.
D. Verification	IV. The 'hatching' period in creative thought process us characterised by restlessness and poorly coordinated activity accompanied by a feeling of unease and frustration through unconscious thought processes.

Codes

	A	B	C	D
(1)	II	III	IV	I
(2)	I	III	IV	II
(3)	III	II	I	IV
(4)	III	IV	I	II

49. Which of the following sets of stage models of health behaviour is in correct chronological order?

I. People are unaware of health issues.

II. People are aware of the issue but never thought about adopting the precaution.

III. People decide against adopting the.

IV. People act on their decision.

Codes

(1) I, II, III, IV (2) I, II, IV, III

(3) II, I, III, IV (4) II, I, IV, III

50. What is considered statistically 'abnormal' for a person to score in an IQ Test?

(1) Below 55 (2) Above 145

(3) Both 1 and 2 (4) None of these

51. Muller-Lyer illusion exists in cultures in which there are

(1) more men than women

(2) more women than men

(3) lots of trees

(4) buildings with lots of corners

52. Functionalism influenced which two major areas in psychology?

(1) Emotion and cognition

(2) Thinking and reasoning

(3) Learning and motivation

(4) Perception and learning

53. Perceived fairness of the amount and rewards among individuals refers to while perceived fairness of the ways used for rewards and pays refers to

(1) organisational justice distributive justice

(2) equity organisational justice

(3) distributive justice; procedural justice

(4) procedural justice; distributive justice

54. Consider the following statements.

I. A set of source can be summarised by a set of central tendency (or average) of the scores.

II. A measure of dispersion (or spread) of the scores.

Codes

(1) Only I (2) Only II

(3) Both I and II (4) None of these

55. Charles Darwin proposed that natural selection leads to the development of characteristics most suited to the survival and reproduction of a species.

His theory has most influenced which branch of psychology?

(1) Humanism

(2) Evolutionary psychology

(3) Cognitive psychology

(4) Behaviourism

56. To be an accurate eyewitness, a person must pass the following stages. Arrange the following in chronological order.

I. Acquisition II. Retrieval

III. Storage

Codes

(1) I, II, III (2) II, I, III
(3) I, III, II (4) III, I, II

57. **The fact that cultural groups with less exposure to carpentered buildings are less susceptible to the Muller-Lyer illusion suggests that**

(1) not all cultures test perceptual hypothesis.
(2) people in technologically advanced cultures are more gullible.
(3) optical illusions can be experienced only by cultures that have been exposed to the concept of optical illusions.
(4) perceptual inferences can be shaped by experience.

58. **Match List I with List II.**

List I (Measures)	List II (Objectives)
A. Mode	I. Purpose of the test
B. Quartile deviation	II. Consistency of test scores
C. Reliability	III. Measure of variability
D. Validity	IV. Measure of central tendency

Codes

	A	B	C	D
(1)	III	IV	II	I
(2)	IV	III	II	I
(3)	III	IV	I	II
(4)	IV	III	I	II

59. **In 'Signal Detection Theory', which of the following determinants are assumed?**

I. Observer's sensitivity
II. Sensory threshold
III. Response bias
IV. Decision bias

Codes

(1) Only I (2) I and III
(3) I, III and IV (4) II and III

60. **Consider the following statements.**

I. According to Jensen, "Intelligence is essentially another activity or function of the individual like blood pressure, temperature, etc.
II. Intelligence test provides accurate result.

Which of the statements given above is/are correct?

(1) Only I
(2) Only II
(3) Both I and II
(4) Neither I nor II

61. **Arrange the following steps of decision-making in order.**

I. Developing and weighing the options
II. Plan and execute
III. Take follow up action
IV. Choosing lest possible option

Codes

(1) I, II, III, IV (2) II, III, IV, I
(3) I, IV, II, III (4) IV, II, III, I

62. **The relative apparent motion of object in the visual field as the viewer moves the head is called**

(1) Image retina system
(2) Accommodation
(3) Motion parallax
(4) The eye-head system

63. **The chronological age that most typically corresponds to a given level of performance is called**

(1) Intelligence Quotient
(2) Maturation
(3) Mental age
(4) None of the above

64. **Which one of the following statistic is used for assessing the test-item bias?**

(1) Item-remainder correlation
(2) Differential item functioning
(3) Construct validity
(4) Multidimensional scaling

65. **Patients with damage to the frontal lobes behave as if they lack control systems that monitor their processing resources appropriately. They are said to suffer from**

(1) Gertsman Syndrome
(2) Dysexecutive Syndrome
(3) Korsakoff's Syndrome
(4) None of the above

66. **Which of the following is not a standard physiological measure of sleep?**

(1) Electrooculogram
(2) Electromyogram
(3) Electrocardiogram
(4) Electroencephalogram

67. **In heightened emotional states, the following functions are not triggered by sympathetic Nervous System activity.**

I. Perspiration
II. Heightened pulse rate
III. Digestion
IV. Pupillary dilation

Codes

(1) Only III (2) III and IV
(3) I, II and III (4) I, III and IV

68. Arrange the following tests with respect to their ability to elicit projective responses from low to high.

I. Sentence Completion Test
II. Rorschach Inkblot Test
III. Rosenzweig Picture Frustration Study
IV. Thematic Apperception Test

Codes
(1) II, IV, III, I (2) I, III, IV, II
(3) IV, II, I, III (4) II, I, IV, III

69. When the action potential reaches the end of the axon terminals, it causes the release of
(1) an electric spark that sets off the next neuron
(2) positively charged ions that excite the next cell
(3) negatively charged ions that inhibit the next cell
(4) neurotransmitters that excite or inhibit the next cell

70. An interval scale of measurement contains
I. properties of normal and ordinal scales
II. true zero point
III. comparable differences between different intervals of the scale
IV. a minimum requirement for use of parametric tests

Codes
(1) I, II, III and IV (2) I and II
(3) I, II and IV (4) I, III and IV

71. Which of the following are not nuclei of Thalamus?
I. Internal lamina
II. Anterior nucleus
III. Ventromedial nucleus
IV. Paraventricular nucleus

Codes
(1) I and II (2) II and III
(3) III and IV (4) I and III

72. The theories of intelligence appeared in which one of the following orders?
(1) Binet-Simon, Thurstone, RB Cattell, Spearman
(2) Binet-Simon, Spearman, Thurstone, RB Cattell
(3) Spearman, Binet-Simon, Thurstone, RB Cattell
(4) RB Cattell, Binet-Simon, Thurstone, Spearman

73. .... makes neurons stand out visibly depicting which neurons are active, whereas .... uses antibodies attached to a dye to identify cellular component such as receptors, neurotransmitters or enzymes.
(1) Immunocytochemistry; Autoradiography
(2) Autoradiography; Immunocytochemistry
(3) Myelin staining; Nissl Staining
(4) Nissl Staining; Myelin Staining

74. Which of the following scaling methods have been developed by Thurstone?
I. Method of paired comparison
II. Method of summated ratings
III. Method of successive intervals
IV. Equal appearing intervals method

Codes
(1) Only II (2) II and III
(3) I, II and IV (4) II, III and IV

75. Given below are two statements, one is labelled as Assertion (A) and the other labelled as Reason (R).

Assertion (A) Subliminal perception implies detection of a stimulus with a magnitude for below the absolute threshold.

Reason (R) Receptors always receive information and that is always perceived.

Codes
(1) Both A and R are true and R is the correct explanation of A.
(2) Both A and R are true, but R is not the correct explanation of A.
(3) A is true, but R is false.
(4) A is false, but R is true.

76. Out of the following theories of intelligence which one is regarded as latest one?
(1) Sternberg's theory
(2) Mayer and Salovey theory
(3) Jensen's theory
(4) Cattell's theory

77. Which of the following do not belong to laws of perceptual grouping?
I. Law of figure and ground
II. Law of good continuation
III. Law of common fate
IV. Law of closure
V. Law of proximity

Codes
(1) I and V (2) II and IV
(3) III and V (4) I and III

78. Which of the following is/are correct in Rogerian therapy?
I. The therapist is supportive and non-directive.
II. It is the client and not the therapist who best understands the problem and in what direction the therapy should proceed.
III. The therapist can sense the client's tensions and incongruent feelings and reflect them back to the client.

Codes

(1) Only I (2) I and II
(3) I and III (4) I, II and III

79. Identify the correct concepts related with Cattell's theory of personality.

I. Dynamic Lattice
II. Specification Equation
III. Orthogonal Rotation
IV. Ergs

Codes

(1) II, III and IV
(3) I, II and IV
(3) II and IV
(4) I, II, III and IV

80. Which of the following tests are considered to be culture-fair tests of intelligence?

I. Cattell's Culture-Fair Test of Intelligence
II. Raven's Progressive Matrices
III. Wechsler's Intelligence Scale for Children
IV. Goodenough-Harris Test

Codes

(1) Only I (2) I and II
(3) I, II and III (4) I, II and IV

81. Given below are two statements, one is labelled as Assertion (A) and the other labelled as Reason (R). Choose your answer using the codes given below.

Assertion (A) Algorithm is a logical rule that guarantees solving a particular problem.

Reason (R) One can find the solution even to complex problems by following step by step procedure.

Codes

(1) Both A and R are true and R is the correct explanation of A.
(2) Both A and R are true, but R is not the correct explanation of A.
(3) A is true, but R is false.
(4) A is false, but R is true.

82. Match List I with List II.

List I (Design)	List II (Full forms)
A. ANOVA	I. Multivariant Analysis of Variance
B. MANOVA	II. Analysis of Variance
C. ANCOVA	III. Analysis of Covariance

Codes

	A	B	C		A	B	C
(1)	I	II	III	(2)	II	I	III
(3)	I	III	II	(4)	II	III	I

83. In an experiment the stimuli were presented to the subjects in certain order and after the presentation of stimuli their order was disturbed. In the test phase the subjects were needed to set them in the presented order. Which of the following methods was used in this experiment?

(1) Recognition (2) Relearning
(3) Reconstruction (4) Recall

84. Given below are two statements, the first labelled as Assertion (A) and the other labelled as Reason (R). Indicate your answer using the codes given below.

Assertion (A) Resolution of Oedipus complex is the main reason for the development of Super Ego.

Reason (R) Resolution of Oedipus complex involves a child's identification with the same gender parent.

Codes

(1) Both A and R are true and R is the correct explanation of A.
(2) Both A and R are true, but R is not the correct explanation of A.
(3) A is true, but R is false.
(4) A is false, but R is true.

85. Choose the right sequence of endocrine system.

(1) Hypothalamus → Cortico releasing hormone → Pancreas → Insulin.
(2) Pituitary gland → Adenocorticotrophic hormone → Adrenal gland → Epinephrine.
(3) Hypothalamus → Adenocorticotrophic hormone → Gonads → Androgens.
(4) Thyroid gland → Cortico releasing hormone → Hypothalamus → Thyroxin.

86. Match List I with List II.

List I (Strategies)	List II (Concepts)
A. Heuristic	I. Step by step
B. Algorithm	II. Sudden occurrence
C. Trial and Error	III. Rule of thumb
D. Insight	IV. Multiple attempts

Codes

	A	B	C	D
(1)	III	I	II	IV
(2)	II	IV	I	III
(3)	III	I	IV	II
(4)	II	IV	III	I

87. Match List I with List II and choose your answer using the codes given below.

List I (Neurotransmitter)	List II (Location)
A. Acetylcholine	I. Mid brain
B. Serotonin	II. Autonomic nervous system
C. Adrenalin	III. Brain stem
D. Dopamine	IV. Neuromuscular Junction

Codes

	A	B	C	D
(1)	I	II	III	IV
(2)	IV	III	II	I
(3)	III	II	I	IV
(4)	II	IV	I	III

88. Read each of the following statements Assertion (A) and Reason (R) and choose your answer using codes given below.

Assertion (A) Pre-operational child is incapable of performing operations.

Reason (R) Pre-operational child cannot mentally re-arrange a sequence of events into reverse order.

(1) Both A and R true and R is the correct explanation of A.
(2) Both A and R are true, but R is not the correct explanation of A.
(3) A is true, but R is false.
(4) A is false, but R is true.

89. Experience of failure followed by .... cognitions lead to depression. Choose your answer using the codes given below.

I. Internal attributions
II. Feeling of controllability
III. Hopelessness
IV. Stable attributions
V. Specific attributions

Codes

(1) I, III and IV (2) I, II and IV
(3) II, III and V (4) III, IV and V

90. Match List I with List II and choose your answer with the help of the codes given below.

List I	List II
A. Multi-store Model	I. Craik and Lockhart
B. Neural Network Model	II. Atkinson and Shiffrin
C. Levels of Processing Model	III. McClleland and Rumelhart
D. Encoding Specificity Principle	IV. Tulving

Codes

	A	B	C	D
(1)	IV	I	III	II
(2)	I	II	IV	III
(3)	III	IV	II	I
(4)	II	III	I	IV

Direction (*Q. Nos. 91-95*) *Read the passage given below and answer the following questions.*

One of the first experimental demonstrations of the effects of stimulus uncertainly in choice RT was provided by Markel continue as a single paragraph.

The result reflected an interesting regularity in the nature of RT, but the general applicability of this regularity did not become fully apparent until. Hick realised that the uncertainty produced by variations in the number of stimulus alternatives could be viewed in information theory terms by expressing the number of alternatives in bits. Consequently, he repeated Merkel's experiment using one to ten lamps arrayed in an irregular circle.

Hick found that in the language of information theory, RT was proportional to stimulus uncertainty. By and of itself, this was not a new discovery on Hick's part, it was merely a confirmation of Merkel's earlier finding , using a different scale for expressing the number of stimulus alternatives. However, by introducing the information metric into this problem, Hick made it possible to map a variety of ways of manipulating stimulus uncertainty into a common scale.

91. Who provided the first experimental demonstrations of the effects of stimulus uncertainty on choice RT?

(1) Markel (2) Hick
(3) Piter (4) Schlosberg

92. Which numerical is found in the stimuli?

(1) Arabic (2) English
(3) Roman (4) Arabic and Roman

93. Who repeated Merkel's experiment?

(1) Hick (2) Molber
(3) Rojer (4) Miller

94. In which procedure Hick repeated Merker's experiment?

(1) One to five lamps arranged in a regular circle
(2) One to ten lamps arranged in an irregular circle
(3) One to five lamps arranged in an irregular circle
(4) One to ten lamps arranged in regular circle

95. Hick found that in the arrangement information theory RT was proportionary to

(1) stimulus uncertainly
(2) stimulus certainly
(3) locus uncertainly
(4) locus certainly

Direction *(Q. Nos. 96-100) Read the passage given below and answer the following questions.*

A researcher hypothesised that a given drug would adversely affect the reaction tiforty subjects were tested for discriminatory reaction time. Each subject was then given a prescribed drug dosage (5 mg/kg body weight) and after appropriate time gap, the subject was retested for discriminatory reaction time. The time-interval between a ready signal and actual presentation of the stimulus was randomly varied from half a second to three seconds. For evaluating the mean difference on the reaction time, the researcher considered various statistical options like the test, analysis of variance, chi-square test, etc. and employed the appropriate techniques.

The mean difference was statistically significant (Mean without drug condition = 240 ms, SD = 20 and mean with drug condition = 210 ms, SD = 18). The statistical examination further revealed that the difference between the two standard deviations was insignificant. During the course of research, the researcher suspected that the effect of drug dosage would be different for discriminatory and simple reaction times.

For this purpose, researcher considered the different experimental designs options such as matched two group design, factorial design, analysis of covariance, variance design, quasi-experimental design etc. Finally, researcher selected the appropriate design to carry out the new investigation.

96. On the basis of above passage, what would you conclude about the variance?

(1) The two conditions have homogeneity of variance.
(2) The two conditions have heterogeneity of variance.
(3) We cannot conclude about the homogeneity of variance from the above data.
(4) It is necessary to apply an additional test to infer about homogeneity of variance.

97. For studying whether the effect of drug would be different for discriminatory and simple reactions, the appropriate design would be

(1) quasi-experimental design
(2) matched two-group design
(3) analysis of covariance design
(4) factorial design

98. For evaluating the mean differences, which of the following techniques would be appropriate?

I. T-test for independent samples
II. Repeated measures ANOVA
III. Chi-square test
IV. Paired samples test

Select the correct answer using the codes given below.

(1) Only IV (2) II and IV
(3) I, II and III (4) II, III and IV

99. On the basis of above information, what can you conclude about the researcher's hypothesis?

(1) The researcher's hypothesis is rejected
(2) The researcher's hypothesis is partially verified
(3) The researcher's hypothesis is accepted
(4) The data are inadequate to evaluate the researcher's hypothesis

100. Which of the following variable is/are not controlled variables?

I. Drug to body weight ratio
II. Foreperiod
III. Type of reaction
IV. Reaction time

Select the correct answer using the codes given below.

(1) Only IV (2) I and IV
(3) II and IV (4) I, II and IV

ANSWERS

1 (2)	2 (2)	3 (4)	4 (4)	5 (1)	6 (3)	7 (1)	8 (1)	9 (3)	10 (1)
11 (4)	12 (3)	13 (3)	14 (1)	15 (4)	16 (4)	17 (2)	18 (4)	19 (4)	20 (4)
21 (3)	22 (4)	23 (2)	24 (2)	25 (3)	26 (3)	27 (2)	28 (4)	29 (3)	30 (2)
31 (4)	32 (2)	33 (2)	34 (3)	35 (1)	36 (4)	37 (3)	38 (2)	39 (2)	40 (2)
41 (3)	42 (2)	43 (4)	44 (1)	45 (1)	46 (2)	47 (1)	48 (1)	49 (1)	50 (3)
51 (4)	52 (3)	53 (3)	54 (3)	55 (2)	56 (3)	57 (4)	58 (2)	59 (2)	60 (4)
61 (3)	62 (3)	63 (3)	64 (2)	65 (2)	66 (3)	67 (1)	68 (2)	69 (4)	70 (4)
71 (3)	72 (3)	73 (1)	74 (2)	75 (3)	76 (1)	77 (4)	78 (4)	79 (2)	80 (4)
81 (2)	82 (2)	83 (3)	84 (1)	85 (2)	86 (3)	87 (2)	88 (1)	89 (2)	90 (4)
91 (1)	92 (4)	93 (1)	94 (2)	95 (1)	96 (4)	97 (1)	98 (3)	99 (2)	100 (3)

Psychology (Paper-2)

Solved Paper, November 2021

General Instructions

1. There are total one hundred questions in this paper. Each question carries 2 marks.
2. All questions are compulsory.

1 Which theory determines poverty as a psychological problem of separated classes in society?

(a) Attribution theory
(b) Depletable self–control theory
(c) Distancing theory
(d) Multiple factor theory of poverty

2 A person's chronological age is 20 years and mental age is 16 years. What would be his IQ?

(a) 120 (b) 100
(c) 80 (d) 110

3 Match List I with List II

List I (Tests)	List II (Psychologists)
A. Creative Achievement Questionnaire	1. Carson-Peterson-Higgins
B. Ideational Behaviour Scale	2. Runco
C. Preference for Active Divergence Scale	3. Basadur
D. Consensual Assessment Technique	4. Amabile

Choose the correct answer from the options given below :

	A	B	C	D		A	B	C	D
(a)	1	2	3	4	(b)	2	1	4	3
(c)	3	4	1	2	(d)	4	3	2	1

4 Match List I with List II.

List I (Theoretical Perspective)	List II (Explanation)
A. Encoding Specificity Hypothesis	1. Does not endorse different memory storage
B. Retrieval Induced Forgetting	2. Supress unwanted memories
C. Schema Theory of Memory	3. Superiority of recognition over recall
D. Level of Processing Theory	4. Effect of meaning and knowledge on memory

Choose the correct answer from the options given below :

	A	B	C	D		A	B	C	D
(a)	2	4	1	3	(b)	3	2	4	1
(c)	1	2	3	4	(d)	4	1	2	3

5 Which of the following are features of Metacognition?

1. Encoding 2. Regulation
3. Monitoring 4. Evaluation

Choose the most appropriate answer from the options given below :

(a) 1, 2 and 3
(b) 1 and 2
(c) 3 and 2
(d) 2, 3 and 4

6 Young adults who return after leaving home for some period, to live in their middle aged parents home are known as

(a) Sandwich children
(b) Benevolent children
(c) Boomerang children
(d) Compliant children

7 Behaviour is a direct result of behavioural intentions, this is explained by which of the following?

(a) Theory of Reasoned Action
(b) Theory of Social Impact
(c) Equity Theory
(d) Correspondent Inference Theory

8 Memory that is thought to contain knowledge, facts, information, ideas that can be recalled or described in words, pictures, or symbols is called

(a) Procedural memory
(b) Episodic memory
(c) Semantic memory
(d) Declarative memory

9 Match List I with List II :

	List I (Type of communication in family therapy)		List II (Description)
A.	Congruent	1.	Carries an air of self-importance
B.	Placating	2.	Placing others above oneself
C.	Blaming	3.	Seeing the world with a lens of objectivity and coolness
D.	Super reasonable	4.	Reasonably flexible with a sense of connection

Choose the correct answer from the options given below :

	A	B	C	D
(a)	3	1	2	4
(b)	2	3	1	4
(c)	4	2	1	3
(d)	4	1	2	3

10 A woman who learns that she has been deprived of promotion to a higher job in a company, may storm into her boss's office and have temper tantrum. It exemplifies

(a) Sublimation
(b) Rationalisation
(c) Reaction Formation
(d) Regression

11 As per Socrates' Greek Philosophy, which of the following is not true about eudaimonia?

(a) It means living well or flourishing
(b) It is more than merely attaining pleasure
(c) Being virtuous is almost identical to eudaimonia
(d) Being virtuous does not guarantee eudaimonia

12 The person's failure to respond to the second stimulus while continuing to respond to the first stimulus is because of

(a) Event Related Potential (ERP)
(b) Psychological Refractory Period (PRP)
(c) Priming effect
(d) Excessive mental effort

13 Pattern of familial transmission of intelligence from one generation to other is investigated in which of the following?

(a) Linkage analysis studies
(b) Adoption studies
(c) Association studies
(d) Segregation analysis studies

14 Give the sequence of Identity Formation in Adolescents.

1. Consolidation
2. Exploration
3. Rapprochement
4. Differentiation

Choose the correct answer from the options given below :

(a) 2, 4, 3, 1 (b) 4, 2, 1, 3
(c) 4, 2, 3, 1 (d) 3, 1, 2, 4

15 Give the correct sequence of stages in the relationship maintenance as suggested by Thibaut and Kelly (1959) in their Social Exchange Theory.

1. Bargaining
2. Commitment
3. Sampling
4. Institutionalisation

Choose the correct answer from the options given below :

(a) 1, 3, 2, 4 (b) 3, 1, 2, 4
(c) 2, 4, 1, 3 (d) 3, 2, 4, 1

16 Ethological approach to motivation mainly explains

1. biological aspects of behaviour
2. evolutionary history of behaviour
3. causation of behaviour in terms of stimulus, hormonal and neurobiological events
4. proximal determinants of behaviour

Choose the most appropriate answer from the options given below :

(a) 1 and 2
(b) 3 and 4
(c) 1, 2 and 3
(d) 2, 3 and 4

17 Discovery and understanding of our own abilities brings happiness but also brings fear of new responsibilities and duties. It is called:-

(a) Fear of failure
(b) Jonah complex
(c) Motives conflict
(d) Fear of success

18 "When individuals believe that moral choices are not dependent on close ties to others and that rules must be enforced in the same manner for everyone and each person should uphold them." The following statement is characteristic of which stage of Moral Development according to Kohlberg?

(a) Social contract orientation
(b) Morality of Interpersonal Cooperation
(c) Social order maintaining orientation
(d) Universal Ethical principle orientation

19 Which of the following nerves carry the sensory messages from skin, eyes and ears to Central Nervous System?

(a) Efferent (b) Afferent
(c) Cranial (d) Peripheral

20 When a target is defined by just one distinctive feature which is available on its feature map and it calls attention to itself is known as

(a) Binding effect
(b) Pop-out effect
(c) Conjunction effect
(d) Orienting effect

21 Given below are two statements, one is labelled as Assertion (A) and the other labelled as Reason (R).

Assertion (A) Lewin asserted that avoidance – avoidance conflicts are relatively more stable.

Reason (R) Opposing forces tend to remain in a state of disequilibrium.

In the light of the above statements, choose the most appropriate answer from the options given below :

(a) Both (A) and (R) are correct and (R) is the correct explanation of (A).
(b) Both (A) and (R) are correct, but (R) is not the correct explanation of (A).
(c) (A) is correct, but (R) is not correct.
(d) (A) is not correct, but (R) is correct.

22 Which one of the following is usually not considered an example of the evaluative dimension of the Osgood Semantic Differential?

(a) Clean — Dirty
(b) Slow — Fast
(c) Good — Bad
(d) Kind — Cruel

23 Some people are able to draw an object, match similar objects and describe the component parts but they fail to recognise the objects that they had just seen or drawn. Which of the following describes this phenomena?

(a) Associative Agnosia
(b) Apperceptive Agnosia
(c) Visual Neglect
(d) Form Agnosia

24 Integration of cognitive aspects of learning with the emotional aspects of experience and learning is known as

(a) Integrated approach to learning
(b) Confluent education
(c) Feeling class approach to education
(d) Motivational approach to learning

25 Which one of the following is a nearest parametric alternative to Kruskal–Wallis test?

(a) Independent samples test
(b) Paired samples t-test
(c) One–way ANOVA for independent groups
(d) One–way ANOVA for repeated measures

26 Which of the following is correct for the Pheromones?

(a) Biochemicals found within the brain which effect a person's behaviour.
(b) Biochemicals which play an important role in transmitting information from neuron to neuron.
(c) Chemical messengers found in the Central Nervous System.
(d) Chemical substances emitted by the person into the environment affecting the behaviour of others.

27 Which of the following tactics for gaining compliance are based on reciprocity?

1. The Door–in–the – face Technique
2. That's – Not–All Approach
3. Playing hard to get
4. Foot–in–the Door Technique

Choose the correct answer from the options given below:

(a) 1 and 2
(b) 1 and 3
(c) 2 and 4
(d) 3 and 4

28 According to Master and Johnson, which of the following is correct sequence of Sexual Response?

1. Excitement 2. Desire
3. Plateau 4. Orgasm
5. Resolution

Choose the correct answer from the options given below :

(a) 1, 3, 4, 5 (b) 2, 1, 4, 5
(c) 2, 1, 3, 4 (d) 1, 2, 3, 4

29 Match List I with List II.

List I (Social Concepts)	List II (Explanations)
A. Elaboration Likelihood Model	1. Gender stereotypes
B. Realistic Conflict Theory	2. Central and peripheral route to persuasion
C. Glass Cliff	3. Idealogical change in core aspect of a group
D. Schism	4. Intergroup competition as a source of prejudice

Choose the correct answer from the options given below :

	A	B	C	D
(a)	1	3	2	4
(b)	3	4	1	2
(c)	2	1	4	3
(d)	2	4	1	3

30 Arrange the following correlations in ascending order in terms of their strength of relationship.

1. –0.75 2. –0.30
3. 0.40 4. 0.68

Choose the correct answer from the options given below :

(a) 2, 3, 4, 1
(b) 2, 1, 3, 4
(c) 1, 2, 3, 4
(d) 4, 3, 2, 1

31 Vouyerstic and exhibitionistic disorders are included in which of the following in DSM-5?

(a) Sexual dysfunctions
(b) Paraphillic disorders
(c) Other conditions that focus on clinical attention
(d) Disruptive impulse control and conduct disorders

32 Which of the following describes the enduring facilitation of synaptic transmission that occurs following activation of synapses by high intensity and high frequency stimulation of pre-synaptic neurons ?

(a) Action potential
(b) Absolute refractory period
(c) Relative refractory period
(d) Long term potentiation

33 The components of 'Working Memory' are

1. Acoustic unit
2. Semantic unit
3. Central executive
4. Episodic buffer

Choose the correct answer from the options given below :

(a) 1 and 2
(b) 1 and 3
(c) 2 and 4
(d) 3 and 4

34 What are the characteristics of 'Emerging persons' in Rogerian approach?

1. Honest and open
2. Indifferent to material comforts and rewards
3. Caring
4. Having profound trust in authority

Choose the most appropriate answer from the options given below :

(a) 1 and 2
(b) 3 and 4
(c) 1, 2 and 3
(d) 2, 3 and 4

35 Which of the following are considered as projective tests of personality?

1. Thematic Apperception Test (TAT)
2. Rotter's Incomplete Sentences Blank (RISB)
3. Guttman's Scalogram Analysis
4. Kent–Rosenoff Free Association Test

Choose the correct answer from the options given below :

(a) 1 and 4
(b) 1, 2 and 3
(c) 1, 2 and 4
(d) 1, 2, 3 and 4

36 The evolution of the various explanations or models of memory occur in the following sequence.

1. Multistore
2. Working memory
3. Level of processing
4. Interference

Choose the correct answer from the options given below :

(a) 4, 1, 3, 2 (b) 4, 3, 2, 1
(c) 1, 2, 3, 4 (d) 2, 3, 4, 1

37 It is possible to accept the world as it is, without experiencing dissatisfaction. This is related to which of the following in Buddhism?

(a) Right thought in eight–fold path
(b) Right mindfulness in eight-fold path
(c) Elimination of craving
(d) Existence of satisfaction/dissatisfaction

38 Which of the following in learning environment are considered to be true about school success?

1. The self image is vital to learning
2. Very high goal setting is necessary to motivate and study
3. Success experience is a function of challenge more than repetition
4. Child's spiritual identity is vital to learning

Choose the correct answer from the options given below :

(a) 1 and 4
(b) 2 and 3
(c) 1, 3 and 4
(d) 2, 3 and 4

39 In the two group design with a continuous dependent variable, which of the following measures of effect size can be employed?

1. Cohen's D
2. Point Biserial correlation
3. Eta Squared
4. Partial Eta Squared

Choose the most appropriate answer from the options given below :

(a) Only 1 (b) 2 and 3
(c) 1, 2 and 3 (d) 1, 2 and 4

40 Arrange the first five elements of 'Flow' in correct sequence.

1. Clarity of Goals
2. Immediate Feedback of Actions
3. Balance between challenges and skills
4. Merger of awareness and actions
5. Exclusion of distractions from consciousness

Choose the correct answer from the options given below :

(a) 1, 2, 3, 4, 5 (b) 1, 3, 2, 4, 5
(c) 2, 3, 1, 5, 4 (d) 3, 2, 1, 4, 5

41 Which of the following statements describe the term 'Diffusion of Responsibility?

(a) People help others in order to reduce their emotional discomfort.
(b) Greater the number of witnesses to an emergency, the less likely the victims are to receive help.
(c) Helping others is a means of increasing one's own status and reputation.
(d) Prosocial acts are motivated solely by the desire to help someone in need.

42 Which among these is correct for Cyber bullying?

1. It involves disinhibition
2. Lesser role of Bystanders
3. Ability of targets to retaliate is more
4. No evidence left behind

Choose the correct answer from the options given below :

(a) 1 and 2
(b) 1, 2 and 3
(c) 2, 3 and 4
(d) 1, 2 and 4

43 Arrange the following as per the Yogic Concept of Cognition.

1. Sensorial transformation is attended by manas
2. Reaction by budhi to the object of cognition
3. Registration of external object on mind
4. Assimilation and discrimination by manas
5. Information to Ahamkara

Choose the correct answer from the options given below :

(a) 3, 1, 5, 2, 4 (b) 3, 1, 4, 5, 2
(c) 1, 3, 4, 5, 2 (d) 3, 1, 2, 4, 5

44 Match List I with List II.

List I (Variable type)	List II (Examples)
A. Artificially discrete variable	1. Reaction time
B. Continuous behavioural variable	2. Gender
C. Continuous organismic variable	3. Selection test result interms of selected, not selected, on waiting list
D. Dummy variable	4. Height

Choose the correct answer from the options given below :

	A	B	C	D		A	B	C	D
(a)	3	1	4	2	(b)	3	4	1	2
(c)	2	4	1	3	(d)	1	3	2	4

45 Visuospatial sketch pad is a component of which of the following?

(a) Long-term memory
(b) Short-term memory
(c) Working memory
(d) Sensory memory

46 In which schools of Indian thought about yoga, 'Prakrti' remains isolated as a principle of ultimate reality into self and is active only in the presence and service of 'Purusa'?

(a) Integral yoga philosophy
(b) Vedanta
(c) Samkhya
(d) Sahaj yoga

47 Given below are two statements.

Statement I Edwards Personality Preference Schedule (EPPS) uses forced choice format.

Statement II The forced choice format is presumed to prevent socially desirable responding.

In the light of the above statements, choose the most appropriate answer from the options given below :

(a) Both Statement I and Statement II are correct
(b) Both Statement I and Statement II are incorrect
(c) Statement I is correct, but Statement II is incorrect
(d) Statement I is incorrect, but Statement II is correct

48 After being robbed by a boy recently the shopkeeper says 'beware of teenagers in our community'.

Which of the following explains his reactions?

(a) Algorithm
(b) Availability Heuristic
(c) Representative Heuristic
(d) Gambler's fallacy

49 Which of the following are true regarding Broca's area?

1. It is located in the frontal lobe.
2. Its function is speech production.
3. Understanding and processing aspects of language are associated with it.
4. It helps people using sign language.

Choose the correct answer from the options given below :

(a) 1 and 2
(b) 3 and 4
(c) 1, 2 and 3
(d) 1, 2, 3 and 4

50 The tendency to believe that a task will take less time than it really will, is known as

(a) Magical Thinking
(b) Planning Fallacy
(c) Optimistic Bias
(d) Fundamental Attribution Error

51 Which among the following does not refer to Social Referencing?

1. Intentional search for information about other's feelings, to help explain the meaning of uncertain circumstances and events.
2. It occurs around the age of 2 – 3 years.
3. Infants make use of facial expressions in social referencing.
4. Infants need to understand the significance of other's behaviour within the context of a specific situation.

Choose the most appropriate answer from the options given below :

(a) Only 2
(b) Only 1 and 3
(c) Only 2 and 3
(d) Only 1 and 4

52 Which of the following categories were given by Skinner for different verbal responses in terms of how they are reinforced?

1. Mand
2. Tact
3. Echoic Behaviour
4. Autoclitic Behaviour

Choose the correct answer from the options given below :

(a) 1 and 2
(b) 3 and 4
(c) 1, 2 and 3
(d) 1, 2, 3 and 4

53 Projective measures, particularly inkblot tests, index, which of the following?

(a) Novelty context of creativity
(b) Meaning context of creativity
(c) Domain specific creativity
(d) General creative potential

54 Jensen's Level I and Level II abilities can be best understood in terms of which of the following?

1. Difficulty and complexity of tasks
2. SES Differences
3. Racial Differences
4. Gender Differences

Choose the most appropriate answer from the options given below :

(a) 1 and 2
(b) 3 and 4
(c) 1, 2 and 3
(d) 2, 3 and 4

55 New Mood Therapy
1. is a cognitive therapy
2. is meant for treatment of depression
3. involves many behavioural interventions
4. was originated by Ellis
5. is action commitment therapy

Choose the correct answer from the options given below :
(a) 1, 2 and 5
(b) 1, 2 and 3
(c) 2 and 5
(d) 2, 3 and 4

56 If a person's distinctive social category makes him or her vulnerable to stereotyping, it is referred to as
(a) Token integration
(b) Neosexism
(c) Ingratiation
(d) Token bias

57 Given below are two statements, one is labelled as Assertion (A) and the other is labelled as Reason (R).

Assertion (A) In fixed interval schedule of reinforcement behaviour is reinforced in a fixed time period

Reason (R) When students get feedback intermittently their level of performance increases.

In the light of the above statements, choose the most appropriate answer from the options given below :
(a) Both (A) and (R) are correct and (R) is the correct explanation of (A).
(b) Both (A) and (R) are correct, but (R) is not the correct explanation of (A).
(c) (A) is correct, but (R) is not correct.
(d) (A) is not correct, but (R) is correct.

58 Which of the following characteristics are applicable to emotions that are considered to occur as a result of interaction among subjective and environmental factors and neural and hormonal processes?
1. Emotions give rise to hedonic experiences
2. Emotions stimulate to generate cognitive explanations
3. Emotions trigger variety of internal neurobiological changes
4. Emotions always elicit rewarding behaviour

Choose the most appropriate answer from the options given below :
(a) 1 and 2
(b) 2 and 3
(c) 1, 2 and 3
(d) 2, 3 and 4

59 In which phase of Enright's model of psychological forgiveness, individual gains a cognitive understanding of the offender in a new light that brings a positive change in view about the offender, self and the relationship?
(a) Uncovering phase (b) Decision phase
(c) Work phase (d) Deepening phase

60 Multivariate Analysis of Variance (MANOVA) is best suited for making groupwise comparisons for several dependent variables. Which of the following are these?
(a) Uncorrelated
(b) Moderately correlated
(c) Very highly correlated
(d) Either uncorrelated or have small negative correlations

61 Match List I with List II.

List I (Depth Cues)	List II (Explanations)
A. Motion Parallax	1. Both eyes fixate on the same point in space
B. Texture Gradient	2. Partial occlusion of a far object by a near object
C. Interposition	3. Graded variation in the shape, size and density of the surface elements
D. Convergence	4. Movement in one part of the image relative to another

Choose the correct answer from the options given below :

	A	B	C	D
(a)	3	2	4	1
(b)	4	3	2	1
(c)	1	4	3	2
(d)	2	1	3	4

62 Which of the following are correct for the Biopsychosocial Model of health?
1. Close interaction between body and mind, though they are separate entities.
2. Active participation of the patient.
3. Health and illness are on the same continuum.
4. Treatment process involves medication, surgery and radiation.

Choose the most appropriate answer from the options given below :

(a) 1, 2 and 3
(b) 1, 2 and 4
(c) 2, 3 and 4
(d) 1, 2, 3 and 4

63 Which one of the following is considered as a culture-fair test?

(a) Bhatia's Battery of Intelligence
(b) Kaufman's Intelligence Tests
(c) Wechsler's Adult Intelligence scale
(d) Naglieri Non-verbal Ability Test

64 Match List I with List II.

List I (Concept)	List II (Description)
A. Situational Poverty	1. Not equipped with tools to move out
B. Generational Poverty	2. Not able to meet the average standard of society
C. Relative Poverty	3. Scarcity of necessities like shelter, running water and food
D. Absolute Poverty	4. Caused by environmental disasters, divorce and other issues like poor health etc

Choose the correct answer from the options given below :

	A	B	C	D
(a)	1	3	4	2
(b)	3	1	4	2
(c)	4	1	2	3
(d)	4	2	1	3

65 Cattell proposed his theory of fluid and crystallised intelligences on the basis of which of the following?

(a) First order factors of abilities
(b) Second order factors of abilities
(c) Third order factors of abilities
(d) Higher order factors of abilities

66 Match List I with List II.

List I (Indices)	List II (Test)
A. Universal Index	1. OATB
B. Disclosure Index	2. MCMI
C. True Response	3. MMPI Inconsistency
D. Coping Deficit Index	4. Rorschach Inkblot Test

Choose the correct answer from the options given below :

	A	B	C	D
(a)	1	2	3	4
(b)	2	1	4	3
(c)	3	4	1	2
(d)	4	3	2	1

67 Which of the following is involved in Type 'a' processes of thinking as described by Wertheimer?

(a) Grouping and reorganisation
(b) Assimilation and conditioning
(c) Blind trial and error
(d) Partially productive methods

68 Which of the following statements is wrong?

(a) Body's requirement of sleep varies with age
(b) Tertiary prevention is action taken to identify and treat an illness or injury early with an aim of stopping or reversing the problem
(c) Endorphins are released during exercise
(d) Excessive alcohol consumption leads to shrinking of frontal lobe of the brain.

69 Arrange the Nafs (Self in Sufism) from lower to higher self.

1. The self pleasing to God
2. The pure self
3. Inspired self
4. Serene self
5. The pleased self

Choose the correct answer from the options given below :

(a) 5, 3, 1, 2, 4
(b) 3, 4, 5, 1, 2
(c) 3, 5, 1, 4, 2
(d) 2, 3, 5, 4, 1

70 Communication of the understanding of the 'internal frame of reference' to client by a therapist pertains to which type of counselling skills?

(a) Reflection
(b) Focusing
(c) Empathy
(d) Social influencer

71 Given below are two statements, one is labelled as Assertion (A) and the other labelled as Reason (R).

Assertion (A) Chances of inheriting the dominant genes are twice in females as compared to males.

Reason (R) Females in comparison to males have two 'X' chromosomes.

In the light of the above statements, choose the most appropriate answer from the options given below :

(a) Both (A) and (R) are correct and (R) is the correct explanation of (A)
(b) Both (A) and (R) are correct but (R) is not the correct explanation of (A)
(c) (A) is correct but (R) is not correct
(d) (A) is not correct but (R) is correct

72 Who of the following emphasised nomothetic approach in personality research?
(a) Allport (b) Eysenck
(c) Jung (d) Galton

73 Arrange in correct sequence, the first five intelligences given by Gardner.
1. Linguistic Intelligence
2. Logico-mathematical Intelligence
3. Spatial Intelligence
4. Kinesthetic Intelligence
5. Natural intelligence

Choose the correct answer from the options given below :
(a) 1, 2, 3, 4, 5 (b) 2, 1, 3, 5, 4
(c) 3, 2, 1, 4, 5 (d) 4, 3, 5, 2, 1

74 Who among the following proposed that different emotional stimuli induce different patterns of ANS activity and that these different patterns produce different emotional experiences?
(a) James–Lange
(b) Cannon–Bard
(c) Singer–Schachter
(d) Plutchik

75 Match List I with List II.

	List I		List II
A.	Cognitive Assessment System	1.	Dass
B.	Hold and Dout Hold Tests	2.	Wechsler
C.	Cognitive Assessment Battery	3.	Cattell
D.	Differential Ability Test	4.	Elliot

Choose the correct answer from the options given below :

	A	B	C	D		A	B	C	D
(a)	1	2	3	4	(b)	2	1	4	3
(c)	3	4	1	2	(d)	4	3	2	1

76 Match List I with List II.

List I (Concept)	List II (Description)
A. Turiyavastha	1. Transcognitive realisation
B. Aparvidya	2. Highest state of consciousness
C. Paravidya	3. Transcendental knowledge
D. Nididhasan	4. Empirical knowledge

Choose the correct answer from the options given below :

	A	B	C	D
(a)	1	3	2	4
(b)	2	3	4	1
(c)	2	1	3	4
(d)	3	2	4	1

77 Which of the following are the correct differences between Parkinson's disease and Huntington's disease?
1. Parkinson's disease is a disorder of middle and old age while Huntington's disease is a disorder of young.
2. Parkinson's disease is a movement disorder while Huntington's disease is an emotional disorder.
3. Unlike Parkinson's disease, Huntington's disease has a strong genetic base.
4. Parkinson's disease is not associated with severe dementia while Huntington's disease is.

Choose the correct answer from the options given below:
(a) 1 and 2
(b) 3 and 4
(c) 1, 3 and 4
(d) 2, 3 and 4

78 Mayer-Salovey-Caruso Emotional Intelligence Test (MSCEIT) measures
1. Perceiving emotions
2. Using emotions to facilitate thought
3. Understanding emotions
4. Implicit motivation

Choose the correct answer from the options given below :
(a) 1 and 2
(b) 3 and 4
(c) 1, 2 and 3
(d) 2, 3 and 4

79 Loftus and Pickrell (1995) asked people to read and think about events which had happened to them in childhood and also instructed to write a description of one event which was actually fictitious. About one third of the participants described the fictitious events as having really happened to them.
This is called
1. Eyewitness memory
2. False memory
3. Flash bulb memory
4. Autobiographical memory

Choose the correct answer from the options given below :

(a) Only 1 and 2 (b) Only 2
(c) Only 2 and 3 (d) Only 1

80 Persons inclined to be verbally aggressive have
(a) low threshold for Behaviour Activation system
(b) low threshold for Flight–Fight system
(c) high threshold for Behaviour Inhibition system
(d) high threshold for Behaviour Activation system

81 Which of the following characterises Cognitive Dissonance?
1. Dissonance often occurs in situations involving forced compliance.
2. Attempts to resolve dissonance are reflected in increased cortical activity.
3. Dissonance cannot be reduced directly but only by adding cognitions that justify our behaviours.
4. Dissonance is stronger when we have little justification for our attitude–inconsistent behaviour.

Choose the correct answer from the options given below :

(a) 1, 2 and 3 (b) 1, 2 and 4
(c) 2, 3 and 4 (d) 1, 2, 3 and 4

82 Which of the following are the performance subtests of WAIS?
1. Digit span 2. Similarities
3. Digit symbol 4. Object assembly

Choose the correct answer from the options given below :

(a) 1 and 3 (b) 3 and 4
(c) 2, 3 and 4 (d) 1, 3 and 4

83 Given below are two statements, one is labelled as Assertion (A) and the other is labelled as Reason (R).

Assertion (A) Cattell incorporated factors Q_1, Q_2, Q_3 and Q_4 in 16 PF.

Reason (R) Some factors appeared only in *L*–data not in *Q* and *T*-data.

In the light of the above statements, choose the most appropriate answer from the options given below :

(a) Both (A) and (R) are correct and (R) is the correct explanation of (A)
(b) Both (A) and (R) are correct, but (R) is Not the correct explanation of (A)
(c) (A) is correct, but (R) is not correct
(d) (A) is not correct, but (R) is correct

84 Which of the following are correctly described influences of Behaviourism?
1. Watson's scientific psychology was designed to predict and control human behaviour.
2. Mary Cover Jones studied the effectiveness of counter conditioning.
3. Skinner claimed to have introduced the term 'Behaviour therapy' and is also credited for it.
4. Lazarus emphasised the extension of Thorndike's Law of effect.

Choose the correct answer from the options given below :

(a) 1 and 4 (b) 2 and 3
(c) 1 and 2 (d) 3 and 4

85 Which of the following type of inversion is observed in reaction formation?
1. Implicit 2. Explicit
3. Conscious 4. Unconscious

Choose the correct answer from the options given below :

(a) 1 and 4
(b) 2 and 3
(c) 2 and 4
(d) 1 and 3

86 Which of the following is/are correctly associated with Plato's idea of 'Chariot that is pulled by two horses'?
1. Desiring soul is the charioteer
2. Rational soul is located in the head
3. Rational soul is governed by restraint and modesty
4. Spirited soul knows the honour.

Choose the correct answer from the options given below :

(a) Only 3
(b) 1 and 2
(c) 2 and 4
(d) 1, 3 and 4

87 Qualities such as calmness, tolerance, sociability, love of comfort and easy goingness depict, which of the following?

(a) Viscertonia (b) Somatotonia
(c) Cerebrotonia (d) Ectomorphia

88 Attitudes can be classically conditioned even without our awareness by which of the following?
1. Subliminal conditioning
2. Observational learning
3. Mere exposure
4. Social networks

Choose the correct answer from the options given below :

(a) 1 and 2
(b) 2 and 3
(c) 1 and 3
(d) 2 and 4

89 Arrange in a sequence the Stop-start Relapse Cycle of Internet Addiction.

1. Regret
2. Rationalisation
3. Relapse
4. Abstinence

Choose the correct answer from the options given below :

(a) 1, 4, 2, 3
(b) 2, 1, 4, 3
(c) 4, 1, 3, 2
(d) 1, 2, 4, 3

90 Interscorer reliability is relevant in

1. projective tests of personality
2. achievement tests with short answers
3. achievement tests with essay type questions
4. self–report personality inventories

Choose the correct answer from the options given below :

(a) 1 and 2
(b) 1 and 3
(c) 1, 2 and 3
(d) 2, 3 and 4

Directions (91-95) *Read the following paragraph and answer the five questions that follow :*

A psychologist was interested in developing English Language Usage test for HSSC students. She wrote 120 questions trying to cover several areas of the language usage. Each question had five alternatives, out of which only one was right. The draft version of the test was given to a sample of 200 students. The test items were analysed in two ways carrying out item-remainder correlation and discrimination index for each item. For the purpose of computing item discrimination index, she labelled those who had a total score below P_{27} as low scorers, and those who had a total score above P_{73} as high scorers. (Assume that P_{27} and P_{73} had non-fractional, i.e. full integer values). The statistical significance of the discrimination index of each item was evaluated by appropriate test. Ninety items were retained in item analysis.

The Ninety-item version was administered to a fresh sample of 400 subjects. Cronbach alpha was computed. The psychologist also wondered if she could compute Kuder Richardson (K-R) reliability for her test. Since the Cronbach alpha was pretty high, i.e 947 and the test was quite long she decided to develop the two parallel forms each of 45 items. She randomly assigned the items to two halves, labelling them as Form A and Form B. For each Form, she assessed average inter-item corelation mean, standard deviation and Cronbach alpha. The two forms satisfied the criteria for parallel forms.

91 Item I was passed by 30 subjects in Low scoring group and by 56 subjects in High scoring group. What would be the discrimination index for item I?

(a) 0.241
(b) 0.481
(c) 0.556
(d) 0.796

92 Which one of the following test can be used for evaluating statistical significance of the discrimination index?

(a) Chi-square test
(b) T-test
(c) F test
(d) Mann-Whitney U test

93 Given below are two statements, one is labelled as Assertion (A) and the other is labelled as Reason (R).

Assertion (A) It is not possible to compute K-R reliability for the above test, since each item has five alternatives.

Reason (R) K-R reliability can be computed, when the items can be dichotomously scored.

In the light of the above statements, choose the most appropriate answer from the options given below :

(a) Both (A) and (R) are correct and (R) is the correct explanation of (A)
(b) Both (A) and (R) are correct but (R) is not the correct explanation of (A)
(c) (A) is correct but (R) is not correct
(d) (A) is not correct but (R) is correct

94 What is the expected Cronbach alpha for the Form A?

(a) .474
(b) .899
(c) .913
(d) .947

95 For computing inter-item correlations, which one of the following is suitable?

(a) Point biserial correlation
(b) Biserial correlation
(c) Rank difference correlation
(d) Phi-coefficient

Directions (Q. Nos. 96-100) *Read the following paragraph and answer the five questions that follow :*

An experimental psychologist wanted to test two hypotheses. The first hypothesis proposed that stress would adversely affect the rate of serial learning. The second hypothesis proposed that the type of material (meaningless vs. meaningful) would moderate the effect of stress. The Psychology formed six groups by manipulating stress (A) at three levels—Low, Moderate and High and Type of material (B) at two levels. The subjects were randomly assigned to these groups from an initial pool of subjects. The list of 15 CVC trigrams constituted meaningless material and the list of 15 three-lettered meaningful words constituted meaningful material. The number of trials required to learn the list was the dependent variable. The data were analysed by suitable analysis of variance. Following are the selected findings.

1. The ratio of largest to smallest standard deviations for the six groups was reasonably close to one.
2. The degrees of freedom for error variance was 135.
3. The F ratio for the effect of stress was 0.95.
4. The effect sizes for each effect were calculated both the obtaining *eta* square and partial *eta* square.

96 Which one of the following F ratio would be used to evaluate second hypothesis?

(a) $F = MS_A / MS_E$
(b) $F = MS_B / MS_E$
(c) $F = MS_{A \times B} / MSE$
(d) $F = MS_A / (MS_{A \times B} + MS_E)$

97 The above data indicates

(a) that the assumption of homogeneity of variance is satisfied
(b) that the assumption of homogeneity of variance is not satisfied
(c) the absence of information related to the assumption of homogeneity of variance
(d) the formal test of homogeneity of variance needs to be carried out

98 The a+-bove findings indicate that the post-hoc comparisons are

(a) Necessary for the effect of stress
(b) Necessary for the effect of type of material
(c) Necessary both for the effect of stress and type of material
(d) Neither necessary for the effect of stress nor the type of material

99 The above results indicate that

(a) the first hypothesis is verified
(b) the first hypothesis is rejected
(c) the first hypothesis is partially verified
(d) the inadequate information for evaluating the first hypothesis

100 The above design can best be labelled as :

(a) Randomised 3 × 2 balanced factorial design
(b) Randomised 3 × 2 balanced factorial design with a covariate
(c) Randomised 3 × 2 unbalanced factorial design
(d) Randomised block design

ANSWERS

1 (c)	2 (b)	3 (a)	4 (b)	5 (d)	6 (c)	7 (a)	8 (d)	9 (c)	10 (d)
11 (d)	12 (b)	13 (a)	14 (c)	15 (b)	16 (c)	17 (b)	18 (c)	19 (b)	20 (b)
21 (c)	22 (b)	23 (a)	24 (b)	25 (c)	26 (d)	27 (a)	28 (a)	29 (d)	30 (a)
31 (b)	32 (d)	33 (d)	34 (c)	35 (c)	36 (a)	37 (c)	38 (c)	39 (c)	40 (a)
41 (b)	42 (b)	43 (b)	44 (a)	45 (c)	46 (c)	47 (a)	48 (c)	49 (a)	50 (b)
51 (a)	52 (d)	53 (b)	54 (c)	55 (b)	56 (a)	57 (b)	58 (c)	59 (c)	60 (b)
61 (b)	62 (d)	63 (d)	64 (c)	65 (b)	66 (a)	67 (a)	68 (b)	69 (b)	70 (a)
71 (a)	72 (b)	73 (a)	74 (a)	75 (a)	76 (*)	77 (b)	78 (c)	79 (b)	80 (a,b,c)
81 (b)	82 (b)	83 (b)	84 (c)	85 (c)	86 (c)	87 (a)	88 (c)	89 (b)	90 (c)
91 (b)	92 (a)	93 (d)	94 (b)	95 (d)	96 (c)	97 (a)	98 (d)	99 (b)	100 (c)

Psychology (Paper-2)
Solved Paper, September 2020

General Instructions

1. There are total one hundred questions in this paper. Each question carries 2 marks.
2. All questions are compulsory.

1. Which one of the following branches of philosophy of science deals with the question of existence?

(a) Post-positivism (b) Structuralism
(c) Ontology (d) Scientific realism

2. Which one of the following terms denotes that there are qualities of experience that cannot be explained in terms of combinations of traditional kinds of sensations?

(a) Zeitgeist (b) Tropism
(c) Gestalt Qualitaten (d) Conarium

3. A researcher is studying group process of software startup developers by staying with them and line them for six months. Which of the following is used by her?

(a) Grounded Theory (b) Ethonography
(c) Narrative analysis (d) Phenomenological research

4. Testing the scientific hypothesis is impossible due to the need of auxiliary assumptions. What is this associated with?

(a) Occam's razor (b) Logical empiricism
(c) Duhem-Quine thesis (d) Incommensurability

5. Making decisions by the use of mental short cuts that focus on one aspect of a problem, while ignoring others refers to which one of the following?

(a) Framing (b) Belief perseverance
(c) Heuristics (d) Mental set

6. A group of sixty newly diagnosed diabetic patients were tested for anxiety using a standardised inventory. They were retested for anxiety again after months using the same inventory. The mean difference in anxiety was evaluated by a suitable *t*-test. The degrees of freedom associated with the *t*-test would be

(a) 120 (b) 118 (c) 59 (d) 58

7. In depth perception, what kind of images are used?

(a) Uni-dimensional image (b) Two-dimensional images
(c) Three-dimensional images (d) Four-dimensional images

8. Total cholesterol is determined by adding which of the following values?

(a) HDL + LDL
(b) HDL + LDL + 30% OF VLDL
(c) HDL + LDL + 10% OF VLDL
(d) HDL + LDL + 20% of Triglycerides

9. Which approach focussed on the nature of a task and its influence on a person's ability in solving problems?

(a) Associationist approach
(b) Information processing approach
(c) Gestalt approach (d) Behaviourist approach

10. Teplov while discussing the strong/weak nervous system believed that the point of 'transmarginal unhibition' is the point beyond which

(a) the magnitude of response decreases as stimulus intensity decreases.
(b) the magnitude of response increases as stimulus intensity decreases.
(c) the magnitude of response increases irrespective of stimulus intensity decrease/increase.
(d) the magnitude of response decreases irrespective of stimulus intensity decrease/increase.

11. In multiple approach-avoidance conflict, one has to choose between which of the following?

(a) Two goals possessing both negative and positive aspects.
(b) More than two goals; each having both positive and negative aspects.
(c) More than two goals; one having negative aspects and others having positive valences.
(d) More than two goals; at least one having positive aspects while others may have negative aspects.

12. Which one of the following models proposes that there are three major functional units of the brain; focussing on sustaining attention; receiving and storing information and planning and self-monitoring?

(a) PASS Model (b) Kar and Parrila's Model
(c) Atkinson and Shiffrin Model
(d) Hunt's Model

13. For an intelligence test in an educational setting, which of the following difficulty value shows maximum discrimination?

(a) 0.8 (b) 0.6 (c) 0.5 (d) 0.3

14. What do you call the attention that is drawn automatically to a stimulus without the intention of the participant?

(a) Divided attention (b) Shadowing
(c) Endogenous attention (d) Exogenous attention

15. Jensen put forward the 'Regression' argument to account for which of the following?

(a) To understand inter-generation changes in intellegence.
(b) To understand intra-generation changes in intelligence.
(c) To understand group differences in intelligence.
(d) To understand the role of genetics in intelligence.

16. What is the retention without conscious recollection of skills and dispositions called?

(a) Iconic memory (b) Implicit memory
(c) Explicit memory (d) Semantic memory

17. Who among the following is credited with proposing the investment theory of creativity?

(a) Gatzels and Jackson (b) Kaufman
(c) Wallach and Kogan (d) Sternberg

18. Client : (Silent and shifting nervously in her chair. She is facing the counsellor, but her eyes scan anxiously about).
Counsellor : It must be difficult for you to decide what you going to do here with me.
This response is an example of

(a) dealing with content speculated to be motivating for non-verbal behaviour by the counsellor.
(b) encourages to deal with non-verbal behaviour.
(c) encourages to understand the feelings.
(d) reflection of feelings.

19. In Bronfenbrenners Model, which one of the following systems is independent of cultural bias?

(a) Micro system (b) Meso system
(c) Exo system (d) Macro system

20. A Harsh father always restricts the curiosity motive of his son and the son develops a general hostility towards his superiors. Which of the following is correct about this?

(a) The father represses the curiosity.
(b) Such change is permanent.
(c) It is the most modifiable response.
(d) It is conditioned hostility.

21. Which of the following principle is violated when a psychologist internationally misrepresents his research results?

(a) Beneficence (b) Fidelity and responsibility
(c) Integrity (d) Confidentiality

22. According to Lazarus, what comes between the stimulus and emotional response to that stimulus to mediate?

(a) Physiological reactions (b) Labeling
(c) Social and situational cues (d) Cognitive appraisal

23. Vaibhasika and Sautrantika are associated with which of the following?

(a) Theravada (b) Cetasikas
(c) Madhyamikavada (d) Sarvastivadin

24. In the famous experiment by Schacter and Singer involving epinephrine, what was found to govern the emotions?

(a) Perceptual cues only (b) Social appraisal only
(c) Both cognitive appraisal and physiological arousal
(d) Both cognitive and social appraisal

25. Which of the following is the correct response pattern for the semantic differential test to measure a trait 'active'?

(a) I am active : SA A N D SD (b) I am active : True/False
(c) Choose one : Active-Trusting
(d) Active...Neutral...Passive

26. Which one of the following is the correct description of old fashioned racism?

(a) A contemporary form of antagonism towards a racial based on prejudice and values rather than on self-interest.
(b) Beliefs in which racial superiority, segregation and formal discrimination.
(c) Attitude towards a racial group, combining egalitarian social values and negative emotion resulting in avoidance of that group.
(d) Well learned sets of association that can be automatically activated, uncontrollable and unintentional.

27. Which of the following is an attitude measure that places a single adjective in the centre of an even number of numerical values?

(a) Edward Scale (b) Thurstone Scale
(c) Stapel Scale (d) Semantic Differential Scale

28. Which one of the following is considered as correct for poverty gap?

(a) Gap between rich and poor.
(b) Gap between developed and developing nations.
(c) Difference between poverty line and actual income level of all those living below that line.
(d) Gap in the infrastructure facilities between developed nations.

29. Who among the following conducted one of the most famous and controversial experiments in the area of obedience?

(a) Sherif (b) Asch (c) Milgram (d) Cialdini

30. Immediately after an action potential, the cells does not produce another action potential due to
(a) absolute refractory period (b) relative refractory period
(c) resting state (d) active state

31. Which one of the following attitude scaling methods is especially unsuitable for scaling a large number of attitude statements?
(a) Paired comparison (b) Equal appearing intervals
(c) Summated ratings (d) Successive intervals

32. The 'Door in the Face Technique' is based on which tactics of compliance?
(a) Tactics based on reciprocity.
(b) Tactics based on commitment or consistency.
(c) Tactics based on friendship or liking.
(d) Tactics based on scarcity.

33. Which neurotransmitter is helpful in synaptic plasticity?
(a) Acetylcholine (b) Glutamate
(c) GABA (d) Dopamine

34. Which technique of studying the brain involves injecting the patient with radioactive glucose?
(a) EEG (b) MRI (c) PET (d) CT

35. What does 'Absolute Poverty' mean?
(a) Poverty in terms of absolute number of people.
(b) Poverty in terms of prevailing price level.
(c) Poverty in terms of absolute level of unemployment.
(d) Basic minimum calorie requirement.

36. What do you call the neurological procedure involving the implantation of a medical device under the skin in the chest that sends electrical impulses to electrodes surgically placed in the specific location in the brain?
(a) Deep Brain Stimulation (DBS)
(b) Repetitive Transmagnetic Stimulation (rTMS)
(c) Electroconvulsive Therapy (ECT)
(d) Vagus Nerve Stimulation (VNS)

37. Antiduretic Hormone (ADH) is released by which of the following?
(a) Adrenal Convex (b) Adrenal Medulla
(c) Anterior Pituitary (d) Posterior Pituitary

38. Which of the following is the correct explanation of "An intolerance for weakness, a punitive attitude and submissive respect for their in-group authorities as reflected in their agreement"?
(a) Social Dominance Orientation (b) Ethnocentrism
(c) Conformity (d) Inequality

39. Who believed that meaning in life can be uncovered by creative, experiential and attitudinal values?
(a) Rollo May (b) Victor Frankl
(c) Friedrick Nietzsche (d) Jean Paul Sartre

40. Who among the following has laid emphasis on examining the relationship of culturally specific practices with development?
(a) Piaget (b) Fodor (c) Vygotsky (d) Kohlberg

41. Which of the following are considered in favour of scientific realism?
1. Corroboration 2. Empiricism
3. Miracle argument 4. Selective optimism
Choose the correct answer from the options given below.
(a) 1 and 2 only (b) 2 and 4 only
(c) 2 and 3 only (d) 1, 3 and 4 only

42. In the independent groups' design, selective subject loss occurs because of which of the following?
1. Subject are lost differently across conditions.
2. Subject characteristics are responsible for subject loss.
3. Subject are lost uniformly across conditions.
4. Subject characteristics are independent of subject loss.
Choose the correct answer from the options given below.
(a) 1 and 2 only (b) 1 and 3 only
(c) 2 and 4 only (d) 3 and 4 only

43. Which one of the following personality test/s employs a 'Lie scale'?
1. Rotter's Locus of control scale.
2. Eysenck Personality Profiler
3. Minnesota Multiphasic Personality Inventory-2
4. Edwards Personal Preference Schedule
Choose the correct answer from the options given below.
(a) 3 only (b) 2 and 3 only
(c) 1, 2 and 4 only (d) 2, 3 and 4 only

44. Which of the following are involved in decreased food intake and weight loss?
1. Insulin 2. Leptin
3. Cholecystokinin 4. Orexin
Choose the correct answer from the options given below.
(a) 1 and 2 only (b) 1, 2 and 3 only
(c) 1, 2 and 4 only (d) 2, 3 and 4 only

45. Which of the following character strengths are included in the VIA classification of strengths?
1. Creativity 2. Forgiveness
3. Resilience 4. Prudence
Choose the correct answer from the options given below.
(a) 1, 2 and 3 only (b) 4, 3 and 1 only
(c) 1, 2 and 4 only (d) 1, and 3 only

46. Which of the following internal roadblocks to effective listening is exemplified by the statement "We have never done it that way before"?
1. Resistance to change
2. Halo Effect 3. Stereotyping
4. Hearing only, not feeling

Choose the correct answer from the options given below.

(a) 1 only (b) 1 and 2 only
(c) 1, 2 and 3 only (d) 1, 2, 3 and 4s

47. Adult neurons rely heavily on which of the following?

1. Glucose 2. Protein 3. Potassium 4. Sodium

Choose the correct answer from the options given below.

(a) 1 only (b) 1 and 2 only
(c) 3 and 4 only (d) 1, 3 and 4 only

48. Which of the following were considered to be appropriate for psychological study by Wundt?

1. Analysis of cultural products
2. Higher mental processes
3. The totality of psychological phenomena
4. Self-observation
5. Physiological type of experimentation

Choose the correct answer from the options given below.

(a) 2, 3 and 4 only (b) 2, 3, 4 and 5 only
(c) 1, 4 and 5 only (d) 1, 3, 4 and 5 only

49. The cognitive theory contends dependency behaviours to be arising, from and being maintained by cognitive distortions and maladaptive thought processes. Which of the following are associated with cognitive distortions?

1. Availability 2. Hindsight bias
3. Flexible attribution 4. Illusion of control

Choose the correct answer from the options given below.

(a) 1, 2, 3 and 4 only (b) 1, 2 and 3 only
(c) 2, 3 and 4 only (d) 3 and 4 only

50. Which of the following is true about Hypovolemia?

1. It causes thirst.
2. It increases the blood pressure.
3. Angiotensin is released during this condition.
4. The volume of blood increases.
5. Blood pressure reduces.

Choose the correct answer from the options given below.

(a) 1, 2 and 3 only (b) 1, 3 and 5 only
(c) 1, 4 and 5 only (d) 2, 3 and 4 only

51. Which of the following are the parts of mental logic theories of reasoning?

1. A set of interference schemes
2. Accumulation of concepts
3. A reasoning program
4. A set of pragmatic principles

Choose the correct answer from the options given below.

(a) 1, 2 and 3 only (b) 1, 2 and 4 only
(c) 1, 3 and 4 only (d) 2, 3 and 4 only

52. Which is true about coefficient alpha?

1. It is a lower bound of a test of parallel items.
2. It is an upper bound of a test of parallel items.
3. It is an average of all combination of split-half reliabilities.
4. It is independent of inter-item correlations.

Choose the correct answer from the options given below.

(a) 3 only (b) 1 and 2 only
(c) 1 and 3 only (d) 3 and 4 only

53. Which of the following statements are true about Unity Thema?

1. It is a compound of interrelated needs linked to press.
2. It is a compound of conflicting needs linked to press.
3. It operates largely as an unconscious force.
4. It operates largely as a conscious force.

Choose the correct answer from the options given below.

(a) 1, 2 and 3 only (b) 1 and 3 only
(c) 1 and 4 only (d) 2 and 4 only

54. What comprises haptic perception?

1. Shape 2. Size 3. Volume 4. Identity

Choose the correct answer from the options given below.

(a) 1, 2 and 3 only (b) 1, 3 and 4 only
(c) 2, 3 and 4 only (d) 1, 2 and 4 only

55. Which of the following are the components of Metacognition?

1. Metacognition knowledge
2. Metacognition experience
3. Metacognition control
4. Metacognition regulation

Choose the correct answer from the options given below.

(a) 1 and 2 only (b) 1 and 4 only
(c) 1, 2 and 3 only (d) 1, 2 and 4 only

56. Which of the following are associated with the path in Sufism?

1. Establishing self and assertion
2. Repentance 3. Renunciation
4. Poverty 5. Annihilation

Choose the correct answer from the options given below.

(a) 2, 3 and 5 only (b) 1, 2 and 4 only
(c) 1, 2, 3 and 4 only (d) 2, 3, 4 and 5 only

57. Which of the following is useful for testing univariate normality of distribution?

1. Q-Q Plot 2. Shapiro-Wilk Test
3. Jarque-Bera Test 4. Scatter Plot

Choose the correct answer from the options given below.

(a) 1 and 2 only (b) 2 and 4 only
(c) 1, 2 and 4 only (d) 1, 2 and 3 only

58. Johnson-Laird (1995) has some contengencies in the scientific study of logic, which comprise
1. relational inferences
2. propositional inferences
3. focus gambling 4. syllogisms

Choose the correct answer from the options given below.

(a) 1, 2 and 3 only (b) 1, 2 and 4 only
(c) 1, 3 and 4 only (d) 2, 3 and 4 only

59. Which of the following are comprised in executive functions?
1. Planning 2. Attention
3. Set shifting 4. Declarative memorys

Choose the correct answer from the options given below.

(a) 1, 2 and 3 only (b) 1, 2 and 4 only
(c) 1, 3 and 4 only (d) 2, 3 and 4 only

60. Mr A is very good at discriminating between progressive and regressive ways of behaviour. His choices are clearly perceived by him and adequately symbolised.

According to Rogers, these are the characteristics of which of the following?
1. Individual tendency towards 'growth'.
2. Tendency to 'self actualise'.
3. His constructive creativity.
4. His self-affirmation.

Choose the correct answer from the options given below.

(a) 1 and 3 only (b) 1, 3 and 4 only
(c) 1 and 2 only (d) 2 only

61. The Psychosocial stage of Intimacy v/s Isolation is preceded and succeeded by which of the following?
1. Generativity v/s Stagnation
2. Identity v/s Identity Confusion
3. Industry v/s Diffusion

Choose the correct answer from the options given below.

(a) 1 only (b) 1 and 3 only
(c) 1 and 2 only (d) 2 and 3 only

62. Which of the following characterise the hardy person?
1. He is high on sense of commitment.
2. He is more likely to act to 'cover-up'.
3. He doesn't avoid problems, yet he is often angry.
4. He is always under the control of his life and events.

Choose the correct answer from the options given below.

(a) 1 and 3 only (b) 1 and 4 only
(c) 1 and 2 only (d) 1, 2 and 4 only

63. Which of the following dimensions are essential to be mastered in multicultural counselling, as per McFadden's transcultural perspective?
1. Cultural-Historical
2. Historical Hostility Management
3. Scientific-Ideological
4. Minority Identity Management
5. Social

Choose the correct answer from the options given below.

(a) 1, 5 and 2 only (b) 2, 4 and 1 only
(c) 2, 4 and 5 only (d) 1, 3 and 5 only

64. Several types of heuristics have been identified by researchers. Which of the these are included in it?
1. Lexicographic Strategy
2. Satisficing Strategy
3. Mental Set
4. Elimination by Aspects

Choose the correct answer from the options given below.

(a) 1, 2 and 3 only (b) 1, 2 and 4 only
(c) 1, 3 and 4 only (d) 2, 3 and 4 only

65. A teacher engages students in hands-on, inquiry-based and relevant learning activities in his class. What does this illustrate?
1. Application of the law of exercise.
2. Application of the law of effect.
3. Creating intrinsic motivation.
4. Creating extrinsic motivation.

Choose the correct answer from the options given below.

(a) 2 only (b) 2 and 3 only
(c) 1 and 3 only (d) 3 only

66. Match List I with List II.

List I	List II
A. Cancer that originates in the blood-forming cells such as stem cells	1. Carcinoma
B. Cancer of the epithelial tissue, cells that line the outer and inner surface of the body such as skin, stomach etc.	2. Sarcoma
C. Cancer that arises from the cells in connective tissue such as bone, muscles	3. Leukaemia
D. Cancer of the sympathetic system which is one of the rare types of cancer	4. Lymphoma

Choose the correct answer from the options given below.

	A	B	C	D
(a)	2	3	1	4
(b)	1	2	4	3
(c)	4	2	3	1
(d)	1	2	3	4

67. **Match List I with List II.**

List I (Sources of Personal Efficacy by Bandura)	List II (Therapeutic Processes)
A. Performance accomplishment	1. Live models, symbolic modelling
B. Vicarious experiences	2. Attribution, relaxation biofeedback, symbolic desensitisation
C. Verbal persuasion	3. Participant modelling, performance exposure
D. Emotional arousal	4. Suggestion, exhortation, self-instruction

Choose the correct answer from the options given below.

	A	B	C	D		A	B	C	D
(a)	3,	2,	4,	1	(b)	1	3	2	4
(c)	2,	3,	1,	4	(d)	3	1	4	2

68. **Match List I with List II.**

List I (Types of Reliability)	List II (Source of Error Variance)
A. Test-Retest	1. Content heterogeneity
B. Alternate Form (delayed)	2. Inter-scorer differences
C. Coefficient alpha	3. Time sampling
D. Kohen's Kappa	4. Content sampling and time sampling

Choose the correct answer from the options given below.

	A	B	C	D		A	B	C	D
(a)	4	2	1	3	(b)	4	1	2	3
(c)	3	4	1,	2	(d)	3	4	2	1

69. **Match List I with List II.**

List I	List II
A. Pratibha	1. Samkhya Philosophy
B. Prajma	2. Nyaya Vaisesika
C. Vak	3. Tantrik Tradition
D. Bhavas	4. Patanjali Yoga System

Choose the correct answer from the options given below.

	A	B	C	D		A	B	C	D
(a)	1	2	4	3	(b)	2	4	1	3
(c)	2	4	3	1	(d)	1	4	2	3

70. **Match List I with List II.**

List I	List II
A. Efficacy	1. Response activated when drugs bind with a receptor
B. Tolerance	2. Repeated exposure with less activation of receptors
C. Down regulation	3. Compensatory reduction in receptor availability
D. Withdrawal	4. Unpleasant physiological responses

Choose the correct answer from the options given below.

	A	B	C	D		A	B	C	D
(a)	2	1	3	4	(b)	1	2	3	4
(c)	3	4	2	1	(d)	4	1	2	3

71. **Match List I with List II.**

List I	List II
A. Happiness results from experiences of personal expressiveness	1. Rayan and Deci
B. Happiness is self-realisation, meaning the expression and fulfilment of inner potentials	2. Diener
C. Happiness reflects an individual's own judgement about the quality of his or her life	3. Aristotle
D. Happiness result from the fulfilment of three basic psychological needs : autonomy, competence and relatedness	4. Waterman

Choose the correct answer from the options given below.

	A	B	C	D		A	B	C	D
(a)	1	2	3	4	(b)	3	4	1	2
(c)	4	3	2	1	(d)	2	1	4	3

72. **Match List I with List II.**

List I	List II
A. Aggression	1. Aggression that is permissible according tot the norms of the individual's social group
B. Anti-social Aggression	2. Aggressive acts that support commonly accepted social norms
C. Pro-social Aggression	3. Any action intended to hurt another person
D. Sanctioned Aggression	4. Aggressive acts that violate commonly accepted social norms

Choose the correct answer from the options given below.

	A	B	C	D		A	B	C	D
(a)	4	2	3	1	(b)	3	4	1	2
(c)	1	2	3	4	(d)	2	1	3	4

73. **Match List I with List II.**

List I (Description)	List II (Type of Reinforcement)
A. A reinforcement that reinforces a response at unpredictable time intervals	1. Fixed-ratio schedule
B. A reinforcement that reinforces a response only after a specified time has lapsed	2. Variable-ratio schedule
C. A reinforcement that reinforces a response after an unpredictable number of responses	3. Fixed-interval schedule
D. A reinforcement that reinforces a response only after a specified number of responses	4. Variable-interval schedule

Choose the correct answer from the options given below.

	A	B	C	D
(a)	1	2	3	4
(b)	2	3	4	1
(c)	3	4	1	2
(d)	4	3	2	1

74.* Match List I with List II.

List I	List II
A. The theory that an individual's self-concept is driven partly from membership in a group	1. Realistic group conflict theory
B. The theory that prejudice arises from a real conflict of interest between groups	2. Social Dominance theory
C. The theory that all societies are organised in group hierarchies and sustained through discrimination	3. Social identity theory
D. The most important social perspective in social psychology	4. Interdependence theory

Choose the correct answer from the options given below.

	A	B	C	D
(a)	2	3	1	4
(b)	3	4	2	1
(c)	1	2	3	4
(d)	3	2	4	1

75. Match List I with List II.

List I (Description)	List II (Concept)
A. A laboratory device for testing depth in infants and young animals	1. Perceptual adaptation
B. Refer to differences in two eyes location of corner angles	2. Horizontal disparity
C. Refer to two points which fall on non-corresponding retinal positions one nearer and the other farther	3. Vertical disparity
D. Perceptional adaptability to adjust to an artificially displaced visual field	4. Visual cliff

Choose the correct answer from the options given below.

	A	B	C	D
(a)	1	2	3	4
(b)	2	3	4	1
(c)	3	4	1	2
(d)	4	3	2	1

76. Which is the correct sequence of speech and language development according to Vygotsky?

1. Naive
2. Primitive
3. Egocentric
4. Ingrowth

Choose the correct from the options given below.

(a) 1, 2, 3, 4 (b) 2, 1, 3, 4 (c) 1, 2, 4, 3 (d) 2, 1, 4, 3

77. In cognitive therapy by Elis, arrange the sequence of the following after recognising the activating event.

1. Discriminating the new emotional/behavioural consequences.
2. Recognising the emotional/behavioural consequences of belief.
3. Understanding the corresponding beliefs.
4. Challenging and counteracting these beliefs.
5. Recognising new feelings.

Choose the correct from the options given below.

(a) 2 3 1 5 4 (b) 3 2 4 1 5
(c) 3 2 1 5 4 (d) 2 3 4 1 5

78. What is the correct sequence of decision making perspective of pro-social behaviour to help a person in distress?

1. Taking personal responsibility
2. Weighing the cost and benefits
3. Perceived a need
4. Deciding how to help

Choose the correct from the options given below.

(a) 1, 3, 2, 4 (b) 2, 1, 3, 4
(c) 1, 2, 3, 4 (d) 3, 1, 2, 4

79. Arrange the following is sequence as per the Extinction Transfer Theory of Aggression.

1. Frustration
2. Residual Arousal
3. Arousing Events
4. Increased Arousal
5. Arousal attributed to Frustration

Choose the correct from the options given below.

(a) 1, 3, 2, 4, 5 (b) 4, 2, 3, 1, 5
(c) 3, 4, 2, 1, 5 (d) 1, 3, 4, 2, 5

80. Arrange in sequence what Yerkes described commonly takes place in "insight learning"

1. Sharpening and frequent recurrent attention to the goal
2. Trial
3. Survey/Inspection
4. Attitude of concentrated attention
5. Critical point

Choose the correct from the options given below.

(a) 2, 3, 1, 4, 5 (b) 2, 4, 3, 1, 5
(c) 3, 4, 2, 1, 5 (d) 2, 3, 1, 5, 4

81. The enhancement of dominant responses is strongest when people think they are being evaluated. What is the correct sequence of this theory?

1. Evaluation apprehension
2. Well learned
3. Presence of other
4. Increased arousal
5. Social facilitation

Choose the correct from the options given below.

(a) 2, 1, 3, 4, 5 (b) 3, 4, 1, 2, 5
(c) 1, 2, 3, 4, 5 (d) 1, 3, 4, 2, 5

* Answer not given in official answer key.

82. What is the correct sequence of transformation in integral yoga?

1. Transformation of physical
2. Transformation of subconscient
3. Transformation of mind
4. Transformation of vital
5. Transformation of inconscient

Choose the correct from the options given below.

(a) 3, 4, 1, 2, 5 (b) 1, 3, 4, 2, 5
(c) 1, 4, 3, 2, 5 (d) 3, 1, 4, 2, 5

83. In which sequence, according to Piaget, the following cognitive milestones are achieved?

1. Object permanence 2. Reversibility
3. Abstraction 4. Centration

Choose the correct from the options given below.

(a) 1, 2, 3, 4 (b) 3, 1, 2, 4 (c) 4, 1, 2, 3 (d) 1, 4, 2, 3

84. Arrange the pairings of US and CS in classical conditioning in terms of onset of US in relation to CS starting from the earliest.

1. Backward 2. Simultaneous
3. Delayed 4. Trace

Choose the correct from the options given below.

(a) 1, 2, 3, 4 (b) 4, 2, 3,1 (c) 3, 4, 2, 1 (d) 4, 3, 1, 2

85. Arrange the stages of personality development in the theory given by Rollo May.

1. Innocence 2. Rebellion
3. Ordinary consciousness of self
4. Creative consciousness of self

Choose the correct from the options given below.

(a) 1, 3, 2, 4 (b) 1, 2, 3, 4 (c) 2, 3, 1, 4 (d) 2, 3, 4, 1

86. Give below are two statements one is labelled as Assertion (A) and the other is labelled as Reason (R).

Assertion (A) Schertzer and Stone (1974) specified that acceptance requires respect for the individual as a person of warmth.

Reason (R) Therapists relate to their patients/clients in a non-judgemental, non-critical and non-punitive way.

In the light of the above statement, choose the correct answer from the options given below

(a) Both A and R are true and R is the correct explanation of A
(b) Both A and R are true, but R is not the correct explanation of A
(c) A is true, but R is false
(d) A is false, but R is true

87. Give below are two statements one is labelled as Assertion (A) and the other is labelled as Reason (R).

Assertion (A) Obtained t-valve will follow theoretical t-distribution if underlying assumptions are fulfilled.

Reason (R) The application of t-test makes an assumption of heterogeneity of variance.

In light of the above statement, choose the correct answer from the options given below.

(a) Both A and R are true and R is the correct explanation of A
(b) Both A and R are true, but R is not the correct explanation of A
(c) A is true, but R is false
(d) A is false, but R is true

88. Give below are two statements one is labelled as Assertion (A) and the other is labelled as Reason (R).

Assertion (A) According to Classical Test Theory (CTT) total variance is equal to the sum of true variance and error variances.

Reason (R) Error variance and true variance are independent of each other as per CTT.

In light of the above statement, choose the correct answer from the options given below.

(a) Both A and R are true and R is the correct explanation of A
(b) Both A and R are true, but R is not the correct explanation of A
(c) A is true, but R is false
(d) A is false, but R is true

89. Given below are two statements one is labelled as Assertion (A) and the other is labelled as Reason (R).

Assertion (A) The NEO-PI-R does not have a response style scale.

Reason (R) NEO-PI-R developers argued that adjustment of social desirability leads to a reduction in a validity.

In light of the above statement, choose the correct answer from the options given below.

(a) Both A and R are true and R is the correct explanation of A
(b) Both A and R are true, but R is not the correct explanation of A
(c) A is true, but R is false
(d) A is false, but R is true

90. Given below are two statements, one is labelled as Assertion (A) and the other is labelled as Reason (R).

Assertion (A) Many companies now enable their employees to share profits or even to participate in company ownership.

Reason (R) Worker's productivity boosts rewards from employers.

In light of the above statement, choose the correct answer from the options given below.

(a) Both A and R are true and R is the correct explanation of A
(b) Both A and R are true, but R is not the correct explanation of A
(c) A is true, but R is false
(d) A is false, but R is true

Directions *(Q. Nos. 91-95) Read the following paragraph and answer the five questions which as follows.*

A researcher wanted to predict academic achievement using Intelligence Test-A (IT-A), Intelligence Test-B (IT-B), Type of school (rural/urban), and conscientiousness as predictors. She used multiple regression analysis. She collected data on 200 students on all variables. The OLS estimator was used. The F = 8.9, P < 0.1 for the entire model. In individual predictor analysis, IT-B was the insignificant predictor. The suitable test indicated homoscedasticity. The model ^{2}=6.64 and adjusted ^{2} = 0.59. Both intelligence tests are significantly correlated with the criterion variable with each other.

91. Which of the following is df for F for the entire model?

(a) 4 ; 195
(b) 4 ; 199
(c) 4 ; 195
(d) 3 ; 199

92. Which of the following is correct about residual variance in the passage?

(a) It is correlated with predictor variable.
(b) It is correlated with criterion variable.
(c) It is systematically distributed.
(d) It is randomly distributed.

93. What kind of a variable is 'type of school' in the passage?

(a) Moderator variable
(b) Mediator variable
(c) Dummy variable
(d) Quasi-continous variable

94. Which of the following is the reason for the insignificance of IT-B?

(a) Heteroscedasticity
(b) Poor predictive power
(c) Small sample size
(d) Multicolinearity

95. What is indicated by ^{2} in the passage?

(a) 64% variance is explained
(b) 80% variance is explained
(c) 32% variance is explained
(d) 36% variance is explained

Directions *(Q. Nos. 96-100) Read the following paragraph and answer the five questions which as follows.*

A psychologist developed a scale for measuring warmth and competence dimensions. As a part of scale development, she factor analysed 25 items to retain 20-items. She chose Exploratory Factory Analysis (EFA). The Bartlett's test = 237.8, p < .001. The overall, Kaiser-Meyer-Olkin test (KMO) is 0.89. The Principal Components Analysis (PCA) was used to extract components. The first eight eigenvalues were 9.9, 6.5, 1.00, 0.85, 0.82 and 0.79. She retained factors on the basis of scree plot and rotated them using varimax criteria. Three items showed cross-loadings, eighteen items loaded on only one of the factors, and remaining items did not load on any factors.

96. Which of the following is correct in case of three items having cross-loading?

(a) They have excellent validity
(b) They are conceptually sound items
(c) The scale has poor reliability
(d) They should not be retained in the final scale

97. In the above example, what percentage of the variance would be explained by the first unrotated factor?

(a) 9.9
(b) 39.6
(c) 65.6
(d) 72.0

98. The Bartlett's test results in the above study suggested that

(a) population correlation matrix is not an identity matrix.
(b) population correlation matrix is an identity matrix.
(c) sample correlation matrix is not an identity matrix.
(d) sample correlation matrix is an identity matrix.

99. Using the Kaiser-Guttman criterion, how many factors would be retained in the above study?

(a) 4
(b) 8
(c) 2
(d) –3

100. Which of the following is correct for the Kaiser-Meyer-Olkin test?

1. It is a test of sampling adequacy.
2. Chi-square test is used to test the significance.
3. Values smaller than 0.5 are desirable.
4. Smaller partial correlation leads to high KMO.

Choose the correct answer from the options given below.

(a) 1 only
(b) 1 and 2 only
(c) 1 and 4 only
(d) 2, 3 and 4 only

ANSWERS

1 (c)	2 (c)	3 (b)	4 (c)	5 (c)	6 (c)	7 (c)	8 (d)	9 (c)	10 (a)
11 (b)	12 (a)	13 (c)	14 (d)	15 (c)	16 (b)	17 (d)	18 (a)	19 (d)	20 (d)
21 (c)	22 (d)	23 (d)	24 (c)	25 (d)	26 (b)	27 (c)	28 (c)	29 (c)	30 (a)
31 (a)	32 (a)	33 (b)	34 (c)	35 (d)	36 (a)	37 (d)	38 (b)	39 (b)	40 (c)
41 (d)	42 (a)	43 (b)	44 (b)	45 (c)	46 (a)	47 (a)	48 (c)	49 (a)	50 (b)
51 (c)	52 (c)	53 (a)	54 (d)	55 (b)	56 (d)	57 (d)	58 (b)	59 (a)	60 (c)
61 (c)	62 (b)	63 (d)	64 (b)	65 (b)	66 (a)	67 (d)	68 (c)	69 (c)	70 (b)
71 (c)	72 (b)	73 (d)	74 (*)	75 (d)	76 (b)	77 (b)	78 (d)	79 (c)	80 (c)
81 (b)	82 (a)	83 (d)	84 (a)	85 (b)	86 (a)	87 (c)	88 (a)	89 (a)	90 (a)
91 (a)	92 (d)	93 (c)	94 (d)	95 (a)	96 (d)	97 (b)	98 (a)	99 (a)	100 (c)

Psychology (Paper-2)

Solved Paper, December 2019

General Instructions

1. There are total one hundred questions in this paper. Each question carries 2 marks.
2. All questions are compulsory.

1. Phi-Phenomenon is best seen between which of the following time intervals?
(a) 50 to 350 milliseconds (b) 110 to 320 milliseconds
(c) 30 to 200 milliseconds (d) 215 to 375 milliseconds

2. Dr. 'X' as a therapist felt a sense of complete understanding towards a father client, whose children behaved exactly the way his own children used to behave. This is
(a) empathy (b) jumping to conclusion
(c) warmth and genuineness (d) sympathy

3. Which of the following would be the best method for studying the relative contribution of heredity and environment?
(a) Comparing identical and fraternal twins reared together.
(b) Comparing identical and fraternal twins reared apart.
(c) Comparing siblings reared together and reared apart.
(d) Comparing identical and fraternal twins: half of whom have been reared apart.

4. Which of the following is the most common anti-obesity hormone?
(a) Leptin (b) Orexin (c) Insulin (d) Ghrelin

5. 'Y' has 'concrete experience' and a 'reflective observation' as dominant learning abilities, views concrete situations from different viewpoints, has broad cultural interests and is imaginative and emotional. His experiential learning style is
(a) assimilating style (b) diverging style
(c) converging style (d) accommodating style

6. Which of the following problem solving technique, involves the analysis of difference between the current situation and the desired set goal, then doing something to reduce this difference?
(a) Heuristics (b) Subgoals
(c) Means and analysis (d) Brain storming

7. Using Hull's theory, Taylor conceptualised that anxiety is an emotionally based drive and therefore, high anxious subjects on Taylor's Manifest Anxiety Scale (MAS) should be conditioned faster than the low anxious subjects. The study verified the hypothesis. This provides evidence for
(a) Concurrent validity of MAS
(b) Construct validity of MAS
(c) Convergent validity of MAS
(d) Lack of validity for MAS

8. Imaginal disputation by using the ability of client to imagine is a method of
(a) REBT
(b) Existential Confrontation
(c) Gestalt Therapy Confrontation
(d) Mindfulness

9. What of the following was described by RB Cattell using S-Technique of Factor Analysis?
(a) Differential effects of stimulus situations on personality
(b) Group formation
(c) Social interactions
(d) Individual differences among people

10. A psychological currency that permits deviation from the group is called
(a) conformity (b) obedience
(c) idiosyncracy credit (d) compliance

11. In a newly developed adjustment inventory using 'Yes/No' format,there were some positively worded items ('Yes' response indicating adjustment) and some negatively worded items ('No' response indicating adjustment). Test developers follow this practice of offset the effects of
(a) Acquiescence (b) Faking
(c) Random responding (d) Socially desirable responding

12. Which of the following is the explanation of Premack Principle?
(a) A primary reinforcement is thought of being related to an organism's survival.
(b) A secondary reinforcer acquires reinforcing value because of pairing with primary reinforcer.
(c) All responses are potential reinforcers.
(d) More frequently occurring activity can be used to reinforce the activity that occurs less often.

13. Which part of brain is responsible for transferring information from short term memory to long term memory?
(a) Amygdala (b) Hypothalamus
(c) Hippocampus (d) Cerebellum

14. According to definition theory, for the development of a concept of an OFFICE, one must
(a) construct an ideal office. (b) visit various offices.
(c) list all essential features of an office.
(d) transform a room into office.

15. Read the conversation and choose the best option.
X-What time is it?
Y-I think it is about 9:30 AM This is
(a) adult-adult transaction
(b) adult-adult complimentary transaction
(c) child-adult complimentary transaction
(d) child-adult transaction

16. Ferminist theory helped in
(a) dealing with gender inequality.
(b) understanding sexual preferences.
(c) human growth and development.
(d) gender issues.

17. Which of the following is excluded from Berkowitz's frustration-aggression hypothesis?
(a) Frustration always leads to aggression.
(b) Social rules may inhibit aggression.
(c) Frustration may result in other behaviour than aggression.
(d) Cognitive factors can overside aggression.

18. Eleven rural, eleven semiurban and eleven urban students were thoroughly interviewed and they were ranked (using a pooled sample of N=33) for their communication skills. Which one of the following statistical technique would be appropriate to explore groupwise difference in communication skills?
(a) Friedman's Test (b) Kruskal Wallis H-Test
(c) Rank Difference correlation
(d) One-way ANOVA for independent samples

19. The bipolar adjectives scale 'Fast-slow' in Osgood semantic differential would belong to
(a) evaluative factor (b) potency factor
(c) general factor (d) activity factor

20. In quota sampling, the probabilityof each element of population being included in the sample
(a) is equal to sampling fraction.
(b) can be specified in advance.
(c) cannot be specified in advance.
(d) is $\frac{1}{K}$ where K is the number of strats.

21. Which of the following school of Buddhism focuses on collective freedom from suffering and feeling the ways of enlightment?
(a) Nirvana (b) Theravada Buddhism
(c) Mahayana Buddhism (d) Vajrayana Buddhism

22. The three psychologists who illustrated the diversity of approaches to functional psychology at Columbia were
(a) Harvey Carr, James Mckeen Cattell and EL Thorndike
(b) James Angell, Harvey Carr and James Mckeen Cattell
(c) EL Thorndike, RS Woodworth and James Angell
(d) James Mckeen Cattell, EL Thorndike and RS Woodworth

23. Which one of the following statement is true regarding the relationship of test length with reliability and validity?
(a) As test length increases, only reliability improves.
(b) As test length increases, only validity improves.
(c) As test length increases, neither reliability nor validity improves.
(d) As test length increases, both reliability and validity improve.

24. According to Decision Stage Model, how many stages are comprised in taking a decision?
(a) Three (b) Four (c) Five (d) Six

25. Which among the following are the levels of processing proposed by Craik and Lockhart?
(a) Symbolic, Semantic and Acoustics
(b) Physical behavioural and Acoustics
(c) Behavioural, Acoustics and Semantic
(d) Physical, Acoustics and Semantic

26. Which device is used for the expression of different letters of a word?
(a) Acoustics (b) Acronyms
(c) Key word system (d) Clustering

27. Which of the following explains the tendency of traits that are encoded on the same chromosome to be inherited together?
(a) Mitosis (b) Meiosis (c) Linkage (d) Gene expression

28. 'Confrontation' in Gestalt therapies involves
(a) what and why questions. (b) what and how questions.
(c) how and why questions.
(d) what, how and why questions.

29. Descartes argued that body and mind interact. According to him which is the site for this interaction?
(a) Pancreas Gland (b) Pineal Gland
(c) Pituitary Gland (d) Adrenal Gland

30. Value of behaviour to the organism, its evolutionary history, and its causation in terms of stimulus, hormonal and neurological events" has been area of study of which of the following?
(a) Evolutionary psychology (b) Psychoanalysis
(c) Ethology (d) Instinct psychology

31. Which part of neuron is covered by Myelin sheath?
(a) Whole of Axon (b) Parts of Axon
(c) Whole of Dendrite (d) Parts of Dendrites

32. If you move a book from your desk to a shelf, you know the form of book is not changing. It may be because of which of the following?

(a) Linear perspective (b) Relative size
(c) Shape constancy (d) Size onstancy

33. Beta endorphin is mobilised from pituitary gland during stress in approximately same quantities as

(a) Adreno Corticotropic Hormone (ACTH)
(b) Corticotropin Releasing Factor (CRF)
(c) Epinephrine (d) Dopamine

34. The phenomenon where by-standers assume that nothing is wrong in an emergency as no one looks concerned is called

(a) diffusion of responsibility (b) pluralistic ignorance
(c) pro-social behaviour (d) by-stander effect

35. Client: "I really don't have much to say (tapping foot)".

Counsellor: "Do you know you are tapping your foot".

Client: "No I guess I am feeling some impatience (pause) even more some confused ......".

Here the counsellor is

(a) trying to create awareness in client.
(b) being a little too harsh.
(c) making an effort to understand client's behaviour at deeper level.
(d) trying to create both awareness and deeper understanding.

36. For becoming a good basketball player one must use

(a) Algorithms (b) Heuristics (c) Concepts (d) Prototypes

37. Which of the following consists of elaborative rehearsal?

(a) Remembering of information to maintain it in STM.
(b) Transferring information from STM to LTM.
(c) Holding information for brief period of time while being used.
(d) Ability to focus on only stimulus.

38. Choose the odd one for pattern of sympathetic activation during emotions.

(a) Increased heart rate (b) Pupil constriction
(c) Increased breathing rate (d) Lowered skin resistance

39. In terms of Psychoanalytic Therapy, the means of keeping the unconscious conflict intact; thereby impeding any attempts to probe into real sources of personality problems is known as

(a) repression (b) suppression (c) denial (d) resistance

40. Which of the following norms suggest people that they ought to behave?

(a) Social Responsibility Norms (b) Reciprocity Norms
(c) Prescriptive Norms (d) Proscriptive Norms

41. Generational-digital or Gen-D factor

1. pertains to reversal of power hierarchy in terms of digital technology.
2. pertains to imparting knowledge downward to younger generation.
3. calls for psycho education of parents and care givers on digital technology usage.
4. calls for the adolescent psycho education on digital technology usage.

Choose the correct option.

(a) Only 1 (b) Only 2 (c) Both 1 and 3 (d) Both 2 and 4

42. According to Goleman, 'Management of Emotions' component of emotional intelligence includes

1. handling feelings, so that they are appropriate.
2. ability to soothe oneself.
3. ability to shake off rampant anxiety, gloom or irritability.
4. recognising feeling as it happens.

Choose the correct option.

(a) 1, 2 and 4 only (b) 2, 3 and 4 only
(c) 1, 2 and 3 only (d) 1, 2, 3 and 4

43. Double standards of mental health with regard to adult females

1. depicted adult female behaviour as less socially desirable and healthy.
2. had set up barriers against the advancement of women in non-traditional roles.
3. pertain to the changing dual personality of women in the current scenario.
4. pertain to the identification of the general standards of healthy behaviour with men only.

Choose the correct option.

(a) Only 4 is correct (b) Only 3 is correct
(c) Only 1 and 2 are correct (d) 1, 2 and 3 are correct

44. Which of the following are the two major symptoms of Alzhiemer's disease?

(a) Neurofibriliary tangles and Amyloid plaques
(b) Collateral sprouting and cerebral ischemia
(c) Amyloid plaques and cerebral ischemia
(d) Neurofibriliary tangles and collateral sprouting

45. Read the following conversation and choose the correct option.

X: "I am so hungry! I am like way starving".

Y: "You might consider a small nutritional snack to suppress your appetite". This is

(a) adult-adult and child-child interaction respectively.
(b) complimentary transactions
(c) child-child and adult-adult, crossed transactions respectively.
(d) child-adult and adult-child crossed transactions respectively.

46. According to Social Impact Theory, the effect of majority on minority rests on three of following factors.

1. Majority's strength
2. Minority's will
3. Immediacy
4. Number of persons

Choose the correct option.

(a) 1, 2 and 3 (b) 1, 3 and 4
(c) 2, 3 and 4 (d) 2, 4 and 1

47. Which of the following correctly describe Nafs (Self or ego) in Sufism?
1. It can be viewed along a continuum.
2. It is not meant to please the God.
3. It refers to negative traits only.
4. It has a potential to function from grossest to highest level.
(a) 1 and 3 are correct (b) 2 and 3 are correct
(c) 2 and 4 are correct (d) 1 and 4 are correct

48. The core emphasis of developmental psychology is represented by which of these sets of pairs?
(a) Individual v/s shared and stability v/s change
(b) Young v/s old and stability v/s change
(c) Individual v/s shared and young v/s old
(d) Cross-sectional v/s longitudinal and self esteem v/s self doubt

49. Which of the following are the advantages of FMRI over PET scan?
1. Nothing has to be injected into the body.
2. Provides both structural and functional information of the same image.
3. Produces three dimensional images of activity over the entire brain.
Choose the correct option.
(a) Only 1 and 2 (b) Only 1 and 3
(c) Only 2 and 3 (d) 1, 2 and 3

50. Which of the following are the main biases in attribution process?
1. Fundamental attribution error
2. Actor-observer effect
3. Situational influence 4. Self serving bias
Choose the correct option.
(a) 1, 2 and 3 (b) 1, 2 and 4 (c) 2, 3 and 4 (d) 1, 3 and 4

51. Which of the following are the elements of language acquisition process?
1. Phonemes 2. Morphemes
3. Syntax 4. Pragmatics
Choose the correct option.
(a) 1, 3 and 4 only (b) 2, 3 and 4 only
(c) 1, 2 and 3 only (d) 1, 2 and 4 only

52. There are many mnemonic devices to help a person to memorise the lists of words and vocabulary items. Identify the correct device series.
1. Categorical Clustering
2. Interactive Images 3. Recognition
4. Pegword System 5. Method of Loci
Choose the correct option.
(a) 1, 2 and 3 (b) 2, 3 and 4
(c) 3, 4 and 5 (d) 1, 2, 4 and 5

53. Consider the three types of investigation in psychological research written in alphabetical order: (a) Controlled laboratory experiments (b) Ex post facto studies (c) Field experiments.
Arrange them in descending order in terms of their ability to control secondary variance usually.
(a) (a), (c), (b) (b) (a), (b), (c)
(c) (c), (a), (b) (d) (b), (c), (a)

54. During 1960s, Hoffman and others criticised the college entrance examination and other nationally administered educational tests, and argued that
1. these favour shrewd and nimble witted.
2. these are over concerned with quality of thought behind it and the expression of skill than answer.
3. these favor subtle, creative and more profound persons.
4. these carry a bad effect in recognition of merit.
Choose the correct options.
(a) Only 1 is correct (b) 1 and 4 are correct
(c) Only 3 is correct (d) 3 and 4 are correct

55. That is the reason of negative voltage of a neuron during resting potential?
(Sodium = Na^+; Potassium = K^+; Chloride = Cl^-; Organic Anions = A^-)
(a) Na^+ and Cl^- ions outside the membrane have more negative charge than K^+ and A^- ions inside.
(b) Na^+ and Cl^- ions outside the membrane have more negative charge than K^+ and A^- ions inside.
(c) Na^+ and A^- ions outside the membrane have more negative charge than K^+ and Cl^- ions inside.
(d) Na^+ and A^- ions outside the membrane have more negative charge than K^+ and Cl^- ions inside.

56. Suler's (2004) concept of 'Online Disinhibition Effect' is characterised by
1. anonymity 2. accessibility
3. hierarchies negation
4. easy escape consequences
Choose the correct option.
(a) 1 and 2 only (b) 1, 2 and 3
(c) 1, 3 and 4 (d) 1, 2 and 4

57. Which are the two basic features of Schema?
1. Influencing memory 2. Promoting forgetting
3. Resisting change 4. Promoting change
Choose the correct option.
(a) 1 and 2 (b) 1 and 3 (c) 1 and 4 (d) 2 and 3

58. Creativity has been conceptualised in terms of which of the following?
1. As person 2. As potential
3. As process 4. As perseverance
Choose the correct option.
(a) 1, 2 and 3 only (b) 2, 3 and 4 only
(c) 1, 3 and 4 only (d) 1, 2, 3 and 4

59. The Eudemonic view of subjective well-beings holds that
1. true happiness is found in expression of virtue.
2. well being refers to 'striving for perfection'.

3. subjective well-being focuses on bodily pleasures like focus on appetite and self interests.
4. well-being consists of fulfilling its 'true-self'.

Choose the correct option.

(a) Only 3 (b) 3 and 4 (c) 1, 2 and 4 (d) Only 1

60. Which of the following are the motivators for helping others?

1. Attitudes 2. Empathy
3. Personal distress 4. Norms and values

Choose the correct option.

(a) 1, 2 and 3 (b) 1, 2 and 4
(c) 1, 3 and 4 (d) 2, 3 and 4

61. The context of marginalisation it is suggested to adopt 'Social Empowerment Model' while dealing with LGBTs because

1. it increases this group's collective and personal self advocacy.
2. they learn that they can lead "fulfilling and satisfying" lives.
3. concerns about LGBTs are social concerns and not the concern for individual.
4. they realise that being gay or lesbian is not a pathological condition.

Choose the correct options.

(a) 1, 2 and 3 are correct (b) 1 and 4 are correct
(c) 2 and 3 are correct (d) 1, 2 and 4 are correct

62. Jensen's level I and level II abilities can be best understood in terms of which of the following?

1. Difficulty and complexity of tasks
2. Socio-economic differences
3. Racial differences 4. Geographical differences

Choose the correct option.

(a) 1, 3 and 4 only (b) 1, 2 and 3 only
(c) 2, 3 and 4 only (d) 1, 2, 3 and 4

63. Which of the following statements are correct?

1. Dilthey opposed reductionism.
2. Dilthey opposed psychophysical parallelism.
3. Dilthey rejected the positivistic approaches to experimental psychology.
4. Dilthey rejected the idea of description.

Choose the correct option.

(a) 1, 2 and 4 are correct (b) 1, 3 and 4 are correct
(c) 2 and 4 are correct (d) 1, 2 and 3 are correct

64. The teacher had marks for 50 students in his class. He computed their mean and standard deviation. considering that the evaluation was too strict, he gave five grace marks to each student. This would

1. increase mean by five.
2. alter standard deviation in an unpredicted way.
3. change the rank order of the students.
4. change the skewness of the distribution.

Choose the correct option.

(a) 1, only (b) 1 and 2 only
(c) 1, 2 and 3 only (d) 1, 3 and 4 only

65. Which of the following are true as per Brentano's concept of Phenomenology?

1. Outer objects can be perceived only.
2. Mental experiences can be perceived only.
3. Feelings and willing be combined in one category.
4. Outer objects can be both perceived and experienced.

Choose the correct option.

(a) 3 and 4 are correct (b) 1 and 3 are correct
(c) 2, 3 and 4 are correct (d) 1 and 2 are correct

66. Match the given concepts in List I with description given in List II.

List I	List II
(a) Turiyavastha	(i) The state of normal consciousness concerned with material world
(b) Prajnavastha	(ii) subconscious faculty concerned with the subtler aspects of human knowledge and experience
(c) Swapanvastha	(iii) State of super consciousness when dichotomy between grossness and subtlety disappears
(d) Jagratavastha	(iv) Steady state of consciousness when essential nature of atman is experienced

(a) (a)-(iii), (b)-(ii), (c)-(i), (d)-(iv)
(b) (a)-(iv), (b)-(iii), (c)-(ii), (d)-(i)
(c) (a)-(iii), (b)-(iv), (c)-(ii), (d)-(i)
(d) (a)-(i), (b)-(iii), (c)-(ii), (d)-(iv)

67. Match the following concepts with the corresponding bodily states.

List I	List II
(a) Rebound Phenomena	(i) REM sleeps
(b) Phantom Limb	(ii) Pain
(c) Scotopic Process	(iii) Vision
(d) Apoptosis	(iv) Cell death

Choose the correct option from those given below.

(a) (a)-(i), (b)-(ii), (c)-(iii), (d)-(iv)
(b) (a)-(ii), (b)-(i), (c)-(iv), (d)-(iii)
(c) (a)-(i), (b)-(iv), (c)-(iii), (d)-(ii)
(d) (a)-(iv), (b)-(i), (c)-(iii), (d)-(ii)

68. Match the following types of aggression with their description.

List I	List II
(a) Hostile Aggression	(i) An instinctual drive involving aggressive actions towards death
(b) Emotional Aggression	(ii) Injury in which the goal is to obtain something of value
(c) Instrumental Aggression	(iii) An act stemming from feelings of anger and aimed at inflicting pain
(d) Thantos	(iv) Injury or harm that is carried out for the explicit goal of hurting some one

Choose the correct option from those given below.

(a) (a)-(i), (b)-(ii), (c)-(iii), (d)-(iv)
(b) (a)-(ii), (b)-(iii), (c)-(iv), (d)-(i)
(c) (a)-(iii), (b)-(iv), (c)-(i), (d)-(ii)
(d) (a)-(iii), (b)-(iv), (c)-(ii), (d)-(i)

69. Match the given concepts with relevant description.

List I	List II
(a) Bottom up	(i) Happiness due to circumstances tends to be temporary because we generally adjust fairly soon to new circumstances
(b) Top down	(ii) Life circumstances influence happiness
(c) Happiness set point	(iii) Happiness begins in ourselves
(d) Hedonic adaptation	(iv) happiness levels are fixed and stable across time

Choose the correct option.

(a) (a)-(ii), (b)-(i), (c)-(iv), (d)-(iii)
(b) (a)-(ii), (b)-(iii), (c)-(i), (d)-(iv)
(c) (a)-(iii), (b)-(ii), (c)-(iv), (d)-(i)
(d) (a)-(ii), (b)-(iii), (c)-(iv), (d)-(i)

70. Match the following diseases with their corresponding descriptions.

List I	List II
(a) Parkinson's Disease	(i) Movement disorder associated with cognitive deficits
(b) Huntington's Disease	(ii) Progressive motor disorder associated with severe dementia
(c) Alzheimer's Disease	(iii) Progressive decline in memory starting with selective forgetting
(d) Korsakoff Syndrome	(iv) A form of dementia which is caused by deficiency of vitamin Thiamine

Choose the correct option from those given below.

(a) (a)-(ii), (b)-(i), (c)-(iv), (d)-(iii)
(b) (a)-(i), (b)-(iv), (c)-(iii), (d)-(ii)
(c) (a)-(i), (b)-(ii), (c)-(iii), (d)-(iv)
(d) (a)-(ii), (b)-(iii), (c)-(iv), (d)-(i)

71. Match the following elements of Immune System with their respective functions.

List I	List II
(a) Neutrophils	(i) Field Marshalls
(b) Immunoglobins	(ii) Cytoxic Action
(c) NK (National Killer) Cells	(iii) Phagocytic Action
(d) CD_4	(iv) Antibody Action

Choose the correct option.

(a) (a)-(iv), (b)-(ii), (c)-(iii), (d)-(i)
(b) (a)-(iii), (b)-(i), (c)-(ii), (d)-(iv)
(c) (a)-(iii), (b)-(iv), (c)-(ii), (d)-(i)
(d) (a)-(ii), (b)-(iv), (c)-(i), (d)-(iii)

72. Match the following leadership styles with their characteristics.

List I	List II
(a) Directive	(i) Leader consults subordinates thereby permitting them to participate in decision making
(b) Supportive	(ii) Leader sets challenging goals and seeks improvement in performance
(c) Participative	(iii) Leader provides specific guidance by establishing work schedules and rules
(d) Achievement oriented	(iv) Leader establishes good relations with subordinates and satisfies their needs

Choose the correct option from the given below.

(a) (a)-(i), (b)-(ii), (c)-(iii), (d)-(iv)
(b) (a)-(ii), (b)-(iii), (c)-(iv), (d)-(i)
(c) (a)-(iii), (b)-(iv), (c)-(i), (d)-(ii)
(d) (a)-(iv), (b)-(i), (c)-(ii), (d)-(iii)

73. Match the following types of memories with their features.

List I	List II
(a) Non-declarative memory	(i) Type of declarative memory containing general knowledge of language and information
(b) Echoic memory	(ii) Type of declarative memory containing personal information not readily available with others
(c) Semantic memory	(iii) Type of LTM for skills, procedures, habits etc
(d) Episodic memory	(iv) Auditory sensation lasting only for 2 to 4 seconds

Choose the correct option from those given below.

(a) (a)-(i), (b)-(ii), (c)-(iii), (d)-(iv)
(b) (a)-(ii), (b)-(iii), (c)-(iv), (d)-(i)
(c) (a)-(iii), (b)-(iv), (c)-(i), (d)-(ii)
(d) (a)-(iv), (b)-(iii), (c)-(ii), (d)-(i)

74. Match the waves with the corresponding frequencies.

List I	List II
(a) Alpha Waves	(i) 4-7 Hz
(b) Beta Waves	(ii) 14-30 Hz
(c) Theta Waves	(iii) 8-13 Hz
(d) Delta Waves	(iv) 0-3 Hz

Choose the correct option from those given below.

(a) (a)-(iii), (b)-(ii), (c)-(i), (d)-(iv)
(b) (a)-(ii), (b)-(iii), (c)-(i), (d)-(iv)
(c) (a)-(iii), (b)-(ii), (c)-(iv), (d)-(i)
(d) (a)-(ii), (b)-(iii), (c)-(iv), (d)-(i)

75. Match the following intelligence/ability tests with the associated features.

List I	List II
(a) Naglier Non-Verbal Ability Test	(i) Provides deviation IQ
(b) Raven's Progressive Matrices (Standard)	(ii) Open-end Test
(c) Torrance Test of Creative Thinking	(iii) Suitable for Children
(d) Wechsler Adult Intelligence Scale	(iv) Adult Culture Fair Test

Choose the correct option from those given below.

(a) (a)-(iii), (b)-(iv), (c)-(ii), (d)-(i)
(b) (a)-(iv), (b)-(ii), (c)-(i), (d)-(iii)
(c) (a)-(iv), (b)-(iii), (c)-(ii), (d)-(i)
(d) (a)-(iii), (b)-(iv), (c)-(i), (d)-(ii)

76. Arrange the following in temporal sequence.

1. Establishment of Psychology Department in Mysore
2. Establishment of Psychology Department in Calcutta
3. Establishment of Psychology Department in Madras
4. Establishment of Psychology Department in Pune
5. First Indian Jounal of Psychology

Choose the correct option.

(a) 2 → 1 → 3 → 5 → 4 (b) 2 → 1 → 5 → 3 → 4
(c) 2 → 3 → 1 → 4 → 5 (d) 1 → 2 → 5 → 3 → 4

77. Arrange the following in sequences as per Atkinson and Shiffrin's Model of memory when the information is processed.

1. Short term memory 2. Elaborative rehearsal
3. Long term memory 4. Attention
5. Sensory memory

(a) 4 → 5 → 1 → 2 → 3 (b) 5 → 1 → 4 → 2 → 3
(c) 5 → 4 → 1 → 2 → 3 (d) 4 → 5 → 1 → 2 → 3

78. Involvement of frontal lobe in intelligence can be understood in terms of which of the following sequence.

(a) Frontal lobe → focusing attention internally → working memory → general reasoning
(b) Frontal lobe → focusing attention internally → response selection → general reasoning
(c) Frontal lobe → short term storage → working memory → general reasoning
(d) Frontal lobe → response selection → working memory → general reasoning

79. Arrange in sequence, the scoring categories for 'Motive to Avoid Success' as given below.

1. Non-contingent negative consequences
2. Interpersonal engagement
3. Relief
4. Absence of instrumental conditioning
5. Absence of others

Which of the given below sequence is correct?

(a) 1 → 2 → 4 → 3 → 5 (b) 1 → 2 → 3 → 4 → 5
(c) 2 → 1 → 3 → 5 → 4 (d) 3 → 4 → 5 → 2 → 1

80. Arrange the following stages of moral development in sequence of their emergence as an individual grows up.

1. Morality of interpersonal cooperation
2. Universal ethical principle orientation
3. Social order maintaining orientation
4. Instrumental purpose orientation

Choose the correct option.

(a) 4 → 1 → 2 → 3 (b) 4 → 1 → 3 → 2
(c) 1 → 2 → 4 → 3 (d) 2 → 3 → 4 → 1

81. In what sequence the social combination rules are followed for group success?

(a) Additive, disjunctive, compensatory, conjunctive
(b) Additive, compensatory, disjunctive, conjunctive
(c) Disjunctive, compensatory, conjunctive, additive
(d) Compensatory, conjunctive, disjunctive, additive

82. Arrange the ego strengths in correct sequence according to Erickson's stages of ego development.

(a) Hope → purpose → competence → fidelity → love → care → wisdom → will
(b) Will → hope → purpose → competence → fidelity → care → wisdom → love
(c) Hope → will → purpose → competence → fidelity → love → care → wisdom
(d) Purpose → hope → will → fidelity → competence → care → wisdom → love

83. Escalation of committment involves following sequence of steps.

1. Occurrence of loss 2. Self-Justification
3. Strengthening by external factor
4. Rational expectation of positive outcome

Choose the correct option.

(a) 4 → 1 → 3 → 2 (b) 4 → 1 → 2 → 3
(c) 1 → 2 → 3 → 4 (d) 1 → 2 → 4 → 3

84. Choose the correct sequence of events following prolonged stress.

1. Corticotropin releasing factor
2. Adrino-corticotrophic hormone
3. Cortisol 4. Immune suppression

Choose the correct option.

(a) 1 → 2 → 3 → 4 (b) 4 → 3 → 1 → 2
(c) 1 → 3 → 4 → 2 (d) 2 → 3 → 1 → 4

85. Arrange in sequence, the network of auditory pathways.

1. Auditory Nerve 2. Cochlear Nuclei
3. Superior Olives 4. Lateral Leminiscus
5. Inferior Colliculi
6. Medial Geniculate Nuclei
7. Primary Auditory Cortex

Choose the correct sequence.

(a) 1 → 3 → 2 → 4 → 5 → 7 → 6 (b) 1 → 2 → 3 → 4 → 5 → 6 → 7
(c) 2 → 1 → 4 → 3 → 7 → 5 → 6 (d) 6 → 7 → 5 → 4 → 3 → 2 → 1

86. Given below are two statements one is labelled as Assertion (A) and the other is labelled as Reason (R).

Assertion (A) MRI provides images of brain activity rather than brain images.

Reason (R) Results in MRI are obtained from the measurement of waves that hydrogen atoms emit when they are activated by radio-frequency waves in a magnetic field.

In the light of the above two statements choose the correct option.

(a) Both A and R are true and R is the correct explanation of A
(b) Both A and R are true, but R is not the correct explantion of A
(c) A is true, but R is false
(d) A is false, but R is true

87. Given below are two statements one is labelled as Assertion (A) and the other is labelled as Reason (R).

Assertion (A) Sensitivity to targets reflects the placement of a flexible criterion and is measured in terms of 'hits minus false alarms'.

Reason (R) When the consequences of making a Miss are very grave, we lower the criterion for considering something as a Hit.

In the light of the above two statements choose the correct option:

(a) Both A and R are true and R is the correct explanation of A
(b) Both A and R are true, but R is not the correct explantion of A
(c) A is true, but R is false
(d) A is false, but R is true

88. Given below are two statements one is labelled as Assertion (A) and the other is lablled as Reason (R).

Assertion (A) High sensation seekers are inclined to get involved in variety of thrill seeking activities.

Reason (R) Engagement in thrill seeking behaviour triggers the release of epinephrine.

In the light of above two statements choose the correct option.

(a) Both A and R are true and R is the correct explanation of A
(b) Both A and R are true, but R is not the correct explantion of A
(c) A is true, but R is false
(d) A is false, but R is true

89. Given below are two statements one is labelled as Assertion (A) and the other is labelled as Reason (R).

Assertion (A) Culture encompasses life styles, values, practices and goals which provide distinct identities to the people and community.

Reason (R) Culture always acts as a constraint in the growth of a community.

In the light of theabove two statements choose the correct option.

(a) Both A and R are true and R is the correct explanation of A
(b) Both A and R are true, but R is not the correct explantion of A
(c) A is true, but R is false
(d) A is false, but R is true

90. Given below are two statements one is labelled as Assertion (A) and the other is labelled as Reason (R).

Assertion (A) Philosophically the word pragmatism emphasises results rather than methods.

Reason (R) A pragmatic view of science accepts methodological approaches to knowledge.

In the light of above two statements choose the correct option.

(a) Both A and R are true and R is the correct explanation of A
(b) Both A and R are true, but R is not the correct explantion of A
(c) A is true, but R is false
(d) A is false, but R is true

Directions *(Q. Nos. 91-95) Read the following paragraph and answer the five questions which as follows.*

The experimental psychologist wanted to explore whether the noise adversely affects the Reaction Time (RT). She also wanted to explore whether the stress level would moderate the effect of noise. She varied noise at three levels-Low (30 decibels), Moderate (60 decibels) and High (90 decibels). She varied stress at two levels-low and high. From the initial pool of college students, subjects were randomly assigned to different groups. However, a few subjects could not turn up to the laboratory due to vacation. In all, two hundred and ninety seven subjects participated in the experiments. Each subject, in each group, was tested for simple RT, disjunctive RT, and choice RT.

The theory and preliminary analyses indicated the three types of RT were moderately correlated. The covariance matrices, showing the covariances among the three types of RTs, were found to be quite similar for all the groups. The Multivariate Analysis of Variance (MANOVA) results were computed to explore the group differences in means. As the most common practice is, four test criteria (Pillai's Criterion. Wilks' Criterion., Hotelling's Criterion, and Roy's Criterion) were obtained. Among the different results obtained in this work, one interesting finding was that the stress moderated the effect of noise level on reaction time.

91. Which one of the following reason best justifies the application of MANOVA in the present work?

(a) There are several groups and more than one Independent Variable (IV).
(b) More than one Dependent Variables (DV) have been employed.
(c) More than one Dependent Variables with moderate inter correlations, have been employed.
(d) The moderating effect of stress on the effect of noise on RT can be demonstrated only through MANOVA.

92. The design employed in the above study can best be labelled as
(a) randomised six group design with single factor.
(b) balanced factorial design.
(c) unbalanced factorial design.
(d) unbalanced factorial design with a covariate.

93. The above information suggests that
(a) the assumption of homogeneity of covariance matrices is not satisfied.
(b) the assumption of homogeneity of covariance matrices is satisfied.
(c) covariance among Dependent Variables (DVs) are zero.
(d) the assumption of homogeneity of variances is not tenable.

94. Which of the following test criterion is more appropriate than the others?
(a) Roy's Criterion (b) Wilk's Criterion
(c) Hotelling's Criterion (d) Pillai's Criterion

95. Which one of the following conclusion can be confidently drawn from the above study?
(a) Main effect of noise is significant.
(b) Main effect of stress is significant.
(c) Noise × stress interaction is significant.
(d) The main effects of noise, stress and interaction effect are significant.

Directions *(Q. Nos. 96-100) Read the following paragraph and answer the five questions which as follows.*

A leading business school in the city had a view that its students must have a good proficiency in English language usage. As an initial step, the school authorities decided to develop a brief language usage test.

The project incharge wrote 30 items. Each item had five alternative answers, one of which was correct. He administered these 30 items to a sample of 250 students. For item analysis, item-remainder correlations were computed. The item analysis retained 25 items.

The twenty-five item version was administered to a fresh sample of 300 students. Three reliability coefficients were computed split half reliability coefficient. Kuder-Richardson (K-R) reliability coefficient, and Cronbach alpha were computed. The Cronbach alpha was found to be 0.7. The test-retest reliability was also computed with a time-interval of eight weeks in two administrations, using the same sample.

The test retest correlation was found to be 0.26, significant at .001 level. The school authorities, pleased with the efforts of the project incharge, asked him to add similar items and develop a 75 item version.

96. Which one of the following correlation is most suitable for computing item-remainder correlations?
(a) Tetrachoric Correlations (b) Phi-Coefficient
(c) Contingency Coefficient (d) Point bi-serial Correlation

97. Given below are two statements-one is labelled as Assertion (A) and the other is labelled as Reason (R)
Assertion (A) The computation of (K-R) reliability is questionable in the above study.
Reason (R) K-R reliability is suitable for tests with dichotomous items.
In the light of the above two statements, choose the correct option.
(a) Both A and R are true and R is the correct explanation of A
(b) Both A and R are true and R is not the correct explantion of A
(c) A is true, but R is false
(d) A is false, but R is true

98. The above information provides an evidence for
(a) unsatisfactory test-retest reliability
(b) sasitfactory test-retest reliability
(c) acceptable internal consistency reliability
(d) unacceptable internal consistency reliability
Choose the correct option.
(a) (a) and (c) (b) (a) and (d) (c) (b) and (c) (d) (b) and (d)

99. Consider the three reliability coefficients:
(a) Split-half reliability coefficient; (b) K-R reliability coefficient (c) Cronbach alpha computed in the above study.
Which one of the following is true in the above context?.
(a) All the three reliability coefficients would be same.
(b) All the three reliability coefficients would be different.
(c) (b) and (c) would be same, but (a) can be different.
(d) (a) and (c) would be same, but (b) canbe different.

100. The project incharge developed a 75-item version by adding similar items, what would be the expected Cronbach alpha?
(a) 0.700 (b) 0.824 (c) 0.875 (d) 0.931

ANSWERS

1 (c)	2 (d)	3 (d)	4 (a)	5 (b)	6 (c)	7 (b)	8 (a)	9 (c)	10 (c)
11 (a)	12 (d)	13 (c)	14 (c)	15 (b)	16 (c)	17 (a)	18 (b)	19 (d)	20 (c)
21 (c)	22 (d)	23 (d)	24 (c)	25 (d)	26 (b)	27 (c)	28 (b)	29 (b)	30 (c)
31 (b)	32 (c)	33 (a)	34 (b)	35 (d)	36 (a)	37 (b)	38 (b)	39 (d)	40 (c)
41 (c)	42 (c)	43 (d)	44 (a)	45 (c)	46 (b)	47 (d)	48 (a)	49 (d)	50 (b)
51 (c)	52 (d)	53 (a)	54 (b)	55 (b)	56 (c)	57 (b)	58 (a)	59 (c)	60 (d)
61 (d)	62 (b)	63 (d)	64 (d)	65 (c)	66 (b)	67 (a)	68 (d)	69 (d)	70 (c)
71 (c)	72 (c)	73 (c)	74 (a)	75 (a)	76 (b)	77 (c)	78 (a)	79 (b)	80 (b)
81 (a)	82 (c)	83 (b)	84 (a)	85 (b)	86 (d)	87 (a)	88 (c)	89 (c)	90 (b)
91 (c)	92 (c)	93 (b)	94 (d)	95 (c)	96 (d)	97 (d)	98 (a)	99 (c)	100 (c)

Psychology (Paper-2)
Solved Paper, July 2018

General Instructions

1. There are total one hundred questions in this paper. Each question carries 2 marks.
2. All questions are compulsory.

1 In Erikson's theory, which psycho-social crises preceed and succeed Autonomy v/s Shame

(a) Basic trust v/s Mistrust and Industry v/s Inferiority.
(b) Initiative v/s Guilt and Industry v/s Inferiority.
(c) Industry v/s Inferiority and Identity v/s Role confusion.
(d) Basic trust v/s Mistrust and Initiative v/s Guilt.

2 Read each of the following statements - Assertion (A) and Reason (R); and indicate your answer using code given below :

Assertion (A) Horner found high level of motive to avoid success or fear of success in females.

Reason (R) As a result of success, the threat of social rejection and fear concerning perceived lack of feminity are aroused in women.

Codes

(a) Both A and R are true and R is the correct explanation of A
(b) Both A and R are true, but R is not the correct explanation of A
(c) A is true, but R is false
(d) A is false, but R is true

3 Match List I with List II and select the correct answer by choosing from codes given below:

List I (Concept)	List II (Explanation)
A. Life Space	1. Unlearned, fixed stereotyped pattern of activity.
B. Instinctual Behaviour	2. Psychological reality depicting the totality of facts that determine behaviour at a moment in true. It counts of environment as perceived by the person.
C. Vacuum Behaviour	3. Tendency to resume the previously unfinished task during intervening period.
D. Task Resumption	4. Behaviour patterns that appear when the sign stimulus is not identifiable.

Codes

	A	B	C	D
(a)	1	2	3	4
(b)	2	1	4	3
(c)	3	4	1	2
(d)	4	3	2	1

4 Read each of the following statements - Assertion (A) and Reason (R) and indicate your answer using codes given below.

Assertion (A) Perceived fairness of the interpersonal treatment is used to determine organisational outcomes.

Reason (R) People expect informational transparency and respect in organisations.

Codes
(a) Both A and R are true and R is the correct explanation of A
(b) Both A and R are true, but R is not the correct explanation of A
(c) A is true, but R is false
(d) A is false but R is true

5 Match List I with List II and select the correct answer by choosing from codes given below.

List I (Concept)	List II (Explanation)
A. Episodic retrieval	1. Physical environment at retrieval matching that at encoding.
B. Context-dependent retrieval	2. Mood at retrieval matching that at encoding.
C. State-dependent retrieval	3. Retrieval stimulated by hints from the external and internal environment.
D. Cue-dependent retrieval	4. Subsequent reactivation of stored memory traces.

Codes

	A	B	C	D
(a)	1	2	3	4
(b)	2	4	3	1
(c)	3	4	2	1
(d)	4	1	2	3

6 Read each of the following statements - Assertion (A) and Reason (R) and indicate your answer using codes given below.

Assertion (A) Rational persuation refers to the use of logical arguments and facts to persuade others for achieving a desired result.

Reason (R) Managers use several techniques to influence others in organisations.

Codes
(a) Both A and R are true and R is the correct explanation of A
(b) Both A and R are true, but R is not the correct explanation of A
(c) A is true, but R is false
(d) A is false, but R is true

7 Match List I with List II and select the correct answer by choosing from codes given below.

List I (Concept)	List II (Description)
A. Counter-conditioning	1. After conditioning, a new CS(B) when paired with already Conditioned Stimulus CS(A) and presented as a compound stimulus, little or no conditioning occurs to CS(B).
B. Blocking	2. Elimination of undesirable behaviour by pairing CS with US other than the one that originally reinforced that behaviour.
C. Overshadowing	3. Inhibition of conditioned response caused by conditioned emotional response.
D. Conditioned Suppression	4. While using compound CS where one of its components is more salient than the other, only the salient component is conditioned.

Codes

	A	B	C	D
(a)	2	1	3	4
(b)	2	1	4	3
(c)	4	3	1	2
(d)	4	3	2	1

8 Match List I with List II and select the correct answer by choosing from codes given below.

List I (Concept)	List II (Explanation)
A. Convergence	1. If you see a distant mountain range on a crystal-clear day, it looks like it was only a few miles away.
B. Frame of reference	2. When the two images are fused into one overall image.
C. Stereoscopic vision	3. When we look at a distant object, the lines of vision from our eyes are parallel. Looking at a nearby object, the eyes turn in.
D. Aerial perspective	4. An internal perspective relative to which events are perceived.

Codes

	A	B	C	D
(a)	1	2	3	4
(b)	3	4	2	1
(c)	2	3	4	1
(d)	4	1	3	1

9 Read each of the following statements - Assertion (A) and Reason (R) and indicate your answer using codes given below.

Assertion (A) Perception remains constant although the proximal sensation changes.

Reason (R) Our perceptual system has mechanisms that adjust our perception of the proximal stimulus.

Codes

(a) Both Aand R are true and R is the correct explanation of A

(b) Both A and R are true, but R is not the correct explanation of A

(c) A is true, but R is false

(d) A is false, but R is true

10 **Match List I with List II and select the correct answer by choosing from codes given below.**

	List I (Concept)		List II (Description)
A.	Physiological Psychology	1.	Studies the psychological effects of brain damage in human patients.
B.	Neuropsychology	2.	Studies the neural mechanisms of behaviour by manipulating the nervous systems of non-human animals in controlled experiments.
C.	Psychophysiology	3.	Studies the relation between physiological activity and psychological processes in human subjects by non-invasive physiological recording.
D.	Cognitive Neuroscience	4.	Studies the neural mechanisms of human cognition, mainly by using functional brain imaging techniques.

Codes

	A	B	C	D		A	B	C	D
(a)	1	2	3	4	(b)	3	4	1	2
(c)	2	1	4	3	(d)	4	3	2	1

11 **Which of the following explains the Threshold Hypothesis regarding Intelligence-Creativity relationship ?**

(a) There is a positive correlation between intelligence and creativity.

(b) There is a positive correlation between intelligence and creativity upto a particular level of intelligence.

(c) There is a positive correlation between intelligence and creativity beyond a particular level of intelligence.

(d) There is a negative correlation between intelligence and creativity beyond a particular level of intelligence.

12 **Match List I with List II and select the correct answer by choosing from codes given below.**

	List I (Concept)		List II (Explanation)
A.	Concordance	1.	Percentage of cases in which, if specific gene is present, a particular trait, characteristic or disease will actually manifest itself in the fully developed organism.
B.	Penetrance	2.	Relationship between twins or other family members with respect to a given trait.
C.	Prevalence	3.	Number of new cases of specific condition or disease that arise during a particular period of time.
D.	Incidence	4.	Frequency of occurrence of a given condition among a certain population at a particular point of time.

Codes

	A	B	C	D		A	B	C	D
(a)	1	2	3	4	(b)	3	4	1	2
(c)	2	1	4	3	(d)	4	3	2	1

13 **Which of the following significant changes have been incorporated in DSM-5 ?**

1. The title of the manual is not DSM-V, but DSM-5, a deliberate shift from traditional Roman numerals used in previous editions toward Arabic numerals.
2. Multiaxial Assessment System - a central feature of DSM since its introduction in DSM - III in 1980, has been dropped altogether from DSM-5.
3. DSM-5 authors have overhauled the manual to emphasise neuropsychological or biological roots of mental disorders.
4. DSM-5 authors have removed 5 of 10 personality disorders previously included in that section. Dropped disorders are paranoid, schizoid, histrionic, dependent and narcissistic personality disorders.

Codes

(a) 1, 2, 3 are correct; 4 is incorrect

(b) 2, 3 and 4 are correct; 1 is incorrect

(c) 1 and 2 are correct; 3 and 4 are incorrect

(d) 3 and 4 are correct; 1 and 2 are incorrect

14 **Which one of the trait theories/models is/are not based on factor analytic methodology ?**

1. Allport's Theory
2. Costa and McCrae's Model
3. Goldberg's Model
4. Eysenck's Theory

Codes

(a) Only 1 (b) 1 and 3 (c) 2 and 3 (d) 2 and 4

15 **The factors that operate with deep levels of processing are**

1. Distinctiveness 2. Sameness
3. Elaboration 4. Physical contours

Codes

(a) 1 and 2 (b) 2 and 3

(c) 2 and 4 (d) 1 and 3

16 Observation learning involves following processes. Arrange them in the correct sequence
1. Attentional processes
2. Retention processes
3. Production processes
4. Motivational processes

Codes:
(a) 1, 2, 3, 4 (b) 1, 4, 2, 3 (c) 4, 1, 2, 3 (d) 1, 2, 4, 3

17 Key issues in the study of environmental effects on intelligence are
1. Reaction Range
2. Proximal and Distal Causation
3. Colinearity
4. Environment Sphere

Codes
(a) 1, 2 and 3 (b) 1, 2 and 4 (c) 2, 3 and 4 (d) 1, 3 and 4

18 Read each of the following statements - Assertion (A) and Reason (R) and indicate your answer using codes given below.

Assertion (A) According to two factor theory, cognitive appraisal of cues in the environment helps the individual label the emotions.

Reason (R) An individual is aroused when he confronts any emotion producing event.

Codes
(a) Both A and R are true and R is the correct explanation of A
(b) Both A and R are true, but R is not the correct explanation of A
(c) A is true, but R is false
(d) A is false, but R is true

19 Whether we can be affected by stimuli that remain outside our conscious awareness has been examined by researches using a technique called
(a) Cuing (b) Visualisation
(c) Imagery (d) Priming

20 Which of the following sequences depicts Erikson's stages of development correctly ?
(a) Oral Sensory → Muscular anal → Locomotor genital → Latency → Adolescence → Adulthood.
(b) Muscular anal → Oral Sensory → Locomotor genital → Latency → Adolescence → Adulthood.
(c) Oral Sensory → Muscular anal → Latency → Locomotor genital → Adolescence → Adulthood.
(d) Muscular anal → Locomotor genital → Oral Sensory → Latency → Adolescence → Adulthood.

21 Match List I with List II and select the correct answer by choosing from codes given below.

List I (Concept)	List II (Explanation)
A. Magnocellular System	1. Discrimination of fine detail and colour.
B. Parvocellular System	2. Specialised for brightness contrast and for movement.
C. Fourier Analysis	3. Neurons that fire most when they receive input from both ears at the same time.
D. Coincidence Detectors	4. Analysis of a complex wave into sine wave components.

Codes

	A	B	C	D
(a)	1	2	3	4
(b)	3	4	1	2
(c)	2	1	4	3
(d)	4	3	2	1

22 Match List I with List II and select the correct answer by choosing from codes given below.

List I (Concept)	List II (Explanation)
A. Inductive thought	1. Thought that is intuitive and haphazard.
B. Logical thought	2. Thought that applies a general set of rules to specific situations.
C. Deductive thought	3. Drawing conclusions on the basis of principles of learning.
D. Illogical thought	4. Thinking in which a principle is inferred from a series of specific examples.

Codes

	A	B	C	D
(a)	1	2	3	4
(b)	2	3	4	1
(c)	3	4	1	2
(d)	4	3	2	1

23 Which of the following personality questionnaires have a lie scale ?
1. Edward Personality Preference Schedule
2. Eysenck Personality Questionnaire
3. Minnesota Multiphasic Personality Questionnaire-2
4. Rotter's Locus of Control Scale.

Codes
(a) 1 and 2 (b) 1 and 3
(c) 2 and 3 (d) 1, 2 and 3

24 Read the following statements and describe which are correct.
1. Archetypes are themes that have existed in all cultures through history.
2. Personal unconscious is the region next to ego which consists of all the forgotten experiences that have lost their intensity.
3. Masculine archetype in men is called animus.
4. Persona is a compromise between demands of the environment and necessities of individuals.

Codes
(a) 1, 2 and 3 are correct ; 4 is not correct
(b) 2, 3 and 4 are correct ; 1 is not correct
(c) 1, 2 and 4 are correct ; 3 is not correct
(d) 1, 3 and 4 are correct ; and 2 is not correct

25 George Sperling (1960) studied iconic memory using.

1. Partial-report procedure
2. Whole-report procedure
3. Self-report procedure
4. Backward procedure

Codes
(a) Only 1 (b) Only 4 (c) 1 and 3 (d) 2 and 4

26 Match List I with List II and select the correct answer by choosing from codes given below.

List I (Sub Test)	List II (Test)
A. Visual Puzzles	1. WAIS - IV
B. Famous people	2. Kaulfman Adult Intelligence Test (KAIT)
C. Matrix Task	3. Cognitive Assessment System (CAS)
D. Matrix Patterns	4. Otis-Lenon Test

Codes

	A	B	C	D		A	B	C	D
(a)	1	2	3	4	(b)	2	1	4	3
(c)	3	4	1	2	(d)	4	3	2	1

27 Which of the following terms explains the Reinforcement which is given only if a specific response is made ?
(a) Concurrent Reinforcement
(b) Incremental Reinforcement
(c) Contingency Contract
(d) Contingent Reinforcement

28 Read each of the following statements - Assertion (A) and Reason (R) and indicate your answer using codes given below.

Assertion (A) A person scored high on Hope of Success (as measured by TAT) and high on Fear of Failure (as measured by Mandler and Sarason's TAQ). As per Atkinson's theory, his resultant achievement motivation will be intermediate.

Reason (R) As per Atkinson, the resultant achievement motivation is a product of Hope of Success and Fear of Failure.

Codes
(a) Both A and R are true and R is the correct explanation of A
(b) Both A and R are true, but R is not the correct explanation of A
(c) A is true, but R is false
(d) A is false, but R is true

29 Read each of the following statements - Assertion (A) and Reason (R) and indicate your answer using codes given below

Assertion (A) Personality factors such as D, J, K and P are not incorporated in Cattell's 16 PF test.

Reason (R) Some personality factors appeared only in Life - data (L-data) measures.

Codes
(a) Both A and R are true and R is the correct explanation of A
(b) Both A and R are true, but R is not the correct explanation of A
(c) A is true, but R is false
(d) A is false, but R is true

30 During which stage most of the creative thinking occurs ?
(a) Preparation (b) Incubation
(c) Illumination (d) Evaluation

31 Match List I with List II and select the correct answer by choosing from codes given below.

List I (Concept)	List II (Explanation)
A. Disjunctive Concept	1. A class of objects that have two or more features is common.
B. Prototype	2. Showing relationship between object and surroundings.
C. Conjunctive Concept	3. Showing the presence of at least one of several possible features.
D. Relational Concept	4. An ideal model referring to a particular concept.

Codes

	A	B	C	D		A	B	C	D
(a)	1	2	3	4	(b)	3	4	1	2
(c)	2	3	4	1	(d)	4	3	1	2

32 Chimpanzee Sarah's one of the most outstanding achievements was the construction of sentences involving
(a) Negation
(b) Conditional relationship
(c) Adult grammar
(d) Unprompted questions

33 In a typical 'Learning' experiment which of the following are used as dependent variables ?

1. Probability of Response
2. Latency
3. Rate of Presentation
4. Trials to Extinction

Codes
(a) 1 and 2 (b) 2 and 4
(c) 1, 2 and 3 (d) 1, 2 and 4

34 **Explanation of the moon illusion given by is, "The horizon seems more distant than the night sky."**
(a) Perceptual learning hypothesis
(b) Expectancy hypothesis
(c) Apparent - distance hypothesis
(d) Frame of reference hypothesis

35 **Absorptive phase of energy mobilisation involves the following events. Arrange them in the correct sequence.**
1. Glucose increases.
2. Parasympathetic activation.
3. Pancreas secretes insulin.
4. Glucose enters the body cells.
5. Glucose is stored in liver and muscles as glycogen.
6. Fat stored in adipose cells as triglycerides.

Codes
(a) 1, 2, 3, 5, 4, 6 (b) 1, 2, 3, 4, 5, 6
(c) 1, 3, 2, 4, 6, 5 (d) 1, 4, 2, 6, 5, 3

36 **In a multiple regression analysis, the three predictors explained 49 per cent variance in the criterion variable. What would be the value of multiple correlation ?**
(a) 0.30 (b) 0.49 (c) 0.51 (d) 0.70

37 **Read each of the following statements - Assertion (A) and Reason (R) and indicate your answer using codes given below.**
Assertion (A) The analysis of time series designs often involve the problem of auto correlation.
Reason (R) Quasi - experiments, as compared to laboratory experiments, do not control secondary variance efficiently.

Codes
(a) Both A and R are true and R is the correct explanation of A
(b) Both A and R are true, but R is not the correct explanation of A
(c) A is true, but R is false
(d) A is false, but R is true

38 **Future oriented performance appraisal techniques consist of**
1. MBO 2. 360° Appraisal
3. Psychological Appraisal 4. BARS

Codes
(a) 1, 2 and 4 (b) 1, 2 and 3 (c) 2, 3 and 4 (d) 1, 3 and 4

39 **In group counselling, what is the correct sequence of stages of group development ?**
1. Forming 2. Norming
3. Mourning 4. Storming
5. Performing

Codes
(a) 2, 3, 1, 5, 4 (b) 1, 4, 2, 5, 3
(c) 1, 3, 5, 2, 4 (d) 4, 1, 2, 3, 5

40 **Read each of the following statements - Assertion (A) and Reason (R) and indicate your answer using codes given below.**
Assertion (A) Pre-operational child is incapable of performing operations.
Reason (R) Pre-operational child cannot mentally rearrange a sequence of events into reverse order.

Codes
(a) Both A and R are true and R is the correct explanation of A
(b) Both A and R are true, but R is not the correct explanation of A
(c) A is true, but R is false
(d) A is false, but R is true

41 **Read each of the following statements - Assertion (A) and Reason (R) and indicate your answer using codes given below.**
Assertion (A) For extraversion, monozygotic twins correlated more than the dizygotic twins.
Reason (R) Extraversion has genetic basis.

Codes
(a) Both A and R are true and R is the correct explanation of A
(b) Both A and R are true, but R is not the correct Explanation of A
(c) A is true, but R is false
(d) A is false, but R is true

42 **During autobiographical recall, we often reveal a .... , as a consequence, our memory of the past may be**
(a) inconsistency bias; distorted
(b) consistency bias; distorted
(c) inconsistency bias; enhanced
(d) consistency bias; enhanced

43 **Persons with a leison at the ventromedial nucleus are likely to**
(a) Overeat (b) Undereat
(c) Eat normally (d) Eat normally or undereat

44 **The percepts are based on**
1. What we sense
2. What we know
3. What we infer
4. What we conform

Codes
(a) 1 and 2 (b) 2 and 3 (c) 1, 2 and 3 (d) 1, 2 and 4

45 **Match List I with List II and select the correct answer by choosing from codes given below**

List I (Concept)	List II (Explanation)
A. Phrenology	1. Field that locates areas of the brain responsible for specific aspects of emotional and behaviour functioning.

List I (Concept)		List II (Explanation)
B. Selective Breeding	2.	An approach to establish genetic - behaviour relationship through mating of successive generations with a particular trait.
C. Plasticity	3.	Ability of parts of neurobiological system to change temporarily and for extended period time.
D. Twin studies	4.	An approach to establish of genetic - behaviour relationship through the comparison degree of similarity among identical twins, fraternal twins and non-twins siblings.

Codes

	A	B	C	D		A	B	C	D
(a)	1	2	3	4	(b)	2	1	4	3
(c)	3	4	1	2	(d)	4	3	2	1

Directions (Q. Nos. 46 to 50) *Read the following paragraph and answer the five questions which follow.*

A researcher in experimental psychology hypothesised that a particular 'Reward System' for fast reactions would improve the reaction time. To verify this hypothesis, he selected forty subjects in the age range of 25 to 35 years from an organisation. Following the standard reaction time experiment, he measured the simple reaction time without the reward system. While taking each trial in the experiment, the time-interval between the ready signal and the onset of stimulus was randomly varied between two to five seconds. In the second part of the experiment, the reward system was introduced and the simple reaction time was measured again for the same subjects. The mean reaction time before the introduction of reward system was 210 milliseconds and the mean reaction time after the introduction of reward system was 250 milliseconds. The difference between the two means was statistically significant at .01 level.

46 In the above study, the researcher's hypothesis is

(a) Correlational hypothesis (b) Directional hypothesis
(c) Non-directional hypothesis (d) Null hypothesis

47 Which of the following statistical techniques can be used for evaluating the mean differences ?

1. Independent samples t-test
2. Paired samples t-test
3. Mann-Whitney U-test
4. Repeated measures ANOVA

Codes

(a) Only 2 (b) 1 and 2 (c) 2 and 4 (d) 1, 2 and 4

48 Which one of the following conclusions can be drawn on the basis of the above study ?

(a) The researcher's hypothesis has been accepted.
(b) The researcher's hypothesis has been rejected.
(c) The researcher's hypothesis has been partially accepted.
(d) Inadequate hypothesis to verify the hypothesis.

49 Read each of the following statements - Assertion (A) and Reason (R) and indicate your answer using codes given below.

Assertion (A) **In the above study, the foreperiods were randomly varied.**

Reason (R) **Random variation of the foreperiods reduces the false reactions.**

Codes

(a) Both A and R are true and R is the correct explanation of A
(b) Both A and R are true, but R is not the correct explanation of A
(c) A is true, but R is false
(d) A is false, but R is true

50 In this experiment, reaction time can be labelled as

1. Continuous variable
2. Dependent variable
3. Stimulus variable
4. Behavioural variable

Codes

(a) Only 2 (b) 1 and 2 (c) 1, 2 and 3 (d) 1, 2 and 4

51 In Vertebrates, myelin is produced in the brain and spinal cord by .... and in rest of nervous system by

(a) Oligodendrocytes ; Schwann cells
(b) Schwann cells ; Oligodendrocytes
(c) Astrocytes ; Microglia
(d) Microglia ; Astrocytes

52 Read each of the following statements - Assertion (A) and Reason (R) and indicate your answer using codes given below.

Assertion (A) **Algorithm is a logical rule that guarantees solving a particular problem.**

Reason (R) **One can find the solution even to complex problems by following step by step procedure.**

Codes

(a) Both A and R are true and R is the correct explanation of A
(b) Both A and R are true, but R is not the correct explanation of A
(c) A is true, but R is false
(d) A is false, but R is true

53 Match List I with List II and select the correct answer by choosing from codes given below.

List I (Personality tests)	List II (Dimensions covered)
A. EPQ-R	1. Need for power
B. NEO-PI-3	2. Psychoticism
C. TAT	3. Anxiety as a state
D. STAI	4. Openness to experience

Codes

	A	B	C	D		A	B	C	D
(a)	2	4	1	3	(b)	4	2	1	3
(c)	2	4	3	1	(d)	1	4	3	2

54 The basic speech sounds are called .... and the meaningful smallest units of speech are called

(a) Phonemes ; Fixation (b) Phonemes ; Lexigram
(c) Morphemes ; Phonemes (d) Phonemes ; Morphemes

55 Which of the following concept/s is/are not found in Freudian Psychoanalysis ?

1. Unconscious motivation
2. Collective unconscious
3. Striving for superiority
4. Instincts

Codes

(a) 1 and 2 (b) 2 and 3
(c) 3 and 4 (d) 1, 2 and 4

56 Tests of declarative memory are termed as .... tests, whereas tests of non-declarative memory are termed as .... tests.

(a) Long term memory ; explicit memory
(b) Short term memory ; implicit memory
(c) Implicit memory ; explicit memory
(d) Explicit memory ; implicit memory

57 Which method is used for memorising a poem ?

(a) Massed practice (b) Distributed practice
(c) Serial memorising (d) Syntactic memorising

58 .... makes neurons stand out visibly depicting which neurons are active; whereas ...... uses antibodies attached to a dye to identify cellular components such as receptors, neurotransmitters or enzymes.

(a) Immunocytochemistry ; Autoradiography
(b) Autoradiography ; Immunocytochemistry
(c) Myelin staining ; Nissl Staining
(d) Nissl Staining ; Myelin Staining

59 Which of the following are predictors of good prognosis in Schizophrenia.

1. Positive symptoms
2. Late onset
3. Acute onset
4. No precipitating factors

Codes

(a) 1, 2 and 3 are correct ; 4 is incorrect
(b) 2, 3 and 4 are correct ; 1 is incorrect
(c) 3, 4 and 2 are correct ; 1 is incorrect
(d) 1, 3 and 4 are correct ; 2 is incorrect

60 The body's response to danger is triggered by the release of .... by the .... glands.

(a) Acetylcholine ; adrenal
(b) Epinephrine and norepinephrine; adrenal
(c) Acetylcholine ; pituitary
(d) Epinephrine and norepinephrine; pituitary

61 Which of the following is the characteristic of Mastery-Oriented Students ?

(a) They see ability as improvable
(b) They feel competent when they succeed
(c) They feel worthless when they fail
(d) They set unrealistically high goals

62 A child's cognitive transition from external influences to internal thoughts occurs in four stages. What is the correct order of this transition?

1. Naive Stage
2. Natural / Primitive Stage
3. Ego-centric speech Stage
4. Ingrowth Stage

Codes

(a) 1, 2, 3, 4 (b) 2, 1, 3, 4
(c) 1, 2, 4, 3 (d) 2, 1, 4, 3

63 Match List I with List II and select the correct answer by choosing from codes given below.

	List I (Psychologist)		List II (Concept)
A.	Bruner	1.	Conservation
B.	Vygotsky	2.	Iconic mode of representation
C.	Sternberg	3.	Scaffolding
D.	Piaget	4.	Componential Analysis

Codes

	A	B	C	D
(a)	2	3	4	1
(b)	4	2	3	1
(c)	2	3	1	4
(d)	3	2	4	1

64 Which of the following issues are addressed in the field of Personality Psychology?

1. Human Universals
2. Individual Differences
3. Uniqueness
4. Modification of Behaviour

Codes

(a) 1 and 2 (b) 2 and 3
(c) 1, 2 and 3 (d) 2, 3 and 4

65 Match List I with List II and select the correct answer by choosing from codes given below.

	List I (Psychologist)		List II (Concept)
A.	Thorndike	1.	Equipotentiality premise
B.	Pavlov	2.	Cortical Mosaic
C.	Wertheimer	3.	Neural Bond
D.	Seligman	4.	Isomorphism

Codes

	A	B	C	D		A	B	C	D
(a)	1	4	3	2	(b)	2	3	4	1
(c)	3	2	4	1	(d)	4	1	2	3

66 In case of visual stimulus "Where" pathways in the brain are mainly responsible for processing :

1. Location
2. Colour
3. Motion
4. Shape

Codes

(a) 1 and 2 (b) 2 and 3
(c) 3 and 4 (d) 1 and 4

67 Which of the following sequences describes the Cranial Nerves in ascending order?

(a) Optic → Trochlear → Abducens → Auditory - Vestibular → Vagus
(b) Trochlear → Optic → Auditory-Vestibular → Abducens → Vagus
(c) Optic → Abducens → Trochlear → Vagus → Auditory - Vestibular
(d) Abducens → Trochlear → Optic → Auditory - Vestibular → Vagus

68 Many psychologists played pivotal role in the emergence of the field of Social Psychology. Arrange them in correct chronological sequence.

(a) F Allport; William McDougall; Kurt Lewin; Muzafer Sherif
(b) Kurt Lewin; William McDougall; Muzafer Sherif; F Allport
(c) William McDougall; F Allport; Kurt Lewin; Muzafer Sherif
(d) F Allport; William McDougall; Muzafer Sherif; Kurt Lewin

69 Kinship Selection Theory suggests that we help others who are related to us because this increases the likelihood that our .... shall be .... to future

(a) character; transferred; population
(b) genes; transmitted; population
(c) genes; transmitted; generation
(d) genes; transferred; population

70 Read each of the following statements - Assertion (A) and Reason (R); and indicate your answer using codes given below.

Assertion (A) Results of experimental studies of bilateral lesion effects are considered more promising than those of unilateral lesions.

Reason (R) Behaviour effects of bilateral lesions are milder than those of unilateral lesions.

Codes

(a) Both A and R are true and R is the correct explanation of A
(b) Both A and R are true, but R is not the correct explanation of A
(c) A is true, but R is false
(d) A is false, but R is true

71 Which of the following are the basic forms of intelligence in Triarchic Theory?

1. Dimensional
2. Componential
3. Contextual
4. Experiential

Codes

(a) 1, 2 and 3 (b) 1, 2 and 4 (c) 2, 3 and 4 (d) 1, 3 and 4

72 In a single factor repeated measures design, the F-ratio, evaluating the effect of independent variable (treatment) is evaluated as

(a) MStreatment/MSsubjects
(b) MStreatment/MStreatment × subjects
(c) MStreatment/(MSsubjects) + (MStreatment×subjects)
(d) MStreatment/MStotal

73 Match List I with List II and select the correct answer by choosing from codes given below

List I (Leadership style)	List II (Description)
A. Task Management	1. Less focus on both production and workers
B. Team Management	2. More Focus on both production and workers
C. Impoverished Management	3. Less focus on production but more on workers
D. Country Club Management	4. More focus on production but less on workers

Codes

	A	B	C	D		A	B	C	D
(a)	1	2	3	4	(b)	4	3	2	1
(c)	3	4	1	2	(d)	4	2	1	3

74 Read each of the following statements - Assertion (A) and Reason (R) and indicate your answer using codes given below.

Assertion (A) Behaviour therapy helps people to respond to life situations in the way they would like to respond.

Reason (R) Positive therapeutic relationship is a necessary but not sufficient condition for effective behaviour therapy.

Codes

(a) Both A and R are true and R is the correct explanation of A
(b) Both A and R are true, but R is not the correct explanation of A
(c) A is true, but R is false
(d) A is false, but R is true

75 Decentration and reversible thought processes are the characteristics of which of the following stage ?

(a) Sensory - Motor
(b) Pre - Operational
(c) Concrete - Operational
(d) Formal Operations

76 Match List I with List II and select the correct answer by choosing from codes given below.

	List I (Concept)		List II (Explanation)
A.	Central executive	1.	Helps us in playing videogames, jigsaw puzzles, etc.
B.	Visuospatial sketchpad	2.	Helps us in solving new problems and plan future activities.
C.	Episodic buffer	3.	Helps us decide what to do next and what not to do.
D.	Phonological loop	4.	Helps us in reading and mathematical calculations.

Codes

	A	B	C	D		A	B	C	D
(a)	1	2	3	4	(b)	3	1	2	4
(c)	4	3	1	2	(d)	2	3	4	1

77 Read each of the following statements - Assertion (A) and Reason (R) and indicate your answer using codes given below.

Assertion (A) Working memory is like a workbench where material is constantly being handled, combined and transformed.

Reason (R) Both new material and old material retrieved from long term memory are held in working memory.

Codes

(a) Both A and R are true and R is the correct explanation of A
(b) Both A and R are true, but R is not the correct explanation of A
(c) A is true, but R is false
(d) A is false, but R is true

78 Read each of the following statements - Assertion (A) and Reason (R) and indicate your answer using codes given below.

Assertion (A) Galton developed anthropometric tests of intelligence.

Reason (R) Psychometric tests were low in reliability and validity.

Codes

(a) Both A and R are true and R is the correct explanation of A
(b) Both A and R are true, but R is not the correct explanation of A
(c) A is true, but R is false
(d) A is false, but R is true

79 Read each of the following statements - Assertion (A) and Reason (R) and indicate your answer using code given below.

Assertion (A) Proprioceptive stimuli result from the firing of the kinesthetic receptors in the muscles, joints and tendons of the body.

Reason (R) A response is conditioned to the stimuli present prior to the ingestion of a primary reinforcer.

Codes

(a) Both A and R are true and R is the correct explanation of A
(b) Both A and R are true, but R is not the correct explanation of A
(c) A is true, but R is false
(d) A is false, but R is true

80 Activation of anterior portions of both hemispheres is associated with the .... of emotions, while activation of the posterior portions of the hemispheres is associated with

(a) expressions; moods
(b) valence; arousal
(c) intensity; expressions
(d) arousal; valence

81 Signal detection theory identifies two distinct processes in sensory detection

1. sensory process
2. decision process
3. motivational process
4. response bias

Codes

(a) 1 and 2 (b) 3 and 4
(c) 1 and 3 (d) 1 and 4

82 Read each of the following statements - Assertion (A) and Reason (R) and indicate your answer using codes given below.

Assertion (A) Visual Simple Reaction Time is more than Auditory Simple Reaction Time.

Reason (R) Visual system involves more complex photochemical processes.

Codes

(a) Both A and R are true and R is the correct explanation of A
(b) Both A and R are true, but R is not the correct explanation of A
(c) A is true, but R is false
(d) A is false, but R is true

83 Creative thinking is different from routine problem solving in respect of

1. Fluency
2. Flexibility
3. Originality
4. Day dreaming

Codes

(a) 1 and 2 (b) 2 and 3 (c) 3 and 4 (d) 1, 2 and 3

84 The Wechsler type deviation IQ of 115 corresponds to which value of percentile rank ?

(a) 68 (b) 84
(c) 90 (d) 9

85 Match List I with List II and select the correct answer by choosing from codes given below.

List I (Term)		List II (Description)
A.	Conformity	1. Rules indicating how individuals are expected to behave in a specific situation.
B.	Compliance	2. Social influence involving direct request from other.
C.	Social norms	3. Social influence wherein individuals change their attitude to go along with existing norms.
D.	Intense indoctorinisation	4. Process in which members of extreme group accept the beliefs and rules in unquestioning way.

Codes

	A	B	C	D		A	B	C	D
(a)	1	2	3	4	(b)	2	3	4	1
(c)	3	4	1	2	(d)	3	4	2	1

86 Spatial processing of location relies on :

1. Dorsal pathway
2. Inferior temporal cortex
3. Subcortical pathway
4. Ventral pathway

Codes

(a) Only 1 (b) Only 4 (c) 2 and 3 (d) 1 and 4

87 Read each of the following statements - Assertion (A) and Reason (R) and indicate your answer using codes given below.

Assertion (A) Jensen has put forward regression argument in favour of his theory.

Reason (R) Children of parents having very high intelligence levels will have below average intelligence scores.

Codes

(a) Both A and R are true and R is the correct explanation of A
(b) Both A and R are true, but R is not the correct explanation of A
(c) A is true, but R is false
(d) A is false, but R is true

88 Handling feelings appropriately, ability to soothe oneself and ability to shake off rampant anxiety are the characteristics of which of the components of emotional intelligence as proposed by Goleman?

(a) Knowing one's emotions (b) Managing emotions
(c) Motivating oneself (d) Handling relationships

89 Which of the following new disorders have been introduced in DSM-5 ?

1. Premenstrual Dysphoric Disorder
2. Mild Neurocognitive Disorder
3. Disruptive Mood Dysregulation Disorder
4. Road Rage Behaviour Disorder

Codes

(a) 1, 2 and 3 are correct ; 4 is incorrect
(b) 1, 2 and 4 are correct ; 3 is incorrect
(c) 1, 3 and 4 are correct ; 2 is incorrect
(d) All 1, 2, 3 and 4 are correct

90 In selection process, Guilford - Zimmerman Test assesses :

(a) Mathematical and Verbal skills
(b) Mental and Personal profile
(c) Extent of temperamental adaptability
(d) Analytical and Verbal Skills

91 'Mechanistic Behaviour Analysis' are characterised as

1. Behaviour is instigated by the onset of external or internal stimuli.
2. Direction of behaviour is determined by S-R bonds or habits.
3. Behaviour directed toward the goal persists till the achievement of goal.
4. Events related to the goal achievement are encoded, categorised, and transformed into a belief.

Codes

(a) 1 and 2 correct ; 3 and 4 are incorrect
(b) 2 and 3 correct ; 1 and 4 are incorrect
(c) 1, 2 and 3 are correct ; 4 is incorrect
(d) 2, 3 and 4 are correct ; 1 is incorrect

92 Guilford (1981) in his modified SOI model mentioned hierarchical structure of intellectual abilities reporting that there are first order factors; second order factors and third order factors.

(a) 150; 85; 20 (b) 120; 80; 20 (c) 150; 85;16 (d) 180; 75; 18

93 Read each of the following statements - Assertion (A) and Reason (R) and indicate your answer using codes given below.

Assertion (A) Children have remarkable ability to create mental representation of the world in the form of language.

Reason (R) Reasoning and problem solving are the ways of manipulating the ideas.

Codes

(a) Both A and R are true and R is the correct explanation of A
(b) Both A and R are true, but R is not the correct explanation of A
(c) A is true, but R is false
(d) A is false, but R is true

94 Read each of the following statements - Assertion (A) and Reason (R) and indicate your answer using codes given below.

Assertion (A) Forgetting of everyday events in young people is not an indication of a poor memory.

Reason (R) Ineffective encoding due to failure to attend to an event while it is happening results in failure to remember.

Codes

(a) Both A and R are true and R is the correct explanation of A
(b) Both A and R are true, but R is not the correct explanation of A
(c) A is true, but R is false
(d) A is false but R is true

95 Read each of the following statements - Assertion (A) and Reason (R) and indicate your answer using codes given below.

Assertion (A) Premack principle, based on Probability-Differential Hypothesis, states that the opportunity to engage in a frequently occurring activity can be used to reinforce less frequently activity.

Reason (R) According to Probability-Differential Hypothesis, restricted access to a response makes that response reinforcing and excessive access to that response makes that response punishing.

Codes

(a) Both A and R are true and R is the correct explanation of A
(b) Both A and R are true, but R is not the correct explanation of A
(c) A is true, but R is false
(d) A is false, but R is true

Directions (Q. Nos. 96-100) *Read the following paragraph and answer the five questions which follow.*

An educational psychologist wanted to develop an achievement test in physics for graduate students. After going through the usual test construction procedure, he retained 100 items; each item having five alternatives, one of them being correct. The psychologist wanted to examine the factor structure of the resulting achievement test. Using a sample of 1,000 subjects, the psychologist obtained the inter-item correlations. He obtained the initial estimates of communality and then decided to factor analyse the inter-item correlations matrix by following the common-factor model. He extracted the unrotated factors and retained the first nine factors for rotation. The nine unrotated factors explained 67.5 per cent of variance. After factor rotation, all the inter-factor correlations were found to be zero. The factor structure of the achievement test of physics was found to be interpretable.

96 The inter-item correlations would be :

(a) Biserial correlations (b) Kendall's tau
(c) Phi-coefficients (d) Point-biserial correlations

97 Read each of the following statements - Assertion (A) and Reason (R) and indicate your answer using codes given below.

Assertion (A) For the factor analysis of item scores, Common-Factor model is quite often more suitable.

Reason (R) Item scores are quite often less reliable than the psychometrically measured trait variables.

Codes

(a) Both A and R are true and R is the correct explanation of A
(b) Both A and R are true, but R is not the correct explanation of A
(c) A is true, but R is false
(d) A is false, but R is true

98 Which one of the following method of factor extraction, the psychologist would not use in the present study ?

(a) Principal axes method
(b) Principal components method
(c) Psychometric (alpha) factor analysis
(d) Maximum likelihood method

99 Which method/s of rotation has/have most probably been used in the present study ?

1. Oblimin 2. Promax
3. Quartimax 4. Varimax

Codes

(a) Only 1 (b) Only 3 (c) 3 and 4 (d) 2, 3 and 4

100 The second-order factor analysis of the nine rotated factors is not recommended in the present study because

(a) there are only nine first-order factors.
(b) the interfactor correlations are zero.
(c) the factors obtained by common-factor model are not subjected to second-order factor analysis.
(d) unrotated factors are more suitable for second-order factor analysis.

ANSWERS

1	*(d)*	2	*(a)*	3	*(b)*	4	*(a)*	5	*(d)*	6	*(a)*	7	*(b)*	8	*(b)*	9	*(a)*	10	*(c)*
11	*(b)*	12	*(c)*	13	*(c)*	14	*(a)*	15	*(d)*	16	*(a)*	17	*(a)*	18	*(b)*	19	*(d)*	20	*(a)*
21	*(c)*	22	*(d)*	23	*(c)*	24	*(c)*	25	*(a)*	26	*(a)*	27	*(d)*	28	*(c)*	29	*(a)*	30	*(b)*
31	*(b)*	32	*(b)*	33	*(d)*	34	*(c)*	35	*(b)*	36	*(d)*	37	*(b)*	38	*(b)*	39	*(b)*	40	*(a)*
41	*(a)*	42	*(b)*	43	*(a)*	44	*(c)*	45	*(a)*	46	*(b)*	47	*(c)*	48	*(b)*	49	*(a)*	50	*(d)*
51	*(a)*	52	*(a)*	53	*(a)*	54	*(d)*	55	*(b)*	56	*(d)*	57	*(b)*	58	*(b)*	59	*(d)*	60	*(b)*
61	*(a)*	62	*(b)*	63	*(a)*	64	*(c)*	65	*(c)*	66	*(d)*	67	*(a)*	68	*(c)*	69	*(c)*	70	*(b)*
71	*(c)*	72	*(b)*	73	*(d)*	74	*(b)*	75	*(c)*	76	*(b)*	77	*(b)*	78	*(c)*	79	*(a)*	80	*(c)*
81	*(a)*	82	*(a)*	83	*(b)*	84	*(b)*	85	*(b)*	86	*(a)*	87	*(c)*	88	*(b)*	89	*(a)*	90	*(c)*
91	*(c)*	92	*(c)*	93	*(b)*	94	*(a)*	95	*(c)*	96	*(c)*	97	*(a)*	98	*(b)*	99	*(c)*	100	*(b)*

NTA UGC

NET/JRF/SET

PSYCHOLOGY

CHAPTER 1

UNIT I : Emergence of Psychology

Psychological Thoughts in Eastern Systems

Psychology as a subject originated in Western world. However, Eastern systems and texts have made immense contribution in enrichment of psychological thoughts and perspectives.

Introduction to Psychology

Psychology is the study of the human mind and its functions, especially those affecting behaviour in a given context. It is the scientific study of human mind and mental processes and how it affects human behaviour.

Though the main stream of psychology originated in the West and is promoted by the majority of 'Western' psychologists, yet the relevance of considering the value of psychological perspectives mentioned in Eastern systems cannot be side lined.

Eastern influence on Western thought goes back to the time of the ancient Greeks and Romans. Alexander the Great in 4th Century BC and the Roman philosopher Plotinus in 242 CE reached India and made efforts to study the philosophies of the region.

Great Psychologists like Carl Rogers, Abraham Maslow, William James and Eric Fromm have shown deep interest in the psychological thoughts presented in the major Eastern systems. Theosophical Movement in the 19th century created a real interest of scholars in Eastern thought (including Buddhism). The insights in understanding human nature as per Indian thoughts is derived from various Indian philosophical traditions like Vedanta, Samkhya, Yoga, Buddhism, Jainism and many more ancient religious texts.

Indian psychology follows the description of self and personality as mentioned in the various Hindu religious texts. In Hinduism as per Taittiryopanishad, soul (atma or bliss) is wrapped inside five layers (Pancha kosha) of Arishadvarga.

The five layers which wraps the soul as per Hindu religious texts are

(i) Annamaya Kosha (food sheath).
(ii) Pranamaya Kosha (vital air sheath or life force).
(iii) Manomaya Kosha (mind as distinctly different from intelligence).
(iv) Vigyanmaya Kosha (intellect sheath).

In this Chapter

- Introduction to Psychology
- Psychological Thoughts in Eastern Systems
- Academic Psychology in India
- Issues in Indian Psychology

(v) Anandmaya Kosha (Bliss sheath–ceaseless joy not connected to body or mind)

Out of these five layers, Annamaya Kosha is the outermost layer of Pancha Kosha and Anandmaya Kosha is the innermost layer of Pancha Kosha.

There is essential continuity between the self and non-self. This implies that the line demarcating self and non-self is not a fixed one. The self may be more or less inclusive on different occasions.

Psychological Thougts in Eastern Systems

It is naturally believed that psychology as a subject originated in Western world. However, a deep reading of Eastern text like Bhagavad Gita, ideas of Buddhism, Sufism and Integral yoga gives an insight into importance of psychological thoughts in the Eastern system.

Bhagavad Gita

Bhagavad Gita is a 700 verse sanskrit scripture that is a part of Hindu Epic Mahabharata. The Gita is set in a narrative framework of a dialogue between Pandava prince Arjun and his guide and charioteer Krishna. Gita is considered to be one of the best contributions of India to the world as it is one of the first revelations from God. Its a doctrine of universal truth.

Gita needs no introduction and is respected in both Eastern and Western culture. As Bhagavad Gita deals with human day-to-day worries, anxieties and inhibitions which people face in their daily day-to-day life. The importance of Gita cannot be over looked in any age . It is relevant for people of any culture, gender, race or religion.

Bhagavad Gita was not written at any temple or religious place but was spoken by Lord Krishna in the battle field of Mahabharata, to Arjuna who was facing a situation of turmoil when, Arjuna was supposed to fight against his respected elders, teachers and other family members.

This makes Gita an efficient text which can provide practical solutions to the daily stress, anxieties, inhibitions and apprehensions that a person faces in his/her daily lives. The nature of self, consciousness, the universe and the supreme which is described in Bhagavad Gita has never been presented by any other philosophical or religious work.

There are 18 chapters in Gita each describing different aspect of the process of self transformation. The aim of the Gita is to teach a person how to establish composure in his internal life and in his activities of the external world, to help a person develop tranquility within and to explain the art and science of doing actions skillfully and selflessly.

The Bhagavad Gita consists of 18 chapters. Each chapter is called a *yoga*. Yoga is the science of the individual consciousness attaining communion with the ultimate consciousness. So, each chapter is highly specialised revealing the path to attain realisation of the ultimate truth.

Various Chapters Describing Process of Self Consciousness

The various chapters describing process of self-consciousness are classified into Karma yoga, Bhakti yoga and Jnana yoga.

Karma Yoga

The first six chapters are classified as the karma yoga as they mainly deal with the science of individual consciousness attaining communion with the ultimate consciousness through actions. *These chapter are*

(i) **Visada Yoga** As the opposing armies stand poised for battle, Arjuna, the mighty warrior, sees his intimate relatives, teachers and friends in both armies ready to fight and sacrifice their lives. Struck by grief and pity, Arjuna fails in strength, his mind becomes confused and he gives up his determination to fight.

(ii) **Sankhya Yoga** In this chapter Krishna explains the fundamental distinction between the temporary material body and the eternal spiritual soul. Krishna explains to Arjuna the nature of selfless service to the supreme and the characteristics of a self-realised person.

(iii) **Karma Yoga** This chapter summarises the role of action of 'Karma' in one's life. It says that by acting for the pleasure of the supreme, without selfish motives, one can liberate from the law of Karma (action and reaction) and attain transcendental knowledge of the self and the supreme.

(iv) **Jnana Yoga** In this chapter Krishna talks about the spiritual knowledge of the soul, of God and of their relationship which is both purifying and liberating. He says that such knowledge is the fruit of selfless devotional action (Karma Yoga).

The lord explains the remote history of the Gita, the purpose and significance of his periodic descents to the material world and the necessity of approaching a guru, a realised teacher.

(v) **Karma-Sanyasa Yoga** This chapter talks about 'action' or 'karma'. Lord says that by outwardly performing all actions but inwardly renouncing their fruits, the wise man is purified by the fine transcendental knowledge and attains peace, detachment, forbearance, spiritual vision and bliss.

(vi) **Dhyana Yoga** Here the lord talks about the power of Ashtanga yoga, a mechanical meditative practice, which controls the mind and senses and centres concentration on parmatma (the super soul, the form of the lord situated in the heart). This practice culminates in samadhi, full consciousness of the supreme.

Bhakti Yoga

The middle six chapters have been designated as the Bhakti yoga, as they principally deal with the science of the individuals consciousness attaining communion with the ultimate consciousness by the path of devotion. *These chapters are*

(vii) **Paramhans a Vijnana Yoga** This chapter talks about the knowledge of the absolute. Lord Krishna tells Arjuna that he is the supreme truth, the supreme cause and sustaining force of everything both material and spiritual. The advanced souls surrender to him in devotion, whereas, impious souls divert their minds to other objects of worship.

(viii) **Akshara Parabrahma Yoga** This chapter talks about how by remembering Lord Krishna in devotion throughout one's life and especially at the time of death one can reach supreme abode, beyond material world.

(ix) **Raja Vidya Raja Guhya Yoga** This chapter talks about the power of bhakti and devotional service in attaining the transcendental self.

(x) **Vibhuti Vistara Yoga** It talks about that the wondorous phenomena showing power, beauty, grandeur or sublimity either in the material world or in the spiritual, are nothing but partial manifestations of Krishna's divine energies and opulence. As the supreme cause of all causes and the support and essence of everything, Krishna is the supreme object of worship for all beings.

(xi) **Visvarupa Darsana Yoga** Lord Krishna grants Arjuna divine vision and reveals his spectacular unlimited form as the cosmic universe. Krishna explains that his own beautiful human like form is the original form of Godhead. One can perceive this form only by pure devotional service.

(xii) **Bhakti Yoga** Bhakti Yoga, pure devotional service to Lord Krishna, is the highest and most expedient means for attaining pure love for Krishna, which is the ultimate end of spiritual existence.

Jnana Yoga

The final six chapters are regarded as the Jnana Yoga, as they are primarily concerned with the science of the individual consciousness attaining communion with the ultimate consciousness through intellect. *These chapters are*

(xiii) **Kshetra Kshetrajna Vibhaga Yoga** This chapter talks about the individual who understands the difference between the body, the soul and supersoul, attains liberation from this material world.

(xv) **Gunatraya Vibhaga Yoga** It talks about the three modes or qualities of material nature *i.e.* goodness passion and ignorance. Lord Krishna explains what these modes are, how they act upon us, how one transcends them and the symptoms of one who has attained the transcendental self.

(xiv) **Purushottam Yoga** The chapter talks about the ultimate purpose of vedic knowledge which is to detach oneself from the entanglement of the material world and to understand Lord Krishna as the supreme personality of Godhead. One who understands Krishna's supreme identity surrenders to him and engages in his devotional service.

(xvi) **Daivasura Sampad Vibhaga Yoga** This chapter tells that those who possess demoniac qualities and who lives playfully, without following the regulations of scripture, attain lower births and further material bondage, but those who possess divine qualities and lines regulated life gradually attain spiritual perfection.

(xvii) **Shraddha Traya Vibhaga Yoga** It talks about three types of faith and its outcomes. Acts performed by those whose faith is in passion and ignorance yield only impermanent material results, whereas acts performed in goodness, in accord with scriptural injunctions, purify the heart and lead to pure faith in Lord Krishna and devotion to him.

(xviii) **Moksha–Upadesa Yoga** Here Krishna explains the meaning of renunciation and the effects of the modes of nature on human consciousness and activity. He explains Brahman realisation, the glories of the Bhagavad Gita and the ultimate conclusion of the Gita.

He explains that the highest path of religion is absolute, unconditional and loving surrender to lord Krishna. This frees one from all sins, brings one to complete enlightenment and enables one to return to Krishna's eternal spiritual abode.

Importance of Bhagavad Gita in Psychology

Bhagavad Gita is not just conversation between Lord Krishna and Arjuna, but its a type of psychiatric counselling between counsellor (Krishna) and a patient (Arjuna). Arjuna, the greatest hero, momentarily becomes so despondent that he wants to lay his ghandiva down and refuses to fight. Krishna, his charioteer, makes a quick diagnosis of Arjuna's mental state as classical reactive depression coupled with severe anxiety neurosis and starts his pyschotherapy session effectively through this great classic, Shrimad Bhagavad Gita.

Arjuna had all the features of anxiety: state-dry mouth, palpitation, sweating, trembling of legs, fear clouded mind etc. Krishna's diagnosis was dead right. The best treatment for that is good psychotherapy and Lord Krishna did a good job. He reminded Arjuna that it was his duty to fight as a warrior; he will let his brother down if he now declines to fight. Krishna tells him to have a detached attachment in life.

Prof **BM Hegde** said , 'I am yet to find a better textbook of psychotherapy than Gita in medical literature'. It also teaches us that life is a struggle with ups and downs like the waves in the sea which one has to survive to live, but it says that if you want to realise God you have to win over your ego. Krishna practised futuristic medicine of making the irrational mind see reason and work properly (psychotherapy). The Gita also gives us a living philosophy for happiness of mind and peace. Detached attachment is a wonderful formula to avoid shoka (sorrow) in life and to move on.

Buddhism

The life and the basic teachings of Lord Buddha is known to us, through stories we have been listening to since childhood. Lord Buddha was born in a royal family in Kapilavastu in the 6th century BC and renounced the world early in life seeing disease, old age, death and other miseries of life.

Throughout his life he endeavoured to seek solution to all miseries of life. He tried to sought answers to his questions from numerous religious teachers of his time, but nothing satisfied him.

He practised great austerities, did intense meditation with his strong will and mind, free from all disturbing thoughts and passions. His aim was to search for the causes of all sufferings in the world. Finally, he accomplished his mission and prince Siddhartha became Buddha or 'enlightened'. The message of his enlightenment laid the foundation of both Buddhist religion and philosophy. Buddhist psychology is both a psychology of transformation and theory of cognition. As a psychology of transformation, it aims to develop the innate psychic potential of every being to its perfection.

The ordinary state of being is 'flawed' or 'pathological' in the sense that one has a limited perception of the world and undergoes innumerable cycles of suffering psychological tensions in attempts to respond and cope with the world. These efforts do not provide ever lasting happiness because the perceptions of self and world are discordant with one's true nature. Buddhist psychology aims to transcend this entrapment. It's main endeavour is to analyse the root cause behind any suffering. Buddhism focuses on personal spiritual development and strives for true nature of life.

Although there are many divisions or schools within Buddhism, *there are two main branches which differ in some areas of focus*

(i) **Theravada Buddhism** It focuses on individual enlightenment and experience as well as monastic life.
(ii) **Mahayana Buddhism** It focuses on collective freedom from suffering and teaching the ways to enlightenment. Zen and Tibetan Buddhism are considered to be the off shots of Mahayana Buddhism .

Key Principles of Buddhism

Buddhism is more than a religion; it is a tradition that focuses on personal spiritual development. For many, it is a philosophy and a humanistic way of life which can be summed up as striving to lead a moral life; being aware of one's thought and actions; and developing wisdom, compassion and understanding. It is all about finding inner peace and controlling one's self desires. The principles of Buddhism are based on four noble truths and eightfold path.

Buddhism's Four Noble Truth

When Siddhartha Gautama achieved his spiritual breakthrough beneath the Bodhi tree, he came to an important realisation concerning the plight of the world and our physical existence within it. He realised particular truths about the world, these are called *the four noble truths. These are*

(i) Existence of suffering (Duhkha).
(ii) Suffering has a cause namely craving and attachment (Duhkha – Samudaya).
(iii) There is a cessation of suffering (Duhkha-Nirodha).
(iv) There is a path to the cessation of suffering (Duhkha-Nirodha Marga).

The Eight Fold Paths in Buddhism

The path to cessation of suffering is an eight fold path, which helps a person to attain the state of nirvana by freeing him from attachments and delusions and helping him to understand the innate truth of all things. This path is open to all monks as well as laymen. The first two segments of the path are referred to as prajna meaning wisdom.

The eight folds in the path of overcoming stress and sufferings are as follows

(i) **Right Views** Understanding the nature of all things as imperfect, impermanent and insubstantial and our self inflicted suffering is result of clinging (attachment) hate and ignorance.

(ii) **Right Resolve/Aspiration** It is to have determination to free oneself from attachment, hatefulness and ignorance.

(iii) **Right Speech** Abstaining from lying, gossiping and hurtful speech in which we can harm others.

(iv) **Right Action/Conduct** It includes 'Pancha-Sila' the five vows for desisting from killing, stealing, sensuality, lying and intoxication.

(v) **Right Livelihood** Making one's living in a honest, non- hurtful way. The last three segments of the path are the ones Buddhism is most famous for and is concerned with samadhi or meditation.

(vi) **Right Effort** Taking control of your mind and its contents, requires efforts to develop good mental habits.

(vii) **Right Mindfulness** Mindfulness refers to a kind of meditation (vipassana) involving an acceptance of thoughts and perceptions, a 'bare attention' to these events without attachment. The mindfulness can be extended to daily life as well and it becomes a way of developing a fuller and richer awareness of life.

(viii) **Right Concentration** One who has guided his life in the last seven rules and freed himself from all passions and evil thoughts is fit to enter into deeper stages of concentration that gradually takes him to goal of his long and arduous journey of cessation of suffering.

Right concentration through four stages is the last step to attain nirvana.

(i) The first stage of concentration is based on reasoning and investigaton regarding the truths and then a joy of pure thinking prevails.

(ii) The second stage is unruffled meditation free from reasoning. There is then a joy of tranquility.

(iii) The third stage of concentration is detachment from even the joy of tranquility but a feeling of a bodily case persists.

(iv) The fourth stage and final stage is detachment from the bodily case too. There are then perfect equanimity and indifference. This is the state of nirvana, perfect wisdom. This is the highest from of Buddhist meditation.

Buddhism and Western Psychology

Many renowned teachers, clinicians and writers in the West such as Carl Jung, Erich Fromm, Joseph Goldstein and Sharon Salzberg among others have attempted to bridge and integrate psychology and Buddhism from time to time, in a manner that offers meaning, inspiration and healing to the common man's suffering. Buddhism and Western psychology have a number of commonalities in theory and in practice which has been mentioned by many experts in the field.

These commonalities can be seen in various branches of modern Western psychology like

Buddhism and Phenomenological Psychology

Abhidhamma Pitaka of Buddhism articulates philosophy, psychology and ethics as well; all integrated into the framework of a program for liberation. The primary concern of the Abhidhamma is to understand the nature of experience and thus the reality on which it focuses is conscious reality.

For this reason Abhidhamma shades off into a phenomenological psychology. Chogyam Trungpa, in his book 'Glimpses of the Abhidhamma' wrote, that many modern psychologists have found the discoveries and explanations of the abhidharma coincide with their own discoveries and new ideas. Thus, abhidhamma which is 2500 yrs old had been redeveloped in the modern times.

The four noble truths and eight fold path of Buddhism provide a way to end suffering. Like Buddhism, psychoanalysis focuses on self-exploration and self-understanding and identifying the cause of suffering. In the psychoanalytic process, the therapist asks patient to give up conscious control over the presentation of his or her inner world.

Buddhism and psychoanalysis share the goal of the alleviation of mental suffering both from a highly personal and individual perspective as well as universalistic perspective. Both are radically experiential rather than primarily philosophical or dogmatic. Both of them employ the technique of moment-to-moment awareness of mental processes to reduce suffering.

Buddhism and Existential Psychology

Buddha said that life is suffering and this suffering is due to attachment, but he believed that this suffering can be extinguished and one can attain the state of nirvana. Similar are the concepts of existentialists, who speaks of ontological anxiety, angst, dread and clinging on to things with the hope of certain benefit. Existentialists talks about freedom which is similar to 'nirvana'. Buddhism emphasise that there is a way to extinguish suffering. For the existerntial psychologist, the therapist must take an assertive role in helping the client become aware of the reality of his or her suffering and its roots.

Likewise, the client must take an assertive role in working towards improvement even though it means facing the fears. They have been working so hard to avoid and especially facing the fear that they will 'Lose' themselves in the process.

Buddhism and Cognitive-Behaviour Therapy Principles

Psychotherapies dealing with cognitive restructuring share core principles with ancient buddhist antedotes to personal suffering.

Fromm distinguishes between two types of meditative techniques that have been used in psychotherapy

(i) Auto suggestion used to induce relaxation

(ii) Meditation "to achieve higher degree of non attachment, of non-greed and of non-illusion; briefly those that serve to reach a higher level of being".
From attributes techniques associated with meditation to Buddhist mindfulness practices.

Two other increasingly popular therapeutic practices using Buddhist mindfulness techniques are Jon Kabat Zinn's Mindfulness Based Stress Reduction (MBSR) and Marsha M Linehan's Dialectical Behavioural Therapy (DBT).

The noble eight fold path of Buddhism has a great connect with the School of Behaviourism, which describe human functions in relation to principles of behaviour which can be manipulated to create positive effects on the life of the clients. Its principles are in sync with right to action, right speech and right livelihood (of eight fold noble path of Buddhism). The training of human mind by cognitive and cognitive behaviourists in order to remove phobias, beliefs and fears, by using techniques of visualisations and positive self talks, are similar to noble eight fold paths which focus on right thinking and right mindfulness.

Buddhism and Other Psychotherapy Principles

Gestalt therapy by Fritz Perls, is heavily based on existentialist principles and significantly Zen Buddhism. Gestalt therapy also works on whole person and encourage right mindfulness, similarly as Buddhism.

Similarly Client Centered therapy by Carl Rogers works on the principle that therapist does not direct the process of therapy, but patient has the resources to deal with their own 'cure' and 'self growth', provided the environment is safe for them. Like the Buddha this non-authoratative approach suggests that the 'patient can be a light to themselves.'

Thus, we can say that Buddha was a unique Psychotherapist and his teachings, writings and wisdom helped millions of people through out the centuries. Today even the Western world has realised the psychological essence of Buddhism. In short the Psychotherapeutic models described by Buddhism are of great value and have, all time applications.

Sufism

Sufism is the mystical or inward aspect of Islam. The word 'sufism' is derived from 'sufi' which means yogi and refers to someone who has reached the 'goal'. Sufism philosophy is to teach people to live simple harmonious lives. The main idea of sufism is that mankind is the most honourable of all living creatures on Earth and so it is bound to carry the divine trust.

It follows that if ego forgets the divine purpose of creation, and view itself as existing independent of its creation, it is betraying that sacred trust. Basically, Sufism teaches that the essence of this universe is spiritual. In modern times, ego continually quests for self satisfaction and self adoration. These practices of Sufism enable people to combat this tendency, seeking to discover the higher or 'true' self.

It views humans beings as religio-psychological beings who began life in the unconscious union with nature . It says that in the process of evolution humans got separated from nature and experienced pain. Sufism is a process of regaining one's naturalness and harmonisation with true nature. It is an inner experience that enables one to get identifications of his object or desire. The main belief in sufism is that the duality turns in to unity, it emphasis on purity of heart.

Essentials of Sufi Psychology

Sufism offers a comprehensive approach to sacred psychology with the ultimate aim of self knowledge and self acceptance.

Three principal aspects of the human being and their relationship comprise the triadic foundation of Sufi Psychology: the nafs (self), qalb (heart) and ruh (soul). Sufis consider that the spiritual heart is the agent of reconciliation between the physical and the metaphysical dimensions of the human being. The spiritual destiny of a human being depends on whether soul or nafs, becomes the eventual winner of the inner battle (jihad) between the tendencies exercised by the nafs and the higher qualities of the soul.

Nafs

Nafs is equivalent to English word 'self'. It has often been translated as 'ego' or 'self lover' which is incorrect. 'Ego' is generally a hypothetical construct which has different definition and function in each School of Psychology. 'Nafs' however is not an abstract or theoretical concept, it is a living, organic reality which could be experienced in day-to-day life situations. It is the agency of human will and is the product of bio-psycho-social development . According to **Frager**, "In sufi psychology the self or nafs, is an aspect of the psyche that begins as our worst adversary but can develop into an invaluable tool."

Nafs-ammarah (the commanding self), encompasses three levels of the nafs prior to the human self in evolutionary terms. *These are*

- The mineral/inorganic self (nafs-al-jamaadi)
- The vegetable/organic self (nafs-al-habaati)
- The animal self (nafs-al-haywaani)

As the principle of embodiment, the human self is the crown of the evolutionary process, presiding over the animal self, vegetable self and the mineral self.

The commanding self (Nafs-al-Ammarah) though intelligent in wordly ways, generally lacks spiritual wisdom. The mineral self generates inertia, the vegetative self creates desires for food and inactivities and the animal self is the source of both sexual and destructive tendencies . Nafs-al- Ammarah seeks material objects, power and is plagued with various ego-desires and narcissistic tendencies.

The nafs often craves for wordly desires and ignores the wisdom of the heart, which is the medium of transformation of the knowledge of the soul. They need spiritual guidance to awaken to its spiritual potential from the state of sleep like ignorance (geflat).

Heart

Sufism is often referred to as the path of the heart. However, Sufism has also developed as one of the most complete teachings and practices for understanding and knowing of self, its growth and evolution in the context of human psycho spiritual developmental process.

In the journey of self-knowledge one must encounter and discover nafs, but nafs being extremely intelligent is unable to see through is own makeup and heart is the wisest place to start.

Javad Nurbakhsh writes, 'The heart is a city between the domain of unity (spirit, ruh) and the land of multiplicity (nafs). If the heart snaps that cord linking it with nafs, it falls under the sway of the spirit, that is to say, it becomes heart in the true sense of the word, polished clean of the corrosion of multiplicity. On the other hand, if the heart becomes dominated by the nafs, it becomes darkened by the tarnish of the nafs multiplicity, taking on its hue.

Thus, it can be concluded that the role of heart in overall process of psycho spiritual transformation is cardinal. In Sufi practice the initial goal is to open the seeker's heart. The open heart helps to transcend and transform the nafs. As the 'nafs' transforms it co-operates with further transformation of consciousness. Desires of the nafs give way to the desires of the heart and finally these remains only one-desire, desire to know God.

Soul

The human soul (ruh) is the innermost dimension (baatin) of the human being and is hidden to the immediate consciousness of the ordinary individual as our surface consciousness (zaheer) is dominated by the activities of nafs. All souls are formless and seek expression and experience in different levels of consciousness. The ascent of soul through various planes of consciousness is called transmigration or metempsychosis (tanaasukh).

Once the spiritual heart is opened, the soul experiences wholeness and true individuality. The next two stations of the soul are the 'secret' and the 'secret of secrets' which are unknown to the ordinary mind and are marked by oneness with ultimate truth and unity with God or the over-soul, respectively.

In its origin individual soul is part of the over-soul or God, yet it's not conscious of its identity with God. Through its journey the soul moves through various states of consciousness and experiences its identity with the various states.

There are numerous veils of illusions that keep human beings in the state of gheflat or sleep like ignorance and unconsciousness. According to traditional saying "there are seventy veils between the human being and God, yet none between God and human being".

The goal of Sufism is to open seeker's heart, which is the gateway to soul. The open heart, first helps to transcend and then transform the 'nafs', and as nafs transforms it no longer acts as a dividing agent but cooperates in further transformation of consciousness.

Sufism and Psychospiritual Transformation

Sufi practice begins with the first stage of psychospiritual transformation or spiritual awakening. After perfecting first stage Nafs-al-Amanarah undergoes a gradual process of transformation known as *fana*, which means ego-annihilation or loss of self centered personality traits.

Once 'nafs' is modified a new self called 'Nafs-al-Lawwama' is experienced. It is the stage of absitenence, where the sufi practioner actively avoids all forms of inferior impulses and tendencies by observing ethical codes of the discipline (adab) until eventually the third stage of non-attachment is mastered.

By means of successive passages into next two stages; 'spiritual poverty; during which heart is perfectly purified and 'patience' longing for divine grace, the sixth stage is attained referred to as 'self-surrender' or reliance on God; through completion of which all tendencies of nafs-al-ammarah are eradicated at the root.

Completion of sixth stage also marks the cessation of all efforts on the part of individual. Beyond this point experience of cosmic self and universal consciousness occur spontaneously or by divine grace.

At the seventh and last stage, called *Contentment*, the self takes its final mode, Nafs-al motma'enna which is a stage of joy and removal of all doubts.

Sufi practice is best attained under the guidance of a learned teacher call 'Sheikh'.

Thus, it can be concluded that psychological thoughts presented in Sufism are quite impactful and it very well portrays the evolution of an individual from an egoistic, self centered being to an stage of higher self and union to god. Sufism is a knowledge of absolute reality, not of logic. This knowledge can be attained only by the 'eye of the heart' that is by means of illumination and contemplation.

Integral Yoga

Integral yoga or purna yoga sometimes also called the *supramental yoga*, refers to the union of all parts of one's beings with the divine and the transmutation of all of their jarring elements into a harmonious state of higher divine consciousness or existence. The nature and practice of integral yoga is defined by Sri Aurobindo in his opus 'The synthesis of yoga.' The integral yoga of Sri Aurobindo, is a yoga of synthesis, intended to harmonise the paths of Karma, Jnana and Bhakti Yoga as described in Bhagavad Gita. It can also be considered as the synthesis between Vedanta and Tantra and even between Eastern and Western approaches to spirituality.

Sri Aurobindo's Integral Yoga and Integral Psychology attracted world wide attention. Sri Aurobindo's perspective provides legitimate spaces for the insights gathered on human existence both from West as well as East and allows us to integrate these and seems to go beyond what the previous systems offer in terms of growth and expansion which are possible for human being.

Sri Aurobindo's Model of Personality

The aspect of personality defined in Western psychology is largely preoccupied with the 'outer consciousness' that is the way a person expresses itself in ordinary life through external, mental and vital form. However, Sri Aurobindo's integral yoga has a different approach of understanding human personality. According to this approach identification with only the outer aspects of our existence keeps one trapped in a state of ignorance, because it keeps them unaware.

According to integral yoga, the outer being is capable of experiencing only a narrow range of stimuli and events related to stimuli impinging from the external world. The inner being consists of the inner mind, inner vital, inner physical and serves as a connection between the psychic and the outer being.

On each level-mental, vital and physical, there is a wider range of experiences possible and vaster energies that can be tapped. The inner being is in contact with the universal planes of consciousness. The process of Sadhana leads to the awakening and activation of the inner being, and with the opening of the 'chakras' the outer being also get an access to the universal bands of consciousness.

Sri Aurobindo, has used the term 'subliminal' for all parts of the being, which are not on the waking surface, especially those referring to the workings of the inner being.

The psychic within us awakens us toward the good, the true, the beautiful and love. The existence of the psychology remains latent (outside of conscious awareness) within most of us, but is responsible for the experience of all that is sublime.

Over the lifetime psychic evolves and keeps us guiding towards the 'light'. A point comes when psychic has evolved sufficiently and it makes its presence felt in outward consciousness. At this stage a sense of lightness, greater freedom from the external world, is felt. A feeling of silence, peace, bliss, love all spontaneous and not a response to anything outside of the person is experienced. From this point where psychic is felt in conscious state, 'Sadhana' helps to progress rapidly towards spiritual awakening taking a person to the higher planes of consciousness.

The Gradients of Consciousness

The lowest form of consciousness is that which is found in inanimate matter as involved in the workings of the atom with the electrons revolving around the nucleus and is referred as 'inconscience'.

The next higher level of consciousness is subconscient. It is the quite submerged part of our being in which there is no wakingly conscious and cohernt thought, will or feeling or organised reaction, but yet receives obscurely the impressions of all things and stores them up in itself and from it too all sorts of Stimuli, of persistent habitual movements, crudely repeated or disguised in strange forms.

Further in the gradient of consciousness is the physical or the body consciousness which is present in animals as well.

The highest that is most commonly found in humans is the level of the mind. In the language of integral yoga the words 'mind' and 'mental' are used to describe the part of nature which is concerned with cognition and intelligence, ideas, mental or thought perceptions, the reactions of thought to things, mental vision and will etc. that are part of human intelligence.

For those human beings who have not gone deeper within themselves mind and consciousness are synonymous. It is when one becomes aware of oneself by a growth in consciousness then one can see different degress, kinds and powers of consciousness– mental, physical, psychic and spiritual.

There is a description of higher ranges of consciousness above mind which become accessible through 'Sadhana'. These include 'higher mind' the first and lowest of the spiritual mental grades, lying above the normal mental level. The mind's characteristic movement is a mass ideation, as seeing of the inner relation between ideas. Truth is seen in wholeness.

Sri Aurbindo describes the sequential involution of the infinite reality into finite matter which he calls "Planes of Consciousness". Listed from lowest to highest order the major planes of consciousness *are as follows*

(i) **Illumined Mind** In this mode the mind begins to operate visually using subtle images rather than dry logic and reason. It is found in poets, musicians and painters.

(ii) **Intuitive Mind** At this level knowledge is gained by intuition. The consciousness of the subject meets the consciousness of the object and vibrates with the knowledge of that which it contacts.

(iii) **Over Mind** This is the state where one begins to live in cosmic consciousness. Those who attain liberation saluation are said to be in this state.

(iv) **Super Mind** This is the highest plane where one joins an all encompassing vision and is able to see truth from all sides.

According to **Sri Aurobindo**, "there are two systems simultaneosouly active in the organisation of the being and its parts. One is concentric, a series of rings or sheaths with the psychic at the centre (Annamaya Kosha, Prananjaya Kosha, Manomaya Kosha, Vijnamaya Kosha, Anandamaya Kosha) and other is vertical an ascension and descent, like a flight of steps, as series of super imposed planes with supermind-overmind as the crucial nodes of transition beyond the human into the divine.

Thus, Sri Aurobindo's depiction of personality and human existence refers to a lesser self-caught up in the demands of the outer being, which can get transformed into the greater self via a process of development. This entails first an inward movement leading to the uncovering of the psychic and then an upward movement through the higher gradations of consciousness taking one towards the supramental level of awareness, and subsequently descent of the higher force into lower parts leading to their transformation.

This simply means that our whole nature gets converted and we are no longer caught up in the narrow egoistic confines of a delimited consciousness, which identifies with experiences limited to the horizons of the outer being. The integral yoga view helps us in getting in touch with the most essential and fundamental aspect of our existence and has potential applications in the area of psychotherapy, parenting attitude towards work, human relationships, education etc.

Academic Psychology In India

Psychology as an academic discipline made a new beginning in the first decade of 20th century. The initial years were marked by the influence of West-oriented academic psychology on Indian psychologists. This prevented the enrichment of academic psychology in India form diverse expertise and life-experiences of Indian psychologists. Thus, psychology in India remained discounted from its own vast storehouse of knowledge inherent in Indian philosophical texts. However, in recent years there is a shift from emphasis on replication of Western studies to socially relevant research and understanding the psychological, social and cultural contexts using qualitative approaches.

Pre-Independence Era

Wilhelm Wundt, known as the *father of modern Psychology* set up the first Psychological laboratory in the University of Leipzig in the year 18. After this numerous developments took place in West in the area of psychology. Impressed and influenced by the growth of psychology in the West, modern psychology was introduced at Calcutta University with the starting of a separate department of Psychology in 1916.

Since then many psychologists from India have been trained abroad and many have been trained in India, following the Western brands of psychology. Indian psychological traditions also flourished significantly during last century with its distinctive emphasis on spiritual self development. There were numerous teacher and disciple pairs who practiced their own bands of theory and practice and made an impact globally.

Contribution of Various Psychologists

One of this pair of teacher disciple in the modern times was (teacher) Ramakrishna Paramhansa-Swami Vivekananda (disciple). Swami Vivekananda's lecture at the world conference on religions in Chicago in 1883, became the landmark in introducing Indian thought in the USA. His thoughts and work for psychology, had a deep impact on William James and his ideas about the higher states of consciousness.

The famous pioneers in interpreting Indian thought in the context of Western philosophy were Krishna Chandra Bhattacharya (1875-1949) and S Radhakrishnan (1888-1975). In terms of articulation of the basic principles and theories for Psychological theory and practice the work of BG Tilak (1856-1920) is most suitable. He interpreted the path of action described in the Bhagavad Gita in light of Post-Kantian Philosophy and Darwinian thought.

But the most important contribution to psychology in the Indian tradition was made by Sri Aurobindo (1872-1950). Though he was not formally trained in psychology, he was a sage in Indian tradition and wrote on basis of his profound experience as a yogi. His most prominent contribution to psychology is his work called the *synthesis of yoga* (Aurobindo 1949-1999) in which he brings together essence of the three basic varieties of yoga namely the paths of knowledge (Jnana Marga), Devotion (Bhakti) and Action (Karma).

Now if we talk about academic psychology that was transplanted from the West, the names of two pioneers names are worth mentioning are : Narendra Nath Sengupta of the Calcutta University, who was trained in experimental Psychology with Hugo Musterberg at Harvard and his successor Givindra Shekhar Bose, who became a self-taught psychoanalyst to be admitted by Freud to membership of the International Association of Psychoanalysis.

As both Western experimental and clinical approaches were imported, many psychologists got trained abroad, and continued influencing psychology in India. However in India the experimental model flourished and psychoanalysis lagged behind. In area of Indian Psychology too, its theoretical side became a small part of philosophy courses in universities, while applied part had no place in academic curriculum.

The contribution of Mahatma Gandhi (1869-1948) who is known as *saint*, freedom fighter, social reformer and great thinker, in the area of 'applied social psychology' is quite impressing. His principle of non-violence (ahimsa) and the movement Satyagraha, are the techniques which have wide application in resolution of social conflicts.

His ideas and practices were a replication of traditional Indian thoughts and culture. His style of leadership shows his deep understanding of what modern psychologists called *group dynamics*. Gandhiji's work reflects the practical orientation of psychology in India.

Post Independence Era

Soon after India gained independence from the British rule, psychology witnessed an explosive growth with departments of psychology opening up in old universities as well as in continually widening circle of new universities and IIT's, and IIM's. There was similar explosion in the number of research publications in Indian as well as international journals.

Separate psychology department were largely set up between 1940-1960. In 1954 Bureau of Psychology was established at Allahabad. The first NIMHANS (National Institute of Mental Health and Neuro Sciences) was set up in Bangalore, in 1955. In 1962, hospital for mental diseases in Ranchi was established.

Though Psychology as an academic discipline was creating its mark in India, but it was totally influenced by Western theories and concepts and these were influencing the research and teaching programmes in most of Indian universities. 'Psychology' was flourishing in India academia, but it was maintaining a distance from its own vast store house of knowledge which was available in the Indian philosophical texts like in Buddhism, Jainism, Bhagavad Gita etc. But now psychology in India is returning to its roots and moving towards a new path.

Development of Academic Psychology in India

- **1947** Girindra Shekhar Bose published journal 'Samiksha'. Guidance Bureau was set up at Bihar and Parsi Panchayat Vocational Guidance Bureau at Bombay was established.
- **1949** Indian Government established psychological research under Defence Ministry with an aim of the inclusion of psychologists on research and selection board.
- **1950** Prof. VK Kothurkar, who was trained at Cambridge University, founded and headed the department of psychology at University of Pune and named it as 'Experimental Psychology'.
- **1950** UNESCO and Ministry of Education in Collaboration with Gardner Murphy, developed a research project to investigate the causes of command violence. Many Indian Psychologists too became the part of this project and published a book named, 'In the minds of mea'. This project gave a lot of interest for research in the scholars.
- **1950's-1960's** During this period 32 Psychology departments were established in universities all over India. These departments pursued research as per their interest area and developed their distinct identity like Rural and Social Psychology (Allahabad), Test Construction (Mysore), Industrial Psychology (Osmania) and Measurement and Guidance (Patna). During this period only applied psychology applications widened in Industrial Psychology, organisational management developing training and job-productively oriented work activities.
- **1955** With the collaborative support of Mc Clelland and Erikson advanced training programmes in clinical psychology were introduced at NIMHANS Bangalore.
- **1957** The Madras psychological society published the first journal of Psychological Research.
- **1961** Department of Psychology started in Allahabad University, and Prof. Durganand Sinha, who was trained at Cambridge University and Patna University became its first head.
- **1964** An independent psychology Department was set up in Delhi University under Prof. HC Ganguli. However, the psychology course at the master's level was introduced in Delhi University in 1957.
- **1964** 'The Madras Psychology Society' published the Indian Journal of Applied Psychology.
- **1953** Indian Psychologist Jadunath Sinha wrote a book on Cognition.
- **1959** Department of Applied psychology established in University of Mumbai.
- **1961** The NCERT reviewed all psychological test made till 1961.
- **1967** The university of Calcutta officially established Applied Psychology under the guidance of Prof. SN Roy.
- **1968** The Indian Association of Clinical Psychologists was started in 1968.
- **1970** Several well organised research centres were established like ANS Institutes of Social Research (Patna), Centre for Study of Developing Societies (New Delhi) NIPCCD, Delhi, National Institute of Health and Family Welfare (Delhi), National Institute of Educational Policy and Administration (New Delhi), NCERT New Delhi Indian Institute of Sciences, (Bangalore), Academic Staff College (Bangalore) and Indian Statistical Institute (Calcutta). Together with this the invention of first Statistical Package for the Social Sciences (SPSS) manual published by Norma H Nie, Dale H Bent and Chadlai Hull's made the research work in psychology an outstanding one.
- **1974** A directory made by compiling 503 psychological tests. The department of Psychology was established at Bangalore University and Bharathiar University.
- **1975** By the end of 1975, 51 of 101 recognised university offered psychology as one of its courses.
- **1976** First publication of journal of Indian psychology (Dalar AK and Misra A. 2010).

The Move of Addressing Social Issues in 1970's

In 1970's it was quite evident that psychology in which most of the theories and ideas are westernised is of no applicability in addressing social issues which are prevalent in Indian society. The only solution is to turn to the rich intellectual heritage of one's own culture *i.e.* Indian traditional thoughts and psychological practices presented in numerous religious and historical texts and writings.

A Clarion call in this direction was given by Durganand Sinha (1965) asking for integration of modern Psychology with Indian thought. He emphasised that Indian Models of psychology would have enormous applications for health psychology, education, organisational management, human and social development.

Being a developing country with millennia old culture, a rich diverse society, a two century long colonial past , India is currently aspiring to emerge as a self reliant and economically strong nation. India has been engaged with rapid growth in the field of higher education to meet the need of trained professionals required in sectors like health, administration, banking, police, military and management. But being a land of diverse cultures and traditions, ecology and language, uneven introduction of technology, the challenge before the planners to ensure social welfare through democratic processes is quite tough. The challenge to relate India's past and modern psychology was a main concern in the early period and continued since then.

It was largely in the 1970's that many psychologists raised the issue of insufficient and inadequate attention to social psychological problems. It was at this time Indian and psychologists realised that they had been indifferent to the vast and rich collection of knowledge inherent in the Indian texts. But the commitment to scientific inquiry was regarded with due respect and the debates related to philosophy of science could not be addressed until the 1980's.

1980's Indigenisation

Modern Psychology did not originate as an indigenous science. It was a transplant from the West and it is yet to be sufficiently indigenised.

Indigenious Psychology is not imported from outside but originates in its native land and grows out of people's responses and interactions in a culture. They form clusters and patterns from their interactions. Some are innovative, some are rational, irrational etc. Psychologists examine them systematically and develop concepts, principles, laws and theories.

Again people act on them, make informed responses and create new information, that psychologists use to refine their theorisation and capture the reality more comprehensively. This is the process of '*indigenious knowledge creation*' resulting into Indigenisation over a period of time.

Indigeneous psychology is closer to cultural psychology. And till 1980's psychology in India was what was imported from West. However, the theories and perspectives of the West do not explain the reality of human psyche in the cultural context of Indian culture.

Whenever a Western theory failed to explain evidence collected in India, Indians blamed Western psychologists for lacking in skill to conduct the study or for wrong sampling methods, or items. When reality clearly contradicted a theory for *e.g.* Indians perceived participative leaders as weak, Indians preferred personalised relationships and Indians respected and obeyed their parents; Indians were advised to change their mindset and behaviour.

So, it was clear at this time (1970-1980's) that Indian psychology was in crisis. There were many inconsistent and unexplained findings, tests and measures were insensitive to Indian culture and findings were irrelevant to people's life and problems.

Later 'self reliance', a new sentiment arose in the Academia of Psychology and a search for cultural heritage started. It was realised that there is a disconnect between psychology and Indian culture and it not worthy to address social problems in India.

This has led to the realisation of the need of an indegenous Psychology and also Emergence of the International Association of Cross-Cultural Psychology. In this forum where psychologists can talk about differences in cross-cultures and not just the similarities resulted in a positive impact on the growth of Indigeneous Psychology in India.

Then, began the search for ancient wisdom for creating authetic Indian Psychology. The earlier attempts include the following

Jadunath Sinha's (1933) work on Perception and Emotion, Akhilanand's (1952) work on how Psycho-spiritual though and mental health, *Aurobindo's* (1986) work on spirituality and nationalism and Radha Krishnan's Philosophical work on '*Synthetic Indian Mindset*'.

During 1970's–1980's many other psychologists joined the search of ancient wisdom. The assumptions made was that it is all time valid and verifiable, thus it must be continued at present.

Indegenisation in Psychology is done from both sources

(i) Western Perspective known as *Exogenous Indigenisation:* Exogenous Indigenisation is integration of modern Psychology with Indian thought.

(ii) Ancient Indian Perspective known as *Endogenous Indigenisation:* Ancient indian perspective put emphasis on experimental and individual centric transformation. It believes on knowing through practicing and explores human possibilities parallels in Western and Indian psychology.

Indian psychologists refined themselves by using multi-dimensional approach, flexible methods and inspiration from Western and ancient Indian sources. Thus, the process of indigenisation initiated. It was happening 'Surely but slowly' (Adair, 1989) in all three perspective *Western, Ancient Indian and Folways*. But in each perspective there were only few frontrunners.

Few front runners of indigenisation who examined Western concepts by Western methods, are

- **Janak Pandey** (1981) found unlike in the West ingratiation is rampant and risk free in India because of hierarchical world view and assymetrical power distribution.
- **Jain** (1987) found, unlike in the West crowding is not negatively experienced in India because officiation, not privacy are valued.
- **L Krishnan** (1997) talks about 'Distributive Justice' in India is not contractual, but it is duty bound (social obligation).
- Similarly, post conventional morality in **Kohlberg's** model in West highlights the individual rights, responsibility and autonomy, where as in India it is to care and duty for others.

  Another shade of Indigenisation where conditions were attached to a concept, or the concept was modified are for example.
- **MC Clelland's** (1975) Concept of need for achievement (H Achv) for individuals was modified, as Udai Paveek (1968) said need for achievement works in India only if it is combined with need for affiliation.
- **Prayag Mehta** (1987) concluded that its not need for achievement for individuals but social need for achievement which is good for India.

  So achievement in Western culture is different than achievement in Indian culture.

  There were numerous other researches done in the field of psychology towards an indigenous approach to various theories and methods. A beginning was made in 1980's and the hard work is still on. Today, Indian psychology is emerging which promises a broad theoretical foundation for the exploration of human consciousness (Yoga) and radical psychological transformation.

  Its applications are found in modern areas like organisational behaviour and social development. Accounts of the states and contents of mental functions regulating responsible human conduct available in vast Indian texts and practices is being rediscovered in a more contemporary context.

1990's Paradiagmatic Concerns

By the mid 1970's the enthusiasm with which the Western educated Indian Psychologists were conducting research was waning. Western Psychology was failing to throw light on Indian social issues.

Sixty years of Western Psychology had not yielded any significant discoveries KG Agarwal (1973) has called psychology in India as 'adoptology'. There was growing disillusimment about the applicability of Western theories and their mindless testing in India.

A strong need was felt to return to cultural roots. D Sinha (1977) urged that the scientific understanding of Indian reality should benefit from its vast treasure of traditional psychological knowledge accumulated over centuries. He called for the development of an indigenious psychology with its own paradigms to understand developmental problems of the region.

In short, psychology in India was seeking its own identity. The need at this time was to make psychology more relevant in Indian context. D Sinha (1986) also stressed on finding appropriate theoretical framework and research methodologies to make subject 'socially relevant' to meet the needs of changing society.

Contemporary Debates

The ongoing debate on the indegenisation of psychology resulted in Indian psychologists showing more interest in studying problems relevant to the country using Indian concepts and theories.

Neki (1973) for example suggested a teacher-pupil model in counselling to break cultural and social barriers.

JBP Sinha (1980) proposed a new leadership style nurturant task master, which is more likely to succeed in Indian work organisations.

Kakar (1982, 1991) studied the role of traditional healers in maintaining mental health in Indian society.

Ramchandra Rao (1983) and **Palsane, Bhavasar Goswami** and **Evans** (1986) developed a concept of stress based on ancient scriptures.

Pande and Naidu (1992) developed a measure to study the concept of detachment and its mental health consequences.

1990s Disciplinary Identity Crisis

The crisis of discipline's identity was of concern. JBP Sinha (1993) made a distinction between bulk and the front of psychological research. Mass produced bulk of the research which was replicative and immitative. But few frontrunners started to take indigenous psychology more seriously.

The Canadian Psychologists, John Adair saw indigenisation as a gradual process and in collaboration with his Indian colleagues, developed a scale to measure the degree of Indigenisation. He concluded on the basis of content analysis of over 300 journal articles that there was a progress in indigenisation of psychology in India, but at a slow pace.

There were numerous research work done to address the social problems of Indian society. Eventually it was realised that Western theories and methods could not be fruitfully applied to study Indian social problems. It was realised that in the absence of any cultural based knowledge and understanding, no real insight and solutions of the Indian social problems are possible.

This led to the development of cross-cultural testing of psychological concepts and theories. Thus Indian psychologists got an opportunity to operate on wider plane and to influence developments in mainstream psychology. But to a large extent cross cultural psychology remained a methodological enterpise and culture remained a peripheral concern (*Misra and Gregen*, 1993). In recent times cross-cultural psychology itself is going through a crisis and the classical conception of culture, that was the basis of most research in this area, is being seriously questioned (Miller, 1998).

All these developments in the field of psychology and that of indigenous psychology firmed the belief that all psychological knowledge is rooted in the prevalent world view of a society and is conditioned by its historical and metatheoretical considerations.

The type of indigenisation as proposed by D Sinha (1994) which is based on a systematic analysis of the culture bound concept and categories, and focuses on the contemporary relevance of cultural heritage and native theories is termed as *'Indian Psychology'*.

This stream has primarily relied on the rich storehouse of knowledge found in Indian scriptures and philosophical texts of the last two to three millennia. The work of Kakar presents research which finely blends both adaptation of the mainstream (Western) psychology and ancient Indian psychology.

The beginning of Indian psychology can be traced in the writings of many eminent thinkers such as Swami Vivekananda and Sri Aurobindo in the early part of last century. The monumental work of Jadunath Sinha (1934/1958/1961) on Indian Psychology can be considered as a landmark informally establishing it as an independent discipline.

The books of Ramachandra Rao (1962) and Raghunath Safaya (1975) gave it further impetus during early years. Some notable publications in 1980's and 1990's are by Paranjpye (1984, 1998) Chakraboity (1995) Saraswathi (1999) and K Ramakrishna Rao (1988, 2002, 2005). There is a rich and growing body of research in this area and many excellent reviews available. The stream of psychology is not only built on theories and perspectives in contemporary idiom, but also involves integration with broader global perspective.

Matthijis Cornelissen (2000, 2005) has requested that Psychological knowledge from ancient Indian spiritual tradition needs to be integrated in the teaching program. He advised that core of psychology curriculum could be Indian theories of self and consciousness.

Indian Psychology in Academia in 2000s

In the beginning of 2000's the academics in India started to change rapidly. The scientific community became more accepting towards psychology rooted in native wisdom and philosophical traditions. Indian psychologists were endeavoring to break free from theoretical and methodological constraints of the discipline to understand with the real issues of development and act as a social catalysts in the change process. Indian psychologists also realised that if they do not take up the challenge they are likely to be marginalised.

Infact the psychologists in many countries of all the continents in the world realised the need for developing indigenous perspective of one's culture and to get the subject free from the dominance of American psychology. Thus, it has become a movement, not a culture specific phenomena limited to a few Asian societies. However, Indian psychology was not only suited to address India's specific psychological issues and problems, but it offers psychological models and theories appropriate to address problems of social conflicts, violence and mental health in other societies also.

Four factors have contributed to this change of attitudes and perceptions of Indian psychology.

(i) First is the failure of Western psychology to deal with its own societal problems. It has been realised that growing problems such as social and family violence, mental health and moral decay cannot be resolved through Western psychology which follows the brute empiricism in psychological research.

A need was felt to bring back spirituality and religiosity in psychological research which were banished from psychology 150 years ago.

(ii) Second, the growing popularity of yoga and other spiritual systems of India in the West. Numerous people with spiritual training and experiences in India have been visiting other countries and have acquired a large following. They have been responsible for disseminating the Indian spiritual tradition. Mahrishi Mahesh Yogi and Swami Rama are some prominent gurus who have been able to draw the attention of academic psychologists. Sri Aurobindo's integral yoga and integral psychology attracted worldwide attention.

Mahesh Yogi transcendental meditation went through rigorous experimental testing at Harvard and many other universities. Swami Rama's medical testing at the meninger foundation laboratory, New York, in which he demonstrated various Yogic feats proved the power of mind over body.

All this has contributed significantly towards evoking interest in the Indian psychological perspectives publications by Sri Aurobindo Ashram in Puducherry and the Himalayan International Institute for Yoga Sciences, Philosophy and Religion in Honesdale Pennsy lvania founded by Swami Rama. These publications have played an important role in popularising Indian Psychology in the world.

(iii) The secular nature of Indian psychology, of consciousness validated the fact that it has more to offer in terms of self growth than any other religious tradition. Psychologists became more interested to examine the indigenous perspectives available in many religious traditions of the East. It was clearly understood that modern psychology has nothing to offer regarding the spiritual transcendental dimension of human nature to understand others or for personal growth (Tart, 1975). Unfortunately most academic psychologists in India have not appreciated this fact and consider Indian Psychology as part of revivalistic movement.

(iv) With India emerging as a major economic power in the world, there is a renewed interest in Indian values, philosophies and practices as well as in strength and resilience of Indian society. The very Indian culture and philosophies which were debunked earlier for India's poverty and backwardness by many Western ideologists (Max Muller for example) are now taken seriously by both Western and Indian psychologists.

Features of Indian Psychology

The newly emerging psychology is rooted in traditional Indian thought and practice.

Some of the features which give Indian psychology a distinct identity are briefly discussed.

- Indian psychology can be deemed as 'universal' as it deals with the perennial issues of human existence which are not bound by any geographical region or time period.

  The questions which were raised by sages and thinkers 100's of years ago, are the same and are relevant even today and in this sense Indian psychology is both ancient and contemporary at the same time. The roots of Indian psychology can be Indian but it was never proposed as the psychology of India. For instance, Buddhist psychology which is an integral part of Indian psychology, was developed in Sri Lanka, Tibet and Japan, among other countries.
- It deals with the 'inner-state' of a person taking consciousness as the primary subject matter of study. Human consciousness is considered to be hierarchial, the highest state being of pure consciousness, bliss and truth. Yoga and meditation are the tools to attain this highest state of pure consciousness. However, it should not be misinterpreted that Indian Psychology is not concerned about human conditions of poverty, injustice and pain. Indian psychology do not dismiss the empirical research in these areas but provides a broader perspective within which their findings should make sense.
- Indian psychology is spiritual in nature, but is based on truthful methods. As its a human science of consciousness its methods are different from the methods of physical sciences but they are not less stringent than any scientific methods. Methods of self observation, direct observation (for example insitution) and others which rely on sensory and mental mediation. These methods rely on blending of first person and second person perspectives. These methods work well within the guru (second person)- Pupil (first

person) tradition. Methods of yoga and meditation have been used for centuries to test, experiment and empirically validate higher mental states.

- Indian psychology is applied and its not just concerned with testing the existing theories and developing generalisable propositions but more importantly, about the practices that can be used for the transformation of human conditions towards perfection. This is the transformation of the person to higher level of achievement and well-being.

In more recent times, efforts to build Indian psychology as a vibrant discipline have intensified. Several conferences (Puducherry 2001, 2002, 2004, Kollam, 2001, Delhi, 2002, 2003, 2007 Visakhapatnam, 2002, 2003, 2006, Bengaluru 2007). have been conducted in this regard which have given impetus to this movement of Indian Psychology. A number of publications of Indian psychology such as Kuppuswami's elements of ancient Indian psychology (1985), Sen's integral psychology (1986), Misra and Mohanty's perspective on Indian psychology (2002) have the potential of serving as textbooks.

More recently, Joshi and Cornelissen's edited volume, Consciousness, Indian Psychology and Yoga (2004); Rao and Marwaha's towards a spiritual Psychology (2006); Rao, Parangjpe and Dalal's Handbook of Indian Psychology (2008) and provide rich resource material for teaching and research in the area. Thus it can be concluded that a movement has started toward contemporarising Indian theories and testing their relevance for enhancing human competencies and well being. Indian Psychology can be seen ushering towards a new era of many exciting possibilities.

Issues in Indian Psychology

Following are the issues crippling Indian Psychology

The Colonial Encounter

The British East Indian Company adopted a policy of funding only European-style education within its territories several years before the subcontinent was formally accessioned to Queen Victoria's empire in 1857. Education in colleges and universities was modeled after Oxford and Cambridge. Modern psychology was introduced at Calcutta University with the starting of a separate department of psychology in 1916. Dalal (2002) has given an excellent overview of the history of psychology since that time onward. During nearly a century that has passed since, Indian psychologists trained abroad as well as those trianed in India almost exclusively followed theWestern brands of pscyhology.

The teaching and research in modern psychology began largely as an extension of the Euro-American tradition in the British period. Its initial emphasis was not so much on questioning and doubting the Western concepts and methods, but on preserving the essential configuration of the discipline and keeping it as similar to the one in the Western world, as possible.

We also note that there existed a tradition of British psychoanalysts who tried to offer interpretations of the Indian psyche to justify the British rule. Citing Christine Hartnack's work Vahali (2011) has discussed at length how early British psychoanalysts tried to create universal psychoanalytic conceptualisations that explain away Indian experiences of selfhood or view them as essentially inferior, less worthy or simply pathological or otherwise deficient. It acted as a tool to justify social oppression and colonial rule.

Post-Colonialism and Psychology

Soon after India gained independence from the British rule, psychology witnessed an explosive growth with departments of psychology opening up in old universities as well as in a continually widening circle of new universities and institutes of technology and management. These was a similar explosion in the number of research publications in Indian as well as international journals. Despite the exceptional growth of the field, there has been acute restlessness about the significance of the accomplishments.

Though there was an expansion of psychology departments within university system since 1970, there were little organisational support for pursuing research projects in these departments. There was no incentive for research, because of the mass entry of students in higher education and chronic campus unrest for political reasons. Research in psychology began to develop outside university system. All this time research institutes like ANS Institute of Social Studies, Patna, Centre for Study of Developing Societies New Delhi and National Institute of Community Development, Hyderabad became centres for research in psychology. There was a rapid but unplanned expansion. However by 1960's the number of psychology departments increased to 32 in Indian Universities, but this development was quite unplanned. No serious thinking preceded in establishing these departments in terms of their need-based specialisation.

Lack of Distinct Disciplinary Identity

With due course of time several departments developed their own distinct identity on the basis of their own areas of research interest but it was mainly was in congruence with the area of interest of their head of the department. The interest and training of one dominant person (or HOD) were decisive factors in the specialisation of that department.

For example Mysore University psychology department was known for 'Test construction', Osmania University department for industrial psychology, Patna University for measurement and guidance, Allahabad University for rural and social psychology etc.

As these departments were mostly dependent on one dominant personality (HOD), and when these scholars departed, the department encountered a major set back and showed shifts in interests/specialisation. Thus, psychology as a discipline report on experiencing distinct identity crisis.

EXAM BASED QUESTIONS

1 Who worked as guide and councellor during ancient times ?
(a) Kings (b) Common people
(c) Lay people (d) Sages and saints

2 What is the main goal of Indian Psychology?
(a) Self efficacy (b) Self realisation
(c) Self propogation (d) Self appraisal

3 In Indian tradition hierarchy of self is
(a) uni layer (b) multi layer
(c) bi layer (d) All of these

4 According to an analysis of selfhood in the model of human being RC Tripathi has concluded that self is viewed as
(a) participant, objective viewer
(b) witness, participant
(c) witness, non-participant
(d) non-participant, dual

5 What is 'Jiva' in Indian Psychology ?
(a) Witness (b) Non-participant
(c) Experiential self (d) Objective

6 What is 'Brahman' in Indian concept of self ?
(a) Experiential self (b) Absolute self
(c) Physical self (d) Inflated self

7 The Indian notion of self encompasses the physical, social, mental as well as
(a) Experiential aspect (b) Dependent aspect
(c) Spiritual aspect (d) Real aspect

8 The multilayered hierarchy of self in Indian context is called
(a) Panch kosha
(b) Panch mukhas
(c) Panch tattva
(d) Panch reti

9 Bhagavad Gita emphasises the importance of
(a) emotional intelligence (b) visuo-spatial intelligence
(c) naturalistic intelligence (d) spatial intelligence

10 Gita upholds the necessity of
(a) Rewards, Puruskar (b) Action, Karma
(c) Self, Vinoda (d) Knowledge, Vidya

11 According to Gita, the way to attain self-realisation can be achieved by
(a) self less action
(b) surrendering onself to God
(c) desireless actions
(d) All of the above

12 Jnana yoga is a path of knowledge, wisdom and
(a) path of righteousness
(b) realisation of Brahman
(c) path of duty
(d) path of action

13 What is the main goal of Buddhism?
(a) Harmonious life
(b) Personal spiritual development
(c) Self actualisation
(d) Cognitive enhancement

14 Who among the following psychologists found that Buddhist teachings have potential for transformation and healing?
(a) Leon Festinger (b) Alfred Adler
(c) Eric Fromm (d) Karen Horney

15 What is the meaning of 'nirvana' as per Buddhist philosophy ?
(a) Transcendenting to higher level of consciousness
(b) Total cessation of dissatisfaction and suffering
(c) To have healthy and virtous life
(d) Gaining knowledge or wisdom

16 What are the two main branches of Buddhism?
(a) Mahayana and Nirvana
(b) Ayantavas and Theraveda
(c) Theravada and Mahayana
(d) Vipassana and Nirvana

17 The existence of suffering, in Buddhism is called
(a) Arusala (b) Vedana
(c) Duhkha (d) Duhkha-nirodha

18 What are the first two segments of Eightfold Path in Buddhism known as
(a) Prajna (b) Pancha-sila
(c) Sila (d) Samadhi

19 Which path in Buddhism are concerned with Meditation or Samadhi ?
(a) Right effort (b) Right action
(c) Right livelihood (d) None of these

20 Which stage in Buddhism appears just prior to attain Nirvana?
(a) Unreffeed meditation
(b) Detachment from joy
(c) Reasoning and investigation
(d) Detachment from body

21 Which part of Buddhism is mostly connected to phenomenological psychology?
(a) Sutta Pitaka (b) Dhamma Sangri
(c) Abhidhamma Pitaka (d) None of these

22 Who wrote the famous book 'Glimpses of Abhidhamma'?
(a) Eric Fromm (b) Dalai Lama
(c) Chogyam Trungpa (d) Daniel Goleman

23 Who wrote 'Buddhist manual of Psychological Ethics'?
(a) Rhys Davids (b) Carl Rogers
(c) Eric Fromm (d) DT Suzuki

24 Which principles of Buddhism are supreme with respect to the concept of anxiety in Existential Psychology?
(a) Duhkha (b) Spiritual illness
(c) Clinging (d) Attachment

25 Who introduced 'MBSR' technique based on Buddhism mindfulness techniques?
(a) Steven C Hayes (b) Jon-Kabat-Zinn
(c) Marsha M Linehan (d) Eric Fromm

26 Who introduced 'DBT' (Dialectical Behavioural Technique) based on Principles of Buddhism?
(a) Steven C Hayes (b) Jon Kabat Zinn
(c) Marsha M Linehan (d) Eric Fromm

27 What does 'MBSR' stands for ?
(a) Inner (b) Subliminal (c) Central (d) Outer

28 Which one of the following is not the principal aspect of Sufi Psychology?
(a) Self (b) Mind
(c) Heart (d) Soul

29 Sufi Psychology believes that spiritual……is the agent of reconciliation between the physical and metaphysical dimensions of human being.
(a) self (b) mind (c) heart (d) soul

30 What is the name given to the inner battle between the 'self' and 'soul' in Sufism?
(a) Nafs (b) Ghalb (c) Run (d) Jihaad

31 In the context of spiritual growth and development the term 'transformation' in Sufism refers to
(a) shift of locus of consciousness
(b) shift in emotional patterns
(c) shift in sense of identity
(d) All of the above

32 What are the characteristics of Nafs-al-Ammara as described in Sufism?
(a) Seeks material objects (b) Power
(c) Narcissitic Tendencies (d) All of these

33 How many planes of consciousness are described in Sufism ?
(a) 8 (b) 7
(c) 9 (d) 5

34 Which one of the following is not a station of heart as described by Sufi master 'Tirmidhi' ?
(a) Spiritual heart (b) Physical heart
(c) Inner heart (d) Conscious heart

35 What is the ascent of soul through various planes of consciousness called in Sufism?
(a) Metem psychosis (b) Evolution
(c) Journey (d) Transcendence

36 What is the commanding self in Sufism called?
(a) Nafs-al-Lawwamah
(b) Nafs-al-Molhamah
(c) Nafs-al-Ammarah
(d) Nafs-al-Mutmainna

37 What is the sleep like ignorance or unsconsciousness called in Sufism?
(a) Zaaher (b) Tanaasukh
(c) Gheflat (d) Samskara

38 Integral yoga is also called the
(a) Higher conscious yoga (b) Higher level yoga
(c) Supramental yoga (d) Subeliminal yoga

39 The main goal of integral yoga is
(a) awareness of divine
(b) integration of physical, mental and spiritual aspects of self
(c) Manifest the divine on Earth
(d) All of the above

40 What are the three types of being according to Sri Aurobindo?
(a) Outer, Central, Inner
(b) Outer, Inner, Psychic
(c) Outer, Inner, Jiva
(d) Outer, Inner, Atman

41 Name two important pioneers of 19th century who interpreted Indian thoughts in context of Western Philosophy ?
(a) RC Tripathi and Sri Aurobindo
(b) Krishna Chandra Bhattacharya and RC Tripathi
(c) Krishna Chandra Bhattacharya and S Radhakrishnan
(d) S Radhakrishnan and Sri Aurobindo

42 The process that leads to the awakening of inner being is called
(a) Sadhana (b) Meditation
(c) Yoga (d) Prayer

43 What is the innermost being, a portion of divine self known as
(a) Brahman (b) Anandamaya kosha
(c) Jivatman (d) Pranamaya

44 Which is the lowest form of consciousness, which is found in inanimate matter?
(a) Sub conscience (b) Higher mind
(c) In conscience (d) Illumined mind

45 Which type of mind is found in poets, musicians and painters ?
(a) Illumined mind (b) Over mind
(c) Higher mind (d) Super mind

46 Which state of mind is related to cosmic consciousness?
(a) Mind and behaviour stress relaxation
(b) Mindfulness behavioural stress reduction
(c) Mindfulness based state reversal
(d) Mindfulness based stress reduction

47 What is 'Supra mentalisation' in integral Yoga ?
(a) Realisation of enlightenment
(b) Realisation of the supermind
(c) Realisation of illumination
(d) All of the above

48 Where was the first psychology department set up in India?
(a) Delhi University (b) Madras University
(c) Calcutta University (d) Allahabad University

49 In which year the first Department of Psychology was set up in India?
(a) 1920 (b) 1916 (c) 1914 (d) 1918

50 Whose lecture became the landmark in introducing Indian thought in USA?
(a) Swami Vivekananda
(b) Ramakrishna Paramhansa
(c) Swami Rama
(d) RC Tripathi

51 Who interpreted the path of action described in Bhagavad Gita in Light of Post Kantian and Drawanian thoughts in 19th century?
(a) S Radhakrishnan
(b) Krishnachandra Bhattacharya
(c) BG Tilak
(d) Sri Aurobindo

52 Name two early pioneers in the area of Academic Psychology, whose work had a great impact in development of psychology in India?
(a) Gopal Shekhar Bose, BG Tilak
(b) Girindra Shekhar Bose, NN Sen Gupta
(c) NN Sengupta, Gopal Shekhar Bose
(d) NN Sen Gupta, BG Tilak

53 Mahatma Gandhi's thoughts and principles.
(a) Illumined mind (b) Over mind
(c) Super mind (d) Intuitive mind

54 Read is a major impact of
(a) Psychiatry (b) Applied Social Psychology
(c) Community Psychology (d) Crisis Psychology

55 When did Indian Government established Psychological research wing in Defence Ministry?
(a) 1952 (b) 1949 (c) 1951 (d) 1950

56 Which university first published the Indian journal of applied Psychology ?
(a) Madras (b) Calcutta (c) Delhi (d) Allahabad

57 Which Indian Psychologist wrote the first book on 'Cognition'?
(a) JBP Sinha (b) Girishwar Misra
(c) Durganand Sinha (d) NN Sen Gupta

58 When was the Indian Association of Climeal Psychologists started?
(a) 1975 (b) 1974 (c) 1972 (d) 1968

59 Indigenous Psychology is closer to
(a) Community Psychology (b) Clinical Psychology
(c) Cultural Psychology (d) Orgnisation Psychology

60 Who has worked on Psycho-spiritual thought and mental health in mid 20th century ?
(a) Jadunath Sinha (b) Akhilanand
(c) Sri Aurobindo (d) S. Radha Krishnan

61 Who modified the concept of need for achievement by Mc Clelland according to Indian Context ?
(a) Janak Pandey (b) L Krishnan
(c) Udai Pareek (d) Jain

62 Who has called Psychology in India as adoptology?
(a) KG Agarwal (b) L Krishnan
(c) Janak Pandey (d) Udai Pareek

63 What was the reason behind the need for indigenisation in Psychology ?
(a) Need for scientific understanding Indian Psychological knowledge
(b) Western theories were not applicable in Indian context
(c) Western psychology was failing to shed light on Indian social issues
(d) All of the above

64 Who was the first psychologist to describe the scientific understanding of Indian traditional concepts ?
(a) Girishwar Misra (b) JBP Sinha
(c) Durganand Sinha (d) RC Tripathi

65 The Indigenisation of Psychology basically has helped the subject and research methodologies to become more
(a) politically applicable (b) socially relevant
(c) culturally suited (d) Both b and c

66 Who among the following has suggested a teacher pupil model in counselling?
(a) Neki (b) Janak Pandey
(c) JBP Sinha (d) Udai Pareek

67 Which famous psychologist said "Indigenisation in India is slow and sluggish"?
(a) Eric Fromm (b) MC Clelland
(c) John Adair (d) Garden Murphy

68 Psychologists in India has started to realise that it is important to accept the philosophical traditions and native wisdom in our culture. This will help them to act as
(a) change makers (b) social catalysts
(c) slow movers (d) dynamic and scientists

69 Psychologists in various countries and continents realised the need for developing indigenous perspective and free Psychology from the dominance of
(a) American Psychology (b) Indian Psychology
(c) European Psychology (d) Contemporary Psychology

70 Who invented Transcendental Meditaion?
(a) Sri Aurobindo (b) Swami Rama
(c) Mahesh Yogi (d) Swami Vivekananda

71 What is the nature of 'consciousness' in Indian psychology which makes it best suited for 'Self Growth'?
(a) Dynamic (b) Static (c) Secular (d) Accepting

72 What has become quite evident for Western psychology which led to the acceptance of Indian psychology worldwide?
(a) It is positivist
(b) Western psychology is purely experimental in nature
(c) Western Psychology has nothing to offer in spiritual transcendental dimension of human nature
(d) All of the above

73 Indian psychology can be addressed as being universal as
(a) It deals with the inner state of a person
(b) It is based on consciousness and spiritual development
(c) It deals with the issues of human existence which are not bound by any geographical region or time period
(d) None of the above

74 Which is the highest state in human consciousness ?
(a) Self efficacy
(b) Self understanding
(c) Self actualisation
(d) Truth or bliss or pure consciousness

75 What are the methods used in Indian psychology to study self and behaviour ?
(a) Self observation
(b) Sensory and mental mediation
(c) Direct observation
(d) All of the above

76 Which methods are used to test, experiment and empirically validate higher mental state?
(a) Self observation
(b) Introspection
(c) Direct observation
(d) Yoga and meditation

77 Who wrote the famous book 'Elements of Ancient Indian Psychology'?
(a) Durganand Sinha (b) Kuppu Swami
(c) Misra and Mohanty (d) JBP Sinha

78 Who authored the famous book "Handbook of Indian Psychology (2008)"?
(a) Joshi and Cornelissen (b) Rao, Pranjpe and Dalal
(c) Misra and Gregen (d) Rao and Marwaha

79 Why did research in psychology began to grow outside university in 1970's ?
(a) Lack of Vision
(b) Prevalence of students and chronic campus unrest
(c) Lack of funding
(d) Lack of Infrastructure

80 What did Prayag Mehta conclude in his famous research on need of achievement in context to Indian society ?
(a) Need for achievement is high in India
(b) Need for achievement is low India
(c) Need for achievement is collective concept in India
(d) Social need for achievement is good for India

81 Match the following

List I (Layer in Jiva)	List II (Description)
A. Annamaya Kosha	1. Cognitive Sheath
B. Pranmaya Kosha	2. Life
C. Manomaya Kosha	3. Mental Sheath
D. Vigyanmaya Kosha	4. Product of food

Codes

	A	B	C	D
(a)	1	2	3	4
(b)	2	4	3	1
(c)	1	3	2	4
(d)	4	2	3	1

82 Match the following

List I (Koshas as per Indian Context)	List II (Description of Sheaths)
A. Atman	1. Food
B. Manomaya	2. Life
C. Annamaya	3. Mental sheath
D. Pranamaya	4. Joyous sheath

Codes

	A	B	C	D		A	B	C	D
(a)	1	2	3	4	(b)	1	3	2	4
(c)	4	3	1	2	(d)	2	3	1	4

83 Match the following

List I (Chapters of Bhagavad Gita)	List II (Classification of the Chapter)
A. First 6 Chapters	1. Jnana Yoga
B. Middle six chapters	2. Bhakti Yoga
C. Last 6 chapters	3. Karma Yoga

Codes

	A	B	C		A	B	C
(a)	1	2	3	(b)	3	2	1
(c)	3	1	2	(d)	2	3	1

84 Match the following

List I (Terms used in Sufism)	List II (Physical Aspect)
A. Nafs	1. Heart
B. Ghalb	2. Soul
C. Ruh	3. Self
D. Jihad	4. Inner battle

Codes

	A	B	C	D
(a)	1	2	4	3
(b)	4	3	1	2
(c)	1	2	3	4
(d)	2	1	3	4

85 Put the following in correct sequence on the basis of emergence.

1. Interal Yoga 2. Sufism
3. Buddhism 4. Bhagavad Gita

Codes

(a) 2, 3, 4, 1 (b) 1, 2, 3, 4
(c) 4, 1, 3, 2 (d) 4, 3, 2, 1

86 Arrange the following in chronological order.

1. Nafs-al-Amanarah 2. Fana
3. Self surrender 4. Non-attachment

Codes

(a) 1, 2, 3, 4 (b) 1, 2, 4, 3
(c) 4, 3, 2, 1 (d) 3, 2, 1 4

87 Arrange the following in chronology.

1. Department of Psychology started in Allahabad.
2. Girindra Shekhar Bose published journal 'Samiksha'.
3. Independent psychology department set up in DU.
4. Department of Applied Psychology established in University of Mumbai.

Codes

(a) 1, 2, 3, 4 (b) 4, 3, 2, 1
(c) 2, 1, 3, 4 (d) 4, 3, 1, 2

88 Arrange the following in sequence based on publication year.

1. Indian psychology and yoga.
2. Rao and Marwaha towards a spiritual psychology.
3. Dalal's Handbook of India Psychology.
4. Sen's integral psychology.

Codes

(a) 4, 1, 2, 3 (b) 1, 2, 3, 4 (c) 3, 2, 1, 4 (d) 1, 4, 3, 2

89 Consider the following statements

1. Jnana Yoga talks about the spiritual knowledge.
2. Sankhya Yoga talks about the role of action of 'Karma'.

Which among the above is/are currect?

(a) Only 1 (b) Only 2
(c) Both 1 and 2 (d) None of these

90 Consider the following statements

1. Abhidhamma Pitaka of Buddhism, articulates philosophy, psychology and ethics as well.
2. Psychoanalysts like karen Thorney and Fritz Peals studied Zen-Buddhism.

Which among the above is/are correct?

(a) Only 1 (b) Only 2
(c) Both 1 and 2 (d) None of these

91 Consider the following statements

1. 'Nafs' is the equivalent word to 'self' or 'ego'.
2. The human soul (ruh) is the innermost dimension of the human being.

Which among the above is/are correct?

(a) Only 1 (b) Ony 2
(c) Both 1 and 2 (d) None of these

92 Consider the following statements

1. The integral yoga of Aurobindo, is a yoga of synthesis, intended to harmonise the paths of Karma, Jnana and Bhakti Yoga.
2. According to integral yoga, the outer being is capable of experiencing only a narrow range of stimuli.

Which among the above is/are correct?

(a) Only 1 (b) Only 2
(c) Both 1 and 2 (d) None of these

93 Consider the following statements

1. Gandhiji's work reflects the practical orientation of psychology in India.
2. Gandhian style of leadership in modern psychology is called 'group dynamics'.

Which among the above is/are correct?

(a) Only 1 (b) Only 2
(c) Both 1 and 2 (d) None of these

94 Consider the following statements

1. Durganand Sinha ask for integration of modern psychology with Indian thought.
2. Modern Psychology originate as an indigenous science.

Which among the following is/are correct?

(a) Only 1 (b) Only 2
(c) Both 1 and 2 (d) None of these

95 Consider the following statements

1. Exogenous Indigenisation is integration of modern psychology with Indian thought.
2. Janak Pandey found that unlike the West ingratiation is rampant and risk free in India.

Which among the following is/are correct?

(a) Only 1 (b) Only 2
(c) Both 1 and 2 (d) None of these

96 Put the stages in right order to attain 'Nirvana' as per Buddhism.

1. Unruffed meditation
2. Detachment from joy
3. Reasoning and investigation
4. Detachment from body

Codes

(a) 2, 3, 4 and 1 (b) 3, 1, 4 and 2
(c) 3, 1, 2 and 4 (d) 1, 2, 3 and 4

Directions (Q. Nos. 97-101) *Read the passage given below and answer the following questions.*

Gestalt therapy by Fritz Perls, is heavily based on existentialist principles and significantly Zen Buddhism. Gestalt therapy also works on whole person and encourage right mindfulness, similarly as Buddhism. Similarly Client Centered therapy by Carl Rogers works on the principle that therapist does not direct the process of therapy, but patient has the resources to deal with their own 'cure' and 'self growth', provided the environment is safe for them. Like the Buddha this non-authoratative approach suggests that the 'patient can be a light to themselves.'

Thus, we can say that Buddha was a unique Psychotherapist and his teachings, writing and wisdom helped millions of people through out the centuries. Today even the Western world has reals the psychological essence of Buddhism. In short the Psychotherapeutic models described by Buddhism or great value and have applications at all times.

97 Gestalt therapy by Fritz Perls is heavily based on

(a) existentialist principles (b) hypothetical construct
(c) biological behaviours (d) None of these

98 Client Centered Therapy was proposed by

(a) Fritz Perls (b) Carl Rogers
(c) Buddha (d) Aurobindo

99 Which among the following is correct about Client Centered Therapy?

(a) Patients can be a light to themselves
(b) self growth
(c) Both a and b
(d) None of the above

100 Who is considered as an unique Psychotherapist?

(a) Carl Roger (b) Fritz Perls
(c) Buddha (d) Krishna

101 Consider the following statements

1. Client Centered therapy is a non-authoritative approach.
2. Gestalt therapy works on whole person and encourage right mindfulness.

Which among the above is/are correct?

(a) Only 1 (b) Only 2
(c) Both 1 and 2 (d) None of these

Directions (Q. Nos. 102-109) *In the questions given below are two statements labelled as Assertion (A) and Reason (R). In the context of the two statements, which one of the following is correct?*

(a) Both A and R are true and R is the correct explanation of A
(b) Both A and R are true, but R is not the correct explanation of A
(c) A is true, but R is false
(d) A is false, but R is true.

102 **Assertion** (A) Self an be considered as a synonym to ego or lower self.

Reason (R) Nafs in sufism is related to 'self'.

103 **Assertion** (A) Nafs is not an equivalent to 'ego' as used in Western Psychology.

Reason (R) Nafs is a lived organic reality which is experienced in day-to-day life situations.

104 **Assertion** (A) Nafs is a static and universal phenomena. It is same in all humans.

Reason (R) 'Nafs' has a unique formation in each individual.

105 **Assertion** (A) Indian psychology is spiritual.

Reason (R) It studies levels of consciousness and works to help a person to attain higher level of consciousness.

106 **Assertion** (A) Indian psychology is only concerned with testing the existing theories and developing generalisable propositions.

Reason (R) Indian psychology is applied.

107 **Assertion** (A) Indian psychology totally dismiss the empirical research done in the area.

Reason (R) It deals with 'inner-state' of a person.

108 **Assertion** (A) Indian psychology is both ancient and contemporary.

Reason (R) The issues of life raised by the ancient safes and saints are similar to those prevalent today.

109 **Assertion** (A) Indian psychology is never proposed as the psychology of India.

Reason (R) Buddhist psychology an integral part of Indian psychology was developed in Srilanka, Tibet and Japan.

ANSWERS

1 (d)	2 (b)	3 (b)	4 (c)	5 (c)	6 (b)	7 (c)	8 (a)	9 (a)	10 (b)
11 (d)	12 (a)	13 (b)	14 (c)	15 (b)	16 (d)	17 (c)	18 (a)	19 (a)	20 (d)
21 (c)	22 (a)	23 (a)	24 (a)	25 (b)	26 (c)	27 (b)	28 (b)	29 (c)	30 (d)
31 (d)	32 (d)	33 (b)	34 (d)	35 (a)	36 (c)	37 (c)	38 (a)	39 (d)	40 (b)
41 (b)	42 (a)	43 (c)	44 (c)	45 (a)	46 (a)	47 (d)	48 (c)	49 (b)	50 (a)
51 (c)	52 (c)	53 (a)	54 (b)	55 (b)	56 (a)	57 (a)	58 (d)	59 (c)	60 (c)
61 (a)	62 (a)	63 (d)	64 (c)	65 (d)	66 (a)	67 (c)	68 (b)	69 (a)	70 (c)
71 (d)	72 (d)	73 (c)	74 (d)	75 (d)	76 (d)	77 (b)	78 (b)	79 (b)	80 (c)
81 (d)	82 (c)	83 (b)	84 (d)	85 (d)	86 (b)	87 (c	88 (a)	89 (a)	90 (c).
91 (c)	92 (c)	93 (c)	94 (a)	95 (c)	96 (c)	97 (a)	98 (b)	99 (c)	100 (c)
101 (c)	102 (d)	103 (a)	104 (d)	105 (a)	106 (c)	107 (c)	108 (a)	109 (a)	

CHAPTER

2

Emergence of Western Psychology

Psychology as a discipline owes its genesis to numerous ancient cultures. Until the middle of 19th century, psychology was widely regarded as a branch of philosophy. It was during the last quarter of 19th century that the Western world began to seriously pursue psychology as a scientific discipline.

Western Psychology

The roots of Western psychology can be traced to Greek philosophy. The word psychology itself is derived from the Greek words 'psyche' which means 'study'. Psychology thus started as a part of philosophy and became an independent discipline much later. While psychology did not emerge as a separate discipline until the late 1800s, its earliest history can be traced back to the time of the early Greeks. During the 17th century, the French philosopher Rene Descartes introduced the idea of dualism, which asserted that the mind and body were two entities that interact to form the human experience. Many other issues still debated by psychologists today, such as the relative contributions of nature v/s nurture, are rooted in these early philosophical traditions.

The journey of emergences of Western psychology is divided into three periods

(i) Greek heritage (ii) Medieval period (iii) Modern period

Greek Heritage

The modern ideas about mind and its functioning were derived from Greek Philosophy. The eminent Greek philosophers who made relevant contribution in field of psychology are Alcmeon, Hippocrates (460-370 BC), Socrates (469-399 BC), Plato (428-348 BC) and Aristotle (384-322 BC). Alcmeon was an ancient Greek physician who laid the foundation of psychology as a science in 6th century BC. He proposed that 'mental life is a function of the brain.' His idea is even relevant today, where we studies the relationship between mental processes and brain in the realm of psychology.

Hippocrates proposed a typology of human personality on the basis of body fluid or humour *i.e.* sanguine (blood), melancholic (black bile), choleric (yellow bile) and phelgmatic (phlegm).

In this Chapter

Socrates recognised mind in addition to soul. He analysed the activities of mind in addition to as well as soul. He had analysed the activities of mind in the form of thinking, dreams, memory and imagination. Plato and Aristotle were the students of Socrates and they further reinforced and strengthened the idea of Socrates. But they do not believe on the concept of soul called *human being*; a rational animal, stressing on human ability to reason and think.

Plato was always interested in knowing the role of mind in controlling human behaviour, thus, he was the one who introduced the concept of dualism in psychology. Though he regarded body and mind to be two distinct, independent identity, but he could not clearly define his stand.

Aristotle, the student of Plato was the believer of the idea that soul and living body are inseparable. He further explained his view point insisting that mind is the result of psychological processes. It is then necessary to understand those psychological processes including the activities of sense organs which help the individual to experience his environment. Aristotle's assumption had a scientific base, thus, it was accessible for verification. It is true that brain controls our conscious experiences and behaviour.

Medieval Period

In Europe, there is a huge gap in the development of psychology and psychiatry between the classical period, where scholars such as Aristotle and Plato first began to study the nature of thought and mind.

Commonly known as the *Dark Ages* from the 6th to the 13th centuries, this period began when the Roman Empire fell into a terminal decline, a period that we automatically associate with superstition and fear. It ended with the work of the great Renaissance men, whose studies into anatomy and willingness to challenge the church laid the groundwork for the Scientific Revolution and the Enlightenment itself, where the great empiricists would finally start to probe the mind.

Scholars such as **St. Augustine, Thomas Aquinas** and **Roger Bacon** made some astute observations about the inner workings of the human mind, providing a foundation for the Renaissance.

In the East, the Byzantine Empire preserved the knowledge of the Greeks and philosophers such as the Jewish Symeon Seth (11th century) and Niketas Stethatos (100-1090 CE) studied the nature of dreams and emotions, as well as studying mental disorders and the brain.

Gradually, psychology moved away from this focus and started to establish itself as a scientific discipline which deals with the underlying human experience and behaviour. Psychology as a separate area of study split away from philosophy a little over 100 years ago.

Modern Period

In 1879, the first Psychological Laboratory was established at the University of Leipzig by the German Philosopher-Psychologist Wilhelm Wundt (1832-1920). The first formal Psychological Laboratory in the United States was set up at Johns Hopkins University in 1883 and within few years most of the major universities had psychology laboratories and departments.

Although still philosophical in part, psychology developed as a new separate field of study in the last years of 19th century and is captured in Wilhelm Wundt's famous text book of 1890 'The Principles of Psychology'.

Around 1890 a steady stream of what since then was considered radical ideas and theories began to appear. While there were pioneers before him, the acknowledged 'Father of Modern Psychology' is Sigmund Freud. Over the past 125 years, the world of psychology has witnessed the development of several approaches to theory and practice in response to Freud's work. Included within the modern framework are names like BF Skinner, Jean Piaget, Carl Rogers, Carl Jung and Erik Erikson.

All saw the ongoing development of the human mind as the product not of duality, but of tasks associated with conscious and unconscious levels of functioning. While each one interpreted their findings differently there seemed to be a shared acceptance of Freud's hypothesis that human thought functioned within its own structure. People achieved maximum functioning or they are dysfunction in relationship to their development.

Wundt, James and other psychologists did experiments to study the mind and its processes. They studied the process by which one becomes aware of some external events and not to others. Several experiments were done in the area of imagery, memory, thinking and emotion.

Different Schools of Thoughts

In the initial years of 20th century the development of psychology as an independent science gained its momentum. Different psychologists had different approaches to study human mind and behaviour. They held quite different views on the nature of mind and proper subject matter of psychology.

This lead to the emergence of different schools of thoughts like *Structuralism, Functionalism, Behaviourism, Gestaltism, Psychoanalysis, Humanistic schools* etc. These schools of psychology set the direction of research on mind and behaviour in the early years of this century.

Structuralism

This is the earliest School of Psychology which grew up around the ideas of Wilhelm Wundt in Germany and was established at Cornell University in the United States by the student of Wundt, Edward B Titchener.

Structuralism focused on the basic elements of consciousness. It focused on the 'units' which make up the mind. They thought that in order to study mind one must study the basic or elementary unit of sensation, image, and emotion which compose it. It sought to analyse human adult mind (the sum total of experience from birth to present) in terms of the simplest definable components and then to find a way in which these components fit together in complex forms.

The major method used by the structuralists to discover these elementary units of mind was introspection. Subjects were trained to objectively report what they experienced in connection to a stimuli disregarding the significance or value of that experience.

They believed that an experience should be evaluated as a fact. *For example* A subject might be presented with a coloured light, an odor, a tone and asked to describe it as minutely as possible such as red, sweet, loud tone respectively. Titchener held the view that 'anatomy of the mind' had little to do with how or why the mind functions.

Though, Wundt is credited to be the founder of structuralism, it was actually his student Edward B Titchener who coined the term 'Structuralism'. Structuralism essentially disappeared when Titchener died. Though it was short lived, it played an important role in the development of early psychology and emergence of experimental psychology.

Functionalism

John Dewey (1873-1954), James K Angell (1869-1949) and Harvey A Carr (1873-1954) are the main functionalists. They proposed that psychology should study what mind and behaviour do. They were interested in studying the adaptive nature of mind and behaviour, which enables human to adjust to changing environment. Basically it emphasised on the study function of mind and behaviour like learning memory, problems solving and motivation that help people and animals to adapt in their environments, rather than the structure of human consciousness which was the core basis of structuralism.

This school of thought examined the ways in which behaviour allows people to satisfy their needs. Functionalists were more interested in the operation of the whole mind rather than of its individual parts which was the focus of structuralism. **William James** was the founder of functional psychology. He believed that introspection could serve as one means by which mental activities can be studied, but James relied on more objective measures, including the use of various recording devices and examinations of concrete products of mental activities and of anatomy and physiology (Gordon 1995). William James wrote the first text book of psychology. He was highly influenced by **Darwin's** evolutionary theory; which states that "all characteristics of a species must serve some adaptive purpose."

Three parts ushered functional psychology into the modern day's psychology . Utilising the Darwinian ideology, the mind was considered to perform diverse biological functions on its own and evolve as well as adapt to varying circumstances. Secondly, the physiological functioning of the organisms result in the development of the consciousness. Lastly, the promise of the impact of functional psychology in the improvement of education, mental hygiene and abnormal states.

Gestalt School

In the early 20th century, a new perspective called *Gestalt psychology* emerged in Germany as a reaction to the structuralism of Wundt. It was founded in 1912 by Max Wertheimer and his colleagues Kurt Koffka (1886-1941) and Wolfgang Kohler (1887-1967). They rejected the principle of structuralism which emphasised that mind is made up of simple elements. They pointed that mind is not made up of combination of simple elements. Instead of looking at the components of the mind, Gestalt psychologists emphasised that the whole of anything is greater than sum of its parts.

The German word Gestalt means 'form' or 'configuration' and the Gestalt psychologists believed that mind is the result of a whole pattern of sensory activities and the relationships or organisations within this pattern.

For Example

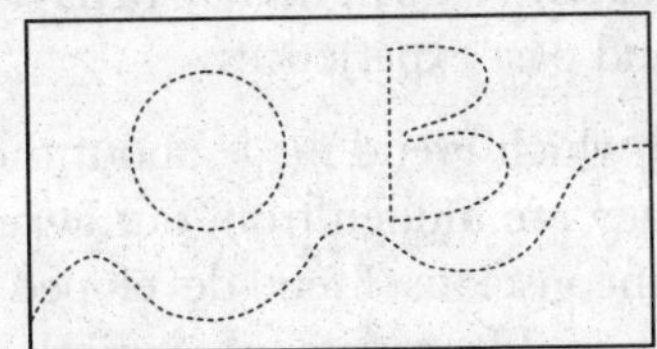

Demonstration of Gestalt Psychology

When we look at the above figure we perceive it as 'O' and 'B' inscribed on a wavy line rather than just dots or elements. The organisation of dots in a meaningful way gives way to our mental experience. Thus, they pointed a very important aspect of mental experience that it is based on the organisation and patterning of elements and is not due to simply the compounding of elements as proposed by structuralists.

The earliest Gestalt's work was mainly in the area of perception, with particular emphasis on visual perception and organisation, as elaborated by the phenomena of illusion. The concept of phi-phenomena is an optical illusion in which the light falling from a series of flashing bulbs on our retina, actually make us experience the movement of light. Similarly in case when we are watching movies in cinema hall, we actually have a series of rapidly moving images of still pictures falling on our retina and we experience movement in it. This phenomena in which stationary objects shown in rapid succession, transcending the threshold at which they can be perceived separately, appear to move, was given by Wertheimer in 1912.

The explanation of this phenomena also strengthens the Gestalt's view that our perceptual experience is more than the elements. Experience is holistic: it is a gestalt.

In the next few decades, Wertheimer, Koffka, Kohler and their students extended the Gestalt approach to the problems of perception, learning, thinking, problem solving, motivation and social psychology. Infact **Kurt Lewin** applied Gestalt principles in his filed theory of personality. The main principle of Gestalt psychology that whole is more than the sum of its parts has played an important role in the other areas including our understanding of the brain and social behaviour.

Behaviourism

This School of Psychology originated around 1910 when John B Watson (1879-1958) at John Hopkins University rejected mind as the subject matter of psychology. He emphasised that psychology must be concerned with the study of only behaviour; the observable or potentially observable behaviour or activities of humans and animals.

He was influenced by the work of **Ivan Pavlov** on classical conditioning and rejected the notion of 'mind' which is not observable and 'introspection' which is not verifiable because it is a subjective notion. In 1913, Watson in his article in psychological review, wrote behaviourist view of psychology as a purely objective and experimental branch of natural science. Its theoretical goal is the prediction and control of behaviour.

Introspection presents no essential parts of its methods, nor is the scientific value of its data dependent upon the readiness with which they lend themselves to interpretation in terms of consciousness. The behaviourist in his efforts to get a unitary scheme of animal response, recognises no dividing line between man and brute. The behaviour of man, with all its refinement and complexity, forms only part of the behaviourist's total scheme of investigation.

Characteristics of Behaviourism

Behaviourism has three important characteristics that define its main idea. These are

- Discard all mentalistic concepts (sensations, images or emotions), stick to stimulus-response terminology. It maintained that complex processes are compounds of more elementary ones. But its elements were the conditioned responses. Behaviourists believed that complex human and animal behaviour is made up of almost all of our of conditioned responses.
- They denied the existence of any inborn or innate behavioural tendencies and laid emphasis on learned behaviour rather than unlearned behaviour.
- For investigation he studied animal behaviour and proposed that there is no difference between man and animal behaviour. He argued that much can be learnt about human behaviour by studying animal behaviour.

They also had belief on the 'Principle of Extreme Environmentalism', which says that environment shapes the behaviour of the organisms. The behaviourist's approach in psychology has a wide application in dealing with various social problems as their principles can be applied in the prediction and control of human behaviour.

Views of Various Psychologists

Behaviourism of Watson was further developed by many influential psychologists like Skinner who applied behaviourism to wide range of situations and further popularised the approach.

BF Skinner was a radical behaviourist and refused to acknowledge any part of mental events in human behaviour. His study was focused on the relationship between reinforcements and response rate or probability. He used his approach to describe environmental and behavioural events.

Another influential behaviourist was **Edward Thorndike.** His work on learning theory has a lot of influences on the Skinner's work on operant conditioning. Thorndike developed his learning theory through studies on animals and developed a very important law of learning called the *law of effect* which states that any behaviour which is followed by pleasant consequences is likely to be continued while any behaviour which is followed by unpleasant consequences are discontinued.

Ivan Pavlov another behaviourist is famous for his work on classical conditioning (which we will study in detail in chapter on learning).

Another influential work in behaviourism was done by **Edward Chace Tolman.** He focused on purposive behaviour. Purposive behaviour is directed towards a goal and terminates once the goal is attained. He also emphasised on the role of intervening variable in human or animal behaviour. Intervening variables occur between environmental and behavioural events. An example of Tolman intervening variable is 'Cognitive maps'. Cognitive maps are the mental representations one makes to make associations in order to reach goals.

One very important concept introduced by Tolman in his learning experiments was that of 'Latent Learning', which says that learning remains latent or hidden until an organism has a reason to use it.

Thus, it can be concluded that behaviourism gave many important and valuable principles in the field of psychology for study and better understanding of human behaviour. The three main theorists of behaviourism -Skinner, Tolman and Watson are vital not only to behaviourism, but to psychology as a whole.

Without behaviourism the further modern advancements would not have been possible in psychology as till date. Behaviourism serves as the basis of further theory building and new developments.

Psychoanalysis

Although behaviourists had a major impact on psychology even after Watson, some other approaches and views of psychology were also developing. The major and the most radical viewpoint about human behaviour was presented by **Sigmund Freud.** Freud viewed human behaviour as a result of urges, drives and past experiences.

The crucial point which Freud made about these urges and drives are that they are hidden from our awareness and in other words are unconscious. Freud developed the theory of personality while in his course of clinical practice. His theory visualised human mind in terms of different levels of consciousness. The thoughts of which they were aware of are in consciousness. Just next to consciousness is subconscious or preconscious which we can recall or retrieve from our memory and beyond the preconscious is unconscious. Unconscious is the deepest level which contains the repressed desires and impuses including primitive and instinctual desires.

Freud believed that human being is constantly struggling to find a suitable and socially acceptable way to express these unconscious impulses and urges. He proposed the techniques like free associations, dream analysis as the ways to approach the unconscious of a person.

The personality structure as defined by Freud consists of three structures, *which are as follows*

(i) **ID** It operates at an unconscious level and focuses solely on basic, instinctual drives and desires. *Eros* and *Thanotos*, the survival instinct and death instinct respectively makes up the Id. It is mainly concerned with the immediate gratification of needs and desires. It follows the **Pleasure Principle.**

(ii) **Ego/Reason** It works on the reality principles and works to meet the Id needs of the 'Id' in a most socially acceptable ways.

(iii) **Super Ego/Conscience** It works on the moral principle and represents the ideal. It creates the feeling of guilt on doing something wrong and encourages us to act in a socially and morally acceptable ways.

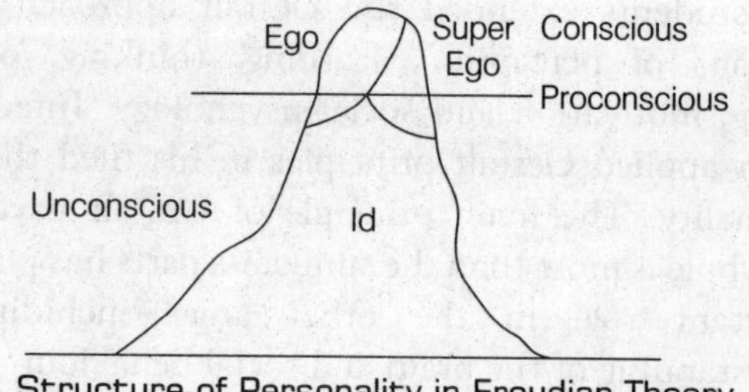

Structure of Personality in Freudian Theory

Freud gave emphasis to childhood traumas as the key to neurotic disorder during adulthood. He believed that people normally progresses through five stages of psychosexual development. Each of his five states focused on different sources of pleasure.

Stage	Age	Activity/Focus
Oral	0-2 yrs	Infant achieves gratification through oral activities such as feeding, thumb sucking etc.
Anal stage	2-3 yrs	Pleasure focuses on bowel and bladder elimination, coping with demands for control.
Phallic stage	3-6 yrs	Pleasure zone is the genitals, coping with incestuous sexual feeling (oedipus-electra complex).
Latency stage	6 to puberty	Dormant sexual feelings, identification process-gender identity.
Genital stage	Puberty	Maturation of sexual interests.

Freud believed that people acquire defences to transform the wishes of Id into an acceptable form. *These defence mechanisms are*

- **Repression** Threatening and disturbing thoughts are pushed out of consciouness.
- **Denial** Blocking of upsetting or overwhelming experiences from awareness.
- **Projection** Attribution of own objectionable impulses to another person.
- **Displacement** A mechanism to satisfy an impulse by acting out on a substitute person in a socially unacceptable way.
- **Regression** Moving backward in development to cope with stress.
- **Sublimation** Satisfying an impulse by acting on a substitute, but in a socially acceptable way.

Freud gave a lot of emphasis to human dreams and studied them intensively. He called dreams a royal road to unconscious. He said that dreams fulfill three purposes. They work as wish fulfillment device, releases unconscious tension and work as guardians of sleep.

However, the traditional psychoanalytic approach is criticised on many grounds. It is said that the concepts are vaguely defined, distinctions are not made, techniques have low reliability and the theory is not testable. Thus, posing a question on efficiency of such approach in study of Human Behaviour.

Other major Psychoanalytic thinkers include Carl Jung who gave the concept of Collective Unconscious and Archetypes. He proposed that human psyche includes conscious as well as a shadow aspect that is unconscious. He proposed that the unconscious of every female includes a masculine, assertive element-the animus and unconscious of every male includes a feminine passive element-the anima. Erik Erikson, Karen Horney, Eric Fromm and Alferd Adler too are well known and influential psychoanalysts.

But psychoanalysis because of its lack of scientific approach has to face a lot of criticisms and led to which development of Humanistic School of Thought.

Humanistic Psychology

Humanistic psychology developed as a response to psychoanalysis and behaviourism. It emphasises on looking at the whole individual and stresses the concepts such as free will, self efficacy and self actualisation.

Humanist thinkers believe that both behaviourism and psychoanalysis have a pessimistic approach as these schools focus on the abnormal behaviour, tragedy and gives no importance to the personal choices of an individual. Humanistic psychology focuses on the whole person and identifies each individual as unique such that the thought processes of every individual can be different.

They focus on individual's free will. Thus, each individual has an ability to make their own choices and select their own path in life. Humanistic psychologists refer to this concept as 'Personal Agency'.

They believe on the goodness of humans beings and thus proposed that human have an innate desire to make world a better place. The emphasis of Humanistic psychology is on persons's perception of self worth, creativity and overreaching human values. They pointed that the mental and social problems that arise are the result of deviations from the natural tendency of humans to be good.

According to **Humanistic psychology**, "people are continually looking for different ways to grow, to become better, to experience self growth and self actualisation."

Abraham Maslow and Carl Rogers are the key psychologists whose ideas have heavy influence on humanistic psychology. Other prominent thinkers were Rollo May and Viktor Frankl.

In 1943, Maslow described his hierarchy of needs in 'A theory of Human Motivation', published in 'Psychological Review'.

In 1951, Carl Rogers published 'Client-Centered Therapy' which described his humanistic client-centered approach to therapy. In 1961, 'Journal of Humanistic Psychology' was published. It was in 1962 that the American Association for Humanistic psychology was formed and by 1971, Humanistic psychology became an 'APA' division.

In 1962, Maslow published, 'Toward a Psychology of Being', in which he described humanistic psychology as the 'Third force' in psychology. The first and second being Behaviourism and Psychoanalysis.

The major strengths of Humanistic psychology lies in the fact that it emphasises the role of the individual in controlling and determining their mental health. It also accounts the importance of environmental influences on our experiences. It also lifts the stigma on therapy and made it more normal and acceptable with a view that even a normal and healthy individual can realise his/her full potential through therapy.

Humanistic psychology has a major impact on education, therapy, healthcare and other areas. Its relevance cannot be denied even today. It endeavours to empower individuals and enhance well-being. The influence of Humanistic psychology can be easily seen on other areas of psychology like-Transpersonal psychology and Positive psychology.

Existential Psychology

Existential psychology represents the philosophical root of the phenomenological approach to personality. Existentialism was at its height in 1930-1950's in Europe. Key figures associated with this school of thought are Jean Paul Sartre, Albert Camus, Friedrich Nietzsche, and Soren Kierkegaard, who were earlier philosophers.

The purpose of Existentialism was to make contact of an individual with the experiences of being Alive and Aware.

According to **Existentialists**, "Human beings have no existence apart from the world. Being in the world or Dasein is man's existence. The basic issue in life is that inevitably it ends in death and we experience angst or anguish because our awareness of death is inevitable." Thus, either human being retreat into nothingness or have the courage to 'BE' and in order to 'BE', we have to live life authentically. Authenticity is about living genuinely with one's angst and achieving meaning despite the temporary nature of one's existence. Life has no meaning, unless you create it.

Views on Existential Psychology

Friedrich Nietzsche, said the only logical response to this void and meaninglessness was to rise about it and become a super man. According to **Existentialists**, "Human beings are all responsible for the choices they make, but the honest choices are also not the good ones always and that make a person feel guilty if he is unable to fulfill all the possibilities in ones' life." Existential guilt, existential anxiety or angst is inescapable.

Ludwig Binswanger an existentialist, proposed that our conscious experience of being alive has three components, biological (umwelt), social (mitwelt) and inner or psychological (eigen melt).

Rollo May

He introduced existential perspective in USA. May saw people living in the world of present experiences and ultimately being responsible for who they become.

He believed that people lack the courage to face their destiny and while in the process of feeling from it they give up much of their freedom. Having negated their freedom, they likewise run from their responsibility and not being willing to make choices, they lose sight of who they are which leads to insignificance and alienation.

He gave concepts of Normal Anxiety, Neurotic Anxiety and Guilt. He wrote the famous book 'Love and Will', in which many of his unique ideas can be found. He also elaborated on forms of love in which sex is defined as a biological urge that can be satisfied through sexual intercourse or some other release of sexual tension.

Eros is a psychological desire of a lasting union with a loved one, Philia is intimate non-sexual friendship between two people and Agape is altruistic brotherly love. He defined certain stages of development, though these were not as strict as that of Freud. Psychosexual stages, rather signify a sequence of major issues in an individual's life. *These stages are*

- **Innocence** Stage of infant, pre-egoic, pre-self conscious.
- **Rebellion** Person wants freedom, but does not have understanding of the responsibilities attached to it.
- **Ordinary** The normal adult has learnt his responsibility, but finds it too demanding so seeks refuge in conformity and traditional values.
- **Creative** The authentic adult, the existential stage, self actualising state.

Rollo May was one of the major proponents of Existentialist philosophy and his ideas had wide influence on numerous psychologists like Eric Fromm, who also focused on self expression and free will.

Viktor Frankl

He was an influential Existential therapist. He developed what is called Logo therapy which is based on the principle that the primary motivational force in human beings is their search for a meaning in life. Frankl's approach is based on three philosophical and psychological concepts.

These are

(i) Freedom of will (ii) Will to meaning

(iii) Meaning of life

He believed that a person has a control over the choices they make in their lives and thus have some control over their fate. He also used the technique of Paradoxical intention in treating his clients in which he encourages the client to exercise and even exaggerate their problem behaviour, in order to realise that they can have control over the problem and thus can overcome it.

He wrote many famous books like 'Man's Search for Meaning', 'The Will to Meaning', 'The Doctor and The Soul' and 'Man's Search for Ultimate Meaning'.

Existentialists believe that individuals have free will and free choices of how to behave. So, they can choose better ways of coping with life's suffering. Existentialism is in fact a blend of philosophy and psychology.

Transpersonal Psychology

Inspite of the popularity of Humanistic psychology, **Maslow** and **Switch** began to get dissatisfied from the conceptual framework, which they created earlier. They were aware of the truth that they have left out an extremely important element; the spiritual element of human psyche (Switch 1976).

The growing interest in Eastern spiritual philosophy, various mystical traditions, meditation and the widespread psychedelic experimentation during 1960s made it quite clear that a comprehensive and cross-culturally valid psychology had to include observations from the areas like Psychedelic experiences, trance phenomena, creativity, religious, artistic and scientific inspirations.

In 1967, Abraham Maslow along with Anthony Switch, Stanislar Grof, James Fadiman, Miles Vich and Sonya Margulie met with a purpose of creating a new psychology that would honour the entire spectrum of human experience including various non-ordinary states of consciousness. They named this new discipline 'Transpersonal psychology'. They launched the Association of Transpersonal psychology and started the Journal of Transpersonal psychology. In 1975, Robert Frager founded the 'Institute of Transpersonal Psychology' in Palo Alto.

Transpersonal psychology integrates spiritual and transcendent experiences within the framework of modern psychology. It encompasses a range of themes including, but not limited to, spiritual self-development, transcendence, beyond ego experiences, peak experiences, mystical experiences, spiritual crises, altered states of consciousness, spiritual practices and so forth.

While the field of Transpersonal psychology formally began in 1960s, it had rooted in early work by Psychologists, including **William James** and **Carl Jung** who were deeply interested in the spiritual aspects of human nature. In addition of understading the spiritual aspects of human nature, Transpersonal psychology also strives to provide a deeper and richer understanding of individuals and help them to achieve their greatest potential.

Lofore and **Shapiro** identified spirituality, higher potential, transcendence and other states of consciousness as the key concepts of Transpersonal psychology. Transpersonal psychology addresses the full spectrum of human psychological and spiritual development from our deepest wounds and needs, to the existential crisis of the human being, to the most transcendent capacities of our consciousness. (Mariana Caplan's, book 'Eyes Wide Open: Cultivating Discernment on the Spiritual Path)'.

Transpersonal psychology has been attracting a lot of attention in modern days as the theories and ideas from this field can be applied to different sub-fields of psychology. Mindfulness meditation is an element of Transpersonal psychology which has become popular these days.

Cognitive Revolution

Cognitive Revolution in psychology is mostly a response to behaviourism which emphasised on objectivity and focused on the overt behaviour for studying human psyche. The focus on the principles of behaviourism had pulled away the attention of psychologists from the mind for a prolonged period of time. Humanistic psychologists emphasised on studying human being as a whole and as a conscious and self aware being.

In 1950s, new disciplinary fields like linguistics, neuroscience and computer science again revived interest in mind as focus of scientific enquiry. This particular perspective was known as the *Cognitive Revolution*. There were numerous publications by psychologists which further triggered the Cognitive Revolution *e.g.* **George Miller's** 1956 article 'The Magical Number Seven, Plus or Minus Two', linguist **Noam Chomski's** rejection of the behaviourist approach in his 1959, review of BF Skinner's 'Verbal Behaviour (1957)', foundational works in the field of artificial intelligence by John McCarthy, Marvin Minsky, Allen Newell and Herbert Simon, 1958 article 'Elements of a Theory of Human Problem Solving' and **Ulric Neisser's** 1967 book 'Cognitive psychology,' which served as a core text in cognitive psychology courses and were the landmark contributions. **Noam Chomski** argued in favour of cognitive studies saying that psychology's focus on behaviour is short sighted, and the field had to incorporate mental functioning if it has to offer any meaningful contributions in understanding human behaviour.

Advent of psychology towards cognitive processes for the study of Human Behaviour also led to several developments in the field, as now European psychology which was never influenced by behaviourism to a great extent like American psychology, witnessed the role of cognitive psychology in reestablishing the line of communication between European and American psychologists.

Furthermore, psychologists began to cooperate with scientists in other fields like linguistics, computer science, neuroscience etc. This inter disciplinary approach was known as cognitive science, and its influence and prominence is quite visible in modern day psychology.

This development of information processing models, psycho linguistics and neuropsychology in the second half of the 20th century produced what has been called the *Cognitive Revolution* in psychology, which transformed nearly all areas of the field.

This approach emphasised on cognitive processes and it claimed that the scientific analysis of mental processes and structures are possible.

The basic assumption of cognitive perspective was

- Only by studying mental processes we can understand what organisms do,
- We can study mental processes in an objective fashion by focusing on specific behaviours but interpreting them in terms of underlying mental processes.

In making these interpretations, cognitive psychologists have often relied on an analogy between the mind and a computer. Incoming information is processed in various ways. It is selected, compared and combined with other information already in memory, transformed, rearranged and so on.

In sum, during the 20th century the focus of psychology expanded. After rejecting conscious experiences as ill-suited to scientific investigation and turning to the study of overt, observable behaviour, Psychologists are once again theorising about covert aspects of the mind, such as thoughts and emotions, but this time with much scientific approach.

Multiculturalism

Multicultural psychology refers to the systematic investigation, analysis and assessment of human behaviour as they are experienced in surroundings where people of different cultural background interact (American Psychological Association, 2003). It studies the impact of culture on individual lives and behaviour.

Multicultural psychology is one of the most recent and dynamic fields in psychology and is crucial for learning the role of culture in psychological study. It is considered to be the fourth force in psychology after psychoanalysis, behaviourism and humanistic psychology.

Multiculturalism, emerged as a prominent area of interest during the Civil Rights Movement that started in 1964 in USA. In this movement the minority ethnic group of people who were initially regarded as inferior were demanding equal treatment especially in shelter, education and employment opportunities. The study of psychology was also affected by this as the provisions which psychology was following till date were not culturally sensitive. Numerous psychologists pushed for necessary changes in the field.

The necessary changes were made and brought in effect. In 2002, the APA's 'Ethical Principles of Psychologists and Code of Conduct' were revised to include the diverse cultural issues (APA, 2003).

The APA (American Psychological Association) has also established specific provisions for the enhancement of multicultural psychology.

Multicultural psychology has been developing since then as a unique field of study. The importance of this field lies in the fact that it takes into account the uniqueness of groups of people on the basis of their belief systems, values, principles and norms that are part of the different cultures they belong to.

Moreover, psychology till then was just focussing on the scientific dimensions in understanding human behaviour. Now, with the advent of multiculturalism a lot of emphasis was put on culture. Further studies in the field were not ignoring the aspect of culture in their research.

The inclusion of different cultural themes in research has led to the elimination of stereotype tendencies.Most of the studies done initially in the field did not consider culture in selecting the participants, thus, the conclusions made were not inclusive.

Furthermore, the world is increasingly becoming globalised and the development of multiculturalism in psychology has made it easy for conducting investigations in diverse societies. 'Multiculturalism' is an asset in the field which deals with human behaviour.

The understanding of multiculturalism has led to the formulation of better and appropriate interventions in the field and has also led to the alleviation of hatred and discrimination. This subspeciality can be seen as enhancing the fields of psychology since cultural differences are viewed as a part of humanity. Thus, it can be said that multicultural psychology is crucial in the development of the broad field of psychology, as it has helped in understanding human behaviours from a cultural perspective where people with different cultural backgrounds co-exist.

The Most Important Approaches (Schools) of Psychology

School of Psychology	Description	Important Contribution
Structuralism	Uses introspection to identify basic elements, structures of psychological experience	Wilhelm Wundt, Edward B Titchener
Functionalism	Attempts to understand why animals and humans have developed the particular psychological aspect they possess	William James
Psychodynamic	Focuses on role of unconscious thoughts, feelings and memories and our early childhood experiences in determining behaviour	Sigmund Freud, Carl Jung Alfred Adler, Erik Erickson
Behaviourism	Study of overt observable behaviour is important	John B Watson, BF Skinner
Cognitive	The study of mental processes including perception, thinking, memory and judgements	Hermann, Ebbighaus, Jean Piaget, Sir Frederic Bertlett
Social cultural	Studies how the social situations and the cultures influence thinking and behaviour	Fritz Heider, Leon Festinger, Stanley Schachter

Founding Paths of Academic Psychology

Academic psychology assist the children with psychological needs and relates directly to their learning style, academic challenges, family environments, learning disabilities and social interactions. *The four founding pillar or famous scholars of academic psychology are Wilhelm Wundt, Sigmund Freud, William James, Wilhelm Dilthey.*

Wilhelm Wundt

Wilhelm Wundt opened the 'Institute for Experiment Psychology' at the University of Leipzig in Germany in 1879. This was the first laboratory dedicated to psychology and its opening is usually thought of as the beginning of modern psychology. Wundt is often regarded as the father of Psychology. Wundt's contribution in the field is regarded to be very important as he made a distinction between the field of philosophy and psychology. The impetus for the establishment of the Wundt's lab was the belief that mind and behaviour like planets, chemicals, human organs could be subject to scientific analysis. Wundt's own research was concerned primarily with the senses, especially vision, but he and his co-workers also studied attention, emotion and memory.

The laboratory set by Wundt became a focus for those with a serious interest in psychology, first for German philosophers and psychology students then for American and British students. All subsequent psychological laboratories were closely modeled in their early years on Wundt's model.

Wundt's background was in physiology and this was reflected in the topics with which the institute was concerned, such as the study of reaction time and sensory processes, and attention. Wundt's aim was to record thoughts and sensations, and to analyse them into their constituent elements in much the same way as a chemist analyses chemical compounds in order to get underlying structure.

His School of psychology was called *voluntarism,* the process of organising mind. During his academic career Wundt trained 186 graduate students (116 in psychology). Edward Titchener, Wundt's student promoted Wundt's theory and described his system as **structuralism**, or the analysis of the basic elements that constituted the mind.

Wundt relied on Introspection to study mental processes. Introspection refers to observing and recording the nature of one's own perceptions, thoughts and feelings. Examples of introspection includes people's subjective reports of how hot or cold they perceive an object to be, or how bright a flash of light seems to be.

Though the method of introspection was inherited from philosophy, Wundt added a new dimension to this concept. Pure self observation was not sufficient. It had to be supplemented by experiments.

He trained psychology students to make observations. Wundt's experiments systematically varied some physical dimension of a stimulus, such as its intensity and used the introspective method to determine how these physical changes modified the participants conscious experience of the stimulus. He used the results to develop a theory of Conscious Thoughts.

The reliance on introspection, particularly for very rapid mental events, proved unworkable; even after extensive training, different people produced very different introspections about simple sensory experiences and few conclusions could be drawn from these differences. Though Wundt's method of introspection did not remain a fundamental tool of psychological experimentation past the early 1920s, this greatest contribution was to show that psychology could be a valid experimental science.

The major contribution of Wundt to psychology was to do his research in carefully controlled conditions *i.e.* experimental methods. Wundt concentrated on three areas of mental functioning - thoughts, images and feelings. These are the basic areas studied under the realm of cognitive psychology. This means that the study of perceptual processes can be traced back to Wundt. Wundt's work stimulated interest in cognitive psychology.

Wundt's Contribution in Psychology

Wundt's contribution to psychology can be summarised in four main points: *These are as follow*

(i) He wrote first text book of psychology (Principles of Physiological psychology, 1873-74).

(ii) He set up the first Laboratory of Experimental Psychology (1875).

(iii) He used the scientific method to study the structure of sensation and perception.

(iv) He showed that introspection could be used to study mental states in replicable laboratory experiments.

It was Wundt's contribution and interest in the field of psychology in late 1800 and early 1900 that saved the future of psychology to be known as a *distinct field of study*. It was Wundt's work and his establishment of a psychological laboratory that cemented psychology's identity as a legitimate discipline. He is therefore often referred to as 'The Father of Experimental Psychology'.

Sigmund Freud

Freud is one of the most influential and well known figures in psychology. Freud (1856-1939) was an Austrian neurologist who was fascinated by patient's suffering from hysteria and neurosis. Hysteria was an ancient diagnosis for disorders, primarily of women with a wide variety of symptoms, including physical symptoms and emotional disturbances, none of which had any apparent physical cause. Freud theorised that many of his patients' problems arose from the unconscious mind. Gaining access to the unconscious then was crucial for the resolution of patient's problems.

'Psychoanalysis' is both a theory of personality and a method of psychotherapy originated by Freud around the turn of 20th century.

At the center of Freud's theory is the concept of unconscious, the thoughts, attitudes, impulses, wishes, motivations and emotions of which we are unaware. Freud believed that the childhood's unacceptable(forbidden or punished) wishes are driven out of conscious awareness and become a part of the unconscious, where they continue to influence our thoughts, feelings and actions.

In 'Classical Freudian Theory', the motivations behind unconscious wishes almost always involved sex or aggression. He said that sexual and aggressive impulses are inperpetual conflict for supremacy with the defences against them. In 1897, he began an intensive analysis of himself. In 1990 his major work 'The Interpretation of Dreams' was published in which Freud analysed dreams in terms of unconscious desires and experiences.

In 1902, Freud was appointed as the Professor of Neuro Pathology at the University of Vienaa and in 1910, the International Psychoanalytic Association was founded by Freud in collaboration with Carl Jung, a close associate. Jung, later broke with Freud and developed his own theories.

After World War First, Freud spent less time in clinical observation and concentrated on the application of his theories to history, art, literature and anthropology. In 1923, he published 'The Ego and The ld', which suggested a new structural model of the mind, divided into the 'id', the 'ego' and the 'super ego'.

In particular Freud combined cognitive notions of consciousness, perception and memory with ideas about biologically based instincts to forge a bold new theory of human behaviour.

The basic assumption of the psychoanalysis was that behaviour stems from unconscious processes meaning, beliefs, fears and desires that a person is unaware of, but that nonetheless influence behaviour. Freud believed that many of the impulses that are forbidden or punished by parents and society during childhood are derived from innate instincts.

Because each of us is born with these impulses, they exert a pervasive influence that must be dealt with in some manner. Forbidding them merely forces them out of awareness into the unconscious. However, they do not disappear. They may manifest themselves as emotional problems and symptoms of mental illness or as socially approved behaviour such as artistic and literary activity.

Freud believed that we are driven by the same basic instincts as animals (primarily hunger, sex, aggression) and that we are continually struggling against a society that stresses on a control of these impulses.

Thus, it can be concluded that psychoanalysis suggested new ways of looking at the human problems like aggression which is viewed as an innate instinct. Freud's thoughts and his perspective has a deep impact on the progress of the field of psychology and also in the research and the learning happening in the field.

William James

William James was an American psychologist and philosopher who is sometimes referred to as the 'Father of American Psychology'. He was the first to offer a course in psychology in United States. He wrote numerous books and emerged as the leading thinker during the later half of the 19th century. His theories were influential in both psychology and philosophy.

His approach in psychology was based on pragmatic philosophy (pragmatism is a philosophy of truth) and his work is still viable to many. Though he called information and thoughts from various sources and schools of thought, he carefully picked and choose only information he believed to be useful.

Pragmatism and Functionalism are the two philosophies used by William James to further his understanding of the world around him. James put forward the pragmatic theory of truth and he used this philosophy to define and re-define, filtering answers to questions through this theory.

Although he was a trained Doctor, but he found his true interest in the workings of the mind. He began his career with a doctorate in physical medicine, but from there he studied psychology and philosophy in the brightest and best of his days.

He founded the 'School of Functionalism', which was a direct result of the 'School of Thought' founded by Wilhelm Wundt known as *Structuralism*. Wundt criticised functionalism as nothing more than literature and James criticised structuralism as 'All School and No Thought'. When criticisms faded functionalism influenced major schools of thought still in use such as cognitive behavioural and behavioural schools. Functionalism focused on human natural tendency for individualism and this heavily influenced how education was structured. James was influenced by his education in physiology and the work of Charles Darwin. Functionalism was a much more systematic approach to study mental processes. He developed Functionalism in search for consciousness and behaviour.

During his life, he was a member of the Theosophical Society and one of the founders of the American Society for Psychical Research. From spiritualism to pragmatic philosophy and the Functionalist School of Psychology, William James has something to add ; he was eventually named the 14th most eminent psychologist of the 20th century.

In his famous book 'The Principles of Psychology', James put forth four main concepts which are 'stream of consciousness, emotion, habit and will'. His book 'The Principles of Psychology' was a comprehensive work covering the entire field of psychology. The book itself did more than providing a compendium of scholarly knowledge for intellectuals, it provided text for teaching and for learning. In addition to above concepts, James also discussed theories and hypotheses about centers of brain receiving specific input from the physical senses. The concept of instinct and the evolution of brain function, particularly the cerebrum is also discussed.

The topic of experimental psychology is covered in the book. He explained the concept of both auditory and visual illusions. He explained that the mind becomes accustomed to recognise something that is repeated and when similar stimuli is presented, an assumption is made and this assumption is 'Illusion'.

Various Concepts of Psychology

The four main concepts like habit, stream of consciousness, emotion and will, make up the bulk of his work. *The explanations of these concepts in his work are given as below*

- **A Stream of Consciousness** The metaphor 'a stream of consciousness' was coined by James. He showed a shift in how consciousness was understood till then. It was no longer a 'chain' of consciousness, strung together like the links of the chain. It was a 'stream'. always flowing and moving forward. According to **James**, "consciousness is continuous and humans could never experience the same idea or thought more than once."

- **Emotion** In emotion, his major contribution was the theory of emotion, known as the *James-Lange Theory*. In his theory he proposed that emotion is the result of the bodily experience and not a result of the stimuli that triggers that bodily experience. When a stimulus triggers bodily reaction, the bodily reaction triggers a emotion. His explanation of emotion has been criticised then and now.

- **Habit** It was understood that habits were formed in response to a desire, a want or need. Habits focus the mind on achieving the desire, want or need. James observed that habits are not always bad, they are good and this ability to form habits shows the power of the mind to focus and achieve.
- **Will** James relied on his personal experiences to express his understanding of free will. To him, "free will was the ability to attend to difficult object and hold it fast before the mind." For him, "free will is an ability to hold on principles even when facing opposition and lack of support."

Though psychology came a long way since then, still great thinkers like William James are viable sources of insight and information. His work in the field of psychology is highly influential and has helped psychology to reach the level of advancement on which it is standing today.

Wilhelm Dilthey

Wilhelm Dilthey was born in Biebrich on the Rhine in 1833, two years after Hegel had died. He was the Professor of philosophy at Basel in 1867, at Kiel from 1869 to 1870, at Breslau from 1871 to 1881 and at Berlin, he succeeded Hermann Lotze in 1882.

He admired Hegel's recognition of the historical dimension of philosophical thought, but rejected the speculative and metaphysical ways. Dilthey's researches revolved around the questions of scientific methodology, historical evidence and history's status as a science. He could be considered as an empiricist. According to **Dilthey**, "the human sciences (humanities and social science), help to define what Dilthey calls the Historical world".

By making use of inner as well as outer experiences, the human sciences preserve a more direct link with our original sense of life than the natural sciences that seek to focus on the way things behave independently of human involvement, although human sciences take account of this involvement.

The natural sciences seek explanations of nature, connecting the discrete representations of outer experience through hypothetical generalisations and causal laws, while the human sciences aim at understanding the fundamental structures of historical life given in lived experience (lived experience refers to a representation of the experiences and choices of a given person and the knowledge that they gain from these experiences and choices). Finding lived experience to be inherently connected and meaningful, Dilthey opposed traditional atomistic and associationlist Psychologies and developed a descriptive psychology that has been recognised as anticipating phenomenology.

Dilthey first thought that this descriptive psychology could provide a neutral foundation for the other human sciences, but in his later Hermeneutical writings, he rejected this idea of a foundational discipline or method. Thus, he ends up claiming that all the human sciences are interpretative and mutually dependent.

The human sciences will henceforth be conceived as primarily concerned with understanding the meaning of human action and interaction. Also he emphasised in his essay 'The Origin of Our Belief in the Reality of the External World and Its Justification' of 1890, that our initial access to the external world is not inferential, but is felt as resistance to the will. The world of our lived experience is not merely a theoretical representation, but is directly presented to us as embodying values that are relevant to our purposes.

Final phase of Dilthey's life until his death in 1911, begins with the realisation in the essay 'The Rise of Hermeneutics' of 1900 that the inner intelligibility of lived experiences does not yet constitute understanding. Self understanding can only evolve as a result of dialogue with the world. The way we express ourselves, whether in communication or in action, is a crucial intermediary in defining ourselves. Understanding can only be reliable, if it proceeds through the interpretation of human objectifications. Thus, we understand ourselves not through introspection, but through history.

He also introduced a distinction between explanatory psychology and descriptive psychology. In his terminology, Explanatory Psychology is the study of psychological phenomena from the point of view of a third person, which involves subordination to a system of causality, while Descriptive Psychology is a discipline that attempts to explicate how different mental processes converge in the structural nexus of consciousness.

Thus, the notable ideas from the desk of Dilthey were numerous like **Hermeneutics** which is the theory and methodology of interpretation, especially interpretation of biblical texts, wisdom literature and philosophical texts, distinction between explanatory and descriptive psychology, distinction beetween explanatory and descriptive sciences and typology of the three basic **Weltanschauungen** (German world for world view).

Issues in Psychology

Psychology emphasises on a strict adherence to experimental method (logical empiricism), logical positivism, operationism and use of inferential statistics. This adherence has given genesis to replication crisis in psychology.

Crisis in Psychology Due to Strict Adherence to Logical Empiricism

Logical Empiricism (LE) is a term that was coined by the Austrian sociologist and economist Otto neurath (1880-1945) to name the philosophical work of the Vienna Circle and related work being pursued by the physicist and philosopher Hans Reich en bach (1891-1953) and his associates. The central thesis of logical empiricism was 'verificationism,' a theory of knowledge which asserted that only statements verifiable through empirical observation are meaningful. The movement flourished in 1920s and 1930s in several European centers.

The reproducibility of experiments is an essential part of the empiricist method. The inability to replicate the studies of others has potentially grave consequences for many fields of science in which significant theories are based on unreproducible experimental work. The strict adherence to experimental-analytical paradigm has created replication crisis in psychology where a number of efforts have been made to re-investigate classic results and to attempt to determine both the reliability of the results and the reasons for the failure of replication if it is found to be unreliable.

The notion of verificationism also created a lot of crisis in the field as according to this doctrine a proposition is 'Cognitively meaningful,' only if there is a finite procedure for conclusively determining whether it is true or false. An intended consequence of this view for most logical empiricists, is that metaphysical, theological and ethical statements fall short of this criterion and so are not cognitively meaningfull.

Empiricism believes that all kinds of knowledge related to existence, can be derived only from experience. There is no place for the pure reason to get knowledge about the world. In short it can be said that, logical empiricism gives negation to intuition and thoughts which are the core inputs of study in psychology.

Logical empiricism has failed dismally to give a faithful account of science, whether natural or social. It failed because it remained anchored to sense data and to phenomenalist metaphysics, overrated the power of induction and underrated that of hypothesis and denounced realism and materialism as metaphysical nonsense. Although it has never been practiced in natural sciences and has been criticised by many philosophers, Natabely Popper's version of (1959) logical empiricism remains the tacit of philosophy for many scientists.

The logical empiricism sought to reduce all experience to sensory experience and to reduce every sensory experience to a conclusive or exact statement. This has proved to be an unattainable goal.

Logical empiricism was opposed by **Hayek**, who proposed that there are two orders through which individuals consider, the world the sensory order and the physical order. The sensory order is what we sense and the physical world is real world of existence beyond our senses. As he believed physical world to be external to mind, he ascribed almost no (if any) properties to it.

Logical empiricism appears to be attractive to those people who do not want to worry about what they cannot observe. It is ultimately a theory about meaning and about the content of theory. It has a great impact on the field of psychology in which the study of subjective feelings, thoughts and intentions make the major part of its studies. Thus following the ideas of logical empiricism has created a sense of crisis in the field.

Indic Influences on Modern Psychology

The Psychologist Cyril Burt once summarised the modern history of psychological science as "psychology first lost its soul, then lost its mind, until it was finally in danger of losing consciousness altogether". Officially, psychology is said to begin in 1879, when Wilhelm Wundt established the first Psychological Lab in Leipzig, Germany. This school of thought was primarily concerned with the senses, especially vision, but he and his co-workers also studied attention, emotion and memory.

Wundt relied on the method of 'introspection' to study mental processes. There was a little progress made during 30-40 years when this school was in existence.

The second psychological school represented a radical break from the introspectionists and was initiated by John Watson in 1913. The behaviourists tend to discuss psychological phenomena in terms of stimuli and responses, giving rise to the term stimulus response (SR) psychology. S-R terminology is still used in psychology today.

In 1950s Cognitive Revolution began with the classic article by George Miller, 'The Magic Number 7, Plus or Minus 2' (It refers to the amount of information that our memory can hold at a time) with the advent of computers and technology.

In 1950s Herbert Simon and his colleagues described how psychological phenomena could be simulated with computers. Many psychological issues were recasted in terms of information processing models, which viewed human beings as processors of information and provided a more dynamic approach to psychology.

All these were the crucial developments in the fields of psychology. It has been observed that university, departments of psychology hold the purely scientific disciplines in much higher esteem than the applied disciplines of psychotherapy, educational psychology etc. The scholars in the filed of psychology are familiar with popular versions of psychology *i.e.* four forces of psychology-psychoanalysis, behavioural therapy, humanistic therapy and transpersonal therapy. Technically these are four divisions of psychotherapy.

It is in the area of Transpersonal theory that the Indic traditions have had the most direct influence on modern psychologists which are as follows

- **Franz Brentano** Brentano was a philosopher as well as a teacher of Sigmund Freud. According to JJ Clarke, Brentano has been familiar with Indian Philosophy as many of his works were inspired by the readings of various Indian texts. It can be a possibility that the Freud's idea of unconsciousness is rooted in Indian philosophy. Clarke noted that Canus and Von Hartmann, two Pre-Freudian popularisers of the notion of the unconscious were influenced by Vedanta.
- **William James** James too was familiar with Vedanta and other branches of Indian philosophy, which is quite evident in his work 'Varieties of Religious Experience.'
- **Roberto Assagioli** Assagioli, a psychiatrist and founder of the Psychotherapeutic technique known as Psychosynthesis had a knowledge of the Upnishads, the Yoga Sutra and various Buddhist texts. He openly acknowledged his debt to these writings.
- **JH Schultz** In the 1920's, JH Schultz, a psychiatrist developed his 'Autogenic training' a fairly, widely used system of visualisation and relaxation, which is largely derived from yogic practices.
- **Caroline Rhys Davids** Caroline Rhys Davids published 'Buddhist psychology' in 1914 and claimed that 'Buddhist thought is very largely an enquiry into mind and its activities and has much to teach in the West.'
- **Carl Jung** There are many studies of Eastern influences on Jung. 'Jung engaged in extensive studies of Taoism, Mahayana and Vajrayana, Buddhism as well as Vedanta and the Yoga Sutras. The book 'Jung and Eastern Thought' by Harold Coward highlights the impact of East on Jung's life, teachings and works.

Various Influencer of Modern Psychology

Gordon Allport was a personality psychologist at Haward; met regularly with Swami Akhilanada of the vedanta society of Boston to discuss Upanishads, Yoga Sutras and other Indian texts.

In 1950s **Michael Murphy** visited Sri Aurobindo Ashram and got deeply inspired and started Esalen on returning to California. Many ideas of humanistic and transpersonal psychology developed at Esalen. DT Surzuki from Japan also propogated Zen Buddhism in America.

Herbert Benoit 1955, a French Psychiatrist, wrote on Psychoanalysis and Zen Buddhism.

In 1960s many Asian teachers became popular in the West, including Swami Satchitanand , Kirpal Singh, Nahana Ponika Thera, Swami Muktananda, Pir Vilayat Khan and many others.

In 1960 only **Eric Fromm** wrote on Psychoanalysis and Zen Buddhism.

In 1965, **Medrad Boss**, a psychiatrist who visited India to study Yoga, was deeply impressed and on his return to Europe wrote on Yoga and Psychotherapy.

Leaders of the Humanistic psychology were also influenced with the Eastern thoughts like **Maslow** referred to Vedanta in his writings on 'Beings vs doing', where as **Roger** was highly influenced by 'Taoism' in the development of his notion of a natural 'Organism' process of self actualisation.

Transpersonal psychology too has a lot of influences from the Eastern thought especially of Buddhism.

Daniel Goleman, a psychologist wrote 'The Varities of Meditative Experience' in 1977, after his visit to India where he studied bout Hindu and Buddhist meditation. He wrote his dissertation after returning from India, under Herbert Benson at Haward. It was Goleman who suggested the use of meditation as a form of 'Stress management'

Another notable person is **Jon Kabat Zinn** who used Buddhist meditation to treat pain in over 10,000 patients at Massachusetts Medical Center, most of who were referred because conventional medical treatments had been effective. He published several excellent research studies in may journals.

Ken Wilber published his first book 'The Spectrum of Consciousness' in 1977. In the same year pioneers in bio feedback technique Elmer and Alyce Green published 'Beyond Bio feedback', in which they described their ground breaking studies of Swami Rama's ability to control parts of his nervous system, which were previously thought to be beyond control of mind.

Renneth Pelletier, 1983 published an excellent book titled 'Toward a Science of Consciousness', which very well summarised the integration of Indian ideas and modern science, including not just psychology, but neuroscience, quantam physics and other disciplines.

In between various other books were published by psychologists, which emphasises the role of Indian philosphy and Buddhism on the filed of psychology.

In 1990 Crook and Fontana published an excellent book 'A Buddhist Influences on Modern Psychology'.

In1991, **Robert Thurman** along with **Dalai Lama** and scientists from several disciplines including neuroscience, psychology, biology, among other convene the first of several **'Mind Science'** conferences at Haward.

Thus, it can be concluded that Eastern thoughts have a major implication on psychology for health psychology, education, organisational management and human and social development studies. Emphasis on Indian psychology would provide a comprehensive foundation and a refreshing new and indigenous orientation to all the branches of psychology.

Timeline showing some of the most Important Psychologists

Date	Psychologist	Description
428-327 BC	Plato	Greek philosopher who argued for the role of nature in psychological development
384-322 BC	Aristotle	Greek philosopher who argued for the role of nature in psychological development
1588-1679	Thomas Hobbes	English philosopher
1596-1650	Rene Descartes	French philosopher
1632-1704	John Locke	English philosopher
1712-1778	Jean-Jacques Rousseau	French philosopher
1801-1887	Gustav Fechner	Developed the idea of Just Noticeable Difference (JND) which is considered to be first empirical psychological measurement
1809-1882	Charles Darwin	His theory of natural selection influenced the functionalist school and field of evolutionary psychology.
1832-1920	William Wundt	He opened the first psychology laboratory and helped developed the field of Structuralism
1842-1910	William James	He contributed to the field of Functionalism
1849-1936	Ivan Pavlov	Russian physiologists contributed to the field of learning by his experiments on classical conditioning
1850-1909	Hermann Ebbinghaus	German psychologist who studied the ability of people to learn nonsense syllables in different conditions
1856-1939	Sigmund Freud	Austrian psychologist who founded the field of psychodynamics
1007-1927	Edward Bradford Titchener	American psychologist who contributed to the field of Structuralism
1878-1958	John B Watson	American psychologist who contributed to the filed of behaviourism
1886-1969	Sir Fredric Bartlett	British psychologist, who studied the cognitive and social processes of remembering
1896-1980	Jean Piaget	Swiss psychologist who developed the theory of cognitive development in children
1904-1990	BF Skinner	Contributed to the School of Behaviourism and gave the concept of Operant Conditioning in learning
1926-1993	Donald Broadbent	Cognitive psychologist, Pioneer in study of attention
20th and 21st centuries	Linda Bartoshuk, Daniel Kahneman, Elizabeth Loftus, George Miller	American psychologist contributed to the cognitive School of Psychology by studying, learning, memory and judgement. Daniel Kahneman won the Noble Prize in Economics for his work on psychological decision making
20th & 21 st centuries	Mahzarin Banaji, Marilynn Brewer, Susan Fisker, Fritz Heider, Kurt Lewin, Stanley Schachter, Claude Steele, Harry Triandis	Contributed to the social cultural school of psychology. Their contributions have included an understanding of how people develop and are influenced by social norms

EXAM BASED QUESTIONS

1 Psychology shares borders with various other fields like
(a) Physiology (b) Anthropology
(c) Sociology (d) Both a and b

2 Who were the main contributors in the scholarly study of Psychology in ancient times?
(a) Indians (b) Westerners
(c) Ancient Greeks (d) None of these

3 Until 1870s psychology was considered to be the branch of which field?
(a) Philosophy (b) Neuroscience
(c) Humanities (d) Sociology

4 In which year psychology began as a distinct field of study?
(a) 1872 (b) 1870 (c) 1879 (d) 1889

5 When was the first time the word 'psychology' was used in texts?
(a) 16th century (b) 17th century
(c) 15th century (d) 18th century

6 Psychology is made of two Greek words 'psyche' and 'logos' which means
(a) soul's study (b) mind's study
(c) soul's doctrine (d) soul's thoughts

7 Who was the early ancient physician who laid the foundation of psychology proposing that "mental life is a function of brain"?
(a) Hippocrates (b) Kant
(c) Alcmeon (d) Sheldon

8 What was the typology proposed by Hippocrates of human personality?
(a) Sanguine, melancholic, choleric, phlegm
(b) Sanguine, euphoric, choleric, phlegm
(c) Sanguine, eudaemonic, choleric, phlegm
(d) Sanguine, melancholic, egoistic, phlegm

9 Who were the two notable students of Socrates?
(a) Plato, Aristotle (b) Hippocrates, Plato
(c) Aristotle, Kant
(d) Plato, James MC Keen Cattell

10 What was the belief of 'Plato' in his understanding of human behaviour?
(a) His belief on the concept of soul
(b) Role of mind in controlling human behaviour
(c) His belief on study of human thinking
(d) His belief on human ability to reason

11 What was the idea behind the Descartes' theory of human behaviour?
(a) Bodily functions control soul
(b) Soul controls the bodily functions
(c) He considered soul and human body to be independent
(d) He considered soul and body to be dependent

12 Who advanced the idea of Plato regarding 'dualism' in human behaviour?
(a) Hippocrates (b) Sheldon
(c) Rene Descartes (d) Aristotle

13 Who gave the famous quote 'Cogito Ergosum'?
(a) Rene Descartes (b) Aristotle
(c) Plato (d) Socrates

14 Who established the first lab of psychology in Leipzig?
(a) Wilhelm Wundt (b) Freud
(c) William James (d) Plato

15 Which famous text book of psychology was authored by Wilhelm Wundt?
(a) Fundamentals of Psychology
(b) Foundation of Psychology
(c) The Principles of Psychology
(d) Psychology an Emerging Science

16 According to many founders of modern day psychology, the first psychologist was
(a) Wundt (b) Weber
(c) Fechner (d) Helmholtz

17 Which of the following researcher had a profound impact on developmental psychology despite the limitations of his methodology?
(a) Sigmund Freud (b) Skinner
(c) Francis Galton (d) John Watson

18 Which of the following school of thought would be most likely to reject the method of introspection to study human experience?
(a) Behaviourism (b) Structuralism
(c) Psychoanalysis (d) Functionalism

19 The study of psychology is most concerned with which field of scientific enquiry?
(a) The science of philosophy
(b) The science of physical process
(c) The science of behaviour and mental process
(d) The science of emotional and mental process

20 Approach which focused on analysis of components of consciousness is called
(a) Functionalism (b) Behaviourism
(c) Structuralism (d) None of these

21 Which school of thought best describes the Darwin's approach to psychology subject matter?
(a) Structuralism (b) Behaviourism
(c) Functionalism (d) Associationism

22 What was the main difference between functionalism and structuralism?
(a) Reductionist approach
(b) Focus on the functions of thoughts, feelings and behaviour than on their forms

(c) Focus on mind and soul studies
(d) Focus on covert form of behaviour

23 Which word is used to describe the phenomena of combination of elementary mental processes to form higher order thoughts?
(a) Functionalism (b) Reductionalism
(c) Associationism (d) Structuralism

24 The method used by Wilhelm Wundt in breaking down the contents of a person's conscious experience was
(a) facilitation (b) investigation
(c) introspection (d) experimentation

25 The psychologist who brought structuralism in United States was
(a) BF Skinner (b) Albert Bandura
(c) William James (d) Edward B Tichener

26 Aristotle's definition of psychology was
(a) study of behaviour (b) study of soul
(c) study of intelligence (d) study of basic body fluids

27 The psychologist who stated that, "human beings are not controlled primarily by rational and conscious processes, but rather by drives and urges of unconscious" was
(a) Aristotle (b) Sigmund Freud
(c) Hippocrates (d) John Dewey

28 Who said, "psychology has a long past but only a short history"?
(a) Hermann Ebbinghaus (b) Skinner
(c) Aristotle (d) Watson

29 What was structuralism centered on?
(a) Investigating the structure of body
(b) Investigating the structure of mind
(c) Investigating the structure of human soul
(d) Investigating the structure of learning

30 "If a child pulls apart a toy , to investigate its component", which school of thought has similar philosophy in psychology?
(a) Structuralism (b) Functionalism
(c) Behaviourism (d) Associationism

31 Which method did Wundt applied to unveil the structure of the mind?
(a) Free association (b) Reductionism
(c) Free recall (d) Introspection

32 What does Introspection involve?
(a) Looking outward toward mainfested behaviour
(b) Looking inward, reflecting on our own internal experiences
(c) Reflecting on the society
(d) Reflecting on one's feeling for others

33 According to functionalists, mind is supposed to be
(a) fluid (b) stable
(c) static (d) Both a and b

34 The main concepts on which the functionalist's approach was based was
(a) to study how mind operates
(b) to study the main components of mind
(c) how the elements of mind work together
(d) Both a and c

35 Functionalists also studied how mental processes promote
(a) functioning (b) adaptation
(c) learning (d) None of these

36 Who influenced the main principles of functionalism?
(a) Charles Darwin (b) Aristotle
(c) Sperry (d) Plato

37 Functionalism influenced which two major areas in psychology?
(a) Emotion and cognition (b) Thinking and reasoning
(c) Learning and motivation (d) Perception and learning

38 What were the research methodologies adopted by functionalists in addition to introspection?
(a) Questionnaires (b) Physiological measures
(c) Testing (d) Both a and b

39 Freud compared human psyche to an iceberg. The invisible portion of this iceberg is known as
(a) Unconscious (b) Id
(c) Consciousness (d) Ego

40 Freud believed that many factors that influence human thoughts and actions are operating entirely from
(a) conscious (b) unconscious
(c) ego (d) superego

41 The word Gestalt is synonymous to
(a) configration (b) perception
(c) mind matters (d) thoughts

42 Who was the first psychologist to lay the foundation of Gestalt School of Psychology?
(a) Kurt Koffka (b) Max Wertheimer
(c) Johann Wolfgang (d) Wolfgang Kohler

43 Which psychological area of human behaviour was initially the main focus of gestalt psychologists?
(a) Learning (b) Perception
(c) Thinking (d) Memory

44 Max Wertheimer discovered which two phenomena in visual perception?
(a) Optical illusion, phi phenomena
(b) Binocular and monocular cues
(c) Depth perception and retinal disparity
(d) Size and colour constancy

45 Which famous psychologist applied gestalt principles to explain his theory of personality?
(a) Kurt Lewin (b) Abraham Maslow
(c) Freud (d) Guildford

46 Necker Cube and Rubin's figure/wase illusion is the example of which property of gestalt psychology?
(a) Emergence (b) Multistability
(c) eification (d) Invariance

47 Incomplete figures are perceived as the known or learned figures by humans. Which property of gestalt school is used in this?
(a) Reification (b) Invariances
(c) Multistability (d) Emergence

48 What is the fundamental principle of gestalt perception?
(a) Law of effect (b) Law of pragnanz
(c) Law of similarity (d) Law of pattern

49 The main focus of humanistic psychologists were
(a) growth and self belief
(b) self belief and self efficacy
(c) growth and self actualisation
(d) growth and learning

50 Who were the early developers of humanistic psychology?
(a) Carl Rogers, Abraham Maslow
(b) Eric Fromm, Sternberg
(c) Fritz Heider, Kurt Lewin
(d) Viktor Frankl, Rollo May

51 What was the name of the therapy introduced by Carl Rogers?
(a) Self actualisation therapy (b) Congruence of approach
(c) Self belief therapy (d) Client centered therapy

52 What are the major concepts that emerged as a result of humanist movement?
(a) Hierarchy of needs (b) Peak experiences
(c) Free will (d) a, b and c

53 What were the main areas of study in trans personal psychology?
(a) Free will
(b) Peak experiences
(c) Spiritual aspects of human life
(d) Both b and c

54 What are the key elements of transpersonal psychology?
(a) Spirituality (b) Self efficacy
(c) Transcendence (d) Both a and b

55 Which of the following is not an area covered under transpersonal psychology?
(a) Spirituality (b) Psychic phenomena
(c) Transcendence (d) Mindfulness

56 What was the main principle of existential therapy?
(a) Congruence between ideal self and social identity
(b) Learning principles
(c) Unconscious needs and desires
(d) Make clients aware that they have choices and thus can control their fate

57 Who proposed the technique of 'Paradoxical intentions' in psychotherapy?
(a) Viktor Frankl (b) Watson
(c) Rollo May (d) Carl Rogers

58 What led to the development of multiculturalism perspective in psychology?
(a) Scientific psychology of West has assumed that people in all cultures have same psychological processes.
(b) To understand the sensory perceptions of different cultures.
(c) To explain the behaviour of person individually.
(d) None of the above

59 What is the main difference in explanation of behaviour by Eastern perspective and Western perspective?
(a) Westerners define interrelationships while Easterners define individuality.
(b) Westerners define behaviour in terms of social situation while Easterners are more concerned about personal traits.
(c) Westerners define behaviour in terms of personal traits while Easterners define in terms of social situations.
(d) None of the above

60 Western culture gives emphasis on
(a) collectivism (b) individualism
(c) social situations (d) interrelationship

61 The cognitive revolution was the response to which school of thought in psychology?
(a) Behaviourism (b) Functionalism
(c) Structuralism (d) Psychoanalysis

62 Who were the main proponents of behaviourism?
(a) Pavlov and Skinner
(b) Viktor Frankl and Rollo May
(c) Koffka and Kohler
(d) Noam Chomsky and Herbert Simon

63 What was the main idea of cognitive revolution?
(a) To study mental events
(b) To study overt behaviour
(c) To study mind as a complex system composed of many interacting parts
(d) To study the covert human behaviour

64 The values, beliefs and practices of groups of people shared through symbols and passed down from generation to generation is called
(a) Group (b) Culture
(c) Race (d) Society

65 What is the combination race and culture called?
(a) Androgyny (b) Race
(c) Culture (d) Ethnicity

66 Who is considered 'The Father of Modern Psychology'?
(a) Wilhelm Wundt (b) Gustav Fechner
(c) Ernt Weber (d) Hermann Von Helmholtz

67 Who is main figure in establishing the School of Thought called 'Structuralism'?
(a) Wilhelm Wundt (b) James Mc Keen
(c) Edward B Titchener (d) G Stanley Hall

68 What are the path breaking contributions of Wundt in the field of psychology?
(a) Setting of first psychological lab
(b) He separated psychology and physiology
(c) He wrote first text book of psychology
(d) All of the above

69 Wundt was keen towards the study of
(a) sensory processes (b) attention
(c) reaction time (d) All of these

70 Freud emphasised that if any of psychosexual stage is not successfully completed then a person will be
(a) resonated (b) fixated
(c) propogated (d) conflicted

71 In the anal stage gratification is derived from
(a) bowel movement (b) eating
(c) sucking (d) oral stimulation

72 Ungratified desires at any stage leads to
(a) aggression (b) conflict
(c) dependency (d) Both a and b

73 Who wrote the book 'The Psycho Pathalogy of Allaily Life'?
(a) William James (b) Sigmund Freud
(c) Wilhelm Dilthey (d) Wilhelm Wundt

74 What were the name given to life and death instinct by Freud?
(a) Eros and thanatos (b) Id and eros
(c) Eros and superego (d) Ego and superego

75 Who is known as 'Father of American Psychology'?
(a) Wilhelm Wundt (b) William James
(c) Wilhelm Dilthey (d) Sigmund Freud

76 Who wrote the book 'The Principles of Psychology'?
(a) Wilhelm Wundt (b) William James
(c) Sigmund Freud (d) Wilhelm Dilthey

77 William James's writings and theories organised around which dual principle?
(a) Pragmatism, functionalism
(b) Pragmatism, structural
(c) Pragmatism, associationism
(d) Functionalism, behaviourism

78 Who gave the concept of 'Stream of Consciousness'?
(a) Dilthey (b) William James
(c) Watson (d) Immanuel Kant

79 Who gave one of the famous theory of emotions in psychology?
(a) Watson (b) Immanuel Kant
(c) William James (d) Sigmund Freud

80 According to Dilthey the human science helps to define
(a) historical world (b) relational world
(c) phenomenal world (d) experiential world

81 Who held the concept of historical consciousness in psychology?
(a) Wilhelm Dilthey (b) William James
(c) Wilhelm Wundt (d) Sigmund Freud

82 Which psychologists was influenced by the science of 'Hermeneutics'?
(a) Sigmund Freud (b) William James
(c) Wilhelm Dilthey (d) Ebbinghaus

83 According to Dilthey, how can self understanding be achieved?
(a) Through inner experiences
(b) Through how we express ourselves
(c) Through introspection
(d) Through history

84 Who introduced a distinction between explanatory and descriptive psychology?
(a) Wilhelm Dilthey (b) Karen Horney
(c) Wilhelm Wundt (d) Kurt Lewin

85 What is the other name of logical empiricism?
(a) Logical positivism (b) Neo empiricism
(c) Pragmatism (d) Both a and b

86 What is logical empiricism?
(a) Movement (b) Doctrine
(c) School of philosophy (d) None of these

87 What was the adopted paradigm of logical positivists?
(a) Objective (b) Subjective
(c) Scientific (d) Philosophical

88 Who was the main figure in the initiation of logical empiricism?
(a) Moritz Schlick (b) Immanuel Kant
(c) Wilhelm Dilthey (d) Kuhn

89 What was the main belief of logical positivists?
(a) Principle of absolutism.
(b) Introspection is the main method to study mental processes.
(c) They believed that science alone can provide universal and certain knowledge.
(d) None of the above

90 Who wrote the 'Manifesto of Logical Positivism' in 1929?
(a) Comte, Mill , Hume
(b) Carnap, Neurath and Hann
(c) Avenarius and Mach
(d) Frege, Peano

91 Who among logical positivists rejected the idea of metaphysics as a science?
(a) Hunn (b) Immanuel Kant
(c) Wittgenstein (d) None of these

92 According to the logical positivists metaphysical statements are not

(a) proved to be false (b) literal nonsense
(c) meaningless (d) have only emotive value

93 Who was the founder of psycho synthesis a psychotherapeutic technique?

(a) William James (b) Roberto Assagioli
(c) Caroline Rhys (d) Carl Jung

94 Who developed autogenic training?

(a) Caroline Rhys (b) Roberto Assagioli
(c) Carl Jung (d) JH Schultz

95 Gordon Allport was largely influenced by

(a) Upanishads (b) Indian texts
(c) Yoga Sutra (d) All of these

96 Which famous psychologist wrote 'Psychoanalysis and Zen'?

(a) Hubert Benoit (b) Christman Humphreys
(c) Michael Murphy (d) Gordon Allport

97 Match the following

List I (Freud's Conception of Human Psyche)	List II (Level of Existence)
A. Ego	1. Unconscious
B. Super-ego	2. Subconscious
C. Id	3. All three Levels

Codes

	A	B	C		A	B	C
(a)	1	2	3	(b)	3	2	1
(c)	2	3	1	(d)	2	1	3

98 Match the following

List I (Freud's Conception of Mind)	List II (Explanation)
A. Conscious mind	1. Outside awareness but accessible
B. Subconscious mind	2. Present awareness
C. Unconscious mind	3. Not accessible

Codes

	A	B	C		A	B	C
(a)	2	1	3	(b)	1	2	3
(c)	3	1	2	(d)	1	3	2

99 Match the following

List I (Component of Personality)	List II (behavioural Manifestation)
A. Id	1. Reality principle
B. Ego	2. Moral principle
C. Super ego	3. Aggresiveness, sea, hunger

Codes

	A	B	C		A	B	C
(a)	3	2	1	(b)	1	2	3
(c)	3	1	2	(d)	2	1	3

100 Match the following

List I (Component of Personality)	List II (Manifestation)
A. Id	1. "I want it now"
B. Ego	2. "I need to do a bit of planning toget it"
C. Super-ego	3. "You can't have it is not right"

Codes

	A	B	C		A	B	C
(a)	1	2	3	(b)	2	3	1
(c)	1	3	2	(d)	3	2	1

101 Match the following

List I (Gestalt Properties)	List II (Examples)
A. Multistability	1. Incomplete figures seen as complete
B. Reification	2. objects are recognised independent of its rotation
C. Invariance	3. 3 legged bilivet

Codes

	A	B	C		A	B	C
(a)	3	1	2	(b)	2	1	3
(c)	3	1	2	(d)	1	2	3

102 Match the following

List I (Psychologist)	List II (Contributions)
A. Viktor Frankl	1. Shadow
B. Rollo May	2. Logotherapy
C. Fritz Pearls	3. Paradoxical intentions
D. Carl Rogers	4. Gestalt therpy

Codes

	A	B	C	D		A	B	C	D
(a)	1	2	3	4	(b)	4	3	1	2
(c)	3	2	4	1	(d)	3	1	2	4

103 Match the following

List I (Psychologist)	List II (Known for)
A. Roberto Assagioli	1. Autogenic training
B. JH Schultz	2. Buddhist psychology
C. Caroline Davids Rhys	3. Zen meditation
D. Friedrich Heiler	4. Psychosynthesis

Codes

	A	B	C	D		A	B	C	D
(a)	1	2	3	4	(b)	4	3	2	1
(c)	2	1	4	3	(d)	3	4	1	2

104 Consider the following statement

1. **Structuralism grew up around the ideas of Wilhelm Wundt.**
2. **John Dancy, James K Angell and Harvery A Carr are also structuralists.**

Which among the above is/are correct?

(a) Only 1 (b) Only 2
(c) Both 1 and 2 (d) None of these

105 Consider the following statements

1. Gestalt psychology emerged in Germany as a reaction to the structuralism of Wundt.
2. Gestalf means 'form' or 'Configuration'.

Which among the above is/are correct?

(a) Only 1
(b) Only 2
(c) Both 1 and 2
(d) None of the above

106 Consider the following statements

1. Behaviourism originated around 1910.
2. The major and the most radical viewpoint about human behaviour was presented by Sigmund Freud.

Which among the above is/are correct?

(a) Only 1
(b) Only 2
(c) Both 1 and 2
(d) None of the above

107 Consider the following statements

1. Humanistic psychology developed as a response to psychoanalysis are behaviourism
2. Key scholars related to Humanistic psychology are Jean Paul Sartre, Albert Camus, Friedrich Nietzsche.

Which among the above is/are correct?

(a) Only 1 (b) Only 2
(c) Both 1 and 2 (d) None of these

108 Consider the following statements

1. Rollo May introduced existential perspective in USA.
2. Viktor Frankl developed Logo therapy.

Which among the above is/are correct?

(a) Only 1 (b) Only 2
(c) Both 1 and 2 (d) None of these

109 Consider the following statements

1. Freud opened the 'Institute for Experiment Psychology' in Germany.
2. Wilhelm Wundt's School of Psychology was called voluntarism.

Which among the above is/are correct?

(a) Only 1 (b) Only 2
(c) Both 1 and 2 (d) None of these

110 Consider the following statements

1. William James is referred as 'father of American Psychology'.
2. 'The Principles of Psychology' was written by Sigmund Freud.

Which among the following is/are correct?

(a) Only 1 (b) Only 2
(c) Both 1 and 2 (d) None of these

111 Consider the following statements

1. The essay 'the Origin of our Belief in the Reality of the External World and its Justification' was written by Wilhelm Dilthey.
2. Wilhelm Dilthey introduced a distinction between explanatory psychology and descriptive psychology.

Which among the following is/are correct?

(a) Only 1
(b) Only 2
(c) Both 1 and 2
(d) None of these

112 Consider the following statements

1. Franz Brentano was a teacher of Sigmund Freud.
2. Caroline Rhys Davids published Buddhist psychology.

Which among the following is/are correct?

(a) Only 1
(b) Only 2
(c) Both 1 and 2
(d) None of the above

113 Consider the following statements

1. Daniel Goleman, a psychologist wrote 'The Varities of Meditative Experience in 1977'.
2. The Spectruum of Consciounes' was written by Ken Wilber.

Which among the above is/are correct?

(a) Only 1
(b) Only 2
(c) Both 1 and 2
(d) None of the above

Directions (Q. Nos. 114-118) *Read the passage given below and answer the following questions.*

Cognitive Revolution in psychology is mostly a response to behaviourism which emphasised on the objectivity and focused on the overt behaviour for studying human psyche. The focus on the principles of behaviourism had pulled away the attention of psychologists from the mind for a prolonged period of time. Humanistic psychologists emphasised on studying human being as a whole and as a conscious and self aware being.

In 1950s, new disciplinary fields like linguistics, neuroscience and computer science again revived interest in mind as focus of scientific enquiry. This particular perspective was known as the *Cognitive Revolution*. There were numerous publications by psychologists which further triggered the Cognitive Revolution, Geore Miller's 1956 article 'The Magical Number Seven, Plus or Minus Two' linguist Noam Chomski's rejection of the behaviourist approach in his 1959 review of BF Skinner's Verbal Behaviour (1957)', foundational works in the field of artificial intelligence by John McCarthy, Marvin Minsky, Allen Newell and Herbert Simon in the 1958 article 'Elements of a Theory of Human Problem Solving' and Ulric Neisser's 1967 book 'Cognitive psychology', which served as a core text in cognitive psychology courses were the landmark contribution. Noam Chomski, argued in favour of cognitive studies saying that psychology focuses on behaviour is short sighted and field had to incorporate mental functioning if it has to offer any meaningful contribution in understanding human behaviour.

114 Cognitive Revolution in psychology is a response to

(a) Functionalism (b) Structuralism
(c) Behaviourism (d) None of these

115 Humanistic psychologists emphasised on studying human being as

(a) a whole (b) as a conscious
(c) self aware (d) All of these

116 The article 'The Magical Number Seven, Plus or Minus Two' was written by

(a) Noam Chomski (b) George Miller
(c) Ulric Neisser (d) None of these

117 The book 'Cognitive Psychology' was written by

(a) Noam Chomski
(b) Ulric Neisser
(c) George Miller
(d) None of these

118 'Verbal Behaviour' (1957) was written by

(a) John McCarthy
(b) Marvin Minsky
(c) Allen Newell
(d) All of these

Directions *(Q. Nos. 119-123) In the questions given below are two statements labelled as Assertion (A) and Reason (R). In the context of the two statements, which one of the following is correct?*

(a) Both A and R are true and R is the correct explanation of A
(b) Both A and R are true, but R is not the correct explanation of A
(c) A is true, but R is false
(d) A is false, but R is true

119 **Assertion** (A) Elements which has same shape are grouped together while perceiving.

Reason (R) Law of proximity states that when an individual perceives an assertment of objects, they perceive objects which are close to each other as forming a group.

120 **Assertion** (A) Individual's perceive objects such as shapes, letters, pictures as being whole when they are not complete.

Reason (R) Law of closure works on human perception.

121 **Assertion** (A) It is perceived as being symmetrical and forming around a point.

Reason (R) Law of common fate explains the above concept.

122 **Assertion** (A) When moon is near the horizon, it looks larger sthan when it is high in sky.

Reason (R) Size-distance principle explains it.

123 **Assertion** (A) The perceived lightness of the particular object changes very little, even with the change in the intensity of light.

Reason (R) Color constancy principle explains the above.

ANSWERS

1 (d)	2 (c)	3 (a)	4 (c)	5 (a)	6 (c)	7 (c)	8 (b)	9 (a)	10 (b)
11 (c)	12 (c)	13 (a)	14 (a)	15 (c)	16 (a)	17 (b)	18 (a)	19 (c)	20 (c)
21 (c)	22 (b)	23 (c)	24 (c)	25 (d)	26 (b)	27 (b)	28 (a)	29 (b)	30 (a)
31 (d)	32 (b)	33 (a)	34 (d)	35 (b)	36 (a)	37 (c)	38 (d)	39 (a)	40 (b)
41 (a)	42 (b)	43 (b)	44 (a)	45 (a)	46 (b)	47 (a)	48 (b)	49 (c)	50 (a)
51 (d)	52 (d)	53 (d)	54 (d)	55 (b)	56 (d)	57 (a)	58 (a)	59 (c)	60 (b)
61 (a)	62 (b)	63 (c)	64 (b)	65 (d)	66 (a)	67 (c)	68 (d)	69 (d)	70 (b)
71 (c)	72 (d)	73 (b)	74 (a)	75 (b)	76 (b)	77 (a)	78 (b)	79 (c)	80 (a)
81 (a)	82 (a)	83 (c)	84 (a)	85 (d)	86 (a)	87 (c)	88 (a)	89 (c)	90 (b)
91 (b)	92 (a)	93 (b)	94 (d)	95 (d)	96 (a)	97 (c)	98 (a)	99. (a)	100 (a)
101 (c)	102 (b)	103 (a)	104 (a)	105 (c)	106 (c)	107 (d)	108 (c)	109 (b)	110 (c)
111 (c)	112 (c)	113 (c)	114 (c)	115 (d)	116 (b)	117 (b)	118 (d)	119 (b)	120 (a)
121 (c)	122 (a)	123 (b)							

Essential Aspects of Knowledge Paradigm

To understand and articulate beliefs about the nature of reality, we study knowledge paradigm. A paradigm is a basic belief system and theoretical framework with assumptions about ontology, epistemology and methodology. In other words, it is our way of understanding the reality of the world and studying it. In psychological studies determination of knowledge paradigm is essential to set out the aspect of study.

Knowledge Paradigm

The term paradigm originated from the Greek word 'Paradeigma' which means 'pattern' and was first used by **Thomas Kuhn** to denote a conceptual framework shared by a community of scientists which provided them with a convenient model for examining problems and finding solutions. In the words of Kuhn, "a paradigm can be described as an integrated cluster of substantive concepts, variables and problems attached with corresponding methodological approaches and tools".

According to Kuhn, the term paradigm refers to a research culture with a set of beliefs, values and assumptions that a community of researchers has in common regarding the nature and conduct of research. According to **Olsen, Lodwick** and **Dunlop**, "A paradigm implies a pattern, structure and framework or system of scientific and academic ideas, values and assumptions".

Components of Knowledge Paradigm

Ontology, Epistemology and Methodology are important components of knowledge paradigm in research. *Let's study about the above components of knowledge paradigm in details*

Ontology

Ontology is the study of 'being' and is concerned with 'what is' i.e. the nature of existence and structure of reality as such or what is possible to know about the world. It is the branch of philosophy concerned with the assumptions we make in order to believe that something that makes sense or is real, or the very nature of reality or essence of the social phenomena we are investigating.

In this Chapter

- *Knowledge Paradigm*
- *Paradigms of Western Psychology*
- *Paradigmatic Controversies*
- *Indian Paradigms on Psychological Knowledge*
- *Science and Spirituality*
- *Primacy of Self Knowledge in Indian Psychology*

It is the philosophical study of the nature of existence or reality of being or becoming, as well as the basic categories of things that exist and their relations. It examines the underlying belief system of the researcher about the nature of being and existence.

Jonathan Grix quoted, "Ontology and epistemology are to research what 'footings' are to a house; they form the foundations of the whole edifice".

According to **Richards**, "Ontology refers to the nature of our beliefs about reality". Researchers have assumptions (sometimes implicit) about reality, how it exists and what can be known about it. It is ontological question that leads a researcher to inquire what kind of reality exists: "A singular, verifiable reality and truth (or) .... socially constructed multiple realities" (Patton 2003).

Philosophical assumptions about the nature of reality are crucial in understanding how the researcher makes meaning of the collected data. The assumptions made helps to orient one's thinking about the research problem, its significance and how one can approach it so as to contribute to its solution. The main characteristic of Ontology is that it helps to provide an understanding of the things that constitute the world, as it is known.

It makes the researcher ask questions such as; Is there reality out there in the social world or is it a construction, created by one's own mind? What is the nature of reality? In other words, is reality objective in nature, or is the result of individual cognition? What is the nature of the situation being studied? Ontology enables the researcher to examine their belief system and philosophical assumptions, about the nature of being, existence and reality.

Epistemology

Epistemology word has its Greek origin in which the word 'episteme', means 'knowledge'. In simple words, epistemology is used to describe how the knowledge is acquired or how the truth or reality is known.

In words of **Cookery** and **McDonald**, "epistemology is what is considered as knowledge with in the world."

According to **Richards**, "Epistemology is the assumptions which the researcher make about the kind and the nature of knowledge." Epistemology addresses the issue as to what is regarded as an acceptable knowledge in a discipline. Epistemology is concerned about the very basis of knowledge, its nature, form and also how it can be communicated to others.

The kind of assumptions which the researcher make about the knowledge, like if the researcher assumes knowledge to be hard, objective and tangible then he/she would be an observer to the research and applying methods of natural science such as testing, measuring etc. Whereas, if knowledge is considered to be personal, subjective and unique, then the researcher is more involved with the subjects and rejects the methods of natural science.

It focuses on the nature of knowledge and comprehensions that the researcher or knower can possibly acquire to extend, broaden and deepen understanding in the field of research.

It is the study of the nature of knowledge and justification. Epistemology in research involves answering the questions such as; Is knowledge something which can be acquired on one hand or is it something which has to be personally experienced? What is the nature of knowledge and the relationship between the knower and that would be known? What is the relationship between me, as the inquirer and what is known? These questions are important because they help the researcher to position themselves in the research context so that they can discover what else is given and what is known.

The most important question which the researcher can ask to understand the epistemological element of a paradigm is how we know and what we know? This question forms the basis of investigating 'truth'. Whereas, the existence of truth is a debatable concept in itself.

But if we consider the factual evidence as truth, then epistemology helps to ask factual questions such as; how do we know the truth? What counts as knowledge? These questions have a lot of weightage as the major criteria for judging higher degree research is its contributions to knowledge.

The four sources of knowledge that aids researcher to articulate the above questions are

(i) **Intuitive Knowledge** It is the form of knowledge which has sources such as beliefs, faith and intuition.

(ii) **Authoritative Knowledge** It is the form of knowledge which is based on the data gathered from known people, books and leaders in organisations.

(iii) **Logical Knowledge** It is the knowledge which is acquired by putting emphasis on reason in order to achieve a new knowledge.

(iv) **Empirical knowledge** It is based on demonstrable, objective facts which are determined through observation and/or experimentation.

Research often makes use of following four ways of knowing

- **Intuitive** When coming up with an initial idea for research.
- **Authoritative** When reviewing the professional literature.
- **Logical** When reasoning from findings to conclusions.
- **Empirical** When engaging in procedures that lead to these findings.

Methodology

Methodology is a broad term which refer to the research, design, methods, approaches and procedures used in a well-planned investigation to find out something. Data gathering, participants, instruments used and data analysis are all part of the broad field of methodology. In sum methodology articulates the logic and flow of the systematic processes followed in conducting a research project in order to attain knowledge about the research problem.

Methodology is mainly concerned with the plan that lies behind the choice and use of particular methods (Crotty, 1998). It is basically concerned with what, why, when, where and how data is collected and analysed. Methodology includes assumptions made, limitations encountered and how they were mitigated or minimised. Methodology is basically a strategy or action plan that justifies the use and choice of certain techniques. Therefore, methods of enquiry are reflections of the researcher's assumptions about the nature of reality and the nature of knowledge.

Paradigms of Western Psychology

Paradigm is a distinct set of concepts or thought patterns including theories, research methods, postulates and standards that are commonly accepted by members of a discipline or group. It is a mental representation of how an entity is structured (the parts and their inter-relationships) and how it functions. *Following paradigms have evolved in Western psychology:*

Positivism

Positivism was first proposed by the French Philosopher **Auguste Comte**. The positivist paradigm adhere to the basic idea that understanding of phenomena in reality must be measured and supported by evidence. The process of studying a phenomena in positivism is done by finding out the relationship between an independent variable and one or more dependent variable and also discovering causal inferences by applying experimental designs to maximise the influence of the independent variable on the dependent variable and events through this process.

This paradigm † tally focuses on understanding the objects by empirical tests and methods such as sampling, measurement, questionnaire, group discussion etc. This leads to high validity and reliability to the insights provided by positivist researchers. Positivist studies thus can be generalised to large scale of population too. For positivists, true knowledge is based on experience of senses and can be obtained by observation and experiment. Positivist researchers adopt scientific method as a means of knowledge generation.

For better decision of using this theoretical approach in research, one must be aware of its advantages and disadvantages, especially when positivism is applied in social research.

Advantages of Positivism

The major advantages of using a positivist approach is

- As it is a paradigm based on evidence, statistics, the methods and methodolgies used are empirical in nature, the result of the same phenomena or event may be allowed to replicate for different groups or subgroups of population in social contexts. As a result it proves to be quite economical in terms of both saving time and investments for using the findings of specific study for future quantitative predictions.
- As data being collected under the view of objectivist epistemology, the findings of research can be reliable and support researchers to make scientific assumptions.
- Reliability which can be estimated by statistical analysis *i.e.* identifying the internal consistency or correlation among the variables, using Cronbach's alpha reliability coefficient and validity of research results is one of the key strength of this approach.
- Application of key methods such as experimental research or survey research and appropriate methods of sampling, instrumentations and statistical treatments of data, for determining quantitative findings will help to provide an intensive answer for any research questions.

Limitations of Positivism

Though positivism has its advantages in helping researchers to continuously develop their understanding about humans and events in the areas of social research based on clear evidence; this paradigm has some limitations too. *Few limitations of positivism are*

- It could be impossible to measure phenomena related to intention, attitudes, thoughts of a human because these concepts profoundly may not explicitly be observed or measured with sense, experience or without evidence.
- Generalisation of research findings is the main focus of positivism, which at times results in neglect of important and pertinant issues. The general findings of research outcomes pose a challenge for researchers to directly apply for understanding the phenomena in particularly local context.
- In some situations the respondents may choose random answers rather than authentic responses or they are not allowed to have flexibility to give their answers which are more relevant to their personal cases. This results in inaccuracy of scientific data collected within the paradigm.

Post-Positivism

Moving to the next paradigm of research 'Post-Positivism' is a meta-theoretical stance that critiques and amends positivism. While positivists believe that the researcher and the researched person are independent of each other, Post-Positivists accept that theories, background, knowledge and values of the researcher can influence what is observed. However, Post-positivists pursue objectivity by recognising the possible effects of the bases.

Post-Positivism is a contemporary paradigm that developed as a result of the criticism of positivism. Like positivists post positivists also believe in the existence of single reality. However, Post-positivists acknowledge that reality can never be fully known and efforts to understand reality are limited owing to human beings sensory and intellectual limitations.

Although the aim of Post-positivists researchers is prediction and explanation, post- positivists also strive to be objective, neutral and ensure that the findings fit with the existing knowledge base. Post-positivists acknowledge and spellout any predispositions that may affect objectivity.

Post- positivism recognises that the way scientists think and work and the way we think in our everyday life are not distinctly different. Scientific reasoning and common sense reasoning are essentially the same process. Between the two there is no difference in kind, there is only a difference in degree. Post-positivism recognises that all observation is fallible and has error and that all theory is revisable. As Post-positivists are critical to the reality that they study, they do not rely on a single method of scientific inquiry. They believed that each method can have errors and these errors can only be avoided by using multiple methods this is called *Triangulation*.

Though positivism and Post-positivism are both grounded on objectivity but there exist a vast difference between both as post-positivists assumes that researchers are never objective and are biased due to their cultural beliefs and thus pure objectivity can never be achieved. This accounts for a vast difference between Positivism and Post-positivism. **Karl Popper** was a notable Post-positivist.

The difference between the two approaches i.e. Positivism and Post-positivism can be summarised as follows

Positivism	Post-Positivism
It is a philosophical stance that highlights the importance of objectivity and the necessity to study observable components.	It is a philosophy that rejects positivism and presents new assumptions in order to unravel the truth.
Empiricism including observation and measurement are considered to be the core of positivism.	Post-positivism considered Empiricism to be faulty.
Positivists are realists.	Post-positivists are critical realists.
Positivists believes that science aims to unravel the truth.	Post-positivists believe that all scientific methods have errors so it is impossible to unravel truth through science.
Positivists considers scientists to be objective.	Post-positivism highlights that there are biases in science as well.

Thus, it can be understood that the core idea of Positivism and Post-positivism creates the difference between them and sets them apart. These both can be considered as philosophies used in science for scientific inquiry and could be considered independent to each other.

Critical Perspective

Critical perspective in research has its origins in critical theory, attributed to **Georg Hegel** (18th century) and **Karl Marx** (19th century) and critical pedagogy, a key figure being **Paulo Freire** (20th century).

These influential figures focused on eliminating injustice in society and addresses inequities and power differentials. Critical theory is in contrast to traditional theory that explores and confirms the status quo, whereas critical theory challenges the status quo and strives for a balanced and democratic society. It is particularly concerned with the issue of power relations within the society and interaction of race, class, gender, education, economy, religion and other social institutions that contribute to social systems.

Horkheimer, one of the founders of the Critical theory suggests their criteria for an adequate critical theory. *These are*

- It must be explanatory about what is wrong with current social reality.
- It must identify the action to change it.
- It must provide both clear norms for criticism and transformation.

The above criteria entitles critical theorists not merely to explore the problem but also to identify the ways and strategies which could ensure a successful implication in the society. Critical theory not only intend to highlight and explain the social factors that cause powerful groups to dominate the weaker sections of society but also strives for a social set up based on equality for all the members.

In order to achieve the predefined target, critical theorists have used various methodologies. It provides choices that allow linking theories and methods as an ongoing process that is contextually bound and not pre-determined. Critical theory is flexible to adopt any methodology or technique, which could help in suggesting betterment in the unbalanced social system.

Tools of Critical Perspective

Critical researchers may use qualitative, quantitative or mixed methods. However, it is mostly seen that critical research is more inclined towards qualitative research designs.

The three typical tools of critical research are

(i) **Ideology Critique** It is a way of critiquing the ideology of the powerful group who use particular values and practices to exercise their power and get control over the suppressed classes. An ideology is an organised collection of ideas. The suppressed classes never realise that they are under the ideological control of the dominant group which is a capitalist society. Critiquing these practices and values uncovers the vested interests of exploiting groups and restores to consciousness of oppressed class.

(ii) **Critical Action Research** This is another tool to uncover the unjust and unfair practices and ideologies prevalent in society and achieve the target of a balanced and just society. Action research is about research that focuses on practice in education. It gives power to those who are operating in context to school, curriculum etc. It attempts to take account of disadvantage that affect teacher community on the basis of gender, ethnicity or bias on any other basis.

(iii) **Critical Discourse Analysis** (CDA) This is another tool used by researcher under the critical paradigm.

Van Digk define CDA as "type of discourse analytical research that primarily studies the way social power abuse, dominance and inequality are enacted, reproduced and resisted by text and talk in the social and political context." The above definition highlights certain characteristics of CDA *which are as follows*

- It is analytical by nature and related to the misuse of power by some social institution on political, social, cultural, ethical or gender basis.
- The task of critical analysts is not just to understand, but to challenge the social inequality that surfaces as the result of Critical Discourse analysis.
- It is of significant potential and importance in the social domain for critical research and brings change in society.
- It has been observed globally in recent researches that problems in systems, resource management, social action, social practices or forces of structure are a result of language and discourse.

Discourse structures create power relations in terms of how our relative status is negotiated through interchange with others. The dynamics of language, power and society are inter-related and worth studying form CDA point of view.

Thus, the 'declared' purpose of CDA is to expose how language is used in the socio-political abuse of power.

Selecting an appropriate research paradigm to conduct an effective research is not an easy task for a researcher, as he might get carried away with the popularity of any one paradigm over others and end up with invalid or vague findings. It is important for the researcher to select an appropriate research paradigm and at the same time broaden their vision by opening up to new concepts and ideas.

Critical paradigm offers new and refreshing perspectives to explore issues and make difference not only to the world of knowledge, but literally to the world itself and these perspectives should be explored and used by modern researchers. Critical theory being more flexible and independent in its pursuit of reality puts heavier responsibility on researcher to observe, perceive, analyse and interpret the data with extra vigilance.

Social Constructionism

Social constructionism may be defined as "a perspective which believes that a great deal of human life exists as it does due to social and interpersonal influences." Although genetically inherited factors and social factors are at work at the same time, social constructionism does not deny the influence of genetic inheritance, but decides to concentrate on investigating the social influences on communal and individual life. Social constructionism is interested in the study of culture and society *i.e.* the shared social aspects of all that is psychological.

Social constructionism regards individuals as integral of cultural, political and historical evolution in specific times and places and thus re-situate psychological processes cross culturally, in social and temporal contexts. Social constructionism hypothesis that apart from inherited and developmental aspects of humanity, all the other aspects of humanity are created, maintained and destroyed in human interactions with others through time. Social constructionism shows the importance of socialisation and enculturation, amongst the people known to us and also the current influence of those whom we know at present, are most active in shaping our mutual existence with others.

Conventional psychology gives major importance to physiological and inherited aspects of human existence. Conventional psychology aims to objectify human acts in an 'objective manner' as it believes that it is possible to exclude the aims, values, presence and biases of researcher. However, social constructionism argues that true objectivity is absent in the human sciences because all methods require one set of subjective humans to rate another set of subjective humans. So, 'the tool for knowing' is inevitably subjective people themselves.

According to **Owen**, "In essence, social constructionism is the claim and viewpoint that the content of our consciousness and the mode of relating we have towards other is taught by our culture and society; all the metaphysical quantities we take for granted are learned from others around us".

Peter Berger and **Thomas Luckmann** (1966) are credited by many for having developed this perspective. While positivists seek 'the truth', the social constructionist framework put forward that 'truth' varies. Truth is based on whom you ask and people change their definitions of truth all the time based on their interactions with other people. This is because according to social constructionism, humans create reality themselves as opposed to simply accepting the existing reality, through their interactions and interpretations of those interactions. Key to the social constructionist paradigm is the idea that social context and interaction frame our realities.

Researchers who are keen to work into this paradigm have an interest in understanding how people come to socially agree or disagree about what is real and true. A significant example of socially constructed behaviour is how different hand gestures vary across different regions of the world.

For example pointing fingers towards someone has different meanings in different cultures and people interpret it differently across cultures. So, what is the 'truth' of pointing finger towards someone? It depends on what the person doing it intended, how the other person interpreted and the social context in which the action has occurred.

Existential Phenomenology

This approach is inspired by the philosophical tradition developed by thinkers such as Buber, Kierkegaard, Nietzsche, Heidegger, Gadamer, De Beauvoir, Sartre, Marcel, Merleau-Ponty and Leninas. Existential phenomen - ology seeks to develop an indepth understanding of human existence.

It challenge approaches in psychology that view human being in a reductionistic manner. This approach utilises the philosophical tradition in psychotherapy and growth. It gives an insight into the richness and diversity of human psychological experience.

Existential phenomenology deepens our understanding of the experiences and perspectives of others through its focus upon the meanings that we make in our lives and the choices that are reflected in our understandings and actions.

Existential phenomenology is Martus Heidegger brand of phenomenology. Phenomenology is the philosophical study of the structures of experience and consciousness. It was founded in the early years of the 20th century by Edmund Husserl and was later expanded upon by a circle of his followers.

Phenomenology provides a theoretical basis for existentalism. Both employ the method of observation and description.

- Observation and description of consciousness.
- Observation and description of human situations.

Phenomenology is essentially a description of appearances. Phenomenology and existentialism takes complementary roles. But, both take the conditions of life as brute facts, rather than having to be proven.

Existential phenomenology takes the human condition in all its wondrous manifestations as the focus of investigation. Existential phenomenology emphasises the unfolding nature of human experience and brings out the fact that world is not only the correlate of consciousness but that without world there will be no consiousness. Consequently, for existential phenomenology the modalities of conscious experiences are also the ways one is in the world.

The core belief of existentialism, 'Dasein' *i.e.* being-in the-world, refers exclusively to human reality in contrast to non-human reality. It lay insistence that human reality is situated in a concrete world context.

In short, man is only man as a result of his actions which are worked out in the world. The word 'existence' is usually used by existentialists to refer only to human reality for what it means to exist is to be always engaged in tasks of the world.

Thus, it can be seen that existential phenomenology is the merger of two streams of thought *i.e.* kierkegaard' existentialism and Husserl's phenomenology . It merged in Heidegger's 'Being and time' and served as foundation of the philosophy 'existential phenomenology'.

Cooperative Inquiry

Cooperative inquiry is a way of working with other people who have similar concerns and interest as researcher, in order to

- understand the world and make sense of life of the researcher and develop new and creative ways of looking at things.
- learn how to act to change things as the researcher wants and finds out to do things in a better way.

Research is always considered to be the work done at universities and research institutes. The researcher asks questions, do interviews and gather data applicable for his studies by studying other people.

The trouble here lies in the fact that there exist a little connection between the researcher and the other people involved. People are treated as passive agents rather than active agents. In traditional research, there exist a big gap between the researcher and the people whom he studies. But through cooperative inquiry the whole scenario is changing as in this approach research is conducted with people rather than on people.

Another problem in traditional research is that the thinking done by researchers is often theoretical rather than practical. Therefore, the research never helped people to find how to act in order to change things in their lives. Thus, the outcome of a good research is not fulfilled as the solutions offered for a better life were just restricted to books and academic papers. However, good research is concerned with revisioning our understanding of our world, as well as transforming practice within it.

So, in traditional research the role of researcher and subject was mutually exclusive. Researcher was the one who was contributing to the thinking that goes into the project while subjects role was to do actions which are to be studied. In cooperative enquiry, the mutually exclusive role are transformed into cooperative roles and involved people work as co-researchers and co-subjects. Everyone is involved in each and every step of a research *i.e.* management of the inquiry, experience and action to be explored, drawing conclusions, taking initiative and exerting influence on the process. Thus, it can be said that cooperative enquiry is not a research on people, but it's a research with people.

Features of Cooperative Inquiry

The defining features of a cooperative inquiry can be summarised as follows

- There exist an intentional interplay between reflection and making sense on one hand and action-experience on the other hand.
- There is the external attention, through agreed procedures to establish the validity of inquiry and its findings. The primary procedure is to use inquiry cycles, moving several times between action and reflection.
- Inquiry method can be both transformative and informative about any human condition that has an open unbound awareness.
- Importance is given to transformative inquiries that involves action where people change their way of being, doing and relating to the world in the direction of greater prosperity.
- There is a radical epistemology for a wide ranging inquiry method that integrates. The four types of knowledge created by cooperative inquiry which are experiential knowledge, presentational knowledge, propositional knowing and practical knowing.
- Experiential knowing in integrated through meeting and encounter, presentational knowing through use of aesthetic, expressive forms, propositional knowing through use of words and concepts and practical knowing through the exercise of diverse skills-intrapsychic,

interpersonal, political, transpersonal and so on. These forms of knowledge are brought to bear upon each other through the use of inquiry cycles, to enhance mutual congruence,with in each inquirer and inquiry group as a whole.

- The full range of human capacities and sensibilities are available as an instrument of inquiry.

Phases in Cooperative Inquiry

Cooperative inquiry is a systematic approach to developing understanding and action. Although every group is different, each one can be seen as engaged in cycles of action and reflection.

The **first phase** in cooperative inquiry is to bring a group of people together who have common interest. The group of co-researchers come together to explore an agreed area of human activity. They discuss their interest area and concerns, agree on the focus of their inquiry and develop together a set of questions or propositions they wish to explore. They also agree upon some set of procedures by which they will observe and record their own and each other's experience.

In **second phase**, the agreed upon actions are applied in the everyday life and work of people. They initiate the actions, observe and record the outcomes of their own and each other's behaviour.

In **third phase**, the co-researchers become fully immersed in their experience. They may become more open to what is going on and may begin to see their experience in new ways. They may deepen into the experience so that superficial understandings are elaborated and developed or they may be led away from the original ideas and proposals into new fields, unpredicted actions and creative insights.

At times the co-researchers get fully immersed in what they are doing and lose the awareness that they are part of inquiry group. This phase is an important phase of inquiry and is what makes cooperative inquiry different from conventional research, because here people are deeply involved in their own experience. Thus, any practical skills or new understandings will grow out of this experience.

In **phase fourth**, the co-researchers re-assemble to consider their original questions in the light of their experience. Now they can change their questions in some ways, reject them and pose new questions and agree on second cycle of action and reflection.

Now they can choose to focus on different aspects of overall inquiry. The group may choose to amend or develop its inquiry procedures, forms of action and ways of gathering data in the light of experience of first cycle.

Paradigmatic Controversies

The paradigmatic controversies in psychology can be explained with the help of following table

Issue of Controversy	Positivism	Post-positivism	Critical Theory	Constructivism
Ontoiogy	Naive realism–'real' reality but apprehendable	Critical realism–'real' reality but only imperfectly and probabilistically apprehendable	Historical realism–virtual reality shaped by social, political, cultural, economic, ethnic and gender values crystalised over time.	Relativism–local and specific constructed realities
Epistemology	Dualist/objectivist; findings true	Modified dualist/objectivist; critical tradition/community; findings probably true	Transactional/subjectivist; value–mediated findings	Transactional/subjectivists; created findings
Methodology	Experimental/manipulative; verification of hypothesis; chiefly quantitative methods	Modified experimental/manipulative; critical mutiplism; falsification of hypothesis; may include qualitative methods	Dialogic/dialectic	Hermeneutic dialectic
Nature of knowledge	Verified hypothesis established as facts or laws	Nonfalsified hypothesis that are probable facts or laws	Structural/historical insights	Individual reconstructions coalescing around consensus
Knowledge accumulation	Accretion–'building blocks' adding to 'edifice of knowledge'; generalisations and cause effect linkages		Historical revisionism; generalisation by similarity	More informed and sophisticated reconstructions; vicarious experience
Goodness or quality criteria	Conventional benchmarks of 'rigor':internal and external validity, reliability and objectivity		Historical situatedness; erosion of ignorance and misapprehensions; action stimulus	Trustworthiness and authenticity
Values	Excluded–influence denied			Included–formative

Issue of Controversy	Positivism	Post-positivism	Critical Theory	Constructivism
Ethics	Extrinsic-tilt toward deception		Intrinsic–moral tilt toward revelation	Intrinsic-process tilt toward revelation
Inquirer posture	'Disinterested scientist' as informer of decision makers, policy makers and change agents	'Transformative intellectual' as advocate and activist	—	'Passionate participant' as facilitator of multivoice reconstruction
Training	Technical and quantitative; substantive theories	Technical, quantitative and qualitative; substantive theories	Resocialisation; qualitative and quantitative; history; values of altruism and empowerment	
Axiology	Propositional knowing about the world is an end in itself, is intrinsically valuable.	Propositional, transactional knowing is instrumentally valuable as a means to social emancipation, which as an end in itself, is intrinsically valuable.		
Accommodation and commensurability	Commensurable for all positivist forms	Incommensurable with positivist forms; some commensurability with constructivist, criticalist and participatory approaches, especially as they merge in liberationist approaches outside the West.		
Action	Not the responsibility of the researcher; viewed as 'advocacy' or subjectivity and therefore a threat to validity and objectivity.	Found especially in the form of empowerment; emancipation anticipated and hoped for; social transformation, particularly toward more equity and justice, is end goal	Intertwined with validity, inquiry often incomplete without action on the part of participants; constructivist formulation mandates training in political action if participants do not understand political systems	
Control	Resides solely in researcher	Often resides in 'tranformative intellectual'; in new constructions, control returns to community	Shared between inquirer and participants	
Relationship to foundations of truth and knowledge	Foundational	Foundational	Foundational within social critique	Antifoundational

Indian Paradigms on Psychological Knowledge

During the past century different paradigms have emerged in the field of Psychology because of its remarkable growth and interest of researchers in its numerous areas. We have already discussed about different Western paradigms, now we will study about various Indian paradigms which leads to enhancement on psychological knowledge.

The significant Indian paradigms on psychological knowledge include Yoga, Bhagavad Gita, Buddhism, Sufism and integral yoga. Buddhism, Bhagavad Gita, Sufism and integral yoga have already been discussed.

Yoga

Within the yogic and Indian Psychology traditions, the means of 'Knowing' have been described with precision. *Three aspects of knowing are*

(i) The refinement of knowing with in the training system of the Patanjali Yoga-Sutras.

(ii) Sri Aurobindo's views of the four types of knowledge.

(iii) Sri Aurobindo's views of the process of intuition.

The eight limbs described in the Patanjali Yoga-Sutras provide ways of readying and purifying the body, emotions and mind for a form of knowing through being or identifying with what is to be known, achieved through 'Samyama', the intensive and conjoint practice of the last three limbs of dharana (concentration), dhyana (contemplation or meditation) and samadhi (absorption).

The several limbs of Patanjali Rajayoga *i.e.* yama, niyama, asana, pranayama, pratyahara, dharana, dhyana and samadhi provide methods for systematically reducing the possible environmental social, bodily, sensory, emotional and cognitive sources of noise or distraction that might serve as impediments to, or distortions of accurate and sensitive knowing.

Sri Aurobindo described four forms of knowledge which are the four cognitive methods of nature. These four forms of knowledge include knowledge by identity, knowledge by intimate direct contact, knowledge by separative direct contact and a wholly separative knowledge by indirect contact.

Sri Aurobindo described a special form of knowing which he called *intuition*. Intuition is a power of consciousness nearer and more intimate to the original knowledge by identity. It is a power arising out of a higher plane of consciousness than the mind. The mind is the source of intuition, thus, it is subject to errors and misperceptions that are inherent in mental view of things. Intuition is verified by sense-perception and is assured by self-evidence.

Yoga helps in developing more accurate introspection in refining the observation of inner experience, the same techniques can be used in preparing and purifying the researcher's antahkarana (internal organ of knowing) for a deeper, more accurate and more satistying study of any object of inquiry. This purification process can allow the researcher to reduce various distractions and biases that might distort what is to be known.

Significance of Yoga

The yogic preparation and purification are more profound in that it addresses a much wider and deeper range of possible distractions or impediments to knowing that exist not only at the cognitive level but also at sensory, bodily, emotional and more subtle levels, as well.

Practising of Patanjali's Ashtanga yoga can help the researcher to adjust his or her very being in ways that can allow more direct forms of knowing the object of research.

Yoga lay emphasis on introspection as the method of knowing. Though in modern psychology introspection is not considered a very reliable source of knowledge, it is still used extensively both in quantitative and qualitative studies. It is clearly seen as the main, if not only way to observe directly what happens inside ourselves.

It is true that in beginning meditators tend to fall into this 'introspectionist' trap. Instead of silencing the mind they move to and fro between their usual thoughts, feelings and sensations and an equally noisy running commentary on these very same thoughts etc. But this is not what meditation is about. The process of self observation used in Yoga is an entirely different nature of introspection.

Indian Tradition and Yoga

According to Indian tradition, the thinking condition at the beginning of mediation is an unfortunate entanglement of our conscious essence, (atman) with the activities of the mind, (manas). The entanglement shows itself in the fact that in the ordinary waking state most people identify with their body, feelings and thoughts. One can find the tendency to conflate consciousness with 'thinking' throughout Western thought, though the development of apparently unconscious machines that can at least imitate human thought is slowly beginning to make space for a more subtle understanding of their relationship.

The main element of Yoga as the knowledge system is the possibility of freeing one's consciousness entirely from the processes that go on inside it. Most schools of Indian thought attribute ignorance as a reason for human sufferings. In the language of the Samkhya, the defining characteristic of ignorance is an erroneous identification of our true self, 'Purusha' with the limited movements of nature, 'Prakriti'.

The cure of ignorance consists of the two main processes that are mentioned virtually in all schools of Yoga. The first is a shift of the center of our consciousness away from Prakriti, to which the processes and the contents of the mind belong, till it is fully centered in the 'Purusha', the ultimate essence of our being. The second process takes place within the domain of Prakriti under influence of the Purusha, it is the purification and ultimate transformation of one's nature.

Thus, it can be concluded that Yoga serves as one of the most important paradigm of knowledge of the Indian traditions and its applications are widespread in the field of therapy and transpersonal psychology too.

Indian Perspective

The Indian perspective takes a qualitative and spiritual position and warrants inner development that may enable direct experience. It calls for a consciousness based paradigm with the scope of direct and experiential knowledge.

Thus, this move can be seen as a matter of contemporary relevance and practical utility. It is more rigorous and inclusive than Western empirical approach as currently practised in Psychological science. It goes beyond the Western approach in many ways as it believes in multiple but interdependent worlds, use of discussive practices, significance of language, reason, perception and sadhana to obtain empirical truth on the one hand and realisation of transcendental reality on the other, are very important for a holistic understanding.

Science and Spirituality (Avidya and Vidya)

The pursuits in the realm of knowledge were classified into two broad categories, *which are as follows*

(i) **Spiritual knowledge** *i.e.* spirituality (para vidya) spiritual knowledge is concerned with the experience of universal reality. It deals with the name (nama) and form (rupa) of ultimate reality in its diverse manifestations. The knowledge of supreme reality was supposed to lead to liberation (moksa).

(ii) **Empirical knowledge** *i.e.* science (apara vidya). Empirical knowledge is bound to specific objects. Empirical or scientific knowledge is pragmatic and deals with the ordinary world.

These two types of knowledge are complementary as it deals with the whole range of existential concerns.

Vidya

The term Vidya is used for science as well as philosophy. Vidyas were classified in four major categories that is Anvishiki, Trayi, Vartta and Dandaniti. The development of these vidyas demonstrates a dialectic of two perspectives, the orthodox and the heterodox.

The development of knowledge systems is conceptualised in the form of 'Sastras'. A Sastra is a system of rules with its own techniques and concepts.

It was required to define itself with respect to its subject matter, purpose, relevance and the class of enquirer who was eligible for its study (anubandha-catu satya).

The Indian attitude towards knowing is grounded in a set of premises as stated below

- Suffering is the result of ignorance. Gaining knowledge leads to end to suffering in one's life.
- Knowledge is considered to be inseparable from the human goals and values.
- The quest for being itself (ontological being), which encompasses both being and becoming is central to the process of knowing.
- Knowledge changes the person engaged in the pursuit of knowledge, as it is supposed to transform the whole person by introducing changes in mental, liguistic and behavioural functioning of the person.
- There is no conflict between science and religion in Indian context. In fact, Indian science has developed in close relationship with dharma.
- Western view emphasises a conflict between man and nature, whereas Indian system assumes that universe is lawful and there is a continuity within the entire kingdom. In Indian tradition, man and nature are interdependent and share co-escistence.

Avidya

In the yogic sense, avidya means something that goes far beyond ordinary ignorance. Avidya is a fundamental blindness about reality. The core ignorance called as *avidya* isn't a lack of information, but the inability to experience your deep connection, to the others, to the source of being and to your true self. Avidya has many layers and levels, which operate in different ways.

All forms of cluelessness and fogged perception are forms of avidya's. But behind each of avidya manifestations is the failure to recognise that essentially you are spirit and that you share this with every atom of the universe.

Primacy of Self Knowledge in Indian Psychology

Self knowledge is a component of the self. It is the knowledge of oneself and one's properties. It is the desire to seek the knowledge that guide the development of self-concept. It informs us of mental representations of ourselves which contain attributes that we pair with ourselves and theories on whether these attributes are stable or dynamic.

Aspects of Self Knowledge

Self knowledge is the expert variety of knowledge by identity and it leads us directly to who we are in the very essence of our being. The little of real self-knowledge that reaches our surface consciousness may never attain to that level of perfection, but in oneself this type of knowledge is intrinsically true and perfect. According to **Indian tradition**, "a perfect knowledge of oneself automatically gives in principle the possibility of perfect knowledge of everything else."

The self knowledge is governed by three aspects

(i) **Cognitive Self** It is referred as known self. It is made up of everything we know or think we know about ourselves. This includes physiological properties such as hair colour, race and height etc. and psychological properties like beliefs, values etc. Its motives guide the search to gain greater clarity and assurance about oneself.

(ii) **Affective Self** It is also known as *felt self*. It refers to the emotional component of self knowledge.

(iii) **Executive Self** It is also known as *active self*. It refers to the behavioural component of self knowledge.

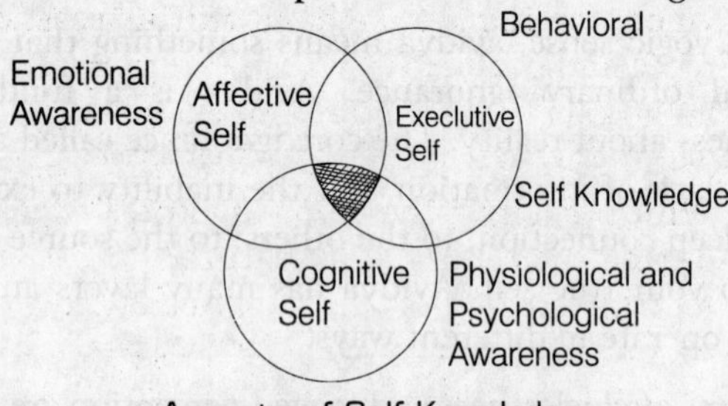

Aspects of Self Knowledge

Indian Psychology and Self Knowledge

Indian psychology is built on self-knowledge rather than on knowledge of statistically generalised facts.

Indian Psychology considers mind (manas) and self (atman) to be different, self being the knower. Mind is considered to be the substance and an instrument of knowledge .

It is believed that knowledge constitutes the nature or quality of self (atman) acting through mind, reaching out to the objects and making them known to the self. The yoga system delineates five modes or states of mental activity consisting of Ksipta (wandering), Mudha (forgetful), Viksipta (distracted), Ekagra (one-pointed) and Niruddha (restrained).

Perception depends on mental modification or citta vrtti and contact between the target object and manas through sense organs. Self (Purusa) is considered as the real cogniser. Knowledge is illumination of a thing not already presented and is caused by the operation of the self. The realisation of the true-self is blocked by mis-conceptions (klesa), such as avidya (ignorance), asmita (egoism), raga (attachment or passion), dvesa (aversion) and abhinivesa (clinging to life), vikalpa (predicate relation) is considered by Yoga Sutra as a way of knowing. Recognition (pratyabhijna) is considered as a form of perception by the Nyaya School of Indian Philosophy.

It occurs because of many factors such as attention, association, practice, indicative, distinguishing features, likeness, ownership or possession, support, sequence, seperation, enmity, superiority, acquisition, cover pleasure and pain, desire and aversion, fear, need, profession, affection and merit and demerit.

These causes of recognition are not mutually exclusive. They refer to the characteristics of objects and events, their contexts and relationships. Some thinkers emphasise on its perceptual aspects and directness of experience, while others emphasise its memory component.

Memory (smriti) refers to the activation of residual impressions or traces of the past experiences (samskaras). Memory is the function of the contact of these Samskara with mind (manas).

The Samskaras gradually become stronger with their repeated manifestation in actions. This has implications for the practice of Yoga. For instance bad and painful Samskaras have to be substituted by good and pleasent Samskaras. The stored up experiences have tendencies for actualisation (vasanas).

The Samskaras are often present at the unconscious level. Thus, while knowledge is a quality of the self it is manifested by mind through its contact with the objects. It should be noted that if the self has to attain knowledge, the mind has to be active and regulate the entire processes.

In order to attain higher levels of consciousness and intimacy to 'Self', the yogic system of Patanjali prescribes the practice of Yoga consisting of eight limbs: restraints (yama), observances (niyama), postures (asana), breathing exercises (pranayama), withdrawal of senses from its objects (pratyahara).

EXAM BASED QUESTIONS

1 Which amongst the following is a basic belief system and theoretical framework to our understanding of the reality?
(a) Ontology (b) Epistemology
(c) Methodology (d) Paradigm

2 Which two components form the foundations of the whole research?
(a) Ontology and Methodology
(b) Ontology and Epistemology
(c) Epistemology and Methodology
(d) Methodology and Paradigm

3 Ontology is the nature of our beliefs about
(a) research (b) subjects (c) reality (d) world

4 Ontology is synonymous to
(a) Philosophy (b) Experimental approach
(c) Metaphysics (d) Sociology

5 The word 'outos' and 'logo' in Ontology means respectively.
(a) Being, study (b) Being, form
(c) Study, being (d) Being, process

6 An important aspect of Ontology, 'subjectivism' is synonymous to
(a) constructionism (b) positivism
(c) interpretivism (d) Both a and b

7 The interpretive paradigm is more likely to be employed in
(a) quantitative research (b) naturalistic research
(c) qualitative research (d) Both b and c

8 The positivist approach is based on sound experimental design and emphasis upon.
(a) qualitative data collection
(b) logical data collection
(c) quantitative data collection
(d) analytical data collection

9 Episteme in the word Epistemology means
(a) Self (b) Experience
(c) Knowledge (d) Reality

10 Epistemology is also known as the
(a) theory of reality (b) theory of knowledge
(c) analysis of reality (d) justification of knowledge

11 According to Positivist Research Paradigm, the epistemology of the research study believes that
(a) reality is only subjective in nature
(b) reality can be measured
(c) reality cannot be measured
(d) None of the above

12 Which type of knowledge is used by researchers, when coming up with an initial research area, topic and problem?
(a) logical (b) authoritative
(c) intuitive (d) empirical

13 Which amongst the following knowledge is gained during the review of literature?
(a) Logical (b) Authoritative
(c) Intuitive (d) Empirical

14 Which amongst the following knowledge is arrived at on the analysis of the primary data findings?
(a) Intuitive (b) Empirical
(c) Authoritative (d) Logical

15 In Constructivist research paradigm, acceptable knowledge is based on
(a) subjective meaning
(b) objective meaning
(c) logical meaning
(d) interpretative meaning

16 A qualitative approach sees social reality between people in the real world as
(a) mutually constructed (b) mutually exclusive
(c) matter of perspective (d) None of these

17 Epistemology attempts to identify what is .... and reflects.
(a) true knowledge, accuracy (b) accuracy, reality
(c) true knowledge, reality (d) true knowledge

18 Epistemology defines the relationship between
(a) knower and facts (b) knower and knowledge
(c) knower and the known (d) None of these

19 A methodology is synonymous to
(a) a procedure (b) a design process
(c) a method (d) Both a and c

20 Descriptive methodology is concerned with the_____ of the completed activities.
(a) organisation (b) structure
(c) assumptions (d) description

21 What is Positivism?
(a) Positivism is an epistemological position that advocates the application of the methods of the natural sciences to the study of social reality.
(b) Positivism involves a dialogical process between theory and the empirical phenomena; this results in the production of 'reflexive narratives' , not explanatory models or theoretical propositions.

(c) Positivism is a way of thinking about the research process and staying positive.
(d) Positivism is an outlook in life about seeing things positively.

22 How many types of reasoning in organisational research are there?
(a) One organisational reasoning research.
(b) Two theory testing and interpretive research.
(c) Three theory testing research, inductive case research and interpretive research.
(d) Four positivism, theory testing research, inductive case research and interpretive research.

23 'Standard Positivism' is associated with which of these philosophers?
(a) Moritz Schlick (b) Karl Popper
(c) Ernt Mach (d) Carl Henpel

24 Which amongst the following term has developed from Empiricism and is closely related to Positivism?
(a) Scientism (b) Naturalism
(c) Reductionism (d) All of these

25 Which is not a tool for Post-positivist research?
(a) Concept of discourse (b) Value of narrative
(c) Concern with power (d) Need to be irreflexive

26 Critical theory is a
(a) social theory (b) religious theory
(c) political theory (d) moral theory

27 Critical perspective involves asking questions about the
(a) validity, reliability
(b) applicability, throughness
(c) rationale and legitimacy
(d) None of the above

28 Which one of the following is a popular critical theory?
(a) Feminist (b) New Historicism
(c) Freudian (d) All of these

29 Social Constructionism is associated with
(a) positivism (b) modernism
(c) post-positivism (d) post-modernism

30 Which kind of social life is emphasised by social theories?
(a) Socially (b) Critically
(c) Politically (d) Contemporary

31 A linked term to Social Constructionism is
(a) post-modernism (b) phenomenological
(c) constructivism (d) innovative

32 The term 'Constructivism' is related to which famous theory in Psychology.
(a) Piaget's theory
(b) Kohlberg's theory
(c) Adler's theory
(d) Erik Ericson theory

33 Basic themes of Existential Phenomenology is
(a) lived experience (b) ontology
(c) modes of being (d) All of these

34 Which type of human experience is described by Existential Phenomenology?
(a) Subjective (b) Sensory
(c) Objective (d) All of these

35 In 'Phenomenology' the word phenomena means
(a) logic (b) belief (c) appearence (d) pattern

36 The main theorists attached to Existential Phenomenology are
(a) Sartre (b) Husserl
(c) Heidegger (d) All of these

37 A phenomenological understanding is primarily descriptive and does not violate integrity of our
(a) intellectual capacity
(b) psychological phenomena
(c) human experience
(d) behavioural phenomenal

38 An Existential Phenomenologist makes a client to be
(a) self- reflective (b) independent
(c) congruent (d) affirmative

39 Existential therapy centers around the search for
(a) values (b) meaning
(c) self-efficacy (d) None of these

40 Existential Phenomenological Psychology challenges the approaches in psychology that view human beings in a
(a) utilitartian manner (b) reductionist manner
(c) deterministic manner (d) positivist manner

41 What is the nature of Existential Phenomenology?
(a) Behaviourist (b) Cognitive
(c) Humanistic (d) Rationalist

42 Who proposed 'Cooperative Inquiry' as a method of research?
(a) John Hopkins (b) Peter Reason
(c) John Heron (d) None of these

43 Cooperative enquiry view is based on
(a) Positivistic (b) Participative
(c) Exemplar (d) Generative

44 According to Cooperative Inquiry each individual has presence in the world as
(a) naive (b) spiritual
(c) distinct (d) Both b and c

45 Cooperative inquiry in it research methods overlaps with
(a) qualitative, quantitative (b) quantitative, naturalistic
(c) qualitative, naturalistic (d) None of these

46 In Cooperative Inquiry people engage in cycles of
(a) action, participation (b) participation, proposition
(c) action, reflection (d) reflection, participation

47 The phase I of Cooperative Inquiry is a phase of
(a) propositional knowing (b) practical knowing
(c) experiential knowledge (d) consciousness

48 Both science and spirituality have .... epistemological contours.
(a) similar (b) distinct
(c) opposite (d) overlapping

49 Spirituality and science both spring from
(a) human mind (b) religion
(c) insatiable human needs (d) worldly affairs

50 Science is based on cognitive processing of information while spirituality is considered to be
(a) behavioural (b) transcognitive
(c) psychological (d) None of these

51 Science is based on
(a) reason (b) experiments
(c) observation (d) None of these

52 Based on the purpose of science it can be classified into two broad categories called
(a) Basic and Applied (b) Natural and Physical
(c) Social and Natural (d) Physical and Social

53 The major researchers related to 'Critical research or Critical theory' are
(a) Max Horkheimer and Karl Popper
(b) Jurgen Habermas and Max Horkheimer
(c) Max Horkheimer and Karl Marx
(d) Both b and c

54 The word 'Samkhya' in Indian philosophical practice means
(a) union of mind and body.
(b) knowledge of reality.
(c) knowledge of self.
(d) knowledge of self and universe.

55 The whole of human experience in this universe is made up of two aspects known as
(a) purusha and prakriti
(b) consciousness and matter
(c) the seer and the seen
(d) All of the above

56 What according to Yoga is the inward perceiving seeing consciousness and is lodged with the individuality of the seer?
(a) Adhibhuta (b) Adhyatma
(c) Purusha (d) Jiva

57 The word used in Yoga for the entire mind structure is called
(a) Antahkarana (b) Mann
(c) Chitta (d) Jiva

58 What does 'chitta-vritti-nirodhah' means in Yoga?
(a) Restraint of worldly stuff
(b) Freedom from anxiety
(c) Restraint to the mind stuff
(d) Subject and object correlation

59 Yoga as per Indian philosophy is a practical means to
(a) self-affirmation (b) self-acceptance
(c) self-realisation (d) self-energiser

60 The word 'Yoga' in its simplest sense means
(a) to integrate (b) to assimilate
(c) to unite (d) to transcend deep

61 Which among the following is one of the means of attaining Nirodhah?
(a) Yama (b) Nada Yoga
(c) Mantra Yoga (d) Laya Yoga

62 Although there is no intrinsic opposition between science and spirituality but there lies a difference in their
(a) ontology (b) epistemology
(c) methodology (d) Both b and c

63 In which traditions mind and self is considered different?
(a) Western Psychology
(b) Indian Psychology
(c) Both a and b
(d) None of the above

64 Which among the following are modes or states of mental activity
(a) Kripta (b) Mudha
(c) Viksipta (d) All of these

65 Who identified and described the four forms of knowing that occur in our ordinary waking consciousness?
(a) Buddha (b) Krishna
(c) Aurobindo (d) None of these

66 Memory is the function of the contact of these samskara with
(a) self (b) atman
(c) mind (d) None of these

67 Arrange the phases of Cooperative Inquiry in sequence of their occurence.
1. Experiences leading to new fields
2. Reframe
3. Reflection
4. Action

Codes
(a) 1, 2, 3, 4 (b) 4, 3, 2, 1
(c) 3, 4, 1, 2 (d) 1, 3, 2, 4

68 Arrange in order The scientific thoughts according to their emergence.
1. Rationalism 2. Positivism
3. Critical research
4. Post-positivism

Codes
(a) 1, 2, 3, 4 (b) 4, 1, 2, 3
(c) 1, 2, 4, 3 (d) 2, 1, 4, 3

69 Consider the following statements

1. Ontology refers to "the nature of our beliefs about reality."
2. Ontology helps to provide an understanding of the things that constitute the world, as it is known.

Which of the above is/are correct?

(a) Only 1 (b) Only 2
(c) Both 1 and 2 (d) None of these

70 Consider the following statements

1. Knowledge which is acquired by putting emphasis on reason is known as Intuitive knowledge.
2. Knowledge which has sources as beliefs, faith and intuition is known as Logical knowledge.

Which of the above is/are correct?

(a) Only 1 (b) Only 2
(c) Both 1 and 2 (d) None of these

71 Consider the following statements

1. Positivism is a philosophical stance that highlights the importance of objectivity and the necessity to study observable components.
2. Post-positivism is a philosophy that rejects positivism and presents new assumptions in order to unravel the truth.

Which among the above is/are correct?

(a) Only 1 (b) Only 2
(c) Both 1 and 2 (d) None of these

72 Consider the following statements

1. Horkheimer was one of the founder of Critical theory.
2. A Critical theory is not compulsorily required to identify the action to change it.

Which among the above is/are correct

(a) Only 1
(b) Only 2
(c) Both 1 and 2
(d) None of these

73 Consider the following statements

1. Social Constructionism regards individuals as integral of cultural, political and historical evolution in specific times and places.
2. Conventional psychology gives major importance to physiological and inherited aspects of human existence.

Which among the above is/are corrent?

(a) Only 1 (b) Only 2
(c) Both 1 and 2
(d) None of these

74 Consider the following statements

1. Cooperative inquiry is a way of working with other people who have similar concerns and interests.
2. Inquiry method can be both transformative and information about any human condition that has an open unbound awareness.

Which among the above is/are correct?

(a) Only 1 (b) Only 2
(c) Both 1 and 2 (d) None of these

75 Consider the following statements

1. The eight limbs described in the Patanjali Yoga-Sutras provide ways of purifying the body, emotions and mind.
2. Within the yogic and Indian psychology tradition the means of 'knowing' have been described with precision.

Which among the above is/are correct?

(a) Only 1 (b) Only 2
(c) Both 1 and 2 (d) None of these

76 Consider the following statements

1. Practising of Patanjali's Ashtanga yoga can help the researcher to adjust his or her very being.
2. It can allow more direct form of knowing the object of research.

Which among the above is/are correct?

(a) Only 1 (b) Only 2
(c) Both 1 and 2 (d) None of these

77 Consider the following statements

1. Most schools of Indian thought attribute ignorance as a reason for human sufferings.
2. Indian traditions and its application are not widespread in the field of therapy and transpersonal psychology.

Which among the above is/are correct?

(a) Only 1 (b) Only 2
(c) Both 1 and 2 (d) None of these

78 Consider the following statements

1. Indian perspective of psychology takes a qualitative and spiritual position and warrants inner development the may enable direct experience.
2. Indian perspective of psychology is more rigorous and inclusive than Western empirical approach.

Which among the above is/are correct?

(a) Only 1 (b) Only 2
(c) Both 1 and 2 (d) None of these

79 Consider the following statements

1. The term Vidya is used for science as well as philosophy.
2. A Sastra is a system of rules with its own techniques and concepts.

Which among the above is/are correct?

(a) Only 1 (b) Only 2
(c) Both 1 and 2 (d) None of these

80 Match the following

List I (Research Paradigms)	List II (Eminent Personality)
A. Epistemology	1. F Bacon
B. Methodology	2. Parmenides
C. Ontology	3. Plato
D. Theory of Knowledge	4. Socrates

Codes

	A	B	C	D		A	B	C	D
(a)	2	1	4	3	(b)	2	1	3	4
(c)	3	1	2	4	(d)	3	1	2	4

81 Match the following

List I (Type of Knowledge)	List II (Main Characteristics)
A. Propositional knowing	1. Artistic rehearsal process
B. Practical knowing	2. Feedback in real time
C. Experiential knowledge	3. Contemporary science
D. Presentational knowledge	4. Doing what is proposed

Codes

	A	B	C	D
(a)	4	3	2	1
(b)	2	1	3	4
(c)	1	3	4	2
(d)	3	4	2	1

82 Match the following

List I (Concept in Research)	List II (Explanation)
A. Inductive research	1. Know-how
B. Deductive research	2. Theory-building
C. Methodological skills	3. Know What
D. Theoretical skills	4. Theory-testing

Codes

	A	B	C	D		A	B	C	D
(a)	4	2	1	3	(b)	2	4	1	3
(c)	2	4	3	1	(d)	1	3	2	4

83 Match the following

List I (Researchers)	List II (Paradigms of Knowledge)
A. Karl Popper	1. Positivism
B. Francis Bacon	2. Empiricism
C. Auguste Comte	3. Natural-philosophy
D. Galileo	4. Post-positivism

Codes

	A	B	C	D
(a)	2	4	1	3
(b)	4	2	3	1
(c)	4	2	1	3
(d)	1	2	3	4

Direction (Q. Nos.84-103) In the questions given below are two statements labelled as Assertion (A) and Reason (R). In the context of the two statements, which of the following is correct?

Codes

(a) Both A and R are true and R is the correct explanation of A
(b) Both A and R are true, but R is not the correct explanation of A
(c) A is true, but R is false
(d) A is false, but R is true

84 Assertion (A) Researcher's position regarding Ontology will determine how, questions and answers about the nature of both social and political reality are to be investigated.

Reason (R) Researcher's Ontological view determines the focus, chosen methods and how data is gathered, interpreted or analysed.

85 Assertion (A) A researcher with subjective ontological assumption believes in awareness of social conditions which can be achieved through interaction with environment and experience.

Reason (R) Researcher with subjective ontological view gather qualitative data.

86 Assertion (A) A researcher can have an objective assumption for his research and gathers quantitative data.

Reason (R) Objective researcher needs to rely on experience and awareness of social conditions for his study.

87 Assertion (A) Positivism and Subjectivism are two important aspects of Ontology.

Reason (R) Positivism says that social entities exist in reality and are external to social factors concerned with their existence.

88 Assertion (A) Subjectivism approach of a researcher is wholly anti-positivist.

Reason (R) In this approach researcher views the world to be interpreted by those engaged in it and understanding their perceptions.

89 Assertion (A) Subjective approach in research does not generate data that is generalisable.

Reason (R) Subjective paradigm generates contextual data/knowledge.

90 Assertion (A) Epistemology is an acquisition of knowledge.

Reason (R) Epistemology is concerned with nature and sources of knowledge.

91 **Assertion** (A) Intuitive knowledge is based on beliefs and faith.

Reason (R) Emotions and feelings do not have significance in this knowledge.

92 **Assertion** (A) In existential therapy, human relationship between patient and therapist takes precedence over therapeutic interventions.

Reason (B) Existential therapy is based on honesty.

93 **Assertion** (A) Western psychology has bits of theories relevant to specific areas, but not an overreaching theory encompassing the entire field.

Reason (R) Western psychology is wholistic in its approach.

94 **Assertion** (A) Indian psychology has implications that are broader than psychology itself.

Reason (R) It can be applied to areas which contemporary psychology fails to address.

95 **Assertion** (A) The goal of science and spirituality is same goal *i.e.* search of truth.

Reason (R) In contemporary world, spiritual quest is the dominant force.

96 **Assertion** (A) Both science and spirituality share a common goal of emanicipation of the human condition from suffering to a state of happiness and well-being.

Reason (R) Both science and spirituality share a common epistemology to reach their goal.

97 **Assertion** (A) The fundamental units for spiritual experiences is the existence of intuitive mode.

Reason (R) For scientific understanding the fundamental unit of study is brain and sensory functioning.

98 **Assertion** (A) Positivism relies on theories that can be observed directly and is objective in nature.

Reason (R) Human thoughts and emotions can be easily measured through positivists methods.

99 **Assertion** (A) Western doctrine of evolution propose that human beings advance from a lower level to a higher level of existence.

Reason (R) Western philosophy states that there is an ascent and therefore, an improvement, from matter to life, life to mind, mind to intellect.

100 **Assertion** (A) 'Yoga' states that it is essential for humans to control their mind in order to achieve higher level of consciousness.

Reason (R) Mind is the root cause of all troubles in one's life.

101 **Assertion** (A) Yoga is a version of stimulus-intensity reduction theory of motivation and is psychological in nature.

Reason (R) Yoga promotes chitta-vritti-nirodhah.

102 **Assertion** (A) There is a need for a meta-theory, which aims at unification of science and spirituality.

Reason (R) The influence of science and spirituality on humans are distinct and there effect on human life is independent of each other.

103 **Assertion** (A) The need of a meta theory between science and spirituality must postulate unity and complementarity between the two.

Reason (R) Spiritual psychology attempts to gain unified understanding of the transcendental and empirical domains of human existence and experience.

Directions (Q. Nos. 104-108) *Read the passage given below and answer the following questions.*

Within the yogic and Indian psychology traditions the means of 'Knowing' have been described with precision. Three aspects of knowing are the refinement of knowing within the training system of the Patanjali Yoga-Sutras, Sri Aurobindo's views of the four types of knowledge and Sri Aurobindo's views of the process of intuition.

The eight limbs described in the Patanjali Yoga-Sutras provide ways of readying and purifying the body, emotions and mind for a form of knowing through being or identifying with what is to be known, achieved through 'Samyama,' the intensive and conjoint practice of the last three limbs of dharana (concentration), dhyana (contemplation or meditation) and samadhi (absorption).

The several limbs of Patanjali Rajayoga *i.e.* yama, niyama, asana, pranayama, pratyahara, dharana, dhyana, samadhi-provide methods for systematically reducing the possible environmental social, bodily, sensory, emotional and cognitive sources of noise or distraction that might serve as impediments to or distortions of accurate and sensitive knowing.

104 **In which traditions 'knowing' have been described with precision.**

(a) Oriental psychology (b) Indian psychology
(c) Western psychology (d) None of these

105 **Patanjali yoga-sutras consist of**

(a) 5 limbs (b) 6 limbs
(c) 7 limbs (d) 8 limbs

106 Patanjali yoga-sutras provide ways of readying and purifying the

(a) body (b) emotions
(c) mind (d) All of these

107 'Samyama', the intensive and conjoint practice includes

(a) dharana (concentration)
(b) dhyana (meditation)
(c) Samadhi (absorption)
(d) All of the above

108 Which among the following are part of Patanjali Raja yoga?

1. Yama 2. Niyama
3. Sanyama
4. Pratyahara

Codes

(a) 1 and 2
(b) Only 3
(c) 1, 2, and 4
(d) All of the above

ANSWERS

1 (d)	2 (b)	3 (c)	4 (c)	5 (a)	6 (d)	7 (d)	8 (d)	9 (c)	10 (b)
11 (b)	12 (c)	13 (b)	14 (d)	15 (a)	16 (a)	17 (c)	18 (c)	19 (b)	20 (d)
21 (a)	22 (c)	23 (a)	24 (c)	25 (a)	26 (a)	27 (c)	28 (d)	29 (d)	30 (a)
31 (c)	32 (a)	33 (d)	34 (a)	35 (a)	36 (d)	37 (c)	38 (a)	39 (b)	40 (d)
41 (c)	42 (c)	43 (b)	44 (d)	45 (a)	46 (c)	47 (a)	48 (b)	49 (a)	50 (b)
51 (c)	52 (a)	53 (d)	54 (b)	55 (d)	56 (b)	57 (c)	58 (c)	59 (c)	60 (c)
61 (a)	62 (d)	63 (b)	64 (d)	65 (c)	66 (c)	67 (c)	68 (c)	69 (c)	70 (d)
71 (c)	72 (a)	73 (c)	74 (c)	75 (c)	76 (c)	77 (a)	78 (c)	79 (c)	80 (c)
81 (d)	82 (b)	83 (c)	84 (a)	85 (a)	86 (c)	87 (b)	88 (a)	89 (a)	90 (a)
91 (c)	92 (a)	93 (c)	94 (a)	95 (c)	96 (c)	97 (b)	98 (c)	99 (a)	100 (a)
101 (a)	102 (c)	103 (b)	104 (b)	105 (d)	106 (d)	107 (d)	108 (c)		
111 (c)	112 (b)	113 (c)	114 (c)						

Research : Meaning, Purpose and Dimensions

The goal of psychological research is to discover, describe, explain the change of behaviour. For this, we need to understand behaviours and the events that are responsible for their occurrence in a language i.e. both precise enough to be understood by others and general enough to apply to a wide variety of situations.

Research

Research is a careful and detailed study of a specific problem, concern or issue using the scientific method. It is defined as a careful consideration of study regarding a particular concern on a problem using scientific methods. The term research is also used to describe "as an entire collection of information about a particular subject or topic." Research is defined as human activity that are based on intellectual application in the investigation of matter. The purpose of research is to discover, interpret and to develop methods and systems for the advancement of human knowledge on a wide variety of scientific matters of our world and the universe.

Definitions of Research

Some of the definitions of research are given below which can help you to understand proper meaning and concept of research.

According to **Earl Robert Babbie**, "Research is a systematic inquiry to describe, explain, predict and control the observed phenomenon. Research involves inductive and deductive methods."

According to **Kerlinger**,"Research is systematic, controlled, empirical and critical investigation of hypothetical propositions about the presumed relationship about various phenomena."

According to **Burns**, "Research is a systematic investigation to find answers to a problem."

In this Chapter

- Research
  - Research Problem
- Variables and Operational Definitions
- Hypothesis
- Sampling
- Research Ethics

According to **John W Creswell**, "Research is a process of steps used to collect and analyse information to increase our understanding of a topic or issue."

Characteristics of Research

- Research is always directed towards the solution of problem.
- Research is always based on empirical or observable evidence.
- Research involves precise observation and accurate description.
- Research is characterised by systematic, objective and logical procedure.
- Research is replicable.
- Research requires skills of writing and reproducing the report.
- Research gives emphasis to the development of theories, principles and generalisations, which are very helpful for the accurate prediction of variables under study.

Purpose of Research

The purpose of research is to discover answers to questions through the application of scientific procedures. The main aim of research is to find out the truth which is hidden and which has not been discovered yet.

Though each research study has its own specific purpose, we may think of research objectives as falling into a number of following broad groupings.

- To get introduced with a process for achieving new insights into the subject. Studies with this purpose are known as *exploratory or formulative research studies.*
- To test a hypothesis for ascertaining causal relationship between two or more variables. These studies are termed as *hypothesis testing research.*
- To findout the features of a particular individual situation or a group perfectly. The studies with this type of purpose are known as *descriptive research studies.*
- To evaluate the frequency with which something occurs or with which it is associated with something else. Thess type of studies with this purpose are known as *diagnostic research studies.*

Purpose of Psychological Research

Psychological researchers want to know and understand human behaviour. It can be about how people think, how they feel, how they behave or some combination of these issues.

Research and the understanding that follows, trickles down from the scientists and alters society. More specifically, psychological research is used to measure, describe and categorise human behaviour.

Dimensions of Research

The dimensions of research are vibrant, they can be classified or categorised on the basis of purpose, context, use and time etc. *The major dimensions of research are given below*

On the Basis of Purpose

On the basis purpose of the study dimension of research can be categorised as

- **Exploration Research** Exploratory research is often the first step in a sequence of studies analysing a social phenomenon that is largely unknown. Exploratory research most often addresses the 'what' question. Exploratory researchers frequently use qualitative techniques to keenly observe and collect data for analysis.
- **Descriptive Research** Descriptive research requires a more developed idea about a social phenomenon. Here, researchers engage in clearly describing or detailing a social setting or relationship. Descriptive research focuses on 'how' and 'who' questions.
- **Explanation** When researchers engage in explanation, they are actively attempting to explain and answer the 'why' question. Thus, explanation builds on already existing knowledge collected about a social phenomenon as a result of more basic exploratory and descriptive studies.

On the Basis of Context

On the basis of context research can be categorised as

- **Idiographic** 'Idio-' in this context means unique, separate, peculiar or distinct, as in the word 'idiosyncrasy'. When we have completed an idiographic explanation, we feel that we fully understand the causes of what happened at a particular instance. At the same time our scope of explanation is limited to the case at hand. While parts of the idiographic explanation might apply to other situations also, our intention is to explain a complete case.
- **Nomothetic** Seeks to explain a class of situations or events rather than a single one. Moreover, it seeks to explain 'efficiently,' using only one or just a few explanatory factors. Finally, it settles for partial rather than full explanation of a type of situation.

On the Basis of Use

- **Basic Research** Basic research is mostly conducted to enhance knowledge. It covers fundamental aspects of research. The main motivation of this research is knowledge expansion. It is a non-commercial research and doesn't facilitate in creating or inventing anything. *For example-* An experiment is a good example of basic research.
- **Applied Research** Applied research focuses on analysing and solving real life problems. This type of research refers to the study that helps solve practical problems using scientific methods. This research plays an important role in solving issues that impact the overall well-being of humans. *For example-* Finding a specific cure for a disease.
- **Problem Oriented Research** As the name suggests, problem-oriented research is conducted to understand the exact nature of the problem and to find out relevant solutions. The term 'problem' refers to having issues or two thoughts while making any decisions.
- **Problem-Solving Research** This type of research is conducted by companies to understand and resolve their own problems. The problem-solving research uses applied research to find solutions to the existing problems.

Research Problem

A research problem, in general, refers to some difficulty, which a researcher experiences in the context of either a theoretical or practical situation and wants to obtain a solution for the same. Conditions for declaring something as a research problem *are*

- There must be an individual or a group, which has some difficulty or the problem.
- There must be some objectives to be attained at. If one wants nothing, one can't have a problem.
- There must be alternative means (or the course of action) for finding out the objectives one wishes to attain.
- There must be some doubt in mind of a researcher with regard to the selection of alternatives. This means that research must answer the question concerning the relative efficiency of the possible alternatives.

Selecting the Problem

The research problem undertaken for study must be carefully selected. The task may be difficult one, although it may not appear to be so. Help may be taken from a research guide in this connection.

However, the following points may be observed by a researcher in selecting a research problem or subject for research.

- Subject which is overdone should not be normally chosen, as it will be a difficult task to throw any new light in such a case.
- Controversial subject should not become the choice of an average researcher.
- Too narrow or too vague problem should be avoided.
- The subject selected for research should be familiar and feasible, so that the related research material or sources of research are within one's reach.
- The importance of the subject, the qualifications and training of a researcher, the costs involved, the time factor are few other criteria that must also be considered while selecting a problem.
- The selection of a problem must be preceded by a preliminary study. This may not be necessary when the problem requires the conduct of a research closely similar to one that has already been done. But when the field of inquiry is relatively new and does not have available set of well developed techniques, a brief feasibility study must always be undertaken.

Techniques Involved in Defining a Problem

The usual approach is that the researcher should himself pose a question (or in case someone else wants the researcher to carry on research, the concerned individual, organisation or any authority should pose the question to researcher) and sort out techniques and procedures for throwing light on the question concerned for formulating or defining the research problem. But such an approach generally does not produce definitive results because the question phrased in such a fashion is usually in broad general terms and as such may not be in a form suitable for testing.

The following steps are followed in understanding problem

- Statement of the problem in a general way.
- Understanding the nature of the problem.
- Surveying the available literature.
- Developing the ideas through discussion.
- Rephrasing the research problems.

The task of defining a research problem, very often, follows a sequential pattern-the problem is stated in general way, the ambiguities are resolved, thinking and rethinking process results in a more specific formulation of the problem, so that it may be a realistic one in terms of the available data and resources and is also analytically meaningful. All this results in a well defined research problem that is not only meaningful from an operational point of view, but also equally capable of paving the way for the development of working hypothesis and for means of solving the problem itself.

Research Biases

One of the challenges, while doing research is to remain free from biases. Most of your ideas and beliefs are probably linked with certain biasness because they are influenced by your opinions or values. A variety of biases that have been found to distort people's impressions of collected data, *are as follows*

- **External Influences** Such as one's culture or the media can influence people to accept a particular view.
- **Personal Bias** It distorts estimating or evaluating processes as a result of personal beliefs, attributes or past experiences.
- **Observer Bias** It operates when some events are taken as meaningful by some and not taken as meaningful by others. It must be kept in mind that researchers raised in certain cultures and societies. They also might have been exposed to certain gender role expectations. These background factors can affect the way that researchers observe and interpret events in their lives.
- **Expectancy Bias** It can affect observations of behaviour by encouraging reactions to the events, being observed. Researchers sometimes expect to find specific outcomes, what they expect to see rather than remaining objective. Unfortunately, if one is not alert to the possibility of expectancy bias, it may seem as though the observed events are being 'discovered' instead of created by the observer's expectations.

Variables and Operational Definitions

Webster says that a variable is 'a thing that is changeable' or 'a quantity that may have a number of different values.' A variable, as the name implies, is something which varies. It is defined as those attributes of objects, events, things and beings, which can be measured *e.g.* intelligence, anxiety, aptitude, income, education etc. which are examples of variables, commonly employed in psychology, education and sociology.

It is also important that the values of the variable be observable. Thus, if what is being studied is a variable, it has more than one value and each value can be observed.

Definitions of Variables

Various research scientists and scholars have tried to provide a more precise and specialised definition of variables. *Some of those definitions are as follows*

According to **Kerlinger,** "Variable is a property that takes as different values."

According to **D'Amato**, "Variables may be defined as those attributes of objects, events, things and beings, which can be measured."

According to **Postman and Egan,** "A variable is a characteristic or attribute that can take on a number of values."

Use of Operational Definitions

The variables are related to the theoretical concepts by means of the operational definitions used to measure the concepts. It is important to know how the study variables are related to a theoretical concept. Because the study variables have some value but the theory is an idea, researcher make certain assumption to relate the two. These assumption are guide ropes that tie a theory to the real world. The variables are tangible : duration, frequency, rate or intensity of bar presses; items checked on a questionnaire; murders committed; book written etc. The theoretical concept is intangible. Suppose a theory reveals that increasing anxiety will increase the affiliation motive. To test out this theory, you may take the theoretical concept of anxiety and affiliation motive and relate them to variables by means of operational definitions.

Psychologists are interested in studying the behaviour or causes of behaviour as variables. Many psychologists have adopted a theoretical viewpoint or model called the S-O-R model to explain all behaviour.

S-O-R Model

The symbols S, O and R represent different categories of variables. S is the symbol of **stimuli** and categorised as stimuli variables. O is the symbol for **organism** variables, finally, R is the symbol for **response** variables.

A stimulus variable is some form of energy in the environment, such as light, to which the organism is sensitive. Organism variables are those that has the changeable physiological and psychological characteristics of the organisms being observed. Response variables refer to some behaviour or action of the organism like pressing a lever and reaction to any stimulus.

Types of Variables

The description of different types of variables are given below

Independent Variables

Independent variables are manipulated by the experimenter. The brightness of a lamp, the loudness of a tone, the number of decompressions given to a rate are all independent variables, because the experimenter thinks, they will cause changes in behaviour.

Increasing the intensity of a tone should increase the speed, with which people respond to the tone. Increasing the number of decompressions given to the mother rat may change the rate of development of her babies, when a change in the level of an independent variable causes a change in behaviour, we say that behaviour is under the control of independent variable.

Dependent Variables

The dependent variable is observed and recorded by the experimenter. It depends on the behaviour of the participant, which in turn, is supposed to depend on the independent variable.
The time it takes to press a switch,the speed of a worm crawling through a maze and the age when a rat climbes are all dependent variables because they are observed and recorded by the experimenter.
One criterion for a good dependent variable is reliability. When an experiment is repeated exactly with same participant, at same levels of independent variable it should yield the same score as previously. Unreliability can occur, if there is some deficit in the way we measure the dependent variable.

Extraneous Variables

Extraneous variables are those variables that operate in the experimental situation in addition to the independent variable and also affect the dependent variable.

Some of the techniques to control extraneous variables are

- **Elimination** It involve eliminating the variable completely. *For example-* If noise is extraneous variable their experiment can be conducted is sound proof situation or settings.
- **Constancy** If elimination is not possible then control over the extraneous variable can be made by holding their values constant in all situation. *For example-* If sex, age etc. are extraneous variables then chosing the subject of same sex, intelligence and age can provide control.
- **Balancing** In this method, participants in control group and experimental group are made equal in all respect. This is done when constancy of conditions are not possible.
- **Counter Balancing** It is used to control extraneous variable occurring as a result of practice or fatigue together called as order effect.
- **Randomisation** It refers to a technique, in which each member of the population or universe has an equal and independent chance of being selected. This technique is applied where the extraneous variable are known.

Confounding Variables

Confounding variable is one that varies with the independent variable. While doing a study if we are not careful then two variables may get combined so that the effect of one cannot be separated from the effect of other. This is known as *confounding*. Confounding makes the conclusion of the study doubtful. It is therefore, necessary that effort should be made to unconfound the variables.

Active Variables

Any variable that can be manipulated is called *active variables*. Example of active variables are reward, punishment, methods of teaching, creating anxiety through instructions and so on.

Attribute Variables

It is that variable which is not manipulated but measured by the experimenter. Variables that are human characteristics like intelligence, aptitudes, sex, socio-economic status, education, field dependence and need for achievement are the examples of attribute variables.

Hypothesis

In conducting research, the next step after the selection of the problem is to formulate a hypothesis. A hypothesis is a testable relationship between two or more than two variables. McGuigan has defined hypothesis as, "a testable statement of a potential relationship between two variables, *i.e.* advanced as potential solution to the problem."

On the basis of this definition, two points can be suggested about a hypothesis. *First,* a hypothesis is a testable statement, which means that it displays the relationship between those variables, which are measurable or potentially measurable. *Second,* a hypothesis exhibits either a general or specific relationship between variables.

Characteristics of Hypothesis

A hypothesis indicates, what we are looking for. It is a proposition, which always looks forward. After testing the hypothesis, the investigator may find it to be correct or incorrect.

If it proves to be correct, the problem is solved and if it proves to be incorrect, the problem is not solved. There are several criterions or characteristics of a good research hypothesis. A good hypothesis is one, which meets such criteria or incorporates the following characteristics to a large extent.

Some of the characteristics are enumerated below

- The hypothesis should be conceptually clear. A good research hypothesis is one which is based upon operationally defined concepts.
- The hypothesis must be testable. It should be formulated in a way that can be tested directly and found to be probably true or probably false.
- The hypothesis should be economical and parsimonious. If several hypothesis are offered to test a research problem, the more economical ones should be preferred to hypothesis involving higher monetory expenses.
- The hypothesis should be related to the existing theory and fact. If the investigator advances a hypothesis, which seems to him of interest, but is not related to the existing body of theory of facts, it cannot be a good research hypothesis.
- The hypothesis should have logical unity and comprehensiveness. If several hypothesis can be formulated regarding the same research problem, the most logical comprehensive one should be preferred.
- The hypothesis should be general in scope. A general hypothesis permits several deductions and thus, explains several facts at a time.
- The hypothesis should be related to available scientific tools and techniques. A hypothesis, about which data cannot be collected because no scientific tools or techniques are available, cannot be a good research hypothesis.
- The hypothesis should be in accord with other hypothesis of the same field. While this is not an essential condition, if any hypothesis satisfies this criterion, it can be claimed to be a good research hypothesis.

Difficulties in Formulating a Hypothesis

Goode and Hatt have pointed out three major possible difficulties in formulation of a good research hypothesis.

(i) The absence of knowledge of a theoretical framework is a major difficulty in formulating a good research hypothesis. If detailed theoretical evidences are not available or if the investigator is not aware of the availability of those theoretical evidences, a research hypothesis cannot be formulated.

(ii) When the investigator lacks the ability to utilise the knowledge of the theoretical framework, a hypothesis cannot be formulated.

(iii) When the investigator is not aware of the important scientific research techniques, he will not be able to frame a good research hypothesis.

A Good Hypothesis

Good hypothesis are made, not born. Researcher often become interested in a question about human behaviour for personal reasons, but the ultimate value of research study depends on the researcher's methodological criteria selected for the hypothesis testing.

Hypothesis plays a key role in formulating and guiding any study. A researcher should consider certain points while formulating a hypothesis.

(i) Expected relationship or differences between the variables.

(ii) Operational definition of variables.

(iii) Hypothesis are formulated following the review of literature.

According to **Russell and Reichenbach**, "the hypothesis should be stated in the logical form on the general implications. 'A' hypothesis can be put in the form of a statement; if A is true then 'B' should follow. *For example-* Verbal development theory of amnesia states that childhood amnesia is caused by the development of language."

Types of Hypothesis

Theoretically, there should be one type of hypothesis on the basis of the investigation *i.e.* research hypothesis. However, because of the conventions in scientific enquiries and the words used in the constructions of the hypothesis, hypothesis can be classified into several types, like; universal hypothesis, existential hypothesis, conceptual hypothesis etc. Broadly, there are two categories of the hypothesis

(i) Null hypothesis (ii) Alternative hypothesis

(i) **Null Hypothesis** In its simplest form, this hypothesis asserts that there is no true difference between two population means and the difference found between sample means is accidental and unimportant. It arises out of fluctuation in sampling and by chance.
Null hypothesis is a useful tool in testing the significance of difference. Traditionally null hypothesis stated that there is zero relationship between the terms of the hypothesis.

(ii) **Alternative Hypothesis** Alternative hypothesis is the hypothesis that specifies those values that the researcher believes to hold true and hopes that the sample data will lead to acceptance of this hypothesis as true.

Errors in Testing Hypothesis

Hypothesis has probability of either being correct or incorrect. It is possible to arrive at a incorrect conclusion about a hypothesis for the various reasons if

- Sampling procedure adopted is faulty.
- Data collection method is inaccurate.
- Study design selected is faulty.
- In appropriate statistical methods used.
- Conclusion drawn are incorrect.

Two common errors exists while testing a hypothesis.

Type I error-Rejection of a null hypothesis when it is true.

Type II error-Acceptance of a null hypothesis when it is false.

Sampling

Sampling is the process of selection of units (*e.g.* people, organisation) from a population of interest so that by studying, the sample may fairly generate results back to the population from which they were chosen. Ideally sample corresponds to the larger population on the characteristics of interest. In the case, the researcher's conclusions from the samples are applicable to the entire population.

Definitions of Sampling

According to **Blalock**, "Sample is a small piece of the population obtained by a probability process that mirrors with known precision, the various patterns and sub-classes of population."

According to **Goode and Hatt**, "A sample, as the name implies, is a smaller representative of a large whole."

According to **Young**, "A statistical sample is miniature picture of cross selection of the entire group or aggregate from which the sample is taken."

Objectives of Sampling

The objective of sampling is to derive the desired information about the population at the minimum cost or with the maximum reliability. Further, the aim in selecting a sample is to achieve maximum precision in estimates within a given sample size and to avoid bias in the selection of sample. Bias in the selection of sample can take place if

- The researcher selects the sample by non random method and influenced by human choice.
- The researcher does not cover the sampling population accurately and completely.
- A section of a sample population is impossible to find as refuses to cooperate.

Sampling Methods

According to **Blalock** most sampling methods could be classified into two categories

(i) Non probability sampling method
(ii) Probability sampling method

Non Probability Sampling Methods

Non probability sampling is one in which there is no way of assessing the probability of the element or group of elements, of population being included in the sample. *Important techniques of non-probability sampling methods are*

(i) **Haphazard, Accidental or Convenience Sampling** Haphazard sampling can produce ineffective, highly unrepresentative samples and is not recommended. When a researcher haphazardly selects cases that are convenient, he or she can easily get a sample that seriously misrepresents the population. *For example* An investigator may take student of class X into research plan because the class teacher of the class happens to be his/her friend. This illustrates accidental or convenience sampling.

(ii) **Quota Sampling** Quota sampling is an improvement over haphazard sampling. In quota sampling, a researcher first identifies relevant categories of people (*e.g.* male and female or under age 30, ages 30 to 60, over age 60 etc.) then decides how many to get in each category. Thus, the number of people in various categories of the sample is fixed. Quota sampling ensures that some differences exist in the sample. In haphazard sampling, all those interviewed might be of the same age, sex or background.

(iii) **Purposive Sampling** Purposive sampling is a valuable kind of sampling for special situations. It is used in exploratory research or in field research. It uses the judgment of an expert in selecting cases or it selects cases with a specific purpose in mind. With purposive sampling,the researcher never knows whether the cases selected represent the population. Purposive sampling is appropriate to select unique cases that are especially informative.

(iv) **Snowball Sampling** Snowball sampling is also known as *network,* chain referral or reputation sampling method. Snowball sampling which is a non probability sampling method is basically sociometric. It begins by the collection of data on one or more contacts usually known to the person collecting the data. At the end of the data collection process (*e.g.* questionnaire, survey or interview), the data collector asks the respondent to provide contact information for other potential respondents. These potential respondents are contacted and provided more contacts. Snowball sampling is most useful when there are very few methods to secure a list of the population or when the population is unknowable.

(v) **Systematic Sampling** Systematic sampling is another method of non-probability sampling plan, though the label 'systematic' is somewhat misleading in the sense that all probability sampling methods are systematic sampling methods. Due to this, it often sounds that systematic sampling should be included under one category of probability sampling, but in reality this is not the case.

Probability Sampling Methods

Probability sampling methods are those that clearly specify the probability or likelihood of inclusion of each element or individual in the sample. Probability sampling is free of bias in selecting sample units.

They help in estimation of sampling errors and evaluate sample results in terms of their precision, accuracy and efficiency. Hence, the conclusions reached from such samples are worth generalisation and comparable to similar population to which they belong.

Major probability sampling methods are

(i) **Simple Random Sampling** A simple random sample requires

- A complete listing of all the elements.
- An equal chance for each elements to be selected.
- A selection process whereby the selection of one element has no effect on the chance of selecting another element.

For example- If we are to select a sample of 10 students from the seventh grade consisting of 40 students, we can write the names (or roll number) of each of the 40 students on separate slips of paper, all equal in size and colour and fold them in a similar way. Subsequently, they may be placed in a box and reshuffled thoroughly.

(ii) **Stratified Random Sampling** In stratified random sampling the population is divided into two or more strata, which may be based upon a single criterion such as sex, yielding two strata-male and female or upon a combination of two or more criteria such as sex and graduation, yielding four strata, namely, male undergraduates, male graduates, female undergraduates and female graduates.

These divided populations are called *subpopulations*, which are non-overlapping and together constitute the whole population.

(iii) **Cluster Sampling** A type of random sample that uses multiple stages and is often used to cover wide geographic areas in which aggregated units are randomly selected and then sample are drawn from the sampled aggregated units or cluster.

Research Ethics

Research ethics address the application of ethical principles or values to the various issues in the field of research. This includes ethical aspects of the design and conduct of research, the way human participants or animals within research projects are treated, whether research results may be misused for criminal purpose. It (also) refers on aspects of scientific misconduct.

Research integrity is recognised as the attitude and habit of the researchers to conduct research according to appropriate legal, ethical and professional frameworks, obligations and standards. The fields of research ethics and research integrity combine general ethical reflections, ethics and law as academic discipline addressing researcher's activities, moral attitudes of researchers, normative policies of stakeholders like sponsors on funding organisations and various ethical expectations of the civil society.

Codes and Policies For Research Ethics

Given the importance of ethics for the conduct of research, multiple agencies, association and universities have adopted specific codes, rules and policies relating to research ethics.

The following is a rough and general summary of some ethical principles

- **Honesty** Honestly report data, results, methods, procedures and publication status. Do not fabricate, falsify or misrepresent data. Do not deceive colleagues, research sponsors or the public.
- **Objectivity** Strive to avoid bias in experimental design, data analysis, data interpretation, peer review, personnel decisions, grant writing, expert testimony and other aspects of research where objectivity is expected or required. Avoid or minimise bias or self-deception. Disclose personal or financial interests that may affect research.
- **Integrity** Keep your promises and agreements; act with sincerity; strive for consistency of thought and action.
- **Carefulness** Avoid careless errors and negligence; carefully and critically examine your own work and the work of your peers. Keep good records of researcher's activities, such as data collection, research design and correspondence with agencies or journals.
- **Openness** Share data, results, ideas, tools and resources. Be open to criticism and new ideas.
- **Respect for Intellectual Property** Honor patents, copyrights and other forms of intellectual property. Do not use unpublished data, methods or results without permission. Give proper acknowledgement or credit for all contributions to research.
- **Confidentiality** Protect confidential communications, such as papers or grants submitted for publication, personnel records, trade or military secrets and patient's records.
- **Responsible Publication** Publish in order to advance research and scholarship, not to advance just your own career. Avoid wasteful and duplicative publication.
- **Responsible Mentoring** Help to educate, mentor and advise students. Promote their welfare and allow them to make their own decisions.
- **Social Responsibility** Strive to promote social good and prevent or mitigate social harms through research public education and advocacy.
- **Non-Discrimination** Avoid discrimination against colleagues or students on the basis of sex, race, ethnicity, or other factors not related to scientific competence and integrity.
- **Competence** Maintain and improve your own professional competence and expertise through lifelong education and learning; take steps to promote competence in science as a whole.
- **Legality** Know and obey relevant laws and institutional and governmental policies.
- **Animal Cares** Show proper respect and care for animals while using them in research. Do not conduct unnecessary or poorly designed animal experiments.
- **Human Subjects Protection** When conducting research on human subjects, minimise harms and risks and maximise benefits; respect human dignity, privacy and autonomy; take special precautions with vulnerable populations and strive to distribute the benefits and burdens of research fairly.

Ethical Issues in Psychological Research

All research conducted by trained psychologists is performed in accordance with strict ethical standards designed to protect the safety, privacy and well-being of all research participants.

The major ethical issues regarding psychological research are

- **Deception** The temporary withholding of information about a study from participants.
- **Informed Consent** A principle requiring that research participants be provided with information about all events and procedures a study will involve before they agree to participate in it.
- **Debriefing** Providing research participants with full information about all aspects of a study refer they have participated in it.

An example to explain these ethical issues regarding psychological research is as follow

Let's assume that you are a participant in a study designed to test the following hypothesis: "The more attractive people are, the better they are in making first impressions on others." To test the hypothesis, the experimenter arrange for you to meet several people. One who is unattrative, another who is average in appearance and a third who is a real knockout and then asks you to rate your liking for each. Suppose that before, the study begins, the psychologist explains the hypothesis to you.

Do you think this knowledge could influence your behaviour? Perhaps one possibility is that, knowing what the psychologist hypothesis you can express even greater liking for the attractive person than you might normally do. Another possibility is that you decide to show the researcher that you are not so easy to predict, so you actually report liking the unattractive person most.

It is in order to avoid such effects that psychologists sometimes choose to withhold information about the hypothesis they are investigating and other details of the research. This process of temporary withholding of information from participants is called *Deception*.

Although this issue remains controversial, most psychologists believe that deception is permissible, provided that two basic principles are followed.

The first involves obtaining **informed consents** providing research participants with as much information as possible about events and procedures, a study will involve before they agree to participate in it. The second principle known as *debriefing,* requires that research participants be given full information about all aspects of a study, including deception, after they have participated in it. These practices in a research make it **ethical** in nature.

EXAM BASED QUESTIONS

1 Which among the following is not right about research?
(a) It requires a detailed study
(b) It does not require a specific problem
(c) It can use scientific method
(d) It requires a problem solving approach

2 "Research is a systematic investigation to find answers to a problem". Who said these words?
(a) Kerlinger (b) John W Creswell
(c) Burns (d) Earl Robert Bobbie

3 Which among the following are the objective of Psychological research?
(a) To learn and understand human behaviour.
(b) To measure, describe and categorise human behaviour.
(c) Both a and b
(d) None of the above

4 Which among the following are the characteristics of research?
(a) Research is replicable.
(b) Research requires skills of writing and reproducing the report.
(c) It is based on empirical evidences.
(d) All of the above

5 Which among the following is not a characteristics of research?
(a) It is based on observable evidence.
(b) It involves precise observation.
(c) It is based on presumptive evidence.
(d) It is directed towards the solution of a problem.

6 The studies with an objective to get introduced with a process for achieving new insights into it are known as
(a) Hypothesis testing research
(b) Exploratory research
(c) Descriptive research
(d) Diagnostic research

7 A study to test a hypothesis of a causal relationship between two or more variables is known as
(a) Hypothesis testing research
(b) Formulative research
(c) Descriptive research
(d) Diagnostic research

8 A study to draw the features of a particular individual's situation or a group perfectly is known as
(a) Diagnostic research (b) Formulative research
(c) Descriptive research
(d) Hypothesis testing research

9 Which among the following is a study to evaluate the frequency with which something occurs or with which it is associated with something else?
(a) Diagnostic research (b) Hypothesis research
(c) Formulative research (d) None of the above

10 Which kind of research most often addresses the 'what' questions?
(a) Exploration research (b) Descriptive research
(c) Explanation research (d) Idiographic research

11 Which research has the purpose to focus on 'how' and 'what' question?
(a) Nomothetic research (b) Basic research
(c) Descriptive research (d) None of the above

12 The research which actively attempt to address and answer the 'why' question is known as
(a) Nomothetic research (b) Explanation research
(c) Idiographic research (d) Applied research

13 A research that seeks to explain a class of situations or events rather than a single one is known as
(a) Basic research (b) Applied research
(c) Nomothetic research (d) Idiographic research

14 **The main motive of Basic research is**
(a) to increase data (b) to reduce hypothesis
(c) to understand situation (d) to enhance knowledge

15 **Research focused to analyse and solve real-life problems are known as**
(a) Problem oriented research
(b) Applied research
(c) Problem solving research
(d) Basic research

16 **Problem oriented research is conducted**
(a) to understand the exact nature of the problem.
(b) to resolve their own problems by companies.
(c) solving issues that impact the overall well-being of humans.
(d) None of the above

17 **'Difficulties', a researcher experiences in the context of either a theoretical or practical situation are known as**
(a) Research experiment (b) Applied research
(c) Research problems (d) None of these

18 **The distinction between observation with intervention and observation without intervention is similar to the distinction between**
(a) natural use traces and controlled use traces
(b) physical traces and archival records
(c) quantitative and qualitative data analysis
(d) correlations and spurious relationships

19 **Researchers must take special safeguards to protect human participants when**
(a) behaviour is observed in the public domain
(b) informed consent is not required
(c) anonymous questionnaires are used
(d) more than minimal risk is present

20 **Which of the following is typically not one of the types of risk that may be present in psychological research?**
(a) Economic (b) Psychological
(c) Social (d) Physical

21 **Researchers who use narrative records seek to provide a verbal summary of observations and to develop a theory that explains behaviour in the narrative records. This approach to data analysis represents**
(a) qualitative data analysis with comprehensive recording of behaviour.
(b) qualitative data analysis with selective recording of behaviour.
(c) quantitative data analysis with comprehensive recording of behaviour.
(d) quantitative data analysis with selective recording of behaviour.

22 **Researchers who conduct observational studies typically use a combination of time sampling and situation sampling to achieve**
(a) nominal scales of measurement
(b) representative samples of behaviour
(c) maximum interobserver reliability
(d) internally valid samples of behaviour

23 **Which of the following is not a characteristic of the naturalistic observation method?**
(a) Observers in a natural setting.
(b) Systematic observation of behaviour.
(c) Major goal being description of behaviour.
(d) Manipulation of events by an experimenter.

24 **The influence that an observer has on the behaviour under observation is called**
(a) Reactivity (b) Observer bias
(c) Demand characteristics (d) Expectancy effect

25 **Before beginning a research project researchers should search the psychological literature about their topic**
(a) in order to develop research hypothesis.
(b) to stop the research, if the study or a similar one has already been done.
(c) to demonstrate that no one has had a similar idea.
(d) All of the above

26 **Which of the following points should be observed while selecting a research problem?**
(a) Controversial subject should not be studied by average researcher.
(b) Too narrow or too vague problem should be avoided.
(c) Both a and b
(d) None of the above

27 **Distorts estimating on evaluating process as a result of personal beliefs represent.**
(a) Expectancy bias (b) Personal bias
(c) Placebo bias (d) External influences

28 **One culture the media can influence people to accept a particular world view. This situation is known as**
(a) Expectancy bias (b) Personal bias
(c) External influence (d) Observer bias

29 **The background factors that affect the way the researcher observe result into**
(a) personal bias (b) observer bias
(c) expectancy bias (d) None of these

30 **Expectancy bias is**
(a) when people strongly want to believe a treatment is successful.
(b) when some events are taken as meaningful by some not by other.
(c) expectation to find specific outcomes.
(d) None of the above

31 **When people strongly want to believe a treatment is successful then it result into?**
(a) Placebo biases (b) Expectancy biases
(c) Personal bias (d) None of these

32 Who said "Variable is a thing that is changeable"?
(a) Kerlinger (b) D'Amato
(c) Webster (d) None of these

33 Which among the following is an example of variable?
(a) Anxiety (b) Aptitude (c) Income (d) All of these

34 According to whom, "variable is a property that takes as different values"?
(a) D'Amato (b) Kerlinger
(c) Webster (d) None of these

35 According to whom, "A variable is a characteristic or attribute that can take on a number of values"?
(a) Postman and Egan (b) Kerlinger
(c) Webster (d) None of these

36 Who said "Variables may be defined as those attributes of objects, events, things and beings, which can be measured"?
(a) Kerlinger (b) D'Amato
(c) Webster (d) Postman

37 Researchers are often unable to control extraneous variables, when they use the case study method. This lesser degree of control makes it difficult to use the case study method to
(a) draw cause-effect conclusions behaviour.
(b) develop predictions of behaviour.
(c) consider alternative theoretical explanation of behaviour.
(d) develop descriptions of behaviour.

38 In an experiment, after completing conditioning once, an injection of a drug affecting neuro transmitter substance was given to the affecting neuro transmitter substance was given to the subject. Then, the subject was conditioned again. In this experiment, what were bio-chemical changes treated as?
(a) Dependent variable (b) Independent variable
(c) Control variable (d) Intervening variable

39 Which of the following is kept open by the experimenter?
(a) Dependent variable (b) Extraneous variable
(c) Intervening variable (d) Organismic variable

40 A variable is best defined as
(a) something which varies despite efforts to control it.
(b) any attribute which is influenced by the experimenter.
(c) any measurable attribute of objects, things or beings.
(d) any attribute which disturbs the experimentation.

41 Which of the following is not a kind of independent variable?
(a) Task variable (b) Environmental variable
(c) Subject variable (d) Experimentel variable

42 S-O-R model represent different categories of
(a) sampling (b) hypothesis
(c) variables (d) None of these

43 Which among the following are part of S-O-R model?
(a) Stimuli variables (b) Organism variables
(c) Response variables (d) All of these

44 Which of the following is correct about Independent variables?
(a) These are manipulated by the experimenter
(b) It is observed and recorded by experimenter
(c) It depends on behaviour of the participant
(d) None of the above

45 Which among the following is/are correct about Dependent Variables?
(a) It is observed by the experimenter
(b) A good dependent variable is reliable
(c) It depends on the behaviour of the participant
(d) All of the above

46 Which among the following is/are the techniques to control Extraneous Variables?
(a) Constancy (b) Elimination
(c) Counter balancing (d) All of the above

47 A technique, in which each member of the population or universe has an equal and independent chance of being selected is known as
(a) Counter balancing (b) Elimination
(c) Randomisation (d) Balancing

48 The main difference between field studies and laboratory studies is that
(a) field study is less expensive, while laboratory study is more expensive.
(b) field study is less explorative, while laboratory study is more explorative.
(c) field study has limited scope to control the variables, while laboratory study has adequate scope to regorously control the variables.
(d) field study can be conducted without sufficient professional experience, while laboratory study cannot be conducted without sufficient professional experience.

49 Type E and type S variables are related to
(a) dependent variable (b) intervening variable
(c) independent variable (d) extraneous variable

50 The categorial variables are known as
(a) continuous variable
(b) qualitative variable
(c) discrete variable
(d) independent variable

51 The number of family members constitutes which of the following variables?
(a) Discrete variable (b) Independent variable
(c) Continuous variable (d) Organismic variable

52 The variable which is not manipulated by experiment, but only measured
(a) active variable (b) control variable
(c) type E variable (d) attribute variable

53 The matched groups design ensures that the groups in the experiment are equivalent
(a) on all subject are variables
(b) only on the matching task variable
(c) on subject variable, but not on context variables
(d) on context variables, but not on nuisance variables

54 When a researcher is studying an individual difference variable, the levels of the independent variable are
(a) manipulated (b) held constant
(c) balanced (d) selected

55 Which of the following types of variables is most likely to be an independent variable in a natural groups design?
(a) Individual differences (subject) variables
(b) Task variables
(c) Nuisance variables
(d) Environmental variables

56 Latene and Darley decided to test the hypothesis that person's perception of the number of other bystanders witnessing an emergency will affect his willingness to help.

Which one of the following had been used as 'dependent variable' in the experiment?
(a) Person's perception
(b) Number of other bystanders
(c) Witnessing an emergency
(d) Willingness to help

57 According to whom hypothesis is "a testable statement, of a potential relationship between two variables"?
(a) Webster (b) Mc Guigan
(c) Darley (d) Latene

58 Which among the following is/are correct about a hypothesis?
(a) It displays relation between measurable variables.
(b) It exhibits a general or specific relationship between variables.
(c) Both a and b
(d) None of the above

59 Which among the following things should be considered while formulating a hypothesis?
(a) Expected relationship between the variables
(b) Operational definition of variables
(c) Hypothesis should be formulated after reviewing the literature
(d) All of the above

60 Who said that "the hypothesis should be stated in the logical form on the general implications"?
(a) Webster (b) Russell (c) Putnam (d) None of these

61 Hypothesis can be classified as
(a) universal hypothesis (b) existential hypothesis
(c) conceptual hypothesis (d) All of these

62 A hypothesis that asserts that there is no true difference between two population means is known as
(a) Alternative hypothesis (b) Null hypothesis
(c) Conceptual hypothesis (d) None of these

63 A hypothesis that specificies those values that are researcher believes to hold true are known as
(a) Alternative hypothesis (b) Null hypothesis
(c) Conceptual hypothesis (d) None of these

64 Which among the following is an error in testing hypothesis?
(a) Sampling procedure adopted faculty
(b) Study design selected is faculty
(c) Inappropriate statistical methods used
(d) All of the above

65 According to whom, "A sample is a smaller representative of a large whole"?
(a) Goode and Hatt (b) Blalock
(c) Young (d) None of these

66 According to Blalock most sampling methods could be classified into categories.
(a) non probability sampling methods
(b) probability sampling methods
(c) Both a and b
(d) None of the above

67 Which among the following is also known as network, chain referral or reputation sampling method?
(a) Systematic sampling (b) Snowball sampling
(c) Purposive sampling (d) Quota sampling

68 A methods that clearly specify the probability or likelihood of inclusion of each element or individual in the sample.
(a) Non-probability sampling
(b) Probability sampling
(c) Both a and b
(d) None of these

69 A type of random sample often used to cover wide geographic areas in which aggregated units are randomly selected is known as
(a) Stratified random sampling
(b) Simple random sampling
(c) Cluster sampling
(d) None of the above

70 Which among the following are ethical principles of research?
(a) Openness (b) Objectivity
(c) Carefulness (d) All of these

71 Maintaining and improving your own professional expertise through lifelong education and learning is known as
(a) Confidentiality (b) Openness
(c) Competence (d) Carefulness

72 Giving proper acknowledgement or credit for all contributions to research is known as
(a) Responsible mentoring
(b) Responsible publication
(c) Respect for intellectual property
(d) Integrity

73 When a scientist which is to generalise about a whole population after study small part of it, he must use
(a) probability sampling techniques
(b) a proper experimental design
(c) panel design
(d) psychometric tests

74 Which one of the following sampling procedures is least suitable for generalising experimental results?
(a) Random sampling
(b) Purposive sampling
(c) Incidental sampling
(d) Stratified or quota sampling

75 When psychologists do not use samples that are representative of the population, they must
(a) be very careful not to over-generalise their findings.
(b) destroy any data they have collected and begin the study again.
(c) request the subjects to behave in a manner consistent with the population.
(d) repeat the same study at least ten times to ensure accuracy.

76 Consider the following statements

A control group is

1. a condition of the independent variable that receives treatment.
2. a condition of the independent variable that does not receive treatment.
3. used for comparison purposes of the statements.

Which of the statements given above is/are correct?
(a) 1 and 2 (b) Only 1 (c) 2 and 3 (d) Only 2

77 In method of serial learning for an experiment relating to the effect of meaningfulness on the rate of learning, the rate of learning can be conceptualised as

1. dependent variable 2. independent variable
3. organimic variable 4. stimulus variable

Select the correct answer using the codes given below
(a) Only 1 (b) Only 2 (c) 3 and 4 (d) 1 and 2

78 Which of the following statements is/are not correct about a research problem or subject?

1. Subject which is overdone should not be normally chosen.
2. Subject selection should be familiar.
3. Controversial subject should be avoided.

Select the correct answer using the codes given below
(a) 2 and 3 (b) Only 3
(c) 1 and 2 (d) None of these

79 In an experimental study of the effects of a new drug on depression a double-blind control technique is used, which of the following persons should not be informed as to which drug, experimental or placebo is being administered to each individual research participant?

1. Research participants in the experimental group.
2. Research participants in the control group.
3. Persons administering the drug.
4. Persons evaluating the drug effect.

Select the correct answer using the codes given below
(a) Only 2 (b) 1 and 3 (c) 1, 2 and 4 (d) All of these

80 Which of the following statements are correct regarding primary research?

1. It is also known as field research.
2. It can be in numerous form that includes questionnaires and telephone interviews.

Select the correct answer using the codes given below
(a) Only 1 (b) Only 2
(c) Both 1 and 2 (d) Neither 1 nor 2

81 Which of the following are the techniques to control extraneous variables?

1. Elimination 2. Balancing
3. Constancy in the condition
4. Randomisation
5. Theoretical consideration
6. Counter balancing

Select the correct answer using the codes given below
(a) 1, 5 and 6 (b) 1, 2, 3 and 6
(c) 1, 2, 3, 4 and 6 (d) All of these

82 Arrange the following in correct sequence related to research process.

1. Identifying the problem
2. Literature search
3. Collection of data
4. Formulating hypothesis
5. Formulating research design
6. Analysis data

Codes
(a) 1, 2, 3, 4, 5, 6 (b) 1, 2, 5, 4, 3, 6
(c) 1, 2, 4, 5, 3, 6 (d) 1, 4, 2, 5, 3, 6

83 Which of the following is not correct about the hypothesis?

1. It is a suggested testable answer to a problem.
2. It is a interogative statement.
3. It is based on operationally defined concepts.
4. It involves higher monetary expenses.
5. It should always be in accord with other hypothesis of the same field.

Select the correct answer using the codes given below
(a) Only 1 (b) Only 2
(c) 2, 4 and 5 (d) 2, 4 and 3

Directions (Q. Nos. 84-93) *In the question given below are two statements labelled as Assertion (A) and Reason (R). In the context of the two statements, which of the following is correct?*

Codes

(a) Both A and R are true and R is the correct explanation of A
(b) Both A and R are true, but R is not the correct explanation of A
(c) A is true, but R is false
(d) A is false, but R is true

84 **Assertion** (A) Observation is a primary method of any scientific enquiry.

Reason (R) Empirical studies are based on experience and experimentalist.

85 **Assertion** (A) Exploratory research is often the first step in a sequence of studies analysing a social phenomenon that is largely unknown.

Reason (R) Exploratory research most often addresses the 'what' question.

86 **Assertion** (A) Attribute variable is not manipulated but measured by experimenter.

Reason (R) Intelligence, aptitudes, sex etc. are example of Attribute variable.

87 **Assertion** (A) The hypothesis must be testable.

Reason (R) Hypothesis should be formulated in a way that can be tested directly and found to be probably true or probably false.

88 **Assertion** (A) Dependent variable is observed and recorded by the experimeter.

Reason (R) It depends on the behaviour of the participant, which in turn, is supposed to depend on the independent variable.

89 **Assertion** (A) Applied research focuses on analysing and solving real-life problems.

Reason (R) Applied research plays an important role in solving issues that impact the overall well-being of humans.

90 **Assertion** (A) According to D' Amato "Variables may be defined as those attributes of objects, events, things, being, which can be measured."

Reason (R) A variable is a characteristic or attribute that can take on a number of values.

91 **Assertion** (A) Elimination involve eliminating the variable completely.

Reason (R) If elimination is not possible then control over the extraneous variable can be made by holding their values constant in all situation.

92 **Assertion** (A) Mc Guigan has defined hypothesis as, a testable statements of a potential relationship between two variables.

Reason (R) Hypothesis should be conceptually clear.

93 **Assertion** (A) Null hypothesis is useful tool in testing the significance of difference.

Reason (R) Null hypothesis is usefull tool in testing the significance of differences between two population means and the difference found between sample means.

94 Match the following

List I (Types of Variable)	List II (Examples)
A. Continous variable	1. Voice pitch
B. Artificially discrete variable	2. Caste
C. Real discrete variable	3. Intelligence
D. Qualitative variable	4. Examination results in terms of pass and fail

Codes

	A	B	C	D		A	B	C	D
(a)	2	1	3	4	(b)	3	4	2	1
(c)	2	4	3	1	(d)	3	1	2	4

95 Match the following

List I (Nature of Variance)	List II (Source of Variance)
A. Systematic variance	1. Methodological artifacts
B. Error variance	2. Effect of IV
C. Extraneous variance	3. Uncontrolled factors

Codes

	A	B	C		A	B	C
(a)	2	1	3	(b)	2	3	1
(c)	1	2	3	(d)	3	1	2

96 Match the following

List I (Types of Research)	List II (Characteristics)
A. Fundamental research	1. Solution of immediate problem
B. Applied research	2. Critical evaluation and exploration of present material
C. Analytical research	3. Relies on experience and observation alone
D. Empirical research	4. Process that are universal

Codes

	A	B	C	D		A	B	C	D
(a)	4	1	2	3	(b)	4	3	2	1
(c)	4	1	3	2	(d)	4	2	1	3

97 Match the following

List I (Variable)	List II (Features)
A. Independent variable	1. Randomisation
B. Dependent variable	2. Counter -balancing
C. Carry over effect	3. Measurement
D. Control of variables	4. Active manipulation

Codes

	A	B	C	D		A	B	C	D
(a)	4	3	1	2	(b)	3	4	2	1
(c)	3	4	1	2	(d)	4	3	2	1

98 Match the following

List I (Types of Research)	List II (Objective)
A. Exploratory research	1. Testing causal relationship
B. Hypothesis testing research	2. Frequency with which it is associated
C. Descriptive research	3. Identifying feature of particular group
D. Diagnostic research	4. To get introduced with a process

Codes

	A	B	C	D		A	B	C	D
(a)	1	2	3	4	(b)	4	1	3	2
(c)	4	3	1	2	(d)	2	3	1	4

99 Match the following

List I (Variables)	List II (Property)
A. Independent variable	1. Physical characteristics of apparatus
B. Dependent variable	2. Variable manipulated by experimenter
C. Task variable	3. Variable recorded by experimenter
D. Extraneous variable	4. Variable controlled by the experiment

Codes

	A	B	C	D		A	B	C	D
(a)	2	3	1	4	(b)	2	4	3	1
(c)	3	1	4	2	(d)	1	2	3	4

Directions (Q. Nos.100-104) *Read the passage given below and answer the following questions.*

Good hypothesis are made, not born. Researcher often becomes interested in a question about human behaviour for personal reasons, the ultimate value of research study depends on the researcher bringing methodological criteria to bear on the selection of the hypothesis to be tested.

Hypothesis plays a key role in formulating and guiding any study. A researcher should consider certain points while formulating a hypothesis.

(i) Expected relationship or difference between the variables.

(ii) Operational definition of variables.

(iii) Hypothesis are formulated following the review of literature.

According to Russell and Reichenbach, "the hypothesis should be stated in the logical form on the general implications. 'A' hypothesis can be put in the form of a statements; if A is true then 'B' should follow. *For example* Verbal development theory of amnesia states that childhood amnesia caused by the development of language."

100 The ultimate value of research study depends on

(a) research bringing methodological criteria
(b) researcher bringing hypothetical criteria
(c) Both a and b
(d) None of the above

101 Hypothesis plays a key role in

(a) formulating study
(b) guiding study
(c) Both a and b
(d) None of these

102 Consider the following statements

1. A researcher should expected relationship or difference between the variables.
2. Operational definition of variable.

Which among the above is/are correct?

(a) Only 1
(b) Only 2
(c) Both 1 and 2
(d) None of these

103 Hypothesis must be formulated following the review of

(a) participant
(b) observer
(c) literature
(d) theory

104 Who said that "the hypothesis should be stated in the logical form on the general implication"?

(a) Russel and Reichenbach
(b) Goode and Hatt
(c) Postman and Egan
(d) None of these

PREVIOUS YEARS' QUESTIONS

July 2018

Directions (Q. Nos.1-4) *Read the following paragraph and answer the four questions which follow:*

A researcher in experimental psychology hypothesised that a particular 'Reward System' for fast reactions would improve the reaction time. To verify this hypothesis, he selected forty subjects in the age range of 25 to 35 years from an organisation. Following the standard reaction time experiment, he measured the simple reaction time without the reward system. While taking each trial in the experiment, the time-interval between the ready signal and the onset of stimulus was randomly varied between two to five seconds. In the second part of the experiment, the reward system was introduced and the simple reaction time was measured again for the same subjects. The mean reaction time before the introduction of reward system was 210 milliseconds and the mean reaction time after the introduction of reward system was 250 milliseconds. The difference between the two means was statistically significant at .01 level.

1 **In the above study, the researcher's hypothesis is**

(a) Correlational hypothesis
(b) Directional hypothesis
(c) Non-directional hypothesis
(d) Null hypothesis

2 **In this experiment, reaction time can be labelled as**

1. Continuous variable
2. Dependent variable
3. Stimulus variable
4. Behavioural variable

Codes

(a) Only 1 (b) 1 and 2 (c) 1, 2 and 3 (d) 1, 2 and 4

3 **Which of the following statistical techniques can be used for evaluating the mean differences ?**

1. Independent samples t-test
2. Paired samples t-test
3. Mann-Whitney U-test
4. Repeated measures ANOVA

Codes

(a) Only 2 (b) 1 and 2 (c) 2 and 4 (d) 1, 2 and 4

4 **Which one of the following conclusions can be drawn on the basis of the above study?**

(a) The researcher's hypothesis has been accepted
(b) The researcher's hypothesis has been rejected
(c) The researcher's hypothesis has been partially accepted
(d) Inadequate hypothesis to verify the hypothesis

November 2017

Directions (Q. Nos. 5-9) *Read the following paragraph and answer the five questions which follow*

A psychologist, working in the area of learning and memory hypothesised that a particular drug would adversely affect the learning rate. One hundred and fifty subjects, 75 boys and 75 girls, studying in the first year of a degree college, in the age range of 18 to 20 years, were available for the study. It was ensured that all the subjects were in the DIQ (deviation IQ) range of 85 to 115. Three groups - A, B and C of equal size were formed by random assignment. Group A received high dosage of drug, Group B received moderate dosage of drug, and Group C received only placebo. A list of 15 CVC trigrams, each having an association value in the range of 50 to 70 was already prepared. Each subject was required to learn the list upto two errorless trials using method of anticipation on a memory drum. The mean trials required to learn the list were 12, 15 and 20 respectively. The intergroup mean differences were statistically significant at .01 level.

5 **Which one of the following conclusions can be drawn on the basis of the above study?**

(a) The researcher's hypothesis has been verified
(b) The researcher's hypothesis has been rejected
(c) The researcher's hypothesis has been partially accepted
(d) Inadequate data to evaluate the hypothesis

6 **In the above study, 'association value' can be labelled as**

1. Continuous variable
2. Controlled variable
3. Organismic variable
4. Stimulus variable

Codes

(a) 1 and 2 (b) 1 and 3
(c) 1, 2 and 3 (d) 1, 2 and 4

7 **Read each of the following two statements Assertion (A) and Reason (R) and indicate your answer using codes given below.**

Assertion (A) In the above study, the subjects have been randomly assigned to the three groups.

Reason (R) The independent variable is manipulated more effectively with random assignment of subjects.

Codes

(a) Both A and R are true and R is the correct explanation of A

(b) Both A and R are true, but R is not the correct explanation of A
(c) A is true, but R is false
(d) A is false, but R is true

8 Match List I with List II in the context of above study and select the correct answer by choosing from the codes given below

List I		List II
A. Independent variable	1.	Intelligence
B. Dependent variable	2.	Drug dosage
C. Controlled variable	3.	Gender
D. Discrete variable	4.	Trials required to learn the list

Codes

	A	B	C	D		A	B	C	D
(a)	4	2	3	1	(b)	4	2	1	3
(c)	2	4	3	1	(d)	2	4	1	3

9 In the above study, the variance caused by drug dosage can be labelled as

(a) primary variance (b) secondary variance
(c) controlled variance (d) error variance

January 2017

Directions (Q. Nos 10-14) *Read the following paragraph and answer the five questions which are follow*

A researcher working in the area of human intelligence wanted to develop a new verbal test of intelligence. For this purpose, he wrote 200 objective multiple-choice items. Each item had four alternatives, one of which was right and the three remaining ones were wrong. He administered this initial version to a sample of 400 subjects. Using P27 and P73 as the cut-off points, he obtained two groups - Low Scoring and High Scoring respectively. The item difficulty index and the item discrimination index were computed for each of the 200 items.

To assess whether each item significantly discriminates between Low scoring and High scoring groups, appropriate statistical significance tests were also employed. This item analysis process retained 150 items. The final version of 150 items was administered to a fresh sample of 750 subjects. The appropriate measures of internal consistency reliability were obtained. The test norms were developed using normalised T scores (mean = 100, SD = 20) and the Wechsler type deviation IQ scores. To assess the dimensionality of verbal intelligence, the researcher also carried out the factor analysis of item scores.

10 Which one of the following test of statistical significance can be employed in the above study to evaluate whether the item significantly discriminates between the Low scoring and High scoring groups? .

(a) Chi-square
(b) Point-biserial correlation
(c) *t* test
(d) Biserial correlation

11 Which of the following reliability coefficients can be computed in the above study to assess the internal consistency?

1. Odd-even reliability coefficient
2. Kuder-Richardsen reliability coefficient
3. Cronbach alpha coefficient
4. Interscorer reliability coefficient

Codes

(a) Only 1 (b) 1 and 3
(c) 1, 2 and 3 (d) 2, 3 and 4

12 For the above test, what is the expected percentile rank for the T score of 120?

(a) 60 (b) 68 (c) 75 (d) 84

13 For the above test, a T score of 80 would correspond to the deviation IQ of

(a) 68 (b) 80 (c) 85 (d) 115

14 In the above study, which type of correlations can be employed to carry out the factor analysis of the test items?

(a) Biserial correlations (b) Phi coefficients
(c) Point biserial correlations (d) Rank order correlations

July 2016

Directions (Q. Nos. 15 to 19) *Read the following paragraph and answer the five questions which follow.*

An environmental psychologist hypothesised that the noise would adversely affect the performance on mental tasks. One hundred and fifty subjects, 75 boys and 75 girls, studying in the twelfth standard, in the age range of 17 to 19 years and in the IQ range of 85 to 115, constituted the initial pool of subjects. Three groups of equal size were formed by random assignment. Group I performed under high noise condition (75 decibels), Group II performed under moderate noise condition (60 decibels) and Group III performed under silent condition. Each subject was instructed to solve 45 simple numerical problems in the allotted time of 90 minutes. The mean number of correctly solved problems were twenty-four, twenty and fifteen respectively. The intergroup mean differences were statistically significant.

15 The variable 'intelligence', in the above study, can be labelled as

1. Behavioural variable
2. Organismic variable
3. Continuous variable
4. Controlled variable

Codes
(a) 1 and 4 (b) 2 and 3 (c) 1, 3 and 4 (d) 2, 3 and 4

16 **Which one of the following conclusion can be drawn on the basis of the above study?**
(a) The researcher's hypothesis has been accepted
(b) The researcher's hypothesis has been rejected
(c) The researcher's hypothesis has been partially accepted
(d) Inadequate data to evaluate researcher's hypothesis

17 **Read each of the following two statements Assertion (A) and Reason (R)and indicate your answer using codes given below.**

Assertion **(A) In the above study, the subjects have been randomly assigned to the three groups.**

Reason **(R) Random assignment of the subjects enables the experimenter to manipulate the independent variable effectively.**

Codes
(a) Both A and R are true and R is the correct explanation of A
(b) Both A and R are true, but R is not the correct explanation of A
(c) A is true, but R is false
(d) A is false, but R is true

18 **Match List I with List II in the context of the above study, select the correct answer by choosing from the codes given below**

List I (Types of Variable)	**List II** (Variables)
A. Independent variable	1. Subject's education
B. Dependent variable	2. Subject's gender
C. Controlled variable	3. Noise level
D. Discrete variable	4. Number of numerical problems correctly solved by subject

Codes

	A	B	C	D		A	B	C	D
(a)	3	4	1	2	(b)	4	3	1	2
(c)	4	3	2	1	(d)	3	4	2	1

19 **In the above study, the researcher's hypothesis would be labelled as**
1. directional **2. non-directional**
3. causal **4. correlational**

Codes
(a) Only 1 (b) 1 and 3
(c) 2 and 3 (d) 2 and 4

December 2015

20 **The factors that influence social behaviour and thoughts in certain ways are called**
(a) Independent variables
(b) Confounding variables
(c) Dependent variables
(d) Mediating variables

21 **Research shows that the following does not contribute to teacher effectiveness.**
(a) Communication skills
(b) Use of ICT
(c) Years of experience
(d) Use of student feedback

December 2014

Directions (Q. Nos 22-26) *Read the passage given below and answer the questions that follow.*

The research process usually begins with the identification and formulation of research problem. Once, the problem is identified, the appropriate hypothesis are developed. The hypothesis are tentative solutions to the problem and represent the conjectural statements of relationship among two or more variables. The hypothesis could be classified in various ways, such as directional vs non-directional, correlational vs causal etc.

Edwards classified the variables in psychological research as stimulus variables, organismic variables and behavioural variables. The variables are classified as the continuous variables and discrete variables, the latter having two subtypes-the real discrete variables and artificially discrete variables. The variables in research need to be properly operationalised. Robinson classified the psychological studies in four categories Laboratory experiments, Field experiments, Ex-post facto field studies and Ex post facto analysis of experiment (slightly modified). The fourth category, on its own, is accorded less respect but is essential for the advancement of Science.

22 **Which of the following hypothesis/hypothes are non-directional hypothesis?**
1. Males and females differ on anxiety.
2. Intelligence and academic achievement are negatively related.
3. Anxiety disrupts academic performance of the students.
4. Stress and work output are related.

Codes
(a) Only 2 (b) 1 and 3
(c) 3 and 4 (d) 1 and 4

23 **Which one of the following is an example of artificially discrete organismic variable?**
(a) Examination result as pass or fail
(b) Nationality
(c) Classification of students as low, average and high intelligent
(d) Gender

24 **Which one of the following cannot be employed as the dependent variable in a psychological experiment?**
1. Heart rate **2. Learning rate**

3. Reaction time
4. Age

Codes

(a) Only 4 (b) 1 and 2
(c) 3 and 4 (d) 1, 2 and 4

25 Arrange the following three types of investigation in ascending order in terms of the researcher's ability (usually) to control secondary variance.

1. Laboratory experiments
2. Field experiments
3. Ex-post facto field studies

Codes

(a) 3, 1, 2 (b) 1, 2, 3
(c) 3, 2, 1 (d) 2, 3, 1

26 After the catastrophic earthquake, the researcher interviewed a group of subjects to understand whether the earthquake has changed their attitude towards fate. This can best be labelled as an example of

(a) ex-post facto field study
(b) field experiment
(c) attitude change experiment
(d) ethological study

ANSWERS

Exam Based Questions

1	(b)	2	(c)	3	(c)	4	(d)	5	(c)	6	(b)	7	(a)	8	(c)	9	(a)	10	(a)
11	(c)	12	(b)	13	(c)	14	(d)	15	(b)	16	(a)	17	(c)	18	(a)	19	(d)	20	(a)
21	(a)	22	(b)	23	(d)	24	(a)	25	(a)	26	(c)	27	(b)	28	(c)	29	(b)	30	(c)
31	(a)	32	(c)	33	(d)	34	(b)	35	(a)	36	(b)	37	(a)	38	(d)	39	(a)	40	(c)
41	(d)	42	(c)	43	(d)	44	(a)	45	(d)	46	(d)	47	(c)	48	(c)	49	(c)	50	(c)
51	(a)	52	(d)	53	(b)	54	(c)	55	(a)	56	(d)	57	(b)	58	(c)	59	(d)	60	(b)
61	(d)	62	(b)	63	(a)	64	(d)	65	(a)	66	(c)	67	(b)	68	(b)	69	(c)	70	(d)
71	(c)	72	(c)	73	(a)	74	(d)	75	(a)	76	(c)	77	(a)	78	(d)	79	(c)	80	(c)
81	(c)	82	(c)	83	(c)	84	(a)	85	(b)	86	(b)	87	(a)	88	(b)	89	(a)	90	(b)
91	(c)	92	(b)	93	(a)	94	(b)	95	(c)	96	(a)	97	(d)	98	(b)	99	(a)	100	(a)
101	(c)	102	(c)	103	(c)	104	(a)												

Previous Years' Questions

1	(b)	2	(a)	3	(c)	4	(c)	5	(b)	6	(d)	7	(c)	8	(d)	9	(a)	10	(a)
11	(c)	12	(d)	13	(c)	14	(b)	15	(d)	16	(b)	17	(c)	18	(a)	19	(b)	20	(d)
21	(b)	22	(d)	23	(c)	24	(a)	25	(c)	26	(a)								

Paradigms of Research

A Paradigm is a world view about how to conduct a research. Paradigm includes the methodology, approach and ontology to conduct the research.
These methodologies are approaches to research that can help the researcher to conduct a systematic research.

Research Paradigm

The term paradigm was first used by Kuhn in his work, 'The Structure of Scientific Resolution'. He defined research paradigm as an integrated cluster of substantive concepts, variables and problems attached with corresponding methodology approaches and tools.

A paradigm provides the researcher with a guideline to follow throughout the research. Before beginning your research you must be fairly familiar with the basics of research paradigms and underlying fundamentals of each of these paradigms. The methodologies can be quantitative or qualitative and within each of these methodology, there are several research techniques. In science, quantitative research methodology is commonly used.

In social science, qualitative research methodology is more common in use. As a combination of both quantitative and qualitative research methodologies, there is mixed-method methodology that is more adaptable and used in both science and social science.

Quantitative Research Approach

Quantitative research is defined as the systematic investigation of phenomena by gathering quantifiable data and performing statistical, mathematical or computational techniques. Quantitative research gathers information from existing and potential customers using sampling methods and sending out online surveys, online polls, questionnaires etc. the results of which can be depicted in the form of numericals.

In this Chapter

Quantitative research is mostly conducted in social science using the statistical methods, to collect quantitative data from the research study. In this research method, researchers and statisticians deploy mathematical frameworks and theories that pertain to the quantity under question. Quantitative research templates are objective, elaborative and many a times, are investigational in nature. The results achieved from this research method are logical, statistical and unbiased.

Characteristics of Quantitative Research

Some distinctive characteristics of quantitative research are

- **Structured Tools** Structured tools such as surveys, polls or questionnaires are used to gather quantitative data. Using such structure methods helps in collecting in-depth and actionable data from the survey respondents.
- **Sample Size** Quantitative research is conducted on a significant sample size that represents the target area. Appropriate sampling methods have to be used while collecting the sample so as to fortify the research objective.
- **Close-Ended Questions** Closed-ended questions are formulated in accordance with the objective of the research. These questions helps in collecting quantitative data and hence are extensively used in quantitative research.
- **Prior Studies** Various factors related to the research topic are studied before collecting feedback from respondents.
- **Quantitative Data** Usually, quantitative data is represented by tables, charts, graphs or any other non-numerical form. This makes it easy to understand the data that has been collected as well as proves the validity of the research.
- **Generalisation of Results** Results of this research method can be generalised to an entire population to take appropriate actions for improvement.

Advantages of Quantitative Research

There are many advantages of quantitative research. Some of the major advantages why researchers use this method in research *are as follows*

- **Collecting Reliable and Accurate Data** As data is collected, analysed and presented in numbers, the results obtained will be extremely reliable. The numbers do not lie. It presents an honest picture of the conducted research without discrepancies and is also extremely accurate. In situations where a researcher predicts conflict, quantitative research is conducted.
- **Quick Data Collection** A quantitative research is carried out with a group of respondents. The survey or other quantitative research method applied to these respondents and the involving statistics, makes the conduction and analyses of results quite straightforward and less time-consuming.
- **Wider Scope of Data Analysis** Due to the statistics, this research method provides a wide scope of data collection.
- **Eliminate Bias** This research method offers no scope for personal comments or biasness in results. The results achieved are numerical and thus, fair in most cases.

Quantitative Research in Psychology

Quantitative psychologists study and develop the methods and techniques used to measure human behaviour and other attributes. Their work involves the statistical and mathematical modeling of psychological processes, the design of research studies and the analysis of psychological data.

Quantitative psychologists are expert in designing methodologies and studies that reveal answers to research questions on topics as diverse as human performance, child development, memory and language retention.

Qualitative Research Approach

The process of collecting data in 'qualitative research' is field based on iteraction *i.e.* the data collected from the study is organised during analysis in such a way that a pattern will emerge.

Unlike quantitative research, it usually starts with the specific procedure and moves towards the general. In this type of research, data patterns generated from analysis inevitably leads to different questions or concepts that the researcher had set prior to data gathering.

The main purpose of this kind of research is to understand and interpret social interactions. It usually studies smaller and purposively selected groups of participants. It does not focus on specific variables, but sees the study as a whole. Qualitative research examines all the aspects of phenomena. Forms of data gathered typically comprise responses to interviews, participants observations, field notes, reflections and other open-ended responses such as words, images or objects.

Assumptions of Qualitative Methods

- Multiple facts are considered in the research which includes views of the researcher, participants of the study, and even the reader or the audience interpreting the results.
- The researcher actively interacts with the participants and one of his/her goals is to reduce the distance between him/her and the people being studied.
- The researcher recognises that the research is not value-free, and that it can be influenced by his values and beliefs.
- Qualitative research is context-bound.
- Categories of interest emerge from the participants of the research, rather than being set by the researcher before conducting the study. An inductive form of logic is followed.
- The objective of the research is to come up with patterns or theories that will explain the phenomenon being studied.

Qualitative Research in Psychology

Qualitative research methods has gained much importance in the discipline of psychology, leaving other human sciences such as sociology and social work far below. Qualitative research is less interested in explaining phenomena than in understanding them and that is why it has relevance in psychology. Qualitative research therefore, helps in attaining an indepth knowledge of human nature, attitude, behaviour and experiences.

Implications of Qualitative Research

Qualitative research has several implications in the discipline of psychology, which are *as follows*

- Helps in textual description of experiences of people.
- Helps in identifying and explaining social norms, religion, roles of gender and socio-economic status.
- Helps in understanding those behavioural phenomena which can not be quantified.
- Helps in collecting data under natural situations.
- Helps in determining those factors which are meaningful and are important to the respondents under study.

The open ended questions used in qualitative research provides an opportunity to unfold those facts which can not be done with the help of 'to the point' close-ended questions.

Mixed Method Research Approach

Mixed method research approach as a method, focuses on collecting, analysing,and mixing both quantitative and qualitative data in a single study or a series of studies. Its central premise is that the use of quantitative and qualitative approaches, in combination, provides a better understanding of research problems than either approach alone.

Mixed methods research is basically defined as the class of research, where the researcher mixes or combines quantitative and qualitative research techniques, methods, approaches, concepts or language into a single study.

Characteristics of Mixed Method Research

The following are the some basic features of the mixed method research

- It is a synthesis of both qualitative and quantitative data.
- The collection of both open and closed-ended data (qualitative and quantitative data) in response to research question.
- Persuasive and rigorous procedures for the qualitative and quantitative methods.
- The integration of two data sources (by merging, connecting and embedding).
- The use of specific mixed method design that involves a concurrent or sequential integration.
- An approach to research that has a philosophical foundation.

Mixed Method Research Process Model

The mixed method research process model comprises eight distinct steps

(i) Interpretation of data; (ii) Analysis of data;
(iii) Collection of data;
(iv) Selection of mixed method or mixed-model research design;
(v) Determining the research question;
(vi) Determining whether a mixed research procedure is appropriate;
(vii) Legitimisation of data; and
(viii) Drawing conclusions and writing the final report.

Role of Mixed Method Research in Psychology

Psychology relies heavily on quantitative based data analysis but benefits from incorporating the advantages of both quantitative and qualitative methodologies into one cohesive framework. Mixed methods ideally includes the benefit of both methods : Quantitative analysis and Qualitative Analysis. Qualitative analysis produce expressive data that provide descriptive details (often in narrative form) to examine the study's research objectives. While, quantitative data may be collected through measures such as self-reports and physiological tests, qualitative data are collected through focus groups, structured or semistructured interviews and other forms.

Research Methods

Research methods are the strategies, processes or techniques utilised in the collection of data or evidence for analysing in order to uncover new information or create better understanding of a topic. 'Research methods' is a broad term. While methods of data collection and data analysis represent the core of research methods, you have a range of additional elements within the scope of your research, *which are discussed below–*

Observation

Observation method consists of collecting facts, which are in the direct knowledge of the investigator. Observation is the perception with the purpose and can also be called as regulated perception.

Pauline Young, has described it as 'Deliberate study through the eyes'.

For observation method to become scientific, the observation must be precise, accurate and systematic.

Qualities of Good Observer

The qualities of good observer are as follows

- Efficient sense organ.
- Ability to estimate rapidly and accurately.
- Must possess sufficient alertness to observe several details simultaneously.
- Mustn't allowed his personal prejudices to bias his observation.
- Must be good in physical condition.
- Must be able to record quickly and accurately the record of his observation.

Roles of an Observer

- A visiting stranger
- Eager learner
- Attentive listener
- Participant observer

Planning an Effective Observation

Measures for effective observation are–

- Sample selected should truly represent population.
- Behaviour observed should be clearly defined.
- Units of behaviour to be observed should be simple and so should be the methods of recording these units.
- Detailed instruction should be given to the observers, so that consistency can be obtained in their observation.
- Too many variables shouldn't be simultaneously observed.
- Excessively long process of observation without being interspread with rest period shouldn't be allowed.
- Observers should be well trained, well equipped and the number of observers should be adequate.
- Condition of observation should remain constant.
- Interpretation should be objectively made.
- Length of observation period, number of observation period and the number and duration of interval period should be clearly stated.

Objectifying Observation

Ways to objectifying observation are–

- The perceptive powers of the observers should be sharpened by regular practice and by teaching them superior methods of observation.
- Selecting individuals with higher emotional stability as observers as they are likely to carry out an unbiased observation.
- By training the observers in writing, the researcher reports and trains them in the interpretation of the information.
- By increasing the richness and accuracy of individual observation by guarding against the errors of perception.
- By equipping the observation with mechanical devices and tools that will allow them to record all the facts under investigation.

Types of Observation

Observation can be categorised into two types based on participation of respondants, *which are given below.*

Naturalistic or Non-Participant Observation

Observing events that occur naturally. It is used where artificial probes or manipulation might destroy all or basic character of the event or phenomenon being studied and where there is no possibility to carry out controlled observation. In naturalistic observation, obtrusive observation procedures are used. These observations are also carried out at places where ethical consideration prevents the researcher from deliberately creating phenomena.

Naturalistic observation have been popularised by ethologists, who study animal behaviour in its natural habitats. Some popular ethologists, who have carried out naturalistic observations are Hess, Harlow, Tinbergen, Lorenz. The key requirement in naturalistic observation is to avoid intrusion. Intrusion occurs when the subject comes to know that they are being observed and the observation is being made in the environment, which the participant regards as research setting. In naturalistic observation, since the observer does not get involved with the subject under study, it can also be called as *non-participation* of observation.

Participant Observation

In participant observation, the investigators have interface with the subjects.

Participant observation are of two types which are as follows

(i) **Undisguised Participant Observation** (UPO) The individual being observed knows the observers who has the intension to collect the information about the social aspect of their behaviour.

(ii) **Disguised Participant Observation** (DPO) In disguised participant observation, the researcher pretend to be members of the social group they are observing and conceal their true identity as researchers.

Use of Observation Method in Psychology

Observation could seem to be an obvious method of carrying out research in psychology. Controlled observation in likely to be carried out in a psychology laboratory. Naturalistic observation is a research method commonly used by psychologists and other social scientists. The technique involves observing, studying the spontaneous behaviour of participants in natural surroundings. The researcher simply records what they see in whatever way they can. With regard to human subjects, Margaret Mead used this method to research the way of life of different tribes living on islands in the South Pacific. Kathy Sylva used it to study children at play by observing their behaviour in a playground in Oxfordshire.

Survey Method

The term 'survey' can be defined as a process which may involve an investigation/examination or assessment in the form of a short paper-and-pencil feedback form to an intensive one-on-one in-depth interview. With the help of the questionnaire or other statistical tools, the method ties together data about people, their thoughts and behaviours.

In a survey research, the researcher collects data with the help of standardised questionnaires or interviews, which is administered on a sample of respondents from a population. The method of survey research is one of the techniques of applied social research, which can be helpful in collection of data both through direct and indirect observation.

Interview

Interview is a kind of face to face interaction which helps in providing more honest answers and responses from the sample, as the interviewer works directly with the respondent or the interviewee. Unlike questionnaires, the interviewer has an opportunity to ask follow-up questions.

These are the best suitable methods for those questions which require opinions or impressions from the respondents.

Interview can be of different types as given below

- **Structured Interview** Structured interviews are those interviews in which the questions that are to be asked from the respondents, are prepared and preplanned in advance by the researcher. The researcher puts forth those prepared questions to the respondents serialwise and notes down the answers given by them.
- **Unstructured Interview** Interviews are said to be unstructured when the researcher conducts an interaction with the respondent in an informal atmosphere. Nothing is preplanned in advance. The response of the sample gives a clue to the researcher to ask the next question.

- **Telephonic Interview** In order to save time and money, the researcher may call the subjects through telephone and ask them questions to collect data. This method helps in saving time and energy, but the interview gets limited to only that part of the population who have the facility of telephones at their residence or offices.

Questionnaire

The second element required for a survey is an instrument to collect data. A questionnaire, is a basic tool of survey research, because it can be tailored to meet the needs of almost any inquiry.

At its simplest, a questionnaire is a list of questions. However, to reduce the possibility of misunderstandings to a minimum and to enable data to be compared, the questions are normally presented in a very structured way. A notable feature of survey research is that, unlike an experiment or interview, there is usually only one opportunity to collect data from each informant. It is therefore important to make the questionnaire as clear and effective as possible.

Merits of Questionnaire

The method of collecting data by mailing the questionnaires to respondents is most extensively employed in various economic and business surveys.

The merits of this method are as follows–

- This is low cost method.
- It is free from the bias of the interviewer, answers are in respondents own words.
- Respondents have adequate time to give well thought out answers.
- Respondents, who are not easily approachable, can also be reached conveniently.
- Large samples can be used and thus, the results can be made more dependable and reliable.

Demerits of Questionnaire

The main demerits of this method are as follows

- It can be used only when the respondents are educated and cooperating.
- The control over questionnaire may be lost once it is sent.
- There is an inbuilt inflexibility because of the difficulty of amending the approach once questionnaires have been dispatched.

Question Formulation and Wording

With regard to this aspect of questionnaire, the researcher should note that each question must be very clear, any sort of misunderstanding can do irreparable harm to a survey. Questions should also be impartial in order not to give a biased picture of the true state of affairs.

In general, all questions should meet the following standards

- It should be easily understood.
- It should be simple *i.e.* should convey only one thought at a time.
- It should be concrete and should conform as much as possible to the respondent's way of thinking. For instance, instead of asking 'How many razor blades did you use annually?' The more realistic question would be to ask, 'How many razor blades did you use last week?'

Main Aspects of Questionnaire

Quite often the questionnaire is considered as the heart of a survey operation. Hence, it should be very carefully constructed. If it is not properly set-up, then the survey is bound to fail.

The general form of a questionnaire can be either structured or unstructured questionnaire. Structured questionnaires are those questionnaires, in which there are definite, concrete and pre-determined questions. The form of the questions may be either closed or open, but should be stated in advance and not constructed during questioning.

Structured questionnaires may also have fixed alternative questions, in which responses of the informants are limited. When these characteristics are not present in a questionnaire, it can be termed as unstructured or non-structured questionnaire.

Uses of Survey Method in Psychology

Surveys are commonly used in psychology research to collect self-report data from participants. A survey may focus on factual information about individuals or it might aim to obtain the opinions of the survey takers.

A survey can be used to investigate the characteristics, behaviours or opinions of a group of people. These research tools can be used to ask questions about demographic information about characteristics such as sex, religion, ethnicity and income. They can also collect information on experiences, opinions and even hypothetical scenarios. For example, researchers might present people with a possible scenario and then ask them how they might respond in that situation.

Experimental Research Method

Experimental research is mainly used in science subjects such as physics, chemistry, medicine, biology etc. Experiment requires two variables, one independent variable and the other dependent variable. It is important that in experimental research the independent variable is manipulated and the effect of manipulation is observed on the dependent variable. In other words, it is a systematic and scientific approach to research in which the researcher manipulates one or more variables, and controls and measures the other variables.

A psychological experiment starts with the formulation of a problem, which is usually best stated in the form of a question. The only requirement that the problem must meet is that it must be meaningful. It must be answerable with the tools that are available to the psychologist.

Beyond this, the problem may be concerned with any aspect of behaviour, whether it is judged to be important or trivial. One lesson we learn from history is that we must not be hasty in judging the importance of the problem, on which a scientist works, for many times what was discarded as being of little importance contributed sizeably to later scientific advances.

Process of Experiment

One of the first steps that the experimenter will take in actually collecting his data is to select a group of subjects. The type of subject he/she studies will be determined by the nature of the problem. If he/she is concerned with psychotherapy, he/she may select a group of mentally disturbed patients.

The assignment of subjects to groups must be made in such a way that the groups will be approximately equivalent at the start of the experiment. The experimenter, next typically administers an experimental treatment to the groups.

Types of Experiments

There are two types of experiments i.e. Laboratory and Field experiments, which are discussed below

Laboratory Experiments

According to **Festinger** and **Katz**, lab experiment is "one in which the investigator creates a situation with the exact conditions, he wants to have and in which he controls some and manipulates other variables."

Thus, laboratory experiment is a study of problem in a situation in which some variables are manipulated and some are controlled in order to have an effect upon the dependent variable.

According to **Kerlinger**, *there are three main purposes of laboratory experiment*

(i) It purports to discover a relationship between the dependent variables and the independent variables under pure, uncontaminated and controlled conditions.

(ii) It helps in testing the accuracy of predictions derived from researches.

(iii) A laboratory experiment helps in building the theoretical systems by refining theories and hypothesis and thus, provides a breeding ground for scientific evaluation of those theories and hypothesis.

Advantages of Lab Experiment

Advantages of lab experiment are as follows

- It studies the problem in pure and controlled situation. Therefore, it has the fundamental requisite for any investigator, that is internal validity.
- Lab experiment is replicable.
- It has a greater degree of precision in manipulating of Independent variables.

Disadvantages of Lab Experiment

Disadvantages of lab experiment are as follows

- It lacks of external validity due to artificiality of situation.
- It is not feasible in all situations.
- It is costly and time taking.
- Behaviour of persons in certain situations may not be studied in laboratory research.

Field Experiments

A field experiment may be defined as a scientific investigation carried out in the field, which involves the direct manipulation of Independent and Dependent Variables.

The field experiment is a scientific investigation carried out in practical manner. Differences between the field experiment and the laboratory experiment lies in the fact that field experiment is carried out in a realistic way.

Advantages of Field Experiment

Advantages of field experiments are as follows

- One of the main advantages of field experiments, is that they involve the manipulation of a situation that is more realistic and practical than the laboratory setting.

- There is greater possibility that the relationships found are true demonstrations of what happens in real life situations.
- When the variables are stronger because of more realistic situations, an experimenter can make better and more sound generalisation.

Disadvantages of Field Experiment

Disadvantages of field experiment are as follows

- Since, a field experiment is carried out in a realistic situation, there is always a possibility that the effects of independent variables is contaminated with uncontrolled environmental variables.
- In many field situation's manipulations of independent variables may be difficult due to non-cooperation of subjects.
- In a field experiment, it is not possible to achieve a high degree of precision or accuracy because of some uncontrolled environmental variables.

Use of Experimental Method in Psychology

How exactly do researchers investigate the human mind and behaviour? While there are a number of different research techniques, the experimental method allows psychological researchers to look at cause and effect relationships. There are a few different types of experiments that psychological researchers might choose to use.

Lab experiments are very common in psychology because they allow the experimenter to control the variables. These experiments can be easier for other researchers to replicate. The problem, of course, is that what takes place in a lab is not always identical to what takes place in the real world.

Sometimes, researchers might opt to conduct their experiments in the field. *For example*– Let's imagine that a social psychologist is interested in researching pro-social behaviour. The experimenter might have a person pretend to faint and observe to see how long it takes onlookers to respond. This type of experiment can be great way to see behaviour in action in realistic settings.

Psychologists, like other scientists, utilise the scientific method when conducting an experiment. The scientific method is a set of procedures and principles that guide how scientists develop research questions, collect data and come to conclusions. *The four basic steps of the process are–*

(i) Forming a hypothesis
(ii) Designing a study and collecting data
(iii) Analysing the data and reaching conclusions
(iv) Sharing the findings

Quasi-Experimental Research Method

All experimental situations in which the researcher/experimenter does not have full control over the assignment of experimental units or the treatment cannot be manipulated, are collectively called *quasi-experimental method*. An quasi-experiment is carried out exactly like a true experiment, except for two important variations.

First, the investigator does not have the ability to assign a subject randomly or control the experimental groups. Rather, actively arranging an experimental situation consisting of a control and an experimental group, the investigator searches for a group of subjects that has been exposed to the particular Independent Variable. He is interested in a second group, similar to the first in other relevant respects, that has not experienced the Independent Variable. Being unable to select subjects randomly greatly increases the possibility that secondary variables may contaminate the investigation.

Aim of Quasi-Experimental Method

The aim of the quasi-experiment is the same as that of a true experiment i.e. to understand a cause-effect relationship. The initial steps involved in an quasi experiment are essentially the same as those employed with experimental designs. First, a problem must be identified and then a hypothesis spelled out in detail and to the point.

Advantages of Quasi-Experimental Method

Quasi-experimental investigations have some advantages over experimental investigations. *These are*

- It is possible to seek answers to certain kinds of questions about the past and unethical situations that could not be dealt with experimental method.
- Time can be saved by dealing with records that have been kept over the years rather than starting fresh.
- School, educational, social and industrial psychologists may especially benefit from using quasi-experimental investigations because schools, business and government agencies generally secure and preserve records over many years.

Disadvantages of Quasi-Experimental Method

Disadvantages quasi-experimental method are as follows

- Without proper randomisations, statistical test can be meaningless. Because randomisation is absent in this method, the casual relationships are difficult to determine.
- Lack of internal validity.

Field Studies

Field studies involve collecting data outside of an experimental or lab setting. This type of data collection is most often done in natural settings of the environment and can be done in a variety of ways for various disciplines. Field studies are known to be expensive, however, the amount and diversity of the data collected can be valuable.

Field studies collect original data through face to face interviews, surveys, or direct observation. This research technique is usually treated as an initial form of research because the data collected is specific only to the purpose for which it was gathered. Therefore, it is not applicable to the general public.

Advantages of Field Studies

The advantages of field studies are –

- It is conducted in a natural environment where there is no tampering of variables and the environment is not doctored.
- Due to the study being conducted in a comfortable environment, data can be collected even about ancillary topics.
- The researcher gains a deep understanding into the research subjects due to the proximity to them and hence the research is extensive, thorough and accurate.

Disadvantages of Field Studies

The disadvantages of field studies are–

- The studies are expensive and time-consuming and can take years to complete.
- It is very difficult for the researcher to distance themselves from a bias in the research study.
- The notes have to be exactly what the researcher says but the nomenclature is very tough to follow.
- It is an interpretive method which is subjective and entirely dependent on the ability of the researcher.
- In this method, it is impossible to control external variables and this constantly alters the nature of the research.

Cross Cultural Studies

Cross cultural studies involve studies carried out in different cultures, with the objective of verifying universality of theory or its specific application.

Choosing Appropriate Topics for Cross-Cultural Study

Many cross-cultural problems will never plague the researcher, if he chooses an appropriate topic for study. Choosing specific rather than general topics for investigation is a good start. General or global issue should be avoided. Since, little is known of the workings of another culture, variables such as social schemat's, religious systems and politics are difficult, not impossible to study. These abstractions are so complex and multidimensional that they are of little use for cross-cultural research.

Understanding Cultural Variables

The problem is that every culture 'should be understood in its own terms'. Such description has been a goal of anthropology and it is called the *emic* part of social science research. Another goal, however is to incorporate aspects of many cultures into a general hypothesis or theory, such as the influence of cultural art style on individual perception. Such theory building has been the goal of psychology and this goal is called the *etic* part of social science research.

The problem of psychologists is that the administering cross cultural studies test standardised in one country, may be imposing an artificial etic and losing the emic or meaningful aspects of the other culture as practiced by their member.

Use of Cross-Cultural Research in Psychology

The main purpose of cross-cultural research in psychology is the elaboration of general and specific objectives to the cultures involved without distorting the common goal. Generalisations, very common in social disciplines, must be supported empirically to satisfy the external validity of the conclusion. The advantage of the cross-cultural approach is that the possibilities for misinterpretation are less.

John Whiting, a leading figure in psychological anthropology and a pioneer in the development of systematic cross-cultural research, *states that the advantages of the cross-cultural method are two fold*

(i) It ensures the findings relating to human behaviour that general rather than being bound to a single culture.

(ii) It increases the range of variation of many variables.

Phenomenology

Phenomenology has its roots in a 20th century. This philosophical movement was based on the work of the philosopher **Edmund Husserl**. As research tool, phenomenology is based on the academic disciplines of philosophy and psychology and has become a widely accepted method for describing human experiences. Phenomenology is a qualitative research method that is used to describe how many human being experience a certain phenomenon.

A phenomenological study attempts to set aside biases and preconceived assumptions about human experiences, feelings, and responses to a particular situation. It allows the researcher to delve into the perceptions, perspectives, understandings and feelings of those people who have actually experienced situations of interest. Therefore, phenomenology can be defined as the direct investigation and description of phenomena as consciously experienced by people.

Characteristics of Phenomenology

Following is a list of the main characteristics of phenomenology research

- It seeks to understand how people experience a particular situation or phenomenon.
- It is conducted primarily through in-depth conversations and interviews; however, some studies may collect data from diaries, drawings or observation.
- Small samples sizes, often 10 or less participants, are common in phenomenological studies.
- Interview questions are open-ended to allow the participants to fully describe the experience from their own view point.
- Phenomenology is centered on the participants' experiences with no regard to social or cultural norms, traditions, or preconceived ideas about the experience.
- It focuses on these four aspects of a lived experience: lived space, lived body, lived time and lived human relations.
- Data collected in qualitative analysis includes an attempt to identify themes or make generalisations regarding how a particular phenomenon is actually perceived or experienced.

Advantages of Phenomenology

Following are some advantages of phenomenology are –

- Can look at change processes over time.
- Helps to understand the experiences, of people
- Help to adjust the new issues and ideas that the emerged in society.
- Contribute to the development of new theories.

Disadvantages of Phenomenology

Phenomenology has many disadvantages which are as follows

- Data gathering can take up a great deal of time and resources.
- The analysis and interpretation of data may be difficult.
- May be harder than positivist approach to control pace, progress and end points.
- Policy-makers may give low credibility to a phenomenological study.

Use of Phenomenology in Psychology

The Phenomenological method in psychology was developed by the American psychologist **Amedeo Giorgi** in the early 1970s. Giorgi based his method on principles laid out by philosophers like Edmund Husserl and Maurice Merleau-Ponty as well as what he had learned from his prior professional experience in psychophysics. Giorgi was an early pioneer of the humanistic psychology movement; Even todays, the use of phenomenology in psychology continues to advocate for the importance of a human science approach to psychological subject matter.

According to Giorgi, The phenomenological psychological attitude is to be assumed while analysing the data in order to ensure that "the results reflect a careful description of precisely the features of the experienced phenomenon as they present themselves to the consciousness of the researcher".

In this sense, the researcher attends to the phenomenon in its "own appropriate mode of self-givenness, thus meeting the demand for scientific objectivity concerning the subjective : the method of phenomenological reduction". This is done so as to reach a level of understanding that is appropriate for psychologists, while also helping the researcher to reach a empathically sensed intuition of the experiences.

Grounded Theory

Grounded theory refers to "the purpose of generation of theory which is based on collection of data from multiple sources." It is the only method of qualitative research which also uses quantitative data when required. The grounded theory approach aims to collect data and interpret the data from the textual base (field notes or video recordings).

After the process of interpreting, the data base is categorised into different variables and then the interrelationship between these variables are analysed and studied. The approach of grounded theory was developed by Glaser and Strauss in 1960's. Grounded theory provides a direction to the researcher and directs them to generate new theories or modify the existing ones.

In the words of **Glaser**, "Grounded theory is multivariate. It happens sequentially, subsequently, simultaneously, serendipitously and scheduled."

Objective of Grounded Theory

The basic objective of the grounded theory are

- Since the approach consists of a series of systematic steps and the data is collected from more than one source, it assures to provide a 'good theory' as the output.
- The grounded theory approach emphasises on the process by which the theory is evaluated. This determines the quality of the theory.
- The grounded theory approach also emphasise on enhancing the theoretical sensitivity.
- One goal of a grounded theory is to formulate hypothesis based on conceptual ideas.
- On the basis of the questions asked the researcher tries to discover the participants' main concern and how they continually try to resolve it.
- It also aims to generate those concepts which explain people's actions regardless of time and place. The descriptive parts of a ground theory are there mainly to illustrate the concepts.

Significance of Grounded Theory

The data or the information collected and the theory generated with the help of grounded theory is significant because

- The ground theorists prepare report on the basis of information collected with the help of various sources which increases the chances of reliability and validity of the theory.
- The ground theory approach gives an opportunity for exploring the facts and analysing the casual reason behind those facts.
- It is an inductive type of research which has its basis or is 'grounded' on the base of observations and the data collected.
- The grounded theory approach also provides a base to specify how a knowledge base should be changed in the light of new information.
- The grounded theory often categorises data which further forms a basis for organising and reporting results.

Focus Group

A focus group is a form of qualitative research in which group of people are asked about their attitude towards a product, concept, advertisement, idea or packaging. Questions are asked in an interactive group setting where participants are free to talk with other group members. In the world of marketing, focus groups are an important tool for acquiring feedback regarding new products as well as various topics.

In the social science especially in psychology, focus groups allow interviewers to study people in a more natural setting than a one-to-one interview. In combination with participant observation, it can be used for gaining access to various cultural and social groups, selecting sites to study, sampling of such sites, and raising unexpected issues for exploration.

Focus groups have a high approach validity since the idea is easy to understand the results are believable. Also, its cost effective. One can get results relatively, quickly and they can increase the sample size of a report by talking with several folks at once.

Use of Focus Group Method

Focus group Method can be used alone or in combination with other methods. The conventional aim of focus groups is to understand, perspective of stories, discourses and experiences which are meaninglessly expressed by people.

The focus group can be used either as a primary means of data collection or as a supplement to a multi-method approach depending on how it fits into the overall research plan. More practical uses of the focus group includes decision-making, intervention, collective empowerment and social change.

In practice, the focus group method is most commonly used for the following–

- To check the validity of conceptual model.
- To supplement other traditional methods.
- To invite a uniquely different perspective on an issue.
- To generate report on a topic.

Types of Focus Group

The variants of focus group include–

- **Two-way Focus Group** One focus group watches another focus group and discusses the observed interactions and conclusions.
- **Dual Moderator Focus Group** One moderator ensures the session progresses smoothly, while another ensures that all the topics are covered.
- **Dueling Moderator Focus Group** Two moderators deliberately take opposite sides on the issue under discussion.

- **Respondent Moderator Focus Group** One or more of the respondents are asked to act as the moderator temporarily.
- **Client Participant Focus Group** One or more client representatives participate in the discussion, either covertly or overtly.
- **Mini Focus Group** It is comprised of 4 to 5 members rather than 8 to 12.
- **Teleconference Focus Group** Telephone networks are used.
- **Online Focus Group** Computers and internet networks are used.

Narrative Research Method

Narrative research is a term that constitutes a group of approaches that in turn rely on the written or spoken words or visual representation of individuals. These approaches typically focus on the lines of individuals based on their narrated stories.

The emphasis in such approaches is on the story, typically both what and how is narrated. Narrative research can be considered both as a research method in itself, but also as a phenomenon under study.

Narrative methods considers 'real world measures' that are appropriate when life problems' are investigated. In a basic linear approach, that encompasses the study of the experiences of a single individual embracing different stories of the life and exploring the significance of those different experiences.

Requirements of Narrative Inquiry

Basic requirements of narrative research are as follows–

- Trust and openness in research relationship
- High levels of ethical and critical engagement
- Mutual and sincere collaboration
- Tolerance of ambiguity
- Valuing of signs, symbols, metaphors
- Using multiple data sources

Advantages of Narrative Research

Following are some advantages of narrative research

- Memorable and interesting knowledge helps in understanding people, their cultures and how they have created change.
- Narrative research tries to make sense of the past and create meanings, as they tell and/or 'show' us what happened to them.
- Shape of a story helps organise information about how people have interpreted events; the values, beliefs and experiences that guide those interpretations; and their hopes, intentions and plans for the future.
- We find complex patterns, descriptions of identity construction and reconstruction, and evidence of social discourses that impact a person's knowledge creation from specific cultural standpoints.
- Knowledge gained in this way is transient, partial and provisional; characterised by multiple views, perspectives, truths and meanings.

Use of Narrative Method in Psychology

Narrative psychology is not a single or well-defined theory. It refers to a range of approaches to examine the role of stories in human life. In narrative psychology, a person's life story becomes a form of identity as how they choose to reflect on, integrate and tell facts and events of their life not only reflects, but also shapes, who they are. It is a social constructivist approach that studies the implications of these stories for individuals and societies.

Psychologists became interested in stories and everyday accounts of life in the 1970s. The term narrative psychology was introduced by Theodore R Sarbin in his 1986 book 'Narrative Psychology:

He claimed that human conduct is best explained through stories and the explanation should be done through qualitative research. Sarbin argued that 'narrative' is a root metaphor for psychology that should replace the mechanistic and organic metaphors which shaped so much theory and research in the discipline over the past century.

Jerome Bruner explored the 'narrative kind of knowing' in a more empirical way in his 1986 book, 'Actual Minds, Possible Worlds'. Bruner makes a distinction between 'paradigmatic' and 'narrative' forms of thought, proposing that they are both fundamental but irreducible to one another.

The narrative approach was also furthered by Dan P McAdams, who put forward a life story model of identity to describe three levels of personalities, leading to exploration of how significant life transitions are narrated and how the 'self and culture comes together in the narrative'.

Case Study

The case study is not itself a research method. Instead, it constitutes an approach to the study of singular entities, which may involve the use of a wide range of diverse methods of data collection and analysis. The case study is, therefore, not characterised by the methods used to collect and analyse data, but rather by its focus upon a particular unit of analysis.

The case study involves an in-depth, intensive and sharply focused exploration of an event. Case studies have a long and varied history. They have been used in many different discipline, including sociology, political theory, history, social anthropology, education and psychoanalysis. Case studies can make use of both qualitative and quantitative research methods.

Characteristics of Case Study

Major characteristics of case study are

- **An Idiographic Perspective** Here, researchers are concerned with the particular rather than the general. The aim is to understand an individual case, in its particularity. This can be contrasted with a nomothetic approach, which aims to identify general laws of human behaviour by averaging out individual variation.
- **Attention to Contextual Data** Study research takes a holistic approach, in which it considers the case within its context. This means that the researcher pays attention to the ways in which the various dimensions of the case relate to or interact with its environment. Thus, while particular cases need to be identified as the focus of the study, they cannot be considered in isolation.
- **Triangulation** Triangulation enriches case study research because it allows the researcher to approach the case from number of different perspective. This, in turn, facilitates an appreciation of the various dimensions of the case as well as its embeddedness within its various contexts.
- **A Temporal Element** Case studies involve the investigation of occurrences over a period of time. According to Yin, "establishing the how and why of a complex human situation is a classic example of the use of case studies." Case studies are concerned with processes that take place over time. This means that a focus on change and development is an important feature of case studies.
- **A Concern with Theory** Case studies facilitate theory generation. The detailed exploration of a particular case can generate insights into social or psychological processes, which in turn, can give rise to theoretical formulations and hypothesis. Freud's psychoanalytic case studies constitute a clear example of the relationship between case studies and theory development. In addition, case studies can also be used to test existing theories or to clarify or extend such theories by looking at deviant or extreme cases.

Research Methods for Psychological Case Study

Many methods can be used in case study research. Some of them are well-known qualitative techniques, such as semi-structured interviewing, participant observation and diaries. Data for case studies can also be generated on the basis of personal or official documents. The data can be analysed in a number of different ways, including grounded theory and interpretative phenomenological analysis.

Smith identifies two further methods, the twenty statements test and Repertory Grids, as suitable analytic techniques for case study research.

Twenty Statements Test (Gordon)

Here, the participant is asked to give 20 answers to the question, about "who or what are you?" Each answer begins with the words 'I am .....' and the participants response can be explored in terms of content or sequence. In addition, the test can be repeated at different points in time to identify self-perception.

Repertory Grids (Kelly)

In this grid, the participant is asked to generate about 10 elements, which he or she then compares with one another. *e.g.* if the elements are 'self as friend', 'self as lover', 'self as parent', 'self as worker' and so on, the participant would be asked in what way any two of them are similar and how they are different from a third (*e.g.* 'self as friend' and 'self as lover' may be described as 'warm' and 'contrasted' when 'self as worker', which is described as 'business-like').

Each comparison generates a construct, that is the terms of reference that the person uses to think about his or her social roles.

This process of comparison continues until the participant finds it difficult to generate new constructs. Finally, the participant rates each element in relation to each construct when the grid is complete, it provides a visual display of patterns and associations between elements and constructs. This, in turn, provides insight into the ways in which the participant constructs personal meanings to make sense of the social world.

Although, these methods can be used qualitatively, they do not constitute what has been referred to as 'big Q' methodology. This is because they work with preconceived categories, which are then filled with content specific to the case under investigation. However, they are idiographic, they focus upon the individual case without reference to a comparison group.

Advantages of Case Study Method

Advantages of case study method are as follows

- Case study allows a lot of detail to be collected that would not normally be easily obtained by other research designs. The data collected is normally a greater depth than can be found through other experimental design.
- Within the case study, scientific experiments can be conducted.
- Case studies can help experimenters adopt ideas and produce novel hypothesis, which can be used for later testing.
- Developed research questions for future research could then be generalised.

Disadvantages of Case Study Method

- One of main criticisms is that, the data collected can't necessarily be generalised to the wider population. This leads to data being collected over longitudinal case studies not always being relevant or particularly useful.
- Case studies are generally on one person, but there also tends to be only one experimenter collecting data. This can lead to bias in data collection, which may further influence results.
- It is very difficult to draw a definite cause/effect from the case study.

Ethnography

Ethnography is a research method which basically intends to study culture through close observation and active participation.

This method is also known as *ethnomethodology* or *methodology of people. It focuses on studying socio cultural phenomena of a community. The ethnographer/researcher collects information regarding the socio-cultural phenomena from a lot of people belonging to the community under study.*

Purpose of Ethnographic Research

The purpose of ethnographic researech are as follows

- It helps in cross cultural analysis.
- It helps in analysing the past events or the history of the culture.
- It helps in studying the behaviour, experiences and attitudes of individuals in a more natural environment.
- Close observation increases the chances of validity in the reports and theory formulated.

Types of Ethnographic Research

There are many types of Ethnographic Research which are as follows-

- **Macro Ethnography** It is the study of broadly defined cultural groupings such as–'the Indians', 'the Turkish etc'. The common perspectives are studied at a more larger level which are found to be common under a more broader strata.
- **Micro Ethnography** It is the study of more specific cultural groupings such as the 'local government' and the 'terrorists.'
- **Emic Perspectives** It is the ethnographic approach under which the viewpoints and responses of the 'ingroup' or the members of the culture under study are noted down.
- **Etic Perspective** It is the ethnographic approach, under which the viewpoints and responses of the 'out groups' or the members who do not belong to the culture under study are studied.

Steps of Ethnographic Research

Following steps are followed in ethnographic research

(i) **Selection** The ethnographic research begins with selection of a culture. The researcher selects the culture/community or population according to his/her interest.

(ii) **Review of Literature** Then the researcher reviews the literature pertaining to the culture to get a brief idea and historical sketch of the culture selected for study.

(iii) **Identification of Variables** The researcher then identifies variables which interest him or her as well as the members of the culture that needs to be explored.

(iv) **Entry** The ethnographer then tries to enter the culture and gain the acceptance of the members of the culture.

(v) **Cultural Immersion** Ethnographers live in the culture for months or even years which they have chosen to study. The middle stages of the ethnographic research involve gaining informants, using them to gain yet more informants in a chaining process.

(vi) **Data Collection** After gaining the confidence of the respondents, the researcher collects information in the form of observational transcripts and interview recordings and tapings.

(vii) **Development of Theory** After analysing the data, the researcher formulates theory on the basis of interpretation of the results and reports achieved.

The ethnographic researcher tries his/her best to avoid theoretical preconceptions and formulates theory on the basis of the perspectives of the members of the culture and observation. The researcher may seek validation of induced theories by going back to members of the culture for their reaction.

Use of Ethnography in Psychology

Ethnography constitutes a major focus in the psychological literature; however, debates continue regarding the usage of this qualitative methods. Despite the fact ethnographic research fall within the purview of post-positivism and constructivism-interpretivism frameworks, positivists, postpositivists and postmodernists who the currently argue over the definition of ethnography and criteria for evaluating ethnographic work.

Despite the conflicts and changes that emerge out of different philosophical approaches to ethnography, ethnographic research have had and continue to have, a major impact on topics often considered to be within the purview of counselling psychology (*e.g.* vocational development).

Stewart advocated the usage of ethnographically informed research in psychology. She noted that ethnographic research are 'compatible' with the 'methodological values' of most psychologists. Although researchers in social work and in social and community psychology advocate the use of ethnographic research, there is paucity of published ethnographies in counselling psychology. Counselling psychologists' focus on relationship and integration of contextual variables with respect to culture is advocated and evidenced throughout much of the literature in our discipline. Greater efforts are needed in counselling psychology to incorporate ethnographically informed research methods in studies with diverse communities.

EXAM BASED QUESTIONS

1 **The word Paradigm was first used by**
(a) Robert Owen (b) Thomas Cock
(c) Kuhn (d) None of these

2 **Mixed-method methodology of research is a combination of**
(a) Qualitative research (b) Quantitative research
(c) Both a and b (d) None of the above

3 **In which kind of research results can be depicted in the form of numericals?**
(a) Mixed-method research (b) Qualitative research
(c) Quantitative research (d) All of these

4 **Which among the methods are used in quantitative research?**
(a) Online surveys (b) Online polls
(c) Questionnaires (d) All of these

5 **Which among the following is correct about the result achieved from the quantitative research?**
(a) Logical (b) Hypothetical
(c) Biased (d) All of these

6 **Which among the following are the advantages of quantitative research?**
(a) Quick data collection
(b) Wider scope of data analysis
(c) Eliminate bias
(d) All of the above

7 **Whose work involves the statistical and mathematical modeling of psychological processes?**
(a) Qualitative psychologist
(b) Quantitative psychologist
(c) Experimental psychologist
(d) None of the above

8 **Generalisation of results is a characteristic of**
(a) Qualitative research (b) Quantitative research
(c) Both a and b (d) None of these

9 **The process of collecting data in 'qualitative research' is field based on**
(a) open-ended response (b) comprehensive words
(c) interactive (d) None of these

10 **Which kind of research recognises that the research is not value-free and that it can be influenced by his values and beliefs?**
(a) Qualitative research (b) Quantitative research
(c) Both a and b (d) None of the above

11 **Which among the following is correct about the relevence of qualitative research in psychology?**
(a) In depth knowledge of human nature
(b) Attitude
(c) Bahaviour and experience
(d) All of the above

12 Which one of the following statements about naturalistic observation is not correct?
(a) The behaviour observed is more likely to be spontaneous than behaviour in a laboratory set-up.
(b) One trained observer is more advantageous than several trained observers.
(c) It is a preferred method of data collection in ethological research.
(d) Observer bias is one of the important problems associated with this method.

13 Which one of the following is an advantage of the method of naturalistic observation over the experimental method?
(a) It leads to better control over the variables to be studied
(b) It is more objective
(c) It is closer to reality
(d) It facilitates the study of cause-effect relationships

14 A researcher, interested in studying the psychological functioning of the group, becomes a member of the group and lives with the group members for a stipulated time period. This is an example of which one of the following?
(a) Naturalistic observation (b) Participant observation
(c) Scientific observation (d) Controlled observation

15 Naturalistic observation is the major method of study used by
(a) psychoanalysts, ethologists, anthropologists and Gestalt psychologists.
(b) psychoanalysts and Gestalt psychologists.
(c) ethologists, anthropologists and gestalt psychologists.
(d) psychoanalysts, anthropologists and Gestalt psychologists.

16 If a cross cultural psychologist wants to study how mothers of Gond tribe deal with the aggressive responses of their children, the most appropriate method for this study would be
(a) field experiment (b) controlled observation
(c) naturalistic observation (d) projective technique

17 Which of the following characteristic of observers would most likely to be associated with high inter observer reliability?
(a) Observers are unclear about what is to be observed
(b) Observers are well trained
(c) Observers are tired or bored
(d) Observers differ in outcome expectancy

18 Which one of the following is a primary advantage of the naturalistic observation?
(a) It is a highly objective research method.
(b) It allows for the better control of secondary variance in the dependent behavioural variable of interest.
(c) It allows for cheaply as compared to other research methods.
(d) It allows to study the behaviour that is more natural, varied and spontaneous than in a laboratory.

19 The influence that an observer has on the behaviour under observation is called
(a) reactivity
(b) observer bias
(c) demand characteristics
(d) expectancy effect

20 Which of the following is not a characteristics of the naturalistic observation method?
(a) Observation in a natural setting
(b) Systematic observation of behaviour
(c) Major goal being description of behaviour
(d) Manipulation of events by an experimenter

21 Which of the following observational methods represents a middle ground between passive non-intervention and the systematic control and manipulation of variables in laboratory methods?
(a) Naturalistic observation
(b) Participant observation
(c) Structured observation
(d) A field experiment

22 The distinction between observation with intervention and observation without intervention is similar to the distinction between
(a) natural use traces and controlled use traces
(b) physical traces and archival records
(c) quantitative and qualitative data analysis
(d) correlations and spurious relationships

23 Researchers who conduct observational studies typically use a combination of time sampling and situation sampling to achieve
(a) nominal scales of measurement
(b) representative samples of behaviour
(c) maximum interobserver reliability
(d) internally valid samples of behaviour

24 Researchers who use narrative records seek to provide a verbal summary of observations and to develop a theory that explains behaviour in the narrative records. This approach to data analysis represents
(a) qualitative data analysis with comprehensive recording of behaviour.
(b) qualitative data analysis with selective recording of behaviour.
(c) quantitative data analysis with comprehensive recording of behaviour.
(d) quantitative data analysis with selective recording of behaviour.

25 'Census' is the example of which method?
(a) Ex-post facto (b) Field study
(c) Sociometry (d) Survey

26 Prepoll forecasts are mainly based on
(a) observation
(b) field experiment
(c) survey
(d) psychological scaling

27 Experiment is defined as 'observation under controlled conditions'. What an experimenter observes?

(a) Changes in independent variable
(b) Changes in dependent variable
(c) Changes in extraneous variable
(d) All of the above

28 In experimental research designs, error variance is sought to be minimised by

(a) random assignment of subjects to groups only
(b) control or systematic manipulation of extraneous variables only
(c) matching techniques only
(d) All of the above

29 The researcher smiles at the friendly subjects, but not at the unfriendly subjects and affects the research results, the results suffer from

(a) subject bias (b) experimental bias
(c) population bias (d) subjective bias

30 Psychologists use a wide variety of research methods. Which one is best?

(a) Experimental study
(b) Correlational study
(c) Case study
(d) There is no single best method

31 Which one of the following statements regarding field experiments is not true?

(a) Field experiments require investigators, who are specially skilled for intervening in social situation.
(b) The greatest difficulty in field experiments lies in the randomisation and manipulation of the independents variable.
(c) Field experiments are concerned with casual relationship, but not with the direction of relationship.
(d) Field experiments are carried out in natural setting.

32 Experimental and quasi-experimental can not be distinguished on the basis of

(a) manipulation of independent variable
(b) random assignment of subjects to experimental conditions
(c) studying casual relationship
(d) applying statistical analysis

33 Which of the following is true about experimental designs?

(a) Internal validity is controlled
(b) Are the weaker designs
(c) Easier to conduct
(d) Control groups are not used

34 Which one of the following is the most essential characteristic of the experimental method?

(a) Active manipulation of the independent variable
(b) Ability to test complex hypothesis
(c) Precise measurement and recording of the dependent variables
(d) Use of sophisticated tools and equipment

35 The most frequently used method in psychology to explore cause and effect relationships between variables is

(a) correlational method
(b) experimental method
(c) natural observation method
(d) participant observer method

36 Maximum replicability is possible, in which of the following method?

(a) Field study
(b) Participant observation
(c) Ex-post facto study
(d) Lab experiment

37 Which one of the following methods is used by researchers to make the most exacting study of naturally occurring behaviour?

(a) Experimental method
(b) Systematic observation
(c) Survey research
(d) Field experiment

38 Which of the following method requires specific efforts to deal with ethical issues?

(a) Field experiment (b) Survey research
(c) Laboratory experiment (d) Participant observation

39 The main difference between field studies and laboratory studies is that

(a) field study is less expensive, while laboratory study is more expensive.
(b) field study is less explorative, while laboratory study is more explorative.
(c) field study has limited scope to control the variables, while laboratory study has adequate scope to regorously control the variables.
(d) field study can be conducted without sufficient professional experience, while laboratory study cannot be conducted without sufficient professional experience.

40 Which one of the following statements regarding field experiments is not true?

(a) Field experiments require investigators, who are specially skilled for intervening in social situation.
(b) The greatest difficulty in field experiments lies in the randomisation and manipulation of the independents variable.
(c) Field experiments are concerned with casual relationship but not with the direction of relationship.
(d) Field experiments are carried out in natural settings.

41 Time series design is the example of

(a) factorial design
(b) experimental design
(c) quasi-experimental design
(d) between group design

42 Which one of the following is a quasi-experimental design?

(a) Panel design (b) Ex-post facto study
(c) Time series design (d) Randomised block design

43 Which one of the following characteristics predominantly discriminates between 'ex-postfac to' research and experimental research?
(a) Control of variables
(b) Number of variables
(c) Value of sample
(d) Use of statistical analysis technique

44 Which of the following characteristics of true experiments is most often lacking in quasi-experiments?
(a) Potential for contamination due to diffusion of treatments.
(b) High degree of control.
(c) Appropriate comparison or control condition.
(d) Implementation of some type of intervention or treatment.

45 Which of the following should not be used in cross-cultural studies?
(a) Psychometric tests (b) Projective tests
(c) Observations (d) Interviews

46 Who said, "Grounded theory is multivariate. It happens sequentially, subsequently, simultaneously, serendipitously and scheduled"?
(a) Glaser (b) Strauss
(c) Robert (d) None of these

47 Which research method emphasises on the process by which the theory is evaluated?
(a) Experimental method
(b) Cross-cultural method
(c) Grounded theory
(d) Ethnography

48 Which among the following is correct about Grounded theory?
(a) It emphasise on enhancing theoretical sensitivity
(b) Formulate hypothesis based on conceptual ideas
(c) Both a and b
(d) None of the above

49 Which research method aim to capture content in the form of understanding, perspective, stories, discourses and experiences not otherwise meaningfully expressed by number?
(a) Ethnography (b) Grounded theory
(c) Focus group (d) Experimental methods

50 Which among the following is correct about focus group method?
(a) To check the validity of conceptual method
(b) A form of qualitative research
(c) Generate conversation worthy of analysis
(d) All of the above

51 The variants of focus group include
(a) dual moderator focus group
(b) dueling moderator focus group
(c) mini focus group
(d) All of the above

52 Which method is also known as methodology of people?
(a) Focus group (b) Case study
(c) Ethnography (d) Cross-cultural method

53 The ethnographic approach under which view points and responses of the 'out groups, are noted down is known as
(a) Macro ethnography (b) Micro Ethnography
(c) Emic perspective (d) Etic perspective

54 Which among the following are the purpose of ethnographic research?
(a) To help in cross-cultural analysis
(b) To analysing the past events
(c) Helps in studying the behaviour
(d) All of the above

55 Which of the following statements are correct regarding primary research?
1. It is also known as field research.
2. It can be in numerous form that includes questionnaires and telephone interviews.

Select the correct answer using the codes given below
(a) Only 1 (b) Only 2
(c) Both 1 and 2 (d) Neither 1 nor 2

56 Which of the following statements is/are correct regarding naturalistic observation?
1. Carried out in a controlled conditions.
2. An obstrusive observation procedures are used.
3. Popularised by ethologist, who study animal behaviour in its natural habitats.

Select the correct answer using the codes given below
(a) Only 1 (b) 2 and 3
(c) All of these (d) None of these

57 Arrange the following in ascending order in terms of control.
1. Field experiment 2. Lab experiment
3. Quasi-experiment 4. Ex-post facto

Codes
(a) 1,2,3,4 (b) 4,3,1,2
(c) 4,1,3,2 (d) 3,4,1,2

58 Lab experiments are higher on which of the following?
1. Internal validity 2. External validity
3. Replicability 4. Subjectivity
5. Precision

Select the correct answer using the codes given below
(a) 2, 3 and 5 (b) 1, 4 and 5
(c) 2, 3 and 4 (d) 1, 3 and 5

59 Which of the following are the types of descriptive research?
1. Field study 2. Case study
3. Ex-post factor 4. Survey research

5. Content analysis 6. Ethnographic study

Select the correct answer using the codes given below

(a) 1, 2, 3 and 4 (b) 2, 3, 4 and 6
(c) 2, 3, 5 and 6 (d) All of these

60 Which of the following are the types of field studies?

1. Exploratory field study
2. Survey field study
3. Hypothesis testing field study
4. Cross sectional field study

Select the correct answer using the codes given below

(a) 1 and 2 (b) 1 and 3 (c) 2 and 4 (d) 1 and 4

61 Arrange the following research methods in order of their increasing potential to find casual relationships.

1. Experiments 2. Field studies
3. Surveys 4. Quasi-experiments

Codes

(a) 1, 2, 3, 4 (b) 3, 2, 4, 1 (c) 3, 4, 2, 1 (d) 1, 3, 2, 4

62 Consider the following statements about

1. Experimental method has introduced the quantitative measurement in psychology.
2. It is low on replicability.

Which of the statements given above is/are correct?

(a) Both 1 and 2 (b) Only 2
(c) Only 1 (d) Neither 1 nor 2

63 Arrange the following types of investigation.

1. Field experiment
2. Laboratory experiment
3. Ex-post facto field study

The typical sequential arrangement of these investigations in descending order in term of the researcher's ability to control secondary variance would be

(a) 1, 2, 3 (b) 2, 1, 3 (c) 2, 3, 1 (d) 3, 1, 2

64 Which of the following statements regarding quasi-experiments are correct?

1. There is no random assignment of subjects in quasi-experiments.
2. There are no independent and dependent variables in quasi-experiments.
3. Quasi-experiments are ex-post facto studies.
4. Casual inferences cannot be made from quasi-experiments.

Select the correct answer using the codes given below

(a) 1 and 3 (b) 2 and 4 (c) 1, 3 and 4 (d) 1, 2 and 3

65 Arrange the following three types of psychological investigation.

1. Field experiment
2. Laboratory experiment
3. Ex-post facto field study

Codes

(a) 3, 2, 1 (b) 3, 1, 2 (c) 2, 1, 3 (d) 2, 3, 1

Directions (Q. Nos. 66-74) *In the question given below are two statements labelled as Assertion (A) and Reason (R). In context of the two statements, which one of the following is correct?*

Codes

(a) Both A and R are true and R is the correct explanation of A
(b) Both A and R are true, but R is not the correct explanation of A
(c) A is true, but R is false
(d) A is false, but R is true

66 **Assertion** (A) A case study is an unavoidable technique in the clinical setting.

Reason (R) If provides a complete picture of the subject for diagnosis and prognosis.

67 **Assertion** (A) The results of experimental method can be employed to formulate universal law.

Reason (R) Experimental method is an objective method.

68 **Assertion** (A) While, carrying out surveys, if possible random samples are preferred to non-random samples.

Reason (R) Random samples usually permit less accurate generalisation from samples to populations.

69 **Assertion** (A) Numerous experimental psychologists now propose that behavioural research must reply on unobtrusive measures of dependent variables for dependable and valid results.

Reason (R) Human participants respond to experimental stimuli according to their own hypothesis, which may have little or no correspondence to the research hypothesis.

70 **Assertion** (A) Factorial experimental designs are less efficient than quasi-experimental designs.

Reason (R) Factorial experimental designs yield information about the main and interaction effects variables.

71 **Assertion** (A) Field experimenters are high on external validity.

Reason (R) Field experiments are carried in real life situations.

72 **Assertion** (A) Field experiment is an experimental research whereas field study is a non-experimental one.

Reason (R) Field experiment is more precise than field study.

73 Assertion (A) Observation is a primary method of any scientific enquiry.

Reason (R) Empirical studies are based on experience and experimentalist.

74 Assertion (A) The researchers in the field of ethology quite often prefer naturalistic observation as a research method.

Reason (R) Naturalistic observation is free from observer bias.

75 Match the following

List I (Research Method)	List II (Meaning)
A. Case study	1. Respondents may distort their response to make them socially acceptable
B. Correlational research	2. Difficulties in generalising to the population at large
C. Observation	3. The behaviours of the persons may change, when they are aware of the process of data collection
D. Survey research	4. The findings show the nature of association, but not cause-and-effect relationship

Codes

	A	B	C	D		A	B	C	D
(a)	2	3	4	1	(b)	1	4	3	2
(c)	1	3	4	2	(d)	2	4	3	1

76 Match the following

List I (Concept)	List II (Method)
A. Time sampling	1. Ex-post facto studies
B. Double blind	2. Case study
C. Natural setting	3. Observation
D. Biographic records	4. Experiment

Codes

	A	B	C	D		A	B	C	D
(a)	4	1	3	2	(b)	2	4	1	3
(c)	3	4	1	2	(d)	4	3	2	1

77 Match the following

List I (Tools)	List II (Types)
A. Experiment	1. Structured v/s unstructured
B. Interview	2. Participant v/s non-participant
C. Observation	3. Etic v/s emic
D. Cross-cultural studies	4. True v/s Quasi

Codes

	A	B	C	D
(a)	1	4	3	2
(b)	1	3	4	2
(c)	4	1	2	3
(d)	4	1	3	2

78 Match the following

List I (Method)	List II (Basic Problem)
A. Correlational research	1. Respondents may disort answers in a socially desirable way
B. Case study	2. Shows only the association, but not the cause-and-effect relationship
C. Observation	3. Problems in generalising to the population at large
D. Survey	4. Behaviour may change, if the persons know that they are being watched

Codes

	A	B	C	D		A	B	C	D
(a)	2	3	4	1	(b)	3	2	4	1
(c)	2	3	1	4	(d)	3	2	1	4

79 Match the following

List I (Method)	List II (Procedure)
A. Experiment	1. Naturalistic observation
B. Field study	2. Control and manipulation of variables
C. Survey method	3. Measurement of scores on two or more fact
D. Correlational study	4. Questionnaire

Codes

	A	B	C	D		A	B	C	D
(a)	1	4	3	2	(b)	2	1	4	3
(c)	1	2	3	4	(d)	3	1	2	4

80 Match the following

List I (Research Method)	List II (Main Precaution for Valid Results)
A. Experiment	1. Obtrusive Procedure
B. Naturalistic observation	2. Contral group
C. Survey	3. Generalisation
D. Case study	4. Sample size

Codes

	A	B	C	D		A	B	C	D
(a)	2	1	4	3	(b)	3	4	1	2
(c)	2	4	1	3	(d)	3	1	4	2

81 Match the following

List I (Method)	List II (Procedure)
A. Experimental method	1. Time sampling
B. Survey method	2. Correlations
C. Observation method	3. Personal Interview
D. Non-experimental method	4. Case histories
	5. Casual relations

Codes

	A	B	C	D		A	B	C	D
(a)	1	3	4	2	(b)	5	2	4	3
(c)	1	2	4	3	(d)	5	3	1	2

Directions (Q. Nos. 82-86) *Read the passage given below and answer the following questions.*

A focus group is a form of qualitative research in which group of people are asked about their attitude towards a product, concept, advertisement, idea or packaging. Questions are asked in an interactive group setting where participants are free to talk with other group members. In the world of marketing, focus groups are an important tool for acquiring feedback regarding new products as well as various topics.

In the social science and urban planning, focus groups allow interviewers to study people in a more natural setting than a one-to-one interview. In combination with participant observation, they can be used for gaining access to various cultural and social groups, selecting sites to study, sampling of such sites and raising unexpected issues for exploration.

Focus groups have a high approach validity since the idea is easy to understand the results are believable. Also, they are low in cost, one can get results relatively, quickly and they can increase the sample size of a report by talking with several folks at once.

Used alone or in combination with other methods, the conventional aims of focus groups is to capture content in the form of understanding, perspective, stories, discourses and experiences not otherwise meaningfully expressed by numbers. The focus group can be used either as a primary means of data collection or as a supplement to a multi-method approach depending on how it fits into the overall research plan.

82 Focus group is a form of

(a) qualitative research (b) quantitative research
(c) mixed method research (d) None of these

83 Which among the following is correct about focus group method?

(a) Questions are asked in interactive group setting
(b) Participants are free to talk with other group members
(c) It allow interviewers to study people in natural setting
(d) All of the above

84 The significance of focus group method is that

(a) idea is easy to understand
(b) low in cost
(c) Both a and b
(d) None of the above

85 The conventional aim of focus group method is to

(a) capture content in form of stories
(b) capture content in form of discourses
(c) capture content in form of understanding
(d) All of the above

86 Which method can be used as a primary means of data collection or as a supplement to a multi method approach?

(a) Cross-cultural method (b) Focus group
(c) Experimental research (d) Ethnography

ANSWERS

1 (c)	2 (c)	3 (b)	4 (d)	5 (a)	6 (d)	7 (b)	8 (b)	9 (c)	10 (a)
11 (d)	12 (b)	13 (c)	14 (b)	15 (c)	16 (c)	17 (b)	18 (d)	19 (a)	20 (d)
21 (c)	22 (a)	23 (b)	24 (a)	25 (d)	26 (c)	27 (a)	28 (b)	29 (b)	30 (a)
31 (c)	32 (b)	33 (a)	34 (a)	35 (b)	36 (d)	37 (d)	38 (c)	39 (c)	40 (c)
41 (c)	42 (b)	43 (a)	44 (b)	45 (c)	46 (a)	47 (c)	48 (c)	49 (c)	50 (d)
51 (d)	52 (c)	53 (d)	54 (d)	55 (c)	56 (b)	57 (b)	58 (d)	59 (d)	60 (b)
61 (c)	62 (c)	63 (b)	64 (c)	65 (a)	66 (a)	67 (b)	68 (c)	69 (a)	70 (d)
71 (b)	72 (b)	73 (a)	74 (c)	75 (d)	76 (c)	77 (b)	78 (d)	79 (b)	80 (a)
81 (d)	82 (a)	83 (d)	84 (c)	85 (d)	86 (b)				

Statistics in Psychology

Statistics is a branch of mathematics devoted to the collection, compilation, display and interpretation of numerical data. Psychologists rely heavily on statistics to help assess the meaning of the measurements they make. Sometimes individual use measurement in psychological test; the measurements involve statistics that describe general properties of people or animals.

Introduction

In psychological research, psychologists use two kinds of statistics, descriptive and inferential. **Descriptive** statistics simply give a general picture of the sources in a given group. They include the measures of central tendency and the measure of variability. Central tendency involves different kinds of averages : the mean, median and mode and **Inferential** statistics use a random sample of data taken from a population to describe and make inferences about the population.

Measures of Central Tendency and Dispersion

When we carry out a psychological experiment, we end up with a voluminous data, usually in the form of two sets of scores, one for each condition. The two sets of scores need to be compared to see if there is a noticeable difference between them. Often, we need to summarise this data so that it can easily be interpreted whether the study was successful or not.

A set of scores can be summarised by

- A set of central tendency (or average) of the scores.
- A measure of dispersion (or spread) of the scores.

A measure of dispersion is a number which indicates how far each individual score (in the raw data set) is from the mean (*i.e.* how far each score in the raw data set deviates from the mean).

In this Chapter

- *Measures of Central Tendency and Dispersion*
- *Normal Probability Curve*
- *Parametric Test*
- *Non-Parametric Test*
- *Power Analysis*
- *Effect Size*

Central Tendency

There are three measures of central tendency and each one plays a different role in determining where the center of the distribution or the average score lies. A measure of central tendency is a single value that describe the way in which a group of data cluster around a central value. To put in other words, it is a way to describe the center of a data set.

There are three measures of central tendency: the mean, the median and the mode.

Mean

In statistics, the mean is the mathematical average of a set of numbers. The average is calculated by adding up two or more scores and dividing the total by the number of scores.

Consider the following number set: 2, 4, 6, 9, 12. The average is calculated in the following manner: 2 + 4 + 6 + 9 + 12 = 33/5 = 6.6. So, the average of the number set is 6.6.

Uses of Mean in Psychology

Once data has been collected, a researcher has a great deal of information. Since the researcher needs to make sense of this information and determine how to present it in a meaningful way. A mean can help do that.

Imagine, for example, that a psychologist is doing research on sleep habits among college students. Psychologist hands out a form to a random sample of 100 university students and asked them track how much they sleep each night for a period of 30 days.

The first thing psychologist might do is take a look at the data collected from each individual student. Psychologist might want to look at things such as the range of data difference between (the smallest amount of sleep the student got and the highest amount of sleep the student reported), but one of the most helpful numbers psychologist might want to look at is the average amount of sleep that the student got per night over the course of the month.

In order to accomplish this, she would start adding each number and then dividing by the total number of data points. In this case, the month had thirty days, so psychologist would add up the hours of each night sleep and then divide that total number by 30. This value represents the mean or average number, of hours of sleep that each particular student reported over the course of the month.

Median

It is another method for determining central tendency and is the preferred method for highly skewed distributions. The median is simply the middle most occurring score.

Formula for finding Median

- If the number of observation (n) is **odd**

$$\text{Median} = \frac{n+1}{2}^{th} \text{ term}$$

- If the number of observation (n) is **even**

$$\text{Median} = \frac{\left(\frac{n}{2}\right)^{th} \text{term} + \left(\frac{n}{2}+1\right)^{th} \text{term}}{2}$$

Using the same distribution as above, the scores '8', '9' and '10' would have a median of '9'. By changing the '10' to a score of '100' you will notice that the median of this new positively skewed distribution does not change. The median remains equal to '9'.

For example– Imagine the following are scores from a memory test obtained from a group of teenagers (age 13 to 19 inclusive);19, 18, 19,20,15, 16, 11, 14, 12, 19, 18, 19, 17, -12 (there are 14 participants in this research study), in order to calculate the median of the data given above the scores are first arranged in ascending order 11, 12, 12, 14, 15, 16, 17, 18, 18, 19, 19, 19, 19, 20 now the middle (median) value of this data set can be established-which, in this case is,

$$\text{Median} = \frac{\left(\frac{n}{2}\right)^{th} \text{term} + \left(\frac{n}{2}+1\right)^{th} \text{term}}{2}$$

[Total number 14 = even number]

$$\text{Median} = \frac{\left(\frac{14}{2}\right)^{th} \text{term} + \left(\frac{14}{2}+1\right)^{th} \text{term}}{2}$$

$$\text{Median} = \frac{7 \text{ th term} + 8 \text{ th term}}{2}$$

$$\text{Median} = \frac{17+18}{2}$$

$$\text{Median} = \frac{35}{2} = 17.5$$

Mode

The mode is the least used measure of central tendency. The mode is simply the most frequently occurring score. For distributions that have several peaks, the mode may be the preferred measure. There is no limit to the number of modes in a distribution.

If two scores tie as the most frequently occurring score, the distribution would be considered bimodal. Three would be trimodal and all distributions with two or more modes would be considered multimodal distributions.

For example Imagine the following are scores from a memory test obtained from a group of teenagers (age 13 to 19 inclusive);19, 18, 19,20,15,16, 11, 14, 12, 19, 18, 19, 17, 12 (there are 14 participants in this research study) in the following set of data: 19, 18, 19,20, 15, 16, 11,14,12,19,18,19,17,12 the mode is 19. This is because the number 19 appears more frequently than any other in this set of data.

Significance of Central Tendency in Psychology

Central tendency is very useful in psychology. It lets us know what is 'normal' or 'average' for a set of data. It also condenses the data to set down to one representative value, which is useful when we are working with large amounts of data. Central tendency also allow us to compare one data set to another.

For example Let's say you have a sample of girls and a sample of boys and you are interested in comparing their heights. By calculating the average height for each sample, you could easily draw comparisons between the girls and boys.

Central tendency is also useful when you want to compare one piece of data to the entire data set. Let's say you received a 60% on your last psychology quiz, which is usually in the 'D' range. You go around and talk to your classmates and find out that the average score on the quiz was 43%. In this instance, your score was significantly higher than those of your classmates. Are you not known about the measures of central tendency, you probably would have been really upset about your grade and assumed that you bombed the test.

Measures of Dispersion

Measures of dispersion describe the spread of data around a central value (mean, median or mode). They tell us how much variability is there in the data. There are two measures of dispersion : Range (where you subtract the lowest score from the highest score) and Standard Deviation (which calculates the spread of scores around the mean).

The three types of measures of dispersion, are as follows

Range

The range substracts the smallest number from the largest in a set of results. The advantage here is that it is easy to find and calculate.

Range formula = maximum value – minimum value

For example Consider the following data set 2, 4, 5, 8, 9, 10.

Range of this dataset = maximum value - minimum value

Maximum value = 10

Minimum value = 2

Range = 10-2

Range = 8

Semi-Interquartile Range

The semi-interquartile range is a measure of dispersion. It is computed as one half the difference between the 75 th percentile [Q 3] and the 25th percentile [Q 1].

$$\text{Its formula} = \frac{Q3 - Q1}{2}$$

Standard Deviation

The standard deviation is a static that measures the dispersion of a data set relative to its mean and is calculated as the square root fo the variance. It symbol is σ.

$$\text{Formula of standard deviation } (\sigma) = \sqrt{\frac{\Sigma^n i = 7\,(x_1 - \bar{x})^2}{N}}$$

N = Number of observation

X_1 = Each value of data

$\bar{X}$ = The mean of X_1

Normal Probability Curve

Normal probability curve is the frequency curve of any normal distribution. It is an ideal symmetrical frequency curve and is supposed to be based, on the data of a population. Normal probability curve, is bell shaped curve and a graph representing a distribution of scores.

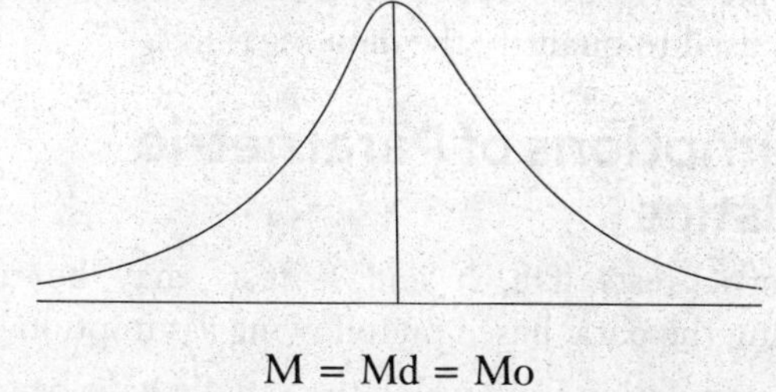

M = Md = Mo

Laplace and **Gauss**, derived the normal probability curve independently, so the curve is also known as ***Gaussian curve*** in the honour of Gauss.

Characteristics of NPC

- Normal Probability Curve is a bell shaped curve.
- All the three central tendencies:mean,median and mode coincide in it and are equal.
- NPC is asymptotic. It approaches but never touches the baseline.
- The NPC is bilateral symmetrical.lt implies size,shape and slope of the curve on one side are identical to that of the other side.
- The curve has its maximum height or ordinate at the starting point *i.e.* the mean of the distributions.
- The first and the third quartile (Q 1 and Q 3) are at equal distance from Q2 or median.
- The point of inflection(where the curvature changes its direction) is at point + – 1 σ, up and below the mean.

Parametric Test

A parametric test is a hypothesis testing procedure based on the assumption that observed data are distributed according to some distribution of well-known form (*e.g.* normal, Bernoulli and so on) upto some unknown parameters on which we want to make inference (say the mean or the success probability). In a parametric test a sample statistic is obtained to estimate the population parameter. This estimation process involves a sample, a sampling distribution of a population, certain parametric assumptions are required to ensure all components are compatible with each other.

Parametric tests are useful as these tests are most powerful for testing the significance or trustworthiness of the computed sample statistics. However, their use is based upon certain assumptions. These assumptions are based on the nature of the population distribution and on the type of scale is used to quantify the data measures.

Assumptions of Parametric Statistics

Parametric tests like, 't and f' tests may be used for analysing the data; based on following assumption

- The population from which the sample have been drawn should be normally distributed.
- The variables involved must have been measured interval or ratio scale. The observation must be independent.
- The inclusion or exclusion of any case in the sample should not unduly affect the results of study.
- These populations must have the same variance or in special cases, must have a known ratio of variance.
- The samples have nearly equal variances.
- The selection of one case in the sample is not dependent upon the selection of any other case.

Parametric Tests Used for Inference

Student's T-test

It was developed by **Prof WS Gosset** in **1908**, who published statistical papers under the pen name of'Student'. Thus, the test is known as *Student's T-test. Student's* T-test finds its applicability when

- Samples are small.
- Population variances are not known.

Uses of Student's T-test

- Two means of small independent samples.
- Sample mean and population mean.
- To proportion of small independent samples.

Assumptions made in the use of t-test

- Samples are randomly selected.
- Dala utilised is quantiative.
- Variable follows normal distribution.
- Sample variances are mostly same in both the groups under the study.
- Samples are small, mostly lower than 30.

Student's T-test for Different Purposes

One Sample T-test

It is used when mean of a single group of observations is compared with a specified value. In one sample t-test, we know the population mean. We draw a random sample from the population and then compare the sample mean and make a statistical decision as to whether or not the sample mean is different from the population.

Formula for one sample t-test $t = \frac{\overline{X} - \mu}{S\sqrt{n}}$

Where, $\overline{X}$ = Sample mean

μ = Population mean)

$S\sqrt{n}$ = Standard error

$$S^2 = \frac{Sum\,(X - \overline{X})^2}{n-1}$$

Where, X = Element of sample

$\overline{X}$ = Sample mean

n – 1 = Degrees of freedom

Two Sample 'T' Test

Unpaired Two Sample 't' test

It is used when two means are compared. Unpaired two sample 't,' test is used when the two independent random samples come from the normal populations having unknown or same variation 'In this, we test the null hypothesis, that the two population means are same *i.e.* $M_1 = M_2$ against an appropriate one sided or two sided alternative hypothesis.

Assumptions

- The samples are random and independent of each other.
- The distribution of dependent variable is normal.
- The variance is equal in both the group.

Formula

$$t = \frac{Mean\,1 - Mean\,2}{SE\,(Mean\,1 - Mean\,2)}$$

SE (*Mean 1- Mean 2*) = $S\sqrt{(1/n_1 + 1/n_2)}$

$$S = \frac{(n_1 - 1)S_1^2 + (n_2 - 1)S_2^2}{(n_1 + n_2 - 2)}$$

Where, S_1^2 and S_2^2 are respectively called Standard deviation's of first and second group.

Paired Two-sample T-test

It is used when we have paired data of observations from one sample only, when individuals give a pair of observation.

Assumptions

- The outcome variable should be continuous.
- The difference between pre and post measurement should be normally distributed.

Formula $t = \frac{\overline{d}}{SD/\sqrt{n}}$

where,

d = Difference between x_1 *and* y_2

$\overline{d}$ = Average of d

SD = Standard deviation for the difference.

n = Sample size

Uses of T-test in Psychological Research

In the case of a one sample t-test, if a researcher in the field of psychology is working on a study where he wants to make sure that at least 65% of students will pass the IQ test, he can use the t-test. So, one sample t-test will be used after the hypothesis has been formulated in this particular case. The parametric test is then calculated by selecting an appropriate formula of t-test. In this case, the appropriate formula will be a t-test for a single mean.

A selection of the level of significance is conducted to check the t-test of the null hypothesis. Usually, the researcher takes 0.05 as the appropriate level of significance while conducting the t-test. The level of significance refers to the minimum probability that there will be a false rejection of the null hypothesis. Now, if the value calculated from the t-test is more than the tabulated value, then the null hypothesis gets rejected at a particular level of significance. Similarly, if the value calculated from the t-test is less than the tabulated value, then the null hypothesis gets accepted at a particular level of significance.

Advantages of Parametric Statistics

- **Don't Require Data** One of the biggest and best advantages of using parametric tests is first of all that you don't need much data that could be converted in some order or format of ranks. The process of conversion is something that appears in rank format and in order to be able to use a parametric test regularly you will end up with a severe loss in precision.
- **Quite Easy to Calculate** Another big advantage of using parametric tests is the fact that you can calculate everything so easily. In short, you will be able to find software much quicker so that you can calculate them fast and quick. Apart from parametric tests, there are other non-parametric tests, where the distributors are quite different and they are actually not all that easy when it comes to testing such questions that are focused related to the means and shapes of such distributions.
- **Provides All the Necessary Information** One of the biggest advantages of parametric tests is that they give you real information regarding the population which is in terms of the confidence intervals as well as the parameters.

- **Other Benefits of Parametric Tests** The parametric test can perform quite well when they have been spread over and each group happens to be different. While these non-parametric tests don't really assume that the data follows a regular distribution, they do tend to have other ideas and assumptions which can become very difficult to meet.

Disadvantages

- **They aren't valid** Parametric tests are not valid when it comes to small data sets. The requirement that the populations are not still valid on the small sets of data, the requirement that the populations which are under study have the same kind of variance and the need for such variables are being tested and have been measured at the same scale of intervals.
- **The Size of Sample is Always Very Big** Another disadvantage of parametric tests is that the size of the sample is always very big, something you will not find among non-parametric tests. That makes it a little difficult to carry out the whole test.
- **What you are studying here shall be represented through the medium itself** The best reasons why you should be using a non parametric test is that they aren't ever mentioned. In fact, they can also do a usual test with some non-normal data and that doesn't mean in any way that your mean would be the best way to measure if the tendency in the centre for the data.

  For example If you look at the centre of any skewed spread out or distribution such as income which could be measured using the median where at least 50% of the whole median is above and the rest is below. In case think you can add some billionaires to the sample, the mean will increase greatly even if the income doesn't show a sign of change.
- **You have ranked data as well as out liners you just can't remove** Typical parametric tests will only be able to assess data that is continuous and the result will be affected by the outliers at the same time. The non-parametric tests may also handle the ordinal data, ranked data will not in any way be affected by the outliners.

Non-Parametric Test

A non-parametric statistical test is based on model that specifies only general conditions and nothing with respect to the distribution from which the sample was drawn. The first meaning of non-parametric covers techniques that do not rely on data belonging to any particular distribution. *These include*

- **Distribution Free Methods** This means that there are no assumptions that the data have been drawn from a normally distributed population. This consists of non-parametric statistical models, inference and statistical tests.
- **Non-Parametric Statistics** In this the statistics is based on the ranks of observations and do not depend on any distribution of the population.
- **No Assumption of a Structure of a Model** In non-parametric statistics, the techniques do not assume that the structure of a model is fixed.
- The assumptions of a classical or standard tests are not applied to non-parametric tests.

Assumptions of Non-Parametric Test

The assumption of non-parametric test are

- Where sample size is quite small. If the size of the sample is as small as $N = 5$ or $N = 6$, the only alternative is to make use of non-parametric tests.
- When assumption like normality of the distribution of scores in the population are doubtful, we use non-parametric tests.
- When the measurement of data is available either in the form of ordinal or nominal scales or when the data can be expressed in the form of ranks or in the shape of + signs or – signs and classification like 'good-bad' etc. we use non-parametric statistics.
- The nature of the population from which samples are drawn is not known to be normal.
- The variables are expressed in nominal form.
- The data are measures which are ranked or expressed in numerical scores which have the strength of ranks.

Non-Parametric Procedures

When classical methods of hypothesis testing are not applicable, an appropriate non-parametric procedure can be selected.

Non-parametric test procedure may be broadly defined as

- Those who test statistic does not depend upon the form of the underlying populations distribution from, which the sample data was drawn.

- Those that are not concerned with the parameters of a population.
- Those for which the data are of 'insufficient strength' to warrant meaningful arithmetic operations.

The one, two and C- sample tests for proportions as well as the chi-square tests for independence and for goodness of fit and the McNemar test for changes fit such a broad definition. Indeed, when testing a hypothesis about a proportion, we have employed, what is called (in the non-parametric literature) the binomial test.

Methods of Non-Parametric Tests

Various test methods are used in drawing statistical inferences in case of related samples. Multiple methods for non-parametric tests *are as follows*

- Sign test
- Wilcoxon Signed test
- Mann - Whitney test
- Kruskal -Wallis test
- Friedman Rank test

Sign Test

The sign test is a non-parametric test that is used to test whether two groups are equally sized or not. The sign test is used when dependent samples are ordered in pairs, where the bivariate random variables are mutually independent.

It is based on the direction of the plus and minus sign of the observation and not on their numerical magnitude. The sign test is considered as weaker test, because it tests the pair value below or above the median and it does not measure the pair difference.

It is particularly useful in situations in which quantitative measurement is impossible or inconvenient, but on the basis of superior or inferior performance it is possible to rank with respect to each other, the two members of each pair. The sign test is used either in the case of single sample from which observation is obtained under two experimental conditions. The researcher wants to establish that the two conditions are different.

Assumptions of Signs Test

- **Data Distribution** The sign test is a non-parametric (distribution free) test, so we do not assume that the data is normally distributed.
- **Two Sample** Data should be from two samples. The population may differ for the two samples.
- **Dependent Sample** Dependent samples should be a paired sample or matched. Also known as *before-after sample*.

Types of Sign Test

- **One Sample** We set up the hypothesis so that '+' and '–' signs are the values of random variables having equal size.
- **Paired Sample** This test uses the '+' and '–' signs in paired sample tests or in 'before-after' study. In this test, null hypothesis is set up so that the sign '+' and '–' are of equal size or the population means are equal to the sample mean.

Wilcoxon Signed Test

The wilcoxon signed test is a non-parametric test statistical hypothesis test used to compare two related samples, matched samples or repeated measurement on a single to assess whether their population mean rank differ.

The Wilcoxon signed rank test relies on the W-statistics. For large samples with n > 10 paired observations the W-statistics approximates a normal distribution. The W-statistics is a non-parametric test, thus, it does not need multivariate normality in the data. Wilcoxon signed-rank is used when comparing two related samples or repeated measurements on a single sample to assess whether their population mean ranks differ.

This procedure known as the *Wilcoxon Signed-Ranks Test*, may be choosen over its respective classical counterpart: the one-sample 't' test or the paired difference 't'-test, when the researcher is able to obtain data measured at a higher level than an ordinal scale, but does not believe that the assumptions of the classical procedure are sufficiently met. When the assumptions of the 't'-test are violated, the Wilcoxon procedure (which makes fewer and less stringent assumptions than does the 't'-test) is likely to be more powerful in detecting the existence of significant differences than its corresponding classical counterpart. Moreover, even under conditions appropriate to the classical 't'-test, the Wilcoxon signed-ranks test has proven to be almost as powerful.

Mann-Whitney Test

The Mann-Whitney 'U' test is a non-parametric test that can be used to analyse data from a two-group independent groups design when measurement is atleast ordinal. It analyses the degree of separation (or the amount of overlap) between the Experimental and Control groups.

Assumptions of Mann-Whitney Test

The Mann-Whitney U test is based on the following assumptions

- Random sample for population.
- Independence within samples and mutual independence between samples.
- Measurement of at least ordinal.

Step-By-Step Procedure

Mann Whitney U Test for small sample case (not more than 20 items in each set), use U if the data is

- in the form of ranks or
- not normally distributed
- there is an obvious difference in the variance of the two groups.

STEP 1 Rank the data (taking both groups together) giving rank 1 to the lowest score and the highest rank to then highest score.

STEP 2 Find the sum of the ranks for the smaller sample.

STEP 3 Find the sum of the ranks for the larger sample.

STEP 4 Find U applying the formula given below

$$U_1\, n_1\, n_2 + \frac{n_1(n_1+1)}{2} - R_1$$

And $$U^1 = n_1\, n_2 + \frac{n_2\,(n_2+1)}{2} - R_2$$

STEP 5 Look up the smaller of U and U′ in table. There is a significant difference if the observed value is equal to or more than the table value.

STEP 6 Conclusion.

Kruskal-Wallis Test

The Kruskal-Wallis test compares the medians of several (more than two) populations to see whether they are all the same or not. The Kruskal-Wallis test is a non-parametric analogue to ANOVA. It can be viewed as ANOVA based on rank transformed data. The initial data are transformed to their associated ranks before being subjected to ANOVA. In other words, it's like ANOVA, except that it is computed with medians and not means. It can also be viewed as a test of medians.

The Kruskal-Wallis test for C independent samples (where C> 2) may be considered an extension of the Wilcoxon rank-sum test for two independent samples discussed. Thus, the Kruskal-Wallis test enjoys the same power properties relative to the analysis of variance 'F'-test as does.

Assumptions of Kruskal-Wallis

The Kruskal-Wallis one way analysis of variance by rank is based on the following assumptions

- Each sample has been randomly selected from the population it represents;
- The samples are independent of one another;
- The dependent variable (which is subsequently ranked) must be continuous random variable.
- The underlying distributions from which the samples are derived are identical in shape.

Step-by Step Procedure

- Rank all the numbers in the entire data set from smallest to largest (using all samples combined); in the case of ties, use the average of the ranks that the values would have normally been given.
- Total the ranks for each of the samples; call those totals T1, T2, ... , Tk, where k is the number of groups or populations.
- Calculate the Kruskal-Wallis H test statistic,

$$H = \frac{12}{n\,(n+1)}\, \Sigma\, \frac{R_1^2}{n_1} - 3\,(n+1)$$

n = the total number of cases

n = the number of cases in a given group

$(\Sigma^1 R)^2$ 2 = the sum of the ranks squared for a given group of subjects.

- Find the H-value.
- Make your conclusion about whether you can reject Ho (null hypothesis) by examining the p-value.

Friedman Rank Test for Related Samples

If the data collected are only in rank form within each block or if normality cannot be assumed a simple, but fairly powerful non-parametric approach called the *Friedman Test* can be utilised. The friedman test is essentially a two way analysis of variance (ANOVA) on ranked data.

Advantages of Using Non-Parametric Test

The use of non-parametric methods offers numerous advantages, *which are explained below*

- Non-parametric methods may be used on all types of data-qualitative data (nominal scaling) data in rank form (ordinal scaling), as well as data that have been measured more precisely (interval or ratio scaling).
- Non-parametric methods are generally easy to apply and quickly to compute when the sample size are small. Sometimes they as simple as just counting how often some feature appears in the data.
- Non-parametric methods make less stringent assumptions (which are more easily met) than do the classical procedures. Hence, they enjoy wider applicability and yield a more general broad based set of conclusions.

- Non-parametric methods permit the solution of problems that involve the testing of population parameters.
- Non-parametric method may be more economical than classical procedures, since the researcher may increase power and yet save money, time and labour by collecting larger samples of data that are more grossly measured (*i.e.* qualitative data or data in rank form).
- Depending on the particular procedure selected, non-parametric methods may be equally (or almost) as powerful as the classical procedures when the assumptions of the later are met and when they are not met may be quite a bit more powerful.

Disadvantages of Non-Parametric Test

Few major disadvantage of non-parametric test are as follows

- It is disadvantageous to use non-parametric methods when all the assumptions of the classical procedures can be met and the data are measured on either an interval or ratio scale. Unless classical procedures are employed in these instances, the researcher is not taking full advantage of the data.
- As the sample size gets larger, data manipulations required for non-parametric procedures are sometimes labourious unless appropriate computer software is available.

Power Analysis

Power analysis is directly related to tests of hypothesis. While conducting test of hypothesis. The researcher can commit two types of errors: Type I error and Type II error. Statistical power mainly deals with type II errors.

It should be noted by the researcher that the larger size of the sample, the easier it is for the researcher to achieve the 0.05 level of significance. If the sample is too small, however, then the investigator might commit a Type II error due to insufficient power.

Power analysis is normally conducted before the data collection. The main purpose underlying power analysis is to help the researcher to determine the smallest sample size that is suitable to detect the effect of a given test at the desired level of significance. The reason for applying power analysis is that, ideally, the investigator desires a smaller sample because larger samples are often costlier than smaller samples. Smaller samples also optimise the significance testing.

Effect Size

Effect size is a statistical concept that measures the strength of the relationship between two variables on a numerical scale. For instance, if we have data on the height of men and women and we notice that, an average, men are taller than women, the difference between the height of men and the height of women is known as the *effect size*.

The greater the effect size, the greater the height (null hypochaeris) difference between men and women will be statistic effect size helps us in determining if the difference is real or if it is due to a change of factors. In hypothesis testing effect size, power, sample size and critical significance level are related to each other. In Meta-analysis, effect size is concerned with different studies and then combines all the studies into single analysis. In statistics analysis the effect size is usually measured in three way

- Standardised mean difference.
- Add ratio.
- Correlation coefficient.

EXAM BASED QUESTIONS

1 Statistics is a branch of mathematics devoted to
(a) collection (b) compilation
(c) interpretation (d) All of these

2 Which among the following types of statistics are used by psychologists during research?
(a) Descriptive (b) Inferential
(c) Both a and b (d) None of these

3 Descriptive statistics includes in it
(a) measures of central tendency
(b) measures of variability
(c) Both a and b
(d) None of the above'

4 Why measuring of central tendency is required in a research?
(a) To get a summarise result
(b) To find out variable
(c) To eliminate the exceptions
(d) None of the above

5 A set of scores can be summarised by
(a) a set of central tendency of the scores
(b) a measures of dispersion of the scores
(c) Both a and b
(d) None of the above

6 A number which indicates how far each individual score is deviated from the mean is known as
(a) Measure of central tendency
(b) Measure of dispersion
(c) Measure of variable
(d) Measure of hypothesis

7 The measure of a single value that describe the way in which a group of data cluster around a central value is known as
(a) Measure of dispersion
(b) Measure of variables
(c) Measures of central tendency
(d) None of the above

8 Adding together of all score and dividing by the number of scores represents the calculation of
(a) median (b) mean
(c) mode (d) All of these

9 Which among the following is a preferred method for a highly skewed distribution?
(a) Mode (b) Mean
(c) Median (d) None of these

10 Which among the following is the least used in measures of central tendency?
(a) Mean (b) Median
(c) Mode (d) None of these

11 Which of the following is correct about the significance of central tendency in psychology?
(a) It condenses the data
(b) It helps in knowing the 'average'
(c) It allow to compare sets of data
(d) All of the above

12 Which among the following comes under the measures of dispersion?
(a) Range (b) Standard deviation
(c) Both a and b (d) None of these

13 Which among the following measure of dispersion substracts the smallest number from the largest in a set of results?
(a) Range (b) Semi-interquartile range
(c) Standard deviation (d) None of these

14 Which range measures the spread of the middle 50% of scores?
(a) Interquartile range (b) Semi-interquartile range
(c) Standard deviation (d) None of these

15 The measure of dispersion of results from the mean result is known as
(a) Semi-interquartile range (b) Range
(c) Standard deviation (d) None of these

16 Which among the following measure of dispersion is unaffected by extreme results?
(a) Semi-Interquartile range (b) Standard Deviation
(c) Range (d) None of the above

17 What is the shape of Normal Probability Curve?
(a) Straight line (b) Oval shape
(c) Bell shaped (d) None of these

18 Who discovered Normal Probability Curve?
(a) David and Paul (b) Laplace and Gauss
(c) Robert Owen (d) None of these

19 Which among the following is/are correct about Normal Probability Curve.
(a) All central tendency coincide in it
(b) NPC is asymptotic
(c) Both a and b
(d) None of the above

20 Which of the following is considered as conventional statistical procedures?
(a) Parametric tests (b) Non-parametric tests
(c) Both a and b (d) None of the above

21 Which of the following is considered as the most powerful and significant for the computed sample statistics?
(a) Non-parametric test (b) Parametric test
(c) Dispersion test (d) None of the above

22 Parameter is
(a) characteristic of a sample
(b) characteristic of a population
(c) assumption of a parametric tests
(d) characteristic of a parametric test

23 Parameter is characteristic of
(a) the sample (b) the population
(c) an individual (d) a test

24 Statistical tests could be used, if the data are
(a) unorganised (b) organised
(c) normal (d) variable

25 The reliable difference between two groups could be obtained, if we use
(a) norms (b) validity
(c) statistical test (d) reliability

26 Statistically reliable difference is known as
(a) chance difference (b) hypothesised difference
(c) random difference (d) real difference

27 Which among the following is not a assumption of Parametric statistics?
(a) Population should be normally distributed
(b) The samples does not have equal variances
(c) Selection of case in the sample are independent
(d) None of the above

28 The meaningfulness of the results of a parametric test depends on the
(a) evenness of sample (b) exception in sample
(c) validity of the assumption (d) None of the above

29 Which of the following test is used to determine if the scores of two groups differ on a single variable?
(a) 'Z' test (b) 'T' test
(c) 'F' test (d) None of these

30 Parametric test called t-test is based on a
(a) Teacher's t statistic (b) Student k statistic
(c) Student's t statistic (d) None of these

31 The distribution of t-test has a shape of
(a) ball shaped (b) bell shaped
(c) square shaped (d) Triangular shaped

32 The parametric test called t-test is useful for testing those samples whose size is less than
(a) 20 (b) 50 (c) 40 (d) 30

33 Which among the following is/are types of t-test?
(a) One sample t-test
(b) Two independent sample t-test
(c) Paired sample t-test
(d) All of the above

34 The distribution free methods is included in
(a) Parametric test
(b) Non-Parametric Test
(c) Wilcoxon signed test
(d) None of these

35 Which among the following are correct about Non-Parametric statistics?
(a) The variables are expressed in nominal form
(b) Where sample size is quite small
(c) Both a and b
(d) None of the above

36 Which among the following are methods of Non-Parametric Tests
(a) Sign test
(b) Wilcoxon signed rank test
(c) Mann-Whitney test
(d) All of the above

37 A test that specifies only very general conditions and name regarding any specific issue of the sample is known as
(a) Parametric test (b) Non-parametric test
(c) Both a and b (d) None of these

38 Which among the following is/are correct about Non-parametric test?
(a) Distribution free methods
(b) Non-parametric statistics
(c) No assumption of a structure of a model
(d) All of the above

39 The assumption of a classical or standard tests are not applied to
(a) parametric test (b) non-parametric test
(c) Both a and b (d) None of the above

40 When classical methods of hypothesis testing is not applicable, then which among the following can be used?
(a) Parametric test (b) Non-Parametric test
(c) Sampling (d) None of the above

41 Which among the following is/are not correct about Non-parametric test?
(a) Not concerned with the parameters of a population
(b) Who test statistic depend upon the form of the underlying population
(c) For which the data are of 'insufficient strength'
(d) All of the above

42 Which test is calculated by ranking all of the participants scores from lowest to highest and adding up the ranks separately for each condition?
(a) Spearman's Rho
(b) Friedman's Anova
(c) Mann Whitney
(d) Pearson's R

43 Which test is calculated by taking the difference between to sets of scores and ranking them from highest to lowest?
(a) Kruskal-Wallis
(b) Independent 't'-test
(c) Wilcoxon Signed test
(d) Spearman's Rho

44 **Under what circumstances would you use a non-parametric test?**
(a) When your data does not meet the assumptions for a parametric test
(b) In a pilot study
(c) When you think your sample size is too big
(d) When you do not really understand a parametric test

45 **The formula for the Kruskal-Wallis is based upon?**
(a) Ranks (b) Categories
(c) Means (d) Deviations

46 **What statistic is used to check the significance of the Kruskal-Wallis 'H'-test?**
(a) Chi-squared (b) Partial n^2
(c) 'T' (d) Mean rank

47 **Which tests would be used to assess whether there is a significant difference between the mean ranks of two conditions?**
(a) Spearman's Rho (b) Friedman
(c) Kruskal-Wallis (d) Wilcoxon

48 **Where in SPSS would you find the Friedman test?**
(a) Compare means-Friedman test
(b) Non-parametric test-Legacy dialogs-K related sample
(c) Compare means - Related samples
(d) Non-parametric test-Legacy dialogs-Friedman test

49 **In SPSS, where will you find an alternative to the independent sample 't'-test?**
(a) Non-parametric test-legacy dialogs-'U'-test
(b) Compare means-'U'-test
(c) Non-parametric tests-legacy dialogs-independent samples
(d) Compare means-independent samples

50 **Effect size is usually measured in**
(a) standardised mean difference way
(b) odd ratio way
(c) correlation coefficient way
(d) All of the above

51 **Statistical power mainly deals with.**
(a) Type I error (b) Type II error
(c) Both a and b (d) None of these

52 **What is the non-parametric alternative to one-way ANOVA?**
(a) Friedman's test (b) Kruskal-Wallis H test
(c) Mann-Whitney U test (d) None of the above

53 **Parametric methods make assumptions about the .... from which sample populations are selected.**
(a) Underlying distribution (b) Sample size
(c) Population size (d) Subject characteristics

54 **Any statement whose validity is tested on the basis of a sample is called**
(a) Null hypothesis
(b) Alternative hypothesis
(c) Statistical hypothesis
(d) Simple hypothesis

55 **Which one among the following is a standardised produce to measure quantitatively and qualitatively one or more aspect of human traits or attributes including achievement and ability, personality and neurological functioning etc ?**
(a) A case study (b) An interview
(c) A test (d) An experiment

56 **Rejection of the null hypothesis is a conclusive proof that the alternative hypothesis is**
(a) true (b) false
(c) neither true nor false (d) partially true

57 **Two types of errors associated with hypothesis testing are Type I and Type II. Type II error is committed when**
(a) we reject a null hypothesis when it is true
(b) we accept a null hypothesis when it is not true
(c) we reject the null hypothesis when the alternative hypothesis is true
(d) None of the above

58 **Which of following is a limitation of case study?**
(a) It does not provide indepth information of the subjects.
(b) It is difficult to generalise from the case study.
(c) It is useful only in clinical and counselling psychology.
(d) It uses diverse methods and sources to collect data about the subjects.

59 **Researchers use both open-ended and closed-ended questions to collect data. Which of the following statements is true?**
(a) Open-ended questions directly provide quantitative data based on the researcher's predetermined response categories.
(b) Closed-ended questions provide quantitative data in the participant's own words.
(c) Open-ended questions provide qualitative data in the participant's own words.
(d) Closed-ended questions directly provide qualitative data in the participant's own words.

60 **Which one of the following test is closest to independent samples 't' test from power consideration point of view?**
(a) Mann-Whitney U test
(b) Signed rank test
(c) Chi-square test
(d) Kolmogorov - Smirnov test

61 **Power analysis is directly related to tests of**
(a) Assumptions (b) Hypothesis
(c) Effect size (d) None of these

62 **A researcher can commit how many types of errors?**
(a) Type I errors (b) Type II errors
(c) Both a and b (d) None of these

63 **If the sample size is too small, then it will causes**
(a) Type II error (b) Type I error
(c) Type III error (d) None of these

64 Consider the following statements

1. A set of source can be summarised by a set of central tendency (or average) of the scores.
2. A measure of dispersion (or spread) of the scores.

Which among the above is are correct?

(a) Only 1 (b) Only 2
(c) Both 1 and 2 (d) None of these

65 Consider the following statements

1. Median is preferred method for highly systematic distributions.
2. The mode is most used measure of central tendency

Which among the above is are correct?

(a) Only 1 (b) Only 2
(c) Both 1 and 2 (d) None of these

66 Consider the following statements

1. The semi-interquartile range measures the spread of the middle 50% of scores.
2. Standard deviation is the measure of dispersion of results from the mean result.

Which among the above is are correct?

(a) Only 1 (b) Only 2 (c) Both 1 and 2 (d) None of these

67 Consider the following statements

1. Normal probability curve is a bell shaped curve.
2. NPC is asymptotic. It approaches but never touches the baseline.

Which among the above is are correct?

(a) Only 1 (b) Only 2
(c) Both 1 and 2 (d) None of these

68 Consider the following statements

1. Conventional statistical procedures are called Parametric tests.
2. Parametric test are trustworthy of the computed sample statistics.

Which among the above is are correct?

(a) Only 1 (b) Only 2
(c) Both 1 and 2 (d) None of these

69 Consider the following statements

1. Non-Parametric methods are generally easy to apply and quickly to compute when the sample size are small.
2. Non-parametric methods permit the solution of problems that do involve the testing of population parameters.

Which among the above is are correct?

(a) Only 1 (b) Only 2 (c) Both 1 and 2 (d) None of these

70 Consider the following statement

1. Range is a measure of central tendency.
2. The smaller the range of values defining a confidence interval, the greater the error in estimation.

Which one of the statements given above is/are correct?

(a) Only 1 (b) Only 2
(c) Both 1 and 2 (d) None of these

71 Arrange the following concepts in sequence.

1. Reliable difference 2. Hypothesis
3. Statistical test 4. Random fluctuation

Codes

	A	B	C	D		A	B	C	D
(a)	3	4	2	1	(b)	2	1	3	4
(c)	1	2	4	3	(d)	4	3	1	2

72 Match the following

List I (Groups)	List II (Test)
A. Single sample	1. Kruskal-Wallis Test
B. Matched groups	2. Wilcoxon Sign Test
C. Two independent groups	3. Chi Square Test
D. More than two groups	4. Mann-Whitney U Test

Codes

	A	B	C	D		A	B	C	D
(a)	3	1	4	2	(b)	3	2	4	1
(c)	4	1	2	3	(d)	4	2	1	3

73 Match the following

List I (Methods)	List I I(Data Suited for)
A. Kruskal Wallis	1. Independent samples
B. Friedman	2. Independent samples
C. Mann Whitney	3. Related samples
D. Wilcoxon	4. Related samples

Codes

	A	B	C	D		A	B	C	D
(a)	1	3	2	4	(b)	4	3	2	1
(c)	3	4	2	1	(d)	3	1	2	4

Directions (Q. Nos. 74-80) *In the question given below are two statements labelled as Assertion (A) and Reason (R). In the context of the two statements, which one of the following is correct?*

Codes

(a) Both A and R are true and R is the correct explanation of A
(b) Both A and R are true, but R is not the correct explanation of A
(c) A is true, but R is false
(d) A is false, but R is true

74 **Assertion** (A) The sign test is a non-parametric test that is used to test whether two groups are equally sized or not.

Reason (R) The sign test is used when dependent samples are ordered in pairs, where the bivariate random variables are mutually independent.

75 **Assertion** (A) Wilcoxon sign test signed rank test is closely related to dependent sample t-test.

Reason (R) Because the dependent samples t-tests analysis if the average difference of two repeated measures is zero.

76 **Assertion** (A) Mann-Whitney 'U' test is a non-parametric test that can be used to analyse data from two group independent groups design when measurement is atleast ordinal.

Reason (R) Each sample has been randomly selected from the population it represent.

77 Assertion (A) Kruskal-Wallis test compares the medians population to see whether they are all the some or not.

Reason (R) The Kruskal-Wallis test is a non-parametric analogue to ANOVA.

78 Assertion (A) Power analysis is normally conducted before the data collection.

Reason (R) The reason for applying power analysis is that, ideally, the investigator desires a smaller sample because larger samples are often costlier than smaller samples.

79 Assertion (A) Effect size is a statistical concept that measures the strength of the relationship between two variables on a numerical scale.

Reason (R) The difference between the height of men and the height of women is known as the effect size.

80 Assertion (A) Non-Parametric Statics is based on the ranks of observations and do not depend on any distribution of the population.

Reason (R) The assumption of a classical or standard tests are not applied to non-parametric tests.

Directions (Q. Nos. 81-85) *Read the passage given below and answer the following questions.*

The Wilcoxon sign test signed rank test is closely related to dependent sample t-test. Because the dependent samples t-tests analyses if the average difference of two repeated measures is zero; it require metric (interval or ratio) and normally distribution data; the Wilcoxon sign test uses ranked or ordinal data. Thus, it is a common alternative to the dependent samples t-test when its assumption are not met. The Wilcoxon signed rank test relics on the W-statistics. For large samples with n > 10 paired observations the W-statistics approximates a normal distribution. The W-statistics is a non-parametric test, thus, it does not need multivariate normality in the data.

Wilcoxon signed-rank is used when comparing two related samples or repeated measurements on a single sample to assess whether their population mean ranks differ.

This procedure known as the Wilcoxon Signed-Ranks Test, may be choosen over its respective classical counterpart- the one-sample 't'. test or the paired difference 't'-test, when the researcher is able to obtain data measured at a higher level than an ordinal scale, but does not believe that the assumptions of the classical procedure are sufficiently met. When the assumptions of the 't'-test are violated, the Wilcoxon procedure (which makes fewer and less stringent assumptions than does the 't'-test) is likely to be more powerful in detecting the existence of significant differences than its corresponding classical counterpart. Moreover, even under conditions appropriate to the classical 't'-test, the Wilcoxon Signed-ranks test has proven to be almost as powerful.

81 Wilcoxon sign test signed rank test is closely related to

(a) Independent sample t-test (b) Dependent sample t-test
(c) Paired sample t-test (d) None of these

82 The Wilcoxon signed rank test relies on the W-statistics. For large sample it require

(a) n>20 (b) n<10
(c) n>10 (d) n<20

83 Which test does not require multivariate normality in the data?

(a) Mann-Whitney test (b) Wilcoxon singed rank test
(c) Friedman Rank Test (d) Kruskal-Wallis test

84 Consider the following about Wilcoxon signed rank test

1. It is used when comparing two related samples.
2. It is also used when comparing two repeated measurements on a single sample.

Which among the above is/are correct?

(a) Only 1 (b) Only 2 (c) Both 1 and 2 (d) None of these

85 Consider the following

1. Wilcoxon signed ranks test has proven unsuccessful in classical t-test.
2. When the assumptions of t-test is violated, Wilcoxon procedure because more powerful.

Which among the above is/are correct?

(a) Only 1 (b) Only 2
(c) Both 1 and 2 (d) None of these

ANSWERS

1 (d)	2 (c)	3 (c)	4 (a)	5 (c)	6 (b)	7 (c)	8 (b)	9 (c)	10 (c)
11 (d)	12 (c)	13 (a)	14 (b)	15 (c)	16 (a)	17 (c)	18 (b)	19 (c)	20 (a)
21 (b)	22 (c)	23 (b)	24 (b)	25 (c)	26 (d)	27 (b)	28 (c)	29 (b)	30 (c)
31 (b)	32 (d)	33 (d)	34 (b)	35 (c)	36 (d)	37 (c)	38 (d)	39 (b)	40 (b)
41 (d)	42 (c)	43 (c)	44 (a)	45 (a)	46 (d)	47 (b)	48 (c)	49 (c)	50 (d)
51 (b)	52 (b)	53 (a)	54 (c)	55 (c)	56 (c)	57 (b)	58 (d)	59 (c)	60 (a)
61 (b)	62 (c)	63 (a)	64 (c)	65 (a)	66 (c)	67 (c)	68 (c)	69 (c)	70 (d)
71 (b)	72 (b)	73 (a)	74 (b)	75 (a)	76 (b)	77 (b)	78 (b)	79 (c)	80 (b)
81 (b)	82 (c)	83 (b)	84 (c)	85 (b)					

Correlation and Regression Analysis

Correlation and regression analysis procedures are used to study the relationship between variables. Correlation is a measure of the strength of a relationship between variables. Regression is used to predict the value of one variable based on the value of different variable. The variables are data which are measured and counted in an experiment.

Correlation

Correlation is a bivariate that measures the strength of association between two variables and the direction of the relationship. In terms of the strength of relationship, the value of the correlation coefficient varies between +1 and -1. A value of ±1 indicates a perfect degree of association between the two variables. As the correlation coefficient value goes towards 0, the relationship between the two variables becomes be weaker. The direction of the relationship is indicated by the sign of the coefficient; a + sign indicates a positive relationship and a - sign indicates a negative relationship.

Here are some examples of statements that represents correlation

- More the income, more the expenditure.
- As the cost increases, the sales decreases.
- More the practise, better the performance.
- As the intelligence increases, the marks obtained increases.
- As the introversion increases, number of friends decreases.

Correlation Analysis

The correlation analysis is the statistical tool used to study the closeness of the relationship between two or more variables. The variables are said to be correlated, when value of one variable is changed it affects the value of other variable. The correlation analysis is used, when the researcher wants to determine the possible association between the variables. To begin *the following steps are to be followed*

In this Chapter

- Determine whether the relation exists and then measure it (the measure of correlation is called as the *Coefficient of Correlation*).
- Test its significance.
- Establish the cause and effect relation, if any.

Below are some of the method given for correlation analysis

Product Moment

The method of product moment was introduced by Karl Pearson in 1886. Product moment is also known as the *Pearson Product - Moment Correlation Coefficient*. The Pearson's product-moment correlation coefficient is usually calculated for two continuous variables. If either or both the variables are not continuous, then other statistical procedures are to be used.

The Pearson's product-moment correlation coefficient (or Pearson's correlation coefficient, for short) is a measure of the strength of a linear association between two variables and is denoted by 'r'.

Basically, Pearson's product-moment correlation attempts to draw a line of best fit through the data of two variables and the Pearson correlation coefficient, (r) indicates how far away all these data points are to this line of best fit.

Value of Pearson's Correlation Coefficient

The Pearson's correlation coefficient (r) can take a range of values from +1 to −1. A value of '0' indicates that there is no association between the two variables.

A value greater than '0' indicates a negative association, that is, as the value of one variable increases, the value of the other variable decreases.

Equations for Pearson's Product Moment Coefficient of Correlation

We shall now learn how to compute the Pearson's correlation coefficient.

Formula

The simplest way to define Pearson's correlation coefficient is

$$r = \frac{Cov_{XY}}{S_X S_Y}$$

Where, the Cov_{XY} is covariance between X and Y,

S_X is standard deviation of X

S_Y is standard deviation of Y.

Since, it can be shown that Cov_{XY} is always smaller than or equal to $S_X S_Y$, the maximum value of correlation coefficient is bound to be 1.

The sign of Pearson's *(r)* depends on the sign of Cov_{XY}.

If the Cov_{XY} is negative, then (*r*) will be negative and if Cov_{XY} is positive then (*r*) will be a positive value.

The denominator of this formula ($S_X S_Y$) is always positive. This is the reason for A −1 to +1 range of correlation coefficient. By substituting covariance equation for covariance, we can rewrite the equation as

$$r = \frac{\Sigma \frac{(X - \bar{X})(Y - \bar{Y})}{n}}{S_X S_Y}$$

By following a simple rule, $a \div b \div c = a \div (b \times c)$, we can rewrite the equation as follows $r = \frac{\Sigma \frac{(X - \bar{X})(Y - \bar{Y})}{n}}{nS_X S_Y}$

Spearman's Rank-Order Correlation

Rank-order correlation procedure is developed by Charles Spearman. It is also known as *Spearman's rho* (r_s). It was developed to compute correlation, when the data is presented on two variables for 'n' subjects.

It can also be calculated for data of 'n' subjects evaluated by two judges for inter-judge agreement. It is suitable for the rank-order data. If the data on '*x*' or '*y*' or on both the variables are in rank-order then Spearman's *rho* is applicable.

It is used to assess a monotonic relationship.

The range of Spearman's *rho* (r_s) is also from −1.00 to +1.00. Like Pearson's correlation, the interpretation of Spearman's *rho* is based on sign of the coefficient and the value of the coefficient. If the sign of r_s is positive then relationship is positive, if the sign of r_s is negative then the relationship is negative.

If the value of r_s is close to zero then relationship is weak and as the value of r_s approaches to ±1.00, the strength of relationship increases. When the value of r_s is zero then there is no relationship between X and Y. If r_s is ±1.00, then the relationship between X and Y is perfect.

Whatever, the value of r_s may take, it does not directly imply causation.

Equation for Spearman's Rank-Order Correlation

There are two methods to calculate Spearman's correlation depending on whether (1) your data does not have tied ranks or (2) your data has tied ranks.

The formula for when there are no tied ranks is $\rho = 1 - \dfrac{6\Sigma d_i^2}{n(n^2-1)}$

Where d_i = difference in paired ranks and n = number of cases.

The formula to use when there are tied ranks is

$$\rho = \frac{\Sigma_i (x_i - \bar{x})(y_i - \bar{y})}{\sqrt{\Sigma_i (x_i - \bar{x})^2 \Sigma_\iota (y_i - \bar{y})^2}}$$

Where, i = paired score

Partial Correlation (r_p)

Partial correlation measures separately the relationship between two variables in such a way that the effects of the other related variables are limited. In other words, in partial correlation analysis, we aim at measuring the relation between dependent variable and a particular independent variable by holding all other variables constant.

Thus, each partial coefficient of correlation measures the effect of its independent variable on the dependent variable. To obtain, it is first necessary to compute the simple coefficients of correlation between each set of pairs of variables as stated earlier. In the case of two independent variables, we shall have two partial correlation coefficients denoted as $r_y x_1 x_2$ and $r_y x_2 x_1$ which are worked out as under

$$r_{y\,x_1 \cdot x_2} = \frac{R^2{}_{y.x_1 x_2} - r^2{}_{y\,x_2}}{1 - r^2{}_{yx_2}}$$

This measures the effort of X_1 on y, more precisely, that proportion of the variation of y not explained by X_2, which is explained by X_1. Also,

$$r_{y\,x_2 \cdot x_1} = \frac{R^2{}_{x_1 x_2} - r^2{}_{y\,x_1}}{1 - r^2{}_{y\,x_1}}$$

in which X_1 and X_2 are simply interchanged, given the added effect of X_2 on y.

Alternatively, we can work out the partial correlation coefficients thus,

$$r_{y\,x_1 \cdot x_2} = \frac{r_{y\,x_1} - r_{y\,x_2} \cdot r\,x_1 \cdot x_2}{\sqrt{1 - r^2{}_{y\,x_2}}\sqrt{1 - r^2_{x_1 x_2}}}$$

and

$$r_{y\,x_2 \cdot x_1} = \frac{r_{y\,x_2} - r_{y\,x_1} \cdot r_{x_1 x_2}}{\sqrt{1 - r^2_{y\,x_1}}\sqrt{1 - r^2_{x_1 x_2}}}$$

These formula of the alternative approach are based on simple coefficients of correlation. The partial correlation coefficients are called *first order coefficients*, when one variable is held constant as shown above; they are known as *second order coefficients*, when two variables are held constant and so on.

Multiple Correlation Coefficient

The multiple correlatis coefficient denote's a correlation of one variable with multiple other variables. The multiple correlation coefficient is denoted as $R_{ABCD....K}$, which denotes that A is correlated with B, C, D , upto K variables.

For example We want to compute multiple correlation between A with B and C, then it is expressed as R_{ABC}. In this case, we create a linear combination of the B and C, which is correlated with A.

To understand multiple correlation coefficient we take academic achievement, anxiety and intelligence as three variables. The correlation between academic achievement with the linear combination of anxiety and intelligence is multiple correlation.

This denotes the proportion of variance in academic achievement explained by intelligence and anxiety. We denote this as R (Academic Achievement, Intelligence, Anxiety) which is a multiple correlation.

Often, it is used in the context of regression, when academic achievement is a criterion variable, and intelligence and anxiety are called as *predictors*.

The multiple R can be calculated for two predictor variable as follows

$$R_{A.BC} = \sqrt{\frac{r^2_{AB} + r^2_{AC} - 2r_{AB} r_{AC} r_{BC}}{1 - r^2_{BC}}}$$

$$R_{B.AC} = \frac{\sqrt{r^2{}_{AB} + r^2_{BC} - 2r_{AC} \cdot r_{BC} r_{AB}}}{1 - r^2_{AC}}$$

$$R_{C \cdot AB} = \sqrt{\frac{r^2_{Ca} + r^2_{CB} + 2r_{AB} \cdot r_{BC} r_{AC}}{1 - r^2_{AB}}}$$

Where,

$R_{A.BC}$ = is multiple correlation between A and linear combination of B and C

r_{AB} = is correlation between A and B

r_{AC} = is correlation between A and C

r_{BC} = is correlation between B and C

Special Correlation Methods

Other than Pearson's 'r' and Spearman's *rho,* the other correlation methods *are as follows*

Biserial 'r'

The symbol of the correlation coefficient is 'r_b'. It is a correlation between, one or more quantative variables, but one of the variable is dichotomous ordinal data and has an underlying continuity. *For example,* Despersion level can be measured on a continous scale, but can be classified dichotomously as high/low.

Point Biserial 'r'

The symbol of the correlation coefficient is 'r_{pb}'. Correlation between one continuous variable and other variable that is a true dichotomous *For example* Correlation between height (continuous) and gender (true dichotomy).

Tetrachoric

The symbol of this correlation coefficient is 'r_t'. Correlation between two continuous variables that have been arbitrarily dichotomised.

For example, correlation of tall versus short (arbitrarily dichotomised) with pass versus fail in a physical fitness test (arbitrarily dichotomised). Another example is correlation between pass/fail an entrance exam and good/poor student.

Phi Coefficient

The symbol of this correlation coefficient is 'ϕ'. Correlation between two true dichotomous variables. *For example,* correlation between male / female and alive / dead.

Use of Correlation Analysis in Psychology

- A psychologist utilises correlation checks to see, if two sets of numbers are related; in other words, are the two sets of numbers corresponding in some way.
- In the case of psychology, the numbers being analysed relate to behaviours (or variables that could affect behaviour) but actually any two variables producing quantitative data could be checked to establish whether a correlations exists.
- Each of the two sets of numbers represents a co-variable. Once data has been collected for each of the co-variables, it can be plotted in a scattergram and/or statistically analysed to produce a correlation coefficient.
- The relationship between two variables will always produce a coefficient between 1 and -1.
- Coefficients with a minus in front of them highlight a negative correlation which means that as one set of numbers is increasing the other set is decreasing or as one decreases the other increases, so the trend in the data from one variable opposes the other.

Regression Analysis

Regression analysis is a set of statistical processes for estimating the relationship among variables. It includes many techniques for modeling and analysing several variables, when the focus is on the relationship between a dependent variables and one or more independent variables.

More specifically, regression analysis helps one to understand, how the typical value of the dependent variable (or 'criterion variable') changes when any one of the independent variables is varied, while the other independent variables are held fixed.

Regression analysis is widely used for prediction and forecasting, where its use has substantial overlap with the field of machine learning. Regression analysis is also used to understand which among the independent variables are related to the dependent variable and to explore the forms of these relationships.

In restricted circumstances, regression analysis can be used

to infer casual relationship between the independent a nd dependent variables. However, this can lead to illusions or false relationships, so caution is advisable.

Assumptions of Regression Analysis

Classical assumptions for regression analysis include

- The sample is representative of the population for the inference prediction.
- The error is a random variable with a mean of zero, conditional on the explanatory variables.

- The independent variables are measured with no error. (Note: If this is not so, modeling may be done instead using errors in variables model techniques).
- The independent variables (predictors) are linearly independent *i.e.* it is not possible to express any predictor as a linear combination of the others.
- The errors are uncorrelated *i.e.* the variance-covariance matrix of the errors is diagonal and each non-zero element is the variance of the error.
- The variance of the error is constant across observations (homoscedasticity). If not, weighted least squares or other methods might instead be used.

Equations of Regression Analysis

Linear regression is a way to model the relationship between two variables. You might also recognise the equation as the slope formula.

The equation has the form $Y = a + bX$, where Y is the dependent variable (the variable that goes on the Y axis), X is the independent variable (plotted on the X axis), b is the slope of the line and a is the y-intercept.

$$a = \frac{(\Sigma y)(\Sigma x^2) - (\Sigma x)(\Sigma xy)}{(n(\Sigma x^2) - (\Sigma x)^2}$$

$$b = \frac{n(\Sigma xy) - (\Sigma x)(\Sigma y)}{n(\Sigma x^2) - (\Sigma x)^2}$$

The first step in finding a linear regression equation is to determine if there is a relationship between the two variables. This is often a judgment call for the researcher. You'll also need a list of your data in x-y format (*i.e.* two columns of data- independent and dependent variable.)

Linear Regression

In linear regression, the model specifications is that the dependent variable 'y_i' is a linear combination of the parameters. In simple words, linear regression for modeling 'n' data points there is only one independent variable: x_i and two parameters β_0 and β_1

Straight line: $y_i = \beta_0 + \beta_1 x_i + \varepsilon_i$

$$i = 1, \ldots n$$

In multiple linear regression, there are several independent variables or functions of independent variables.

Adding a term in x_i^2 to the preceding regression gives

Parabola : $y_i = \beta_0 + \beta_1 x_i + \beta_2 x_i^2 + \varepsilon_i$

$$i = 1, \ldots n.$$

This is still linear regression; although the expression on the right hand side is quadratic in the independent variable x_i it is linear in the parameters, β_0, β_1 and β_2. In both cases, ε_i is an error term and the subscript '*i*' indexes a particular observation.

Multiple Regression

Multiple Regression refers to a set of techniques for studying the straight line relationship among two or more variables. Multiple regression estimates the B's in the equation.

$$Y_j = \beta_0 + \beta_1 x_2 j + \ldots \beta_p X_{pj} + E_j$$

The 'x' represents the independent variables. Y is the dependent variable. The subscripts represents the observation (row) number. The β's are unknown regression coefficients. Their estimates are represented by p's. Each β represents the original unknown (population) parameter, while p is an estimate of this β. The E_j is the error of observation.

When the equation is solved hierarchically, then the predictors are entered one after another depending on the theory or simply depending on their statistical ability to predict the Y. The multiple regression is very useful technique in psychological research.

Factor Analysis

Factor analysis is a method for determining the number and nature of the underlying variables among large numbers of observations. More succinctly, it is a method for determining '*k*' underlying variables (factors) from '*n*' sets of measures, '*k*' being less than '*n*'. It may also be called a method for extracting common factor variance from sets of measures.

Factor analysis serves the cause of scientific parsimony. It reduces the multiplicity of tests and measures to greater simplicity. A factor is a hypothetical entity *i.e.* assumed to underlie tests, scales, items and indeed, measures of almost any kind. A number of factors have been found to underlie intelligence. *For example-* Verbal ability, numerical ability, abstract reasoning and others. Similarly, aptitude, attitude and personality factors have been isolated and identified.

Merits of Factor Analysis

The main merits of factor analysis can be stated as follows–

- The technique is helpful in pointing out important and interesting relationships among observed data that were there at the time, but not easy to see from the data alone.

- The technique can reveal the latent factors (*i.e.* underlying factors not directly observed) that determine relationships among several variables concerning a research study. *For example-* if people are asked to rate different cold drinks (say limca, coca cola, fanta and so on) according to preference, a factor analysis may reveal some salient characteristics of cold drinks that underlie the relative preferences.
- The technique may be used in the context of empirical clustering of products.

Demerits of Factor Analysis

Apart from considering its merits, one should also be aware of several limitations of factor analysis.

Important ones are as follows

- Factor analysis, like all multivariate techniques, involves laborious computations involving heavy cost burden. With computer facility available these days, there is no doubt that factor analysis has become relatively faster and easier, but the cost factor continues to be the same *i.e.* large factor analysis are still quite expensive.
- The results of a single factor analysis are considered generally less reliable and dependable, for very often, a factor analysis starts with a set of imperfect data. The factors are merely blurred averages, difficult to be identified. To overcome this difficulty, it has been realised that analysis should be done at least twice. If we get more or less similar results from all rounds of analysis, our confidences concerning such results increases.
- Factor analysis is a complicated decision tool that can be used only when one has thorough knowledge and enough experience of handling this tool. Even then, at times, it may not work well and may disappoint the user.

To conclude, we can state that inspite of all the said limitations, factor analysis not only helps the investigator make sense of intertwined data, but also points out some interesting relationships that may not be obvious from a more superficial examination.

Use of Factor Analysis

Professor BN Mukherjee (Computer and Science Unit of Indian Statistical Institute, Calcutta, 1975) has outlined seven conditions under, which factor analysis should be used.

These are–

- Factor analysis should be used for data reduction, when the researcher wants to combine different aspects of variance related to original variables. If the investigator is interested in classifying a set of variables in relation to each other to identify sub-groups of observed variables that are similar, then cluster analysis and not factor analysis is the appropriate method.
- Factor analysis should be used in test development programme of studying the factorial structure of a battery of tests and the extent to which certain tests are factorially 'pure'.
- Principal component analysis or principal axes solution may be used for deriving a set of orthogonal variables, which could be used in applied predication using multiple regression technique. Thus, factor analysis may be quite useful in subsuming a large number of factors into a smaller group.
- Factor analysis or principal component analysis can be used to combine and scale several measures of a unidimensional domain (such as extraversion or neuroticism or verbal fluency), so as to produce maximum discrimination among individuals along a single dimension.
- Factor analysis reveals the minimum number of independent dimensions that are required to define adequately the domain under investigation.
- Factor analysis is preferred, when the total underlying dimensions are less than the number of variables taken in the study. This is particularly required, when the observed variables are infested with measurement error.

Important Methods of Factor Analysis

There are several methods of factor analysis, but they do not necessarily give same results. Factor analysis is not a single unique method, but a set of techniques.

Important methods of factor analysis are–

- The centroid method
- The principle components method
- The maximum likelihood method

Before we describe these different methods of factor analysis, it seems appropriate to understand some basic terms relating to factor analysis *which are as follows*

- **Factor** A factor is an underlying dimension that accounts for several observed variables. There can be one or more factors, depending upon the nature of study and the number of variables involved in it.
- **Factor Loading** Factor loading are those values, which explain how closely they are related to each one of the factors discovered. They are also known as *factor-variable correlations.*

- **Communality** Communality, symbolised as h^2, shows how much of each variable is accounted for by the underlying factor taken together.
  h^2 of the ith variable
  = (ith Factor loading of Factor A)^2
  + (ith Factor loading of Factor B)^2 + ...
- **Eigen Value** When we take the sum of squared values of factor loadings relating to a factor, then such sum is referred to as Eigen value or latent root. Eigen value indicates the relative importance of each factor in accounting for the particular set of variables being analysed.
- **Total Sum Squares** When Eigen value of all factors are added, the resulting value is the total sum of squares. The value, when divided by the number of variables results in an index that shows how the particular solution accounts for and what all the variables taken together represent.
- **Rotation** Rotation, in the context of factor analysis, is something like staining a microscope slide. Just as, different stains on it reveal different structures in the tissue, different rotations reveal different structures of the data.
- **Factor Scores** Factor scores represents the degree, to which each respondent gets high scores on the group of items that load high on each factor. Factor scores can help explain what the factors mean with such scores, several other multivariate analysis can be performed.
  Method of factor analysis are as follows

Centroid Method of Factor Analysis

This method of factor analysis, developed by LL Thurst was used until about 1950, before the advent of large capacity high speed computers. The centroid method tends to maximise the sum of loadings. This method, which extracts the largest sum of absolute loading for each factor in turn. It is defined by linear combinations, in which all weights are either + 1.0 or– 1.0.

Various steps involved in this method are as follows–

- This method starts with the computation of a matrix of correlations (R), wherein unities are placed in the diagonal spaces. The product moment formula is used for finding out the correlation coefficients.
- If the correlation matrix so obtained, happens to be positive manifold then centroid method requires that the weights of all variable be + 1.0.
- The first centroid factor is determined by the sum of the coefficients in each column of the correlation matrix worked out.
- To obtain second centroid factor, one must first obtain a matrix of residual coefficient. For this purpose, the loadings for the two variables on the first centroid factor are multiplied. This is done for all possible pairs of variables. The resulting matrix of factor cross products may be named as Q_1.
- After the second centroid factor is obtained, cross products are computed forming matrix Q_2. This is than subtracted from R_1 resulting in R_2.

Principal Components Method of Factor Analysis

This methods of factor analysis, developed by H Hotelling, seeks to maximise the sum of squared loading of each factor. Accordingly, PC method of factor analysis explains more variance than would the loadings obtained from any other method of factoring.

The aim of the principal component method is the construction out of a given set of variables.

$Xjs\ (J = 1, 2, \ldots, k)$ of new variable (Pi) called *principal components*, which are linear combinations of the Xs.

$$P_1 = a_{11}X_1 + a_{12}X_2 + \ldots + a_{1k}X_k$$
$$P_2 = a_{21}X_1 + a_{22}X_2 + \ldots + a_{2k}X_k$$
$$P_k = a_{k1}X_1 + a_{k2}X_2 + \ldots + a_{kk}X_k$$

The method is being applied mostly by using standardised variables *i.e.* $= Z_j = (X_j - \bar{x}_j)^2 / \sigma_j$

The a_{ij}'s are called loading and are worked out in such a way that the extracted principal components satisfy two conditions *which are*

(i) Principal components are uncorrelated and
(ii) The first principle component (P_1) has the maximum variance, the second principle component (P_2) has the next maximum variance and soon.

Following steps are usually involved in principle components method

- Estimates of a_{ij}'s are obtained with which X's are transformed into orthogonal variables *i.e.* the principal components. A decision is also taken with regard to the question "how many of the components to retain into the analysis"?
- We than proceed with the regression of Y on these principal components.
  i.e. $Y = \hat{Y}_1\hat{P}_1 + \ldots + \hat{Y}_m P_m \ (m < k)$
- From the $\hat{a}_{ij}$ and $\hat{Y}_{ij}$, we may find b_{ij} of the original model, transferring back from the p's into the standardised X's.

Alternative method for finding the factor loadings is as under

- Correlation coefficients between the pairs of k variables are worked out and may be arranged in the form of a correlation matrix, *R*, as under.

Correlation Matrix, R Variables

Variables	$X_1\ X_2\ X_3 \ldots X_4$
X_1	$Y_{11}\ Y_{12}\ Y_{13} \ldots Y_{1\kappa}$
X_2	$Y_{21}\ Y_{22}\ Y_{23} \cdots Y_{2\kappa}$
X_3	$Y_{31}\ Y_{32}\ Y_{33} \cdots Y_{3\kappa}$
$\vdots$	$\vdots$
X_k	$Y_{\kappa 1}\ Y_{\kappa 2}\ Y_{\kappa 3} \cdots Y_{\kappa\kappa}$

The main diagonal spaces include unity, since such elements are self-correlations. The correlation matrix happens to be a symmetrical matrix.

- Presuming the correlation matrix to be positive manifold, the first-step is to obtain the sum of coefficient in each column, including the diagonal element.
- To obtain factor B, one seeks solutions for ν_b and the actual factor loadings for second component factor, B.
- This very procedure is repeated over again to obtain the successive PC factors (*i.e.* C, D etc).

Maximum Likelihood Method

Maximum likelihood, also called the *Maximum Likelihood method*, is the procedure of finding the value of one or more parameters for a given statistic which makes the known likelihood distribution a maximum. The maximum likelihood estimate for a parameter (μ) is denoted by $\hat{\mu}$.

Rotation of the Reference Axis

For the purpose of simplifying the interpretation of the obtained factors and also to increase the number of high and low positive loadings in the column of factor analysis, a procedure is used which is known as *Factor Rotation.*

There are two basic methods

(i) Orthogonal rotation (ii) Oblique rotation

Orthogonal rotation method is employed, when we have factors that are not correlated with one another, while the oblique rotation method is employed when the obtained factors are related to one another. Factor analysts like Guilford prefer orthogonal rotation, while Thurstone and Cattell prefer oblique rotation.

Interpreting the Factor

After the statistical computations of factoring and rotation have been completed, the next problem faced by the investigator would be of interpreting the factors. This is achieved by inspecting the pattern of high and low loading of each factor on the subtests/variables. It is to be remembered that the higher the loading, the most important the factor is on the given test.

Let us elaborate the interpretation of a factor with some example. Take factor I.

S. No.	Name of the Variable	Loadings
1.	One-upmanship lifestyle	0.876
2.	Exploitative lifestyle	0.869
3.	Domineering lifestyle	0.755
4.	Conservatism	0.656
5.	Political, social and economic gain	0.494
6.	Marriage and interpersonal relations	0.444
7.	Religiosity	0.439
8.	Individualistic lifestyle	– 0.657
9.	Defiant lifestyle	– 0.658

It is observed that the above factor is a very complex factor, consisting of nine variables in all. Among these variables are five lifestyles, two dimensions of caste prejudice and conservatism. The highest positive loading is that of one-upmanships coping style. This positive loading indicates an individual or operator, who uses his wits to get the better of people. The second highest positive loading on the exploitative lifestyle indicates attempt to get ahead by exploiting others.

The positive loadings on the domineering authoritarian lifestyle reflect the attitude 'I know what is best' and 'You should do what I say'. Positive loadings on conservatism reflect the desire to preserve old beliefs, customs and traditions and to vehemently oppose processes or change. Positive loading on Political Social and Economic Gain (PSEG) and Marriage and Interpersonal Relations (MIR) reflect the existence of religious orientation, with an emphasis on the concrete and literal qualities of religious belief. The negative loadings of the individualistic and defiant resistive on the factor indicates that such individuals do not have the desire to be a distinctively different individual and neither do they possess the 'to hell with you' attitude. In the light of above discussion, this factor may be named as the 'going against people' factor.

EXAM BASED QUESTIONS

1 Which among the following is a measure of the strength of a relationship between variables?
(a) Regression (b) Correlation
(c) Factor analysis (d) None of these

2 Which among the following is used to predict the value of one variable ?
(a) Regression (b) Correlation
(c) Factor analysis (d) None of these

3 Which among the following analysis is used when the researcher wants to determine the possible association between the variables?
(a) Factor analysis (b) Regression analysis
(c) Correlation analysis (d) All of these

4 "More the practise, better the performance" the statements represents
(a) Regression (b) Correlation
(c) Factor analysis (d) Ethnography

5 Establishing 'the cause and effect relation' is .... step for measuring the correlation.
(a) 1st (b) 2nd (c) 3rd (d) 4th

6 The method of product moment was introduced by
(a) Patman (b) Robert Owen
(c) Michael Sandel (d) Karl Pearson

7 'Correlation Coefficient' is also known as
(a) Pearson' product-moment
(b) spearman's rank-order
(c) Both a and b
(d) None of the above

8 Which among the following is a measure of the strength of a linear association between two variables and is denoted by 'r'?
(a) Spearman's rank-order
(b) Phi coefficient
(c) Pearson's product- moment
(d) None of the above

9 The Pearson's correlation coefficient, 'r', can take a range of values from
(a) +1 to −1 (b) −1 to 0
(c) 0 to +1 (d) −2 to +2

10 In formula, $r = \frac{Cov_{xy}}{S_X S_Y}$, 'S' stands for
(a) Covariance (b) Standard deviation
(c) Product moment (d) None of these

11 Rank-order correlation procedure is developed by
(a) Spearman (b) Pearson
(c) Both a and b (d) None of these

12 'rho' or 'r_s' is used to represent
(a) Rank - order
(b) Product moment
(c) Point biserial
(d) Tetrachoric

13 Which among the following are used to assess monotonic relationship?
(a) Product moment (b) Rank-order
(c) Point biserial (d) Tetrachoric

14 The range of Spearman's rho (r_s) is from
(a) +1.00 to −1.00 (b) −1.00 to +1.00
(c) 0 to +1.00 (d) −1.00 to 0

15 When the value of r_s is zero then
(a) there is no relationship between X and Y
(b) relationship is weak
(c) relationship is strong
(d) None of the above

16 Spearman's rho is calculated as
(a) transforming original data into categories.
(b) by using original scores, no transformation are needed.
(c) by transforming original scores into deviations.
(d) by transforming original scores into ranks.

17 The correlation between X and Y variable is 0.80. It means X and Y have a common variation of
(a) 50% (b) 20% (c) 36% (d) 64%

18 In a psychological study, the results are statistically significant when likelihood of their occurrence by change is
(a) zero (b) high (c) moderate (d) low

19 A psychologist investigating child abuse wants to test the hypothesis that those parents, who abuse their children were frequently mistreated themselves by their parents when younger. Which one of the following methods is suitable for this purpose?
(a) Case study (b) Introspection
(c) Correlation method (d) Survey method

20 In SPSS, where do you find the option for Spearman's rho?
(a) Non-parametric tests (b) Correlation
(c) Explore (d) Regression

21 In a correlation research, the variables can be controlled by
(a) experimenter's manipulation and observation.
(b) experimenter's observation and selection.
(c) selection and statistical techniques.
(d) experimenter's manipulation and statistical techniques.

22 A research investigator randomly selected. Some, students and administered their tests of verbal intelligence and verbal creativity. He desires to find out whether an individual's creativity can be predicted on the basis of his intelligence. For this study, the most suitable method of psychology would be
(a) descriptive (b) correlation
(c) experimental (d) developmental

23 Statistical method for identifying groups of abilities or behaviours or traits that are related to one another is termed as
(a) Multiple regression analysis
(b) Factor analysis
(c) Regression equation (d) Multiple correlation

24 The research strategy in which psychologists try to discover a relationship between two factors by measuring each factor separately and then comparing results is called
(a) Observation (b) Correlation
(c) Experimentation (d) Unobstrusive study

25 Correlation between X and Y is 0.80. Its X and Y have common variation of
(a) 80% (b) 20% (c) 36% (d) 64%

26 Surveys play an important role in a type of research that is intended to assess the covariation of naturally occurring variables. This general type of research is called
(a) Experimental research (b) Correlational research
(c) Analytical research (d) Qualitative research

27 In which kind of correlation analysis, we aim at measuring the relation between dependent variable and a particular independent variable by holding all the variables constant?
(a) Maltiple Correlation (b) Partial Correlation
(c) Special Correlation (d) None

28 Each partial coefficient of correlation measures the effect of its
(a) independent variable (b) dependent variable
(c) both a and b (d) None of these

29 When one variable is held constant, partial correlation coefficients is known as
(a) First order coefficients (b) Second order coefficients
(c) Third order coefficients (d) Fourth order coefficients

30 Which among the following measures separately the relationship between two variables in such a way that the effects of the other related variables are limited?
(a) Multiple correlation (b) Partial correlation
(c) Rank-order correlation (d) None of these

31 When one coefficient is held constant, then the partial coefficients are known as
(a) First order coefficient (b) Second order coefficient
(c) Third order coefficient (d) None of these

32 $R_{ABCD......K}$ is used to represent
(a) Multiple correlation (b) Partial correlation
(c) Rank order (d) Product method

33 The correlation between academic achievement with the linear combination of anxiety and intelligence is called
(a) Partial correlation (b) Multiple correlation
(c) Both a and b (d) None of these

34 'r_b' is used as a symbol to represent
(a) Tetrachoric coefficient (b) Point biserial coefficient
(c) Biserial coefficient (d) Phi coefficient

35 'r_{pb}' is used as a symbol to represent
(a) Point biserial coefficient (b) Biserial coefficient
(c) Tetrachoric coefficient (d) Phi coefficinet

36 'ϕ' is used as a symbol to represent
(a) Tetrachoric coefficient (b) Phi coefficient
(c) Point biserial coefficient (d) Biserial coefficient

37 Tetrachoric coefficient is represented as
(a) ϕ (b) r_{pb} (c) r_b (d) r_t

38 Biserial correlation coefficient is represented by
(a) r_{pb} (b) r_f (c) r_b (d) ϕ

39 Correlation between height and gender is an example of
(a) Biserial (b) Point Biserial (c) Tetrachoric (d) Phi

40 Correlation between male/female and alive/dead is an example of
(a) Phi (b) Tetrachoric
(c) Biserial (d) Point Biserial

41 Which is a set of statistical processes for estimating the relationship among variables?
(a) Correlation analysis (b) Special correlation analysis
(c) Regression analysis (d) Factor analysis

42 Which among the following analysis is used for prediction and forecasting?
(a) Regression analysis (b) Factor analysis
(c) Correlational analysis (d) None of these

43 Which among the following can be used to infer casual relationship between dependent and independent variable?
(a) Correlational analysis (b) Factor analysis
(c) Regression analysis (d) None of these

44 In which type of regression, dependent variable 'y_i' is a linear combination of the parameters?
(a) Multiple regression (b) Partial regression
(c) Linear regression (d) None of these

45 'y_i' is used to represent
(a) Independent variable (b) Linear regression
(c) Dependent variable (d) Straight line

46 When we have multiple predictors rather than a single predictor variable, the regression carried out is called as
(a) Dependent variable (b) Linear regression
(c) Independent variable (d) Multiple regression

47 Which among the following analysis is used for determining the number and nature of the underlying variables among larger numbers of measures ?
(a) Factor analysis (b) Correlational analysis
(c) Regression analysis (d) None of these

48 Which among the following serves the purpose of scientific parsimony?
(a) Factor analysis (b) Correlational analysis
(c) Regression analysis (d) None of these

49 Which among the following are factor/rs that have been found to underlie intelligence?
(a) Verbal ability (b) Abstract reasoning
(c) Numerical ability (d) All of these

50 Who outlined seven conditions under which factor analysis should be used?
(a) Parker (b) B N Mukherjee
(c) P S Pradhan (d) None of the above

51 Which among the following are important methods of factor analysis?
(a) Centroid method
(b) Principle compenents method
(c) Maximum likelihood method
(d) All of the above

52 Centroid method of factor analysis was developed by
(a) Cattell (b) Thurstone
(c) Guilford (d) BN Mukherjee

53 Principle component method of factor analysis was developed by
(a) Thurstone (b) Cattell
(c) H Hotelling (d) Guilford

54 The method to decide about the important factors to be interpreted/retained from the external factors is
(a) Factor leading
(b) Communality
(c) Scree test
(d) None of these

55 After analysis of variance, which mechanism is adopted by a researcher to find out that interaction is statistically significant?
(a) Analysis of the medians for each condition of the experiment.
(b) Main effects of each independent variable.
(c) Simple main effects.
(d) Analytical comparisons involving each independent variable.

56 A factor loading is
(a) a correlation coefficient between a variable and a factor (cluster or variables).
(b) the correlation between binomial variable and variable, which has a continuous distribution of scores.
(c) the correlation of a variable.
(d) empirically based hypothetical variable consisting of items, which are strongly associated with each other.

57 A factor loading of 0.80 means, generally speaking that
(a) there is no relationship between that variable and the factor.
(b) the variable is moderately related with the factor.
(c) the item correlates well with the factor, though not perfectly.
(d) the item is poorly related to the factor.

58 A empirically based hypothetical variable consisting of items, which are strongly associated with each other and upon which individuals differ is known as what?
(a) A factor (b) A factor loading
(c) Rotating (d) Factor analysis

59 Which of the following statements is correct?
(a) In extracting factors, we want to account for as little variance as possibile, while keeping the number of factors extracted as small as possible.
(b) In extracting factors, we want to account for as little variance as possible, while keeping the number to factors extracted as large as possible.
(c) In extracted factors, we want to account for as much variance as possible, while keeping the number of factors extracted as large as possible.
(d) In extracted factors, we want to account for as much variance as possible, while keeping the number of factors extracted as small as possible.

60 In a rank-order correlation
(a) variables are in an ordinal scale
(b) normality of distribution is assumed
(c) variables are converted to an interval scale
(d) number of cases is always less than 12

61 Consider the following statements
1. A correlation exists, when two different measures of the sample people, events or things vary together.
2. A scatterplot that appears to have no shape or reveals no trend whatsoever is associated with a correlation coefficient of 0.50.

Which one of the statements given above is/are correct?
(a) Only 1 (b) Only 2
(c) Both 1 and 2 (d) None of these

62 Consider the following statements
1. In partial correlation, relationship between two variables are calculated .
2. In multiple correlation, relationship between two or more than two independent variables are calculated.

Which one of the statements given above is/are correct?
(a) Only 1 (b) Only 2
(c) Both 1 and 2 (d) None of these

63 Consider the following statements
1. The standard deviation tells us approximately how far scores vary from the mean on the average.
2. Dividing the standard deviation by the square root of the sample size yields the range.

Which one of the statements given above is/are correct?
(a) Only 1 (b) Only 2
(c) Both 1 and 2 (d) None of these

64 Consider the following statements
1. If a correlation coefficient is close to 0.0, we know that our ability to make predictions for the variables is poor.

2. Perhaps, the best way to get a fell for a data set is to draw a graph of the data.

Which one of the statements given above is/are correct?

(a) Only 1
(b) Only 2
(c) Both 1 and 2
(d) None of these

Directions (Q. Nos. 65-70) *In the questions given below are two statements labelled as Assertion (A) and Reason (R). In the context of two statements, which one of the following is correct?*

Codes

(a) Both A and R are true and R is the correct explanation of A
(b) Both A and R are true, but R is not the correct explanation of A
(c) A is true, but R is false
(d) A is false, but R is true

65 Assertion (A) In general, the reliability of a test increases with the number of items on the test.

Reason (R) Obtaining a correlation coefficient (R) of 1.42 indicates an error in calculation.

66 Assertion (A) A reliable test is one that measures what it is supposed to measure.

Reason (R) A correlation coefficient of +0.46 indicates a stronger relationship than that of coefficient 0.56.

67 Assertion (A) Out of the five correlation coefficients, 0.80, 0.70, 0.50 and 0.00 and –0.20, between X and Y variables, the strongest relationship is indicated by a correlation coefficient of 0.70.

Reason (R) The correlation coefficient of 0.70 indicates that as X increases, Y also tends to increase.

68 Assertion (A) Causal inferences are problematic, when based only on correlational evidence.

Reason (R) A correlation of 0.05 between scores on two measures designed to assess the same construct would indicate good convergent validity.

69 Assertion (A) A probability sample is when individuals are probably available and willing to respond to a survey.

Reason (R) Scores on two questionnaires designed to measure different constructs should demonstrate a low correlation.

70 Assertion (A) A spurious relationship occurs, when a third variable explains the relationship between two correlated variables.

Reason (R) A reliable test is a perfect measurement principle.

71 Match the following

List I (Correlation methods)	List II (Symbols)
A. Biserial	1. r_{pb}
B. Point biserial	2. r_b
C. Tetrachoric	3. r_t
D. Phi	4. ϕ

Codes

	A	B	C	D
(a)	1	2	3	4
(b)	2	1	3	4
(c)	1	3	4	2
(d)	2	4	3	1

72 Match the following

List I (Author)	List II (Methods)
A. Pearson	1. Factor analysis
B. Spearman	2. Product moment
C. B N Mukherjee	3. Rank-order

Codes

	A	B	C		A	B	C
(a)	1	2	3	(b)	3	2	1
(c)	2	3	1	(d)	1	3	2

73 Match the following

List I (Methods)	List II (Range)
A. Product moment	1. –1.00 to +1.00
B. Rank order	2. +1.00 to –1.00
C. Multiple correlation	3. ABCD ....K

Codes

	A	B	C		A	B	C
(a)	1	2	3	(b)	3	2	1
(c)	2	1	3	(d)	3	1	2

Direction (Q.Nos. 74-78) *Read the passage given below and answer the following questions.*

Rank-order correlation procedure is developed by Charles Spearman. It is also known as *Spearman's rho* (r_s). It was developed to compute correlation, when the data is presented on two variables for 'n' subjects.

In can also be calculated for data of 'n' subjects evaluated by two judges for inter-judge agreement. It is suitable for the rank-order data. If the data on '*x*' or '*y*' or on both the variables are in rank-order then Spearman's *rho* (*rs*) is applicable.

It is used to assess a monotonic relationship.

The range of Spearman's *rho* (r_s) is also from –1.00 to +1.00. Like Pearson's correlation, the interpretation of Spearman's rho is based on sign of the coefficient and the value of the coefficient.

If the sign of r_s is positive then relationship is positive, if the sign of r_s is negative then the relationship is negative. If the value of r_s is close to zero then relationship is weak and as the value of r_s approaches to ± 1.00, the strength of relationship increases. When the value of r_s is zero then there is no relationship between X and Y. If r_s is ± 1.00, then the relationship between X and Y is perfect

74 Rank order correlation procedure is developed by
(a) Pearson
(b) Guilford
(c) Spearman
(d) None

75 Spearman's rho is symbolised as
(a) r_b (b) r_r (c) r_p (d) r_s

76 Spearman's rho is used to assess
(a) monotonic relationship
(b) eliatonic relationship
(c) tritonic relationship
(d) None of the above

77 If the value of r_s is close to zero the relationship is
(a) strong (b) weak (c) moderate (d) stable

78 The range of spearman's rho is from
(a) + 1.00 to – 1.00 (b) – 1.00 to + 1.00
(c) 0 to + 1.00 (d) – 1.00 to 0

ANSWERS

1 (b)	2 (a)	3 (c)	4 (b)	5 (c)	6 (d)	7 (a)	8 (c)	9 (a)	10 (b)
11 (a)	12 (a)	13 (b)	14 (b)	15 (a)	16 (d)	17 (a)	18 (d)	19 (c)	20 (b)
21 (c)	22 (b)	23 (d)	24 (b)	25 (a)	26 (b)	27 (b)	28 (c)	29 (a)	30 (b)
31 (a)	32 (a)	33 (b)	34 (c)	35 (a)	36 (b)	37 (d)	38 (c)	39 (b)	40 (a)
41 (c)	42 (a)	43 (c)	44 (c)	45 (d)	46 (d)	47 (a)	48 (a)	49 (d)	50 (b)
51 (d)	52 (b)	53 (c)	54 (c)	55 (c)	56 (a)	57 (c)	58 (a)	59 (b)	60 (a)
61 (a)	62 (c)	63 (a)	64 (c)	65 (b)	66 (a)	67 (d)	68 (c)	69 (d)	70 (c)
71 (b)	72 (c)	73 (c)	74 (c)	75 (d)	76 (a)	77 (b)	78 (b)		

CHAPTER

8

Experimental Designs

Experimental design is the branch of statistics that deals with the design and analysis of experiment. It includes various technique such as ANOVA, Randomised block design, Latin square etc.

Introduction of Experimental Design

Experimental design is a way to plan experiments carefully in advance, so that your results are both objective and valid. The terms 'Experimental Design' and 'Design of Experiments' are used interchangeably. However, the medical and social sciences tend to use the term 'experimental design', while engineering, industrial and computer sciences favour the term 'design of experiments'.

Scholars have compared the design of an experiment to an architect's plan for the structure of a building. The designer of experiments perform a role similar to that of the architect. The prospective owner of a building gives his basic requirements to the architect, who then exercising his ingenuity, prepares a plan or a blue-print, outlining the final shape of the structure. Similarly, the designer of the experiment has to do the planning of the experiment, so that the experiment on completion fulfills the objectives of research.

According to **Myers**, "The design is the general structure of the experiment, not its specific content."

According to **Lindquist**, "Research design is the plan, structure and strategy of investigation conceived, so as to obtain answer to research question and to control variance."

The first part of the statement emphasises only upon the objective of research *i.e.* to obtain answer to research question. The most important function of the design is the strategy to control variance.

In this Chapter

Experimental Design as Variance Control

Variance is a measure of dispersion or spread of a set of scores. It describes the extent to which the scores differ from each other. Variance and variation though used synonymously are not identical terms. Variation is a more general term, which includes variance as one of the statistical methods of representing variation.

The problem of variance control has three aspects that deserve full attention. The three aspects of variance are *systematic variance, extraneous* variance and *error variance.* Main functions of experimental design are to maximise the effect of systematic variance, control extraneous source of variance and minimise error variance. *The three aspect of variance are as follows*

Systematic Variance

Systematic variance is the variability in the dependent measure due to manipulation of the experimental variable by the experimenter. An important task of the experimenter is to maximise variance. This objective is achieved by making the levels of the experimental variable/s as unlike as possible.

Extraneous Variance

In addition to the independent variable and the dependent variable, which are main concern in any experiment. Extraneous variables are encountered in all experimental situations that can influence **a dependent variable**.

There are five basic procedures for controlling the extraneous source of variance. *These procedures are*

(i) **Randomisation** Randomisation in the experiment means random selection of the experimental units from the larger population of interest by the experimenter and/or random assignment of the experimental unit or subjects to the treatment condition. Random assignment means that every experimental unit has an equal chance of being placed in any of the treatment condition or groups. Random selection and random assignment are different procedure.

It is possible to select a random sample from a population, but then assignment of experimental units to group may be biased.

(ii) **Elimination** Another procedure for controlling the unwanted extraneous variance is through elimination of the variable by choosing the experimental units in such a way that they become homogeneous, as far as possible. Elimination procedure for controlling the extraneous source of variance is primarily a non-experimental design control procedure.

(iii) **Matching** Another procedure, which is also a non-experimental design procedure, is control of extraneous source of variance through matching. The procedure is to match subjects on that variable, which is substantially related to dependent variable. However, matching as a method of control, limits the availability of subjects for the experiment. Beside this, the method of matching biases the principle of randomisation. Further, matching the subjects on one variable may result in their mismatching on other variable.

(iv) **Additional Independent Variables** Sometimes, the experimenter may consider elimination in expedient or unpractical way. He may not eliminate the extraneous variable from the experiment and thus, build it right into the design as a second independent variable.

(v) **Statistical Control** In this approach, no attempt is made to restrain the influence of secondary variables. In this technique, one or more **concomitant** variables are measured and the dependent variable is statistically adjusted to remove the effects of the uncontrolled source of variation.

Error variance

Error variance usually indicates how much random fluctuation is expected within scores and often forms part of the denominator of test statistics, such as the F ratio in an analysis of variance. It is also known as *residual error* or *residual variance*. Error variance is uncontrollable variance. The source of error variance can be guessing, momentary inattention, bad mood...etc.

Blocing If all subjects are treated as big group, variability may be very huge. By dividing the experimental conditions into several 'blocks' the researcher can localise error variance *i.e.* in each block the within-group variability is smaller.

Improve the Reliability of Measure If the instrument has a high reliability coefficient, there will be less measurement error variance is reduced. Reliability will be discussed in the section 'Measurement'.

ANOVA

The test of significance of the difference between two mean is very important technique of inferential statistics, which is used to test the null hypothesis and help to draw concrete conclusion, but its scope is very limited. It is only applicable to the two sets of scores or the scores obtained from two samples taken from a single population or from two different population. Generally 'CR' or 't'-test of significance is used, but when we have more than two groups, then 'F'-test is more suitable and it is known as one way Analysis of Variance (ANOVA).

Basic Principles of ANOVA

The basic principles of Analysis of Variance (ANOVA) is to test differences among the means of the population by examining the amount of variation within each of the samples, relative to the amount of variation between the samples. While using ANOVA, we assume that each of the sample is drawn from a normal population and that each of these population has the same variance. We also assume that all factors other than the one or more being tested are effectively controlled. Thus, in other words, mean that we assume the absence of many factors that might affect our conclusions, concerning the factor(s) to be studied.

In short, we have to make two estimates of population variance *i.e.* one based on between samples variance and the other based on within sample variance. Then, the said two estimates of population variance are compared with 'F'-test, wherein we work out.

$$F = \frac{\text{Estimate of population variance based on between sample variance}}{\text{Estimate of population variance based on within sample variance}}$$

$$= \frac{\delta^2 \text{ between the groups}}{\delta^2 \text{ within the groups}}$$

The technique of analysis of variance was first devised by **Sir Ronald Fisher**, an English statistician, who applied it in the field of agriculture. Since then, it has found wide application in many areas of experimentation.

The value of 'F' to be compared to the F-limit for given degrees of freedom. If the F- value work out is equal or exceeds the F-limit value, then we may say that these are significant differences between the sample means.

Techniques of ANOVA

ANOVA has two main techniques of analysis, which are as follows

One Way ANOVA

Under the one way ANOVA, we consider only one factor and then observe the reason for said factors, several possible types of samples can occur within that factor. We then determine, if there are differences within that factor.

The technique involve the following steps

(i) Obtain the mean of each sample *i.e.*, obtain

$$x_1, x_2, x_3, \ldots .. x_k$$

where, k are samples.

(ii) Work out the mean of the sample means as follows

$$x = \frac{x_1 + x_2 + x_3 + \ldots .. + x_k}{\text{Number of Sample } (k)}$$

(iii) Take the deviations of the sample means from the mean of the sample means and calculate the square of such deviations, which may be multiplied by the number of items in the corresponding sample and then obtain their total. This is known as the sum of squares for variance between the samples.

Symbolically, this can be written as

$$\text{MS between} = \frac{SS \text{ between}}{(k-1)}$$

where, $(k-1)$ represents degrees of freedom (df) between samples.

(iv) Obtain the deviation of the values of the sample items for all the samples from corresponding means of the samples and calculate the squares of such deviations and then obtaining their total. This total is known as the sum of squares for variance within samples.

Symbolically, this can be written as

$$\text{SS within} = \Sigma(x_{1i} - \bar{x}_1)^2 \pm \Sigma(x_{2i} - \bar{x}_2)^2 + \ldots + \Sigma(x_{ki} - \bar{x}_k)^2$$

$$i = 1, 2, 3 \ldots \ldots$$

(v) Divide the result of (5) step by the degrees of freedom within samples to obtain the variance or mean square (MS) within sample.

Symbolically, this can be written as

$$\text{MS within} = \frac{SS \text{ within}}{(n-k)}$$

where, $(n-k)$ represents degrees of freedom within samples.

$n =$ Total number of items in all the samples *i.e.* $n_1 + n_2 + \ldots .. + n_k$

$k =$ number of sample.

(vi) To check, the sum of squares of deviations for total variance can also be worked out by adding the squares of deviations, when the deviations for the individual items in all the samples have been taken from the mean of the sample means.

Symbolically, this can be written as

$$\text{SS for total variance} = \Sigma(x_{ij} - \bar{\bar{x}})$$

$$i = 1, 2, 3 \ldots .$$

$$j = 1, 2, 3 \ldots .$$

This total should be equal to the total of the result of the (3) and (5) steps explained above *i.e.*

SS for total variance = *SS* between + *SS* within

The degrees of freedom for total variance will be equal to the number of items in all samples minus one *i.e.* $(n - 1)$.

The degrees of freedom for between and within must add upto the degree of freedom for total variance *i.e.* $(n - 1) = (k - 1) + (n - k)$

This fact explains the additive property of the ANOVA technique.

(vii) Finally, F-ratio may be worked out as

$$\text{F-ratio} = \frac{\text{MS between}}{\text{MS within}}$$

This ratio is used to judge whether the difference among several sample means is significant or is just a matter of sampling fluctuations. For this purpose, we look into the table, giving the value of F, for given degree of freedom at different levels of significance.

If the worked out value of 'F', as stated above is less than the table value of F, the difference is taken as insignificant *i.e.* due to chance and the null-hypothesis of no difference between sample means stands. In case, the calculated value of F happens to be either equal or more than its table value, the difference is considered as significant and accordingly, the conclusion may be drawn.

The higher the calculated value of 'F' is above the table value of 'f', the more definite and sure can be about conclusion.

Setting-up Analysis of Variance Table

For the sake of convenience, the information obtained through various steps above can be put as under.

Analysis of Variance Table for One Way ANOVA

Source of Variation	**Sum of Squares** (SS)	**Degree of Freedom** (*df*)	**Mean Square** (MS) (This is SS divided by *df*) **and is an estimation of variance to be used in F-ratio**	**F-ratio**
Between samples or categories	$n_1 (X_1 - \bar{X})^2 + \ldots + n_k (\bar{x}_k - \bar{x})^2$	$(k - 1)$	$\frac{SS \text{ between}}{(k-1)}$	$\frac{MS \text{ between}}{MS \text{ within}}$
Within samples or categories	$\Sigma (x_{1i} - \bar{x}_1)^2 + \ldots + \Sigma (x_{ki} - \bar{x}_k)^2$ $i = 1, 2, 3\ldots$	$(n - k)$	$\frac{SS \text{ within}}{(n-k)}$	
Total	$\Sigma (x_{ij} - \bar{x}_k)^2$ $i = 1, 2,\ldots$ $j = 1, 2,\ldots$	$(n - 1)$		

Merits of One Way ANOVA

The analysis of variance technique has the following advantages

- It is an improved technique over the 't'-test or 'z' test, it evaluates both types of variance 'between' and 'within'.
- This technique is used for ascertaining the difference among several groups or treatments at a time. It is an economical device.
- It can involve more than one variable in studying their main effects and interaction effects.
- In some of the experimental design. *For example* simple random design and levels *X* treatment designs are based on one -way analysis of variance.
- If 't' is not significant, 'F'-test must be followed to analyse the difference between two means.

Demerits of One Way ANOVA

The analysis of variance technique has following limitations also

- We have seen that analysis of variance techniques is based on certain assumptions. *For example* normality and homogeneity of the variance among the groups. The departure of the data from these assumptions may affect adversely on the inferences.
- The 'F' value provides global finding of difference among groups, but it can not specify the inference. Therefore, for complete analysis of variance, the 't'-test is followed for specifying the statistical inference.
- It is time-consuming process and requires the knowledge and skills of arithmetical operations as well as the high vision for interpretations of the results.
- For the use of 'F'-test, the statistical table of 'F' value is essential, without it results cannot be interpreted.

Two Way ANOVA

Two way ANOVA technique is used, when the data are classified on the basis of two factors. *For example* the agricultural output may be classified on the basis of different varieties of seeds and also on the basis of different varieties of fertilizers used. A business firm may have its sales data classified on the basis of different salesmen and also, on the basis of sales in different regions.

The ANOVA technique is little different in case of repeated measurement, where we also compute the interaction variation. Now, we shall explain the two way ANOVA technique in the context of both the said designs with the help of examples.

ANOVA with Two Way Design and No Repeated Values

As we do not have repeated values, we cannot directly compute the sum of squares within samples as we had done in the case of one way ANOVA.

Therefore, we have to calculate this residual or error variation by subtraction, once we have calculated the sum of squares for total variance and for variance between varieties of one treatment and also for variance between varieties of the other treatment.

The various steps involved are as follows

- Use of coding device, if it simplifies the task.
- Take the total of the values of individual items in all the samples and call it T.
- Work out the correction factors as under

$$\text{Correction factor} = \frac{(T)^2}{n}$$

- Find out the square of all the item values one by one and then take its total. Subtract the correction factor from this total to obtain the sum of squares of deviations for total variance.

Symbolically, we can write it as

Sum of squares of deviations for total variance or total SS

$$= \Sigma x_{ij}^2 - \frac{(T)^2}{n}$$

- Take the total of different columns and then, obtain the square of each column total and divide such square values of each column by the number of items in the concerning column and take the total of the result thus, obtained. Finally, subtract the correction factor from this total to obtain the sum of squares of deviations for variance between columns.
- Take the total of different rows and then, obtain the square of each row total and divide that squared values of each row by the number of items in the corresponding row and take the total of the result thus, obtained.

  Finally, subtract the correction factor from this total to obtain the sum of squares of deviations for variance between rows (or *SS* between rows).
- Sum of squares of deviations for residual or error variance can be worked out by subtracting the result of the sum of 5th and 6th steps from the result of 4th step steped above.

  In other words

  Total SS – (*SS* between columns + *SS* between rows) = SS for residual or error variance
- Degree of freedom (df) can be worked out as under.

  df for total variance = $(c\,r - 1)$

  df for variance between columns = $(c - 1)$

  df for variance between rows = $(r - 1)$

  df for residual variance = $(c - 1)(r - 1)$

  Where c = number of columns

  r = number of rows
- ANOVA table can be set-up in the usual fashion as shown below

  SS residual = Total *SS* – (*SS* between columns + *SS* between rows)

Analysis of Variance Table for Two Way ANOVA

Source of Variation	Sum of Squares (SS)	Degree of Freedom (df)	Mean Square (MS)	F-ratio
Between columns treatment	$\Sigma \frac{(T_j)^2}{n_j} - \frac{(T)^2}{n}$	(c – 1)	$\frac{SS \text{ between columns}}{(c-1)}$	$\frac{MS \text{ between columns}}{MS \text{ residual}}$
Between rows treatment	$\Sigma \frac{(T_i)^2}{n_i} - \frac{(T)^2}{n}$	(r – 1)	$\frac{SS \text{ between rows}}{(r-1)}$	$\frac{MS \text{ between rows}}{MS \text{ residual}}$
Residual or error	Total SS – (SS between columns + SS between rows)	(c – 1)(r – 1)	$\frac{SS \text{ residual}}{(c-1)(r-1)}$	
Total	$\Sigma X_{ij}^2 - \frac{(T)^2}{n}$	(cr – 1)		

Thus, MS residual or the residual variance provides the basis for the F-ratio concerning variation between columns treatment and between rows treatment. MS residual is always due to the fluctuations of sampling and hence, serves as the basis for the significance test. Both the F-ratios are compaired with their corresponding table values, for given degrees of freedom at a specific level of significance, as usual and if it is found that the calculated F-ratio concerning variation between columns is equal to greater than its table value, then the difference among columns means is consider significant. Similarly, the F-ratio concerning variation between rows can be interpreted.

Merits of Two Way ANOVA

The following are the advantages of two way analysis of variance

- This technique is used to analyse two types of effects *i.e.* main effects and interaction effects.
- More than two factors effects are analysed by this technique.
- For analysing the data obtained on the basis of factorial designs, this technique is used.
- This technique is used to analyse the data for complex experimental studies.

Demerits of Two Way ANOVA

The following limitations are found in this technique

- When there are more than two classification of factors of study, F-ratio value provides global picture of difference among the main treatment effects.
- The inference can be specified by using 't'-test in case, when F-ratio is found significant for a treatment.
- This technique also follows the assumptions, on which one way analysis of variance is based. If these assumptions are not fulfilled, the use of this technique may give us spurious results.
- This technique is difficult and time-consuming.
- As the number of factors are increased in a study, the complexity of analysis is increased and interpretation of results become difficult.
- This technique requires high level arithmetical and calculative ability. Similarly, it also requires high level of imaginative and logical ability to interpret the obtained results.

Factorial ANOVA

The factorial ANOVA has two or more independent variables that split the sample in four or more groups. The simplest case of a factorial ANOVA uses two binary variables as independent variable, thus creating four group within the sample.

For some statisticians, the factorial ANOVA doesn't only compare differences but assumes a cause-effect relationship, this infers that are or more independent, controlled variables (the factors) cause the significant difference of one on more characteristics. The way this works is that the factors sort the data points into one of the groups, causing the difference in the mean value of the groups.

Dependent Variable		Independent Variable	
		1	2+
	1	One-way ANOVA	Factorial ANOVA
	2+	Multiple ANOAVA	MANOVA

For Example Let us claim blonds women have on average longer hair than brunette women as well as men of all hair colors. We find 100 undergraduate students and measure the length of their hair.

A conservative statistician would then state that we measured the hair of 50 female (25 blondes, 25 brunettes) and 25 male students and we conducted an analysis of variance and found that the average hair of blonde female undergraduate students was significantly longer than the hair of their fellow students. A more aggressive would claim that gender and hair color have a direct influence on the length of a person's hair.

Randomised Block Designs

A randomised block design is an experimental design, where the experimental units are in groups called blocks. The treatments are randomly allocated to the experimental units inside each block. When all treatments appear at least once in each block, we have a completely randomised block design. Otherwise, we have an incomplete randomised block design.

Suppose, that we are planning to conduct an agricultural experiment on the effect of the concentration of a fertilizer on the growth rate of a certain crop. A large rectangular field has been allocated for the purpose of this research.

This field is sub-divided into small plots, each sufficiently large to contain only a single growing plant, while allowing adequate space between adjoining plots to ensure isolation of each from all the others. The simplest procedure, which might be used in assigning the different concentration of fertilizer would be, of course, to apply the different concentration to different large segment of the field, each segment containing several plots.

But, this procedure would be rejected as unsatisfactory on the obvious grounds that the different segments may differ greatly in soil fertility and any observed differences in growth rate of the plants that received the different concentration of fertilizer could just an easily be due to soil by employing randomisation to determine which concentration of fertilizer is applied to which large segment, since chance factor will still determine which large segment receives which amount of concentration of fertilizer.

A better procedure would be use randomisation for assigning different concentration to each separate plots in the field. This would ensure that the error variance due to soil heterogeneity would be distributed according to chance both between and within the different levels of the independent variable. Thus, it should be apparent, it the basis of the simple random group designs. *After initial process of randomisations, following step are follows*

Reducing Heterogeneity

Fortunately, in the present case, it is known that the major factors leading to soil heterogeneity are such as to make plots near one another, more equally fertile than those separated by some considerable distance. Such things, as the location of nearby stream, the distribution of natural chemicals in the soil, the angle of incidence of available sunlight and the shading produced by trees and hills etc. are all more likely to influence the fertility of adjacent plots more similarly than they would influence plots more widely separated.

The simplest application of the blocking principles in this case would be to divide the field into six segments or blocks, each of which contains six plots. Within each of these blocks, the six amounts of concentration of fertilizer are assigned randomly, one to a plot. The actual fashion in which the six blocks are formed may depend upon special features to the local environment and terrain.

Appropriateness of Error Estimate

To illustrate the fact that this variability is exactly what will provide the appropriate error term in the randomised block design, each experiment involving three blocks. In one of these experiments, considerable fluctuation in the influence of the independent variable among the three blocks is depicted. The trend of growth rates across concentration is less variable from block to block. It should be noted that both sets of hypothetical data indicate substantial differences between blocks in the overall level of growth rate and that the average trend of growth rate across concentration was about the same.

Even though, the average effect of the concentration of fertilizer variable is approximately the same. To the extent, which the different blocks differ in the way, in which the independent variables has its influence, we should properly be less inclined to reject a null hypothesis which states that the independent variables has no influence. To the extent, the effect of the independent variables is similar from block to block, we may be more confident of its reliability.

Repeated Measures Design

In a repeated measures designs, each group member in an experiment is tested for multiple conditions over time or under different conditions. *For example* A group of people with Type II diabetes might be given medications to see if it helps control their disease and then they might be given nutritional counselling. A blood test to measure glucose levels is given to the patients after each treatment.

Repeated measures designs may be categorised into two type; which are as follows

(i) An *ordinary repeated measures* is where patients are assigned a single treatment and the results are measured over time (*e.g.* at 1, 4 and 8 weeks).

(ii) A *Crossover design* is where patients are assigned all treatments and the results are measured over time.

The most common crossover design is "two-period, two treatment". Participants are randomly assigned to receive either A and B or B and then A.

One important fact that sets crossover design apart from the "usual" type of experiment is that the same patients are in the control group and all of the treatment groups. A patients is measured by how well they respond to treatments against themselves; the "control" is the original status of the patient. For example, a patient undergoing nutritional counseling is measured before treatment (the control part) and after treatments (exprimental part).

Benefits of Repeated Measures Designs

- *Mejor benefit of repeated measures design are listed below*
- **More statistical Power** Repeated measures designs can be very powerful because they control for factors that cause variability between subjects.

- **Fewer Subjects** Thanks to the greater statistical power, repeated measures design can use fewer subjects to detect a desired effect size. Further sample size reductions are possible because each subject is involved with multiple treatments. *For example,* If an independent groups design requires 20 subjects per experimental group, a repeated measures design may only require 20 total.
- **Quicker and Cheaper** Fewer subjects need to be recruited, trained and compensated to complete an entire experiment.
- **Assess An Effect Over Time** Repeated measures designs can track an effect overtime, such as the learning curve for a task. In this situation, it's often better to measure the same subject at multiple times rather than different subjects at one point in time for each.

Limitations of Repeated Measure Designs

Some limitation of repeated measures design, are as follows

- May not be feasible when sample size is big.
- May not be realistic assessment of treatment effects.
- Analysis become complex and more difficult usually it requires to take into account association between observation taken from some individual.

Latin Square Designs

Latin Square designs are similar to randomised block designs, these designs are carefully constructed to allow the removal of two blocking factors. They accomplish this while reducing the number of experimental units that are needed to conduct the experiment.

Following is an example of a four treatment Latin Square. The experimental layout is as follows

Columns

Rows	Col 1	Col 2	Col 3	Col 4
Row 1	Aa	Bb	Cc	Dd
Row 2	Bd	Ca	Db	Ac
Row 3	Cb	Dc	Ad	Ba
Row 4	Dc	Ad	Ba	Cb

In the above table, the four treatments are represented by the four letters : A, B, C and D. The letters are arranged in such a way, so that each letter occurs only once within each row and each column. Notice that a simple random design would requires $4 \times 4 \times 4 = 64$ experimental units. This Latin Square has only 16 experimental units - a reduction of 75%.

The influence of a fourth factor may also be removed from the design by introducing a second set of letters, this time lower case. This design is known as the *Graeco-Latin* Square.

Columns

Rows	Col 1	Col 2	Col 3	Col 4
Row 1	Aa	Bb	Cc	Dd
Row 2	Bd	Ca	Db	Ac
Row 3	Cb	Dc	Ad	Ba
Row 4	Dc	Ad	Ba	Cb

Four factors at four levels each would normally requires 256 experimental units, but this design only requires 16, a reduction in experimental units of almost 94%.

The **Graeco-Latin** Square is formed by combining to orthogonal Latin Squares. Graeco-Latin Squares are available for all numbers of treatments except six.

Cohort Studies

A cohort study is used in the medical fields and social sciences, is an observational study used to estimate how often disease or life events happen in a certain population. 'Life events' might include incidence rate, and relative risk or absolute risk. A cohort is a defined group, like 'nurses', '10-19 year-olds,' or 'college students'. Participants are chosen with due process, rather than randomly.

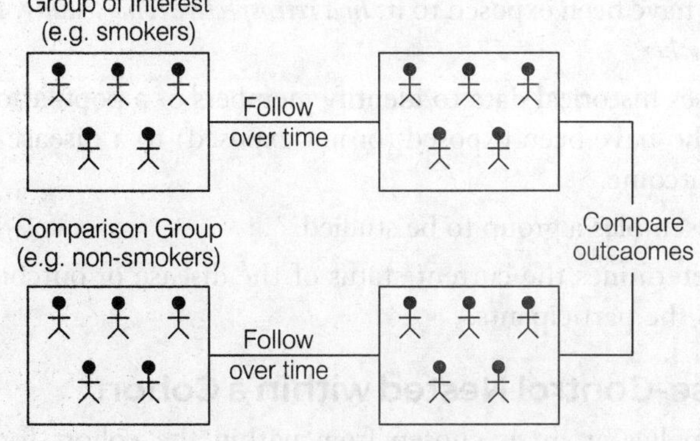

The study usually has two groups : 'exposed' and 'not exposed'. If the exposure is rare *e.g.* exposure to an industrial solvent), then the cohort is called a *special exposure cohort*.

Both groups are followed to see who develops a disease and who does not. *For example* You could look at **cigarette** smokers who gets breast cancer and non-smokers does not.

Classification of Cohort Studies

Cohort studies can be grouped in several ways

Prospective Cohort Study

A prospective cohort study takes a group of similar people (a cohort) and studies them overtime. At the time, the baseline data is collected, none of the people in the study have the condition of interest. This is in contrast to a retrospective cohort study. The famous Framingham Heart Study; is one example of a prospective cohort study; the researchers have studied the data 'three generations of Framingham residents' in order to understand the causes of heart disease and stroke.

Although, none of the participants actually have the disease of interest in a prospective cohort study, some of the cohort are expected to develop the disease in the future. *For example* a cohort of thirty year-old people in a certain town might be studied to see who develops lung cancer.

Half of the cohort might be smokers and half may not. This enables comparisons between the two groups.

Retrospective Cohort Study

A retrospective cohort study (also known as a historic study or longitudinal study) is a study, where the participants already have a known disease or outcome.

The study looks back into the past to try to determine, why the participants have the disease or outcomes and how they may have been exposed to it. *In a retrospective cohort study, the researcher*

- uses historical data to identify members of a population; who have been exposed (or not exposed) to a disease or outcome.
- assembles a group to be studied.
- determines the current status of the disease or outcome in the participants.

Case-Control Nested within a Cohort

A smaller group is chosen from within the cohort for a deeper look. These investigations may include genotyping, collecting tissue samples or other factors.

Case-Cohort

Similar to case-control nested within a cohort. The difference is that in a case-cohort study, participants are evaluated for outcome risk factors at any time before the first outcome (*i.e.* the first incidence of disease).

Time Series Analysis

Time series is a sequence of well-defined data points measured at consistent time intervals over a period of time. Data collected on an **ad-hoc** basis or irregularly does not form a time series. Time series analysis is the use of statistical methods to analyse time series data and extract meaningful statistics and characteristic about the data. Time series anaylsis helps us to understand what are the underlying forces leading to a particular trend in the time series data points and helps us in forecasting and monitoring the data points by fitting appropriate model to it.

Benefits and Applications of Time Series Analysis

Time series analysis aims to achieve various objectives and the tools and models used, varies accordingly. *The various types of time series analysis include*

- **Descriptive Analysis** to determine the trend or pattern in a time series using graphs or other tools. This helps us identify cyclic patterns, overall trends, turning points.
- **Spectral Analysis** also referred to as frequency domain and aims to separate periodic or cyclical components in a time series. *For example,* identifying cyclical changes in sales of a product.
- **Forecasting** used extensively in business forecasting, budgeting etc. based on historical trends.
- **Intervention Analysis** used to determine, if an event can lead to a change in the time series. *For example.* an employee's level of performance has improved or not after an intervention in the form of training to determine the effectiveness of the training program.
- **Explanative Analysis** studies the cross correlation or relationship between two time series and the dependence of one on another. *For example* the study of employee turnover data and employee training data to determine, if there is any dependence of employee's training programs on employee's turnover rates over-time.

MANOVA

Multivariate analysis of variance (MANOVA) is an extension of the univariate analysis of variance (ANOVA). In ANOVA, we examine for statistical differences on one continous dependent variable by an independent grouping variable. The MANOVA extends this analysis by taking into account multiple continuous dependent variables and bundles them together into a weighted linear combination or composite variable. The MANOVA will compare, whether or not, the newly created combination differs by the different groups, or levels of the independent variable. In this way, the MANOVA essentially tests whether or not, the independent grouping variable simultaneously explains a statistically significant amount of variances in the dependent variable.

Assumptions of MANOVA

The assumptions of MANOVA are as follows

- **Independent Random Sampling** MANOVA assumes that the observations are independent of one another. There is not any pattern for the selection of the sample and that the sample is completely random.
- **Level and Measurement of the Variables** MANOVA assumes that the independent variables are categorical and the dependent variables are continuous or scale variables.
- **Absence of Multicollinearity** The dependent variables cannot be too correlated to each other.
- **Normality** Multivariate normality is present in the data.
- **Homogeneity of Variance** Variance between groups is equal.

Key Concepts and Terms

The key concepts and terms of MANOVA are as follows

- **Levene's Test of Equality of Variance** Used to examine, whether or not, the variance between independent variable groups are equal; also known as homogeneity of variance. Non-significant values of Levene's test indicate equal variance between groups.
- **Box's M-Test** Used to know the equality of covariance between the groups. This is the equivalent of a multivariate homogeneity of variance. Usually, significance for this test is determined at $\alpha = .001$ because this test is considered highly sensitive.
- **Partial Eta Square** Partial eta square (n^2) shows how much variance is explained by the independent variable. It is used as the effect size for the MANOVA model.
- **Post Hoc Test** If there is a significant difference between groups, then post hoc tests are performed to determine, where the significant differences lie (*i.e.* which specific independent variable level significantly differs from another).
- **Multivariate F-Statistics** The F- statistic is derived by essentially dividing the means sum of the square (SS) for the source variable by the source variable Mean Error (ME or MSE).
- **SPSS** Can be performed using the analysis menu, selecting the 'GLM' option and then choosing the 'Multivariate' option from the GLM option.

ANCOVA

Analysis of Covariance (ANCOVA) is used in examining the differences in the mean values of the dependent variables that are related to the effect of the controlled independent variables while taking into account the influence of the uncontrolled independent variables.

Analysis of covariance is used to test the main interaction effects of categorical variables, controlling for the effects of selected after continuous variable, which covary with the dependent. The control variables are called the *covariates*.

Uses of ANCOVA

The uses of ANCOVA are as follows

- **In Experimental Design** To control the factors, which cannot be randomised, but which can be measured on an interval scale.
- **In Observational Designs** To remove the effects of variables, which modify the relationship of the categorical independents to the interval dependent.
- **In Regression Models** To fit regression where there are both categorical and interval independents.

Assumptions of ANCOVA

The assumptions of ANCOVA are as follows

- The independent variable may be categorical, except atleast one must be a covariate (interval level). Likewise, atleast one independent must be categorical.
- The dependent variable is continuous.
- The covariate are continuous and interval level are assumed to be measured without error.
- The form of the relationship between the covariate and the dependent must be known and most computer

programs assume this relationship is linear, adjusting the dependent mean based on linear regression.

- The covariate coefficients are the same for each group formed by the categorical variables and measured on the dependents. The more this assumption is violated, the more conservative ANCOVA becomes.
- The error term is independent of the covariates and the categorical independents. Randomisation in experimental designs assures this assumption will be met.

Key Concepts of ANCOVA

Key concepts of ANCOVA are as follows

- **Covariate** An interval level (*i.e.* continuous) independent variable. If there are no covariates, ANOVA must be used instead of ANCOVA and if there are covariates, ANCOVA is used instead of ANOVA. Covariates are commonly used as control variables. *For instances*, use of a baseline pre-test score can be used as a covariate to control the initial group differences on math ability or whatever is being assessed in the ANCOVA study *i.e.* in ANCOVA, we look at the effects of the categorical independents on an interval dependent variable, after effects of interval covariats are controlled.
- **F-Test** The F-test of significance is used to test each, main and interaction effect, for the case of a single interval dependent and multiple groups formed by a categorical independent. F is between groups variance divided by within groups variance. If the computed p-value is small, then significant relationship exist.
- **T-Test** A T- test of significance of the difference in the means of the difference single interval dependent, for the case of two groups formed by a categorical independent.

Single-Subject Designs

Single-subject designs are thought to be a direct result of the research of **BF Skinner**, who applied the techniques of operant conditioning to subjects and measured the outcomes at various point in time. Because of this, single-subject designs are often considered the design of choice when measuring behavioural change or when performing behavioural modification. Rather than comparing groups of subjects, this design relies on the comparison of treatment effects on a single subject or group of single subjects.

An important aspect of this type of study is the gathering of pretest information, often called a *baseline measure.* It is important to measure the dependent variable or behaviour prior to administering any treatment. Without this information, it is difficult and likely impossible to determine, if any change has occurred.

Also often associated with the design are periods of measurement to determine not only a change but the degree of change through the process of behavioural modification.

Types of Single-Subject Design

Single-subject design is sub divided in two types

Reversal Designs

The most basic single-subject research design is the reversal design, also called the *ABA design*. During this first phase, 'A' a base line is established for the dependent variable. In a reversal design, the participant is tested in a baseline condition, then tested in a treatment condition and then return to baseline. If the dependent variable changes back with the return to baseline, this provides strong evidence of a treatment effect.

Multiple-Baseline Designs

In a multiple baseline design, baselines are established for different participants, different dependent variables or different settings and the treatment is introduced at a different time on each baseline. If the introduction of the treatment is followed by a change in the dependent variable on each baseline, this provides strong evidence of a treatment effect.

EXAM BASED QUESTIONS

1 **The term 'Experimental Designs' are used by**
(a) medical and social science
(b) engineering
(c) industrial
(d) computer science

2 **The term 'Design of Experiments' is used by**
(a) medical science (b) social science
(c) engineering (d) None of these

3 **Who said that, "the design is the general structure of the experiment, not its specific content"?**
(a) Myers (b) Graeco
(c) Both a and b (d) None of these

4 **According to whom, "Research design is the plan, structure and strategy of investigation conceived so as to obtain answer to research question and to control variance"?**
(a) Myers (b) Graeco
(c) Lindquist (d) None of these

5 **Which one of the following is an advantage of the method of naturalistic observation over the experimental method?**
(a) It leads to better control over the variables to be studied
(b) It is more objective
(c) It is closer to reality
(d) It facilitates the study of cause-effect relationships

6 **In an experiment, after completing conditioning once, an injection of a drug affecting neuro transmitter substance was given to the affecting subject. Then, the subject was conditioned again. In this experiment, what were bio-chemical changes treated as?**
(a) Dependent variable (b) Independent variable
(c) Control variable (d) Intervening variable

7 **The most frequently used method in psychology to explore cause and effect relationships between variables is**
(a) correlational method
(b) experimental method
(c) natural observation method
(d) participant observer method

8 **Which of the following is not a kind of independent variable?**
(a) Task variable (b) Environmental variable
(c) Subject variable (d) Experimental variable

9 **Which of the following is true about experimental designs?**
(a) Internal validity is controlled
(b) Are the weaker designs
(c) Easier to conduct
(d) Control groups are not used

10 **In an experiment, a measured difference between groups of subjects that is highly unlikely to have come about by chance is said to be**
(a) statistically meaningless (b) unreliable
(c) statistically insignificant (d) statistically significant

11 **Which of the following is not a part of heuristic strategy?**
(a) Random search (b) Means and analysis
(c) Planning strategy (d) Backwards searching

12 **Which among the following are the main functions of experi...ental design?**
(a) Maximise the effect of systematic variance
(b) Control extraneous source of variance
(c) Minimise error variance
(d) All of the above

13 **Which among the following is not a procedure for controlling the extraneous source of variance?**
(a) Randomisation (b) Repetition
(c) Matching (d) Elimination

14 **In which procedure, there has an equal chances of being placed in any of the treatment condition or groups?**
(a) Elimination (b) Matching
(c) Randomisation (d) None of these

15 **In which approach, no attempt is made to restrain the influence of secondary variables?**
(a) Matching (b) Elimination
(c) Statistical control (d) Randomisation

16 **If in an experiment, neither the subject nor the experimenter knows, which subjects are in experimental group and which are in control group, then the design is known as**
(a) Double blind subject study
(b) Double blind study
(c) Double blind deception study
(d) Double blind experimental study

17 **Which one of the following is the most essential characteristic of the experimental method?**
(a) Active manipulation of the independent variable.
(b) Ability to test complex hypothesis.
(c) Precise measurement and recording of the dependent variables.
(d) Use of sophisticated tools and equipments.

18 **Which among the following is correct to a linear regression?**
(a) A real line is drawn through the data points, where total error is minimised.
(b) The line of best fit maximises the distance between the scores and the regression line.
(c) The line fits the data in the best place possible.
(d) The line tells us by how much Y is predicted to changes as a result of a change in X.

19 In the independent groups design, the only factor that should differentiate the separate groups at the start of the experiment is the
(a) dependent variable
(b) independent variable
(c) characteristics of the participants
(d) conditions under which all subject are tested

20 Which among the following is right fullform of ANOVA?
(a) Aspiration of Variance (b) Approval of Variance
(c) Area of Variance (d) Analysis of Variance

21 Who was the first to devise the technique of Analysis of Variance ANOVA?
(a) Henry (b) Myers
(c) Ronald Fisher (d) Lindquist

22 In an experiment, if the subject are randomly assigned of different conditions, then the measures are correlated by using
(a) ANOVA (b) ANCOVA
(c) DFA (d) X^2Test

23 Find out formula of correction factor, when value of individual item is referred as T.
(a) $\frac{T}{n}$ (b) $\frac{T^2}{n}$
(c) $\frac{n^2}{T}$ (d) $\frac{T^2-n}{n^2}$

24 In randomised block design, when all treatments appear atleast once in each block then, we have
(a) completely randomised block
(b) incompletely randomised block
(c) Both a and b
(d) None of the above

25 In a repeated measures design, how many ypes?
(a) Three (b) Two
(c) One (d) Four

26 Which among the following are correct about Repeated Measures?
(a) Have the advantage of statistically controlling variance.
(b) Members of a matched pair are treated as though they were the same person.
(c) Both a and b
(d) None of the above

27 Which among the following is similar to randomised block designs?
(a) Cohort studies
(b) Latin square designs
(c) MANOVA
(d) Time series analysis

28 Which among the following is/are correct about Latin Square design?
(a) It is formed by combining to orthogonal latin squares.
(b) It is available for all numbers of treatments except six.
(c) Both a and b
(d) None of the abvove

29 "The row factor and the column factor affect the response independently of one another." This assumption belongs to
(a) Cohort studies (b) Latin square design
(c) Time series analysis (d) MANOVA

30 Cohort study can be used in
(a) medical fields (b) social science
(c) Both a and b (d) None of these

31 Which among the following can be considered as a Cohort group?
(a) Nurses (b) College students
(c) Trades (d) All of these

32 Cohort is called a 'special exposure cohort" when
(a) exposure is prevalent
(b) exposure is rare
(c) exposure as industrial solvent
(d) None of the above

33 Data collected on an ad-hoc basis or irregularly does not form a
(a) Cohort study (b) Time Series analysis
(c) MANOVA (d) None of these

34 When the same subjects are matched on some basis across conditions, we call it a
(a) Repeated Measure design
(b) Randomised Group design
(c) Elimination design
(d) None of these

35 How Latin Square design is different from Randomised block design?
(a) Removal of one blocking variables
(b) Removal of two blocking factors
(c) Removal of three blocking variables
(d) None of the above

36 Which among the following is right about Cohort Studies?
(a) It is an observational study
(b) It is used in the fields of medical science and social science
(c) Both a and b
(d) None of the above

37 In which kind of experimental design, participants are chosen for a reason, rather than randomly?
(a) Latin square design (b) Cohort design
(c) Time series (d) MANOVA

38 Framingham's heart study is an example of
(a) Prospective Cohort Study
(b) Retrospective Cohort Study
(c) Both a and b (d) None of the above

39 Which among the following is also known as longitudinal study?
(a) Retrospective cohort study
(b) Prospective cohort study
(c) Time series
(d) None of the above

40 Spectral analysis is a type of
(a) time series analysis
(b) latin square analysis
(c) repeated measures design analysis
(d) randomised block design

41 In which experimental design, multiple continuous dependent variables are taken into account?
(a) ANCOVA (b) MANOVA
(c) ANOVA (d) None of these

42 Which among the following is also known as 'Analysis of Covariance'?
(a) ANCOVA (b) MANOVA
(c) ANOVA (d) None of these

43 Which among the following is correct about MANOVA?
(a) Multiple continuous dependent variables
(b) Statistically significant amount of variance
(c) Both a and b
(d) None of the above

44 Which among the following are assumptions of MANOVA?
(a) Normality
(b) Homogeneity of variance
(c) Absence of multicollinearity
(d) All of the above

45 Levene's test of equality of variance is related to
(a) MANOVA (b) ANCOVA
(c) ANOVA (d) None of these

46 Which among the following analysis is used to examine the difference in the mean values of the dependent variables?
(a) Time series (b) ANOVA
(c) ANCOVA (d) MANOVA

47 ANCOVA is used to remove the effects of variables, which modify the relationship of the categorical independents to the interval dependent. This statement is right for
(a) experimental design (b) observational design
(c) regression model (d) None of these

48 Which among the following is used in regression model, to fit regressions where there are both categorical and interval independent?
(a) MANOVA (b) ANCOVA
(c) ANOVA (d) Latin square

49 An interval level independent variable is known as
(a) F-test (b) T-test
(c) covariate (d) None of these

50 When number of independent variables in an experiment are increased, what will be the changes in the treatment and error components of total variance?
(a) Error component will decrease and treatment component will increase.
(b) Error component will decrease and there will be no effect on treatment component.
(c) Error component will increase and treatment component will increase.
(d) Error component will increase and there will be no effect on treatment component.

51 When physiological changes are treated as independent variable in learning experiment?
(a) A drug is injected to the subject before learning.
(b) A drug is injected to the subject after learning.
(c) Physiological changes resulting from learning are recorded.
(d) Physiological changes correlated when forgetting are recorded.

52 Which of the following can not be inferred from correlations ?
(a) Cause and effect relationship
(b) Covariance between variables
(c) Direction of relationship
(d) Percentage of explained variance

53 Coefficient of stability in reliability is determined by
(a) Split - half method
(b) Kuder - Richardson formula
(c) Test - retest method
(d) Parallel form method

54 When a researcher wants to validate a new test against an established theory, he is aiming at
(a) content validity (b) concurrent validity
(c) construct validity (d) factorial validity

55 Method of summated ratings was developed in attitude scale construction by
(a) Thurstone (b) Bogardus
(c) Likert (d) Thorndike

56 Time series design is the example of
(a) factorial design
(b) experimental design
(c) quasi experimental design
(d) between group design

57 A method of research used in psychology to explore cause and effect relationship between variables is
(a) correlational method
(b) scheduled interview
(c) case study
(d) biographical enquiry

58 Which of the following is an example of counter balancing design?
(a) Within design (b) Time series design
(c) Latin square design (d) Expost facto design

Directions (Q. Nos. 59-64) *Read the passage given below and answer the following questions.*

A researcher hypothesised that a given drug would adversely affect the reaction **tiforty** subjects were tested for discriminatory reaction time. Each subject was then given a prescribed drug dosage (5 mg/kg body weight) and after appropriate time gap, the subject was retested for discriminatory reaction time. The time-interval between a ready signal and actual presentation of the stimulus was randomly varied from half a second to three seconds. For evaluating the mean difference on the reaction time, the researcher considered various statistical options like the test, analysis of variance, chi-square test, etc. and employed the appropriate techniques.

The mean difference was statistically significant (Mean without drug condition = 240 ms, SD = 20 and mean with drug condition = 210 ms, SD = 18). The statistical examination further revealed that the difference between the two standard deviations was insignificant. During the course of research, the researcher suspected that the effect of drug dosage would be different for discriminatory and simple reaction times. For this purpose, researcher considered the different experimental designs options such as matched two group design, factorial design, analysis of covariance, variance design, quasi-experimental design etc. Finally, researcher selected the appropriate design to carry out the new investigation.

59 **On the basis of above information, what can you conclude about the researcher's hypothesis?**
(a) The researcher's hypothesis is rejected
(b) The researcher's hypothesis is partially verified
(c) The researcher's hypothesis is accepted
(d) The data are inadequate to evaluate the researcher's hypothesis

60 **For evaluating the mean differences, which of the following techniques would be appropriate?**
1. T-test for independent samples
2. Repeated measures ANOVA
3. Chi-square test
4. Paired samples test

Select the correct answer using the codes given below
(a) Only 4 (b) 2 and 4
(c) 1, 2 and 3 (d) 2, 3 and 4

61 **Which of the following variable is/are not controlled variables?**
1. Drug to body weight ratio
2. Foreperiod
3. Type of reaction
4. Reaction time

Select the correct answer using the codes given below
(a) Only 4 (b) 1 and 4 (c) 2 and 4 (d) 1,2and4

62 **On the basis of above passage, what would you conclude about the variance?**
(a) The two conditions have homogeneity of variance.
(b) The two conditions have heterogeneity of variance.
(c) We cannot conclude about the homogeneity of variance from the above data.
(d) It is necessary to apply an additional test to infer about homogeneity of variance.

63 **For studying whether the effect of drug would be different for discriminatory and simple reactions, the appropriate design would be**
(a) quasi-experimental design
(b) matched two-group design
(c) analysis of covariance design
(d) factorial design

64 **For a scale, norms were developed using T scores (Mean = 50, SD = 10). A subject got a T score of 60. What would be his PR?**
(a) 16 (b) 34
(c) 60 (d) 84

65 **In method of serial learning for an experiment relating to the effect of meaningfulness on the rate of learning, the rate of learning can be conceptualised as**
1. dependent variable
2. independent variable
3. organimic variable
4. stimulus variable

Select the correct answer using the codes given below
(a) Only 1 (b)Only 2 (c) 3 and 4 (d)1 and 2

66 **In an experimental study of the effects of a new drug on depression, a double-blind control technique is used, which of the following persons should not be informed as to which drug, experimental or placebo is being administered to each individual research participant?**
1. Research participants in the experimental group
2. Research participants in the control group
3. Persons administering the drug
4. Persons evaluating the drug effect

Select the correct answer using the codes given below
(a) Only 2 (b) 1 and 3
(c) 1, 2 and 4 (d) All of these

67 **Group designs involve, which of the following?**
1. Randomised group design
2. Complete design
3. Factorial design
4. Matched group design

Select the correct answer using the codes given below
(a) 1,2 and 3 (b) 1, 3 and 4
(c) 1 and 3 (d) All of these

68 Consider the following statements
1. Experimental method has introduced the quantitative measurement in psychology.
2. It is low on replicability.

Which of the statements given above is/are correct?
(a) Both 1 and 2 (b) Only2
(c) Only 1 (d) Neither 1 nor 2

69 Which of the following pairs is/are correctly matched?

1. Systematic variance : effect of independent variable
2. Extraneous variance : methodology artifacts
3. Control of variables : randomisation

Codes

(a) Only 1 (b) 1 and 3
(c) 1 and 2 (d) All of these

70 Consider the following statements

In the experimental method, the psychologist attempts to

1. systematically vary the independent variable.
2. make a detailed case study of the individual.
3. observe whether the experimental manipulation has of these statements.

Which of the statements given above is/ are correct?

(a) 1 and 3 (b) 1 and 2
(c) 2 and 3 (d) All of these

71 Which of the following tests is/are classified as non-parametric?

1. F-test 2. Signed-rank test
3. T-test 4. U-test

Which of the statements given above is/are correct?

(a) 1 and 3 (b) 2 and 4
(c) 2 and 3 (d) 3 and 4

72 Consider the following statements

1. ANOVA is used to analyse two types of effects *i.e.* main effects and interaction effects.
2. ANOVA technique is difficult and time consuming.

Which of the statements given above is/are correct?

(a) Only 1 (b) Only 2
(c) Both 1 and 2 (d) None of these

73 Consider the following statements

1. Time series analysis used extensively in business forecasting, budgeting etc. based on historical trends.
2. Spectural analysis aims to separate periodic or cyclical components in a time series.

Which of the statements given above is/are correct?

(a) Only 1 (b) Only 2
(c) Both 1 and 2 (d) None of these

74 Consider the following statement about ANCOVA

1. The covariate are continuous and interval level are assumed to be measured without error.
2. The dependent variable is continuous.

Which of the statements given above is/are correct?

(a) Only 1 (b) Only 2
(c) Both 1 and 2 (d) None of these

75 Arrange the following steps of One Way ANOVA.

1. Work out the mean of the sample
2. Obtain the mean of each sample
3. Obtain the deviation of values

Codes

(a) 3, 2, 1 (b) 2, 1, 3 (c) 3, 1, 2 (d) 2, 3, 1

76 Arrange the following steps of ANOVA with Two Way Design.

1. Work out the correlation factor
2. Use of coding device
3. Finding the square of all the item

Codes

(a) 1, 2, 3 (b) 2, 3, 1 (c) 2, 1, 3 (d) 3, 2, 1

77 Arrange the following processes in order in which they occur in test construction.

1. Item analysis 2. Validity
3. Reliability 4. Norms

Codes

(a) 1,2,3,4 (b) 2,1,3,4
(c) 1,3,2,4 (d) 4,3,1,2

Directions (Q. Nos. 78-84) *In the question given below are two statements labelled as Assertion (A) and Reason (R). In the context of the two statements, which one of the following is correct?*

Codes

(a) Both A and R are true and R is the correct explanation of A
(b) Both A and R are true, but R is not the correct explanation of A
(c) A is true, but R is false
(d) A is false, but R is true

78 **Assertion** (A) While carrying out surveys, if possible random samples are preferred to non-random samples.

Reason (R) Random samples usually permit less accurate generalisation from samples to populations.

79 **Assertion** (A) A case study is an unavoidable technique in the clinical setting.

Reason (R) It provides a complete picture of the subject for diagnosis and prognosis.

80 **Assertion** (A) Random assignment of subjects to two or more groups in an experiment is a suitable way of creating equivalent groups.

Reason (R) Randomisation acts as control for individual differences.

81 **Assertion** (A) One may do his research in a laboratory or a hospital or natural habitat or any other setting and may still be an experimental psychologist.

Reason (R) In psychological experiments, causal relationships between variables are studied under controlled conditions.

82 **Assertion** (A) Numerous experimental psychologists now propose that behavioural research must reply on unobtrusive measures of dependent variables for dependable and valid results.

Reason (R) Human participants respond to experimental stimuli according to their own hypothesis, which may have little or no correspondence to the research hypothesis.

83 Assertion (A) The results of experimental method can be employed to formulate universal law.

Reason (R) Experimental method is an objective method.

84 Assertion (A) Randomisation is like an insurance.

Reason (R) It insures the independence of the measurement.

85 Match the following

List I(Design)		List II (Full forms)
A. ANOVA	1.	Multivariant analysis of variance
B. MANOVA	2.	Analysis of variance
C. ANCOVA	3.	Analysis of covariance

Codes

	A	B	C		A	B	C
(a)	1	2	3	(b)	2	1	3
(c)	1	3	2	(d)	2	3	1

86 Match the following

List I (Variances)	List II (Features)
A. Systematic variance	1. Randomisation
B. Extraneous variance	2. Methodology artifacts
C. Control of variables	3. Effect of independent variables

Codes

	A	B	C		A	B	C
(a)	1	2	3	(b)	3	2	1
(c)	3	1	2	(d)	1	3	2

87 Match the following

List I (Analysis)	List II (Features)
A. Descriptive analysis	1. To determine trend
B. Spectral analysis	2. Used in business forecasting
C. Forcasting	3. Frequency domain
D. Explanative analysis	4. Cross correlation

Codes

	A	B	C	D		A	B	C	D
(a)	1	2	3	4	(b)	2	3	4	1
(c)	1	3	2	4	(d)	4	3	2	1

88 Match the following

List I (Test)		List II (Characteristics of Variance)
A. Levene's test	1.	Equality of covariance
B. Box's m test	2.	Hemogeneity of variance
C. Post hoc test	3.	Significant difference in variable
D. · Partial eta square	4.	Explaining independent variable

Codes

	A	B	C	D		A	B	C	D
(a)	2	1	3	4	(b)	4	3	1	2
(c)	1	2	3	4	(d)	4	2	3	1

89 Match the following

List I (Test)		List II (Effects)
A. Covariate	1.	Single interval dependent
B. F-test	2.	Test interaction effect
C. T-test	3.	Interval-level independent variable

Codes

	A	B	C		A	B	C
(a)	1	2	3	(b)	3	2	1
(c)	2	3	1	(d)	1	3	2

ANSWERS

1 *(a)*	2 *(c)*	3 *(a)*	4 *(c)*	5 *(c)*	6 *(d)*	7 *(b)*	8 *(d)*	9 *(a)*	10 *(c)*
11 *(d)*	12 *(d)*	13 *(b)*	14 *(c)*	15 *(c)*	16 *(b)*	17 *(a)*	18 *(b)*	19 *(b)*	20 *(d)*
21 *(c)*	22 *(b)*	23 *(b)*	24 *(a)*	25 *(b)*	26 *(c)*	27 *(b)*	28 *(c)*	29 *(b)*	30 *(c)*
31 *(d)*	32 *(b)*	33 *(b)*	34 *(a)*	35 *(b)*	36 *(c)*	37 *(b)*	38 *(a)*	39 *(a)*	40 *(a)*
41 *(b)*	42 *(a)*	43 *(c)*	44 *(d)*	45 *(a)*	46 *(c)*	47 *(b)*	48 *(b)*	49 *(c)*	50 *(c)*
51 *(b)*	52 *(c)*	53 *(c)*	54 *(c)*	55 *(c)*	56 *(b)*	57 *(b)*	58 *(b)*	59 *(b)*	60 *(c)*
61 *(c)*	62 *(d)*	63 *(a)*	64 *(b)*	65 *(a)*	66 *(c)*	67 *(b)*	68 *(c)*	69 *(b)*	70 *(a)*
71 *(d)*	72 *(c)*	73 *(c)*	74 *(a)*	75 *(b)*	76 *(c)*	77 *(a)*	78 *(c)*	79 *(a)*	80 *(a)*
81 *(b)*	82 *(a)*	83 *(b)*	84 *(a)*	85 *(b)*	86 *(b)*	87 *(c)*	88 *(a)*	89 *(b)*	

Psychological Testing : Test Construction and Standardisation

Psychological testing, also known as Psychometrics, is the systematic use of tests to qualify psychological behaviour, abilities and problems and to make predictions about psychological performance.

Concept of Psychological Testing

Psychological tests are written, visual, or verbal evaluations administered to assess the cognitive and emotional functioning of children and adults. Psychological tests are used to assess a variety of mental abilities and attributes, including achievement and ability, personality and neurological functioning.

Psychologists and other qualified mental health professionals use psychological tests and assessments to measure specific psychological ideas and beliefs in individuals.

Psychological tests are used to assess many areas of a person, including

- Traits such as introversion or extroversion.
- Certain conditions such as depression or anxiety.
- Intelligence, aptitude and achievement such as verbal intelligence and reading achievement.
- Attitudes and feelings such as how individuals feel about the treatment that they received from their therapists.
- Interests such as the careers and activities that a person is interested in.
- Specific abilities, knowledge or skills such as cognitive ability, memory and problem-solving skills.

In this Chapter

- Concept of Psychological Testing
- Test Construction
- Test Standardisation

Types of Tests

Tests have been developed to measure many different human characteristics. Psychological tests can be classified by the ways in which

- They are constructed, scored and administered
- In terms of behaviour or characteristics they are designed to assess

Psychological Tests on the Basis of Construction Scoring and Administration

These tests are based on whether they can administer large number of people or an individual at time. It helps to determine whether tests are scored objectively or subjectively. *The various psychological tests on basis of construction, scoring and administration are*

- **Test Administration Perspective** It includes group tests and individual tests. Group tests are designed in such a way that they can be administered to a large number of people at the same time. It can be used in large scale testing programme in industry.

  Individual tests are administered to one person at a time. These tests are used more frequently for vocational guidance, counselling and clinical purposes.
- **Computer Assisted Testing** In this, type of testing questions appear one at a time on computer screen and job applicant presses a key corresponding to an answer selected. It is designed for both large scale group testing and individual testing. Computerised tests is more efficient less costly and provides standardised reports free from personal biases and errors.
- **Speed and Power Tests** Speed test has a fixed time limit at which point everyone taking the test must stop. It consists of a set of items having more or less uniform level of difficulty.

  Power test has no time limit and subjects are allowed as much time as they need to finish the test. It contains more difficult items and the set of its constituent items are arranged in increasing order of difficulty.
- **Paper and Pencil Tests** The items or questions are in printed form and answer are pointed on a separate answer sheet. The paper and pencil tests include standard group tests of intelligence, interest and personality.
- **Objective and Subjective Scoring** The psychological tests that are objectively scored are used in assessing persons performances in industrial or organisational settings. Subjectivety in test scoring leads to personal prejudices and attitudes in assessment of performance.

Psychological Tests on the Basis of Behaviour or Characteristics Assessed

These psychological tests are commonly used for measurement of mental abilities and cognitive abilities. They can either be used as assessments for screening at corporate or educational institutes, or they can be used for clinical purposes for diagnosis of a psychological problem so as to prescribe the best possible treatment for the problem. *The various psychological tests on the basis of behaviour or characteristics assessed by them are as follows–*

- **Achievement Tests** An achievement test is a measure of one's developed knowledge or skill in a particular field e.g. Mathematics. Usually a standardised test which provides insight into the respondent's knowledge and skills in a particular field of expertise or a particular grade level is used.

  The person being tested is given a series of tasks at the end of which the person will be graded according to standardised guidelines. *Two achievement tests commonly used are*
- Peabody Individual Achievement Test
- Wechsler Individual Achievement Test
- **IQ Tests** Intelligence Quotient (IQ) tests measure intelligence and other cognitive faculties. These tests are used to measure intelligence, or your ability to understand your environment, interact with it and learn from it. *The three types of intelligence tests which are most often used are*
  - (i) Stanford-Binet Intelligence Scale (SB)
  - (ii) Wechsler Adult Intelligence Scale (WAIS)
  - (iii) Wechsler Intelligence Scale for Children (WISC)
- **Attitude Tests** These tests try to assess the individual's reaction towards a certain event, object or towards another person. *For instance*, in the marketing field, attitude ranks or scales are used to find out a group's or an individual's preferences for items or brands. Usually, either a Likert or a Thurstone scale is used in these types of tests, *these scales are as follows–*
  - (i) **Likert Scales** The Likert scale is a 5 or 7 point survey scale that ranges from one extreme attitude to another, such as 'extremely likely' to 'not at all likely' or 'strongly agree' to 'strongly disagree'. Typically, it includes a moderate or neutral midpoint. Likert scales (named after their creator, American social scientist Rensis Likert) are quite popular because they are one of the most reliable ways to measure opinions, perceptions and behaviours.

(ii) **Thurstone Scale** The Thurstone scale was the first formal technique to measure an attitude. It was developed by Louis Leon Thurstone in 1928 as a means of measuring attitudes towards religion. It is made up of statements about a particular issue and each statement has a numerical value indicating how favourable or unfavourable it is to be judged. People check each of the statements to which they agree and a mean score is computed, indicating their attitude.

The Thurstone scale is fundamentally based on the Likert scale, except that it not only takes the value of each item into consideration while evaluating the final attitude score, but also takes care of neutral items.

- **Neuropsychological Tests** These consist of a series of carefully designed tasks which are known to trigger one's psychological function linked to a typical nerve pathway or a specific brain structure. These kinds of tests are conducted to check the proper cognitive functioning of the brain.

Some typical examples of these tests are–

(i) Benton Visual Retention Test
(ii) Wisconsin Card Sorting Test
(iii) Halstead Reitan Neuropsychological Test Battery

- **Personality Tests** Personality tests are designed to reveal some of the characteristic patterns of an individual's personality which includes his/her characteristic ways of thinking, feeling or behaving.

These are either projective (answers are more subjective and unrestricted to any scale or measure) or objective tests (mainly consisting of true/ false responses; responses which are restricted to a scale). Proper interpretation of the projective tests requires a high degree of training and experience. *The three types of personality tests which are most often used are–*

(i) Minnesota Multiphasic Personality Inventory (MMPI) (objective type)
(ii) Thematic Apperception Test (TAT) (projective type)
(iii) Rorschach, also known as the 'Inkblot test' (projective type)

- **Observation** (Direct) **Tests** Such tests are mostly used in research work. In these tests, the behaviour of the respondent is observed as he/she completes certain tasks and activities.

For example– To determine parent-child relationship or assessing the basic symptoms of ADHD (Attention-Deficit/ Hyperactivity Disorder) in a child with the help of a test conducted inside a controlled class environment.

- **Aptitude/Interest Tests** Aptitude tests helps to indicate the respondent's aptitudes such as spatial, numerical, clerical or mechanical aptitudes. Interest tests are designed to find out the participant's areas of interest, the results of which are usually used for career counselling. *Some aptitude tests are*

(i) Armed Services Vocational Aptitude Battery
(ii) Bloomberg Aptitude Test

Test Construction

Test construction refers to the various ways in which items in a psychological measure are created and decided upon. It is the set of activities involved in developing and evaluating a test of some psychological function.

Development of good psychological test requires the test constructor to decide about the major objectives of the test and the population for whom the test is intended. The conditions under which the test can be used are also specified.

Test construction involves a number of steps which include specifying the construct of interest; deciding test's function (diagnosis, description of skill level, prediction of recovery); choosing a method (performance, behavioural observation, self report); designing item content; evaluating reliability and validity of test and modifying the test to maximise its utility. Any test will consist of a number of items on which the respondent is tested. Two important aspects of the construction are item writing and item analysis.

Item Writing

An item can be defined as a single question or task that is not usually broken down into any smaller units. *For instance*-a mechanical puzzle may be an item. Item writing is a creative art, but the person writing the items must have certain capabilities. *These are*

- **Command on Subject Matter** One must have good knowledge of all facts, principles, misconceptions and mis-beliefs in that particular field so that he/she may be able to write good and appropriate items.
- **Awareness of Respondents' Level** He/She should be aware of the intelligence level of the respondents so that he may adjust the difficulty level of the items for proper adjustment with their ability level.

- **Familiarity with Different Types of Items** He/She should be aware of the characteristics of good items and the common probable errors in writing items.
- **Excellent Knowledge of the Language** He/She should know the different meanings of words so that confusion in writing the items may be avoided. He must be able to convey the meaning of the items in the simplest possible language.
- **Cultivate a Rich Source of Ideas** He/She can source these from textbooks, journals, discussions, questions from interview and other instructional materials.

After writing down the items, they must be reviewed by a group of subject experts for their suggestions, which must then be incorporated into the items. A good item must have the characteristics of clarity in meaning, moderate difficulty level, positive discrimination, not encouraging guesswork and having independence in its meaning from other items.

Various Guidelines for Item Writing

The various guidelines for item writing are as follows

- **Clarity** No item should be a test of the examinee's ability to understand the language. Each item must be able to discriminate between those who are competent and those who are not, which is possible only when the items have been written in a simple and clear language. This happens particularly in objective items because each such item provides an isolated bit of knowledge. If the objective item is a vague one, it will create difficulty in understanding and the validity of the item will be adversely affected.
- **Avoid Non-Functional or Stereotyped Words** Words which do not contribute to making the appropriate and correct choice of a response by the examinees should not be used. Similarly, stereotyped words either in the stem (beginning part of the item that presents item as a problem to be solved) or in the alternative responses should not be used because these facilitate rote learners in guessing the correct answer, so that the candidates who really know the correct answer are discriminated against. It is better to paraphrase stereotyped words to ensure that examinees who really understand the subject are given their due.
- **Avoid Irrelevant Accuracies or Clues** If irrelevant accuracies are unintentionally incorporated in any item they may mislead the examinee and also show the poor critical ability of the item writer. Similarly, irrelevant clues decrease the difficulty level of the item because they provide an easy route to the correct answer. Specific determiners such as never, always, all, none etc. must also be avoided.
- **Avoid Interlocking Items** These are also known as interdependent items. They can be answered only by referring to other items. Thus, when responding correctly to an item is dependent upon the correct response to any other item, the item is an example of an interlocking or interdependent item. Such items should not be used.
- **Adaptable Difficulty Level** The item must not be too easy or too difficult for the examinees. The level of difficulty of the item should be adaptable to the level of understanding of the examinees. In certain forms of objective items such as multiple choice and matching items, when the response alternatives are made homogeneous, the difficulty value of the item is increased. But when the response alternatives are made heterogeneous, except the correct alternative, the level of difficulty is decreased.

Item Analysis

Item analysis is a set of methods used to evaluate test items. Items can be analysed qualitatively in terms of their content and form as well as quantitatively in terms of their statistical properties.

The analysis is important because–

- Both the validity and reliability of any test depend ultimately on the characteristics of its items. High reliability and validity can be built into a test in advance through analysis of each item.
- Tests can be improved through the selection, substitution or revision of items which have been analysed and found lacking in any aspect.
- Item analysis makes it possible to shorten a test and at the same time to increase its validity and reliability.

Indices Used in Item Analysis

Item should be analysed for their difficulty and discrimination. This can be done by calculating their item difficulty index and item discrimination index. *The procedures for these are–*

Item Difficulty Index

The difficulty of an item is defined as the proportion of persons who answer it correctly. Thus, for an easy item, the proportion will be high (nearer to 1.00), whereas for a difficult item it will be low. In the process of test construction, we measure item difficulty so as to choose items of suitable difficulty level. Items that are too easy or too difficult do not affect the variability of test scores and do not contribute to the reliability or validity of the test. The closer the difficulty of an item approaches 1.00 or 0.00, the less information it gives about differences between the test takers. However, if the difficulty level of an item approaches 0.50, it shows that the item differentiates very well.

In a psychological test, normally items are arranged in order of increasing difficulty, so that test takers begin with relatively easy items and proceed to items of increasing difficulty.

As items within a test tend to be inter-correlated, the more homogeneous the test, the higher these inter-correlations will be. Moreover the higher the item inter-correlations, the wider would be the variations in item difficulty.

The item difficulty index (p) is defined by the equation

$$p = \frac{R}{N}$$

where

R = Number of right responses

N = Total number of candidates attempting that item.

However, if only a portion of examinee are taken into consideration, the item difficulty index (p) can be calculated as

$$p = \frac{U_P + L_P}{U + L}$$

Where,

U_p = Right responses in upper group

L_p = Right responses in lower group

U = Number of examinees in upper group

L = Number of examinees in lower group

For instance– assume that 50 people take a test. Then the upper and lower groups can be formed from the top 14 and bottom 14 examinees are on the total test score. If 12 of the examinees are in the upper group and 7 of those in the lower group pass item A, the p = (12 + 7)/(14 + 14) = 0.68 for item A.

Item Discrimination Index

It refers to the degree to which an item differentiates correctly among test takers in the behaviour that the test is designed to measure. The extreme group method is used to calculate item discrimination.

The upper group is made up of 25%-33% who are the best performers in the test and the bottom group consists of 25%-33% who are the poorest performers in the same test. The most appropriate percentage is to use the top and bottom 27% of the distribution. A higher discrimination index indicates that the item discriminates more. The item discrimination index (D) is defined by the equation

$$D = \frac{U_P - L_P}{U}$$

Where,

U_p = Number of rights in upper group

L_p = Number of rights in lower group

U = Total number of examinees in upper group suppose in a particular item A, right responses in upper and lower group are 12 and 7 respectively and total number of examinees in upper group are 14, then item discrimination index is

D = (12 – 7)/ 14 = 0.37 for item A.

Item discrimination indices must always be interpreted in the context of the type of test which is being analysed. Items with low discrimination indices are often ambiguously worded and should be modified suitably. Tests with high internal consistency consist of items with mostly positive relationships with the total test score. In practice, values of the discrimination index will rarely be more than 0.50 because of differences between the item distributions and total score distributions.

Item Characteristic Curves (ICCs)

Item Characteristic Curves (ICCs) are displayed as graph of the probability of passing items conditional on specific value of the latent distribution. It describes the relationship between a latent ability and the performance on a test item.

It is a plot of the probability that a test item is answered correctly against the examinee's underlying ability on the trait being measured. For item characteristic curves, the *x*-axis reflects a wide range of trait levels and *y*-axis reflects probabilities ranging from 0 to 1.

An item characteristic curve is described via the following two properties

(i) **Difficulty of the Item** It describes where the item functions along the ability scale.

(ii) **Discrimination** It describes how well an item can differentiate between examinees having abilities below the item location and those having abilities above the item location.

The steepness or slope of the item characteristic curve describes the discriminating power of the item. The steeper the curve, the better the item can discriminate. The flatter the curve, the less the item is able to discriminate as the probability of correct response at low ability levels is nearly the same as it is at high ability levels.

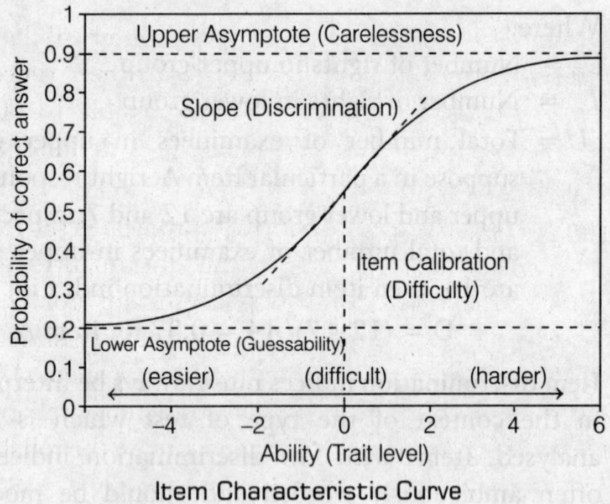

Test Standardisation

Standardisation of a test means that uniform procedures have been used in administrating and scoring the test for all candidates. If the scores obtained by different persons are to be compared, testing conditions must be the same for all. For this to be ensured, the directions to examinees must be very carefully made for any new test. It also includes the exact materials employed for the test, time limits, oral instructions, preliminary demonstrations, methods of handling queries from test takers and any other detail of the testing situation.

For a test to be scientifically sound, the items should be objective (item objectivity) and the scoring of the test should also be objective (scoring objectivity).

- **Item Objectivity** It means that the items should be phrased in such a manner that they are interpreted in exactly the same way by all examinees. For ensuring the objectivity of items, they must have uniformity of order of presentation (either ascending or descending).
- **Scoring Objectivity** It means that the scoring method of the test should be a standard one so that complete uniformity can be maintained when the test is scored by different experts at different times. Then only we can be sure that the test will have sufficient reliability and validity.

Reliability

A test must be reliable, which means that the results obtained should be consistent when the test is administered once or more than once on the same sample with a reasonable gap. Consistency in results obtained in a single administration is called the index of internal consistency of the test. Consistency in results obtained upon testing and retesting is called the index of temporal consistency.

Reliability includes both internal consistency as well as temporal consistency. For a test to be called sound, it must be reliable because reliability indicates the extent to which the scores obtained in the test are free from internal defects of standardisation which are likely to produce errors of measurement.

Sometimes we do not get the same score in successive administrations of a psychological test. *Some possible reasons for this are*

- **Test Taker's Temporary Psychological or Physical State** Test performance can be influenced by a person's psychological or physical state at the time of testing. *For instance*–differing levels of anxiety, fatigue or motivation may affect the applicant's test results.
- **Environmental Factors** Differences in the testing environment, such as room temperature, lighting, noise or even a different test administrator, can influence an individual's test performance.
- **Form of the Test** Some tests have more than one version or form. Items differ on each form, but each form is supposed to measure the same trait. Different forms of a test are known as parallel forms or alternate forms. These forms are designed to have similar measurement characteristics, but they contain different items. Because the forms are not exactly the same, a test taker might do better in one form than on another.
- **Multiple Raters** In certain tests, scoring is determined by a rater's judgments of the test taker's performance or responses. Differences in training, experience and frame of reference among raters can produce different test scores for the test taker.

These reasons are sources of chance or random measurement error in the assessment process. The degree to which test scores are unaffected by measurement errors is an indication of the reliability of the test. Reliable assessment tools produce dependable, repeatable and consistent information about people. In order to meaningfully interpret test scores and make useful employment or career-related decisions, we need reliable tools.

Reliability Coefficient

The reliability of a test is indicated by its reliability coefficient denoted by the letter 'r'. It is expressed as a number ranging between 0 and 1.00, with r = 0 indicating no reliability and r = 1.00 indicating perfect reliability. Generally, one will find the reliability of a test as r = .80 or r = .93. A larger reliability coefficient indicates that the test is more reliable.

Reliability Coefficient Value	Interpretation
0.90 and up	excellent
0.80 - 0.89	good
0.70 -0.79	adequate
below 0.70	may have limited applicability

However, do not select or reject a test solely based on the size of its reliability coefficient. To evaluate a test's reliability, one should consider the type of test, the type of reliability estimate reported and the context in which the test will be used.

Types of Reliability

There are several types of reliability, each influenced by different sources of measurement error. Test developers have the responsibility of reporting the reliability estimates that are relevant for a particular test. The acceptable level of reliability will differ depending on the type of test and the reliability estimate used. *The types of reliability are–*

- **Test-Retest Reliability** It indicates the repeatability of test scores with the passage of time. It also reflects the stability of the characteristic or construction being measured by the test. Some qualities of a person are more stable than others. *For instance–* an individual's reading ability is more stable over a particular period of time than that individual's anxiety level. Therefore, we expect a higher test-retest reliability coefficient on a reading test than on a test that measures anxiety. For constructs that are expected to vary over time, an acceptable test-retest reliability coefficient may be lower than is suggested in the above table.
- **Alternate or Parallel Form Reliability** It indicates how consistent test scores are likely to be if a person takes two or more forms of a test. A high parallel form reliability coefficient indicates that the different forms of the test are very similar, which means that it makes almost no difference in which version a person takes the test. On the other hand, a low parallel form reliability coefficient suggests that the different forms are probably not comparable; they may be measuring different things and therefore should not be used interchangeably.
- **Inter-rater Reliability** It indicates how consistent test scores are likely to be if the test is scored by two or more raters. On some tests, raters evaluate responses to questions and determine the score. Differences in judgments among raters are likely to produce variations in test scores. A high inter-rater reliability coefficient indicates that the judgment process is stable and the resulting scores are reliable. Inter-rater reliability coefficients are usually lower than other types of reliability estimates. However, it is possible to obtain higher levels of inter-rater reliabilities if raters are appropriately trained.
- **Internal Consistency Reliability** It indicates the extent to which items on a test measure the same quality. A high internal consistency reliability coefficient for a test indicates that the items on the test are very similar to each other in content (*i.e.* they are homogeneous). The length of a test can affect internal consistency reliability. *For instance–* a very lengthy test can increase the reliability coefficient artificially.

Tests that measure multiple characteristics are usually divided into distinct components. Manuals for such tests typically report a separate internal consistency reliability coefficient for each component in addition to one for the whole test. Test manuals and reviews report several kinds of internal consistency reliability estimates. Each type of estimate is appropriate under certain circumstances. The test manual should explain why a particular estimate is reported.

Standard Error of Measurement (SEM)

The SEM gives the margin of error that we should expect in an individual test score because of imperfect reliability of the test. The SEM represents the degree of confidence that a person's true score lies within a particular range of scores. *For example* – a SEM of '2' indicates that a test taker's true score probably lies within 2 points in either direction of the score the individual receives on the test. This means that if an individual receives a score of 91 on the test, there is a good chance that the person's true score lies somewhere between 89 and 93. The SEM is a useful measure of the accuracy of individual test scores. If the SEM is small, the test score measurement is more accurate.

When evaluating the reliability coefficients of a test, we should go through the test manual for information relating to

- **Types of Reliability Used** The test manual should indicate why a certain type of reliability coefficient was reported and mention the sources of random measurement error relevant for the test.
- **How Reliability Studies are Conducted** The manual should indicate the conditions under which the data is obtained. One condition is the length of time that passed between administrations of a test in a test-retest reliability study, as reliability coefficient tends to reduce if the time between test administrations increases.
- **Characteristics of the Sample Group** The manual should indicate the important characteristics of the group used in gathering reliability information, such as education level, occupation etc. This will allow us to compare the characteristics of the people we want to test with the sample group. If they are similar, then the reported reliability estimates will probably hold true for our population as well.

Validity

Validity is another prerequisite for a test to be sound. Validity indicates the extent to which the test measures, what it intends to measure, when compared with some outside independent criteria.

Validity refers to what characteristic the test measures and how well the test measures that characteristic. Accordingly, a test's validity is established with reference to a specific purpose and with reference to a specific group. This information is given in the test manual.

Generally, validity of a test is dependent upon the reliability because a test which yields inconsistent results (poor reliability) will not correlate with some outside independent criteria.

Some properties of the validity of a test are

- It tells us if the characteristic being measured is related to job qualifications and requirements.
- It gives meaning to the test scores. Validity evidence indicates that there is linkage between test performance and job performance. It can tell us what we may conclude or predict about someone from the score on the test. If a test has been demonstrated to be a valid predictor of performance on a specific job, persons scoring high on the test are more likely to perform well on the job than persons who score low on the test, all else being equal.
- It describes the degree to which we can make specific conclusions or predictions about people based on their test scores. Thus, it indicates the usefulness of the test.

Difference between Reliability and Validity

Validity will tell us how good a test is for a particular situation; reliability will tell us how trustworthy a score on that test will be. We cannot draw proper conclusions from a test score unless we are sure that the test is reliable. Even when a test is reliable, it may not be valid. So we should ensure that any test we select is both reliable and valid for our situation.

As a test's validity is established for a specific purpose, it may not be valid for a different purpose. *For instance*, the test we use to make valid predictions about someone's technical proficiency on the job may not be valid for predicting the same person's leadership skills or absenteeism rate.

Similarly, a test's validity is established for a specific group of persons. These groups are called reference groups. The test may not be valid for a different group of persons. *For instance–* a test designed to predict the performance of managers in situations requiring problem solving will not help in making predictions about the performance of clerical employees.

If, *for instance–* the kind of problem-solving ability required for the two positions is different, or the reading level of the test is not suitable for clerical applicants, the test results may be valid for managers, but not for clerical employees.

Thus, we must determine whether the test being given to a target population or target group is suitable for them before administering it.

Types of Validity

Validity may be either internal or external. Internal validity means that the effects observed in a test are due to the changes in the test itself and not some other factor. It can be improved by controlling extraneous conditions, using standardised instructions, counter balancing and eliminating demand characteristics and investigator effects.

External validity is the extent to which the results of a study can be generalised to other settings (ecological validity), other people (population validity) and over time (historical validity). It can be improved by setting tests in a more natural setting and using random sampling to select participants.

We may assess the validity of a test in the ways given below

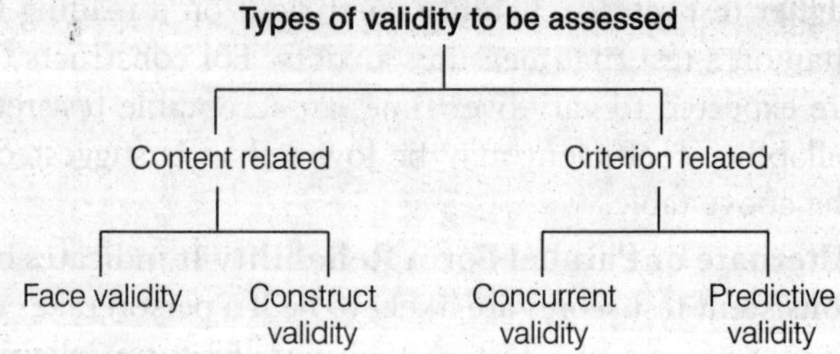

Content Validity

Many psychological tests are designed to measure a construct, an attribute, a trait as a characteristic *i.e.* abstracted from observable behaviors. *For example* the Fundamental Interpersonal Relations Orientation Behaviour (FIROB) is used frequently by organisations to improve their interaction with others and measure interpersonal needs.

Content validity is the extent to which the items on a test are representative of the construct the test measures. If a midterm exam *i.e.* intended to assess your understanding of the material covered during the first half of a course contains a representative sample of the material covered during the first half of the course, the exam demonstrates evidence of content validity.

The components of content validity are as follows

(i) **Face Validity** It means whether the test appears (at face value) to measure what it claims to measure. The purpose of high face validity tests is clear to even simple persons who take the test. Conversely, tests whose purpose is not clear have low face validity. It can be measured by asking people to rate the validity of a test as it appears to them. *For instance–* the rater could use a Likert scale to assess face validity with the meanings given below–

- The test is highly suitable for the given purpose
- The test is very suitable for that purpose
- The test is adequately suitable
- The test is inadequate for that purpose
- The test is irrelevant and so it is unsuitable for that purpose

While computing face validity, we should take the precaution to select suitable people to rate a test such as a questionnaire, an interview, an IQ test etc. *For instance–* individuals who actually take the test would be well placed to judge its face validity.

It is important that opinions of experts in the field should not be considered for face validity of a test, as they are having additional information than what appears on the face. The computation of face validity is correct if a reasonable level of agreement exists among raters. But face validity is only a crude and basic measure of validity.

(ii) **Construct Validity** It refers to the extent to which a test captures a specific theoretical construct or trait. To test for construct validity, it must be demonstrated that the phenomenon being measured actually exists. So, the construct validity of a test for intelligence *for instance–* is dependent on a model or theory of intelligence.

Criterion-Related Validity

In addition to measuring construct, many psychological test are developed to predict events and behaviours. *For example–* the SAT was developed to help predict success in college. Many employment tests are designed to predict success in the job. Criterion related validity is a validation method that is used to determine whether a test indeed predicts, what it claims to predict.

A test has evidence of criterion related validity, when it demonstrates that its scores are systematically related to a relevant criterion. The necessary level of accuracy of the test's predication of the criterion depends on how the predication will be used.

The components of criterion related validity are as follows–

(i) **Concurrent Validity** It is the degree to which a test corresponds to an external criterion that is known concurrently (*i.e.* occurring at the same time). *For instance,* a new IQ test or personality test might be compared with an older but similar test known to have good validity already.

(ii) **Predictive Validity** It is the degree to which a test accurately predicts a criterion that will occur in the future. *For instance–* a prediction may be made on the basis of a new intelligence test that high scorers who are twelve years old will be more likely to obtain university degrees several years later. If the prediction is borne out ultimately, then the test has good predictive validity.

Norms

Another important step in the standardisation of a test is the establishment of norms for the test. A norm is the average performance of an identified group of examinees on the test. When standardising a test, it is administrated to a large, representative sample of the type of persons for whom it is designed.

This group, known as the standardisation sample, helps to establish the norms. Norms are established for personality tests in a similar manner to those for aptitude tests. In both types of tests, the norm corresponds to the average performance of the representative sample on a given test.

Types of Norms

Norms may be developmental level norms or those specifying the relative position within a specific group. Developmental level norms are a method to attach meaning to scores and to indicate how far an individual has progressed along the normal developmental path. *The two types of development level norms are–*

(i) **Age Equivalent Norms** This is the average performance of a standard sample at a certain age level. It is most suitable for a trait or ability which increases systematically with age, *e.g.* height, weight, cognitive abilities, intelligence etc. *The limitations of this norm are that–*

- It is not a fully standard and uniform unit for measurement for the overall period.
- Some of the traits cannot be explained by age norms, though they are related to age. *For instance–* maze learning will not develop after adolescence and IQ will not increase after 16 years, but vocabulary can.

(ii) **Grade Equivalent Norms** Just as in age equivalent norms, the criterion here is the grade or standard in which a student is studying. These norms are made for achievement tests and educational tests. *For instance–* if the average number of problems solved correctly in a maths test by a 4th Grade student in a standardisation sample is 23, then the raw score of 23 corresponds to a grade equivalent to 4th Grade. *The limitations of this norm are–*

- The same students in different subjects are not comparable, *e.g.* the Maths norm cannot be compared with the norm for Social Sciences.
- It is not suitable for higher grades or for subjects in which there is rapid growth in lower grades.

Norms specifying the relative position within a specific group are essentially of two types *which are–*

(i) **Percentile Norms** This is the most popularly used norm. The percentile value indicates the value below which a given percentage of observations in a group of observations fall. *For instance–* if 30% of the total respondents in a test obtain less than 18 problems correct in a Maths test, then the raw score of 18 corresponds to the 30th percentile (P_{30}), *i.e.* the test taker has a percentile rank of 30 and percentile score of 18. Thus, a lower percentile rank for a person indicates a poorer performance.

It is different from a percentage score; the percentage is a raw score, whereas the percentile is a derived score. Percentiles are simple to understand, easy to calculate and can be understood to mean the rank of the person in a group of 100.

(ii) **Standard Score Norms** A standard score is calculated by transforming the raw score into one on a common scale. A standard score is based on a normal distribution with a mean and a standard deviation. On many standardised assessments, the standard score is based on a distribution with a mean of 100 and a standard deviation of 15.

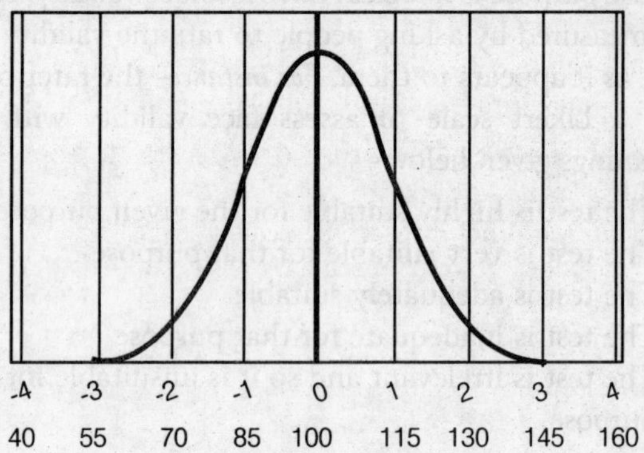

A score of 100 on such a test means that the respondent has scored in the middle of the distribution. A Standard Score of 85 indicates that the respondent has scored one standard deviation below the mean of the normative sample. The standard deviation is an indication of the variability of scores in a population. There is an increasing trend to use these norms as it is easier to interpret standard scores.

Depending upon the purpose and use, a test constructor prepares any of the above norms as norms of his test. As norms help in interpretation of the scores, no meaning can be made of the score obtained on the test in their absence.

A test must also be practicable from the point of view of the time taken in its completion, length, scoring etc. In other words, the test should not be lengthy and the scoring method must neither be difficult nor one which can only be done by highly specialised persons.

EXAM BASED QUESTIONS

1 In psychology testing .... test are used.
(a) random (b) standardised
(c) asystematic (d) None of these

2 Different areas of psychological functioning include
(a) feelings and attitude (b) mental condition
(c) personal interest (d) All of these

3 Which of the following are used to measure intelligence?
(a) Stanford Binet intelligence scale
(b) Wechsler intelligence scale for children
(c) Both a and b
(d) None of the above

4 Rorschach test, Thematic apperception test and MMPI are used to measure?
(a) Intelligence (b) Attitude
(c) Personality (d) Achievement

5 When are neuro-psychological test conducted?
(a) After a trauma/injury (b) After a seizure episode
(c) Regularly (d) All of these

6 Achievement test can be assessed through
(a) peabody individual achievement test
(b) wechsler individual achievement test
(c) Both a and b
(d) None of the above

7 Which among the following test is a measurement of mental and cognitive abilities?
(a) Achievement (b) Aptitude
(c) Personality (d) Intelligence

8 Development of good psychological test requires thoughtful and sound application of established principle of
(a) test construction (b) psychology principle
(c) Both a and b (d) None of these

9 Capabilities of a good item writers are
(a) command of subject matter
(b) familiarity with different types of items
(c) excellent knowledge of the language
(d) All of the above

10 General guideline for item writing include
(a) clarity (b) beautiful writing
(c) non-functional words (d) high difficulty level

11 What all should be avoided in item writing?
(a) Non-functional words
(b) Irrelevant accuracies/clues
(c) Interlocking items
(d) All of the above

12 What makes the development of test easier?
(a) Careful definition (b) Review of construct
(c) Both a and b (d) None of these

13 Test questions can be in the form of
(a) statement
(b) picture
(c) incomplete statement
(d) All of the above

14 MCQ's are used more often because
(a) the familiar format (b) easy to fill up
(c) Both a and b (d) None of these

15 ...... personality inventory, uses the true/false format and converts it into multiple choice questions.
(a) Andrew (b) Holdon
(c) Holdman (d) Hogan

16 Forced choice test is used for
(a) personality (b) attitude
(c) Both a and b (d) None of these

17 In item analysis of test construction, P is considered as proportion of right answers and q as proportion or wrong answers. The product of p and q will always lie between.
(a) −1to +1 (b) 0 to +1
(c) 0 to 0.25 (d) 0.05 to 0.95

18 To make the test effective the test constructor must study all the items one by one. This is known as
(a) test analysis (b) test writing
(c) test requirement (d) None of these

19 Item validity and difficulty levels are determined
(a) successively
(b) simultaneously
(c) one by one
(d) None of the above

20 Which of the following is an important tool of item analysis, in item difficulty and item discrimination?
(a) ICT (b) ICP (c) ICC (d) IDC

21 ICC is a .... curve
(a) 2 dimensional
(b) 3 dimensional
(c) 4 dimensional
(d) All of the above

22 What is plotted on X axis in ICC curve?
(a) Probablity of correct response
(b) Total score
(c) Both a and b
(d) None of the above

23 The steepness of ICC shows the
(a) item difficulty
(b) item validity
(c) item discriminating power
(d) item analysis

24 **Items should be phrased in such a manner that they are interpreted in exact same way by all the examinees. This is known as**
(a) reliability (b) scoring objectivity
(c) item objectivity (d) validity

25 **A psychological test can be considered as standard, when it establishes**
(a) reliability and variability
(b) reliability and validity
(c) validity, norm and variability
(d) reliability, validity and norm

26 **Which of the following characteristics applies to measurement that consistently discriminates between high and low scores?**
(a) Validity (b) Reliability
(c) Precision (d) Accuracy

27 **Consistency in result obtained in a single administration is called the**
(a) index of internal consistency of test
(b) index of external consistency of test
(c) Both a and b
(d) None of the above

28 **Reason for not getting same score in successive administration of a psychological test depends on**
(a) test taker's temporary psychological state
(b) environmental factors
(c) form of test
(d) All of the above

29 **The Reliability coefficent 'r' alway's lie between**
(a) 1–100 (b) 0–1.00 (c) 1–10 (d) 1–50

30 **Test-retest method gives the estimate of test's**
(a) stability (b) duration
(c) Both a and b (d) None of these

31 **Test-retest reliability depends on**
(a) time interval between two test
(b) time taken to prepare two test
(c) Both a and b
(d) None of the above

32 **When participants take benefit from the first test, the phenomena is known as**
(a) Beginner' Luck (b) Practice effect
(c) Experience (d) None of these

33 **What does low parallel from reliability coefficient indicates?**
(a) Different form of test are not comparable
(b) Different form of test are same
(c) Tests can be used interchangeably
(d) All of the above

34 **How do we obtain higher level of inter rater reliability coefficient?**
(a) By asking the rater to do so
(b) By training the raters
(c) Both a and b
(d) None of the above

35 **What can affect the internal consistency reliability?**
(a) Quality of question (b) Length of test
(c) Rater's mood (d) None of these

36 **What gives the margin of error that is expected in a test score due to imperfect reliability of the test?**
(a) Standard error of measurement
(b) Area of error
(c) Deviation from standard
(d) All of the above

37 **Factors influencing reliability coefficient of a test include**
(a) types of reliability used
(b) how reliability studies were conducted
(c) characteristic of the sample group
(d) All of the above

38 **....... refers to what characteristic the test measures and how well the test measures that characteristic.**
(a) Reliablity (b) Validity
(c) Norms (d) Stability

39 **Validity of a test is dependent upon**
(a) reliablity (b) stability
(c) norms (d) None of these

40 **Properties of the validity of a test are**
(a) it tells us if the characteristic measured is related to job qualification and requirement
(b) validity evidence indicates there is a linkage between test performance and job performance
(c) it defines degree to which we can make specific conclusion about people based on their test scores
(d) All of the above

41 **Test's validity is established for a specific group of person. These groups are called**
(a) trial group (b) peer group
(c) reference group (d) review group

42 **Higher levels of both reliability and validity requires the inter correlation range between**
(a) 0.10 to 0.85 (b) 0.10 to 0.81
(c) 0.10 to 0.60 (d) 0.10 to 0.69

43 **Validity can be**
(a) internal (b) external
(c) Both a and b (d) None of these

44 **External validity deals with**
(a) replaceability (b) generalisability
(c) stability (d) objectivity

45 **An important step when interpreting findings using a physical trace measure is to seek converging evidence for the finding. This is reflected by which of the following?**
(a) Reliability
(b) Rationale
(c) Causal inference
(d) Validity

46 The results of an externally valid study are ones that
(a) apply to a narrow range of subjects, conditions and settings
(b) apply to a wide range of subjects, conditions and settings
(c) are likely to replicate, if the study is repeated
(d) are likely to be difficult to interpret unambiguously

47 When a study is free of confounding it is said to have
(a) external validity (b) internal validity
(c) integrity (d) reproducibility

48 The validity of the test can be measured by?
(a) To ask the rater to rate the test
(b) By assessing test by the help of an expert
(c) Both a and b
(d) None of the above

49 .... refers to the extent to which a test capture a specific theoretical construct or trait.
(a) Face Validity (b) Concurrent Validity
(c) Predictive Validity (d) Construct Validity

50 It is a validation method that is used to determine whether a test indeed predicts what it claims to predict. Which method is this?
(a) Content Validity
(b) Face Validity
(c) Criterion Related Validity
(d) Concurrent Validity

51 A psychologist develops a new test of numerical ability. He correlates this test's scores of the students. With the marks obtained by them in mathematics in their examination held recently. The correlation is quite high. This indicates
(a) high interval consistency of the test
(b) high predictive validity of test
(c) high test retest reliability of the test
(d) high concurrent validity of the test

52 Concurrent validity is evaluated by showing
(a) how well the content of the test samples the class of situations or subject matter about, which conclusions are to be drawn
(b) how well the test scores corresponds to already accepted measures of performance or status made at the same time
(c) how well the test corresponds to some meaningful trait or construct the helps us in understanding and individual
(d) how well the test sure helps in predicting some future but comes

53 .... is the degree to which a test accurately predicts a criterion that will occur in the future.
(a) Predictive Validity
(b) Content Validity
(c) Concurrent Validity
(d) Face Validity

54 Standardisation sample help us to establish a
(a) reliability (b) validity
(c) norm (d) None of these

55 Limitation of age equivalent norm is
(a) it is not a fully standard and uniform unit for measurement
(b) some of the traits can not be measured by age norms
(c) Both a and b
(d) None of the above

56 .... are the norms specifying the relative position within a specific group are
(a) Percentile norms
(b) Standards score norms
(c) Both a and b
(d) None of the above

57 Match the following

List I (Measures)	List II (Objectives)
A. Mode	1. Purpose of the test
B. Quartile deviation	2. Consistency of test scores
C. Reliability	3. Measure of variability
D. Validity	4. Measure of central tendency

Codes

	A	B	C	D		A	B	C	D
(a)	3	4	2	1	(b)	4	3	2	1
(c)	3	4	1	2	(d)	4	3	1	2

58 Match the following

List I (Types of Validity)	List II (Brief Explanations)
A. Concurrent validity	1. Gives theoretically expected results
B. Construct Validity	2. Correlates high with a test measuring the same trait
C. Face validity	3. Forecasts the trait-related performance
D. Predictive	4. Gives overall impression that the test measures the intended trait

Codes

	A	B	C	D		A	B	C	D
(a)	2	3	4	1	(b)	4	1	2	3
(c)	2	1	4	3	(d)	4	3	2	1

59 Match the following

List I (Types of Reliability)	List II (Briefs)
A. Alternative from reliability	1. Internal consistency
B. Inter scorer reliability	2. Temporal stability
C. Odd-even reliability	3. Agreement between scores obtained by two versions of the same test
D. Test-retest reliability	4. Agreement among scores give by different scores

Codes

	A	B	C	D		A	B	C	D
(a)	4	3	2	1	(b)	3	4	2	1
(c)	4	3	1	2	(d)	3	4	1	2

60 Match the following

List I (Type of Reliability)	List II (Measures the Consistency)
A. Test-retest	1. Individual items of a test
B. Inter-rater	2. Same test over time
C. Parallel form	3. Same test conducted by different people
D. Internal consistency	4. Different versions of a test which are designed to be equivalent

Codes

	A	B	C	D		A	B	C	D
(a)	2	3	1	4	(b)	1	4	3	2
(c)	2	4	3	1	(d)	2	3	4	1

61 Match the following

List I (Type of Test)	List II (Example)
A. Neuropsychological test	1. Inkblot test
B. Achievement test	2. Wisconsin card sorting test
C. Personality test	3. Peabody individual test

Codes

	A	B	C		A	B	C
(a)	2	3	1	(b)	3	2	1
(c)	1	2	3	(d)	2	1	3

62 Choose the correct option

1. A standard score is calculated by transformaing raw score into one on a common scale.
2. A standard score is based on normal distribution with a mean and standard deviation.

Which of the above statements is/are correct?

(a) Only 1 (b) Only 2
(c) Both 1 and 2 (d) None of these

63 Consider the following statements

1. Self perception theory suggest that subjects act as problem solver.
2. The correlation between creativity and general mental ability is zero.

Which of the statements given above is/are incorrect?

(a) Only 1 (b) Only 2
(c) Both 1 and 2 (d) None of these

64 Consider the following statements

1. The total set of attitude of a individual is called attitude conglomeration.
2. The semantic differential techniques measure the social learning of the subject.

Which of the statements given above is/are incorrect?

(a) Only 1 (b) Only 2
(c) Both 1 and 2 (d) None of these

65 Consider the following statements

1. A test constructor must have command over the subject matter.
2. It does not matter if test constructor is awar of respondent's intelligence level.

Which of the above statement is/are correct?

(a) Only 1 (b) Only 2
(c) Both 1 and 2 (d) None of these

66 Which of the following should be considered in item writing?

1. Adaptable difficulty level
2. Clarity
3. Avoid inter-locking items
4. Use of stereotyped words
5. Use of irrelevant clues

Codes

(a) 4 and 5 (b) 1, 2 and 3
(c) 1, 4 and 5 (d) 2, 3 and 4

67 Consider the following statements

1. Item analysis makes it possible to shorten a test.
2. Item analysis decreases test's validity and reliability.

Which of the above statement is/are correct?

(a) Only 1 (b) Only 2
(c) Both 1 and 2 (d) None of these

68 Consider the following statements

1. Test retest reliablity indicates repeatability of test score with the passage of time.
2. Alternate form of reliablity indicates now consistent test scores are likely to be if a person takes two or more form of test.

Which of the above statement is/are correct?

(a) Only 1 (b) Only 2
(c) Both 1 and 2 (d) None of these

69 Consider the following statements

1. Item difficulty index is measured using $\dfrac{U_P - L_P}{U}$
2. Item discrimination index is measured using $\dfrac{U_P + L_P}{U + L}$

Which of the above statement is/are correct?

(a) Only 2 (b) None of these
(c) Both 1 and 2 (d) Only 1

70 Psychological test are used to assess many areas of a person. Which of the following are assessed by psychological test?

1. Traits such as introversion and extroversion
2. Certain conditions such as depression or anxiety.

Codes

(a) Only 1 (b) Only 2
(c) Both 1 and 2 (d) None of these

Directions (Q. Nos. 71-75) *Read the passage given below and answer the following questions.*

Objectivity is another important characteristic of psychological test, besides standardisaton. The purpose of standardising a test and giving it uniformity, administration scoring and interpretation is to make psychological test as objective as possible. No test is purely objective in practice because subject element do enter into it. However, sound the research methodology may be inspite of this the goal of test construction is to move more and more toward objectivity and such objectivity is the goal of the construction and has been achieved to a considerable extent in most tests.

Objectivity can be achieved in the following two ways. *First* by estabishing uniformity in testing situation which includes factors like time limit, instruction, materials to be used an preliminary demonstration. Objectivity also covers, the control of factors in the physical environment like lightening, ventilation, noise etc. *Second* method obtaining objectivity refers to uniformity in scoring which means scoring the test performance according to specific answer or specimen of answers. Group tests present one of the best example of objective scoring. Such test scoring is done either by a stencil, electronic matching or by a computer.

71 Which of the following test present one of the best example of objective scoring?
(a) Individual test (b) Group test
(c) Interview method (d) Mass scale method

72 **Assertion** (A) In practical psychological test cannot be purely objective.
Reason (R) Subjective elements always enter into psychological test
Codes
(a) Both A and R are true and R is the correct explanation of A
(b) Both A and R are true, but R is not the correct explanation of A
(c) A is true, but R is false
(d) A is false, but R is true

73 Which of the following is important characteristic of psychological test?
(a) Objectivity (b) Subjectivity
(c) Rationality (d) Validity

74 In how many ways objectivity can be achieved?
(a) 1 (b) 2 (c) 3 (d) 4

75 Which of the following is not an object of scoring in group test?
(a) Computer
(b) Electronic machine
(c) Stencil
(d) Data method

76 Arrange the following steps involved in test construction in chronological order
1. specifying construct of interest
2. evaluating reliability and validity of test
3. choosing a method
4. deciding test's function
5. designing item content
Codes
(a) 1, 4, 3, 5, 2 (b) 1, 3, 4, 5, 2
(c) 1, 4, 3, 2, 5 (d) 1, 3, 4, 2, 5

77 Arrange the following in chronological order.
1. Hindustan binet performance scale.
2. Binet and terman group test
3. Verbal intelligence test.
Codes
(a) 1, 2, 3 (b) 3, 2, 1 (c) 2, 1, 3 (d) 2, 3 1

78 Arrange the following in chronological order.
1. Freeman 2. Guilford
3. Stevens
Codes
(a) 1, 2, 3 (b) 3, 2, 1
(c) 3, 1, 2 (d) 1, 2, 3

79 Arrange the following in chronological order.
1. Sharp 2. Flamagan
3. Garrett
Codes
(a) 1, 2, 3 (b) 3, 2, 1 (c) 3, 1, 2 (d) 1, 3, 2

80 Arrange the following in chronological order.
1. Woodard 2. Heaton
3. Dust
Codes
(a) 1, 2, 3 (b) 2, 1, 3 (c) 1, 3, 2 (d) 2, 3, 1

81 Arrange the following in chronological order.
1. Kuder 2. Cronbach
3. Cohen
Codes
(a) 1, 2, 3 (b) 3, 1, 2 (c) 2, 1, 3 (d) 3, 1, 2

82 Arrange the following in chronological order.
1. Richardson 2. Nanda 3. Borich
Codes
(a) 1, 2, 3 (b) 3, 2, 1 (c) 2, 1, 3 (d) 3, 1, 2

Directions *(Q. Nos. 83-91) In the questions given below are two statements labelled as Assertion (A) and Reason (R). In the context of the two statements, which one of the following is correct?.*
Codes
(a) Both A and R are true and R is the correct explanation of A
(b) Both A and R are true, but R is not the correct explanation of A
(c) A is true, but R is false
(d) A is false, but R is true

83 Assertion (A) Group tests are used in large scale testing program in industry.

Reason (R) Group tests can be administered to a large number of people at same time.

84 Assertion (A) Lengthening of the test increase reliability as well as validity.

Reason (R) Validity does not change rapidly with the increase in the length.

85 Assertion (A) Word association test expose some of the deeper personality trait.

Reason (R) It assist in differentiating different psychological disorder.

86 Assertion (A) The purpose of data was to identify man, who would prove to be poor prospect for military service.

Reason (R) Undesirable personality and behavioural characteristic play a role.

87 Assertion (A) Inkbolt test is a device for differentiating among various kind of psychological test.

Reason (R) It is the most extensive test of that time.

88 Assertion (A) The reliability is sufficient, but not the necessary condition for validity.

Reason (R) This is true for heterogenous test.

89 Assertion (A) When there are extreme scores in a series, which affect the mean, we use median as a measure of central tendency.

Reason (R) Extreme scores in a series do not affect the median.

90 Assertion (A) Split-half technique should not be employed to determine the reliability of speed tests.

Reason (R) Speed test are of low difficulty level. When difficulty level is low, an odd-even split will give a correlation close to one.

91 Assertion (A) The most important step in constructing a questionnaire, is to pretest the draft of the questionnaire.

Reason (R) Valid test are characterised by consistency.

ANSWERS

1 *(b)*	2 *(d)*	3 *(c)*	4 *(c)*	5 *(a)*	6 *(c)*	7 *(b)*	8 *(a)*	9 *(d)*	10 *(a)*
11 *(d)*	12 *(c)*	13 *(d)*	14 *(a)*	15 *(d)*	16 *(c)*	17 *(a)*	18 *(a)*	19 *(b)*	20 *(c)*
21 *(a)*	22 *(b)*	23 *(c)*	24 *(a)*	25 *(d)*	26 *(b)*	27 *(a)*	28 *(d)*	29 *(b)*	30 *(a)*
31 *(a)*	32 *(b)*	33 *(a)*	34 *(b)*	35 *(b)*	36 *(a)*	37 *(d)*	38 *(b)*	39 *(a)*	40 *(d)*
41 *(c)*	42 *(c)*	43 *(c)*	44 *(b)*	45 *(d)*	46 *(b)*	47 *(b)*	48 *(a)*	49 *(d)*	50 *(c)*
51 *(d)*	52 *(b)*	53 *(a)*	54 *(c)*	55 *(c)*	56 *(c)*	57 *(b)*	58 *(c)*	59 *(d)*	60 *(d)*
61 *(a)*	62 *(c)*	63 *(b)*	64 *(c)*	65 *(a)*	66 *(b)*	67 *(a)*	68 *(c)*	69 *(b)*	70 *(c)*
71 *(b)*	72 *(a)*	73 *(a)*	74 *(b)*	75 *(d)*	76 *(a)*	77 *(a)*	78 *(b)*	79 *(c)*	80 *(b)*
81 *(a)*	82 *(a)*	83 *(a)*	84 *(b)*	85 *(c)*	86 *(a)*	87 *(d)*	88 *(a)*	89 *(c)*	90 *(d)*
91 *(c)*									

Areas of Psychological Testing and Attitude Scales

Psychological tests are used to assess a variety of mental abilities and attributes, including achievement and ability, personality and intelligence, creativity, aptitude and neurological functioning.

Areas of Testing

Psychological assessment contributes important information to the understanding of individual characteristics and capabilities. This is done through collection, integration and interpretation of information about an individual's intelligence, creativity, aptitude, personality, interest and neuro-psychological condition.

Intelligence

Human intelligence or mental quality consists of the abilities to learn from experience, adapt to new situations, understand and handle abstract concepts and use knowledge to manipulate one's environment.

Generally, a person's intelligence level is understood as his ability to solve a problem, power of reasoning and thinking, learning ability, decision-making etc.

These abilities and capacities can be combined into three basic functions

(i) **Learning** Acquiring, retaining and using knowledge.

(ii) **Recognising Problems** Identifying possible problems in the environment that need to be addressed.

(iii) **Solving Problems** Using what has been learned to come up with a useful solution to a problem which has been noticed.

Measurement of Intelligence

Various individual tests have been used to test the intelligence of an individual. The two main individual intelligence tests are the Stanford-Binet Intelligence Test and the Wechsler Intelligence Scale for Children (WISC)/ Wechsler Adult Intelligence Scale (WAIS) for adults.

In this Chapter

- Areas of Testing
- Attitude Scales
- Computer-Based Psychological Testing

Stanford-Binet Intelligence Test

This test was originally developed in 1905 as the Binet-Simon Intelligence Scale by French psychologists **Alfred Binet** and **Theodore Simon**. It was administered to children to evaluate their performance (*i.e.* their mental age) at a given chronological age. *Its features and history of development are*

- The mental age/ chronological age ratio, called a *mental quotient*, was used to evaluate a child's learning potential.
- Lewis Terman of Stanford University revised the Binet-Simon scale in 1916. The revised scale, called the *Stanford-Binet Intelligence Scale*, retained the concept of mental and chronological ages but introduced the concept of the Intelligence Quotient (IQ), which allowed comparison between children of different ages. Intelligence quotient can be expressed by the formula

  Intelligence Quotient (IQ) = (Mental age / Chronological age) × 100
- It is a cognitive ability and intelligence test which is also used to diagnose developmental or intellectual deficiencies in young children.
- The test measures five weighted factors: knowledge, quantitative reasoning, visual-spatial processing, working memory and fluid reasoning.
- The revision of this test in 1986 made it useful for testing adults as well as children. The latest revision of this test was released in the year 2003.
- In this test, a person's score for correct answers is compared to a table of scores of test takers of the same age, with the average score always scaled to 100, meaning that

  mental age = chronological age.

Scores between 90 and 110 are labelled as 'normal', above 130 as 'superior' and below 70 as 'mentally deficient' or 'retarded'.

Wechsler Intelligence Tests

David Wechsler developed the Wechsler Adult Intelligence Scale (WAIS) in 1939, revised as the WAIS-R. A subsequent revision was conducted in the USA in 1997. The present scale is the 3rd edition known as the WAIS-III. Wechsler also developed the Wechsler Intelligence Scale for Children (WISC) in 1949, revised as the WISC-R.

The revised forms of these scales are widely used. They contain two sub-scales, verbal (6 sub-tests) and performance (5 sub-tests), which provide a verbal IQ and a performance IQ.

The details of the sub-tests for the adult scale are

Verbal

(i) **Information** A set of 29 questions which measure general knowledge are given.

(ii) **Digit Span** Test takers are given sets of digits to repeat initially forwards then backwards. This is a test of immediate auditory recall and freedom from distraction.

(iii) **Vocabulary** Test takers are asked to define 35 words. It measures expressive word knowledge and correlates very highly with the full scale IQ.

(iv) **Arithmetic** Test takers are given 14 mental arithmetic brief story type problems. It tests distractibility as well as numerical reasoning.

(v) **Comprehension** Test takers are given 16 questions which focus on issues of social awareness.

(vi) **Similarities** Test takers are asked to say how two seemingly dissimilar items might infact be similar. It is a measure of concept formation.

Performance

(i) **Picture Completion** Test takers are asked to complete 20 small pictures that all have one vital detail missing. It is a test of attention to fine details.

(ii) **Picture Arrangement** Test takers are shown 10 sets of small pictures; they are required to arrange them in a logical sequence.

(iii) **Block Design** Test takers have to put sets of blocks together to match patterns given on cards.

(iv) **Digit Symbol** Test takers are asked to copy a coding pattern.

(v) **Object Assembly** Test takers are asked to complete four small jig-saw type puzzles.

The subscales in the verbal and performance tests are combined for the total IQ. Test score combinations may also reveal other strengths and weaknesses to a skilled examiner. The mean IQ for each age group on this test is 100 with a standard deviation of 15. The WAIS scales have impressive reliability and validity.

Extreme Levels of Intelligence Scores

The extreme levels of intellectual functioning are known as *mentally retarded* (*i.e.* developmentally disabled) and gifted.

- **Mentally Retarded** Children identified as mentally retarded (also described as developmentally disabled) have IQ scores of 70 or below. Severity of disability and corresponding IQ scores are mild (50 to 70), moderate (35 to 50), severe (20 to 35) and profound (below 20). Some, but not all, of the causes of mental retardation are known and include Down Syndrome (a genetic disorder), Phenylketonuria (PKU: a birth defect) etc.

- **Gifted** Such children usually fall within the upper 2% to 3% of the IQ score distribution (*i.e.* with IQ between 130 and 145). **Louis Terman's** well-known longitudinal study of the gifted found that such children are generally superior to average IQ peers in health, achievement and adjustment to life stresses. Currently, gifted children are identified not only by IQ but also by superior potential in any of the six areas of general intelligence, specific aptitudes (*e.g.* mathematical), creativity, leadership, performing arts and athletics.

Creativity

Creativity tests, mostly devised during the last 30 years, are aimed at assessing the qualities and abilities that constitute creativity. These tests evaluate mental abilities in ways that are different from conventional intelligence tests. Persons with the highest scores on creativity tests do not necessarily have the highest IQs. Creative people tend to have IQs that are atleast average if not above average, but for higher than an IQ of 120, there is hardly any correlation between performance on intelligence and creativity tests.

Most creativity tests in use today are based partially on the theory of creativity evolved by **JP Guilford** in the 1950s. Guilford said that the ability to think of more than one solution to a problem lay at the core of creativity. He called this process 'divergent thinking'. The reverse process *i.e.* the tendency to narrow all options to a single solution, was called 'convergent thinking'.

Guilford identified three components of divergent thinking

(i) **Fluency** The ability to quickly find multiple solutions to a problem.

(ii) **Flexibility** Being able to simultaneously consider a variety of alternatives.

(iii) **Originality** Referring to ideas that differ from those of other people.

Measurement of Creativity

Early tests designed to assess an individual's aptitude for divergent thinking included the **Torrance** (1962) and **Meeker** (1969) tests. *Some tests which are used to test creativity at present are*

(i) **Alternative Uses Task** This is Guilford's test of divergent thinking. It is used to measure how respondents are able to come up with alternative uses for a certain product (*e.g.* a chair, paperclip, cup etc.) *based on four factors*

- **Originality** The novelty of the alternative use
- **Fluency** The number of uses the respondent was able to come up with
- **Flexibility** The categories which the alternative uses fall into
- **Elaboration** The amount of detail the respondent provided regarding alternative uses of the item

(ii) **Remote Associates** This tests convergent thinking *i.e.* finding the 'one right' answer to the problem. This test gives the respondents three words which are in one way or the other related. The respondents task is to find what links or associates these words together.

(iii) **Incomplete Figures** This is Torrance's test of creative thinking. It is easy to administer and can be completed in a short period of time. The test begins with giving the respondents an incomplete figure which they must draw and build an object upon. Uncommon subject matter, implied stories, humour and original perspective all earn high marks in this test.

(iv) **Artistic-Assessment Tests** These creativity tests are administered in special domains or areas. They are used to measure the creativity of an artwork, dance, design and similar fields.

(v) **Self-Assessment Tests** They allow respondents to assess their creative intelligence by answering questions such as how they feel about a certain situation and whether they have that certain creative trait. One popular test in this category is called the *Khatena-Torrance's Creative Perception Inventory which contains two sub-categories*

- Something About Myself (SAM), which gauges the respondent's artistic abilities, self-strength and individuality.
- What Kind of Person Are You? (WKoPAY), which measures imagination, self-confidence and inquisitiveness.

Neuropsychological Tests

Neuropsychological tests are specifically designed tasks used to measure a psychological function known to be linked to a particular brain structure or pathway. This is done by systematic administration of clearly defined procedures in a formal environment. Neuropsychological tests are usually administered to a single person working with an examiner in a quiet office environment which is free from distractions.

Most neuropsychological tests presently being used are based on traditional psychometric theory. Thus, a person's raw score on a test is compared to a large general population normative sample that should ideally be drawn from a population comparable to the person being examined.

These tests are used when there is evidence to suggest neurological problems such as ADHD, dyslexia, autism spectrum, non verbal learning disorder, alcohol or drug related damage, brain injury or concussion or other neurologic conditions. Although standard psychological testing can diagnose a condition such as ADHD based upon behaviour, neuropsychological testing can specify the origin, severity and development of a disorder and then customise recommendations to create a specific treatment plan.

Some common neuropsychological tests are

- Ammons Quick Test (QT)
- Bender Visual Motor Gestalt (BVMG) Test
- Halstead-Reitan Neuropsychological Test Battery (HRNB)

Aptitude

An aptitude test is designed to assess a person's level of competency to perform a certain type of task. Such aptitude tests are often used to assess academic potential or career suitability. Such tests may be used to assess either mental or physical talent in various areas. Whereas, achievement tests evaluate a person's level of skill or knowledge at any given time, aptitude tests determine how capable a person might be for performing a certain task.

Some examples of aptitude tests are

- A test assessing an individual's aptitude to become a fighter pilot.
- A career test evaluating a person's capability to work as an air traffic controller.
- Aptitude tests given to high school students to determine which type of career may suit them.
- A computer programming test to determine how a job candidate might solve hypothetical problems.
- A test designed to test a person's physical abilities needed for a job such as a police officer or fire fighter.

Aptitude tests are commonly used for

- Numerical Reasoning
- Verbal Reasoning
- In-Tray/ E-tray Exercises
- Inductive Reasoning
- Mechanical Reasoning
- Diagrammatic Reasoning/ Abstract Reasoning
- Spatial Reasoning
- Situational Judgement
- Mental Arithmetic
- Number Sequences
- Verbal Analogies
- Vocabulary
- Watson Glaser Critical Thinking
- Syllogisms
- Maths Word Problems
- Logical Reasoning

Common Aptitude Tests

- **In-Tray/ E-tray Exercises** They test a candidate's ability to manage and respond to a series of different tasks, to negotiate conflicting demands and analyse different priorities in a business situation. The candidate is given a particular job role to test his aptitude for business.
- **Watson Glaser Critical Thinking** It is used for selecting candidates of graduate, professional and managerial level. It tests the understanding of the importance of evidence when making conclusions, the ability to differentiate between inferences, abstractions and generalisations by applying logic and the ability to combine all these skills when making decisions.
- **Syllogisms** These provide information about a candidate's deductive and logical reasoning skills. A syllogism consists of a logical argument composed of three parts, two premises (a major one and a minor one) and one conclusion inferred from the provided premises.
- **Maths Word Problems** These provide information about a candidate's reading comprehension skills, ability to visualise information and numerical aptitude.

Personality Assessment

Personality tests are designed to assess characteristic patterns of an individual's personality which includes his/her characteristic, ways of thinking, feeling or behaving. Psychologists measure personality through objective tests (such as self-reports) and projective test.

Objective Tests

Objective tests or self-reports are those tests which are not influenced by the examiner's own beliefs; thus they are independent of rater bias. Commonly used objective personality tests are the Myers-Briggs Type Indicator, Neo Pi-R, MMPI/ MMPI-2, 16 PF and Eysenck Personality Questionnaire. In an objective test, a set of questions is marked and compared against standardised scores similar to school exams.

However, they are dependent on the willingness and ability of the examinees to be open, honest and self-reflective enough to accurately represent and report their true personality. They may use multiple-choice items or numbered scales, which represent a range from 1 (strongly disagree) to 5 (strongly agree).

Some objective personality tests are as follows

- **Myers-Briggs Type Indicator** (MBTI) It is based on Carl Jung's theory of personality. It measures individuals across four dimensions *i.e.* attitude (extrovert/ introvert), perception (sensing/ intuition), judgement (thinking/ feeling) and lifestyle preferences (judging/ perceiving). This test has been criticised for its lack of statistical validity and low reliability.
- **Revised NEO Personality Inventory** (NEO PI-R) It is designed to measure personality traits using the five factor model, in which the five dimensions of personality lie along a continuum of opposing poles which include openness to experience, conscientiousness, extraversion, agreeableness and neuroticism.
- **Minnesota Multiphasic Personality Inventory** (MMPI) It is the most widely used personality inventory for both clinical and nonclinical populations. It is commonly used to help with the diagnosis of personality disorders. The responses are scored to produce a clinical profile of the test taker composed of 10 scales, *These scales are*
  - (i) Hypochondria
  - (ii) Depression
  - (iii) Hysteria
  - (iv) Social deviance
  - (v) Masculinity versus femininity
  - (vi) Paranoia
  - (vii) Obsessive/ compulsive qualities
  - (viii) Schizophrenia
  - (ix) Hypomania
  - (x) Social introversion

  The MMPI-2 (the 1989 revised version) has 567 true/ false questions which may take a maximum of two hours to complete. It was once again revised in 2008 as MMPI-2-RF with the number of questions reduced to 338, but MMPI-2 is still most popularly used.
- **Sixteen Personality Factor Inventory** (16 PF) It measures personality according to Cattell's 16 factor theory of personality. The 16PF is also used to help diagnose psychiatric disorders and help with forecasting and therapy planning. It provides measurements of anxiety, adjustment, emotional stability and behavioural problems. It can also be used for career and occupational selection.
- **Eysenck Personality Questionnaire** It is based on Eysenck's model of personality. The questionnaire was developed from extensive research. It focuses on psychoticism, extraversion and neuroticism.

Projective Tests

Projective test are based on psychoanalytic theories of personality and use ambiguous stimuli to reveal inner aspects of an individual's personality. They are dependent on the rater's or examiner's beliefs. They are based on Freudian psychology (psychoanalysis) and they try to expose people's unconscious perceptions.

Projective tests may expose certain aspects of personality that are not measurable by an objective test; *for instance*, they are more reliable at uncovering unconscious personality traits or features. However, they are criticised for having poor reliability and validity, lacking scientific evidence and relying too much on the subjective judgment of a clinical technician.

The popular projective tests are

(i) **Thematic Apperception Test** (TAT) It consists of 30 cards (including one blank card) depicting ambiguous drawings. Test takers are asked to tell a story about each picture, including the background that led up to the story and the thoughts and feelings of the characters. The results are thought to indicate a person's personality characteristics and emotional functioning.

(ii) **Rorschach Inkblot Test** (RIT) It consists of ten inkblots which were created by Herman Rorschach by dribbling ink on paper and then folding over the paper to create a symmetrical design. During the test, participants are shown the inkblots and asked what each one looks like. The test administrator then asks questions about the responses, such as which part of the inkblot was linked to each response. This test can be used to examine a person's personality characteristics and emotional functioning. It can also measure unconscious attitudes and motivations.

Validity and Reliability of Objective Tests and Projective Tests

Validity refers to whether or not a test ctually measures the construct that it is meant to measure and Reliability refers to the degree to which a test produces stable and consistent results. As objective tests are relatively free from rater bias, or the influence of the examiner's own beliefs, they have more validity than projective tests. However, objective tests require the test takers to be open, honest and self-reflective enough to accurately represent and report their true personality. This limits their reliability, as those takers who are not open and honest will create a false impression of their personality. *Some exceptions to this are*

- The MMPI tries to take care of this problem by including validity and reliability scales in addition to its clinical scales. *For instance*, if test takers respond 'yes' to a number of unrealistically positive items such as 'I have never told a lie', they may be trying to 'fake good' or appear better than they actually are.
- The Eysenck Personality Questionnaire was developed after long years of research on factor analysis and conduct of a large number of laboratory experiments. Thus, it has excellent reliability and validity. Additionally, there is a large body of research that demonstrates the practical uses of the Eysenck measure.

On the other hand, projective tests are highly sensitive to the examiner's beliefs. The Rorschach Inkblot test has gone through standardisation procedures; so it is reasonably effective in measuring depression, psychosis and anxiety. But in the TAT, which involves open-ended story telling, standardisation of test administration is not there. Thus, the TAT is low on validity and reliability.

Infact, projective tests are often considered best used for information only and not as a true measure of personality. As these two types of projective test have failed in cross-cultural personality assessments, other personality assessments that explore factors such as race, language and level of adaptation to culture have been developed, such as Hoy-Watkins test, developed in 2008.

Interest Inventories

The term 'interest' means a special attitude that engages the individual and motivates him to move toward the object of interest. Thus, an interest inventory measures a person's liking for a particular task without reference to the individual's actual ability to perform the task (achievement) or potential for doing so in the future (aptitude).

Most commonly, the interest inventory is designed to help a person to decide about his future education and career. It is a questionnaire that has been developed for the purpose of assessing an individual's patterns of interest in or preference for a variety of activities.

We should examine patterns of interest because

- Interest in a particular activity provides some motivation for engaging in that activity. Thus, the person concerned might have the degree of motivation necessary for following an activity.
- The scores obtained from an interest inventory are helpful in pointing out which groups of persons an individual resembles the closest.
- A relationship exists between a person's domain of interest and the occupational field that person may choose or has chosen.

Tools for Measuring Interest

The tools for measurement of interest are of two types

(i) **Formal** These are specialised and standardised measuring instruments such as interest inventories, interest test batteries etc.

(ii) **Informal** These include the person's own statement, a record of his activities and observation by parents and the teachers. Usually the informal methods supplement the formal methods.

Methods of Interest Inventories

Three significant formal methods employed are

(i) **Strong Vocational Interest Blank** Prof Strong of Stanford University designed and standardised this checklist, which contains 400 separate items including 100 occupations, 49 recreations, 36 school subjects, 48 activities and 47 peculiar interests, besides others.

The individual is asked to indicate whether he likes, dislikes or is indifferent to each of them on a three point scale. The test reveals the interest maturity of the individual, his masculinity/ femininity and his occupational level. It is useful for both educational and vocational guidance.

(ii) **Kuder Preference Record** This test, prepared by G Frederic Kuder, comprises of nine separate scales of occupations *i.e.* mechanical, computational, scientific, persuasive, artistic, literary, musical, social and clerical.

Kuder presupposed three major interests *i.e.* mechanical, literary and artistic. So, when the same task is presented to the subject with three related activities, the subject will select the activity that relates one of the three interests that he possesses.

For instance, three choices are given about one item *i.e.* building a bird house, writing articles about birds and drawing sketches about birds. If the subject opts for the first, his interest is mechanical and similarly for the other two choices, he is literary and artistic. There are many other such items in this test. A detailed scoring system is employed for analysis and interpretation. A percentile of 75 or above is considered significantly high. If a person goes beyond P75 in any of the areas, all the occupations in that area are attractive for him.

(iii) **Thurstone's Vocational Interest Schedule** Thurstone administered a comprehensive test to 3400 college students who expressed their Likeness (L), Indifference (I) and Dislike (D) to each of the items in the test. He analysed their test scores. Through the techniques of factor analysis, he arrived at 8 factors of interest *i.e.* Commercial Interest, Legal, Athletic, Academic, Descriptive, Biological, Physical Science and Art.

Other interest inventories which are sometimes used may have more than nine scales of occupations. Some of these are specialised for women only.

Limitations of Interest Inventories

All interest inventories have one or more limitations. *Some of these limitations are*

- Some of the tests reveal ability (*i.e.* achievement) instead of interest. So these tests are not fully valid or reliable.
- The tests assume that the test taker possesses a particular interest. But the test will only tell us the interest *i.e.* present at the time of testing, not at any other time afterwards. The interests revealed may not remain permanent. Moreover, interests are also cultivable. At the time of testing a particular interest may not have developed fully, but it may develop afterwards. It has been seen that some interests develop after the test taker actually starts working.
- The interest inventories reveal facts on the basis of the report given by the test taker. As some people do not reveal facts correctly, the accuracy of the report is not guaranteed.
- The questions in the inventories deal with certain types of activities. Not all of them will lead to clear-cut vocations. Further, overlapping exists between one activity and another. Actually an occupation is not one's interest but a combination of activities or interests.
- The predictive aspect of the inventories has also been tested. On investigation, proctor found that these have 25% permanence in school studies. Prof Strong found correlation with future vocation as 0.75 *i.e.* less than + 1.

Inspite of the above limitations, interest inventories are very useful in determining the future trends of the individual's vocational life.

Attitude Scales

Attitude can be defined as an enduring disposition to consistently respond in a given manner. However, as attitudes are related to self-image and social acceptance, people's responses to questions about their attitude on any issue may be affected by what attitudes are socially desirable. To create a positive self-image, people may not reveal their true attitudes, but answer in a way which they feel will be socially acceptable.

Three components of an attitude are

- **Affective** The feelings or emotions toward an object
- **Cognitive** Knowledge and beliefs
- **Behavioural** A predisposition to action, intentions, behavioural expectations

In social research, scaling techniques are used to measure attitude and behaviour. One can make judgment about any characteristic of an individual and place him at a suitable point on a scale which is measuring that characteristic. A scale represents a series of ordered steps at fixed intervals used as a standard of measurement.

Scales are used to rank people's judgments of objects, events or other people from low to high or from poor to good. Thus, attitude scales are designed to measure people's opinions on social issues.

An attitude scale is a special type of questionnaire designed to produce scores indicating the intensity and direction (for or against) of a person's feelings about an object or event. Such scales are used in attitude change experiments. In this, one group of people is asked to fill out the scale twice, once before some event, such as reading a persuasive argument and again afterwards.

A control group fills out the scale twice without reading the argument. The control group is used to measure exposure or practice effects. The change in the scores of the experimental group relative to the control group, whether their attitudes have become more or less favourable, indicates the effects of the argument.

Characteristics of Attitude Scales

Some important characteristics of attitude scales are

- These are used for measuring social attitudes of an individual towards a matter, thing, an object or system by responses to items in a questionnaire.
- On the basis of his responses, he is assigned a score which indicates the position.
- Some relevant and indirect statements can also be used to reveal the attitude.
- The scale also specifies the crucial shades of opinions.
- The simplest such scale has the respondent classifying the object/ issue/ product into one among two dichotomous categories.
- Attitude measurement scales can be categorised into unidimensional and multidimensional.
- Examples of single dimensional attitude measurement scales are graphical and numerical scales, summated scales, paired comparisons and equal-appearing intervals.

Types of Attitude Scales

Researchers have developed a variety of attitude rating scales to measure the intensity of an attitude's affective, cognitive and behavioural components. These scales may require a respondent to rank, rate, sort and choose when we assess an attitude. *The three commonly used attitude scales include semantic differential scale, stapel's scale and likert scale.*

Semantic Differential Scale

This scale measures respondents attitudes about the strengths and weaknesses of a concept or construct. With this scale, researchers select a pair of dichotomous adjectives to describe the concept under investigation. Typically, researchers use a scale from 1 to 7. The mean of each pair is calculated and then plotted on a table.

An example of construction of such a scale is

Below is a list of characteristics of a department store. For each pair of adjectives, place an 'X' at the point that you believe best reflects your experience at this department store.

	1	2	3	4	5	6	7	
Clean	—	—	—	—	—	—	—	Dirty
Dark	—	—	—	—	—	—	—	Wel lit
Poor quality	—	—	—	—	—	—	—	High quality
Innovative	—	—	—	—	—	—	—	Conservative
Convenient	—	—	—	—	—	—	—	Inconvenient

The Semantic Differential Scale Summary Chart of a typical response by a visitor to the department store may look as given below.

	1	2	3	4	5	6	7	
Clean	—	—	—	—	—	—	—	Dirty
Dark	—	—	—	—	—	—	—	Well lit
Poor quality	—	—	—	—	—	—	—	High quality
Innovative	—	—	—	—	—	—	—	Conservative
Convenient	—	—	—	—	—	—	—	Inconvenient

This scale is regularly used in marketing research because it is an efficient way to examine the differences in image attributes among a variety of brands or companies. *However, its limitations are*

- As there are no general scales, valid and reliable scales using suitable adjectives must be developed for each survey or research project.
- Researchers should be careful about a 'halo' effect, which will bias a respondent's answers. It means that a respondent's overall impression affects his views on a single adjective pair. To counteract the 'halo' effect, researchers do not place all the positive adjectives on the same side of the scale. In the above example, the positive adjectives 'clean', 'innovative' and 'convenient' have been put on the same side of the scale as the negative adjectives 'dark' and 'poor quality'.

Stapel's Scale

This scale was developed by **J Stapel**. It is a uni-polar scale which requires respondents to rate a concept on a scale of -5 to +5 on how closely an adjective given at the centre of the scale represents the concept. The major advantage of Stapel's scale is that the researcher does not have to create bipolar pairs.

An example of construction of such a scale is

Select a suitable positive number for the phrase that best represents attributes of the ABC mobile phone. If the phrase does not represent the ABC mobile phone, select a suitable negative number that reflects your attitude towards the phone.

High quality	Well designed	Easy to use
+ 5	+ 5	+ 5
+ 4	+ 4	+ 4
+ 3	+ 3	+ 3
+ 2	+ 2	+ 2
+ 1	+ 1	+ 1
− 1	− 1	− 1
− 2	− 2	− 2
− 3	− 3	− 3
− 4	− 4	− 4
− 5	− 5	− 5

Likert Scale

This scale allows respondents to state how strongly they agree or disagree with an attitude. The scale is named after Rensis Likert, who developed it.

Although the Likert scale was developed as a five-point scale ranging from 'strongly disagree' to 'neutral' to 'strongly agree', sometimes we may see a six-point or seven-point variation of it being used. A six-point Likert scale has three levels of disagreement and three levels of agreement with no neutral point. The seven-point Likert scale adds a neutral point.

An example of construction of such a scale is

My children love eating mangoes during summers

Strongly disagree	Disagree	Neutral	Agree	Strongly agree

Computer-Based Psychological Testing

Computers have been important to applied psychology since their introduction during the 1960s. The application of computerised methods has broadened subsequently in both scope and depth. Computers are mainly used in psychological testing for interpreting the test scores. This is called Computer-Based Test Interpretation (CBTI).

CBTI programs are used for a variety of psychological tests, such as clinical interviews or problem rating, but are most frequently used in psychological and neuropsychological assessments. *These programs are either empirically based or clinically based.*

- **Empirically Based Programs** These are also called *Actuarial Assessment programs*. They use statistical analysis, linear regression equations and Bayesian rules to interpret the data. These are all empirically based.
- **Clinically Based Programs** These are also called *Automated Assessment programs*. They consist of a series of if-then statements and rely on information from expert clinicians and research.

Although CBTI programs have high test-retest reliability, they are criticised for not being able to assess inter-rater reliability and internal consistency reliability. Extensive studies have not confirmed the validity of CBTI programs due to the varying reports of individual programs. However, CBTI programs are very efficient because they

- Save time
- Reduce human error
- Are cost effective
- Are objective/ reliable

However, their use is limited because they are not always used by adequately trained evaluators or are not integrated with multiple sources of data.

Advantages of CBTI

CBTI programs arguably have many benefits over traditional hand-scored assessments and clinician interpretations which may contribute to their popularity. *For example*

- CBTI programs save time and eliminate human responding and scoring errors.
- CBTI programs are often more comprehensive than clinician interpretation.
- Tend to be more reliable than clinician interpretation and are cost effective.
- They are more objective which may allow clients to easily accept feedback.

Disadvantages of CBTI

Despite these benefits, there are significant limitations of CBTIs to consider. *For example*

- CBTI reports may suggest an unwarranted impression of scientific precision and reports may be too general to provide differential information.
- CBTIs may promote exceedingly cavalier attitudes towards clinical assessment and interpretation and as they are increasingly available to inadequately trained evaluators, the potential for misuse is high.
- Clinicians are cautioned to educate themselves before using CBTI programs, not to blindly interpret computer-generated reports as true or use CBTIs as a way to circumvent their responsibilities.

EXAM BASED QUESTIONS

1 The three basic functions of intelligence do not include

(a) retaining knowledge (b) recognising problems
(c) solving problems (d) learning

2 Which one of the following is generally not used in the measurement of intelligence?

(a) Group tests (b) Non-verbal tests
(c) Projective tests (d) Individual tests

3 Guilford had originally divided intelligence at second order level into

(a) two parts (b) 120 parts
(c) more than a dozen parts (d) seven parts

4 Which one of the following is not used for measuring intelligence?

(a) Reaction time experiments
(b) Projective tests
(c) Psychometric tests
(d) Performance tests

5 Among the following which one is not a theory of intelligence?

(a) Coci's biological theory (b) Anderson's theory
(c) James-Lange theory (d) Gardner's theory

6 The theory mentioning 120 factors of intelligence was propounded by

(a) Guilford (b) Cattell
(c) Spearman (d) Thurstone

7 Structure of the intellect model was given by

(a) Jensen (b) Spearman
(c) Thurstone (d) Guilford

8 The theory of Level I and Level II intelligence was proposed by

(a) Jensen (b) Guilford
(c) Torrance (d) Eysenck

9 Intelligence Quotient (IQ) is a

(a) norm
(b) raw score
(c) score of verbal intelligence
(d) score of non-verbal intelligence

10 Among the following, which is not a performance test of intelligence?

(a) Picture arrangement (b) Finger-dexterity
(c) Object assembly (d) Picture completion

11 The chronological age that most typically corresponds to a given level of performance in an IQ test is called

(a) Intelligence quotient (b) Maturation
(c) Mental age (d) None of these

12 In the Stanford-Binet Intelligence Test, a person with C A of 40 years has the M A of 20 years. The person was intellectually

(a) below average (b) average
(c) above average (d) a genius

13 The concept of mental age in calculating IQ was given by

(a) Cattell (b) Galton
(c) Spearman (d) Binet

14 There are five sub-tests in the performance battery of WAIS. Identify the correct order in which they are administered.

(a) DS, PC, BD, OA, PA (b) PC, BD, OA, PA, DS
(c) DS, PC, BD, PA, OA (d) OS, PC, PA, BD, DA

15 Weschler Adult Intelligence scale is used to assess

(a) social intelligence (b) abstract intelligence
(c) global intelligence (d) emotional intelligence

16 Which one of the following sub-tests is not part of Wechsler Adult Intelligence scale?

(a) Information (b) Vocabulary
(c) Creativity (d) Digit symbol

17 Wechsler Adult Intelligence scale has eleven sub-tests out of which

(a) five are performance and six are verbal
(b) seven are verbal and four are performance
(c) four are verbal and seven are performance
(d) six are performance and five are verbal

18 For an intelligence test, while computing item-remainder correlations for item analysis, we compute

(a) Phi-coefficient (b) Spearman rho
(c) Tetrachoric correlation (d) Point-biserial correlation

19 The IQ score for a developmentally disabled person categorised as 'severe' will be

(a) between 50 and 70
(b) between 50 and 35
(c) between 35 and 20
(d) below 20

20 Culture-Fair Intelligence Test developed by Cattell is a

(a) performance test (b) power test
(c) speed test (d) None of these

21 Cattell's Culture Fair Intelligence Test is an example of

(a) verbal test
(b) speed test
(c) power test
(d) speed cum power test

22 Which one of the following statements indicates the true relation between intelligence and creativity?
(a) Intelligence and creativity have a high correlation.
(b) Intelligence and creativity have a low correlation.
(c) Intelligence and creativity have a moderate correlation.
(d) Intelligence and creativity have higher correlation at the lower level than at a higher level of intelligence.

23 In which a person begins with multiple ideas and reaches one solution?
(a) Vertical thinking (b) Brainstorming
(c) Divergent thinking (d) Convergent thinking

24 Creativity is measured on the dimension of
(a) originality (b) applicability
(c) flexibility (d) All of these

25 A type of thinking in which a person searches for multiple ideas or solutions is known as
(a) divergent thinking (b) vertical thinking
(c) ideational fluency (d) convergent thinking

26 The factor which detracts us from solving a problem is
(a) flexibility (b) divergent thinking
(c) set (d) goal

27 Which of the following cannot be the necessary characteristic of a creative person?
(a) Self assertive (b) Independent in judgment
(c) Follows rules (d) Prefers complexity

28 Which one of the following is Torrance's test of creative thinking?
(a) Something About Myself (SAM)
(b) Incomplete figures
(c) Remote associates
(d) Artistic-Assessment

29 Which one of the following is not a neuropsychological test?
(a) Bender Visual Motor Gestalt (BVMG) Test
(b) Halstead-Reitan Neuropsychological Test Battery (HRNB)
(c) Autism Spectrum Test (AST)
(d) Ammons Quick Test (AQT)

30 Which among the following is/are neurological problem?
(a) ADHD
(b) dyslexia
(c) autism
(d) All of the above

31 Which among the following is/are neurological test?
(a) Ammons Quict Test
(b) Beder Visual Motor Gestalt
(c) Halstead-Reitan Neuropsychological Test Battery (HRNB)
(d) All of the above

32 The Watson Glaser Critical Thinking Test is used for testing
(a) intelligence (b) aptitude (c) attitude (d) personality

33 The actual power to perform a mental or physical task which is gained by training is known as
(a) achievement (b) ability (c) attitude (d) aptitude

34 Which one of the following tests does not measure aptitude?
(a) GATB (b) TAT (c) FACT (d) DAT

35 Which one of the following dimensions is not measured by Revised NEO Personality Inventory?
(a) Extraversion (b) Conscientiousness
(c) Neuroticism (d) Psychoticism

36 Which one of the following factors is not included in the 'big five' dimensions of personality?
(a) Extraversion (b) Neuroticism
(c) Agreeableness (d) Dominance

37 Which one of the following traits is not a part of the 'big-five' personality traits?
(a) Self assertiveness (b) Conscientiousness
(c) Openness to experience (d) Agreeableness

38 A psychotic person would probably score the highest on which MMPI-2 scale?
(a) Depression (b) Hysteria
(c) Schizophrenia (d) Mania

39 NEO Pi-R Personality Inventory is based on which approach?
(a) Behaviouristic (b Cognitive
(c) Trait (d) Psycho-dynamic

40 The Eysenck Personality Inventory (EPI) has the dimension(s) of
(a) extraversion only
(b) extraversion and neuroticism only
(c) neuroticism only
(d) extraversion, neuroticism and lie only

41 The Trait Theory of Personality was developed by
(a) Freud (b) Kurt Lewin (c) Eysenck (d) Allport

42 The personality theory of Eysenck does not include
(a) extraversion (b) openness
(c) psychoticism (d) neuroticism

43 The most commonly used and popular method for personality measurement is
(a) projective (b) psychometric
(c) sociometric (d) ethnographic

44 The Thematic Apperception Test was devised by
(a) AH Maslow (b) CR Rogers
(c) H Rorschach (d) HA Murray

45 The TAT is low on validity and reliability
(a) low on both validity and reliability
(b) high on both validity and reliability
(c) low on validity but high on reliability
(d) high on validity but low on reliability

46 Location in Rorschach test is concerned with
(a) whole/ part (b) fantasy/ emotion
(c) colour/ movement (d) figure/ landscape

47 Among the following, which one is not a projective test?
(a) Minnesota Multiphasic Personality Inventory
(b) Somatic Inkblot Systems
(c) Thematic Apperception Test
(d) Rorschach Inkblot Test

48 In Rorschach Inkblot Test, responses reflect our inner
(a) conflicts (b) experiences
(c) feelings (d) conflicts and feelings

49 An interest inventory measures a person's
(a) ability to perform a particular task
(b) liking for a particular task
(c) potential to perform a particular task in the future
(d) chances of success in performing a particular task

50 The accuracy of the reports on interest inventories is not guaranteed because
(a) some people do not reveal facts correctly
(b) some interests develop after the test taker actually starts working
(c) Both a and b
(d) Neither a nor b

51 Which one of the following is not a formal tool used for measurement of interest?
(a) Kuder Preference Record
(b) Thurstone's Vocational Interest Schedule
(c) Strong Vocational Interest Blank
(d) Predictive Test Inventory

52 The measurement of weight of children is an example of a/ an
(a) interval scale (b) ratio scale
(c) nominal scale (d) ordinal scale

53 Which one of the following is not an important characteristic of attitude scales?
(a) The simplest scale has the respondent classifying the object into one out of two categories
(b) Some relevant and indirect statements can also be used to reveal the attitude
(c) They can be categorised into unidimensional and multidimensional
(d) None of the above

54 Arbitrary zero is the characteristic of the
(a) ratio scale (b) ordinal scale
(c) interval scale (d) nominal scale

55 Which one of the following is a uni-polar scale?
(a) Ammons Quick Test
(b) Stapel's Attitude Scale
(c) Eysenck Personality Questionnaire
(d) Kuder Preference Record

56 The method of summated ratings was developed in attitude scale construction by
(a) Thurstone (b) Bogardus
(c) Likert (d) Thorndike

57 Which one of the following is not correctly matched?
(a) Osgood : Semantic Differential
(b) Likert : Rating Scale
(c) Bogardus : Social distance
(d) Guttman : Equal-appearing intervals

58 Likert scale is a type of
(a) Intelligence test (b) Aptitude test
(c) Attitude scale (d) None of the above

59 Which test measure respondents attitudes about the strengths and weaknesses of a concept or construct?
(a) tapel's Scale
(b) Semantic differential scale
(c) Likert Scale
(d) None of the above

60 Which scale allow respondents to state how strongly they agree or disagree with an attitude?
(a) Stapel's scale
(b) Likert scale
(c) Semantic differential scale
(d) None of the above

61 CBTI programs are used for
(a) neuropsychological assessments
(b) problem rating
(c) clinical interviews
(d) All of the above

62 The two types of CBTI programs are
(a) empirically based and actuarial assessment
(b) clinically based and automated assessment
(c) actuarial assessment and automated assessment
(d) None of the above

63 Why is use of CBTI programs limited?
(a) Because they are used by trained evaluators
(b) Because they are not integrated with multiple sources of data
(c) Both a and b
(d) Neither a nor b

64 CBTI programs are very efficient because they
(a) save time and reduce human error
(b) are able to assess inter-rater reliability
(c) are able to assess internal consistency reliability
(d) have high validity and reliability

65 CBTI programs are mainly used for
(a) testing and classify attitudes
(b) testing and determining dimensions of personality
(c) interpreting the test scores in psychological testing
(d) All of the above

Directions (Q. Nos. 66-81) *In the questions given below are two statements labelled as Assertion (A) and Reason (R). In the context of the two statements, which one of the following is correct?*

Codes

(a) Both A and R are true and R is the correct explanation of A
(b) Both A and R are true, but R is not the correct explanation of A
(c) A is true, but R is false
(d) A is false, but R is true

66 Assertion (A) Intelligent people are more creative.

Reason (R) Intelligence and creativity are positively related.

67 Assertion (A) A 40 years old man may have the same IQ as that of a 20 years old.

Reason (R) The 40 years old man could have been somewhat retarded to start with.

68 Assertion (A) Paired comparison scaling is not suitable for scaling a large number of items.

Reason (R) With a large number of items, the number of possible pairs of items would be very large and experimentally inconvenient.

69 Assertion (A) Personality traits measured by 16 PF are source traits.

Reason (R) Cattell used oblique rotation to identify personality traits.

70 Assertion (A) Scales are an indirect method of measuring attitudes.

Reason (R) Scales can measure all aspects of human behaviour.

71 Assertion (A) Creativity self-assessment tests allow respondents to assess their creative intelligence by answering questions.

Reason (R) Khatena-Torrance Creative Perception Inventory is one such test.

72 Assertion (A) Most neuropsychological tests presently being used are based on traditional psychometric theory.

Reason (R) Neuropsychological tests cannot test for disorders such as neurological problems such as ADHD, dyslexia and autism spectrum.

73 Assertion (A) Aptitude tests are often unable to assess academic potential or career suitability.

Reason (R) Numerical Reasoning, Verbal Analogies and Number Sequences are aptitude tests.

74 Assertion (A) Objective tests or self-report measures of personality are generally free of bias by raters.

Reason (R) These tests rely on an individual's personal responses.

75 Assertion (A) The MBTI test of personality is based on Freud's theory of personality.

Reason (R) It is designed to measure personality traits using the five factor model.

76 Assertion (A) Responses to the MMPI-2 are scored to produce a clinical profile of the test taker composed of 10 scales.

Reason (R) These scales include hysteria, paranoia and schizophrenia.

77 Assertion (A) The Sixteen Personality Factor Inventory is based on Eysenck's theory.

Reason (R) This test is not useful for career and occupational selection.

78 Assertion (A) The Rorschach Inkblot Test consists of twelve inkblots which were created by Herman Rorschach.

Reason (R) This test is useful for examining a person's personality characteristics and emotional functioning.

79 Assertion (A) Objective tests of personality have more validity than projective tests.

Reason (R) They are relatively free from the influence of the examiner's own beliefs or rater bias.

80 Assertion (A) Interest inventories are not fully valid or reliable.

Reason (R) Some of the tests reveal achievement instead of interest.

81 Assertion (A) The usual educational evaluation is aimed at maximising examiner variance.

Reason (R) Examiner variance is reduced with higher inter-scorer reliability.

82 For personality assessment, different projective techniques are used, both pictorial and non-pictorial. *These are*

1. Figure Drawing Test
2. Rorschach Inkblot Test
3. Word Association Test
4. Thematic Apperception Test

Which two of the above are non-pictorial tests?

(a) 2 and 4 (b) 1 and 4
(c) 1 and 3 (d) 3 and 4

83 **Arrange the following tests with respect to their ability to elicit projective responses from low to high.**

1. Sentence Completion Test
2. Rorschach Inkblot Test
3. Rosenzweig Picture Frustration Study
4. Thematic Apperception Test

Codes

(a) 2, 4, 3, 1 (b) 1, 3, 4, 2
(c) 4, 2, 1, 3 (d) 2, 1 4, 3

84 **Arrange the following in the order in which they were developed.**

1 Bar-On's EQ-i questionnaire
2 Binet's test of intelligence
3 Eysenck's Personality Inventory
4 Thematic Apperception Test

Codes

(a) 1, 2, 4, 3 (b) 3, 1, 2, 4
(c) 2, 4, 3, 1 (d) 4, 3, 1, 2

85 **An interval scale of measurement contains**

1. properties of normal and ordinal scales
2. true zero point
3. comparable differences between different intervals of the scale
4. a minimum requirement for use of parametric tests

Codes

(a) 1, 2, 3 and 4 (b) 1 and 2
(c) 1, 2 and 4 (d) 1, 3 and 4

86 **Which of the following scaling methods have been developed by Thurstone?**

1 Method of paired comparison
2 Method of summated ratings
3 Method of successive intervals
4 Equal appearing intervals method

Codes

(a) Only 2 (b) 2 and 3
(c) 1, 2 and 4 (d) 2, 3 and 4

87 **The theories of intelligence appeared in which one of the following orders?**

(a) Binet-Simon, Thurstone, RB Cattell, Spearman
(b) Binet-Simon, Spearman, Thurstone, RB Cattell
(c) Spearman, Binet-Simon, Thurstone, RB Cattell
(d) RB Cattell, Binet-Simon, Thurstone, Spearman

88 **Which of the following are needed for creativity?**

1. Focused recall
2. Identification of problem
3. Contrary recognition
4. Observing specific rules

Codes

(a) 1, 3 and 4 (b) 1, 2 and 4
(c) 1, 2 and 3 (d) 2, 3 and 4

89 **Which of the following tests are considered to be culture-fair tests of intelligence?**

1. Cattell's Culture-Fair Test of Intelligence
2. Raven's Progressive Matrices
3. Wechsler's Intelligence Scale for Children
4. Goodenough-Harris Test

Codes

(a) Only 1 (b) 1 and 2
(c) 1, 2 and 3 (d) 1, 2 and 4

90 **Identify the correct chronological sequence of the approaches used in assessment of intelligence.**

1. Culture Fair Testing
2. Psychometric Approach
3. Biological Approach
4. Chronometric Analysis

Codes

(a) 4, 3, 2, 1 (b) 4, 2, 3, 1 (c) 1, 2, 3, 4 (d) 2, 1, 3, 4

91 **Identify the correct concepts related with Cattell's theory of personality.**

1. Dynamic Lattice
2. Specification Equation
3. Orthogonal Rotation
4. Ergs

Codes

(a) 2, 3 and 4 (b) 1, 2 and 4
(c) 2 and 4 (d) 1, 2, 3 and 4

92 **Which of the following can be employed to assess the vocational interests of the subjects in guidance and counselling?**

1 EPPS 2 SVIB
3 DAT 4 GATB

Codes

(a) 2, 3 and 4 (b) 3 and 4
(c) 1 and 2 (d) Only 2

93 **Match the following**

List I (Test Name)	List II (Its Inventor)
A. TAT	1. Cattell
B. PF Test	2. Rosenzweig
C. Draw a man	3. Murray
D. 16 PF	4. Bender

Codes

	A	B	C	D		A	B	C	D
(a)	4	1	2	3	(b)	3	2	4	1
(c)	1	4	3	2	(d)	2	3	1	4

94 **Match the following**

List I	List II
A. Aptitude	1. Two factor theory
B. Hereditary	2. WAIS
C. Spearman	3. Special ability
D. Measurement of intelligence	4. Genes

Codes

	A	B	C	D		A	B	C	D
(a)	3	4	1	2	(b)	4	3	2	1
(c)	3	1	2	4	(d)	1	2	3	4

95 Match the following

List I (Author)	List II (Test)
A. Murray	1. Word Association Test
B. Eysenck	2. Culture Fair Intelligence Test
C. Cattell	3. Thematic Apperception Test
D. Kent-Rosanoff	4. Maudsley Personality Inventory

Codes

	A	B	C	D
(a)	2	3	1	4
(b)	3	2	1	4
(c)	4	3	2	1
(d)	3	4	2	1

96 Match the following

List I (Types of Thinking)	List II (Characteristics)
A. Autistic thinking	1. Reasoning
B. Realistic thinking	2. Drawing facts
C. Convergent thinking	3. Unusual uses
D. Creative thinking	4. Fantasy

Codes

	A	B	C	D		A	B	C	D
(a)	1	3	4	2	(b)	3	1	2	4
(c)	2	1	3	4	(d)	4	3	2	1

97 Match the following

List I (Test)	List II (Associated with)
A. Eysenck Personality Questionnaire	1. Objective
B. MMPI -2 -RF	2. Projective
C. TAT	3. Developed in 2008
D. 16 PF	4. Cattell's theory

Codes

	A	B	C	D
(a)	3	4	1	2
(b)	4	3	2	1
(c)	3	1	2	4
(d)	1	3	2	4

98 Match the following

List I (Methods)	List II (Characteristics)
A. Thurstone's Vocational Interest Schedule	1. Formal
B. Record of the subject's activities	2. Informal
C. Strong Vocational Interest Blank	3. Eight factors of interest
D. Kuder Preference Record	4. Checklist contains 400 separate items

Codes

	A	B	C	D		A	B	C	D
(a)	3	4	1	2	(b)	3	2	4	1
(c)	3	2	1	4	(d)	1	2	3	4

99 Match the following

List I (Behavioural)	List II (Property)
A. Attitude	1. Component of attitude
B. Affective	2. Designed to measure people's opinions
C. Attitude scales	3. Emotions toward an object
D. Behavioural	4. Measured by scaling techniques

Codes

	A	B	C	D		A	B	C	D
(a)	4	3	2	1	(b)	3	2	4	1
(c)	3	2	1	4	(d)	1	2	3	4

100 Match the following

List I (Scale)	List II (Characteristics)
A. Stapel's Scale	1. May have 5, 6 or 7 points
B. CBTI scale	2. Ratings vary from -5 to +5
C. Likert Scale	3. A 'halo' effect will bias a respondent's answers
D. Semantic Differential Scale	4. Not an attitude scale

Codes

	A	B	C	D		A	B	C	D
(a)	1	4	2	3	(b)	3	2	4	1
(c)	2	4	1	3	(d)	3	4	2	1

Directions (Q. Nos 101-105) *Read the passage given below and answer the following questions.*

Employers choose to use psychometric testing during their recruitment process to help give a better overall evaluation of candidate's and their suitability for the job that they are applying for. Psychometric testing could help to gauge the future performance of candidate's and also improve employee retention by making successful hiring decisions.

Preparing for an assessment centre or online aptitude test can be stressful due to the fact that you don't know what to expect. The best way to familiarise yourself is with practice aptitude tests, available from commercial organisations, which mimic the tests used by employers and recruiters. Such tests offer realistic test simulations with fully worked solutions.

In-Tray and E-Tray exercises are used in combination with other selection techniques, such as psychometric tests (numerical reasoning, verbal reasoning etc.), group exercises, presentations, case study interviews and role play exercises. This means that the performance in all exercises included in the selection procedure are taken into account. So don't worry if you didn't perform your best in one of the tests; performance on others may make up for this. However, it must be noted that due to the character and workplace relevance of this exercise it is widely regarded as a reliable tool for selection purposes and performance on this specific exercise could be an important factor in the decision making process.

101 **Psychometric testing is used during the recruitment process by employers to**
(a) evaluate the candidate's suitability for the job
(b) gauge the past performance of candidates
(c) weed out candidates with personality problems
(d) All of the above

102 **The best way for a candidate to familiarise himself with aptitude tests is to**
(a) mimic the tests used by employers
(b) practice on tests available from commercial organisations
(c) take help from an assessment centre
(d) All of the above

103 **In-Tray and E-Tray exercises are widely regarded as a reliable tool for selection purposes because**
(a) of their on-line nature
(b) of their use by recruiters
(c) of their relevance to the work place
(d) All of the above

104 **Which one of the following is not a selection technique used by recruiters?**
(a) Psychometric tests
(b) Attitude tests
(c) In-Tray and E-Tray exercises
(d) Role play exercises

105 **Aptitude tests available from commercial organisations offer**
(a) case study interviews
(b) questions without answers
(c) group exercises
(d) realistic test simulations

ANSWERS

1 (a)	2 (c)	3 (b)	4 (b)	5 (c)	6 (a)	7 (d)	8 (b)	9 (d)	10 (b)
11 (c)	12 (a)	13 (d)	14 (c)	15 (b)	16 (c)	17 (a)	18 (d)	19 (c)	20 (a)
21 (a)	22 (d)	23 (d)	24 (d)	25 (a)	26 (b)	27 (a)	28 (b)	29 (c)	30 (d)
31 (d)	32 (b)	33 (b)	34 (b)	35 (d)	36 (d)	37 (a)	38 (c)	39 (c)	40 (b)
41 (c)	42 (b)	43 (a)	44 (d)	45 (a)	46 (a)	47 (a)	48 (c)	49 (b)	50 (c)
51 (d)	52 (h)	53 (d)	54 (a)	55 (b)	56 (c)	57 (d)	58 (c)	59 (b)	60 (a)
61 (d)	62 (c)	63 (b)	64 (a)	65 (a)	66 (d)	67 (a)	68 (a)	69 (c)	70 (c)
71 (b)	72 (d)	73 (d)	74 (a)	75 (d)	76 (b)	77 (d)	78 (d)	79 (a)	80 (a)
81 (d)	82 (c)	83 (b)	84 (c)	85 (d)	86 (b)	87 (c)	88 (c)	89 (d)	90 (b)
91 (b)	92 (d)	93 (b)	94 (a)	95 (d)	96 (c)	97 (d)	98 (b)	99 (a)	100 (c)
101 (a)	102 (b)	103 (c)	104 (b)	105 (d)					

Applications of Psychological Testing

Psychological tests find numerous applications in the field of education, health, military, counselling and industry. These tests by assessing various mental abilities and attributes of an individual helps in the development of these fields.

Psychological Testing

Psychological tests are formalised measures of Mental functioning. Most of the psychological tests are objective and quantifiable. However, certain projective tests may involve some level of subjective interpretation, also known as *inventories, measurements, questionnaires* and *scales*. Psychological tests are administered in a variety of settings, including preschools, primary and secondary schools, colleges and universities, hospitals, militaries and other agencies. They come in a variety of formats, including written, verbal and computer administered.

Psychological tests are used to assess a variety of mental abilities and attributes, including achievement ability, personality and neurological functioning. Personality tests are administered for a wide variety of reasons, from diagnosing psychopathology (*e.g.* personality disorder, depressive disorder) to screening job candidates.

They may be used in an educational setting to determine personality strengths and weaknesses. For children, academic achievement, ability and intelligence tests may be used as tools in school placement, in determining the presence of a learning disability or a developmental delay, in identifying giftedness, or in tracking intellectual development. Intelligence testing may also be used with teens and young adults to determine vocational ability (*e.g.* in career counselling).

In this Chapter

- *Psychological Testing*
- *Psychological Testing in Clinical Setting*
- *Psychological Testing in Organisation and Business*
- *Psychological Testing in Education*
- *Psychological Testing in Counselling*
- *Psychological Testing in Military*
- *Psychological Testing in Career Guidance*

Psychological Testing in Clinical Setting

Clinical assessment has a long history in the field of mental health. Psychological assessment helps in determining mental health of an individual. The use of psychological test in clinical setting is guided by three models of mental health, *which are as follows.*

(i) **Information Gathering Model** It is used by the practitioner of mental health when they use psychological tests to collect information for the diagnosis of mental problem.

(ii) **Therapeutical Model** It involves the use of psychological tests to provide new experiences and information to the client, which he can use for self discovery, personal growth and development. So, in the therapeutic model, tests basically act as a tool of intervention to bring out positive changes in the patient.

(iii) **Differential Treatment Model** It represents the use of test for conducting research and evaluating the outcome of the intervention programmes.

These three models provide a complete psychological intervention when they are combined in the same order as presented above.

Clinical assessment is a way of diagnosing and planning treatment for a patient that involves evaluating someone in order to figure out what is wrong. Psychological tests enable mental health professionals to make diagnoses more reliably, validly and quickly which allows the clinician to focus on appropriate treatment. Once a course of treatment has begun, the psychological tests can help the clinician to –

- monitor effectiveness of treatment.
- monitor a persons response to medications.
- track progress during course of treatment to determine if a person is receiving correct dosage and is responding correctly to medication.

There are many types of psychological assessments, which are as follows.

(i) **Intelligence and Achievement Tests** These tests are designed to measure certain specific kinds of cognitive funtioning (IQ). These tests such as Wechlser tests attempts to measure traits such as general knowledge, verbal skill, memory, attention span, logical reasoning and visual/spatial perception.

(ii) **Personality Tests** Tests of personality aim to describe patterns of behaviour, thoughts and feelings. It helps in analysis of personality disorders. These include objective and projective tests. Objective tests, such as Minnesota Multiphasic Personality Inventory, are based on restricted answers such as yes/no, true/ false or rating scale the allow for computation of scores. Projective tests such as Rorschach Inkblot test are based on ambiguous stimuli which allow scope of open- ended answers.

(iii) **Neuropsychological Tests** These tests are used to measure psychological function known to be linked to a particular brain structure or pathway. They are useful for screening patients for signs of neurological disorder and determine whether a particular treatment is working properly or not.

(iv) **Clinical Observation** Clinical psychologists are trained to gather data by observing behaviour. The clinical interview is a vital part of assessment which can employ either a structured or an unstructred format.

A clinical interview is a discussion in which psychologist asks specific, open-ended questions in order to assess a client's thoughts, behaviours and feelings. Such assessment focus on certain areas such as general appearance and behaviour, mood, perception, comprehension, orientation, insight, memory and content of communication.

Psychotheraphy

Psychotherapy involves a formal relationship between a professional and a client (individual, couple, family or small group) that employs a set of procedures to form a therapeutic alliance, explore nature of psychological problems and determine new ways of thinking, feeling or behaving.

The variour psychotherapies include

- **Psychodynamic Psychotherapy** This developed out of psychoanlysis of Sigmund Freud. It involves examination of transference and defences, appreciation of power of the unconscious and focus on how early developments in childhood have shaped client's current psychological state.
- **Humanistic Psychotherapy** This involves realisation of inbuilt potentials and resources of an individual to help build a stronger personality and self- concept.
- **Behavioural and Cognitive Psychotheraphy** It is based on how an individual thinks (cognition), feels (emotion) and acts (behaviour). It involves discovering and identifying the biased, dysfunctional ways of reacting to help clients transcend these in ways that will lead to increased well-being.

- **Systems or Family Therapy** It involves working with couples and families and emphasising family relations as an important factor in psychological health. It involves improving communication, establishing healthy roles, creating alternative narrative and addressing problematic behaviours.
- **Existential Psychotherapy** It deals with the fundamental issues of life, such as death, loneliness and freedom. It emphasises on client's ability to be self-aware, freely make choices, establish personal identity and social relationships and cope with natural anxiety of living.
- **Gestalt Therapy** It was developed by Fritz Perls in 1950s. It is designed to increase self-awareness.
- **Transpersonal Therapy** It is concerned with helping clients achieve their highest potential.

Psychological Testing in Organisation and Business

Industrial and organisational psychology is the field that applies psychological principles to work related issues. In case of business organisations, psychological tests are used mainly at two stages-first in the pre-employment phase and second, in the form of various performance appraisal tools done after the employment. Psychological evaluations can be used in employee screening, succession planning, managerial selection, pre-employment decisions and employee counselling situations.

Formal testing begins with an interview wherein information regarding the suitability of a candidate is assessed by the interviewer, in which the interviewer follows a standardised format of questions in a set order. The information received by formal interviews is systematic and its validity is high. Successful candidates can be assessed by using psychological tests for their polytonality traits, cognitive skill, ethical values, and social and interpersonal skills. Psychological tests and various rating scales are very useful instruments for the performance appraisal of employees.

Apart from this, psychological tests can be used for management development programmes, leadership development trainings and other areas of training and development. Psychological tests assess intellecutual level, problem solving ability, creative abilities, personality and emotional functioning, managerial style, decision-making ability, organisational skills, leadership abilities and adaptability. *There are several applications to psychometric tests in an organisational context which are–*

- Recruitments
- Organisational Planning
- Employee Engagement
- Training and Development
- Performance Evaluation

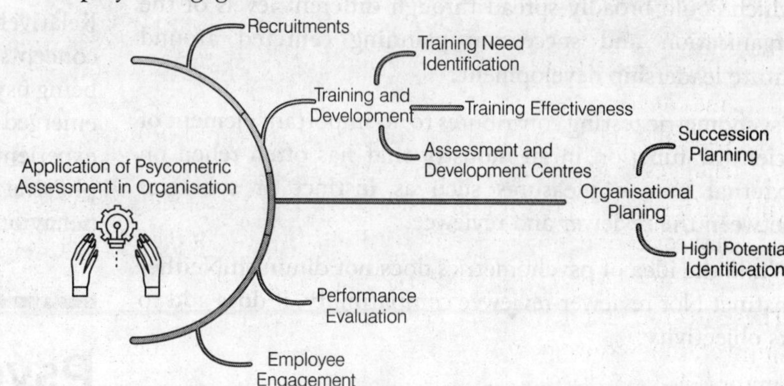

Application of Psychometric Assessment in Organisation

Psychological Test in Recruitment

There's wide variation in workforce performance across jobs. This makes it important to understand the differences among individuals that systematically affect job performance, ensuring candidates with the greatest probability for success being hired. Psychological assessment can protect the organisation by eliminating candidates that are not suitable for organization. It helps to recognise talent, potential, abilitities and deficiencies of an individual.

Psychological Test in Training and Development

Psychological tests give a better understanding of person's work performance and personality issues and to design a plan for their training.

Training need identification that utilises psychometric tests that must remain focused on the effectiveness of the enterprise as a whole. It targets discrepancies that reveal the skills or knowledge required to bridge gaps. The test must take into account factors such as new environmental policies, changing workforce dynamics, demographics and the economy. When working through a training, identification of the need ranks fairly high in importance. A prime focus on each kind of training - albeit task based, industry based or job based is necessary to determine the best course of action for the enterprise.

Psychological Test in Organisational Planning

When it comes to organisational planning, a lot of weight is given to employees at different stages of their employee lifecycle.

It mostly covers segments of high potential identification, which could broadly spread through different levels of the organisation and succession planning centered around future leadership development.

Psychometric testing contributes to an important element of scientific function in an industry that has often relied on external human measures such as instinct or synergies between the reviewer and reviewee.

While the idea of psychometrics does not diminish Neither instinct Nor reviewer-reviewee compatibility, it does add to its objectivity.

Psychological Test in Performance Evaluation

It is important to note that in the matter of performance evaluation, job performance is subject to social and organisational influences.

This is indicative of something known as *effective job behaviour*, but what constitutes good from poor performance relies entirely on organisational context.

For example– The armed forces place a ton of importance on performance metrics such as military bearings. It signified the appearance and mentality of a serviceman, covering meticulous attributes such as ironed uniforms, properly worn equipment, manner of behaviour in and out of formation and more.

Likewise, a mechanic would be evaluated a little differently than military personnel by a car dealership. So, experts suggest the inclusion of descriptions based on job complexity for the purpose of appraisal namely situational factors that interact or influence behaviour, job outcomes and job behaviour. Psychological tests help to monitor individual's growth over time, better understands a person's work performance and discovers whether an employee is suitable for promotion or managerial work.

Psychological Test in Employee Engagement

In an organisational context, there is often the case of employee burnout which is a situation of emotional exhaustion, lack of personal attribution or accomplishment and depersonalisation. Around the early 1980s, psychometric research led to the development of the Maslach-Burnout Inventory (MBI) designed to measure burnout.

Typically restrained to the evaluation of human services, research later led to the making of the MBI-General Survey (MBI-GS), a newer version to include all employees and not merely those in industries of people work.

Relatively little attention has been directed toward concepts considered antipodes of burnout; an exception being psychological presence be invested fully. The thought emerged from role theory and is often defined as an experiential state that channels energies into cognitive, physical and emotional labours using personally engaging behaviours.

Psychological Testing in Education

Psychological tests play an important role in educational settings and their role is likely to continue to increase in future. Assessment has always been an integral part of education.

However, current educational environment demands a great emphasis on the psychological aspects of the teaching-learning process. The scientific understanding of behaviour and mental processes as derived from psychology, can be operationalised for effective and empowering education that is needed in 21st century through the use of appropriate psychological tests.

Educators as Assess-Mentors

Assessment is generally taken as synonymous to evaluation in the areas of psychology and education, which has essentially become a passive concept. The modern requirements are that of educators playing a more positive role in assessing their students and offering counselling, guidance or mentoring to them as well. This will make assessment a more likely and fruitful enterprise and so ultimately assessment is to be finally replaced by assess-mentoring.

Assess-mentoring is a science, which involves careful and objective measurement of behavioural, psychological and educational attributes of the students and mentoring the students by providing them with active feedback and support, based on the previously mentioned type of assessment. Such assessment begins at the entrance test level and includes the assessment of abilities, personality assessment and assessment of career, guidance and placements.

Importance of Psychological Tests in Schools

Many parents, teachers and school administrators regard psychological testing in schools as an advantageous practice that supports children in achieving success in school. If children have undiagnosed psychological, emotional or behavioural difficulties, psychological testing can detect these challenges and help schools place students in the best learning environments to meet their needs. Psychological testing can also be used to benefit kids with previously diagnosed conditions and to place them in classrooms where they can be challenged and motivated to grow both intellectually and personally. *The key benefits of using psychological test in school are–*

Identifies Weaknesses and Strengths

Norm-referenced and group-administered achievement tests are the most common types administered in schools. The test results are used to determine a child's potential for achievement and to identify strengths and weaknesses. Once a test administrator determines the test results, he can pinpoint areas where the student needs further instruction. If a child's test reveals he needs to enhance his math skills, but his ability to comprehend mathematics is subpar, he may be put into a specialised math class designed to bring him up to the level of his peers.

Supports Individualised Lesson Plans

Psychological testing in schools can identify students with disabilities or delayed skills and determine their eligibility for receiving individualised lesson plans free of charge to families. The Individualised Education Program or IEP allows parents to work with educators to craft lesson plans that help the child become successful in school.

The student may also get a number of special support services, depending on the outcome of his psychological test. If a child's test determines that he is a visual learner with emotional problems, a specialised series of lesson plans can be applied to the child's education to make him more successful as he works through his challenges.

Enables Placement Decisions

Schools will always try to place disabled students in a class of their non-disabled peers. This is known as a *Least Restrictive Environment* or LRE.Federal law dictates that disabled students must be educated with their non-disabled peers whenever possible. The school psychologist, school administration and parents take the test results into account when determining the best way to meet the child's academic and emotional needs. When a child demonstrates handicaps in reading and shows severe insecurities in larger groups of his non-disabled peers, he may be placed in a smaller classroom of remedial learners until further testing reveals that he is able to move into a traditional classroom.

Monitors Progress

Psychological testing in schools allows for Curriculum-Based Measurement or CBM, in which a student's academic progress is monitored from elementary school through high school. Test outcomes are used to monitor the learning abilities and decision-making abilities of students in both general and special education. CBM helps estimate a student's improvement rate, identifies those who are dragging in progress. Therefore it requires alternative methods of learning and helps to design more effective individualised lessons for students with special challenges. By using psychological tests to monitor a student's progress, children are able to learn in ways according to their current conditions.

Psychological Testing in Counselling

The counselling process is a continuous and cyclical model in which the counsellor and client set goals, formulate action plans and assess progress towards goal. Psychological tests have helped in the process of counselling. The integration and informed application of principles derived from basic psychological sciences such as differential, vocational, developmental and social psychology have led to development of counselling psychology.

Counselling psychologists try to gain understanding of how each individual thinks, feels and acts to help individual to make informed choices in field of education, career and social relations. It helps them attain emotional moral, mental, aesthetic and spiritual well-being. Counselling psychology research and practice is concerned with the influence of social cognitive process on

- People's attitudes *e.g.* in-group bias
- Perceptions *e.g.* fundamental attribution error and unrealistic optimism
- Decision-making *e.g.* judgemental overconfidence and illusory correlation.
- Individual behaviour e.g. conformity, obedience and social facilitation.

Thus, psychological counselling helps in better health, adjustments, better family relation, undertanding of one's interests and informed career decisions.

Assessment Procedures Used by Counselling Psychologists

Testing and assessment are not the same; much psychological assessment does not involve the formal use of objective or projective techniques. More than 80% of counselling psychologists report that they use interviews and observation to collect data about clients. Counselling psychologists regard using the interview as an assessment technique which is central to their professional identity and they believe that it is one of their most important job functions.

The tests used most frequently by counselling psychologists include objective and projective personality tests, individually administered tests of cognitive functioning, vocational interest tests and brief scales to assess specific symptomology. The specific assessment procedures used by counselling psychologists vary somewhat as a function of the setting, client characteristics and reason for seeking services.

Projective techniques are used with greater frequency in psychiatric settings whereas interest, aptitude and objective personality tests are used more frequently in counselling and community mental health centers. Some tests are designed for use with specific age ranges, so counselling psychologists who work with adult clients use tests that are different from the tests used by those who work with children and adolescents.

Test Used for Psychologistic Counselling

Overall, the tests that are most frequently used by counselling psychologists to measure cognitive functioning are the Wechsler Adult Intelligence Scale-III (WAIS-III), Wechsler Intelligence Scale for Children-Ill (WISC-III), and the Stanford-Binet Intelligence Scale, Fourth Edition (SB). The Minnesota Multiphasic Personality Inventory-2 (MMPI-2) is the most widely used test for objective personality assessment.

The Bender-Gestalt Visual-Motor Test (Bender-Gestalt) and various forms of the Draw-A-Person Test (DAP) provide projective assessments of personality and cognitive functioning. The most frequently used projective personality tests are the Rorschach Inkblot Test (Rorschach), Thematic Apperception Test (TAT), various forms of the Sentence Completion Tests (SCT) and the House-Tree-Person Test (HTP). Although not ranked in the top 10 in terms of overall usage, university professors strongly advise counselling psychology students to learn to use the Strong Interest Inventory (SII) a vocational interest test, in addition to the MMPI-2 and WAIS-III.

Psychological Testing in Military

Psychological testing and assessment is one of the most important contributions of psychology to the military. Advances in the field of psychological testing have led to the development of an area of psychology called *military psychology*.

Military psychology refers to the research, design and application of psychological theories and data for understanding, predicting and countering behaviours in friendly and enemy forces or in civilian population. It utilises multiple psychology sub- disciplines to encourage resiliency among military troops and counteract forces for military victories.

The psychological tests helps in describing, explaining, predicting and modifying military behaviours. Weeks, months and years of active military service can often lead to emotional and mental stress, for both military personnel and their loved ones. War can seriously affect thoughts and actions. Infact, some studies have shown that the majority of enlisted men and women are affected by some type of mental or emotional disorder or illness.

The military men and women aren't the only ones that suffer. Family members and loved ones are often affected by being separated for long periods of time which can add to the mental anguish. Psychological testing, hence, focuses specifically on treatment of stress and fatigue of military personnel and their families. This might involve performing psychiatric evaluations; assessing and treating mental and emotional disorders; and offering counselling services.

Psychological tests can help to assess, diagnose, treat and recommend duty status which is most suitable for optimal well-being of individual, group and organisation. The results of these tests can provide expert care and consultation to preserve behavioural health of the fighting force. These tests can be used in interview of subjects, interrogation of prisoners and examination of those who may provide information of operational or intelligence value which would enhance outcomes of friendly military operations or reduce friendly and enemy casualties.

Practical Demonstration

The term 'personality testing' is used in a broad sense to include paper-and-pencil psychiatric screening devices. The most prominent trend has been development of screen tests for use in neuropsychiatric selection. These are paper-and-pencil tests of the inventory type and have proved remarkably successful. Two of the most successful tests are the Personal Inventory (PI) and the Cornell Selectee Index. They detect 50 to 90% of the neuropsychiatrically unfit at a cost of from 3 to 25% of false-positives. This represents greater success than in civilian situations and is one of the outstanding contributions in the war work. The psychological test should not be substituted for the clinical interview, but one should supplement the other.

Indian Institutes having Psychology Testing

The famous Military Institute of India for psychlological research and testing *are*

DIPR

Dedicated to Military Psychology, Defence Institute of Psychological Research (DIPR) is the nodal agency and technical headquarters for the selection of officers for the armed forces. DIPR is the only institute in the country that provides technical assistance to the armed forces in ensuring person-job fit.

The focus of research in the institute is on finding optimum solutions to problems pertaining to the selection of officers, placement and categorisation of men, with a view to optimise the efficiency of the armed forces and to devise suitable standardised tests for personality, intelligence and aptitude assessment.

Another focus area of research is on refining the techniques of psychological warfare, ideological convictions, motivation, attitude, morale, leadership behaviour, job satisfaction and organisational climate. Developing a better understanding of human factors in man-machine systems and studying the effects of extreme environmental conditions on the psychological adjustment, efficiency and well-being of service personnel forms the essence of many research studies undertaken by the institute.

Armed Force Medical College

The department of Psychiatry was established in 1970 by Professor Maj SB Chatterjee

Facility which exists in the department is inpatient psychiatric service, outpatient treatment, child guidance clinic, memory clinic, deaddiction clinic etc. The Psychometry lab of this department caters to clinical and diagnostic evaluation of patients as well as personality profiling and behavior modification of entrant medical students.

Newer neuromodulatory techniques like Repetitive Transcranial Magnetic Stimulation are being used as an adjunct treatment for resistant cases.

Psychological Testing in Career Guidance

The assessment of different measures, such as an individual's interests or personality, can influence career development and counselling, giving both the individual and the career counsellor useful information for decision-making. Psychological tests are designed to help individuals understand how a variety of their personal attributes like preferences,motivations, aptitudes and skills, impact their potential success and satisfaction with different career options and work environments. They are designed to discover the skills, aptitude and talents of an individual.

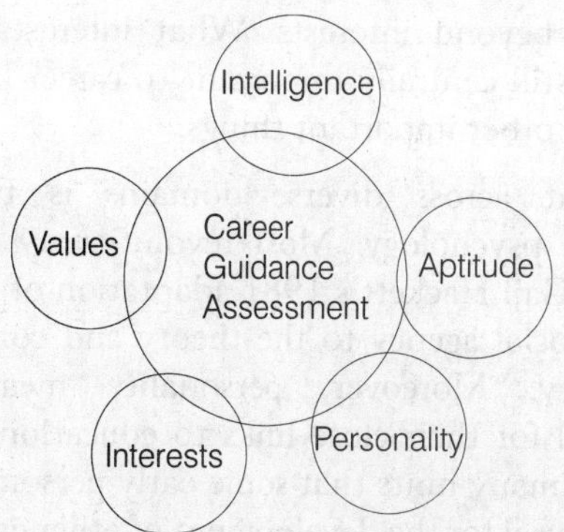

Personal Attributes Measured Using Psychological Tests

These tests can play a critical role in development of career of a person. It can be a useful tool in assessing the areas of strengths and limitations of an individual. Assessment of these attributes can help individuals or organisations such as university career service centers, career counsellors, outplacement companies, corporate human resources staff, executive coaches, vocational rehabilitation counsellor. Thus, psychological testing in field of career guidance has proven to introduce more career options, increase satisfaction in one's career plan and increase the understanding of oneself. *This section discusses three central points regarding career assessment, which are as follow*

(i) Career assessment has a long and distinguished history forged by some of the leading test developers in psychology.
(ii) The reliability, validity and usefulness of career assessment measures are unsurpassed in psychology.
(iii) Comprehensive and multivariate assessment with a variety of high-quality and specific measures will best reflect the individuality that underlies career development.

History of Career Guidance Test

Modern psychological assessment began just over 100 years ago when Alfred Binet created the first intelligence test in 1905. Some 15 years later at Carnegie Institute of Technology, a number of pioneering psychologists were devising ways to measure vocational interests. From that work emerged in 1927 EK Strong's Vocational Interest Blank, a powerful and practical measure that has been revised and expanded over its 80 years history by leading psychologists. Today, the Strong Interest Inventory (Strong) is an icon of career assessment and it illustrates many important ways by which individuality can be measured to give meaning to career decisions.

Also, in the past 30-40 years, the kinds of constructs that can be usefully measured in career inventories have greatly expanded beyond interests. What interests (or disgusts) a person is still centrally important to career life, but there are also many other important things.

Assessment across diverse domains is the keystone of vocational psychology. Most revolutionary has been Nancy Betz and Gail Hackett's 1981 adaptation of Albert Bandura's ideas of social agency to the theory and constructs of career self-efficacy. Moreover, personality measures are now recognised for their close links to educational and work life. There are many hints that some early personality dispositions may be causal for the development of other career inclinations, such as interests, self-efficacy and satisfaction.

Utility of Career Assessment Test

The quality of measures in career assessment is as good as any area of psychological assessment. The meaning of a measure for career counselling derives from its reliability and validity.

Meaning rests on scale quality. The pioneers in career assessment 70 years ago, such as Strong, Frederic Kuder, and DG Paterson, were astutely attentive to reliability and validity.

Developers of career measures since then have stood on the shoulders of these giants. Strong launched the empirical, criterion-based occupational scale and showed with decades-long longitudinal studies that interests of adults are quite stable. Kuder pioneered the concept of internal consistency underlying content scales with high homogeneity.

In the late 1960s, David Campbell merged these kinds of scales in the Strong as he brought John Holland's content-based concepts to Strong's empiricism. In the current 2005 revision of the Strong, the internal consistency reliabilities for those Holland scales are all 90 or more.

Tools for the Career Counsellor's Toolkit

Here are several kinds of measures that are likely to be useful in career assessment, dependent to some degree on the setting. These are all subjective self-report measures. Some of these inventories have very long histories; others are recently developed or are still being refined and have yet to be widely accepted. Some counsellors in some settings may equally need objective measures of cognitive skills or even behavioural samples.

- Comprehensive interest inventory with broad and specific measures.
- Comprehensive personality inventory identifying strengths in normal people.
- Comprehensive confidence inventory with broad and specific measures.
- Measure of work and life values.
- Measure of career indecision.
- Life satisfaction or well-being measure.
- Job or college satisfaction measure.
- Measure of career maturity.
- Measure of career decision-making self-efficacy.
- Career goal-setting inventory.

EXAM BASED QUESTIONS

1 Psychological test can be
(a) objective (b) subjective
(c) Both a and b (d) None of these

2 The use of psychological test in clinical setting is guided by
(a) Information Gathering model
(b) Therapeutic model
(c) Differential Treatment model
(d) All of the above

3 Which model is used to collect information for the diagnosis of mental problem?
(a) Therapeutic model
(b) Differential Treatment model
(c) Information Gathering model
(d) None of the above

4 Which among the following represent the use of test for conducting research and evaluating the outcome of the intervention programmes?
(a) Differential Treatment model
(b) Information Gathering model
(c) Therapeutic model
(d) None of the above

5 It is a way of diagnosing and planning treatment for a patient that involves evaluating someone in order to figure out what is wrong?
(a) Career assessment
(b) Educational assessment
(c) Clinical assessment
(d) None of these

6 Which of the following depict the significance of psychological tests to a clinician?
(a) Monitor effectiveness of treatment
(b) Monitors person response to medications
(c) Determine correct dosage of medicine for a person
(d) All of the above

7 Which of the psychological assessment helps to measure cognitive functioning?
(a) Neuropsychological test
(b) Intelligence and achievement test
(c) Personality tests
(d) Clinical observation

8 Sigmund freud gave the concept of
(a) Psychoanalysis (b) Humanistic therapy
(c) Behavioural therapy (d) None of these

9 Which of the following psychotherapy was developed by Fritz Parls?
(a) Existential Psychotherapy
(b) Transpersonal therapy
(c) Gestalt therapy
(d) Humanistic therapy

10 Which of the following psychotherapy involves emphasis on family relations in promoting psychological health
(a) Transpersonal therapy
(b) System therapy
(c) Existential therapy
(d) Psychodynamic therapy

11 Existential psychotherapy deals with
(a) family relations
(b) issues of life such as death, loneliness and freedom
(c) way of thinking of an individual
(d) None of the above

12 When is/are the psychological testing used in business setting?
(a) Pre employment phase
(b) Performance appraisal in post employment phase
(c) Both a and b
(d) None of the above

13 Psychometric tests in an organisation help in
(a) recruitment
(b) organisational planning
(c) performance evaluation
(d) All of these

14 What an HR must know?
(a) Variation in work force performance.
(b) Differences among individuals systematically affect job performance.
(c) Both a and b
(d) None of the above

15 Psychological test for Training and Development must take into account factors such as
(a) new environmental policies
(b) changing work force dynamics
(c) demographic of economy
(d) All of the above

16 Job performance evaluation is based on
(a) Social influences
(b) organisational influences
(c) Both a and b
(d) None of these

17 When was the Maslach-Burnout Inventory (MBI) developed?
(a) 1990s (b) 1980s
(c) 1920s (d) 1950s

18 The modern requirements state that educators play a more positive role of
(a) assessing their students
(b) offering counselling
(c) guidance and mentoring
(d) All of the above

19 Which among the following are the most common types of test administered in school?
(a) Norm-reference test (b) Group-administred test
(c) Both a and b (d) None of these

20 Which among the following allows parents to work with educators for craft?
(a) IEP (b) LRE
(c) CBM (d) None of these

21 When school try to place disabled student in a class of their non-disabled peers it is known as
(a) Individualised Education Program
(b) Least Restrictive Environment
(c) Curriculum Based Measurement
(d) None of the aboves

22 In which psychological testing student's academic progress is monitored from elementary school to high school?
(a) Curriculum-Based Measurement
(b) Least Restrictive Environment
(c) Individualised Education Program
(d) None of the above

23 The test used to measure cognitive functioning are
(a) Wechsler Adult Intelligence Scale-III
(b) Standford-Binet Intelligence Scale
(c) Minnesota Multiphasic Personality Inventory-2
(d) All of the above

24 The most frequently used projective personality tests are
(a) Rorschach Inkblot Test
(b) Thematic Apperception Test
(c) House-Tree-Person Test
(d) All of the above

25 Strong Interest Inventory (SII) is a
(a) Projective personality test
(b) objective personality test
(c) Vocational interest test
(d) None of the above

26 What are the successful candidates assessed for?
(a) Cognitive skill (b) Ethical value
(c) Interpersonal skill (d) All of these

27 Psychological tests are used for
(a) management development programme
(b) leadership development programme
(c) Both a and b
(d) None of the above

28 What is the modern requirement of educator?
(a) To offer counselling (b) To offer guidance
(c) To mentor (d) All of these

29 Assessment includes the assessment of
(a) abilities (b) personality
(c) career (d) All of these

30 Psychological testing in case of military consists of
(a) Psychiatric evaluation
(b) treating mental and emotional disorder
(c) offering counselling services
(d) All of the above

31 Personality test involves which of the following test?
(a) Personal Inventory (b) Cornell Selecte Index
(c) Both a and b (d) None of these

32 What does DIPR stand for?
(a) Delhi Institute of Physiological Research
(b) Defence Institute of Physiological Research
(c) Delhi Institute of Psychological Research
(d) Defence Institute of Psychological Research

33 DIPR is institute dealing with
(a) Military Psychology (b) Military training
(c) Career Guidance (d) All of these

34 DIPR works on the techniques of
(a) Psychological warfare
(b) Ideological conviction
(c) Motivation
(d) All of the above

35 When was department of Psychiatry established in Armed Force Medical College?
(a) 1970 (b) 1960
(c) 1980 (d) 1940

36 What facilities are provided by Dept. of Psychiatry of Armed Force Medical College?
(a) Inpatient psychiatric service
(b) Out patient treatment
(c) Child guidance clinic
(d) All of the above

37 Albert Bandura's ideas are related in
(a) Political agency (b) Social agency
(c) Both a and b (d) None of these

38 Who pioneered the concept of internal consistency?
(a) DG Paterson (b) David Campbell
(c) Fredric Kuder (d) None of these

39 Choose the correct sequence
1. Therapeutic model
2. Differential treatment model
3. Information gathering model

Codes
(a) 1, 2, 3 (b) 3, 1, 2 (c) 3, 2, 1 (d) 2, 3, 1

40 Write in chronological order
1. Moving Embeded Figures Test
2. Minnesota Child Development Inventory
3. Columbia Mental Maturity Scale
4. Perceptual Acuity Test

Codes
(a) 3, 2, 1, 4 (b) 2, 1, 3, 4
(c) 4, 3, 1, 2 (d) 3, 1, 4, 2

41 Which of the following is incorrect? Practical demonstration of psychological test in education includes

1. Career Interest Inventory
2. Standard Progressive Matrices
3. TAT

Codes

(a) Only 1 (b) Only 2
(c) Only 3 (d) Both 1 and 2

42 Consider the following statements

1. DIPR only deals with the research on military psychology.
2. Dept. of psychiatry have post graduate programmes.

Codes

(a) Only 1 (b) Only 2
(c) Both 1 and 2 (d) None of these

43 In business organisation

1. Psychological testing is done in pre employment state.
2. Psychological testing can be done as performance appraisal tool.

Codes

(a) Only 1 (b) Only 2
(c) Both 1 and 2 (d) None of these

44 Consider the following statement

1. Definition of health is limited to physical mental and social well-being.
2. Three stage strategy is applicable for various counselling.

Codes

(a) Only 1 (b) Only 2
(c) Both 1 and 2 (d) None of these

45 Consider the following statements

1. Psychological test assess a variety of mental abilities and attributes.
2. Psychological test can be taken in limited format.

Codes

(a) Only 1 (b) Only 2
(c) Both 1 and 2 (d) None of these

46 Consider the following statements

1. There are four models guiding clinical setting.
2. The model can be used individually.

Codes

(a) Only 1 (b) Only 2
(c) Both 1 and 2 (d) None of these

47 Consider the following statements

1. Training need identification that utilises psychometric test must remain focused on the effectiveness of the enterprise as a whole.
2. A hiring person must know that there's wide variation in workforce performance across jobs.

Codes

(a) Only 1 (b) Only 2
(c) Both 1 and 2 (d) None of these

48 Consider the following

1. Introduce more career options.
2. Increase satisfaction in one's career plan.
3. Increase understanding of oneself.

Which of the above are benefits of psychological testing in career guidance?

(a) 1 and 2 (b) 2 and 3 (c) 1 and 3 (d) 1, 2 and 3

49 Which of the following are benefits of psychological tests in the field of military?

1. Assigning duty status.
2. Preserve biological health of fighting force.
3. Interregation of prisoners.

Codes

(a) 2 and 3 (b) 1, 2 and 3 (c) 1 and 3 (d) 1 and 2

50 Consider the following statements

1. Counselling is non-cyclic and periodic model.
2. Counselling helps to make informed choices in field of education, career and social relations.

Which of the above statements are correct?

(a) Only 1 (b) Both 1 and 2
(c) Only 2 (d) None of these

Directions (Q. Nos. 51-58) *In these questions, there are two statements given, one is labelled as Assertion (A) and the other is labelled as Reason (R). You have to select the correct answer from the codes.*

Codes

(a) Both A and R are true and R is the correct explanation of A
(b) Both A and R are true, but R is not the correct explanation of A
(c) A is true, but R is false
(d) A is false, but R is true

51 **Assertion** (A) Psychological tests of specific attitudes and skills are now at a reasonably advanced stage of development.

Reason (R) They have been in the process of evolution and improvement for many years.

52 **Assertion** (A) Personality tests are being used in some business organisation.

Reason (R) To educate them about the organisation.

53 **Assertion** (A) 6PF test measures anxiety extraversion, independence, self control and tough mindedness.

Reason (R) It gives most complete coverage of personality in a brief time.

54 **Assertion** (A) Myres-Briggs type indicator is used in case of business setting.

Reason (R) This test is used in recruitment process.

55 Assertion (A) While carrying out the research, psychologist must keep his interest in mind.

Reason (R) The subject must not be used as a guinea pig.

56 Assertion (A) The concept of psycholanalysis was given by Sigmund Freud.

Reason (R) Gestalt therapy was developed by Fritz Perls.

57 Assertion (A) Projective tests allow for open-ended answers and are based on ambiguous stimuli.

Reason (R) Rorschach Inkblot test is an objective test.

58 Assertion (A) Psychological tests helps in development of career of a person.

Reason (R) Psychological tests are designed to discover skills, aptitudes and talents of an individual.

59 Match the following

	List I (Tests)		List II (Functions)
A.	Intelligence test	1.	Meaures functioning of brain
B.	Personality Tests	2.	Clinical interview
C.	Neuropsychological Tests	3.	Measures cognitive functioning
D.	Clinical Observation	4.	Analysis of Personality disorder

Codes

	A	B	C	D		A	B	C	D
(a)	4	3	2	1	(b)	4	3	1	2
(c)	3	4	1	2	(d)	3	4	2	1

60 Match the following

	List I (Test)		List II (Function)
A.	Maslach-Burnout Inventory	1.	Measure burnout
B.	Individualised Education Program	2.	For disabled student
C.	Least Restrictive Environment	3.	Enable placement decisions
D.	Curriculam-Based Measurement	4.	Monitoring progress

Codes

	A	B	C	D		A	B	C	D
(a)	1	2	3	4	(b)	4	3	2	1
(c)	3	2	1	4	(d)	4	1	2	3

61 Match the following

	List I (Test)		List II (Associated with)
A.	MMPI-2	1.	Projective assessment
B.	DAP	2.	Cognitive functioning
C.	HTP	3.	Projective personality
D.	TAT	4.	Personality assessment

Codes

	A	B	C	D		A	B	C	D
(a)	1	2	3	4	(b)	2	1	4	3
(c)	1	4	3	2	(d	2	4	3	1

62 Match the following

	List I (Program)		List II (Full forms)
A.	I E P	1.	Least Restrictive Environment
B.	LRE	2.	Individualised Education Program
C.	CBM	3.	Curriculum-Based Measurement

Codes

	A	B	C		A	B	C
(a)	3	2	1	(b)	2	3	1
(c)	3	1	2	(d)	2	1	3

63 Match the following

	List I (Text)		List II (Full forms)
A.	DAP	1.	Strong Internet Inventory
B.	TAT	2.	Draw-A-Person Test
C.	SII	3.	Sentence Completion Tests.
D.	SCT	4.	Thematic Apperception Test

Codes

	A	B	C	D		A	B	C	D
(a)	1	2	3	4	(b)	2	4	1	3
(c)	2	3	4	1	(d)	1	3	2	4

64 Match the following

	List I (Test)		List II (Author)
A.	16PF	1.	Raven
B.	TAT	2.	Raymond B Cattel
C.	Career Interest Inventory	3.	Henry Murray
D.	SPM	4.	Gillian Hyde and Geoff Tricpy

Codes

	A	B	C	D
(a)	2	1	3	4
(b)	1	4	3	2
(c)	2	1	4	3
(d)	2	3	4	1

ANSWERS

1 (c)	2 (d)	3 (c)	4 (a)	5 (c)	6 (d)	7 (b)	8 (a)	9 (c)	10 (b)
11 (b)	12 (c)	13 (d)	14 (c)	15 (d)	16 (b)	17 (b)	18 (d)	19 (c)	20 (a)
21 (b)	22 (a)	23 (b)	24 (d)	25 (c)	26 (a)	27 (c)	28 (d)	29 (d)	30 (d)
31 (c)	32 (d)	33 (a)	34 (d)	35 (a)	36 (d)	37 (b)	38 (c)	39 (b)	40 (d)
41 (c)	42 (d)	43 (c)	44 (b)	45 (a)	46 (d)	47 (c)	48 (d)	49 (b)	50 (b)
51 (a)	52 (c)	53 (a)	54 (c)	55 (d)	56 (b)	57 (c)	58 (a)	59 (c)	60 (a)
61 (b)	62 (d)	63 (b)	64 (d)						

CHAPTER 12

Nervous and Sensory Systems

Psychology is destined to study the behaviour of humans, which depends upon the processing in their brain and other parts. Thus, studying and understanding the nervous and sensory systems and their aspects is extremely necessary for analysing the psychological behaviour of humans.

In this Chapter

Neurons

Neurons are the specialised cells present within the body that perform the task of transmission of information.

The neuron differs from other cells as it is specialised for information processing. To some degree, all functions that sustain life, as well as those that make us human are coordinated and depend on the communication of neurons. Neurons are anatomically independent as they do come very close to each other, but they do not touch each other. The nervous system, thus, consists of separate units rather than a single continuous structure.

Structure of Neurons

Neurons vary in form, but all neurons possess the basic structural units like a cell body, an axon and dendrites.

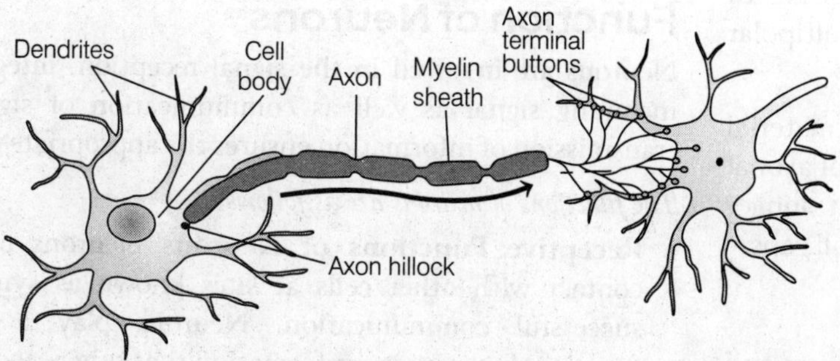

Basic Structure of Neuron

Cell Body

The functioning and survival of the neuron depend on the integrity of the cell body. The cell body controls and maintains the neuronal structure. These cell bodies are gray, the term gray matter is used to describe those areas of the brain which are dense in cell bodies such as the cortex. The cell body contains mitochondria, amino acids and DNA and it has the same properties of other cells in the body. Protein synthesis cannot occur in the axon, so all axonal proteins come from the cell body.

Dendrites

Neurons generally receive chemical transmissions from one another through dendrites. These are the feathery extensions that branch from the neuron and carry information toward the cell body. There are often thousands of dendrites per neuron. The profuse branching of dendrites allows them to receive communication from a large number of axonal terminals across the synapse. The shape of dendritic 'trees' are often among the most characteristic morphological features of a neuron.

Dendrites are tiny and are usually shorter than the axon, but they can have upto thousands of synapses or contacts with other neurons. Dendrites comprise most of the receptive surface of a neuron.

Axon

The axon extends away from the cell body. Its primary function is to transmit electrochemical information from the cell body to the synapse through microtubules along its length.

Axons are less than 1 mm in length. Large motor neurons of long axons, some of them reaching to the lower end of the spinal cord or the foot muscles, whereas other neurons, including those that coordinate activity within a specific region of the CNS, have short axons.

Unipolar axons proceed from one region in the CNS to another without branching. In bipolar or multipolar axons, the branching is elaborate.

Many axons are surrounded by a sheath of fatty material known as a *myelin sheath* that increases the speed of axonal transmission. This is especially important in longer neurons. The myelin sheath is interrupted by small gaps.

Glial Cells

The glial cells surround neurons and provide support and insulation between them. Glial cells are the most abundant cell types of the central nervous system. They are also known as *supporting cells* of the nervous system. *The main functions of glial cells are*

- to surround neurons and hold them in place,
- to supply nutrients and oxygen of the neurons
- to insulate one neuron from another.

Glial cells are found throughout the CNS and PNS. *The three main types of glial cells in the CNS are*

(i) **Astrocytes** are fibrous, star-shaped cells with many small 'feet' or processes that interpose themselves between neuronal cell bodies, dendrites and the vasculature providing structural support. Astrocytes respond to brain injury by swelling or proliferating to fill a damage space. With injury astrocytes can also degenerate and form scar tissue.

(ii) **Oligodendrocytes** in the CNS and Schwann cell in the PNS are myelin forming glial cells that envelope axons and neurons. These cells perform a vital function in wrapping the nerve cell with a lipid layer of myelin and increasing the speed with which a neurons conduct its impulse along an axon.

(iii) **Microglia** are small cells within the CNS that undergo rapid proliferation in response to tissue destruction, migrating toward the site of injured or dead cells, where they act as scavengers and metabolise tissue debris.

Axon Terminals

Near the end of the axon are branches with slightly enlarged ends called *axonal terminals or terminal buttons*. The site of inter neuronal contact where neurochemical information is transmitted from one neuron to another, is called a *synapse*. The terminal button is the presynaptic portion of the neuron, the place where electrical nerve impulses causes the release of a neurotransmitter. This chemical in turn affects another neuron or muscle in either an excitatory or an inhibitory manner. Signals that travel along the axon are electrical and the transfer of neurotransmitters across synapses, from one neuron to another, is chemical.

Function of Neurons

Neurons are involved in the signal reception, integration of incoming signal as well as communication of signal. This transmission of information ensures the appropriate response.

The functions of neurons are as follows

- **Receptive Functions of Neurons** Neurons come into contact with other cells at sites known as synapses for successful communication. Neurons play a receptive function by receiving information that originated from the stimuli. This ensures effective transmission of information and appropriate response to stimuli.

- **Integrative Functions of Neurons** The integrative function of neurons occurs in dendrites as well as cell body of neuron. It involves integration of excitatory and inhibitory responses in order to determine whether certain information should be transmitted.
- **Impulse Initiation** Nerve impulses are initiated when memberance potential of neuron is sufficiently depolarised and reach a certain threshold. This allows some of the neurons to initiate impulses and information to specific target.
- **Transmission** Transmission from one neuron to another is electrical or chemical.

Neurons send signal using action potentials. An action potential is a shift in the neurons electric potential caused by the flow of ions in and out of neural membrane.

Action potential can trigger both chemical and electrical synapses, *which are as follows*

- **Chemical Synapses** In a chemical synapse, the action potential affects other neurons through a gap between neurons called a *synapse*. Synapses consist of a presynaptic ending, a synaptic cleft and a postsynaptic ending.

  When an action potential is generated, it is carried along the axon to a presynaptic ending. This triggers the release of chemical messengers is called *neurotransmitters*. These molecules cross the synaptic cleft and bind to the receptors present in the postsynaptic ending of a dendrite.

  Neurotransmitters can excite the postsynaptic neuron, causing it to generate an action potential.

  Alternatively, they can inhibit the postsynaptic neuron, in which case it doesn't generate an action potential.
- **Electrical Synapses** Electrical synapse is the mechanical and electrically conductive link between two neighbouring neurons. They occur when two neurons are connected through a gap junction. This gap is much smaller than a synapse and includes ion channels which facilitate the direct transmission of positive electrical signal.

  As a result, electrical synapses are much faster than chemical synapses. However, the signal diminishes from one neuron to the next making electrical synapses less effective at transmission.

Types of Neurons

In terms of function, scientists classify neurons into three broad types

(i) **Sensory Neurons** These neurons are activated by external physical or chemical stimuli. This involves sensory activation of any of the five senses.

(ii) **Motor Neurons** Motor neuron are the neurons in spinal cord that connects organs muscles and different types of glands in the body. They transmit impulses from central nervous system to organs, glands and muscles. Thus, it controls movement of different types of muscles as well as activity of organs and glands in body.

(iii) **Inter Neurons** These are found only in CNS and connect one neuron to another. They receive information from one neuron and transmit this information to another neuron.

Neural Impulse

Neural impulse originate as electrical events of a very short duration that travel from dendrites to the axon terminals. A nerve impulse is brief and sharp. It is called *Spike*. It is a rapid reversible change in the electrical charges inside and outside a neuron.

This electrical change is a matter of excitation of the neuron caused by electrical energy from stimulus. A nerve cell comparable to a battery, has negative and positive poles, which on being interconnected by an electric wire, produces electric current.

Likewise, the outer and inner sides of cell' memberance has a positive potential , *i.e.* highly positively charged with sodium ions ((Na^+) and a negative potential, *i.e.* less positively charged by potassium ions (K^+) respectively, when it is in resting stage (rest potential). On being excited by a stimulus, it makes the inside of the cell memberane a little less negative.

At a critical point (threshold), the membrane surrounding the neuron will change its polarity. The channels (small pores) open briefly allowing charged particles of sodium ion (Na^+) floating into the cell, which are positively charged. Thus, the inside of the neuron becomes more positive than the area outside the cell for a short duration (about a millisecond). This brief change to inside positive is called the *Action Potential* or *Neural Impulse*.

Origin of Neural Impulse

Neurons are information carriers of the nervous system. The interneurons are largely found in spinal cord and brain. It receives impulses conducted through afferent neurons and passes it onto the motor neurons to conduct the impluses conducted through afferent neurons and passes it onto the neuron to conduct the impulses down to the organs or response. Thus, it connects the two neurons or brings about an association between them.

Thus, the function of the neuron is to generate neural energy, which is known as neural impluses and with the help of axon fibres it transmits neural impulses from one place to another in the nervous system.

The brief charge to inside positively is the 'neural impulse'.

After the nerve impulse has occurred, the neuron is restored to its original resting charge by an outward flow of potassium ion and is ready to fire again. The electrical nerve impulses travel along axon exciting the next region and does so as it continously moves down the axon. The function of neural conductivity is regulated by certain functions and laws. The details, describing how the propagation of neural impulse happens is described below.

Propagation of the Impulse

A neuron receives most of its messages from other neurons, from sensory receptors through synapses on its dendrites and cell body. These messages do not ordinarily produce action potentials, which begin at the axon Hillock, where the threshold for activation is lower.

The axon is a countinuous structure with action potentials being transmitted from one segment to the next along the length of the axon. At the same time the ion channels in the first segment close for Na^+ions. The Na^+ions that entered this first segment are attracted to a region where there are fewer Na^+ions and a more negative charge is generated inside of the next segment of the axon. When these ions reach the next segment, the resulting depolarisation brings this second segment of the axon to the threshold level. More sodium channels open consequently.

Due to this more Na^+ions enter and these Na^+ions are attached to the next segment and thus, the action potential continues along the length of the axon. Before the threshold is reached in a given segment; there is a change in membrane potential because of the Na^+ions that have entered the segment. This depolarisation that has not reached threshold can be called as a *graded depolarisation*.

The speed of impulse transmission is not the same for all neurons and is independent of stimulus intensity which is an aspect of all or none law. So, if the stimulus exceeds the threshold potential, the nerve or muscle fibre will give a complete response, otherwise there is no response. Larger neurons transmit messages faster than smaller neurons; myelinated axons have a faster transmission rate than unmyelinated axons and the greater the number or synapses, the slower the message travels. When an action potential occurs, Na^+ions flow along the inside of the cell membrane, depolarising the segment of the membrane that lies just ahead. The thicker the axon, the faster the local membrane will depolarise. And the faster the segments are depolarised, the faster the neural impulse will travel along the axon.

The polarity of the first segment returns to normal as K^+ ions leave the cell. The movement of Na^+ ions into the next portion of the axon causes the polarity of that part to change with the inside becoming positively charged. These changes in polarity (the action potential) continue along the axon until reaching the presynaptic terminals.

Synaptic Transmission

The communication within neurons happens at the synapse which is the gap between two neurons or between a neuron and a target cell, like a muscle or a gland. At the synapse, the firing of an action potential from one neuron *i.e.* the presynaptic or sending neuron, causes *i.e* the transmission of a signal to another neuron, the postsynaptic or receiving neuron, making the postsynaptic neuron either more or less likely to fire its own action potential.

Synaptic transmission involves the release of neurotransmitters. Neurotransmitters carry information from the presynaptic or sending neuron to the postsynaptic or receiving neuron.

Synapses are usually formed between nerve terminals *i.e.* axon terminals of the sending neuron and the cell body or dendrites of the receiving neuron. Inside the axon terminal of a presynaptic neuron are many synaptic vesicles. These are membrane bound spheres that are filled with neurotransmitters.

There is a small gap between the axon terminal of the presynaptic neuron and the membrane of the postsynaptic cell and this gap is called the *synaptic cleft*.

When an action potential, or nerve impulse, arrives at the axon terminal, it activates voltage gated calcium channels in the cell membrane. Ca^{2+}, which is present at a much higher concentration outside the neuron than inside, rushes into the cell. The Ca^{2+} allows synaptic vesicles to fuse with the axon terminal membrane, releasing neurotransmitter into the synaptic cleft.

The neurotransmitter molecules diffuse across the synaptic cleft and bind to receptor proteins on the postsynaptic cell.

Activation of postsynaptic receptors leads to the opening or closing of ion channels in the cell membrane. This may be depolarising making the inside of the cell more positive or hyperpolarising making the inside of the cell more negative-depending on the ions involved.

Excitatory and Inhibitory Postsynaptic Potentials

When a neurotransmitter binds to its receptor on a receiving cell, it causes ion channels to open or close. This can produce a localised change in the potential across the membrane of the receiving cell.

- In some cases, the change makes the target cell more likely to fire its own action potential. In this case, the shift in membrane potential is called an *excitatory postsynaptic potential* or EPSP. An EPSP is depolarising it makes the inside of the cell more positive, bringing the membrane potential closer to its threshold for firing an action potential. Sometimes, a single EPSP isn't large enough to bring the neuron to threshold, but it can sum together with other EPSPs to trigger an action potential.
- In other cases, the change makes the target cell less likely to fire an action potential and is called an *inhibitory postsynaptic potential* or IPSP. IPSPs tend to keep the membrane potential of the postsynaptic neuron below threshold for firing an action potential. IPSPs are important because they can counteract, or cancel out, the excitatory effect of the EPSPs.

Neurotransmitter

Neurotransmitters are often referred to as the body's chemical messengers. They are the molecules used by the nervous system to transmit messages between neurons or from neuron to muscle.

A neurotransmitter can work in two ways *i.e.* excitatory or inhibitory and neuromodulators

(i) **Excitatory Transmitter** promotes the generation of action potential in the receiving neurons, while **inhibitory transmitter** prevents it. A neurotransmitter being excitatory or inhibitory depends on the receptor it binds to.

(ii) **Neuromodulators** affect a large number of neurons simultaneously once. Therefore, they regulate the population of neuron and operate over a slower time course than excitatory and inhibitory neurotransmitters.

Types of Neurotransmitter

There are several types of neurotransmitters which are as follows

Amino Acid Neurotransmitters

The neurotransmitters in the vast majority of fast acting, directed synapses in the central nervous system are amino acids (the molecular building blocks of proteins). The four most widely acknowledged amino acid neurotransmitters are glutamate, asparate, glycine and Gamma- Amino Butyric Acid (GABA). The first three are common in the protein we consume, where as GABA is synthesised by a simple modification of the structure of glutamate. Glutamate is the most prevalent excitatory neurotransmitter in the mammalian central nervous system and GABA is the most prevalent inhibitory neurotransmitter.

Monoamine Neurotransmitters

Monoamines are another class of small molecule neurotransmitters. Each is synthesised from a single amino acid, hence, the name monoamine. Monoamine neurotransmitters are slightly larger than amino acid neurotransmitters and their effects tend to be more diffused. The monoamines are present in small groups of neurons whose cell bodies are mostly, located in the brain stem.

These neurons often have highly branched axons with many varicosities, from which monoamine neurotransmitters diffuse into the extracellular fluid. There are four monoamine neurotransmitters ; dopamine, epinephrine, norepinephrine and serotonin. They are sub-divided into two groups, catecholamines and indolamines, on the basis of their structures.

Dopamine, norepinephrine and epinephrine are catecholamines and each is synthesised from the amino acid tyrosine. In contrast to other monoamines, serotonin is synthesised from the amino acid tryptophan and is classified as an indolamine.

Soluble-Gas Neurotransmitters

Another class of small molecule neurotransmitters are the soluble gases which include nitric oxide and carbon monoxide. The soluble gases do not act like the other neurotransmitters. They are produced in the neural cytoplasm and once produced, they immediately diffuse through the cell membrane into the extracellular fluid and then into nearby cells.

These can easily pass through the cell membrane because they are soluble in lipids. Once in other cells, these stimulate the production of a second messenger and in a few seconds are deactivated by being converted to other molecules. Soluble gas neurotransmitters have been shown to be involved in retrograde transmission to regulate the activity of pre-synaptic neurons.

Acetylcholine

Acetylcholine is a small molecule neurotransmitter. It is created by adding an acetyl group to a chlorine molecule. Acetylcholine is the neurotransmitter at neuromuscular junctions, at many of the synapses in the autonomic nervous system and at synapses in several parts of the central nervous system. Acetylcholine is broken down in the synapse by the enzyme acetylcholinesterase. Neurons that release acetylcholine are said to be cholinergic.

Some of the common neurotransmitters with their effect are

Neurotransmitter	Location	Effects
Acetylcholine	Found throughout the central nervous system, in the autonomic nervous system and at all neuromuscular junctions.	Involved in muscle action, learning and memory.
Norepinephrine	Found in neurons in the autonomic nervous system.	Primarily involved in control or alertness and wakefullness.
Dopamine	Produced by neurons located in a region of the brain called the substantia nigra.	Involved in movement, attention and learing. Degeneration of dopamine producing neurons has been linked to Parkinson's disease. Too much dopamine has been linked to schizophrenia.
Serotonin	Found in neurons in the brain and spinal cord.	Plays a role in the regulation of mood and in the control of eating, sleep and arousal. Has also been implicated in the regulation of pain and in dreaming.
GABA (Gamma amino-butyric acid)	Found throughout the brain and spinal cord.	GABA is the major inhibitory neurotransmitter in the brain. Abnormal levels of GABA have been implicated in sleep and eating disorders.

Nervous System

Nervous system is a complex network of neurons that regulates bodily processes and is ultimately responsible for all aspects of conscious experience.

The nervous system is divided into two main parts as central nervous system and peripheral nervous system.

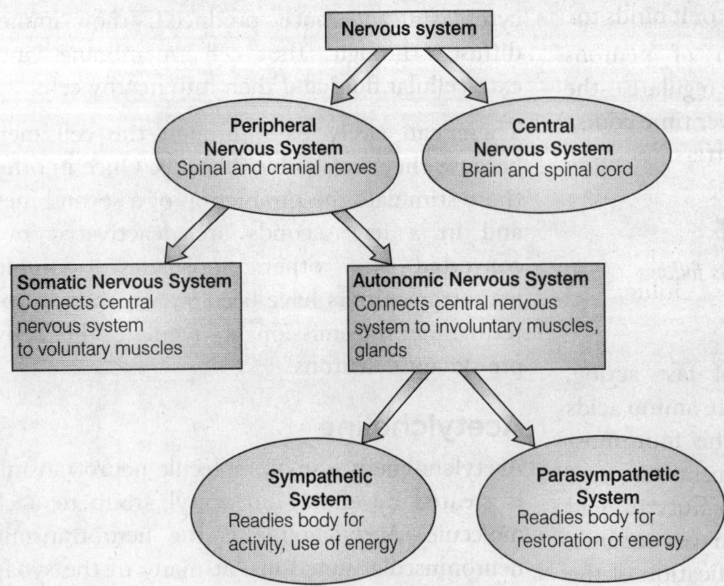

Types of Nervous System

Central Nervous System

The central nervous system consists of the brain and spinal cord and serves as the integrating and command centre of the nervous system. The brain plays the central role in the control of most of the bodily functions, including awareness, movements, sensations, thoughts, speech and memory.

Some reflex movements can occur through spinal cord pathways without the participation of any of the brain structures. The spinal cord is connected to a section of the brain called the *brainstem* and runs through the spinal canal. Cranial nerves exit the brainstem and nerve roots exit the spinal cord to both sides of the body. The spinal cord carries signals (messages) back and forth between the brain and the peripheral nerves.

Brain

The brain is the central control module of the body and also coordinates various activities. From physical motion to the secretion of hormones, the creation of memories and the sensation of emotion everything is controlled by the brain. To carry out these functions, some sections of the brain have dedicated roles.

However, many higher functions like reasoning, problem-solving, creativity involve different areas working together in networks.

Specific Regions of Brain

Some specific brain regions are as follows

(i) **Cerebrum** It constitutes of the most developed part in humans and is mainly involved in specialised functions like intelligence, learning skills, memory, speech etc.

The cerebrum is roughly split into four lobes

- **Temporal Lobe** It is important for processing sensory input and assigning it emotional meaning. It is also involved in laying down long-term memories. Some aspects of language perception are also housed here.
- **Occipital Lobe** It is a visual processing region of the brain, housing the visual cortex.
- **Parietal Lobe** The parietal lobe integrates sensory information including touch, spatial awareness and navigation. Touch stimulation from the skin is ultimately sent to the parietal lobe. It also plays a part in language processing.
- **Frontal Lobe** It is positioned at the front of the brain. The frontal lobe contains the majority of dopamine-sensitive neurons and is involved in attention, reward, short-term memory, motivation and planning.

(ii) **Basal Ganglia** It is involved in the control of voluntary motor movements, procedural learning and decisions about which motor activities to be carried out.

(iii) **Cerebellum** It is mostly involved in precise motor control, language processing and attentiveness.

(iv) **Broca's Area** This is a small area on the left side of the brain (sometimes on the right in left-handed individuals) and is important in language processing.

(v) **Corpus Callosum** It is a broad band of nerve fibers that join the left and right hemispheres. It is the largest white matter structure in the brain and allows the two hemispheres to communicate.

(vi) **Medulla Oblongata** It extends below the skull, and is involved in involuntary functions, such as vomiting, breathing, sneezing and maintaining the correct blood pressure.

(vii) **Hypothalamus** The hypothalamus secretes a number of neurohormones and regulates the body temperature, thirst and hunger.

(viii) **Thalamus** It is positioned in the center of the brain. The thalamus receives sensory and motor input and relays it to the rest of the cerebral cortex. It is involved in the regulation of consciousness, sleep, awareness and alertness.

(ix) **Amygdala** These are two almond-shaped nuclei deep within the temporal lobe. These are involved in decision-making, memory and emotional responses; particularly negative emotions.

Spinal Cord

The spinal cord runs almost along the full length of the back and carries information between the brain and body, but it also carries out other tasks. From the brain stem where the spinal cord meets the brain, 31 spinal nerves enter the cord. Motor commands from the brain travel from the spine to the muscles and sensory information travels from the sensory tissues, such as the skin toward the spinal cord and finally up to the brain.

The spinal cord contains circuits that control certain reflexive responses, such as the involuntary movement the arm might make if finger touches a flame. The circuits within the spine can also generate more complex movements such as walking. Even without input from the brain, the spinal nerves can coordinate all of the muscles necessary to walk.

Peripheral Nervous System

The Peripheral Nervous System (PNS) is the connection between the Central Nervous System and the rest of the body. It creates the signals that control the functions of the body.

The PNS can be broken down into the Autonomic Nervous System, which controls bodily functions without conscious control and the sensory-somatic nervous system, which transmits sensory information from the skin, muscles and sensory organs to the CNS and sends motor commands from the CNS to the muscles.

Autonomic Nervous System

The Autonomic Nervous System serves as the relay between the CNS and the internal organs. It controls the lungs, the heart, smooth muscle and exocrine and endocrine glands. The Autonomic Nervous System controls these organs largely without conscious control. It can continuously monitor the conditions of these different systems and implement changes as needed. Signaling to the target tissue usually involves two synapses: a preganglionic neuron (originating in the CNS) synapses to a neuron in a ganglion that, in turn, synapses on the target organ.

The autonomic nervous system consists of two parts

- **Sympathetic Nervous System** This is activated during a 'fight or flight' situation in which great mental stress or physical danger is encountered. Neurotransmitters such as norepinephrine and epinephrine are released, which increases heart rate and blood flow in certain areas like muscle, while simultaneously decreasing activities of non-critical functions for survival, like digestion. The systems are independent to each other allowing the activation of certain parts of the body, while others remain rested.

- **Parasympathetic Nervous System** Primarily using the neurotransmitter acetylcholine (ACh) as a mediator, the parasympathetic system allows the body to function in a 'rest and digest' state. Consequently, when the parasympathetic system dominates the body, there is increase in salivation and activities like digestion, while heart rate and other sympathetic responses decrease. Unlike the sympathetic system, humans have some voluntary control in the parasympathetic system. The most prominent examples of this control are urination and defecation.

Somatic Nervous System

The somatic nervous system is made up of cranial and spinal nerves and contains both sensory and motor neurons. Sensory neurons transmit sensory information from the skin, skeletal muscle, and sensory organs to the CNS. Motor neurons transmit messages about desired movement from the CNS to the muscles to initiate muscle contraction. Without the somatic nervous system, an animal would be unable to process any information about its environment (*e.g.* what it sees, feels, hears and so on) and could not control motor movements.

The cranial and spinal nerves which make up somatic nervous system are as follows

(i) **Cranial Nerves** Humans have 12 cranial nerves. These nerves emerge from or enter the skull. Some of the cranial nerves are
   - **Olfactory Nerve** Transmits information about smell from nose to brainstem.
   - **Oculomotor Nerve** Controls opening and closing of eyelid and some eye movements.
   - **Glossopharyngeal Nerve** Has role in both taste (sensory) and swallowing (motor).

(ii) **Spinal Nerves** Humans have 31 spinal nerves. These emerge from vertebral column and transmit sensory and motor information between spinal cord and rest of the body.

The spinal nerves are as follow

- **Cervical Spinal Nerves (C1-C4)** The first four cervical spinal nerves, C1 through C4, split and recombine to produce a variety of nerves that serve the neck and back of head. Spinal nerve C1 provides motor innervation to muscles at the base of the skull. C2 and C3 form many of the nerves of the neck, providing both sensory and motor control. These include the greater occipital nerve, which provides sensation to the back of the head and the lesser occipital nerve, which provides sensation to the area behind the ears. The phrenic nerve is a nerve essential for our survival which arises from nerve roots C3, C4 and C5. It supplies the thoracic diaphragm, enabling breathing.
- **Brachial Plexus** (C5- T1) The last four cervical spinal nerves, C5 through C8 and the first thoracic spinal nerve, T1, combine to form the brachial plexus, a tangled array of nerves, splitting, combining and recombining, to form the nerves that subserve the upper-limb and upper back. It is responsible for cutaneous and muscular innervations of the entire upper limb, with two exceptions: the trapezius muscle innervated by the spinal accessory nerve (CN XI) and an area of skin near the axilla innervated by the intercostobrachial nerve.
- **Lumbosacral Plexus** (L 1-Co1) The anterior divisions of the lumbar nerves, sacral nerves and coccygeal nerve form the lumbosacral plexus, the first lumbar nerve being frequently joined by a branch from the twelfth thoracic. For descriptive purposes this plexus is usually divided into three parts: lumbar plexus, sacral plexus and pudendal plexus. It works with the sacral plexus to give autonomic, motor and sensory fibers to the lower extremities.

Neuroplasticity System

Neuroplasticity is the capacity of neurons and neural networks in the brain to change their connections and behaviour in response to a new information, sensory stimulation, development, damage or dysfunction. Although neural networks exhibit modularity and carry out specific functions, they retain the capacity to deviate from their usual functions and to reorganise themselves. Rapid change or reorganisation of the brain's cellular or neural networks can take place in many different forms and under many different circumstances.

Developmental plasticity occurs when neurons in the young brain rapidly sprout branches and form synapses. Then, as the brain begins to process sensory information, some of these synapses strengthen and others weaken. Eventually, some unused synapses are eliminated completely, through a process known as synaptic pruning, which leaves behind efficient networks of neural connections. Other forms of neuroplasticity operate by almost same mechanism but, under different circumstances and sometimes only to a limited extent. These circumstances include changes in the body, such as the loss of a limb or sense organ that subsequently alters the balance of sensory activity received by the brain. In addition, neuroplasticity is employed by the brain during the reinforcement of sensory information through experience, such as in learning and memory and following actual physical damage to the brain, when the brain attempts to compensate for lost activity.

In addition to the changes in the way the brain works and functional adaptations, neuroplasticity offers potential avenues for psychological change as well. We already use medications and chemicals to change the way our brain works and psychology has certainly put forth tons of effort to learn how to change the way the brain works by modifying our thought patterns. Researchers are trying to find ways to make permanent, significant changes to our brain structure and function through simple activities that we often do in a normal day.

Sensory System

Sensory system consists of sensory receptors, neural pathway and those parts of the brain involved in sensory perception. Commonly recognised sensory system are those for vision, hearing, touch, taste, smell and balance. But, senses are not limited to these as humans possess more or less, about ten different types of senses.

Skin have separate warmth, cold and pain senses. Furthermore, sense organ in the muscle, tendons and joints tell us about position of our limbs and the state of tension in the muscle. These form a sense called *kinesthesis*. Sensation is a human's detection of stimuli. Detection of sensation allows the human body to be aware of changes (stimuli) that occur in the environment or inside the body. These senses make the Central Nervous System to produce reaction for the stimuli and maintain body homeostasis.

General Sensation

The general senses are pain , temperature, touch, pressure, vibration and proprioception. Receptors for these sensations are distributed throughout the body. General sensations are received by General Sensory Receptors which when stimulated, send a sensation to the Central Nervous System. *General Sense Receptors are basically of three types*.

(i) **Exteroceptors** Provide info about external environment.
(ii) **Proprioceptors** Provide info about sketetal muscles and joints.
(iii) **Interoceptors** Provide info about visceral organs and functions.

Specific Sensation

Specific senses detect the sensation of taste, smell, hearing, equilibrium and sight, only through specific sense organs present in the head region. This phenomenon is known as *cephalisation.* HE Torebjork said "Specific sensations are evoked by activity in single identified sensory units in man."

Receptors

Receptors are the stimuli receiving organs of the body. These are called *sense organs.* Sense organs are in fact windows through which information about various objects of the world is gathered. These are the primary organs of contact with the physical environment, because our cognition or awareness about the world depends upon sense organs.

The stimuli from the external world stimulates or activates the receptor mechanism of the sense organs and produce nerve impulses of information about the present stimulating conditions. The impulses are carried over through afferent fibers to the corresponding sensory area in the brain. Thus, aware of the present stimulus. Thus, the windows or the receptors are the senses, which function as primary channel of mental awareness, which is termed as sensation.The major sense organs are the eyes, ears, nose, tongue and skin. Each of the aforementioned organs is capable of being stimulated by specific stimuli and produce specific sensations.

Types of Receptors or Sense Organs

Pschologists in fact, do not know exactly, how many sensory organs one possesses. There are certainly more than traditionally known five sense organs *i.e.* eyes, ears, nose, skin and tongue. The other senses which are hidden within the body are involved in knowing the position of one's body in space, its movement, internal changes and physiological tensions, when one is hungry, thirsty or tired.

All these sensory organs can be broadly classified into the following three categories

Exteroceptors

Exteroceptors are related to receiving information or getting stimulated from stimuli present in the external world. There are five known exteroceptors-the eyes, the ears, the nose, the skin and the tongue. Appropriate external stimulus stimulates the receptor cells within the organs as a result of which sensory nerve impulses are produced and conveyed to the appropriate sensory area in the brain and thus, the individual becomes aware of the external stimuli. For example, wave lengths of light enters into eyes and the receptors within the eyes get stimulated from where the sensory impulses of visual features of the objects are transmitted to the visual area in the brain and then visual sensation takes place.

Similarly, various frequencies of sound waves are received by the hair cells present inside the ears and the resultant nerve impulses are conveyed to the auditory area in the brain and thus, we have auditory sensation. Similar mechanism takes place with olfactory, tactile and taste sensation.

Interoceptors

Interoceptors are related to the visceral organs of the body such as lungs, intestines, heart etc. These get stimulated from changes taking place in our visceral or internal organs of the body and produce sensations of the changes taking place in our internal environment, *i.e.* within the body *viz.* stomach pain, chest pain, headache, palpitation etc. Since, these receptors are found inside the body organs and are stimulated by internal stimuli only, they are termed interoceptors.

Proprioceptors

Proprioceptors are found in the peripheral regions of the body and are responsible for kinesthetic sensations. It should be clear that the muscles themselves are not the receptors, rather they are the effectors or organs or response. But the muscles also contain receptor structures, which give sensations whenever muscles make any movement to respond.

Sensory Processes

Sensory processes refers to the way the nervous system receives messages from the senses and turns into responses. *The sensory processes are as follows*

Sensory Processes : Vision

Light enters the eye through the pupil, travels through the cornea, the lens and the interior of the eye ball to strike the rod and cones cells of the retina at the back of eye ball. Transduction of the physical energy into receptor potentials occurs in the rod and cones cell.

Nerve impulses are then generated in certain cells of the retina, the ganglion cell. These impulses travel to the brain along the optic nerve and their pattern signals a visual event in the environment. The rays of light are bent or refracted by cornea and lens to bring them to focus on retina. Most of the light bending or refraction, in the eye is done by cornea; the lens, by changing its shape which simply adds enough to the basic corneal refraction to bring the light from near objects to a sharp focus on the retina.

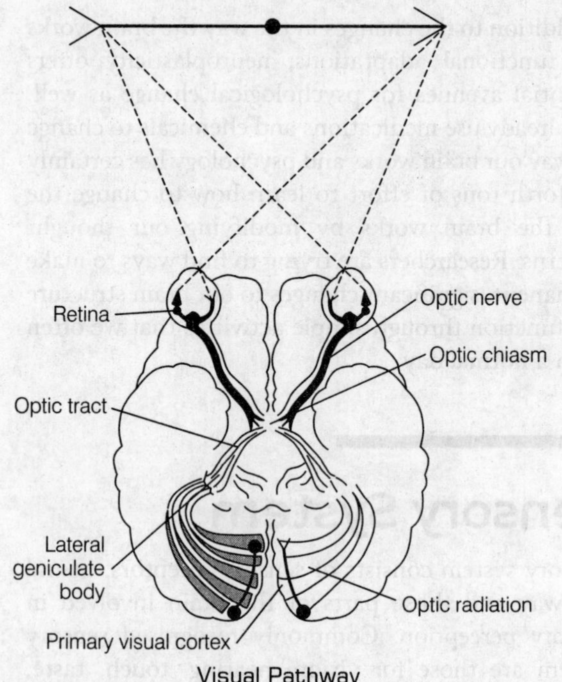

Visual Pathway

Ganglion cells have axons that leave the retina through the optic disc to make up the optic nerve. The patterns of nerve impulse in these fibers carry information about the light that struck the rods and cones. Human eye contains about 120 million rods and about 6 million cones. The axons of the ganglion cells in the optic nerve reach the lateral geniculate body of the thalamus.

There, they make connection/synapses with cells of the lateral geniculate body. Then, fibre from the lateral geniculate cell carry nerve impulses to the primary visual sensory area at the back of the brain.

Sensory Processes : Hearing

The ear has three principle parts, the external ear, which collects the physical energy; the middle ear, which transmits the energy and the inner ear, where the transduction of energy into nerve impulses actually occurs.

The pinna of the external ear collects energy which travels through a small air filled duct called the auditary canal to the eardrum. Alteration in the pressure of the sound wave moves the eardrum back and forth.

The oscillation of the eardrum, in turn moves three small bones, the ossicles, so that vibration is conducted through the middle ear to the entrance of the cochlea in the inner ear. The bones of middle ear are connected like series of levers. Hence, energy is transmitted mechanically and an implication takes place through the middle ear.

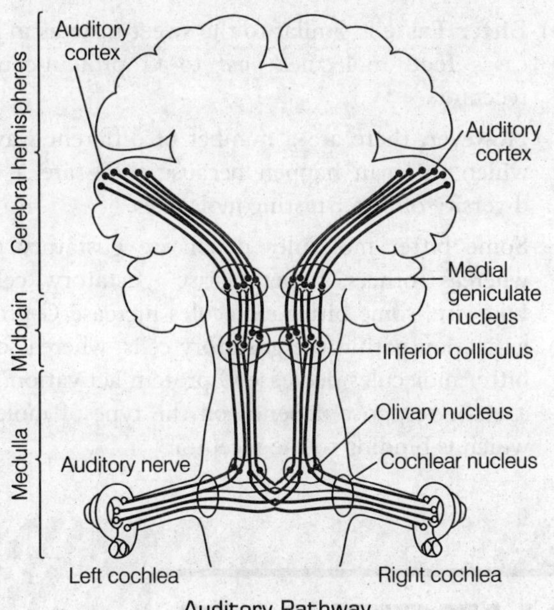

Auditory Pathway

As the ossicles move back and forth, one of them, the stapes presses on oval window which seals off the end of the vestibular canal of the cochlea.

The waves in the cochlea reach the organ of corti, which lies on the basilar membrane. The pressure wave in the cochlear canals produce bending movement of hair cell of the organ of corti. When these hair cells are bent, receptor potential is initiated, thus starting a process to generate nerve impulse.

The nerve impulses initiated in the cochlea travel into the brain and then along certain nerve fibre within the brain. These fibres and the nerve cells from which they originate, make up what is called the *auditory pathway*.

Sensory Processes : Smell

The receptor for smell respond to chemical substances, especially volatile ones. Smell receptors are located high up in the nasal passage, leading from nostril to throat.

They lie in two small passage, one on left and one on right. The sensitivity of the smell receptor is impressive. Humans can detect incredibly small amounts of odorous substances.

Once the odorant particle binds to the specific receptor, olfactory transduction is initiated. Individual odour molecules affect various parts of the olfactory system in the brain and combine to form a representation of smell. Since, most odour molecules have individual features, the number of possible combinations allow the olfactory system to detect impressively broad range of smells.

Sensory Processes : Skin

Three skin senses are usually distinguished *i.e.* pressure, Temperature Sensation (cold and warmth) and pain.

- **Pressure or Touch** The sensation of being slightly touched is known as *pressure* or *touch*. A gradient of pressure, not uniformly distributed, is the stimulus for touch experience. Meissner Corpuscle serves as the pressure sensor in the hairless region of the body. The basket nerve ending does the same thing for the root of hair. Even free nerve endings convey touch impulses.
- **Temperature Sensation** Experiences of cold and warmth are elicited by changes in the normal gradient of skin temperature *i.e.* by changes in the difference between the temperature of the skin surface and the temperature of the blood circulating beneath it.
- **Pain** A lot of things can produce pain, from a needle prick to a hard blow on the skin. Pain is caused by damage of body tissue. Receptors stimulated by the tissue damage are free nerve endings. The free nerve endings of the pain spots must be specialised in some way to respond to painful stimuli and not to other stimuli.

Sensory Processes : Taste

The sense of taste is transduced by taste buds, which are clusters of 50-100 taste receptor cells located in the tongue, soft palate, epiglottis, pharynx and esophagus. The tongue is the main sensory organ of the gustatory system. The tongue contains papillae, or specialised epithelial cells, which have taste buds on their surface. Each taste bud has a flask-like shape and is formed by two types of cells: supporting cells and gustatory cells.

The gustatory cells are sensitive to the chemicals present within foods that are ingested and they release neurotransmitters based on the amount of the chemical present in the food. Neurotransmitters from the gustatory cells can activate sensory neurons in the facial, glossopharyngeal and vagus cranial nerves.

Four tastes can be recognised: Salty, sour, sweet and bitter.

(i) **Salty Taste** refers to the perception of the sodium ions (Na^+) in the saliva. When we eat something salty, the salt crystals dissociate into the component ions *i.e.* Na^+ and Cl^-, which dissolve into the saliva in the mouth.

The Na^+concentration becomes high outside the gustatory cells, creating a strong concentration gradient that drives the diffusion of the ion into the cells. The entry of Na^+ into these cells results in the depolarisation of the cell membrane and leads to the generation of a receptor potential.

(ii) **Sour Taste** is the perception of H^+ in the saliva. The hydrogen ions enter the cell and trigger depolarisation. Sour flavours are essentially, the perception of acids in our food. Increasing hydrogen ion concentrations in the saliva (lowering saliva pH) triggers progressively stronger graded potentials in the gustatory cells.

(iii) **Sweet Taste** is the sensitivity of gustatory cells to the presence of glucose dissolved in the saliva. Other monosaccharides such as fructose, or artificial sweeteners such as aspartame, saccharine, or sucralose also activate the sweet receptors. The affinity for each of these molecules varies and some will taste sweeter than glucose because they bind to the G protein-coupled receptor differently.

(iv) **Bitter Taste** is similar to the sweet taste as in both cases food molecules *bind* to G protein-coupled receptors.

However, there are a number of different ways in which this can happen because there are a large diversity of bitter-tasting molecules.

Some bitter molecules depolarise gustatory cells, whereas others hyperpolarise gustatory cells. Likewise, some bitter molecules increase G protein activation within the gustatory cells, whereas other bitter molecules decrease G protein activation. The specific response depends on the type of molecule which is binding to the receptor.

EXAM BASED QUESTIONS

1 What is the basic function of neurons?
(a) Receiving information (b) Moving information
(c) Processing information (d) All of these

2 What is the function of cell body of neuron?
(a) Survival of neuron
(b) Maintaining neuronal structure
(c) Both a and b
(d) None of the above

3 Axon contains
(a) mitochondria (b) amino acid
(c) RNA (d) All of these

4 Neuron receive chemical transmission from one another through
(a) axon (b) dendrites
(c) cell body (d) None of these

5 How many synapses can one dendrite make?
(a) Thousand (b) Hundred
(c) Millions (d) Ten

6 Long axon is present in
(a) Sympathetic nerves (b) Para sympathetic nerves
(c) Motor neurons (d) Afferent neurons

7 Where does the Unipolar axon proceed from one region to another without branching?
(a) CNS (b) PNS (c) Spinal cord (d) Brain

8 Which of the following is function of myelin sheath?
(a) Decreases rate of signal transmission
(b) Insulator
(c) Both a and b
(d) None of these

9 Axonal terminal are also known as
(a) Terminal button (b) Axon end
(c) Terminal block (d) None of these

10 Neurotransmitters are released at the
(a) Synapse (b) Terminal button
(c) Both a and b (d) None of these

11 Action potential can trigger
(a) chemical synapse (b) electrical synapse
(c) Both a and b (d) None of these

12 The microscopic space between two neurons is called a(n)
(a) enkephalins (b) acetylcholine
(c) catecholamine (d) synapse

13 When an action potential is generated, it is carried along the axon to the
(a) presynaptic ending (b) postsynaptic ending
(c) dendrite (d) None of these

14 Action potential triggers the release of chemical messengers known as
(a) Synapse (b) Neurotransmitters
(c) Both a and b (d) None of these

15 Direct transmission of positive electrical signal is done through
(a) synapse (b) neurotransmitter
(c) ion channel (d) None of these

16 A nerve cell carrying information from your eyes, ears, fingers etc. toward the CNS is called a(n)
(a) Motor neuron (b) Effector cell
(c) Connector neuron (d) Sensory neuron

17 Which neuron conveys commands to the muscle organ and glands?
(a) Motor neuron
(b) Sensory neuron
(c) Afferent neuron
(d) Efferent neuron

18 Glial cells are found throughout the
(a) CNS (b) PNS
(c) Both a and b (d) None of these

19 Which of the following respond to brain injury by swelling or proliferating to fill up the damage space?
(a) Astrocyte (b) Microglia
(c) Schwann cell (d) None of these

20 Neural impulse originate as electrical event of very short duration that travel from
(a) synapse to axon (b) synapse to dendrites
(c) axon to dendrites (d) dendrites to axon

21 Electrical event of very short duration travelling from dendrite to axon terminal is
(a) Synaptic transmission (b) Neurotransmission
(c) Neural impulse (d) None of these

22 Which of the following is true of ion distribution across the axon membrane?
(a) Chloride ions are more concentrated inside the axon membrane.
(b) Potassium ions are more concentrated outside the cell membrane.
(c) The action potential is the balance point between diffusion and electrostatic pressure.
(d) Sodium ions are more concentrated outside the axon membrane.

23 Which one of the following is true of neural impulses in a single neuron?
(a) The strength of a neural impulse is the same each time the neuron fires.
(b) The strength of a neural impulse decreases as the strength of the incoming message gets stronger.
(c) The strength of a neural impulse increases as the strength of the incoming message gets stronger.
(d) The neuron may fire during the absolute refractory period.

24 Which of the following is true regarding the Action Potential (AP)?
(a) The AP is conducted along the dendrite.
(b) The AP is conducted faster in unmyelinated nerve cells.
(c) The AP is an all-or-none electrical event.
(d) The AP amplitude is higher for an intense signal.

25 As compared to the outside, the inside of a resting neuron is
(a) slightly negative
(b) largely negative
(c) slightly positive
(d) largely positive

26 The difference in electrical charge between the inside and the outside of the axon membrane is defined as the
(a) membrane potential (b) local potential
(c) glial potential (d) action potential

27 Which among the following chemical ions are involved in the generation of action potential?
(a) Na^+ (b) cl^-
(c) K^+ (d) All of these

28 Which potential is defined as the difference in electrical charge between the inside and the outside of an undisturbed axon membrane?
(a) resting membrane (b) local
(c) None of these (d) action

29 A change in the axon membrane potential from-70 mV to-90 mV would be termed as
(a) Repolarisation (b) Threshold potential
(c) Action potential (d) Hyperpolarisation

30 A neuron membrane potential moves from −90 mV to −80 mV in response to a brief stimulation. We would term this change in potential as an
(a) repolarisation (b) resting potential
(c) action potential (d) hyperpolarisation

31 What will be recorded from a nerve cell, whose membrane potential rises above threshold?
(a) Action potential
(b) Local potential
(c) Downward shift of the threshold of excitation
(d) Upward shift of the membrane threshold

32 What is the voltage level at which an action potential is triggered in a patch of axon membrane?
(a) Resting membrane potential
(b) Hyperpolarisation event
(c) Threshold of excitation
(d) Rate level

33 Which of the following is consistent with the 'all-or-none' law?
(a) The action potential will diminish to near 0 mV, when transmitted down a long axon.
(b) The action potential fires at the same rate regardless of the inputs to the neuron.
(c) The action potential is conducted more rapidly down the axon as it reaches the axon terminal.
(d) The action potential is produced whenever the membrane potential reaches threshold.

34 Depolarisation of the axon membrane that are below the threshold of activation
(a) involve activation of the sodium-potassium pump.
(b) remain the same size at each point along the membrane.
(c) are just smaller versions of the action potential.
(d) decrease in size as they sweep along the membrane.

35 Neurotransmitters are referred to as body's
(a) chemical messengers (b) insulator
(c) defender (d) None of these

36 Neurotransmitters can function as
(a) excitatory (b) inhibitory
(c) modulatory (d) All of these

37 Which neurotransmitters are synthesised from a single amino acid?
(a) Amino acid (b) Monoamine
(c) Soluble gas (d) Acetylcholine

38 Which amino acid neurotransmitters are present in the food we consume?
(a) Glutamate (b) Aspartate
(c) Glycine (d) All of these

39 Inside the axon-terminal, there are membrane bound spheres filled with neurotransmitter. Name of these spheres is
(a) synaptic vessicles (b) synaptic cleft
(c) synaptic sphere (d) All of these

40 Which lobe is important for processing sensory inputs and assigning its emotional meaning?
(a) Occipital lobe (b) Temporal lobe
(c) Parietal lobe (d) Frontal lobe

41 Occipital lobe helps in
(a) laying down memories (b) sensory information
(c) visual inputs (d) All of these

42 Which part of the brain is mostly involved in motor control?
(a) Cerebellum (b) Cerebrum
(c) Hypothalamus (d) Basal Ganglia

43 Broca's area is involved in
(a) reflex action (b) motor movement
(c) language processing (d) involuntary function

44 Which nerve fibre joins the left and right hemisphere?
(a) Corpus callosum (b) Medula oblongata
(c) Amygdala (d) Thalamus

45 Hypothalamus secretes a number of
(a) neurotransmitter (b) neurohormones
(c) Both a and b (d) None of these

46 How many spinal nerve enter the spinal cord?
(a) 21 (b) 31
(c) 30 (d) 20

47 The autonomic nervous system contains two branches called the
(a) Spinal nerves and cranial nerves
(b) Somatic and spinal systems
(c) Sympathetic and parasympathetic systems
(d) Parasympathetic and spinal systems

48 The word 'spike' is used to denote
(a) synapse (b) neural impulse
(c) dendrites (d) None of these

49 What does the autonomic nervous system control?
(a) Lungs
(b) Heart
(c) Exocrine and endocrine gland
(d) All of the above

50 Which neurotransmitter is released in sympathetic nervous system?
(a) Norepinephrine (b) Epinephrine
(c) Both a and b (d) None of these

51 Which neurotransmitter is used in parasympathetic nervous system?
(a) Acetylcholine (b) Nitric oxide
(c) Dopamine (d) Carbon monoxide

52 Somatic Nervous system consists of
(a) spinal nerve and cranial nerve
(b) somatic and spinal system
(c) sympathetic and parasympathetic system
(d) parasympathetic and spinal system

53 Which cranial spine nerve provide motor innervation to muscle at the base of the skull?
(a) C1 (b) C2, C3 (c) C5 (d) C4

54 What is the function of Brachial plexus?
(a) Motor control
(b) Muscular innervation
(c) Sensation to occipital nerve
(d) None of the above

55 Which of the following form the lumbosacral plexus?
(a) C5-T1 (b) C1-C4 (c) CN X1 (d) L1-CO1

56 Which of the following statement is false?
(a) Sympathetic nervous system is activated during fight or flight situation.
(b) Autonomic system can be divided into sympathetic and parasympathetic.
(c) Autonomic nervous system include the brain.
(d) Parasympathetic nervous system is activated to rest and digest.

57 Which is the specialised protein molecule located in the axon membrane that can open or close?
(a) Receptor (b) Voltage transporter
(c) Auto receptor (d) Ion channels

58 Autonomic nervous system is a part of the
(a) Central nervous system
(b) Peripheral nervous system
(c) Somatic nervous system
(d) None of the above

59 Which system gets activated during a 'fight and flight' situation?
(a) Parasympathetic nervous
(b) Sympathetic nervous system
(c) Cervical spinal nervous system
(d) None of the above

60 Which system allows the body to function in a 'rest and digest' state?
(a) Sympathetic nervous system
(b) Peripheral nervous system
(c) Automatic nervous system
(d) Parasympathetic Nervous system

61 Sensory system consists of
(a) sensory receptor (b) neural pathway
(c) part of brain (d) All of these

62 Which receptor responds to mechanical pressure?
(a) Mechanoreceptor (b) Chemoreceptor
(c) Thermoreceptor (d) Thermomagnetic receptor

63 Phonoreceptor is sensitive to which organ?
(a) Merkel's corpuscles (b) Golgi mazzoni
(c) Free nerve ending (d) Corti of ear

64 Where is the nerve impulse generated in retina?
(a) Ganglion cell (b) Cornea
(c) Rod and cones (d) All of these

65 Which the part of ear helps in hearing?
(a) External ear (b) Middle ear
(c) Inner ear (d) All of these

66 Three small bones oscillated after eardrum are known as
(a) Cochlea (b) Stapes (c) Ossicles (d) Organ of corti

67 Where are nerve impulses generated in the ear?
(a) Cochlea (b) Stapes
(c) Ossicles (d) Organ of corti

68 Which is usually detected by skin?
(a) Pressure (b) Temperature
(c) Pain (d) All of these

69 What serves as pressure sense in hairless regions of the body?
(a) Meissner corpuscles (b) Merkel's corpuscles
(c) Both a and b (d) None of these

70 Sour taste is the perception of which ion?
(a) Na^+ (b) K^+ (c) H^+ (d) Cl^-

71 What is the correct sequence of events in communicating a stimulus (such as stepping on a tack) to another neuron?
(a) Stimulus, electrical impulse, neurotransmitter, receptor site
(b) Electrical impulse, receptor site, neurotransmitter, stimulus
(c) Receptor site, electrical impulse, stimulus, neurotransmitter
(d) Receptor site, stimulus, electrical impulse, neurotransmitter.

72 Which of the following is the correct sequence for processing of information in the primary visual pathway?
(a) Retina, dorsal lateral geniculate (lgn), striate cortex
(b) Retina, striate cortex, extrastriate cortex, inferior temproal cortex
(c) LGN, Retina, striate cortex, primary visual cortex
(d) Retina, lgn, inferior temporal cortex, amygdala

73 Which of the following is true of the primate retina?
(a) There are three different rod types within the retina.
(b) The retina contains about 55 different neuron types.
(c) The retina contains one type of cone.
(d) Photoreceptors directly form synapses with ganglion cells.

74 Which of the following is true of the visual transduction process?
(a) In the dark, the photoreceptor releases a transmitter that inhibits the bipolar cell.
(b) Light depolarises the photoreceptor.
(c) Action potentials are recorded from the bipolar cell after light exposure.
(d) Action potentials are recorded from the photo receptors after light exposure.

75 Which of the following is true of the manner in which visual information is carried from retina to be cortex?
(a) Information from the temporal ganglion cells projects to the opposite hemisphere.
(b) Information from the nasal ganglion cells projects to the ipsilateral hemisphere.
(c) Information from one side of the visual field is transmitted to the opposite hemisphere.
(d) Visual information remains on the same side of the brain as it moves from retina to cortex.

76 The taste buds are formed by
(a) supporting cells
(b) gustatory cells
(c) Both a and b
(d) None of the above

77 Consider the following statements
1. Neuroplasticity is capacity of neurons and neural networks in brain to change their behaviour is response to sensory stimulation.
2. Synaptic pruning is responsible for complete elimination of unused synapses.

Which of the above statement is/are correct?
(a) Only 1 (b) Only 2
(c) Both 1 and 2 (d) None of these

78 Match the following

List I (Neurons)	**List II** (Functions)
A. Cell body	1. Maintain the neuron
B. Dendrites	2. Transmit electrochemical information
C. An axon	3. Transmit chemical information
D. Terminal synaptic buttons	4. Transmission of neuro chemical information from one neuron to other

Codes

	A	B	C	D		A	B	C	D
(a)	1	2	3	4	(b)	1	3	2	4
(c)	4	2	1	3	(d)	3	1	2	4

79 Match the following

List I (Nervous System)	List II (Associated With)
A. Central	1. Connects central nervous system to voluntary muscles
B. Somatic	2. Readies body for restoration of energy
C. Parasympathetic	3. Brain and spinal cord

Codes

	A	B	C		A	B	C
(a)	1	2	3	(b)	3	1	2
(c)	3	2	1	(d)	1	3	2

80 Match the following

List I (Neurotransmitter)	List II (Effect)
A. Acetylcholine	1. Regulation of mood
B. Nor-epinephrine	2. Learning and memory
C. Serotonin	3. Control of alertness

Codes

	A	B	C		A	B	C
(a)	2	3	1	(b)	2	1	3
(c)	3	1	2	(d)	3	2	1

81 Match the following

List I (Sense Receptor)	List II (Function)
A. Exteroceptor	1. Info about skeletal muscle and joints
B. Interoceptor	2. Info about visceral organs
C. Proprioceptor	3. Info about external environment

Codes

	A	B	C		A	B	C	D
(a)	3	2	1	(b)	3	1	2	
(c)	2	3	1	(d)	2	1	3	

82 Which of the following pairs is/are correctly matched?

1. Central nervous system – Brain
2. Somatic nervous system – Spinal cord
3. Para sympathetic nervous system – Neural fiber

Codes

(a) 1 and 2 (b) 2 and 3
(c) 1, 2 and 3 (d) Only 1

83 Which of the following is/are correct?

1. Calcium ion required for release of neurotransmitter
2. Ionotropic receptor involve the direct opening of ion chennal
3. Large myelinated fiber conduct action potential more rapidly

Codes

(a) 1 and 2 (b) 2 and 3
(c) 1 and 3 (d) All of these

84 Which of the following pairs is/are correctly matched?

1. Ophthalmic – Spinal cord
2. Vertebral – Eye
3. Carotid – Neck

Codes

(a) Only 1 (b) Only 2 (c) Only 3 (d) None of these

85 Which of the following pairs is/are correctly matched?

1. Brain – CNS
2. Spinal cord – ANS
3. Neuron – Dendrite

Codes

(a) Only 1 (b) Only 2
(c) Only 3 (d) None of these

86 Consider the following statements

1. In a myelinated axon, ions enter or leave the axon membrane only at the node of ranvier.
2. Vesicle speeds up the velocity, with which an axon can conduct an action potential.

Which of the statements given above is/are correct?

(a) Only 1 (b) Only 2
(c) Both 1 and 2 (d) Neither 1 nor 2

87 Consider the following statements

1. Visual information from the retina is carried by ganglion cell axons to the thalamic dorsal lateral geniculate nucleus.
2. The retino-spinal pathways are important for the synchronisation of behavioural activity to that of the light-dark cycle.

Which of the statements given above is/are correct?

(a) Only 1 (b) Only 2
(c) Both 1 and 2 (d) None of these

88 Consider the following statements

1. Bipolar neurons are the most common type in the central nervous system.
2. The cell membrane is formed by a dual layer of lipid molecule.

Which of the statements given above is/are correct?

(a) Only 1 (b) Only 2
(c) Both 1 and 2 (d) Neither 1 nor 2

89 Consider the following statements in respect of the glial cells.

1. They help in regulating neuronal metabolism.
2. They help in myelinisation.
3. They help in cell proliferation.
4. They speed up nerve impulse.

Which of the statements given above is/are correct?
(a) 1, 2 and 3 (b) 3 and 4
(c) 1 and 2 (d) All of these

90 Consider the following statements
1. The central nervous system consists of brain.
2. Spinal cord is not a part of central nervous system.

Which of the statements given above is/are correct?
(a) Only 1 (b) Only 2
(c) Both 1 and 2 (d) Neither 1 nor 2

Directions (Q. Nos. (91-94) *Read the passage given below and answer the following questions.*

Neurons can organise their rate of electrical activity in two fundamental ways. First, groups of neurons can fire in synchronised oscillations by taking cues from other cells, also known as pacemaker cells or K neurons. Cortical neurons also take cues from other brain structure such as the thalamus, which can act as powerful pace maker, even when there is no external sensory input. *For example*, during non-rapid eye movement, the thalamus generates rhythmic, self-sustaining discharge patterns that prevent organised information from reaching the cortex.

Thus, one's brain is asleep, demonstrating large, rhythmic data waves. Second, nervous may fire in a consistent rhythmic pattern in response of collective behaviour, such as large group of people clapping in as synchronised way without a cheer leader being present.

91 In how many ways neurons can organise their rate of electrical activity?
(a) One fundamental way (b) Two fundamental way
(c) Three fundamental way (d) Four fundamental way

92 From which brain structure cortical neuron takes cues?
(a) Thalamus (b) Hypothalamus
(c) Frontal lobe (d) Side lobe

93 During which period the thalamus generates rhythmic self-sustaining discharge pattern that prevent organised information from reaching the cortex?
(a) Rapid eye movement
(b) Non-rapid eye movement
(c) Theta activity
(d) Gama activity

94 The K neurons are otherwise called as
(a) neuron cell (b) somatic cell
(c) pacemaker cell (d) thalamus cell

Directions (Q. Nos. 95-100) *In the questions given below are two statements, labelled as Assertion (A) and Reason (R). In the context of the two statements, which one of the following is correct?*

Codes
(a) Both A and R are true and R is the correct explanation of A
(b) Both A and R are true, but R is not the correct explanation of A
(c) A is true, but R is false
(d) A is false, but R is true

95 **Assertion** (A) The message, which the neuron receives from other neuron does not produce action potential.
Reason (R) The neuron receives message from sensory receptors through synapses on its dendrites and cell body.

96 **Assertion** (A) Auditory neurons are sensitive to the differences in the arrival times of an auditory stimulus.
Reason (R) Sound that occurs directly in front will arrive at the right and left ears at same time.

97 **Assertion** (A) Nervous system facilitates the spread of infectious agents from one hemisphere to the other.
Reason (R) There is free circulation within the nervous system.

98 **Assertion** (A) CNS include the brain.
Reason (R) CNS is part of our nervous system.

99 **Assertion** (A) Neurons show a resting potential or membrane potential when they are inactive.
Reason (R) They show a slight electrical imbalance between the inner and outer surface of the membrane.

100 **Assertion** (A) Determination of sound identity is carried out by the auditory cortex.
Reason (R) Low pitched sounds are detected by the use of place coding by the cochlea.

PREVIOUS YEARS' QUESTIONS

July 2018

1 In case of visual stimulus 'Where' pathways in the brain are mainly responsible for processing

1. location 2. colour
3. motion 4. shape

Codes

(a) 1 and 2 (b) 2 and 3
(c) 3 and 4 (d) 1 and 3

2 In vertebrates, myelin is produced in the brain and spinal cord by .... and in rest of nervous system by.........

(a) oligodendrocytes; schwann cells
(b) schwann cells; oligodendrocytes
(c) astrocytes; microglia
(d) microglia; astrocytes

3 Read each of the following statements Assertion (A) and Reason (R) and indicate your answer using code given below :

Assertion (A) Visual simple reaction time is more than auditory simple reaction time.

Reason (R) Visual system involves more complex photochemical processes.

Codes

(a) Both A and R are true and R is the correct explanation of A
(b) Both A and R are true, but R is not the correct explanation of A
(c) A is true, but R is false
(d) A is false, but R is true

4 Which of the following sequences describes the Cranial Nerves in ascending order?

(a) Optic → Trochlear → Abducens → Auditory → Vestibular → Vagus
(b) Trochlear → Optic → Auditory → Vestibular → Abducens → Vagus
(c) Optic → Abducens → Trochlear → Vagus → Auditory → Vestibular
(d) Abducens → Trochlear → Optic → Auditory → Vestibular → Vagus

November 2017

5 In which parts of brain the feeling of hunger and full are felt?

(a) Hypothalamus; Cerebral cortex
(b) Lateral hypothalamus; Ventromedial hypothalamus
(c) Lateral hypothalamus; Cerebral cortex
(d) Cerebral cortex; Ventromedial hypothalamus

6 Where is Broca's area located?

(a) Frontal lobe (b) Occipital lobe
(c) Parietal lobe (d) Temporal lobe

7 An important factor which enables one to adapt to inverted vision is

(a) orientation (b) active movement
(c) new learning (d) frame of reference

8 Which of the following is associated with memory for emotionally charged events?

1. Thalamus 2. Hypothalamus
3. Amygdala 4. Temporal lobe

Codes

(a) 1 and 2 (b) Only 3 (c) 2 and 4 (d) Only 4

9 Read each of the following two statements Assertion (A) and Reason (R) and indicate your answer using codes given below

Assertion (A) Increase in synaptic strength is due to the simultaneous stimulation of pre synaptic and post synaptic neurons.

Reason (R) Long term potentiation can be induced in the laboratory by stimulating the pre-synaptic neurons with pulses of high frequency of electricity for few seconds.

Codes

(a) Both A and R are true and R is the correct explanation of A
(b) Both A and R are true, but R is not the correct explanation of A
(c) A is true, but R is false
(d) A is false, but R is true

10 Which is the correct sequence of parts of ear through which sound travels in the ear?

(a) Tymphanic membrane → Stapes → Incus → Malleus → Cochlea
(b) Tymphanic membrane → Incus → Stapes → Malleus → Cochlea
(c) Malleus → Incus → Stapes → Cochlea → Tymphanic membrane
(d) Tymphanic membrane → Malleus → Incus → Stapes → Cochlea

11 Afferent and efferent nerves are found in which of the following?

(a) Sympathetic Nervous System
(b) Para-Sympathetic Nervous System
(c) Somatic Nervous System
(d) Central Nervous System

January 2017

12 Network of auditory pathways can be arranged in which of the following sequence

(a) Auditory Nerve → Cochlear Nuclei → Superior Olives → Lateral Leminiscus → Inferior Colliculi → Medical Geniculate Nuclei → Primary Auditory Cortex

(b) Cochlear Nuclei → Auditory Nerve → Lateral Leminiscus → Superior Olives → Inferior Colliculi → Medial Geniculate Nuclei → Primary Auditory Cortex
(c) Auditory Nerve → Cochlear Nuclei → Lateral Leminiscus → Inferior Colliculi → Superior Colliculi → Medial Geniculate Nuclei → Auditory Cortex
(d) Cochlear Nuclei → Auditory Nerve → Inferior Colliculi → Superior Colliculi → Lateral Leminiscus → Medial Geniculate Nuclei → Auditory Cortex

13 Read each of the following two statements Assertion (A) and Reason (R) and indicate your answer using codes given below

Assertion (A) Patients with amygdala damage are unable to recognise fear in other's facial expression.

Reason (R) Looking at fearful faces activates amygdala.

Codes
(a) Both A and R are true and R is the correct explanation of A
(b) Both A and R are true, but R is not the correct explanation of A
(c) A is true, but R is false
(d) A is false, but R is true

14 Which of the following are not nuclei of Thalamus?
1. Internal lamina 2. Anterior nucleus
3. Ventromedial nucleus
4. Paraventricular nucleus

Codes
(a) 1 and 2 (b) 2 anc 3 (c) 3 and 4 (d) 1 and 3

July 2016

15 When the action potential reaches the end of the axon terminals, it causes the release of
(a) an electric spark that sets off the next neuron
(b) positively charged ions that excite the next cell
(c) negatively charged ions that inhibit the next cell
(d) neurotransmitters that excite or inhibit the next cell

16 Arrange the parts of CNS in ascending order.
1. Thalamus 2. Medulla oblongata
3. Spinal cord 4. Frontal lobe

Codes
(a) 1, 2, 3, 4 (b) 2, 1, 3, 4
(c) 4, 2, 1, 3 (d) 3, 2, 1, 4

17 In heightened emotional states, the following functions are not triggered by sympathetic Nervous System activity.
1. Perspiration 2. Heightened pulse rate
3. Digestion 4. Pupillary dilation

Codes
(a) Only 3 (b) 3 and 4
(c) 1, 2 and 3 (d) 1, 3 and 4

18 Amit met with an accident and later turned into impulsive, irresponsible and less concerned with the consequences of his actions. He must have suffered damage in
(a) parietal lobe (b) frontal lobe
(c) occipital lobe (d) temporal lobe

December 2015

19 **Assertion** (A) Action potentials normally travel along axons in one direction.

Reason (R) The portions of an axon over which an action potential has just travelled are left momentarialy refractory.

Codes
(a) Both A and R are true and R is the correct explanation of A
(b) Both A and R are true, but R is not the correct explanation of A
(c) A is true, but R is false
(d) A is false, but R is true

20 In which lobe of the cerebral cortex, the primary olfactory cortex lies?
(a) Frontal lobe (b) emporal lobe
(c) Occipital lobe (d) Parietal lobe

21 Which of the following is the final destination for much of the brain's information about emotion before action is taken?
(a) Amygdala
(b) Anterior consulate cortex
(c) Pre-frontal cortex
(d) Hypothalamus

June 2015

22 The parasympathetic nerves project from
(a) the lumber and thoracic regions of the spinal cord
(b) the brain and sacral region of the spinal cord
(c) the brain and the lumbar region of the spinal cord
(d) the lumbar and the sacral regions of the spinal cord

23 **Assertion** (A) A synapse does not necessarily result into action potential in post synaptic neuron.

Reason (R) Synapses produce inhibitory post synaptic potential also in post synaptic neuron.

Codes
(a) Both A and R are true and R is the correct explanation of A
(b) Both A and R are true, but R is not the correct explanation of A
(c) A is true, but R is false
(d) A is false, but R is true

December 2014

24 **Assertion** (A) A major function of the perceptual system is to keep the appearance of objects, the same inspite of change in the stimuli.

Reason (R) The posterior brain system selects objects on the basis of location, shape or colour and the anterior system is responsible for guiding the process.

Codes

(a) Both A and R are true and R is the correct explanation of A
(b) Both A and R are true, but R is not the correct explanation of A
(c) A is true, but R is false
(d) A is false, but R is true

25 During resting potential, cell membrane is

1. almost permeable to sodium.
2. almost permeable to potassium.
3. almost impermeable to sodium.
4. almost impermeable to potassium.

Codes

(a) 1 and 4 (b) 2 and 3
(c) 1 and 2 (d) 3 and 4

26 Match List I with List II and select the correct answer by choosing from the codes given below

List I (Parts of Human Brain)		**List II** (Functions)
A. Thalamus	1.	Plays a special role in memory
B. Medulla	2.	Involved in mediating emotions
C. Hippocampus	3.	Helps in control sleeps and wakefulness
D. Amygdala	4.	Helps the organism to maintain upright position

Codes

	A	B	C	D		A	B	C	D
(a)	3	4	1	2	(b)	4	3	1	2
(c)	4	1	2	3	(d)	1	4	3	2

June 2014

27 Which of the following cells do produce myelin in the Central Nervous System?

(a) Schwann cells (b) Astrocytes
(c) Microglia (d) Oligodendrocytes

28 Autonomic Nervous System is concerned with the regulation of …… .

1. smooth muscles
2. skeletal muscles
3. cardiac muscles
4. glands

Codes

(a) 1 and 2 (b) 1, 2 and 3
(c) 1, 3 and 4 (d) All of these

29 Arrange the following in correct sequence through which the sound waves reach to receptors.

1. Oval window
2. Incus
3. Stapes
4. Malleus
5. Tympanic membrane

Codes

(a) 5, 4, 2, 3, 1 (b) 5, 4, 3, 2, 1
(c) 5, 4, 1, 3, 2 (d) 5, 3, 2, 4, 1

30 **Assertion** (A) A positive charge applied to the inside of the membrane of the neuron produced depolarisation.

Reason (R) Inside of the membrane was positively charged.

Codes

(a) Both A and R are true and R is the correct explanation of A
(b) Both A and R are true, but R is not the correct explanation of A
(c) A is true, but R is false
(d) A is false, but R is true

ANSWERS

Exam Based Questions

1 (b)	2 (c)	3 (d)	4 (b)	5 (a)	6 (c)	7 (a)	8 (b)	9 (a)	10 (a)
11 (c)	12 (d)	13 (a)	14 (b)	15 (c)	16 (d)	17 (a)	18 (c)	19 (a)	20 (d)
21 (c)	22 (d)	23 (d)	24 (c)	25 (a)	26 (a)	27 (d)	28 (c)	29 (d)	30 (a)
31 (a)	32 (a)	33 (c)	34 (d)	35 (a)	36 (d)	37 (b)	38 (a)	39 (a)	40 (b)
41 (c)	42 (a)	43 (c)	44 (a)	45 (b)	46 (b)	47 (c)	48 (b)	49 (d)	50 (c)
51 (a)	52 (a)	53 (a)	54 (b)	55 (d)	56 (c)	57 (d)	58 (b)	59 (b)	60 (d)
61 (d)	62 (a)	63 (d)	64 (a)	65 (d)	66 (c)	67 (a)	68 (d)	69 (a)	70 (c)
71 (a)	72 (a)	73 (c)	74 (d)	75 (c)	76 (c)	77 (c)	78 (b)	79 (b)	80 (a)
81 (a)	82 (d)	83 (d)	84 (d)	85 (a)	86 (a)	87 (a)	88 (b)	89 (d)	90 (a)
91 (b)	92 (a)	93 (b)	94 (c)	95 (b)	96 (b)	97 (b)	98 (b)	99 (b)	100 (c)

Previous Years Questions

1 (d)	2 (a)	3 (b)	4 (c)	5 (b)	6 (a)	7 (b)	8 (d)	9 (b)	10 (d)
11 (c)	12 (a)	13 (c)	14 (c)	15 (d)	16 (d)	17 (a)	18 (b)	19 (a)	20 (b)
21 (c)	22 (b)	23 (b)	24 (b)	25 (b)	26 (a)	27 (d)	28 (c)	29 (a)	30 (c)

Physiological Psychology

Physiological psychology is a subset of neuroscience methods. It is used across the disciplines in order to seek answers to diverse questions related to psychology, both mental and behavioural. Many techniques can be classified as a part of physiological psychology. Every technique has its own strengths and weaknesses. Knowing all of them allow the researcher to know which one to choose for a particular experiment.

Introduction of Physiological Psychology

Physiological psychology is the study of the physiological basis of how we think, connecting the physical operation of the brain with that what we actually say and do. It is thus concerned with brain cells, brain structures and components, brain chemistry and how all this leads to speech and action. It is also, important for understanding how we take in information from our five senses.

Modern psychology grew out of medical explorations of the brain and one of the first psychology text books was called 'Principles of Physiological Psychology'. Much early knowledge was gained through observing how behaviour changes when different parts of the brain are damaged. Modern scanning system, such as MRI and PET have given further insights as activation of parts of the brain can be seen without the more intrusive former methods.

Methods of Physiological Psychology

Stimulation

Stimulation involves feeding a signal into some part of a circuit and measuring its consequences at some other point. Since, the brain is not being altered in any other way, the way the brain is organised would not seem to affect the interpretation of stimulation studies. Stimulation will work for both interactive and modular systems.

In this Chapter

- *Introduction of Physiological Psychology*
- *Invasive Techniques*
- *Non-Invasive Techniques*

Stimulation can either be electrical or chemical. Electrical stimulation is delivered through electrodes. Chemical stimulation is delivered through fine tubes, cannular, lowered into the intended stimulation site. Usually, stimulation devices are positioned using a stereotaxic device. Whether one uses electrical or chemical stimulation there is inevitably a gradient of intensity of stimulation as one moves away from the source.

The traditional stimulation approach, using large sources of stimulation is imprecise. Recognising these problems, many people engaged in electrical stimulation work have moved to micro-stimulation. This involves stimulating through micro-electrodes of the sort used in single unit recording studies, with very low currents at a level calculated to affect a small population of adjacent cells or fibers.

Following are the steps of stimulation that are discussed below

Problems in Interpretation

Even if one has a stimulus of psychologically realistic intensity, that does not necessarily mean that one can readily interpret the effects of stimulation, because there are still two problems. The first is that the brain is organised with a considerable amount of parallel wiring, so that information about the same event may be encoded in the activity of a number of cells not necessarily adjacent to each other. The second is that the electrical activity of the brain is temporally patterned, when a cell is active or inactive is as important as how much it is active.

Conditions for Interpretable Data

Stimulation provides readily interpretable data under two conditions. One is if local elements are arranged in parallel with independent access to the output mechanisms. The other is, if a system is organised, so that the amount of activity in its neurons is more important than their spatial or temporal pattern. The first condition is satisfied in parts of the motor system, in which cells in the brain project directly on to motor neurons in the spinal cord, so that a small group of cells in the CNS have a direct line to a small group of muscles and perhaps in visuomotor centres in the brainstem.

Analogous Studies Outside the CNS

Stimulation has been the method of choice for most researchers studying the peripheral mechanisms of eating and drinking. By producing precisely controlled changes in the concentration of nutrients or salts in the blood, it has been possible to explore the role of factors like blood glucose level or cellular dehydration in eating and drinking. Within the last decade, analogous methods have been used to study the role of the gastro-intestinal tract in satiation.

Recording

Physiologists capitalised on this instrumentation to demonstrate that the electrical activity of the brain and its nerve cells was a function of what the individual was doing or not doing or how sensory receptors were stimulated. A wide range of electrical recording techniques are currently available, although not all are suitable for studying behavioural processes. The most important distinction is between those that register the activity of large numbers of cells and those that record action potential from individual units.

The simplest of the first type to record, but most difficult to interpret, is the Eletroencephalogram (EEG), in which the activity of the brain is monitored continuously through the scalpel. This is used widely to determine the functional state of the brain,but is difficult to relate to the operations of different areas. More useful in this respect are 'event-related potential', which are extracted from the EEG by signal-averaging techniques. They rely on the fact that although the EEG is very noisy there are, embedded within it, consistent changes in voltage that are time-locked to specific events like the presentation of stimuli or the performance of movements.

Invasive Technique

Invasive technique involves the introduction of instrument into the body or body cavities. Invasive method is not comfortable and requires a lot of skill set to operate. Thus, non-invasive techniques are preferred over invasive techniques nowadays.

The invasive methods include

- Anatomical method
- Lesion method
- Microelectrode method
- Chemical method
- Degenerative method

Anatomical Method

Anatomical method involves studying of different parts of any organised body. It is aimed at discovering their situation, structure and economy.

Before advent of sophisticated techniques, the anatomy and function of the human brain have been visualised by microscopy for more than a century.

For most kinds of microscopic investigations, the tissue to be imaged must be this enough for light to pass through it and portions of it must be of different colours or transparency so that important features are distinguishable. *A variety of histological* (having to do with the study of the minute structrue of tissues) *procedures have been devised to meet these objectives*

(i) **Fixation** In most instances, the tissue to be examined must first be prepared by fixation, a procedure to preserve the features of interest. Fixation is often accomplished by using an agent - such as formalin-to harden the tissue. Freezing is another useful approach to stabilise neural tissue.

(ii) **Thinning of Tissue** Once hardened, the tissue is sliced very thinly to render it nearly transparent. One typical procedure is to first embed the tissue in a substance such as paraffin to facilitate holding the specimen. It then can be cut by using a **microtome**, a specialised automatic slicing machine that produces thin, regular sections, in the fixed and embedded tissue. The resulting thin sections may then be mounted on glass slides in preparation for viewing.

Such microscopic sections are now thin enough for light to pass through them, but in most cases they lack sufficient contrast to make different features of the tissue apparent.

(iii) **Visualising Cells and Cell Components** Following techniques can be used to visualize cell and cell components

(a) **Staining** is a procedure to selectively darken or colour particular featrues of the sectioned tissue. By choosing an appropriate stain, different featrues of the tissues are highlighted. *Some of the stains are as follows*

- **Golgi Silver Stain** has the property of completely staining a few individual cells in the specimen. Because only a few cells are stained, they stand out with exquisite clarity. The Golgi method is probably the best histological procedure for visualising single nerve cells.
- **Nissl Staining** is useful for visualising the distribution of cell bodies in the specimen.
- **Myelin Stains** selectively colour myelin protective coating, a procedure that is useful for mapping, connecting pathways in brain tissue.

(b) **Selective Damage of Nerve Cell Bodies** One classical approach of determining where cells in a particular location make their connections is to selectively damage those nerve cell bodies. Since, the cell body supplies all the metabolic needs of the cell, the axons then die and begin to degenerate.

Silver staining of the tissue-a procedure perfected by Walle Nauta-turns the dying axons dark brown. In this way, specific pathways can be traced through the nervous system.

(c) **Radioactive Labelling** Pathways can also be traced in experimental animals by injecting radioactively labelled amino acids in the vicinity of the cell bodies of interest. The labelled amino acids are taken up by the cell and transported along the axons. After sufficient time for the transport to be completed, the brain is removed and sections are made. Each section is coated with a sensitive emulsion.

The radioactive level then exposes the emulsion that can be developed at a later time, in much the same way as photographic film is developed. This is one example of autoradiography, a term for procedures in which the section in effect takes a radiograph of itself, highlighting areas of intense radioactive label.

(d) **Enzyme Horseradish Peroxidase** Pathways can also be mapped in the reverse direction from the ends of the axon back to the cell body by injecting the enzyme horseradish peroxidase. The tips of the axon pick up the enzyme and it is transported back to the cell body. Along the way, the enzyme causes reactions in the interior of the axon that may be subsequently visualised by a special staining procedure.

(e) **Monoclonal Antibodies** These are being developed to recognise and mark particular cellular proteins. Antibodies are proteins produced by lymphocytes-a type of white blood cell - that bind to particular target molecules.

Thus, antibodies could be used to locate particular targets, but the problem is to obtain sufficient quantities of identical antibodies to carry out the search. This is accomplished by cloning the antibody. In cloning, a single antibody-producing lymphocyte is joined to a lymphocyte tumor cell. The lymphocyte tumor cell divides indefinitely, producing a strain of identical-cloned-lymphocytes, all of which produce the desired antibody.

Monoclonal antibodies-antibodies produced by the same cloned lymphocytes-may then be used to map highly specific biochemical characteristics of specific neural populations.

Chemical Method

The chemical analysis can be carried out on a much localised basis, by specifically introducing the chemical to a particular brain region.

Tools of Chemical Methods

This can be done through cannula or microdialysis.

Cannula

Researchers interested in the relationship between drugs and behaviour have utilised various methods for the administration of discrete amounts of chemicals directly into cerebral structrues through cannula. The ease of construction, economy of materials and simplicity of use make this technique highly suitable for small laboratories with limited facilities.

The end of the cannula to be inserted into the brain is cut at an angle, so that the pointed tip causes a minimum of distortion to the surrounding tissue. The other end is sealed by touching it to a match flame or a hot soldering iron. The animal is anesthetised and the head of the animal is shaved for preparing for surgery.

Once the mid-saggital incision has been made and the connective tissue cleared, the anterior-posterior and lateral dimensions of the target structrue from Bregma are measured on the exposed skull. A hand drill is used to make a small hole in the skull, which exactly fits the outer dimensions of the cannula. Care must be taken that the insertion angle of the cannula is at right angles to the top of the skull.

Cranioplast is then used to cement the cannula firmly to the screw and the skull. For intracerebral (IC) administration of chemicals, the rat is wrapped in a towel or placed in a small restraining device. The sealed end of the polyethylene cannula is cut off and the injection is made by inserting a microsyringe into the cut cannula tip.

Rats implanted in this manner have been used for four months with no problems of a blocked cannula, even if the intracerebral injections are spaced as far apart as 2-4 weeks. The loss of animals due to blockade of the cannula can be avoided by constructing a cleaner that matches the length of the stainless steel portion.

Microdialysis

The technique of microdialysis enables the monitoring of neurotransmitters and other molecules in interstitial tissue fluid. This method is widely used for sampling and quantifying neurotransmitters, neuropeptides and hormones in the brain and periphery.

Depending on the availability of an appropriate analytical assay, virtually any soluble molecule in the interstitial space fluid can be measured by microdialysis. This technique is used either to sample a substance from an external solution or to deliver a substance to the external solution (*e.g.* retrodialysis) or both.

Elements of Microdialysis

The elements of mirodialysis are as follows

(i) **Probe** A principal element of microdialysis is the probe, which is used to capture molecules from the extracellular space. All microdialysis probes are composed of a length of tubular dialysis membrane through which a solution, usually devoid of the analyte of interest, is constantly perfused. The dialysis membrane is semipermeable and permits free transport of some but not all solutes. Permeability of dialysis membrane is limited to compounds with molecular mass <20,000 Da.

(ii) **Concentration Gradient** A complete characterisati on of the transport of an analyte during microdialysis involves a description of the concentration gradient in the external medium (*e.g.* tissue), the concentration gradient across the membrane and the concentration gradient across the annular width of the microdialysis probe.

It is important to note that the concentration gradient is influenced not only by the physical attributes of the analyte (*i.e.* molecular weight, hydrophobicity and tertiary structrue), but also by the physical composition of the medium in which transport occurs. During microdialysis, substances move from an area of higher concentration to an area of lower concentration.

The extraction fraction (*i.e.* probe efficiency or relative recovery) defines the proportional difference in concentration between the highest concentration of substance and the lowest concentration of the substance (*i.e.* 'undisturbed' extracellular concentration versus dialysate concentration).

Knowing the extraction fraction is essential for determining the external concentration of a substance relative to its concentration in the dialysate.

Methods of Microdialysis

Once the probe is inserted into an external medium (*i.e.* tissue) and perfusion begins, substances on the outside surface of the dialysis membrane diffuse through the membrane into the probe along their concentration gradient.

The perfusate is infused slowly and continuously through the length of the dialysis probe into the outflow tubing where it can be collected for subsequent analyte quantification. The presence of the microdialysis probe impacts the external medium surrounding it.

As low-molecular-weight solutes are removed from the external medium by the probe, a zone around the probe becomes depleted of solute. Depletion is not completed because the external medium is continuous and large, so that the solutes can be partially replaced by diffusion from areas of higher concentration that are undisturbed by the probe.

Moreover, the perfusion itself may induce changes in the surrounding brain tissue, which may influence the release and metabolism of the sampled transmitter. Therefore, a description of the microdialysis process should include an account of the changes in concentration of the analyte in the tissue around the probe.

Diffusion of a given analyte involves transport of that analyte down its concentration gradient from the undisturbed tissue into the perfusate.

The direction of movement is set by the experimenter, who biases the procedure, so that the concentration of the analyte under study is higher on one side of the probe membrane.

Lesion Technique

The lesion method aims at establishing a correlation between a circumscribed region of brain damage, a lesion and a pattern of alteration in some aspect of an experimentally controlled cognitive or behavioural performance. The brain-damaged region is conceptualised as a part of a large-scale network of cortical and sub cortical sites that operate in concert by virtue of their interlocking connectivity to produce a particular function. Given a theoretical framework for how such networks are constituted and carry out that particular function, a lesion is thus a probe to test a specific hypothesis.

- A lesion probe allows the investigator to decide whether damage to a component of the putative network, responsible for function x, alters the network behaviour according to a prediction made for it.
- The subjects for the lesion method may be humans or animals. The lesions may have been produced by neurologic disease alone or incurred in the process of treating it.

The lesion approach provided the first association between unilateral brain disease and contra lateral sensory and motor disabilities. Bouillau's and Broca's finding of a correlation between speech and focal damage to the frontal lobe are reasonable signposts to mark the modern era of lesion studies. Two key developments made human lesion studies rewarding again. *First,* lesion studies in nonhuman primates brought major advances to the understanding of the neural basic of vision and memory, as demonstrated among others by Mishkin and Colleagues. *Second,* the advent of CT and MRI began to permit human lesion studies in vivo.

It is apparent now that the lesion method is indispensable to cognitive neuroscience, especially when it comes to human studies. The new lesion method is not concerned with localising functions, nor it is a contest for localising lesions. It is a means to test, at systems level hypothesis regarding both neural structure and cognitive processes. The lesion method does have its limitations. Not every anatomic region of the human nervous system can be properly sampled by natural lesions and the size of the lesions provides a natural limit to the structures, the method can probe with confidence. And yet, in its modern incarnation, the approach provides data currently unavailable through other means.

Degenerative Technique

Neural degeneration provides surprising insight into nervous organisation because of a unique property of nervous tissue: injured neurons are not replaced when they die. In the degenerative technique the normal brain is compared with a brain undergoing degeneration. In such a way we gain insights to various disorders which happen due to degeneration of brain. Ageing also causes the degeneration of brain.

It has been widely found that the volume of the brain and its weight declines with age at a rate of around 5% per decade after age 40 with the actual rate of decline possibly increasing with age particularly over age 70. The manner in which this occurs is less clear. The shrinking of the grey matter is frequently reported to stem from neuronal cell death, but whether this is solely responsible or even the primary finding is not entirely clear.

It has been suggested that a decline in neuronal volume rather than number contributes to the changes in an ageing brain and that it may be related to sex with different areas most affected in men and women. Additionally, there may be changes in dendritic arbour, spines and synapses. Dendritic sprouting may occur thus maintaining a similar number of synapses and compensating for any cell death. Conversely a decrease in dendritic synapses or loss of synaptic plasticity has also been described. The role of white matter in the ageing brain also needs to be considered.

White matter may decline with age, the myelin sheath deteriorating after around the age of 40 even in normal ageing and it has been suggested that the late myelinating regions of the frontal lobes are most affected by White Matter Lesions (WML), although not all studies support this view. Leukoariosis/WML increase with age and may indicate subclinical ischemia. *Brain degeneration also occurs in case of diseases like Alzheimer and Parkinson.*

Alzheimer's Disease

In Alzheimer's disease, damage is widespread, as many neurons stop functioning, lose connections with other neurons and die. Alzheimer's disrupts processes vital to neurons and their networks, including communication, metabolism and repair and initially affects entorhinal cortex and hippocampus part of brain.

Eventually, many other areas of the brain are damaged. Over time, a person with Alzheimer's gradually loses his or her ability to live and function independently. Ultimately, the disease is fatal.

The hallmarks of Alzheimer's disease are

(i) Accumulation of amyloid plaques between nerve cells (neurons) in the brain. Amyloids are protein fragments which are broken down and eliminated in a healthy brain while tend to accumulate in form of hard, insoluble plaques in case of Alzheimere's disease.

(ii) Abnormal protein which leads to collapse of the microtubule structrues. The microtubule structures are responsible for transporting nutrients and other important substances from one part of never cell to other.

Parkinson's Disease

Parkinson's Disease (PD) is a degenerative, progressive disorder that affects nerve cells in deep parts of the brain called the basal ganglia and the substantia nigra.

Nerve cells in the substantia nigra produce the neurotransmitter dopamine and are responsible for relaying messages that plan and control body movement. For reasons not yet understood, the dopamine-producing nerve cells of the substantia nigra begin to die off in some individuals. When 80 percent of dopamine is lost, PD symptoms such as tremor, slowness of movement, stiffness and balance problems occur.

Body movement is controlled by a complex chain of decisions involving inter-connected groups of nerve cells called ganglia. Information comes to a central area of the brain called the striatum, which works with the substantia nigra to send impulses back and forth from the spinal cord to the brain. The basal ganglia and cerebellum are responsible for ensuring that movement is carried out in a smooth, fluid manner.

These impulses are passed from neuron to neuron, moving quickly from the brain to the spinal cord and finally to the muscles. When dopamine receptors in the striatum are not adequately stimulated, parts of the basal ganglia are either under or over-stimulated. In particular, the subthalamic nucleus (STN) becomes overactive and acts as a brake on the Globus Pallidus Interna (GPI), causing shutdown of motion and rigidity. When the GPI is overstimulated, it has an over inhibitory effect on the thalamus, which decreases thalamus output and causes tremor.

The action of dopamine is opposed by another neurotransmitter called acetylcholine. In PD the nerve cells that produce dopamine die. High levels of glutamate, another neurotransmitter, also appear in PD as the body tries to compensate for the lack of dopamine.

Microelectrode Studies

Microelectrodes have emerged as an important tool used by scientists to study biological changes in the brain and in single cells. Microelectrodes as chemical sensors have furthered the field of neurobiology by reporting on changes that occur on the sub-second time scale.

Microelectrodes have been used in a variety of fields including their use by electrophysiologists to characterise neuronal action potentials and development of neural prosthetics. Microelectrodes is an electrode used in electro physiology either for recording neural signals or for electrical stimulation of nervous tissue. They have played a major role in many important neurobiological findings.

Sensors for measuring neurobiological events must be both small and rapid. Microelectrodes are thus ideal for this type of application since they possess dimensions in the micron range. Microelectrodes can be fabricated in a variety of ways, either through insulation of a carbon fiber with a glass capillary, or utilising carbon fiber nanoelectrodes. The small size of the electrode minimises the double-layer capacitance, thus make it possible to make recordings on the subsecond time scale. Microelectrodes are not inherently selective; however, the selectivity of the microelectrodes can be enhanced either through application of techniques such as FSCV or chemical modification of the electrode surface.

Electrochemical detection utilising microelectrodes requires that the detected species be electroactive. Several neurochemical transmitters can be electrochemically detected, such as dopamine and serotonin and many other molecules derived from the amino acids tyrosine and tryptophan. Additionally, there are other processes, such as transient changes in physiological pH, which can be detected electrochemically using FSCV.

Microelectrodes are also capable for measuring changes in concentration of several biologically relevant gases such as nitric oxide, oxygen and carbon monoxide. In the case of FSCV, multiple analytes can be detected simultaneously and when combined with sophisticated data analysis procedures, the individual concentrations can be accurately measured as a function of time.

Many biological changes, particularly at the protein level, occur on the order of minutes, however, many biological changes also occur on the order of milliseconds. Early neurobiological techniques such as microdialysis were limited to measuring tonic changes, or changes that occur over several minutes. This limitation prevented further study of neurobiological mechanisms, which can alter chemical communication within a matter of a few milliseconds. These changes can be monitored with microelectrodes either through amperometry or voltammetry.

Microelectrodes are now widely used in numerous biological preparations, ranging from single cell to awake, behaving animals. This versatility permits neuroscientists to probe a variety of neurobiological mechanisms such as exocytosis, neuron receptor functionality and the chemical changes that occur in addiction to drugs of abuse.

Non-Invasive Technique

Non-invasive technique includes neuroimaging or brain scanning. It consist of usage of various techniques to directly or indirectly image the structrue, function or pharmacology of the brain. It is a relatively new discipline within medicine, neuroscience and psychology. Physicians who specialise in the performance and interpretation of neuroimaging in the clinical setting are known as neuroradiologists.

Neuroimaging falls into two broad categories

(i) **Structural Imaging**, which deals with the structure of the brain and the diagnosis of large-scale intracranial disease (such as a tumor), as well as injury.

(ii) **Functional Imaging**, which is used to diagnose metabolic diseases and lesions on a finer scale (such as Alzheimer's disease) and also for neurological and cognitive-psychology research. Functional imaging allows the brain's information processing to be visualised directly because activity in the involved area of the brain increases metabolism and 'lights up' on the scan.Three most common types of brain scans are EEG, PET, MRI.

EEG

Electroencephalography (EEG) is used to show brain activity in certain psychological states, such as alertness or drowsiness. It is useful in the diagnosis of seizures and other medical problems that involve an over abundance or lack of activity in certain parts of the brain.

To prepare for an EEG, electrodes are placed on the face and scalp. After placing each electrode in the right position, the electrical potential of each electrode can be measured.

According to a person's state (waking, sleeping, etc.), both the frequency and the form of the EEG signal differ.

Mechanism of EEG

The brain's electrical charge is maintained by billions of neurons. Neurons are electrically charged (or 'polarised') by membrane transport proteins that pump ions across their membranes. Neurons are constantly exchanging ions with the extracellular milieu, *e.g.* to maintain resting potential and to propagate action potentials. Ions of similar charge repel each other and when many ions are pushed out of many neurons at the same time, they can push their neighbours, who push their neighbours and so on, in a wave. This process is known as volume conduction.

When the wave of ions reaches the electrodes on the scalp, they can push or pull electrons on the metal in the electrodes. Since, metal conducts the push and pull of electrons easily, the difference in push or pull voltages between any two electrodes can be measured by a voltmeter. Recording these voltages overtime gives us the EEG.

The electric potential generated by an individual neuron is far too small to be picked up by EEG or MEG (Magnetoencephalography). EEG activity therefore always reflects the summation of the synchronous activity of thousands or millions of neurons that have similar spatial orientation. If the cells do not have similar spatial orientation, their ions do not line up and create waves to be detected. Pyramidal neurons of the cortex are thought to produce the most EEG signal because they are well-aligned and fire together.

Because voltage field gradients fall off with the square of distance, activity from deep sources are more difficult to detect than currents near the skull.

Scalp EEG activity shows oscillations at a variety of frequencies. Several of these oscillations have characteristic frequency ranges, spatial distributions and are associated with different states of brain functioning (*e.g.* waking and the various sleep stages). These oscillations represent synchronised activity over a network of neurons.

The neuronal networks underlying some of these oscillations are understood (*e.g.* the thalamocortical resonance underlying sleep spindles), while many others are not (*e.g.* the system that generates the posterior basic rhythm). Research that measures both EEG and neuron spiking finds the relationship between the two is complex, with a combination of EEG power in the gamma band and phase in the delta band relating most strongly to neuron spike activity.

Uses of EEG

A routine clinical EEG recording typically lasts 20-30 minutes (plus preparation time), usually involves recording from scalp electrodes.

The uses of EEG are as follows

Routine EEG

Routine EEG is typically used in clinical circumstances like

- to distinguish epileptic seizures from other types of spells, such as psychogenic non-epileptic seizures, syncope (fainting), sub-cortical movement disorders and migraine variants,
- to differentiate 'organic' encephalopathy or delirium from primary psychiatric syndromes such as catatonia,
- to serve as an adjunct test of brain death,
- to in certain instances, in patients with coma and
- to determine whether to wean anti-epileptic medications.
- to monitor the depth of anesthesia, as an indirect indicator of cerebral perfusion in carotid endarterectomy,
- to monitor amobarbital effect during the Wada test.

Recording EEG While

Seizure is Occurring at times, a routine EEG is not sufficient to establish the diagnosis and/or to determine the best course of action in terms of treatment. In this case, attempts may be made to record an EEG while a seizure is occurring.

This is known as an ictal recording, as opposed to an inter-ictal recording which refers to the EEG recording between seizures. To obtain an ictal recording, a prolonged EEG is typically performed accompanied by a time-synchronised video and audio recording.

This can be done either as an outpatient (at home) or during a hospital admission. While in the hospital, seizure medications are usually withdrawn to increase the odds that a seizure will occur during admission. For reasons of safety, medications are not withdrawn during an EEG outside of the hospital. Ambulatory video EEGs therefore have the advantage of convenience and are less expensive than a hospital admission, but the disadvantage of a decreased probability of recording a clinical event.

Advantages of EEG

- They are functionally fast, relatively cheap and safe way of checking the functioning of different areas of brain.
- High precision time measurements.
- Today's EEG technolgy can accurately detect brain activity at a resolution of a single millisecond.
- EEG electrodes are simply stuck onto the scalp. It is therefore a non-invasive procedure.
- EEG equipment is relatively inexpensive compared with other devices and is simple to operate.

Disadvantages of EEG

- The main disadvantage of EEG recording is poor spatial resolution.
- The EEG signal is not useful for pin-pointing the exact source of activity. In other words, they are not very exact.
- EEG waveform does not allow researchers to distinguish between activities originating in different but closely adjacent locations.

PET

A Positron Emission Tomography (PET) scan is an imaging test that allows doctor to check for diseases in the body. The scan uses a special dye containing radioactive tracers. These tracers are swallowed, inhaled, or injected into a vein in arm depending on what part of the body is being examined. Certain organs and tissues then absorb the tracer.

Mechanism of PET

The system detects pairs of gamma rays emitted indirectly by a positron-emitting radio ligand, most commonly fluorine-18, which is introduced into the body on a biologically active molecule called a radioactive tracer. Different ligands are used for different imaging purposes, depending on what the radiologist/researcher wants to detect.

Three-dimensional images of tracer concentration within the body are then constructed by computer analysis. In modern PET computed tomography scanners, three-dimensional imaging is often accomplished with the aid of a computed tomography X-ray scan performed on the patient during the same session in the same machine.

If the biologically active tracer molecule chosen for PET is fludeoxyglucose (FDG), an analogue of glucose, the concentrations of tracer imaged will indicate tissue metabolic activity as it corresponds to the regional glucose uptake. Use of this tracer to explore the possibility of cancer metastasis (*i.e.* spreading to other sites) is the most common type of PET scan in standard medical care (representing 90% of current scans). Metabolic trapping of the radioactive glucose molecule allows the PET scan to be utilised.

Uses of PET

PET has wide range of application in medial diagnosis.

Oncology

PET scanning with the tracer Fluorine-18 (F-18) Fluorodeoxyglucose (FDG), called FDG-PET, is widely used in clinical oncology. This tracer is a glucose analog that is taken up by glucose-using cells and phosphorylated by hexokinase (whose mitochondrial form is greatly elevated in rapidly growing malignant tumors).

Because the oxygen atom that is replaced by F-18 to generate FDG is required for the next step in glucose metabolism in all cells, no further reactions occur in FDG. Furthermore, most tissues (with the notable exception of liver and kidneys) cannot remove the phosphate added by hexokinase. This means that FDG is trapped in any cell that takes it up until it decays, since phosphorylated sugars, due to their ionic charge, cannot exit from the cell.

This result in intense radiolabeling of tissues with high glucose uptake, such as the normal brain, liver, kidneys and most cancers. As a result, FDG-PET can be used for diagnosis, staging and monitoring treatment of cancers, particularly in Hodgkin's lymphoma, non-Hodgkin lymphoma and lung cancer.

Neuroimaging

PET neuroimaging is based on an assumption that areas of high radioactivity are associated with brain activity. What is actually measured indirectly is the flow of blood to different parts of the brain, which is, in general, believed to be correlated and has been measured using the tracer oxygen-15. Because of its 2-minute half-life, 0-15 must be piped directly from a medical cyclotron for such uses, which is difficult.

Standard FDG-PET of the brain, which measures regional glucose use, can be used to make early diagnosis of Alzheimer's diseases and differentiate Alzheimer's disease from other dementing processes. This is because the brain is normally a rapid user of glucose and brain pathologies such as Alzheimer's disease also greatly decrease brain metabolism of both glucose and oxygen in tandem.

The advantage of FDG-PET for these uses is its much wider availability. Some radioactive tracers used for Alzheimer's are florbetapir F18, flutemetamol F18 and florbetaben F18, which are all used to detect amyloid-beta plaques (a potential biomarker for Alzheimer's) in the brain.

Cardiology

PET scans reveal areas of decreased blood flow in the heart. This is because healthy heart tissue will take in more of the tracer than unhealthy tissue or tissue that has decreased blood flow. Different colours and degrees of brightness on the scan will indicate different levels of tissue function, helping the doctor to decide best way to move forward.

Musculoskeletal Imaging

PET has been shown to be a feasible technique for studying skeletal muscles during exercises like walking. One of the main advantages of using PET is that it can provide muscle activation data about deeper lying muscles such as the vastus intermedialis and the gluteus minimus, as compared to other muscle studying techniques like electromyography, which can be used only on superficial muscles (*i.e.* directly under the skin). A clear disadvantage is that PET provides no timing information about muscle activation because it has to be measured after the exercise is completed. This is due to the time it takes for FDG to accumulate in the activated muscles.

MRI

Magnetic Resonance Imaging (MRI) is a type of scan that uses strong magnetic fields and radio waves to produce detailed images of the human body. MRI scanner is a large tube that contains powerful magnets. The patient lies inside the tube during the scan.

MRI scan can be used to examine almost any part of the body, including the

- brain and spinal cord
- bones and joints
- breasts
- heart and blood vessels
- internal organs, such as the liver, womb or prostate gland

The results of an MRI scan can be used to help diagnose conditions, plan treatments and assess how effective previous treatment has been.

Mechanism of MRI

Most of the human body is made up of water molecules, which consist of hydrogen and oxygen atoms.

At the centre of each hydrogen atom is an even smaller particle called a proton. Protons are like tiny magnets and are very sensitive to magnetic fields. When the patient lies under the powerful scanner magnets, the protons in his/her body lineup in the same direction, in the same way that a magnet can pull the needle of a compass.

Short bursts of radio waves are then sent to certain areas of the body, knocking the protons out of alignment.

When the radio waves are turned off, the protons realign. This sends out radio signals, which are picked up by receivers.

These signals provide information about the exact location of the protons in the body. They also help to distinguish between the various types of tissues in the body, because the protons in different types of tissues realign at different speeds and produce distinct signals. In the same way that millions of pixels on a computer screen can create complex pictures, the signals from the millions of protons in the body are combined to create a detailed image of the inside body.

Uses of MRI

MRI has a wide range of applications in medical diagnosis.

Neuroimaging

MRI is the investigative tool of choice for neurological cancers over CT, as it offers better visualisation of the posterior cranial fossa, containing the brainstem and the cerebellum. The contrast provided between grey and white matter makes MRI the best choice for many conditions of the central nervous system, including demyelinating diseases, dementia, cerebrovascular disease, infectious diseases, Alzheimer's disease and epilepsy. Since many images are taken milliseconds apart, it shows how the brain responds to different stimuli, enabling researchers to study both the functional and structural brain abnormalities in psychological disorders.

MRI is also used in guided stereotactic surgery and radiosurgery for treatment of intracranial tumors, arteriovenous malformations and other surgically treatable conditions using a device known as the N-localiser.

Cardiovascular

Cardiac MRI is complementary to other imaging techniques, such as echocardiography, cardiac CT and nuclear medicine. Its applications include assessment of myocardial ischemia and viability, cardiomyopathies, myocarditis, iron overload, vascular diseases, and congenital heart disease.

Magnetic Resonance Angiography (MRA)

MRA generates pictures of the arteries to evaluate them for stenosis (abnormal narrowing) or aneurysms (vessel wall dilatations, at risk of rupture). MRA is often used to evaluate the arteries of the neck and brain, the thoracic and abdominal aorta, the renal arteries and the legs (called a 'run-off').

A variety of techniques can be used to generate the pictures, such as administration of a paramagnetic contrast agent (gadolinium) or using a technique known as 'flow-related enhancement' (*e.g.* 2D and 3D time-of-flight sequences), where most of the signal on an image is due to blood that recently moved into that plane.

Liver and Gastrointestinal

Hepatobiliary MR is used to detect and characterise lesions of the liver, pancreas and bile ducts. Focal or diffuse disorders of the liver may be evaluated using diffusion-weighted, opposed-phase imaging and dynamic contrast enhancement sequences. Extracellular contrast agents are used widely in liver MRI and newer hepatobiliary contrast agents also provide the opportunity to perform functional biliary imaging.

Anatomical imaging of the bile ducts is achieved by using a heavily T2-weighted sequence in Magnetic Resonance Cholangiopancreatography (MRCP). Functional imaging of the pancreas is performed following administration of secretin. MR enterography provides non-invasive assessment of inflammatory bowel disease and small bowel tumors. MR-colonography may play a role in the detection of large polyps in patients at increased risk of colorectal cancer.

EXAM BASED QUESTIONS

1 Physiological psychology is a subset of
(a) neuroscience (b) aneurysm studies
(c) cardiovascular study (d) muscle dystrophy

2 In which field does physiological psychology can be used?
(a) Mental
(b) Behavioural
(c) Both a and b
(d) None of the above

3 Which amongst the following involves the introduction of instrument into the body?
(a) Non-invasive (b) Invasive
(c) Both a and b (d) None of these

4 Which among the following is invasive method of physiological psychology?
(a) Anatomical method (b) Lesion method
(c) Chemical method (d) All of these

5 Microscopes are used in
(a) anatomical method
(b) degeneration technique
(c) lesion method
(d) chemical method

6 Which chemical is used for fixation?
(a) Acetylcholine (b) Potassium
(c) Formalin (d) Formaldehyde

7 Which among the following is used to cut thin slice of embedded tissue?
(a) Microtome (b) Microelectrode
(c) Microdialysis (d) None of these

8 Golgi silver staining is used to stain
(a) cerebral cortex (b) cell body
(c) nerve cell (d) All of these

9 Which stain is used for visualising cell body?
(a) Myelin stain (b) Nissl stain
(c) Golgi silver staining (d) Formaldehyde staining

10 Who came up with the staining that turns dying axon dark brown?
(a) Walle Nauta (b) William Nauta
(c) Walle Nottingham (d) William Nottingham

11 Reverse pathway *i.e.* from axon to cell body can be mapped by
(a) trypsin (b) maltase
(c) horse radish peroxidase (d) amylase

12 Administration of discrete amount of chemical directly into cerebral structrue is done by
(a) cannula (b) cone
(c) injection (d) None of these

13 Insertion of the cannula should be at .... from top of the skull.
(a) acute angle (b) obtuse angle
(c) right angle (d) any angle will do

14 Microdialysis is used in quantifying and sampling
(a) neuro transmitter (b) neuropeptide
(c) hormones (d) All of these

15 Permeability of dialysis membrane is limited to molecular mass
(a) < 20,000 Da (b) < 10,000 Da
(c) 20,000 Da (d) > 10,000 Da

16 End of cannula is sealed by
(a) match flame (b) hot souldering iron
(c) Both a and b (d) None of these

17 Microdialysis membrane is .... of analyte of interest.
(a) devoid (b) present
(c) partially present (d) partially devoid

18 The structure of the microdialysis membrane is
(a) Circular (b) Tubular
(c) Cuboidar (d) None of these

19 Main mechanism of microdialysis is
(a) osmosis (b) transportation
(c) diffusion (d) transduction

20 During microdialysis substance move from
(a) higher concentration area to lower concentration area
(b) lower concentration area to higher concentration area
(c) doesn't move
(d) neither move

21 What is damaged in case of lesion?
(a) Cortical region (b) Subcortical region
(c) Both a and b (d) None of these

22 Which amongst the following is a probe to test specific hypothesis?
(a) Lesion (b) Cannula
(c) Mark (d) All of these

23 The subject of lesion method may be
(a) human (b) animal
(c) Both a and b (d) None of these

24 Who found correlation between speech and frontal lobe?
(a) Bouillau and Broca (b) Mishkin
(c) Boillau and Mishkin (d) Broca and Mishkin

25 Lesion studies on non-primate have given information about
(a) vision and memory (b) vision and taste
(c) vision and hearing (d) taste and memory

26 Neural degeneration occurs in case of
(a) ageing (b) alzheimer
(c) parkinson (d) All of these

27 In old age .... of brain decreases.
(a) volume (b) weight
(c) Both a and b (d) None of these

28 The decrease in volume/weight of brain in old age is linked to shrinking of
(a) nerve cell (b) gray matter
(c) cerebral cortex (d) hypothalamus

29 In old age there are changes in
(a) dendritic arbour (b) spine
(c) synapses (d) All of these

30 What does WML stands for?
(a) White matter lesion
(b) White matter leukocyte
(c) White monocyte leukocyte
(d) White monocyte lesion

31 Alzheimer's affect
(a) etorhinal cortex (b) hippocampus
(c) Both a and b (d) None of these

32 In Alzheimer, there is accumulation of
(a) amyloid plaques (b) hardened grey matter
(c) tau protein (d) All of these

33 Neurofilrillary tangles consists of
(a) tau protein (b) amyloid protein
(c) grey matter (d) neuron

34 Parkinson's disease affect
(a) basal ganglia (b) substantia nigra
(c) Both a and b (d) None of these

35 Parkinson's disease's symptom include
(a) tremor (b) slowness of movement
(c) balance problem (d) All of these

36 Overstimulation of .... causes tremor.
(a) STN (b) WML
(c) GPI (d) None of these

37 Which neurochemical can be detected by microelectrode?
(a) Dopamine (b) Serotonin
(c) Tryptophan (d) All of these

38 Microelectrode can detect relevant
(a) gas (b) organs
(c) liquid (d) None of these

39 Microelectrode can detect the biological changes in matter of
(a) minute (b) seconds (c) hour (d) days

40 What does EEG detects?
(a) over activity (b) Lack of activity
(c) Both a and b (d) None of these

41 EEG is measured using
(a) electrodes (b) magnets
(c) ligands (d) All of these

42 Which of the following neurous of cortex produce most EEG?
(a) Pyramidal (b) Cuboidal
(c) Tubular (d) Cylindrical

43 EEG is used to detect
(a) parkinson's (b) alzheimer's
(c) seizures (d) brain tumor

44 PET scan uses
(a) electrode (b) radioactive tracer
(c) magnet (d) scanner

45 Which ligand is introduced in body during PET scan?
(a) Chlorine - 4 (b) Helium - 20
(c) Fluorine -18 (d) All of these

46 FDG stands for
(a) fluorodeoxyglucose (b) flourodideoxy glucose
(c) flouro deglucose (d) flouro diglucose

47 What is measured in neuro imaging using PET scan?
(a) Nerve cell (b) Blood flow
(c) Organs (d) None of these

48 Radioactive tracer for alzheimer is
(a) florbetapir F18 (b) flulemetamol F18
(c) florbetaben F18 (d) All of these

49 FDG, PET can be used for
(a) oncology (b) neuroimaging
(c) Both a and b (d) None of these

50 What does MRI measure?
(a) Signal from proton (b) Signal from electron
(c) Signal from neutron (d) None of these

51 In which type of scan strong magnetic fields and radio waves are used?
(a) EEG (b) MRI
(c) PET (d) None of these

52 MRI scan can be used to examine
(a) breasts (b) bones
(c) joints (d) All of these

53 Cardiovascular Cardiac MRI is complementary to
(a) echocardiography
(b) Cardiac CT
(c) nuclear medicine
(d) All of the above

54 Write in correct sequence.

1. End of cannula to be inserted is cut at an angle.
2. Cannula is inserted in right angle.
3. Other end of cannula is sealed.
4. A small hole is drilled into skull.

Codes

(a) 1 2 3 4 (b) 2 3 1 4 (c) 3 1 2 4 (d) 1 3 4 2

55 Write in correct sequence.

1. Embeded tissue is cut using microtome.
2. Tissue is fixed using formalin.
3. Tissue is stained.
4. Tissue is embeded in paraffin.

Codes

(a) 3 2 1 4 (b) 2 4 1 3 (c) 1 3 2 4 (d) 3 1 2 4

56 Which of the following statements fall within the scope of physiological psychology.

1. Effects of the stimulation of limbic system on approach and avoidance.
2. Effect of lesions in frontal lobe on manipulation of symbols and numbers.
3. Effect of excessive smoking on blood pressure and functioning of heart.
4. Effect of hyperthyroidism on development of general mental ability.

Which of the statements given above are correct?

(a) 1, 2 and 3 (b) 1, 3 and 4
(c) 1, 2 and 4 (d) 2, 3 and 4

57 Math the following

List I (Brain Imagings/ Recordings)	List II (Functioning Principles)
A. Electroencephalography	1. Increased delivery of radioactive water
B. Magneto-encephalography	2. Venous oxygen concentration
C. Position Emission Tomography (PET)	3. Magnetic fields within the brain
D. Magnetic Resonance Imaging (MRI)	4. Electrical activity from the scalp

Codes

	A	B	C	D		A	B	C	D
(a)	1	2	4	3	(b)	1	3	4	2
(c)	4	3	1	2	(d)	4	2	1	3

58 Which of the following is correct statement?

1. Lesion is a probe to test specific hypothesis.
2. Lesion is created by researcher on healthy human brain.

Codes

(a) Only 1 (b) Only 2
(c) Both 1 and 2 (d) None of these

59 Which of the following is a correct statement?

1. Serotonin producing cells are dying in parkinson.
2. Volume of brain increase with age.

Codes

(a) Only 1 (b) Only 2
(c) Both 1 and 2 (d) None of these

60 Match the following

List I (Technique)	List II (Measuring equipment)
A. EEG	1. Magnet
B. PET	2. Electrodes
C. MRI	3. Radioactive tracer

Codes

	A	B	C		A	B	C
(a)	1	2	3	(b)	2	3	1
(c)	3	2	1	(d)	2	1	3

61 Match the following

List I (Condition)	List II (Part affected)
A. Alzheimer's	1. Grey matter
B. Parkinson's	2. Amyloid plaque
C. Old age	3. Dopamine neurons

Codes

	A	B	C		A	B	C
(a)	2	3	1	(b)	1	3	2
(c)	1	2	3	(d)	3	1	2

62 Match the following

List I (Stain)	List II (Part)
A. Golgi Silver	1. Cell body
B. Nissl	2. Myelin
C. Myelin	3. Nerve cell

Codes

	A	B	C		A	B	C
(a)	1	2	3	(b)	2	1	3
(c)	3	2	1	(d)	3	1	2

63 Match the following

List I (Researcher)	List II (Contribution)
A. Bouillau and Broca	1. Stain that turn dying axon brown
B. Miskhkin and colleague	2. Neural basic of vision and memory
C. Walle Nauta	3. corretation between speech and frontal lobe

Codes

	A	B	C
(a)	3	2	1
(b)	3	1	2
(c)	2	1	3
(d)	3	2	1

64 Which is the incorrect pairing?

(a) Microelectrode - Electrochemical
(b) Microdialysis - Permeable membrane
(c) Cannula - Drill
(d) Lesion - Neurological disorder

Directions (Q. Nos. 65-74) *Given below are two statements one labelled as Assertion (A) and other labelled as Reason (R). Following are the codes given below. Choose the correct option.*

(a) Both A and R are True (b) Both A and R are False
(c) A is true, but R is false (d) A is false, but R is true

65 Assertion (A) In alzheimer's neuron stop working, loose connection with other neuron and die.
Reason (R) In alzheimer's disease the tau protein is abnormal and microtubule structrue collapse.

66 Assertion (A) Parkinson's disease is a degenerative, progressive disorder.
Reason (R) Amyloid palques are formed incase of parkinson's disease.

67 Assertion (A) PET scanning with chlorine is widely used in oncology.
Reason (R) The tissues with high glucose uptake are radio labelled.

68 Assertion (A) At times routine EEG is not sufficent for diagnosis of seizure.
Reason (R) EEG in some cases is recorded when a seizure is occurring.

69 Assertion (A) MRI detects the electron.
Reason (R) MRI can't be used on internal organs.

70 Assertion (A) PET scan reveals decrease blood flow to heart.
Reason (R) Unhealthy heart doesn't take up radioactive tracer.

71 Assertion (A) Pathways can be detected by autoradiography.
Reason (R) In this the axon are injected by horse radish peroxides.

72 Assertion (A) The probe of microdialysis allow all the analyte to diffuse.
Reason (R) The perfusate is infused slowly across the length of dialysis.

73 Assertion (A) The lesion method links absence of part of brain to its function.
Reason (R) Lesion approach has been used by many researchers.

74 Assertion (A) Electrochemical detection using microelectrode requires the detected species to be electroactive.
Reason (R) Several molecules derived from amino acid tyrosine and tryptophan are thus detected by microelectrodes.

Directions (Q. Nos. 75-78) *Read the passage given below and answer the following questions.*

In Alzheimer's disease, damage is widespread, as many neurons stop functioning, lose connections with other neurons and die. Alzheimer's disrupts processes vital to neurons and their networks, including communication, metabolism and repair.

At first, Alzheimer's disease typically destroys neurons and their connections in parts of the brain involved in memory, including the entorhinal cortex and hippocampus . It later affects areas in the cerebral cortex responsible for language, reasoning and social behaviour. Eventually, many other areas of the brian are damaged. Over time, a person with Alzheimer's gradually loses his or her ability to live and function independently. Ultimately, the disease is fatal.

One of the hallmarks of Alzheimer's disease is the accumulation of amyloid plaques between nerve cells (neurons) in the brain. Amyloid is a general term for protein fragments that the body produces normally. Beta amyloid is a fragment of a protein snipped from another protein called Amyloid Precursor Protein (APP). In a healthy brain, these protein fragments would break down and be eliminated. In Alzheimer's disease, the fragments accumulate to form hard, insoluble plaques.

Neurofibrillary tangles are insoluble twisted fibers found inside the brain's nerve cells. They primarily consist of a protein called tau, which forms part of a structure called a microtubule. The microtubule helps transport nutrients and other important substances from one part of the nerve cell to another. In Alzheimer's disease the tau protein is abnormal and the microtubule structures collapse.

75 Consider the following statements
1. **Alzheimer damage is widespread, it stops neuron functioning.**
2. **Alzheimer disrupts communication, metabolism and repair.**

Which among the above is/are correct?
(a) Only 1 (b) Only 2
(c) Both 1 and 2 (d) None of these

76 The accumulation of amyloid plaques between never cells in the brain happen in
(a) Parkinson's disease
(b) Alzheimer's disease
(c) Both a and b
(d) None of the above

77 Neurofibrillary tangles are insoluble twisted fibers found inside the
(a) nefrons
(b) nerve cells
(c) vessel
(d) microtubule

78 In Alzheimer's disease
(a) Tau protein is abnormal
(b) microtubule structures collapse
(c) Both a and b
(d) None of the above

PREVIOUS YEARS' QUESTIONS

July 2018

1 **Persons with a leison at the ventromedial nucleus are likely to**

(a) overeat (b) undereat
(c) eat normally (d) eat normally or undereat

2 **............... makes neurons stand out visibly depicting which neurons are active; whereas .... uses antibodies attached to a dye to identify cellular component such as receptors, neurotransmitters, or enzymes.**

(a) Immunocytochemistry ; Autoradiography
(b) Autoradiography ; Immunocytochemistry
(c) Myelin staining ; Nissl Staining
(d) Nissl Staining : Myelin Staining

November 2017

3 **Match List I with List II and select the correct answer by choosing from the codes given below.**

	List I (Technique)		**List II** (Description)
A.	CT	1.	Detects increase in oxygen levels during neural activity
B.	MRI	2.	Measures variation in hydrogen concentration in brain tissue
C.	PET	3.	Form 3-D image of brain by combining X - rays of cross sections of brain
D.	FMRI	4.	Image produced by emission from injected substances that have been made radioactive

Codes

	A	B	C	D
(a)	4	1	3	2
(b)	3	2	4	1
(c)	4	2	3	1
(d)	3	1	4	2

July 2016

4 **Which of the following techniques can be used to study activities in a living human brain?**

1. Computerised Tomography
2. Ablation and Lesioning
3. Stereotoxic Procedures
4. Functional Magnetic Resonance Imaging

Select the correct answer using the codes given below

(a) 1 and 2 (b) 3 and 4
(c) 2, 3 and 4 (d) 1, 3 and 4

ANSWERS

Exam Based Questions

1 (a)	2 (c)	3 (b)	4 (d)	5 (a)	6 (c)	7 (a)	8 (c)	9 (b)	10 (a)
11 (c)	12 (a)	13 (c)	14 (d)	15 (a)	16 (c)	17 (a)	18 (b)	19 (c)	20 (a)
21 (c)	22 (a)	23 (c)	24 (a)	25 (a)	26 (d)	27 (c)	28 (b)	29 (d)	30 (a)
31 (c)	32 (a)	33 (a)	34 (c)	35 (d)	36 (c)	37 (d)	38 (a)	39 (b)	40 (c)
41 (a)	42 (a)	43 (c)	44 (b)	45 (c)	46 (a)	47 (b)	48 (d)	49 (c)	50 (a)
51 (b)	52 (d)	53 (d)	54 (b)	55 (b)	56 (c)	57 (d)	58 (a)	59 (d)	60 (b)
61 (a)	62 (d)	63 (a)	64 (b)	65 (a)	66 (c)	67 (d)	68 (a)	69 (b)	70 (a)
71 (c)	72 (d)	73 (a)	74 (a)	75 (c)	76 (b)	77 (b)	78 (c)		

Previous Years' Questions

1 (c)	2 (a)	3 (d)	4 (d)

Muscular and Glandular System and Biological Behaviour

The muscular system is the biological system of humans that produces movement. The endocrine system, along with the nervous system, functions in the regulation of body activities. These two system together manipulate and direct the biological motives, emotions and behaviour of humans in significant manner.

Muscular System

The muscular system is an organ system, involved majorly in the movement of the body. There are about 700 muscles that are connected to the bones of the skeletal system, which roughly make up half of the human body weight. Every muscle is a different organ made up of skeletal muscle, tissue, blood vessels, nerves and tendons. Muscle tissues are found in the heart, blood vessels and digestive system.

Types of Muscles

There are three kinds of muscle tissues namely cardiac, visceral and skeletal.

(i) **Cardiac Muscle** This muscle is present only in heart and responsible for supplying blood to all over the body. It is also an involuntary muscle since it cannot be controlled. When brain signals adapt the rate of contraction, cardiac muscle stimulates by itself to contract. The natural pace of the heart is made up of cardiac muscle tissue and it stimulates other cardiac muscle cells to shrink. The cardiac muscle cells are straight which reveals that they seem to have dark and light stripes when seen under a microscope. The protein fibers arrangement within the cells is responsible for these dark and light stripes.

(ii) **Visceral Muscle** These muscles are found in the organs like intestines, blood vessels and stomach. It is the weakest of all muscle tissues and makes organs contract to move substances through the organ. It is said to be involuntary muscle because it cannot be directly controlled by the conscious mind. It is also known as *smooth muscle* since it has a very smooth, uniform appearance when viewed under the microscope.

In this Chapter

- *Muscular System*
- *Glandular System*
- *Biological Basis of Motivation*
- *Biological Basis of Emotions*
- *Genetics and Behaviour*

(iii) **Skeletal Muscle** It is the only voluntary muscle tissue that can be controlled in conscious condition. Every physical action that a human does (*e.g.* walking, writing) needs skeletal muscle. The skeletal muscle is responsible for moving the body parts that are connected to the bone. Skeletal muscles from many ancestor cells lump themselves together to produce straight, long fibers. These skeletal muscles are strong just like cardiac muscles. The name is derived from the fact that these are connected to the skeleton in atleast one region.

Functions of Muscular System

The main functions of the muscular system are as follows

(i) **Mobility** The muscular system's main function is to allow movement. When muscles contract, they contribute to gross and fine movement. Gross movement refers to large, coordinated motions and includes: walking running, swimming. Fine movement involves smaller movements, such as writing, speaking, facial expressions.

The smaller skeletal muscles are usually responsible for this type of action. Most muscle movement of the body is under conscious control. However, some movements are reflexive, such as withdrawing a hand from a source of heat.

(ii) **Stability** Muscle tendons stretch over joints and contribute to joint stability. Muscle tendons in the knee joint and the shoulder joint are crucial in stabilisation. The core muscles are those in the abdomen, back and pelvis and they also stabilise the body and assist in tasks, such as lifting weights.

(iii) **Posture** Skeletal muscles help keep the body in the correct position when someone is sitting or standing. This is known as *posture*. Good posture relies on strong, flexible muscles. Stiff, weak or tight muscles contribute to poor posture and misalignment of the body. Long term, bad posture leads to joint and muscle pain in the shoulders, back, neck and elsewhere.

(iv) **Circulation** The heart is a muscle that pumps blood throughout the body. The movement of the heart is outside of conscious control and it contracts automatically when stimulated by electrical signals. Smooth muscle in the arteries and veins plays a further role in the circulation of blood around the body. These muscles maintain blood pressure and circulation in the event of blood loss or dehydration. They expand to increase blood flow during times of intense exercise when the body requires more oxygen.

(v) **Respiration** Breathing involves the use of the diaphragm muscle. The diaphragm is a dome-shaped muscle located below the lungs. When the diaphragm contracts, it pushes downward, causing the chest cavity to get bigger. The lungs then fill with air. When the diaphragm muscle relaxes, it pushes air out of the lungs. When someone wants to breathe more deeply, it requires help from other muscles, including those in the abdomen, back and neck.

(vi) **Digestion** Smooth muscles in the gastrointestinal or GI tract control digestion. The GI tract stretches from the mouth to the anus. Food moves through the digestive system with a wave like motion called *peristalsis*. Muscles in the walls of the hollow organs contract and relax to cause this movement, which pushes food through the esophagus into the stomach. The upper muscle in the stomach relaxes to allow food to enter, while the lower muscles mix food particles with stomach acid and enzymes. The digested food moves from the stomach to the intestines by peristalsis. From here, more muscles contract to pass the food out of the body as stool.

(vii) **Urination** The urinary system comprises both smooth and skeletal muscles, including those in the bladder, kidneys, ureter and urethra. The muscles and nerves must work together to hold and release urine from the bladder. Urinary problems, such as poor bladder control or retention of urine, are caused by damage to the nerves that carry signals to the muscles.

(viii) **Childbirth** Smooth muscles in the uterus expand and contract during childbirth. These movements push the baby through the vagina. Also, the pelvic floor muscles help to guide the baby's head down the birth canal.

(ix) **Vision** Six skeletal muscles around the eye control its movements. These muscles work quickly and precisely and allow the eye to

- Maintain a stable image
- Scan the surrounding area
- Track moving objects

Damage to the eye muscles can cause impaired vision.

(x) **Organ Protection** Muscles in the torso protect the internal organs at the front, sides and back of the body. The bones of the spine and the ribs provide further protection. Muscles also protect the bones and organs by absorbing shock and reducing friction in the joints.

(xi) **Temperature Regulation** Maintaining normal body temperature is an important function of the muscular system. Almost 85% of the heat a person generates in their body comes from contracting muscles. When body heat falls below optimal levels, the skeletal muscles increase their activity to make heat. Shivering is one example of this mechanism. Muscles in the blood vessels also contract to maintain body heat. Body temperature can be brought back within normal range through the relaxation of smooth muscle in the blood vessels. This action increases blood flow and releases excess heat through the skin.

Glandular System

The endocrine system, along with the nervous system, functions in the regulation of body activities. The endocrine system acts through chemical messengers called *hormones* that influence growth, development and metabolic activities. The action of the endocrine system is measured in minutes, hours or weeks and is more generalised than the action of the nervous system.

There are two major categories of glands in the body exocrine and endocrine.

Exocrine Glands

Exocrine glands have ducts that carry their secretory product to a surface. These glands include the sweat, sebaceous and mammary glands and the glands that secrete digestive enzymes.

Endocrine Glands

The endocrine glands do not have ducts to carry their product to a surface. They are called *ductless glands*. The word endocrine is derived from the Greek terms 'endo,' meaning within and 'krine,' meaning to separate or secrete. The secretory products of endocrine glands are called *hormones* and are secreted directly into the blood and then carried throughout the body where they influence only those cells that have receptor sites for that hormone.

Various endocrine glands present in the body are

Hypothalamus

The hypothalamus is located in the lower central part of the brain. This part of the brain is important in regulation of satiety, metabolism and body temperature. In addition, it secretes hormones that stimulate or suppress the release of hormones in the pituitary gland.

Many of these hormones are releasing hormones, which are secreted into an artery (the hypophyseal portal system) that carries them directly to the pituitary gland. In the pituitary gland, these releasing hormones signal secretion of stimulating hormones. The hypothalamus also secretes a hormone called *somatostatin*, which causes the pituitary gland to stop the release of growth hormone.

Pituitary Gland

The pituitary gland is located at the base of the brain beneath the hypothalamus and is no larger than a pea. It is often considered the most important part of the endocrine system because it produces hormones that control many functions of other endocrine glands. When the pituitary gland does not produce one or more of its hormones or not enough of them, it is called *hypopituitarism*.

The pituitary gland is divided into two parts: the anterior lobe and the posterior lobe.

The anterior lobe produces the following hormones, which are regulated by the hypothalamus

- **Growth Hormone** Stimulates growth of bone and tissue. Its deficiency in adults results in problems in maintaining proper amounts of body fat and muscle and bone mass. It is also involved in emotional well-being.
- **Thyroid-Stimulating Hormone** (TSH) Stimulates the thyroid gland to produce thyroid hormones. The lack of thyroid hormones either because of a defect in the pituitary or the thyroid itself is called *hypothyroidism*.
- **Adrenocorticotropin Hormone** (ACTH) Stimulates the adrenal gland to produce several related steroid hormones.
- **Luteinising Hormone** (LH) and **Follicle-Stimulating Hormone** (FSH) Control sexual function and production of the sex steroids, estrogen and progesterone in females or testosterone in males.
- **Prolactin Hormone** Stimulates milk production in females.

The posterior lobe produces the following hormones, which are not regulated by the hypothalamus

- **Antidiuretic Hormone** (vasopressin) Controls water loss by the kidneys.
- **Oxytocin** Contracts the uterus during childbirth and stimulates milk production.

The hormones secreted by the posterior pituitary are actually produced in the brain and carried to the pituitary gland through nerves. They are stored in the pituitary gland.

Thyroid Gland

The thyroid gland is located in the lower front part of the neck. It produces thyroid hormones that regulate the body's metabolism. It also plays a role in bone growth and development of the brain and nervous system in children.

The pituitary gland controls the release of thyroid hormones. Thyroid hormones also help maintain normal blood pressure, heart rate, digestion, muscle tone and reproductive functions.

Parathyroid Glands

The parathyroid glands are two pairs of small glands embedded in the surface of the thyroid gland, one pair on each side. They release parathyroid hormone, which plays a role in regulating calcium levels in the blood and bone metabolism.

Adrenal Glands

The two adrenal glands are triangular-shaped glands located on top of each kidney. The adrenal glands are made up of two parts. The outer part is called the *adrenal cortex* and the inner part is called the *adrenal medulla*. The outer part produces hormones called *corticosteroids*, which regulate the body's metabolism, the balance of salt and water in the body, the immune system and sexual function. The inner part or adrenal medulla, produces hormones called *catecholamines* (*e.g.* adrenaline). These hormones help the body cope with physical and emotional stress by increasing the heart rate and blood pressure.

Pineal Gland

The pineal body or pineal gland, is located in the middle of the brain. It secretes a hormone called *melatonin*, which may help regulate the wake-sleep cycle of the body.

Reproductive Glands

The reproductive glands are the main source of sex hormones. In males, the testes, located in the scrotum, secrete hormones called *androgens*; the most important of which is testosterone. These hormones affect many male characteristics (*e.g.* sexual development, growth of facial hair and pubic hair). In females, the ovaries, located on both sides of the uterus, produce estrogen and progesterone as well as eggs. These hormones control the development of female characteristics (*e.g.* breast growth) and they are also involved in reproductive functions (*e.g.* menstruation, pregnancy).

Pancreas

The pancreas is an elongated organ located toward the back of the abdomen behind the stomach. The pancreas has digestive and hormonal functions. One part of the pancreas, the exocrine pancreas, secretes digestive enzymes. The other part of the pancreas, the endocrine pancreas, secretes hormones called *insulin* and *glucagon*. These hormones regulate the level of glucose (sugar) in the blood.

The Main Hormone Systems in the Human Body

Endocrine Gland	Hormone(s)	Main Actions
Adrenal contex	Glucocorticoids (including cortisol and cortisone)	Adapts the body to long-term stress
Adrenal Medulla	Adrenaline (Epinephrine)	Increases sympathetic arousal and stimulates the breakdown of glycogen
Ovaries	Oestrogen and progesterone	Female sexual development and control of the menstrual cycle
Pancreas gland	Insulin and glucagon	Involved in regulation of blood sugar
Pineal gland	Melatonin	Control of circadian rhythms
Pituitary gland (anterior part)	Vasopressin and oxytocin	Control of water balance and female sexual behaviour
Pituitary gland (posterior part)	Master control of other endocrine glands. Also produces growth hormone and prolactin	Wide range of functions. Growth and protein synthesis. Milk production
Testes	Testosterone	Male sexual development and behaviour
Thyroid gland	Thyroxine and triodothyronine	Increases metabolic rate

Biological Basis of Motivation

Biological theory of motivation says that motivational level are regulated by neural pattern recognition events. The biological motives are embedded in physiological state body. There are many such biological motives like hunger, thirst, sleep, desire for sex, pain avoidance and need of oxygen. *Few of the biological motives are discussed below.*

Hunger Motivation

The hypothalamus region of brain plays an important role in regulation of hunger motivation. This is done by two regions of hypothalamus-lateral and ventromedial.

Lateral hypothalamus is an excitatory region for hunger motivation. Within the hypothalamus are nerve cell, which when activated produces sensation of hunger. They do so by producing two protein that cause hunger: Neuropeptide Y (NPY) and Agouti-Related Peptide (AgRP).

Ventromedial hypothalamus is involved in cessation of eating *i.e.* satiety. They do so by two different kind of protein that inhibits hunger: Cocaine and Amphetamine-Regulated

Transcript (CART) and Melanocyte Stimulating Hormone (MSH). These two sets of nerve cells initiate and send hunger signal to other area of hypothalamus. So, a person's hunger at any moment depends on balance of the activity between these two sets of neuron.

Short-Term Regulation of Hunger and Food Intake

Short-term regulation of hunger and food intake involves neural signals from the GI tract, blood levels of nutrients, GI tract hormones and psychological factors.

Neural Signals from the GI Tract

The brain evaluates the contents of the gut through vagal nerve fibers that carry signals between the brain and the Gastrointestinal tract (GI tract). Stretch receptors work to inhibit appetite upon distention of the GI tract by sending signals along the vagus nerve afferent pathway and inhibiting the hunger center.

Nutrient Signal

Blood levels of glucose, amino acids and fatty acids provide a constant flow of information to the brain that may be linked to regulating hunger and energy intake. Nutrient signals that indicate fullness and therefore inhibit hunger include rising blood glucose levels, elevated blood levels of amino acids and blood concentrations of fatty acids.

Hormone Signals

The hormones insulin and Cholecystokinin (CCK) are released from the GI tract during food absorption and act to suppress feeling of hunger. CCK helps in suppressing hunger because of its role in inhibiting neuropeptide Y. Glucagon and epinephrine levels rise during fasting and stimulate hunger. Ghrelin, a hormone produced by the stomach, is a hunger stimulant. Leptin, a hormone produced by adipose tissue acts as hunger suppressant.

Psychological Factors

Two psychological processes appear to be involved in regulating short-term food intake: liking and wanting. Liking refers to the palatability or taste of the food, which is reduced by repeated consumption.

Wanting is the motivation to consume the food, which is also reduced by repeated consumption of a food and may be due to change in memory-related processes. Wanting can be triggered by a variety of psychological processes. Thoughts of a food may intrude on consciousness and be elaborated on, for instance, as when one sees a commercial or smells a desirable food.

Long -Term Regulation of Hunger and Food Intake

Hunger regulation is a complex process involving gastrointestinal tract, hormones and both central and autonomic nervous systems. Effectors and sensors work to regulate hunger in long term.

Effector

The arcuate nucleus of the hypothalamus, is the main regulatory organ for the human hunger. Many brain neurotransmitters affect appetite, especially dopamine and serotonin. Dopamine acts primarily through the reward centers of the brain, whereas serotonin primarily acts through effects on Neuropeptide Y (NPY)/Agouti-Related Peptide (AgRP) [stimulate appetite] and Proopiomelanocortin (POMC) [induce satiety] neurons located in the arcuate nucleus. Similarly, the hormones leptin and insulin suppress appetite through effects on AgRP and POMC neurons.

Hypothalamocortical and hypothalamolimbic projections contribute to the awareness of hunger and the somatic processes controlled by the hypothalamus include vagal tone (the activity of the parasympathetic autonomic nervous system), stimulation of the thyroid (thyroxine regulates the metabolic rate), the hypothalamic-pituitary-adrenal axis and a large number of other mechanisms. Opioid receptor-related processes in the nucleus accumbens and ventral pallidum affect the palatability of foods.

The Nucleus Accumbens (NAc) is the area of the brain that coordinates neurotransmitter, opioid and endocannabinoid signals to control feeding behaviour.

The few important signalling molecules inside the NAc shell modulate the motivation to eat and the affective reactions for food. These molecules include the dopamine, Acetylcholine, opioids and cannabinoids and their action receptors inside the brain, DA, muscarinic and MOR and CB1 receptors respectively.

Sensor

The hypothalamus senses external stimuli mainly through a number of hormones such as leptin, ghrelin, PYY 3-36, orexin and cholecystokinin; all modify the hypothalamic response. They are produced by the digestive tract and by adipose tissue (leptin). Systemic mediators, such as tumor necrosis factor-alpha (TNFα), interleukins 1 and 6 and Corticotropin-Releasing Hormone (CRH) influence appetite negatively; this mechanism explains why ill people often eat less.

Leptin, a hormone secreted exclusively by adipose cells in response to an increase in body fat mass, is an important component in the regulation of long term hunger and food intake. Leptin serves as the brain's indicator of the body's total energy stores. When leptin levels rise in the bloodstream they bind to receptors in ARC. *The functions of leptin are to*

- Suppress the release of Neuropeptide Y (NPY), which in turn prevents the release of appetite enhancing orexins from the lateral hypothalamus. This decreases appetite and food intake, promoting weight loss.
- Stimulate the expression of Cocaine and Amphetamine Regulated Transcript (CART).

Though rising blood levels of leptin do promote weight loss to some extent, its main role is to protect the body against weight loss in times of nutritional deprivation. Other factors also have been shown to affect long-term hunger and food intake regulation including insulin. In addition, the biological clock (which is regulated by the hypothalamus) stimulates hunger.

Processes from other cerebral loci, such as from the limbic system and the cerebral cortex, project on the hypothalamus and modify appetite. This explains why in clinical depression and stress, energy intake can change quite drastically.

Thirst Motivation

Several different conditions can produce thirst and motivate drinking behaviour. Although thirst is often caused by a biological need, it can, like hunger, also result from a psychological need. *Two theories have been given to describe thirst motivation.*

The Dry Mouth Theory

In 1934, **Walter B Cannon** proposed that we become thirsty and drink, when our mouth is dry and that wetting the tissue of the mouth quenches the thirst. Although this may seem to be a good hypothesis, the evidence does not support it. *For example* Just a few sips of water eliminate a dry mouth, but we usually drink much more to satisfy our thirst.

In addition, neither the removal of the salivary glands, which causes a permanently dry mouth, nor the administration of drugs that cause excessive salivation have any influence on the amount of water consumed, when thirsty. Sham drinking studies, in which an animal drinks, but the water does not reach its stomach, indicate that wetting the mouth only temporarily reduces thirst. Thus, factors other than a dry mouth appear to determine the amount of water we drink.

Double-Depletion Hypothesis

According to it, thirst is triggered by cellular dehydration and hypovolemia (reduction of blood volume). The dehydration of cells and reduction of blood volume results in generation of nerve impulses by osmoreceptors (nerve cells in anterior or front of hypothalamus). These nerve impulses act as a signal for thirst. *This thirst can be*

Osmotic Thirst

Body fluids contain a small amount of sodium chloride (NaCl or table salt). Increase in salt intake affect the extracellular fluids first, so that the NaCl concentration outside the cells becomes greater than the concentration inside the cells. This greater NaCl concentration creates a higher osmotic pressure outside than inside the cells, the pressure draws water from the cells to decrease the concentration of NaCl in the extracellular fluid, thereby equalising the osmotic pressure. The resulting cellular dehydration activates two processes that work to restore normal intracellular water levels.

The kidneys concentrate the urine and the animal becomes thirsty and drinks fluids. The type of thirst caused by increased osmotic pressure because of increased salt levels in the extracellular fluid is called *osmotic thirst*.

Hypovolemic Thirst

Hypovolemic thirst, occurs, when we lose extracellular fluids. Fluid loss results from sweating during exercise (sweat is salty because both salts and fluids are lost), diarrhea or bleeding, either from an injury or from heavy menstrual flow. Like osmotic thirst, hypovolemic thirst activates internal changes that cause both water retention and increased fluid intake.

Sleep Motivation

Sleeping is a compulsory biological activity of human life processes. Its psychological implications are of great importance for understanding human behaviour.

Stages of Sleep

Sleep is divided into two broad types: non-rapid eye movement (non-REM or NREM), sleep and rapid eye movement (REM) sleep. Non-REM and REM sleep are so different that physiologists identify them as distinct behavioural states. Non-REM sleep occurs first. It is followed by a transitional period sleep called *slow-wave sleep* or *deep sleep*. During this phase, body temperature and heart rate fall and the brain uses less energy. REM sleep, also known as *paradoxical sleep*, represents a smaller portion of total sleep time. It is the main occasion for dreams (or nightmares) and is associated with desynchronised and fast brain waves, eye movements, loss of muscle tone and suspension of homeostasis.

The sleep cycle of alternate NREM and REM sleep takes an average of 90 minutes, occurring 4-6 times in a good night's sleep.

There are five stages of sleep : Non-REM sleep (stage 1, 2, 3 and 4) and REM sleep. Periods of wakefulness occur before and intermittently throughout various sleep stages or as one shifts sleeping position. Wake is the period when brain activity is at its highest and muscle tone is active.

EEGs play an important role in scientific study of sleep. *The stages of sleep are*

Stage	Characteristics
Stage 1	Light sleep; transition between waking and sleep; person can be awakened easily; eyes move slowly and muscle activity slows.
Stage 2	Eye movement stop, brain waves become slower and occasional bursts of rapid waves called sleep spindles.
Stage 3	Extremely slow brain waves called delta waves are interspersed with smaller and faster waves.
Stage 4	Brain produces delta waves exclusively and sleep lasts for approximately 30 minutes. Stage 3 and 4 are known as deep sleep stages where there is no eye movement or muscle activity.
REM sleep	Breathing becomes rapid, irregular and shallow; eyes jerk rapidly and limb muscles are temporarily paralysed.

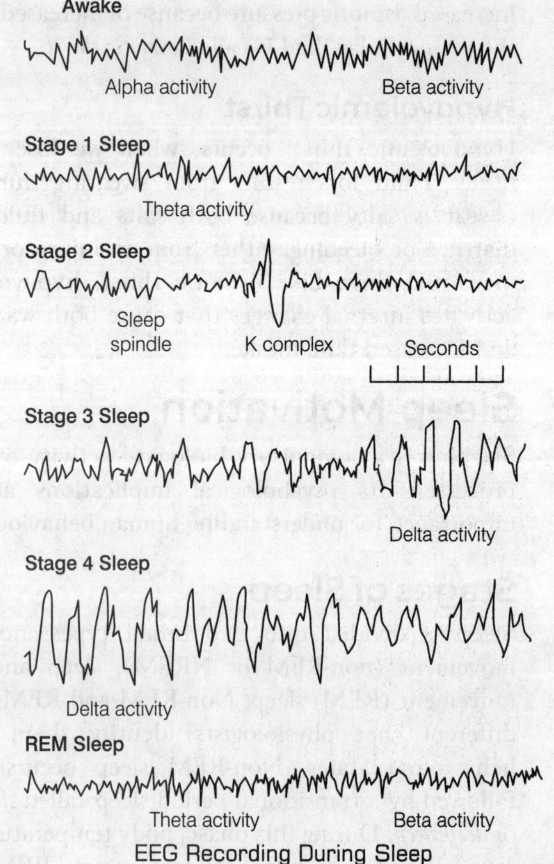

EEG Recording During Sleep

Physiological Mechanism of Sleep

Neurons in the brain and brainstem produce a variety of neurotransmitters which control whether one is asleep or awake. When the alerting areas of the brain are most active, they send arousal signals to the cerebral cortex while at the same time inhibiting activity in other areas of the brain that are responsible for promoting sleep, resulting in a period of stable wakefulness. When the sleep-promoting areas of the brain are most active, they inhibit activity in areas of the brain responsible for promoting wakefulness, resulting in a period of stable sleep.

The Ventrolateral Preoptic Nucleus (VLPO or VLPN) of the hypothalamus is one area of the brain that is particularly involved in the switch between wakefulness and sleep. Neurons in this small area help to promote sleep by inhibiting activity in areas of the brainstem that maintain wakefulness. Likewise, in a process of 'mutual inhibition', during waking hours, those areas of the brain that are active in maintaining wakefulness by stimulating the cerebral cortex also work to inhibit the neurons of the VLPO. Thus, the VLPO is often referred to as the 'sleep switch'.

Following neurotransmitters are involved in driving wakefulness and sleep

- **Histamine** sometimes referred to as the 'master' wakefulness-promoting neurotransmitter, exhibits high activity during wakefulness, decreasing activity during non-REM sleep and its lowest levels during REM sleep.
- **Serotonin** promotes wakefulness, increases sleep-onset latency (the length of time it takes to fall asleep) and decreases REM sleep.
- **Acetylcholine** activity in the reticular activating system of the brainstem stimulates activity in the forebrain and cerebral cortex, encouraging alertness and wakefulness, although it also appears to be active during REM sleep.

- **Dopamine** promotes wakefulness and sometimes sleep (it is also involved in the process of dreaming), so its role is still far from clear.
- **Orexin** (also called *hypocretin*) regulates arousal, wakefulness and appetite. Activation of orexin triggers wakefulness, while low levels of orexin at night serve to drive sleep. A deficiency of orexin results in sleep-state instability, leading to many short awakenings and mixed-up REM and non- REM sleep states typical of sleep disorders like narcolepsy.

Melatonin, also called *sleep hormone*, is converted from serotonin in the pineal gland in the brain, under directions from the body's internal circadian clock. Melatonin production increases in the evening, themically causing drowsiness and helping to lower body temperature and then decreases back to its normal negligible daytime levels by the early morning.

When sleep is called for, the normal signals of wakefulness are interrupted at the thalamus, which serves as the 'gatekeeper' to the cerebral cortex, effectively disconnecting the cortex from most internal and external signals. It is largely the thalamus that imparts the regular slow brain waves of deep slow-wave sleep to the cortex, rather than the more unsynchronised cortical firing typical of the waking state and REM sleep.

REM sleep in particular is regulated in the pons region of the brainstem, where a population of neurons are selectively active during REM sleep. At the same time as acetylcholine neurotransmitters activate this part of the brainstem, two other areas in the pons are simultaneously inhibited in order for REM sleep to occur.

Inhibitory signals are also sent from the pons to the spinal cord to bring about the temporary atonia or muscle paralysis that is characteristic of REM sleep. As a result of this, the release of neurotransmitters such as norepinephrine, serotonin and histamine, which normally stimulate motor neurons to create muscle activity, is completely shut down.

The switching between non-REM and REM sleep during each sleep cycle is regulated by several complex interactions between various 'REM-on' and 'REM-off' neurons, employing different neurotransmitters in various different regions of the mid-brain and hind-brain, all of which are necessary for the various characteristics of REM sleep to play out.

The homeostatic pressure to sleep is largely regulated by a neurotransmitter and neuromodulator called *adenosine*, which builds up throughout the day and acts to inhibit many of the processes associated with wakefulness.

During night, after the body has received a certain amount of restorative non-REM sleep, adenosine levels start to decline. At this point, the systems responsible for wakefulness start to become more active (*i.e.* become less inhibited by adenosine) and conditions gradually become more favourable to awakening.

Towards the end of the night, the secretion of the stress hormone cortisol begins to increase in preparation for the anticipated stress of the day, usually capped by a particularly large increase (upto 50%) about 20-30 minutes after waking, known as the *cortisol awakening response*.

Sexual Motivation

Sexual behaviour is considered a biological motive as it depends on physiological conditions. *The following characteristics of sexual motivation differentiates it from other biological drives*

- Sex is not necessary for an individual's survival.
- Sexual behaviour is not aroused by lack of substances in the body.
- In higher animals, sexual motivation is under the influence of sensory information from environment.

Masters and Johnson divided sexual response into four phases excitement, plateau, orgasm and resolution. *The intensity of sexual urge is dependent upon sex hormones; external stimuli and cultural learning.*

Sex Hormones

The organisational and activational role of sex hormones are responsible for sexual motivation.

Organisational Role of sex Hormones

It refers to the effect of sex hormones on the structure of the body and the brain especially the regions of hypothalamus that regulate hormone release. While a person's sex is inherited, the organisation of the body and brain as either male or female depends on presence of appropriate sex hormones during early life in womb.

Genes on sex chromosomes start sexual development off in one direction or the other. Under their influence, a fetus with female sex chromosomes will develop ovaries which secrete estrogen (female sex hormone) while a fetus with male sex chromosome will develop testes which secrete testosterone (male sex hormone). These hormones then direct further sexual development of body and brain. Later in life, the sex organs grow rapidly and hormone release increases markedly. Secondary sexual characteristics like breast development, body shape, pitch of voice and amount and texture of facial hair etc. develop under influence of estrogens or testosterone at puberty.

Activational Role of Sex Hormones

In males, a certain level of testosteron must be present for sexual behaviour to occur at all. Increase above this threshold have little or no effect on male sexual motivation and behaviour. In human females, the activation of sexual behaviour by estrogen is problematical. Some studies have shown a peak of sexual interest at midpoint of menstrual cycle when estrogen levels are high while others indicated that greatest sexual interest occurs immediately following menstruation when estrogen levels are relatively low. After menopause, when there is an overall reduction in amount of estrogen cirulating in blood, there is little change in women's sexual drive.

Internal Stimuli

External stimuli play an important role in activating sexual motivation in higher primates and humans. Looks, dressing style, voices, odor etc. drive sexual behaviour.

Cultural Learning

Much of the variability in human sexual behaviour seems due to people's early learning experiences. Wide variation exist from person to person in stimuli which will activate sexual behaviour and in ways that sexual motivation is expressed. This all depends on learning experiences.

Biological Basis of Emotions

Emotions can be explained in biological and neurological terms. The limbic system, autonomic nervous system and reticular activating system all interact to assist the body in experiencing and processing emotions.

The Limbic System

The limbic system also known as *paleomommalian cortex* is a collection of brain structures that plays a role in unconscious bodily functions as well as emotion, learning, memory and behaviour. It is the part of the brain that feels and reacts and although it is generally under control of the thinking part of the brain, it can react to stimuli on its own.

The limbic system is the area of the brain most heavily implicated in emotion and memory. The processes of the limbic system control our physical and emotional responses to environmental stimuli. This system categorises the experience of an emotion as a pleasant or unpleasant mental state. Based on this categorisation, neurochemicals such as dopamine, noradrenaline and serotonin increase or decrease, causing the brain's activity level to fluctuate and resulting in changes in body movement, gestures and poses. Its structures include the hypothalamus, thalamus, amygdala and hippocampus.

- The *hypothalamus* plays a role in the activation of the sympathetic nervous system, which is a part of any emotional reaction.
- The *thalamus* serves as a sensory relay center and its neurons project signals to both the amygdala and the higher cortical regions for further processing.
- The *amygdala* plays a role in processing emotional information and sending that information on to cortical structures. The left and right amygdala play a central role in our emotional responses, including feelings like pleasure, fear, anxiety and anger. The amygdala also attaches emotional content to our memories and so plays an important role in determining how robustly those memories are stored.
- The *hippocampus* integrates emotional experience with cognition. It is essentially the memory centre of our brains. Here, our episodic memories are formed and catalogued to be filed away in long-term storage across other parts of the cerebral cortex. Connections made in the hippocampus also help us associate memories with various senses. The hippocampus is also important for spatial orientation and our ability to navigate the world. The hippocampus is one site in the brain where new neurons are made from adult stem cells. This process is called *neurogenesis* and is the basis of one type of brain plasticity.

Other parts of the limbic system include the olfactory bulbs, anterior nuclei, fornix, column of fornix, mammillary body, septum pellucidum, habenular commissure, cingulate gyrus, parahippocampal gyrus, limbic cortex and limbic midbrain areas.

Hormonal Regulation of Behaviour

In terms of their behaviour, one can think of humans and other animals conceptually comprising three interacting components

(i) input systems (sensory systems),
(ii) integrators (the central nervous system) and
(iii) output systems, or effectors (*e.g.* muscles).

Hormones do not cause behavioural changes. Rather, hormones influence these three systems so that specific stimuli are more likely to elicit certain responses in the appropriate behavioural or social context.

In other words, hormones change the probability that a particular behaviour will be emitted in the appropriate situation. This is a critical distinction that can affect how we think of hormone-behaviour relationships.

This scientific study of the interaction between hormones and behaviour is known as *behavioural endocrinology*.

This interaction is bidirectional *i.e.* hormones can influence behaviour and behaviour can sometimes influence hormone concentrations. Hormones coordinate the physiology and behaviour of individuals by regulating, integrating and controlling bodily functions.

These are the chemical messengers released from endocrine glands that travel through the blood system to influence the nervous system to regulate behaviours such as aggression, mating and parenting of individuals.

Examples of hormones that influence behaviour include steroid hormones and peptide hormones. *The prominent hormones that influence behaviour are*

Hormone	Effect on Behaviour
Steroid Hormones	
Cortisol	Act indirectly on the quality of maternal care by evoking an increase in the mother's general level of arousal, thus increasing her responsiveness to infantgenerated cues.
Estrogen	It is a group of primary female sex hormones synthesised in the ovaries and are responsible for sexual behaviour in females. It also regulates general behaviour in humans as it has been found to play a role in behavioural inhibition and controlling dangerous or unwanted behaviours in them.
Testosterone	It promotes a sense of separateness, aggression, sexual motivation and behaviour in males, assertiveness and self-confidence and violent, criminal or psychotic behaviour.
Protein and Peptide Hormone	
Kisseptin	It drives sexual behaviour by influencing sex hormone secretion. Also it regulates social behaviour as it acts as an antidepressant in males, reduces fear in males, can induce or reduce anxiety in males, increases male brain activity in processing parts of the brain for sex drive and increases activity in brain for male bonding.
Adrenaline (Epinephrine)	It is known as the *fight or flight* hormone and increases overall muscular function, increases awareness, excitability, desire and emotion.
Oxytocin	It stimulates milk letdown and uterine contractions during birth and promotes social bonding.
Prolactin	It influences behaviour associated with parental care.

Genetics and Behaviour

Every cell of body have a genetic blueprint that enables it to perform its essential functions. This information is contained in chromosomes, thread like structures found in the nuclei of nearly all cells. Chromosomes are composed of DNA, (Deoxyribo Nucleic acid).

The DNA is composed of several simpler component arranged in the form of double helix. Chromosomes contain thousands of genes, segments of DNA that serves as basic units of heredity. Our genes working in complex combination and together with forces in the environment, ultimately determine many aspect of our biological make up.

Most cells in the human body contain 46 chromosomes existing in pair. When such cells divide, the chromosome pairs splits, then after the cells have separated each chromosome replicate itself so that the full number is restored. This cell division is known as mitosis. In contrast sperm and ova, male and female sex cell contains only 23 chromosomes. Thus, when they join to form a fertilised ovum, from which new human being will develop, the full number (46) is attained.

Chromosomal Anomalies

Chromosomal anomalies refers to disorders caused due to absence or excess or abnormal arrangements of one or more chromosomes.

Numerical Abnormalities

The chromosomal anomalies that occur due to absence or excess of one or more chromosomes are called *numerical abnormalities*.

This gain or loss of chromosome occur due to failure of segregation of chromotids during cell division cycle.

This is called *aneuploidy* (an abnormal number of chromosomes). The total number of chromosomes in a normal human cell is 46 (23 pairs). Out of these 22 pairs are autosomes and one pair of chromosomes are sex chromosome. Sometimes, though rarely, either an additional copy of a chromosome may be included in an individual or an individual may lack one of any one pair of chromosomes. These situations are known as *trisomy* or *monosomy* of a chromosome, respectively.

Trisomy A trisomy, a form of aneuploidy, is a type of polysomy in which there are three copies of a particular chromosome, instead of the normal two. *For example* If an individual is born with three 21 chromosomes rather than the ususal pair, the individual is said to have trisomy 21.

Trisomy can occur in both autosomal and sex chromosomes. Autosomal trisomy can be associated with birth defects, intellectual disability and shortened life expectancy. The most common types of autosomal trisomy that survive to birth in humans are Trisomy 21 (Down syndrome), Trisomy 18 (Edwards syndrome), Trisomy 13 (Patau syndrome), Trisomy 9 and Trisomy 8 (Warkany syndrome 2) Trisomy of sex chromosomes can also occur and include XXX (Triple X syndrome), XXY (Klinefelter syndrome) and XYY. Compared to trisomy of the autosomal chromosomes, trisomy of the sex chromosomes normally has less severe consequences. Individuals may show few or no symptoms and have a normal life expectancy.

Monosomy Monosomy is a form of aneuploidy with the presence of only one chromosome from a pair. Thus, there is a total of 45 chromosomes in each cell of the body rather than 46. When a portion of one chromosome in a pair is missing, it is said to be partial monosomy. Human conditions due to monosomy *are as follows*.

- **Turner Syndrome** People with Turner syndrome typically have one X chromosome instead of the usual two sex chromosomes. Turner syndrome is the only full monosomy that is seen in humans all other cases of full monosomy are lethal and the individual will not survive development.
- **Cri du Chat Syndrome** A partial monosomy caused by a deletion of the end of the short arm of chromosome 5.
- **1p36 Deletion Syndrome** A partial monosomy caused by a deletion at the end of the short arm of chromosome 1.

Structural Abnormalities

When the chromosome's structure is altered, it can take several forms *which are as follows*

(i) **Deletions** A portion of the chromosome is missing or deleted. Known disorders in humans include Wolf-Hirschhorn syndrome, which is caused by partial deletion of the short arm of chromosome 4 and Jacobsen syndrome, also called the *terminal 11q deletion disorder.*

(ii) **Duplications** A portion of the chromosome is duplicated, resulting in extra genetic material. Known human disorders include Charcot-Marie-Tooth disease type 1A, which may be caused by duplication of the gene encoding peripheral myelin protein 22 (PMP22) on chromosome 17.

(iii) **Translocations** A portion of one chromosome is transferred to another chromosome. *There are two main types of translocations*

- **Reciprocal Translocation** Segments from two different chromosomes have been exchanged.
- **Robertsonian Translocation** An entire chromosome gets attached to another at the centremere. In humans these only occur with chromosomes 13, 14, 15, 21 and 22.

(iv) **Inversions** A portion of the chromosome has broken off, turned upside down and reattached, therefore the genetic material is inverted.

(v) Insertions A portion of one chromosome has been deleted from its normal place and inserted into another chromosome.

(vi) **Rings** A portion of a chromosome has broken off and formed a circle or ring. This can happen with or without loss of genetic material.

(vii) **Isochromosome** Formed by the mirror image copy of a chromosome segment including the centromere.

Chromosome instability syndromes are a group of disorders characterised by chromosomal instability and breakage. They often lead to an increased tendency to develop certain types of malignancies.

Nature Nurture Theory

Our genetic destiny is not necessarily written in stone; it can be influenced by several factor, such as social factors as well as the environmental influences among which we live. Long standing debates have taken place over the idea of which factor is more inportant, genes or environment. The psychologist use many different method to address it. Two of these, have been most useful-twin studies and adoption studies.

Twin Studies

Twin studies are helpful in disentangling the relative roles of genetic and environmental factor in a given form of behaviour. Identical twins share all the same genes while fraternal twins do not. Under normal conditions, however, both kinds of twins are raised in environment that, if not identical are very similar. The twins are raised in same home, attend same school and so on. Thus, if a given aspect of behaviour is strongly influenced by genetic factor, then the identical twins will resemble each other more closely than fraternal twins.

Adoption Studies

Adoption studies look at the impact of nurturing on children who are raised by parents who are not their biological parents.

As there is no biological connection between the parent and the child, if the child grows up to share the parent's traits (or the traits of their step-brothers or step-sisters who are biologically related to the parents), then these traits are probably produced by nurture.

Adoption studies have to use adopted children as their sample and this is a group that may not be very representative of other children. For one thing, these children have been separated from the biological parents, perhaps through tragic circumstances or because their biological parents, 'gave them up' due to difficult circumstances. Child Psychologists like John Bowlby argue that children are bodly affected if they are separated from their mother during a critical period in infancy. If this happens to adopted children, it would make them even less representative of children in general.

EXAM BASED QUESTIONS

1 What kind of muscle is present in Heart?
(a) Smooth muscle (b) Cardiac muscle
(c) Skeletal muscle (d) All of these

2 Visceral muscles are present in
(a) intestine (b) blood vessel
(c) stomach (d) All of these

3 Which muscle is urinary system composed of ?
(a) Smooth muscle (b) Skeletal muscle
(c) Both a and b (d) None of these

4 How many skeletal muscle are there in the eye to control its movement?
(a) Ten (b) Twelve
(c) Six (d) Seven

5 Hypothalamus controls
(a) satiety (b) metabolism
(c) body temperature (d) All of these

6 Where is pituitary gland located?
(a) Base of the brain
(b) Lower central part of brain
(c) Lower front part of neck
(d) None of these

7 Which hormone plays a role in regulating calcium levels in the blood and bone metabolism?
(a) Thyroid hormone
(b) Para thyroid hormone
(c) Luetinising hormone
(d) Antidiuretic hormone

8 This gland are triangular shaped and located on top of each kidney. Which gland is this?
(a) Pineal body (b) Pancreas
(c) Adrenal gland
(d) Thyroid gland

9 What function does pineal gland serves?
(a) Regulating sleep and wake cycle of body
(b) Regulating salt and water balance of body
(c) Adapt the body to long term stress
(d) Regulation of blood sugar

10 Which amongst the following controls the feeling of hunger?
(a) Cerebellum (b) Hypothalamus
(c) Pituitary (d) Cerebral cortex

11 Protein that causes hunger are
(a) Neuropeptide Y (NPY)
(b) Agouti-Related Peptide (AGRP)
(c) Both a and b
(d) None of the above

12 .... carry signals between brain and GI tract.
(a) Vagal nerve (b) Cranial nerve
(c) Sensory nerve (d) None of these

13 Which nutrient play a role in inhibiting hunger?
(a) Glucose (b) Amino acid
(c) Fatty acid (d) All of these

14 .... level rises during fasting and stimulates hunger.
(a) Glucagon (b) Epinephrine
(c) Both a and b (d) None of these

15 .... is the area of brain that coordinates neurotransmitter, opiod and endocannabinoid signals to control feeding behaviour.
(a) Opoid receptor (b) Nucleus accumbens
(c) Hypothalamocortical (d) None of these

16 Leptin is secreted by
(a) adipose cell (b) thyroid gland
(c) GI tract (d) pituitary gland

17 The dry mouth theory was given by
(a) Walter B Cannon (b) Walter Buchanan
(c) Walter C Cannon (d) Walter H Cannon

18 Body fluid contains a small amount of
(a) KCI (b) NaCl (c) $NaNO_3$ (d) HNO_3

19 Hypovolemic thirst can be induced by
(a) excercise (b) diarrhea (c) bleeding (d) All of these

20 .... occurs under the closed eyelids of sleeping subjects.
(a) Rapid eye movement (b) Random eye movement
(c) Rapid brain collapse (d) Rapid wakefulness

21 What is the psycho physiological basis for defining stages of sleep?
(a) EEG (b) EOG
(c) EMG (d) All of these

22 Which of the following neurotransmitter is known as 'master' wake fulness promoting neurotransmitter?
(a) Histamine (b) Dopamine (c) Serotonin (d) Orexin

23 Which of the following is known as sleep switch?
(a) Pituitary gland
(b) Ventromedial hypothalamus
(c) Ventromedial preoptic nucleus of hypothalamus
(d) None of the above

24 Which of the following regulates homeostatic pressure to sleep?
(a) Orexin (b) Melatonin
(c) Adenosine (d) All of these

25 Bizzare and illogical dreams occur in
(a) REM sleep (b) SWS sleep
(c) Both a and b (d) None of these

26 In an infant what kind of movement are there when they are in REM sleep?
(a) Spasmodic movement of hands
(b) Movement of facial muscle
(c) Facial expression
(d) All of the above

27 Sleep plays a role in the development of the
(a) circulatory system (b) nervous system
(c) endocrine system (d) None of these

28 Reticular formation is made up of
(a) group of capillaries (b) group of arteries
(c) group of neuron (d) None of these

29 Function of reticular formation include
(a) autonomic activity (b) motor reflex
(c) sensory analysis (d) All of these

30 Neurotransmitter having a role in sleep are/is
(a) Adrenaline (b) Serotonin
(c) Both a and b (d) None of these

31 When cholinergic agonist is injected into ......, it increases REM sleep.
(a) GTF (b) LTN (c) PTN (d) PGO

32 Reciprocal interaction model was given by
(a) Jouvet (b) MC Charlie and Hobson
(c) Charles (d) None of these

33 Which of the following is known as sleep horomone?
(a) Melatonin (b) Orexin
(c) Serotonin (d) Dopamine

34 Which of the following imparts regular slow brain wave of deep slow wave sleep to cortex?
(a) Hypothalamus (b) Thyroid gland
(c) Pituitary gland (d) Thalamus

35 Who divided sexual response into four phases?
(a) Master and Johnson (b) Epstein
(c) Bermer (d) None of these

36 Which of the following factor influences sexual motivation?
(a) Sex hormones (b) All of these
(c) External stimuli (d) Cultural learning

37 Which of the following is incorrect?
(a) Sex is not necessary for survival of species.
(b) Sex is not necessary for individual's survival.
(c) Sexual motivation is under influence of sensory information from environment.
(d) None of the above

38 Which of the following are sex hormones?
(a) Estrogen (b) Testosterone
(c) Both a and b (d) None of these

39 Which of the following is responsible for activation of sympathetic nervous system?
(a) Thalamus
(b) Hippocampus
(c) Amygdala
(d) Hypothalamus

40 Which of the followingt serves as a sensory relay centre?
(a) Hippocampus (b) Thalamus
(c) Amygdala (d) Hypothalamus

41 Which of the following integrates emotional experience with cognition?
(a) Hippocampus (b) Amygdala
(c) Septum pellucidum (d) None of these

42 Which of the following attaches feeling of fear to our emotions?
(a) Thalamus (b) Amygdala
(c) Hypothalamus (d) All of these

43 What is the memory centre of our brains?
(a) Hippocampus (b) Hypothalamus
(c) Thalamus (d) Amygdala

44 Amygdala plays an important role in?
(a) Physical responses
(b) Emotional responses
(c) Both a and b
(d) None of these

45 What is the component of hormonal regulation of behaviour?
(a) Input system (b) Integrators
(c) Output system (d) All of these

46 Which among the following is/are controlled by Limbic system?
(a) Emotion (b) Learning
(d) Memory (d) All of these

47 Which among the following is/are part of Limbic system?
(a) Hypothalamus (b) Thalamus
(c) Amygdala (d) All of these

48 What play a rule in processing emotional information and sending that information on to cortical structures ?
(a) Hippocampus (b) Thalamus
(c) Amygdala (d) Hypothalamus

49 Which of the following hormone promotes social bonding?
(a) Adrenaline (b) Vassopressine
(c) None of these (d) Oxytocin

50 Nature v/s nurture controversy can be solved by
(a) twin studies (b) adoption studies
(c) Both a and b (d) None of these

51 What is carried in chromosome ?
(a) Genetic information (b) Hard wave information
(c) Nerves (d) None of these

52 How many chromosomes do human cells contain?
(a) 42 (b) 46 (c) 44 (d) 48

53 Numerical abnormality of chromosome is known as
(a) diploidy (b) triploidy
(c) aneuploidy (d) All of these

54 Trisomy of 21 chromosome causes
(a) down syndrome
(b) huntington disease
(c) phenyl ketonuria
(d) Jacobsen syndrome

55 Charcot Marie Tooth disease is caused by ……… of gene.
(a) deletion (b) duplication
(c) translocation (d) inversion

56 Which of the following pairs is/are correctly matched?

1.	Sleep spindle	:	Stage 2 sleep
2.	Dreaming	:	Stage 5 sleep
3.	Full sleep cycle	:	90 minute

Codes
(a) 1 and 2
(b) 2 and 3
(c) 1 and 3
(d) All of these

57 Which of the following pairs is/are correctly matched?

1. Hypothalamus	:	Regulate hunger
2. Amygdala	:	Heart rate
3. Medulla	:	Emotion

Codes
(a) Only 1 (b) Only 2
(c) Only 3 (d) All of these

58 Which of the following pairs is/are correctly matched?

1. Orexins	:	Hypocretins
2. Adrenaline	:	Noradrenaline
3. Insulin	:	Glucagon

Codes
(a) Only 1 (b) 1 and 2
(c) All of these (d) None of these

59 Which one of the following pairs is correctly matched?

(a) NPY	:	Insulin
(b) Ghrelin	:	CART
(c) CCK	:	Ghrelin
(d) NPY	:	AGRP

60 Which of the following pairs is/are correctly matched?

1.	Beta wave	:	Most synchronous brain wave
2.	Suprachiasmatic	:	Responsible for monitoring circadian rhythm
3.	Theta wave	:	Present when we are awaking

Codes
(a) Only 1 (b) Only 2
(c) Only 3 (d) None of these

61 Arrange the following in chronological order.
1. Glands 2. Ductless gland
3. Hormones
Codes
(a) 2, 1, 3 (b) 1, 2, 3
(c) 3, 2, 1 (d) 3, 1, 2

62 The limbic system contains
1. Amygdala 2. Thalamus
3. Hippocampus
Select the correct answer using the codes given below
(a) 1 and 3 (b) 1 and 2
(c) 2 and 3 (d) All of these

63 Consider the following stateements
1. A key function of specialised lipid molecules located in the nerve cell is to detect the presence of hormones outside the cell.
2. Gamma wave present when we are awake.
Which of the statements given above is/are incorrect?
(a) Only 1
(b) Only 2
(c) Both 1 and 2
(d) Neither 1 nor 2

64 Consider the following statements
Adrenal insufficiency causes
1. increased blood volume
2. decreased plasma K level
3. hyperglycaemia
4. reduce excretion of 17 ketosteroids

Which of the statements given above are correct

(a) 1 and 4 (b) 1, 2 and 3
(c) 2, 3 and 4 (d) 2 and 3

65 Arrange in chronological order
1. Plateau 2. Orgasm
3. Resolution 4. Excitement

Codes
(a) 1, 2, 3, 4 (b) 4, 1, 2, 3
(c) 2, 3, 1, 4 (d) 3, 1, 2, 4

66 Match the following

List I (Glands)	List II (Hormones)
A. Thyroid gland	1. Produce growth hormone
B. Testes	2. Melatonin
C Pituitary gland	3. Thyroxine
D. Pineal gland	4. Testosterone

Codes

	A	B	C	D
(a)	1	2	3	4
(b)	4	3	2	1
(c)	2	4	3	1
(d)	3	4	1	2

67 Match the following

List I (Organs)	List II (Functions)
A. Oral cavity	1. Bile secretion
B. Liver	2. Storage of bile
C Gall bladder	3. Moistanong
D. Duodenum	4. Secretion of CCK

Codes

	A	B	C	D		A	B	C	D
(a)	4	2	3	1	(b)	1	3	2	4
(c)	3	1	2	4	(d)	1	3	4	2

68 Match the following

List I (Hormones)	List II (Main Actions)
A. Progesterone	1. Regulate blood sugar
B. Glucogen	2. Female sexual development
C Melatonin	3. Control of circadian rhythm
D. Oxytocin	4. Control of water balance

Codes

	A	B	C	D		A	B	C	D
(a)	1	2	4	3	(b)	3	4	2	1
(c)	2	1	3	4	(d)	4	3	1	2

69 Match the following

List I (Stage of sleep)	List II (Characteristic)
A. Stage 1	1. Theta activity
B. Stage 2	2. Sleep spindles and K complex in addition to theta activity
C. Stage 3	3. Delta activity predominates
D. Stage 4	4. Addition of delta activity

Codes

	A	B	C	D		A	B	C	D
(a)	2	1	3	4	(b)	4	2	3	1
(c)	1	3	4	2	(d)	1	2	4	3

70 Match the following

List I (Concept)	List II (Given by)
A. Dry mouth theory	1. Verney
B. Osmotic thirst	2. Walter B Canon
C. Hypovolemic thirst	3. Epstein
D. Psychological mechanism of sleep	4. Bremer

Codes

	A	B	C	D		A	B	C	D
(a)	1	2	4	3	(b)	2	1	3	4
(c)	3	4	1	2	(d)	4	3	2	1

Directions (Q. Nos. 71-75) *Read the passage given below and answer the following questions.*

The endocrine system is another important communication system and consists of a number of glands scattered throughout the body that secret chemicals called hormones may be circulating through the body at any one time and these are secreted from a number of organs. *For example* The thyroid, the thymus, the adrenal glands and the gonalds, including the testes and ovaries.

71 The anterior pituitary gland release into the blood which hormone

(a) ardeno corticotropin (b) thyroid
(c) oestrogen (d) testosterone

72 The endocrine system is what type of system?

(a) Neuron (b) Metabolic
(c) Communication (d) Sympathetic system

73 In which side of the brain pituitary gland located?

(a) Underside of the brain (b) Outside of the brain
(c) Back of hind brain (c) Side of medulla

74 The pituitary consists of how many glands?

(a) One (b) Two
(c) Three (d) Four

75 Which of the following hormone is released by the posterior part of pituitary?

(a) Oxytocin
(b) Insulin
(c) Glycogen
(d) Melatonin

Directions (Q. Nos. 76-80) *Read the given below passage and answer the following questions*

The loss of extracellur fluid produces hypovolemic thirst. Early physiological evidence suggested that angiotensin activates neurons in the preoptic and anterior areas of the hypothalamus that detect hypovolemic (or volumetric) thirst and this activation motivates drinking *e.g.* when Epstein and Colleagues (1970) injected angiotensin into the preoptic and anterior hypothalamic areas of rats, they observed drinking even in satiated animals moreover, increasing the quantity of injected angiotensin caused the rats to drink more.

These results suggest that under natural conditions, the amount of fluid consumed corresponds to the amount last, because the level of angotensin released is proportional to the amount of depleted extra cellular fluid. The loss of body fluids creates both thirst and a craving for substances, such as Nacl, that are lost as a result of hypovolemia. Salt deprived rats develop a preference for salty tasting. Solution, preferring salty fluids to salty food (Bertino and Tordoff, 1988). In humans, salt depletion causes moderate sensory changes.

76 **What is the result of salt deptetion in humans?**
(a) It leads to memory loss
(b) It leads to moderate sensory change
(c) It leads to low blood pressure
(d) It leads to high blood pressure

77 **The loss of extracellular fluid produce what?**
(a) Hypovolemic thirst (b) Sensation in stomach
(c) Irritation in mouth (d) Increase heart beat

78 **Who conducted research on hypothalamus thirst?**
(a) Epstein (b) Jackson
(c) Thomas (d) Leptin

79 **Which element is lost as a result of hypothalamus thirst?**
(a) $CaCl_2$ (b) H_2O
(c) NaCl (d) KCl

80 **What cause the rat to drink more?**
(a) Angiotensin (b) Pepsin
(c) Regin (d) Testotorin

Directions (Q. Nos. 81-85) *Read the passage given below and answer the following questions*

Early research on the brain's control of hunger and satiety suggested that the Lateral Hypothalamus (LH) controlled the initiation of eating and the Ventromedical Hypothalamus (VHM) controlled the inhibition of eating or resulted satiety. Lesion studies on rats found that damage to the LH produced an animal that would not eat, whereas damage to the VMH caused a rat to over eat. Stimulation of the two areas produced the complementary effects : LH stimulation in eating and VMH stimulation resulted cause an animal to stop eating.

Thus, the LH became known as the *hunger center* and the VMH as the *satiety center*. This view is now known to be an over simplification. More recent studies show that two fiber tracts, rather than two fiber tracts, rather than two localised structures, are involved in the initiation and lessation of feeding, but first let us examine the information that was accumulated on the role of the LH and VHM.

81 **Which structure is involved in the initiation and cessation of feeding?**
(a) Two fiber tracts (b) Two localised structure
(c) Hypothalamus (d) Ventricles

82 **Which of the following control the initiation of eating?**
(a) Ventro medical hypothalamus
(b) Ateral hypothalamus
(c) Hyperphagia (d) Aphagia

83 **What control the inhibition satiety?**
(a) Lateral hypothalamus
(b) Ventro medical hypothalamus
(c) Adipsia (d) Aphassia

84 **Which is known as hunger centre?**
(a) LH (b) VMH (c) MH (d) VSH

85 **What is known as satiety centre?**
(a) LH (b) VMH (c) MH (d) VSH

Directions *(Q. Nos. 86-95) In the questions given below are two statements labelled as Assertion (A) and Reason (R). In the context of the two statements, which one of the following is correct?.*

Codes
(a) Both A and R are true and R is the correct explanations of A
(b) Both A and R true, but R is not the correct explanation of A
(c) A is true, but R is false
(d) A is false, but R is true

86 **Assertion** (A) Insulin promotes use of glucose.
Reason (R) Glucose is the primary source of energy by the body.

87 **Assertion** (A) Neurons in the arcuate nucleus of the hypothalamus produce neuropeptide 4.
Reason (R) Energy defecit produce due to food deprivation.

88 **Assertion** (A) Greater concentration of NaCl creates a higher osmotic pressure outside than insides the cell.
Reason (R) Osmotic pressure have no role in fluid circulation.

89 Assertion (A) No degree of clitoral or penile erection found in REM sleep.

Reason (R) Cerebral activity increases in REM sleep.

90 Assertion (A) Hormones help in regulation of human behaviour.

Reason (R) Hormones coordinate physiology and behaviour of individuals by integrating and controlling bodily functions.

91 Assertion (A) Twin study is better than adoption study.

Reason (R) It helps to determine whether genetics or environment affect behaviour.

92 Assertion (A) Visceral muscle have smooth appearance, when viewed under microscope.

Reason (R) Visceral muscle are also called smooth muscle.

93 Assertion (A) Monosomy is absence of one member of a pair of chromosome.

Reason (R) Down syndrome is an example of monosomy.

94 Assertion (A) Increase in solutes will draw water from the cell and lead to cell shrinkage.

Reason (R) Water is lost through evaporation or if the organism consumes a salty meal.

95 Assertion (A) Ghrelin is released from the stomach, when it and the duodenum are empty of food.

Reason (R) Injection of ghrelin stimulates eating, while food intake suppresses ghrelin level.

PREVIOUS YEARS' QUESTIONS

November 2017

1 Sex chromosome anomaly (XXY) results into the development of

(a) Klinefelter's syndrome (b) down syndrome
(c) turner's syndrome (d) phenylketonuria

2 Which of the following is the evidence that REM sleep specifically enhances consolidation?

A. REM increases after learning.
B. REM deprivation interferes with learning.
C. Performance improves following REM sleep.

Codes

(a) A and B (b) A and C (c) B and C (d) All of these

3 The correct order of the stages of Master's and Johnson's sexual response cycle is

(a) plateau, excitement, orgasm, resolution
(b) excitement, plateau, orgasm, resolution
(c) excitement, orgasm, plateau, resolution
(d) excitement, plateau, orgasm, refractory

4 Which part of Central Nervous System controls much of the Endocrine System by regulating the Pituitary Gland ?

(a) Amygdala (b) Hypothalamus
(c) Hippocampus (d) Medulla

January 2017

5 Read each of the following two statements Assertion (A) and Reason (R) and indicate your answer using codes given below.

Assertion (A) A large proportion of Down Syndrome cases can be identified in prenatal diagnosis through the use of amniocentesis.

Reason (R) The amniocentesis procedure reveals that the fetus does not have the defect and the parents are spared months of needless anxiety.

Codes

(a) Both A and R are true and R is the correct explanation of A
(b) Both A and R are true, but R is not the correct explanation of A
(c) A is true, but R is false
(d) A is false, but R is true

6 Sensory specific satiety takes place in

(a) Papillae
(b) Thalamus
(c) Nucleus of Solitary Tract (NST)
(d) Insula

7 Read each of the following two statements - Assertion (A) and Reason (R) and indicate your answer using codes given below.

Assertion (A) Pituitary gland is frequently referred to as the master gland.

Reason (R) Most of pituitary hormones are tropic hormones.

Codes

(a) Both A and R are true and R is the correct explanation of A
(b) Both A and R are true, but R is not the correct explanation of A
(c) A is true, but R is false
(d) A is false, but R is true

8 Read each of the following two statements Assertion (A) and Reason (R) and indicate your answer using codes given below.

Assertion (A) Differences between intelligence levels of monozygotic twins are attributed to environmental influences.

Reason (R) Monozygotic twins have identical genetically determined reaction range.

Codes

(a) Both A and R are true and R is the correct explanation of A
(b) Both A and R are true, but R is not the correct explanation of A
(c) A is true, but R is false
(d) A is false, but R is true

ANSWERS

Exam Based Questions

1 *(b)*	2 *(d)*	3 *(c)*	4 *(c)*	5 *(d)*	6 *(a)*	7 *(b)*	8 *(c)*	9 *(a)*	10 *(b)*
11 *(c)*	12 *(a)*	13 *(d)*	14 *(c)*	15 *(b)*	16 *(a)*	17 *(a)*	18 *(b)*	19 *(d)*	20 *(a)*
21 *(d)*	22 *(a)*	23 *(c)*	24 *(c)*	25 *(a)*	26 *(d)*	27 *(b)*	28 *(c)*	29 *(d)*	30 *(c)*
31 *(a)*	32 *(b)*	33 *(a)*	34 *(d)*	35 *(a)*	36 *(b)*	37 *(a)*	38 *(c)*	39 *(d)*	40 *(b)*
41 *(a)*	42 *(b)*	43 *(a)*	44 *(b)*	45 *(d)*	46 *(d)*	47 *(d)*	48 *(c)*	49 *(d)*	50 *(c)*
51 *(a)*	52 *(b)*	53 *(c)*	54 *(a)*	55 *(b)*	56 *(c)*	57 *(a)*	58 *(a)*	59 *(d)*	60 *(b)*
61 *(b)*	62 *(d)*	63 *(c)*	64 *(c)*	65 *(b)*	66 *(d)*	67 *(c)*	68 *(c)*	69 *(d)*	70 *(b)*
71 *(a)*	72 *(c)*	73 *(a)*	74 *(b)*	75 *(a)*	76 *(b)*	77 *(a)*	78 *(a)*	79 *(c)*	80 *(a)*
81 *(a)*	82 *(b)*	83 *(b)*	84 *(a)*	85 *(b)*	86 *(b)*	87 *(b)*	88 *(c)*	89 *(d)*	90 *(a)*
91 *(d)*	92 *(d)*	93 *(c)*	94 *(a)*	95 *(a)*					

Previous Year's Questions

1 *(a)*	2 *(d)*	3 *(b)*	4 *(b)*	5 *(a)*	6 *(c)*	7 *(a)*	8 *(a)*

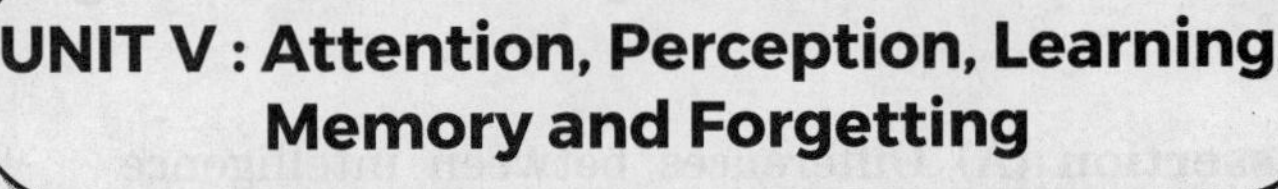

Attention and Perception

Attention refers to the process of selectively responding to a stimuli. From a large number of stimuli that are available in external world, attentional processes limit reception of stimuli selectively. These processes filter information selectively for further processing which finally leads to perception.

Attention

Attention is the term used for the perceptual processes that select certain inputs for inclusion in our conscious experience or awareness at any given time. Attention is the cognitive process of selectively concentrating on one aspect of the environment while ignoring other things. *For examples* Listening carefully to what someone is saying while ignoring other conversations in the room. In other words, attention is the first step in the observation. It implies 'focusing the consciousness on a stimulus.' It is a process of preferentially responding to a stimulus or a range of stimuli.

Attention can be split, as when a person drives a car and talks on a cell phone at the same time. Sometimes attention shifts to matters unrelated to the external environment, a phenomenon referred to as 'mind-wandering' or 'spontaneous thought'. The concentration provided by the process of attention helps us in the clarity of the perception of the perceived object or phenomenon. Thus, attention is not merely a cognitive factor but is essentially determined by emotions, interest, attitude and memory.

Thus, attention is a process which is carried out through cognitive abilities and helped by emotional and behavioural factors to select something out of the various stimuli present in one's environment and bring it in the centre of one's consciousness in order to perceive it clearly for deriving the desired end.

In this Chapter

Definitions of Attention

According to **William James**, "Everyone knows what attention is, focalisation and concentration of consciousness are of its essence. It implies withdrawal from somethings in order to deal effectively with others and is a condition which has a real opposite in the confused, dazed, scatterbrained state." (Principles of Psychology, 1890).

According to **Titchner**, "Attention is a state of sensory clearness with a margin and a focus. Attention is the aspect of consciousness that relates to the amount of effort exerted in focusing on certain aspects of an experience, so that they become relatively vivid."

According to **Dumville**, "Attention is the concentration of consciousness upon one object other than upon another."

According to **Ross**, "Attention is the process of getting an object or thought clearly before the mind."

According to **Morgan**, "Attention is being keenly alive to some specific factors in our environment. It is a preparatory adjustment for response."

Thus, attention is essentially process and not a product. It helps in our awareness or consciousness of our environment, which is of selective kind, because in a given time, we can concentrate or focus our consciousness on a particular object only.

Forms of Attention

Attention can be classified on basis of will of an individual, an individual's response to stimuli, or process- oriented views.

On the basis of will and efforts of an individual, attention can broadly be divided into two forms

(i) **Voluntary Attention** When the attention is drawn at the will and deliberate efforts of individual, it becomes voluntary attention. It demands the conscious efforts on our part, so it is least automatic and spontaneous like that of involuntary attention. Attention paid at the time of solving an assigned problem of mathematics, answering question in an examination hall and so on come under voluntary attention category.

(ii) **Involuntary Attention** When the attention is drawn without the will and efforts of an individual, it is termed as involuntary attention. In case of involuntary attention, we attend to an object or condition without making any conscious effort *e.g.* a mother's attention towards her crying child, an individual's attention towards the members of the opposite sex, towards bright colours and so on.

The attention which is aroused by the instincts is called *enforced involuntary attention*. A young man, when we remark on his sex instinct or his curiosity, becomes quite attentive in his task. The other subtype of involuntary attention, produced by the sentiments is called *spontaneous involuntary attention*. It is the result of properly developed sentiment towards the object or idea of a person around which our sentiments are formed with.

On the basis of an individual's response to stimuli, attention can be divided into two forms

(i) **Overt Attention** The act of directing sense organs towards a stimulus source is known as overt attention.

(ii) **Covert Attention** The act of mentally focusing on particular stimuli is known as *covert attention*. Covert attention is thought to be a neural process that enhances the signal from a particular part of the sensory neuron.

There are studies that suggest the mechanisms of overt and covert attention may not be as separate as previously believed. Though humans and primates can look in one direction but attend in another, there may be an underlying neural circuitry that links shifts in covert attention to plan to shift gaze. *For example* If individuals attend to the right hand corner field of view, we want to move eyes in that direction and have to actively suppress the eye movement that linked to this shift in attention.

The current view is that visual covert attention is a mechanism for quickly scanning the field of view for interesting locations. This shift in covert attention is linked to eye movement circuitry that sets up a slower saccade (saccade is a quick, simultaneous movement of both eyes between two or more phases of fixation in same direction) to that location.

On the basis of process orient attention can be divided into two forms

(i) **Selective Attention** It is concerned mainly with selection of a limited number of stimuli or objects from a large number of stimuli. The selection of stimuli is based on external factors like size, intensity and motion of stimuli and internal factors like social needs, interest, attitude and preparatory set.

(ii) **Sustained Attention** It is concerned with concentration *i.e.* ability to maintain attention on an object or event for longer duration. It is influenced by sensory modality, clarity of stimuli, temporal uncertainty and spatial uncertainty.

Determinants of Attention

Determinants of attention can broadly be divided into two types

External Factors or Conditions

These conditions are generally those characteristics of outside situation or stimuli which make the strongest aid for capturing our attention. *The external factors include*

- **Nature of the Stimulus** Different stimuli have varying influence on an individual. All types of stimuli are not able to bring the same degree of attention. *For example*; A picture attracts attention more readily than words. Among the pictures, too, the pictures of beautiful things and persons invite more attention than pictures of normal category. In this way an effective stimulus should always be chosen for capturing maximum attention.
- **Intensity and Size of the Stimulus** In comparison with the weak stimulus, the strong stimulus attracts more attention of an individual. Our attention becomes easily directed towards a loud sound, a bright light or a strong smell. A large building will also be more readily attended to than a small one.
- **Contrast, Change and Variety** Change and variety strike attention more easily than sameness and absence of change *e.g.* we do not notice the ticking sound of a clock put on the wall until it stops ticking, that is any change in the attention to which you have been attracted immediately captures your attention. The factor, contact or change is highly responsible for capturing attention of the organism and contributes more than the intensity, size or nature of the stimulus.
- **Repetition of Stimulus** Repetition is a factor of great importance in securing attention. Because one may ignore a stimulus at first instance, but if it is repeated for several times it captures our attention *e.g.* a misspelled word is more likely to be noticed if it occurs twice in the same paragraph than 'if it occurs only once.' While giving lecture the important aspects of the speech are often repeated so that the attention of the audience can be easily directed to the valuable points.
- **Movement of the Stimulus** The moving stimulus catches our attention more quickly than a stimulus that does not move. We are more sensitive to objects that move in our field of vision, *e.g.* advertisers make use of this fact and try to catch the attention of people by playing digitally electronic messages or the pictures on the hoardings.

Internal or Subjective Factors

These factors influence the individual to respond to objective factors, to attend to those activities which fulfill his/her desires and motives and suit his interest and attitude. It is the mental state of the perceiver.

Some of the subjective factors are

- **Interest** Interest is said to be the mother of attention. We attend to objects in which we have interest. We would like to watch a movie or a serial in TV because we are interested in the subject around which the movie or serial revolves. In any get-together if any subject of our interest is discussed that attracts our attention easily and makes us participate in the discussion. In our day-to-day life we pay attention to the stimulus we are interested in.
- **Motives** Our basic needs and motives to a great extent determine our attention. Thirst, hunger, sex, curiosity, fear are some of the important motives that influence attention *e.g.* small children get attracted towards eatables.
- **Mind-Set** Person's readiness to respond determines his attention. If we are expecting a stimulus, occurrence of that stimulus along with many other stimuli may not come in the way of attending to that particular stimulus. At a time when students are expecting the examination time table by the end of the semester the time table put out on the notice board along with other notices would attract their attention easily.
- **Moods and Attitudes** An individual's attention is also influenced by the moods and attitudes. Whenever, we are disturbed or in angry mood, we tend to notice even the most trivial mistakes of others. Likewise our favourable and unfavourable attitudes also determine our attention.

Subjective and objective factors are interrelated. How much or in what way we attend to a stimulus depends on both subjective and objective factors.

History of the Study of Attention

Yearwise history of attention has been given below

1850s to 1900s

In James' time, the method more commonly used to study attention is introspection. However as early as in 1858 **Franciscus Donders** used mental chronometry to study attention and it was considered a major field of intellectual inquiry by such diverse authors as Sigmund Freud, Walter Benjamin and Max Nordau. One major debate in this period was whether it was possible to attend two things at once (split attention).

Walter Benjamin described this experience as 'reception in a state of distraction.' Some thinkers felt that they were unable to do so and other thinkers felt that they could. This disagreement could only be resolved through experimentation.

1900s to 1950s

From the 1900s to the 1950s, the field of attention was relatively inactive as the dominant psychological paradigm at the time was behaviourism. Behaviourism was rooted in positivism, an epistemology that rejects the study of and the making of assumptions about, processes that cannot be observed directly such as cognition, gravitational forces in Physics etc. Thus, cognitive processes do not govern attention and attention is best viewed as a form of behaviour that can be understood through purely objective experimental analysis.

1950s to Present

In the 1950s, research psychologists renewed their interest in attention when the dominant epistemology shifted from positivism to realism during what has come to be known as the 'Cognitive Revolution (Harre, 2002). The Cognitive Revolution admitted unobservable cognitive processes like attention as legitimate objects of scientific study.

In the 1960s, Anne Treisman began developing the highly influential feature integration theory (first published under this in a paper with G Gelade in 1980). According to this model, attention is responsible for binding different features into consciously experienced wholes. Although this model has received much criticism, it is still widely accepted or held up with modifications as in Jeremy Wolfe's visual search paradigm.

In the 1960s, Robert Wurtz at the National Institutes of Health, began recording electrical signals from the brains of Macaque monkeys who were trained to perform attentional tasks. These experiments showed for the first time that there was a direct neural correlate of a mental process (namely, enhanced firing in the superior colliculus).

In the 1990s, neuroscientists began using MRI to image the brain in attentive tasks. The results of these experiments have shown a broad agreement with the psychophysical and monkey literature.

Present Status

Attention remains a major area of investigation within psychology and neuroscience. Many of the major debates of James time remain unresolved. *For example* Although most scientists accept that attention can be split, strong proof has remained elusive. And there is still no widely accepted definition of attention more concrete than that given in the James quote above. This lack of progress has led many observers to speculate that attention refers to many separate processes without a common mechanism.

Areas of active investigation involve determining the source of the signals that generate attention, the effects of these signals on the tuning properties of sensory neurons and the relationship between attention and other cognitive processes like memory. Some speculative research has shown that even flies may be able to attend using their poppy seed sized brain in much the same way neurologically as humans do.

Models of Attention

Selective attention is a cognitive process in which a person attends to one or a few sensory inputs while ignoring the other ones. Selective attention can be comparable to the manner by which a bottleneck restricts the flow rate of a fluid.

The bottleneck doesn't allow the fluid to enter into the body of the bottle all at once; rather, it lets the fluid to enter in certain amounts depending on the flow rate, until all of it has entered the bottle's body. Selective attention is necessary for us to attend consciously to sensory stimuli in such a way that we will not experience sensory overload.

There are three models that are associated to selective attention. These are the models of attention by Broadbent, Treisman and Deutsch and Deutsch. They are also referred to as bottleneck models of attention because they explain how we cannot attend to all sensory input at one time in the conscious level.

Broadbent Filter Model

In 1958, **Donald Broadbent** proposed the Filter Model of Attention, which states that there is a sensory buffer where all sensory stimuli enter at any given time. One of the sensory inputs is chosen based on the physical attributes of the stimuli.

This input is then allowed to pass through a filter. Broadbent believed that the filter is necessary for the prevention of overloading the information processing system. Those sensory inputs that are not selected are temporarily kept in the sensory buffer until they undergo processing. However, if they are not processed, these sensory inputs that remain in the sensory buffer may decay or fade away.

Broadbent made an experiment using a dichotic listening task, in which he sent one message to the right ear of a person and a different message to the other ear. The research gave rise to Broadbent's conclusion that people would repeat the messages as they are sent ear-by-ear, rather than in the order by which they were heard.

Treisman's Attenuation Theory

Anne Treisman proposed her selective attention theory in 1964. Her theory is based on the earlier model by Broadbent. Treisman also believed that this human filter selects sensory inputs on the basis of physical characteristics. However, she argued that the unattended sensory inputs (the ones that were not chosen by the filter and remain in the sensory buffer) are attenuated by the filter rather than eliminated.

Attenuation is a process in which the unselected sensory inputs are processed in decreased intensity. For instance, if you selectively attend to a ringing phone in a room where there's TV, a crying baby and people talking, the later three sound sources are attenuated or decreased in volume. However, when the baby's cry goes louder, you may turn your attention to the baby because the sound input is still there, not lost.

Selective Filter Model

Klapper states that the media can only be effective or have an impact on an audience once it has undertaken 3 stages. This theory ensures that the audience has an active role in how they choose to apprehend or understand the message given and what, if any, effect it has on them.

The three stages that an audience must respond to are

(i) **Selective Exposure** The audience has a choice to engage with the media and what types of media they chose to consume. Media messages can have no effect on us if no one sees or hear them. However, the audience choices depends upon their interests, education, work commitments and so on.

(ii) **Selective Perception** The audience can then choose whether they wish to accept the message being conveyed. The audience may not accept the message; some people may take notice of some media content but decide to reject or ignore others.

(iii) **Retention** The audience has to then remember the message in order for it to have an effect on them. The messages have to stick in the mind of those who have accessed the media content. However research indicates that most people have a tendency to remember only the things they broadly agree with or conversely highly disagree with.

Deutsch and Deutsch Model

In 1963, Deutsch and Deutsch proposed a Late Selection Model which explained that all information, both attended and unattended, undergo analysis for meaning. After such analysis, selection of a sensory input takes place. One factor that has a major effect on selecting the input is the relevance of the information during the time of processing.

Clinical Model of Attention

Many times clinical models differ from investigation models. One of the most used models for the evaluation of attention in patients with very different neurologic pathologies is the model of Sohlberg and Mateer. This hierarchic model is based in the recovering of attention processes of brain damage patients after coma. Different kinds of activities are described in the model; connecting with the activities which patients could do as their recovering process advanced.

These activities include the following

- **Focused Attention** This is the ability to respond discretely to specific visual, auditory or tactile stimuli.
- **Sustained Attention** This refers to the ability to maintain a consistent behavioural response during continuous and repetitive activity.
- **Selective Attention** This level of attention refers to the capacity to maintain a behavioural or cognitive set in the face of distracting or competing stimuli. Therefore, it incorporates the notion of 'freedom from distractibility.'
- **Alternating Attention** It refers to the capacity for mental flexibility that allows individuals to shift their focus of attention and move between tasks having different cognitive requirements.
- **Divided Attention** This is the highest level of attention and it refers to the ability to respond simultaneously to multiple tasks or multiple task demands.

This model has shown to be very useful to evaluate attention in very different pathologies, correlates strongly with daily difficulties and it is specially helpful to design stimulation programs such as the APT (Attention Process Training); a rehabilitation program for neurologic patients.

Perception

The study of perception is the attempt to understand those aspects of observation of the world of things and people that depend on the nature of observer.

Such understanding is obviously important to the physiologist and it was once thought, to be important to the philosopher concerned with the question of how we can be sure about the truth of our ideas. Despite these different interests, perceptual study remains predominantly psychological.

Therefore, perception is a complex mental cognitive process through which we have immediate and meaningful knowledge of the present stimulus in the environment.

It is the process where by sensory cues and relevant past experiences are organised to give more structured and meaningful picture under possible circumstances. Hence,

Perception = Sensation + Meaning

Perception depends upon

- Stimulus
- Organismic factors such as mental set
- The receptor and the neural function

Meaning and Definitions of Perception

Perception is the process through which the information from outside environment is selected, received, organised and interpreted to make it meaningful to you. This input of meaningful information results in decisions and actions. Perception governs meaning, as it influences how we and others see the world. Perception is tempered by point of view and experience because of which no two people see things the same way if left to their own devices because of this. One person might see a fancy sports car and another might see an accident waiting to happen. One person might see a cell phone as a necessary communication device and another might see the same device as a time waster.

And while one person might see a random set of paint brush strokes, another might see a masterpiece. Our perception is governed by the information we have access to and the way we interpret it. That's why the area of perceptual organisation is so important.

According to **S P Robbins**, "Perception may be defined as a process by which individuals organise and interpret their sensory impressions in order to give meaning to their environment."

According to **Joseph Reitz**, "Perception includes all those processes by which an individual receives information about his environment seeing, hearing, feeling, tasting and smelling. The study of these perpetual processes shows that their functioning is affected by three classes of variables-the objects or events being perceived, the environment in which perception occurs and the individual doing the perceiving."

In simple words we can say that perception is the act of seeing what is there to be seen. But what is seen is influenced by the perceiver, the object and its environment. The meaning of perception emphasises all these three points.

Nature of Perception

Perception refers to the interpretation of sensory data. In other words, sensation involves detecting the presence of a stimulus, whereas, perception involves understanding what the stimulus means.

For example When we see something, the visual stimulus is the light energy reflected from the external world and the eye becomes the sensor. This visual image of the external thing becomes perception, when it is interpreted in the visual cortex of the brain. Thus, visual perception refers to interpreting the image of the external world projected on the retina of the eye and constructing a model of the three dimensional world. From the above explanation it becomes clear that perception is something more than sensation. It correlates, integrates and comprehends diverse sensations and information from many organs of the body by means of which a person identifies things and objects, referred to by the sensations.

Perception is determined by both physiological and psychological characteristics of the human being, whereas, sensation is conceived with only the physiological features. Thus, perception is not just what one sees with the eyes it is a much more complex process by which an individual selectively absorbs or assimilates the stimuli in the environment, cognitively organises the perceived information in a specific fashion and then interprets the information to make an assessment about what is going on in one's environment.

Perception is a subjective process, therefore, different people may perceive the same environment differently based on what particular aspects of the situation they choose to selectively absorb, how they organise this information and the manner in which they interpret it to obtain a grasp of the situation.

To understand what perception does, one must understand the difference between the proximal (approximate = close) stimulus and distal (distant) stimulus or object.

- Distal stimuli are objects and events out of the world about the individual.
- Proximal stimuli are the patterns of stimuli from these objects and events that actually reach senses (are, ears etc.)

Most of the time perception reflects the properties of the distal objects and events very accurately, much more accurately, than one might expect from apparently limited, varying, unstable pattern of mind's proximal stimulations. The problem of perception is to understand how the mind/brain extracts accurate stable perceptions of objects and events, from such apparently limited, inadequate information.

Importance of Perception

The importance of perception is highlighted by following

- Perception is very important in understanding the human behaviour, because every person perceives the world and approaches the life problems differently, whatever we see or feel is not necessarily the same as it really is. It is because what we hear is not what is really said, but what we perceive as being said. When we buy something, it is not because it is the best, but because we take it to be the best. Thus, it is because of perception, we can find out why one individual finds a job satisfying while another one may not be satisfied with it.
- If people behave on the basis of their perception, we can predict their behaviour in the changed circumstances by understanding their present perception of the environment. One person may be viewing the facts in one way which may be different from the facts as seen by another viewer.
- With the help of perception, the needs of various people can be determined, because people's perception is influenced by their needs. Like the mirrors at an amusement park, they distort the world in relation to their tensions.
- Perception is very important for the manager who wants to avoid making errors when dealing with people and events in the work setting. This problem is made more complicated by the fact that different people perceive the same situation differently. In order to deal with the subordinates effectively, the managers must understand their perceptions properly.

Thus, for understanding the human behaviour, it is very important to understand their perception *i.e.* how they perceive the different situations. People's behaviour is based on their perceptions of what reality is, not on reality itself. The world as it is perceived is the world that is important for understanding the human behaviour.

Characteristics of Perception

It has long been recognised by behavioural scientists that the interests, values and beliefs that employees entertain influence their perceptions of the reality of their work places and their behaviour. An individual's perception of his or her capabilities may result in overly ambitious goals and frequent failure or under attainment.

Usually, extreme perceptual variations result from the following characteristics

(i) **Selectivity** Perception is selective. No one is capable of receiving all the stimuli with regard to a particular circumstance. As a result, people select those things that are most interesting and relevant to them personally and factors that are most consistent with their experience.

(ii) **Closure** Although, perception is selective, human beings fill in gaps and behave as if they have complete knowledge of a situation, person or event. The result is often a failure to recognise the complexity of the entire situation and the inaccurate evaluation of perceptual phenomena through processes such as.

- **Stereotyping** Stereotyping is an over-generalised belief about a particular category of people. *For example* A college student may be considered to be like all other college students because he or she shares the one characterstic of attending a college even if in all other ways, the individual may be clearly different from a fellow students.
- **Hallo effect** Here, a person is evaluated on the basis of a single trait. *For example* The stars of the company tennis team may be given higher performance evaluations on the job than are justified by actual work behaviour.

(iii) **Context** Perception occurs within a setting or an environment known as a *context*. This context is made up of physical factors, such as the amount of lighting, noise and so on. It also relates to emotional and social environments.

The perceptual context is important because through past experience, we have a point of reference. This context includes a number of elements within the environment, such as attitudes, emotions and physical properties. When distortions occur, perceptual accuracy is reduced.

Approaches to the Study of Perception

The psychologists have evolved different approaches to study perception. The most common approaches to study perception are Gestalt approach and Physiological approach.

Gestalt Approach

Gestalt approach to study perception was given by German scientists Max Wertheimer, Wolfgang Kohler and Kurt Koffka. This approach is based on understanding and perceiving the whole sum of an object rather than its components. It evolved against the atomistic concept of psychology which was built on the belief that scientific understanding is result of lack of concern about basic human details.

Gestalt approach is based on perceiving reality in its simplest form. It is based on human nature being inclined to understand objects as an entire structure rather than sum of its parts. *The principles governing this approach are*

- **Principle of Totality** The conscious experience must be considered globally by taking into account all physical and mental aspects of individual simultaneously. This is because nature of mind demands that each component be considered as part of system of dynamic relationships.
- **Principle of Psycho physical Isomorphism** A correlation exists between conscious experience and cerebral activity.
- **Phenomenon Experimental Analysis** In relation to the totality principle any psychological research should take phenomena as starting point and not be solely focused on sensory qualities.
- **Biotic Experiment** It established a need to conduct real experiments that sharply contrasted with and opposed classical laboratory experiments.

The Physiological Approach

Physiological approach is based on study of Neural Mechanism of perception and behaviour. Modern research is designed to focus on determining the relationship between the stimulus and electrical signals called *nerve impulses* and on determining the relationship between these nerve impules and perception. This approach to study perception is empirical and practical.

Johannes Muller in 1842, proposed the doctrine of specific nerve energy, which states that our perception depends on 'nerve energy' reaching the brain and that the specific quality, we experience, depends on which nerves are stimulated.

The physiological approach to study perception involves understanding the process of perception. Perception begins with activation of receptors in eye, ear, skin, nose, etc. This activation results in transmission of electrical signals to brain, where perception occurs.

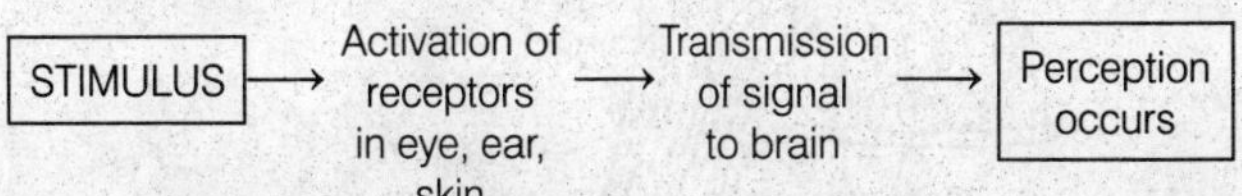

Physiological Approach to Study Perception

Overall Structure of the Visual System

As light enter and the eye, it passes through the cornea (the transparent front of the eye), then through a hole called the *pupil* and then through the lens. The cornea and the lens focus light onto the retina, a thin network of neurons, which consists of the rod and cone receptors and four other types of neurons.

The small depression in the retina, which is called the *fovea*, contains only cone receptors. The rest of the retina, which is called the *peripheral retina*, contains both rod and cone receptor. The receptors face away from the light is, so that they can be in contact with a layer of cells called the *pigment epithelium* which contains nutrients and chemicals called *enzymes* that are vital to the receptors functioning in various ways. The rods and cones generate electrical signals in response to light. These signals are then transmitted through the other four kinds of neurons the bipolar cells, horizontal cell, amacrine cells and ganglion cells.

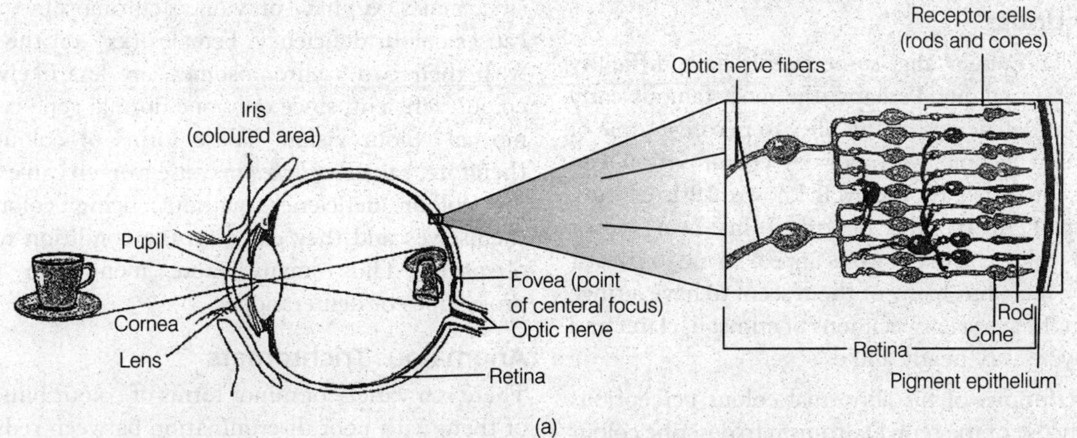

Cross sections of the human eye and retina

Electrical signals in the ganglion cells leave the back of the eye by way of the optic nerve. Optic nerve contain optic nerve fibres that transmit electrical energy out of retina.

Since, there are no receptors in the place where the optic nerve leaves the eye this area is called the *blind spot*.

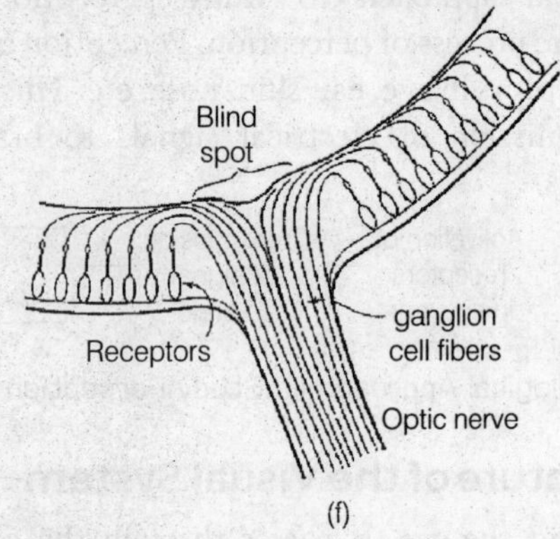

(f)

There are no receptors at the place where the optic nerve leaves the eye. This enables the receptor's ganglion cell fibers to flow into the optic nerve. The absence of receptors in this area creates the blind spot.

Most of the impulses in the optic nerve reach a nucleus in the thalamus called the *Lateral Geniculate Nucleus* (LGN) and from there travel to the visual receiving area in the occipital lobe of the brain (also called the *visual cortex* or *striate cortex*). The journey of these nerve impulses does not, however end in the occipital lobe. Signals from the visual receiving area travel to areas in the extrastriate cortex in two different pathways, the ventral pathway to the temporal lobe and the dorsal pathway to the parietal lobe. One of the problem characterized as the inability to clearly distinguish different colors of the spectrum is discussed below:

Colour Blindness

It has long been known' that some people have difficulty perceiving certain colour. Perhaps, the most famous early report of colour deficiency, an inability to perceive some of the colours that people with normal colour vision can perceive, was provided by the well known 19th century chemist **John Dalton**, who described his own colour perceptions as follows "All crimsons appear to me to consist chiefly of dark blue, but many of them seem to have a tinge of dark brown. I have seen specimens of crimson, claret and mud, which were very nearly a like".

Dalton's descriptions of his abnormal colour perceptions led to the early use of the term Daltonism to describe colour deficiency. Subjects which are colour deficient perceive either different numbers from a person with trichromatic vision or no numbers at all. Another way to determine the presence of colour deficiency is by using the colour matching procedure to determine the minium number of wavelengths needed to match any other wavelength in the spectrum. *This procedure has revealed the following three types of colour blindness*

(i) A monochromat can match any wavelength in the spectrum by adjusting the intensity of any other wavelength. Thus, a monochromat needs only one wavelength to match any colour in the spectrum.

(ii) A dichromat needs only two wavelengths to match all other wavelengths in the spectrum.

(iii) An anomalous trichromat needs their wavelengths to match any wavelength just as a normal trichromat does. However, the anomalous trichromat mixes these wavelengths in different properties from a trichromat and an anomalous trichromat is not as good at discriminating between wavelengths that are closed together.

Colour blindness is catagories into the following

Monochromatism

Monochromatism is a rare form of colour blindness that is usually herditary and occurs in only about 10 people out of 1 million. Monochromats usually have no functioning cones; therefore their vision has the characteristics of rod vision in both dim and bright lights. Monochromats see everything in shades of lightness and can therefore be called *colour blind*.

Dichromatism

Dichromats experience some colours, though a lesser range than trichromats. There are three major forms of dichromatism; protanopia, deuteranopia and tritanopia. The two most common kinds, protanopia and deuteranopia are inherited through a gene located on the x chromosome, since males (xy) have only one x chromosome, a defect in it causes colour deficiency. Females (xx), on the other hand, with their two x chromosomes, are less likely to become colour deficient, since only one normal gene is required for normal colour vision. These forms of colour vision are therefore, called *sex linked* because women can carry the gene for colour deficiency without being colour deficient themselves and they can pass the condition to their male offspring. Thus, many more men than women are protanopes or deuteranopes.

Anomalous Trichromats

There is a variety of minor forms of colour blindness, many of them with poor discrimination between reds and greens but with no absolute loss of red or green sensitivity. Such minor defects are fairly common throughout the population and quite wide spread differences exist in matching *e.g.* spectral yellow by a mixture of red and green, so called Rayleigh match.

Perceptual Organisation

Perceptual organisation is a process by which one structure the input from his sensory receptors. Perceptual organisation is the process of grouping visual elements together (organisation) so that one can more readily determine the meaning of the visual as a whole (perception).

Perceptual organisation allows one to make rapid sense of the things that he sees. But more than that, it can be used to lead the viewer to the conclusion that suits our purpose. The concept of perceptual organisation has become enriched by the contributions of Gestalt psychology.

Gestalt Psychology

Gestalt psychology was founded by German thinkers Max Wertheimer, Wolfgang Kohler and Kurt Koffka and focused on how people interpret the world. The Gestalt perspective formed partially as a response to the structuralism of Wilhelm Wundt, who focused on breaking down mental events and experiences to the smallest elements.

Max Wertheimer noted that rapid sequences of perceptual events, such as rows of flashing lights, create the illusion of motion even when there is none. This is known as the *phi phenomenon.* Motion pictures are based on this principle, with a series of still images appearing in rapid succession to form a seamless visual experience.

According to **Gestalt psychology**, "the whole is different from the sum of its parts. Based upon this belief, Gestalt psychologists developed a set of principles to explain perceptual organisation or how smaller objects are grouped to form larger ones."

These principles are often referred to as the 'laws of perceptual organisation.' However, it is important to note that while Gestalt psychologists call these phenomena 'laws', a more accurate term would be 'principles of perceptual organisation'.

Much of the evidence supporting the idea that the whole is different from the sum of its parts comes from pictures such as the one in the figure, which shows that our perception of one part of a stimulus depends on the presence of other parts of the stimulus.

We interpret the horse in the figure (a) as rearing back, but we interpret the identical horse in figure (b) as moving forward. The presence of the rider in one case and of the lead horse in the other changes our interpretation of the horse's movement.

(a) A rearing horse, (b) One horse following another

Figure and Ground

Gestalt psychologists indicate that cerebral processes are always oriented towards perception of a good figure or pragnanz. Thus, everything is perceived in an organised form and the most primitive organisation takes place in the form of figure ground segregation. When one looks at a surface, certain aspects of surface clearly stand out as separate entities whereas others do not. The part which has a definite shape and a location in space is known as *figure* and the part which has no shape, seems to continue behind the figure and has no definite location is known as *ground*.

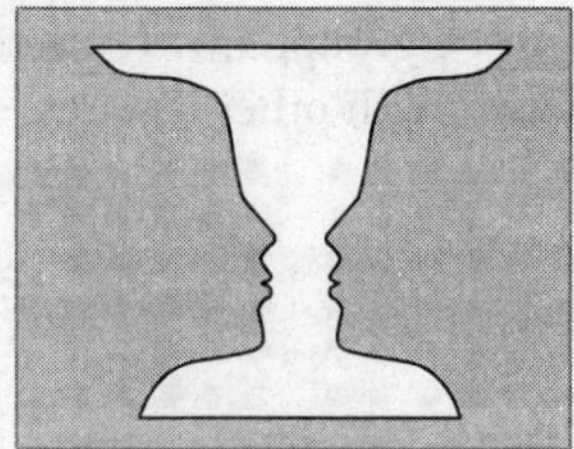
A version of Rubin's reversible face-vase figure

For example In the face-vase figure, the white part of figure looks like a flower pot and black part looks like two faces.

Some of the properties of the figure and ground are that

- The figure is more 'thinkable' and more memorable than ground.
- The figure is seen as being in front of the ground.
- The ground is seen as unformed material and seems to extend behind the figure.
- The contour separating the figure from the ground appears to belong to the figure.

The Law of Perceptual Organisation

Gestalt psychologists have given several laws to explain how and why different stimuli in visual field are organised into meaningful whole objects. These laws are known as the *laws of perceptual organisation.*

These laws are as follows

Law of Good Figure

Pragnanz, roughly translated from the German, means 'good figure.' The Law of Pragnanz; the central law of Gestalt psychology (also called *the law of good figure* or *the law of simplicity*) states; every stimulus pattern is seen in such a way that the resulting structure is as simple as possible.

The familiar olympic symbol in this figure (a) is an example of the law of simplicity at work. We see this display as five circles and not as other, more complicated, shapes such as the ones in figure (b).

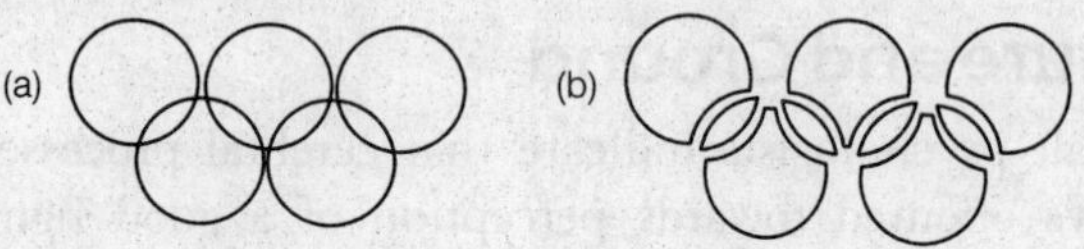

Law of Similarity

Similar things appear to be grouped together. Most people perceive figure (a) as either horizontal rows of circles, vertical columns of circles or both. But when we change some of the circles to squares, as in the figure (b), most people perceive vertical columns of squares and circles.

This perception illustrates the law of similarity. This law causes the circles to be grouped with other circles and the squares to be grouped with other squares.

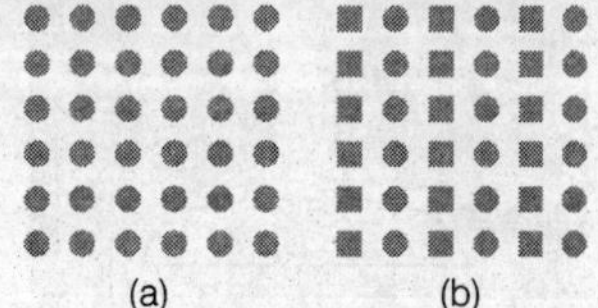

Grouping also occurs for auditory stimuli, *e.g.* notes that have similar pitches and that follow each other closing in time can become perceptually grouped to form a melody.

Law of Connectedness

Things that are physically connected are perceived as a unit. In given figure, we perceive a series of dumbells rather than pairs of dots, even though the dots separated by the spaces are close together than the ones connected by the lines.

Grouping by Connectedness

This is the law of connectedness.

Law of Continuity

This law states that we tend to perceive objects as belonging together if they appear to form a continuous pattern. *For example* In given figure one is more likely to identify two lines a-b and c-d crossing than to identify four lines meeting at center p.

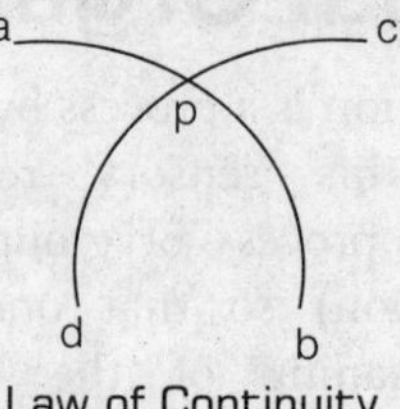

Law of Continuity

Law of Proximity or Nearness

Things that are near to each other appear to be grouped together. Our perception of figure (a) as horizontal rows of circles illustrates the law of proximity or nearness. And although every other circle is changed to a square in figure (b), we still perceive horizontal rows as in this case the law of proximity overpowers the law of similarity.

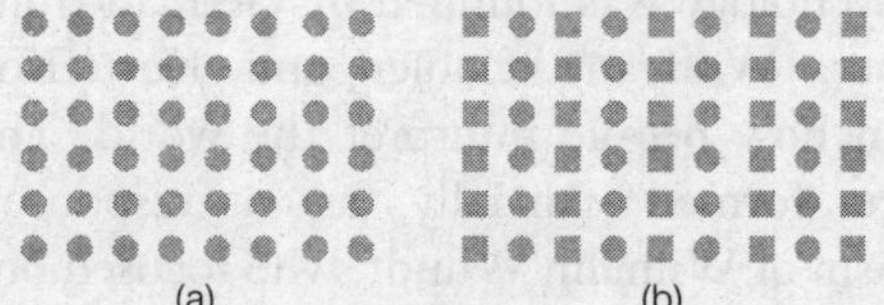

Two examples of the law of nearness
(a) Perceived as horizontal rows of circles.
(b) Still perceived as horizontal rows, even though half of the circles have been changed to squares.

Law of Common Fate

The law of common fate states that things that are moving in the same direction appear to be grouped together. Although, dance choreographers may not be familiar with the Gestalt laws, they are well aware that one way to create perceptual grouping is to choreograph groups of dancers moving together.

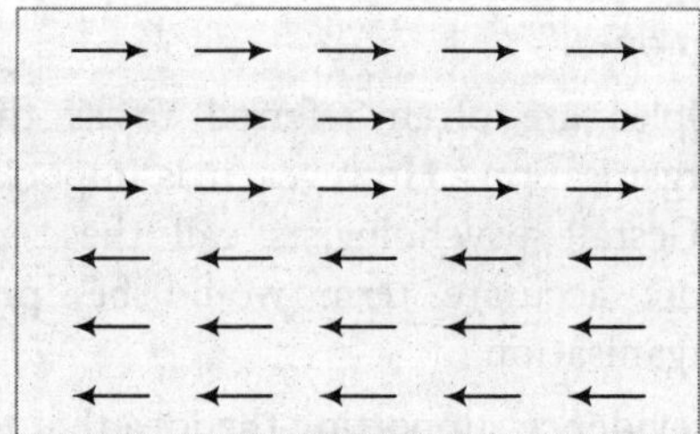

The Law of Common Fate

Law of Closure

It states that individuals perceive a complete object even though parts of it may be missing. *For example* The given figures a and b are perceived as circle and square though gaps are present in the shapes.

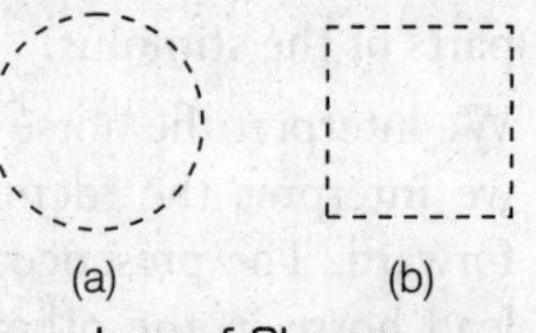

Law of Closure

Perceptual Constancy

The pattern of light reaching the visual system from an object undergoes continual changes as the spatial orientation of the object relative to the viewer changes. This can occur both by spatial displacement of the object and by movements of the observer. Accompanying the spatial changes are changes in the distribution of light striking the viewer's retinae; these are seen as variation in the projected size, shape and intensity. However, inspite of these changes in stimulation, the stable and enduring qualities of the object are perceived.

The book, before you, does not look rectangular when viewed from one angle and trapezoidal when viewed from another angle of observation. Normally the book is perceived as rectangular from every angle of observation. Neither does a person's size appear to contract or expand very much as the person moves away or advances.

Yet the law of spatial geometry dictates certain changes in the retinal image corresponding to the relative displacement of the physical stimulus. Clearly, perception in this instance is based on more than the size and shape of the retinal image. This tendency to perceive physical objective as stable or unchanging in the presence of variation in physical stimulation is termed as perceptual constancy.

The types of perceptual constancies that one experiences in his/ her visual domain are as follows

Brightness Constancy

Brightness refers to the surface quality, the degree of glow of an object or surface, ranging from black to white. The degree of whiteness, greyness or blackness of an object remain constant even though amount of physical energy reflected from them changes considerably. This tendency of an object to maintain relatively constant or stable brightness inspite of changes in the amount of illumination striking it is known as *brightness constancy*. By tradition the term brightness constancy has been applied as general label for lightness and whiteness constancy and for neutral or aeromatic colour constancy.

Thus *e.g.* we perceive a patch of snow in dark shadow as white and a chunk of coal in sunlight as black, yet the physical intensity of the light reflected from the surface of the coal may be greater than that from the snow. In searching for an explanation of this phenomenon, it is necessary to consider the surface property called *albedo or reflectance*.

The albedo is the proportion of the incident light that is reflected from an object or surface. One of the important variables for lightness constancy when viewing under ordinary conditions is the ratio of the intensity of light reflected from objects relative to the intensity of light reflected from the background (with the proviso that light *i.e.* illuminating an object also falls on regions surrounding it). Proportion of incident light that is reflected by stimuli remains constant. The result is that within limits the lightness of the objects doesn't change when there are changes in overall level of illumination.

The Coplanar Ratio Hypothesis

Brightness determined by the relationship of luminescence and not by absolute intensity levels. Gilchrist has demonstrated that certain relational contrast effects occur between surface only if they appear coplanar. Luminance ratios will not determine surface brightness if the surface examined is separated in depth. If one surface appears to be located farther or nearer to the viewer than other, the contrast effect is reduced or absent.

The significance of this finding is that brightness constancy cannot be understood solely on the basic of retinal processes or luminance discontinuities; instead the perception of surface brightness depends on luminance ratios of surfaces perceived to lie next to one another in the same plane.

Shape Constancy

An addition, an object may appear to possess the same shape even when the angle, from which it is viewed, changes radically. This stability in shape of familiar objects despite changes in pattern changes in pattern of retinal image resulting from differences in their orientation is known as *shape constancy*.

A typical window frame or a door appears to be more or less rectangular no matter at what angle it is viewed. Yet geometrically it casts a rectangular image only when it is viewed from a certain position directly in front of the viewer.

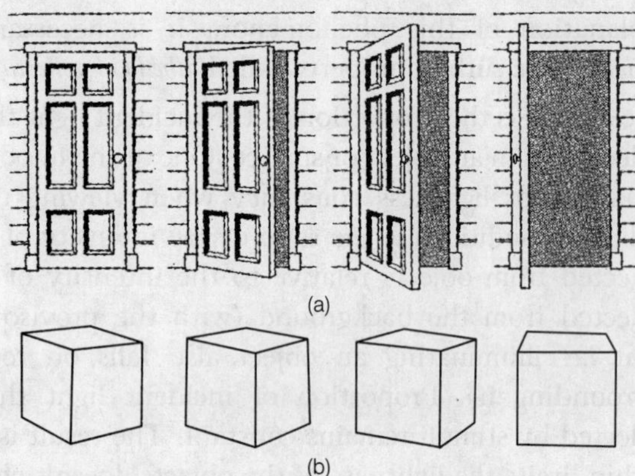

Shape Constancy (a) Various projected images from an opening door are quite different, yet a rectangular door is perceived. (b) Similarly, various trapezoidal projections yield the perception of the faces of a cube.

Experimentally, shape constancy is typically assessed when a subject estimates the shape of objects such as a circular plate or disk tilted or slanted at an angle. It is found that the estimated shape in the following figure, obtained by having subjects draw the shape of a tilted disk or match it against a series of ellipses, is more circular than the elliptical shape projected on the observer's retina (Thouless).

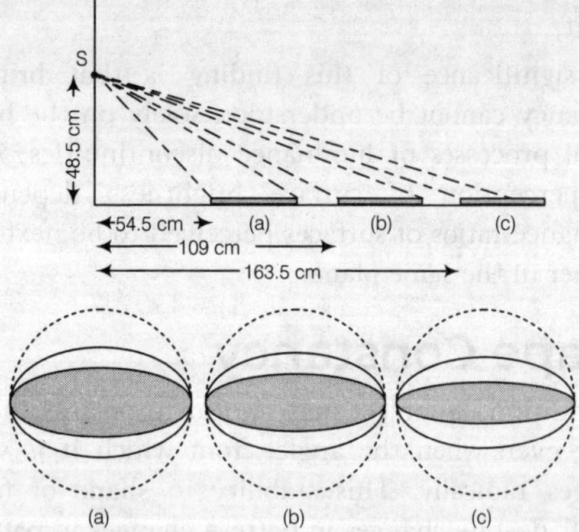

Shape constancy is shown in the reproduction of the tilted disks, (a), (b) and (c), whose projected shapes are indicated by the black figures. The broken line shows the physical shape and the continuous line gives the reproduced shape. The reproduced shape indicates that the perceived shape is more

Size Constancy

The principle of size constancy states that perceived size of an object remains same when distance is varied, even though size of image it casts on retina changes greatly.

The diagram in the figure illustrates some relevant geometrical relations in image formation, such as the size of the retinal image varies inversely with the distance from which an object is viewed. The size of an object's image on the retina may undergo considerable changes with variations in the objects distance from the viewer, but the size changes go relatively unnoticed in conditions of normal viewing.

An important fact about the perceived size of an object in normal viewing conditions is that, it does not depend solely on the size of the image it casts on the retina. In short, perceived size does not regularly follow retinal size. Indeed, over a considerable range of distances, perceived size is some what independent of retinal size. The failure of perceived size to vary with retinal size is owing to the operation of size constancy.

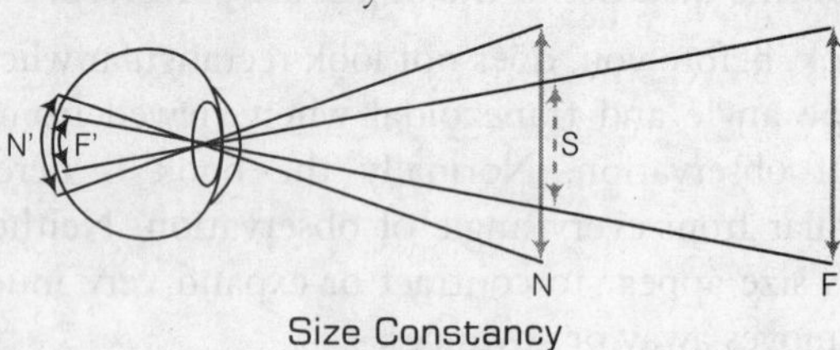

Size Constancy

A schematic diagram showing the relative size of two retinal images, 'N' and 'F', from the same sized objects, N and F, but located at different distances. Object F is twice as far from the eye as object N; hence, its image on the retina is half as large.

This is in accordance with the fact that the size of the retinal image is inversely proportional to the distance of the object from the eye. Notice that the smaller retinal image case by object F could also be produced by the smaller object, S, (smaller by one-half) located at the position of object N.

Holway and Boring Experiment

Holway and Boring conducted psychophysical experiment to examine two hypothesis of size perception.

(i) Law of size constancy indicates that the perception of the size of an object is relatively constant regardless of its variable distance to the observer.
(ii) Law of visual angle indicates that the size of object should be determined by the size, it projects on the retina.

The psychophysical experiments examined the validity of these two hypothesis and concluded that in a perfectly isolated environment, the perceived size of the object follows the law of visual angle.

However, with the presence of depth cues, (such as vanishing lines, shading, diminishing context pattern), the size constancy takes place and allows the observer to correctly perceive the intrinsic size of the object.

The result confirms size-distance invariance hypothesis and provides a practical way to measure the effect of scene context on depth perception.

Size Constancy with Infants

(Peek-a-boo's Experiment)

Most of the recent experiments have indicated that size constancy is possible with human infant between six and sixteen weeks of age (Bower). The method of testing for constancy utilised operant conditioning techniques of 'Peeka-boo' where the experimenter briefly popped her head out in front of the infant, smiled and nodded, saying 'Peeka-boo' and then quickly disappeared from the infant's view. It was found that the infant responded more on the basis of the stimuli's physical size and distance, than on their retinal size or apparent distance. Further research that controlled for various monocular and binocular cues indicated that motion parallex and binocular disparity (Bower, Broughton) provided the distance information necessary for size constancy.

Illusion

According to dictionary, illusion is defined as "A perception of a thing which misrepresents it or gives it qualities not present in reality." But this is a Layman definition of illusion, which does not reflect the insight of scientist, who study perceptual processes.

Illusion are wrong or incorrect perception. The instances in which perception yields false interpretations of physical reality is known as *illusion*. These are not perception in true sense because in perception the stimulation is correctly interpreted, whereas in illusions the stimulation is wrongly interpreted.

Illusion therefore demonstrates that what we experience depends upon processes, which go for beyond the sensory input. Illusions don't correspond to the objective situation as shown by physical measurement. There are illusions, which may concern most of the feature of the physical world, such as distance motion shape size and direction etc.

Kinds of Illusion

Following are kinds of illusion

Poggendorf Illusion

One of the earliest illusions involving angles was the Poggendorf illusion, reported in 1860. This was formed by a vertical rectangle or column with a diagonal line lying behind it. The two visible portion of the line do not seem to be segments of the same line.

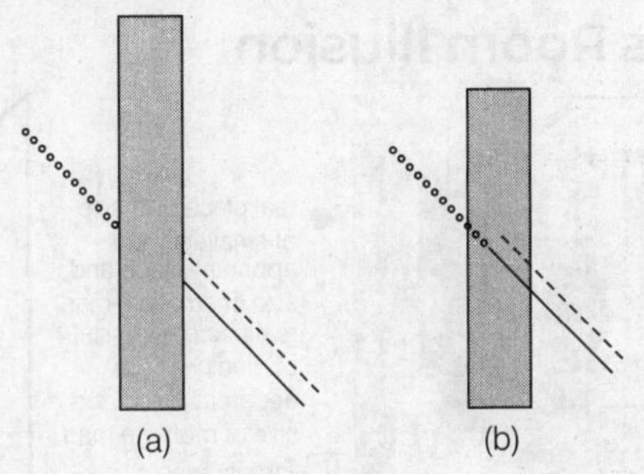

Poggendorf Illusion

A straight dot line and continuous line is obscured by a grey rectangle. In figure (a) the dashed line rather than continuous line, appears to be continuation of dotted line which is clearly shown not to be the case in figure (b). Instead there is an apparent position shift of lower portion of line.

Zollner Illusion

The long diagonal lines are metrically parallel but appear to be non-parallel. The short cross-hatch lines appear to be neither horizontal nor vertical lines in planes that represent the treads and risers of a stairway. The whole figure seems to represent a three-dimensional situation. Consequently, the long diagonal lines do not seem to be parallel.

In an over all three dimensional situation, they do not represent parallel elements. Some pairs have coverage to a for vanishing point and some to a near vanishing point.

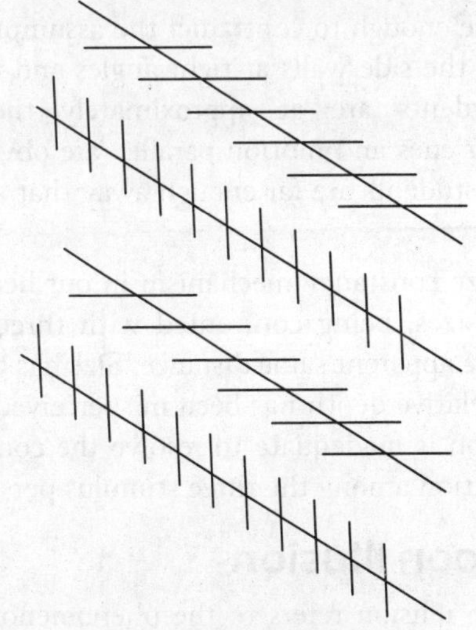

The Zollner Illusion

Ames Room Illusion

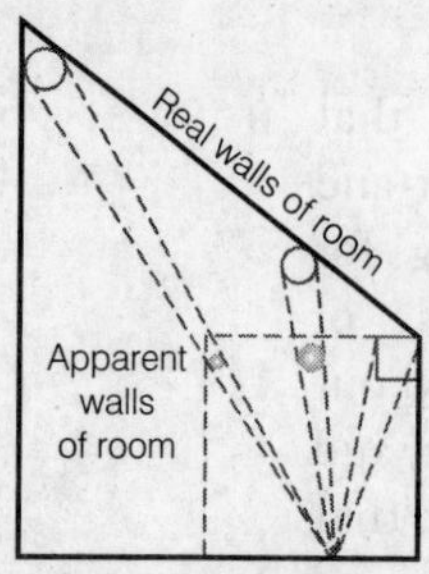

Ames Trapezoidal Room Illusion

The figure shown above illustrates the nature of the illusion first developed by Adelbert Ames in the 1940s, when viewed monocularly from a peephole located as in shown figure, the room appears rectangular, the floor appears level and the three students appear to be of grossly different sizes. The explanation usually given is consistent with size-distance theory. As a matter of fact, the 'smallest' man is actually about twice as far away as the 'largest' man. Hence, the retinal image of the 'smallest' man is only about half as large as that of the 'largest'. It is as if relative retinal size were providing the basic of our size percept. However, relative retinal size works as a cue to objective size. While other depth cues indicate that the object is the same distance away. Indeed, this seems to be the case here.

A real rectangular room and any number of trapezoidal ones could give this same retinal pattern. Given our extensive experience with an environment full of right angles and rectangular rooms our visual brains apparently assume that the room is rectangular. The available monocular cues to depth are not precise enough to contradict the assumption that the back wall joins the side walls at right angles and that therefore the three students are at approximately the same distance (Binocular cues and motion parallex are obviously absent and the three students are far enough away that accommodation is not effective).

So, the size constancy mechanism in our heads gives us three different sizes, being confronted with three different retinal sizes at the apparent same distance. Size has been misperceived because relative depth has been misperceived. Available depth information is inadequate to resolve the conflict as to appear depth relation among the three stimulus persons.

The Moon Illusion

The Moon illusion refers to the phenomenon that the Moon appears larger when it is viewed at the horizon than at the Zenith, although the projected images in both cases are identical when the Moon is on the horizon. It appears much larger than when it is higher in the sky. This enlargement of the horizon Moon compared to the elevated Moon as in figure is called the *Moon illusion*.

An artist's conception of the Moon illusion showing the Moon on the horizon and high in the sky

A number of attempts have been made to explain this phenomenon.

Some of the ekperiments were conducted that leads to emergence of few hypothesis that are discussed below:

- **Angle of Regard Hypothesis** Boring proposed that the apparent size of the Moon is affected by the angles of the eyes relative to the head. That is the Moon illusion is produced by changes in the position of the eyes in the head accompanying changes in the angle of elevation of the Moon.
- **Apparent Distance Hypothesis** An explanation of the Moon illusion based on perceptual factors can be traced to Ptolemy, the second century astronomer and geometrician. He proposed that an object seen through filled space such as the Moon viewed across terrain at the horizon is perceived as being farther away than an object located physically at the same distance or seen through empty space as in the case of the Moon at its zenith. In brief, the projected images of the Moon in both cases are of identical size, but the horizon Moon appears farther away.

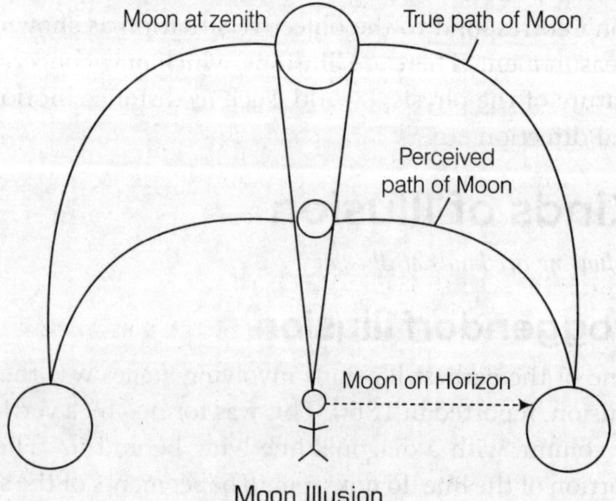

Moon Illusion

- **Relative Size Hypothesis** More recently, Restle has offered an alternative explanation of the Moon illusion that does not depend on apparent distance. Rather, it concerns the visual field in a manner similar to the visual field explanation of the horizontals vertical illusion. The basic assumption of this hypothesis is that the perceived size of an object depends not only on its retinal size, but also on the size of its immediate visual surround.

Ponzo Illusion

The figure depicts an illusion first presented by Ponzo in 1912. The two horizontal lines in each picture are actually of the same length. But they are not perceived as of the same length. Though, the upper horizontal line has the same objective length as the lower one, it appears longer. An explanation consistent with size distance theory is that the upper line is seen as longer because the size constancy mechanism has conclude that it is farther away. The converging lines, after all do provide a linear perspective cue to depth.

Ponzo Illusion

Depth might also be suggested by the greater height in plane of the upper line as well. Hence, the size constancy mechanism concludes that out of the two objects which project same retinal image, the more distant object is larger.

Vertical-Horizontal Illusion

This illusion first introduced by Oppel is illustrated in the figure given below.

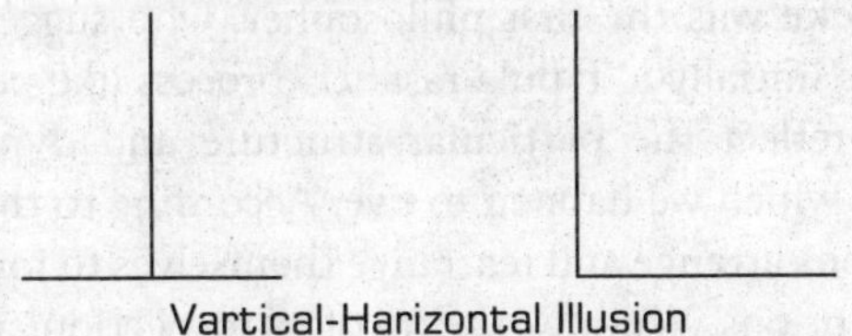

Vertical-Harizontal Illusion

The vertical line in the above figure looks a bit longer than the horizontal line even though they are objectively of the same length. A misapplied constancy explanation of the size illusion can be offered too. There are at least two cues to depth in this instance.

For one perspective might suggest that the vertical line represents a relatively longer horizontal line extending away from the observer. Interposition might also act as a depth cue in that the horizontal line might suggest a surface lying in front of the vertical line.

Muller-Lyer Illusion

This is perhaps the most famous of the various ink-on-paper illusion which presents the version introduced by Muller-Lyer. Though, the vertical shafts in figure are the same length the shaft on the right with the inward-pointing 'arrowheads' appears to be longer than the other shaft and its outward painting. A misapplied constancy explanation has been proposed for the illusion as well.

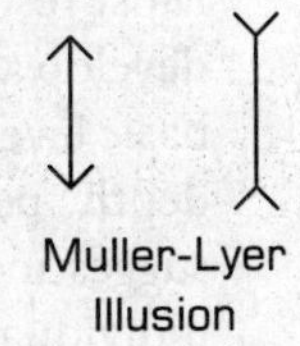

Muller-Lyer Illusion

The shaft with the inward-pointing arrowheads is supposedly seen as farther away because it is perceived as if it were as 'more distant' inside corner as in the left hand part.

On the other hand, the shaft with the out ward-pointing arrowheads is seen as closer since it represents a 'less distant' outside corner as in the right-hand part. If linear perspective cues to relative depth were indeed to operate in the suggested manner, then the size constancy mechanism could well decide that the father shaft is the longer one.

Theory of Illusions

A number of theories have been advanced to explain illusory effects. But none of the theories appears to be adequate in all respects and many of them are even farfetched. One of the more recent attempts to explain illusions involves the concepts of size and shape constancy.

In addition to the constancy theory, there are six major theories attempting to account for illusions

(i) **The Eye-Movement theory** relies on something the observer does overtly *i.e.* moving his eyes along the line of figure movement in one direction is assumed to be more strenuous than in the other; therefore, lines lying in such a direction will be overestimated.

(ii) **The Empathy theory** relies on the elicitation of an aesthetic or emotional bias in the observer.

(iii) **The Good-Figure theory** assumes that figures may either suggest or fully express some characteristic and that the observer tends to see the figure in a way that makes for the full expression of this characteristic.

(iv) **The Confusion theory** suggests that the observer is unable to extract fully the item in question from the presentation as a whole. Hence, some of the properties of the whole cling to the item itself.

(v) **The Perspective theory** assumes that line drawings are not simply seen as items in a single plane, but suggest three-dimensional scenes, with the law of perspective operating. The Moon illusion has been described in terms of the perspective theory.

(vi) **The Inappropriate Constancy Scaling Theory** developed by Gregory, states that when perceptual constancy fails, illusions take place. To maintain perceptual constancy, the brain analyses several information just like a computer.

Taking the distance of the object retinal size and the nature and characteristic of the object and several other depth cues etc. into consideration the brain takes a decision with regard to the probable size and distance of the object. But at times, the brain does not get sufficient information to arrive at a definite conclusion. In such cases, constancy is not maintained and illusions take place. However, there is not a single explanation for all types of illusions.

Perception of Form, Depth and Movement

Visual system allow us to resolve forms of an object, track a moving object and perceive depth.

Perception of Form

Form perception refers to the ability to distinguish an object from its general background. It is the ability to visually perceive objects in world in response to the patterns of light that they caste on the retina. It is the recognition of a figure on a ground.

An individual is able to separate forms from general ground in visual perception on basis of

- Contours
- Organisation

Contours in Form Perception

Contours are formed whenever a marked difference occurs in brightness or colour of background. Thus, it gives shape to the objects by marking one object off from another or marking an object off from general ground.

For example If one looks at a piece of paper that varies continuously in brightness from white at one border to black at opposite border, he will perceive no contour and paper will appear uniform. However, if the change is marked rather than gradual, then an individual will see paper divided into two parts, a light part and a dark part. In perceiving division at place where brightness gradient changes abruptly, a contour is perceived.

Organisation In Form Perception

When several objects are present in visual field, an individual tends to perceive them as organised into patterns or grouping. These patterns can be recognised on basis of Bottom-up Approach or Top-down approach.

Bottom-up approach suggests that the ability to recognise specific pattens such as letter of alphabet, is based on simpler capacities to recognise and combine correctly lower level features of objects, such as lines, edges, corners and angles. According to it, pattern recognition is constructed from simpler perceptual abilities through series of discrete steps. Top-down approach suggests that expectancies play a critical role in shaping perceptions of an individual. An individual often proceed in accordance with what his past experience tells him to expect, without analysing every feature of the encountered stimuli.

Perception of Depth

The visual ability to perceive the world in three dimensions is known as *distance* or *depth perception*.

To have a better understanding of the phenomenon of depth one ought to consider the philosophies of empiricism and nativism. Empiricism claims that the mind at birth is like a blank state, while nativism claims that it is like a veined marble.

John Locke was the first philosopher, who suggested that the mind was initially a 'tabula rasa' *i.e.* process like perception and thought reflect the particular structure and dynamics of the world, in which we happen to live. According to the empiricists, impressions arrange and rearrange themselves to form the core of our perceptions. Wundt's theory of introspectionism is bolstered by empiricism. Pavlov's work on conditioning, Guthrie's theory of contiguity and Broadbend's account of mental functioning in terms of information processing are all built on philosophy of empiricism. Another piece of nativism evidence comes from the field of perception.

Studies done in Gibson's experiment with a visual cliff suggest that depth perception is partly learned and partly innate. Basically, a visual cliff is a glass-topped table with a checkered surface directly beneath the glass one side and the checkered surface 4 ft below on the other side. This makes the glass look like a tabletop on one side and a cliff or drop-off on the other. Most resent research has shown that depth perception begins to develop as early as two weeks of age. It is very likely that atleast a basic level of depth perception is innate. Yet, the development of depth perception is not complete until about six months, suggesting that it depends on both brain maturation and individual experience.

In perceiving depth, an individual of information depends on two main sources of information called *depth cues*.

Depth Cues

A variety of depth cues act as an aid to perceive three-dimensional space. Depth cues are features of the environment and message from the body that supply information about distance and space. Some cues require two eyes (binocular depth cues), whereas others will work with just one eye (monocular depth cues).

Binocular Cues

Binocular cues of depth perception are effective when objects are viewed by both eyes. The depth information is based on coordinated efforts of both eyes, so they are known as *physiological cues*.

Binocular cues for depth perception stem from following sources

- **Retinal/Binocular Disparity** Retinal disparity occurs because the two eyes are separated from each other horizontally by a distance of about 6.5cm. This distance results in slightly different image of same object on the retina of each eye. This difference between the two images is called *retinal disparity*. The brain interprets a large retinal disparity to mean a close object, as disparity is less for distant object, as disparity is less for distant objects and more for near objects.
- **Convergence** On seeing a nearby object, our eyes converge inward to bring image of fovea of each eye. A group of muscles send messages to brain regarding degree to which eyes are turning inward and these messages are interpreted as cues to perception of depth. The degree of convergence decreases as object moves further away from observer.
- **Accommodation** It refers to a process by which we focus image on retina with help of ciliary muscle. If the object gets away (more than 2 meters), the muscle is relaxed. As the object moves nearer, the muscle contracts and thickness of lens increases. The signal about the degree of contraction of muscle is sent to brain which provides cue for distance.

Monocular Depth Cues

Monocular depth cues can be perceived with just one eye. These are also known as *psychological cues*.

The monocular depth cues found in painting, drawing and photographs that impart information about space depth and distance are known as *pictorial depth cues*.

Monocular depth cues as follows

(i) **Linear Perspective** This cue is based on the apparent convergence of parallel lines in the environment. If you stand between two railroad tracks, they appear to meet at the horizon.

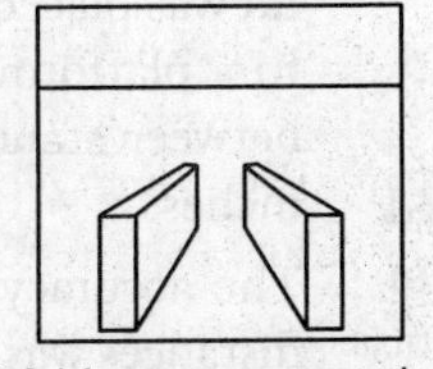

(a) Linear perspective

(ii) **Relative Size** If an artist wishes to depict two objects of the same size at different distances the artist makes the more distant object smaller.

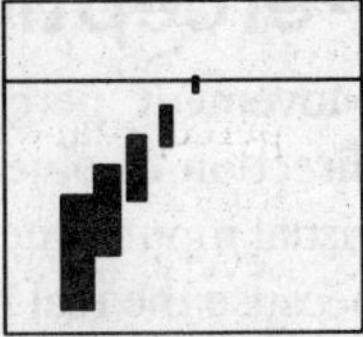

(b) Relative size

(iv) **Height in the Picture Plane** Objects that are placed higher in a drawing tend to be perceived as more distant.

(v) **Light and Shadow** Most object are lighted in ways that create clear patterns of light and shadow. Highlights and shadows provide us with information about an object's distance.

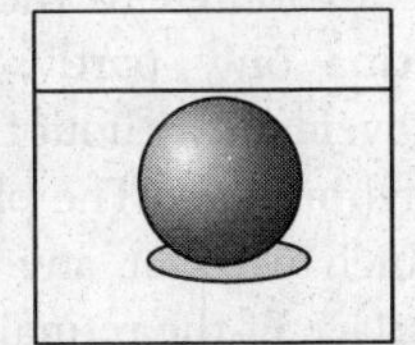

(c) Light and shadow

(vi) **Overlap** Overlap occurs when one object partially blocks another object. The overlapped object is considered farther away, whreas object that covers it appears nearer.

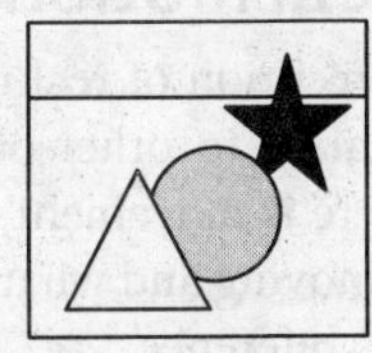

(d) Overlap

(vii) **Texture Gradient** Changes in texture also contribute to depth perception. It represents a phenomenon by which visual field having more density of elements is seen farther away. If you stand in the middle of a cobble stone street, the street will look coarse near your feet. However, its texture will get smaller and finer, if you look at it from the distance.

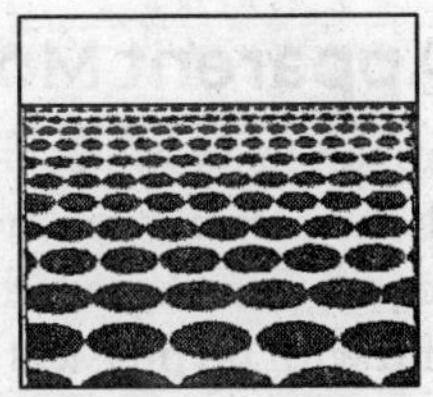

(e) Texture gradients

(viii) **Aerial Perspective** Smog, fog, dust and haze add to the apparent distance of an object. This makes distant, objects look hazy, washed out in colour and lacking detail. Aerial haze is often most noticeable when it is missing.

(ix) **Relative Motion** Relative motion also known as *motion parallax* can be seen by looking out a window and moving your head from side-to-side. Nearby objects appear to move a sizable distance. Tree and house move slightly in relation to background. Hill and mountain do not move at all.

Perception of Movement

Movement perception is process of inferring speed and direction of objects that move in a visual scene given some visual input. One may say that we perceive motion of objects because the real motion correspondingly stimulates different parts of the retina serially. The serial nature of sensation in retina gives the impression of actual movement of the object. This phenomenon also holds true because of some laws of perceptual organisation. However, movement perception can be attributed to these serially changing stimulation in the retina only partly, because sometimes we also perceive movement without the actual movement of the object in the environment. The phenomenon is called *apparent motion,* in which without any energy movement across the receptor surface of the retina, we still perceive movement.

Based on this, *there are two types of motions*

Real Motion

Perception of real movement is based on change of position relative to other objects within the visual field. Whenever there is movement, the perceptual system must decide what is moving and what is stationary with respect to some frames of reference *e.g.* perceiving the train, which remains stationary in the station as moving while sitting on the train moving adjacent to it.

Apparent Motions

Apparent motions are illusions movement, in which there is the perception of motion without any actual movement of object. In other words with our eyes, head and body steady and with no physical movement of an object, we see motions. Psychologists have studied several kinds of apparent movement. These include auto-kinetic effect, stroboscopic motion and the Phi-phenomenon.

Auto-Kinetic Effect

It is the tendency to perceive a stationary point of light in a dark room as moving. *For example* If a person stares at or fixates on a small stationary spot of light in a completely darkroom the spot will eventually appear to move. However, it has been observed that auto kinetic effect is somewhat influenced by suggestion and subjects' prejudice.

Stroboscopic Motion

It is a visual illusion, in which the perception of motion is generated by a series of stationary images that are presented in rapid succession. It is a kind of motion that we see in movies and television. The so-called motion pictures do not consist of images that really move.

Phi-Phenomenon

It is the perception of movement as a result of sequential presentation of visual stimuli. We all have seen the light decoration in the streets during the festival of Durga Puja. It appears as if a light is moving in a row from one end to the other. Actually, the light does not move in a row.

A large number of bulbs are alternatively connected in a row. This quickness in the presentation of light gives the impression of movement of light. Instead of perceiving a series of stationary lights, we perceive a linear movement of light across the row. This illusory movement of light is called the *phi-phenomenon*.

Role of Learning and Motivation in Perception

Basic perceptual processes are same for everyone. However, individual differences in learning and motives make one person's perceptions different from those of another.

Perception and Learning

Whether perception is among the innate characteristics of the organism or is an outcome of the individual's interaction with the environment is among the fundamental questions, with which experimental psychology began.

It would be expected therefore that certain features of perception would manifest at birth and since the higher animals especially are characterised by a capacity to learn, the other features of perception would emerge and improve with practice.

Unlearned Distance Discrimination

During an experiment in 1934, **Lashley** and **Russell** raised thirteen rats in complete darkness from birth for a 100 days. Visual stimulation was restricted to a few seconds of very dim illusion each day. When the cages were opened for feeding on the first day in full light each rat was placed on a jumping stand and encouraged to jump to a platform on which food was available. The distance between stand and platform was varied between 24 and 40 inches.

The accuracy of a rats discrimination of the intervening distances was measured by the force exerted by its leap. To leap 40 inches required a greater force than to leap 24 inches. From the result it was clear in showing that after being reared without visual stimulation the rats did discriminate between different distances between jumping stand and platform. That is distance discrimination in this situation does not depend on visual experience.

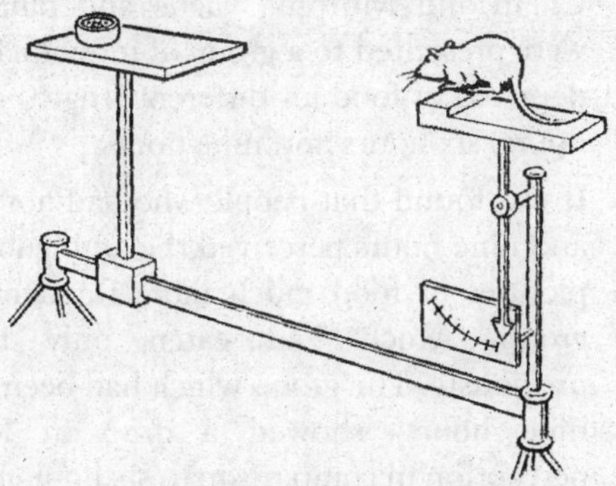

Lashley and Russell experiment; rats reared in darkness discriminate distance between jumping stand and platform as accurately as normally-reared rats.

Visual Cliff Experiment

In Gibsons experiment of 'visual cliff' after showing that a variety of young animals exhibit a marked tendency to avoid the cliff Gibson and Walk used the same procedure as Lashley and Russell. Cats were reared for 90 days without pattern vision and then placed on the runway.

Gibson and Walk's visual cliff; a young animal avoids the 'deep' side of a runway across a cliff. Cats reared without pattern vision also avoid the deep side.

These experimental animals exhibited the same tendency as light reared cats to prefer the shallow side and to avoid the deep side of the runway. The early study by Lashley and Russell and the recent experiments of Gibson, Walk and other investigators show convincingly that depth or distance discrimination occurs without prior practice in the light.

Motion Parallax and Distance Discrimination

Gibson, Walk and Bower have obtained further evidence that the stimulus basic of unlearned distance discrimination is motion parallax, the difference in the extent and velocity of movement of the retinal projections of objects at different distances as the eyes or head move. Bower cited evidence for the role of motion parallax by covering one eye of his infant subjects a procedure, which eliminated retinal disparity.

Unlearned Perceptual Constancy

The capacity to resolve the equivocal size of an objects retinal projection is dependent on information for the distance between observer and object. It is so convincingly demonstrated by Lashley and Russell and by Gibson and Walk, distance discrimination is not learned visually, it could be expected that resolution of size to an approximation to object size would also occur without prior exposure to visual stimulation.

A series of experiments by Bower in the last few years suggests strongly that both size and shape constancy occur at early stage of infant development, explained in peckaboo experiment earlier. There is evidence therefore of size constancy soon after birth. Bower has also demonstrated the occurrence of shape constancy with similar method.

Classes of Learned Perception

An individual depends on visual stimulus information in learning about discriminate patterns and on proprioceptive information in making an appropriate response. Information for discrimination derives in the first instance from the external environment and for appropriate responding from the individuals movements and postures.

Without appropriate sensory information neither task could be learned. An individual with deficiencies of the visual system would have difficulty in learning to discriminate visually as would an individual with deficiencies of the kinesthetic muscular sensory systems in learning a complex motor skill. In other words, individual learns to discriminate between stimuli generated by their own responses as they do between external stimuli. From this view point, a distinction between 'Perceptual' and 'Motor' learning is unwarranted, for both are dependent on sensory information.

It is convenient to distinguish three classes of situation, in which changes in perception occur with practice, discrimination learning, relationship learning and learning to resolve stimulus equivocalities.

(i) The first class refers to progressive refinement or improvement in discriminating between *e.g.* wavelengths spatial separations, chemical concentrations and tonal frequencies.

(ii) The second class refers to progressive changes in behaviour when the relationship between input from two sensory modalities are modified as would occur if a prism of lens were placed infront of the eyes.

(iii) The third class refers to changes in the resolution of equivocal stimuli through prior exposure to certain resolving information.

These three classes of perceptual situation seem to encompass most cases, in which changes in perception occur with practice.

Perceptual Resolution and Learning

The basic of perceptual resolution of equivocal sensory projection of object property such as orientation, size, shape and reflectance at the receptors is so ambiguous that their perception in terms of approximations to the true value of the property is dependent on additional information from proprioceptive or exteroceptive systems.

Depending on the nature of the information, the equivocal projection is resolved to a close approximation to the objective value of the property (perceptual constancy) or to a poor approximation (perceptual illusion). If there is no source of resolving information then perceptual instability occurs.

The information, on which perceptual resolution depends may, under certain condition, be learned, so that resolution in the direction of either constancy or illusion can occur in the absence of the information itself. This aspect of the relation between learning and perception has been recognised for a considerable time as 'the role of past experience in perception'.

Motivational Influences on Perception

Motivation influences on perception (as well as on other processes such as thinking dreaming memory and so on) are postulated in psychoanalytic theory as formulated by Sigmund Freud and his followers and have by now become and accepted part of general psychological lore.

The research on motivation-perception is of two broad sorts : one where the task involves target identification or recognition, the other where the subjects make judgements about some aspect of a stimulus that is well above threshold. Throughout, the effort is to determine whether perceptual functioning can be influenced by motivational variables where 'Motivational' is broadly defined to include

- The primary physiological drives, such as hunger thirst and pain.
- The so called acquired, or social drives such as need for achievement.
- The Psychoanalytically defined impulses conflict and defences.

Biological Motives

Several interesting experiments have been conducted to see how needs like hunger, sex etc influence perception. In an experiment by Levine Chein and Murphy, vague and blurred pictures were presented to a group of individuals, who were deprived of food for different lengths of time three hours, six hours and nine hours.

It was found that people who had not eaten for six and nine hours perceived the ambiguous images as pictures of food much more frequently than the group, which had eaten only three hours previously. The group which had been deprived for nine hours, showed a drop in food related perception in comparison to six hour group as if the hunger had gone beyond a peak of intensity and had died.

Psychological Motives

It is in common knowledge that reward and punishment influence the learning process. But, it is less easy to understand how one's perception of an object can be influenced in a similar manner.

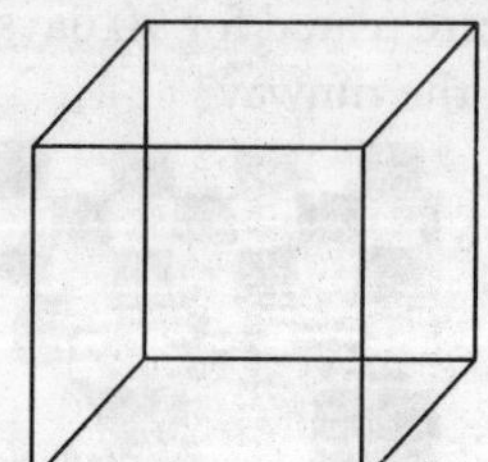

Necker cube-an ambiguous figure consisting of a cube whose edges

Solley and Santos used drawings of 'Necker Cubes' as in following manner (as in the above figure). In the altered cubes to the left and right only one perspective could be seen when seen for one second. The cube in the center, could be seen as having either perspective. The experimenter verbally rewarded the perception of one of the altered cube.

It was found that as the experiment progressed *i.e.* as the amount of verbal reward increased the subject perceived the natural cube more and more only in the perspective, for which they have been rewarded. This incidentally also provides evidence for the role of learning in perception.

EXAM BASED QUESTIONS

1 James (1890) differentiated between which types of attention?

(a) Various forms of top-down attention
(b) Auditory (top-down) and visual (bottom-up)
(c) Various forms of bottom-up attention
(d) Active (top-down) and passive (bottom-up)

2 What was the focus of attentional research in the late 1980s?

(a) Evolutionary theory and biology
(b) Controlled processes and verbal reports
(c) Cognitive neuroscience, patient data and computer modeling
(d) Humans as single channel processors

3 The active selection of information is achieved using which of the following?

(a) Top-down processing
(b) Attentional spotlight or zoom lens
(c) Saccades and inhibition of return
(d) Inhibition of return and zoo

4 Simon and Chabris (1999) demonstrated that which type of attention can result in missing potentially interesting information?

(a) Focused (b) Tactile
(c) Parallel (d) Distributed

5 Treisman and Gelade (1980) proposed which theory of attention?

(a) Feature integration theory
(b) Limited capacity theory
(c) Early selection theory
(d) Filter theory

6 Cherry (1953) investigated which phenomenon?

(a) Focused auditory attention
(b) Cocktail party phenomenon
(c) Visual disparity
(d) Focused visual attention

7 How many inputs pass through the attentional filter in Broadbent's (1958) model?

(a) Multiple (b) Three
(c) One (d) Two

8 At which stage does filtering occur in early selection models?

(a) It does not occur
(b) Before perceptual processing
(c) Prior to semantic processing
(d) After lexical processing

9 Attenuation originally featured in whose model of attention?

(a) Treisman
(b) Broadbent
(c) James
(d) Deutsch and Deutsch

10 Which form of processing is used in Deutsch and Deutsch (1963) model?

(a) Serial processing
(b) Parallel processing
(c) Top down processing
(d) Cascading processing

11 Shadowing becomes more difficult when information is presented to both ears at the same time. What is the implication of this finding?

(a) It implies that semantic information is being processed
(b) Attenuation does not occur
(c) Lack of understanding regarding the instructions
(d) Broadbent's model of attention is accurate

12 Chun and Wolfe (2000) endorsed which definition of attention?

(a) Simple processes with early selection
(b) Late selection of salient facts
(c) Early selection of important information
(d) Attention is a multi-faceted term referring to a range of actions and foci

13 What proportion of participants could identify their name in an unattended conversation according to Conway, Cowan and Bunting (2001)?

(a) All
(b) One-third
(c) Only younger adults (1/4 of the sample)
(d) Only women (1/2 of the sample)

14 What other theory did Conway, Cowan and Bunting incorporate into explaining the cocktail problem?

(a) Working memory (b) Spreading activation
(c) Filter theory (d) Connectionism

15 Schouten, Kalsbeek and Leopold identified which type of task impaired performance during divided attention?

(a) No tasks impaired performance
(b) High capacity tasks
(c) Low capacity tasks
(d) Procedural tasks

16 Spelke, Hirst and Neisser identified that complex tasks could be conducted simultaneously after which of the following?

(a) Injections of adrenaline (b) IQ tests
(c) Extensive practice (d) Sensory deprivation

17 The delay in response which occurs when two signals requiring two responses are presented in rapid succession is known as

(a) Psychological refractory period
(b) Transduction
(c) Induction
(d) Deduction

18 **Who argued that we have limited processing resources which must be shared between tasks?**
(a) Treisman (b) Deutsch
(c) Broadbent (d) Knowles

19 **Kahneman included which factors in his theory of attention?**
(a) Motivation and arousal
(b) Individual differences and early selection
(c) Attenuation
(d) Direct perception and emotion

20 **Which two forms of processing are differentiated in the two-process model of attention?**
(a) Between attention and attenuation
(b) Between computational and neural processing
(c) Between controlled and automatic processes
(d) Between visual and auditory attention

21 **Which theory would predict that the American flag have a green, black and yellow after image?**
(a) Substractive colour mixing
(b) Opponent process theory
(c) Additive color mixing
(d) Trichromatic theory

22 **The illusion of movement created by presenting visual stimuli in rapid succession is called**
(a) convergence (b) retinal dispraity
(c) motion parallax (d) the phi phenomenon

23 **In a painting, train tracks may look as if they go off into the distance because the artist draws the tracks as converging lines a pictorial cue to depth known as**
(a) Interposition (b) Texture gradient
(c) Convergence (d) Linear perspective

24 **Sanam has just finished a long exhausting 6 mile run. She and her friend Lamal are gasing at a hill they need a climb to get back to their car Jamal asks Sanam, "Gee how steep do you think that hill is"? Based on research by Proffitt and his colleagues Sanam is likely to**
(a) make a reasonably accurate estimate of the hill's slant, as most people do.
(b) underestimate the hill's slant, as most people do.
(c) coverestimate the hill's slant, but to a lesser degree than she would have before her exhausting run.
(d) overestimate the hill's slant to an even greater degree than she would have before her exhausting run.

25 **The fact that cultural groups with less exposure to carpentered buildings are less susceptible to the Muller-Lyer illusion suggests that**
(a) not all cultures test perceptual hypothesis.
(b) people in technologically advanced cultures are more gulliable.
(c) optical illusions can be experienced only by cultures that have been exposed to the concept of optical illusions.
(d) perceptual inferences can be shaped by experience.

26 **Attention is aroused by**
(a) subtle differences in stimuli
(b) bright stimuli
(c) contrast or change in stimulation
(d) subliminal stimuli

27 **Broadbent's model suggests that early selection of items to be attended is done on the basis of**
(a) physical characteristics
(b) semantic characteristics
(c) interest
(d) need

28 **The fact that we can walk and chew gum at the same time illustrates that**
(a) our attention depends on different motor systems
(b) we use selective attention
(c) we use divided attention
(d) we use sequential attention

29 **Perception alters the view of the world by**
(a) diminishing irrelevant or redundant information
(b) ignoring a large amount of potential sensory information
(c) falling to take into account regularities of matter and energy
(d) Both a and b

30 **Which two processes are always involved in perception?**
(a) Attention and subliminal stimuli
(b) Subliminal stimuli and sensation
(c) Sensation and interpretation
(d) Internal sensation and distraction

31 **Relationship of distal to proximal representations of an object, indicating the degree to which physical attributes any given perception, is known as**
(a) Brunswik ratio (b) Stevens power
(c) Variable ratio (d) Sensitivity ratio

32 **A hungry person tends to perceive the smell of a food substance much quicker than a satiated person. Which theory of perception may be used to explain this event?**
(a) The new look theory (b) Probabilistic theory
(c) Sensory-tonic field theory (d) Psychophysical theory

33 **Which one of the following is not an auditory cue for localising sound source?**
(a) Binaural time difference
(b) Binaural distance difference
(c) Binaural phase difference
(d) Binaural intensity difference

34 **Auditory comprehension of semantic information, vocal inflection, gesture and metaphors in the area of language are handled by which one of the following?**
(a) Right hemisphere (b) Left hemisphere
(c) Frontal lobe (d) Temporal lobe

35 Rahul wears glasses to correct the farsight, the farsightedness in her left eye. If he does not wear his glasses
(a) the lens would focus images in front of the retina in his left eye
(b) the pupil in his left eye would dilate and let in too much light energy
(c) the lens would focus images behind the retina in his left eye
(d) the pupil in his left eye would constrict and not left in sufficient light energy

36 The retinal area that, when stimulated affects the firing of a visual cell is referred to as the
(a) cell's focal point (b) fovea for that cell
(c) visual field (d) cell's receptive field

37 If you want to see a star better at night, what should you do?
(a) Look directly at it, because the cones will focus better at night.
(b) Look off to the side, using the cones in the periphery of the retina.
(c) Look directly at it because the rods can see sharply at night.
(d) Look off to the side, using the rods in the periphery of the retina.

38 Which of your senses does not adopt to a constant stimulus at the level of the receptor cells?
(a) Vision (b) Touch
(c) Hearing (d) Smell

39 You have a piece of candy that you are holding in your mouth. After a while, the candy does not taste as strong as it did when you first tasted it. What has happened?
(a) Sensory adaption (b) Subliminal perception
(c) Threshold adaption (d) Perceptual defense

40 Which of the following represents the correct path of light through the eyes?
(a) Iris, cornea, lens, retina
(b) Cornea, vitreous humor, iris, lens, aqueous humour, ratina
(c) Cornea, pupil, lens, vitreous humour, ratina
(d) Cornea, lens, pupil, iris, retina

41 Hearing impaired people are less likely to take advantage of new technology to help them hear, if they
(a) have been hearing impaired since, birth
(b) were born able to hear for a time
(c) still remember what it was like to hear
(d) see their impairment as a disability rather than a difference

42 The eardrum is also called the
(a) pinna (b) oval window
(c) tympanic membrane (d) cochlea

43 The purpose of active perception is to
(a) distinguish self-produced patterns of stimulation from externally produced ones.
(b) guide our sensory sampling based on our physical needs.
(c) eliminate the need to make decisions based on sensory stimulation.
(d) reduce the overall quantity of sensory information.

44 After sometime has passed, you can no longer smell the odour of the paper mill that you noticed, when you first walked in your classroom. Which is the most likely reason for this?
(a) The smell has gone away
(b) You have adapted to the smell, even though it is still there
(c) Your nose falls asleep
(d) You fall asleep

45 Which of the following properties of sound would be the most similar to the colour or hue of light?
(a) Pitch (b) Loudness
(c) Purity (d) Timber

46 The receptor on our taste buds work most like a
(a) receptor in the ears (b) receptor in the eyes
(c) receptor sites on neurons (d) receptor in the skin

47 The thin membrane stretched over the opening to the inner ear is the
(a) pinna (b) oval window
(c) tympainc membrane (d) cochlea

48 The olfactory receptor cells are located in the
(a) tops of the nasal passages
(b) auditory passage
(c) roof of the mouth
(d) lining of the outer nose

49 The 'bumps' on the tongue that are visible to the eye are the
(a) taste buds (b) papillae
(c) taste receptors (d) olfactory receptors

50 Which type of retinal cell forms the optic nerve?
(a) Rods (b) Cones
(c) Ganglion cells (d) Bipolar cells

51 Which sets of colour are the primary colours, when mixing lights?
(a) Red, yellow and blue (b) Red, blue and green
(c) Blue, green and yellow (d) Red, green and yellow

52 Which type of retinal cell is responsible for peripheral vision?
(a) Rods (b) Cones
(c) Ganglion cells (d) Bipolar cells

53 Which of the following is responsible for controlling how much light enters the eye?
(a) Cornea (b) Lens
(c) Retina (d) Iris

54 Which of the following terms refers to the psychological effect of the length of light waves?
(a) Colour (b) Brightness (c) Pitch (d) Amplitude

55 The sense of taste is closely related to the sense of
(a) sight (b) hearing (c) smell (d) touch

56 Dark adaptation is a process in which the eyes get more sensitive to
(a) green light
(b) coloured lights
(c) light with bright illumination
(d) light with low illumination

57 In our estimate of the actual size of objects, our brain takes two factors into account. These are
(a) constancies and illusions
(b) object size and apparent distance
(c) object size and retinal size
(d) retinal size and apparent distance

58 The Young-Helmholtz theory of colour vision states that
(a) black and white are true colour qualities and not just the presence or absence of light.
(b) the human eye contains three kinds of cones, each kind being sensitive to one of the three primary colours.
(c) the retina contains two kinds of receptor, one being sensitive to colours and the other being not sensitive to colours.
(d) the visual system reaches a state of equilibrium when no external visual stimulus is present.

59 Each colour that a human being is capable of experiencing can vary in
(a) hue, reflection and brightness
(b) hue, reflection and saturation
(c) reflection, brightness and saturation
(d) hue, brightness and saturation

60 What is approximate visual field covered by each human eye?
(a) 130 degrees (b) 160 degrees
(c) 180 degrees (d) 220 degrees

61 Pain sensation in the skin, muscles tendons and joints that are carried on large nerve fibers are called
(a) Visceral pain (b) Somatic pain
(c) Referred pain (d) Indigenous pain

62 Following Young-Helmholtz theory of colour vision, if a given stimulus innervates 4R, 9G and 13B cones, than the perception is of less saturated greenish-blue because
(a) all RG and B are mixed to produce intermediate colour.
(b) G and B units are mixed to produce greenish-blue which is saturated by R units.
(c) 4 units of each produce greenish-blue and the remaining units desaturate the colour.
(d) 4 units of each produce white leaving 5G and 9B to produce greenish-blue desaturated bye white.

63 Which of the following is the most general of the Gestalt principles describing how individual elements are grouped into higher order figure?
(a) Continuity (b) Proximity
(c) Similarity (d) Simplicity

64 The tendency to perceive an object in its entirely even when some details are missing, is known as the law of
(a) proximity (b) common region
(c) closure (d) good continuation

65 Which one of the following figures is an example of proximity principle of perceptual organisation?
(a)
(b)
(c)
(d)

66 A person looks at two circle. One is black and the other is white. The retinal images are also different for the two circles, inspite of these differences, the person perceives the two circles as being identical in form. This is a case of
(a) perception of Ganzfeld (b) transposition of form
(c) from parallax (d) law of similarity

67 Which one of the following inferences can be drawn from the given figure?

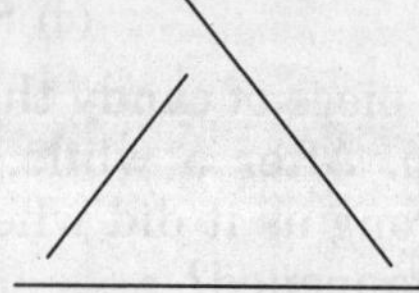

(a) Similar lines are grouped into one unit
(b) Lines are in different directions
(c) Proximity of lines makes it one unit
(d) Incomplete figures are seen as complete

68 One has tendency to organise things to make a balanced or symmetrical figure that includes all parts. This is known as the law of
(a) similarity (b) continuation
(c) closure (d) good figure

69 Rubin is to figure ground segregation as Koffka is to
(a) phi-phenomenon
(b) perceptual organisation
(c) brightness contrast
(d) perceptual constancy

70 What is 'the tendency of a stimulus situation to be perceived in approximately the same way under varying circumstances' called
(a) Perceptual invariance
(b) Perceptual vigilance
(c) Perceptual constancy
(d) Perceptual defense

71 When two close friends are talking other people may not be able to follow their conversation because it has many gaps, which the friends mentally fill in from their shared experience. Which Gestalt principle is illustrated by the friends ability to fill in these conversational gaps?

(a) Ambiguity (b) Similarity
(c) Closure (d) Common fate

72 Constancy phenomenon refers to the

(a) fact that through constant perception of objects we know what their real characteristics are.
(b) fact that the real characteristics of the objects remain constant.
(c) tendency to perceive characteristics of an object to remain more or less unchanged despite marked variations in stimulation.
(d) fact that the essential characteristics of objects do not change in perception.

73 When evening approaches and daylight gives way to artificial light, we notice little change in the colours of objects around us. The perceptual ability that enables us to discount such variations in light is called

(a) Perceptual vigilance (b) Perceptual defense
(c) Perceptual constancy (d) Perceptual readiness

74 When does perceptual constancy occur?

(a) When sensation and perception of an object change with each other constantly.
(b) When perception of an object remains same even when sensation changes.
(c) When sensation and perception of an objects remains constant when the distance changes.
(d) When sensation of an object remains same and only perception changes constantly.

75 If a blue paper is placed in yellow illumination, it would appear as blue in yellow light

(a) colour adaptation (b) colour phenomenon
(c) colour constancy (d) colour mixture

76 An object will be perceived more in agreement with the size of the image it casts on the retina if

(a) illumination is increased (b) depth cues are present
(c) depth cues are absent (d) illumination is decreased

77 A rock band recently covered (re-made) a classic country song. Though, the band uses different kinds of instruments and a different tempo, colby still recognises it due to

(a) the law of continuity
(b) haring opponent process theory
(c) perceptual constancy
(d) transduction

78 To perceive the size of an object remaining the same even though the retinal image changes is called

(a) Perceptual closure (b) Size constancy
(c) Retinal disparity (d) Psychophysics

79 You observe two cars of identical make and mode. Although, one roars away and its image on your retina is changed, you still perceive the cars as identical. This phenomenon is

(a) size constancy
(b) shape constancy
(c) concept constancy
(d) form constancy

80 As a door opens toward you, you perceive it as a rectangular door rather than going through actual image changes on the retina (from rectangular to trapesoid). This is an example of

(a) perceptual closure (b) shape constancy
(c) ambiguous stimuli (d) retinal disparity

81 Even though, the retinal image of an object may change drastically, the object appears unchanged. This is the principle underlying

(a) perceptual closure (b) shape constancy
(c) ambiguous stimuli (d) retinal disparity

82 The tendency to perceive a quarter as being round even when it is viewed at an angle is called

(a) Size constancy (b) Shape constancy
(c) Brightness constancy (d) Colour constancy

83 An old comedy routine in a television had a character who would line up the heads of people, who were very far away from him between his fingers. Then, he would pinch his fingers together and say gleefully. "I am crushing your head," The comedian was playing around with which perceptual constancy?

(a) Size constancy (b) Shape constancy
(c) Brightness constancy (d) Color constancy

84 According to Gestalt Psychologists, the following pattern would be perceived as to units based on the law of

(a) similarity (b) contrast
(c) closure (c) proximity

85 According to Gestalt theory insight is the

(a) 'aha' moment in problem-solving
(b) reorganised problem structure
(c) gradual accretion of a problem solution
(d) main component of means end analysis

86 Phi phenomenon is seen best between

(a) 50 to 250 milli second
(b) 110 to 320 milli second
(c) 30 to 200 milli second
(d) 215 to 375 milli second

87 The ability to perceive depth is mainly

(a) a direct result of the fact that the surface of retina is three dimensional.
(b) due to specialised receptors on the retina.
(c) accomplished through the use of a variety of perceptual cues.
(d) a result of perceptual illusion.

88 The most important monocular cues for depth perception are
(a) partial overlap and size
(b) shading and texture gradients
(c) linear perspective and motion parallax
(d) All of the above

89 The film star wars created illusion of depth by quickly changing images of the sizes of planets and starships using the pictorial depth cue called
(a) Convergence (b) Accommodation
(c) Linear perspective (d) Relative size

90 The ability to see three dimensional space to accurately judge distances is called
(a) Size constancy (b) Shape constancy
(c) Depth perception (d) Perception organisation

91 Which of the following is not a cue for depth perception?
(a) Integration (b) Relative size
(c) Motion parallax (d) Interposition

92 The binocular depth cue that depends on the distance between the eye refers to
(a) illusion (b) movement
(c) convergence (d) retinal disparity

93 A binocular depth cue resulting from the movement of the eye muscles is
(a) accommodation (b) retinal disparity
(c) convergence (d) stereoscopic cue

94 When we perceive an apple from a distance of 6 or 16 feet, it makes no difference in our perception. Choose the correct reason from the following options.
(a) Perceptual assimilation (b) Perceptual contract
(c) Perceptual constancy (d) Perceptual vigilance

95 When we look at a figure for sometime and then look at another figure, the perception of the second figure is referred to as
(a) after image (b) illusion
(c) the figural after effect (d) distorted perception

96 It is noted that windows look rectangular regardless of the angle at which you view them. The top of a glass looks circular even though its retinal is elliptical. This is called
(a) Size constancy (b) Shape constancy
(c) Stimulus constancy (d) Object constancy

97 Dinner plates on a table are seen as round even though from the angle of viewing is oval. This is an example of
(a) size constancy (b) shape constancy
(c) brightness constancy (d) colour constancy

98 In films and television programmes, principle of visual perception used is
(a) stroboscopic (b) stereoscopic
(c) binocular parallax (d) gamma movement

99 Colour blindness is related to
(a) rods (b) cones (c) brightness (d) saturation

100 Dark adaptation is a process in which eyes get more sensitive to
(a) green light
(b) colour light
(c) light with bright illumination
(d) light with low illumination

101 Given a new pair of glasses, we feel slightly disoriented and dizzy. Within a day or two we get adjusted. This is called
(a) Perceptual adaptation (b) Perceptual learning
(c) Perceptual constancy (d) Perceptual organism

102 The moon at the horizon looks bigger than the moon at the zenith, because the perceived distance at the horizon is greater than at the zenith. It supports the
(a) cue theory (b) constancy principle
(c) distance principle (d) gestalt principle

103 Which one of the following is most commonly experienced when a stimulus is ambiguous information is missing elements are combined in unusual ways or familiar patterns are not apparent?
(a) Proximity (b) A correct rejection
(c) A false alarm (d) Common fate

104 The moon illusion is best explained by
(a) the effects of depth cues on apparent distance
(b) the perceptual closure effect
(c) magnification caused by the denser atmosphere along the horizon
(d) convergence

105 If you stand in the middle of a cobblestone street, the street will look course near your feet and her if you into the distance. This is called
(a) Texture gradient (b) Linear perspective
(c) Relative size (d) Relative motion

106 Illusion are
(a) distortions of existing stimuli
(b) the same as hallucinations
(c) the result of innate mechanisms
(d) not based on external reality

107 Illusions differ from hallucination in that
(a) illusions are based on perceptions that have no external reality.
(b) hallucinations are simply misjudgements of sensory information.
(c) illusions are based on perceptual learning.
(d) hallucinations are the result of past experience.

108 An illusion
(a) is the same thing as a hallucination
(b) exists only in the brain cells of the viewer
(c) is a distorted perception of an actual stimulus
(d) corresponds directly to reality

109 **Illusionary contents can be explained by which of the following?**
(a) Nativistic approach
(b) Top- down approach
(c) Bottom-up approach
(d) Both top-down and bottom-up approach

110 **Isaac is in a room that is almost completely dark. He notices, while lying in bed that if he tries to focus on the faint little red light on the fire detector, it seems to disappear. When he asks his mother why this happens, she explains that the eye receptors that understand colour do not function well in very dim light. To which receptors is she referring?**
(a) Rods (b) Cones
(c) Cylinders (d) Ganglion

111 **Which one of the following statements regarding feature detectors is not correct?**
(a) They respond only to a very specific aspect of stimulus.
(b) They are single neurons found in the CNS/sense organs.
(c) They are involved in pattern recognition.
(d) They are first order neurons involved in sensory perception.

112 **Which statement about colour blindness is true ?**
(a) There are more men who has colour blind than woman.
(b) All colour-blind people see only in black and white.
(c) Some colour blind people see only in blue.
(d) Some colour-blind people see only in blue and red.

113 **Which of the following statements about olfactory receptor is false?**
(a) Olfactory receptors are replaced every few years.
(b) There are at least 1000 types of olfactory receptors.
(c) Signals from the receptors go directly to the olfactory bulbs in the brain.
(d) Olfactory receptors have hair like projection called cilia.

114 **According to Gestalt theory, which of the following statements is correct?**
(a) Perceptual organisation is natural.
(b) Perceptual organisation is acquired.
(c) Perceptual organisation is partially natural and partially acquired.
(d) Perceptual organisation is a false notion.

115 **Which of the following statement is not correct?**
(a) Retinal disparity is a cue for depth perception, which is frequently used by the artists.
(b) Retinal disparity is a cue for depth perception, which can be utilised by a person with only one good eye.
(c) Retinal disparity is a cue for depth perception, which is muscular rather than visual.
(d) Retinal disparity is a cue, which is very sensitive aid to the perception of distance, but requires both eyes.

116 **Consider the following Psychologists who studied 'attention' at different times.**
1. Franciscus Donders **2. Walter Benjamin**
3. Donald Broadbent **4. Anne Treisman**
Which of the following codes is in correct chronological order?
(a) 1 2 3 4 (b) 4 3 2 1 (c) 2 4 1 3 (d) 3 1 4 2

117 **Which of the following is the correct chronological order of given Gestalt psychologists.**
(a) Wertheimer , Koffka , Kohler , Lewin
(b) Kohler, Wertheimer, Koffka , Lewin
(c) Lewin, Kohler, Koffka, Wertheimer
(d) Koffka, Lewin, Wertheimer, Kohler

118 **Consider the following in the perceptual process.**
1. Organisation **2. Sensory input**
3. Interpretation **4. Selective attention**
Which one of the following is the correct sequence of the above in perceptual process?
(a) 1, 4, 2 and 3 (b) 2, 3, 1 and 4
(c) 1, 3, 2 and 4 (d) 2, 4, 1 and 3

119 **In the experiments on size constancy, different conditions are used.**
Which one of the following is the correct sequence of the following conditions in the decreasing order of the constancy values?
(a) Monocular with tunnel-Monocular with artificial pupil-Monocular-Binocular.
(b) Binocular-Monocular-Monocular with artificial pupil-Monocular with tunnel.
(c) Monocular with tunnel -Binocular-Monocular with artificial pupil-Monocular.
(d) Binocular-Monocular with tunnel -Monocular with artificial pupil-Monocular.

120 **Which one of the following is the correct sequence of neural structures involved in saccadic eye movement generation from the lowest to the highest?**
(a) Brainstem-visual cortical colliculus areas-superior colliculus -frontal eye field area 8.
(b) Frontal eye field area 8-superior colliculus-visual cortical area-brainstem.
(c) Brainstem-superior colliculus-frontal eye field area 8-visual cortical areas.
(d) Superior colliculus-frontal eye field area 8-brainstem visual cortical area

121 **Which one of the following pairs is correctly matched?**
(a) Perceptual vigilance : Sensitivity to all stimuli
(b) Perceptual illusion : Perceiving all information as positive
(c) Perceptual set : Seeking attitude supportive information
(d) Perceptual defence : Misperceiving or avoiding attitude discrepant information

122 Which of the following pairs is/are correctly matched?

1. Emotion : Solley
2. Motivation : Sandford
3. Expectation : Bruner

Codes

(a) 1 and 2 (b) 2 and 3 (c) All of these (d) Only 3

123 Which of the following pairs is/are correctly matched?

1. Allport : Attitudes
2. Haigh : Motivation
3. Minturn : Emotion

Codes

(a) Only 1 (b) 1 and 2 (c) 2 and 3 (d) None of these

124 Which of the following pairs is/are correctly matched?

1. J von Kries : Duplicity theory of vision
2. Colour deficiency : Max schultce
3. J Mueller: Doctrine of specific energy nerve

Codes

(a) 1 and 2 (b) 2 and 3 (c) 1 and 3 (d) 1, 2 and 3

125 Which of the following pairs is/are correctly matched?

1. Kohler : Isomorphism
2. Truman : Law of pragnanz
3. Koffka : Phi-phenomen

Codes

(a) Only 1 (b) Only 2 (c) Only 3 (d) 1 and 2

126 Consider the following statements

1. Perception is not directly observable.
2. Perception is followed by sensation.
3. Perception can be modified.
4. Perception is inherited.

Which of the following statements given above is/are correct?

(a) Only 2 (b) Only 1
(c) 2 and 3 (d) 1 and 3

127 Which of the following are included in the Gestalt principles of perceptual organisation?

1. Figure-ground proximity, continuity
2. Proximity, continuity, good form
3. Continuity, good form, closure
4. Good form, closure, facilitation

Select the correct answer using the codes given below

(a) 1 and 2 (b) 3 and 4
(c) 1, 2 and 3 (d) 2 and 3

128 Perception of figure and ground depends on

1. size of two areas
2. completeness of two areas
3. brightness of two areas
4. exposure time

Select the correct answer using the codes given below

(a) 1, 2 and 4 (b) 2, 3 and 4
(c) 1, 2 and 3 (d) Only 2

129 Ponzo illusion increases with

1. age
2. learning
3. size of the stimulus
4. brightness of the stimulus

Codes

(a) 1 and 2 (b) 3 and 4 (c) 2 and 4 (d) 3 and 2

130 Consider the following statements

1. Mixing paints yields subtractive colour mixing because the pigments observe most wavelengths, selectively reflecting other wavelength.
2. Rohan has been wearing red welding goggles for the past 30 minutes. Based on the opponent process theory of colour vision, when eric takes off the red goggles he should expect that objects will temporarily appear to be red.

Which of the statements given above is/are correct?

(a) Only 1 (b) Only 2
(c) Both 1 and 2 (d) Neither 1 nor 2

131 Match the following

List I		List II
A. Yellow-blue colour blindness	1.	Sensory information store
B. Interest	2.	Latent attention
C. Attention	3.	Interest in action
D. Prepotency	4.	Exceedingly rare

Codes

	A	B	C	D		A	B	C	D
(a)	1	2	3	4	(b)	4	2	3	1
(c)	2	1	4	3	(d)	3	1	4	2

132 Match the following

List I		List II
A. Sensation	1.	Presentative
B. Perception	2.	Objects and event out of the world
C. Distal stimuli	3.	Presentative as well as representative
D. Proximal stimuli	4.	Stimuli actually reach sense

Codes

	A	B	C	D		A	B	C	D
(a)	4	2	1	3	(b)	2	4	1	3
(c)	1	3	2	4	(d)	1	3	4	2

133 Match the following

List I (Concept)		List II (Associated with)
A. Motion parallex	1.	Perception of thing as changing
B. Memory	2.	Research on cochlea
C. Perceptual constancy	3.	Basic factor in perception
D. Non-bekesy	4.	Depict depth

Codes

	A	B	C	D		A	B	C	D
(a)	4	3	1	2	(b)	3	4	1	2
(c)	1	2	4	3	(d)	2	1	4	3

134 Match the following

List I (Theory)	List II (Concept)
A. Spinal gate control theory	1. Motion sickness is due to disruption of the sensory input to visual and vestibular systems
B. Young Helmholtz theory	2. The perception of spoken language is a result of the knowledge of the articulatory gestures involved in speech
C. Motor theory	3. There are three sets of receptor cones that respond differently to different wavelengths
D. Sensory conflict theory	4. Theory of pain that focuses on afferent nerve impulse transmission from the skin to the spinal cord

Codes

	A	B	C	D		A	B	C	D
(a)	4	3	2	1	(b)	1	2	3	4
(c)	3	2	1	4	(d)	3	1	2	4

135 Match the following

List I (Principles of Perception)	List II (Brief Explanation)
A. Similarity	1. Objects in motion together appear to stand out from their surroundings
B. Continuity	2. Elements that continue a pattern are likely to be seen as part of the pattern
C. Common fate	3. Objects that are like one another tend to be grouped together
D. Proximity	4. Elements found close together lend to be perceived as a unit

Codes

	A	B	C	D		A	B	C	D
(a)	3	2	1	4	(b)	1	3	4	2
(c)	2	4	3	1	(d)	4	1	2	3

136 Match the following

List I (Law of organisation)	List II (Characteristic)
A. Continuity	1. Tendency to perceive a whole object even where none exists
B. Common fate	2. Objects in motion together appear to stand out from their surroundings
C. Proximity	3. Elements that continue a pattern are likely to be seen as part of the pattern
D. Closure	4. Elements found close together tend to be perceived as a unit

Codes

	A	B	C	D		A	B	C	D
(a)	1	4	2	3	(b)	2	4	1	3
(c)	3	1	2	4	(d)	3	2	4	1

137 Match the following

List I (Researchers)	List II (Fields of Research)
A. Gestalt	1. Pandemonium
B. Selfridge	2. Isomorphism
C. Biederman	3. Apparent movement
D. Wertheimer	4. Geons

Codes

	A	B	C	D		A	B	C	D
(a)	4	3	2	1	(b)	2	1	4	3
(c)	3	2	1	4	(d)	1	4	2	3

138 Match the following

List I (Concept)	List II (Associated with)
A. Gestalt	1. Principles of organisation
B. Illusion	2. Fooling of the perception
C. Figure and ground	3. Shape perception
D. Three dimentional vision	4. Depth perception

Codes

	A	B	C	D		A	B	C	D
(a)	1	2	3	4	(b)	2	1	4	3
(c)	3	2	1	4	(d)	4	3	1	2

139 Match the following

List I (Researchers)	List II (Fields of Research)
A. Hebb	1. Transactional functionalism
B. Adler	2. Adaptation level
C. Ames	3. Goal perception
D. Koffka	4. Cell assembly

Codes

	A	B	C	D		A	B	C	D
(a)	2	3	4	1	(b)	3	2	1	4
(c)	4	3	1	2	(d)	1	4	2	3

140 Match the following

List I (Concept)	List II (Associated with)
A. Gestalt psychology	1. Muller-Lyer Illusion
B. Arrow headed line and feather headed line	2. Linear motion
C. The perception of the actual physical movement of object	3. Whole is more than some of its part
D. Melody	4. Frequency of sound cuave

Codes

	A	B	C	D		A	B	C	D
(a)	2	1	4	3	(b)	1	2	3	4
(c)	3	1	2	4	(d)	1	3	4	2

141 Match the following

List I (Research)	List II (Associated with)
A. Holway	1. Psychophysical experiment
B. Gilchrist	2. Figure and ground
C. Edgar Rubin	3. The complanar ratio hypothesis
D. Weirtheimer	4. Gestalt psychologist

Codes

	A	B	C	D		A	B	C	D
(a)	4	2	1	3	(b)	4	2	3	1
(c)	1	3	2	4	(d)	3	1	2	4

142 Match the following

List I (Perceptual Constancy)	List II (Statements)
A. Brightness constancy	1. Seeing a friend you are meeting from a distance
B. Shape constancy	2. Seeing distance objects like cars, trees and people as normal
C. Size constancy	3. Seeing coin as found even when flipped into air
D. Relative size constancy	4. Perceiving sweater as dark green whether indoor or outdoor

Codes

	A	B	C	D		A	B	C	D
(a)	4	3	1	2	(b)	3	4	2	1
(c)	3	4	1	2	(d)	4	3	2	1

143 Match the following

List I (Type of Illusion)	List II (Nature of Constancy Failure)
A. Moon illusion	1. Shape constancy
B. Apparent direction of external objects in relation to moving self	2. Relative position constancy
C. Muller-Lyer illusion	3. Cultural constancy
D. Parallelogram illusion	4. Distancy constancy

Codes

	A	B	C	D		A	B	C	D
(a)	4	2	3	1	(b)	2	4	3	1
(c)	4	2	1	3	(d)	2	4	1	3

144 Match the following

List I (Researcher/ concept)	List II (Associated with)
A. Thomas Reid	1. Mind is capable of perceiving space
B. Helmholtz	2. Theory of space perception
C. Rundolf Lotze	3. Difference between sensation and perception
D. Visual acuity	4. Ability to discriminate fine difference

Codes

	A	B	C	D		A	B	C	D
(a)	4	1	2	3	(b)	4	1	3	2
(c)	2	3	1	4	(d)	3	2	1	4

145 Match the following

List I (Concept)	List II (Associated with)
A. Cochlea	1. Primitive feature of music
B. Rhythm	2. Snail-shaped
C. Phi-phenomenon	3. Stroboscopic motion
D. The law of proximity	4. Principle of organisation of perception

Codes

	A	B	C	D
(a)	2	1	3	4
(b)	4	3	1	2
(c)	4	2	3	1
(d)	1	4	2	3

Directions (Q. Nos. 146-165) *In the questions given below are two statements labelled as Assertion (A) and Reason (R). In the context of the two statements which one of the following is correct.*

Codes

(a) Both A and R are true and R is the correct explanation of A

(b) Both A and R are true, but R is not the correct explanation of A

(c) A is true, but R is false

(d) A is false, but R is true

146 **Assertion** (A) Hue is detectable at relatively low intensities, if the surrounding is coloured.

Reason (R) Colour detectability is higher in the figure sector than in the ground portion of the visual field.

147 **Assertion** (A) People in a cinema hall can be readily grouped into high, middle and low income categories.

Reason (R) Perceptual grouping may be done on the principles of proximity and similarity.

148 **Assertion** (A) The principles of perceptual organisation like proximity, similarity continuation, closure all contribute to from perception.

Reason (R) In a very general way, figures that 'belong together' are grouped together.

149 **Assertion** (A) Size constancy in visual perception develops as a function of age.

Reason (R) Size is acquired through learned usage of distance information.

150 **Assertion** (A) Perception occurs within a setting or an environment known as a context.

Reason (R) This context is made up of physical factor.

151 **Assertion** (A) Gestalt approach has been unsuccessful in explaining most of the facts of our pereceptual world.

Reason (R) Gestalt approach is based purely on hypothetical constructs isomorphism.

152 **Assertion** (A) Proximity is the perceptual tendency to group together objects that are near each other.

Reason (R) Proximity depends upon the depth cues.

153 Assertion (A) The most basic cue to depth arises from the geometric fact that an object of fixed actual size will project a progressively smaller image on to the retina as viewed from more distant.

Reason (R) The retinal area covered by the object increases at a faster rate than its size.

154 Assertion (A) Optic flow and motion parallax are sufficient to support high precision depth perception even when no other depth cues are available.

Reason (R) The success of lmax theaters is testament to the power of dynamic depth cues.

155 Assertion (A) Binocular disparity created by movement of the observer or by movement of objects in the environment.

Reason (R) The two eyes are observing the scene from slightly different positions.

156 Assertion (A) Perceptual hypothesis is an inference, about which distal stimuli could be responsible for the proximal stimuli sense.

Reason (R) Perceptual hypothesis is related to brain action.

157 Assertion (A) A distal stimulus is an object like a book which one look at.

Reason (R) A distal stimulus is different from proximal stimulus.

158 Assertion (A) In pattern recognition people take longer to differentiate similar letters than dissimilar letters.

Reason (R) Similar letters have many similar features.

159 Assertion (A) The phenomena of perceptual organisation, movement, depth and perceptual constancies support what we, but not how to explain.

Reason (R) Perceptual ability is innate, we are designed to perceive the way we do.

160 Assertion (A) Perceptual constancy occurs, when perception remains same, while sensation changes.

Reason (R) Perceptual constancy indicates that high level constructive processes are working during perception

161 Assertion (A) Visual perception is largely based on our experience with the visual environment.

Reason (R) In Ames' illusions the individual is forced to violate one set of assumptions about the spatial environment to preserve another.

162 Assertion (A) Colour of coal appears black inspite of changes in illumination.

Reason (R) Colour constancy is to some extent learnt.

163 Assertion (A) Gestalt psychologists provided evidence for problem-solving by insight.

Reason (R) The internal thinking works like explicit trial and error.

164 Assertion (A) Different people, exposed to the same stimulus, experience entirely different things.

Reason (R) Our internal representation of the world is filled with objects. Our perceptual processes rarely fail to successfully create objects out of physical input to the visual system.

165 Assertion (A) The visual illusions may be due to optical- retinal and cognitive components.

Reason (R) Distortion of depth and distance cues and misapplication of size constancy do not distort perception.

Directions (Q. Nos. 166-170) *Read the passage given below and answer the following questions*

One of the first experimental demonstrations of the effects of stimulus uncertainly in choice **RT** was provided by Markel continue as a single paragraph.

The result reflected an interesting regularity in the nature of RT, but the general applicability of this regularity did not become fully apparent until. **Hick** realised that the uncertainty produced by variations in the number of stimulus alternatives could be viewed in information theory terms by expressing the number of alternatives in bits. Consequently, he repeated Merkel's experiment using one to ten lamps arrayed in an irregular circle.

Hick found that in the language of information theory, RT was proportional to stimulus uncertainty. By and of itself, this was not a new discovery on Hick's part; it was merely a confirmation of Merkel's earlier finding , using a different scale for expressing the number of stimulus alternatives. However, by introducing the information metric into this problem, **Hick** made it possible to map a variety of ways of manipulating stimulus uncertainty into a common scale.

166 Who provided the first experimental demonstrations of the effects of stimulus uncertainty on choice RT?

(a) Markel (b) Hick
(c) Piter (d) Schlosberg

167 Which numerical is found in the stimuli?

(a) Arabic (b) English
(c) Roman (d) Arabic and Roman

168 **Who repeated Merkel's experiment?**
(a) Hick (b) Molber
(c) Rojer (d) Miller

169 **In which procedure Hick repeated Merker's experiment?**
(a) One to five lamps arranged in a regular circle
(b) One to ten lamps arranged in an irregular circle
(c) One to five lamps arranged in an irregular circle
(d) One to ten lamps arranged in regular circle

170 **Hick found that in the arrangement of information theory RT was proportionary to**
(a) stimulus uncertainly (b) stimulus certainly
(c) locus uncertainly (d) locus certainly

PREVIOUS YEARS' QUESTIONS

July 2018

1 **Which of the following explains the threshold Hypothesis regarding intelligence - creativity relationship ?**
(a) There is a positive correlation between intelligence and creativity.
(b) There is a positive correlation between intelligence and creativity upto a particular level of intelligence.
(c) There is a positive correlation between intelligence and creativity beyond a particular level of intelligence.
(d) There is a negative correlation between intelligence and creativity beyond a particular level of intelligence.

2 **Observation learning involves following processes. Arrange them in the correct sequence**
1. Attentional processes
2. Retention processes
3. Production processes
4. Motivational processes

Codes
(a) 1 → 2 → 3 → 4 (b) 1 → 4 → 2 → 3
(c) 4 → 1 → 2 → 3 (d) 1 → 2 → 4 → 3

3 **The percepts are based on**
1. What we sense 2. What we know
3. What we infer 4. What we conform

Codes
(a) 1 and 2 (b) 2 and 3
(c) 1, 2 and 3 (d) 1, 2 and 4

4 **Key issues in the study of environmental effects on intelligence are**
1. Reaction Range
2. Proximal and Distal Causation
3. Colinearity
4. Environment Sphere

Codes
(a) 1, 2 and 3 (b) 1, 2 and 4
(c) 2, 3 and 4 (d) 1, 3 and 4

5 **The factors that operate with deep levels of processing are**
1. Distinctiveness 2. Sameness
3. Elaboration 4. Physical contours

Codes
(a) 1 and 2 (b) 2 and 3 (c) 2 and 4 (d) 1 and 3

6 **Read the following statements labelled as Assertion (A) and Reason (R) and indicate your answer using the codes given below**

Assertion (A) Perception remains constant although the proximal sensation changes.

Reason (R) Our perceptual system has mechanisms that adjust our perception of the proximal stimulus.

Codes
(a) Both A and R are true and R is the correct explanation of A
(b) Both A and R are true, but R is not the correct explanation of A
(c) A is true, but R is false
(d) A is false, but R is true

7 **Match List I with List II and select the correct answer by choosing the codes given below**

List I (Concept)	List II (Explanation)
A. Convergence	1. If you see a distant mountain range on a crystal-clear day, it looks like as, it was only a few miles away.
B. Frame of reference	2. When the two images are fused into one overall image.
C. Stereoscopic vision	3. When we look at a distant object, the lines of vision from our eyes are parallel. Looking at a nearby object, the eyes turn in.
D. Aerial perspective	4. An internal perspective relative to which events are perceived.

Codes

	A	B	C	D		A	B	C	D
(a)	1	2	3	4	(b)	3	4	2	1
(c)	2	3	4	1	(d)	4	1	3	2

8 **Read the following statements labelled as Assertion (A) and Reason (R) and indicate your answer using the codes given below**

Assertion (A) According to two factor theory, cognitive appraisal of cues in the environment helps the individual label the emotions.

Reason (R) An individual is aroused when he confronts any emotion producing event.

Codes

(a) Both A and R are true and R is the correct explanation of A
(b) Both A and R are true, but R is not the correct explanation of A
(c) A is true, but R is false
(d) A is false, but R is true

9 **Whether we can be affected by stimuli that remain outside our conscious awareness has been examined by researches using a technique called**

(a) Cuing (b)Visualisatlon
(c) Imagery (d) Priming

10 **Match List I with List II and select the correct answer by choosing the codes given below**

List I (Concept)		List II (Description)
A. Physiological psychology	1.	Studies the psychological effects of brain damage in human patients.
B. Neuropsychology	2.	Studies the neural machanisms of behaviour by manipulating the nervous systems of non-human animals in controlled experiments.
C. Psychophysiology	3.	Studies the relation between physiological activity and psychological processes in human subjects by non-invasive physiological recording.
D. Cognitive neuroscience	4	Studies the neural mechanisms of human congnition, mainly by using functional brain imaging techniques.

Codes

	A	B	C	D		A	B	C	D
(a)	1	2	3	4	(b)	3	4	1	2
(c)	2	1	4	3	(d)	4	3	2	1

November 2017

11 **Which theory of emotion implies that every emotion is associated with a unique physiological reaction?**

(a) James - Lange theory
(b) Cannon - Bard theory
(c) Two factor theory
(d) Opponent - process theory

12 **According to Gibson's theory of perception**

(a) We directly perceive the environment. We do not need the aid of complex thought processes.
(b) We do not directly perceive the environment. We need the aid of complex thought processes.
(c) We perceive the environment using our intelligence.
(d) We do not connect what we perceive, to what we have stored in our mind.

13 **Motivation is best understood as a state that**

(a) reduces a drive
(b) aims at satisfying a biological need
(c) energises an organism to act
(d) energises and directs behaviour

14 **Which of the following depth cue is based on muscular feedback?**

(a) Texture gradients
(b) Motion parallax
(c) Accommodation
(d) Light and shadow

15 **Which of the following sequence is correctly arranged?**

(a) Incoming information → Rehearsal buffer → Selective attention
(b) Rehearsal buffer → Selective attention → Incoming information
(c) Selective attention → Rehearsal buffer → Incoming information
(d) Incoming information → Selective attention → Rehearsal buffer

16 **Binocular cues depend on**

1. combination of the images in the left and right retinas
2. the way two eyes work together
3. image in either right or left eye
4. difference between the images in the two eyes

Codes

(a) 1, 2 and 4 (b) 1, 3 and 4
(c) 3, 1 and 2 (d) 2, 3 and 4

17 **Which of the following theories represent thc mechanistic metaphor of motivation?**

1. Psychoanalytic
2. Ethological
3. Sociobiological
4. Expectancy - value

Codes

(a) 1, 2 and 3 (b) 2, 3 and 4
(c) 1, 3 and 4 (d) 1, 2, 3 and 4

18 **Match List I with List II and select the correct answer by choosing from the codes given below**

List I (Concept)		List II (Description)
A. Intrinsic motivation	1.	"I am really not feeling too good today. I may not be able to perform well."
B. Achievement motivation	2.	"I love to drive very fast, no matter what happens."
C. Self-handicapping	3.	"For me, accomplishing difficult tasks and meeting high standards of excellence is the top most priority."
D. Sensation - seeking	4.	"I go for swimming everyday. I just love it. I take out time from my tight study schedule."

Codes

	A	B	C	D		A	B	C	D
(a)	1	2	3	4	(b)	2	1	4	3
(c)	4	3	1	2	(d)	3	4	2	1

19 Match List I with List II and select the correct answer by choosing from the codes given below

List I (Concept)	List II (Explanation)
A. Inattentional blindness	1. Medium point of one's personal frame of reference
B. Habituation	2. Ingrained patterns of organisation and attention
C. Adaption level	3. Failure to perceive a stimulus that is in plain view, but not the focus of attention
D. Perceptual habits	4. Tendency to respond less to predictable and unchanging stimuli

Codes

	A	B	C	D		A	B	C	D
(a)	3	4	1	2	(b)	2	1	4	3
(c)	3	2	4	1	(d)	4	3	2	1

20 Read each of the following two statements labelled as Assertion (A) and Reason (R) and indicate your answer using the codes given below

Assertion (A) Some people perceive wolf as dog.

Reason (R) External features in a category of concepts are associated with each other.

Codes
(a) Both A and R are true and R is the correct explanation of A
(b) Both A and R are true, but R is not the correct explanation of A
(c) A is true, but R is false
(d) A is false, but R is true

21 Read each of the following two statements labelled as Assertion (A) and Reason (R) and indicate your answer using the codes given below

Assertion (A) Generally, performance is optimal when arousal is low.

Reason (R) On easy tasks performance becomes optimal.

Codes
(a) Both A and R are true and R is the correct explanation of A
(b) Both A and R are true, but R is not the correct explanation of A
(c) A is true, but R is false
(d) A is false, but R is true

22 Read each of the following two statements labelled as Assertion (A) and Reason (R) and indicate your answer using codes the given below

Assertion (A) Teacher's motivating style determines student's motivation for reading.

Reason (R) To enhance student's interest in reading, teacher may offer a reward for reading along with helpful feedback.

Codes
(a) Both A and R are true and R is the correct explanation of A
(b) Both A and R are true, but R is not the correct explanation of A
(c) A is true, but R is false
(d) A is false, but R is true

January 2017

23 A study shows that children from poor families drew large circles to represent a coin than the children from rich families. This is an example of
(a) perceptual constancy (b) perceptual distortion
(c) perceptual set (d) perceptual adaptation

24 The inputs from our sensory receptors are structured by
(a) selective principles (b) gestalt principles
(c) analytical principles (d) learning principles

25 The tendency for parallel lines to appear to converge on each other is termed as
(a) motion parallax (b) ponzo illusion
(c) linear perspective (d) aerial perspective

26 Length and intensity of lightwave play an important role in
(a) perception of colour and brightness
(b) perception of colour and illumination
(c) perception of constancy and brightness
(d) perception of brightness and illumination

27 Match List I with List II and select the correct answer by choosing the codes given below

List I (Concept)	List II (Explanation)
A. Rods	1. Two optic nerves from two retina join each other for a short distance
B. Cones	2. Do not distinguish colours
C. Blind spot	3. Good detail vision
D. Optic chiasm	4. Optic nerves exit the eyes

Codes

	A	B	C	D		A	B	C	D
(a)	2	3	1	4	(b)	2	3	4	1
(c)	3	2	1	4	(d)	1	2	3	4

28 Read the following two statements labelled as Assertion (A) and Reason (R) and Indicate your answer using the codes given below.

Assertion (A) People belonging to a particular group have some common perceptual patterns.

Reason (R) Personal experiences influence one's perception.

Codes

(a) Both A and R are true and R is the correct explanation of A
(b) Both A and R are true, but R is not the correct explanation of A
(c) A is true, but R is false
(d) A is false, but R is true

29 Read the following two statements labelled as Assertion (A) and Reason (R) and indicate your answer using the codes given below

Assertion (A) An infant often acts as if objects stop existing when they are moved out of his perceptual range.

Reason (R) The infant has not yet developed the object concept.

Codes

(a) Both A and R are true and R is the correct explanation of A
(b) Both A and R are true, but R is not the correct explanation of A
(c) A is true, but R is false
(d) A is false, but R is true

30 Read the following two statements lebelled as Assertion (A) and Reason (R) and indicate your answer using codes given below

Assertion (A) People often attain their visual experiences after many years of blindness.

Reason (R) Most of the knowledge of the world had come to them through the sense of touch.

Codes

(a) Both A and R are true and R is the correct explanation of A
(b) Both A and R are true, but R is not the correct explanation of A
(c) A is true, but R is false
(d) A is false, but R is true

July 2016

31 The light passes through the eye in which of the following sequence?

(a) Cornea, Pupil, Lens, Retina
(b) Cornea, Lens, Pupil, Retina
(c) Lens,Cornea, Pupil, Retina
(d) Pupil, Cornea, Lens,Retina

32 The difference in images in the two eyes is greater for objects that are close and smaller for distant objects is an example of

(a) binocular disparity
(b) convergence
(c) accommodation
(d) relative size

33 According to Trichromatic theory of colour vision, which of the following are the three types of cones?

(a) Red,yellow and blue
(b) Red, blue and green
(c) Yellow, blue and green
(d) Yellow, red and blue

34 Muller-Lyer illusion is likely to occur more in cultures characterised by

(a) people living in rectangular and square buildings
(b) people living in buildings which are round and have few corners
(c) people living in open spaces
(d) people living in caves

35 Match List I with List II and select the correct answer by choosing the codes given below

List I (System)		List II (Components)
A. Visual system	1.	Hammer, pinna, oval window
B. Auditory system	2.	Cornea, vitreous humour, aqueous humour
C. Neural system	3.	GABA, serotonin, dopamine
D. Messenger system	4.	Glial cells, myelin, neurillemma

Codes

	A	B	C	D
(a)	1	2	3	4
(b)	2	3	4	1
(c)	3	2	1	4
(d)	2	1	4	3

36 Read the following two statements labelled as Assertion (A) and Reason (R) and indicate your answer using the codes given below

Assertion (A) The creators of three dimensional movies simulate convergence by photographing a scene with two cameras placed a few inches apart.

Reason (R) Convergence is a binocular cue for perceiving depth by the extent to which the eyes converge inwards when looking at an object.

Codes

(a) Both A and R are true and R is the correct explanation of A
(b) Both A and R are true, but R is not the correct explanation of A
(c) A is true, but R is false
(d) A is false, but R is true

December 2015

37 The James-Lange Theory and the Cognitive Theory of Emotion disagree on whether

(a) specific brain centers are involved in specific emotions
(b) bodily feedback determines which emotion is felt
(c) individuals can judge their emotions accurately
(d) there is no any biological involvement in human emotions

38 Match List I with List II and select the correct answer by choosing the codes given below

List I (Cues)	List II (Perceptions)
A. Linear perspective	1. Our two eyes observe objects from slightly different positions
B. Aerial perspective	2. Parallel lines appears to converge at distance
C. Atmospheric perspective	3. Objects below the horizon appear near
D. Retinal disparity	4. Further away objects are less distinctly seen

Codes

	A	B	C	D		A	B	C	D
(a)	1	2	3	4	(b)	2	3	4	1
(c)	3	4	1	2	(d)	4	3	2	1

39 Read the following two statements labelled as Assertion (A) and Reason (R) and indicate your answer using the codes given below.

Assertion (A) A tree shall appear in same perceived size whether one views it from near or far point.

Reason (R) The size of retinal image remains invariant.

Codes

(a) Both A and R are true and R is the correct explanation of A
(b) Both A and R are true but R is not the correct explanation of A
(c) A is true, but R is false
(d) A is false, but R is true

June 2015

40 Visual cliff is a laboratory method for testing depth perception in

(a) infants (b) children
(c) adults (d) old age people

41 Which one of the following biases play an important role in stereotyping and prejudice?

(a) False consensus (b) Illusory correlation
(c) Priming (d) Confirmation

42 While travelling in a train, nearby objects appear to move faster in the opposite direction than do far away objects, this phenomena is called

(a) phi-phenomena (b) motion parallax
(c) autokinetic movement (d) perception of movement

43 Suppose Merry wants to know, if she can learn Spanish by playing some language tapes while she sleeps. Her question concerns the general topic of .... and according to the text, the answer would most likely be.......

(a) subliminal perception; may be
(b) signal detection; no
(c) subliminal perception; no
(d) signal detection; may be

44 Our brains construct our perceptions because

1. sensations are disassembled into information bits.
2. neuro muscular cues from the greater inward turn when the eyes view a near object.
3. brain reassembles information into its own functional model.
4. perception is merely projecting the world onto our brain.

Codes

(a) 1, 2 and 3 (b) 2, 3 and 4
(c) 1, 3 and 4 (d) 1, 2 and 4

45 People vary in their perceptual-cognitive styles, which may be due to

1. the degree to which their perceptions are flexible.
2. aspects of their personality.
3. rigid belief.
4. field dependence or independence.
5. motives.

Codes

(a) 1, 2, 3 and 4 (b) 2, 3, 4 and 5
(c) 3, 4, 5 and 1 (d) 5, 1, 2 and 4

46 Read the following two statements labelled as Assertion (A) and Reason (R) and indicate your answer using the codes given below.

Assertion (A) Retinal disparity is an important monocular cue in depth perception.

Reason (R) Convergence is a muscular cue in depth perception.

Codes

(a) Both A and R are true and R is the correct explanation of A
(b) Both A and R are true, but R is not the correct explanation of A
(c) A is true, but R is false
(d) A is false, but R is true

47 Read the following two statements labelled as Assertion (A) and Reason (R) and indicate your answer using the codes given below:

Assertion (A) In operant conditioning, the rat presses the bar spontaneously.

Reason (R) Shaping is a procedure in which rewards gradually guide an animal's behaviour toward a desired goal.

Codes

(a) Both A and R are true, and R is the correct explanation of A
(b) Both A and R are true, but R is not the correct explanation of A
(c) A is true, but R is false
(d) A is false, but R is true

December 2014

48 **The perception that one is worse off relative to those with whom one compares oneself refers to**
(a) constant deprivation (b) continuous deprivation
(c) marginal deprivation (d) relative deprivation

49 **From among the following who theorised mostly on the concept of 'achievement motivation'?**
(a) Rogers, CR (b) Julian Rotter
(c) David McClelland (d) Frankl, VE

50 **Match List I with List II and select the correct answer by choosing the codes given below**

List I (Theories)	List II (Explanations)
A. Doctrine of specific nerve energies	1. The basilar membrane vibrates as a whole to the frequency of the sound wave.
B. Frequency theory	2. The sensation elicited by stimulus depends primarily on the nerve excited and secondarily on the stimuli.
C. Purkinje effect	3. Refers to the tendency to perceive the simplest and the most stable figure of all possible alternatives.
D. Law of Pragnanz	4. The illumination decreases owing to the shift from photopic cone vision to scotopic rod vision.

Codes

	A	B	C	D		A	B	C	D
(a)	2	1	4	3	(b)	3	4	1	2
(c)	2	1	3	4	(d)	3	4	2	1

51 **Match List I with List II and select the correct answer by choosing the codes given below**

List I (Theories)	List II (Descriptions)
A. James-Lange	1. Triggering the feeling of pleasure and pain simultaneously.
B. Cannon-Bard	2. Emotional experience comprise of the physiological arousal and its cognitive labelling.
C. Opponent-process	3. Emotion arising stimulus simultaneously triggers physiological responses and the subjective experience of emotion.
D. Two-factor	4. Emotional experience refers to our awareness of our physiological responses to emotion arousing stimuli.

Codes

	A	B	C	D		A	B	C	D
(a)	4	3	2	1	(b)	4	2	3	1
(c)	3	2	4	1	(d)	3	4	1	2

52 **Read the following two statements labelled as Assertion (A) and Reason (R) and indicate your answer using the codes given below**

Assertion (A) Motion Parallax is the relative apparent motion of objects in the visual field as the viewer moves his head.

Reason (F) Motion Parallax is a monocular spatial cue.

Codes
(a) Both A and R are true and R is the correct explanation of A
(b) Both A and R are true, but R is not the correct explanation of A
(c) A is true, but R is false
(d) A is false, but R is true

53 **Read the following two statements labelled as Assertion (A) and Reason (R) and indicate your answer using the codes given below.**

Assertion (A) Freud's theory holds that many behaviours are caused by unconscious motivation. Personality is determined by biological drives of sex and aggression.

Reason (R) Personality differences results from variations in learning experiences.

Codes
(a) Both A and R are true and R is the correct explanation of A
(b) Both A and R are true, but R is not the correct explanation of A
(c) A is true, but R is false
(d) A is false, but R is true

June 2014

54 **After several visits to the doctor for chemotherapy, Anita finds that she begins to feel nauseous just sitting in the waiting room. According to classical conditioning, Anita's feeling of nausea in the absence of chemotherapy is**
(a) an unconditioned stimulus
(b) an unconditioned response
(c) a conditioned stimulus
(d) a conditioned response

55 **An oil painting itself can include all of the following cues to depth perception except**
(a) linear perspective
(b) retinal disparity
(c) texture gradient
(d) relative image size

56 **Arrange the following into correct sequence as per James-Lange Theory.**
1. Emotion producing situation
2. Feeling of emotion
3. Elicitation of emotional responses
4. The brain receives sensory feedback from the muscles and other organs

Codes
(a) 1 2 3 4 (b) 1 4 2 3
(c) 2 3 4 1 (d) 1 3 4 2

57 Which of the following do not belong to laws of perceptual grouping?

1. Law of figure and ground
2. Law of good continuation
3. Law of common fate
4. Law of closure
5. Law of proximity

Codes

(a) 1 and 5 (b) 2 and 4 (c) 3 and 5 (d) 1 and 3

58 Match List I with List II and select the correct answer by choosing the codes given below

List I (Function of Perception)	List II (Perceptual Issue)
A. Attention	1. Where is the something (object)?
B. Localisation	2. What do characterise that thing (the object)?
C. Recognition	3. Is there something?
D. Abstraction	4. What is that thing?

Codes

	A	B	C	D		A	B	C	D
(a)	4	1	3	2	(b)	2	1	3	4
(c)	2	1	4	3	(d)	3	1	4	2

Directions (Q. 59 and 60) *In the questions given below are two statements labelled as Assertion (A) and Reason (R). In the context of the two statements, which one of the following is correct?*

59 Assertion (A) Larger the image of an object on the retina, the closer it is judged to be. In addition, if an object is larger than other objects, it is often perceived as closer.

Reason (R) Retinal disparity provides an important cue for depth perception.

Codes

(a) Both A and R are true and R is the correct explanation of A
(b) Both A and R are true, but R is not the correct explanation of A
(c) A is true, but R is false
(d) A is false, but R is true

60 Assertion (A) Subliminal perception implies detection of a stimulus with a magnitude for below the absolute threshold.

Reason (R) Receptors always receive information and that is always perceived.

Codes

(a) Both A and R are true, and R is the correct explanation of A
(b) Both A and R are true, but R is not the correct explanation of A
(c) A is true, but R is false
(d) A is false, but R is true

ANSWERS

Exam Based Questions

1	(d)	2	(c)	3	(b)	4	(a)	5	(a)	6	(b)	7	(c)	8	(c)	9	(a)	10	(b)
11	(a)	12	(d)	13	(b)	14	(a)	15	(b)	16	(c)	17	(a)	18	(d)	19	(a)	20	(c)
21	(b)	22	(d)	23	(d)	24	(d)	25	(d)	26	(c)	27	(b)	28	(c)	29	(d)	30	(c)
31	(a)	32	(c)	33	(b)	34	(b)	35	(c)	36	(d)	37	(d)	38	(c)	39	(a)	40	(c)
41	(a)	42	(c)	43	(b)	44	(b)	45	(a)	46	(c)	47	(b)	48	(a)	49	(b)	50	(c)
51	(b)	52	(a)	53	(d)	54	(a)	55	(c)	56	(d)	57	(d)	58	(b)	59	(d)	60	(c)
61	(b)	62	(d)	63	(d)	64	(c)	65	(b)	66	(d)	67	(d)	68	(d)	69	(b)	70	(c)
71	(c)	72	(c)	73	(c)	74	(b)	75	(c)	76	(c)	77	(c)	78	(b)	79	(a)	80	(b)
81	(b)	82	(b)	83	(a)	84	(a)	85	(a)	86	(a)	87	(c)	88	(d)	89	(d)	90	(c)
91	(a)	92	(d)	93	(c)	94	(c)	95	(c)	96	(b)	97	(b)	98	(c)	99	(b)	100	(d)
101	(a)	102	(a)	103	(a)	104	(a)	105	(a)	106	(a)	107	(c)	108	(c)	109	(b)	110	(b)
111	(d)	112	(a)	113	(a)	114	(c)	115	(d)	116	(a)	117	(a)	118	(d)	19	(b)	120	(d)
121	(d)	122	(c)	123	(a)	124	(c)	125	(a)	126	(c)	127	(c)	128	(c)	129	(c)	130	(a)
131	(b)	132	(c)	133	(a)	134	(a)	135	(a)	136	(d)	137	(b)	138	(a)	139	(c)	140	(c)
141	(c)	142	(d)	143	(c)	144	(d)	145	(a)	146	(a)	147	(a)	148	(a)	149	(a)	150	(b)
151	(b)	152	(c)	153	(c)	154	(b)	155	(a)	156	(c)	157	(c)	158	(a)	159	(a)	160	(b)
161	(a)	162	(b)	163	(b)	164	(c)	165	(c)	166	(a)	167	(d)	168	(a)	169	(b)	170	(a)

Previous Yearr' Questions

1	(c)	2	(b)	3	(c)	4	(b)	5	(b)	6	(a)	7	(d)	8	(a)	9	(b)	10	(a)
11	(a)	12	(a)	13	(d)	14	(c)	15	(d)	16	(a)	17	(a)	18	(c)	19	(a)	20	(a)
21	(a)	22	(a)	23	(c)	24	(b)	25	(c)	26	(a)	27	(b)	28	(a)	29	(a)	30	(a)
31	(a)	32	(a)	33	(b)	34	(d)	35	(d)	36	(b)	37	(b)	38	(b)	39	(c)	40	(a)
41	(b)	42	(b)	43	(c)	44	(c)	45	(d)	46	(d)	47	(d)	48	(d)	49	(c)	50	(a)
51	(b)	52	(b)	53	(b)	54	(d)	55	(b)	56	(d)	57	(d)	58	(d)	59	(b)	60	(c)

Theories and Perspectives on Perception

The way an individual selects, organises and interprets sensory input to achieve a firm hold of the surroundings is influenced by culture, ecology, perceptual style and approach adopted for recognising the pattern. The way in which given information is perceived depends on the environment and lifestyle of an individual.

Signal Detection Theory (SDT)

One of the early goals of psychologists was to measure the sensitivity of our sensory systems. This activity which led to the development of the idea of a threshold, the least intense amount of stimulation needed for a person to be able to see, hear, feel, or detect the stimulus.

However, this concept suffered from a demerit that even though the level of stimulation remained constant, people were inconsistent in detecting the stimulus. Thus, the signal detection process is influenced by factors other than the sensitivity of sense receptor. There is no single, fixed value below which a person never detects the stimulus and above which the person always detects it. An approach to resolving this dilemma is provided by Signal Detection Theory which abandons the idea of a threshold.

Signal Detection Theory is a psychological theory regarding a threshold of sensory detection. This theory suggests that there are no absolute thresholds for sensations.

Components of SDT

The following three components form basis of signal detection theory:

(i) **Internal Activity** Internal activity refers to the neural activity going on in the body all the time, so is called (neural) NOISE.

(ii) **External Activity** External activity refers to all the activity coming in through the senses. But when it comes into the body, internal noise does not stop, the external adds to the internal= NOISE + SIGNAL

(iii) **Cut-off Point** It refers to the decision-making point for detecting a stimulus.

In this Chapter

Assumptions of Signal Detection Theory

Signal detection theory rests upon following assumptions

(i) SDT recognises that observers are both sensors and decision makers, and that these are distinct processes that can be measured using separate indices, sensitivity and response bias/criterion.

(ii) In making a decision regarding the occurrence of an event, an observer adopts a decision criterion that sets the minimum value of the evidence variable that is required for the person to make a 'yes' response.

(iii) Neurons are constantly sending information to the brain, even when no external stimuli are present. This is called internal *neural noise*. The level of neural noise fluctuates constantly. When a faint external stimulus called a *signal* occurs, it creates a neural response which adds to internal noise. In the environment, this can take the form of acoustic noise (e.g. static) or any physical properties of stimuli that render the signal to be detected less salient. The brain must decide whether the neural activity it is getting reflects noise alone, or whether there was also a signal.

(iv) The noise that occurs is normally distributed. When a signal is present, it has the effect of shifting the distribution upward along the scale of the evidence variable. Perceptual sensitivity is independent of the criterion the observer sets (*i.e.* the response bias).

Processes Involved in Signal Detection Theory

The Signal Detection Theory is a major theoretical advance that combines detection theory with statistical decision theory. *The detection performance is based on a sensory process and a decision process.*

(i) **The Sensory Process** transforms the physical stimulus energy into an internal representation. The sensory process is characterised by a sensitivity parameter. Sensitivity is the ability to distinguish the presence of a signal from its absence.

(ii) **The Decision Process** decides what response to make based on this internal representation. The response can be a simple yes or no ("yes, the stimulus was present" or "no, the stimulus was not present") or a more elaborate response, such as a rating of the confidence that the signal was present. The decision process is characterised by a response criterion or response bias parameter.

Bias is extent to which one response is more probable than other. It is independent of insensitivity.

Signal Detection Theory involves treating detection of the stimulus as a decision-making process, part of which is determined by the nature of the stimulus, by how sensitive a person is to the stimulus, and by cognitive factors. Thus, a person will be able to detect more intense sounds or lights more easily than less intense stimuli. Further, a more sensitive person requires less stimulus intensity than a less sensitive person would.

Finally, when a person is quite uncertain as to whether the stimulus was present, the individual will decide based on what kind of mistake in judgment is worse: to say that no stimulus was present when there actually was one or to say that there was a stimulus when, in reality, there was none.

For example, suppose a person is expecting an important visitor, someone that it would be unfortunate to miss. As time goes on, the person begins to 'hear' the visitor and may open the door, only to find that nobody is there. This person is 'detecting' a stimulus, or signal, that is not there because it would be worse to miss the person than to check to see if the individual is there, only to find that the visitor has not yet arrived.

In a typical sensory experiment that involves a large number of trials, an observer must try to detect a very faint sound or light that varies in intensity from clearly below normal detection levels to clearly above. The person responds positively (*i.e.* there is a stimulus) or negatively (*i.e.,* there is no stimulus). There are two possible responses, "Yes" and "No." There are also two different possibilities for the stimulus, either present or absent.

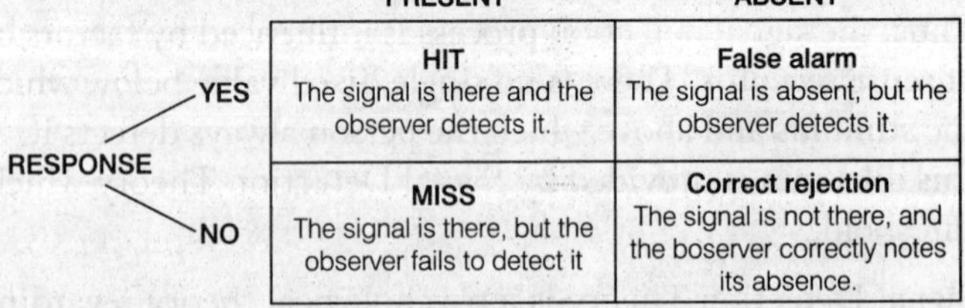

RESPONSE	PRESENT	ABSENT
YES	HIT The signal is there and the observer detects it.	False alarm The signal is absent, but the observer detects it.
NO	MISS The signal is there, but the observer fails to detect it	Correct rejection The signal is not there, and the boserver correctly notes its absence.

One of the Tool developed in SDT is described beelow:

Relative Operating Characteristic (ROC) Curve

The ROC curve is an analytic tool developed in SDT, which provides graphical and statistical representations of important decision factors: discrimination ability (area under the ROC curve) and decision thresholds (points plotted on the ROC curve or slope of the ROC curve). The

ROC graph is a plot of the proportion of hits against the proportion of false alarms for a specified number of decisions. The advantage of ROC curves is that they capture all aspects of Signal Detection theory in one graph. The more the curve bends up to the right, the better the sensitivity.

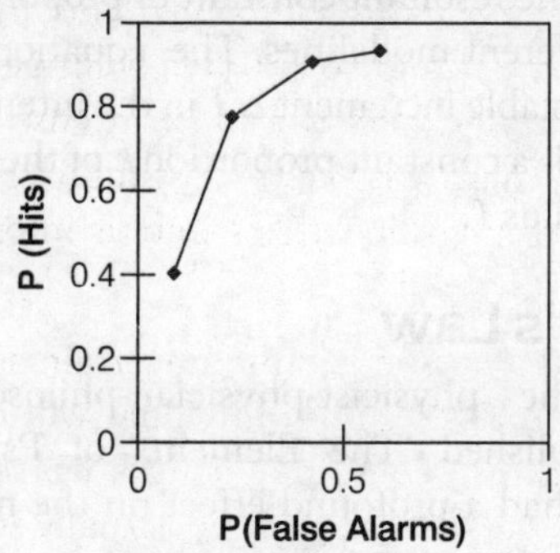

Applications of Signal Detection Theory

Following are the applications of signal detection theory

(i) **Military applications** SDT is employed to optimize the-use of radar, sonar, seismic detectors, and laser radar, as well as in evaluating human performance in activities ranging from visual observation techniques to air combat.

(ii) **Psychology and Human Factors** In the field of psychological research, SDT has been applied to a broad range of psychological processes, including perception, memory, forecast accuracy, human vigilance and even the detection of social cues.

(iii) **Medical Diagnosis** In radiology, SDT is utilised both to assess the practitioner's interpretation of radiographic output and to evaluate the diagnostic accuracy of various radiographic technologies. *For example,* SDT methodology has helped to determine that computed tomography is diagnostically superior to radio nuclide scanning for tumor detection.

(iv) **Psychiatric Diagnosis** SDT methodology has been used extensively in the assessment and development of tests and measures to facilitate psychiatric diagnosis.

(v) **Dentistry** SDT methodology has been used to evaluate endodontic techniques as well as to compare the effectiveness of different imaging and diagnostic procedures.

(vi) **Clinical Chemistry** Chemists utilize SDT to identify and assess various chemical parameters. *For example,* SDT has been used to identify chemical indicators of organ rejection and to distinguish cancerous lesions.

(vii) **Engineering** SDT has found important uses in engineering in such areas as acoustical engineering, electrical engineering, and telecommunications.

(viii) **Forensic Sciences** SDT in the forensic sciences contributes to deepening the understanding of decision-making in forensic examinations, improving the quality and accuracy of the conclusions resulting from those examinations, evaluating the effectiveness of alternative technologies and procedures and quantifying and analysing the diagnostic capabilities of forensic examiners, their instruments, and their procedures.

Multidimensional Signal Detection Theory (MSDT)

It is an extension of Signal Detection Theory to more than one dimension, with each dimension representing a different source of information along with the 'signal' that is registered.

The development of MSDT was motivated by psychologists who wanted to study information processing of more realistic, multidimensional stimuli *e.g.* the shape and colour of geometric objects or pitch, loudness and timbre of tones.

The typical questions of interest are the dimensions (*e.g.* colour and shape of an object) processed independently or does the perception of one dimension (*e.g.* colour) depend on the perception of the second (shape) and if so, what is the nature of their dependence?

MSDT is also known as General Recognition Theory (Ashby and Town send 1986) or Decision Bound Theory (e.g. Ashby and Maddox 1994)

Aspects of Multidimensional Signal Detection Theory

In Multidimensional Signal Detection Theory (MSDT), each of several m-dimensional stimuli is represented by an m-dimensional joint density and decision bounds demarcate the associated responses. Each joint density yields (a) marginal densities for each dimension and (b) conditional densities for each dimension conditioned on the observer's response to the other dimension(s).

These two types of densities give rise to sensitivity, d and response bias, β, parameters for each dimension-marginal and conditional d's and +β s.

These parameters are related to three types of dimensional independence defined in MSDT

(i) **Perceptually Separable** (PS) If perception of a dimension is the same regardless of how the stimuli vary on the other dimension(s).

(ii) **Perceptually Independent** (PI) If, within a single stimulus, the perception of one dimension is stochastically independent of the perception of the other dimension(s).

(iii) **Decisionally Separable** (DS) If the decision process for one dimension is unaffected by the other dimension(s).

The Differential Threshold

The differential threshold is a measure of the smallest difference between two stimuli that can be detected. It is traditionally defined as the difference in the magnitude between two stimuli, usually a standard and a comparison stimulus *i.e.* detected 50% of the time. Like the absolute threshold the differential threshold is a statical concept of some questionable validity.

Point of Subjective Equality (PSE)

A psychophysical measure related to the differential threshold is a measure of the estimate that the magnitude of two stimuli are perceptually equal. It is called the Point of Subjective Equality (PSE). PSE's have a wide range of applicability.

The PSE is defined as the magnitude of a comparison stimulus that is equally likely to be judged greater or less than the magnitude of a standard stimulus. In practice, the PSE lies half way between the stimulus just noticeably smaller than the standard and the one just noticeable larger.

Weber's Law

Some of the background on this issue is quite significant in the history of the measurement of sensation. In 1834, **EH Weber**, a German physiologist, investigated the ability of subjects to perform discrimination tasks, what he noted was that discrimination is a relative rather than an absolute judgement matter. That is, the amount of change, increase or decrease in a stimulus necessary to detect it as different is proportional to the magnitude of the stimulus.

There is a fundamental principle of relative sensitivity involved referred to as Weber's fraction symbolised as follows

$$\frac{\Delta I}{I} = K$$

Where I is the magnitude of the stimulus intensity at which the threshold is obtained, ΔI is the differential threshold value or the increment of intensity which, when added to the stimulus intensity I, produces a just noticeable difference in d and k is the resultant constant of proportionality, which differs for different modalities. The equation states that the smallest detectable increment ΔI in the intensity continuum of a stimulus is a constant proportion k of the intensity of the original stimulus I.

Fechner's Law

In 1860, the physicist-physician-philosopher **Gustav Fechner** published 'The Elements of Psychophysics' a treatise that had a profound effect on the measurement of sensation and perception.

In it, he proposed that the differential threshold or the individual as described by Weber could be used as a standard unit to measure the subjective magnitude of sensation to the magnitude of the stimulus. He began with the assumption that for a given sensory modality, all individuals represent subjectively equal units of sensation.

Under the assumption that all individuals are psychologically equal, it follows that as the number of individual grows arithmetically, stimulus intensity increases geometrically. This arithmetic to geometric progression reduces mathematically to a logarithmic relation *i.e.* the magnitude of a sensation is a logarithmic function of the stimulus or

$$S = K \log I$$

This states that the subjective magnitude or sensation (s) is proportional (k, a constant, which includes the Weber function) to the logarithm of the physical intensity of the stimulus (I).

Steven's Power Law

More recent considerations of this issue contend that the relation between stimulus magnitude and sensory magnitude is not logarithmic. Indeed one paper disputing Fechner's logarithmic equation is pointedly filled: "To honor Fechner and repeal his law".

The mathematical relationship called the *power law* or Steven's power law shows a reasonably good applicability for a wide range of data relating to the magnitude of sensation. According to the Power Law, sensory or subjective magnitude grows in proportion to the physical intensity of the stimulus raised to a power which can be mathematically stated as,

$$S = KI^b$$

Where 'b' is an exponent that is constant for given sensory dimension and set of experimental conditions and S, I and K stand for sensation, intensity and a constant, respectively.

By using a power law formulation it is possible to show that the sensory modalities and perceptual task differ from each other in the extent to which the rate of sensation changes with changes in intensity.

Subliminal Perception

Subliminal Perception or cognition is a subset of unconscious cognition where the forms of unconscious congition also include attending to one signal in a noisy environment while unconsciously keeping track of other signals (*e.g.* one voice out of many in a crowded room) and tasks done automatically (*e.g.* driving a car).

It is the registration of awareness. Greenwald believed his own study and the review of large number of other studies has found a clear cut support for subliminal perception. Hence, the dominant view is that subliminal perception is the genuine phenomena worth of empirical investigation.

Greenwald and **Benstein** in their respective studies found that effects of subliminal studies turned out to be as subliminal as stimuli themselves. In other words, it generally produces weak effects.

These effects can be detected only by very precise measurement under carefully controlled laboratory condition, in which subjects were asked to focus their undivided attention on the visual and auditory materials that contain subliminal stimulus. Also, these effects are theoretically interesting and they appear unlikely to have much practical importance.

Greenwald et al evaluated the efficacy of the subliminal self help taps designed to improve memory and self esteem.

Subliminal Message

Subliminal messages are defined as signals below the Absolute Threshold Level (ATL) of our conscious awareness, On the other hand stimuli perceived by conscious mind is supraliminal stimuli.

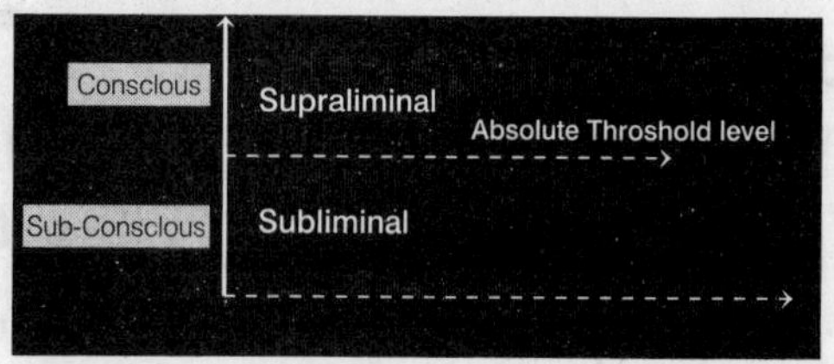

The subliminal messages target two senses-visual and auditory.

(i) **Visual Subliminal Messages** The messages that target visual senses are visual subliminal messages. *These are classified as*
- **Sub visual** The messages that are flashed very quickly (usually few milliseconds) that viewers don't perceive them are called *subvisual*.
- **Embeds** The static messages embedded in an unchanging visual environment hiding in our plain sight are known as **embeds.**

(b) **Auditory Subliminal Messages** The messages that target auditory senses are auditory subliminal messages. *These are classified as–*
- **Subaudible** The low volume messages inserted into louder audio files so that they cannot be heard are called *subaudible messages.*
- **Backmasking** The video message recorded backwards so that original message is disguised when playing it forward is known as *backamsking.*

Factors Related to Subliminal Perception

Following factors influence subliminal perception

- **Message Complexity** A message with low complexity is more likely to be processed sub-consciously than more complex messages. The usage of single worded messages or simple graphical messages can be used to increase the effectiveness of subliminal stimuli.
- **Familiarity** The familiarity with the message can increase the sub-conscious processing of the message. A familiar message increases the effectiveness of subliminal stimuli. For example, subliminal banner effectiveness can be increased when the targeted consumer knows brand or product.
- **Goal Relevance** The extent to which a certain goal or message is relevant determine its influence on subliminal effectiveness. A relevant message is more likely to be processed sub-consciously than less relevant message.

Methodologies of Subliminal Perception

Experimenters have been quite ingenious in the variety of methods they have devised in their attempts to demonstrate subliminal perception. For the purpose of evaluation, *these various experimental approaches have been classified into the following basic methodologies*

Subliminal Conditioning

In subliminal conditioning, the experimenter attempts to condition a non-verbal response to a stimulus whose intensity is lower than capable of eliciting a discriminated verbal report.

The conditioned response may be either voluntary or an autonomic response, although the latter is more typical (*e.g.* galvanic skin response, heart rate, pupillary contraction). From an over all evaluation the numerous studies, that have attempted to demonstrate subliminal conditioning, have been unsuccessful.

Subliminal Stimulation and Behaviour

Since the effect of the subliminal stimulation is expected to be distorted or transformed or to appear in a symbolic rather than the identical form of the stimulation, the detection of this subliminal influence poses severe methodological problem.

Numerous sources of artifact are present in such experimental designs, as have been pointed out by Johnson and Erikson. Interpretation of these experimenters in most cases is to ensure that the stimulation was indeed incidental or to specify the criterion by which they determined that the stimulation was subliminal.

In many of the experiments it is quite obvious that the stimuli were not subliminal and the subject's lack of awareness of the stimulation was due to the nature of the experiment, which directed his attention to other stimuli.

In this case the experiments are more concerned with incidental stimulation than with subliminal stimulation and bear a strong resemblance both methodologically and conceptually to the traditional work on incidental memory.

Information Processing Approach

Information Processing Approach is based on the idea that humans process the information they recive, rather than merely responding to stimuli. It sees the individual as a processor of information, in much the same way as computer takes in information and follows a program to produce an output. The information processing approach is based on a number of assumptions, *including*

- Information made available by the environment is processed by a series of processing systems (*e.g.* attention, perception, short-term memory).
- These processing systems transform or alter the information in systematic ways.
- The aim of research is to specify the processes and structures that underlie cognitive performance.
- Information processing in humans resembles that in computers.

Essentially, a computer codifies (*i.e.* changes) information, stores information, uses information and produces an output (retrieves info). The idea of information processing was adopted by cognitive psychologists as a model of how human thought works.

For example The eye receives visual information and codes information into electric neural activity which is feedback to the brain where it is stored and coded. This information can be used by other parts of the brain relating to mental activities such as memory, perception and attention. The output (*i.e.* behaviour) might be *e.g.* to read what you can see on a printed page.

Hence, the information processing approach characterises thinking as the environment providing input of data, which is then transformed by our senses.

The information can be stored, retrieved and transformed using 'mental programs', with the results being behavioural responses. Cognitive psychology has influenced and integrated with many other approaches and areas of study to produce *e.g.* social learning theory, cognitive neuropsychology and artificial intelligence.

Information Processing and Attention

When we are selectively attending to one activity, we tend to ignore other stimulation, although our attention can be distracted by something else, like the telephone ringing or someone using our name. Psychologists are interested in what makes us attend to one thing rather than another (selective attention); why we sometimes switch our attention to something that was previously unattended (*e.g.* Cocktail Party Syndrome) and how many things we can attend to at the same time (attentional capacity). One way of conceptualising attention is to think of humans as information processors who can only process a limited amount of information at a time without becoming overloaded.

Broadbent and others in the 1950s adopted a model of the brain as a limited capacity information processing system, through which external input is transmitted.

Information Processing Models

Information processing models consist of a series of stages or boxes which represent stages of processing. Arrows indicate the flow of information from one stage to the next.

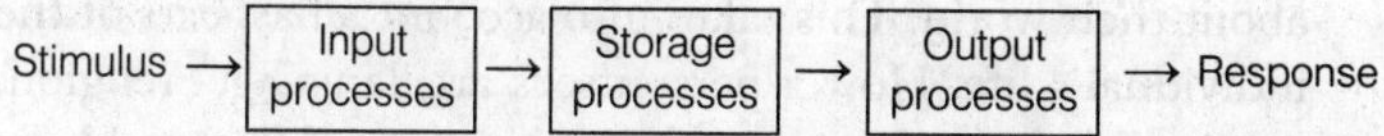

Input processes are concerned with the analysis of the stimuli. Storage processes cover everything that happens to stimuli internally in the brain and can include coding and manipulation of the stimuli. Output processes are responsible for preparing an appropriate response to a stimulus.

A number of models of attention within the Information Processing Framework have been proposed including:

- Broadbent's Filter Model (1958).
- Treisman's Attenuation Model (1964).
- Deutsch and Deutsch's Late Selection Model (1963).

However, there are a number of evaluative points to bear in mind when studying these models and the information processing approach in general. *These include*

(i) The information processing models assume serial processing of stimulus inputs. Serial processing effectively means one process has to be completed before the next starts. Parallel processing assumes some or all processes involved in a cognitive task(s) occur at the same time. There is evidence from dual task experiments that parallel processing is possible. It is difficult to determine whether a particular task is processed in a serial or parallel fashion as it probably depends

- On the processes required to solve a task.
- The amount of practice on a task.
- Parallel processing is probably more frequent when someone is highly skilled *e.g.* a skilled typist thinks several letters ahead, a novice focuses on just 1 letter at a time.

(ii) The analogy between human cognition and computer functioning adopted by the information processing approach is limited. Computers can be regarded as information processing systems in so far as they

- Combine information presented with stored information to provide solutions to a variety of problems.
- Most computers have a central processor of limited capacity and it is usually assumed that capacity limitations affect the human attentional system.

But,

- The human brain has the capacity for extensive parallel processing and computers often rely on serial processing.
- Humans are influenced in their cognitions by a number of conflicting emotional and motivational factors.

(iii) The evidence for the theories/models of attention which come under the information processing approach is largely based on experiments under controlled, scientific conditions. Most laboratory studies are artificial and could be said to lack ecological validity. In everyday life, cognitive processes are often linked to a goal (*e.g.* you pay attention in class because you want to pass the examination), whereas in the laboratory the experiments are carried out in isolation from other cognitive and motivational factors. Although these laboratory experiments are easy to interpret, the data may not be applicable to the real world outside the laboratory.

Using the Information Processing Approach in the Classroom

Following steps are required to be taken for using Information Processing Approach in the classroom

(i) Gain the students' attention.
- Use cues to signal when you are ready to begin.
- Move around the room and use voice inflections.

(ii) Bring to mind relevant prior learning.
- Review previous day's lesson.
- Have a discussion about previously covered content.

(iii) Point out important information.
- Provide handouts.
- Write on the board or use transparencies.

(iv) Present information in an organised manner.
- Show a logical sequence to concepts and skills.
- Go from simple to complex when presenting new material.

(v) Show students how to categorise (chunk) related information.

- Present information in categories.
- Teach inductive reasoning.

(vi) Provide opportunities for students to elaborate on new information.

- Connect new information to something already known.
- Look for similarities and differences among concepts.

(vii) Show students how to use coding when memorising lists.

- Make up silly sentence with first letter of each word in the list.
- Use mental imagery techniques such as the keyword method.

(viii) Provide for repetition of learning.

- State important principles several times in different ways during presentation of information .
- Have items on each day's lesson from previous lesson.
- Schedule periodic reviews of previously learned concepts and skills.

(ix) Provide opportunities for over-learning of fundamental concepts and skills.

- Use daily drills for arithmetic facts.
- Play form of trivial pursuit with content related to class.

Culture and Perception

Culture influences greatly how an individual perceives the world.

Domination of Culture Over an Individual

Group action which, means working with other people, is the dominant factor in society. In business, some individuals may be individual proprietors (running their own single employee business), but they still have to sell products or services to other people. An individual can be single in terms of relationship, but there are many areas in that person's life where they are part of a group.

One membership that all people share is that of culture. Cultural membership is better explained as people who share common features and knowledge that are demonstrated in elements such as artistic accomplishments, language, religion, food and social characteristics. culture involves how a person lives, speaks, interacts with others and what individuals create, but perception considers how that individual sees the world, Thus culture plays a critical role in how people see the world. This is called *cultural perception.*

Cultural perception is how people gather information, learned within their specific culture, to inform themselves about their world. This takes into account all aspects of the individual's life. How a person sees art, language, religion, etc. is all informed by how those elements of the world are seen within the context of their culture.

Culture Shapes an Individual

It means that the culture in which the individual was raised will paint how they see the world.

If the overall culture is restrictive and skeptical of others, it could lead the individual to have the same view. However, as an individual matures and sees the value of other cultures, they may have a more expansive view, especially if the culture, the individual is originally from, values experiences from other cultures.

Interpersonal influence and adjustment play a crucial role in structuring social interactions across cultures. However, not much is known about whether their consequences are culturally contingent.

Overall, the findings support a culturally contingent situation and cognition approach, which highlights not only interpersonal fundations of perceptual styles, but also the role which culture plays in prescribing meaning to interpersonal interactions.

Theories Describing Cultural Variations in Perception

The cultural variations in perception is influenced by following theories

Ecological and Semantic Approach

- **Ecological Approach** It explain cultural variations in perception by referring to the habitat the natural and social environments as well as economy and associated livelihood of a given culture.
- **Semantic Approach** It explains that people perceive the world not by accessing the raw reality but by referring to the meaning that has been historically maintained and inter-subjectively shared by members of a given culture, thus creating a socio-cultural reality.

Independent v/s Interdependent View of Self

- **Independent View of Self** involves conception of the self as an autonomous, independent person. The focus is mainly on self-related goals and needs and their self-perception primarily comprises unique personal traits and attributes with de-emphasis on others.
- **Interdependent View of Self** perceives an individual not as separate from the social context but as more connected and less differentiated from others. The focus is on inter-personal domain, the opinions or reactions of others and how their public self appears to the rest of society.

High Context Versus Low Context Cultures

The concept of high context and low context cultures was popularised by Edward T Hall.

- **Low Context Cultures** are those in which little of the meaning is determined by the context as the message is encoded in the explicit code. In this the verbal messages are elaborated, detailed, highly specific as well as redundant. In this the person is independent of circumstances or of personal relations who can move from group to group, from setting to setting without significant changes.
- **High Context Cultures** are those in which less has to be said or written because more of the meaning is in the physical environment or already shared by people. In this most of the information is either in the physical context or internalised in the person. It decreases the perception of self as separate from the group. In this the person is connected, fluid and conditional.

Individualism V/S Collectivism

- **Individualism** perceives people as autonomous individuals with distinctive features striving for singularity. It places the highest value on personal goals and individual freedom to express true self. It evaluates communication using direct and explicit styles.
- **Collectivism** perceive people to be humble, conform to others, wishes, attend to others' needs and consider how their own actions reflect on the in-group's image, balance and collective well-being. It evaluates communication using indirect or implicit style.

Implications of Cultural Variations in Perception

The differences in culture, *leads to variations in perception which has following implications*

(i) Cross cultural examination of human perception describes
   - mechanisms that are universally shared by humans.
   - mechanisms that are socio-culturally shaped through experience and can differ substantially across cultures.
   - extent to which perception is flexibly structured and influenced by systems associated with experience.

(ii) Cultural malleability in perception can influence neural activity of higher and lower cognitive purposes and underlying brain functions and neural substrates.

(iii) It helps in comprehensively explaining relationship between perception and social cognition such as casual attribution, self perception, judgement, inference and categorisation.

Various Examples of Culture and Perception

A few striking examples of impact of culture on perception and how individuals raised in diverse cultures can sense the world differently.

- **Marshall Segall** and his associates (Segall, Campbell and Herskovits, 1966) analysed that inhabitants of forest or rural areas can sense crooked and slanted lines more accurately when compared to the residents of the urban areas. It brings to light that the rural and urban people sense the same event differently because of their diverse cultural learning.
- In another case, the Africans dwelling in dense forests, constantly experienced verticality and developed a tendency to over estimate it. The Westerners, living in an environment characterised by right angles, grew a tendency to underestimate the length of lines characterised by enclosure *e.g.* arrow head. **Hudson**, 1960 confirmed and approved this outcome in several of his studies.
- In the Indian scenario **D Sinha** and **RC Mishra** have carried out several studies on pictorial perception. They used a variety of pictures with people from diverse cultural settings, such as hunters and gatherers, living in forests, farmers living in the rural areas and the employed people in urban areas. They analysed that interpretation of pictures is strongly related to cultural experiences of people.

  While people in general could recognise familiar objects in pictures, the people, less exposed to pictures had difficulty in the interpretation of actions or events depicted in them (Mishra 1997, 2000).

- According to **Nisbett** and **Miyamoto** (2005), Americans have more analytical visual perception than Asians, who adopt more holistic approach. While Americans pay attention to details, the Asians rely on larger picture. Americans examine object in isolation while Asians are more sensitive to context.

Perceptual Style

Human beings have five senses-sight, hearing, touch, taste and smell. The way an individual takes in information through these five senses and make this information meaningful to himself is known as *perceptual style.* There are seven specific perceptual styles through which people perceive the world around them, with each relying on one sense more than the others.

The seven perceptual styles are as follows

Perceptual Style	Major Sense Organ Involved	Characteristics
Visual Style	Eye	This perceptual style involves observing people and situations. The information is extracted by seeing things and not just hearing them. Slides, pictures, demonstrations, graphs, tables and overhead transparencies are useful ways of extracting information in this style.
Print Oriented Style	Eye	This perceptual style involves obtaining information by reading and writing. Reading books, magazines, or journal articles helps in retaining information.
Aural Style	Ears	This perceptual style involves extracting information by listening carefully and rarely speaking. Listening to audiotapes of popular speakers or books is way to obtain information via aural style.
Kinesthetic Style	Touch	This perceptual style involves concentrating and obtaining information by making movements such as fidgeting, knitting, doodling, or wood carving. Kinesthetically oriented people while speaking often use hand motions to describe what they are saying,
Haptic Style	Touch	This perceptual style involves gaining information through the sense of touch by feeling objects or touching things.
Interactive Style		This perceptual style involves extracting information by verbalising the thoughts and feelings. Small-group discussions, lively question-and-answer sessions, and debates are techniques that involve obtaining information through interactive style.
Olfactory Style	Smell and Taste	This perceptual style involves extracting information through the sense of smell or taste. The smell and taste are associated with specific past memories to obtain information.

Pattern Recognition

Pattern recognition is the process of recognising patterns by using machine learning algorithm. Pattern recognition can be defined as the classification of data based on knowledge already gained or on statistical information extracted from patterns and/or their representation. Pattern recognition when information from the environment is received and entered into short-term memory, causing automatic activation of a specific content of long term memory.

Pattern recognition is driven by following theories

(i) **Template Matching Theory of Pattern Recognition** The theory defines perception as a fundamentally recognition-based process. This theory assumes that every perceived object is stored as a 'template' into long-term memory. The incoming information is compared to these templates to form one single conceptual understanding.

(ii) **Prototype Matching Theory of Pattern Recognition** This theory compares incoming sensory input to one average prototype. It proposes that exposure to a series of related stimuli leads to the creation of 'typical' prototype based on their shared features. Thus, it reduces the number of stored templates by standardising them into a single representation. The prototype supports perceptual flexibility, because unlike in template matching, it allows for variability in the recognition of novel stimuli.

(iii) **Feature Analysis Theory of Pattern Recognition** This theory proposes that the nervous system sorts and filters incoming stimuli to allow the human (or animal) to make sense of the information. In the organism, this system is made up of feature detectors, which are individual neurons, or groups of neurons, that encode specific perceptual features. The most basic feature detectors respond to simple properties of the stimuli. Further along the perceptual pathway, higher organised feature detectors are able to respond to more complex and specific stimuli properties. When features repeat or occur in a meaningful sequence, one is able to identify these patterns because of the feature detection system.

(iv) **Recognition by Components (RBC) Theory of Pattern Recognition** This theory, first proposed by Irving Biederman, focuses on the bottom-up features of the stimuli being processed. It states that humans recognise objects by breaking them down into their basic 3D geometric shapes called geons (i.e. cylinders, cubes, cones, etc.). RBC suggests that there are fewer than 36 unique geons that when combined can form a virtually unlimited number of objects. *According to this theory an individual identifies an object because of following two properties*

- **Edges** enable the observer to maintain a consistent representation of the object regardless of the viewing angle and lighting conditions.
- **Concavities** are where two edges meet and enable the observer to perceive where one geon ends and another begins.

The RBC principles of visual object recognition can be applied to auditory language recognition as well. In place of geons, language researchers propose that spoken language can be broken down into basic components called phonemes. *For example,* there are 44 phonemes in the English language.

(v) **The Bottom up Theory of Pattern Recognition** According to bottom up theory of pattern recognition, our ability to recognise specific patterns, such as letters of the alphabet, is based on simpler capabilities to recognise and combine correctly lower level features of the objects, such as lines, edges, corners and angles. As per this theory, the pattern recognition is constructed from simpler perceptual abilities through a series of discrete steps.

(vi) **Top-down Theory of Pattern Recognition** According to top-down approach, our expectancies play a critical role in shaping our perceptions. One doesn't always analyse every feature of most stimuli, one encounters because one often proceeds in accordance with what one's past experience tells one to expect.

Though top-down processing is mostly very efficient, yet at times it can deviate one's attention from the main focus. *For Example* Most of us, at one time or another, experience rushing over to another person who appears to be known to us only to find that he/she is a stranger in reality. It indicates that our tendency to process information quickly from the top-down approach can result in errors.

Ecological Perspective on Perception

Perception begins with physical stimulation and ends with perceptual experience. JJ Gibson was a perceptual psychologist, who recognised the importance of studying perception in natural environment. Gibson championed an approach that he called the ecological approach to perception, which considers, how perception occurs in natural environment.

Thus, the ecological perspective on perception describes influence of environment of an organism on its perceptually guided behaviour.

Gibson Postulated the following four principles

(i) The proper way to describe the stimulus is not in terms of the image on the retina, but in terms of information in the environment, called the *optic array*.
(ii) The important information for perception is created by movement of the observer.
(iii) The key information in the optic array that is created by this movement is invariant information-information; that remains constant as the observer moves.
(iv) This invariant information leads directly to perception.

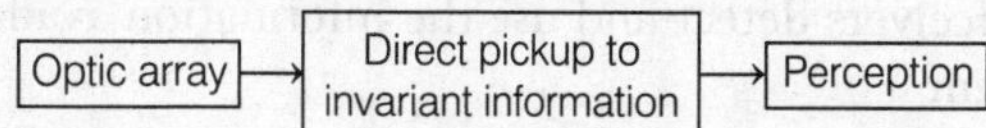

The ecological approach has several advantages over the mechanistic approach and the representational theory of perception. First of all, the concept of perceiver-environment reciprocity avoids the dilemma of (private) mind-(public) world interaction by conceiving perceivers and environments as forming a mutually supportive system. Moreover, the ecological approach establishes this conception without reducing the problem to physical-neurobiological terms, as do contemporary mechanistic approaches.

Gibson's Ecological Program

Gibson's ecological program is designed to overcome the difficulties by rooting the perceiver and the environment in a fully integrated system of mutual constraint, instead of treating them as two distinct domains of existence in (inexplicable) mechanical interaction.

This theory states that physical stimuli initiate patterns of excitation in the sensory receptors on the retina, yielding collections of *immediately* experienced sensations in the material body. On this account, perception is the 'mediate' procedure of constructing representations on the basis of these elementary, atomic sensations. In opposition to this view, Gibson argues that perception is wrongly conceived as a private event in the perceiver's mind.

Representational theories of perception appeal to frameworks fixed in advance of the perceiver's moving, ecological relation to the environment. Models that transcend the perceiver-environment system are both problematic and unnecessary. The structures generated in perceiver-environment systems serve as *stimulus information* for the direct perception of the environment. In Gibson's terminology, perception is the detection of invariant structures in the flow of stimulus information, which is sparked when the active perceiver moves through the environment.

Ecological Optics

Ecological optics analyses the information for vision. This analysis consists of two components.

(i) The *first* is a structural analysis of the environment to be perceived and the information available in the environment.

(ii) The *second* component is a similar analysis of how perceivers detect and use the information available to them.

These two components are complementary. Environmental information is itself a product of the perceiver's bodily involvement with the environment. This interaction generates a 'flow' of information, which underlies and guides all perceptual activity. Hence, the dynamic encounter of the moving perceiver and the environment is the basis of the theory of direct perception.

The viability of a theory of direct perception depends on demonstrating that there is an information in the environment that is capable of specifying its source. Hence, to claim that environmental information does not need to be reconstructed or embellished by inferential processes is to claim that stimulation is uniquely and invariably tied to its source.

Debates in Ecological Optics

Like all branches of optics, ecological optics claims that light is the stimulus for vision. Only light can meaningfully stimulate the eye of the observer. However, the claim that light in the environment is structured and that these structures serve as information about the environment is controversial.

The reason for this, Gibson explains, is that "It has been asserted with some plausibility both that light carries information about the world and that it does not." This debate is as old as the history of visual theory itself. On the one hand, theorists as historically remote as **Ptolemy and Kepler** have argued that objects constantly send off little images of themselves in all directions and that these images serve as the active information for perception. This was the dominant view until descartes produced his radical critique of the doctrine of intentional species in

'The World and the Dioptrics.' Thereafter, it became a foregone conclusion that nothing gets into the eye but the rays of light, propagated from 'points' in geometrical space. Cartesian light rays are perfectly homogenous 'pencils' of moving particles (and therefore lack any internal structure needed to carry appearance of visible qualities of the object to the eye of the perceiver).

Upon entering the eye, the light rays converge to a series of points on the retina. Each point in the stimulated region mechanically produces a sensation from which the mind infers determinate properties of the external world. This is the basis of Descartes's theory of indirect perception.

According to **Gibson**, "this theory is needlessly complex and attributes too much responsibility to the inferential status of the intellect. The difficulties inherent in this view can be overcome by Gibson's doctrine of ecological specificity."

EXAM BASED QUESTIONS

1 Signal detection theory states that there are two discrete states of the world resulting in which four possible classes of joint events?

(a) Hits, noise, signals, misses
(b) Correct rejection, incorrect rejection, noise, signals
(c) Hits, false alarms, misses, correct rejections
(d) Response, state, signal, correct rejection

2 It is possible during a psychophysical trial that the same stimulus strength will cause different answers from the same participant, what offers an explanation as to why our threshold detections are not discrete?

(a) Signal Detection theory
(b) Noisy Wiring theory
(c) Stimulus Discrimination theory
(d) Judgement Bias theory

3 Which of the following words does not describe perception?

(a) A passive process
(b) A psychological process
(c) No direct contact with the physical world
(d) Using sense organs

4 Measuring detection thresholds, a favoured practice of Fechner, can be carried out by three methods, which of the following is not one of them?

(a) Absolute method
(b) Limit method
(c) Adjustment method
(d) Constant stimuli method

5 What percentage correct performance is necessary in psychophysical trials to determine a threshold of perception (discriminatory or detection)?

(a) 75% (b) 90% (c) 50% (d) 67%

6 Parapsychology is

(a) a pseudopsychology dealing with the prediction of the future.
(b) the study of psychic phenomena or psi events.
(c) limited to the study of extrasensory perception.
(d) a non-scientific field concerned with clairvoyance, magic and witchcraft.

7 The information surrounding a stimulus is known as the

(a) Adaptation level (b) Context
(c) Aura
(d) Internal frame of reference

8 The responsiveness shown in form of deceased threshold is known as

(a) Perceptual defence (b) Perceptual vigilance
(c) Subliminal perception (d) Supraliminal perception

9 Jacob has been working at his computer for the past two hours and the hum sound that he found so annoying, when he started no longer bother him. The change in Jacob's sensitivity to the noise from the computer illustrate the process known as

(a) Perceptual invariance
(b) Perceptual assimilation
(c) Adjusting just noticeable difference
(d) Sensory adaptation

10 Relationship of distal to proximal representation of an object, indicating the degree to which physical attributes determine any given perception is known as

(a) Brunswick ratio (b) Detection theory
(c) Purism (d) Propensity

11 The perceived size an after image is directly proportional to the distance of the surface, on which the after image is viewed. This is known as

(a) Garcia law (b) Emmert's law
(c) Weber's law (d) Fechner's law

12 A field that focuses primarily on the psychology of work and adaptation of work and adaptation of machines for human use is

(a) engineering psychology
(b) systems psychology
(c) social psychology
(d) environmental psychology

13 The Muller-Lyer illusion exists in cultures, in which there are

(a) more men than women (b) more women than men
(c) lots of trees
(d) buildings with lots of corners

14 Size judgement is based on

(a) clarity at the object (b) object size
(c) etinal image (d) distance information

15 After visual input has been processed in the primary visual cortex, signals are proceed further along a number of pathways. The dorsal stream processes information about

(a) form and colour (b) motion and depth
(c) brightness and contours (d) complexity and contrast

16 Painting and drawings that lead to ambiguous interpretation often invert the

(a) figure and ground
(b) sensation and perception
(c) top and bottom
(d) open process closed processing

17 Which of the following occurs when one object seems to block another object?

(a) Convergence (b) Liner perspective
(c) Overlap (d) Texture gradient

18 Which of the following properties of sound would be the most similar to the brightness of light?
(a) Pitch (b) Loudness
(c) Purity (d) Timber

19 Which of the following is incorrect about Signal Detection Theory?
(a) It is a framework for interpreting data.
(b) Two or more stimulus classes are sampled repeatedly.
(c) Performance in task is limited by observer's sensitivity.
(d) SDT restricts performance to be predicted across paradigms.

20 Which of the following is correct about MSDT?
(a) It is not related to Signal Detection Theory.
(b) There are three types of sensitivity.
(c) MSDT is also known as General Recognition Theory.
(d) It involves detection of a tonal signal in a background of gaussion noise.

21 What is the theory of colour vision first proposed by Thomas Young and later by Herman Von Helmoltz called?
(a) Trichromatic theory (b) Dichromatic theory
(c) Opponent process theory (d) Complimentarity theory

22 According to event processing hypothesis of time perception, which one of the following statements is correct?
(a) The basic of time perception is biological.
(b) Filled time is perceived shorter than fulfilled time.
(c) Short time intervals are overestimated as compared to long time intervals.
(d) Perception of time depends upon the stimulus changes that have been experienced in that time interval.

23 If you incorrectly perceive that two lines are the same length when they are not, you are experiencing a/an
(a) Muller-lyer effect (b) Phonzo effect
(c) Illusion (d) Delusion

24 The first time Albert had to put together a child's bicycle it took a long time. But several bicycles later his speed increased at constructing them. His improved speed and skill can attributed to
(a) bottom-up processing (b) top-down processing
(c) perceptual expectancy (d) perceptual set

25 Ruby was listening to a tape recording of a famous speech that was played backward. She just heard gibberish until a classmate said the phrase 'meet me in St Louis' was clearly spoken. The tape was rewound and as Ashlynn listened this time, she also clearly heard the same phase. Ruby's ability to detect the phrase the second time through the tape illustrates
(a) the opponent-process model of perception
(b) the top-down processing model of perception
(c) the bottom-up processing model of perception
(d) the electric model of perception

26 Manner in which people process information varies. Some people want an answer to the problem immediately and thus quickly seize upon the answer that satisfies them and freeze that answer. Which one of the following phenomenon this pertains to?
(a) Primacy effect
(b) Need for cognition
(c) Need for control
(d) Need for closure

27 What alarm rate do Signal Detection Theory use?
(a) Hit (b) Miss
(c) Both a and b (d) None of these

28 According to SDT, performance in task is limited by observer's
(a) resistivity (b) sensitivity
(c) variability (d) All of these

29 ROC, an analytical technique stands for
(a) receiver operating characteristic
(b) rapid operating characteristic
(c) random operating curriculum
(d) rationale objective characteristic

30 SDT first sprouted from research on
(a) telephone (b) sick patient
(c) radar (d) None of these

31 d and β stands for .... and .... respectively.
(a) simulation, observation
(b) sensitivity, response bias
(c) marginal, conditional
(d) perceptually separable, perceptually independent

32 How are N and SN effects distributed?
(a) Normally (b) Parabolic
(c) Both a and b (d) None of these

33 In Weber's Law, $\frac{\Delta I}{I} = K$, ΔI stands for?
(a) Noticeable difference
(b) Point of subjective equality
(c) Constant proportion
(d) Diffrential threshold

34 $S = K \log I$ is formula for a law of perception given by?
(a) Fechner (b) Steven Power
(c) Sigmund Froud (d) None of these

35 What kind of effect to subliminal perception provide?
(a) Weak effect (b) Strong effect
(c) High effect (d) Down effect

36 What are the methodologies to evaluate subliminal perception?
(a) Subliminal conditioning
(b) Subliminal stimulation and behaviour
(c) Both a and b
(d) None of the above

37 What is the term for events that seem to defy accepted scientific law?

(a) PSE (b) PSI (c) DEL (d) WY

38 The use of computer as a tool for thinking how the human mind handles information is known as

(a) Computer analogy (b) Computer homology
(c) Computer matching (d) None of these

39 Treisman gave which of the following model?

(a) Filter model (b) Attenuation model
(c) Late selection model (d) All of these

40 Which amongst the following assumes that some or all processes involved in a cognitive task occurs at the same time?

(a) Serial processing (b) Parallel processing
(c) Both a and b (d) None of these

41 Which amongst the following play a crucial role in structuring social interactions accrose culture?

(a) Interpersonal influences (b) Adjustments
(c) Both a and b (d) None of the above

42 What play a crucial role in shaping and structuring social interactions?

(a) Exerting influences (b) Interpersonal influences
(c) Cultural perception (d) None of the above

43 According to whom, "Americans have more analytical visual perception than Asian, who adopt more holistic approach"?

(a) Nisbett Miyamoto (b) Marshall Segall
(c) D Sinha and RC Mishra (d) None of these

44 Which perceptual style see the world as an objective reality?

(a) Goal (b) Flow
(c) Adjustment (d) Activity

45 People with which kind of perceptual style approach life as a singular experience, a journey towards the future?

(a) Vision (b) Method (c) Goal (d) Flow

46 Which perceptual style stride through life focused on the accomplishment of specific results and well defined objective?

(a) Method (b) Activity (c) Goal (d) Flow

47 According to which theory, the pattern recognition is constructed from simpler perceptual abilities through a series of discrete steps?

(a) Bottom up theory (b) Top-down theory
(c) Both a and b (d) None of these

48 Pattern recognition can be categorised as

(a) Bottom up theory (b) Top down theory
(c) Both a and b (d) None of these

49 The formula for optimum beta defines where beta should be set, it is determined by

(a) the ratio of the probability with which noise and signals occur in the environment.
(b) the ratio of probabilities of X given signal and noise.
(c) which placement produces the fewest errors in the long run.
(d) aggregated sensory evidence concerning the presence or absence of a signal.

50 The alternative name for the Receiver Operating Characteristic (ROC) curve is

(a) integral dimensions (b) standard normal curve
(c) bowed curve (d) isosensitivity curve

51 When using fuzzy logic to determine membership in a set, ... is used to describe the degree of membership in that set.

(a) signal function
(b) mapping function
(c) crisp definition
(d) event membership values

52 Detection of the sound of a bell ringing is referred to as a .... Once you interpret the stimulus as the sound of your alarm clock, it is referred to as a ....

(a) perception; sensory adaptation
(b) sensation; perception
(c) perception; sensation
(d) sensory code; perception

53 A .... is the region of space where stimuli affect the activity of a cell in a sensory system.

(a) Merkel's disc (b) receptive field
(c) rod (d) photon

54 The photoreceptors we need to appreciate a blue sky on a sunny day are the ...., whereas the photoreceptors we use to detect the stars outside at night are the ....

(a) cones; hair cells
(b) Meissner's corpuscles; rods
(c) cones; rods
(d) rods; cones

55 The .... theory of colour vision is the idea that colour vision is based on a system of paired opposites of colour.

(a) trichromatic (b) opponent-process
(c) duplex (d) binocular

56 The amount of information transmitted by the human operator to the response is a quantity designated as

(a) HS (b) SH (c) HT (d) TH

57 Which of the following is false about ecological perspective on perception?

(a) Ecological approach has advantage over mechanistic approach.
(b) Theory states that physical stimuli initiate patterns of excitation in the sensory receptor on retina.
(c) Ecological optics analysis the information for vision.
(d) It states expectancy play critical role in shaping our perception.

58 Which of the following statements is/are correct?
1. Subliminal perception is not that people may respond to stimulation below the threshold of awareness.
2. They are affected by stimuli of which they are unaware.

Select the correct answer using the codes given below
(a) Only 1 (b) Only 2
(c) Both 1 and 2 (d) None of these

59 Consider the following statements

A person, put in a dark solitary room for several hours, seems to have lost his perception of time because of
1. loss of all sensory threshold.
2. absence of any primary sensory cue.
3. appearance of temporal illusion.

Which of the statements given above is/are correct?
(a) Only 3 (b) 1 and 2
(c) 2 and 3 (d) 1, 2 and 3

60 Consider the following statements
1. Absolute threshold is the stimulus intensity that is reported 100% of the time.
2. The two eyes are about 65 mm apart.

Which of the statements given above is/are incorrect
(a) Only 1 (b) Only 2
(c) Both 1 and 2 (d) None of these

61 Consider the following statements
1. Micro electrode always monitor a complex cell.
2. After visual information is processed in the primary visual cortex, it is routed through what and where path way.

Which of the statements given above is/are not correct?
(a) Only 1 (b) Only 2
(c) Both 1 and 2 (d) Neither 1 nor 2

62 Consider the following statements
1. Overall, it appears that we perceive changing stimuli better than constant ones.
2. The wavelength of light mainly affects our perception of brightness.

Which of the following statements given above is/are correct?
(a) Only 1 (b) Only 2
(c) Both 1 and 2 (d) Neither 1 nor 2

63 Consider the following statements
1. Information made available by the environment is processed by a series of processing systems.
2. The aim of research is to specify the processes and structures that underlie cognitive performance.

Which of the statements given above is/are correct?
(a) Only 1 (b) Only 2
(c) Both 1 and 2 (d) None of these

64 Consider the following statements
1. PSE is defined as that magnitude of a comparison stimulus that is equally likely to be judged greater or less than the magnitude of a standard stimulus.
2. In practice, the PSE lies halfway between the stimulus just noticeably smaller than the standard and the one just noticeable larger.

Which of the statements given above is/are correct?
(a) Only 1 (b) Only 2
(c) Both 1 and 2 (d) None of these

65 Consider the following statements
1. People with the method perceptual style approach life as a singular experience, a journey towards the future.
2. People with vision perceptual style approach life in a practical, matter-to-fact manner.

Which of the statements given above is/are correct?
(a) Only 1 (b) Only 2
(c) Both 1 and 2 (d) None of these

66 Consider the following statements
1. Signal Detection theory sprouted form World War Second research on radar into a probability-based theory in the early 1950s.
2. JJ Gibson was a perceptual psychologist, who recognised the importance of studying perception in industrial environment.

Which of the statements above is/are correct?
(a) Only 1 (b) Only 2
(c) Both 1 and 2 (d) None of these

Directions (Q. Nos. 67-86) *In the questions given below are two statements labelled as Assertion (A) and Reason (R). In the context of two statements, which one of the following is correct?*

Codes
(a) Both A and R are true and R is the correct explanation of A
(b) Both A and R are true, but R is not the correct explanation of A
(c) A is true, but R is false
(d) A is false, but R is true

67 **Assertion** (A) Research on subliminal perception has been sporadic.

Reason (R) Initially the scientists considerd the idea as non sense.

68 **Assertion** (A) Subliminal stimulation has indirect effects on subsequent behaviour.

Reason (R) Subliminal stimulation leads to precise discrimination.

69 **Assertion** (A) Vigilance behaviour can be explained through the basic principle of attention.

Reason (R)Vigilance behaviour that are novel have biological importance for the person.

70 **Assertion** (A) Subjective threshold implies that each participant provide his/her own idiosyncratic definition of threshold.

Reason (R) Higher levels of visibility are typically associated with subjective threshold.

71 Assertion (A) Affter word war second, research into vigilance performance with the introduction of radar performance decrement was serious.

Reason (R) It could endanger life.

72 Assertion (A) Perceptual style determines what are natural capacities, skill and abilities.

Reason (R) Perceptual style is innate.

73 Assertion (A) Female have higher RT for taboo word than male.

Reason (R) They resort to more selective responding.

74 Assertion (A) Cognitive interpretation is the different way people look at same image.

Reason (R) People have different way of perception.

75 Assertion (A) Unconscious perception will be used to lower all cases when responses are governed by stimuli of which the recipient is unaware.

Reason (R) Subliminal perception will be reserved for those cases where the stimulus is, in fact, below some independently determined limen.

76 Assertion (A) Consciousness of a stimulus depends not only upon the general level of cortical activation, but upon a component of activation produced by the stimulus itself.

Reason (R) Reticular system is used by the cortex as a device for employing or attenuating chosen signals.

77 Assertion (A) Signal detection theory was first developed in a medical context.

Reason (R) Signal detection theory is now used in cognitive science, diagnostic medicine.

78 Assertion (A) SDT is a model for theory as to how organism make fine discrimination.

Reason (R) This is done through an analytical technique called receiver operating characteristic (ROC).

79 Assertion (A) Point subjective equality have a limited range of applicability.

Reason (R) PSE, a psychophysical measure related to the differential threshold is a measure of estimate of the magnitude of two stimuli which are equal.

80 Assertion (A) Individuals' experiences are tainted by their culture.

Reason (R) Culture in which individual are raised does not paint their ideas.

81 Assertion (A) Nisbett and Miyamoto say Americans have more analytical visual perception than Asian.

Reason (R) They think Asian obtain more holistic approach.

82 Assertion (A) Perception is similar for different persons.

Reason (R) Perceptual similarity results in psychological uniqueness.

83 Assertion (A) Sublimal perception is the registration of awareness.

Reason (R) Greenwald and others support sublimal perception.

84 Assertion (A) Extra sensory perception is the ability to perceive events in a way that cannot be explained by known sensory capacities.

Reason (R) Parapsychology studies extra sensory perception.

85 Assertion (A) The development of computer did not influence psychology.

Reason (R) Computer gave analogy to psychologist upon which they can compare human mental processing.

86 Assertion (A) Rural and urban people have different cultural upbringing.

Reason (R) Rural people live a comfortable life compared to urban.

87 Match the following

List I (Researcher)	List II (Contribution)
A. Uri Geller	1. Impact of culture on perception
B. Greenwald	2. Ecology perspective on perception
C. Gibson	3. Extra sensory perception
D. Marshall	4. Subliminal perception

Codes

	A	B	C	D
(a)	4	1	2	3
(b)	1	2	3	4
(c)	2	3	4	1
(d)	3	4	2	1

88 Match the following

List I (Concepts)	List II (Descriptions)
A. Telepathy	1. Ability to perceive future
B. Clair voyance	2. Ability to communicate directly with another person's mind
C. Precognition	3. Ability to exert influence over inanimate object by will power
D. Psycho kinesis	4. Ability to perceive event appearing unaffected by distance

Codes

	A	B	C	D		A	B	C	D
(a)	3	4	2	1	(b)	1	2	3	4
(c)	2	4	1	3	(d)	4	1	2	3

89 Match the following

List I (Laws)	List II (Formulas)
A. Weber's Law	1. $S = K I^b$
B. Fechner's Law	2. $\frac{\Delta 1}{1} = K$
C. Steven's Power Law	3. $S = K \log 1$

Codes

	A	B	C		A	B	C
(a)	1	2	3	(b)	2	3	1
(c)	3	2	1	(d)	3	1	2

90 Match the following

List I (Concept)	List II (Explanation)
A. Differential threshold	1. Measure of the estimate that the magnitude of two stimuli are perceptually equal
B. Subliminal perception	2. Measure of smallest difference between two stimuli that can be detected
C. Point of subjective equality	3. It is registration of awareness
D. Extra sensory perception	4. Ability to perceive event in ways that cannot be explained

Codes

	A	B	C	D		A	B	C	D
(a)	2	3	1	4	(b)	4	3	2	1
(c)	3	4	1	2	(d)	1	2	3	4

91 Match the following

List I (Law)	List II (Description)
A. Weber's Law	1. Sensory on subjective magnitude grows in proportion to the physical intensity of the stimulus
B. Steven's Power Law	2. The amount of change, increases/decreases in a stimulus necessary to detect it as different is proportional to magnitude of stimulus
C. Fechner's Law	3. The magnitude of a sensation is a logarithmic function of the stimulus

Codes

	A	B	C		A	B	C
(a)	2	1	3	(b)	3	2	1
(c)	1	2	3	(d)	3	1	2

92 Match the following

List I (Psychologists)	List II (Theory)
A. Peterson and Birdsall	1. General recognition theory
B. Neyman and Pearson	2. Engineering theory
C. Ashby and Townsend	3. Energy detection model
D. Davegreen et all	4. Statistical inference

Codes

	A	B	C	D		A	B	C	D
(a)	1	3	2	4	(b)	1	2	3	4
(c)	2	4	1	3	(d)	4	3	1	2

93 Match the following

List I (Model/Cycle)	List II (Given by)
A. Filter Model	1. Deutsch and Deutsch
B. Attenuation Model	2. Neisser
C. Late Selection Model	3. Broadbent
D. Perceptual Cycle	4. Treisman

Codes

	A	B	C	D		A	B	C	D
(a)	1	2	3	4	(b)	3	2	1	4
(c)	4	2	3	1	(d)	3	4	1	2

94 Match the following

List I	List II
A. Gain the students attention	1. Provide handouts
B. Bring to mind relevant prior learning	2. Use cues to signal when you are ready to begin
C. Point out important information	3. Review previous day's lesson
D. Present information in an organised manner	4. Show logical sequence to concept and skills

Codes

	A	B	C	D		A	B	C	D
(a)	2	3	1	4	(b)	1	2	3	4
(c)	4	3	2	1	(d)	3	2	1	4

95 Match the following

List (Concept)	List II (Description)
A. Activity	1. People approach life in a practical way,
B. Flow	2. People see the words as an objective reality
C. Method	3. People jump into life with both feet
D. Adjustment	4. People are insensitive advocate for the natural rythm of life

Codes

	A	B	C	D		A	B	C	D
(a)	3	4	1	2	(b)	2	3	1	4
(c)	4	1	3	2	(d)	1	4	2	3

96 Match the following

List I	List II
A. Show students how to categorise related information	1. Have items on each day's lesson from previous lesson
B. Show student how to use coding when memorising lists	2. Connect new information to something already known
C. Provide repetition of learning	3. Present information in categories
D. Provide opportunity for students to elaborate on new information	4. Make up silly sentence with first letters of each word in the list

Codes

	A	B	C	D		A	B	C	D
(a)	3	4	1	2	(b)	2	3	4	1
(c)	1	3	2	4	(d)	4	2	1	3

97 Arrange the following in chronological order
1. Perceptual Cycle 2. Filter Model
3. Late Selection Model 4. Attenuation Model

Codes
(a) 2 4 3 1 (b) 3 2 4 1 (c) 1 2 4 3 (d) 1 3 4 2

98 Arrange the work of researcher in chronological manner.
1. Greenfield and Anderson
2. Fiske
3. Cartwright
4. Greenfield, Inesi, Magee and Galinsky

Codes
(a) 1 2 4 3 (b) 3 4 2 1
(c) 3 2 1 4 (d) 1 2 3 4

Directions (Q. Nos. 99-103) *Read the passage given below and answer the questions that follow.*

Since the effect of the subliminal stimulation is expected to be distorted or transformed or to appear in a symbolic rather than the identical form of the stimulation, the detection of this subliminal influence poses severe methodological problems. Numerous sources of artifact are present in such experimental designs as have been pointed out by Johnson and Erikson, interpretation of these experimenters in most cases to ensure that the stimulation was indeed incidental or to specify the criterion by which they determined that the stimulation was subliminal.

In many of the experiments, it is quite obvious that the stimuli were not subliminal and the subjects lack of awareness of the stimulation was due to the nature of the experiment, which directed his attention to other stimuli. In this case the experiments are more concerned with incidental stimulation than with subliminal stimulation and bear a strong resemblance both methodologically and conceptually to the traditional work on incidental memory.

99 What is the cause of the subject's lack of awareness of the stimulation?
(a) Nature of behaviour of subject
(b) Nature of experiment
(c) Subject's cultural background
(d) Subject's memory skill

100 To which of the following experimenters are concerned?
(a) Incidental stimulation (b) Subliminal stimulation
(c) Subject's nature (d) Type of stimulation

101 Subliminal stimulation has what effect on sub sequence behaviour?
(a) Direct effect (b) Indirect effect
(c) No effect (d) Proportional effect

102 Subliminal stimulation leads to which of the following?
(a) Precise discrimination
(b) Distortion of an conscious process
(c) Fantacy
(d) Dream

103 Which of the following is effect of subliminal stimulation?
(a) Distorted (b) Clear
(c) Fabricated (d) Transperant

PREVIOUS YEARS' QUESTIONS

July 2018

1 Signal Detection Theory identifies two distinct processes in sensory detection

1. sensory process
2. decision process
3. motivational process
4. response bias

Codes

(a) 1 and 2 (b) 3 and 4
(c) 1 and 3 (d) 1 and 4

November 2017

2 In 'Signal Detection Theory', which of the following determinants are assumed?

1. Observer's sensitivity
2. Sensory threshold
3. Response bias
4. Decision bias

Codes

(a) Only 1
(b) 1 and 3
(c) 1, 3 and 4
(d) 2 and 3

January 2017

3 Match List I with List II and choose the correct answer from the codes given below

List I (Concept)	List II (Definition)
A. Hit	1. Signal is present but response is No
B. Miss	2. Signal is present and response is Yes
C. False Alarm	3. Signal is absent and the response is No
D. Correct Rejection	4. Signal is absent but the response is Yes

Codes

	A	B	C	D
(a)	4	1	3	2
(b)	2	1	4	3
(c)	2	1	3	4
(d)	4	3	2	1

July 2016

4 Signal detection depends upon

(a) motivation and expectations
(b) signal intensity and noise
(c) sensitivity and response criterion
(d) absolute and relative thresholds

5 Which of the following does not present with symptoms of mental retardation?

(a) Cri du chat syndrome (b) Down's syndrome
(c) Fugue (d) Trisomy 21

December 2015

6 Four important elements in the Theory of Signal Detection are

(a) errors, hits, speed and accuracy
(b) speed, accuracy, power and false alarm
(c) hit, miss, correct rejection and false alarm
(d) acuity, efficacy, speed and power

June 2015

7 According to Signal Detection Theory, detection of stimuli depends on

1. their physical energy
2. internal factors like relative costs
3. absolute threshold
4. internal factors like benefits with detecting their presence

Codes

(a) 1, 2 and 3 (b) 2, 3 and 4 (c) 3, 1 and 4 (d) 1, 2 and 4

December 2014

8 Match the items of List I (Theories) with List II (Descriptions) and mark your answer with the help of the codes given below.

List I (Theories)	List II (Descriptions)
A. Theory of Signal Detection	1. Sensory subjective magnitude grows in proportion to the intensity of the stimulus raised to a power
B. The Fechner Law	2. The minimal amount of stimulus energy required for a detection of a stimulus
C. Absolute Threshold	3. Evaluation of the separate effects of the observer's sensory capacity and response bias
D. Stevens Power Law	4. Larger and larger input in stimulus energy are required to obtain a corresponding sensory effect

Codes

	A	B	C	D
(a)	1	2	3	4
(b)	1	2	4	3
(c)	3	4	2	1
(d)	3	2	1	4

June 2014

9 Assertion (A) Information reaching the meaning level of processing and elaboration has the best chance of being retained.

Reason (R) According to information processing theories of memory, information is transferred from stage to stage until some of it is finally lodged in long-term memory.

Code

(a) Both A and R are true and R is the correct explanation of A

(b) Both A and R are true, but R is not the correct explanation of A

(c) A is true, but R is false

(d) A is false, but R is true

ANSWERS

Exam Based Questions

1 (a)	2 (a)	3 (a)	4 (a)	5 (a)	6 (a)	7 (b)	8 (b)	9 (d)	10 (a)
11 (b)	12 (a)	13 (d)	14 (d)	15 (b)	16 (a)	17 (c)	18 (b)	19 (d)	20 (c)
21 (a)	22 (b)	23 (c)	24 (b)	25 (b)	26 (d)	27 (c)	28 (b)	29 (a)	30 (c)
31 (b)	32 (a)	33 (b)	34 (a)	35 (a)	36 (c)	37 (b)	38 (a)	39 (b)	40 (b)
41 (c)	42 (b)	43 (a)	44 (c)	45 (a)	46 (c)	47 (a)	48 (c)	49 (a)	50 (d)
51 (d)	52 (b)	53 (d)	54 (d)	55 (a)	56 (c)	57 (a)	58 (c)	59 (d)	60 (a)
61 (b)	62 (a)	63 (c)	64 (c)	65 (d)	66 (a)	67 (a)	68 (c)	69 (c)	70 (b)
71 (a)	72 (a)	73 (a)	74 (b)	75 (b)	76 (b)	77 (d)	78 (a)	79 (d)	80 (c)
81 (a)	82 (b)	83 (a)	84 (a)	85 (d)	86 (c)	87 (d)	88 (c)	89 (b)	90 (a)
91 (a)	92 (c)	93 (d)	94 (a)	95 (a)	96 (a)	97 (a)	98 (c)	99 (b)	100 (c)
101 (b)	102 (b)	103 (a)							

Previous Years' Questions

1 (c)	2 (b)	3 (b)	4 (c)	5 (c)	6 (c)	7 (d)	8 (c)	9 (b)

Learning Process

Learning is a key process in human behaviour. All living is learning. It is relatively a permanent change in behaviour that results from experience. The psychology of learning focuses on a range of theories related to how people learn and intract within their environment.

Introductions of Learning Process

Learning is a relatively permanent change in behaviour, knowledge and thinking skills that occurs through experience. To learn effectively it is important to adapt one's study habits according to one's needs and approaches i.e. choosing techniques that work for one. It is also equally important to evaluate them from time to time to determine if one needs to try something new.

It is a process that people go through to acquire new knowledge and skills and ultimately influence their attitudes, decisions and actions. It is also a set of activities carried out to achieve educational objectives. It is a process in which an individual or group uses, adapts, reproduces or appropriates the structures.

It consists of several mental processes. The completion of learning process includes active testing, concrete experience, reflective observation and abstract hypothesis.

Characteristics of Learning

Yoakman and Simpson have described the following important characteristics of learning.

- **Learning is Growth** The individual grows as he lives. This growth implies both physical as well as mental development of the learner. The individual gains experience through various activities. An individual grows through living and learning.
- **Learning is Adjustment** Learning enables the individual to adjust himself properly, with the new situations. The individual faces new problems and new situations throughout his life and learning helps him solve the problems encountered by him. That is why; many psychologists describe "learning as a process of progressive adjustment to the ever changing conditions, which one encounters." It is through learning that one could achieve the ability to adjust adequately to all situations of life.

In this Chapter

- *Learning Process*
- *Classical Conditioning*
- *Instrumental Learning*
- *Reinforcement*
- *Behaviour Modification*
- *Cognitive Approaches in Learning*
- *Neurophysiology of Learning*

- **Learning is Purposeful** All kinds of learning is goal- oriented. The individual acts with some purpose, he learns through activities. He gets himself interested, when he is aware of his objectives to be realised through these activities. Therefore all learning is purpose oriented in nature.
- **Learning is Experience** The individual learns through experiences. Human life is full of experiences. All these experiences provide new knowledge, understanding, skills and attitudes. Learning is not mere acquisition of the knowledge, skills and attitudes. It is also the reorganisation of experiences or the synthesis of the old experiences with the new.
- **Learning is Intelligent** Mere cramming without proper understanding does not make learning. Thus, meaningless efforts do not produce permanent results. Any work done mechanically cannot yield satisfactory learning outcomes. Learning therefore must be intelligent.
- **Learning is Active** Learning is given more importance than teaching. It implies self-activity of the learning. Without adequate motivation he cannot work whole-heartedly and motivation is therefore at the root of self-activity. Learning by doing is thus an important principle of education and the basis of all progressive methods of education like the project, the montessori (learning through natural interests) and traditional system.
- **Learning is Both Individual and Social** Although learning is an individual activity, individual mind is consciously or unconsciously affected by the group activities. Individual is influenced by his peers, friends, relatives, parents and classmates and learns their ideas, feelings and attitudes in some way or the other. The social agencies like family, church, markets and clubs exert immense influence on the individual minds. As such, learning becomes both individual as well as social.
- **Learning is the Product of the Environment** The individual lives in interaction with the society. Environment plays an important part in the growth and development of the individual. The physical, social, intellectual and emotional development of the child is moulded and remoulded by the objects and individuals in his environment. Therefore, it is emphasised that child's environment should be made free from unhealthy and vicious matters to make it more effective for learning.
- **Learning Affects the Conduct of the Learner** Learning is called the *modification of behaviour*. It affects the learner's behaviour and conduct. Every learning experience brings about changes in the mental structure of the learner. Therefore attempts are made to provide such learning experiences, which can mould the desired conduct and habits in the learners.

Fundamental Theories of Learning

Fundamental learning theories are an organised set of principles which explain how individuals acquire, retain and recall knowledge.

The principles of these fundamental theories can be used as guidelines to help select instructional tools, techniques and strategies that promote learning.

Although there are many different approaches to learning, *there are three basic types of learning theories.*

(i) **Behaviourism Theory of Learning** It originates from the work of BF Skinner and the concept of operant conditioning. Behaviourism theorists believe that learning actually occurs when new changes in behaviour are acquired through associations between stimuli and responses. Thus, association leads to a change in behaviour. *Examples and applications of behaviourist learning theory are*

- Drill
- Repetitive practice
- Bonus points (providing an incentive to do more)
- Participation points (providing an incentive to participate)
- Verbal reinforcement (saying 'good job')
- Establishing rules

Behaviourism instruction does not prepare the learner for problem solving or creative thinking. Learners do what they are told and do not take the initiative to change or improve things. The learner is only prepared for recalling basic facts, automatic responses or performed tasks.

(ii) **Cognitivism Theory of Learning** It is based on the thought process behind the behaviour. It is based on the idea that humans process the information they receive, rather than merely responding to stimuli. The changes in behaviour are observed, but only as indicator to what is going on in the learner's head.

The learner's mind is like a mirror from which new knowledge and skills are reflected. Cognitivism or cognitive information processing is used when the learner plays an active role in seeking ways to understand and process information that he or she receives and relates it to what is already known and stored within memory. Cognitive learning theories are usually credited to Jean Piaget.

Learning through cognitivism involves the reorganisation of experiences, either by attaining new insights or changing old ones. Thus, learning is a change in knowledge which is stored in memory and not just a change in behaviour. *Examples and applications of cognitive learning theory are*

- Classifying information
- Linking concepts (associate new content with something known)
- Providing structure (organising one's lecture in efficient and meaningful ways)
- Discussions
- Problem solving
- Analogies
- Imagery/Providing pictures

(iii) **Constructivism Theory of Learning** It is based on the premise that we all construct our own perspective of the world, based on individual experiences and internal knowledge.

Learning is based on how the individual interprets and creates the meaning of his or her experiences. Knowledge is constructed by the learner and since everyone has a different set of experiences and perceptions, learning is unique and different for each person.

This theory is used to focus on preparing people to solving problem, so the learner requires a significant base of knowledge to successfully interpret and create ideas. Under constructivism, outcomes are not always predictable as learners are constructing their own knowledge.

Examples and applications of constructivism are

- Case studies
- Research projects
- Problem based learning
- Discovery learning
- Collaborative learning/group work

Thorndike's Theory of Learning

Edward Lee Thorndike (1874-1949) is generally considered to have been the foremost educational psychologist of the world. He contributed immensely to research and theory in the field of learning and genetic psychology.

He first stated the elements of his theory of learning in 1913 revealing that connections are formed in the nervous system between stimuli and response. The connections so formed are illustrated by the symbols S-R. Another word used to describe these connections is 'bond' and hence, this theory is sometimes called *Bond Theory of Learning*.

He writes, "Learning is connecting. The mind is man's connection system."

According to **Thorndike**, "learning takes place by trial and error. When no ready-made solution of a problem is available to the learner, he adopts the method of trial and error. He keeps eliminating errors or irrelevant responses which do not serve the purpose and finally discovers the correct solution". In trial and error method also, there are systematic and relevant responses, activities are not random. The stages through which the learner has to pass are, goal, hindrances, random movements or multiple response, chance success, selection and fixation.

Thorndike's theory of learning by trial and error, also termed as 'connectionism' is mainly based on three laws.

(i) **Law of Readiness** According to **Thorndike**, "first primary law of learning is the 'law of readiness' which implies that learning takes place when an action tendency is aroused through preparatory adjustment, set or attitude". Readiness means a preparation for action. If one is not prepared to learn, learning cannot automatically come to him. *For example* In order to learn typing, unless the typist prepares himself to start, he won't succeed to a level of satisfaction.

(ii) **Law of Exercise** The second law of learning is the law of exercise. It means that drill or practice helps in increasing efficiency and durability of learning. According to Thorndike's S-R bond theory, the connections are strengthened with trial or practice and *vice-versa*. The law of exercise, therefore, is also understood as the 'law of use and disuse' where connections or bonds made in the brain cortex are weakned or loosened.

For example Learning to drive a motor car, typewriting singing or memorising a poem or mathematical table, music etc. need exercise repetition of various movements and actions many times.

(iii) **Law of Effect** The third law is the law of effect which states that trials or steps leading to satisfaction strengthen the bond or connection. Satisfying states lead to consolidation of the connection while dissatisfaction, annoyance or pain result in weakening of the connections.

It signifies that if the responses satisfy the subject, they are learnt and selected while the unsatisfactory responses are eliminated. Teaching therefore, must be pleasing. The educator must obey the tastes and interests of his pupils. In other words, greater the satisfaction, stronger will be the motive to learn. Thus, intensity is an important condition of the law of effect.

Guthrie's Contiguity Theory of Learning

Guthrie's contiguity theory specifies that "a combination of stimuli, which has accompanied a movement, will on its recurrence tend to be followed by that movement." According to him, all learning is a consequence of association between a particular stimulus and response. He further argues that stimuli and responses affect specific sensory motor patterns; what is learned are the movements and not the behaviour.

It contiguity theory, rewards or punishment do not play any important role in learning since they occur after the association between stimulus and response has been made. Learning takes place in a single trial. However, since each stimulus pattern is slightly different, many trials may be required to produce a general response. One interesting principle that arises from this position is called *postremity*.

It specifies that we always learn the last thing we do in response to a specific stimulus situation.

Edwin Guthrie through his contiguity theory suggests that forgetting is due to interference rather than the passage of time. Stimuli becomes associated with new responses. Previous conditioning can also be changed by being associated with inhibiting responses such as fear or fatigue. The role of motivation is to create a state of arousal and activity which produces responses that can be conditioned.

Three different methods can help in forgetting an undesirable old habit and replacing it. *They are as follow*

(i) **Fatigue Method** Using numerous repetitions, a subject becomes so fatigued that it is unable to reproduce the old response and thus introduces a new response or simply doesn't react.

(ii) **Threshold Method** First, a very mild version of the stimulus below the threshold level is introduced. Its intensity is then slowly increased until the full stimulus can be tolerated without causing the undesirable response.

(iii) **Incompatible Stimuli Method** The response is unlearned by placing the subject in a situation where it cannot exhibit the undesirable response.

Principles of Contiguity Theory

Following principles have been laid under the contiguity theory

- For conditioning to occur, the organism must actively respond.
- Since learning involves the conditioning of specific movements, instruction must present very specific tasks.
- Exposure to many variations in stimulus patterns is desirable in order to produce a generalised response.
- The last response in a learning situation should be correct since it is the one that will be associated.

Example of Contiguity Theory

The classic experimental paradigm for contiguity theory is cats learning to escape from a puzzle box.

Guthrie used a glass panelled box that allowed him to photograph the exact movements of cats. These photographs showed that cats learned to repeat the same sequence of movements associated with preceding escape from the box. Improvement comes about because irrelevant movements are unlearned or not included in successive associations.

CL Hull's Theory of Learning

CL Hull occupies a very significant position among neo-behaviourist psychologists. It was Hull, who could turn Darwinian. Hull was influenced by both the Watsonian S-R and Woodworth's S-O-R (Stimulus-Organism-Response) formula of behaviour events. The S-O-R formula of behaviour is much like a PC computer, where 'S' stands for the stimulus input, which the 'O' *i.e.* organism receives and processes the information to determine the kind of responses (R) *i.e.* output. Likewise, in a PC, the information is fed by operating the keyboard, the Central Process Unit (CPU) of the computer system processes the fed information and the output is displayed on the visual disc screen of the computer.

Hull having understood the significance of S-O-R formula, incorporated the same to explain learnt behaviour. Hull calls the organism related variables as the intervening variables, which are internal states of the organism such as the 'drive state' that can be inferred. To explain learning phenomenon along S-O-S paradigm, Hull envisaged hypothetico-deductive method, which in fact has three steps.

At the first-step, a system of definition or concept is set in order. At the second-step, some postulates are formulated on the basis of definitions or concepts in the first-step. At the third and final-step, several theorems or corrolaries are deduced. Thus, on the basis of the entire set of definitions, postulates and corollaries or theorems, a formal systematic and integrated scientific theory emerged, which is known as *mathematics-deductive theory* or *model of learning.* This model is based on vast number of empirical data and use of mathematical constructs, which has the characteristic of being tested and verified. Hence, a scientific model of learning could be advanced.

Hull's theory is probabilistic in nature because, it is possible for an experimenter to assign a probability of a response to occur on the basis of number of reinforced trials. This is what we intend to predict in a model of learning. In Hull-Spencer theory,

The probability of a response is the product of two general factors

(i) Drive motivation and other features of learning situation.

(ii) Habit strength, *i.e.* the degree of association built up or extinguished in previous trial.

Hull-Spencer's notion of learning is expected in a simple equation as mentioned below

F (tendency/respond)
= Drive (D) × Habit strength (H)

$$F = D \times H.$$

This equation means that in a particular learning or extinction situation, the probability of tendency to respond is the product of habit. For measuring motivational or drive state, level hours of deprivation is used as parameter. *Assuming this, a law of habit formation was framed, which is expressed as follows*

$$H = 1 - 10^{0.03} N$$

In this equation, N is the number of reinforced trials and 0.03 is empirically determined constant.

Critical Comments on CL Hull's Theory

- Hull has severely been criticised for introducing mathematics to explain the key points and concepts of his theory. This has made the explanation complex enough and obscure to comprehend. It seems, he was obsessed with mathematics, otherwise his theory could have been nicely explained.
- Some critics have charged Hull with dualism of thought as on the one hand, he claims himself as behaviouralist while, on the other, he has explained his theory with the help of intervening variables of the organism. His dependence upon inferred organismic state and wider use of intervening variables are subjective and hence, not compliant to objective demonstration.
- Though, Hull claims that his system is highly logical, it suffers from many logical flaws. Kock observes several difficulties owing to which, he finds himself at a loss to arrive at a particular conclusion in a logical way.
- According to **Osgood**, "Hull's theory suffers from backward effect. Hull assumes that reinforcement reduces drive level and therefore one learns the reinforced trials. But, the truth is otherwise."
- The organism emits a response, which subsequently is reinforced. Then, how can reinforcement work backward in time.
- Hull has laid emphasis on response learning only and ignored place learning. For this reason, Woodworth considers Hull's theory only partially correct.

Evaluation of Hull's Theory

Despite the criticisms as stated above, Hull occupies a very significant position among the learning theorists for some salient features of his system, which are distinct and unique in itself.

The distinct characteristics are as follow

- The attribute of quantification is one such characteristic feature that distinguishes his theory from all other theories of learning. The concepts of intervening variables such as response, latency, response probability, response intensity, reactive inhibitions, conditioned inhibitions etc. are all relevant as well as quantitatively measurable.
- From the scientific point of view, the testability and verifiability of this theory are two most distinct features that meet the scientific criteria.
- In addition, Hull's theory contains heuristic (self discovery) value and the attributes of objectivity. To quote Osgood, much of the experimental literature in the field during the recent years has been aimed either in criticism or in support of some aspects of Hull's theory. This remark sufficiently proves that Hull's constructs have heuristic value and hence, are an important contribution to the area of learning.

In essence, though the theory suffers from certain limitations and criticisms, yet the scientific orientations, mathematical interpretation and heuristic values that it contains, are some important features of this theory and hence, its contributions cannot be ignored. These, along with some other salient features of Hull's system have in fact, influenced the contemporary psychology of learning in many ways. This clearly speaks of the strength and potentiality of Hull's system in the area of learning.

Classical Conditioning

Classical conditioning is the basic form of learning in which one stimulus comes to serve as a signal for the occurrence of second stimulus. During classical conditioning, organisms acquire information about the relations between various stimuli. A stimuli is a physical event capable of affecting behaviour.

Classical conditioning gets its name from the fact that it is the kind of learning situation that existed in the early "classical experiments of Ivan P Pavlov, the nobel prize wining Russian physiologists. He established many of the basic principles of this form of conditioning. Classical conditioning process is sometimes known as *Pavlovian conditioning*."

Pavlov's Classical Dog Experiment

Pavlov designed an apparatus that could measure how much a dog's mouth waters in response to food. At the beginning of his experiment, Pavlov noted that no Salvia flows when he rang the bell. He then trained the dog by sounding the bell and immediately presenting food. After the sound he tested the effects of the training by measuring the amount of Salvia that flows when he rang the bell and did not present food.

He found that some salvia was produced in response to the bell alone. He resumed the training and paired the food and the bell a few more times and then tested by ringing the bell alone. After training the dog, he found that the dog's mouth produced salvia in response to the ringing of the bell. This was learned by the dog through training, this is known as the *conditioned response*. This experiment will be referred to multiple times during the description of the procedure of conditioning. Only then it would be easy to understand.

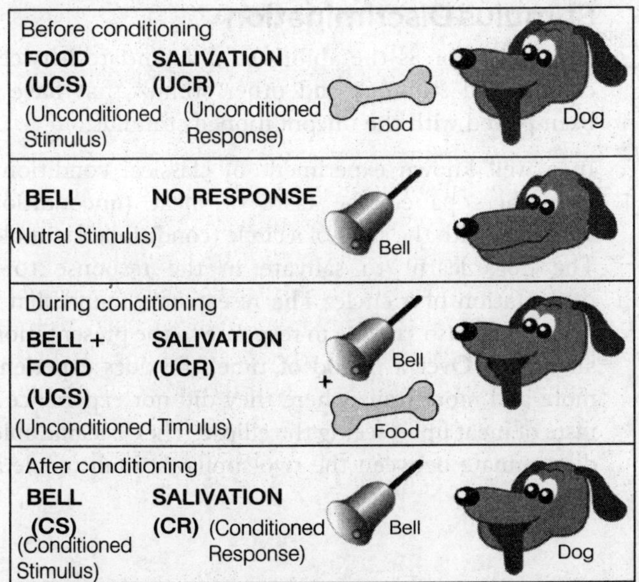

Proceduce of Pavlov's Experiments

Classical conditioning involves placing a neutral signal before a naturally occurring reflex. In Pavlov's experiment, the neutral signal was the sound of a bell and the naturally occurring reflex was the saliva in response to the food. By associating the neutral stimulus with the natural stimulus (Presenting the food), the sound of the bell could produce the salivation.

Classical conditioning involves forming an association between two stimuli resulting in a learned or conditioned response. *There are three phases of this process.*

Phase 1 : Before Conditioning

The first part of the classical process requires a naturally occurring stimulus that will automatically bring out a response. During this phase, the Unconditioned Stimulus (UCS) results in an Unconditioned Response (UCR). *For example* In Pavlov's experiment presenting food to the dog (UCS), naturally triggers a response, which is the formation of saliva in the dog's mouth. This process of salivation is the Unconditioned Response (UCR).

In this phase, there is a neutral stimulus that produces no effect yet, it produces an effect later when it is paired with the UCS.

The two critical components of this phase of classical conditioning are

(i) **Unconditioned Stimulus** (UCS) It naturally and automatically brings out a response. *For Example* When we smell out favourite food, our mouth may become watery. The food here is the unconditioned stimulus.

(ii) **Unconditioned Response** (UCR) It is the response that occurs naturally in response to the unconditioned stimulus *For example* The coming of saliva in the mouth after seeing our favourite food is the Unconditioned Response (UCR).

Phase 2 : During Conditioning

During the second phase of classical conditioning, the previous neutral stimulus is repeatedly paired with the unconditioned stimulus. As a result of this pairing or linking, an association between the previously neutral stimulus and the UCS is formed. At this point, the neutral stimulus becomes the conditioned stimulus.

For example In Pavlov's experiment when the sound of the bell was linked paired to the smell of the food given to the dog then only the ringing of the bell (earlier neutral stimulus now conditioned stimulus) produced a Conditioned Response (CR).

The conditioned response was the salivation of mouth and conditioned stimulus was the ringing of the bell.

Phase 3 : After Conditioning

Once the association has been made between the unconditioned stimulus and conditioned stimulus then presenting the conditioned stimulus alone will bring out a response even without the conditioned response is the learned response to the previously neutral stimulus.

For example The Conditioned Response (CR) is the salivation of the mouth. Whereas, the neutral stimulus was the ringing of the bell. When the neutral stimulus (ringing bell) was linked to the unconditioned stimulus then the neural stimulus became the conditioned stimulus. Now even when the smell of the food is absent, only the ringing of the bell would generate the salivation of the mouth.

Phenomenon in Pavlov's Experiment

Behavioural psychologists describes a number of different phenomenons associated with classical conditioning. Some of these involve the initial establishment of response while others describe the disappearance of a response. *The following phenomenons are associated with classical conditioning*

Acquisition

Acquisition is the initial stage of learning. It occurs when a response is first established and gradually strengthened. During the acquisition a neutral stimulus is repeatedly paired with an unconditioned stimulus. After an association is made, the subject will begin to show a particular behaviour in response to previously neutral stimulus, which is now known as *conditioned stimulus*. At this point, we say that the response has been acquired.

Extinction

Extinction is when the occurrences of a conditioned response disappears or decreases. In classical conditioning, this happens when a conditioned stimulus is no longer paired with an unconditioned stimulus. A number of factors can influence how resistant a behaviour is to extinction. The strength of original conditioning plays an important role in it. The longer the conditioning has taken place and the magnitude of the conditioning process makes the response more resistant to extinction. Behaviours that are very well established may also become resistant to extinction.

Spontaneous Recovery

Sometimes a learned response can suddenly reemerge after the period of extinction. Spontaneous recovery is the reemergence of the conditioned response after a rest period or period of lessened response. The phenomenon of spontaneous recovery demonstrates that extinction is not the same as unlearning. The response might disappear but it does not mean that it has been forgotten or eliminated.

After a conditioned response has been extinguished, spontaneous recovery may gradually increase as the time passes. However, the response that reoccurs is not the same strength as the original response unless additional conditioning takes place.

Stimulus Generalisation

Stimulus generalisation is the tendency for the conditioned stimulus to bring out similar responses after the response has been conditioned.

For example If a child has been conditioned to fear a stuffed white rat, it will invoke a fear of objects similar to the conditioned stimulus such as a white toy or any furry white object.

Stimulus generalisation can influence responses to the conditioned stimulus. Once a person has been trained to respond to a stimulus, very similar stimuli may produce similar response as well. This can be problematic particularly in cases where the individual needs to be able to distinguish between stimuli and the response only to a very specific stimulus. *For example* If a person is afraid of spiders, then He/She will be afraid of spiders of all sizes and even photographs of spiders.

Stimulus Discrimination

Discrimination is the ability to differentiate between a conditioned stimulus and other stimuli that have not been paired with the unconditioned stimulus.

In a well known experiment of classical conditioning, researchers paired the taste of meat (unconditioned stimulus) with the sight of a circle (conditioned stimulus). The dogs learnt to salivate in the response to the presentation of a circle. The researchers found that the dogs would also salivate in response to the presentation of an ellipse. Over a period of time, the dogs experienced more and more trails where they did not experience the taste of meat upon seeing the ellipse. They became able to discriminate between the two similar stimuli (circle and ellipse).

Issues in Pavlov's Experiment

Pavlov's theory of classical conditioning has helped us understand how people learn to associate stimulus to a particular response. It emphasises upon learning from the environment and is based on scientific and empirical evidence. But the process of conditioning has a number of disadvantages too. *Following issues are related to the process of conditioning*

- Classical conditioning does not take into account free will. Classical conditioning suggests that everything can be learnt through the environment. Whereas, if doesn't take into account the free will of the individual. The individual has control over his actions and may not always be influenced by the environmental factors.
- It does not take into account uniqueness in human beings. An individual can be conditioned to respond to certain stimuli but the individual can change his mind to respond in a certain way, not influenced by the environmental factors.
- There is no predictive quality to classical conditioning. Different people respond to different stimulus in different ways. *For example* Smell of one food all of the time can cause one person to feel hungry whereas other may become ill due to it.
- It does not differentiate between creating and learning. Classical conditioning doesn't help someone to create new behaviours. It is a learning process which connects a natural response to the stimulus that is present in the environment. Whereas, creating new behaviour is a natural outcome. It is difficult to measure as the response can provide different levels of success in each situation.
- It doesnot take into account variables that can change the possible outcomes.
  There are various changes that occur in stable environments which impacts how someone reacts. Individual experiences, perspectives and habits are just as essential to final outcomes as other factors.
- The effect of classical conditioning is temporary classical conditioning can create positive response to different stimulus. But as the time passes, the response fades.
- It does not take into account the effects of genetics on learning.

Genetics plays an important role in the process of learning. The brain starts to develop during the embryonic stage. It continues to evolve as the child grows older. But in the embryonic stages, the brain develops under the direction of certain genetic programs.

Other issues concerning conditioning process includes

- Individuals can learn by observations rather than learning through conditioning.
- Conditioning alone doesnot take into account all human behaviour.
- Different species have different capacities for learning by conditioning.
- Studies conducted an animals may be unethical and cannot be generalised on humans.

Instrumental Learning

Instrumental conditioning is another term for operant conditioning, a learning process first described by BF Skinner. In instrumental learning, reinforcement or punishment are used to either increase or decrease the probability of occurrence of a behaviour again in the future.

For Examples

- If a student is rewarded with praise every time she raises her hand in class, he or she becomes more likely to raise his/her hand again in the future. If he/she is also scolded when he/she speaks out of turn, he/she becomes less likely to interrupt the class. In these examples, the teacher is using reinforcement to strengthen the hand-raising behaviour and punishment to weaken the talking out of turn behaviour.
- Instrumental conditioning is often used in animal training as well. *For example* Training a dog to shake hands would involve offering a reward every time the desired behaviour occurs.

Thorndike's work had a tremendous effect on BF Skinner's later research on operant conditioning. Skinner even created his own version of Thorndike's puzzle boxes which he referred to as an operant chamber, also known as a *Skinner box*.

Skinner identified two key types of behaviours. The first type is **respondent behaviours**. These are simply actions that occur reflexively without any learning. If you touch something hot, you will immediately draw your hand back in response. Classical conditioning focuses on these respondent behaviours.

Skinner realised that while classical conditioning could explain how respondent behaviours could lead to learning, it could not account for every type of learning. Instead, he suggested that it was the consequences of voluntary actions that lead to the greatest amount of learning.

The second type of behaviours is what Skinner referred to as **operant behaviours**. He defined these as any and every voluntary behaviour that acts upon the environment to create a response. These are the voluntary behaviours that are under our conscious control. These are also actions that can be learned. The consequences of our actions play an important role in the learning process.

Phenomenons in Instrumental Learning

When learning takes place, it involves occurrence of certain processes and phenomenons. These phenomenons include reinforcement, extinction, generalisation, discrimination and spontaneous recovery.

Reinforcement

Reinforcement is the operation of administering a reinforcer by the experimenter. Reinforcers are stimulus that increase the rate or probability of responses that precedes. The responses that are reinforced increases in rate of occurrence, whereas, the responses that are not reinforced decreases. Reinforcers may be primary or secondary. A primary reinforcer is biologically important as it determines organism's survival. *For example* Food for an hungry organism.

A secondary reinforcer is one which has acquired characteristics of the reinforcer because of person's experience with the environment. Praise, grades, money etc. are generally the secondary reinforcers.

Extinction

Extinction means disappearance of a learned response due to removal of reinforcements from the situations in which the response generally occurred. The learned behaviour gradually disappears if the conditioning processes are not continued. Learning shows resistence to extinction. This means that even when the learned response is not reinforced, it would continue to occur for sometime. But if the trials are conducted without reinforcements then the response gradually decreases and ultimately stops occurring.

It has been generally found that with increasing number of reinforced trials, resistance to extinction increases and learned response reaches its highest level. At this level, the performance is stabilised and after that the number of trials do not make a difference in the strength of the response. The resistance to extinction increases with increasing number of reinforcements and beyond a certain point, increasing reinforcements reduces the resistence to extinction.

If the reinforcement is delayed during acquisition trials, the resistance to extinction increases. Reinforcement makes the response less resistant to extinction, whereas, partial reinforcement makes a response more resistance to extinction.

Generalisation and Discrimination

The process of generalisation and discrimination occurs in all kinds of learning. The phenomenon of responding similarly to similar stimuli is known as *generalisation*. A learned response occurs by a new stimulus in the phenomenon of genralisation. Discrimination is complementary to generalisation. Discrimination is a response due to difference occurrence of generalisation means failure of discrimination. Discriminative response depends upon the discrimination capacity of the organisms or individual.

Spontaneous Recovery

Spontaneous recovery occurs after a learned response is finished. As some time passes without any reinforcements, the response gets extinguished and doesnot occur again. But it has been seen that the conditioned response occurs again after passage of a considerable amount of time. The amount of spontaneous recovery depends on the duration of the time lapsed after the extinction. The longer the duration of time lapsed, the greater the recovery of learned response, such recovery occurs suddenly.

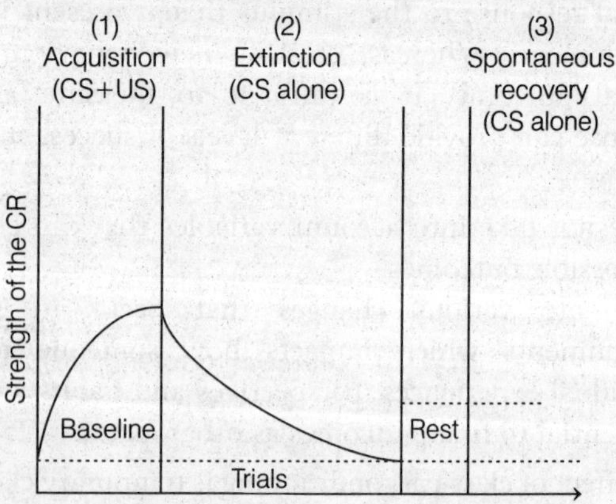

Basic Paradigms Associated with Instrumental Learning

There are many paradigms related to instrumental learning. *They have been explained in brief below*

- **Acquisition Paradigm** In acquisition paradigm, an outcome is typically paired with making a response in the presence of a stimulus.

- **Extinction Paradigm** In extinction paradigm, the pairing typically ceases within this broad framework (particularly with respect to acquisition), several additional paradigms may be distinguished.
- **Appetitive or Approach Paradigm** In appetitive or approach learning, the animal makes a response that results in a desired reward. This is the type of learning involving reinforcement. But it is not the only paradigm based on reinforcement.
- **Omission Training** Another paradigm that deserves particular note is omission training, in which an animal has to suppress or withhold a response in order to get its reward. *For example* Sheffield trained dogs to salivate in the presence of a tone associated with food and then shifted them to omission training. In this latter phase, the dogs had to avoid salivating to the tone for several seconds to get the food. Omission training is initially typically difficult and displays a relatively slow learning curve. However, there are several studies suggesting that in the long run, it will be as effective as extinction in decreasing the frequency of a response.
- **Escape Paradigm** Another paradigm based on reinforcement is escape learning. In escape learning, the animal learns a response that gets it away from punishment, either by turning off the punisher, or by allowing the animal to leave the area where the punishment was administered. Escape learning is closely associated with another paradigm, avoidance learning.
  In avoidance learning, the punishment is intermittent rather than continuous. If the animal makes the proper response before the punishment comes on, it will succeed in cancelling that punishment.
- **Punishment Training Paradigm** Punishment training (or aversive learning), of course, involves the administration of an unpleasant, aversive outcome following a response. Thus, punishment training, omission training and extinction all have in common reducing the level of a given response, whereas, appetitive learning, escape learning and avoidance learning attempt to increase response level.
- **Transfer Training Paradigm** Another paradigm, transfer training will prove important, especially when we focus on discrimination. In transfer training, we look at the effects of learning one task on another. Transfer might be non-existent (zero), positive (facilitation: the learning is faster) or negative (inhibition: there is interference). In addition, transfer effects might be proactive (in which we look at the effect of an earlier task on the learning or performance of a later task) or retroactive (in which we saw how the later task influences performance of the earlier one).
- **Shaping Paradigm** A final paradigm involves shaping. Normally, approach learning applies to responses that are not especially frequent to start with, since we want to track an increase in frequency as one of our measures of learning. Thus, we find ourselves in the following situation: we sit in the lab, watching our animal subject, waiting for it to make the desired response so that we can administer the reinforcer.
  Shaping is a very powerful technique, not only because of its ability to 'coax' low frequency responses out of an animal, but also and especially because of its ability to mould a response that is not normally part of the animal's skills. Thus, by combining shaping and chaining, instrumental conditioning allows us to train totally new responses, rather than just transfer stimulus control of an old response to a new stimulus.

Operant v/s Instrumental Learning

Finally, it is important to note a distinction that is sometimes made between what is termed instrumental conditioning and operant conditioning.

Instrumental Learning

In instrumental conditioning, the emphasis is on a discrete trial, a situation in which there is a clear starting point and a clear terminus. We may measure how long it takes the animal to make the response during the trial or we may measure the relative probability of the animal's success.

So, to take Thorndike's puzzlebox apparatus, the start of the trial occurs when a cat is placed in the puzzlebox and it ends when the cat has made the escape response. How long this takes is what we are interested in. Similarly, in maze learning, the trial starts with the animal being placed in the start box and ends when the animal has found its way to the goal box.

In a third example, choice discrimination, the trial starts when the animal is exposed to two stimuli and ends when the animal makes a response relevant to one of them. Our interest in this situation typically involves whether the animal has chosen the correct stimulus.

Operant Learning

There are no discrete trials in operant conditioning, on the other hand. A standard apparatus for operant conditioning involves a Skinner Box, a chamber with something that can be manipulated (a key to peck; a bar to press; a lever to move); various discriminative stimuli that may be turned on or off (lights; noises) and means to automatically administer reinforcements or punishments (food or shock dispensers connected to the bar.

Reinforcement

Contiguity is the oldest principle of association; reinforcement is the newest. **Aristotle** recognised that association occurred because of temporal and spatial contiguity. Reinforcement, as a principle of association, is a development of the 20th century.

A reinforcer may be either positive or negative. A positive reinforcer may be identified as any state an organism will undertake to approach or achieve. A negative reinforcer may be defined as any state an organism will undertake or reduce or to avoid.

But these definitions describe only the incentive function of reinforcers. They define reinforcement in terms of approach and avoidance and say nothing about the relation of reinforcement to association or learning.

Reinforcers

Reinforcers may also be defined in terms of their effects on associational connections. Thus, a positive reinforcer is sometimes defined as one which produces a strengthening of a stimulus response connection or one which increases the probability of occurrence of the response. A negative reinforcer may similarly be defined as one which weakens a stimulus response connection or decreases the probability of a response. While the incentive property of reinforcers are denied by no one, the issue of whether reinforcers operate to strengthen associational connections is an issue of debate that is difficult to resolve. The term positive reinforcement and negative reinforcement are closely associated with reward and punishment.

They cannot be used interchangeably with the latter terms, however, reward and punishment are general terms that can be used by any learning theorist regardless of his position. Thus, one can be a strict behaviourist and assert that contiguity is the necessary and sufficient condition of learning and still talk about the effects of reward and punishment. The use of the word reinforcement implies incentive properties as a minimum and an influence on associative strength as an additional option.

In using the terms, most reinforcement theorists assume that positive and negative reinforcers are inseparably associated. A drive state, such as hunger, is regarded as a negative reinforcer and the food reward that relieves the state as a positive reinforcer. An unpleasant state, such as fear, is a negative reinforcer; a reduction in fear is a positive reinforcer. Among reinforcement theorist, however, the term negative reinforcement is rarely used. Instead, the tendency is to use the terms drive or aversive stimulus to suggest a role in the instigation of action and occasionally the term negative incentive to emphasis the tendency to avoid such a stimulus.

Explanations of Reinforcement

A basic explanation of the nature of reinforcement is that, it is a reduction of a biological need. This need-reduction theory is generally identified with Hull, who specified that the reduction is a stimulus that is characteristic of a biological need. It is what actually constitutes reinforcement.

All of the stimuli closely associated with actual need reduction can acquire reinforcing properties and instances of reinforcement without reduction in a secondary reinforcers. If reinforcement has no obvious connection with hunger, thirst, fear or sexual needs, then additional drives or needs can be postulated.

Skinner says that any stimulus that increases the probability of response is a reinforcer by definition. If a stimulus is identified as a reinforcer in one situation, it can be used as a reinforcer in another situation, a condition that makes the definition general.

Types of Reinforcement

Following are the types of ireinforcements

Primary Reinforcer

A primary reinforcer is a reinforcer that satisfies a biological need. Food, water, oxygen and warmth are examples of possible primary reinforcers. Physical affection and cuddling may also address biological needs, thus serving as primary reinforcers. There may be individual differences in what constitute primary reinforcers *e.g.* sex will be reinforcing to some individuals, but not to others and a certain drug will be a primary reinforcer for a drug addict, but not for a non addicted individual.

Secondary Reinforcer

A secondary reinforcer, also known as a *conditioned reinforcer*, is a previously neutral stimulus, that has become reinforcing to an organism through repeated association with another reinforcer. Examples of secondary reinforcers, which do not satisfy any obvious biological necessities, are praise, grades, money and feelings of success.

Some psychologists believe that secondary reinforcers are learned through the processes of classical conditioning. A neutral stimulus is paired with an existing reinforcer Unconditioned Stimulus (UCS) that brings out some form of biological satisfaction Unconditined Response (UCR). That neutral stimulus becomes a Condistioned Stimulus that elicit the same satisfaction Conditioned Response (CR).

The relative influences of primary and secondary reinforcers on our lives probably depend a great deal on economic circumstance. When such biological necessities as food and warmth are scarce, these primary reinforcers and the secondary reinforcers closely associated with them, may be major factors in reinforcing behaviour.

On the other hand, in times of economic well being, when cupboards are full and houses are warm, such secondary reinforcers as praise, grades and feelings of success are more likely to play a major role in the learning process.

In addition to the distinction between primary and secondary reinforcers, a distinction can also be made between positive and negative reinforcement.

Let's examine these two forms of reinforcement and look at how they are different from punishment.

Positive Reinforcement

Positive reinforcement involves the presentation of a stimulus after the response. Food, praise, a smile and success are all positive reinforcers.

Negative Reinforcement

Negative reinforcement increases the response through the removal of a stimulus, usually an aversive or unpleasant one. *For example* Rats will learn to press a bar in order to terminate an electric shock; removal of the aversive shock is a negative reinforcer. As another example, many newer cars sound a loud buzzer, if the keys are still in the ignition, when the drivers door is opened; removal of the keys from the ignition is negatively reinforcer because the buzzer stops.

The removal of anxiety or guilt can be an extremely powerful negative reinforcer. A child may confess to an offence committed days or even weeks earlier because she has been feeling guilty about the transgression all that time and needs to get it off the mind.

Anxiety may drive one student to complete a term paper early, thereby removing an item from his 'things to do' list. At the same time, another student confronted with the same term paper might drag until the last minute, thereby removing anxiety-although only temporarily about the more difficult aspects of researching and writing that paper.

Punishment

Both positive reinforcement and negative reinforcement increase the responses they follow. Punishment, on the other hand, is likely to decrease these responses, punishment is different from negative reinforcement. There are actually two different forms of punishment, frequently referred to as punishment I and punishment II.

Punishment I involves the presentation of a stimulus, usually an aversive one. Scolding and spanking are examples of this form of punishment. Punishment II involves the removal of a stimulus, usually a pleasant one *e.g.* include fines for misbehaviours and loss of privileges. The following figure illustrates the differences among positive reinforcement, negative reinforcement, punishment I and punishment II.

Schedules of Reinforcement

Skinner tried several different rules of reinforcement schedules, for deciding which responses to reinforce and he found that the choice of schedule had important consequences for how his animals responded. Here, there are some of the schedules, he used and then looked at their effects on behaviour.

The simplest schedule is to reinforce a response every time it occurs. This schedule is known, as a *Continuous Reinforcement* (CRF) schedule. In the real world, though, behaviour is rarely reinforced consistently. *For example* Children are not praised everytime they tell the truth and factory workers are not paid every time they tighten a screw, instead, most behaviour is reinforced on intermitted or partial, reinforcement schedules.

Two types of partial reinforcement schedules have been studied, most commonly ratio schedules and interval schedules.

Ratio Schedule

In a ratio schedule, reinforcement depends on the number of responses that have been emitted. *For example* In piece work a worker's wages depends solely on the number of units completed, regardless of how long the job takes.

Interval Schedule

In an interval schedule, on the other hand, the passage of time, since the last reinforcement rather than the number of responses, determines whether the next response will be reinforced or not.

For example Whether someone searches his mail, the next time they go to mailbox, will depend on how long it has been, since the last time they searched the mail, not on how often they visited the mailbox in the interim. Note that obtaining mail in this example still requires a response.

Further complicating matters, ratio and interval schedules can be subdivided according to whether the requirement for reinforcement is fixed or variable. In a Fixed Interval (FI) schedule, the interval that must elapse before a response can be reinforced is always the same, whereas in a Variable Interval (VI) schedule this interval is varied. Ratio schedules are subdivided in a similar way. In a Fixed Ratio (FR) schedule, the number of responses required for reinforcement is always the same. In a Variable Ratio (VR) schedule, the number of responses required to obtain reinforcement varies across successive reinforcement.

Simple Reinforcement Schedules

Various reinforcement schedules are given below

Fixed Ratio

On this schedule, the ratio of responses to reinforcements is fixed and regular so that *e.g.* every fifth response that the subject makes produces reinforcement. This schedule is analogous to piece work pay rates in industry, where one may be paid a certain amount or given a certain bonus for every fifth electronic device assembled. Fixed-ratio schedules of reinforcement produce a high rate of responding with, a pause in the rate after the delivery of the reinforcement.

The development of characteristic fixed-ratio behaviour in a rate across successively more stringent ratio is shown in the figure below.

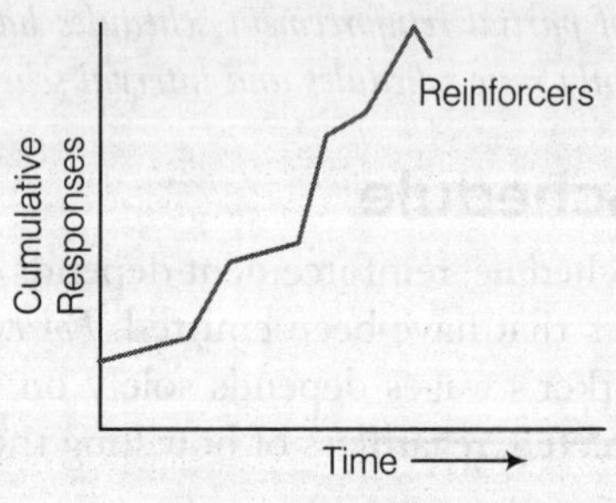

Fixed Interval (FR)

The high rate of responding obtained in fixed-ratio schedules seems reasonable, since there is a direct contingency between the subject's rate of responding and the delivery of reinforcement; the faster the subject responds, the sooner the reinforcement is obtained.

Variable Ratio

In a Variable Ratio (VR) schedule, there is also a relationship between the number of responses the subject makes and the delivery of reinforcement, but the relationship is varied rather than fixed. *For example* The first reinforcement may be delivered after 10 responses, the next after 20 responses, the third after 10 responses, etc.

The VR schedule is characterised by the average number of responses it takes to produce a reinforcement. *For example* If the three ratio values given just above were the only values used and they were presented in an irregular order, then the schedule could be characterised as a VR-15, since on the average, it would take 15 response to produce a reinforcement. A more complete description of a VR schedule would include a specification, of the actual ratios reinforced and their sequence of presentation.

The behaviour associated with VR schedules is similar to the behaviour produced by FR schedules in that there is generally a high rate of sustained responding interrupted by occasional pauses. However, on VR schedule these pauses are less frequent and are not correlated with the delivery of a reinforcement. An example of performance on a VR schedule is presented in the figure below.

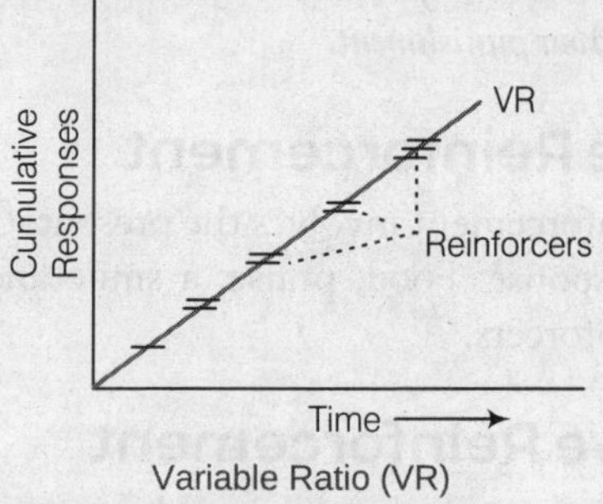

Variable Ratio (VR)

Fixed Interval

In a Fixed Interval (FI) schedule, the delivery of a reinforcement depends upon both the passage of a time interval and the occurrence of a response. *For example.* In a Fixed-Interval one-minute schedule (FI-1'), the first response after the passage of one minute produces a reinforcement. In FI schedules, the subject may ideally obtain reinforcement by making only one response each interval; responses, that occur before the interval has passed, have no bearing on the availability of reinforcement. Although, the behaviour produced by FI schedules does not match the theoretical ideal, it is influenced in a systematic fashion by the passage of the time period.

Generally, there is a pause after the delivery of the reinforcement and then a gradual increase in the rate of responding as the availability of a reinforcement draws near, behaviour produces a pattern termed a scallop on a cumulative record as shown in the figure.

In comparison with Fixed ratio schedules, Fixed internal schedules produce lower overall rates of responding and the transition from the pause after reinforcement to responding tends to be less abrupt on FI than on FR schedules.

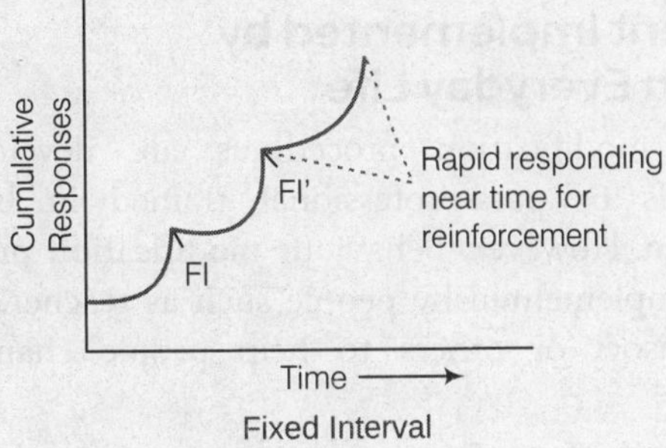

Fixed Interval

The rate of responding on FI schedules is related to the length of the interval, the longer the interval the lower is the overall rate of responding. This lower overall rate of responding is in turn, quite likely related to the length of the pause after reinforcement, which appears to increase directly with the length of the fixed interval. In speculating about the processes controlling the typical FI behaviour, it seems quite likely that the subjects from a temporal discrimination, with the delivery of reinforcement serve as a cue that another reinforcement will not be forth coming for some period of time.

Variable Interval

A Variable Interval (VI) schedule is similar to a FI schedule except that the length of time between the availability of successive reinforcements is varied rather than fixed. *For example* The first reinforcement may be produced by the first response following a one minute interval, the second reinforcement by the first response following a three minute interval, the third by the first response following a two minute interval, etc.

Such a schedule with different time intervals occurring a random order may be designated by the length of the average interval. In the example given just above, if only one-two and three-minute intervals were used and if they were presented in a random order and used equally often, then the schedule could be designated as VI-2.

In the VI, as in the VR schedule, the irregular changes in the availability and delivery of reinforcement deprive the subject of any cue that it can reliably use to predict the occurrence of the next reinforcement. And in the VI as the VR schedule, the subjects behaviour is less regular; there is no consistent pattern, like scalloping, associated with VI schedules. Instead, the typical steady-state behaviour produced by VI schedules is characterised by generally consistent rate of responding as demonstrated in the figure given below.

These four basic schedules of intermittent reinforcement include conditions, in which the delivery of reinforcement is either directly related to the number of responses or depends on the passage of time as well as on a response and either of these schedules may be regular or irregular.

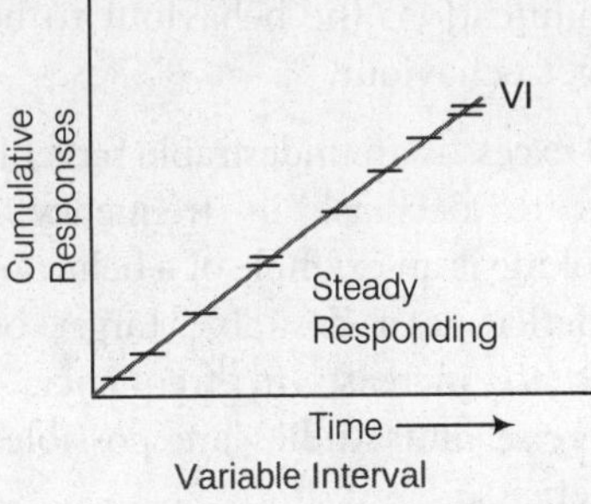

Variable Interval

In general, ratio schedules produce higher rates of responding than interval schedules and fixed schedules produce more stereotyped and regular behaviour patterns than varied schedules. The exact relationship between schedules depends on the parameters of schedules.

Behaviour Modification

Behaviour modification is the field of psychology concerned with analysing and modifying any undesirable human behaviour.

- **Analysing** means identifying the functional relationship between the environment and a particular behaviour to understand the reasons for behaviour or to determine, why a person behaved as he or she did.
- **Modifying** means developing and implementing procedures to help people change their behaviour. It involves altering environmental events, so as to influence behaviour.
- **Behaviour Modification Procedures** are used by professionals or para-professionals to help a person change socially significant behaviours, with the goals of improving some aspect of the person's life. An alternative term for behaviour modification is known as *applied behaviour analysis*.

Characteristics of Behaviour Modification

The following are some characteristic that define behaviour modification

Focus on Behaviour

Behaviour modification procedures are designed to change behaviour, not a personal characteristic or trait. *For example* Behaviour modification is not used to change autism, rather, behaviour modification is used to change problem behaviours exhibited by autistic children.

Behavioural excess and behavioural deficits are targets for change with behaviour modification procedures. In behaviour modification, the behaviour to be modified is called the target behaviour.

A behavioural excess is an undesirable target behaviour the person wants to decrease in frequency, duration or intensity. Smoking is an example of a behavioural excess. A behavioural deficit is a desirable target behaviour the person wants to increase in frequency, duration or intensity. Exercise and studies are possible examples of behavioural deficits.

Procedures based on Behavioural Principle

Behaviour modification is the application of basic principles originally derived from experimental research with laboratory animals. The scientific study of human behaviour is called the experimental analysis of human behaviour or applied behaviour analysis. Behaviour modification procedures are based on research in applied behaviour analysis that have been conducted for more than 40 years.

Emphasis on Current Environmental Events

Behaviour modification involves assessing and modifying the current environmental events that are functionally related to the behaviour. Human behaviour is controlled by events in the immediate environment and the goal of behaviour modification is to identify those events. Once these controlling variables have been identified, they are altered to modify the behaviour.

Successful behaviour modification procedures alter the functional relationships between the behaviour and the controlling variables in the environment to produce a desired change in behaviour. Sometimes, labels are mistakenly identified as the causes of behaviour. *For example* A person might say that an autistic child engages in problem behaviours, because the child is autistic.

Description of Behaviour Modification Procedures

Behaviour modification procedures involve specific changes in environmental events that are functionally related to the behaviour. For the procedures to be effective each time they are used the specific changes in environmental events must occur each time they are used. By describing procedures precisely, researchers and other professionals make it more likely that the procedures will be used correctly each time.

Treatment Implemented by People in Everyday Life

Behaviour modification procedures are developed by professionals or para-professional trained in behaviour modification. However, behaviour modification procedures often are implemented by people such as teacher, parents, job supervisors or others to help people change their behaviour.

People, who implement behaviour modification procedures should do so only after sufficient training. Precise descriptions of procedures and professional supervision make it more likely that parents, teachers and others will implement procedures correctly.

Measurement of Behaviour Change

One of the merit of behaviour modification is its emphasis on measuring the behaviour before and after intervention to document the behaviour change resulting from the behaviour modification procedures.

De-emphasis on Past Events as Cause of Behaviour

As stated earlier, behaviour modification places emphasis on current environmental events as the causes of behaviour. However, knowledge of the past might also provide some useful information about environmental events related to the current behaviour. *For example* Previous learning experiences have been shown to influence current behaviour.

Rejection of Hypothetical Underlying Causes of Behaviour

Although, some fields of psychology such as Freudian psychoanalytic approaches, might be interested in hypothesised underlying cause of behaviour, such as unresolved conflicts.

Skinner has called such explanations explanatory fictions because they can never be proven or disproven and thus, are unscientific. These supposed underlying causes can never be measured or manipulated to demonstrate a functional relationship to the behaviour they are intended to explain.

Applications of Behaviour Modification

The application of behaviour modification to the alleviation of various social problems is of primary concern. Specific issues such as energy consumption, pollution control, welfare of citizens, worker's performance, crime, social integration can be solved through the application of behaviour modification techniques.

The following are the applications of behaviour modification

- **Reducing Energy Consumption** A system is devised to monitor energy consumption. Behaviour modification techniques are used to provide reinforcers such as food, saving to modify the consumption of energy in the households. Similarly, consumption of fuel, gas, oil can be reduced.
- **Controlling Pollution** Techniques of behaviour modification have been used to control littering and pollution in mass transit systems, public places etc. Positive reinforcements like providing rewards for reducing litter were used to stop the throwing of garbage etc. in the public places.
- **Improving Welfare** Positive reinforcements such as utensils, rugs, toys, stoves etc. are used to improve the attendance of citizens in self-help group meetings and other such welfare programs. It can also be used to improve student's participation in educational programs.
- **Worker's Performance** Worker's performance can be improved by using monetary reinforcement contingencies to decrease absenteeism and decreasing productivity of workers.
- **Social Integration** Behaviour modification offers a way to structure reinforcement contingencies to facilitate social integration among the individuals of different faith and races.

Cognitive Approaches in Learning

Cognition refers to mental activity including thinking, remembering, learning and using language. When cognitive approach to learning and teaching is applied, the focus is centered on the understanding of information and concepts. If the connections between concepts can be understood, information can be broken down and logical connection can be rebuilt, then our retention of material and under standing will strengthen.

Latent learning, observational learning, verbal learning and discrimination learning form main components of cognitive learning. *The some have been explained briefly below*

Latent Learning

The concept of latent learning relates to the fact that under specified conditions, organisms can learn correct response tendencies, without immediately executing them in overt behaviour and proper reward incentives not being there. Simply stated latent learning signifies learning that is not revealed or reflected in performance.

It is learning, which does not alter performance in any way, having no immediate effects on it. More theoretically inclined psychologists of the expectancy persuasion, wanting to challenge the law of effect, further stipulated that not only it is learning, which occurs without manifesting itself in overt performance, but also, it is what accrues without any reward or reinforcement.

For instance, it is obvious that no one will perform an act without some incentive even though one is skilled to perform that act. This, however, leads one to believe that even for knowing or learning, some incentive is necessary since, in the usual laboratory experiment, the two learning and performance, are inextricably mixed up. Latent learning experimentation may be viewed as an elaborate attempt to extricate the effective conditions of either.

Experiments on Latent Learning

Apparently, men acquire quite a good bit of knowledge merely by going through a course of experience although they may not get anything else from it. Similarly, rats may learn something about a place like a maze merely by exploring it although they may not be rewarded for it. This is generally the expectancy position.

With food available in the goal box, the mazewise animals quickly learn to transverse the right path from start to finish, avoiding blind alleys at all choice points.

Latent learning experimenters from Blodgett and Tolman and Honizk have generally followed the procedure of just exposing the latent learning group of subjects to the experimental maze situation and of suddenly introducing reward at the end of some specified latent period and watching, if the performance level, immediately and more or less abruptly, catches with that of a control group, which is continuously rewarded.

Test of latent learning is usually made by comparing maximum reduction in errors between two consecutive trials of the control group with the decrease in error scores immediately on introducing food.

Past Experience in Latent Learning

It has also been found that past history and experience of the organism especially, if it had the opportunities of exercising its exploration drive, of taking wide eyed interest in the world of objects and environment and of overcoming the timid experiences in strange surroundings, determines whether the latent learning effects will be displayed by it.

Motivation in Latent Learning

Motivation sustains, energises and directs behaviour, in latent learning as elsewhere. More specifically, the exploratory drive maintains the free wondering, which probably provides opportunities for learning-spatial relationships like relative placements of start and finish, through paths and blocking dead-end-learning that becomes evident as soon as rewards are introduced. With multiple motives and ever changing pluralistic situations, diverse results are only to be expected.

Tolman's View on Latent Learning

In Tolman's view of learning, there is no effect on reinforcement of responses, but emphasis on certain noticeable signs leads to certain significates, validation or falsification of hopeful ideas and more or less probable hypothesis. What cognitive structures, cognitions or sign-significate expectancies the stuff of learning an animal may have, depends upon his specific motives, concerns and interests.

Motives, incentives are essentially 'emphasisers'. Even punishment may be correct choice, probably the only function of which is known to facilitate learning. Quite conceivably, punishment may be beneficial or injurious according as the learner's view or cognitions about it.

In some instances atleast its value as a striking reminder and emphasiser of the correct path cannot be denied. Vividness of signs, significates or both is almost effectively facilitative of learning. The twin pleasure-pain motivational principles, which have been exercising man's thinking over millennia, teach emphasis and quality through their accent.

Sign-significate or 'what leads to what' expectancies are strengthened on being confirmed and weakened on being non confirmed or disconfirmed. Confirmation occurs, when environmental events actually happen as expected. Expectancies are established in proportion to the confirmation they receive, which increases their probability value. When they do not receive confirmation to that extent, their probability value is decreased.

The distinction between confirmation and reinforcement can be illustrated by Tolman's own example regarding how likes and dislikes about eating places may be acquired: they are not learned on the basis of need reduction, but through confirming experiences that past visits to a particular place have always led to delicious foods, at reasonable prices and so on.

According to **Tolman**, "the strengthening mechanism is just plain confirmation of expectancies and not any stamping in of correct response through reinforcement".

Observation Learning

The **social learning** or **modeling theory** developed by **Albert Bandura** especially emphasises the important roles played by derived, symbolic and self-regulatory processes in psychological functioning. Virtually all learning phenomena resulting from direct experiences can occur on a derived basic through observation of other people's behaviour and its consequences for the observer.

Accordingly, an individual may acquire intricate response patterns simply by observing the performances of appropriate models. Emotional responses can be conditioned observationally by witnessing the affective reactions of others undergoing painful or pleasurable experiences; fearful and avoidant behaviour can be extinguished through observation of modelled approach behaviour toward feared objects without any adverse consequences to the performer. Inhibitions can be induced by witnessing the behaviour of other punished. Finally, the expression of well-learned responses is extensively controlled by the modeling stimulus.

While many theories of learning depict learning and behavioural change in terms of associational processes, *i.e.* coupling and recoupling of stimuli to responses, Bandura's research demonstrates that behavioural changes produced through instrumental conditioning, classical conditioning, extinction and punishment are, largely, cognitively modified. Operant conditioning is difficult to achieve without awareness of the responses required for reinforcement under some circumstances.

The schedules of reinforcement that people believe to be in effect are much more powerful than the actual reinforcement in regulating their behaviour. Paired stimulation usually does not result in classical conditioning subjects, which are unaware of the stimulus contingencies. Emotional conditioning can be attained by substituting symbolically produced arousal for physically aversive events as the unconditioned stimulus. In most instances, a symbolic self-stimulation system intervenes between external stimuli and response.

Persons can regulate their own behaviour to some extent by visualising self-generated consequences, with the many changes accompanying conditioning operations explained in terms of self-control processes.

Conditioning outcomes are viewed as "Reflecting the operation of mediating mechanisms rather than the direct coupling of stimuli with responses evoked by other events." Modelling theory is compatible with humanistic approaches, including humanistic value theory and morality.

Critical Study of Observational Learning

Bandura broke away from early social learning's interest in psychoanalytic concepts and its preoccupation with how imitation is maintained by reinforcement. *He made social learning theory a more convincing explanation of learning by contributing three key concepts.*

(i) **Observational Learning** It can be much broader than copying another person's behaviour. The child can symbolically construct a new behaviour by listening to another person or simply by reading. Complex new behaviours as well as simple modifications of previously acquired behaviours can be learned in this way. Furthermore, overt behaviour is not even necessary in order for learning to occur. As Bandura summarises the influences of models, they can serve as instructers, motivators, inhibitors, disinhibitors, social facilitator, and emotion arousers.

(ii) **Children are Self-regulatory** Although reinforce ment is not necessary for learning, it is helpful for self-regulation. Children observe, behaviours occuring around them. It lead to reinforcement and punishment and these observations are used as sources of information to help them informing rules, evaluate their performance, develop standards of conduct, set goals and decide in which situations to use the observed behaviour.

(iii) **Reciprocal Determinism Provides a Model of Behaviour Change** This is a source of influence to the person, his behaviour and his environment interaction. The environment does not always exert the greatest control. The most novel feature of this three-pronged model is that children's behaviour helps shape their environment, which in turn acts on them.

During development, children become more skilled at the four component processes of observational learning: attention, retention production and motivation.

Advantages of Learning Approach

- Bandura's theory is testable, flexible and integrative. It is flexible in that it continues to change in light of research outcomes. It is integrative in that it brings together several areas that, by themselves, are somewhat limited. These areas include operant conditioning, information processing, reinforcement processes and socialisation processes.
- Social learning theory holds great promise for correcting several shortcomings of Piagetian and information-processing theory, currently the most influential cognitive approaches.

The theory provides a way to conceptualise why the child's behaviour or demonstrated knowledge might vary from situation to situation. Second, it shows that focusing on physical concepts and ignoring the social context, in which they are acquired has resulted in an incomplete view of how concepts are learned.

There are two essential directions for further developing social learning theory. *First,* the interface between cognitive development and observational learning must be worked out in greater detail before the theory can be considered a truely developmental theory.

Second, the theory could become much more powerful in predicting and exploring behaviour, if it is acquired a broader ecological base. The theory has shown us that processes of social learning can guide development; the next step is to discover how the processes are tied to the environments typically found at various points in development, in various types of families and in various socio-economic niches.

Verbal Learning

In the literatue of learning theory, memorising kind of behaviour is referred to as verbal learning. In everyday language, we would refer to it as rote learning; that activity we engage, in when called upon to memorise foreign language vocabulary, word-for-word formulae and definitions and those helpful lectures.

The development of learning theory sometimes shows, what might be described as the theory's search for its own fountain of youth. Verbal learning, which is nothing more or less than the study of rote learnings, interests us for reasons. The first reason is a theoretical one. Learning a list of words in the form of foreign language vocabulary, or memorising a set of lines verbatim, can illustrate chaining of multiple associations and serve as a vehicle for the further development of the principals of learning. The second reason is a practical one. Whether desirable or not, rote learning represents a large bulk of formal learning in the early school years and later.

Early works on verbal learning are discussed below:

Reconstructive Memory

This reconstructive view of memory is attributed largely to the early work of **Sir Frederik Bartlett**. Numerous other studies have shown that, when memory for meaningful material is involved, it is often hard to tell whether correct recall is in fact reproduction or a reconstruction.

In other words, from the experimenter's point of view, the only difference between apparent verbatim recall and reconstructions based simply on remembered outlines may be only that the experimenter knows, which were presented and which were not. The so called verbatim response may have been the product of reconstruction.

Ebbinghaus and the Non-Sense Syllable

The study of verbal learning examines the processes involved in rote, verbatim memorisation of verbal materials. To overcome the problems inherent in the study of verbal memory, which is ordinarily a creative, reconstructive process, early students of verbal learning followed Ebbinghaus's lead by concentrating on meaningless materials such as nonsense syllables.

Three measures of retention were devised

- **Free Recall** The most direct measure of retention, free recall, simply involves reproducing, in correct order, as much of a learned list as possible from memory.
- **Savings** Even after one is no longer able to recall list under free-recall conditions, there may still be some residue of the initial learning. The savings method can discover the level of this trace by having the subject re-learn the forgotten material.
- **Recognition** If free recall is the most demanding, recognition is the least. This requires only that the person to be able to select from a larger group of items.

Discrimination Learning

Discrimination learning involves differential responding in the face of alternative stimuli. Discriminative control of behaviour is, in a sense, the opposite of generalisation of learning. It is learning not to generalise. In discrimination learning, in place of a generalised spread of a conditioned response to other test stimuli, there is constriction exclusively to some signal. Discriminations between stimuli are learned on the basis of differential responding and reinforcement. Thus, a given response to a specified stimulus may be appropriately reinforced, but the same response to any other stimuli may not only be not rewarded, but may be even punished.

For example A mother teaches her child to show his head, eyes, ears, nose etc. If he correctly identifies he is rewarded with affectionate head-pats; if he points wrongly, he receives a rather stern forbidding 'No'. In due course, he learns to distinguish between his right and left hand and so on.

Essentially, all this illustrates discrimination learning. Discrimination behaviour is learned at all stages, from the elementary to the most sophisticated levels. The basic maxim of discrimination learning is 'reinforce responding to one stimulus and does not reinforce or extinguish the response to the other. Discrimination is accomplished through systematic reinforcement and non-reinforcement.

Transposition Tests

Arising out of discrimination learning, experiments known as transposition tests, are interesting as well as significant from a theoretical point of view. In a size discrimination experiment of this sort, it is found that transposition test is involved discrimination learning mediating generalisation.

Generalisation test trials with the high and low tones were scattered during the course of conditioning trials. Consistently with the requirements of generalisation paradigm the high and low test tones were never presented together with the US (airpuff). So far, the setup is no different from the usual tests of primary generalisation. Demonstration of mediated generalisation, however, comes through asking the subjects to also make distinctive manual reactions to different tone stimuli.

The different manual responses may be pushing a lever, when either the high or the intermediate (CS) tones are sounded and pulling it when the low tone is given. Presumably tones sharing the common manual response are thereby rendered more alike and become more sharply distinguished from the other associated with a different movement. General result was that more eyeblinks were given to a test stimulus, when it shared similar manual response with the CS than when the test stimulus had a different response attached to it.

Learning Sets (Learning-to-Learn)

Learned discriminations are involved in transfer tests through generalisation. They may operate over long succession of tests as well and essentially through the same mechanism-discrimination and generalisation. Over a long series of discrimination learning tasks, remarkable improvement occurs in organism's ability not only to make a given individual discrimination, but also in its general ability to master any similar problem. Overall improvement in learning efficiency occurs in all manner of tasks from simple to complex.

This phenomenon of increased efficiency or generalised improvement in learning each new task of a certain class, has been mentioned as development of learning sets. In his well known study concerning formation of learning sets, in each new task of a sequence of about 300 discrimination problems, monkeys learned to choose from among two objects, the one which was positive or correct. Surprisingly enough, although all the tasks were about equally difficult, later discrimination were made more and more rapidly until, in the end, unfailing discrimination and selection of the positive object ensured in just one or two trials.

Apparently, not only did the animal learn each new task afresh, but while doing so, he has also learned how to learn other similar tasks. Additionally, he has acquired many useful details of the technique of attacking similar problems.

Learning sets have been demonstrated across many species including young humans and have been used in rank ordering them along an evolutionary scale. Even within humans, normal children are found to excel in comparison with defectives, on learning sets or learning-to-learn tasks.

Neurophysiology of Learning

Different species need to learn the same kinds of lessons including how events in the world are related to each other and what the consequences are of the organism's own actions. But do all organisms accomplish this learning through the same neural mechanisms? If we zoom in for a closer look, will we find the biology of learning is the same from one species to the next? *The following suggests the proof for the above*

- The biological mechanisms that allow learning in mammals are somewhat different from the mechanisms crucial for reptiles, amphibians or invertebrates.
- Even within a single species, the biological mechanisms needed for learning can vary and seem to depend on the CS, the US and the procedure.
- The brain circuits underlying fear conditioning (with electric shock as the US) are centered in the amygdala. The brain circuits underlying eyeblink conditioning (with a puff of air to the eye as the US) are centered in the cerebellum. Conditioning with a long delay between the CS and US typically involves the hippocampus, while conditioning with a shorter delay may not.

Even with these variations, some biological principles do apply to all cases of learning. In all cases, learning depends on neural plasticity which is the capacity for neurons to change the way they function as a result of experience. In all cases, the plasticity involves changes at the synapse *i.e.* changes in the way neurons communicate with each other. These changes, in turn, can involve any of three adjustments: some neurons, after learning, end up sending a stronger signal than they did before.

Other neurons become more sensitive to the signals they've been receiving all along. And third, learning can lead to the creation of entirely new connections among neurons- new synapses-allowing for new lines of communication within the nervous system.

Evidence for these points comes from many sources, including studies of the marine mollusk Aplysia. Because the nervous systems of these creatures contain a mere 20000 neurons, they're good candidates for detailed analysis.

Researchers have been able to document that, after conditioning, the Aplysia's sensory neurons the neurons that receive the CS literally release more neuro transmitter into the synapse than they did before the conditioning trials. This is a crucial part of why, at the end of learning, these neurons are able to trigger a response, the CR-that they couldn't trigger at the start.This process, which can be documented in many species in addition to Aplysia, produces an increase in the neural signal being sent and is called *presynaptic facilitation*.

Other forms of neural plasticity, in other organisms, involve postsynaptic changes *i.e.* they influence the receiving side of the synapse. A particularly important mechanism in this category is long-term potentiation because the mechanism involves an increase in the responsiveness of a neuron (an increase in the neuron's potential for firing) and long-term because this potentiation lasts for days, perhaps even weeks.

LTP (Long-Term Potentiation) is produced when one neuron activates another neuron over and over. The repeated stimulation causes the post-synaptic neuron to become more sensitive to this input than it was before, so it's more likely to respond to this input in the future. In addition, the increased responsiveness can spread to other nearby neurons. Here's an example, Let's suppose that within some brief period of time neuron A repeatedly causes neuron C to fire. This will cause neuron C to become more responsive to A than it was initially. But, of course, C also has other synapses that receive input from other neurons, such as neuron B in the figure.

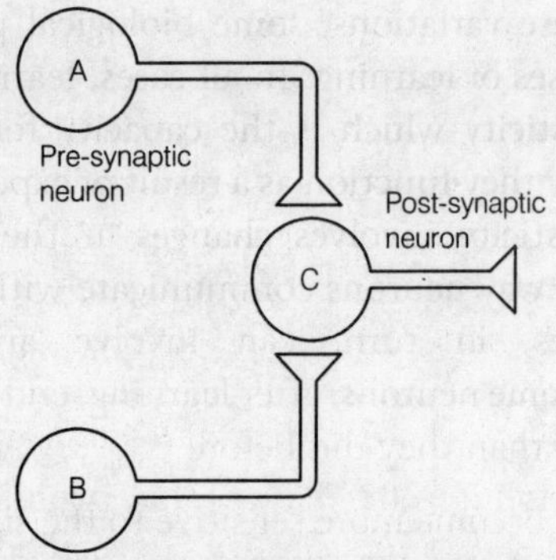

Synapses changes in LTP

These receptors, too, will become more sensitive as a result of neuron as repeated activity, provided that these other neurons fire at the same time as neuron A. In this way, LTP provides a cellular mechanism through which associations in our example, the association between A's and B's activity can be detected and recorded in the brain.

Presynaptic facilitation and LTP both involve changes in how efficiently a synapse functions. The first involves changes in how neurons send signals and the second involves changes in how neurons receive signals. A third form of neural plasticity involves the creation of entirely new synapses.

These changes seem to take place largely on the dendrites of the postsynaptic neurons; the dendrites can grow new dendritic spines. These spines are the 'receiving stations' for most synapses; so, growing more spines means that, as learning proceeds, the neuron is gaining new lines of communication with its cellular neighbours.

EXAM BASED QUESTIONS

1 What does the learning process influence?
(a) Attitude (b) Decisions (c) Actions (d) All of these

2 Which of the following is not a characteristic of learning?
(a) Growth (b) Adjustment
(c) Luxury (d) Intelligence

3 Which of the following is not a fundamental theory of learning?
(a) Behaviourism (b) Cognitivism
(c) Constructivism (d) None of these

4 By whom was 'Trial and error theory of learning' formulated?
(a) Thorndike (b) Guthrie
(c) Hull (d) Kohler

5 On which of these laws is Thorndike's theory of 'connectionism' based?
(a) Law of Readiness (b) Law of Exercise
(c) Law of Effect (d) All of these

6 With whom is 'Contiguity theory of learning' associated?
(a) Thorndike (b) Guthrie
(c) Hull (d) Pavlov

7 What is 'learned' according to contiguity theory of learning?
(a) Behaviour (b) Emotions
(c) Movements (d) Power

8 The pattern, which specifies that we always learn the last thing we do in response to a specific stimulus situation, is known as
(a) postremity (b) connectivity
(c) longivity (d) activity

9 Which theory of learning suggests that 'forgetting is due to interference rather than passage of time'
(a) Trial and error theory (b) Contiguity theory
(c) Reinforcement theory (d) Constructivism theory

10 Which of the following factors can help in forgetting an undesirable old habit and replacing it with the desired one?
(a) Fatigue method
(b) Threshold method
(c) Incompatiable stimuli method
(d) All of the above

11 Which one of the following gave the formulation that internal derives are generally viewed as relatively useless explanatory constructs similar to personality traits?
(a) Thorndike (b) Skinner
(c) Hull (d) Tolman

12 **Which of the following gives the correct mathematical formula of Hull's goal to develop a theory of learning that could be expressed mathematically to explain and understand human behaviour?**
(a) sEr = V x D x K x J x sHr - sIr - Ir - sOr - sLr
(b) sLr = V x D x K x J x sHr - sIr - Ir - sOr - sEr
(c) sHr = V x D x K x J x sEr - sIr - Ir - sOr - sLr
(d) sIr = V x D x K x J x sHr - sEr - Ir - sOr - sLr

13 **'Goal gradient,' concept in problem-solving was introduced by**
(a) Kohler (b) Kendler
(c) Birch (d) Hull

14 **Watching televised violence may enhance the tendency to get involved in violent acts, especially in the play behaviour of children. This is best explained by**
(a) Freudian concept of release of energy
(b) Frustration-aggression hypothesis
(c) Social learning theory
(d) Milgrams study on 'obedience to authority'

15 **According to Kohler learning is a**
(a) behavioural change process
(b) trial and error process
(c) perceptually organising process
(d) conditioning process

16 **The temporal relation that is unable to establish conditioning is**
(a) forward conditioning
(b) delayed conditioning
(c) trace conditioning
(d) backward conditioning

17 **Learning which is complete in one trial relates to**
(a) classical conditioning
(b) productive learning
(c) instrumental conditioning
(d) contiguity theory

18 **Choose the correct option about spontaneous recovery**
(a) spontaneous recovery can never be extinguished.
(b) spontaneous recovery is a slow process.
(c) spontaneous recovery occurs before extinction.
(d) spontaneous recovery can be extinguished with certain unreinforced trials.

19 **Which of the following is not correct regarding classical conditioning?**
(a) Generalisation is due to spread of excitation over cortex.
(b) Without reinforcement spontaneous recovery diminishes.
(c) Extinction is due to abolition of original response.
(d) None of the above

20 **Skinner's term for generalisation is**
(a) transfer (b) induction
(c) irradiation (d) association

21 **For Skinner, which of the following is most important aspect of study?**
(a) Number of response (b) Time of last response
(c) Number of errors (d) Latency of response

22 **An animal does not learn a new response rather it is selected out from the reservoir of responses . The statement is related to**
(a) trial and error learning (b) classical conditioning
(c) insight (d) latent learning

23 **Experiencing a discrimination problem due to an early exposure to stimuli is described as**
(a) perceptual learning (b) latent learning
(c) configural learning (d) sensory preconditioning

24 **In conditioning experiments, the extinction of conditioned response takes place due to**
(a) lack of motivation
(b) absence of unconditioned stimulus
(c) inhibition
(d) excitation

25 **Generally which one of the following CS-US relationships leads to faster conditioning ?**
(a) The CS is presented several minutes before the US.
(b) The CS and the US are both presented simultaneously.
(c) The CS is presented half a second to half a minute before the US.
(d) The US is delayed for several minutes.

26 **Which one of the following is the correct sequence of steps involved in a typical classical conditioning procedure?**
(a) US, CS, CS, US, CR (b) CR, US+CS, US, CS
(c) US, US+CS, CS, CR (d) CS, US, CR, US+CS

27 **Which one of the following expression best illustrates the dog's salivation at the sight of the light?**
CS = conditioned stimulus
US = unconditioned stimulus
IR = irrelevant response
UR = unconditioned response
CR = conditioned response
(a) CS → IR → US → UR (b) CS → UR
(c) US → CR (d) CS → CR

28 **A conditioned response is established by a series of contiguous pairings of CS and US. This is referred to as the law of**
(a) practice (b) generalisation
(c) acquisition (d) spontaneous recovery

29 **Which of the following statements about conditioning is false according to Pavlov?**
(a) The CS and UCS must come close together in time.
(b) The CS must come immediately after the UCS.
(c) The neutral stimulus and UCS must be paired several times before conditioning takes place.
(d) All of the above

30 **The prologue is about Stephanie's fear of white coats as a child. The fact that she was not only afraid of white coats worn by doctors and nurses but also those worn by photographers is an example of**
(a) extinction (b) spontaneous recovery
(c) stimulus discrimination (d) stimulus generalisation

31 **When a conditioned response briefly reappears after it has been extinguished, this is called**
(a) spontaneous recovery (b) higher order conditioning
(c) extinction (d) stimulus generation

32 **The use of a strong CS to create a second CS is called**
(a) spontaneous recovery (b) higher-order conditioning
(c) extinction (d) stimulus generalisation

33 **Who among the following defined learning as relatively permanent change in behaviour which is a result of experience excluding changes due to injury and physiological adjustment?**
(a) GA Kimble and N Garmezy
(b) ML Munn and LD fernald
(c) B Inhelder and J Piaget
(d) RM Ganga an LJ Briggs

34 **Learning is the result of the formation of 'cell assemblies'. The concept has been proposed by**
(a) Pavlov (b) Lashky (c) Hebb (d) Skinner

35 **By providing information on the functioning of involuntary systems such as heart rate and stomach contraction a person can be trained to regulate them. This is called**
(a) systematic desensitisation
(b) bio-feedback
(c) self-reinforcement
(d) para-systematic chain-reaction

36 **Which one of the following problems is associated with the way a child may perform in school?**
(a) Attention-deficit (b) Hyperactivity
(c) Dyslexia (d) All of these

37 **Which of the following sequence explains higher order conditioning?**
(a) Clap-bell-salivation
(b) Clap-salivation
(c) Bell- lemon juice-salivation
(d) Lemon juice-salivation

38 **A student does a good job on Math problems for homework and the teacher awards a sticker. This demonstrates the use of**
(a) extinction (b) reinforcement
(c) spontaneous recovery (d) antecedents

39 **Reinforcement in operant conditioning is most effective when it is**
(a) response contingent (b) stimulus contingent
(c) US-CS contingent (d) NS-CS contingent

40 **Which one of the following behaviours is typically reinforced on a variable ratio schedule?**
(a) Inserting coins into a gambling machine
(b) Checking the mail box to see if mail has arrived
(c) Studying for surprise or unexpected quizzes
(d) Inserting coins into a vending machine to get a candy bar

41 **What type of reinforcement schedule ensures fastest rate of conditioning?**
(a) Ratio Schedule (b) Continuous Schedule
(c) Interval Schedule (d) Intermittent Schedule

42 **In Thorndike's puzzle box experiments, the cats were rewarded by**
(a) getting out of the box (b) getting food
(c) being petted and praised (d) Both a and b

43 **What phenomenon occurs when a response is followed by experiencing something pleasurable?**
(a) Positive reinforcement (b) Negative reinforcement
(c) Punishment (d) Generalisation

44 **Cindy hates to clean up after dinner. One night, she volunteers to bathe the baby before cleaning up. When she finishes with the baby and returns to the kitchen, her husband has cleaned everything up for her. Which of the following statements is most likely true?**
(a) Cindy will start cleaning up the kitchen before she bathes the baby.
(b) Cindy's husband has positively reinforced her for bathing the baby.
(c) Cindy's husband has negatively reinforced her for bathing the baby.
(d) Cindy will never bathe the baby again.

45 **The term conditioned reinforcer is synonymous to**
(a) primary reinforcer
(b) positive reinforcer
(c) secondary reinforcer
(d) negative reinforcer

46 **Which schedule is most resistant to extinction?**
(a) Fixed ratio (b) Variable interval
(c) Variable ratio (d) Fixed interval

47 **'Scalloping effect' is the important feature of which schedule.**
(a) Fixed ratio (b) Variable ratio
(c) Variable interval (d) Fixed interval

48 **What is meant by fixed-ratio schedule of positive reinforcement?**
(a) Reinforcement is given after a variable number of responses.
(b) The response must occur a certain number of times before reinforcement is given.
(c) Reinforcement is given for every occurrence of a particular response.
(d) No reinforcement is given until a certain interval of time has elasped.

49 In a variable ratio schedule of reinforcement
(a) the passage of time determines delivery of reinforcement.
(b) the number of responses determines delivery of reinforcement.
(c) the period of non-reinforcement is different after each reinforced response.
(d) the ratio of time interval determines the occurrence of reinforcement.

50 Which one of the following schedules is most effective for maximising acquisition?
(a) Continuous (b) Variable interval
(c) Fixed ratio (d) Variable ratio

51 Words of praise illustrate
(a) secondary reinforcement
(b) intermittent reinforcement
(c) primary reinforcement
(d) successive approximation

52 Rats learn to press a panel for food as they go through a discrimination learning sequence. Noise-press the panel-food; no noise-press the panel-no food. A lever is now introduced, which when depressed, produces a 5 second noise for the experimental animals. Control subjects, although they had the same previous discrimination learning, do not get any such operationally produced noise.
The final result indicated that the experimental group pressed the lever more than twice as the control group.
In this experiment, the function of noise in increasing the frequency of lever pressing is
(a) a differential reinforcer (b) a secondary reinforcer
(c) a consecutive reinforcer
(d) an intermittent reinforcer

53 Tolman believed that information from environment was worked over and elaborated into a tentative pattern, indicating routes, paths and environmental relationships. Tolman was referring to
(a) cognitive maps (b) mental rotation
(c) memory traces (d) eidetic images

54 A rat is placed on a grid in which an electric charge is introduced which gradually increases until in the midst of its random jumping etc. it happens to press a bar which terminates the shock. Few exposures to such a situation made the animal to learn bar pressing to discontinue the painful shock. This type of training is called
(a) avoidance training (b) omission training
(c) punishment training (d) escape training

55 Which of the following might serve as a secondary reinforcer?
(a) Sex (b) Grades
(c) Food (d) A pain-relieving drug

56 A team coach who benches a player for poor performance is using
(a) aversive conditioning (b) modeling
(c) negative reinforcement (d) punishment

57 Which of the following a consequence which increases the likelihood that the preceding behaviour will occur again?
(a) Reinforcement (b) Discriminative stimulus
(c) Punishment (d) Conditioned stimulus

58 To be effective, punishment should be
(a) delivered later in the day
(b) immediate and sever
(c) explained in detail to the child
(d) paired with reinforcement

59 Rachana was annoyed by the dinging sound her car made when her seatbelt was not fastened, so she decided to fasten her seatbelt before she started the car to avoid hearing the dinging sound. What learning phenomenon is associated with the removal of such an aversive stimulus?
(a) Positive reinforcement
(b) Negative reinforcement
(c) Positive punishment
(d) Negative punishment

60 Habituation and sensitisation both refer to a change in response as a result of learning. Which of the following statements best expresses the relationship between the types of changes in response denoted by the two terms?
(a) The two terms refer to the same type of change in response.
(b) The two terms refer to similar kinds of changes in response.
(c) The two terms refer to different sorts of changes in response.
(d) The two terms refer to opposite changes in response.

61 What phenomenon did Ivan Pavlov initially set out to study?
(a) Canine audition (b) Canine vision
(c) Associative learning (d) Salivary reflex in digestion

62 What type of learning occurs when there is no obvious reinforcement?
(a) Shaping (b) Operant
(c) Latent (d) Insight

63 A cardinal assumption of stimulus generalisation theory of Pavlov is that
(a) locus of generalisation gradients is in the testing rather then in the training phase.
(b) generalisation gradients might be the result of variations in discriminative thresholds.
(c) a process that develops automatically during conditioning along with the spread of associative strength.
(d) stimulus generalisation occurs due to 'failure of association'.

64 **In instrumental conditioning**

(a) reinforcement is given irrespective of the production of an appropriate response.
(b) reinforcement is given before the on set of the response.
(c) appropriate response is immediately followed by reinforcement.
(d) reinforcement is not given.

65 **Freezing of response occurs in**

(a) respondent conditioning
(b) instrumental conditioning
(c) vicarious trial and error
(d) Both respondent conditioning and trial and error method

66 **Which one of the following statements explains the incidental learning ?**

(a) Learning without actually trying to attain a goal.
(b) Learning in the absence of ostensible reinforcement.
(c) Learning without the knowledge of the relationship between the response and the reinforcement.
(d) Learning in the absence of changes in the perception or discriminations.

67 **Which one of the following methods is applicable in formation of habits?**

(a) Reciprocal conditioning
(b) Operant conditioning
(c) Second-order conditioning
(d) Differential conditioning

68 **When response is unpredictable upon environment to product a consequence, it is termed as**

(a) insight (b) trial and error
(c) operant conditioning (d) classical conditioning

69 **With the help of classical conditioning, emotional responses**

(a) are learned best
(b) are equal to other responses
(c) are learned very slowly
(d) are learned only when US (unconditioned sitmulus) is powerful

70 **A stimulus or event, when its termination contingent to a response increase the likelihood the occurence of the response is a**

(a) primary reinforcer (b) negative reinforcer
(c) secondary reinforcer (d) positive reinforcer

71 **Cognition refers to**

(a) behaviour *i.e.* observable and external
(b) behaviour *i.e.* directly measurable
(c) the mental events that take place while a person is behaving
(d) memories

72 **In Tolman's maze study, the fact that the group of rats receiving reinforcement only after the 10th day of the study solved the maze far more quickly than did the rats who had been reinforced from the Ist day can be interpreted to mean that these particular rats**

(a) were much smarter than other rats
(b) had already learned the maze in the first nine days
(c) had the opportunity to cheat by watching the other rats
(d) were very hungry and therefore learned much more quickly

73 **How can the principle of partial reinforcement be used to manage the behaviour of children?**

(a) Shaping (b) Behaviour modification
(c) Continuous reinforcement (d) Learned helplessness

74 **Applied behaviour analysis**

(a) is the process of shaping
(b) is useful only for teaching autistic children
(c) is different from behaviour modification
(d) cannot be used with animals

75 **Elizabeth's parent want her to put her clothes in the hamper. At first, they praise her for putting the clothes together in one pile. Then, they praise her forgetting the clothes on the same side of the room as the hamper. When she gets the clothes on the top of the hamper she gets praise. Finally, her parents praise her when she put her clothes in the hamper. This is an example of**

(a) negative reinforcement (b) punishment
(c) extinction (d) shaping

76 **Marcella starts whining in the grocery store because she wants some candy. Her father refuses to give her candy and ignores her whining, what will happen?**

(a) Generalisation (b) Extinction
(c) Spontaneous recovery (d) Discrimination

77 **The first time Giorgio sees a duck, his mother tells him, 'that's a duck can you say duck?' He repeats the word gleefully. The next day he is watching a cartoon and sees a chicken on the television. He points at the chicken and says 'duck'! This is an example of**

(a) generalisation (b) extinction
(c) spontaneous recovery (d) discrimination

78 **Ella is teaching her parrot a new word. Every time the parrot says a sound *i.e.* close to the new word. She gives it a treat. But the parrot keeps repeating other words, it has learned in the past, trying to get a treat what way. The parrot is exhibiting**

(a) generalisation (b) extinction
(c) spontaneous recovery (d) discrimination

79 **When a conditioned stimulus (CS) is no longer followed by the unconditioned stimulus (UCS), the CS gradually loses the ability to evoke Conditioned Response (CR). This phenomenon is known as**

(a) reconditioning (b) backward conditioning
(c) discrimination learning (d) extinction

80 Which of the following is not an element involved in observational learning?
(a) attention (b) retention
(c) reproduction (d) perception

81 Which of the following psychologists is well known for their work of investigating latent learning?
(a) Watson (b) Kohler (c) Skinner (d) Tolman

82 What is learning that is not demonstrated until one is motivated to perform the behaviour called?
(a) Learning by insight (b) Observational learning
(c) Classical learning (d) Latent learning

83 A procedure by which the application or removal of a stimulus decreases the strength of a behaviour are both examples of
(a) negative reinforcement (b) punishment
(c) positive reinforcement (d) secondary reinforcement

84 Two schedules of reinforcement that produce the highest rates of response are
(a) continuous and fixed interval
(b) fixed interval and variable interval
(c) variable interval and variable ratio
(d) fixed ratio and variable ratio

85 Learning that is affected by consequences is called
(a) classical conditioning
(b) self-regulated learning
(c) behavioural self-management
(d) operant conditioning

86 Jared's father is ill and cannot prepare his famous chili recipe, which Jared has watched his father make many times. When his father tells Jared that he must cook the chili, he panics at first. But then Jared finds that he knows how to put the recipe together anyway. His ability to prepare the recipe is an example of
(a) latent learning (b) learned helplessness
(c) insight learning (d) discovery learning

87 Jared realised that he had learned how to prepare his father's famous chili recipe by watching his father in the kitchen for many years. This kind of learning is called
(a) discovery larning
(b) helplessness learning
(c) insight learning
(d) observational learning

88 A child bitten by a white dog is not afraid of black dogs. This is an example of
(a) discrimination (b) spontaneous recovery
(c) shaping (d) generalisation

89 A Pigeon is placed in a cage with two pellets containing grains. One of the pellets is round in shape and the other is square. If the pigeon pecks the round pellet it is given a mild shock, but it can eat the grains from the square pellet. Soon it learns to peck only the square pellet.
The above experiment is an example of
(a) classical conditioning (b) escape behaviour
(c) stimulus discrimination (d) stimulus generalisation

90 A child has learned to avoid a furry, black cat. However, she still plays with her grandmother's short haired tabbycat. Her response demonstrates
(a) negative transfer (b) extinction
(c) discrimination (d) successive approximation

91 The process through which a response is taught by rewarding successive approximations to the final desired response is
(a) extinction (b) fading
(c) shaping (d) secondary reinforcement

92 A dog that gets rewarded for the first bark it makes in each ten minute period is being reinforced on a .... schedule of reinforcement.
(a) continuous (b) fixed interval
(c) variable interval (d) fixed ratio

93 Extinction in operant conditioning is also subject to .... of a response.
(a) successive approximations
(b) shaping
(c) automation
(d) spontaneous recovery

94 You toss a newly purchased felt mouse across the floor. Your cat chases it excitedly, clutches it in her paws and rolls around with it. Several tosses later, your cat yawns pointedly and settles herself for a nap. The change in your cat's behaviour illustrates
(a) adaptation (b) habituation
(c) conditioning (d) sensitisation

95 Punishment is more effective when
(a) it occurs long after the misdeed
(b) it is a clear consequence of a specific behaviour
(c) rewards of the misdeed outweigh the negativity of the punishment
(d) the negative consequences of the punishment are weak

96 Which of the following pair fills the blanks?
Classical conditioning applies mostly to ......
Operant conditioning applies mainly to ......
(a) involuntary behaviour; voluntary behaviour
(b) voluntary behaviour; involuntary behaviour
(c) voluntary behaviour; voluntary behaviour as well
(d) involuntary behaviour; involuntary behaviour as well

97 In associative learning, we learn that certain events occur together. Two forms of associative learning are classical conditioning, in which the organism associates...... and operant conditioning, in which the organism associates ....
(a) two responses; a responses and a consequence
(b) two stimuli; two responses
(c) two stimuli; a response and a consequence
(d) two responses; two stimuli

98 Which of the following pairs is/are correctly matched? Learning about events in our own lives is called......... learning. Learning about facts is called ......

(a) semantic; episodic learning
(b) semantic; semantic learning
(c) episodic; episodic learning
(d) episodic; semantic learning

99 In Pavlov's study, the US was ...... the neutral stimulus was ...... and finally, the CS was.......

(a) meat; the assistant; meat
(b) meat; the assistant; the assistant
(c) the assistant; meat; meat
(d) meat; meat; the assistant

100 In applied behaviour analysis which of the following steps are taken

(a) skills are broken down into their smallest steps and then reinforced.
(b) punishment by application is often used to control behaviour.
(c) investigators develop new theories of learning rather than actually solving problems.
(d) basic form of learning used in instrumental conditioning.

101 'Eureka! I've got it!' The sudden awareness of a problem's solution is termed...... learning.

(a) insight (b) non-associative
(c) latent (d) discovery

102 Depending upon the task characteristics, there is a gradual transition from simpler forms of learning to the level of higher complex ones. These different forms are

1. Establishment of simple S-R relationships
2. Acquiring motor and verbal skills
3. Concept formation
4. Problem-solving

The correct order of learning sequence is

(a) 1, 4, 2, 3 (b) 1, 2, 3, 4 (c) 2, 4, 1, 3 (d) 2, 3, 4, 1

103 Arrange the following theories in order of proposal

1. Classical Conditioning (Pavlov)
2. Social Development Theory (Vygotsky)
3. Stage Theory of Cognitive Development (Piaget)
4. Erikson's Stages of Development (Erikson)

Codes

(a) 2, 1, 3, 4 (b) 1, 2, 3, 4 (c) 4, 3, 2, 1 (d) 3, 2, 4, 1

104 Which of the following is a correct sequence of conditioned emotional response becoming phobia

1. Stimulus generalisation and higher-order conditioning
2. Desensitisation
3. Amygdala producing fear
4. Conditional emotional response

Codes

(a) 1, 2, 3, 4 (b) 2, 3, 4, 1 (c) 4, 3, 1, 2 (d) 1, 3, 2, 4

105 Arrange the steps in order in Pavlov's experiment

1. Selecting stimulus and response
2. Establishing classical conditioning
3. Testing for Conditioning

Codes

(a) 1, 2, 3 (b) 3, 1, 2 (c) 2, 1, 3 (d) 1, 3, 2

106 Arrange the following on classical conditioning in corrects sequence

(a) US, UR, NS, No response, NS associated with US, CS, CR
(b) NS, No response, NS associated with US, CS, CR, US, UR
(c) NS associated with US, CS, CR, US, UR, NS, No response
(d) CR, US, UR, NS, No response, NS associated with US, CS

107 Arrange the sequence of factors in the order of importance that alter the effectiveness of consequences in learning.

(a) Satiation, Immediacy, Contingency, Size
(b) Contingency, Size, Satiation, Immediacy
(c) Size, Satiation, Contingency, Immediacy
(d) Immediacy, Contingency, Size, Satiation

108 Arrange the sequence in operant conditioning to change human behaviour in experimental studies.

1. State goal
2. Monitor behaviour
3. Reinforce desired behaviour
4. Reduce incentives to perform undesirable behaviour

Codes

(a) 2, 1, 3, 4 (b) 1, 3, 4, 2 (c) 4, 3, 2, 1 (d) 1, 2, 3, 4

109 Any discriminative stimulus can serve as a reinforcer for the behaviour that precedes it, which of the following sequence is correct ?

(a) S (string), R (string pull), S (light), R (bar press), S (food)
(b) S (light), R (bar press), S (food), S (string), R (string pull)
(c) S (food), S (string), R (string pull), S (light), R (bar press)
(d) R (bar press), S (food), S (string), R (string pull), S (light)

110 Which one set of the following is the correct sequence of vicarious learning process meant for behaviour modelling practice?

(a) Motivation, Motoric Production, Retention, Attention
(b) Attention, Motoric Production, Retention, Motivation
(c) Attention, Retention, Motoric Production, Motivation
(d) Retention, Attention, Motivation, Motoric Production

111 Which one of the following pairs is correctly matched?

	Conditioning Process	Type of Conditioning
(a)	Reinforcing a spontaneously emitted response	: Instrumental
(b)	Using a conditioned stimulus as an unconditioned one	: Generalised
(c)	Reinforcing only one of the two simultaneously presented conditioning stimuli	: Higher-order
(d)	Stimulus resembling the conditioned one elicing the conditioned response	: Differential

112 Which of the following pairs is correctly matched?

(a) Social reinforcer	Primary reinforcement
(b) Token reinforcer	Secondary reinforcement
(c) ICS Secondary	Reinforcement
(d) Negative reinforcer	Punishment

113 Which of the following pairs is wrongly matched?

(a) Escape	:	End aversive stimulus
(b) Avoidance	:	Making a response to postpone discomfort
(c) Aggression	:	Common response to frustration
(d) None of the above		

114 Which of the following pairs is correctly mached?

(a) Cognitive map	:	Internal representation of an area
(b) Latent learning	:	Remains hidden until reinforcement is provided
(c) Rote learning	:	Learning by memorisation or rules
(d) All of the above		

115 In an experiment in which Watson tried to classically condition an emotional response in a child, which of the following is not correct?

(a) Neutral stimulus	:	White rat
(b) Unconditioned stimulus	:	Noise
(c) Unconditioned response	:	Startle/cry
(d) None of the above		

116 Consider the following statements regarding Thorndike's 'Law of Effect'

1. It is only a case of law of exercise.
2. It emphasises only on situational reinforcers but does not refer to cognitive aspects of learning.
3. It cannot be applied in achievement-oriented learning.
4. It ignores the functional effect of persons-environment interaction in learning.

Which of the statements given above is/are correct?

(a) Only 1 (b) 2, 3 and 4
(c) 2 and 3 (d) 3 and 4

117 Consider the following statements about focus of behavioural theories of learning

1. stimulus and response units.
2. principle of contiguity.
3. comprehension of underlying principle.
4. organisation of stimuli.

Which of the statements given above is/are correct ?

(a) 1 and 2 (b) 2 and 3 (c) 1 and 4 (d) 3 and 4

118 Which of the following are dependent variables in a conditioning experiment ?

1. Latency of response 2. Rate of response
3. Amplitude of response 4. Direction of response

Select the correct answer using the codes given below

(a) 1 and 2 (b) 3 and 4 (c) 1, 2 and 3 (d) 2, 3 and 4

119 Which of the following statements are correct regarding extinction and spontaneous recovery ?

1. If reinforcement is delayed during acquisition trials, subsequent resistance to extinction will tend to increase.
2. As the effort required to produce a response increases, resistance to extinction decreases.
3. Resistance to extinction decreases as the amount of reinforcement used during acquisition trials increases.
4. The amount of spontaneous recovery depends upon the time interval; the shorter the interval the greater the spontaneous recovery.

Select the correct answer using the codes given below

(a) 1, 2 and 4 (b) 1, 3 and 4 (c) 2 and 3 (d) 1, 2 and 3

120 Consider the following statements.

Decrease in the likelihood of the response R is contingent upon

1. positive reinforcement if R occurs.
2. omission of reinforcement if R occurs.
3. omission of reinforcement if R does not occur.
4. punishment if R occurs.

Which of the statements given above is/are correct?

(a) 1 and 2 (b) 3 and 4 (c) 1 and 3 (d) 2 and 4

121 Which of the following pairs are correctly matched?

1. Learning which involves reorganisation	:	Insight learning
2. Learning to make a particular response to a wrong signal to avoid a noxious stimulus	:	Active avoidance
3. Learning, in which reinforcement is contingent on a particular response	:	Latent learning
4. Learning to apply a label to a group of stimuli that have one common aspect, but vary in a number of other aspects	:	Appreceptive learning

Codes

(a) 1 and 2 (b) 1 and 3 (c) 2 and 3 (d) 2 and 4

122 Cognitive theory of learning developed on the basis of experiments designed to test the relative role of motor habits versus sign learning. Under which of the following headings can the experiments be placed?

1. Place learning
2. Role of drive
3. Latent learning
4. Whole versus part learning
5. Reward expectancy

Select the correct answer using the codes given below

(a) 1, 2, 3 and 4 (b) 1, 2 and 5
(c) 1, 3 and 5 (d) 2, 3, 4 and 5

123 Classical conditioning is the basis of
1. explosive therapy
2. flooding
3. omission therapy
4. systematic desensitisation

Select the correct answer using the codes given below
(a) 1 and 2 (b) 1 and 3 (c) 2 and 4 (d) 2 and 3

124 Which of the following are the characteristics of operant conditioning?
1. Stimulus-response association.
2. Law of contiguity in learning.
3. Law of effect.
4. Difference in UR and CR.

Select the correct answer using the codes given below
(a) 1 and 2 (b) 2 and 3 (c) 1, 3 and 4 (d) 2, 3 and 4

125 In which of the following schedules of reinforcement resistance to extinction occurs?
1. Variable ratio schedule
2. Fixed-ratio schedule
3. Fixed-interval schedule
4. Variable interval schedule

Select the correct answer using the codes given below
(a) 1 and 4 (b) 1 and 3
(c) 3 and 4 (d) 1 and 2

126 Match the following

List I (Condition/Situation)	List II (Principles/Authors)
A. A mother allows a child to go out to play only after he has finished his homework	1. Premack principle
B. Conditioning of authonomic behaviour	2. Guthrie
C. Whenever a response occurs that response is immediately and completely associated with all stimuli present at that instant	3. Neal Miller
D. Partial reinforcement in conditioning	4. Retardation in extinction

Codes

	A	B	C	D		A	B	C	D
(a)	3	1	4	2	(b)	1	3	2	4
(c)	1	3	4	2	(d)	3	1	2	4

127 Consider the following principles
1. Law of effect
2. Law of contiguity
3. Law of reinforcement
4. Law of vicarious reinforcement

The correct sequence in which these principles were postulated is
(a) 1, 2, 4, 3 (b) 2, 1, 4, 3 (c) 2, 1, 3, 4 (d) 1, 2, 3, 4

128 Match the following

List I (Psychologist)	List II (Theory)
A. BF Skinner	1. Statistical learning theory
B. EL Thorndike	2. Systematic desensitisation
C. Estes	3. Transfer through common elements
D. Wolpe	4. Operant conditioning

Codes

	A	B	C	D
(a)	3	4	2	1
(b)	4	3	1	2
(c)	4	3	2	1
(d)	3	4	1	2

129 Match the following

List I (Key Phrases)	List II (Theorists)
A. Habit Strength	1. E L Thorndike
B. Trial and error	2. I P Pavlov
C. Contiguity	3. C L Hull
D. Contingencies	4. B F Skinner

Codes

	A	B	C	D		A	B	C	D
(a)	3	1	2	4	(b)	1	3	2	4
(c)	3	1	4	2	(d)	1	3	4	2

130 Match the following

List I (Theorists)	List II (Theory)
A. Thorndike	1. S-R theory without reinforcement
B. Tolman	2. S-R reinforcement theory
C. Guthrie	3. Sign-Gestalt theory
D. Lewin	4. Field theory

Codes

	A	B	C	D		A	B	C	D
(a)	2	3	4	1	(b)	3	2	4	1
(c)	3	2	1	4	(d)	2	3	1	4

131 Match the following

List I (Conditions)	List II (Response)
A. CS and UCS are presented at the same time and continue till the onset of CR	1. Trace
B. CS terminates before the onset of UCS	2. Simultaneous
C. UCS precedes CS	3. Delayed
D. CS is presented first and overlaps the onset of UCS	4. Backward

Codes

	A	B	C	D
(a)	2	1	3	4
(b)	1	2	3	4
(c)	1	2	4	3
(d)	2	1	4	3

132 Match the following

List I (Principle)	List II (Description)
A. Generalisation	1. Reacting to similar odours
B. Extinction	2. Not reacting to a previously powerful stimulus
C. Discrimination	3. Not reacting to a new odour
D. Spontaneous Recovery	4. Having a reaction come back

Codes

	A	B	C	D
(a)	1	2	3	4
(b)	4	3	2	1
(c)	4	3	1	2
(d)	3	4	2	1

133 Match the following

List I (Elements)	List II (Examples)
A. Unconditioned stimulus	1. Bell after conditioning
B. Unconditioned response	2. Bell before conditioning
C. Conditioned stimulus	3. Reflex salivation to the US
D. Neutral stimulus	4. Meat powder

Codes

	A	B	C	D
(a)	1	2	3	4
(b)	4	3	2	1
(c)	4	3	1	2
(d)	3	4	2	1

134 Match the following

List I (Phenomenon)	List II (Description)
A. Unconditioned Response (UR)	1. A response that takes place in an organism whenever an unconditioned stimulus occurs
B. Unconditioned Stimulus (US)	2. A stimulus that invariably causes an organism to respond in a specific way
C. Conditioned Stimulus (CS)	3. An originally neutral stimulus that is paired with an unconditioned stimulus and eventually produces the desired response in an organism when presented alone
D. Conditioned Response (CR)	4. After conditioning, the response an organism produces when only a conditioned stimulus is presented

Codes

	A	B	C	D
(a)	1	3	2	4
(b)	2	1	3	4
(c)	3	2	1	4
(d)	1	2	3	4

135 Match the following

List I (Phenomenon)	List II (Description)
A. Reinforcer	1. A stimulus that follows a behaviour and decreases the likelihood that the behaviour will be repeated
B. Positive reinforcer	2. Any event whose reduction or termination increases the likelihood that ongoing behaviour will recur
C. Negative reinforcer	3. Any event whose presence increases the likelihood that ongoing behaviour will recur
D. Punisher	4. A stimulus that follows a behaviour and increases the likelihood that the behaviour will be repeated

Codes

	A	B	C	D
(a)	1	3	2	4
(b)	4	3	2	1
(c)	3	2	1	4
(d)	3	2	1	4

136 Match the following

List I (Principles)	List II (Given by)
A. Schedules of Reinforcement	1. EL Thorndike
B. Modeling	2. A Bandura
C. Conditioning	3. BF Skinner
D. Law of effect	4. Ivan Pavlov

Codes

	A	B	C	D
(a)	1	3	4	2
(b)	2	1	3	4
(c)	3	2	4	1
(d)	4	3	2	1

137 Match the following

List I (Phenomenon)	List II (Description)
A. Acquisition	1. Paying attention
B. Retention	2. Pull-up information later and act
C. Reproduction	3. Actually perform the behaviour observed
D. Motivation	4. Reinforcement and punishment

Codes

	A	B	C	D
(a)	3	4	2	1
(b)	4	3	2	1
(c)	4	3	1	2
(d)	1	2	3	4

138 Match the following

List I (Experiment)	List II (Psychologist)
A. Operant conditioning chamber	1. Bandura
B. Dog, Bell, Saliva experiment	2. BF Skinner
C. Doll Experiment	3. Whorf
D. Eskimo and Chinese language	4. Pavlov

Codes

	A	B	C	D
(a)	3	4	2	1
(b)	2	4	1	3
(c)	2	4	1	3
(d)	1	2	3	4

139 Match the following

List I (Phenomenon)	List II (Performed by)
A. Positive reinforcement	1. Food given
B. Negative reinforcement	2. Pain stops increase
C. Punishment	3. Pain begins
D. Punishment (response cost)	4. Food removed

Codes

	A	B	C	D		A	B	C	D
(a)	3	4	2	1	(b)	4	3	2	1
(c)	4	3	1	2	(d)	1	2	3	4

140 Match the following

List I (Theories of Learning)	List II (Authors)
A. Attribution Theory	1. Mayer
B. Cognitive Load Theory	2. Weiner
C. Cognitive Theory of Multimedia Learning	3. Tolman
D. Gestalt Psychology	4. Sweller

Codes

	A	B	C	D		A	B	C	D
(a)	3	4	2	1	(b)	2	4	1	3
(c)	4	3	1	2	(d)	1	2	3	4

141 Match the following

List I (Experimenter)	List II (Subjects)
A. Skinner	1 Chimpanzee
B. Kohler	2. Cat
C. Thorndike	3. Rat
D. Pavlov	4. Dog

Codes

	A	B	C	D		A	B	C	D
(a)	3	1	2	4	(b)	1	2	3	4
(c)	1	2	4	3	(d)	3	1	4	2

142 Match the following

List I (Given by)	List II (Theory)
A. Skinner and Ferster	1. Drive reduction theory
B. Watson and Raynor	2. Frustration response theory
C. Hull and Spence	3. Schedules of reinforcement
D. Amsell and Rousell	4. Classical conditioning

Codes

	A	B	C	D		A	B	C	D
(a)	4	3	2	1	(b)	3	4	2	1
(c)	4	3	1	2	(d)	3	4	1	2

143 Match the following

List I (Theorist)	List II (Principle)
A. Pavlov	1. Trial and error learning
B. Skinner	2. Insightful learning
C. Thorndike	3. Classical conditioning
D. Kohler	4. Operant conditioning

Codes

	A	B	C	D		A	B	C	D
(a)	3	4	2	1	(b)	4	3	1	2
(c)	3	4	1	2	(d)	4	3	2	1

144 Match the following

List I (Theory)	List II (Description)
A. Social learning theory	1. Affects the willingness of others to perform the behaviours they learned
B. Vicarious reinforcement and vicarious punishment	2. Emphasises the ability to learn by observing a model
C. Observational (or vicarious) learning	3. The ability to become increasingly more effective in solving problems
D. Learning set	4. Learning by observing other people's behaviour

Codes

	A	B	C	D		A	B	C	D
(a)	1	3	2	4	(b)	4	3	2	1
(c)	2	1	4	3	(d)	1	2	3	4

145 Match the following

List I (Schedule)	List II (Description)
A. Variable-ratio schedule	1. Correct response is reinforced after a fixed length of time, since the last reinforcement
B. Variable-interval schedule	2. The correct response is reinforced after a fixed number of correct responses
C. Fixed-ratio schedule	3. The correct response is reinforced after varying lengths of time following the last reinforcement
D. Fixed-interval schedule	4. A varying number of correct responses must occur before reinforcement is presented

Codes

	A	B	C	D		A	B	C	D
(a)	1	3	2	4	(b)	4	3	2	1
(c)	2	1	4	3	(d)	1	2	3	4

146 Match the following

List I (Associated to)	List II (Phenomenon)
A. Pigeons	1. Reinforcement
B. Sea Slugs	2. Change of nervous system with related to learning
C. Rats	3. Non-associative learning
D. Non-human Primates	4. Language and thought

Codes

	A	B	C	D		A	B	C	D
(a)	1	3	2	4	(b)	4	3	2	1
(c)	2	1	4	3	(d)	1	2	3	4

147 Match the following

List I (Psychologist)	List II (Related to)
A. Bandura	1. Demonstrated the conditioning of fear in children
B. Pavlov	2. Demonstrated learning through social observation
C. Watson	3. Credited with the discovery of conditioning
D. Skinner	4. The leading behaviourist after World War Second

Codes

	A	B	C	D		A	B	C	D
(a)	1	2	3	4	(b)	2	3	1	4
(c)	4	3	1	2	(d)	3	1	2	4

148 Match the following

List I (Phenomenon)	List II (Related to)
A. Reinforcement	1. Strengthening a behaviour
B. Shaping	2. Modifying behaviour
C. Weakening a response	3. Counter conditioning
D. Recurring of a response	4. Spontaneous recovery

Codes

	A	B	C	D		A	B	C	D
(a)	4	3	2	1	(b)	1	2	3	4
(c)	2	3	4	1	(d)	3	2	4	1

149 Match the following

List I (Conditioning)	List II (Occurs)
A. Trace conditioning	1. When CS and US occurs together
B. Delayed conditioning	2. CS appears first, it disappears then US appears
C. Simultaneous conditioning	3. CS appears first, but also present when the US appears
D. Backward conditioning	4. When US is presented first and after the disappearance of US, CS is presented

Codes

	A	B	C	D		A	B	C	D
(a)	2	1	3	4	(b)	1	2	3	4
(c)	4	3	1	2	(d)	3	1	4	2

150 Match the following

List I (Theory)	List II (Description)
A. Structuralism	1. Emphasised the purpose of mental processes
B. Functionalism	2. Emphasised the elements of mental experience
C. Behaviourism	3. Emphasised the unconcious determinants of behaviour
D. Gestalt Psychology	4. Emphasised the organisation of perception

Codes

	A	B	C	D		A	B	C	D
(a)	1	2	3	4	(b)	2	1	3	4
(c)	4	3	1	2	(d)	3	1	2	4

151 Match the following

List I (Phenomena)	List II (Concepts/Principles in Operant Conditioning)
A. More preferred activity used to reinforce less preferred one	1. Conditioned reinforcer
B. Withdrawl of an aversive state following a response	2. Positive reinforcement
C. Introduction of an aversive state following a response	3. Premack Principle
D. Events acting as positive reinforces through their association with primary reinforcers	4. Punishment
	5. Negative reinforcement

Codes

	A	B	C	D		A	B	C	D
(a)	1	5	2	3	(b)	3	5	4	1
(c)	1	4	5	2	(d)	5	4	3	1

152 Match the following

List I (Phenomenon)	List II (Concepts)
A. Rules regarding delivery of reinforcement	1. Shaping
B. Approximation of desired behaviour	2. Punishment
C. Process of weakening or decreasing rate of response	3. Reinforcement
D. Voluntary response	4. Schedules of reinforcement
	5. Operant

Codes

	A	B	C	D		A	B	C	D
(a)	5	1	2	3	(b)	4	3	5	2
(c)	4	1	2	5	(d)	5	3	1	2

153 Match the following

List I (Schedule)	List II (Description)
A. Variable ratio schedule	1. Reinforcement is given after a predetermined number of responses
B. Variable interval schedule	2. Reinforcement is given at the end of predetermined time periods
C. Fixed interval schedule	3. Reinforcement is given after any number of responses
D. Fixed ratio schedule	4. Reinforcement is given at the end of varying time periods

Codes

	A	B	C	D		A	B	C	D
(a)	3	2	4	1	(b)	3	4	1	2
(c)	3	4	2	1	(d)	4	3	2	1

154 Match the following

List I (Learning)	List II (Description)
A. Escape learning	1. Learning occuring without behaviour changing in a corresponding way
B Avoidance learning	2. Learning to make a response to terminate
C. Learned helplessness	3. Animal learn they are helpless from a stimulus and not prevent the stimulus in future
D. Latent learning	4. Make a certain response to prevent an aversive event from even starting

Codes

	A	B	C	D		A	B	C	D
(a)	4	3	2	1	(b)	2	4	3	1
(c)	3	4	1	2	(d)	2	3	1	4

155 Match the following

List I (Formula)	List II (Explanation)
A. S^ER	1. Conditioned inhibition
B. S^HR	2. Net reaction potential
C. S^IR	3. Habit strength
D. I_R	4. Reactive inhibition

Codes

	A	B	C	D		A	B	C	D
(a)	3	2	4	1	(b)	2	3	1	4
(c)	2	3	4	1	(d)	3	2	1	4

Directions *(Q. Nos. 156-185) In the question given below are two statements labelled as Assertion (A) and Reason (R). In the context of the two statements, which one of the following is correct?*

Codes

(a) Both A and R are true and R is the correct explanation of A
(b) Both A and R are true, but R is not the correct explanation of A
(c) A is true, but R is false
(d) A is false, but R is true

156 **Assertion (A)** According to Thorndike's law of effect, behaviours that result in unpleasantness are more likely to occur again.

Reason (R) He drew on Gestalt psychology to argue that animals could learn the connections between stimuli and did not need any explicit biologically significant event to make learning occur.

157 **Assertion** (A) Laboratory methods employed in the experimental analysis of behaviour are based upon BF Skinner's philosophy of radical behaviourism.

Reason (R) Everything that organisms do is behaviour (including thinking) and all behaviour is lawful which allows itself to be experimentally studied.

158 **Assertion** (A) The most commonly used tool in animal behavioural research is the operant conditioning chamber also known as a Skinner Box.

Reason (R) The interior of the chamber contains some type of device that serves the role of discrimi native stimuli, atleast one mechanism to measure the subject's behaviour as a rate of response.

159 **Assertion** (A) Classical conditioning entails the learning of new behaviour through association where two stimuli are linked together to produce a new learned response.

Reason (R) There are four basic components of a classical conditioning process (unconditioned stimuli, conditioned stimuli, unconditioned response and conditioned response).

160 **Assertion** (A) The term radical behaviourism is also used to refer to the school of psychology known as the experimental analysis of behaviour.

Reason (R) Skinner saw that classical conditioning didn't account for the behaviour most of us are interested in, such as riding a bike or writing a book. His observations led him to propose a theory about how these and similar behaviours are called operants.

161 **Assertion** (A) Habituation involves neuronal changes in the central nervous system, whereas adaptation involves changes only in the peripheral sensory systems.

Reason (R) Habituation and sensitisation both refer to a opposite changes in response as a result of learning.

162 **Assertion** (A) Pavlov believed that animals and people evolved the capacity for classical conditioning because it had an adaptive value.

Reason (R) Once rats get sick on a particular bait poison, they quickly learn to avoid its smell or taste called bait shyness.

163 **Assertion** (A) Through taste aversion, Blue Jays learn that the distinctive colour pattern of monarch butterflies predicts getting sick and so, Blue Jays avoid eating monarch butterflies.

Reason (R) Classically conditioned taste aversion has survival value for animals.

164 **Assertion** (A) Bandura found that children who had watched the film of an adult modeling aggressive behaviour played more aggressively than children, who had not seen the film.

Reason (R) The entire learning process appeared to take place in the children's minds without their performing any observable responses or receiving any noticeable rewards.

165 **Assertion** (A) Unconditioned stimulus will be food, which when presented to dog will elicit the salivation reflex *i.e.* will make a dog salivate.

Reason (R) A neutral stimulus is some stimulus that triggers or elicits a physiological reflex such as salivation or eye blink.

166 **Assertion** (A) Human beings have the capacity for complex learning.

Reason (R) Second order conditioning follows the principle of associating a new stimulus with a natural or existing conditioned stimulus.

167 **Assertion** (A) Prem's experience of being classically conditioned to feel anxious when he smelled a particular after shave, which is different from his own brand.

Reason (R) Pavlov found that these phenomena were associated with classical conditioning.

168 **Assertion (A)** Skinnerian radical bhavioursalism is no longer criticised or considered controversial since many new areas have since been researched.

Reason (R) Epstein (1991) carried forward Skinner's radical behaviourism and attempted to study the emergence of novel behaviours. He found that principles of multi controlling, stimuli autochaining and resurgence can explain creative behaviour.

169 **Assertion** (A) In classical conditioning, conditioned stimulus should be immediately followed by unconditional stimulus; in instrumental conditioning the response must be closely followed by reward.

Reason (R) Conditioning, both classical and . instrumental, depends on reward.

170 **Assertion** (A) In classical conditioning, the neutral stimulus becomes the conditioned stimulus.

Reason (R) It is associated with the unconditioned stimulus.

171 **Assertion** (A) If a response in the presence of a stimulus leads to a satisfying effect, the association between the stimulus and the response is strengthened.

Reason (R) Thorndike's law of effect prove this.

172 **Assertion** (A) On a cumulative recorder, a rapid response rate produce a/an smooth slope.

Reason (R) Discriminative stimuli are cues that influence operant behaviour by indicating the probable consequences of a response.

173 **Assertion** (A) Food is a primary reinforcer.

Reason (R) Food satisfy biological need.

174 **Assertion** (A) Intermittent reinforcement occurs when every instance of a designated response is reinforced.

Reason (R) Partial reinforcement occurs when a designated response is reinforced only some of the time.

175 **Assertion** (A) Even after Pavlov's assistant stopped bringing food to the dogs during visits, the dogs salivated weeks later when they saw the assistant.

Reason (R) Extinction occurs after repeated presentation of the CS without the UC.

176 **Assertion** (A) When a response is conditioned under intermittent reinforcements, it is more difficult to extinguish such a response in comparison to the response conditioned under continuous reinforcement.

Reason (R) On reinforced trials, the interfering frustrative responses become extinguished.

177 **Assertion** (A) Positive reinforcement occurs when a response is strengthened.

Reason (R) Positive reinforcement is followed by the presentation of a desirable stimulus.

178 **Assertion** (A) Negative reinforcement occurs when a response is strengthened as the result of the removal of an unpleasant stimulus.

Reason (R) People often incorrectly confuse punishment with negative reinforcement.

179 **Assertion** (A) Problem associated with the application of physical punishment as a disciplinary procedure include emotional side effect.

Reason (R) Physical punishment decreases aggressive behaviour.

180 **Assertion** (A) Observational learning occurs when an organism's responding is influenced by the observation of models.

Reason (R) Models are important in observational learning.

181 **Assertion** (A) When a behaviour is strengthened indirectly through vicarious conditioning the process at work is observational learning.

Reason (R) Conditioning is directly related to learning.

182 **Assertion** (A) Social critics have expressed concern about the amount of violence on Television since TV is popular.

Reason (R) Majority of research into the impact of media violence on behaviour has focused on the role of observational learning.

183 Assertion (A) A variable ratio schedule is an example of intermittent reinforcement.

Reason (R) If a rat was rewarded for pressing a lever every five times on average, we would call this a variable ratio schedule of reinforcement.

184 Assertion (A) Primary reinforcers are essential for survival.

Reason (R) Good grades are an example of primary reinforcer.

185 Assertion (A) Partial reinforcements schedules (fixed-interval, fixed-ratio, variable-interval and variable-ratio) produce slower acquisition of the target behaviour than does continuous reinforcement.

Reason (R) They also produce greater resistance to extinction.

Directions (Q.Nos. 186-190) *Read the passage given below and answer the following questions.*

Pavlov and his students noticed that a dog conditioned to the sound of one tone also responded somewhat to the sound of a different tone that had never been paired with food. Likewise, a dog conditioned to salivate when rubbed would also salivate somewhat when scratched (Windholz, 1989) or when stimulated on a different body part.

This tendency to respond to stimuli similar to the CS is called *generalisation*. Generalisation can be adaptive as when toddlers are taught to fear moving cars in the street respond similarly to trucks and motorcycles. So, automatic is generalisation that one Argentine writer who underwent torture still recoils with fear when he sees black shoes; his first glimpse of his torturers when they approached his cell. Generalisation has been brought to the laboratory in studies comparing abused with non-abused children. Shown an angry face on a computer screen, abused children's brain-wave responses are dramatically stronger and longer lasting (Pollak and others, 1998).

Because of generalisation, stimuli that are similar to naturally disgusting or appealing objects will, by association, evoke some disgust or liking. Normally desirable foods, such as fudge are unappealing when presented in a disgusting form as when shaped to resemble dog feces (Rozin and others, 1986). We perceive adults with child-like facial features (round face, large forehead, small chin and large eyes) as having childlike warmth, submissiveness and naivete (Berry and Mc Arthur, 1986). In both cases, people's emotional reactions to one stimulus generalise to similar stimuli.

186 Consider the following statements

1. In operant conditioning, generalisation is the tendency to respond to stimuli similar to the CS.
2. Organism's response to similar stimuli is also reinforced in classical conditioning.

Which of the statements given above is/are incorrect?

(a) Only 1 (b) Only 2
(c) Both 1 and 2
(d) Neither 1 nor 2

187 Which of the following about generalisation is false?

(a) Generalisation helps organisms to adapt new events by responding to a range of stimuli similar to the CS.
(b) Adaptation requires us to respond similarly to stimuli that are equivalent in function.
(c) Because of stimulus generalisation, the CR can also be elicited by stimuli that are similar to the CS.
(d) To train the animal to generalise among stimuli, one stimulus (CS+) is presented with the US, while another (CS–) is presented without the US.

188 Which of the following is the best example of generalisation?

1. A bird that learns to avoid a bad-tasting butterfly will also avoid other butterflies of similar appearance.
2. Babies can identify their mother's voice from those of other women.
3. Child has been conditioned to fear a stuffed white rabbit, the child will exhibit fear of objects similar to the conditioned stimulus.

Select the correct answer using the codes given below

(a) 1 and 2
(b) 2 and 3
(c) 1 and 3
(d) None of the above

189 Based on the theory of generalisation, a dog who is treated cruelly by its male owner learns to be afraid of that man. Which of the following is wrong?

(a) The CS is the sight, sound, etc. of the man
(b) The UCS is the cruel treatment
(c) The UCR is the distress elicited by the cruel treatment
(d) UCS is fear of the man

190 After Watson and Rayner classically conditioned a small child named Albert to fear a white rat, the child later showed fear in response to a rabbit, a dog and a sealskin coat. Little Albert's fear of objects resembling the rat illustrates

(a) extinction
(b) generalisation of the conditioned response
(c) spontaneous recovery
(d) discrimination between two stimuli

Directions (Q.Nos. 191-195) *Read the passage given below and answer the following questions.*

Positive reinforcement is the presentation of an event (*e.g.* food or money)that strengthens or increases the likelihood of a behaviour. Punishment occurs when a response is followed by an event such as pain. You put your hand on a hot stove, burn yourself and learn to stop doing that. Punishment is also called passive avoidance learning because the individual learns to avoid an outcome by being passive (*e.g.* by not putting your hand on the stove).

Try not to be confused by the term negative reinforcement. Negative reinforcement is a kind of reinforcement (not a punishment) and therefore, it increases the frequency of a behaviour. It is negative because the reinforcement is the absence of something. *For example* You learn to apply sun-screen to avoid skin cancer and you learn to brush your teeth to avoid tooth decay. Negative reinforcement increases the behaviour and decreases the undesirable outcome.

Negative reinforcement is also known as escape learning, if the response stops an outcome or avoidance learning, if it prevents the outcome altogether. For more researchers use the terms escape learning and avoidance learning than the potentially confusing term negative reinforcement. Pigeons in Skinner's experiment had these response patterns to the different schedules. Just like people, the pigeons produced higher response rates when reinforcement was linked to the number of responses in a ratio schedule as opposed to the amount of time in an interval schedule. The pigeons also produced more consistent responding with an unpredictable or variable schedule as opposed to a predictable or fixed schedule.

191 **Based on the passage above about reinforcement, three of the following are examples of positive reinforcement. Which one is not?**

(a) When Asha's teacher praises her in class for her oral report, Alice is embarrassed and vows never to act so smart in front of her friends again.
(b) When Bhaskar changes the way he throws the javelin, he finds that it goes further than it ever has before and so he continues to use the new technique.
(c) When Chitra tells a funny joke, her classmates laugh. Cordell soon becomes the class clown, telling jokes at every opportunity.
(d) When Dinesh discovers that he can leave physical education class early by complaining about a stomach ache, he begins to get these stomach aches about once a week.

192 **Which of the following is an example of negative reinforcement?**

(a) Priya's friends think she is cool because she has the audacity to swear in class.
(b) Divya completes her English paper two days early so she won't have it hanging over her head.
(c) Tom's teacher scolds him, when she finds a copy of Playboy hidden behind the textbook, he is supposed to be reading.
(d) Bindu gets the attention of all the boys when she wears tight, skimpy outfits to school.

193 **Negative reinforcement brings about the increase of a behaviour through the ...... of a stimulus.**

(a) addition
(b) removal
(c) Both a and b
(d) Neither a nor b

194 **When a teenager gets poor grades, his father takes away his cellphone. This consequence is a**

(a) positive reinforcer
(b) negative reinforcer
(c) positive punishment
(d) negative punishment

195 **Consider the following statements**

1. Predictable reinforcements are less stressful than unpredictable reinforcements.
2. Primary reinforcers do not require prior experience to be reinforcing.

Select the correct answer using the codes given below

(a) Only 1 (b) Only 2
(c) Both1 and 2 (d) Neither 1 or 2

Directions (Q. Nos. 196-198) *Read the passage given below and answer the following questions.*

In Tolman's experiment, three groups of rats were taught to run a maze. The rats that were never shown food in the maze appeared not to have learned it.

However, when food appeared they could find it just as quickly as rats that had always been shown food.

196 **This demonstrates the effect of**

(a) latent learning
(b) observational learning
(c) operant conditioning
(d) insight learning

197 **The operationalised dependent variable in Tolman's experiment was**

(a) the number of groups of rats
(b) whether rats were shown cheese originally
(c) the amount of electric shocks the rats were given
(d) the time it took the rats to solve the maze

198 **Tolman used rats in his experimentation. When using animals in psychological research**

(a) ethics do not apply.
(b) ethics only apply to animals that are domestic not wild.
(c) ethical principles apply to animals and humans.
(d) ethical principles apply to animals and humans, but are not charged for breaking ethics against animals.

PREVIOUS YEARS' QUESTIONS

July 2018

1 Chimpanzee Sarah's one of the most outstanding achievements was the construction of sentences involving

(a) negation (b) conditional relationship
(c) adult grammar (d) unprompted questions

2 In a typical learning experiment which of the following are used dependent variables?

1. Probability of response 2. Latency
3. Rate of presentation 4. Trials to extinction

Codes

(a) 1 and 2 only (b) 2 and 4 only
(c) 1, 2 and 3 only (d) 1, 2 and 4 only

3 Creative thinking is different from routine problem solving in respect of

1. Fluency 3. Flexibility
3. Originality 4. Day dreaming

Codes

(a) 1 and 2 (b) 2 and 3 (c) 3 and 4 (d) 1, 2 and 3

4 Read each of the following statements Assertion (A) and Reason (R) and indicate your answer using codes given below

Assertion (A) Children have remarkable ability to create mental representation of the world in the form of language.

Reason (R) Reasoning and problem solving are the ways of manipulating the ideas.

Codes

(a) Both A and R are true and R is the correct explanation of A
(b) Both A and R are true, but R is not the correct explanation of A
(c) A is true, but R is false
(d) A is false, but R is true

5 According to Bandura, which of the following is the correct sequence of processes involved in observation learning?

(a) Attention → Retention → Cognitive Rehearsal → Corrective Action
(b) Attention → Cognitive Rehearsal → Corrective Action → Retention
(c) Attention → Corrective Action → Cognitive Rehearsal → Retention
(d) Corrective Action → Attention → Cogntive Rehearsal → Retention

6 Read each of the following two statements Assertion (A) and Reason (R) and indicate your answer using codes given below

Assertion (A) Autoshaping involves S-S learning.

Reason (R) Some behaviours are innate reponses to a stimulus and because of temporal contiguity between them, they acquire stimuls related properties.

Codes

(a) Both A and R are true and R is the correct explanation of A
(b) Both A and R are true, but R is not the correct explanation of A
(c) A is true, but R is false
(d) A is false, but R is true

7 Read each of the following two statements Assertion (A) and Reason (R) and indicate your answer using codes given below

Assertion (A) The names of objects, days of the week, the seasons and other general facts are all quite lasting and we do not forget them.

Reason (R) Most of our basic factual knowledge about the world is almost totally immune to forgetting.

Codes

(a) Both A and R are true and R is the correct explanation of A
(b) Both A and R are true, but R is not the correct explanation of A
(c) A is true, but R is false
(d) A is false, but R is true

8 Read each of the following two statements Assertion (A) and Reason (R) and indicate your answer using codes given below

Assertion (A) To use a computer, we must learn to pay attention to specific stimuli, such as icons, commands and signals.

Reason (R) Learning creates perceptual habits that affect our daily experience.

Codes

(a) Both A and R are true and R is the correct explanation of A
(b) Both A and R are true, but R is not the correct explanation of A
(c) A is true, but R is false
(d) A is false, but R is true

July 2016

9 Read each of the following two statements Assertion (A) and Reason (R) and indicate your answer using codes given below

Assertion (A) Organisms learn to perform responses that produce positive reinforcers.

Reason (R) Positive reinforcement strengthens responses that permit escape from or a avoidance of stimulus.

Codes
(a) Both A and R are true and R is the correct explanation of A
(b) Both A and R are true, but R is not the correct explanation of A
(c) A is true, but R is false
(d) A is false, but R is true

10 Match List I with List II and select the correct answer by choosing from the codes given below

List I (Thinking)	List II (Related to)
A. Autistic thinking	1. Planning
B. Creative thinking	2. Fantansy
C. Deterministic thinking	3. Illusion
D. Cognitive thinking	4. Dreams

Codes

	A	B	C	D
(a)	1	2	3	4
(b)	4	3	2	1
(c)	4	1	2	3
(d)	1	4	3	2

11 Words learned under water are recalled
(a) better on land than under water
(b) better above land (sky) than on land
(c) better above land (sky) than under water
(d) better under water than on land

12 Read the following statment and decide "If a rat that had previously learned to traverse a maze or a runway to obtain food is placed directly into a non-empty goal box, it will stop traversing the maze or runway on subsequent trails."What it examplifies?
(a) Letent learning (b) Place learning
(c) Response extinction (d) Latent extinction

June 2015

13 Partial reinforcement is considered better than continuous reinforcement because
(a) the learning occurs rapidly
(b) the learning occurs slowly
(c) the extinction occurs rapidly
(d) the extinction occurs slowly

14 Self-modelling means
(a) a type of learning in which individuals watch themselves behaving in a situationally appropriate manner and then show the same behaviours later on.
(b) type of learning in which individuals learn new behaviour.
(c) type of learning in which individuals learn to develop self-beliefs.
(d) type of learning in which individuals learn through guides-participation from significant others.

15 Read each of the following two statements Assertion (A) and Reason (R) and indicate your answer using the codes given below

Assertion (A) People who learn more and more lists of words on successive days have more and more difficulty in learning each new list next day.

Reason (R) People have limited capacity to learn verbal material.

Codes
(a) Both A and R are true and R is the correct explanation of A
(b) Both A and R are true, but R is not the correct explanation of A
(c) A is true, but R is false
(d) A is false, but R is true

16 Match itmes of List I with the items of List II. Select the correct response from the answer codes given below

List I (Learning)	List II (Explaination)
A. Latent learning	1. Learning a response to terminate an aversive stimulus
B. Cognitive learning	2. Occurrence of learning is not evident in behaviour until later
C. Escape learning	3. A change in the way of processing informations as a result of experiences
D. Avoidance learning	4. Learning a response to avoid an averisve stimulus

Codes

	A	B	C	D		A	B	C	D
(a)	3	2	4	1	(b)	2	3	1	4
(c)	1	4	2	3	(d)	4	3	1	2

17 Match List I with List II and select the correct answer by choosing correct codes given below

List I (Concepts)	List II (Explanations)
A. Situated learning	1. Internalise knowledge and skills developed in interaction with others
B. Social negotiation	2. Aspect of learning process that relies on collaboration with others and respect for different perspectives
C. Appropriate	3. Skills are tied to the settings in which they are learned and are difficult to apply in new settings
D. Cognitive apprenticeship	4. A relationship in which a less experienced learner acquires knowledge and skills in interaction with expert

Codes

	A	B	C	D		A	B	C	D
(a)	1	2	3	4	(b)	3	4	1	2
(c)	3	2	1	4	(d)	1	4	3	2

18 According to Tolman, the three parts of learning that work together as Gestalt are
1. significant 2. habit strength
3. sign 4. means-end-relationship
5. drive strength

Codes

(a) 2, 3 and 5 (b) 3, 4 and 5 (c) 1, 2 and 3 (d) 1, 3 and 4

19 **Match List I with List II and select the correct answer by choosing from the codes given below**

List I (Procedures)		List II (Behavioural Outcomes)
A. Positive reinforcement	1.	Learn to perform responses that produce pleasant outcome
B. Negative reinforcement	2.	Learn to suppress responses that lead to unpleasant outcome
C. Positive punishment	3.	Learn to suppress responses that lead to loss or postponement of desired stimulus
D. Negative punishment	4.	Learn to perform responses that permit to avoid or escape an unpleasant event

Codes

	A	B	C	D		A	B	C	D
(a)	4	3	2	1	(b)	1	2	4	3
(c)	2	1	3	4	(d)	1	4	2	3

June 2014

20 **Arjun gets annoyed when his mother nags him to do his homework. When he finlly does it, his mother stops nagging. Now he does the homework without any nagging. Here 'nagging' has served as a**

(a) punishment by application

(b) positive reinforcement

(c) negative reinforcement

(d) punishment by removal

21 **Put the steps involved in observational learning in sequence of its occurrence.**

1. Reproduction 2. Attention
3. Motivation for later use 4. Retention

Codes

(a) 4, 2, 1, 3 (b) 1, 4, 3, 2 (c) 2, 4, 1, 3 (d) 3, 1, 2, 4

22 **Learned helplessness may appear when stress causes**

1. anxiety
2. anger and aggression
3. withdrawal and apathy
4. feeling of uncontroliability

Codes

(a) 1 and 2 (b) 2 and 3 (c) 2 and 4 (d) 3 and 4

23 **Assertion** **(A) Children with learning disability are allowed to type or tape record their assignments.**

Reason **(R) Omitting handwriting as a criterion for evaluating reports/copies is a way of helping children with learning disability.**

Codes

(a) Both A and R are true and R is the correct explanation A

(b) Both A and R are true, but R is not the correct explanation A

(c) A is true, but R is false

(d) A is false, but R is false

ANSWERS

Exam Based Questions

1 *(d)*	2 *(c)*	3 *(d)*	4 *(a)*	5 *(d)*	6 *(b)*	7 *(c)*	8 *(a)*	9 *(b)*	10 *(d)*
11 *(c)*	12 *(a)*	13 *(d)*	14 *(c)*	15 *(a)*	16 *(a)*	17 *(d)*	18 *(d)*	19 *(c)*	20 *(b)*
21 *(d)*	22 *(a)*	23 *(d)*	24 *(b)*	25 *(c)*	26 *(c)*	27 *(d)*	28 *(c)*	29 *(b)*	30 *(d)*
31 *(a)*	32 *(b)*	33 *(b)*	34 *(a)*	35 *(b)*	36 *(d)*	37 *(a)*	38 *(b)*	39 *(a)*	40 *(a)*
41 *(d)*	42 *(d)*	43 *(c)*	44 *(c)*	45 *(c)*	46 *(c)*	47 *(d)*	48 *(b)*	49 *(b)*	50 *(d)*
51 *(a)*	52 *(a)*	53 *(a)*	54 *(d)*	55 *(c)*	56 *(d)*	57 *(a)*	58 *(d)*	59 *(b)*	60 *(d)*
61 *(d)*	62 *(c)*	63 *(c)*	64 *(c)*	65 *(b)*	66 *(c)*	67 *(b)*	68 *(c)*	69 *(d)*	70 *(a)*
71 *(c)*	72 *(b)*	73 *(b)*	74 *(a)*	75 *(d)*	76 *(b)*	77 *(a)*	78 *(c)*	79 *(d)*	80 *(d)*
81 *(d)*	82 *(d)*	83 *(d)*	84 *(a)*	85 *(d)*	86 *(a)*	87 *(d)*	88 *(a)*	89 *(c)*	90 *(c)*
91 *(b)*	92 *(b)*	93 *(d)*	94 *(b)*	95 *(b)*	96 *(a)*	97 *(c)*	98 *(d)*	99 *(b)*	10 *(a)*
101 *(a)*	102 *(b)*	103 *(b)*	104 *(c)*	105 *(a)*	106 *(a)*	107 *(a)*	108 *(d)*	109 *(a)*	110 *(c)*
111 *(a)*	112 *(b)*	113 *(d)*	114 *(d)*	115 *(d)*	116 *(b)*	117 *(a)*	118 *(c)*	119 *(b)*	120 *(d)*
121 *(a)*	122 *(a)*	123 *(c)*	124 *(d)*	125 *(a)*	126 *(b)*	127 *(d)*	128 *(c)*	129 *(a)*	130 *(d)*
131 *(d)*	132 *(a)*	133 *(c)*	134 *(d)*	135 *(b)*	136 *(c)*	137 *(d)*	138 *(b)*	139 *(d)*	140 *(b)*
141 *(a)*	142 *(d)*	143 *(c)*	144 *(c)*	145 *(b)*	146 *(d)*	147 *(b)*	148 *(b)*	149 *(a)*	150 *(b)*
151 *(c)*	152 *(c)*	153 *(b)*	154 *(b)*	155 *(b)*	156 *(c)*	157 *(a)*	158 *(b)*	159 *(b)*	160 *(b)*
161 *(a)*	162 *(a)*	163 *(a)*	164 *(a)*	165 *(c)*	166 *(b)*	167 *(a)*	168 *(a)*	169 *(b)*	170 *(a)*
171 *(a)*	172 *(d)*	173 *(a)*	174 *(b)*	175 *(b)*	176 *(a)*	177 *(a)*	178 *(b)*	179 *(c)*	180 *(b)*
181 *(c)*	181 *(a)*	183 *(c)*	184 *(b)*	185 *(b)*	186 *(c)*	187 *(d)*	188 *(c)*	189 *(d)*	190 *(b)*
191 *(a)*	192 *(b)*	193 *(b)*	194 *(d)*	195 *(b)*	196 *(a)*	197 *(d)*	198 *(c)*		

Previous Years' Questions

1 *(b)*	2 *(b)*	3 *(c)*	4 *(c)*	5 *(a)*	6 *(a)*	7 *(a)*	8 *(b)*	9 *(c)*	10 *(c)*
11 *(d)*	12 *(d)*	13 *(d)*	14 *(a)*	15 *(c)*	16 *(b)*	17 *(c)*	18 *(d)*	19 *(d)*	20 *(c)*
21 *(c)*	22 *(d)*	23 *(a)*							

Memory and Forgetting

Human memory is like the memory of a computer. The memory allows us to store information for later use. We have sensory memory, short term memory and long term memory. There are many reasons that we forget. Some information never makes it to the long term memory and some is permanently stored in the short term memory.

Introduction

Memory is a psychological process that goes beyond simply remembering important information. It is influenced by our beliefs, expectations, fears and anticipations. This is one reason that memory is so unreliable. As our consciousness evolves, so does the reference point for the information, which we have stored. Information is reviewed through new lenses, causing the focus of our memories to shift. As a result of which even something as fine as our present moment, emotions can have a substantial impact on our ability to recall anything with accuracy.

Memory can be described in three dimensions : persistence, intensity and accuracy. Perceived truthfulness can also be considered as fourth variable of memory. In general, emotionally charged situations produce memories, which are persistent, intense and unreliable, but the emotional involvement causes us to evaluate those memories as having a high degree of perceived truthfulness.

Forgetting is also associated with the memory. Forgetting is the inability to recall information. This can occur either because of retrieval cue or encoding failures or as a part of the process of decay. While forgetting is simply a part of life, there are a number of things that we can do to improve our memories and become better at recalling information. Various aspects of memory and forgetting have been discussed below in detail.

In this Chapter

- *Memory*
- *Stages of Memory*
- *Forgetting*

Memory

Memory is the retention of information over time. It is a crucial aspect of cognition, as it provides the basis for all cognitive processes. The term 'memory' has been derived from the Latin word 'memoria', which means historical account or long remembrance. Modern approach to memory has gone far beyond the simple yet significant beginnings made by **Hermann Ebbinghaus**.

The contemporary psychologists take an information processing view of memory, which relies on the computer as a model. Like computers, the human mind receives information from the external world, stores it in some form for a period of time and recalls it. Therefore, memory can be defined as process by which we encode, store and retrieve information. Memory refers to retaining and recalling information over a period of time, depending upon the nature of cognitive task required to perform. It is conceptualised as a process consisting of three independent, though interrelated stages. These are encoding, storage and retrieval. Any information received by us necessarily goes through these stages.

Memory Processes

The memory process includes the following.

Encoding

The Human memory is used for accomplishing three basic tasks. These are encoding, storage and retrieval. These are used to enter information to the memory, retain and option information at the time it is needed.

It is the process of getting information into memory. If information or stimuli never gets encoded, it will not be remembered. Encoding is the first stage of memory process. It occurs when information is translated into a form that can be processed mentally. Information from the environment is constantly reaching one's senses in the forms of stimuli. Encoding allows one to change the stimuli, so that one may put it into one's memory.

It can be considered similar to librarians classifying books before placing them on the shelf. As librarians encode/label books for users to locate them easily, an individual encodes information before placing the information into his/her memory. Encoding requires paying attention to information and linking to existing knowledge in order to make the new information meaningful and thus easier to remember.

Factors Influencing Encoding

Various factors influencing encoding are as follows

Massed and Spaced Practice

Researchers after Ebbinghaus have investigated the most effective way to use learning time in order to maximise the amount that will be remembered. Their research shows that it is more effective to have a series of shorter learning sessions than to have one long period, even if both of them involve the same amount of time in the end. Moreover, this principle that spaced practice is more effective than massed practice applies both to physical skills and to the learning of factual or abstract information. It seems that, if we allow our memories and time to settle, then we can recall things more effectively.

In spaced learning, the practice trials are interspaced with rest period. In massed learning, the material to be learned is mastered in a single session.

Spaced learning is generally regarded as better to be the period of rest because it

- Prevents the boredom and fatigue from setting in
- Brings back motivation and enthusiasm
- Also helps to remove the interfering association that might develope during the course of learning

Primacy and Recency Effects

Another aspect of encoding memories concerns the way how the material is presented. Ebbinghaus is generally credited with having discovered primacy and recency effects, although this may not be strictly accurate.

Murdock (1962) showed people a set of 20 words, one at a time and gave them either one or two seconds to look at each one. Then, they were asked to write down as many of the words as they could remember. Murdock found that most of the words that the research participants remembered had occupied the first or the last few places in the list and not the middle of the list, which were easily forgotten.

Several explanations have been put forward to explain primacy and recency effects. One of them is the idea that we may pay more attention to the first few items in a list because they are new to us. Another explanation for recency effects comes from the idea that remembering some information can interfere with our memory for other material. This model proposes that we remember later items better because the information does not suffer from interference; nothing comes after it, so we do not confuse it with anything else. There are other possible explanations, **Glanzer** and **Cunitz** (1966), proposed that primacy and recency effects result from the words being retrieved from different memory stores.

Many psychologists believe that we have two different kinds of memory stores; a Short Term Memory(STM), which fades quickly, lasting for only a few seconds and a Long Term Memory (LTM) store, which retains information for longer periods of time. Primacy effects come about because the words have been stored in long-term memory, whereas recency effects result from word being retrieved from short term memory.

Imagery and Semantic Coding

Once the information is acquired, it also needs to be represented in the mind and this is a part of the encoding stage as well. One of the best-known methods of representing information is in sensory images, such as sounds or pictures. When we do this, it is as if we can hear the sound or see the picture when the memory comes back. For instance, the memory of someone's favourite song is stored in this way. Other memories might be coded in different kinds of sensory modes *e.g.* the taste of lemon is one, which people can often remember quite clearly.

One way that we can often tell which kind of imagery people are using is by the mistakes that they make. **Conrad**, used this technique by showing research participants a list of letters and asking them to remember which letters they had seen. Although, most of the research participants were able to get the lists right, when they did make errors, these were from substituting a letter, which sounded similar-like a J instead of a K or a T instead of B.

The conclusion was that they were using acoustic imagery rather than visual imagery. But, if a participant had put a C instead of an O, this would have suggested that he was using visual imagery instead. One may find it interesting to see, which kinds of coding you prefer to use by looking at the mistakes, which you make when you are remembering telephone numbers or similar information.

Experimental Study

Bower (1972), asked people to memorise lists of word-pairs. One group were asked to remember the word-pairs by forming mental images, which would link the two, like imagining a shoe dropped in a pot of paint for the word-pair 'Shoe-paint'. Another group were asked to use semantic coding (coding by meaning), forming a sentence which would link the pairs, like 'she put on her shoes and went to pick up the paint'.

A third group were asked to imagine the objects separated in space, rather than connected such as imagining a shoe in a shoe shop and a pot of paint by a wall. Bower found that the group which used semantic coding remembered the most word-pairs, closely followed by the group, which had used connected imagery.

Those who had used disconnected imagery did not recall many of the word-pairs at all. There are individual differences in the type of mental representation that people prefer to use although each of us can use each kind to some extent.

The Generation Effect

The term generation effect describes the observed phenomenon that when an individual is more likely to remember information individual retrieves or generates (during study) than information that he simply receives and attempts to memorise. Thus, one is more likely to remember the 12 cranial nerves from flashcards, which demand action on his/her part, than from studying a list. The effect is an experimental demonstration of the generally accepted idea that we often learn best by doing.

Generating information from memory is thought to be a more powerful encoding event than merely processing externally presented information because both elaboration and greater attention are required for generation. Support for this interpretation and greater attention are required for generation. Support for this interpretation comes from neuroimaging experiments, which have demonstrated that the left frontal lobe region, which shows a level of processing effect, is also more active when generating than when reading words.

Transfer appropriate processing further suggests that generation is a particularly effective way to learn because the processes that are engaged during the initial generation at encoding are likely to overlap with those required to generate the information from memory at retrieval.

Encoding Specificity Principle

The encoding specificity principle says that for retrieval cues to be effective, they need to be encoded along with the 'to be remembered material'.

This means that, if you want to remember something at a certain place and time, you should pay close attention to the conditions that are likely to be present, when you need to remember. You must engage in what psychologists call transfer appropriate processing *i.e.* you should study the material using the same kind of mental processes that will be required during retrieval. Because of the importance of retrieval cues, performance on a memory test will always depend on the match between the mental process used during studying and the mental processes required by the test.

Storage

It consists of retention of information overtime. It is believed that one can gather information in three main storage areas : sensory memory, short-term memory and long-term memory. These areas vary according to time frames. The period of time, the information retained, is anywhere from a fraction of second to a few years.

Sensory information stores information only for a brief second. Short-term memory can hold information longer, but it is only usually about 30-45 seconds. Long-term memory, however, can last a lifetime.

Retrieval

It is the process of recalling stored information from memory. Basically, it is getting information out of one's long-term memory and returning it to one's conscious mind.

The ability to access and retrieve information from memory allows one to use the memories to answer the questions, perform tasks, make decisions and interact with other people.

The third stage of memory according to the Ebbinghaus approach, is retrieval. The first stage, you will recall was encoding; the second stage is storage and this is the third. In some senses, it is the most important storage. Afterall, we cannot know whether someone has really remembered something unless they show us that they have, by retrieving that information from memory in some way. But there seem to be several different types of retrieval.

Among many other findings, Ebbinghaus identified four different forms of retrieval from the list which he and his research assistant had memorised.

The strongest of these was recall, when they could remem ber the word that would come next without any prompting.

On other occasions, although a word could not be recalled, it could be recognised as having formed part of the list, once it had been seen again. Ebbinghaus identified recognition as a second, though weaker form of memory. A third form of remembering was reconstruction.

Ebbinghaus found that even if he was unable to recall or even recognise a set of trigrams. He still might be able to reconstruct the list in the order in which he had originally learned it showing that there were still some traces of the original learning left.

The fourth and the weakest form of retrieval can be termed as relearning. It occurs when we go through the moments like "Oh! I used to know this." We may not be able to recall the information, but we know that it is there and therefore, we remember it through learning it again.

Factors Influencing Retrieval Process

The process of getting access to the stored information is called retrieval.

Important factors which influence the retrieval process are

- **Retrieval Cues** It facilitates retrieval of information. *For example* State dependent memory and context dependent memory are the memory based on retrieval cues.
- **Reconstructive Process** It was given by Bartlett which refers to the modification of the already stored information. Reconstructive memories are difficult to retrieve.
- **Elaborative Rehearsal** It facilitates better retrieval of information. Elaborative processing provides deeper processing.
- **Schema** Mental representation of people, object, situation or events aquired through experience is known as schema. Schema establishes expectancies that result in the selection of feature of the event to be encoded.

Stages of Memory

In late 1960s, many researchers in the field of memory believed that *Human Memory Model* is based on the connectionist approach. **Martindale** (1991), viewed that information processing explanation of memory is a well researched framework for examining human learning and memory.

Information processing view of memory uses computer as a model of understanding memory systems. Like the computer, the human mind takes in information, performs operation on it to change its form, stores the information, retrieves it when needed and generates responses. The three basic tasks that are performed in this process are encoding, storage and retrieval. Several important models of memory, which rest firmly on this (information processing) approach have been proposed. Of these, the model proposed by **Atkinson** and **Shiffrin** is the most influential one.

According to this model, there are three kinds of memory systems or stages

(i) Sensory memory (sensory register)
(ii) Short term memory and
(iii) Long term memory

These storehouses vary in terms of their functions and the length of time for which they retain information.

Sensory Memory

When a stimulus is first encountered, it is entered into sensory memory. This involves the retention of a literal copy of the stimulus *i.e.* if a chair is present, sensory memory codes for the shape of the object, its size, its colour and its location in space.

If a sound is encountered, the physical property of the sound, such as its loudness, tone, pitch and location in space are held in sensory store. The relevant code is therefore termed as a physical and sometimes a structural code.

Sensory memory is essentially preconscious. As it was first researched, it also appeared to be pre-identification or precategorical *i.e.* no code reflecting the meaning of the stimulus was found at this level. If a chair was encountered, the shape and location of the chair would be stored. In contrast, no information reflecting the meaning of the stimulus was found at this level.

Entry of material into sensory store does not depend on attention. Stimuli within the visual or auditory field automatically enter the system at this level. Such entry appears to occur in parallel *i.e.* whatever stimuli are present, enter at the same time, rather than sequentially. Information is lost from sensory memory through decay. Material vanishes from the system whether new material is entered or not.

Neisser labelled sensory memory for visual stimuli as iconic store with a visual array being called the icon. Auditory sensory memory was called the echoic store. These terms are now widely used within the field.

Research into Sensory Memory

In 1859, **Sir William Hamilton** was curious to know how much information can be perceived or apprehended at a single glance. He found that he was able to estimate the presence of upto six and sometimes seven marbles accurately. A larger number could not be accurately judged, unless they formed simple groups of two or three. Our ability to establish information in the briefest of glances became known as the *span of apprehension.* The estimates of this span varied slightly from researcher to researcher.

But so far, there are two kinds of sensory memory, which have been studied extensively *one of them is iconic (visual) and the other is echoic (hearing) sensory memory.*

Iconic Memory Studies

Various studies and experiments have been conducted to study the iconic memory. The most prominent of these experiments is the study of George Sperling.

It has been described by the following phenomenon.

After Images Phenomenon

Let an image store at some form fixedly for 30 seconds or so, then look away at a blank wall. If you maintain a fairly constant fixation and if the illumination and reflectance conditions for your blank wall are appropriate, you should see an afterimage having the same from as the thing you stared at. Everyone experiences afterimages on many occasions, though we rarely pay attention to them. Although, visual persistence and afterimages have long been studied by perceptual psychologists, an important study by George Sperling in 1960, was very influential in producing systematic consideration of these phenomena as examples of sensory memory.

Sperling's Experiment

Over 30 years ago, a graduate student in psychology named George Sperling developed a clever set of procedures for studying the properties of iconic memory using an apparatus called a tachistoscope, which presents visual displays for carefully controlled durations.

Sperling showed people arrays of 12 letters arranged in rows. *For example* X L W F; J B O V; K C Z R
Sperling reasoned from his observation that there were two possibilities. **First**, despite what the subjects believe, might be limited because only 4 to 5 letters can actually be read from the display in a short presentation time. **Second**, the entire display might be read and stored accurately, but its memory fades before subjects have time to report everything they have seen. Again, it was the second alternative that matched what the subjects reported, people were convinced that they saw an image of the entire display, but claimed that it faded before everything could be recovered for recall.

Partial Report Technique

To test between these alternatives, Sperling devised a way to sample selectively from the icon rather than asking subjects to recall everything form the display, he asked them to report only the letters shown in a particular row. After the display was turned off, he presented a tone.

If the pitch of the tone was high, medium or low, the task was to report the top, middle or bottom row of the display, respectively, **Sperling** called this new condition partial report because only a portion of the display needed to be recalled. Performance on these partial report trials was then compared to the original whole report condition, which required the recall of all 12 letters. As Sperling anticipated, performance improved dramatically in the new condition-subjects reliably reported almost all of the row letters correctly.

Sperling assumed that iconic memory simply decayed away with the passage of time. However, current evidence indicates that people may perform poorly after a delay because they become confused about where items were presented in the display. Thus, information is not lost from iconic memory in the way that a television picture is lost after the set is turned off ; instead, the image becomes more inexact-subjects may simply forget the item's spatial location rather than the item itself.

In real life, information that has just entered iconic memory will be pushed out very quickly by new information, this process is called as *Masking* (Cowan , 1988). Research suggests that after only a quarter of a second, old information is replaced by new information. In real sense, it is very rare to have Eidetic imagery or the ability to access a visual imagery or the ability to access a visual memory over a long period time. This ability is popularly known as *photographic memory*.

Functions of Iconic Memory

Iconic memory provides a smooth stream of visual information to the brain, which can be extracted over a longer period of time for consolidation into more stable forms. *The following are the functions of the iconic memory*

- It enables integrating visual information along a continuous stream of images. *For example* While watching a movie.
- It plays an important role in the ability to detect change in a visual scene.
- Iconic memory plays a key role in the ability to provide continuity of experience during saccadic eye movements. These rapid eye movements occur in approximately 30 ms and each one lasts for approximately 300 ms.

Echoic Memory

Ulric Neisser's term, echoic memory refers to persistence of audition. It is considered equivalent to what Robert Crowder and John Morton call precategorical acoustic storage. The basic hypothesis is that there is an auditory or perhaps a phonetic analogue of visual iconic memory such that the nodes activated by an auditory stimulus remain activated for some time after the stimulus is over.

Experimental Study

Darwin, Turvey and **Crowder**, using sounds presented at three different locations, estimated echoic store as persistent for about 4 seconds. **Glucksberg** and **Cowan** required their participants to attend to material being presented to one ear, while unattended or ignored information was presented to the other ear.

Control of attention of this kind is possible and participants do not typically retain any information concerning the meaning of the items on the ignored channel, while it remains ignored.

At a given signal, they were asked to switch attention to the other ear and determine whether a digit had just been presented on that channel.

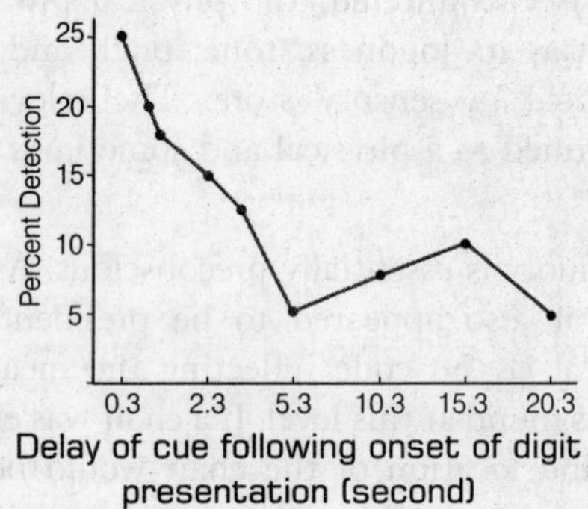

They were able to report digits presented upto 4 seconds before the signal with performance leveling at about 5 seconds. Information had thus been retained in echoic memory over a period of 4 to 5 seconds. The trace appeared to deteriorate rapidly, however, across that interval. The above figure shows the percentage of digit recalled as a function of the delay between the presentation of the digit and the signal.

In the Glucksberg and Cowan study, auditory information was constantly received on the unattended channel. This may have produced interference with the target digit. If the target is followed by silence, the echoic trace continues longer, perhaps for as long as 20 seconds. Echoic memory is very useful when a person wants to have meaningful conversation with others.

It allows the person to remember what someone said just long enough to recognise the meaning of a phrase. *For Example* Echoic memory allows a musician to tune a musical instrument. The memory of the tuning fork's tone is persistent in echoic memory long enough for the person.

Short Term Memory

Short term memory is memory that holds information received from the sensory register for up to about 30 seconds. The length of retention depends upon a number of factors. *The short term memory has mainly three key aspects*

(i) **Limited capacity** (only 7 ± 2 items can be stored at a time).

(ii) **Limited duration** (storage is very fragile and information is lost with distraction or passage of time).

(iii) **Encoding** (it is primarily acoustic).

There are two ways in which the capacity of the short term memory is tested. One is the span and other is the recency effect. The idea that the short term can hold upto 7 ± 2 items was put forward by Miller. He thought that the short term memory could hold 7 items because it only had a certain number of slots in which the items could be stored.

The short term memory shows primacy and recency effects. Superior recall of items at the beginning of the list, called the *primacy effect*, is usually attributed to lack of interference from proceeding items, which makes the early list items more likely to enter long term memory. The better recall of items at the end of the list, called the *recency effect*, which occurs because those later items are still available in short term memory.

Chunking Despite the small size of short-term memory, we can increase the amount of information it can handle by efficiently compacting more information into each item stored. This process is called *chunking. For example* Any time you combine sets of digits in a telephone number to remember it, you are chunking the information to improve your recall. By relying on our tendency to chunk information, telephone companies were able to increase the total number of possible phone number without making them significantly harder to remember. The new information in a single chunk was presented in the form of the exchange : the set of three digit in a phone number that comes before the final four digit block.

Brown-Peterson Test

The duration and capacity of short-term memory depend on what kind of information must be held in mind. *For example* It is easy to remember a list of letters that compose a single word for a long time despite distraction, showing that a chunk of one word enters long-term memory as a single item. Even though the Brown-Peterson test is intended to measure short-term memory alone, it is clear that some items can enter long-term memory and become immune to interference.

Also, studies about repeatedly testing subjects with words as cues have found that performance typically deteriorates for short lists of words as cue from the same category. Such deterioration is blamed on proactive inhibition from earlier items preventing proper encoding of later items. However, when a list of words from a new category is presented, performance suddenly rises.

Short Term Memory Transitions into Long Term Memory

William James (1890), was the first to recognise a distinction between short term and long term memory. The distinction, best captured later in a model developed by Atkinson and Shiffrin, is that these two forms of memory operate in succession so that information from the very short term store is sent into a short term memory buffer just large enough to hold about seven chunks of information. The contents of short term memory can be rehearsed and eventually are stored in long term memory. (As shown in the figure).

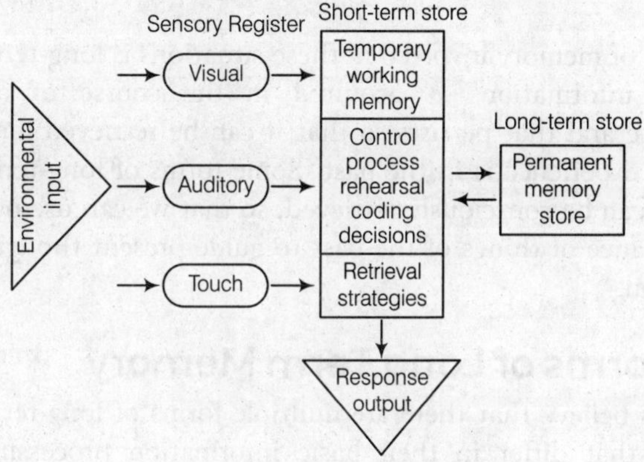

The Atkinson-Shiffrin Model

According to this model, the purpose of short term memory is to rehearse items, so they have a better chance of being stored in long term memory. The pattern of remembering items best near the beginning and end of a series, as shown in serial position curves, matches this model. The primacy effect is caused by superior rehearsal of the first few items, which are held and rehearsed longer before the interference of successive items eventually bumps them out of short term memory. However, other studies have shown that rehearsal by itself does not always improve long-term retention.

Glenberg and Colleagues separated the effects of rehearsal and attention by presenting a four digit number, asking subjects to rehearse an unrelated word for 2, 6 or 18 seconds and then finally asking for recall of the number. Subjects were told that the experiments aimed to assess their ability to recall the number and the word rehearsal was just a distracter.

When the researcher asked that subjects to recall the words they had been rehearsing, they found that subjects performed quite poor and relatively unaffected by the length of time spent rehearsing. Thus, it seems that instead of relying on rehearsal alone, the extent to which items reach long term memory depends on the processing depth of the material. When words are studied at a semantic level, they are better recalled from long term memory.

Long Term Memory

The ability to remember the people, place and things encountered in the course of daily life is a fundamental form of cognition that guides behaviour. Although the consequences of memory failure are sometimes limited to social embarrassment, that is not always the case; memory is essential to the functioning and even the survival of human and other animals. Without memory, we could never learn from our experience and would operate aimlessly, without plans or goals, motor skills and language ability would be lost. Even, the sense of personal identity we all possess would be gone.

The kind of memory involved in these situations is long-term memory information *i.e.* acquired in the course of an experience and that persists so that it can be retrieved long after the experience is in the past. Some forms of long-term memory can be consciously retrieved, so that we can use our remembrance of things of the past to guide present thought and action.

The Forms of Long Term Memory

Theorists believe that there are multiple forms of long-term memory that differ in their basic information processing properties and in the brain structures that support them. These various forms of memory are thought to fall into two general class, described as declarative and non-declarative.

Declarative memory refers to forms of long-term memory that can ordinarily be consciously recollected and declared or described to other people, such as memory for facts, ideas and events. Declarative memory encompasses episodic memory, the memory of events in our own personal past and semantic memory our general knowledge about things in the world and their meaning.

Two forms of long term memory are as follows

- **Declarative Memory** is highly flexible, involving the association of multiple pieces of information into a unified memory representation. Thus, we may have different routes to retrieval of a given memory. Both forms of declarative memory, episodic and semantic, depend on the operation of the medial temporal lobes.
- **Non-Declarative Memory** refers to non-conscious form of long-term memory that are expressed as a change in behaviour without any conscious recollection. Tests of non-declarative memory termed 'implicit memory tests' do not require description of the contents of memory, but rather reveal memory implicitly through observed changes in performance, such as the gradual acquisition of a motor skill.

In comparison to declarative memory, non-declarative memory tends to be more restricted in the ways that this knowledge can be retrieved. The various forms of non-declarative memory do not depend on the medial temporal lobe structures that are important for declarative memory. Rather, the various forms of non-declarative memory are implemented in different brain regions.

Level of Processing Model for Long Term Memory

In general, the information processing theories of memory view memory process in terms of discrete stages each with its own characteristics. Further, information is transferred from one stage to another till some of it is finally stored in long-term memory. **Craik and Lockhart** in contrast to this general view have proposed a new model. They proposed that it is possible to analyse the input (incoming information) at more than one level. *There are three level of processing*

(i) **First Level** (Shallowest) This level of processing is a sensory level of processing through which we merely become aware of incoming information. In this first level, input is registered in our sensory memory and the physical structural aspects of information are processed.

(ii) **Second Level Intermediate** (Phonetic) In this level of processing, one might consider and attend to phonetic sounds that are attached to input. In this level, the structural features are transferred into at least one meaningful word.

(iii) **Third Level Deepest** (Semantic) In order to ensure that the input is retained for a longer period, it is important that it gets analysed and understood in terms of meaning that it carries.
That's why it is called as semantic level of processing. In this level, an elaborate knowledge or cognition of the stimulation situation is obtained. Analysis at the deepest level gives the best memory because deeper is the processing, better is the consolidation of memory traces and deeper is the memory traces, lesser is the chance of decaying.

Some of the information in the short term memory is neither retrieved nor lost but is passed to the long term memory through the process of rehearsal.

It is important to note that mere rehearsal trials at the first level (sensory or perceptual level) of processing is not enough. Rather, the quality of rehearsal is much more important. Rehearsal trials are conducted many times.

However, two types of rehearsals are mostly used. These are maintenance rehearsal and elaborate rehearsal.

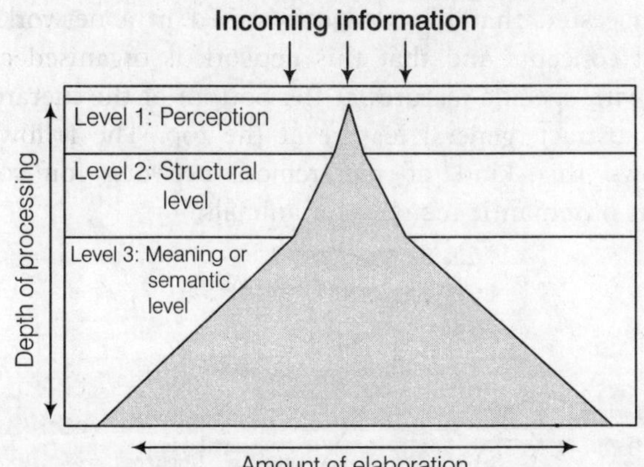

The relationships among levels of processing, elaboration of information and memory. The amount of information retained is shown by the shaded portion of the figure.

Let us discuss the term Rehearsal and its types in detail

Rehearsal

Rehearsal provides a means of maintaining information in short term memory as well as storing information in long term memory. Several studies have shown that more frequently rehearsed items are better remembered than less frequently rehearsed ones.

Rehearsal leads to storage in long term memory, if the rehearsal facilitates the association of the new information with existing information. Repetition of the information by maintenance rehearsal is sufficient to keep the information in short term memory, but insufficient to move it into long term memory. Elaborate rehearsal does facilitate storage in long term memory. *For example* In a study by **Craik and Watkins**, college students were asked to perform two tasks simultaneously: They had to keep one word in their short term memories while at the same time examining additional words to see, if they met certain criteria.
In this situation, the amount of rehearsal did not influence the extent to which the subjects were able to recall the words they had rehearsed; apparently the second task kept them busy enough that they were unable to make associations with the rehearsed words.

Learning information primarily through repetition is sometimes called rote learning. In rote learning, there is little or no attempt to make the information meaningful or to understand it in terms of things one already knows. If such information is stored in long term memory at all, it is not stored in association with similar information, but instead is relatively unconnected and isolated information stored in this unorganised fashion become difficult to retrieve. Although, rehearsal is probably used most frequently by younger children, students must be helped to understand that mere repetition is an inefficient means of storing information for the long run, infact it may not work at all.

Elaboration

When individuals receive new information, they often use what they have already learned about the world to help them understand that information *i.e.* to learn it meaningfully. Sometimes the new information is incomplete, missing pieces need to be filled in.

When new information resembles previously experienced events, then assumptions interpretations and inferences drawn from those previous events are likely to be imposed on the new information and learned right along with it. Elaboration, then, is a process of learning more than the information, actually presented. It is called as learning between lines.

- **Elaboration as a Form of Construction** As a constructive process people use the sensations, they receive to construct a perception of that event. Elaboration is constructive as well. It is a process of using both new information and one's existing knowledge about the world to construct a meaningful interpretation of that new information.
- **Elaboration Involves Frequently the Use of Schemas** Jean Piaget used the concept of schema to refer to a mental unit representing a class of similar actions or thoughts. More recently, psychologists have been using the same term in a somewhat different sense. In contemporary cognitive theory, the term schema usually refers to an organised body of knowledge about a specific topic. An individual's mental script of an event will influence what information is 'learned' from a given instance of that event.
- **Elaboration provides Same Information in Different Ways** Anderson and his colleague found in his study that students' interpretations of a particular story depended on their background, physical education majors more frequently viewed it as a wrestling match, while music education majors were more likely to interpret it as a prison escape. Obviously people elaborate the same information in different ways depending on their previous experience and their expectations about the new information.
- **Elaboration Sometimes Leads to the Storage of Distorted Information** Bartlett found that many of his students recalled distorted versions of 'the war of the ghosts'. When people use previously acquired facts and beliefs to elaborate on new information they may alter the new information erroneously.

- **Elaboration Usually Leads to Better Retention of Information** Although, elaboration can sometimes lead to distortions and errors in what is learned, generally, elaborated information is more effectively learned and remembered than non-elaborated information. Most elaborations reflect correct assumption and interpretations of an event, not incorrect ones.

Elaboration facilitates long-term memory for several reasons. **First**, elaborated information may be less likely to be confused with other similar information stored in long-term memory. **Second**, elaboration may provide additional means through which the information can later be retrieved in a sense it provides more places to 'poke' for the information. And **Third**, elaboration may help with inferences about what the information was likely to have been when the information itself cannot be accurately recalled.

Types of Declarative Memory

Let us discuss the type of declarative memory in detail.

Semantic Memory

This semantic memory is the storehouse of general knowledge which includes our knowledge of words, as its name suggests and it also includes our knowledge of concepts, scenes, geography, mathematics and every other class of knowledge, verbal and non-verbal, for all factual information that can be brought to conscious awareness and expressed explicitly.

Semantic memory is the component of cognitive memory that contains information not bound to any particular event and it is organised by conceptual properties rather than by the order of experienced events.

Tulving defines semantic memory as

Semantic memory is the memory necessary for the use of language. It is a mental thesaurus, organised knowledge a person possesses about words and other verbal symbols, their meaning and references, about relation among them and about rules, formulae and algorithms for the manipulation of these symbols, concepts and relations.

Semantic memory does not register perceptible properties of inputs, but rather cognitive referents of input signals. The semantic system permits the retrieval of information that was not directly stored in it from the system, leaves its components unchanged, although any act of retrieval constitutes an input into episodic memory.

Semantic Memory : As a Hierarchy of Concepts

One of the earliest, most influential modern models of semantic memory suggested that knowledge is stored in a network of interrelated concepts and that this network is organised as a hierarchy, with specific features at the bottom of the hierarchy and more abstract, general feature at the top. The following figure shows this kind of hierarchical network for some components of semantic memory for animals.

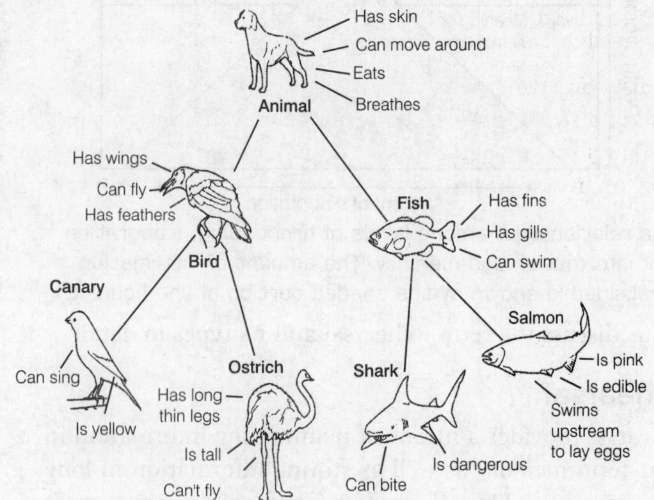

Collins and Quillian's Hierarchical Network

This is an efficient way to store knowledge. The system does not have to explicitly store information for each examplar *i.e.* each particular item to be remembered. Instead, it can more efficiently store common characteristic of several models at higher levels of the hierarchy. This model was tested in famous experiments by Collins and Quillian. They predicted that if semantic knowledge is organised as a hierarchical network, the amount of time required to answer questions should be related to the number of steps in the hierarchy that must be covered to find the answer.

This kind of model could be expressed by a simple mechanism connecting items according to the strength of the association between them. This notion presumes that features within a level occur together more frequently and therefore are more closely associated than features stored at different levels. *For example* the feature yellow is closely associated with canaries. Yellow appears virtually every time we think of canary. If indeed association between concepts underlie the construction of hierarchical organisations, exceptions to the orderly hierarchy sequence should occur when strong associations between features cover large hierarchy distance.

Ripps and Colleagues found that some statements about common associations, that cover large distances in a conceptual category, were verified more quickly than other statements that involve looser associations, among concepts stored closed together in the hierarchy.

Semantic Memories as Distributed Networks

A modern approach to understanding the organisation of semantic memory involves distributed network models. In these models, concepts are represented as patterns of activation across a network of interconnected units. Each unit can be concieved as representing some feature of a concept. The units do not have to correspond to a nameable feature or concept; instead they may represent merely some aspect of a feature that cannot be named.

In distributed network model, knowledge is encoded in the different strengths of connection between units. Typically, the units are organised into modules that correspond to one type of information, such as visual or auditory or serve a particular function, like input or output. Units within a module are typically more richly interconnected than those between modules. Thus, a variety of network models can be created to simulate dissimilar systems and performs various functions. *For example* Farah and McClelland creates a model of semantic memory with three molecules corresponding to verbal inputs, visual inputs and semantic representations, each composed of separate modules for visual and functional units.

In this model, visual and verbal inputs are both connected to the semantic representations, but they are not connected to each other. An important characteristic of these models is that they exhibit graceful degradation, a gradual rather than catastrophic delay of function when part of the model is compromised.

Episodic Memory

Where were you at 8.00 pm yesterday evening? What is your earliest memory? When did you last see the sea? All these questions demand a special kind of memory, one that allows you to access specific memories located at a particular point in time; they require episodic memory. The term episodic memory was devised by Endel Tulving to emphasise the difference between the recollection of specific events and semantic memory, generalised knowledge of the world. It is episodic memory that allows what Tulving calls 'mental time travel,' allowing us to travel back and 'relive' earlier episodes and to use this capacity to travel forward and anticipate future events.

Episodic memory is characterised in humans by our subjective sense of having experienced an event before and our ability to travel back mentally in time and relive the experience. Such memories contain information about what happened, along with when and where it happened.

Episodic memory refers to the memories of the events that we have experienced personally. Episodic memory usually has an emotional content. When past personal experiences are recalled, the earlier events are experienced partly at the conscious level. Episodic memory can be surprisingly detailed.

It is also true that the episodic memory is prone to forgetting. Hence, episodic memory may not always be a reliable reproduction of earlier personal experiences. The crucial feature of episodic memory is the capacity to remember specific events. For this, you need some kind of mental filling system that will allow you to distinguish that event from similar events on other occasions.

Types of Episodic Memory

Types of episodic memories include

(i) **Episodic Memories of Specific Events** These involves memories of particular moments from an individual's personal history.

(ii) **Episodic Memory of Personal Facts** These include memories that are related to personal lives such as when one bought a car or when did he got married.

(iii) **Episodic Memory of General Events** This includes the general feelings and events that one has experienced over the years or a particular period of time.

(iv) **Flashbulb Memory** These are vivid and detailed snaps of particularly important news that one has encountered. These news may be highly personal or even related to some general public event.

Episodic memories, together with semantic memories is a part of division of memory is part of the declarative memory. Episodic memories allows us to recall personal experiences as well as shared experiences with others.

Procedural Memory

Procedural memory is a type of long term memory which involves information as how to perform different actions and skills. It is essentially the memory of how to do certain things. Procedural memories start forming from very early in the life and become so ingrained in the individual that they become almost automatic. *For example* A person does not need to think consciously about how to perform motor skills. It is easy to demonstrate actions stored in the procedural memory, explaining how and where one has learned them can be much more difficult.

Once a particular action is learned, we do not need to consciously remind ourselves of how the memory process works. The procedural memory takes over and allows us to perform a skill without thinking about it.

Formation of Procedural Memories

Procedural memories form when connections are made between synapses at the end of the neuron. The more frequent an action is performed, the more often signals are sent through those same synapses over the time, these synaptic routes become stronger and actions themselves become unconscious and automatic.

A number of brain structures are also associated with the formation and maintenance of procedural memories. The cerebellum is associated with coordinating movements and fine motors skills required for many activities such as drawing, painting, playing an instrument, writing etc. The limbic system in the brain is known for coordinating many processes involved in memory and learning.

The procedural memory forms a person's character. Learning certain behaviours and emotional responses causes them to become automatic responses to specific situations. This can reinforce good habits where it makes it difficult to shed bad habits.

Differences Between STM and LTM

Short term and long term memory surely interact. *For example* Semantic features of information stored in long-term memory can still affect short-term retention of all new information. However, analysis of the recency effect also has suggested that the content of short term memory differs qualitatively from the material stored in long-sterm memory. Short-term memory tends to rely on perceptual qualities of stimuli, whereas long term memory depends more on stimuli meaning.

This distinction was demonstrated by Kintch and Buschke, who had subjects study a list of words that included several pairs of either homophones or sy nonyms and then immediately freely recalled the word.

The response patterns formed a typical serial position curve, which the researchers analysed to differentiated errors due to the homophones, acoustic similarities from error caused by synonyms and semantic similarities. In recency part of the serial position curve, which describes recall rates for the last list items, they found more mistakes based on acoustic similarities between homophones.

On the other hand, the primary part of the curve showed that for the early list items, the subjects made more errors based on the 'synonyms' related meanings. Thus, memory for the early list items relied on phonetic information.

Forgetting

Forgetting is complete or partial loss of information stored in long term memory. It is a failure to retrieve information from long term memory store. Much of the information is lost, but enough remains, so that we have sketchy record of our lives. Sometimes, what we think is forgotten in real sense is not forgotten because it was never encoded and stored in the first place.

Many students complain that they do not remember the contents after attending the class or forget after reading the text. This happens due to lack of attention, some information does not reach short term memory from the sensory register or due to inadequate encoding and rehearsal, the information may not have been transferred from short term to long term memory. Information was not stored in long-term memory because rehearsal was not sufficiently elaborate.

Many times, we forget as memory does not match events which had occurred. This happens due to the constructive processes *i.e.* during encoding, the to-be-remembered information, especially, if it is a complex life event or something you have read, is modified. Certain details are focussed the material may be simplified or it may be changed in many other ways, so that what is encoded and stored is far from a literal copy of the input. Constructive processes of encoding distorts which are stored in the memory and distortions are remembered. We remember the gist or meaning of what we have read or heard, but not the actual words themselves. Inferences constructed at the time, the information was encoded for storage, are remembered or portions of encoded infomations are remembered.

Theories of Forgetting

The past hundred years of memory research have seen several psychological explanations for forgetting. Some theories about forgetting have been very specific, concerning the decay of the memory trace, brain damage or disease, motivated forgetting or interference from other material. In other cases, the reasons why we forget, are to do with other characteristics of memory. There is a considerable amount of work for instance, which shows how important context, cues and processing are for remembering and so forgetting can sometimes be seen as arising from inadequacy in this respect.

Interference Theory of Forgetting

The most common conceptualisation of forgetting has been that it is caused by interference. Originally learned materials cannot be reproduced. They are forgotten because, in the meanwhile, new responses get associated with the old stimuli. These subsequently learned responses interfere with the recall of the old ones. Forgetting is due to subsequent learning of new materials. Verbal learning theorists (*e.g.* Mc Geoch, 1942; Melton and Irwin, 1940; Postman and Underwood, 1973; Underwood, 1948) proposed that in some situations, the learning of one set of verbal material interferes with ability to recall another set and such interference is a major cause of forgetting verbal information.

Imagine that you have to learn a list of 20 words. You are then asked to learn another list of 20 more words. Now try to remember the first list. Learning the second list has probably made it more difficult to recall the first list; to some extent, you have forgotten which words are in which list. The interference theory of forgetting might best be described as a theory of confusion: an individual has learned numerous responses and gets them mixed up. Using more conventional behaviourist terminology, verbal learning theorists called this phenomenon response competition. Crowding of response tendencies, competition and conflict among them, stimulus and response generalisation and resulting confusions are used as explanatory devices and principles in interference theory of forgetting. There may be blocking of memory on account of conflicting associations.

Basic Mechanisms of Interference

The basic mechanism of interference theory can best be appreciated if we remember that it was developed to account for the forgetting of lists of paired verbal units. There are two sets of interference mechanisms. The first set is addressed to considerations of how an organism might get 'mixed-up', about which environmental events belonging to which memory. In the case of humans, they learned two lists of the kind just described. This mix-up might occur as 'response competition'. Although, two responses have been paired with the same stimulus words, one pairing occuring in the first list and another in the second list. Only one response can be given if only one list is tested for retention. So, if the incorrect response happens to be dominant at the moment of the test, forgetting is inferred.

Interference can be explained with the help of following two concepts

Retroactive Inhibition

Retroactive interference is the form of interference when memories restrain the capacity of remembering the old information.

Retroactive inhibition is held as the **paradigm** or **conceptualisation** for the proper understanding of forgetting. Often, large amount of forgetting can be produced in the laboratory by interpolating known and controllable activities between the original learning and its subsequent recall. Retroaction has been called the best explanation of forgetting. However, it is useful to know that the retroactive inhibition interpretation has its limitations. Postman's early description of retroactive inhibition as the adverse effect of retention of an activity interpolated between learning and recall is still the best definition of the concept of retroactive inhibition.

Miller and Pilzecker, who named the phenomenon found that retention of a previously learned lesson and a second learning activity is interpolated between original learning and its recall if the subject is resting during that retention interval.

Retroactive Inhibition

Groups	Activity		
	I	II	III
Experimental	Learn A	Learn B	Recall A
Control	Learn A	Unrelated activity	Recall A

The classical retroactive inhibition paradigm, provides about the only typical illustration of direct interference, however, the adverse effect of interpolated activity occurs even when it is just similar to the original task without involving specifically conflicting associations. Obviously, retroactive inhibition interpretation cannot handle all instances of forgetting. Retroactive inhibition formulation demands quite strict similarity between original and interpolated learning, whereas real life activities bear no corresponding similarity reactions.

Proactive Interference

Proactive interference is the form of interference when old memories restrain the capacity to remember new information. A major inadequacy of retroactive interference position is perhaps its inability to account for the usual shape of the curve of forgetting. Why should interference result in rapid retention loss in the beginning and slower decrease afterwards?

However, the general interference position has the capacity to accommodate further improvements and to enrich itself, so that it can handle more facts more adequately. After accumulation of substantial experimental evidence of fairly recent origin and a plea by Underwood, it is now conceded that forgetting may be brought about through conflicting associations, which have been acquired before the lesson in question is learned. Thus, Proactive Inhibition (PI) has been admitted as an additional source of interference and we have to recognise that forgetting can be brought about by inferring associations learned either prior to or subsequent to the task under consideration.

Proactive Interference

Groups	Activity		
	I	II	III
Experimental	Learn A	Learn B	Recall B
Control	Rest or unrelated activity	Learn B	Recall B

A very definite relationship that has emerged from experiments on proactive inhibition is that greater the number of prior lessons an individual has studied and remembered, the faster is the forgetting of the task learned last. Heavy proactive inhibition accumulates even when there is no formal similarity between the constituents of the series learned successively within the laboratory.

Retrieval Failure Theory

A situation, where the memories are there but can't be accessed, gives rise to retrieval failure theory of forgetting. The basic reasons for this failure in memory retrieval are related to encoding failures and lack of retrieval cues. The main reason behind failing to remember the information is that the information never entered into the long term memory in the first place actually. *For example* Researchers **Nickerson and Adams** conducted an experiment by drawing the back side of a penny and then compared it to an actual penny. They were surprised to note that the actual details were in a notable contrast and they had very poorly recalled the back of a penny.

As we don't require to know what the back of a penny looks like to distinguish it from other coins, our focus is mainly on the information we need like the overall size, shape and colour of the coin. We aren't able to recall what the back of a penny really looks like because that information was never actually encoded into memory in the first place.

Other researchers like **Tulving** (1974) have suggested that sometimes information is actually present in memory, but it can't be recalled unless retrieval cues are present. These cues are elements that were present at the time when the actual memory was encoded. *For Example* The idea is used in a practical may be police when conducting interviews with eyewitnesses. They often use a technique called the cognitive interview which asks eye witnesses to recall every detail and thnke about the context of the crime. The Idea is to increase reale by recreating the situation it was witnessed in

The Retrieval Cue

The perfume was present when that memory was created, so smelling it again can trigger the retrieval of those moments.

- **Cues in Retrieval Theory** Tulving further categorised these cues into two types, namely context (external) cues and state (internal) dependent cues.
- **Context (External) Cues** Retrieval cues may be based on context; the setting or situation in which information is encoded and retrieved. *For example* A particular room, driving along a motorway, a certain group of people, a rainy day and so on.
- **State Dependent (Internal) Cues** The basic idea behind state dependent retrieval is that memory will be best when a person's physical or physiological state is similar at encoding and retrieval. *For example* If someone tells you a joke on saturday night after few drinks, you will be more likely to remember it when you are in a similar state at a later date after a few more drinks.

To sum up, as per the retrieval failure theory, forgetting occurs when information is available in LTM (Long-Term Memory) but it's not accessible. Accessibility depends mainly on retrieval cues. Forgetting is greatest when context and state are very different at encoding and retrieval. In this situation, retrieval cues are absent and the likely result is cue-dependent forgetting.

Decay Theory of Forgetting

It is a theory of forgetting that refers to the loss of memory overtime. Neurons are activated, when any information enters the brain and those memories stay in our heads as long as the neurons are active. Frequent recall of the information and rehearsal are two ways to keep the neurons active.

But, if the activation is not maintained the memory decays and fades *i.e.* why the phenomenon is referred to as decay theory. It suggests that memories are like traces. The memories, we make, leave traces on our brain. As the time passes, these traces will fade. Decay theory refers specifically to the forgetting that occurs in our short term memory.

Decay theory also proposes that memory fades due to mere passage of time. Information is therefore less available for later retrieval as time passes and memory as well as the memory strength wears away.

This theory is popular because it seems to fit with common sense views of the way the memory works. One of the most influencial attempts to explain forgetting in terms of decay of the memory was put forward by Hebb in 1949. However, it is very difficult to prove experimentally that decay actually occurs.

Motivated Forgetting Theory

Motivated forgetting is a concept that arose in early theories of psychology and it may be associated with repressed memories of many psychologists.

The motivated forgetting theory states that instead of interference or lack of consolidation, forgetting occurs because we are motivated to do so. Some experiences or memories are so painful or upsetting that thinking about them would produce overwhelming anxiety. They are, therefore, repressed and consequently become inaccessible. As a result of this, we are not able to remember or retrieve the memory even if we try to remember. One way of accessing the repressed memories is through the use of Freudian techniques.

For example Free association, where the patient is asked to tell the analyst every single thought that comes into his or her head, no matter how trivial, it may be. However, repressed memories can be accessed by the person himself/herself through a dream or through parapraxes (slips of the tongue). When the event or memory is finally recalled, it usually produces an unpleasant emotional reaction such as fear or guilt in the individual.

Once the emotional tension associated with memory has been released, the memory can be retrieved. Retrieval usually occurs during therapy. Freud also suggested that people frequently have imperfect or no memory recall of traumatic events or of things associated with unpleasant feelings. *For example* A person is highly motivated to forget a doctor's appointment, if he fears the doctor.

There is plenty of evidence that many trauma victims don't have full memories of traumatic events. Many sufferers of post-traumatic stress disorder experience significant memory loss. According to Freud, this loss arose out of an unconscious desire to repress the memory and keep the person seemingly comfortable in the present. This repression can also be termed 'a basic defence mechanism.'

Freudians also argued that even if recollections couldn't be assessed, they still caused disturbances for the individual in the present. The way to care people of the pain of these memories was to go back, find the experiences and relieve them. In theory, individuals who were able to remember unconsciously hidden material were eventually more comfortable.

The trouble with this theory is that people can recall false memories under hypnosis or even when they are fully conscious. This may be because the original memory wasn't accurate or because a person wishes to please the therapist. Remembering untrue things is called 'confabulation.' It is not intentional or conscious, so in a way it might be called 'motivated inaccurate remembering.'

EXAM BASED QUESTIONS

1 **Which of the following influences a psychological process called memory?**
(a) Beliefs (b) Expectations
(c) Fears (d) All of these

2 **Which of the following can be considered as a dimension of the memory?**
(a) Accuracy (b) Intensity
(c) Persistence (d) All of these

3 **Which of the following is a process of memory?**
(a) Encoding (b) Storage
(c) Retrieval (d) All of these

4 **Which process occurs when information is translated into a form that can be processed mentally?**
(a) Encoding (b) Storage
(c) Retrieval (d) Forgetting

5 **Name the phenomenon in which an individual is more likely to remember information, he/she retrieves or generates during study than information that he/she simply receives and attempts to memorise?**
(a) The spacing effect (b) The generation effect
(c) Episodic encoding
(d) Consolidation

6 **The first memory structure involved in the encoding of information is**
(a) procedural memory (b) sensory memory
(c) STM (d) LTM

7 **Which one of the following is the most important characteristic of sensory memory?**
(a) It can hold all incoming information for a very short period.
(b) It can hold only a limited amount of visual information, but unlimited amount of auditory information.
(c) It holds its contents only iconically.
(d) It alters the incoming information with the passage of time.

8 In a typical experiment, a subject is presented with a list of items. After the presentation of the list, the subject is merely asked to report as many of the items as possible, without regard to order, within some specified period of time. This technique places greatest emphasis on the simple availability of the materials. This is an example of

(a) cued recall (b) controlled recall
(c) free recall (d) serial recall

9 The more distinctive a stimulus, the more likely one is to recall it later; this is referred to as

(a) rebound effect (b) von-restorff effect
(c) halo effect (d) soap opera effect

10 A procedure in which several trials containing the same list of items are successively given and subjects are asked to recall items in any order they wish to on each trial, is called

(a) repetitive free recall method
(b) single trial free recall method
(c) multi-trial free recall method
(d) continuous free recall method

11 Recency effect in free recall decreases with increase in

(a) length of the list
(b) exposure time
(c) number of previously learned lists
(d) delay prior to recall

12 According to Ebbinghaus, in remote association, every item is associated with every other item in the list and the strength of the association is inversely proportional to the distance between the items. This was explained in terms of

(a) trace conditioning (b) forward learning
(c) inter-dependency of items (d) serial learning

13 Retroactive inhibition is most pronounced, when the first and the second task has

(a) stimulus similarity and response similarity
(b) stimulus similarity and response dissimilarity
(c) stimulus dissimilarity and response similarity
(d) stimulus dissimilarity and response dissimilarity

14 Which one of the following statements is correct?

(a) Retroactive and proactive interference are less than that in recall.
(b) Retroactive and proactive interference are more than that in recall.
(c) Retroactive interference is less, but proactive interference is more than that in recall.
(d) Retroactive interference is more, but proactive interference is less than that in recall.

15 Consolidating or soaking of memory traces is known as

(a) recognition (b) preservation
(c) reminiscence (d) transduction

16 Which of the following is considered as the first stage of memory process?

(a) Storage (b) Retrieval
(c) Encoding (d) None of these

17 Which among the following is required during Encoding?

(a) Paying attention to information
(b) Linking to existing knowledge
(c) Both a and b
(d) None of the above

18 Who proposed that primary and recency effects results from the words being retrieved from different memory stores?

(a) Ebbinghaus (b) Glanzer and Cunitz
(c) Waltzer (d) None of these

19 Short term memory can hold information upto

(a) 10-15 Seconds (b) 20-35 Seconds
(c) 50-60 Seconds (d) 30-45 Seconds

20 Which among the following is a process of recalling stored information from memory?

(a) Storage (b) Retrieval
(c) Encoding (d) Dectding

21 Which of the following is given by Bartlett which refers to the modification of the already stored information?

(a) Schema (b) Elaborative Rehearsal
(c) Retrieval Cues (d) Reconstructive Process

22 Mental representation of peoples, objects, situation or events acquired through experience is known as

(a) Elaboration rehearsal (b) Reconstructive process
(c) Retrieval Cues (d) Schema

23 Subjects tend to perform better after gaining more experience through practice is known as

(a) massed practice (b) transfer
(c) learning to learn (d) None of these

24 Which one of the following models proposed that processing of information proceeds from one to another storage system successively?

(a) Process model of memory
(b) Structure model of memory
(c) Feature-comparison model
(d) Sampling memory model

25 The concept of magical number 7±2 was proposed by

(a) EL Schwartz (b) J Brown
(c) BJ Underwood (d) GA Miller

26 The concept of Magical Number 7±2 has reference to

(a) semantic memory (b) iconic memory
(c) immediate memory (d) episodic memory

27 Self reference effect has been found by

(a) Craik and Lockhart (b) Posner
(c) Paivio
(d) Rogers and Kuiper

28 The memory which consists of facts, principles, relations and strategies and which is organised knowledge about the world including the verbal world of words and how they are used, is known as
(a) iconic memory (b) echoic memory
(c) semantic memory (d) episodic memory

29 What is the process by which recent exposure to stimuli such as people, ideas or even mere words influence the interpretation of new information
(a) Amnesia (b) Script
(c) Impression-formation (d) Priming

30 When a person looks at a phone number and goes to the phone to dial that number, the number is most probably stored in his
(a) iconic memory (b) echoic memory
(c) short-term memory (d) metamemory

31 An experiment is done by the researcher with three clusters given to the subject, who has to recall after varied intervals. After listening the letters, these are to be counted backward. The research is interested in
(a) Sensory memory (b) STM
(c) LTM (d) a and b

32 In the short term memory experiment of Peterson and Peterson, recall is a
(a) linearly increasing function of time interval
(b) linearly decreasing function of time interval
(c) positively acceleration function of time interval
(d) negatively acceleration function of time interval

33 Which one of the following is a control process of short term memory?
(a) Retrieval (b) Attention
(c) Recognition (d) Recall

34 Which one of the following was propounded by Waugh and Norman as a model of short term memory?
(a) Single process model
(b) Dual process model
(c) Simultaneous processing model
(d) Multifactor model

35 Short term memory lasts approximately for
(a) less than two seconds (b) 3 to 10 seconds
(c) 15 to 20 seconds (d) 1 to 2 minutes

36 Sternberg's research on short term memory has a focus on the processes involving
(a) classical or instrumental
(b) parallel or serial
(c) primary or secondary
(d) discriminative or non-discriminative

37 The memory that lasts about twenty seconds and is maintained by acoustic rehearsal is
(a) sensory memory (b) long-term memory
(c) short-term memory (d) procedural memory

38 One way to interfere with information held in short term memory is
(a) to engage in semantic rehearsal
(b) to engage in acoustic rehearsal
(c) to count backward from one hundred by three
(d) to use a mnemonic device

39 Memories are permanently stored in
(a) LTM (b) Sensory
(c) STM (d) Mnemonic devices

40 Information is primarily transferred from short term memory to long term memory through the process of
(a) elaboration (b) verbal rehearsal
(c) clustering (d) sensory-coding

41 Which of the following is not a major reason for information loss in long term memory?
(a) Faculty organisation
(b) Displacement of old information by coming information
(c) Interference
(d) Inappropriate retrieval strategy

42 Long term memory is more likely to result from
(a) passive process of repetition
(b) elaborative rehearsal
(c) maintenance rehearsal
(d) maintenance cue

43 Which of the following statements is incorrect?
(a) Episodic memory is less highly organised than semantic memory.
(b) Episodic memory is part of the long-term memory organisation.
(c) Episodic memory may become a part of semantic memory.
(d) Episodic memory is more susceptible to forgetting than semantic memory.

44 Adams (1967), suggested certain distinction between STM and LTM. Which one of the following statements is incorrect?
(a) STM has a smaller storage capacity than LTM.
(b) Acoustic interference is primarily responsible for STM, but not for LTM.
(c) Semantic interference is also equally responsible for forgetting in STM.
(d) Due to certain lesions in hippocampal region individual fails to transfer information from STM to LTM.

45 Self addressing memory is related to
(a) STM (b) Sensory register
(c) LTM (d) Both a and c

46 Studies of long term memory have revealed several kinds of evidence for the difficulties in retrieving. One such known phenomenon is
(a) retro-active inhibition
(b) pro-active inhibition
(c) tip of the tongue phenomenon
(d) amnesia

47 What is the most important difference between short term memory and long term memory experiments?
(a) There is no rehearsal in short term memory, but rehearsal is essential in long term memory experiments.
(b) The exposure time per item is at least double in long term memory as compared to short term memory experiments.
(c) The time between exposure of an item and recall is very limited in short term memory, but in long term memory experiments are substantially long.
(d) The material used in short term memory experiments is meaningless, but the material used in long term memory experiments is meaningful.

48 The memory, in which events are stored in terms of autographical reference?
(a) Multiple memory (b) Episodic memory
(c) Semantic memory (d) Long term memory

49 Mental representation of objects, states and qualities of the world and also of how these things are related to each other are called
(a) Episodic memories (b) Procedural memories
(c) Eidetic images (d) Semantic memories

50 Which of the following is not a type of long term memory?
(a) Procedural memory (b) Acoustic memory
(c) Episodic memory (d) Semantic memory

51 Which one of the following provides correct description of the term 'flashbulb memories'?
(a) Vivid memory of what happens to us all of a sudden.
(b) Memories of what we were doing at the time of an emotion-provoking event.
(c) Remembering a thing of past experiences by certain current revelation.
(d) Memory occurring in the most tranquil moments of life at once.

52 When a highly unexpected and emotionally intense event takes place, the extreme episodic memory that results is called
(a) Semantic memory (b) Eidetic memory
(c) Autobiographical memory (d) Flashbulb memory

53 Vivid, detailed account of a memory with reference to one's location, activity, reaction, informant and aftermath at the time of occurrence of an event is termed as
(a) Semantic memory (b) Procedural memory
(c) Flashbulb memory (d) TOT phenomenon

54 Bartlett's concept of schema was borrowed from
(a) behaviourism and Thorndike's law of effect.
(b) psychoanalysis and Freud's 'Psychopathology of everyday life'.
(c) neurology and Henry Head's conception of knowledge location.
(d) computer science and Minsky's concept of 'frame'.

55 The most powerful exponent of interference theory is
(a) Jenkins and Dallenbach (b) Zeigarnik
(c) Ebbinghaus (d) Both a and c

56 When retrieving a long-term memory, bits and pieces of information are gathered from various areas and put back together in a process called
(a) Consolidation (b) Automatic processing
(c) Constructive processing (d) Reintegration

57 A problem with using memory trace decay theory to explain forgetting from long term memory is that
(a) older memories always get lost, while newer memories always remain.
(b) older people cannot remember events in their childhood.
(c) older people can still remember things from their early years.
(d) there is no physical change in the brain when forming long-term memories.

58 When the interpolated learning tends to interfere with previous learning, it is known as
(a) Retroactive inhibition (b) Proactive inhibition
(c) Over learning (d) Msassed learning

59 Systematic decay of the memory traces
(a) do not seem to increase with the mere passing of time
(b) account for most of what we forget
(c) increase greatly with the passage of time
(d) are attributable to repression in most instances

60 Decay theory of memory loss seems to be most appropriate for
(a) memory based on visual images
(b) long term memory
(c) short term memory and sensory memory
(d) muscular memory

61 What kind of code is/are used for items stored in short term memory?
(a) Visual code (b) Semantic code
(c) Acoustic code (d) All of these

62 Interference theory of forgetting proposes two processes through which interference produces a detrimental effect on memory. These processes are
(a) unlearning and response similarity
(b) response chaining and response competition
(c) response similarity and response chaining
(d) response competition and unlearning

63 Cue-dependent theories of memory suggest that you would do best on your chemistry test, if you could be tested
(a) in the room where you studied
(b) in a chemistry laboratory
(c) with a large group of chemistry majors
(d) with students who share your interests

64 According to the interference theory of forgetting,
(a) memory capacity is limited, so when new information is brought in, older memories must be removed.
(b) new learning can inhibit the retrieval of stored memory and *vice-versa.*
(c) forgetting is directly related to the complexity and meaningfulness of the incoming information.
(d) cues present at the time of learning interfere with memory retrieval.

65 Interference theories of forgetting suggest that retention will be best when study is followed by
(a) sleep
(b) light reading or watching TV
(c) studying similar subject matter
(d) studying different subject matter

66 Why are mnemonic devices effective?
(a) To remember material, you must first pay attention to it.
(b) Memory depends on the strength of the memory trace and how often it is rehearsed.
(c) Memory depends on retrieval strategies.
(d) None of the above

67 Which of the following is the best explanation for why you would be unable to remember the correct answers, if you panic during an exam?
(a) Anxiety causes extraneous thoughts that interfere with retrieval.
(b) You have repressed them because the test anxiety was unbearable.
(c) The answers are actively blocked by the subconscious.
(d) The capacity of your long-term memory has been reduced.

68 Often, memories appear to be available but not accessible, this is known as
(a) The tip-of-the-tongue phenomenon
(b) Sensory memory failure
(c) Engram decay
(d) Interference

69 Motivated forgetting in perception is due to
(a) repression (b) displacement
(c) sublimation (d) reaction formation

70 Which one of the following terms denotes that memories of threatening experiences or events that are sometimes pushed into unconscious?
(a) Inhibition (b) Suppression
(c) Repression (d) Trace decay

71 Memory which involves the sum total of each person's general abstract knowledge about the world is called
(a) Episodic memory (b) Procedural memory
(c) Semantic memory (d) Long term memory

72 Organised bodies of information stored in memory are called
(a) Norms (b) Cognitions
(c) Schema (d) Traits

73 Which of the following terms term 'chunking'
(a) systematic ways of encoding information
(b) the method of Loci
(c) number and letter-word systems
(d) rehearsal of an image in mind

74 At the time of input, the material is elaborated, simplified and changed; these modifications at the time of input are called
(a) Red integration (b) Reconstructive processes
(c) Constructive process (d) Confabulation

75 Surprising events of short duration which fixes in the form of photographic clarity are called
(a) Episodic memory (b) Flashbulb memory
(c) Photographic memory (d) Both a and c

76 Which one of the following is the correct sequence involved in the memory process?
(a) Retrieval, recognition, learning and retention
(b) Learning, retention, recognition and retrieval
(c) Learning, retention, retrieval and recognition
(d) Recognition, learning, retention and retrieval

77 Which one of the following is the correct sequence of stages of memory?
(a) Storage-organisation-recall
(b) Recall-encoding-decoding
(c) Encoding-decoding-storage
(d) Encoding-storage-retrieval

78 In the serial position curve for ten words, the most remembered to least remembered items would follow the sequence of
(a) last, first, central and seventh
(b) last, first, central and second
(c) first, second, fifth and last
(d) first, last, second and seventh

79 Identify the correct order in the multistore model of human memory.
(a) LTM, sensory register, STM, rehearsal buffer
(b) Sensory register, STM, rehearsal buffer, LTM
(c) Rehearsal buffer, sensory register, STM, LTM
(d) STM, sensory register, rehearsal buffer, LTM

80 Arrange the followings in correct sequence of encoding a new word for transfer to long-term memory.
1. Conceptual category 2. Physical attributes
3. Semantic features 4. Acoustic quality

Codes
(a) 3, 4, 2, 1 (b) 2, 1, 3, 4
(c) 3, 1, 2, 4 (d) 2, 4, 3, 1

81 **Arrange the following with regard to information processing model.**

1. Short term memory 2. Sensory register
3. Retrieval buffer 4. Long term memory

Codes

(a) 1, 2, 4, 3 (b) 3, 1, 2, 4
(c) 2, 1, 3, 4 (d) 4, 1, 2, 3

82 **Arrange the following in correct chronological order.**

1. Recall 2. Relearning
3. Reconstruction 4. Recognition

Codes

(a) 1, 4, 2, 3 (b) 1, 4, 3, 2
(c) 4, 1, 3, 2 (d) 4, 1, 2, 3

83 **Arrange the following processes involved in information processing model of memory in correct chronological order.**

1. Sensory input 2. Long-term storage
3. Retrieval 4. Rehearsal buffer

Codes

(a) 1, 3, 2, 4 (b) 1, 2, 3, 4 (c) 1, 3, 4, 2 (d) 1, 4, 2, 3

84 **Arrange the following in a sequence of stage of remembering.**

1. Learning 2. Defining
3. Recalling 4. Recognising pairs

Codes

(a) 1,2,3,4 (b) 2,1,4,3 (c) 1,2,4,3 (d) 1,4,2,3

85 **Arrange the following theories in chronological order**

1. Theory of retroactive inhibition
2. Two factor theory
3. Response competition theory
4. Decay theory

Codes

(a) 1, 3, 2, 4 (b) 1, 4, 2, 3 (c) 1, 3, 4, 2 (d) 4, 1, 3, 2

86 **Which of the following is/are the differences between semantic and episodic memories?**

1. Semantic memory is concerned with the knowledge of the meaning and rules of words, episodic memory is concerned with life events.
2. Semantic memory is short term, episodic memory is long-term.
3. Semantic memory is disorganised, episodic memory is organised.
4. Episodic memory is more likely to being forgotten as compared to semantic memory.

Select the correct answer using the codes given below

(a) Only 1 (b) 1, 3 and 4 (c) 2 and 3 (d) 1 and 4

87 **Consider the following statements : Episodic memories**

1. are experienced as having occurred at a unique time.
2. are remembered as series of events.
3. are remembered as a highly veridical record of the episode, although this may not be so.
4. require no conscious effort to retrieve and appear involuntarily.

Which of the statements given above is/are correct?

(a) 1 and 4 (b) 1, 2 and 3
(c) 2, 3 and 4 (d) All of these

88 **Which of the following are the components of the Atkinson-Shiffrin model?**

1. Short term storage 2. Address register
3. Long term storage 4. Sensory register

Select the correct answer using the codes given below

(a) 2 and 3 (b) 1, 2 and 4
(c) 1, 3 and 4 (d) All of these

89 **Consider the following statements Semantic memory**

1. is necessary for use of language.
2. is a mental thesaurus.
3. stores temporal and spatial relations.
4. has a short life.

Which of the statements given above is/are correct?

(a) 1 and 2 (b) 2 and 3
(c) 1 and 3 (d) 1, 2 and 3

90 **Which of the following are the conditions necessary for a Short Term Memory (STM) process to produce a Long Term Memory(LTM) ?**

1. STM runs its own course without disruption.
2. There is rehearsal of information.
3. STM undergoes consolidation.
4. There is interruption of learning.

Select the correct answer using the codes given below

(a) 1 and 2 (b) 1, 2 and 3
(c) 2 and 3 (d) 1, 3 and 4

91 **Consider the following statements.**

1. Information stored in long term memory is acquired in the course of experience.
2. Some forms of long term memory can be unconsciously retrieved.
3. Short term memory depends more on stimuli meaning.
4. Long term memory tend to rely on perceptual qualities of stimuli.

Which of the statements given above is/are correct?

(a) Only 1 (b) 2 and 3
(c) 1 and 2 (d) 1 and 4

92 **Consider the following statements.**

1. George sperling developed tachistoscope to study the properties of iconic memory.
2. Sperling discovered that the fleeting image of the iconic memory will stay for a long time.
3. Echoic memory is equivalent to precategorical acoustic storage.
4. Echoic storage has s shorter life than the iconic storage.

Which of the statements given above is/are correct?
(a) 1 and 2 (b) 1 and 3
(c) 2 and 4 (d) 3 and 4

93 Which of the following pairs is/are correctly matched?

1. Shallow processing	Structural encoding emphasises the physical structure of the stimulus
2. Intermediate processing	Semantic encoding emphasises the meaning of verbal input
3. Deep processing	Phonemic encoding emphasises what a stimulus sounds like
4. Level of processing	Craik and Lockhart

Codes
(a) 1 and 4 (b) 2 and 3 (c) 3 and 4 (d) Only 4

94 Consider the following statements
1. Atkinson was the first to recognise a distinc tion between short term and long term memory.
2. William James developed a model that capture the distinction between LTM and STM.
3. Rehearsal is a method of storing information in long-term memory.
4. Maintenance rehearsal is sufficient to keep the information in short term memory, but insufficient to move it into long term memory.

Which of the statements given above is/are correct?
(a) 1 and 2 (b) 2 and 3 (c) 3 and 4 (d) 1 and 4

95 Consider the following statements.
1. Chunking is a process, in which the capacity of short-term memory increase by efficiently compacting more information into each item stored.
2. We can easily remember a lot of telephone numbers with the help of chunking.
3. Superior recall of items at the beginning of the list is called recency effect.
4. The better recall of items at the end of the list is called primacy effect.

Which of the statements given above is/are correct?
(a) 1 and 4 (b) 2 and 3 (c) 1 and 2 (d) 3 and 4

96 Match the following

List I (Psychological State)	List II (Mental Process Involved)
A. Perception	1. Stimulus awareness
B. Thinking	2. Stimulus generalisation
C. Concept formation	3. Symbolic manipulation of past stimulation
D. Illusion	4. Stimulus misrepresentation

Codes

	A	B	C	D		A	B	C	D
(a)	1	2	3	4	(b)	3	4	2	1
(c)	1	3	2	4	(d)	3	4	1	2

97 Match the following

List I (Value)	List II (Descriptor)
A. Upto 250 seconds	1. Miller: 'magic number' of memory span
B. 300 milli-seconds	2. Visual sensory register
C. 7±2	3. Short-term store
D. 20 to 30 seconds	4. Sperling maximum inter-stimulus internal

Codes

	A	B	C	D		A	B	C	D
(a)	4	2	1	3	(b)	3	1	2	4
(c)	4	1	2	3	(d)	3	2	1	4

98 Match the following

List I (Tests of Retention)	List II (Process involved)
A. Method of saving	1. Multiple choice items
B. Recall	2. Relearning
C. Recognition	3. Description of events
D. Testimony	4. Fill in the blanks

Codes

	A	B	C	D		A	B	C	D
(a)	4	2	3	1	(b)	4	2	1	3
(c)	2	4	1	3	(d)	2	1	4	3

99 Match the following

List I (Propounder)	List II (Concept)
A. Herman Ebbinghaus	1. Primacy effect
B. Luchin's	2. Information processing view of memory
C. Glanzer	3. Recency effect result from STM
D. Atkinson	4. Keyword system for remembering information

Codes

	A	B	C	D
(a)	2	1	3	4
(b)	1	2	4	3
(c)	3	4	1	2
(d)	4	3	2	1

100 Match the following

List I (Concept)	List II (Researchers)
A. Flashbulb memory	1. Broadbent
B. Organisation as in library	2. Brown and Kulik
C. VLTM	3. Bahrick and Bahrick
D. STM	4. Wickens

Codes

	A	B	C	D
(a)	2	1	4	3
(b)	2	1	3	4
(c)	1	2	3	4
(d)	4	1	3	2

101 Match the following

List I (Factors)		List II (Author's work)
A. TOT	1.	Tulving's work on retrieval cues
B. Flashbulb memory	2.	Loftus's work on eye-witness testimony
C. Misinformation effect	3.	Brown and Kulik's work on the role of emotion in recall
D. Encoding specificity hypothesis	4.	Brown and McNeill's work on recall

Codes

	A	B	C	D		A	B	C	D
(a)	2	1	4	3	(b)	4	3	2	1
(c)	2	3	4	1	(d)	4	1	2	3

102 Match the follwing

List I (Type of memory)	List II (Learning principle)
A. Episodic memory	1. Cognitive learning
B. Semantic memory	2. Insight learning
C. Episodic-semantic memory	3. Simple conditioning
D. Flashbulb memory	4. Instrumental conditioning

Codes

	A	B	C	D		A	B	C	D
(a)	3	1	2	4	(b)	1	3	4	2
(c)	3	1	4	2	(d)	1	3	2	4

103 Match the following

List I (Researchers)		List II (Studied)
A. Waugh and Norman	1.	Study of STM displacement
B. Craik and Lockhart	2.	Model of cognitive cycle
C. Neisser	3.	Levels of processing model
D. Morris	4.	Problem with the two process theory of memory

Codes

	A	B	C	D		A	B	C	D
(a)	1	2	3	4	(b)	1	3	2	4
(c)	3	1	2	4	(d)	3	2	1	4

104 Match the following

List I		List II
A. Verbal learning theorists	1.	Mc Geoh
B. Mc Geoh	2.	Two factor theory
C. Melton	3.	Response competition theory
D. Retroactive inhibition	4.	Miller and Pilzecker

Codes

	A	B	C	D
(a)	4	3	2	1
(b)	2	1	3	4
(c)	1	3	2	4
(d)	1	2	4	3

105 Match the following

List I (Propounder)		List II (Theory)
A. Watkins	1.	Interference theory
B. Postman and Stark	2.	Cue overload
C. Mc Geoh	3.	List suppression
D. Underwood	4.	Unlearning

Codes

	A	B	C	D		A	B	C	D
(a)	2	1	4	3	(b)	1	2	4	3
(c)	2	3	1	4	(d)	3	2	1	4

Directions (Q. Nos. 106-120) *In the questions, given below are two statements labelled as Assertion (A) and Reason (R). In context of the two statements, which one of the following is correct ?*

Codes

(a) Both A and R are true and R is the correct explanation of A
(b) Both A and R are true, but R is not the correct explanation of A
(c) A is true, but R is false
(d) A is false, but R is true

106 **Assertion** (A) Recall is the verbal reproduction of previously learnt material.

Reason (R) Recognition in the identification of learnt material from a combination of learned and unlearned materials.

107 **Assertion** (A) Semantic memory is the sum total of our general abstract knowledge.

Reason (R) Procedural memory is declarative memory, stores information regarding how things are done.

108 **Assertion** (A) Memory trace is a byproduct of perception and comprehension.

Reason (R) Retention is directly related to the processing of the meaning.

109 **Assertion** (A) Hippocampus plays an important role in transforming information from STM to LTM.

Reason (R) Hippocampus is a crucial connection between LTM to STM.

110 **Assertion** (A) Information is transferred to LTM from STM.

Reason (R) Information maintained in the rehearsal buffer is prevented from decaying in STM.

111 **Assertion** (A) Recall reflects retrieval from LTM only.

Reason (R) The arithmetic task causes the loss of the all words in STM.

112 **Assertion** (A) After only a quarter of second, old information is replaced by new information.

Reason (R) Information that has just entered iconic memory will be pushed out very quickly by new information.

113 **Assertion** (A) In the serial position curve, maximum items are remembered from the middle of the list.

Reason (R) The primacy and the recency effects explain the nature of serial position curve.

114 **Assertion** (A) Flashbulb memories are apparently long-lasting and unchanged over time.

Reason (R) In flashbulb memory, the circumstances, in which the person first receive the news was encoded including the place.

115 **Assertion** (A) People remember unpleasant events more than pleasant ones.

Reason (R) Anxiety-provoking memories are repressed.

116 **Assertion** (A) In proactive inhibition, early learning interferes with later learning.

Reason (R) If a person goes to sleep immediately after learning, forgetting will be less.

117 **Assertion** (A) Retroactive inhibition is influenced by interface between the items of the original and the interpolated list at the time of recall.

Reason (R) More similar the interpolated activity B is to the learning A, the less is the amount recalled and the greater is the retroactive inhibition.

118 **Assertion** (A) Retroactive inhibition is an example of negative transfer.

Reason (R) Forgetting decreases with lapse of time.

119 **Assertion** (A) Forgetting occurs due to withering of the memory traces over time.

Reason (R) Withering takes place when the information remains unused over the time.

120 **Assertion** (A) The nature of encoding influences forgetting.

Reason (R) Proactive interference occurs because of storage failure.

Directions (Q. Nos. 121-125) *Read the passage given below and answer the following questions.*

Morris argued that the main problem of the two-process approach to memory was that it did not really take into account the overall functions of memory for the individual. *For example* The idea that STM only has a limited capacity is not a problem in a laboratory studies, where people are mostly being asked to learn lists of words or short sentences. In everyday life, though we are dealing with much more relevant information, which would not happen as separate, intrinsically meaningless bits, but as part of whole sequence of interaction.

Taking part in a conversation and listing to what the other person says *e.g.* would involve the use of short-term memory, but at those times we need to retain far more than seven items of information simultaneously and we do it quite sucessfully.

121 What type of memory one generally use while taking part in a conversation?

(a) LTM
(b) STM
(c) Episodic memory
(d) Semantic memory

122 How many items one need to retain simultaneously during a conversation?

(a) 5 items
(b) 6 items
(c) 7 items
(d) 8 items

123 What is the main problem of two process approach to memory?

(a) It doesn't take into account the overall process of memory
(b) It takes into account the overall process of memory
(c) It focuses on STM
(d) It focuses on LTM

124 Which of the following is not a problem in laboratory study?

(a) LTM has a limited capacity
(b) STM has a limited capacity
(c) Semantic memory has a limited capacity
(d) Episodic memory has a limited capacity.

125 What type of information do we deal with in everyday life?

(a) Relevent information happens as separate, intrinsically meaningless bits
(b) Less relevant information
(c) Information in meaningful bits
(d) Information as a collection

Directions (Q. Nos. 126-130) *Read the passage given below and answer the following questions.*

More recently, Tulving has increased his emphasis on the distinction that episodic memory involves remembering specific personal past experiences, whereas semantic memory involves simply knowing impersonal facts independent of recollecting where these facts were accrued. This characterisation focuses on what he calls the autonoetic component of episodic memory; the awareness of personal experience that involves yourself as the central feature in the memory.

Episodic memories are defined by being experienced or more properly, re-experienced. Thus, Tulving characterises episodic memory as mental time travel. He assumes that the capacity for episodic memory is predicated on an ability to perceive subjective time, the feeling of time passing and knowledge of times past and the notion that there will be events in the future. As such, episodic memory is a fundamental part or our sense of subjective time. This temporal property of episodic memory contrasts with semantic memory's noetic property or simply the conscious knowing of facts. This difference between episodic and semantic memory has created the 'remember versus know' distinction central to many current investigation of episodic memory.

126 Episodic memory involves which of the following?

(a) Impersonal facts
(b) Specific personal past experiences
(c) Mental time travel
(d) Sense of subjective time

127 What to you understand by 'remember vs know' distinction?

(a) Sense of subjective time vs conscious knowing of facts
(b) To learn vs to retrieve
(c) Recognition vs recall
(d) Learning vs recognition

128 What is autonoetic component of episodic memory?

(a) Experienced and re-experienced
(b) Impersonal facts
(c) Conscious knowing of facts
(d) Awareness of personal experience

129 Which of the following is/are correct about episodic memory?

1. It involves remembering specific personal past experience.
2. It involoves knowing impersonal facts.
3. It involves awarness of personal experience

Codes

(a) Only 1
(b) Only 2
(c) 1 and 3
(d) None of these

130 Which of the following is/are correct about semantic memory?

1. It involves knowing impersonal facts.
2. It involves mental time travel.
3. It involves ability to percieve subjective time.

Select the correct answer using the codes given below

(a) Only 1 (b) 1 and 2
(c) 2 and 3 (d) All of these

PREVIOUS YEARS' QUESTIONS

July 2018

1 Which method is used for memorising a poem?

(a) Massed practice
(b) Distributed practice
(c) Serial memorising
(d) Syntactic memorising

2 Tests of declarative memory are termed as ...... tests, whereas tests of non-declarative memory are termed as...... tests.

(a) long-term memory ; explicit memory
(b) short-term memory ; implicit memory
(c) implicit memory ; explicit memory
(d) explicit memory ; implicit memory

3 During autobiographical recall, we often reveal a ...... as a consequence, our memory of the past may be ....

(a) inconsistency bias; distorted
(b) consistency bias; distorted
(c) inconsistency bias; enhanced
(d) consistency bias; enhanced

4 George Sperling (1960) studied iconic memory using

1. Partial-report procedure
2. Whole-report procedure
3. Self-report procedure
4. Backward procedure

Codes

(a) 1 only
(b) 4 only
(c) 1 and 3
(d) 2 and 4

5 Match List-I with List-II and select the correct answer by choosing from the code given below

List I (Concept)	List II (Explanation)
A. Episodic retrieval	1. Physical environment at retrieval matching that at encoding
B. Context-dependent retrieval	2. Mood at retrieval matching that at encoding
C. State-dependent retrieval	3. Retrieval stimulated by hints from the external and internal environment
D. Cue-dependent retrieval	4. Subsequent reactivation of stored memory traces.

Codes

	A	B	C	D		A	B	C	D
(a)	1	2	3	4	(b)	2	4	3	1
(c)	3	4	2	1	(d)	4	1	2	3

6 Read each of the following statements labelled as Assertion (A) and Reason (R) and indicate your answer using the codes given below

Assertion (A) Working memory is like a workbench where material is constantly being handled, combined and transformed.

Reason (R) Both new material and old material retrieved from long-term memory are held in working memory.

Codes

(a) Both A and R are true and R is the correct explanation of A
(b) Both A and R are true, but R is not the correct explanation of A
(c) A is true, but R is false
(d) A is false, but R is true

7 Read each of the following statements labelled as Assertion (A) and Reason (R) and indicate your answer using the codes given below

Assertion (A) Forgetting of everyday events in young people is not an indication of a poor memory.

Reason (R) Ineffective encoding due to failure to attend to an event while it is happening results in failure to remember.

Codes

(a) Both A and R are true and R is the correct explanation of A
(b) Both A and R are true, but R is not the correct explanation of A
(c) A is true, but R is false
(d) A is false, but R is true

November 2017

8 The most commonly overlooked and obvious reason for forgetting is

(a) encoding specificity
(b) encoding failure
(c) lack of sleep
(d) faulty eating habits

9 In a verbal memory experiment, the two independent variables 'meaningfulness of material' and 'retention interval' were employed each varied at three levels. The number of words correctly recalled was the dependent variable. The sum of squares due to meaningfulness of material is 270. The Mean square for the meaningfulness of material would be

(a) 30.0 (b) 67.5
(c) 90.0 (d) 135.0

10 The levels of processing proposed by Craik and Tulving follow the specific sequence in progressive order of depth ;
Choose the correct.

(a) Acoustic → Semantic → Physical
(b) Physical → Acoustic → Semantic
(c) Semantic → Physical → Acoustic
(d) Acoustic → Physical → Semantic

11 Which of the following is true for Tip of the Tongue (TOT) state?

1. Feeling of knowing
2. Feeling that memory is available
3. Retrievable memory
4. Maintenance recoding

Codes

(a) 1 and 2 (b) 1 and 3 (c) 2 and 4 (d) 3 and 4

12 Match List I with List II and select the correct answer by choosing from the codes given below.

List I (Concept)	List II (Explanation)
A. Procedural memory	1. Memory for facts, words, dates, names of objects
B. Declarative memory	2. Combining several letters, words, phrases into one 'stack' of information
C. Episodic memory	3. Memory for typing, driving, riding a bicycle
D. Recoding	4. Memory about 'what', 'where' and 'when' of our lives

Codes

	A	B	C	D
(a)	1	2	3	4
(b)	3	1	4	2
(c)	4	3	2	1
(d)	2	4	3	1

13 Read each of the following statements labelled as Assertion (A) and Reason (R) and indicate your answer using the codes the given below.

Assertion (A) You can remember vividly what you wore on your first date.

Reason (R) Memories of emotionally significant events cannot be accurate at all.

Codes

(a) Both A and R are true and R is the correct explanation of A

(b) Both A and R are true, but R is not the correct explanation of A

(c) A is true, but R is false

(d) A is false, but R is true

January 2017

14 Information in short term memory enters long term storage through

(a) selective attention (b) elaborate rehearsal

(c) learning (d) information processing

15 People often cannot remember where they heard, what they heard. Sometimes people think they saw things they did not see or heared things they did not hear. This is the case of

(a) bias (b) misattribution

(c) suggestibility (d) blocking

16 Geeta studied for sociology exam and then studied for psychology exam. Certain concepts and theories are similar in psychology and sociology. While taking sociology exam, she finds that she keeps getting confused with psychology theorists. Geeta's problem is most likely due to

(a) decay of memory trace (b) proactive interference

(c) retroactive interference (d) encoding failure

17 Which of the following sequence is correct in case of the curve of forgetting?

(a) Percent recall of words is greatest immediately after learning → Percent recall decreases rapidly within the first hour → Percent recall further decreases rapidly after 30 days

(b) Percent recall of words is greatest immediately after learning → Percent recall decreased rapidly within the first hour → Forgetting levels off after the first hour

(c) Percent recall of words is greatest after two days → Forgetting levels off within 10-15 days → Percent recall decreases further after 30 days

(d) Percent recall of words is greatest after 2 days → Percent recall decreases rapidly 20 days → Forgetting levels off after 30 days

18 Memory retrieval is

1. reconstructive 2. constructive
3. unconscious 4. symbolic

Codes

(a) Only 1 (b) Only 2 (c) 1 and 2 (d) 3 and 4

19 Short-term memory holds information for

1. 50 seconds 2. 30 seconds or less
3. more than 60 seconds
4. between 50 to 60 seconds

Codes

(a) Only 3 (b) Only 1 (c) Only 2 (d) 1 and 4

20 Match List I with List II and select the correct answer by choosing from the codes given below.

List I (Concept)	List II (Explanation)
A. Engram	1. Engaging in conscious recollection
B. Explicit memory	2. Changes in dendrites and in the sensitivity of synapse through repeated stimulation
C. Long-term potentiation	3. Recollecting something without being consciously aware
D. Implicit memory	4. The physical trace of memory in the brain

Codes

	A	B	C	D		A	B	C	D
(a)	1	2	3	4	(b)	4	1	2	3
(c)	2	3	4	1	(d)	3	1	2	4

21 Match List I with List II and select the correct answer by choosing from the codes given below.

List I (Explanation)	List II (Concept)
A. Remembering meaning of words, properties of objects	1. Sensory memory
B. Helping information to be brought back to mind when it cannot be recalled spontaneously	2. Semantic memory
C. Remembering specific experiences of the past	3. Retrieval cues
D. Retaining representation of sensory input for brief periods of time	4. Episodic memory

Codes

	A	B	C	D		A	B	C	D
(a)	1	2	3	4	(b)	2	3	4	1
(c)	3	2	1	4	(d)	4	2	3	1

22 Read each of the following two statements labelled as Assertion (A) and Reason (R) and indicate your answer using the codes given below.

Assertion (A) The information processing approach is rooted in structuralism.

Reason (R) It attempts to identify the basic capacities and processes we use in cognition.

Codes

(a) Both A and R are true and R is the correct explanation of A

(b) Both A and R are true, but R is not the correct explanation of A

(c) A is true, but R is false

(d) A is false, but R is true

23 Read each of the following two statements labelled as Assertion (A) and Reason (R) and indicate your answer using the codes given below.

Assertion (A) Words that are logically connected have been found to be recalled more easily than the words that were concretely connected.

Reason (R) The deeper the level of processing, the higher the level of recall achieved.

Codes
(a) Both A and R are true and R is the correct explanation of A
(b) Both A and R are true, but R is not the correct explanation of A
(c) A is true, but R is false
(d) A is false, but R is true

July 2016

24 Which one of the following does not contribute to memory?
(a) Interesting/disinteresting learning material
(b) Goal behind learning
(c) Gender
(d) Some rest after learning

25 Culture exerts strong effect on memory through the operation of cultural schema. One's memory is influenced by learning in
(a) own culture effect
(b) culture effect due to enculturation
(c) acculturation effect
(d) socialisation effect

26 The model of memory most frequently cited consists of Short Term Memory (STM) which serve(s) as gateway to Long Term Memory (LTM). This model was propounded by
(a) Ebbinghaus (b) Craik and Lockhart
(c) Tulving (d) Atkinson and Shiffring

27 Which one of the following is the right explanation of flashbulb memory?
(a) New, important, helpful social events
(b) Unspecific, important, common events
(c) Specific, surprising, unimportant events
(d) Unspecific, important, common events

28 Mechanistic and cognitive approaches to motivation differ in the extent to which ...... are invoked to account for the initiation, direction, intensity and persistance of goal directed behaviour.
(a) dynamic traits (b) drives
(c) higher mental processes (d) instincts

29 Facial feedback hypothesis means
1. your facial expression affects other's emotions.
2. other's facial expression affects your emotions.
3. facial expression provides feedback to the brain about emotions.

Codes
(a) Only 1 (b) 1 and 2 (c) Only 3 (d) 1 and 3

30 Match List I with List II and select the correct answer by choosing from the codes given below.

List I (Concept)	List II (Explaination)
A. Reintegrative memory	1. Familiarity that we have met before
B. Recall	2. There is some residue from the past to learn easily
C. Recognition	3. Activity of some performance learned in the past
D. Relearning	4. To check detils of the recovery of events in the personal past

Codes

	A	B	C	D		A	B	C	D
(a)	4	3	1	2	(b)	4	1	3	2
(c)	1	2	4	3	(d)	1	4	2	3

31 Read each of the following two statements labelles as Assertion (A) and Reason (R) and indicate your answer using the codes given below.

Assertion (A) People have tendency to recall expriences that are consistent with their current moods.

Reason (R) Moods and memories are congruent.

Codes
(a) Both A and R are true and R is the correct explanation of A
(b) Both A and R are true, but R is not the correct explanation of A
(c) A is true, but R is false
(d) A is false, but R is true

32 Read each of the following two statements labelled as Assertion (A) and Reason (R) and indicate your answer using the codes given below.

Assertion (A) Information is transferred from STM to LTM.

Reason (R) Information maintained in the rehearsal buffer is prevented from decaying in STM.

Codes
(a) Both A and R are true and R is the correct explanation of A
(b) Both A and R are true, but R is not the correct explanation of A
(c) A is true, but R is false
(d) A is false, but R is true

December 2015

33 Which memory is the result of instrumental/ motor learning processes?
(a) Semantic memory (b) Episodic memroy
(c) Sensory memory (d) Procedural memory

34 Entry of information into long term memory depends upon
1. maintenance rehearsal
2. elaborative rehearsal
3. method of loci
4. primary memory

Codes
(a) 1 and 2 (b) 1 and 3
(c) 2 and 4 (d) 2 and 3

35 Which of the following are not mnemonic devices?
1. Categorical clustering
2. Pegword system
3. Consolidation
4. Rehearsal

Codes
(a) 1 and 2 (b) 2 and 3
(c) 1 and 3 (d) 3 and 4

36 Match List I with List II and select the correct answer by choosing from the codes given below.

List I (Concept)		List II (Explaination)
A. Sensory memory	1.	Information that passes through a gate and transferred to short-term memory
B. Attention	2.	Information subjected to deep processing
C. Short-term memory	3.	Temporary storage of sensory information
D. Elaborative rehearsal	4.	Brief storage of information

Codes

	A	B	C	D
(a)	1	2	3	4
(b)	3	1	4	2
(c)	3	4	1	2
(d)	4	3	2	1

37 Match List I with List II and select the correct answer by choosing from the codes given below.

List I (Concept)		List II (Explaination)
A. Encoding failure	1.	Information that is not accessed evades from the storage over a time
B. Proactive interference	2.	Information is not attended to encoding
C. Decay	3.	Newer information interferes with the retrieval of older information
D. Retroactive interference	4.	Older information already in memory interferes with the learning of new information

Codes

	A	B	C	D		A	B	C	D
(a)	1	2	3	4	(b)	1	3	4	2
(c)	2	3	4	1	(d)	2	4	1	3

38 Read each of the following two statements labelled as Assertion (A) and Reason (R) and indicate your answer using the codes given below.

Assertion (A) Iconic store is a discrete visual sensory store.

Reason (R) Information is believed to be stored in the form of visual codes.

Codes
(a) Both A and R are true and R is the correct explanation of A
(b) Both A and R are true, but R is not the correct explanation of A
(c) A is true, but R is false
(d) A is false, but R is true

39 Read each of the following two statements labelled as Assertion (A) and Reason (R) and indicate your answer using the codes given below.

Assertion (A) The forgetting of a memory is caused by the disappearance of its engram over a period of time.

Reason (R) Once the engram has disappeared, the memory no longer exists anywhere in the memory system.

Codes
(a) Both A and R are true and R is the correct explanation of A
(b) Both A and R are true, but R is not the correct explanation of A
(c) A is true, but R is false
(d) A is false, but R is true

June 2015

40 Bartlett described memory as a
(a) constructive mental process
(b) reproductive mental process
(c) active mental process
(d) a process of retention

41 Memory for surprising and consequential events (emotional public events) are known as
(a) Photographic memory (b) Flash bulb memory
(c) Iconic memory (d) Implicit memory

42 Which one of the following is not correct in regard of semantic memory?
(a) It is relatively stable
(b) There is interference in it
(c) It is free from acquisition context
(d) It has chunking

43 According to Interference Theory, which one of the following causes forgetting?
(a) Failure of storage (b) Failure of encoding
(c) Failure of retrieval (d) Response competition

44 What is not typical of Atkinson and Shiffrin Model of Memory?

(a) STM is engaged in complex cognitive activities
(b) STM is gateway to LTM
(c) It is a sequential model
(d) STM controls and enhances information to LTM

45 Which of the following is correctly arranged?

(a) Sensory memory/Short term memory/Forgetting
(b) Long term memory/Sensory memory/Short term memory
(c) Sensory memory/Short term memory/Long term memory
(d) Episodic memory/Short term memory/Long term memory

46 Which of the following fit into declarative memories?

1. Semantic memory 2. Short term memory
3. Episodic memory 4. All of the above

Codes
(a) 1 and 3 (b) 2 and 4
(c) 1, 2 and 3 (d) 1, 2, 3 and 4

December 2014

47 A view of memory suggesting that the greater the effort expended in processing information will be recalled later it represents

(a) neural network models of memory
(b) levels of processing model of memory
(c) multiple components model of memory
(d) three stage model of memory

48 Organising items into familiar, manageable units, often automatically, is termed as

(a) Priming (b) Chunking
(c) Shaping (d) Encoding

49 Short-term memories are stored in which part of the brain?

(a) Cerebellum (b) Amygdala
(c) Hippocampus (d) Prefrontal cortex

50 Match List I with List II and select the correct answer by choosing from the codes given below.

List I (Memory Modules)		List II (Descriptions)
A. Episodic memory	1.	Memory system that retains information we cannot readily express verbally
B. Semantic memory	2	Memory for factual information that we acquired at a specific time
C. Autobiographical memory	3.	Memory system that stores general abstract knowledge about the world
D. Procedural memory	4.	Memory for information about events in our own life

Codes

	A	B	C	D		A	B	C	D
(a)	3	4	1	2	(b)	4	2	3	1
(c)	2	3	4	1	(d)	1	2	4	3

51 Read each of the following two statements labelled as Assertion (A) and Reason (R) and indicate your answer using the codes given below.

Assertion (A) Both, context dependent memory and state dependent retrieval refer to the ease with which one can recall information in a similar context or state as when it was acquired.

Reason (R) According to encoding specificity principle retrieval of information is successful to the extent that the retrieval cues match the cues the learner used during the learning phase.

Codes
(a) Both A and R are true and R is the correct explanation of A
(b) Both A and R are true, but R is not the correct explanation of A
(c) A is true, but R is false
(d) A is false, but R is true

June 2014

52 A network of associated facts and concepts that make out general knowledge of the world is referred to as

(a) episodic memory (b) explicit memory
(c) implicit memory (d) semantic momory

53 Which set of processes is involved in storing of information in long-term memory?

1. Chunking 2. Long term potentiation
3. Consolidation 4. Monitoring

Codes
(a) 2 and 3 (b) 1, 2 and 4
(c) 3 and 4 (d) 1, 3 and 4

54 Arrange the following states of memory in order of their occurrence.

1. Chunking
2. Sensory register
3. Consolidation
4. Elaborative rehearsal
5. Selective attention

Codes
(a) 5, 2, 1, 4, 3 (b) 3, 2, 5, 1, 4
(c) 1, 5, 2, 4, 3 (d) 2, 1, 5, 3, 4

55 According to Sternberg's Theory, which of the following are associated with 'performance component' of the cognitive processes?

1. Perceptual processing
2. Retrieval from long term memory
3. Storage of information in memory
4. Problem solving skills
5. Formulation of strategies for problem-solving

Codes

(a) 1 and 2
(b) 1, 2 and 3
(c) 2, 3 and 4
(d) 3 and 4

56 **Match the following**

List I (Phenomenon)	List II (Condition)
A. Loss of memory of events that occurred prior to a loss inducing events	1. Mental contamination
B. Loss of memory of events that occurs after a loss inducing events	2. Retrograde amnesia
C. Blocking of information in memory we don't try to remember, produced by our retrieval of other related information	3. Anterograde amnesia
D. Mental processing that is not readily under our control, influence our judgements, emotions or behaviour	4. Retrieval inhibition

Codes

	A	B	C	D		A	B	C	D
(a)	4	1	3	2	(b)	1	3	4	2
(c)	2	1	4	3	(d)	2	3	4	1

57 **Assertion (A) In a memory experiment participants were found to use both verbal and visual encoding while performing the given task.**

Reason (R) Episodic buffer, a component of working memory is used to integrate and to store briefly the information from phonological loop and visuo-spatial sketch-pad.

Codes

(a) Both A and R are true and R is the correct explanation of A
(b) Both A and R are true, but R is not the correct explanation of A
(c) A is true, but R is false
(d) A is false, but R is true

ANSWERS

Exam Based Questions

1 (d)	2 (d)	3 (d)	4 (a)	5 (b)	6 (b)	7 (a)	8 (c)	9 (b)	10 (a)
11 (d)	12 (c)	13 (b)	14 (c)	15 (b)	16 (c)	17 (c)	18 (b)	19 (d)	20 (b)
21 (d)	22 (d)	23 (c)	24 (b)	25 (d)	26 (c)	27 (d)	28 (c)	29 (d)	30 (c)
31 (b)	32 (d)	33 (b)	34 (b)	35 (c)	36 (b)	37 (c)	38 (c)	39 (a)	40 (b)
41 (b)	42 (a)	43 (a)	44 (c)	45 (c)	46 (c)	47 (c)	48 (b)	49 (d)	50 (b)
51 (b)	52 (d)	53 (c)	54 (c)	55 (a)	56 (c)	57 (c)	58 (a)	59 (c)	60 (c)
61 (d)	62 (d)	63 (a)	64 (b)	65 (a)	66 (c)	67 (a)	68 (a)	69 (a)	70 (c)
71 (c)	72 (c)	73 (a)	74 (d)	75 (b)	76 (c)	77 (d)	78 (d)	79 (b)	80 (d)
81 (c)	82 (d)	83 (d)	84 (a)	85 (a)	86 (d)	87 (b)	88 (c)	89 (a)	90 (a)
91 (a)	92 (b)	93 (a)	94 (c)	95 (c)	96 (c)	97 (a)	98 (c)	99 (a)	100 (b)
101 (b)	102 (c)	103 (b)	104 (c)	105 (c)	106 (b)	107 (c)	108 (b)	109 (a)	110 (b)
111 (a)	112 (a)	113 (d)	114 (a)	115 (d)	116 (b)	117 (a)	118 (c)	119 (a)	120 (c)
121 (b)	122 (c)	123 (a)	124 (b)	125 (a)	126 (b)	127 (a)	128 (c)	129 (a)	130 (a)

Previous Years' Questions

1 (a)	2 (c)	3 (c)	4 (d)	5 (d)	6 (c)	7 (c)	8 (b)	9 (d)	10 (b)
11 (a)	12 (b)	13 (c)	14 (b)	15 (b)	16 (c)	17 (b)	18 (c)	19 (c)	20 (b)
21 (b)	22 (a)	23 (a)	24 (c)	25 (a)	26 (d)	27 (a)	28 (c)	29 (c)	30 (a)
31 (a)	32 (b)	33 (d)	34 (d)	35 (d)	36 (b)	37 (d)	38 (c)	39 (a)	40 (a)
41 (b)	42 (c)	43 (d)	44 (a)	45 (c)	46 (a)	47 (b)	48 (b)	49 (d)	50 (c)
51 (a)	52 (d)	53 (a)	54 (a)	55 (a)	56 (d)	57 (a)			

CHAPTER 19

UNIT VI : Thinking, Intelligence and Creativity

Theoretical Perspectives on Thought Processes

In this chapter, we will elaborately discuss one of the important section of cognitive psychology that is thought processes. The objective here in this is to focus on multiple, theoretical perspective on thought processes like associationism, gestalt, information processing and feature integration model. This chapter will also include the concept formation, types of reasoning, the language and thought relation.

Introduction

Cognitive psychology involves the study of internal mental processes, all things that go on inside our brain, including perception, thinking, memory, attention, language, problem-solving and learning. There are numerous practical applications for this cognitive research, such as providing help in coping with memory disorder, increasing decision-making accuracy, finding ways to help people to recover from brain injury, treating learning disorder and structuring educational curriculum to enhance learning.

In this Chapter

- *Thought Process*
- *Concept Formation*
- *Reasoning*
- *Language and Thought*

Thought Process

Thought process is also known as *thinking*. Thinking is a process of manipulating information, as when we form concepts, engage in problem-solving, reason and make decisions though, the act of thinking produces thoughts. Thinking, can be defined as a mental activity that goes on in the brain when a person is processing information, organising it, understanding it and communicating it to others.

Thought process is a polymorphus process. It includes organisation of information and knowledge, evaluation, decision-making, judgement, comparision, reasoning etc.

In thought process symbols such as ideas, images, meaningss etc. are implicitly manipulated with a view to arrive at a solution to the problem. Thus, thinking can be defined as a higher order covert mental process of cognition characterised by the use of symbols as representation of objects and events, which is directed towards solution of the problem that initiates this higher order process of cognition.

Definitions of Thinking

Various scholars have tried to define thinking in their own way. *Here are some definitions*

According to **Lee Ross**, "Thinking is a mental activity in its cognitive aspect or mental activity with the regard to psychological aspects."

According to **Henry Garrett**, "Thinking is a behaviour which is often implicit and hidden and in which symbols are ordinarily employed."

According to **Gilmer,** "Thinking is a problem-solving process in which we use ideas or symbols in place of overt activity."

According to **SM Mohsin** "Thinking is an implicit problem-solving behaviour."

Kinds of Thinking

Thinking is basically of two types

Creative Thinking

Creative thinking is the ability to look at things differently and find new ways of solving problems. Creative thinking skills are definitely not just for 'creative types' like artists and musicians, everyone can benefit from creative thinking from time to time.

Stages of Creative Thinking

There are mainly four stages of creative thinking which as follows

(i) **Preparation** In this stage the thinker formulates the problem and collects the facts and materials considered necessary for finding new solutions.

(ii) **Incubation** During this period some of the ideas that were interfering with the solution will tend to fade. The overt activity and sometimes even thinking about the problem is absent in this stage. But the unconscious thought process involved in creative thinking is at work during this period.

(iii) **Illumination** Following the period of incubation the creative ideas occur suddenly. Consequently the obscure thing becomes clear.

(iv) **Verification** Though the solution is found in illumination stage, it is necessary to verify whether that solution is correct or not. Hence in this last stage evaluation of the solution is done.

Autistic thinking It is a type of mental activity in which focus is directed inward and the thinking is subjective (as opposed to objective). Autistic thinking is comprised of inner thoughts and individual reality. Daydreaming and fantasies are common elements of autistic thinking. It is not realistic thinking which is based on reality and real world execution.

Realistic Thinking

Itmeans looking at all aspects of a situation (the positive, the negative and the neutral) before making conclusions. In other words, realistic thinking means looking at yourself, others and the world in a balanced and fair way.

Thought Formation

The processes of thought formation are as follows

Understanding Thought

The understanding of thought is formed through the three stages. *These stages are as follows*

(i) **Analysis** Analysis of the characteristics of similar objects. These objects; we look at the elements one by one.

(ii) **Comparison** Comparing features to find traits which are similar, which is not the same, which is always there and ones which do not always exist, which are essential and which are not essential.

(iii) **Abstraction** After analysis and comparison, essential and similar trait are accepted.

Opinion Formation

Formation of opinion is to put the relationship between two terms or more. The opinions expressed in the language called the *sentence*, which consists of basic sentence. Furthermore, *the opinion can be divided into three kinds*

(i) **Affirmative Opinion** An opinion which declares a state of something. *For example* franzel was clever as well as cool.

(ii) **Negative Opinion** An opinion that clearly explains the absense of qualities and things. *For example* Mikkha is ugly and so skinny.

(iii) **Modalities** An opinion that describes the possibility of somethings on the basis of fact. *For example* It might rain today.

Conclusion of Thought Formation

The decision is the result of the act makes sense to form a new opinion based on the opinions that already exist. *There are three kinds of conclusions i.e.*

(i) **Inductive Inference** The decisions that are taken from the opinion. It is like setting an opinion toward a particular public opinion.

(ii) **Deductive Conclusions** Deductive decision drawn from the general to the specific, so it is in contrast to inductive inference.

(iii) **Conclusion Analogical** This is a decision that is analogical obtained by comparing or customise with specific opinions that already exist.

Theories of Thought Processing

Thought process is an implicit process. It is a chain of processes, which comprises of figures, semantics, images, words, behavioural contents, gestural symbols etc. Number of psychologists have tried to sketch out a theoretical model to explain the thought processing. *Some major theories of thought process are as follows*

Associationism

According to Empiricists, all the complexities of human cognition can be explained in terms of relation between ideas that is association. Associations between ideas in the mind are brought about by experience of the things that produce ideas in mind. Associations can vary in strength, depending on how often the associated ideas occur together and how often they occur separately apart from one another they are all basically similar.

Associationism is a theory that connects learning to thought based on principles of the organism's causal history. Since its early roots, associationists have sought to use the history of an organism's experience as the main sculptor of cognitive architecture. In its most basic form, associationism has claimed that pairs of thoughts become associated based on the organism's past experience. *For example* A basic form of associationism (such as Hume's) might claim that the frequency with which an organism has come into contact with Xs and Ys in one's environment determines the frequency with which thoughts about Xs and thoughts about Ys will arise together in the organism's future.

Early View on Associationism

Early experimental psychologists had the specific goal of converting this empiricist theory of knowledge and philosophy of mind into an exact scientific account of human thought. The introspectionists attempted to find by looking into their own minds, the basic building blocks of thought and to observe the processes that combined and recombined them.

However, the associationist's legacy was most strongly felt in the movement that grew up particularly in the United States as a reaction to the failings of introspectionism-behaviourism.

Aristotle's Concept of Associationism

Aristotle (350 BC) the Greek scientist, who studied in Plato's academy in Athens, came up with four laws of associationism. Although, it is said that the original inspiration was taken from Plato's work. Various laws clarify a lot of concepts related to the association of our thought process with our past experiences *which are explained below*

- **Law of Similarity** When we are reminded of, or recall one thing from the past experiences, similar instances will also be recalled.
- **Law of Contrast** When we are reminded of, or recall things from the past experiences, instances exactly opposite to them, will also be recalled.
- **Law of Contiguity** When we are reminded of, or recall things from the past experiences, we also recall actions or other associations with that objects that were originally experienced along with that entity.
- **Law of Frequency** If a series of events keep occurring frequently, the probability of recalling similar associated instances will increases.

Gestalt Psychology

Gestalt means that the essence or shape of an entity in hollistic form. This theory claims that "The whole is greater than the sum of the parts". The operational principle of Gestalt psychology is that the brain is holistic, parallel and analog with self-organising tendencies. This theory believes and stipulates that perception is the product of complex interactions among various stimuli. Gestalt theory allows for the break up of elements from the whole situation into what it really is.

Major Gestalt Psychologists

There were a number of thinkers who had an influence on Gestalt psychology. *Some of the best-known Gestalt psychologists included.*

- **Max Wertheimer** He was regarded as one of the founder of Gestalt psychology, Wertheimer is also known for his concept of the phi-phenomenon. The phi-phenomenon involves perceiving a series of still images in rapid succession in order to create the illusion of movement.

- **Kurt Koffka** He is known as one of the key founder of Gestalt psychology, Kurt Koffka had diverse interests and studied many topics in psychology including learning, perception and hearing impairments.
- **Wolfgang Kohler** Kohler famously summarised Gestalt theory by saying, "The whole is different than the sum of its parts." He was also known for his research on problem-solving, his criticisms of the introspection used by the structuralists to study the human mind and his opposition to behaviourism.

Information Processing

Information processing refers to aquisuition, recording, organisation and dissemination of information.

The advent of digital computers and information theory in the late 1940s led to a new way of thinking about mental processes, the information processing approach. Information processing can be explained with the help of Multi Store Model of Memory, *which is discussed below*

Multi Store Model of Memory

The Multi Store Model of Memory (also known as the *Modal Model*) was proposed by Atkinson and Shiffrin and is a structural model. They proposed that memory consisted of three stores: a Sensory Register, Short Term Memory (STM) and Long Term Memory (LTM). Information passes from store to store in a linear way and has been described as an **Information Processing Model** (like a computer) with an input, process and output.

The Memory Stores

Each store is a unitary structure and has its own characteristics in terms of encoding, capacity and duration. *The memory stores are divided into three types*

(i) **Encoding** is the way information is changed so that it can be stored in the memory. There are three main ways in which information can be encoded (changed): visual (picture), acoustic (sound), semantic (meaning).

(ii) **Capacity** concerns how much information can be stored.

(iii) **Duration** refers to the period of time information can last in the memory stores.

Sensory Memory

It is a brief memory of things we have seen and things we have heard, which help us to make sense of the world. *It has following characteristic*

- **Duration** 1/4 to 1/2 second
- **Capacity** All sensory experience
- **Encoding** Sense specific (e.g. Different stores for each sense)

Short Term Memory

It is a temporary and limited capacity store once the short term memory is full any incoming information displaces the oldest information. *It has following characteristics*

- **Duration** 0-18 seconds
- **Capacity** 7 +/- 2 items
- **Encoding** Mainly auditory

Long Term Memory

This memory is said to have on unlimited capacity and duration which last a life time. *Its main characteristics are as follows*

- **Duration** Unlimited
- **Capacity** Unlimited
- **Encoding** Mainly Semantic (but can be visual and auditory)

Feature Integration Model

Feature Integration model is a perceptual and attentional theory that explains how an individual combines pieces of observable information about an object in order to form a complete perception of the object. This theory was developed by Gelade and Treisman and focuses on the visual search component of stimuli perception. During a visual search a person uses cues like colour, shape and size to distinguish objects from one another.

Stages of the Model

There are two stages that comprise the feature integration theory/model.

(i) **The first stage** is the pre-attention stage in which the individual focucses on one distinguishing attribute of the object. The pre-attention phase is an automatic process which happens unconsciously.

(ii) **The second stage** is focused attention in which an individual takes all of the observed features and combines them to make a complete perception. *For example* If you were looking for a penny in a handful of quarters, it would be easy to spot and only require pre-attention focus. If you were looking for a nickel in a handful of quarters, it would be more difficult to spot because of the same colour and similar size-focused attention would be required to spot this nickel.

Concept Formation

Concepts are mental categories for objects, events, experiences or ideas that are similar to one another in one or more respects. They allow us to represent a great deal of information about diverse objects, events or ideas in a highly efficient manner. Concepts simplify the complex world of our experience which is full of diversities and wide ranging variations.

A concept is the sum total of what we know about the object. It refers to a generalised idea about the objects, persons or events. It stands for a general class and not for a particular objects, person or events. It is a common definition given on the basis of similarities or commonness found in different object, persons or events.It is a mental disposition that helps in understanding the meaning of the objects perceived earlier. In one sense, it is a general mental image of the object, person or events experienced or perceived earlier.

Types of Concept

Psychologists often distinguish concept into four types. *These are as follows*

- **Concrete or Perpetual Concept** It enables on individual to register information directly through five senses, that are sight, smell, tough taste and hearing.
- **Abstract Concept** This concept helps person in visualising and conceiving ideas. Moreover, it play in critical role in understanding or believing which cannot be seen.
- **Defined or Associated Concept** As the name suggest, if indicates and expresses syntactic station between different thing.
- **Complex Concept** In this concept, there is complex relationship between different concept.

Rules of Concept Formation

- A concept is not static, it always keep's on changing. *For example* In early age child considers even the walls and doors to be living things. Then, he understands they are non-livings.
- The concept is not common for all, different persons may have different concept about the same object/events.
- Concept is an integral part of thought process.
- Concept can be formed without the use of language.
- Concept formation is the association of certain stimuli and responses.
- Concept is the process of discrimination of common features.
- Concepts are very useful in recognising, naming and identifying the object, persons or events.

Types of Concept Formation

As concept formation is an ambigious process, we can categorize it on various types on the basis of its source and base. *Various types of concept formation are as follows*

(i) **Direct Experience** It is the first type of concept formation, in which the learner develops concept through direct experience with the particular objects, persons or events. It is developed from the early childhood onwards. *For example* The concept about cow.

(ii) **Indirect Experience** Here the learner develops concept through pictures, photos and reading descriptions hearing from other. *For example* The concept about Kangaroo.

(iii) **Faulty Concepts** The concepts or the general ideas we have about the objects, persons or events are not always adequate and accurate. Small children have so many concepts that are quite wrong and inadequate. *For example* One's anxiety over the crossing of way by a cat or one's feeling of hatred towards the person belonging to other caste or religion is the result of faulty concepts. Faulty concepts should not be allowed to develop in children.

Strategies of Concept Formation

Following strategies can be utilised in concept formation

- **Brainstorming** It is a strategy for generating creative ideas and solutions. It is a thinking that is definitely out side the box. It is one of the best strategy for concept formation.
- **Debate** It involves formal discussion on a particular topic. People argue with each other and in this process participant gets clearity about the subject and finally lead to concept formation.
- **Cooperative Learning Groups** These are heterogenous with respect to people characteristic. In group discussion they share information with each other and sort out doubts. Through group learning people can easily form concepts.
- **Interviewing** Interviewing, a meeting during which information is obtained by one person from another.

These are some of the strategies of concept formation beside this there are many more stragies are there such as demonstration in drill and practice, teaching etc.

Process of Concept Formation

The process of concept formation has three important phases. *These are as follows*

(i) **Perception** Experiences or learning in any form is the starting point of the process of concept formation. Our perceptions or imaginary experiences, formal or informal learning provide opportunities for getting mental images of the objects, persons or events.

(ii) **Abstraction** The mind analyses the perceived images and synthesises what is common to all, neglecting what is particular. This process of observing similarities and commonness in named as abstraction.

(iii) **Generalisation** After making such observation in the form of abstraction for a numbers of times, the child is able to generalise or form a general idea about the common properties of some objects or events. On account of this generalisation, he will develop a concept about these things or events.

Role of Concept in the Thinking

A concept is a mere representation of a understanding. It refers to a class of objects, ideas or events that share common properties. Concept formation helps us in organising our knowledge, so that whatever we need to access our knowledge, we can do it with in less time and effort. For making our thought process quick and efficient, we form concepts and categorise objects and events concepts usually fall into hierarchies or level of understanding.

The levels are classified as super ordinate (the highest level), basic (an intermediate level) and subordinate while speaking we mostly use basic level concepts. Children also learn basic level concepts first and then the other levels.

Most of the concepts people use in thinking are neither clear nor unambiguous. They are fuzzy. They overlap one another and are often poorly defined. *For example* Under which category would you put a small stool? Would you put it under the category of 'chair' or under the category of 'table'?

Therefore, in the above example of the stool, you would try to compare it with a standard study chair (if you consider it as the typical example of chair) and a small study table (if you consider it as the typical example of a table) and then match the properties of the stool with these two concepts. If it matches with a chair, you would put it under the category of chair otherwise under the category of table.

Reasoning

One task we often face in our every day life is reasoning; drawing conclusion from available information. More formally, in reasoning we make cognitive transformation of appropriate information in order to reach specific conclusion. It is one of the best forms of controlled thinking consciously towards the solution of a problem. It is realistic in the sense that the solution is sought always in reference to the reality of the situation. We can solve many problems in our dreams and imaginations, but they are unrealistic solutions.

Reasoning is used not only when we want to solve an immediate problem, but also when we anticipate future problems. Reasoning plays a significant role in one's adjustment to the environment. It not only determines one's cognitive activities, but also influences the behaviour and personality.

Definitions of Reasoning

Some scholars have tried to provide a standard definitions of reasoning, which are as follow

According to **Sherman**, "Reasoning is a process of thinking during, which the individual is aware of a problem identifies, evaluates and decides upon a solution."

According to **Garrett**, "Reasoning is a stepwise thinking with a purpose or goal in mind."

According to **Gates**, "Reasoning is the term applied to highly purposeful, controlled and selective thinking."

According to **Skinner**, "Reasoning is the word used to describe the mental recognition of cause and effect relationships, it may be the prediction of an event from an observed cause or this inference of a cause from an observed event."

Thus, reasoning is a highly specialised thinking which helps an individual to explore mentally the cause and effect relationship of an event or solution of a problem by adopting some well-organised systematic steps based on previous experience combined with present observation.

Types of Reasoning

The various types of reasoning are as follows

(i) **Deductive Reasoning** It is a reasoning method that deals with certainty. It is a reasoning method that deals with certain conclusions (logically certain inferences).

It is often called top-down reasoning because it generally starts with a certain rule about a class of things, compares to a certain fact about a specific thing and then reasons down towards a certain conclusion about a specific thing. It is a type of analysis that is closely related to rationalism, as it looks at what is logically and necessarily true about a given system.

(ii) **Inductive Reasoning** This reasoning method deals with probability. Inductive reasoning is a reasoning method that deals probable conclusions. It reasons from specific facts and towards probable conclusions that don't necessarily follow from the premises. It looks for patterns in data, reasoning by consistency. It is often called bottom-up reasoning because it generally starts with specific facts/observations/measurements and/or probable rules and reasons towards a generalisation.

It is a type of synthesis *i.e.* closely related to empiricism, because it compares data points that are generally obtained through observation/measurement to better understand how data does and doesn't connect. Since induction deals with likelihoods, it can produce logically strong and cogent arguments with false conclusions.

(iii) **Abductive Reasoning** This reasoning method deals with guesswork, abductive reasoning is a method of reasoning that formulates a hypothesis, a type of probable conclusion that doesn't necessarily follow from the premises.

It reasons by analogy, comparing an interesting observation to a certain rule, probable rule, certain fact, probabbe fact, or another observation to make an educated guess about what might be the case. Since, abduction deals with guesswork, abductive reasoning simply produces a good guess.

Role of Reasoning in Psychology

Reasoning is an activity of human brain and automatically become an integral part of human psychology. Understanding human behaviour can't be accomplished without inclusion of reasoning within the practice. The psychology of reasoning is the study of how people reason, often broadly defined as the process and make decisions. It overlaps with psychology, philosophy, linguistics, cognitics cognitive science, artificial intelligence, logic and probability theory.

Psychological experiments on how humans and other animals reason have been carried out for over 100 years. An enduring question is whether or not people have the capacity to be rational. What does it mean to be rational? Current research in this area addresses various questions about reasoning, rationality, judgements, intelligence, relationships between emotion and reasoning and development.

Language and Thought

The correlation between language and thought has been the focus of many psychologists in the past century and is still open for discussion nowadays. Many have indeed referred to the debate as a chicken-egg situation, to point to the famous impossibility of determining which one of the two processes shapes the other. How are language and thought related? Is language shaping our cognitive processes? Are we talking about a mutual influence? Is there a universal language system or is language completely relative?

The important issues and perspective within the language and thought synergy are as follow

The Traditional View

Both realism and constructivism are compatible with the traditional view about the relation between language and thought. This view, which can be traced back at least as far as the ancient Greek philosopher **Aristotle**, is that (thought is prior to language) and that languages have the properties they have so that they can express the kinds of thoughts people have. In modern times, it is a view that is reflected in different ways in the works of thinkers the developmental psychologist **Jean Piaget**, the linguistist **Noam Chomsky** and the artificial intelligence researcher **Roger Schank.**

In Piaget's influential theory of cognitive development, a child's thinking passes through a fixed sequence of stages. At the broadest level, there are four stages sensory motor, pre-operational, concrete operational and formal operational; though each is divided into a number of sub-stages. At each stage, the child's thought has characteristic properties. So, in the pre-operational stage, children do not realise that when objects or sets of objects are transformed, certain of their properties remain invarient.

They do not realise, *e.g.* that when a ball of plasticine is rolled out the amount of plasticine in it remains the same. So, in Piaget's theory, the way of thinking changes first, then language changes so that the child can express the new way of thinking.

One of the main goals of **Chomsky's linguistic theory** is to discover properties that all human languages have in common and that any other human language that has existed or might exist had or would have to have. These properties reflect the structure of the human mind. Chomsky himself prefers to express these properties formally and to claim that they reflect the structure of a special part of the mind called the language faculty. He also believes that this faculty is largely separated from the part of the mind that gives us our ability to think. Other linguists do not necessarily adhere to this 'modular' view of the mental location of these so called linguistic universals as Chomsky.

Conceptual Dependency

Roger Schank is an artificial intelligence researcher whose goal was to write computer programs that could understand texts in the sense that they could paraphrase them, translate them and answer inferential questions about them. One aspect of his theory was that the meaning of all sentences should be represented in an universal notation, which he called conceptual dependency. Conceptual dependency provides a way of representing the ideas that people have. One of its important properties is that ideas expressed in natural language should be readily convertible into conceptual dependency and *vice versa.* Language is the way through which they can express the ideas that we represent to ourselves in the conceptual dependency notation.

Vygotsky Model on Developing Relation Between Thought and Language

In the *first stage,* thought and speech are unrelated. The kinds of thought that very young children have are much the same as those of the higher animals. An ability to use language is not required for such thoughts. In the second stage, thought and speech become connected. At first what the child says is only loosely related to what it does in order to solve problems. A further features of the second stage is that, at its beginning, the child's verbal comments tend to follow the actions to which they relate.

The talking to oneself that monologue the child engages in during this second stage is what Piaget called egocentric *speech*. Such speech is readily observed in children from about two to six years old, but Vygotsky and Piaget had strongly opposing views on its function.

Thus, in Vygotsky's third stage in the developing relation between thought and language egocentric speech has become internal speech and complex thoughts are made possible by the fact that they can make use of a linguistic medium. However, Vygotsky was careful in identifying thought with internal speech. He always allowed the possibility that some kinds of thought did not depend on internal speech.

The Sapir-Whorf Hypothesis

A more radical alternative to traditional ideas about language and thought is the diametrically opposed view that language is logically prior to thought and that the kind of thought a person can have are determined by the language they speak. Whorf and Sapir believed that speakers of different languages thought in different ways at both at specific as well as at general level. One of his best known examples Eskimos have different words for snow.

These words are names for types of snow that are important in the Eskimos way of life *e.g.* types of snow that are suitable for building different parts of igloo. Whorf argued that the existence of these different words in the Eskimo language led Eskimos to think about snow in a way different from the Europeans.

Learning Theory Approach

Anyone who spends even a little time with children will notice the enormous strides that they make in language development throughout childhood. However, the reasons for this rapid growth are far from obvious. Psychologists have offered two major explanations, one based on learning theory and the other based on innate processes.

The learning theory approach suggests that language acquisition follows the principles of reinforcement and conditioning discovered by psychologists, who study learning. *e.g.* a child who says 'mama' receives hugs and praise from her mother, which reinforces the behaviour of saying 'mama' and makes its repetition more likely. This view suggests that children first learn to speak by being rewarded for making sounds that approximate speech. Ultimately, through a process of shaping, language becomes more and more like adult speech. To support the learning theory approach to language acquisition, research shows that the more parents speak to their young children, the more proficient the children become in language.

The learning theory approach is less successful in explaining how children acquire language rules. Children are reinforced not only when they use language correctly, but also when they use it incorrectly.

Against the problem of learning theory approach, Chomsky argued that humans are born with an innate linguistic capability that emerges primarily as a function of maturation. According to his analysis, all the world's languages share a common underlying structure called a *universal grammar*. Chomsky suggested that the human brain has a neural system, the language-acquisition device that not only lets us understand the structure language provides, but also gives us strategies and techniques for learning the unique characteristics of our native language.

EXAM BASED QUESTIONS

1 Congnitive psychology involves the study of
(a) perception (b) thinking
(c) memory (d) All of these

2 Polymorphus process stands for
(a) action process (b) thought process
(c) working process (d) None of these

3 Who said that "Thinking is a behaviour which is often implicit and hidden and in which symbols are ordinarily employed"?
(a) Mohsin (b) Gilmer (c) Garrett (d) Ross

4 According to whom, "Thinking is an implicit problem-solving behaviour"?
(a) Ross (b) Gilmer (c) Garrett (d) Mohsin

5 Which kind of thinking is concerned with self-gratification?
(a) Realistic thinking (b) Autistic thinking
(c) Analytical thinking (d) Abstraction thinking

6 Which among the following is not correct about realistic thinking?
(a) It is productive
(b) It is determined by requirements of objective situation
(c) It does not give any regard to reality
(d) Directed towards solution of a real problem

7 Which among the following are types of opinion formation?
(a) Affirmative opinion (b) Negative opinion
(c) Modalities (d) All of these

8 Which type of conclusion draw decision from the general to the specific?
(a) Conclusion analogical (b) Deductive conclusion
(c) Inductive inference (d) None of these

9 Who believed that all the complexities of human cognition can be explained in terms of relation between ideas that is of association?
(a) Behaviourist (b) Empiricists
(c) Experimentalist (d) None of these

10 The idea of a 'unicorn' is related to
(a) Feature integration model
(b) Gestalt
(c) Associationalism
(d) Information processing

11 When we are reminded of, or recall thing from the past experiences, instances exactly opposite to them, will also be recalled. This is known as
(a) Law of Contrast (b) Law of Contiguity
(c) Law of Similarity (d) None of these

12 Which theory claims that "The whole is greater than the sum of the parts"?
(a) Associationism (b) Gestalt
(c) Information processing (d) None of these

13 Phi-phenomenon is discovered or introduced by
(a) Kurt Koffka (b) Wolfgang Kohler
(c) Max Wertheimer (d) None of these

14 Who had proposed Multi Store Model of Memory?
(a) Shiffrin and Kohler (b) Wertheimer
(c) Newell (d) Atkinson and Shiffrin

15 There are how many memory store in Multi Store Model of Memory?
(a) 2 (b) 3 (c) 4 (d) 5

16 The view that 'Thinking is nothing, but implicit speech' is expressed by
(a) structuralists (b) gestaltists
(c) behaviourists (d) psychoanalysts

17 Which of the following pairs is correctly matched?
(a) Artificial Intelligence : Roger Schank
(b) Influential theory : Goleman
(c) Semantic differential : Piaget
(d) Linguistic relativity : Vygotsky

18 Much of creative thinking is
(a) conscious reasoning
(b) problem-solving
(c) unconscious rearrangement of symbols
(d) deduction

19 Which of the following is involved in the creative thinking of phenomenon?
(a) Problem-solving (b) Induction
(c) Insight (d) Reasoning

20 One of the essentials of thought processes is
(a) concept (b) image
(c) language (d) All of these

21 In convergent thinking, the number of correct solutions found is
(a) one (b) two
(c) three (d) many

22 According to Schweder, "the nature of thinking pattern of Indians is which one of the following"?
(a) Holistic (b) Collective
(c) Individual (d) Moral

23 A child who gives many answers in response to a question resorts to the process of
(a) convergent thinking (b) latent thinking
(c) divergent thinking (d) critical thinking

24 **Some important tools of thinking are**
(a) perception, learning and memory
(b) objects, concepts and symbols
(c) memory, symbols and perception
(d) objects, learning and concepts

25 **A type of thinking in which a person searches for multiple ideas or solutions is**
(a) divergent thinking (b) vertical thinking
(c) ideational fluency (d) convergent thinking

26 **Rosch proposes that in everyday usage, concepts are encoded according to**
(a) analysing the problem
(b) searching for solution
(c) establishing a mental set
(d) represent the problem

27 **Who developed the theory of feature integration model?**
(a) Kohler (b) Gelade (c) Koffka (d) Shannon

28 **Concepts defined by specific rules on features are called**
(a) formal concept (b) natural concept
(c) conjunctive concept (d) disjunctive concept

29 **Which of the following forms the hierarchy of natural concept?**
(a) Superordinate concept (b) Basic level type
(c) Subordinate concept (d) All of these

30 **A type of concept around which other similar concepts are organised, such as 'dog', 'cat' or 'pear'.**
(a) Subordinate concept (b) Basic level type
(c) Superordinate concept (d) Natural concept

31 **Implicit thinking involves mainly**
(a) motor activity (b) sensory activity
(c) reflex activity (d) glandular activity

32 **Rational concept is that which involves**
(a) a combination of several attributes
(b) relationship among elements in a situation
(c) at least one element from a number of elements
(d) all the elements

33 **Which among the following are inhibiting factors in concept formation?**
(a) Perceptual incongruities (b) Mental set
(c) Functional fixedness (d) All of these

34 **Which one of the following authors has not been associated with researches on concept formation?**
(a) Heidbreder (b) Reed
(c) Cannon Bard (d) Bruner

35 **Concept formation refers to**
(a) the organisation of phonemes and morphemes into meaningful thought.
(b) the application of transformation rules to basic sentence.
(c) inductive as opposed to deductive thinking.
(d) organising experiences into meaningful categories.

36 **If 98 out of 100 people respond 'Golden Retriever' when asked to name what dog best represents the concept 'dog' then a golden retriever would be called**
(a) Denotative concept (b) Protype
(c) Relational concept (d) Feature

37 **Mental images**
(a) represent abstract ideas
(b) consist entirely of unconscious information
(c) have a picture like quality
(d) always prototype

38 **Which of the following areas refers to the meaning of words?**
(a) Phonology (b) Semantics
(c) Morphology (d) Pragmatics

39 **Amar received his paper back from his English teacher, Ms Taylor. She informed him that adverbs follow the verbs they modify in sentence order. What level of language analysis does this represent?**
(a) Syntax (b) Semantics
(c) Morphology (d) Pragmatics

40 **What does a 'critical period' in language development refer to?**
(a) Period during which the brain is receptive to language learning.
(b) Period during which children are proficient in their first language.
(c) Period during which children must receive stimulation to learn language.
(d) Period during which the brain forms neural connections for language learning.

41 **Research with animals such as rats and monkeys with concept attainment problems indicates that**
(a) animals can learn concepts even though they do not have the ability to use language.
(b) animals higher up on the phylogenetic scale can learn concepts, those lower on the scale cannot.
(c) it is impossible without the use of language to learn to abstract a common property.
(d) animals think and communicate with language.

42 **Which one of the following depicts the correct sequence of concepts hierarchically?**
(a) Negative concept, Conditional concept, Disjunctive concept
(b) Conditional concept, Disjunctive concept, Negative concept
(c) Conditional concept, Negative concept, Disjunctive concept
(d) Negative concept, Disjunctive concept, Conditional concept

43 **Using both positive and negative instances in developing a concept is advantageous because**
(a) we can lengthen the post feedback interval
(b) we increase the precision or defining limits of concept

(c) we can counter balance positive and negative instances
(d) we can downplay the role of memory

44 A concept that is made up of several characteristics is known as
(a) Disjunctive concept (b) Relational concept
(c) Discrete concept (d) Conjunctive concept

45 Representations used in thinking include
(a) mnemonic devices
(b) kinsthesis
(c) concepts
(d) primary figments of the imagination

46 What type of concept is 'uncle'?
(a) Conjunction (b) Relational
(c) Relative (d) Disjunctive

47 Words or ideas representing a class of object are called
(a) Abstractions (b) Attributes
(c) Thoughts (d) Concepts

48 The other name for the realistic thinking could be
(a) autistic thinking (b) critical thinking
(c) reasoning (d) deductive thinking

49 Which of the following examples does not reflect inductive reasoning ?
(a) Probabilistic conclusions
(b) Processes involved in concept formation
(c) Heuristics
(d) Decision-making

50 Which one of the following hypothesis emphasises the role of language in thinking?
(a) Thinking is active imagination carried on in words.
(b) Process of thinking is sun-vocal talking or implicit speech when the larynx is in a state of low tonus.
(c) Linguistic relativity determines the nature of thinking.
(d) Thinking can occur without words as we can thinking about things, for which we do not have name.

51 According to the generative or transformation theory of language, it is possible to
(a) have same meaning to different sentence.
(b) have sentences with different deep structures that have a common surface structure.
(c) have sentences with different surface structure that have a same deep structure.
(d) have same connotations for the same surface structure.

52 Which of the factor is involved in the dynamics of speech?
(a) Emotions communicated by speech
(b) Loudness
(c) Fundamental pitch of the voice
(d) All of the above

53 Which one of the following statements describes the most appropriate relationship between language and thought?
(a) Thinking is active imagination carried out by language.
(b) Thinking is nothing, but silent speech.
(c) Thinking is a mental activity and language gives it objective shape.
(d) Thinking denotes language relativity.

54 A phenomenon that involves a disturbance of language and/or speech caused by brain damage is known as
(a) Aphasia (b) Dementia
(c) Haphalgesia (d) Analgesia

55 Which of the following pairs is correctly matched?
(a) Language : Symbols
(b) Category : Analysis
(c) Concept : Searching a solution
(d) Incubation : Establishing mental sets

56 Prosodic cues such as stress, pitch, pause and intonation play an important role in language perception. These are called as
(a) Social factors (b) Semantic factors
(c) Metalinguistic factors (d) Suprasegmental factors

57 To test linguistic relativity hypothesis, a relationship between which one of the following pairs is demonstrated by the experiment 'on the effect of labels on recall'?
(a) Codability and cognition
(b) Communicability and cognition
(c) Language and memory
(d) Language and thinking

58 Who among the following is the Psychologist whose hypothesis, in most extreme form, maintains that language is necessary for thought?
(a) Piaget (b) Vygotsky
(c) Whorf (d) HH Clark

59 Language involves the use of
(a) mark (b) symbols
(c) signs (d) picture

60 Language is a special form of
(a) thinking (b) communication
(c) problem-solving (d) heuristics

61 According to Piaget, egocentrism in the thinking of young children is best explained as
(a) self-centred thinking (b) logical thinking
(c) illogical thinking (d) limited thinking

62 Which of the following is not one of the basic levels of structural analysis for language?
(a) Syntax (b) Linguistic relativity
(c) Heuristic (d) Morphology

63 Consider the following statements about Noam Chomsky
1. He called himself a cartesian linguist.
2. He analysed syntax.
3. He wrote about transformational grammar.
4. He developed an artificial language called Yerkish.

Which of the statements given above are correct?
(a) 1 and 2 (b) 1 and 4
(c) 1, 2 and 3 (d) 2, 3 and 4

64 Arrange the following in chronological order about the stages in language development.
1. Phonemes 2. Morphemes
3. Pragmatism 4. Syntax

Codes
(a) 1, 2, 3, 4 (b) 2, 1, 3, 4
(c) 2, 3, 4, 1 (d) 1, 2, 4, 3

65 Which of the statement given above is/are correct?
1. A concept referring to a objective having atleast one of a number of feature is a conjunctive.
2. Going from general principles to specific situations is called deductive thought.

Select the correct answer using the codes given below
(a) Only 1 (b) Only 2
(c) Both 1 and 2 (d) None of these

66 Arrange the following in correct sequence to control irrational thoughts
1. Develop awareness 2. Self Reward
3. Evaluate
4. Prepare compatible thoughts

Codes
(a) 1, 3, 4, 2 (b) 1, 2, 3, 4 (c) 2, 4, 1, 3 (d) 2, 1, 3, 4

67 Consider the following statements
1. Concept can be learned only when we can discriminate the appropriate feature.
2. Thinking is some sort of linner speech.

Which of the statemetnts given above is/are not correct?
(a) Only 1 (b) Only 2
(c) Both 1 and 2 (d) None of these

68 Consider the following statements
1. Perceptual thinking depends on ungoes.
2. Relaxation theory is also called as 'surplus energy theory'.
3. Gathering information is first step of decision-making.

Which of the statements given above is/are correct?
(a) 1 and 2 (b) 1 and 3
(c) Only 1 (d) All of these

69 Consider the following statements
1. Language can be spoken, signed or written.
2. Humans make new sentences each time they speak. This refers to the concept that language is creative.

Which of the statements given above is/are correct?
(a) Only 1
(b) Only 2
(c) Both 1 and 2
(d) Neither 1 nor 2

70 The ease or difficulty of concept learning depends on
1. complexity of the stimuli.
2. nature of strategies played.
3. conditions present during course of learning.

Codes
(a) Only 1 (b) 1 and 3
(c) 2 and 3 (d) All of these

71 Consider the following statements about the strategies of concept formation.
1. Successive scanning is less efficient, but more cognitively manageable.
2. Simultaneous scanning is more efficient, but less cognitive manageable.
3. Conservative focusing is efficient and more cognitively manageable.
4. Conservative focusing is always the most successful strategy.

Which of the statements given above are correct?
(a) 1, 2 and 3 (b) 2, 3 and 4
(c) 1 and 4 (d) All of these

Directions (Q.Nos. 72-87) *In the questions given below are two statements labelled as Assertion (A) and Reason (R). In the context of the two statements, which one of the following is correct?*

Codes
(a) Both A and R are true and R is the correct explanation of A
(b) Both A and R are true, but R is not the correct explanation of A
(c) A is true, but R is false
(d) A is false, but R is true

72 **Assertion** (A) Anchoring is a type of heuristic.
Reason (R) In Anchoring, we try to make guess and use that as the basis for our estimate.

73 **Assertion** (A) Dedective reasoning involves creativity.
Reason (R) It doesn't allow us to learn new things.

74 **Assertion** (A) Myth of genius hinders problem-solving.
Reason (R) Problem-solving needs basic intelligence.

75 **Assertion** (A) The language comprehension skills of humans exceed that of chimpanzees.
Reason (R) The language production skills of humans exceed that of chimpanzees.

76 **Assertion** (A) Amy is a 5 years old from a socio-economically disadvantaged background. Her cousin Amanda is the same age, but comes from higher socio-economi background.

Reason (R) Amy is exposed to about 1000 words per hour while, Amanda is exposed to approximately 2000 words per hour.

77 **Assertion** (A) Children from lower SES backgrounds are exposed to fewer words than children from higher SES backgrounds.

Reason (R) The initial language deficits of poor children are explained by environmental differences.

78 **Assertion** (A) Smaller the number of defining attributes, greater will be the difficulty in acquiring concepts.

Reason (R) Attributes are discriminable feature of an event that insusceptible of some discriminable variation from event to event.

79 **Assertion** (A) Recognition of the presence of only one attributes or a few attributes eliminates the need of additional attributes redundancy.

Reason (R) Attribute redundancy facilitates the concept identification.

80 **Assertion** (A) In creative thinking, certain imageless elements may appear in the process.

Reason (R) Linguistic relativity suggests that language peculiarities determine content of thought.

81 **Assertion** (A) Language development is dependent on certain cognitive information, processing and multinational disposition.

Reason (R) Language is also acquired through imitation of models.

82 **Assertion** (A) Indian studies highlight the role of cultural factors in individual differences in language and communication skills.

Reason (R) Children from different environments tend to differ in their conception of language resulting in expressive and referential styles of acquisition.

83 **Assertion** (A) According to Noam Chomsky (1965), phrase structure is merely surface structure and deep structure only can capture meaning.

Reason (R) Transformational grammar contends that meaning is derived from deep structure, accepting changes in surface structure.

84 **Assertion** (A) People in different cultures have different language, acquisition devices or deep structures.

Reason (R) According to Chomsky, the deep structure of language is innate.

85 **Assertion** (A) Divergent thinking involves flexibility of ideas.

Reason (R) Flexibility leads to multiple usages of producing vague alternatives.

86 **Assertion** (A) Artificial intelligence can be used to solve any type of problem.

Reason (R) Artificial intelligence involves processes similar to human brain.

87 **Assertion** (A) Persons living in a desert have many words associated with camel.

Reason (R) One's language determines the nature of one's thought.

Directions (Q. Nos. 88-93) *Read the passage given below and answer the question that follow.*

The Whorf hypothesis is the view that language shapes cognition *i.e.* concepts and ways of thinking depend on language. People who speak significantly different languages, then, view the world differently.

Also called the hypothesis of linguistic relativity or the Sapir-Whorf hypothesis, the Whorf hypothesis was named after the early 20th century linguist Benjamin Whorf, who claimed that, because the Hopi language expressed statements about time in importantly dissimilar ways than other languages, the Hopi held a different conception of time than other peoples. Related to linguistic relativity is linguistic determinism, the view that language necessitates how one thinks (thinking outside the bounds of one's language is impossible).

Some psychologists believe the Whorf hypothesis helps explain cognition; like linguistic determinism, however, it is highly controversial. *e.g.* Whorf reasoned that because the Inuit (Eskimos) have many names for snow, they must be able to perceive many more kinds of snow than Americans, for whom snow conditions are less important. On the basis of these kinds of observations, Whorf formulated the theory of linguistic relativity.

88 Which of the following statements best expresses the linguistic relativity hypothesis?

(a) Language is equivalent to thought
(b) Language influences thought
(c) Thought determines language
(d) Language is unrelated to thought

89 According to a common myth, Eskimos have multiple words for 'snow' that influence the complexity of their thoughts about it. Which hypothesis addresses this myth?

(a) Confirmation bias
(b) Functional fixedness
(c) Cognitive control
(d) Linguistic relativity

90 Consider the following statements

1. Researchers discovered that although languages differ in their number of colour categories.
2. People in different cultures seem to perceive colours in similar ways even, if they do not have names for different colours.

Which of the statements given above is/are correct?

(a) Only 1 (b) Only 2
(c) Both 1 and 2 (d) Neither 1 nor 2

91 Which of the following is incorrect about linguistic relativity ?

(a) Evidence for the linguistic relativity hypothesis has been derived from cross-cultural studies
(b) The Whorf hypothesis is the view that language shapes thought
(c) Both a and b
(d) Neither a nor b

92 Which of the following is correct from the following statements?

(a) Linguistic relativity opens the window to the realisation that all languages do not translate to each other
(b) Linguistic categories limit and determine cognitive categories is the weak part of the hypothesis
(c) Linguistic categories and usage influence though and certain kinds of non-linguistic behaviour is the strong part
(d) None of the above

93 Who proposed the linguistic relativity hypothesis?

(a) Sapir and Whorf (b) Eric Lenneberg
(c) Noam Chomsky (d) Steven Pinker

Directions (Q. Nos. 94-98) *Read the passage given below and answer the following questions.*

Kasparov's unique brain, together with his years of experience, allowed him to play chess using heuristics. Heuristics are rules of thumb or clever and creative mental shortcuts, that reduce the number of operations and allow one to solve problems easily and quickly. In the late 1990s, Kasparov's clever and creative shortcuts or heuristics, had given him the advantage over the fixed and not so creative algorithms of computer programs. However, computers now have been programmed with new algorithms that increase their speed of 'thinking' from analysing 100000 chess moves per second to 2.5 million.

As a result of this increased speed, human chess grand masters, whose thinking focuses on using clever heuristics, no longer have a clear advantage over a computer's 'thinking' ability (Boyce, 2002). Besides being used to solve chess problems, heuristics are often used in daily life to make decisions or draw conclusions (Bailensonet al, 2000).

A commonly used heuristic is called the availability heuristic. The availability heuristic says that we rely on information that is more prominent or easily recalled and overlook other information that is available, but less prominent or notable. *e.g.* the murder rate in the United States actually decreased in the late 1990s. However, during this time, network cover age of homicides increased 473%, which made news of murders more available and according to the availability heuristic, led people to conclude that murder rates had become epidemic (Comarow, 2001).

Using the availability heuristic to make a decision means taking a mental shortcut. Although heuristics allow us to make quick decisions, they may result in bad decisions, since we make them using shortcuts, which limits the amount of information we use (F Bower, 1997).

94 Which of the following most likely makes use of heuristics?

(a) A chemical equation for the synthesis of sulphuric acid.
(b) A recipe for making cookies on the back of a box of cornflakes.
(c) An article by a Nobel Prize winner titled 'How to Succeed in Science'.
(d) A computer program for keeping track of inventory at a department store.

95 Frank lost a contact lens in the kitchen, he is searching for it by examining each linoleum tile in turn to see, if the lens is contained within the square. Gemma similarly lost a lens in the kitchen; she is looking for it near the base of the fridge and around the stove, the two appliances she remembers using when she was last in the kitchen. Which statement best describes the problem-solving strategies of these two individuals?

(a) Both Frank and Gemma are using algorithms.
(b) Both Frank and Gemma are using heuristics.
(c) Frank is using a heuristic, whereas Gemma is using an algorithm.
(d) Frank is using an algorithm, whereas Gemma is using a heuristic.

96 Each of the following is a reason to use a heuristic rather than an algorithm, except

(a) sometimes no algorithm is available to solve a particular problem.
(b) heuristics often require less time and effort to apply than do algorithms.
(c) heuristics produce successful problem solutions with sufficient frequency to justify their use.
(d) heuristics yield the single best solution to a problem.

97 Consider the following statements

1. The use of heuristics is a 'best guess' that does not guarantee a solution.
2. Using the availability heuristic to make a decision means taking a mental shortcut.

Which of the above statements is/are correct about heuristics?
(a) Only 1 (b) Only 2
(c) Both 1 and 2 (d) Neither 1 nor 2

98 A rule that guarantees the solution to a problem when it is correctly applied is termed a(n)
(a) heuristic (b) mental set
(c) algorithm (d) schema

99 Match the following

List I (Scholar)	List II (Idea)
A. Edward de Bono	1. Divergent thinking
B. Hodson	2. Brain storming
C. Osborne	3. Lateral thinking
D. Trewatha and Newport	4. Decision-making

Codes

	A	B	C	D		A	B	C	D
(a)	3	1	2	4	(b)	3	2	1	4
(c)	2	3	4	1	(d)	1	3	2	4

100 Match the following

List I (Concept)	List II (Meaning)
A. Concrete	1. Recognising two items as equivalent
B. Identity	2. Recognising an item as the same one diffspatio temporal perspective
C. Classifactory	3. Identifying instance and non-instance of the concept
D. Formal	4. Learner recognises an item

Codes

	A	B	C	D		A	B	C	D
(a)	4	2	3	1	(b)	4	2	1	3
(c)	2	4	3	1	(d)	2	4	1	3

101 Match the following

List I (Type of Thinking)	List II (Concept)
A. Perceptual thinking	1. Abstract thinking
B. Conceptual thinking	2. Insightful thinking
C. Reflective thinking	3. Divergent thinking
D. Creative thinking	4. Concrete thinking

Codes

	A	B	C	D		A	B	C	D
(a)	2	3	4	1	(b)	4	3	2	1
(c)	4	1	2	3	(d)	3	2	1	4

102 Match the following

List I (Psychologist)	List II (Concept)
A. Mc Kellar	1. Assimilation and accommodation
B. Freud	2. Rational thinking
C. Piaget	3. Pre-conscious, conscious and unconscious
D. Guilford	4. Divergent thinking

Codes

	A	B	C	D		A	B	C	D
(a)	1	2	3	4	(b)	2	3	1	4
(c)	3	4	2	1	(d)	4	1	3	2

103 Match the following

List I (Types of Thinking)	List II (Characteristics)
A. Reasoning	1. Free association of ideas, associations are random
B. Reverie	2. Sequence of association of ideas are controlled
C. Autistic	3. Projection of life into inanimate objects
D. Animism	4. Dominated by the thinker's needs

Codes

	A	B	C	D		A	B	C	D
(a)	2	4	1	3	(b)	3	1	4	2
(c)	2	1	4	3	(d)	3	4	1	2

104 Match the following

List I (Scholar)	List II (Concept)
A. Pavlov	1. Law of effect
B. Thorndike	2. Behaviourism
C. Guilford	3. Divergent thinking
D. Chomsky	4. Language and thought

Codes

	A	B	C	D
(a)	3	1	4	2
(b)	3	2	1	4
(c)	2	1	3	4
(d)	2	4	1	3

105 Match the following

List I (Intelligence)	List II (Propounder)
A. Emotional intelligence	1. Ian Marshall
B. Spiritual intelligence	2. Goleman
C. Multiple intelligence	3. Howard Gardner
D. Practical intelligence	4. Sternberg

Codes

	A	B	C	D
(a)	2	1	3	4
(b)	2	3	1	4
(c)	3	2	1	4
(d)	1	4	2	3

106 Match the following

List I (Approaches to Perception)	List II (Characteristics)
A. Template matching	1. Conceptually driven
B. Prototype matching	2. Abstract pattern
C. Bottom up	3. Extremely inflexible
D. Top-down	4. Data driven

Codes

	A	B	C	D
(a)	3	2	4	1
(b)	1	2	4	3
(c)	2	1	3	4
(d)	4	3	1	2

107 Match the following

List I (Concept)	List II (Meaning)
A. Heuristics	1. Manipulating Information
B. Mental set	2. Guidelines
C. Inductive reasoning	3. Fixating
D. Thinking	4. Specific to the general

Codes

	A	B	C	D
(a)	1	3	4	2
(b)	3	4	2	1
(c)	2	3	4	
(d)	4	1	2	3

PREVIOUS YEARS' QUESTIONS

July 2018

1 Match List I with List II and choose the correct answer from the codes given below

List I (Concept)	List II (Explanation)
A. Inductive thought	1. Thought that is intuitive and haphazard
B. Logical thought	2. Thought that applies a general set of rules to specific situations
C. Deductive thought	3. Drawing conclusions on the basis of principles of learning
D. Illogical thought	4. Thinking in which a principle is inferred from a series of specific examples

Codes

	A	B	C	D
(a)	1	2	3	4
(b)	2	3	4	1
(c)	3	4	1	2
(d)	4	3	2	1

2 During which stage most of the creative thinking occurs?

(a) Preparation (b) Incubation
(c) Illumination (d) Evaluation

3 Match List I with List II and choose the correct answer from the codes given below

List I (Concept)	List II (Explanation)
A. Disjunctive Concept	1. A class of objects that have two or more features in common
B. Prototype	2. Showing relationship between object and surroundings
C. Conjunctive Concept	3. Showing the presence of at least one of several possible features
D. Relational Concept	4. An ideal model referring to a particular concept

Codes

	A	B	C	D
(a)	1	2	3	4
(b)	3	4	1	2
(c)	2	3	4	1
(d)	4	3	1	2

November 2017

4 Concepts allow us to identify things without

(a) learning
(b) relearning
(c) recognition
(d) remembering

5 Below given are some concepts. Indicate which is the correct sequence in terms of levels of increasing abstraction? Concepts are

1. Negation concept
2. Alternative denial concept
3. Disjunction concept

Codes

(a) 1, 2 and 3 (b) 1, 3 and 2
(c) 2, 1 and 3 (d) 3, 2 and 1

6 The following statements represent the work of Noam Chomsky, choose the correct one from the codes given below.

1. He called himself a Cartesian linguistic.
2. He analysed syntax.
3. He wrote about transformational grammar.
4. He developed an artificial language called 'Yerkish'.

Codes

(a) 1, 2 and 3 (b) 1, 2 and 3
(c) 2, 3 and 4 (d) 1, 3 and 4

January 2017

7 Gestalt Psychologist Max Wertheimer attempted to train children to think in a logical and systematic way where he used several figures such as

1. Squares and rectangles
2. Parallelogram
3. Triangles
4. Circles

Codes

(a) 1 and 2 (b) 2 and 3
(c) 3 and 4 (d) 1, 2 and 3

July 2016

8 Match List I with List II and indicate your answer using the codes given below

List I (Concepts)	List II (Explanations)
A. Artificial concepts	1. Representation of objects
B. Natural concepts	2. Clearest objects in the physical world
C. Prototypes	3. Defined by set of rules
D. Visual images	4. Not based on precise properties

Codes

	A	B	C	D		A	B	C	D
(a)	2	3	4	1	(b)	3	4	2	1
(c)	3	2	4	1	(d)	4	3	1	2

9 Thinking is a complex set of collaborations between .... and .... representations and processes.

(a) linguistic; semantic (b) linguistic; verbal
(c) semantic; non-linguistic (d) linguistic; non-linguistic

10 Which is the correct sequence of the stages involved in creative thinking?

(a) Preparation; orientation ; illumination; incubation; verification
(b) Preparation; incubation ; illumination; orientation; verification
(c) Orientation; preparation; incubation; illumination; verification
(d) Orientation; preparation; illumination; incubation; verification

December 2015

11 Which of the following is a characteristic of Chomsky's Theory?

(a) Development of language is between 3 and 5 years of age
(b) Language development is dependent on the reinforcements received by the child
(c) Children acquire mistakes in language by observing their parents and others around them
(d) Children have an innate mental grammar

June 2015

12 Which one of the following can be primarily employed to assess/creativity?

(a) Abstract thinking
(b) Convergent thinking
(c) Divergent thinking
(d) Symbolic thinking

June 2014

13 Arrange the following stages of language development in order of their occurrence.

1. Semantic development.
2. Production of meaningful speech.
3. Phonological development.
4. Grammar/Syntax.

Codes

(a) 3, 1, 4, 2 (b) 1, 4, 3, 2
(c) 3, 1, 2, 4 (d) 1, 3, 4, 2

ANSWERS

Exam Based Questions

1 (d)	2 (b)	3 (c)	4 (d)	5 (b)	6 (c)	7 (d)	8 (b)	9 (b)	10 (c)
11 (a)	12 (b)	13 (c)	14 (d)	15 (b)	16 (c)	17 (a)	18 (c)	19 (b)	20 (b)
21 (a)	22 (b)	23 (c)	24 (b)	25 (a)	26 (b)	27 (b)	28 (a)	29 (a)	30 (b)
31 (a)	32 (b)	33 (b)	34 (c)	35 (d)	36 (b)	37 (c)	38 (b)	39 (a)	40 (a)
41 (a)	42 (d)	43 (b)	44 (d)	45 (c)	46 (d)	47 (d)	48 (c)	49 (c)	50 (c)
51 (c)	52 (d)	53 (a)	54 (a)	55 (a)	56 (a)	57 (d)	58 (c)	59 (b)	60 (b)
61 (b)	62 (b)	63 (c)	64 (d)	65 (b)	66 (a)	67 (d)	68 (c)	69 (c)	70 (d)
71 (d)	72 (a)	73 (d)	74 (b)	75 (b)	76 (a)	77 (a)	78 (a)	79 (b)	80 (b)
81 (b)	82 (b)	83 (b)	84 (d)	85 (a)	86 (d)	87 (a)	88 (b)	89 (d)	90 (c)
91 (c)	92 (a)	93 (a)	94 (c)	95 (d)	96 (d)	97 (c)	98 (a)	99 (a)	100 (b)
101 (c)	102 (b)	103 (c)	104 (c)	105 (a)	106 (a)	107 (c)			

Previous Years' Questions

1 (a)	2 (b)	3 (c)	4 (b)	5 (a)	6 (a)	7 (d)	8 (b)	9 (d)	10 (c)
11 (d)	12 (c)	13 (a)							

Problem Solving, Decision-Making and Metarecognition

Problem solving is a mental process to overcome obstacles that stand in the way of accomplish a goal. The term 'decision-making' denotes an information processing activity of a decision-maker that begins with the recognition of a situation and ends with the implementation of the solution and the monitoring of its effects. Metacognition refers to a persons's ability to be aware of what they are thinking about and choosing a helpful thought process.

Problem

A problem is a situation you want to change, a risk you want to reduce or an opportunity you want to seize.

The following are common types of problem

(i) **Personal Problem** Problems that originate within the person or because of his/her situation. Personal problem includes relationship issues, health troubles, phobias, loneliness, anger etc.

(ii) **Social Problem** Problems that originate in the society and affect society as a whole or large number of individuals. For instance poverty, relationship, unemployment, drugs etc are examples of social problem.

(iii) **Political Problem** These types of problem involves cooperation or competition between nations, organisations etc. Such problems have high probability to turn into conflict.

(iv) **Technical Problem** Problems that aren't social in nature such fixing machine.

(v) **Decision-Making Problem** Problems that require a choices between strategies or option.

In this Chapter

- Problem Solving
- Decision-Making
- Metacognition

Problem Solving

Problem solving is a mental process that involves discovering, analysing and solving problems. The ultimate goal of problem solving is to oversscome obstacles and find a solution to set things in order.

According to **George Polya**, "Solving a problem means finding a way out of a difficulty, a way around an obstacle , attaining an aim that was not immediately understandable. Solving problem is the specific achievement of intelligence and intelligence is the specific gift of mankind. Solving problems can be regarded as the most characteristically human activity."

According to **Baron**, "Problem solving involves efforts to develop or choose among various responses in order to attain desired goals."

Witting and **Williams** defined problem solving as "the use of thought processes to overcome obstacles and work towards goals".

Methods of Problem Solving

Following are some of the methods of problem solving

Critical Thinking

It refers to the ability to analyse information objectively and make a reasoned judgment. Critical thinking involves the evaluation of sources such as data, facts, observable phenomenon and research findings. Good critical thinkers can draw reasonable conclusions from a set of information and discriminate between useful and less useful details to solve a problem or to make a decision.

Intuition

Intuition is essentially the brain on autopilot, performing the actions of processing information without the person's conscious awareness that it is operating. It is non-conscious thinking.

Most of us are used to make intuitive decisions in our daily life. As soon as subjective judgment is involved, rational reasoning is very difficult to apply. Typical examples where intuition can play an important role in making decisions are; choosing your life partner, selecting the right car to buy, evaluation of a job, decision about an education, selecting a meal when eating out, selecting the next book to read, decide how to dress for today and so on.

Brainstorming

Brainstorming is a conference technique by which a group attempts to find a solution for a specific problem by amassing all the ideas spontaneously by its members. **Alex Fosborn** is the father of this technique who detailed it in his book titled '**Applied Imagination**' published in **1963**.

Collective Intelligence

Collective intelligence is shared or group intelligence that emerges from the collaboration, collective efforts and competition of many individuals and helps in problem solving. The primary difference between individual intelligence and collective intelligence is the social dimension and the ability of a group to achieve unity of purpose, action and thought. Beside them, there are many more methods of problem solving.

Strategies of Problem Solving

Problem solving involves many strategies which are as follows

Heuristics

Heuristics refers to mental strategy based on rule-of thumb. There is no guarantee that it will always work out to produce the best solution. However, the rule of thumb strategy does help to simplify complex problems by narrowing the possible solutions. It makes it easier to reach the correct solution using other strategies.

Heuristic strategy of problem solving can also be referred to as the mental shortcut. For instance, you need to reach the other part of the city in a limited amount of time. You'll obviously seek for the shortest route and means of transportation. The rule of thumb allows you to make up your mind about the fastest route depending on your past commutes. You might choose subway instead of hiring a cab.

Algorithm

In psychology, one of these problem-solving approaches is known as *an algorithm*. An algorithm is a defined set of step-by-step procedures that provides the correct answer to a particular problem.

By following the instructions correctly, you are guaranteed to arrive at the right answer. While often thought of purely as a mathematical term, the same type of process can be followed to ensure finding the correct answer when solving a problem or making a decision.

Trial and Error

Trial and error is a problem solving method in which multiple attempts are made to reach a solution. It is a basic method of learning that essentially all organisms use to learn new behaviours. Trial and error is trying a method, observing if it works and if it doesn't trying a new method. This process is repeated until success or a solution is reached.

Edward Thorndike, a researcher who studied learning theory by using cats and a specially made 'puzzle box.' He studied how cats learned to escape from the box and concluded it was through trial and error. This was a shift from the theory of insight learning which proposes that problem solving happens in a sudden flash of understanding rather than through trial and error.

Insight

Insight is something that just occurs suddenly. Researchers suggest that insight can occur if you've dealt with similar problems in the past. For instance, knowing that you've solved a particular algebra question in the past will make it much easier for you to solve the similar questions at present. However, it's not always necessary that the mental processes be related with past problem. In fact, most cases of mental processes leading to insight happen outside of consciousness.

Steps in Problem Solving

In order to correctly solve a problem, it is important to follow a series of steps. Many research refers to this as the problem solving cycle, which includes developing strategies and organising knowledge. While this cycle is portrayed sequentially, people rarely follow rigid series of steps to find solution. Instead, they often skip steps or even go back through steps multiple times until the desired solution is reached.

(i) **Identifying the Problem** While it may seem like an obvious step, identifying the problem is not always as simple as it sounds. In some cases, people might mistakenly identify the wrong source of a problem, which will make attempts to solve it inefficient or even useless.

(ii) **Defining the Problem** After the problem has been identified, it is important to fully define the problem so that it can be solved.

(iii) **Forming a Strategy** The next step is to develop a strategy to solve the problem.

(iv) **Organising Information** Before coming up with a solution, we need to first organise the available information.

(v) **Allocating Resource** Since, we don't always have unlimited capital and time to solve a problem. So, appropriate resource should be allocated to solve it.

(vi) **Monitoring Progress** Effective problem solvers tend to monitor their progress as they work towards a solution.

(vii) **Evaluating the Results** After solution has been reached, it is important to evaluate the result to determine, if it is the best possible solution to the problem.

Obstacles in Problem Solving

Problem solving is not a flawless process. There are a number of different obstacles that can interfere with our ability to solve a problem quickly and efficiently. Researchers have described a number of these obstacles, *which are as follows*

- **Functional Fixedness** This term refers to the tendency to view problems only in their customary manner. Functional fixedness prevents people from fully seeing all of the different options that might be available to find a solution.
- **Irrelevant or Misleading Information** When you are trying to solve a problem, it is important to distinguish between information that is relevant to the issue and irrelevant data that can lead to faulty solutions. When a problem is very complex, the easier it becomes to focus on misleading or irrelevant information.
- **Assumptions** When dealing with a problem, people often make assumptions about the constraints and obstacles that prevent certain solutions.
- **Mental Set** Another common problem-solving obstacle is known as a *mental set*, which is the tendency people to use solutions that have worked in the past rather than looking for alternative ideas. A mental set can often work as a heuristic, making it a useful problem-solving tool. However, mental sets can also lead to inflexibility, making it more difficult to find effective solutions.

Decision-Making

In psychology, decision-making is regarded as the cognitive process resulting in the selection of a course of action among several alternatives. Decision-making process is of identifying and choosing alternatives based on the values, preferences and belief of the decision maker.

For some of the complex and important decisions, we are more likely to invest a lot of time, research, effort and mental energy to come at right conclusion.

Definitions of Decision-Making

Following are some definitions of decision- making, given by scholars

According to **George R Terry**, "Decision-making is the selection based on some criteria from two or more possible alternative".

According to **Franklin G Moore**, "Decision-making is blend of thinking, deciding and acting".

According to **Haynes and Massie**, "Decision-making is a process of selection from a set of alternative courses of action which is thoughtful to fulfill the objective of the decision problem more satisfactorily than others".

According to **Mary Cushing Niles**, "Decision-making takes place in adopting objectives and choosing the means and again when a change in the situation creates a necessity for adjustments".

Characteristics of Decision-Making

- Decision-making can be based on rationale, judgement and emotion's.
- It chooses the best option that aligns the outcomes with organisational goals. Hence, it focuses on a predetermined goal.
- It relies on dependable and true information, data and feedback. The value of the decision is dependent on the quality of information. Hence, generally, management uses different software to gather and keep relevant organisational information.
- It is an intellectual process and requires mental judgement. Decision-making needs maturity, skills and knowledge.
- They can be articulated through words or can be inferred from certain behaviour. The person taking decision has the liberty to select any substitute or alternative.
- This process involves time. The process encompasses a collection of information and searches for various alternatives. Various steps are required to be completed in order to make decisions.
- It is a countinuous process. It encompasses all the organisational processes.
- It deals with uncertainty as the outcome of each course of actions is unknown.
- It is rational process and is done only after considering the prose and cons of various alternatives.

Types of Decision-Making

There are several types of decision-making, which are as follows

(i) **Programmed Decision-Making** These are day to day decisions taken by the psychologist after considering all facts and figures. In this type there are certain set criteria to come at conclusion.

(ii) **Non-Programmed Decision-Making** These type of decision are undertaken by psychologist to resolve exclusive and uncommon problem of an individual. These decision are highly significant and play a critical role in sorting issue .

(iii) **Irreversible Decision-Making** It has unique characteristic, once decisions are finalised then they cannot be upturned or changed.

(iv) **Reversible Decision-Making** This type of decision are flexible in nature which means that they can be changed after their implementation.

(v) **Individual Decision-Making** When the decision makers makes a decision on his own then it is called *individual decision-making*.

(vi) **Group Decision-Making** Here, the decisions are made by a group of persons. This type of decision-making is done when the problem is complex and vast and it also requires specialist knowledge of different individuals.

(vii) **Authorative Decision-Making** It is a type style of making which are to taken by person sitting at top. Decision are forced of others.

(viii) **Consultative Decision-Making** This is a form of facilitative decision-making. However, here the final decision is made by the higher authority only. The decision maker will ask for the advice from all the stake holder but the decision will be make by him individually.

Methods of Decision-Making

According to **Patterson Grenny** and **Suitabler**, *there are four common ways of making decisions*

- **Command Style Decision-Making** It is also known as *authoritarian type of Decision-Making method*, in this type a person take decision on various issues without consulting any one. This type of method is not preferred today as they are not able to make as longlasting and sustainable decision. *For example* In traditional family male head of family takes important decision and all others have to follow.
- **Consult Style Decision-Making** One of the most preferred decision-making. At the time of decision-making all stakeholders are invited and consult with each other over issue and finally arrive of consensus based decision. (Accepted to all Stakeholders).

- **Vote Style Decision-Making** Voting is best suited to situation where efficiency is the highest value and you are selecting from number of good option. Decision decided on the basis of majority. Some time there can be narrow gap between favour and against of the decision-making. Best part of this method is that everyone get equal representation.
- **Consensus Style Decision-Making** this method can be both a great blessing and a frustrating curse. Consensus means that one talk until everyone honestly agrees to one decision. This method can produce tremendous unity and high quality decision.

Model of Decision-Making

The decision-making process though a logical one is a difficult task. *All decisions can be categorised into the following model*

Rational Decision-Making Model

Rational decision-making is usually based around a logical assessment of the pros and cons of various alternatives. It usually involves gathering information on possible options and choosing the most logical and sensible approach.

There are many different models of rational Decision-Making. However, many follow a typical pattern, which involves defining what you are trying to achieve, generating alternatives, researching these alternatives, choosing your preferred option and then taking action.

One such model is the **D.E.C.I.D.E.** model, proposed by Guo. *This suggests going through the following stages*

- *D = define the problem*
  What is the decision you need to make?
- *E = establish the criteria*
  What factors are important in this decision?
- *C = consider all the alternatives*
  What are your options?
- *I = identify the best alternative*
  Which is the best option?
- *D = develop and implement a plan of action*
  How are you going to put the best option into practice?
- *E = evaluate and monitor the solution*

Other rational models use scoring to weight the various criteria. One example of this is the Pugh matrix (proposed by Pugh). This involves coming up with the criteria you will use to make the decision and then weighting each one according to its importance. You then give each option a score based on how well it meets the weighted criteria.

Bounded Rationality Model or Administrative Man Model

Decision-making involve the achievement of a goal. Rationality demands that the decision-maker should properly understand the alternative courses of action for reaching the goals.

He should also have full information and the ability to analyse properly various alternative courses of action in the light of goals sought. There should also be a desire to select the best solutions by selecting the alternative which will satisfy the goal achievement.

Herbert A. Simon defines rationality in terms of objective and intelligent action. It is characterised by behavioural nexus between ends and means. If appropriate means are chosen to reach desired ends the decision is rational.

Bounded Rationality model is based on the concept developed by Herbert Simon. This model does not assume individual rationality in the decision process.

Instead, it assumes that people, while they may seek the best solution, normally settle for much less, because the decisions they confront typically demand greater information, time, processing capabilities than they possess. They settle for "bounded rationality or limited rationality in decisions.

This model is based on certain basic concepts .

- **Sequential Attention to Alternative Solution** Normally, it is the tendency for people to examine possible solution one at a time instead of identifying all possible solutions and stop searching once an acceptable (though not necessarily the best) solution is found.
- **Heuristic** These are the assumptions that guide the search for alternatives into areas that have a high probability for yielding success.
- **Satisficing** Herbert Simon called this 'satisficing' that is picking a course of action that is satisfactory or 'good enough' under the circumstances. It is the tendency for decision makers to accept the first alternative that meets their minimally acceptable requirements rather than pushing them further for an alternative that produces the best results.

Satisficing is preferred for decisions of small significance when time is the major constraint or where most of the alternatives are essentially similar. Thus, while the rational or classic model indicates how decisions should be made (*i.e.* it works as a prescriptive model), it falls somewhat short concerning how decisions are actually made (*i.e.* as a descriptive model).

Neuroscientific (Neurocognitive) Model

In cognitive neuroscience, decision-making refers to the cognitive process of evaluating a number of possibilities and selecting the most appropriate thereof in order to achieve a specific goal, or task. This faculty is a fundamental component of executive functions, although recent studies shows that a complex brain network is involved including motor areas.

Implicit Favourite Model

The implicit favourite model or Retrospective Approach to decision-making was developed by **Spielberg**. In this model, the decision maker is both irrational and biased in this decision maker makes a decision on without evaluating the alternatives. This approach is applicable in non-programmed decisions. The decision maker makes a decision what he thinks is best suited. In this approach, the manager first chooses an alternative solution to the problem and highlights its strength and compare with other alternatives and then identifies its drawbacks. The implicit favourite decision-making model provides the decision maker a means to evaluate other solutions against a perceived best decision.

Once all other solutions are found to be less favorable than the implicit favourite, the implicit favourite solution is selected. This is done with a view to proving that the alternative selected by him is the best solution to the given problem. However, another alternative which seems to be similar to the implicit favourite is short listed and is taken as second confirmation candidate. This approach can be observed in the purchase of various favourite items in which a customer gives arguments in favour of his choice on the basis of norms such as price, quality, appearance, easily availability, after-sales service etc. to reject other items of same utility.

Decision-Making Process

Following steps are involved in decision-making process

(i) **Identify the Decision** This deals with the identification of the decision to be made. It also define what outcome are desired to be achieved. Whether it is a strategic decision or routine decisions and what will be the impact of this decision on the organisation. It encompasses identifying the nature of a decision to be made, which can be short-term or long-term or reversible or irreversible.

(ii) **Gather Information** This step deals with the collection of information from various sources. The various decision is to be and with regard to what type of information is reqired and from where the data will be collected. After identifying the sources of input, the decision make has to identify how he can rearch to the sources. In this step, the manager has to deal with the internal (reports, internal, surveys, facts documents etc) as well as external (published acticles, internet, libraries, government agencies etc) environment to collect the data.

(iii) **Identify Alternatives** The thirds step is to identify various alternatives for decision-making. On the basis of the data collected, the manager lays down all the possible course of action. Sometimes he uses past knowledge or information to build new alternatives. Hence, all the desirable and feasible alternatives are identified here.

(iv) **Weight the Evidence** As the decision-making is equipped with all the possible action plans, he then weights each of them. Keeping are requirement of step I in mind the judges whether the states plan will give the desired results. The decision maker uses his emotions and intelligence while evacuating the course of actions. He will rank the alternatives on the basis of priority and desirability.

(v) **Select Among Alternatives** In this step, the decison maker will choose among the ranked action plans. This choice is based on cost benefit analysis. Various pros and cons are looked upon before selecting the said alternative. The decision maker can choose a blend on one or two alternates.

(vi) **Take Action** Here, the decision maker actually takes the action and implements the chosen alternative in the organisation.

(vii) **Review Decision** After the decision is made, the decision maker must review the decision and see whterher the desired consequences have been achieved or not. If the decision lacks certain consequences then the decision maker should repeat step 1.

Metacognition

Metacognition refers to higher order thinking that involves active control over the cognitive processes engaged in learning.

Metacognition plays a critical role in learning, it is important, to study metacognitive activity and development, to determine how students can be taught to apply their cognitive resources through metacognitive control. The term 'metacognition' is most often associated with **John H Flavell**, who proposed that metacognition consists of both metacognitive knowledge and metacognitive experiences or regulation.

Metacognition is often simply defined as 'thinking about thinking'. In actually, defining metacognition is not that simple. Although the term has been part of the vocabulary of educational psychologists for the last couple of decades and the concept for long as humans have been able to reflect on their cognitive experiences, there is much debate over exactly what metacognition is.

Historical Development of Metacognition

The conceptual basis of cognition and metacognition were considered by **James** as he began to describe the mechanics of the mental machine. **Dewey** recognised and described the cognitive processes of self monitoring and self regulation and provided an early conceptual design of metacognition. Most references directed to the ascent studies of metacognition, single out from the work of **Piaget**, a swiss psychologist and philosopher.

Some of Piaget's later research with older children described an evolving ability on the part of these learners to verbalise the actual step by step processes utilised to complete assigned tasks. Piaget terms this awareness and narrative ability as 'consciousness of cognizance', which we call metacognition for this function.

Flavell a cognitive researches, professor of psychology, introduced the term, metacognition. Flavell was the first to recognise that specific strategies for remembering, categorising and recalling, needed information, which can be consciously directed by learners. Metacognition is defined as "cognition about cognition or knowing about knowing".

Metacognitive Knowledge

Metacognitive knowledge refers to the awareness individuals possess about themselves and other people as cognitive processors. According to **Flavell** "Metacognitive knowledge consists of sets of beliefs about personal attributes and strategies. All these aspects are relevant not only to learning in general, but also the specific forms of learning which are mediated by technological devices".

Flavell further divided metacognitive knowledge into three categories which are as follows

(i) **Knowledge of Person Variables** It refers to general knowledge about how human beings learn and process information, as well as individual's knowledge of one's own learning processes.

(ii) **Knowledge of Task Variables** It include knowledge about the nature of the task as well as the type of processing demands that it will place upon the individual.

(iii) **Knowledge of Strategy Variables** It include knowledge about both cognitive and metacognitive strategies, as well as conditional knowledge about when and where it is appropriate to use such strategies.

Types of Metacognitive Knowledge

Metacognitive awareness/knowledge involves three kinds of content knowledge, *which are as follows*

(i) **Declarative Knowledge** It is the fatcual information that one knows; it can be declared spoken or written. An example is knowing the formula for calculating momentum in physics class (Momentum = Mass times velocity).

(ii) **Procedural Knowledge** It is knowledge of how to do something of how to perform the steps in a process. *For example* knowing the mass of an object and its as the effects of solution processes and regulate the stream of solution activity that represents, according to **Kluwe** (1982).

Metacognitive Procedural, Kluwe uses the term executive processes involve both monitoring and regulating other thought processes and therefore correspond with Flavell's (1979) Metacognitive Strategies and Brown's (1978) Metacognitive Skills.

(iii) **Conditional Knowledge** It is knowledge about when to use a procedure, skill or strategy and when not to use it; why a procedure works and under what conditions; any why one procedure is better than another.

For example Students need to recognise that an exam word problem requires the calculation of momentum as part of its solution. In Anderson's Act Theory, however, conditional knowledge is regarded as an intrinsic part of procedural knowledge, which is represented by condition action rules.

Flavell's Model of Metacognition

Flavell in his theory of metacognition offered a model of metacognition with four components, *which are as follows*

(i) **Metacognitive Knowledge** It refers to the personal perspectives of one's own learning abilities as well as others.

(ii) **Metacognitive Experience** It is the conscious consideration of intellectual experiences that accompany any success or failure in learnings.

(iii) **Metacognitive Goals or Tasks** of metacognition are the actual objectives of cognitive endeavour, such as reading and comprehension of a passage.

(iv) **Metacognitive Action or Strategies** It refer to the utilisation of specifics techniques that may assist in understanding.

Metacognitive Regulation

Metacognitive experiences involves the use of metacognitive strategies or metacognitive regulation, metacognitive strategies and sequential processes that one uses to control cognitive activities and to ensure that a cognitive goal (*e.g.* understanding a text) has been met. These processes help to regulate and answer learning and consist of monitoring and evaluating.

Planning involves suitable selection of strategies and the right assignment of resources. Monitoring includes awareness of understanding and task performances, while evaluating refers to the assessment of the final result of task and the efficiency carried out during task performance.

Thus, metacognitive regulations is the regulation of cognition and learning experiences through a set of activities that help people control their learning.

For example After reading a paragraph in a text, a learner may question herself about the concept discussed in the paragraph. Her cognitive goal is to understand the text. Self questioning is a common Metacognitive Comprehension Monitoring Strategy. It she finds that she cannot answer her own questions, or that she does not understand the material discussed, she must then determine what needs to be done to ensure that she meets the cognitive goal of understanding the text.

She may decide to go back and reread the paragraph with the goal of being able to answer the questions she had generated if, after rereading through the text she can new answer the questions, she may determine that she understands the material. Thus, the metacognitive strategy of self questioning is used to ensure that the cognitive goal of comprehension is met.

EXAM BASED QUESTIONS

1 A..........is a situation you want to change, a risk you want to reduce or an opportunity you want to seize.
(a) decision-making (b) problem
(c) Both a and b (d) None of these

2 Problems that originate within the person or because of his/her situation are known as
(a) Personal problem (b) Political problem
(c) Decision-making problem (d) Social problem

3 Which of the following can not be included under personal problem?
(a) Loneliness (b) Anger
(c) Poverty (d) Relationship issues

4 Completion between nation falls within which of the following category?
(a) Personal problem (b) Technical problem
(c) Social problem (d) Political problem

5 which of the following is a mental process that involves discovering, analysing and solving problem?
(a) Decision-Making (b) Problem solving
(c) Metacognition (d) Metaregulation

6 According to George Polya problem solving means
(a) finding way around an obstacle.
(b) it is specific achievement of intelligence.
(c) attaining an aim that was not immediately understandable.
(d) All of the above

7 Who said that, "Problem solving involves efforts to develop or choose among various responses in order to attain desired goals"?
(a) George Polya (d) Baron
(c) Williams (d) Witting

8 Human problem solving consists of
(a) problem orientation (b) problem solving skills
(c) Both a and b (d) None of these

9 Problems can be classified as
(a) ill-defined (b) well-defined
(c) Both a and b (d) None of these

10 What refers to be ability to analyse information, objectively and make reasoned judgment?
(a) Critical thinking (b) Intuition
(c) Brainstorming (d) Collective intelligence

11 Intuition can be described as
(a) group intelligence that emerge from collaboration
(b) type of conference technique
(c) performing action without person's conscious that it is operating
(d) None of the above

12 Which of the following strategy based on the rule of thumb?
(a) Insight (b) Trial and error
(c) Heuristic (d) Algorithm

13 Which one of the following problem solving strategies, though time consuming guarantees solution?
(a) Trial and error
(b) Use of algorithm
(c) Use of heuristics
(d) Study of the problem in parts

14 Which type of problem may be solved successfully by the application of an algorithm?
(a) Well-defined problems (b) Ill-defined problems
(c) Both a and b (d) Neither a nor b

15 Among the following methods which one is based on multiple attempts to reach a solution?
(a) Trial and error (b) Algorithm
(c) Brainstorming
(d) Critical thinking

16 Renowned experiment of 'Puzzle box' with cat, is related with which of the following strategy?
(a) Heuristic (b) Insight
(c) Trial and Error (d) Intuition

17 Among the following which is not included as a method of problem?
(a) Critical thinking (b) Brainstorming
(c) Intuition (d) Algorithm

18 Alex Fosborm is acknowledged as father of which of the following technique?
(a) Collective Intelligence (b) Brainstorming
(c) Insight (d) Intuition

19 A problem solving heuristic is
(a) guaranteed to find a solution, if one exists.
(b) a strategy that guides a search through the problem.
(c) likely to be less effective than a strategy such as means-end analysis.
(d) needed for unfamiliar problems, but not for familiar problems.

20 Insight is a one of the strategy of problem solving it refers to
(a) involves many step
(b) mental shortcut
(c) insight is something that occurs suddenly
(d) None of the above

21 In problem solving, the first step is
(a) Identifying the problem
(b) forming a strategy
(c) Defining a problem
(d) Allocating resources

22 Which of the following is not true about steps in problem solving?
(a) It has multiple step
(b) Forming strategy is first step in the process
(c) Evaluation is compulsory for sustainable solution
(d) All of the above

23 Which of the following is most critical step in problem solving?
(a) Identifying the problem
(b) Allocating resources
(c) Formulation of strategy
(d) Evaluating the result

24 Problem solving process has many obstacles, among the given option which is not an obstacle in the process?
(a) Functional fixedness (b) Mental set
(c) Critical thinking (d) Assumption

25 Name the process which is regarded as the cognative process resulting in the selection of a course of action among several alternative?
(a) Problem solving (b) Decision-making
(c) Both a and b (d) None of these

26 George R Terry is associated with which of the following fields?
(a) Intelligence (b) Metacognition
(c) Decision-making (d) Problem solving

27 Whose 'decision-making' is a blend of thinking, deciding and acting?
(a) Franklin G Moore (b) Haynes and Massie
(c) George R Terry (d) Mary Cushing Nites

28 Choose the characteristic of decision-making?
(a) An intellectual process
(b) A continuos process
(c) It analysis bulk of information
(d) All of the above

29 Decision-making can be
(a) programmed (b) non-programmed
(c) Both a and b (d) None of these

30 The type of decision-making by psychologist to resolve exclusive and uncommon problem of an individual is known as
(a) Non-programmed decision-making
(b) Programmed decision-making
(c) Irreversible decision-making
(d) Consulative decision-making

31 Salient feature of consultative decision-making is
(a) decisions are taken by people upper in hierarchy
(b) all stakeholders are consulted
(c) when decision are irreversible
(d) has a set of criteria

32 According to Patterson, Greeny and Suitzles, there are how many way of decision-making?
(a) 1 (b) 2 (c) 3 (d) 4

33 Which among the following is authoritarian type of decision-making?
(a) Consult type Decision-Making
(b) Consensus style Decision-Making
(c) Command style decision-making
(d) Vote decision-making

34 If we compare different methods of decision-making then which will be most efficient and sustainable?
(a) Vote type (b) Consensus type
(c) Consult type (d) Command type

35 When there large number of stakeholder then which type of decision-making method is adopted?
(a) Vote type (b) Consult type
(c) Command type (d) None of these

36 D.E. C.I. D. E. Model was proposed by
(a) Herbert A Simon (b) Guo
(c) George Polya (d) Baron

37 In D.E.C.I.D.E. Model 'D' stands for
(a) Deciding course of action
(b) Delimination
(c) Define the problem
(d) Discussion on problem

38 Bounded rationality model is based on the concept developed by which of the following scholar?
(a) Herber A Simon (b) Franklin G Moore
(c) Haynes (d) Massie

39 Among the following option, which is not included in the concept of on which bounded rationality model is based?
(a) Heuristic
(b) Algorithm
(c) Satisficing
(d) Sequential attention to alternative solution

40 Neuroscientific (neurocognitive) model is related with which of the following fields?
(a) Decision-Making (b) Problem solving
(c) Metacognition (d) Intelligence

41 Implicit favourite mode is also known as
(a) Neurocognitive model
(b) Administrative model
(c) Retrospective approach
(d) Rational Decision-Making model

42 Retrospective model to decision-making was propounded by
(a) Guo (b) Spielberg
(c) Baron (d) George R Terry

43 Which of the following is the first step in decision-making process?
(a) Weigh the evidence
(b) Select among alternative
(c) Identify the decision
(d) Take action

44 Flavell's divided metacognitive knowledge into three categories, these are

(a) Person variable (b) Task variable
(c) Strategy variable (d) All of these

45 The general knowledge about how human beings learn and process information is known as

(a) Person variable (b) Task variable
(c) Strategy variable (d) None of these

46 Who among the following used the term executive processes to denote kind of procedural knowledge?

(a) Flavell (b) Kluwe
(c) Anderson (d) None of these

47 Which among the following is not a component of metacognition?

(a) Actions (b) Goals
(c) Metacognitive experience
(d) Metacognitive understanding

48 Which among the following are the actual objectives of cognitive endeavour?

(a) Metacognitive experience
(b) Metacognitive knowledge
(c) Metacognitive goals
(d) Metacognitive actions

49 Arrange the following steps of problem-solving in order

1. Defining the problem
2. Identifying the problem
3. Allocating resources
4. Monitoring progress

Codes

(a) 4, 3, 2, 1 (b) 2, 1, 3, 4 (c) 1, 2, 3, 4 (d) 3, 4, 2, 1

50 Arrange the following steps of decision-making in order

1. Developing and weighing the options
2. Plan and execute
3. Take follow up action
4. Choosing lest possible option

Codes

(a) 1, 2, 3, 4 (b) 2, 3, 4, 1 (c) 1, 4, 2, 3 (d) 4, 2, 3, 1

51 Which of the following strategies facilitate problem solving?

1. Algorithms 2. Mental set
3. Planning fallacy 4. Heuristics
5. Analogy

Codes

(a) 1, 2 and 4 (b) 2, 3 and 4 (c) 1 and 5 (d) 1, 4 and 5

52 Which of the following procedures are useful in the process of problem solving?

1. Algorithms 2. Heuristics
3. Sub-goaling 4. Restructuring

Select the correct answer using the codes given below

(a) 1, 2, 3 and 4 (b) 2 and 3
(c) 1 and 4 (d) 2, 3 and 4

53 What among the following define a problem space?

1. An inital state 2. A goal state
3. A set of operations

Codes

(a) 1 and 3 (b) 1 and 2 (c) 2 and 3 (d) 1, 2 and 3

54 Match the following

List I (Strategies)	List II (Concepts)
A. Heuristic	1. Step by step
B. Algorithm	2. Sudden occurrence
C. Trial and Error	3. Rule of thumb
D. Insight	4. Multiple attempts

Codes

	A	B	C	D		A	B	C	D
(a)	3	1	2	4	(b)	2	4	1	3
(c)	3	1	4	2	(d)	2	4	3	1

55 Match the following

List I (Methods)	List II (Concepts)
A. Command style	1. Most efficient
B. Consult style	2. Majority decision
C. Vote style	3. Advice from stakeholder
D. Consensus style	4. Authoritarian in nature

Codes

	A	B	C	D		A	B	C	D
(a)	4	3	2	1	(b)	2	1	4	3
(c)	2	1	3	4	(d)	4	3	1	2

56 Match the following

List I (Explanations)	List II (Concepts)
A. A tendency to repeat mechanically prior solutions of old problems that are no longer optimal for current problem solving	1. Algorithm
B. A set of rules that eventually guarantee success in problem solving, if the rules are appropriately used	2. Heuristics
C. A kind of recognition difficulty in problem solving due to prior experience	3. Einstellung
D. Strategies based on past experience to solve a problem	4 Functional fixedness

Codes

	A	B	C	D		A	B	C	D
(a)	4	2	3	1	(b)	3	1	4	2
(c)	4	1	3	2	(d)	3	2	4	1

57 Match the following

List I (Techniques)	List II (Concepts)
A. Concept formation	1. Strategy
B. Deductive reasoning	2. Attaining goal
C. Problem solving	3. General to specific
D. Algorithm	4. Mental categories

Codes

	A	B	C	D
(a)	2	1	3	4
(b)	3	4	1	2
(c)	1	2	3	4
(d)	4	3	2	1

58 Match the following

List I (Scholars)	List II (Decision-Making)
A. George R Terry	1. Adopting objective and choosing the means
B. Flanklin Gmoore	2. Based on some criteria
C. Haynes and Massie	3. Blend of thinking, deciding and acting
D. Mary Cushing Nites	4. Selection from set of alternative

Codes

	A	B	C	D
(a)	4	1	2	3
(b)	2	3	1	4
(c)	2	3	4	1
(d)	1	4	3	2

Directions (Q. Nos. 59-67) *In the question given below are two statements labelled as Assertion (A) and Reason (R). In the context of the two statements, which one of the following is correct?*

(a) Both A and R are true and R is the correct explanation of A
(b) Both A and R are true, but R is not the correct explanation of A
(c) A is true, but R is false
(d) A is false, but R is true

59 **Assertion** (A) Problem solving is a mental process.

Reason (R) Problem solving involve discovering, analysing and solving problem.

60 **Assertion** (A) Problem solving involves efforts to develop or choose among various responses in order to attain desired goal.

Reason (R) Metarecognition refers to a person's ability to be aware of what they thinking.

61 **Assertion** (A) Personal problem originate in the society and affect society as a whole.

Reason (R) Unemployment, drugs etc are examples of a social problem.

62 **Assertion** (A) Critical thinking is one of the method of problem solving.

Reason (R) In it group attempts to find a specific problem.

63 **Assertion** (A) Hueristic strategy of problem solving can also be referred as the mental shortcut.

Reason (R) In Trial and error method multiple attempts are made to reach a solution.

64 **Assertion** (A) An algorithm is most used strategy in problem solving.

Reason (R) It consists of step by step procedure that provide correct answer.

65 **Assertion** (A) First step in problem solving is identification. of problem.

Reason (R) In problem solving we have unlimited time and money.

66 **Assertion** (A) Problem solving is flawless process.

Reason (R) Problem solving obstackle includes-functional fixedness, assumption etc. (d)

67 **Assertion** (A) Decision-making is process of identifying, choosing and implementing alternative .

Reason (R) Decision-making is blend of thinking, deciding and acting.

Directions (Q. Nos. 68-72) *Read the passage given below and answer the following questions.*

The implicit favourite model developed by Spielberg. In this model, the decision maker is both irrational and biased, in this decision maker makes a decision on without evaluating the alternatives. This approach is applicable in non-programmed decisions. The decision maker makes a decision what he thinks is best suited. In this approach, the manager first chooses an alternative solution to the problem and highlights its strength and compare with other alternatives and then identifies its drawbacks. The implicit favourite decision-making model provides the decision maker a means to evaluate other solutions against a perceived best decision.

Once all other solutions are found to be less favourable than the implicit favourite, the implicit favourite solution is selected. This is done with a view to proving that the alternative selected by him is the best solution to the given problem. However, another alternative which seems to be similar to the implicit favourite is short listed and is taken as second confirmation candidate. This approach can be observed in the purchase of various favourite items in which a customer gives arguments in favour of his choice on the basis of norms such as price, quality, appearance, easily availability, after-sales service etc. to reject other items of same utility .

68 Implicit favourite model has been developed by

(a) Baron (b) Spielberg
(c) George Polye (d) Williams

69 What are two qualities of decision maker in implicit favourite model?

1. Rational 2. Biased
3. Irrational 4. Confident

Codes

(a) 1 and 2 (b) 1, 2 and 3
(c) 2 and 3 (d) All of these

70 The decision maker makes decision

(a) What he thinks is best suited
(b) After evaluating all the facts
(c) Both a and b
(d) None of the above

71 Implicit favourite mode is implement in which type decision-making?

(a) Individual
(b) Programmed
(c) Peresible
(d) Non- programmed

72 Which of the following statement is not true in the context of passage?

(a) There are many alternative in Decision-Making.
(b) Implicit model is applicable to non-programed decision.
(c) Decision maker is rational and biased.
(d) None of the above

ANSWERS

Exam Based Questions

1	(b)	2	(a)	3	(c)	4	(d)	5	(b)	6	(d)	7	(b)	8	(b)	9	(c)	10	(a)
11	(c)	12	(c)	13	(b)	14	(a)	15	(a)	16	(c)	17	(d)	18	(b)	19	(b)	20	(c)
21	(a)	22	(b)	23	(c)	24	(c)	25	(b)	26	(c)	27	(a)	28	(d)	29	(c)	30	(a)
31	(b)	32	(d)	33	(c)	34	(b)	35	(a)	36	(b)	37	(c)	38	(a)	39	()	40	(a
41	(c)	42	(b)	43	(c)	44	(d)	45	(a)	46	(b)	47	(d)	48	(c)	49	(b)	50	(c)
51	(d)	52	(a)	53	(d)	54	(c)	55	(a)	56	(a)	57	(d)	58	(b)	59	(a)	60	(b)
61	(d)	62	(c)	63	(b)	64	(a)	65	(c)	66	(d)	67	(a)	68	(b)	69	(c)	70	(a)
71	(d)	72	(c)																

CHAPTER 21

Intelligence and Creativity

Intelligence is the capacity to acquire and apply knowledge. It includes the ability to benefit from past experience, act purposefully, solve problems and adapt to new situations. Creativity is defined as the tendency to generate or recognise ideas, alternatives or possibilities that may be useful in solving problems, communicating with others and entertaining ourselves as well as others.

Intelligence

Intelligence is one of the most talked about subject in psychology, there is no standard definition of what exactly constitute intelligence. Some researcher have suggested that intelligence is a single, general ability, while other believes that intelligence encompasses a range of aptitude, skills and talent.

Cognitive approaches to intelligence seeks to discover the internal processes that account for intelligent behaviour. There is some evidence to suggest that performance on traditional tests of mental ability might be related to the speed of processing among neurons in the brain. The multiple intelligence approach of **Howard Gardner** and the triarchic theory of **Robert Sternberg** suggests that the concept of intelligence must be defined broadly. We cannot rely entirely on things such as academic ability to define intelligence.

Definitions of Intelligence

According to **Wechsler**, "Intelligence is the aggregate or global activity of the individual to get purposefully, to think rationally and to deal effectively with the environment."

According to **Alfred Buiet**, "Intelligence is the capacity of an individual to reason well, to judge well and to be self critical."

According to **Freeman**, "Intelligence can be defined as the faculty with which the subject-matter of experience can be organised into new patterns."

In this Chapter

- *Intelligence*
  - *– Theories of Intelligence*
- *Creativity*
  - *– Theories of Creativity*
- *Relationship Between Intelligence and Creativity*

According to **Stoddard**,"Intelligence is the ability to undertake activities characterised by, difficulty, complexity, abstracters, economy, adaptiveness to a goal, social value, emergence of originals and to maintain such activities."

Theories of Intelligence

Intelligence is a complex concept to define and understand. Its broadness makes it difficult for psychologist to come up with a determined understanding of the concept. Psychologists have presented their understanding of the concept of intelligence in psychology through various theories of intelligence.

Spearman's Two-Factor Theory of Intelligence

Charles Spearman published an epoch-making study in 1904, which indeed proved to be the crucial step toward quantitative testing of theories, as opposed to simple quantification or measurement. He used the techniques of correlational analysis and factor analysis, both of which had been developed earlier by Karl Pearson, in relation to the scores obtained by groups of children on various intelligence tests. His historical significance can be seen in the development of the factor analytical method and in its explicit use for the first time.

Spearman proposed a *Two Factor Theory* of intelligence. According to him, intelligence consists of two factors : General (g) and Specific (s). This theory maintains that all intellectual activities share a common factor that we call 'g' factor, which is characterised by mental energy. The theory assumes that 'g' factor is a common factor found in all different kinds of activities we do and this is the reason that we find a close relationship between different human activities as shown in figure *e.g.* a good test on memory, reasoning and other abilities parallel a similarly high score on each of these ability tests.

This high positive correlation between different abilities is attributed to the presence of 'g' factor in almost similar amount in all these activities or abilities. From the above discussion, following findings can be arrived.

In view of this, it may be concluded that what we call intelligence is the 'g' factor, which varies from person to person, where an activity involves more of motor and physical action and is routinised the 's' factor assumes a greater role.

The g factor according to Spearman can be taken as the general cortical of neural energy at the disposal of the individual.

According to Spearman, 'g' is involved in apprehension of experience education of relations and education of correlates. Spearman also held that 'g' is innate and is influenced by a number of factor like age, sex, heredity etc. Spearman also suggested the existence of 'group factors' like verbal ability, numerical ability etc. which enter a group of related and similar activities though, he did not emphasise them much.

The credit for arriving at the first systematic and scientific formulation of a theory of intelligence goes to Spearman. His theory changed the nature of tests of intelligence.

Significance of Two-Factor Theory

Spearman's theories of intelligence are very stimulating and his contribution to the psychology of intelligence can be regarded important mainly for two major reasons.

- **First**, he developed the mathematical model for studying 'g' and for that purpose he laid the foundation of factor analysis. The logic and method of correlational analysis was afterward followed by other researchers for developing multi-factorial theories of intelligence.
- **Second**, major importance of Spearman's work is that it established a scholarly tradition in the investigation of human abilities.

According to **Nunnally**, "Spearman was concerned much more with understanding human abilities than with just measuring them. Spearman had many interesting theories about G, its biological basis, the influence of culture, the interactions of G with manifestations of abilities in daily life, and the relation of G to speed, fatigue and other variables."

Criticism of Spearman's Two-Factor Theory

One of the standard criticisms of the factor analytic approach is that it was purely psychometric and failed to provide a cognitive theory. One of the sharpest critics of spearman's two-factor theory was **EL Thorndike**, who believed that the intercorrelations studied by Spearman were too small to test the question of a common factor. He objected very strongly to the idea of the existence of a characteristic such as general intelligence.

Among the other critics of Spearman, GH Thomson has argued that the intercorrelations between tests are actually the result of common samplings of independent factors. Thomson has accordingly proposed a sampling theory, which maintains that every test samples a certain range of elementary abilities; some with a wide range and some with a narrow range.

Thurstone's Theory of Intelligence

LL Thurstone offered a new factor model in the nineteen thirties. He was one among the leading psychologist who criticised the Charles Spearman's two factor theory. Using improved techniques of statistical analysis, he came to vastly different conclusions from Spearman about nature of intelligence. Thurstone generalised Spearman's methods and formulas, translated them into matrix algebra and carried out large scale studies, using as many as fifty-seven tests on one group of subjects. On the basis of these studies he concluded that instead of Spearman's 'g' factor, seven primary abilities fitted the data much better.

He postulated a number of primary mental abilities

- **Numerical Ability** 'N' the ability to deal with number and manipulate them.
- **Reasoning, Ability** 'R' the ability to apply logic like induction, deduction and arrive at conclusion.
- **Verbal Fluency** 'W' competence in language and the use of words, fluently, the ability to translate procedures, factors and ideas into languages, which in turn promotes better reasoning.
- **Verbal Comprehension** 'V-A' part from the ability to use and deal with words, the ability to understand material presented in the form of words.
- **Perceptual Ability** 'P' the ability to perceive situations which are complex with a variety elements and organise them in order to arrive at a meaningful perception.
- **Memory** 'M'-The ability to remember facts, situations, experiences etc. which often become relevant to solve a problem or answer a question in the present.
- **Spatial Ability's** This relates to the ability to organise space and the stimulation coming from different directions, coordinate the same integrate one's behaviour.

Today, Thurstone's theory is not used as often in its original form, but it has served as a basis for many subsequent theories of intelligence, including hierarchical theories and modern theories such as Gardner's. Thus, to the extent that a theory is judged by its heuristic value, Thurstone's has been one of the most important in the field.

Factor Analysis and Work on Intelligence

Thurstone was responsible for the standardised mean and standard deviation of IQ scores used today, as opposed to the Intelligence Test System originally used by Alfred Binet. He is also known for the development of the Thurstone scale. Thurstone work in factor analysis led him to formulate a model of Intelligence center around.

'Primary Mental Abilities', which were independent group factors of intelligence that different individuals possessed in varying degrees. He opposed the notion of singular general intelligence that factored into the scores of a all psychometric tests and was expressed as a mental age. In 1935 Thurstone, together with EL Thorndike and JP Guilford founded the Journal Psychometrika and also the psychometric society, going on to become the society's first President in 1936.

Jensen's Theory on Intelligence

AR Jensen presented yet another view of intelligence. According to **Jensen**, "Intelligence is essentially another activity or function of the individual like blood pressure, temperature etc." Thus, as sphygmanometer and a thermometer give us measures of blood pressure or body temperature intelligence tests also give us a measure of intelligence and therefore there is no need to multiply the same.

Level of Intelligence

Arthur Jensen has advanced a theory of two levels of intelligence Level I and level II.

- Level-I denotes associative learning (*e.g.* learning and memory). These activities involve minimal transformation of the stimulus input prior to the out come or response.
- Level-II refers to a general class of abilities involving effective transformation or manipulation of stimuli as evidenced in higher order learning such as reasoning and problem solving.

Factors of Intelligence

According to Jensen, there are two factors of intelligence breadth and attitude.

- The first includes general information, vocabulary etc. which are directly dependent on a person's experience, exposure and opportunities, which a person has had environmental influences, as well as attitudes and interest acquired by an individual in the course of his life have these own influence on the breadth of a persons intelligence.
- The other factor attitude, however, according to Jensen is more innate and less dependent on environmental influence, again leaving a resemblance to Cattell's concept of fluid intelligence.

Non-Genetic Variance

Genotype-Environment Co-variance

From an evolutionary stand point, the genetic inheritance or innateness of fitness characteristics is essential. Jensen advocated that in humans intelligence and the ability to learn are such characteristics. Jensen argued that genetic variance, genotype-environmental covariance and GXE interaction are the major components of variance.

The variance attributed to shared or between -families, environmental factors, which is considerable throughout childhood gradually shrinks to near-zero between early adolescence and maturity. He supported during this period most of the environmental variance is converted into genotype environmental covariance, as persons elicit, seek selects and modify those elements of the available cognitive social cultural milieu that are most compatible with there genotypically conditioned proactivities.

He viewed that it is important to distinguish between Genotype Environment (GE) covariance and genotype environmental interaction. They are entirely different concepts, but each may account for some part of the phonetype variance in a trait.

Components of Behaviour Genetics

GE covariance is the result of the non-random occurrence of different genotypes in different environments. In other words, genotypes and environments may be correlated. Persons whose genotype is favourable for the development of a certain trait are more likely than chance to grow up in an environment that is favourable to the development of the trait.

The correlation of genotypes and environments for a given traits in the populations increase the phenotypic variance over what it would be, if the correlation were zero. Assuming for simplicity that there is no GE interaction, the total Phenotypic (P) Variance (V) is the sum of the Genetic (G) variance and the environmental (E) Variance plus twice the covariance of G and E or as it is expressed in biometrical genetics. $Ve = Vg + Ve + 2\ C$ *or GE.*

GE interaction is a component of the phenotypic variance that is due to different genotypes reacting differently to the same environmental condition *i.e.* an environmental condition that favours the phenotypic development of individuals who have genotype.

Criticism of Jensen's Veiw on Intelligence

One serious fallacy in Jensen's argument concerns the confusion between within group variance and between group variance. Burt's heritability estimate was an attempt to explain how intelligence varies within a single population. It was looking at within group variance and seeking to explain how that happens. But Jensen was looking at difference between two entirely different populations between group variance. The two types of figures are entirely different and to try to use one to explain the other is completely inappropriate.

Gould gives the example of height, to make this point. Within any given human population , the heritability of height is about 95% tall parents tends to produce tall children and short parents produce short children. That is common within all populations.

But differences in nutrition make a great deal of difference to human height, so if we compare say people in an improvised village in South America with middle class Americans, we would find large differences between the two populations. We would not conclude though that these differences are inherited. And yet *i.e.* precisely what Jensen did. He took a figure obtained to describe individual differences within a single group and used it to account for differences between group.

Cattell Horn Carroll Theory

The theory of Intelligence that is most used in IQ test is the Cattell Horn Carroll (CHC) theory, a combination of the Cattell Horn theory of fluid and crystallised intelligence and Carroll's theory and Saratum theory. Both the Catell Horn and Carroll models essentially started from the same point Spearman's 'g' factor theory.

Though, they took different paths they ended up with remarkably consistent conclusion about the spectrum of broad cognitive abilities. *Aforementioned components are explained below*

- **Crystallised General Ability** From the view point of Cattell crystallised general ability, show itself in judgemental skills that have been acquired by cultural experience , vocabulary, good use of synonyms, numerical skills, mechanical knowledge of a well-stocked memory and even habits of logical reasoning, which refers to accumulated knowledge. He is high on the subtests that traditionally have been built into intelligence tests vocabulary size analogies and classifications involving cultural knowledge of objects in the problem.

  Crystallised ability stretches across the whole range of cultural acquisitions. Mechanical knowledge, which is negligible or even negative on fluid ability has a measurable effect on crystallised ability.

- **Fluid Ability** According to **Cattell**, "fluid ability, has little relation to a well stocked memory. They are culture fair perceptual and performance tests and those specially developed tests of judgement and reasoning, which have been considered relatively culture free." They involve solutions to tests of classifications, analogies, matrices, topology and problem that do not involve much educational acquisition, which is inherites abilities to think and reason.

  Fluid ability does have a role in numerical reasoning and even in verbal skills. It is fairly powerful in spatial reasoning and very powerful in inductive reasoning.

  Horn identified four additional abilities and by mid 1990s his model included 9 to 10 broad abilities. The initial dichtomy had grown, but not is hierarchy. Horn retained the name Gf - GC theory, but the diverse board abilities were treated as equals, not as part of any hierarchy. These included visualisation (GV), short term memory by (GSM), long term memory (GLX) and processing speed (GS).

Stratum Theory

Carroll developed a hierarchical theory based on his depth survey of factor analytic studies composed, of three levels or strata of abilities

(i) **Stratum III** (general), a spearman live g, which considered to be a valid construct based on. Overwearing evidence from factor analysis.

(ii) **Stratum II** (broad), composed of 8 broad factors that correspond closely to Horn's broad abilities.

(iii) **Stratum I** (narrow), composed of about 70 fairly specific abilities organised by the broad factor with which each is most closely associates.

Comparision Between Cattel Horn and Carroll's Theory

In recent years, Carroll's chemical theory and the Horn-Cattell GF -GC theory have been merged into the Cattell Horn Carroll (CHC) theory. The CHC theory has been particularly influential in the development of neart IQ tests, most notably the fifth edition of the standard Binet, the Kaufman assortment battery for children seemed edition.

The CHC model incorporates both the concept of general intelligence and the concept of many different aspects of intelligence are considered to be related to a common 'g' although and the concept of many different aspects of intelligence. Largely because of the confluence of CHC theory, really all curve IQ test have shifted focus from a small number of part screens to a contemporary emphasis on anywhere from 4 to 7, cognitive abilities about, which is better still go on.

The CHC model procedure has ten different factors of intelligence: GF, GQ, GC Grw, GV, GSM, GA, Gir, GS and Gt of there 10 only 7 are measured by today IQ text: GQ grown in domain of academic achievement and therefore, measured by individually administered achievement tests and Gt is not measured by any standardised test of anything.

The CHC theory has only two strata stratum II, which consists of the 10 abilities identified above and startum, which includes more specific abilities similar to Carroll's original theory.

Gardner's Theory of Multiple Intelligences

According to Gardner, intelligence is much more than IQ because a high IQ in the absence of productivity does not equate to intelligence. In terms of his definition: "Intelligence is a bio-psychological potential to process information that can be activated in a cultural setting to solve problems or create products that are of value in a culture." Consequently, instead of intelligence being a single entity described psychometricians.

To achieve this goal Gardner established several criteria for defining intelligence. In identifying capabilities to be considered for one of the 'multiple intelligences' the construct under consideration had to meet eight criteria rather than resting on the results of a narrow psychometric approach.

To qualify as 'intelligence' the particular capacity under the study was considered from multiple perspectives consisting of eight specific criteria drawn from the biological sciences, logical analysis, developmental psychology, experimental psychology and psychometrics.

The criteria to consider candidate intelligences are

- The potential for brain isolation by brain damage
- Its place in evolutionary history
- The presence of core operations
- Susceptibility to encoding
- A distinct development progression
- The existence of idiot-savants, prodigies and other exceptional people
- Support from experimental psychology
- Support from psychometric findings

From the above criteria, Gardner initially formulated a list of seven intelligences. In 1999, he added naturalist intelligence as the eight. He has also considered inclusion of existential intelligence as the ninth intelligence in his theory. The first two have been typically valued in schools; the next three are usually associated with the arts; the next two are what Gardner called *personal intelligences*, while the newly added final two are related to aesthetics and philosophical views of life.

Each of these intelligences are briefly described below

- **Linguistic Intelligence** This intelligence includes the ability to effectively use language to express oneself rhetorically or poetically and as a means to remember information. Writers, poets, lawyers and speakers are among those that Howard Gardner sees having a high linguistic intelligence.
- **Logical-Mathematical Intelligence** In Howard Gardner's words, the intelligence entails the ability to detect patterns, reasons deductively and think logically. This intelligence is most often associated with scientific and mathematical thinking.
- **Musical Intelligence** This intelligence involves skill in the performance, composition and appreciation of musical patterns. It encompasses the capacity to recognise and compose musical pitches, tones and rhythms. According to **Gardner,** "musical intelligence runs in an almost structural parallel to linguistic intelligence."
- **Bodily-Kinesthetic Intelligence** It is the ability to use mental abilities to coordinate bodily movements. In theory, people who have bodily-kinesthetic intelligence should learn better by involving muscular movement and are generally good at physical activities such as sports or dance.
- **Spatial Intelligence** Spatial intelligence involves the potential for recognising and manipulating the patterns of both wide spaces such as those negotiated by pilots or navigators and confined spaces such as those encountered by sculptors, architects or championship chess players.
- **Interpersonal Intelligence** This area has to do interaction with others. In theory, people who have a high interpersonal intelligence tend to be extrovert, characterised by their sensitivity to others' moods, feelings, temperaments and motivations and their ability to cooperate in order to work as part of group.
- **Intrapersonal Intelligence** This entails the capacity to understand oneself, to appreciate one's feelings, fears and motivations. In Howard Gardner's view it involves having an effective working model of ourselves and to be able to use such information to regulate our lives.
- **Naturalistic Intelligence** This intelligence has to do with nature, nurturing and relating information to one's natural surroundings. Such a person demonstrates expertise in recognition and classification of the numerous species-the flora and fauna, of her or his environment. Careers which suit those with this intelligence include naturalists, farmers and gardeners.
- **Existential Intelligence** This is an ability to contemplate phenomena or questions beyond sensory data, such as the infinite and infinitesimal, career which suits those with this intelligence include cosmologists and philosophers.

According to Gardner each of these 'intelligence' has a specific set of abilities that can be observed and measured. Gardner nominated three additional candidate intelligence: Naturalist, Spiritual and Existential intelligence and evaluated them in the context of the eight criteria he had established in his research and outlined earlier in this unit.

Sternberg's Triarchic Theory

Robert Sternberg's triarchic theory of intelligence is a good example of a recent eclectic approach. Sternberg was trained as a cognitive psychologist and his theory contains important elements of the cognitive approach. He is convinced that it is important to understand the mental operation that are involved in the planning and execution of specialised tasks. But he also believes that any complete account of intelligence must address behaviour outside of the laboratory. *For example* What is the form of intelligence that enables people to apply their mental processes creatively to problems that arise in the external environment? He accepts the idea that there may be multiple kind of intelligence. The term triarchic means roughly 'ruled by threes'.

Sternberg's conceptualisation of intelligence is divided into three major parts

Analytic Intelligence

Sternberg believes that any complete theory of intelligence must refer in some way to basic analytic skills. Some people are simply better than others at processing information, they are good at representing problems in the right way and can generate effective strategies for solutions.

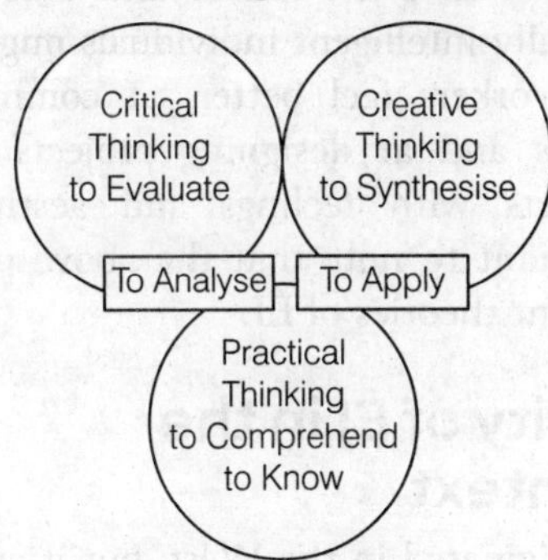

Analytic Intelligence

People with high degree of analytical intelligence tend to perform well on conventional tests that tap reasoning and logical mathematical ability. Because most psychometric tests of intelligence require these kinds of abilities, people, who are high in analytic intelligence tend to be assigned a high g for general intelligence. If you know someone, who perform well in school or who claims to be highly intelligent based on a standardised test, he or she is likely to score highly on analytic intelligence.

Creative Intelligence

Sternberg proposes a second kind of intelligence, creative intelligence, that expresses how well people are able to cope with new or novel tasks. Being analytic and processing information well, does not guarantee that you will be creative or be able to apply the skills you have masters in a new context. The world is full of people, who are good in school or who perform well on assigned tasks, but can not seem to think their way out of a paper bag. They lack creativity and seem to have trouble anything, what they have learned. A child who quickly and effortlessly learns to read after acquiring the rudiments of language *e.g.* is a child, who is presumably high in creative intelligence.

Practical Intelligence

Finally, people differ in practical intelligence, which taps how well they fit into their environments. People with lots of practical intelligence solve the problems that are uniquely possed by their cultural surroundings. They mould themselves well into existing settings and they can select new environments, if required that provide a better fit or niche for their talents. In a nut shell, these individuals have 'street smart'- they size up situations well and act accordingly. You probably know someone, who seems to lack analytical skills, who fails school or drops out, but still manages to succeed quite well in life. They work well with the tools of the environment and manage to do what it takes to succeed.

Sternberg's triarchic theory fits the current trend towards a broadening of the concept of intelligence.

Triarchic Theory of Intelligence

Analytic Intelligence	Creative Intelligence	Practical Intelligence
Meta Component	Novel Task	Adaptation
Performance Component	Automated Task	Selection
Knowledge Acquisition Component		Shaping

Goleman's Theory of Emotional Intelligence

Accordingly to **Goleman** EI consists of, "Abilities such as being able to motivate oneself and persist in the face of frustrations, to control impulse and delay gratification, to regulate one's moods and keep distress from swamping the ability to think, to empathise and to hope."

The main areas are

- Knowing one's emotions.
- Managing emotions.
- Motivating oneself.
- Recognising emotions in others.
- Handling relationships.

But Goleman seems to confuse EI with character. He said, there is an old-fashioned word for the body of skills that emotional intelligence represents: character. Also, he does not credit the original authors in many areas.

Mayer and Salovey revised their earlier model saying the former one 'omits thinking about feelings'. The new model presents a hierarchy of mental abilities.

Accordingly, the revised model consists of the following abilities

- **Perception, Appraisal and Expression of Emotion** The core capacities are identifying feelings and thoughts through proper and appropriate words in itself as well as in others and discriminating between real and unreal emotional expression.
- **Emotional Facilitation of Thinking** The core abilities are using emotions in thinking by giving proper attention to useful information, using emotions in appropriate judgement and memory concerning feelings. This ability also includes emotional facilitation to be optimistic, using emotion in tasks requiring reasoning as well as creativity.
- **Understanding and Analysing Emotions, Employing Emotional Knowledge** The core capacities are understand the differences between emotions, the consequences of the emotions, identifying complex feelings, understanding the transitions of emotions.
- **Reflective Regulation of Emotions to Promote Emotional and Intellectual Growth** The central ideas are one's 'ability to stay open to feelings' including pleasant and unpleasant, capacity to be in and out of emotion depending on the importance through proper judgement, capacity to 'monitor emotions' in terms of how much reasonable and clear they are, and "Ability to manage emotion in oneself and others by moderating negative emotions and enhancing pleasant ones, without repressing or exaggerating information they may convey."

So, this model conceptualises EI completely opposite to Baron's, in terms of cognitive *vs* non-cognitive. Mayer, call their 1997, model as ability model and the other ones, that is, Baron and Goleman's as mixed model.

It seems that the model of **Mayer** and **Salovey** has both emotion and intelligence perspective with more emphasis on intelligence, but all the others are more of emotion perspective with a negligible amount of intelligence. **Roberts**, **Zeidner** and **Matthews** suggests an emotion-less, intelligence perspective of EI. Empathy is common to the proposed ability model as well as mixed model of EI.

It can be either personality trait or intelligence depending on the type of measure used. **Petrides** and **Furnham** believe that "It is the type of measurement rather than the theory that determines the nature of the model."

Application of EI to Different Contexts

Goleman made a provocative claim that if IQ contribute upto 20% of life success, the remaining has to be filled in by EI. The front cover of Time magazine carried the question 'what is your EQ?' and reported, It is not your IQ. It is not even number.

Goleman claimed that EI would contribute to success at home, at school and at work. He further expresses that less rudeness or aggressiveness will be seen more among youth was high EI and right decisions about 'drugs, smoking and sex' is associated with it.

EI is an advantage in any area of life, whether in intimate relationships and romance or picking up the non-verbal rules that help success of organisational politics.

According to Elies et al, more than 20 formal programmes in the entire curriculum of the school has been tested. The ideas used in these programmes are very much closed to the current models of EI-Then Mayer and Salovey feel that "More emotionally intelligent individuals might succeed at making these workers feel better, at communicating in interesting ways and at designing projects that involve infusing products with feelings and aesthetics." It is however, important to note that the above prediction are based on different theories of EI.

Applicability of EI in the Indian Context

Models of EI originated in the West, but it can be applied effectively in the Indian context as we have seen enough evidence of the usefulness of several measures of IQ and personality, which also originated in the West.

However, one has to take several precautions in such venture. Translations of scales standardised in foreign culture or just because the items are understandable in India, do not mean that the conceptions of EI or the most culturally relevant items to measure these conceptions would be the same across cultures.

Similarly, equal means for different ethnic groups do not guarantee that the EI measure is equally appropriate or valid across cultural or ethnic groups. It is very much important to provide reliability and validity within each group.

In India, it is also worth examining whether, the factors in the models of EI can remain together, under the umbrella of a global EI. The factors should correlate moderately if such a global EI has to be established, because if the correlations are high then will indicate that the factors are more or less the same.

Again, if the factors are slightly correlated the difference among the factors are in such a way that they cannot be clubbed together to explain individual differences. However, correlational studies might not be enough to explain the existence of such a phenomenon in real life world.

PASS Theory by Das, Kar and Parrila

The Planning, Attention-Arousal, Simultaneous and Successive (PASS) theory of intelligence, first proposed in 1975 and later elaborated by Das, Nagliberi and Kirby (1994) and Das, Kar and Parrila (1996) challenged 'g-theory' on the grounds that the brain is made up of interdependent, but separate, functional systems.

The PASS theory of intelligence proposes that cognition is organised in three systems and four processes. The first process is *Planning*, which involves executive functions responsible for controlling and organising behaviour, selecting and constructing strategies and monitoring performance.

The second is the *Attention* process, responsible for maintaining arousal levels and alertness and ensuring focus on relevant stimuli. The two processes, *Simultaneous* processing and *Successive* processing is engaged for determination of the relationship between items integration into whole units of information is required. Example of this include recognising figures, such as a triangle within a circle *v/s* a circle within a triangle. Successive processing is required for organising separate items in a sequence such as remembering a sequence of words or actions exactly in the order in which they had just been presented, these four processes are hypothesised to functions of four areas of the brain.

Planning is broadly located in the front part of our brains, the frontal lobe. Attention and arousal are combined functions of the frontal lobe and the lower parts of the cotex, although the parietal lobes are also involved in attention as well. Simultaneous processing and successive processing occur in the posterior region or the back of the brain.

Assessment of PASS Processes

The PASS theory provides the theoretical framework for a measurement instrumental called the Das-Naglieri Cognitive Assessment System (CAS) published in 1997, the test is designed to provide a nuanced assessment of the individuals intellectual functioning, providing information about cognitive strengths and weaknesses in each of the four processes.

This emphasis on processes (rather than abilities) is said to make it useful for differential diagnosis; unlike traditional full scale IQ tests, the PASS is capable of diagnosing learning disabilities and Attention Deficit Disorder, Autism, Mental Retardation Cognitive Change in Ageing and Down Syndrome and more recently changes due to brain impairment in stroke, its usefulness as a theory and measurement instrument for planning and decision-making in management has also been demonstrated.

Remediation and Cognitive Enhancement

One unusual property of the PASS theory of cognitive processes is that it has proven useful for both intellectual assessment (*e.g.* the CAS) and educational intervention. The theory provides the theoretical framework for the **PASS Reading Enhancement Programme (PREP)**, a remediation curriculum designed to improve the planning, attention and information processing strategies that underlie reading. A related school readiness program aims at improving the foundations of cognitive process (COGENT) in preparation for schooling. Both are evidence based intervention programs.

Creativity

Creativity, we tend to assume, is different from intelligence it is inborn, mysterious, unanalysable, unteachable. To see, if this is true, let us look at what psychologists have learned about creativity by studying the work of artists, inventors and scientists by studying creativity in the laboratory. **Perkins** argues that "Creativity products are novel and successful in achieving their purpose." Novelty is what makes creative problem solving different from ordinary problem solving. *Perkins* suggests that the effort to do something novel is infact the main feature that distinguishes creative genius from ordinary intelligence. Invention is not something that just happens without making the effort and most of us do not make the effort very often.

Test of Creativity

Two approaches have been used by psychologists to test creativity. The first approach was inspired by the work of Guilford, who tried to classify mental abilities in much the same way that chemical elements are classified in the periodic table. One of his classification was divergent production, a category of tasks, for which there are many 'right' answers, so that the tester might not know them all in advance. The question, 'How many uses can you think of a brick?'

It is a typical divergent production item. Answers can be scored for appropriateness and quantity.

Another approach is that of Mednick, who argued that "truely creative person is not merely one, who produces a great variety of ideas." Rather, says Mednick, true creativity is the ability to think of an idea *i.e.* improbable, unusual or remote, yet exactly right for the situation. Mednick devised a word-finding test called the Remote Associates Test (RAT).

According to **Wallach**, "what does predict creative accomplishment is past creative accomplishment. If graduate schools want to admit students, who will make creative contributions to some field, they would be wise to admit students, who have already done something creative in the field."

Stages of Creative Thought

It is ironic that no dominant theory has emerged during the past twenty years that might unify the desperate and sometimes conflicting studies of creativity. The absence of a unified theory points out both the inherent difficulty of the topic and the lack of widespread scientific attention nevertheless, creativity is widely heralded as an important part of everyday life and education.

A long ago in the history of cognitive psychology, *Wallas described the creative process as having four sequential stages*

(i) **Preparation** Formulating the problem and making initial attempts to solve it.
(ii) **Incubation** Leaving the problem while, considering other things.
(iii) **Illumination** Achieving insight to the problem.
(iv) **Verification** Testing and/or carrying out the solution.

Wallas's four-stage model of the creative process has given us a conceptual framework to analyse creativity, *which are as follows*

Stage 1: Preparation

This stage prepares a person to acquire. The relevant and necessary facts, experience and skills for the task and to ask the right question.

Poincare mentioned in his notes that he had been working intensively on the problem for 15 days. During that period he seemed to have thought of several tentative solutions, which he tried out and for one reason or another, discarded. However, to suggest that the period of preparation was 15 days is, of course, wrong. All of his professional life as a mathematician and probably a good portion of his childhood could be considered part of the preparation stage.

Stage 2: Incubation

In this stage one leaves the problem alone to develop in the unconscious mind. **Pornos**, offers several hypothesis about the incubation phase. One suggestion is that the incubation period allows us to recover from the fatigue associated with problem solving. Also, interruption of an arduous task may allow us to forget in appropriate approaches to a problem. We have already seen that functional fixedness can impede problem solving and it is possible that during incubation people forget old, unsuccessful solutions to problems another reason incubation may help in the creative process is that during this period we may actually work on the problem unconsciously.

Stage 3: Illumination

In this stage a person gets a crucial idea or any sudden appearance or insight, when relaxing or dreaming. Incubation does not always lead to illumination when it does, however, the sensation is unmistakable. Suddenly, the light bulb is turned on. The creative person may feel a rush of excitement as all the bits and pieces of ideas fall into place.

All of the pertinent ideas complement each other and irrelevant thoughts are discarded. This history of creative breakthroughs is replete with example of the illumination stage. This discovery of the structure of the DNA molecule, the composition of the benzene ring the invention of the telephone, the conclusion of a symphony and the plot of a novel are all examples of how a moment of illumination has flooded the mind with a creative solution to a vexing old problem.

Stage 4 : Verification

Following the euphoria that sometimes accompanies an insightful discovery, the idea is tested. This is the mopping up stage of the creative processes, in which the creative product is examined to verify its legitimacy. Often a solution first thought to be creative is only an intellectual fool's gold, when examined carefully. This stage may be rather brief as in the case of rechecking one's calculations or seeing whether an invention works; however in some cases verification may require a lifetime of study, testing and retesting.

View of Torrance on Creativity

From the evidence accumulated in the Minnesota studies of creative thinking in the early school years it seems that much in our present educational system tends to alienate boys. Especially the highly creative ones, from their peers and teachers. Educators might do well to consider giving parallel streatment to the development of the thinking abilities alongwith the development of the memory and conformity to behavioural norms.

This would involve, among other things, rewarding creative thinking. If boys in the early school years were rewarded for some of the things, in which they appear to excel, they might possibly be more willing to master some of the language and other conforming skills about, which there is concern. *According to Torrence, there are characteristics of creativity. Children show*

- They have reputation for having wild and silly ideas;
- Work characterised by its productivity of ideas of beaten track;
- humour and playfulness.

Principles

He presumed the following factors regarding highly creative children

- Sanctions against divergency.
- Creative children may not be well rounded.
- Creative children prefer to learn on their own.
- Creative children like to attempt difficult task.
- Creative children are searching for a purpose.

Torrance suggests that following five principles, which believed that can be applied to child.

Be Respectful to Unusual Questions

The first, principle, is 'be respectful of unusual questions. Nothing is more rewarding to a child, who tasks questions than to find the answer to his questions. Questions reflect a 'mind hunger' and this hunger must be satisfied lest the mind be starved. Although the need should be met immediately, these is much that we can do to enrich the period between the question and the answer.

This means that we need to teach them the skills of inquiry. The parents or teacher, who sets out to be respectful of the questions children ask must be prepaired for some socks, children will ask many questions, which they cannot answers. This should be accepted as normal and desirable. Teachers and parents should not feel threatened and should find enjoyment in a mutual searching for solutions to the questions children raise.

Be Respectful to the Unusual Ideas of Children

This second principle is 'be respectful of the unusual ideas of children' children, who are stimulated by the creative approach will see many relationships and significances that their children miss. They will express ideas, which their teachers will not be able to evaluate. Thus, it is extremely difficult for the teacher properly to reward such thinking and it is our more creative talented youngsters, who suffer most such unrewarded effort.

Show Children that their Ideas have Value

The third principle is 'Show children that their ideas have value.' The trouble is that many teachers and other adults do not feel that children are capable of thinking of ideas that have value. Such individuals obviously will not be able to reward creative thinking in children. He would only suggest that such individuals be on the alert for a while to recognise new ideas among children. Children can be shown that their ideas have value, if communicate them to proper grounds or individuals, if we display them, if we give credit for them and the like.

Provide Opportunities for Self-Initiated Learning and Give Credit for It

An old principle of learning is, "Excite and direct the self-activities of the learner and tell him nothing that he can learn for himself." One mark of the highly creative individual is his self starting ability. The strong curiosity of the child and his exploratory tendencies suggest that all or almost all children have this self-starting ability. The problem of parents and teacher is to keep it alive.

Provide for Periods of Non-Evaluated Practice or Learning

We do not have to evaluate everything. There needs to be periods, when the individual can learn without threat of being evaluated. External evaluation is always a threat and creates a need for defensiveness. This makes some portion of the individual's experiencing or sensing denied to awareness. Thus, there is lacking the openness, which is so necessary in the production of new ideas we have conducted experiments to try to valid this principle.

Torrance Test on Creative Thinking (TTCT)

Like many other creative tests, the Torrance test measure a variety of areas or aspects of creative thinking. Scores on the TTCT can be obtained in each of these areas. However, like individual ability tests for the handicaped and tests of learning disability, the TTCT does not quite meet the standards of the Binet and Wechsler scales in terms of standardisation, reliability and validity.

In sum, the Torrance test typical of creativity tests. Applied practitioners demand such a tool for their work and although in consistent available data reflect its merit and fine potential. As with so many other tests, however, more work is needed. Results from the new creativity tests must be viewed as tentative and with caution.

Guilfords's View on Creativity

Guilford gave most consideration to the abilities and other traits of individuals that make some of them creative and some not. He assumed that these traits should help us to recognise, which persons are likely to have the potentialities of becoming creativity productive. The same knowledge, should help us in taking steps that should increase creative output in ourselves and in others and other steps that may remove obstacles in the way of creative productivity.

Basic Traits and Creativity

There are a number of approaches to the investigation of the traits or characteristics, in which creative individuals are most likely to excel. Some investigators appear to regard the phenomenon of creativity as a single dimension of personality. He viewed that the creative disposition is made up of many components and that its composition depends upon where you find it. Practically all investigators recognise that there are many potentially contributing conditions.

According to **Guilford**, "creative individuals think with greater fluency, with more flexibility and with greater originality. The tests designed to measure fluency present very simple tasks and the quantity of output determines the scores." Flexibility in thinking means a change of some kind a change in the meaning, interpretation or use of something, a change in understanding of the task a change of strategy in doing the task or a change in direction of thinking, which may mean a new interpretation of the goal.

Guilford gives closer attention to the various factors of fluency, flexibility, originality and elaboration.

Fluency Factors

It turns out that in verbal tests alone there are three differentiated fluency factors.

(i) **Ideational fluency** has to do with the rate of generation of a quantity of ideas. The idea produced may be as simple as a single word, as complex as the title for a picture or a story or as phrases and short sentences that convey unitary thoughts. It is easy to see where an operation such as that in tests of ideational fluency fits into problem-solving of many kinds.

(ii) Another kind of fluency is called *associational fluency*. It pertains to the completion of relationships, in distinction from the factor of ideational fluency, which involves giving ideas that fits a class. The factor of associational fluency may have more general utility.

(iii) A third kind of fluency is called *expressional fluency*. It has to do with the facile construction of sentences. We ask the examine to write as many four word sentences as he can, all different, with no world used more than once.

Flexibility Factors

One type of flexibility Guilford recognised as *spontaneous flexibility* because the tests that measure, it do not even suggest that the examine be flexible, without his knowing it, he can make a good score if he varies his kinds of responses. If we tell the examinee to list all the uses he can think of for a common brick, the total number of uses listed is a good score for his status on the factor of identical fluency.

But we also score his performance in terms of the number of times he changes category of uses. *For example* The person who responds with build a house, build a school, build a factory etc. does not change his class of uses.

The person who makes a low spontaneous flexibility score is rigid in the sense that he perseverates within one or a very few classes.

A second kind of flexibility has been called *adaptive flexibility*, for the reason that in tests in which it was first found, the examinee, to succeed, must make changes of some kind changes in interpretation of the task, in approach or strategy or in possible solutions.

Originality Factor

The current interpretation of the factor of **originality** is that it is adaptive flexibility in dealing with verbal information.

Elaboration Factor

In the course of the investigations of abilities involved in planning, he proposed other kind of ability called *elaboration*. In one test, given the base outlines of a plan, the examinee is asked to produce the detailed steps needed to make the plan work. The more details, he adds, the better is his score. It was eventually recognised that the abilities of fluency, flexibility and elaboration are similar in that the tests of them call for a variety of answers.

Relationship Between Creativity and Intelligence

The relationship between intelligence and creativity is that both of them are functions of the brain that process information to determine a solution or an answer to a problem. Intelligence and creativity are different abilities but they are closely linked with each other. The general belief is that people with high IQ are generally more creative and people who are highly creative have high IQ's. This is'nt necessarily true. Following theories will shed light on relationship between intelligence and creativity.

Getzel's View on Creativity and Intelligence

For many years, it was assumed that creativity and intelligence were closely related. The incidence of highly creative individuals such as Churchill, Edison and Einstein, who at sometimes experience difficulty in school.

One of the most widely published studies were done by Getzel and Jackson, who produced evidence that creativity and intelligence were largely independent traits.

Their study was first systematic study to distinguish between creativity and intelligence was on adolescents. This study attracted wide attention among scientists and the later researchers constantly remembered the results of the study. Creativity in particular mental ability, which is clear from the paper and pencils tests of the adolescents. These tests included verbal and numeral science object space relationship etc. According to these studies creativity depends upon the number, novelty and variety of responses to a given stimuli. They maintained that traditional intelligence tests measure convergent and traditional mental process involving memory. As against this creative tests measure divergent, introvert and creative mental processes. Infact, these two processes are so intimately related that it is difficult to find out persons who are higher in one and not, so in the other.

In the course of this study Getzel and Jackson selected two groups of subjects, in which one group the level of intelligence was high, but creativity was not so much present. In the other group, the level of creativity was high, but the level of intelligence was not a high as that (this study led to conclusion that the traditional tests of intelligence are not sufficient tests of mental processes), low correlation was found between creativity and intelligence.

The scientists, however, maintained that creativity and intelligence are different since, they observed that among the creative and intelligence group there was a clear distinction of personal values, imaginative productivity, aims of career and the family background. This study has been widely criticised on the basis of its method and other factors.

Study by Getzel and Jackson

There were five creativity measures some of which were taken or adopted from test made up by Gilford and by Cattell, an a others specially constructed by Getzel and Jackson.

The measures as follows

- **Word Association** Meaning and use required of common words, with multiple meanings example, bold, sack. Scored both for number of defination and number of radically different meanings.
- **Uses for Things** As many different uses as possible to be given for objects such as brick, paper chip. Scored for number of uses and originality of uses.
- **Hidden Shape** It in simple geometrical figures, each followed by four complex figures. Subject required to find the geometric form hidden in the more complex pattern.
- **Fables** Four fables were presented, in which the last line were missing. The subject was required to provide three different endings to each stories. One moralistic, one humorous and one sad.
- **Make up Problems** Four complex paragraphs containing many numerical statements were presented. Subject required to make up as many mathematical problem as possible from them. Scored on number from appropriateness and originality of problems.

Interesting and important similarity and differences were found by Getzels and Jackson between the high creativity and high IQ groups. Most striking, perhaps was the finding that the high creativity group equal the high IQ group in scholastic achievement inspite of having an average IQ 23 points lower. There were high correlation between some of the individual tests and both verbal and numerical achievement for the whole samples of experiment.

The three tests, which showed up best in this way were word association, make up problems and hidden shapes in that order. Getzel and Jackson attempted to find out whether this unexpectedly high degree of scholastic achievement on the part of the high creativity group could be ascribed to higher strength of motivation. They found however, no difference between the two groups on Mc Clelland's need for achievement measures, therefore concluded that the explanations lay not in any motivational difference, but the predictive limitations of the conventional intelligence test. Another striking findings in this study was that teachers appeared to approve more strongly of the high IQ group than of the high creativity group.

A third respect, in which the groups were found to differ was in their attitudes to success in adult life. In the high IQ group, the correspondence between the qualities they valued for themselves and the qualities, which they thought would be conductive to success in adult life was quite close.

Wallach and Kogan's View

Further light on these conflicting findings has also been thrown by a recent extensive research report by Wallach and Kogan. They begin by reviewing earlier reports of the distinction between intelligence and creativity, of Getzel and Jackson. They made their conclusion from these survey is that the distinction between creativity and intelligence has not been adequately supported by empirical evidence and that the correlation between measures of creativity or generally lower than those between a typical test of creativity and one of intelligence.

Wallach and Kogan report a fair degree of success in establishing separate measures of creativity and intelligence in these conditions

- **High Creativity High Intelligence** These children can exercise within themselves both control and freedom, both adult like and child like kinds of behaviour.
- **High Creativity and Low Intelligence** These children are in angry conflict with themselves and with their school environment and are be set by feelings of unworthiness and in adequacy. In a stress-free context, however, they can blossom forth cognitively.
- **Low Creativity and High Intelligence** These children can be described as addicted to school achievement. Academic failure would be perceived by them as catastrophic, so that they must continually strive for academic excellence in order to avoid the possibility of pain.
- **Low Creativity and Low Intelligence** Basically bewildered these children engage in various defensive maneuver ranging from useful adaptation such as intensively social activity to regression such as passivity or psychomatic symptoms. Thus, work progressed from the definition and operationalisation of two types of cognitive activity to an investigation of their correlates in such areas as observable social and achievement relevant behaviours, ways of forming concepts, pshysiognomic sensitivities and self described levels of general anxiety, text anxiety and defensiveness.

EXAM BASED QUESTIONS

1 David Wechsler defines intelligences as
(a) the psychological potential to solve problems.
(b) what intelligence tests measure.
(c) being able to behave in a consistent way.
(d) the global capacity of act Purposefully, think rationally and deal effectively with the environment.

2 The belief that intelligence is a general ability is a result of the work of
(a) Binet
(b) Gardner
(c) Sternberg
(d) Spearman

3 The heritability estimate for intelligence, according to Jensen is between
(a) 0.10 to 0.25
(b) 0.30 to 0.40
(c) 0.60 to 0.80
(d) 0.90 to 0.95

4 Jensen's work on heritability of intelligence has come in for criticism for
(a) fudging of data.
(b) using inappropriate research design.
(c) drawing conclusions on the basis of culturally biased tests.
(d) using inappropriate statistics.

5 The concept of Inspection Time (IT) in relation to intellion to intelligence was provided by
(a) AR Jensen (b) CR Brand
(c) HJ Eyesenck (d) S Sternberg

6 Improvements in nutrition of the expectant mothers or improvements in obstetrical care can directly improve the child's
(a) general intelligence
(b) fluid intelligence
(c) crystallised intelligence
(d) specific intelligence

7 Which one of the following is the correct chronological order of theorists, who proposed their theories of intelligence ?
(a) Spearman, Jensen, Piaget, Guilford
(b) Spearman, Piaget, Guilford, Jensen
(c) Piaget, Spearman, Guilford, Jensen
(d) Guilford, Jensen, Spearman, Piaget

8 Reasoning involves the operation of reading (the recognition, knowledge, memory of words), the contents of the passage being read (the meanings of the words themselves) and the products of the reading (the understanding that the passage provides). This approach is most probably based on the intelligence theory known as
(a) Sternberg's triarchic theory
(b) Vernon's three kinds of intelligence : A, B and C
(c) Thurstone's theory of primary mental abilities
(d) Guilford's structure of intelligence model

9 Which one of the following theoretical foundations considers intelligence to be a 'genetic potentiality'?
(a) Intelligence B of Hebb
(b) Crystallised Intelligence of Cattell
(c) Fluid Intelligence of Cattell
(d) 'g' factor of Spearman

10 The notion that the Reaction Time (RT) is related to intelligence, was popularised by
(a) Cattell (b) Jensen
(c) Eysenck (d) Sternberg

11 Other name for Group Factor Theories is
(a) group intelligence (b) cube model
(c) structure of intellect (d) primary mental abilities

12 In terms of revised two factor theory, verbal comprehension consisting general knowledge vocabulary, similarities, etc is
(a) general factor (b) specific factor
(c) verbal factor (d) group factor

13 Which of the following is not the component of pass model?
(a) Planning
(b) Simultaneous scanning
(c) Attention
(d) Successive processing

14 Which of the following is not the component of product defined by Guilford?
(a) Unit (b) Class
(c) Symbol (d) Relations

15 Cattell's culture fair test is based on
(a) g factor (b) fluid intelligence
(c) crystallised intelligence (d) All of these

16 Who is considered as the father of Cybernetics?
(a) Waltzer (b) Margaret Mead
(c) Wiener (d) Lorenz

17 Contextual intelligence is given by
(a) Greenberg (b) Rassalang
(c) Sternberg (d) Gardner

18 EQ was popularised by
(a) Weiner (b) Gardner
(c) Goleman (d) None of these

19 Who view that intelligence is inherited?
(a) Francis Galton (b) Jensen
(c) Flunn (d) Thompson

20 Which one of the following statements is true in genotypic-phenotypic problems ?
(a) Genotypic factors alone influence intelligence while phenotypic factors influence personality traits
(b) Genotypic factors influence personality traits while ecological factors influence intelligence
(c) Neither genotypic nor phenotypic factors influence intelligence or personality traits
(d) Both genotypic and phenotypic factors influence intelligence and personality traits

21 What is the importance of correlation coefficient?
(a) It provide a measure of the strength of relationship between two variables
(b) It can help to pick up a strong variable
(c) It helps to compare between many variable
(d) It helps to eliminate the week variable

22 Even though identical twins tend to have very similar IQs, one usually scores slightly higher than the other. This is because intelligence is
(a) a part of one's inheritance
(b) a function of one's motivation and learning
(c) an outcome of the interaction of heredity and environment
(d) dependent on factors other than heredity and environment

23 With advanced computer technology Artificial Intelligence (AI) is as competent as human intelligence in solving complex problems. But in comparison to human intelligence AI is still lagging behind in
(a) information processing
(b) computing multi-variate analysis
(c) experiencing and understanding environment
(d) appreciating design works

24 Evoked potentials are larger, quicker and more complex in people with
(a) low IQ (b) average IQ
(c) high IQ (d) hearing impairment

25 Which of the following is not a creative thought according to Wallas?
(a) Preparation (b) Illumination
(c) Certification (d) Verification

26 The study of creativity starts from four major foci. Which of the following is not a foci?
(a) Creative people (b) Creative process
(c) Creative thought (d) Product of creativity

27 According to Perkins, which one of the following is not includes in creative invention?
(a) Directed remembering (b) Unconscious processing
(c) Contrary recognition (d) Noticing

28 Which one of the following is the correct sequence of steps involved in creative thinking?
(a) Preparation, Incubation, Inspiration, Verification
(b) Inspiration, Incubation, Preparation, Verification
(c) Observation, Concentration, Inspiration, Verification
(d) Incubation, Preparation, Inspiration, Verification

29 Graham Wallach articulated the traditional view of the creative process as four ordered stages. Which one of the following is the correct order of these states?
(a) Incubation, Illumination, Preparation, Verification
(b) Illumination, Preparation, Verification, Incubation
(c) Preparation, Incubation, Illumination, Verification
(d) Preparation, Incubation, Verification, Illumination

30 Artistic children frequently show
(a) unusual and repetitive responses of environment
(b) high amount of creativity
(c) hyper activity
(d) low degree of emotional control

31 An effective method of stimulating creativity in class room situations involves
(a) emphasis on children's divergent thinking
(b) supportive behaviour of the teacher
(c) emphasis on convergent behaviour
(d) giving sufficient freedom to the students

32 The strategy of creative thinking that emphasises free wheeling of ideas as well as deferred evaluation is known as
(a) synectics (b) attributes listing
(c) brainstorming (d) morphological analysis

33 Incubation, a stage in creative thinking, involves
(a) new solution
(b) unconscious thought-process
(c) insight process
(d) verbal thinking

34 Some of the significant contribution to creativity testing came from
(a) Medrick and Medrick (b) Getzels and Jackson
(c) Wallach and Kogan (d) Barron

35 Who among the following as identified Boundary Pushing, Inventing, Boundary Breaking and Aesthetic Organising as four types of creativity?
(a) Irving Taylor (b) B Ghiselin
(c) W Eisner (d) F Barron

36 Which one of the following statements indicates true relationship between intelligence and creativity ?
(a) Intelligence and creativity have high correlation.
(b) Intelligence and creativity have low correlation.
(c) Intelligence and creativity are moderately correlated.
(d) Intelligence and creativity have higher correlation at lower levels than at higher levels of intelligence.

37 Which of the following pairs is/are incorrectly matched?

1. Emotional Intelligence : Munn
2. Spiritual Intelligence : Goleman
3. Mesital testing : Schuman

Codes
(a) 1 and 2 (b) 2 and 3
(c) All of these (d) None of these

38 Which of the following pairs is/are incorrectly matched?

1. Deviation IQ : Wechsler
2. Jean Piaget : Sensory motor stage theory
3. Vernon : Hierarchical theory of intelligence

Codes
(a) 2 and 3 (b) 1 and 3
(c) All of these (d) None of these

39 Which of the following pairs is/are incorrectly matched?

1. Fernald : Emotional Intelligence
2. Bhatia : Giftedness
3. Polarisation : Decision-making in groups tend to show regular shift

Codes
(a) Only 1 (b) Only 2
(c) Only 3 (d) None of these

40 Which of the following pairs is/are incorrectly matched?

1. Thorndike : CAVD tests of intelligence
2. Piaget : Logical reasoning
3. Group cohesiveness : The measure of how attractive a group to its member

Codes
(a) 1 and 2 (b) 2 and 3
(c) 1 and 3 (d) All of these

41 Consider the following statements

1. Highly creative boys exhibit more uniqueness and originality in their drawing than highly creative girls.
2. Highly creative boys have more internal tension than girls.

Which of the statements given above is/are correct?
(a) Only 1 (b) Only 2
(c) Both 1 and 2 (d) None of these

42 Consider the following statements

1. Creative children have repetation for having wild and silly ideas.
2. The work of creative children are characterised by its productivity of ideas of beaten track.

Which of the statements given above is/are correct?
(a) Only 1 (b) Only 2
(c) Both 1 and 2 (d) None of these

43 Consider the following statements

1. Torrance test of creativity thinking is the most popular among creative test.
2. The Torrence test meet the standard of the Binet and Wechsler scale.

Which of the statements given above is/are correct?
(a) Only 1 (b) Only 2
(c) Both 1 and 2 (d) None of these

44 Consider the following statements

1. Creative disposition depends upon many components.
2. Creative individual think with greater fluency, with more flexibility.

Which of the statements given above is/are correct?
(a) Only 1 (b) Only 2
(c) Both 1 and 2 (d) None of these

45 Which of the following pairs is/are correctly matched?

1. Ideational fluency : Quantity of ideas
2. Associational fluency : Facile construction of sentence
3. Expressional fluency : Completion of relationship

Codes
(a) Only 1 (b) Only 2
(c) Only 3 (d) 1 and 3

46 Which of the following pairs is/are correctly matched?

1. Fluency : The ability to produce large ideas
2. Flexibility : The ability to produce uncommon response
3. Originality : The ability to produce a variety of ideas

Codes
(a) Only 1 (b) 1 and 2
(c) 1, 2 and 3 (d) 1 and 3

47 Which of the following pairs are incorrectly matched?

1. Guilford : Divergent thinking
2. Getzel : Measure of creativity
3. Jackson : Word association test

Codes
(a) 1 and 2 (b) 2 and 3
(c) 1 and 3 (d) All of these

48 Which of the following pairs is/are correctly matched?

1. Guilford : Cognition
2. Johnson : Divergent thinking
3. Thomson : Group factor

Codes
(a) 1 and 2
(b) 2 and 3
(c) Only 3
(d) All of the above

49 Which of the following pairs is/are correctly matched?

1. Thorndike : Anarchic Theory
2. Spearman : Bifactor Theory
3. Roger : Electic Theory

Codes
(a) 1and 2 (b) 2 and 3
(c) 1 and 3 (d) Only 3

50 Which of the following pairs is/are correctly matched?

1. Kofka	:	Fluid intelligency
2. Thurstone	:	Harmony mental ability
3. Kelley	:	Multifactor theory

Codes
(a) 1 and 2 (b) 2 and 3
(c) 1 and 3 (d) None of these

51 Which of the following pairs is/are correctly matched?

1. Vernon	:	X factor
2. Cattell	:	Crystallised intelligence
3. Sternberg	:	Triarchic theory

Codes
(a) Only 1 (b) Only 2
(c) Only 3 (d) All of these

52 Arrange the following in chronological order.
1. Gardner 2. Guilford
3. Hunt
Codes
(a) 1, 2, 3 (b) 2, 1, 3 (c) 1, 3, 2 (d) 2, 3, 1

53 Arrange the following in chronological order.
1. Sternberg 2. Mehrabian
3. Persaud
Codes
(a) 1, 2, 3 (b) 3, 2, 1 (c) 1, 3, 2 (d) 3, 1, 2

54 Arrange the following in chronological order.
1. Mayer 2. Goleman
3. Thurstone
Codes
(a) 1, 2, 3 (b) 3, 2, 1
(c) 1, 3, 2 (d) 2, 1, 3

55 Arrange the following in chronological order.
1. Salovey 2. Geher
3. Mayer et al
Codes
(a) 1, 2, 3 (b) 3, 2, 1 (c) 2, 1, 3 (d) 2, 3, 1

56 What is the correct sequence of stages in creative thinking?
1. Illumination 2. Preparation
3. Incubation 4. Revision
5. Evaluation
Codes
(a) 1, 3, 2, 5, 4 (b) 3, 2, 1, 5, 4
(c) 5, 2, 1, 4, 3 (d) 2, 3, 1, 5, 4

57 Consider the following statements
1. Fluid intelligence reflects the capacity or potentiality.
2. Crystallised intelligence is the capacity or potentiality translated into actual ability as a result of practice.

Which of the statements given above is/are correct?
(a) Only 1 (b) Only 2
(c) Both 1 and 2 (d) Neither 1 nor 2

58 Consider the following statements
1. Spearman and Thurstone were measurement psychologist.
2. Cattle had a more inclusive and total perspective view of human behaviour.

Which of the statements given above is/are correct?
(a) Only 1 (b) Only 2
(c) Both 1 and 2 (d) Neither 1 nor 2

59 Consider the following statements
1. According to Jensen, "Intelligence is essentially another activity or function of the individual like blood pressure, temperature, etc.
2. Intelligence test provides accurate result.

Which of the statements given above is/are correct?
(a) Only 1 (b) Only 2
(c) Both 1 and 2 (d) Neither 1 nor 2

60 Consider the following statements
1. Guilford's concept of intellect is not just an ability, but a major functional unit of the mind.
2. Intellect is a part of functional unit of the mind which deals with problems like perceptual thinking, learning, problem solving etc.

Which of the statements given above is/are correct?
(a) Only 1 (b) Only 2
(c) Both 1 and 2 (d) Neither 1 nor 2

61 Which of the following pairs is/are correctly matched?

1. Guilford	:	Divergent production model
2. Mednick	:	Remote associates test
3. Poin care	:	Illumination test

Codes
(a) Only 1 (b) 2 and 3
(c) 1 and 2 (d) 1 and 3

62 Consider the following statements.
1. Guilford classify mental abilities the same way chemical element classified in periodic table.
2. Mednick said that true creativity is the ability to think a remote idea.

Which of the statements given above is/are correct?
(a) Only 1 (b) Only 2
(c) 1 and 2 (d) None of these

63 Consider the following statements
1. Breadth factor of intelligences include general information, vocabulary.
2. Breadth depends on a person's experience, exposure and opportunities.

Which of the statements given above is/are correct?
(a) Only 1 (b) Only 2
(c) Both 1 and 2 (d) Neither 1 nor 2

64 Consider the following statements
1. Environmental influences, as well as attitudes and interests acquired by an individual in the course of life have no influence on the breadth of a person's intelligence.
2. Attitude factor of intelligence is more innate and less dependent on environmental influences.

Which of the statements given above is/are correct?
(a) Only 1 (b) Only 2
(c) Both 1 and 2 (d) Neither 1 nor 2

65 Which of the following pairs is/are correctly matched?
Guilford's three category of intellect
1. Operation : Capability like thinking
2. Contents : Idea and meaning
3. Product : Image, word and symbol

Codes
(a) 1 and 2 (b) Only 1
(c) 2 and 3 (d) 1, 2 and 3

66 Consider the following statements
1. Intelligence is involved more in actions that are not learnt and not repetitive.
2. Intelligent action calling for a solution to a problem and adopt to environmental condition.

Which of the statements given above is/are correct?
(a) Only 1
(b) Only 2
(c) Both 1 and 2
(d) Neither 1 nor 2

67 Consider the following statements
1. Cattell's fluid intelligence is a basic capacity to analyse, remember, understand and arrive at inductive and deductive finding.
2. Cattell's crystallised intelligence takes the form of specific abilities like verbal ability, numerical ability.

Which of the statements given above is/are correct?
(a) Only 1 (b) Only 2
(c) Both 1 and 2 (d) Neither 1 nor 2

68 Consider the following statements
1. Crystallised intelligence is "channelised or conditioned fluid intelligence" developed as a result of experience.
2. People with less fluid intelligence are likely to gain more of crystallised intelligence.

Which of the statements given above is/are correct?
(a) Only 1 (b) Only 2
(c) Both 1 and 2 (d) Neither 1 nor 2

69 Consider the following statements
1. 'g' is involved in apprehension of experience, education of relations and education of correlates.
2. 'g' is innate and influenced by age, sex, heredity etc.

Which of the statements given above is/are correct?
(a) Only 1 (b) Only 2
(c) Both 1 and 2 (d) Neither 1 nor 2

70 Which of the following pairs are correctly matched?
1. Numericalability : Ability to deal with numbers
2. Reasoningability : The ability to apply logic
3. Spatial ability : Ability to organise space

Codes
(a) 1 and 2 (b) 2 and 3
(c) 1 and 3 (d) 1, 2 and 3

71 Which of the following pairs is correctly matched?
1. Verbal fluency : The ability to understand material presented in the form of words.
2. Verbal comprehension : Competence in language and use of words.
3. Perceptual ability : The ability to perceive situation.

Codes
(a) Only 1 (b) Only 2
(c) Only 3 (d) Neither 1 nor 2

72 Consider the following statements
1. In brainstorming, one person's idea is based upon another person's idea (Osborn).
2. Taylor et al supported the idea of Osborn.

Which of the statements given above is/are correct?
(a) Only 1 (b) Only 2
(c) Both 1 and 2 (d) None of these

73 Consider the following statements
1. The 'g' factor depend's on the general cortical or neural energy at the disposal of the individual.
2. The 'g' factor doesn't play in activities called neogenetic.

Which of the statements given above is/are correct?
(a) Only 1 (b) Only 2
(c) Both 1 and 2 (d) Neither 1 nor 2

74 Consider the following statements
1. The neogenetic activity depends less on memory.
2. Role of cerebral activity becomes less and less with practice.

Which of the statements given above is/are correct?
(a) Only 1 (b) Only 2
(c) Both 1 and 2 (d) Neither 1 nor 2

75 Emotional intelligence as personality characteristic requires people to have, which of the following abilities?

1. Ability to handle anger
2. Ability to manage anxiety
3. Ability to understand others feelings

Select the correct answer using the codes given below

(a) 1, 2 and 3 (b) 1 and 2
(c) 2 and 3 (d) 1 and 3

76 Which of the following abilities are measured in tests of creativity?

1. Fantasy 2. Flexibility
3. Originality 4. Elaboration
5. Colourfulness of imagery

Codes

(a) 1, 2 and 4 (b) 1, 3 and 5
(c) 3, 4 and 5 (d) 2, 3 and 4

77 Consider the following statements

1. Contextual factor have no direct effect on the thought process of the problem solver.
2. Among the two similar solution in the problem solvers mind, one is highly creative and one is hardly creative.

Which of the statements given above is/are correct?

(a) Only 1 (b) Only 2
(c) Both 1 and 2 (d) None of these

78 Which of the following pairs are correctly matched?

	Authors	Domain
1.	Cattell	Fluid intelligence
2.	Spearman	Principles of cognition
3.	Guilford	Structure of intellect
4.	Raven	Infant

Codes

(a) 1 and 2 (b) 2 and 3
(c) 1 and 3 (d) 3 and 4

79 Consider the following statements

The exact role of genetic factors in determining intelligence is hard to establish because

1. one cannot say much on the basis of a study of one or two genes.
2. controlled studies on human beings are not easy to conduct.
3. very few identical twins are available for such studies.

Which of the statements given above is/are correct?

(a) 1,2 and 3 (b) 2 and 3
(c) Only 1 (d) 1 and 2

80 Consider the following areas included in the test of crystallised intelligence comprise

1. Verbal skills
2. Numerical skills
3. Rote memory
4. Ability to notice visual details

Select the correct answer using the codes given below

(a) 1 and 2 (b) 3 and 4
(c) 1 and 3 (d) 1, 2 and 3

81 Which of the following pairs is/are not correctly matched?

1. Cattell	:	Structure of intellect
2. Spearman	:	Principles of cognition
3. Guilford	:	Infant scales
4. Raven	:	Fluid intelligence

Codes

(a) 1, 2 and 3 (b) 2, 3 and 4
(c) 1, 3 and 4 (d) Only 2

82 Which of the following pairs are correctly matched?

1. Sternberg	:	Practical intelligence
2. Newton	:	Creative intelligence
3. Einstein	:	Experiential intelligence

Codes

(a) 1 and 2
(b) 2 and 3
(c) All of the above
(d) None of the above

Directions (Q. Nos. 83-95) *In the questions given below are two statements labelled as Assertion (A) and Reason (R). In the content of the two statements, which one of the following is correct?*

Codes

(a) Both A and R are true and R is the correct explanation of A
(b) Both A and R are true, but R is not the correct explanation of A
(c) A is true, but R is false
(d) A is false, but R is true

83 **Assertion** (A) All creative children are children with exceptional intelligence.
Reason (R) Creativity generally involves an incubation period.

84 **Assertion** (A) According to Wallach and Kogan, creativity and intelligence are considered two distinct modes or thinking.
Reason (R) There are sub stantial correlation among intelligence tests as well as among creativity tasks while there are not substantial correlations between intelligence tests and creativity tasks.

85 **Assertion** (A) By using computer models in decision-making many problems in an organisation can be solved.
Reason (R) Thinking is complex informations processing and involves the use of symbols.

86 **Assertion** (A) Imagination is necessary element of creative activity in art and literature.
Reason (R) Imagination helps the individual to indulge in fancy dreams at a higher level.

87 **Assertion** (A) According to Torrance the highly creative child in a small group often work by himself.
Reason (R) Highly creative person is an independent thinker.

88 **Assertion** (A) There is a psychological difference between children high in intelligence and not concomitantly high in creativity.
Reason (R) According to Gelzel and Jackson creativity and intelligence were largely independent traits.

89 **Assertion** (A) A 40-years old man may have the same IQ as that of a 20 years old.
Reason (R) The 40-years old man could have been somewhat retarded to start with.

90 **Assertion** (A) Creative solution to problems are difficult to find in particular circumstance.
Reason (R) They require the synthesis of a large quantity of material.

91 **Assertion** (A) A creative solution to a problem depends on mental process of individual.
Reason (R) Contextual factor has no role in the solution

92 **Assertion** (A) In problem-solving, Artificial Intelligences (AI), uses all algorithmic means, but can never adopt non-algorithmic strategy.
Reason (R) AI lacks the faculty of experience and comprehension.

93 **Assertion** (A) The old people have remarkable vocabulary and storage of knowledge.
Reason (R) Crystallised intelligence of a person increases upto the age of seventy.

94 **Assertion** (A) The person, who makes a low spontaneous flexibility score is rigid.
Reason (R) He perseverates within one or a very few classes.

95 **Assertion** (A) Incubation period allows people to recover from the fatigue associated with problem-solving.
Reason (R) During incubation period, people forget old, unsuccessful solution to a problem.

96 Match the following

List I	List II
A. Normal triplett	1. Social facilitation
B. Social facilitation	2. Bicycle race
C. Cottrxell	3. Scientic measurement of intelligence
D. Alfred Binet	4. Evaluation apprehension theory

Codes

	A	B	C	D		A	B	C	D
(a)	1	2	3	4	(b)	1	2	4	3
(c)	2	4	3	1	(d)	4	2	1	3

97 Match the following

List I	List II
A. Mental age	1. Intelligence is the property of recombining our behaviour
B. Wells	2. Develop the most widely used test for adult
C. Wechsler	3. Absolute level of intelligence
D. Deviation IQ	4. Standard score

Codes

	A	B	C	D		A	B	C	D
(a)	1	3	2	4	(b)	3	1	2	4
(c)	2	4	1	3	(d)	4	3	1	2

98 Match the following

List I	List II
A. Random sequence of ideas without external cue or internal control	1. Fantasy
B. Thinking of another private and pleasant world with a theme of one's own	2. Free association
C. Thinking on a disturbed premise in an irrelevant way, but having special significance to the individual	3. Creative thinking
D. Thinking which has a theme, is rational and directly related to some problem in the external world	4. Delusion

Codes

	A	B	C	D		A	B	C	D
(a)	1	2	3	4	(b)	2	3	1	4
(c)	4	2	3	1	(d)	2	1	4	3

99 Match the following

List I	List II
A. Preparation	1. Ideas are ascertained, checked and reassured by themselves and by other confirming the validity of their hypothesis
B. Incubation	2. 'Happy thoughts' do not occur to lazy persons; they arise in well prepared and well stocked minds
C. Illumination	3. The climax of the process of creative thinking dawns the saving-guiding idea, which is the forerunner of the final solution
D. Verification	4. The 'hatching' period in creative thought process is characterised by restlessness and poorly coordinated activity accompanied by a feeling of unease and frustration through unconscious thought processes

Codes

	A	B	C	D		A	B	C	D
(a)	2	4	3	1	(b)	2	3	4	1
(c)	3	2	1	4	(d)	3	4	1	2

100 **Match the following**

	List I (Stages of Creative Thought)		List II (Conceptual idea)
A.	Illumination	1.	Insight itself
B.	Incubation	2.	Period away from the problem
C.	Verification	3.	Checking done
D.	Preparation	4.	Extensive, fruitless

Codes

	A	B	C	D		A	B	C	D
(a)	1	2	3	4	(b)	2	1	4	3
(c)	3	4	1	2	(d)	4	3	2	1

101 **Match the following**

	List I		List II
A.	Spatial Ability	1.	Ability to Perceive Situations
B.	Perceptual Ability	2.	Ability to organise Space
C.	Reasoning Ability	3.	Ability to deal with number
D.	Numerical Ability	4.	Ability to apply Logic

Codes

	A	B	C	D		A	B	C	D
(a)	2	1	4	3	(b)	1	2	3	4
(c)	4	3	1	2	(d)	3	4	2	1

102 **Match the following**

	List I (Throriests)		List II (Theory)
A.	Arthur Jensen	1.	Hierarchical model
B.	Francis Galton	2.	Information processing
C.	Philip E Vernon	3.	Reaction time studies
D.	Gardner H	4.	Multiple intelligence

Codes

	A	B	C	D		A	B	C	D
(a)	4	3	1	2	(b)	2	3	1	4
(c)	4	1	3	2	(d)	2	1	3	4

103 **Match the following**

	List I (Theories of Intelligence)		List II (Psychologists)
A.	Two factor theory	1.	Thurstone
B.	Multifactor theory	2.	Thompson
C.	Group factor theory	3.	Spearman
D.	Sampling theory	4.	Thorndike

Codes

	A	B	C	D		A	B	C	D
(a)	4	3	2	1	(b)	3	4	1	2
(c)	3	4	2	1	(d)	4	3	1	2

104 **Match the following**

	List I (Theories and Models for Intellect)		List II (Psychologists)
A.	Primary mental abilities	1.	Thompson
B.	Sampling theory	2.	Vernon
C.	Structure of intellect model	3.	Thurstone
D.	Hierarchical organisation of abilities	4.	Guilford

Codes

	A	B	C	D		A	B	C	D
(a)	3	1	2	4	(b)	4	3	1	2
(c)	3	1	4	2	(d)	4	3	2	1

105 **Match the following**

	List I (Theories of Intelligence)		List II (Theorists)
A.	Sampling theory	1.	RL Thorndike
B.	Hierarchical theory	2.	LL Thurstone
C.	Group factor theory	3.	G Thomson
D.	Multifactor theory	4.	C Burt and PE Vernon

Codes

	A	B	C	D		A	B	C	D
(a)	4	3	2	1	(b)	3	4	1	2
(c)	3	4	2	1	(d)	4	3	1	2

106 **Match the following**

	List I (Theories of Intelligence)		List II (Psychologists Associated with them)
A.	Two factor theory	1.	Thorndike
B.	Information processing theory	2.	Thurstone
C.	Multifactor theory	3.	Spearman
D.	Group factor theory	4.	Sternberg

Codes

	A	B	C	D		A	B	C	D
(a)	3	2	1	4	(b)	4	3	2	1
(c)	3	4	1	2	(d)	1	4	3	2

107 **Match the following**

	List I (Types of intelligence)		List II (Descriptions)
A.	Fluid intelligence	1.	Broad cognitive ability
B.	Crystallised intelligence	2.	Involves reasoning and concept formation
C.	'g' factor	3.	Involves previously learned information
D.	's' factor	4.	Special interest

Codes

	A	B	C	D		A	B	C	D
(a)	5	3	1	2	(b)	2	1	4	5
(c)	5	1	4	2	(d)	2	3	1	5

108 **Match the following**

	List I (Theories of Intelligence)		List II (Theorists)
A.	Two factor theory	1.	Guilford
B.	Group factor theory	2.	Cattell
C.	Structure of intellect	3.	Spearman
D.	Crystallised intelligence	4.	Thompson

Codes

	A	B	C	D		A	B	C	D
(a)	1	2	3	4	(b)	3	4	1	2
(c)	1	4	3	2	(d)	3	2	1	4

109 Match the following

List I (Theories)	List II (Authors)
A. The theory of crystallised and fluid intelligence	1. Guilford
B. The 'g' factor theory	2. Thurstone
C. The theory of primary mental abilities	3. Cattell
D. The tridimensional theory	4. Spearman

Codes

	A	B	C	D		A	B	C	D
(a)	3	4	1	2	(b)	4	3	2	1
(c)	4	3	1	2	(d)	3	4	2	1

Directions *(Q. Nos. 110-114) Read the following passage and answer the following questions*

Factor analysis is a method of calculating from the various correlation coefficients of measured individual performances the number and the general nature of the influence that account for observed relations. Through such an analysis, spearmen found the tests that bore most heavily on his general intelligence factor that had to do with reasoning and judgement. He therefore defined this factor as the capacity to educe relations and correlates.

Factor analysis also tells us how much of the individual variation in some particular performance is accounted for by each of the several factors that combine to produce that kind of behaviour. Spearman concluded that about a 9 : 1 ratio to special abilities in determining mathematical learning rate, about 7 : 1 in accounting for the size of ones of properly used vocabulary, about 2 : 1 in determining musical ability and about 1 : 4 in judging drawing ability..

Decades later, louis Thurstone developed a multiple factor analysis. This improvement over Spearman's method led to Thurstone's discovery and definition of a dozen primary abilities, among them verbal comprehension, word fluency, number, space and reasoning. On the contrary, advances in factor analysis rectified the only known statistical and structural flow in spearman's work. General intelligence now emerged from multiple-factors analysis as a single second-order factor, based on the intercorrelation among primary factors. second-order factor, based on the interorrelation among primary factors. The general intelligence concept was strengthened, for the pyramids of primary factors provided a far more reliable base than did the grains of innumerable small variables.

Cattell found that the breadth of a factor and number of factors depend-upon what tests an experimenter uses to gather his data. From the 20, primary abilities surveyed by John French. John Hern obtained some four or five broad abilities, such as fluid intelligence, crystallised intelligence, speed and visualisation. But the bravo stone of all such abilities and the once with a semantic claim to the label 'Intelligence' are fluid and crystallised.

110 Which among the following tells us how much of the individual variation in some particular performance is accounted for?

(a) Primacy ability (b) Reasoning
(c) Factor analysis (d) None of these

111 According to Spearman what is the ratio of special abilities in determining mathematical learning rate?

(a) 9 : 1 (b) 7 : 1 (c) 2 : 1 (d) 1 : 4

112 What is ratio for determining musical ability?

(a) 9 : 1 (b) 1 : 4 (c) 1 : 5 (d) 2 : 1

113 Which among the following is correct about General Intelligence concept?

(a) Emerged from multiple- factor analysis
(b) Strengthened for the pyramids of primary factors
(c) Both a and b
(d) None of the above

114 Who found that the breadth of a factor and the number of factor depends upon what test an experiments uses to gather his data?

(a) Thurstone (b) Cattell
(c) Spearman (d) None of the above

PREVIOUS YEARS' QUESTIONS

July 2018

1 Which of the following are the basic forms of intelligence in Triarchic Theory?

1. Dimensional 2. Componential
3. Contextual 4. Experiential

Codes

(a) 1, 2 and 3 (b) 1, 2, and 4
(c) 2, 3 and 4 (d) 1, 3 and 4

November 2017

2 The 1986 Symposium on intelligence identified the main loci of intelligence

1. Intelligence within the individual.
2. Intelligence within the environment.
3. Intelligence within the interaction between the individual and environment.
4. Intelligence to be measured by psychometric measures.

Codes
(a) 1 and 2 (b) 3 and 4 (c) 1, 2 and 3 (d) 2, 3 and 4

3 **Read each of the following two statements - Assertion (A) and Reason (R); and indicate your answer using codes given below.**
Assertion (A) Spearman proposed the existence of specific factor of intelligence.
Reason (R) It was observed that tetrad differences are always equal to zero.
Codes
(a) Both A and R are true and R is the correct explanation of A
(b) Both A and R are true, but R is not the correct explanation of A
(c) A is true, but R is false
(d) A is false, but R is true

4 **Defined intelligence as the ability to 'see relations and to educe correlates'.**
(a) Binet (b) Spearman (c) Terman (d) Boring

5 **Match List I with List II and select the correct answer by choosing from the codes given below.**

List I (Concept)	List II (Description)
A. Successful Intelligence	1. Ability to cope with the problems of day-to-day life
B. Practical Intelligence	2. Ability to achieve one's goals of life across given cultural contexts, capitalising on strengths and correcting weaknesses to adapt with the environment
C. Mating Intelligence	3. Ability to cope with novel problems and situations
D. Creative Intelligence	4. Ability to understand the outcomes of mind's reproductive system

Codes

	A	B	C	D		A	B	C	D
(a)	1	2	3	4	(b)	2	1	4	3
(c)	3	4	2	1	(d)	4	3	1	2

January 2017

6 **Read each of the following two statements Assertion (A) and Reason (R) and indicate your answer using codes given below**
Assertion (A) In cross-sectional research to study development process of intelligence, age and cohorts are confounded.
Reason (R) According to Flynn effect, each successive generation of people is more intelligent than the preceding one.
Codes
(a) Both A and R are true and R is the correct explanation of A
(b) Both A and R are true, but R is not the correct explanation of A
(c) A is true, but R is false
(d) A is false, but R is true

7 **Chronometric measurement of intelligence involves the use of which of the following?**
(a) Reaction time apparatus
(b) Flicker-Fusion apparatus
(c) ECG Bio-feedback apparatus
(d) EMG Bio-feedback apparatus

8 **Read each of the following two statements Assertion (A) and Reason (R) and indicate your answer using codes given below.**
Assertion (A) In terms of SOI model, intelligence can be taken as a superset of creativity.
Reason (R) Divergent production is just one of the operations of intellect.
Codes
(a) Both A and R are true and R is the correct explanation of A
(b) Both A and R are true, but R is not the correct explanation of A
(c) A is true, but R is false
(d) A is false, but R is true

9 **Which of the following is true of the threshold hypothesis regarding intelligence creativity relationship ?**
(a) There is a 'U' type relationship between intelligence and creativity.
(b) There is 'inverted U' type relationship between intelligence and creativity.
(c) The relationship between the two is 'ill-defined' above a specific level of intelligence.
(d) The relationship between the two is ill defined below a specific level of intelligence.

July 2016

10 **Match List I with List II and select the correct answer by choosing from the codes given below.**

List I	List II
A. Mental Age	1. Stern
B. Intelligence Quotient	2. Binet
C. Mental Tests	3. Spearman
D. Tetrad Equation	4. JM Cattell

Codes

	A	B	C	D		A	B	C	D
(a)	1	2	3	4	(c)	2	1	4	3
(b)	3	2	1	4	(d)	4	3	2	1

11 **Creativity has been conceptualised in terms of following.**
1. Creativity as a product
2. Creativity as a process
3. Creativity as a potential
4. Creativity as perseverance

Codes

(a) 1 and 2 (b) 2 and 3
(c) 1, 2 and 3 (d) 1, 2 and 4

12 **According to Triarchic Theory of Intelligence, arrange the correct functional sequence of→ metacomponents**

(a) Identification of problem →defining the givens, goals and obstacles →choosing appropriate strategy → selection of lower order processes→selection of mental representation →allocation of mental resources →monitoring→evaluation
(b) Identification of problem →defining the givens, goals and obstacles →selection of lower order processes→ choosing appropriate strategy →selecting a mental representation →allocating mental resources → monitoring→evaluation
(c) Identification of problem →choosing appropriate strategy → defining givens, goals and obstacles → allocating mental resources→ monitoring→ selecting mental representation→ evaluation
(d) Defining the givens, goals and obstacles → identification of problem → selection of lower order processes→ choosing appropriate strategy→ selecting a mental representation→ allocating mental resources → monitoring→ evaluation

13 **Read each of the following two statements Assertion (A) and Reason (R) and indicate your answer using codes given below.**

Assertion (A) As per Guilford's SOI model, intelligence can be taken as superset of creativity.

Reason (R) Creativity involves divergent production that is just one of five operations of intellect.

Codes

(a) Both A and R are true and R is the correct explanation of A
(b) Both A and R are true, but R is not the correct explanation of A
(c) A is true, but R is false
(d) A is false, but R is true

December 2015

14 **Match List I with List II and indicate your answer using the codes given below**

List I (Types of variables)	List II (Examples)
A. Continuous variable	1. Examination results in terms of pass and fail
B. Real discrete variable	2. Voice pitch
C. Artificially discrete variable	3. Intelligence
D. Qualitative variable	4. Nationality

Codes

	A	B	C	D		A	B	C	D
(a)	3	4	1	2	(b)	3	1	4	2
(c)	2	4	1	3	(d)	2	1	4	3

15 **Which of the following are not identified by Thurstone ?**

1. Induction 2. Spatial
3. Symbolic 4. Semantic

Codes

(a) 1 and 2 (b) 3 and 4 (c) 1 and 3 (d) 1, 2 and 3

16 **A 19 years old boy was administered the Wechsler Intelligence Scale for children by the clerical staff of a busy psychologist who later wrote the test report. A xerox copy of the test material was shared with the child's parents to ensure that he performs well. The following ethical principles of testing were violated**

1. Use of appropriate test
2. Professional qualification of tester
3. Copyright
4. Culture fair testing

Codes

(a) 1 and 3 (b) 2 and 3
(c) 1, 2 and 3 (d) All of these

June 2015

17 **History of Intelligence Testing can be described in following sequence.**

(a) Galton, JM Cattell, Benet-Simon, Wechsler
(b) JM Cattell, Stern-Terman, Benet-Simon, Wechsler
(c) Wister, Benet-Simon, Spearman, RB Cattell
(d) Galton, JM Cattell, Spearman, Wechsler

18 **Deterioration Quotient (DQ) was first used in which intelligence tests?**

(a) Benet-Simon Test
(b) Galton-Cattell Test
(c) Raven Progressive Matrices
(d) Wechsler Adult Intelligence Test

19 **The best home environment for intellectual development is one**

(a) in which child is encouraged to work out problems with guidance and support from parents.
(b) in which parents dictate the child what to do.
(c) in which child is left on his own.
(d) in which father is absent to impose his authority.

20 **On a Wechsler type intelligence scale, the subject has a deviation IQ 115. What would be his T score (Mean = 50, SD = 10)?**

(a) 60 (b) 65 (c) 68 (d) 84

21 **Intelligence is necessary but not sufficient condition for creativity. It represents**

(a) Threshold Theory (b) Certification Theory
(c) Interference Theory (d) Collaborative Theory

22 **Which is the correct sequence of stages involved in creative thinking?**

(a) Preparation – Orientation – Illumination – Verification – Incubation

(b) Preparation – Incubation – Illumination – Orientation Verification
(c) Orientation – Preparation – Incubation – Illumination – Verification
(d) Orientation – Preparation – Illumination – Incubation – Verification

December 2014

23 **Sternberg's Triarchic theory identifies ...... types of components; ...... are used to plan, control and monitor in problem solving.**
(a) Three, meta components
(b) Four, performance
(c) Problem solving, knowledge
(d) Several, acquisition components

24 **Read each of the following two statements Assertion (A) and Reason (R) and indicate your answer using the codes given below.**

Assertion (A) Environments that influence educational and cultural opportunities enhance crystallised intelligence.
Reason (R) Crystallised intelligence is developed through stimulating fluid intelligence.
Codes
(a) Both A and R are true and R is the correct explanation of A
(b) Both A and R are true, but R is not the correct explanation of A
(c) A is true, but R is false
(d) A is false, but R is true

25 **Read each of the following two statements Assertion (A) and Reason (R) and indicate your answer using the codes given below.**

Assertion (A) Creative people usually have a broad range of knowledge about lot of subjects and are good at using mental imagery.
Reason (R) Creative people are often unconventional and value their autonomy.
Codes
(a) Both A and R are true and R is correct explanation of A
(b) Both A and R are true, but R is not the correct explanation of A
(c) A is true, but R is false
(d) A is false, but R is true

26 **On a Wechsler type intelligence scale Arish has a deviation IQ of 115. If the norms of this test are expressed in terms of normalised T scores (mean = 50, SD = 10), what would be the T score of Arish?**
(a) 40 (b) 60 (c) 65 (d) 84

June 2014

27 **Which of the following is not consequence of Spreaman's Theory?**
(a) The correlation between different measures of intelligence will be positive
(b) The correlation between measures of intelligence will be equal to $r_{1g} \times r_{2g}$, where 1 and 2 represent the two different measures and g represents general factor.
(c) The correlation between to measures of intelligence will be equal to $r_{1g} + r_{2g}$, where 1 and 2 represent the two different measures and g represents general factor.
(d) The law of tetred difference will mold for four measures of intelligence.

28 **Cartell's Culture Fair Intelligence Test (CFIT) is presumed to meaure**
(a) Crystallised intelligence (b) Fluid intelligence
(c) Verbal fluency (d) Convergent thinking

ANSWERS

Exam Based Questions

1	(d)	2	(d)	3	(c)	4	(c)	5	(a)	6	(b)	7	(b)	8	(d)	9	(d)	10	(a)
11	(d)	12	(d)	13	(b)	14	(c)	15	(b)	16	(c)	17	(c)	18	(c)	19	(a)	20	(d)
21	(a)	22	(c)	23	(c)	24	(c)	25	(c)	26	(b)	27	(c)	28	(a)	29	(a)	30	(b)
31	(a)	32	(c)	33	(b)	34	(c)	35	(a)	36	(d)	37	(d)	38	(c)	39	(c)	40	(d)
41	(c)	42	(c)	43	(a)	44	(c)	45	(a)	46	(a)	47	(d)	48	(c)	49	(a)	50	(b)
51	(d)	52	(b)	53	(a)	54	(b)	55	(a)	56	(d)	57	(c)	58	(c)	59	(d)	60	(c)
61	(c)	62	(c)	63	(c)	64	(b)	65	(b)	66	(c)	67	(c)	68	(a)	69	(c)	70	(d)
71	(c)	72	(a)	73	(a)	74	(c)	75	(a)	76	(d)	77	(c)	78	(c)	79	(b)	80	(b)
81	(a)	82	(c)	83	(d)	84	(c)	85	(b)	86	(a)	87	(a)	88	(a)	89	(c)	90	(a)
91	(c)	92	(c)	93	(a)	94	(b)	95	(b)	96	(b)	97	(b)	98	(d)	99	(a)	100	(a)
101	(a)	102	(b)	103	(a)	104	(c)	105	(c)	106	(c)	107	(d)	108	(b)	109	(d)	110	(c)
111	(a)	112	(d)	113	(c)	114	(b)												

Previous Years' Questions

1	(a)	2	(c)	3	(c)	4	(b)	5	(b)	6	(a)	7	(a)	8	(a)	9	(c)	10	(b)
11	(a)	12	(b)	13	(a)	14	(a)	15	(b)	16	(c)	17	(a)	18	(d)	19	(a)	20	(a)
21	(a)	22	(c)	23	(a)	24	(a)	25	(b)	26	(b)	27	(c)	28	(b)				

Personality

Psychologists regard personality as a person's unique long term pattern of thinking emotions and behaviour. In other words, personality refers to the consistency in who you are, have been and will become. It also refers to the special blend of talents, hopes, values, love, hate and habits that make each person a unique in the own way.

Introduction to Personality

The word 'personality' has been derived from the latin word 'persona' which means a mask worn by an actor while performing a character on the stage. Thus, personality is referred as the characteristic pattern or style of behaviour of the person revealed from his external appearance.

Psychologists differ among themselves on the meaning of personality. When psychologists use the term 'personality' they are referring to something more than the role play. Although, a single definition is not acceptable by all personality theorists. It is explained that 'Personality' is a pattern of relatively permanent traits and unique characteristics that both give both consistency and individuality to a person's behaviour. Few other psychologists define personality as the reasonably stable patterns of emotions, motives and behaviour that distinguish one person from another.

Among all the research areas in the science of psychology, personality is notable in the way, it effortlessly meshes with the "Fabric of our life, our everyday situation, problem and relationship". The way personality psychologist define personality has changed over the years, reflecting theoretical and empirical advancements made in the study of personality.

Definitions of Personality

The definition of some prominent personality psychologist are as follow

According to **Ramond B Cattell**, "That which permits a prediction of what a person will do in a given situation."

In this Chapter

According to **David Mc Clelland**, "The most adequate conceptualisation of a person's behaviour in all its detail."

According to **JP Guilford**, "A person's unique pattern of traits."

According to **Gordon W Allport**, "The dynamic organisation within the individual of those psychological system that determine his characteristic behaviour and thought."

Common Features of Personality

The word personality conveys a sense of consistency, internal causality and personal distinctiveness and explanation of content and process of personality. *Common feature of personality are as follows*

- Personality is not just an accumulation of bits and pieces; it has organisation.
- Personality is not static it's active, it has process of some sort.
- Personality is a psychological concept, but it's tied to the physical body.
- Personality is a causal force ; it helps determine how the person relates to the world.

Uniqueness of the Individual

Most definitions of personality include some statements about the uniqueness of an individual's personality. The uniqueness can be explained from various theoretical viewpoints held by different personality psychologist. A biological viewpoint with its emphasis on genetics and local processes, might consider differences in bodily processes.

A dispositional trait viewpoint might assert that certain human qualities are stable even as they are displayed across diverse setting (*e.g.* being conscientious at work and while hiking in the mountains). *Different viewpoint on uniqueness of personality are as follows*

- **A learning viewpoint**, with its emphasis on the effect *e.g.* experience of behaviour might consider distinctive reinforcement pattern.
- **Cognitive Viewpoint** would emphasis or individual differences in the interpretation of environmental cues and the behavioural expectation and consequences associated with these cues (*e.g.* being cooperative at work, but aggressive when playing tennis.)
- **Phenomenological View point** might emphasis on subjective experience and self-determination (*e.g.* your career as an expression of your passion).
- **Evolutionary Viewpoint** would emphasise on the adaptive significance of certain personality characteristics. (*e.g.* aggresive behaviour serves as protection of territory and food sources).
- **Cross Cultural Viewpoint** might highlight the impact of social norm and local custom in the expression of individual differences.
- **Freudian Viewpoint**, with its focus on internal forces, might emphasise early childhood experience (*e.g.* parents children interaction).

Consistency of Behaviour

Personality psychologist generally assume some degree of continuity in individual's personality. Features common to personality is a concern for the consistency of behaviour across the time and situation. The degree of behavioural consistency is influenced by the extent, to which situational factors as well as one's personality determine thought, feeling and behaviour.

Content and Process of Personality

The content and process features of personality are interrelated. The basic make up of the human personality directly influences how the personality operates. *For example* Somc pcrsonality psychologists assume that various traits make up the basic content of human personality and also influence behaviour.

They would explain the aggressive style of the office tyrant across a variety of situations as resulting from a personality that contains a combination of the traits of aggressiveness and hostility.

Combining common features to formulate a definition of personality is significant because it determines how a personality psychologist views the development, measurement and modification of the human personality.

Objectives of Personality

Some major objectives behind personality theories are

- Understand and discuss the concept of personality.
- Understand different definitions of personality.
- Understand the characteristics and features of personality.
- Understand and discuss in your own words different dimensions of personality.
- Will be able to write an essay on the concept and various aspects of personality.

Determinants of Personality

Personality is something that we partially inherit from our parents, it is a product of the environment in which we are brought up. Thus, we see that there are two most important factors which are prominent in the making of personality or in other words that will shape or influence our personality are

(i) Biological (ii) Socio-cultural

Biological Determinant

Biological determinants also called as physical determinants, emphasise that physique and body functioning are directly responsible for personality development. *Some of these factors are*

(i) **Body Build** It influences personality directly by determining what an individual can and cannot do, as well as what the individual's reaction will be to all those whose body builds are superior or inferior.

Some of the known body builds are

- Ectomorph
- Endomorph
- Mesomorph

Ectomorphs are persons who are tall and thin in their body builds. They have been generally found to be superior to Endomorphs who have round and soft body builds. The superiority is especially in speed and endurance. Likewise, mesomorphs who are strong and muscular in their body builds have been found to be superior to both ectomorphs and endomorphs in activities like speed, endurance and agility.

(ii) **Physical Attractiveness** It is another physical component that affects the development of personality. **Brislin** and **Lewis** (1968) have commented that it is very much rewarding to be with someone who is physically attractive.

Generally, it has been found that the people tend to be more tolerant in their attitudes and judgements of an attractive person. That is the reason why a pretty child is less likely to be punished or criticised for troublesome behaviour than a simple looking homely child.

(iii) **Homeostasis** It is another important determinant. It refers to the maintenance of a stable internal environment through relatively having normal temperature, normal level of blood sugar, normal level of blood pressure, proper water balance, etc. When any of these conditions is upset, disequilibrium starts and result into disturbances in homeostasis.

Homeostasis disturbances has a significant impact upon personality both directly and indirectly. Directly, the effect of homeostasis is seen in relaxed, controlled and socially acceptable behaviour patterns of the person who is feeling well both physically and psychologically. When the level of homeostasis is disturbed, behaviours like irritability, indigestion, insomnia and other uncomfortable states often result.

(iv) **Physical Defects** These are other determiners. The first scientific study showing the impact of physical defect upon personality has come from Alfred Adler's theory of organ inferiority. Today several studies have been conducted to examine the direct and indirect impact of physical defects upon personality. Obesity is one of the popular physical defects.

Obesity proves to be a handicap in social relationship because the obese person is unable to keep up with his companion. Obesity also affects the personality indirectly. Awareness of unfavourable attitude towards obesity makes the person feel not only inferior but also they develop the feeling of being socially scorned. Not only this, some researchers have also pointed out that massively obese individuals become more disturbed perhaps because of less self-satisfaction and cumulative adverse comment from others.

Socio-Cultural Determinant

Freud regarded an individual primarily as a complex energy system that maintains itself by the means of transactions with the external world. Personality is based on the existence of a well defined universal human instinctual endowment and a definite universal ontogenetic progress through maturational stage oral, anal, genital. Freud originally gave the name libido to instinctual source of human behaviour.

This Freudian approach was subjected to a new synthesis by a number of American Anthropologists such as Ruth-Benedict, Margaret Mead, Linton Kardiner and Cora Du Bois. This new synthesis focuses on adoptional rather than Freudian instinctual basis of personality. They laid stress on the use of psychodynamics in the social science. Subsequently by anthropological field work paved path in order to demonstrate the relation between culture and personality. These scholars form a school of anthropological thought known as culture and personality school of thought.

Margaret Mead, through her studies has emphasised the impact of culture on personality formation. Margaret Mead argued that a child born in a particular culture where he/she (brings up and there by he/she)enters into a performed cultural environment, which plays a significant role in his/her personality formation.

Ruth Benedict another lady anthropologist of America has dealt with the impact of personality on culture. She exposed the complex relationship between culture and personality of the individual. In her key work *Patterns of Culture,* Benedict developed the concept of culture pattern. She believed that culture was the product of human choices rather than cultural determinism. According to Ruth Benedict, "Culture can be viewed as existence of cultural configurations integrated under the domination of one general master pattern."

Scholars like **Linton** and **Kardiner** are the advocates of third approach as they believe that culture and personality are assistant to and influenced by each other. "The individual and his society and psychological frontier of society." It explained the basis personality form by diversity of subject matter in each culture.

Approaches to the Study of Personality

Personality has been studied in a number of different ways. Some have developed broad theories to explain the origins and makeup of personality. Others have focused only on one or two issues, such as the influence of heredity on personality.

Most of these broad theories can be grouped into following categories

(i) Type and trait theory
(ii) Psychoanalytical
(iii) Neo-freudian
(iv) Humanistic theories
(v) Social learning theory
(vi) Existential
(vii) Transpersonal psychology
(viii) Cognative theory

Type and Trait Theory

Type and trait theories of personality both focus on people's personal characteristics. However, various type theorists and trait theorists differ in the way they use those characteristics to describe people. We will begin to examine these differences by talking briefly about George and Crystal and considering what 'types' of people they are.

Type Theories

The term type is used to identify a certain collection of traits that make up a broad, general personality classification.

A type is simply a class of individuals said to share a common collection of characteristics. *For example* Introverts could be described as people who share characteristics such as shyness, social withdrawal and a tendency not to talk much; while extroverts share a tendency to be outgoing, friendly and talkative. Usually, sharp topologies do not work well scientifically. A major reason is that almost dimension of personality friendliness, sociability and so on is distributed according to a normal bell shaped curve.

Some people do not fall naturally into distinct personality types, psychologists who want to develop type theories have to take special steps. One approach has been to develop theories about specific types by treating each type as a personality dimensions. Individuals can then be scored or rated to determine their position on each dimension; that is how close they come to fitting one of the types. One theorist who used this approach was HH Eysenck.

Eysenck's Hierarchy Theory (Type Theory)

Eysenck's identified the major components of personality as a small number of personality types. Each type is made up of a set of personality characteristics.

For example People who fit Eysenck's extroverted type are said to have such characteristics as sociability, liveliness and excitability. Each one of these characteristics according to Eysenck, can be broken down into certain habitual response patterns that apply to several situations; each of these habitual response patterns can be broken down further into specific responses within specific situations.

The personality theory of Hans Eysenck has strong psychometric and biological components. However, Eysenck contended that psychometric sophistication alone is not sufficient to measure the structure of human personality and that personality dimensions arrived at through factor analytic methods are sterile and meaningless unless they have been shown to possess a biological existence.

Criteria For Identifying Factor

Eysenck listed four criteria for identifying a factor.

(i) Psychometric evidence for the factor's existence must be established. A corollary to this criterion is that the factor must be reliable and replicable.
(ii) The factor must also possess heritability and must fit an established genetic model. This criterion eliminates learned characteristics, such as the ability to mimic the voice of the well-known people or a religious or political belief.
(iii) The factor must make sense from a theoretical view. Eysenck employed the deductive method of investigation, beginning with a theory and then gathering data that are logically consistent with that theory.

(iv) The fourth criterion for the existence of a factor is that it must possess social relevance *i.e.* it must be demonstrated that mathematically derived factors have a relationship (not necessarily causal) with such socially relevant variables as drug addiction, proneness to unintentional injuries, outstanding performance in sports, psychotic behaviour.

Trait Theories

In this approach, we assumes behaviour to be determined by relatively stable traits which are fundamental units of one's personality.

Traits predispose one to act in a certain way, regardless of the situation. This means that traits should remain consistent across situations and over time, but may vary between individuals. It is presumed that individuals differ in their traits due to genetic differences.

Allport's Trait Approach

Allport is regarded as one of the most important and influential personality theorists. According to **Fort Allport**, "Traits are the building blocks of personality as well as the source of individuality".

He is known as idiographic trait theorist who has a strong belief that each person has some unique as well as some common characteristics that together form a unique combination of traits. Fort Allport trait is something that exits but remains invisible. It is located somewhere in the nervous system.

We infer the existence of a trait by observing consistencies in the behaviour of the person. Dissimilar stimuli tend to arouse a trait readiness within the person and then trait manifests itself through the varieties of different responses. All these responses are equivalent in the sense that they serve the function of expression of trait. To illustrate this, let us take an example of an employee working in the university office. His shyness is inferred from his inability to establish friendship with others, his avoidance of social gatherings of the employees, his enjoyment with solitary entertainment activities and his unwillingness to participate in discussion etc.

Common and Individual Traits

Allport recognised two major categories of traits

(i) **Common Traits** are those traits which we share in common with many others in our culture. *For example* Being quiet, showing due respect to seniors and making polite behaviour to others are the traits we share with others in Indian culture. This illustrates the common traits.

(ii) **Individual Traits** Individual traits or also called *personal dispositions* are those traits which are unique to the person concerned and Allport regarded individual traits to be more important than common traits. *According to him, there are three types of individual traits.*

- **Cardinal Traits** A cardinal trait is a trait which is so pervasive, dominant and outstanding in life that every behaviour seems traceable to its influence. Most people do not have cardinal traits but those who have them, are well-known by those traits. *For instance,* Mahatma Gandhi was having the cardinal traits of peace-loving and strong faith in non-violence for which he is well known.
- **Central Traits** These are the basic building blocks that shape most of our behaviour although they are not as overwhelming as cardinal traits. In fact, trait like friendliness, dominance, self-centeredness would be the example of central trait. Every person has several central traits and there are five to ten most outstanding traits in each person around which a person's life focuses.
- **Secondary Traits** Secondary traits are traits which are less conspicuous, less consistent, less generalised and less relevant to the definition of personality. *For example* Food habits, hair style and specific attitudes are examples of secondary traits. All these traits are dynamic in the sense that they possess motivational power. Those individual traits or dispositions which are intensely experienced are said to be more motivational. Those individual traits which are less intensively experienced though possessing more motivational power are said to be more stylistic.

Cattell's Trait Approach

Raymond Cattell considered personality to be a pattern of traits providing the key for understanding and predicting a person's behaviour. According to Cattell, "Traits are relatively permanent and broad reaction tendencies of personality." They serve as the building blocks of personality.

He distinguished various traits which are as follows

- **Surface Traits and Source Traits** The observable qualities of a personality like kindness, honesty, helpfulness, generosity etc. are named as *surface traits.* Allport has called these qualities or traits as *central traits*. Using questionnaires and observations, Cattell studied several thousand people and he reported certain cluster of surface traits that appeared together from time to time. He further reported that these were the clear evidence of some deeper, more general underlying personality factors and he referred to these as source traits.

Source traits make up the most basic structure of personality and are the underlying factors that are responsible for the inter-correlation among surface traits. Although source traits are smaller in number than surface traits, yet they are better predictors of human behaviour. We all possess the same source traits but we do not possess them in the same amount. *For example* Intelligence is an example of source trait and every one of us possesses this but we all do not possess intelligence in the same amount.

- **Constitutional and Environmental Traits** Cattell also distinguished between constitutional traits and environmental mold traits. Constitutional traits are those traits which are determined by nature or biology, whereas environmental mold traits are those which are determined by nurture that is by experience gained in interaction with environment. Most surface traits, for Cattell, reflect a mixture of both heredity (nature) and environment (nurture). However, he further points out that there are some source traits which derive solely from within the individual (biology of the individual) and there are some source traits which derive solely from source derived only from environmental factors.

  Through a complicated statistical technique is called MAVA (Multiple Abstract Variance Analysis), he was able to assess the degree to which various traits are determined either by environmental or genetically determined factors. MAVA is based upon the comparisons between people of the same family either reared together or reared apart or between members of different families reared either together or apart.

- **Ability, Temperament and Dynamic Traits** Cattell has further subdivided traits into ability traits, temperament traits and dynamic traits. *Ability traits* refer to the person's skill in dealing with the environment and the goals set therein. Intelligence is an example of ability trait. *Temperament traits* refer to stylistic tendencies that largely show how a person moves towards a goal. Being moody, irritable, easygoing are examples of temperament trait. *Dynamic traits* are the person's motivation and interest which set the person in action toward the goal.

  A person may be characterised as being power-seeking, ambitious or sports-oriented. This reflects the dynamic trait. The important dynamic traits in Cattell's system are of three types *i.e.* attitudes, ergs and sentiments.

Five Factor Model (Trait Theory)

This trait approach to personality is the Five Factor Model (FFM) also known as the *Big Five*. As its name implies, according to this model, there are five broad personality factors, each of which is composed of constellation of traits. Based on his own researches as well as researches of others in 1981, Goldberg pointed out that it is possible to prepare a model for structuring individual differences among traits of personality.

Big Five was meant to refer to the finding that each factor subsumes a large number of specific traits. In fact, the Big Five are almost as broad and abstract as Eysenck's superfactors. *Those big five dimensions of personality using the names assigned by MC Crae and Costa, are as under*

(i) **Extraversion** (E) This factor assesses the quality and intensity of interpersonal interaction. High scorer in this factor is characterised by being sociable, active, talkative, person-oriented, optimistic, fun-loving and affectionate, whereas low scorer is characterised by being reserved, sober, aloof, task oriented, retiring and quiet. Thus, this factor contrasts extraverted traits with introverted traits.

(ii) **Conscientiousness** (C) This factor mainly assesses the person's degree of organisation, persistence and motivation in goal directed behaviour. In other words, this factor describes task and goal directed behaviours and the socially required impulse control behaviour. This factor easily differentiates individuals who are dependable, organised, hard working, responsible, reliable and thorough (high scorers) from those who are undependable, disorganised, unreliable, impulsive, irresponsible, lazy and negligent (low scorers).

(iii) **Agreeableness** (A) This factor assesses the person's quality of interpersonal orientation ranging from compassion to antogonism in thinking, feeling and action. High scorer on this factor would be characterised by soft-hearted, good-natured, trusting, helpful, straightforward and forgiving whereas the low scorer would be characterised by cynical, suspicious, uncooperative, vengeful, irritable and manipulative.

(iv) **Openness** (O) This factor assesses proactive seeking and appreciation of experience for its own sake as well as tolerance for and exploration for something new and unfamiliar. High scorers would be characterised by being good-natured, warm, sympathetic and cooperative, whereas low scorers would be charactersied by being unfriendly, aggressive, unpleasant, cold and even hostile.

(v) **Neuroticism** (N) This personality dimension is measured on a continuum ranging from emotional stability or neuroticism. People who have high neuroticism scores are often persistent worriers. They are more fearful and often feel ancious, overting their problems and exaggerating their significance. Rather than seeing the positive in a situation, they may dwell on its negative aspects.

Neuroticism can result in a person coping less successfully with common stressor's in their day to day lives. Instead, they often become frustrated with others and may feel angry it events donot occurs as they wish.

Psychoanalytical Theory

Psychoanalysis is a school founded and developed by **Sigmund Freud**. Psychoanalysis as a school of psychology emphasised upon unconscious mind into which individual pushes or represses all of his or her threatening urges and desires.

Freud laid more stress upon the childhood experiences, believing that personality was formed in the first 6 years of life and that, if there were significant problems, those problems must have begun in those early years. Freud stressed on sex and aggression which he considered the two basic instincts of person's behaviour.

Freud's theory is so interesting because of the following reasons

(i) The cornerstones of psychoanalysis are sex and aggression, are two subjects of continuing popularity.

(ii) The theory was spread beyond its viennese origins by an ardent and dedicated group of followers.

(iii) Freuds brilliant command of language enabled him to present his theories in a stimulating and exciting manner.

Basic Assumptions

There are mainly four basic theoretical assumptions serve to link together the various components of Freud's comprehensive view of personality, *which are as follows*

Psychic Determinism

Psychic determinism refers to Freud's belief that behaviour doesn't just happen by chance, but is governed by some purpose or meaning; from this assumption Freud theorised that such everyday events like jog, dream, slip of tongue are expression of psychic determination. Even seemingly innocent or meaningless behaviour are influenced by psychic determinism *e.g.* if you miss a turn while, driving you may be expressing the unconscious desire to avoid something or someone.

Influence of Unconscious Mind

Freud assumed that powerful forces in the unconscious region of mind governs the human behaviour. Freud said that, these forces are unconscious because they contain thought, idea, desire and impulses that individual find threatening, shameful or unacceptable. But these forces are still a part of personality, automatic process of information is a possible explanation of power of unconscious mind which can influence our thought, feeling and behaviour without our conscious awareness.

Dynamic Nature of Personality

This assumption explains that several different element worked together in a homeostatic fashion that is one, in which balance and stability are maintained among different aspects of an individuals personality *e.g.* one can experience homeostatic by taking a break after studying for a couple of hour, walking to a local coffee shop to chat with friend and than resuming studies. Thus, the dynamic process of homeostatic is the creation of *state of arousal* that motivates an individual to take action to *stabilise and restore* balance among different motivational aspect within the individual.

- State of arousal being stressed by studying too long.
- Action, such as chating with friends.
- Stabilise and restore balance social *v/s* studious.

Personality as a Closed System

Freud views personality as a closed system that operate on a fixed amount of psychic energy or libido. In such a system, the limited amount of energy shifted continuously from one part to another in a dynamic and interactive manner in an attempt to maintain a sense of internal balance, while studying when one take a break he or she can actually save psychic energy by relaxing a bit and not wasting a lot of energy trying to concentrate, while tired.

Basic Assumptions of the Psychodynamic View Point

Basic Assumption	Explanation	Example
Psychic Determinism	There is a psychic reason for all of our thoughts, feelings and actions; nothing just happens.	Without being aware of it, certain individuals tend to be attracted to others who have a particular emotional problem, such as alcoholism.
Influence of the Unconscious Mind	Our behaviour is determined by factors outside of conscious awareness.	A shopper's decision to select a red coat rather than a blue one reflects an unconscious desire to be perceived as daring.
The Dynamic Nature of Personality	The nature of our personality includes a number of elements interacting with each other.	As an effective manager, your personality style must include being firm, compassionate and fair when dealing with subordinates.
Personality as a Closed System	The fixed amount of psychic energy used to operate personality is shifted from one part to another.	When playing volleyball, you shift your emotions from being rational when developing a set-up to a team member to aggression when spiking the ball on an opposing player to friendly when shaking hands with the opposing players after the game.

Topological Structural : Regions of Mind

Freud's map of the mind had three regions

(i) **Conscious Mind** As the tip of the iceberg the conscious mind is characterised by sensory awareness and is limited to what people one capable of *i.e.* hearing, touching, sensing, tasting, smelling at any particular time. This is very similar to short-term memory or memory system in which information is held while, being in use. It is the only level of mental life directly available to us. In other words, what we perceive through our sense organs, if not too threatning, enters into conscious mind.

(ii) **Pre-Conscious Mind** It is located below the level of conscious awareness. It contain peace of information that can be brought into conscious awareness, when needed. According to Freud, preconscious mind had not so much influence on behaviour.

(iii) **Unconscious Mind** The largest and most influential region of mind postulated by Freud is unconscious mind. This holds unacceptable memory or urges, desires or impulses that could seriously threaten a persons sense of self, if they were expressed directly at the conscious level of awareness. The threatening information is kept out of the pre-conscious mind and prevented from eventually being expressed at the conscious level of mind by the primary sensorship point, which Freud said is located between the unconscious and pre-conscious stages.

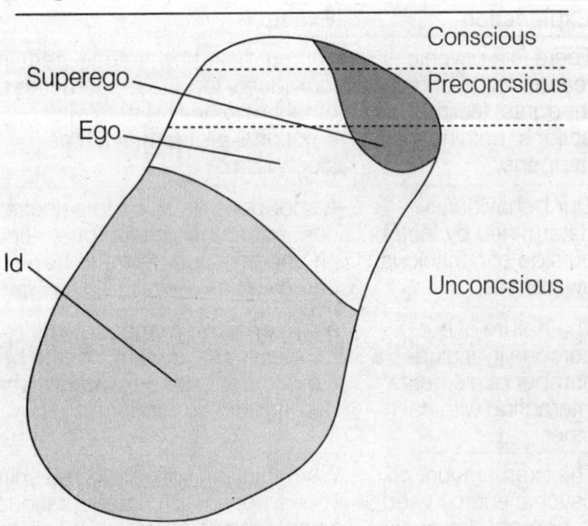

Fruid's map of Mind

Psychic Energy and Theory of Instinct

Freud believed that the operation of personality is powered by force of psychic energy fueled by instinct. As defined by Freud, an instinct is a mental representation or bodily need.

Characteristic of Instinct

Freud postulated that instinct have four major features- a source, an aim, an object and an impetus. Throughout life the source of an instinct is the bodily need, it represents and its aim to gratify the need. Both sources and aim remain constant over time. The object of an instinct includes things that can satisfy the instinct *e.g.* food is object for hunger instinct. The impetus refers to strength or force of the instinct.

Nature of Instinct

Freud sub-divided psychic instinct into two categories defined as life instinct and death instinct. **Life instinct** or **eros** used psychic energy for preserving the organism and achieving pleasure through activities such as reducing a state of hunger or thirst, taking action to avoid danger, reducing sexual arousal, resting when sleepy and seeking company when bored or lonely.

Freud also postulated **death instinct or phanotos**. Freud believe death instinct represent the individuals desire to complete the life cycle by returning to an earlier inactive and tension free state. Freud represented death instinct symbolically, by postulating a set of instinct that could be used to explain the destructive, aggressive and dark side of human nature. But because the life instinct exert, so much pressure and generally make it difficult for people to express their death instinct. They are expressed through arguing, fighting, murder etc.

Id, Ego and Super Ego

The structural elements of personality

Freud introduced his concept of three structure operating within the regions of mind. The Id, Ego and Super Ego. These provisions or regions have no territorial existence, but are merely hypothetical.

Id : If It Feels Good, Then Do It

The Id is the core of personality because it is believed to be present and fully functional at birth. It is located completely in the unconscious region of mind and therefore having no actual contract with the actual world thus, it operates within its own sense of reality. Because of its location in the unconscious mind, it reflects as those characteristic associated with the unacceptable urges, desires, memories and impulse found in the unconscious region. The expression of this impulses and desires is based on the pleasurable principle or hedonistic principle.

Ego : The Master of Reality

To deal more effectively with a demand created by impulses and unfulfilled desires, the Id then channalised some more psychic energy into forming and developing an ego. Ego helps to meet the needs and wishes of Id by creating a buffer between it and the real world. Ego locates in three regions of mind thats, why it connects the Id at the unconscious region of mind with the external world with the conscious region or conscious awareness of mind.

Therefore, ego enables to be aware of the unconscious desire of the id and the external condition under which it must operate to meet them. Ego meets the desire of Id by operating on 'reality principle'.

Super Ego : The Moral Authority of Personality

Super ego is the moral commander of personality and conceptualise as an individual centre of moral standard. It grows out of ego and like ego; it has no energy of its own. It is guided by the idealistic principle. Characteristic of super ego include the ego ideal and conscience.

Though Freud didn't distinguished between this two characteristic, ego ideals develops as a part of super ego that reward as behaviour that is consider right appropriate and morally acceptable whereas conscience results from punishment all behaviour that is considered wrong, in appropriate and morally unacceptable. This two parts of super ego are used to help maintain a morally acceptable level of behaviour.

Characteristics of Personality Structures

Characteristics	Personality Structures		
	Id	Ego	Super Ego
Level of location within the mind	Unconscious	Conscious Preconscious Unconscious	Conscious Preconscious Unconscious
Purpose	The source of psychic energy associated with basic instincts and desires	To meet the needs of the id within the contest of reality and morality	To maintain an acceptable standard of moral behaviour when the ego is meeting the id's needs
Basic Processes	Pleasure principle and primary process actions	Reality principle and secondary process actions	Ego ideal and conscience
Outcome of excessive influence on personality	An overly impulsive individual seeking immediate gratification (*e.g.* a thief or rapist)	An individual overly concerned with reality (*e.g.* lacking the ability to fantasise)	An overly moralistic and righteous person (*e.g.* a fundamentalist preacher or political zealot)

Ego-Defence Mechanism

Ego-defence mechanism are a series of unconscious action taken by the ego as a form of self defence are designed immediately to reduce anxiety *e.g.* forgetting a dentists appointment and to help balance psychic balance.

Thus, defence mechanism are characterised by their unconscious operation to remove an unpleasant emotional state, while having no effect on external reality and creating a potential for distortion in the perception of reality.

Some common ego defence mechanism are discussed below

- **Repression** It occurs when the ego unconsciously removes threatening impulses, desires and memories from conscious awareness. The process of repression occurs at an unconscious level, the individual is not even aware that it is happening. It repression drives may also find an outlet in dreams, slip's of tongue or through other defence mechanism.
- **Denial** It occurs when the ego distorts reality to deal with threatening impulses and information easier. *For example* People engage in unsafe sexual practices cope with the unpleasant possibility of getting AIDS by employing denial, claiming, it wouldn't happen to me.
- **Reaction Formation** The defence mechanism of reaction formation involves dealing with unacceptable impulses by expressing just the opposite feeling. *For example* People who are emotionally unstable and unable to accept their own strong sexual desire may devote much of their time and considerable psychic energy in urging strong protest against pornography and birth control clinic.
- **Displacement** It is a defence mechanism used by the ego to shift the expression of an impulses from an unacceptable or threatening target to a more acceptable or less threatning one, classical example of displacement is the woman, who after being chewed out by her boss comes home and begins to express the anger towards the boss by yelling at her husband, who yells at his child, who then kicks the doll.
- **Regression** It is a defence mechanism by which the individual attempts to cope with a threatening situation by reacting to earlier, less mature behaviour pattern. *For example* The screaming and yelling of a surgeon at the surgical staff each time, she begins to have difficulty during an operation.
- **Rationalisation** With the defence mechanism of the rationalisation, an individual makes up what are supposed to be rational or logical explanation to justify unexpectable behaviour. *For example* A man might justify cheating on his income taxes while everybody else doing it.

- **Undoing** It is a defence mechanism involves an individual engaging in some sort of behaviour (*e.g.* saying I am sorry) designing to compensate or make amend for unacceptable feeling or actions expressed (*e.g.* after having lustful feeling about a co-worker an office supervisor may go home with a gift for his spouse to at one for this feeling).
- **Sublimation** The defence mechanism of sublimation involves converting unacceptable impulses into actions serving a more socially acceptable purpose. Becoming a sex therapist and teaching courses in human sexuality might be an acceptable way of expressing unconscious sexual desires, while helping others with their sexual problem.

Psycho-Sexual Development

Freud viewed personality development as moving through a series of stages. Each stages reflect the body area through which libido or sexual energy is discharged during that period.
According to Freud between birth and the age of 5 or 6 child passes through three stages of psycho sexual development. Oral and phallic.

These are combinedly known as *infantile stages*. Between ages 6 or 7 and 11 or 12, is the forth stage known as *latency stage*. Freud postulates sexual impulse tends to be repressed and sublimated during this stage. The last stage is known as the *genital stage*. Each stage (except latency stage) is characterised by primary aerogenous zone, which refers to the region of body that are sexually sublimated.

Oral Stage : Learning to Cope with the Significance Losses

This stage extend from birth to second year of life. Freud believed an excessive amount of libido was concentrated around the oral region. The infant gets pleasure out of sucking and taking food. This is called *oral erotic period*.

Child gets pleasure from biting after appearing of teeth and is known as *oral sadistic phase.* The basic feature of this stage is that the baby shows total dependency upon others for its care. Therefore, a person who is fixated at this stage is to dependent, pessimistic and argumentative. Smoking cigarettes, biting a pencil, chewing gum are all examples of fixation at oral stage.

Anal Stage : Learning When and Where

Freud refers to second psychosexual stage as anal stage and it extends roughly from 2nd year to 3rd year of life. The primary erogenous zone shift from the oral to anal region. The principle source of pleasure associated with the anal stage is the reduction of tension that accompanies reducing bodily tension by urinating and defecating. The conflict arises, when parents begins to make demands on the infant to regulate his source of pleasure during the process of toilet training. Freud believed that difficulty in the course of toilet training also had implication for future personality development. Personality characteristic arises from fixation during this period by how toilet training is approached by parents and caretaker.

Phallic Stage

Phallic stage begins during the 3rd year and continue through 5th year. Erogenous zones for the phallic stage is the general region. Observation of sex organ is a common tendency found in children at this stage. Children often manipulate their sex-organ and want to know about the cause of birth and sex. The male child recognise and touch his penis with a great interest. He is able to recognise the difference he has from his little sister. Freud said that the girl child become penis envy, when realises that she does not possess the penis like his father or brother.

The dominant conflict found in the phallic stage is oedipus complex in boys and 'electra complex' in girls. These complexes, according to Freud is biologically rooted and found in all human beings. The sexual attachment of son with his mother is called *oedipus complex* and daughter with father called *electra complex*. Castration anxiety arises along with oedipal complex in which the child fears that his father may castrate him. The anxiety help to resolve the oedipus complex as the boy don't want to lose his penis. The girl hate her mother who denied her a penis and love his father.

Latency Stage

Children of age between 5 to 11 years believed to be in this stage. All sexual urge and instinct of children are repressed in this stage. Both boys and girls prefers to mix with same sex. In this stage, a kind of sex antagonism arises. Intellectual interest and athletics became prime importance for libido. As no new erogenous zone emerges in this period, some psychologist viewed that this stage does not qualify for one of the stage of psychosexual stage.

Genital Stage

Arousal of sexual interest occurs with the start of puberty, which is directed towards opposite sex. Some secondary sex characteristics appears in both boy and girl as the sex organ matures and endocrine gland become active. Marriage and courtship are the result of the changes. The genital period which continues throughout the years of maturity never completely replace the earlier four stages together called *pregenital stage*.

Neo-Freudian

Neo-Freudian psychologists were thinkers who agreed with many of the fundamental tenets of Freud's psychoanalytic theory but changed and adapted new approach to incorporate their own beliefs, ideas and opinions.

There are number of Neo-Freudian thinkers who broke the Freudian Psychoanalytical to develop their own psychodynamic theories.

Some of these individuals were individually part of Freud's inner circle including Carl Jung, Alfred Adler and Karen Horney.

Carl Jung

Freud and Jung once had a friendship, but Jung broke away to form his ideas. Jung referred to his theory of personality as analytical psychology. He introduced the concept of collective unconscious. He described this as an universal structure shared by all member of the same species containing all of the instincts and archetypes that influence human behaviour.

Jung still placed great emphasis on the unconscious, but his theory placed a higher emphasis on his concept of the collective unconscious rather than the personal unconscious. Like many of other neo-Freudians, Jung also focused less on sex than Freud.

Alfred Adler

Adler believed that Freud's theories focused too heavily on sex as the primary motivator for human behaviour. Instead, Adler placed a lesser emphasise on the role of the unconscious and a greater focus on interpersonal and social influences. His approach, known as individual psychology was centered on the derive that all people have to compensate for their feelings of inferiority.

Karen Horney

Horney was one of the first women trained in psychoanalysis and she was only one who criticised Freud's depictions of women as inferior to men. Horney objected to Freud's portrayal of women as suffering from 'penis envy'. Instead she suggested that men experience 'womb envy' because they are unable to bear children. Her theory focuses on how to behave, depends upon different neurotic needs.

Humanistic Approach

The humanistic viewpoint is characterised by a belief that people are good, active, creative individuals who live in the present and base their actions on the subjective perception of experience. This viewpoint stresses the positive, healthy aspects of personality and the uniqueness of the individual. People are seen as active agents in the perception and modification of their own reality and are assumed to be motivated to move towards personal growth and self fulfilment.

Carl Rogers and Abraham H Maslow best represent the humanistic tradition in the study of personality.

Carl Roger's Theory

Carl Roger's theory given out of his caient centered approach to psychotherapy and behaviour change. Like psychoanalysis, the theory grew from efforts to help troubled people, but Roger's theory does not involve complex personality structures or stages of development.

Roger emphasised phenomenal field. This is of reference; it may or may not correspond to external reality.

Basic Assumption

The assumptions of his theory clearly illustrate the emphasis Roger placed on the person as being the center of attention in the study of personality. Subjective experience refers to the unique way each person views the world and his or her experience in it. As a result of ones own unique perception, ones response to these subjective experience will also be unique.

Concept of Carl Roger's Theory

Self Actualisation

Roger rejected the deterministic nature of both psychoanalysis and behaviourism and maintained that we behave as we do because of the way we perceive our situation. Roger believed that humans have one basic motive, that is the tendency to self actualise *i.e.* to fulfill one's potential and achieve the highest level of human beings.

Like a flower that will grow to its full potential, if the conditions are suitable, similarly people will flourish and reach their full potential if their environment is good enough. However, unlike a flower, the potential of the individual human is unique and we are meant to develop in different ways according to our personality. Roger believed that people are inherently good and creative.

This means that self actualisation occurs when a person's 'ideal self' congruent with their actual behaviour. Roger described individual who is actualising as a full functioning person. The main determinant of whether we will become self actualised in childhood experience.

The Fully Functioning Person

Roger believed that every person could achieve their goal. This means that the person is in touch with the her and then, his or her subjective experience and feelings, continuously growing and changing.

In many ways, Roger regarded the full functioning person as an ideal and one that people do not ultimately achieve. It is wrong to think of this as an end or completion of life's journey, rather it is a process of always becoming and changing.

Personality Development

Roger's personality theory is the motion of self or self concept. This is defined as "the organised, consistent set of perceptions and beliefs about oneself". The self is our inner personality which is influenced by the experience of their life.

According to Rogers, we want to feel, experience and behave in ways which are consistent with our self image and which reflect what we would like to be like, our ideal self. The closer our self image and ideal self are to each other, the more consistent or congruent we are and the higher our sense of self worth.

A person is said to be in a state of incongruence, if some of the totality of their experience is unacceptable to them and is denied or distorted in the self image. The humanistic approach states that the self is composed of concepts unique to ourselves. *The self concept includes three components.*

(i) Self worth (ii) Self image (iii) Ideal self

Abhraham Maslow's Theory

Maslow developed a theory of personality that has influenced a number of different fields. This wide influence is due to the high level of practicality of Maslow's theory. His theory accurately describes many realities of personal experience. Humanists do not believe that human beings are pushed and pulled by mechanical forces, either of stimuli and reinforcement or of unconscious instinctual impulses.

Humanist focuses on personality as a potential element. They believe that human strive for an upper level of capabilities. Humans seek the theories creativity, when it reaches the consciousness and wisdom. This has been labelled 'fully functioning person', 'healthy personality' or a Maslow calls this level, 'self actualising person.'

Maslow's Holistic Dynamic Theory

Abhraham Maslow formulated his viewpoint of personality in reaction to the pessimistic psychodynamic explanation of the unconsciously controlled individual and to behaviourism and its emphasis on the role of environmental factors as principal determinants of behaviour.

Maslow felt that individuals are motivated by the desire for self enhancement and self actualisation in a manner that goes well beyond satisfying base unconscious needs and simply reacting to external stimuli. He emphasised the creative, spontaneous and optimistic side of human nature over its dark, more pessimistic side. *Basic concept of this theories are given below*

The Nature and Structure of Human Needs

The basic concpets of Maslow's viewpoint include his conceptualisation of the nature and structure of human needs and their motivational impact on the individual. The principal objective of these needs is the motivation of the individual to reach a state of self actualisation. For Maslow the state of self actualisation involves people's attempt to reach their full potential by using their talents and abilities to the fullest extent, while trying to achieve personal growth, satisfaction and fulfilment.

The Hierarchy of Needs

Maslow organised human needs into five main groups in a hierarchical fashion. The logic of the hierarchy of needs is that the need at the lower end of the hierarchy exert more power in that they exert a greater sence of urgency to be satisfied than the need at the next level. Progressing up the hierarchy of needs results in the individual coming closer to achieving the state of self actualisation. *The hierarchy of needs are as follows*

(i) **Physiological Needs** The most basic need directly related to the survival of the individual, they are food, water, sleep, elimintation, such needs are extremely potent and when unfulfiled can dominate the life of individual.

(ii) **Safety Needs** The desire for stability is like creating an environment for living that is free from the threat of danger. They include the need for order, predictability and structure.

(iii) **Belongingness and Love Needs** The desire to be with others directly concerned with the basic desire to feel accepted by and have meaningful interpersonal relationship with others. Belonging to various social organisation, community service group as well as member of a family give one a sence of acceptance and belongingness.

(iv) **Esteem Needs** The desire to be recognised by others have respect of other and sence of self respect. Achieving status and recognition within significant group and being perceived as a worthy and able member of among them.

(v) **Self Actualisation** Developing the individual's full potential involves the individual's desire to develop his or her ability to their fullest potential. Such development involves obtaining a deeper sence of ones own desires and ability and maximising their expression in an attemp to bring them together.

The expression of the self actualisation also might involve designing clothes, working on body building or gardening. While, the self actualisation needs at the highest level of the hierarchy. It is also the least powerful. Individual must be extremely motivated from within to achieve the need.

Social Learning Theory

Social learning theory, theorised by Albert Bandura, postuated that people learn from one another, through observation, imitation and modeling. The theory has often been called as a bridge between behaviourist and cognitive learning theories because it encompasses attention, memory and motivation.

Bandura try to explain how children learn in social environment by observing and then imitating the behaviour of others.

He believed that learning could not be explained by reinforcement, but he believed that the presence of other's will also affect them. He noticed that the consequences of an observed behaviour often determined, whether or not children adopted the behaviour themselves.

Bandura performed the experiment in which he wanted child who attacks Bobo Doll. Child when hit, the doll fell over and then bounce back. Then, child was let loose and imitated the aggressive behaviour of the adult. However, when they observe adult acting aggressively and then being punished, Bandura noted that the children were less willing to imitate the aggressive behaviour themselves.

Bandura's Principles of Social Learning

The principle of Bandura's social learning are as follows

(i) **Attention** We cannot learn if we are not focused on the task. If we see something as being novel or different in some way, we are more likely to make it the focus of their attention. Social contexts help to reinforce these perceptions.

(ii) **Retention** We learn by internalising information in our memories. We recall that information later when we are required to respond to a situation that is similar the situation within which we first learned the information.

(iii) **Reproduction** We reproduce previously learned information (*e.g.* behaviour, skills, knowledge) when required. However, practice through mental and physical rehearsal often improves our responses.

(iv) **Motivation** We need to be motivated to do anything. Often that motivation originates from our observation of someone else being rewarded or punished for something they have done or said. This usually motivates us later to do, or avoid doing, the same thing.

Learning Theory (Pavlov and Skinner)

Pavlov was a behaviourist. This means that his theories focused on observable behaviour,because behaviour can be measured and thought cannot. Pavlov viewed individual differences in personality as the result of learning and different environmental experiences. Scientific evidence is the keyword in his theory.

Pavlov studied reflexes, that is the automatic behaviours that are caused by a stimulus from the environment. Some reflexes, such as blinking our eyes when a puff of air comes in it, or the sucking of a baby when something is put in his/ her mouth. This automatic behaviour can be manipulated this is called *conditioning*.

Conditioning has been defined as a form of learning in which capacity of eliciting a response is transferred from one stimulus to another. In the conditioning process, an unconditioned stimulus is given to a person.

This stimulus causes a reflex on its own. In order to explain Pavlov's learning theory of personality, first we will focus our attention on the process and principles of classical conditioning and see how these processes and principles are found to be helpful in the development and change of personality.

Process of Classical Conditioning

In order to examine the process of classical conditioning in a systematic manner, Pavlov first performed a simple operation on his dog, in which a rubber tube was inserted into salivary gland so that the precise amount of saliva secreted during the experiment could be measured.

After making these initial preparations a neutral stimulus (*e.g.* a bell) was presented for a brief period of time, followed quickly by a second stimulus known to elicit salivation response and called *unconditioned stimulus* (*e.g.* Meat Powder). Each pairing of Conditioned Stimulus (CS) and Unconditioned Stimulus (UCS) served as conditioning trials and a number of such pairings were conducted in rapid succession. As a result of repeated pairing the CS (bell) acquired the ability to evoke the salivation. Because the salivation to the bell (CR) began to occur only after the conditioning, it was termed conditioned response (CR). On the other hand the salivation response to the meat powder which seems to occur automatically was termed Unconditioned Response (UCR).

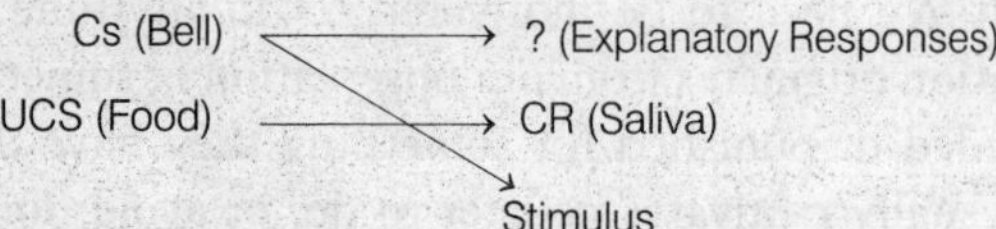

Pavlov further stated that a conditioned stimulus can serve as the basis for further conditioning, which is demonstrated by Pavlov. In the experiment of first order conditioning, food was removed from the situation, and a new stimulus (*e.g.* light) was paired with bell. This new stimulus also acquired the property of eliciting the response.

Skinner (Radical Behaviourism)

BF Skinner theory of personality, like other learning theories of personality did not grow out of the therapeutic situation, rather it emerged from the works carried out in laboratory setting. Skinner derived his principles of learning from the study of individual subjects in precisely controlled condition. He focused on the study of individual subjects instead of generalised group which reflected his belief that lawful control can be seen in individual behaviour.

He attempted to develop general laws by studying individual. Skinner in his theory of personality, emphasised some particular aspects of human nature like determinism, elementalism, changeability, objectivity, reactivity and knowability.

According to Skinner, for studying the personality one has to study and discover the relationship between the behaviour of the organism and its reinforcing consequences. Skinner's theory is based on the assumptions that behaviour is lawful, it can be predicated and it can be controlled.

Existential Theories

Existential psychologists were highly influenced with the philosophical idea of existence. According to existentialists human beings have no existence apart from the world.

In other words, existential psychologists aims at understanding of a person in his total existential reality. This movement in psychology has a strong antencedent forces. Person like Sown Kierkegaard, Staue, Karl Jasper and Martin Heidegger were important forces, whose viewpoint led to the development of existential psychology. *Psychologist associated with existential theories are discussed below.*

Ludwig Biswanger

Ludwig Biswanger, an existential psychologist. He said that, we can understand our experiences at three different levels. That is, that the conscious experience of being alive has three components: biological (Umwelt), social (Mitwelt) and inner or psychological experience (Eigenwelt).

(i) **Umwelt** In order to understand how existence feels we need to be aware of our physical sensation such as pain, pleasure, hunger, warmth, cold etc.

(ii) **Mitwelt** In order to understand how existence feels we need to be aware of our social relations. What we think and feel as a social creature who exists in a world with other people. Your thoughts and feelings about others and the thoughts and feelings you receive from them is your experience of Mitwelt.

(iii) **Eigenwelt** This could be simply classified as introspection. In order to understand how existence feels we need to be aware of the inner workings of ourselves. This is all about our attempt to understand ourselves; the experience of experience itself.

Rollo May

The existential perspective was introduced in the USA by Rollo May. He believed that individuals can only be understood in terms of their subjective sense of self. He felt that abnormal behaviour is often just used for protecting the centre this is the subjective sense of self against perceived threats. The person may give up on self growth if he or she feels his **centre is** threatened and retreat to the secure, centre. May was concerned with people's loss of faith in values. If we lose our commitment to a set of values; we will feel lonely and empty. Life will be meaningless. Ultimately we need to take responsibility for ourselves and find meaning in our lives.

Viktor Frankl

Viktor Frankl from his experience of Nazi camp observed that people, who had hopes of being reunited with loved ones, or who had projects, they felt a need to complete, tended to have better chances that those who had lost all home. During his time in the camps, he observed people who survived horrific circumstances, but were able to resist **despair**. He felt that those who were able to do so were people who found some spiritual meaning in their lives. He believed that the prime motive of human behaviour is the will to meaning. In order to find a meaning in our troubled existence we need to discover meaning through values and we have a moral duty to discover these values. And we discover our values through work, through love for others and through confrontation with our own suffering.

Frankl devised a treatment to help people how find the meaning in their lives. It is called *Logotherapy* from the word Logos = Greek for meaning. Logotherapy views psychological problems as symptomatic of the person having lost meaning in life. Once meaning is rediscovered, the problems tend to resolve. This is done by confronting patients with their responsibility for their existence and by helping them choose values

Transpersonal Psychology

Transpersonal psychology in the field of psychology which integerates psychological concepts theories and methods with the subject matter and practices of the spiritual discipline. It uses both quantitative and qualitative methods. Its central concepts are non-duality, self transcendence and optimum human development and mental health and its core practices includes meditation and ritual.

According to the Association for Transpersonal Psychology, the mission of the field is to promot ecospiritual human transformation through transpersonal inquiry and action. Unlike religion, transpersonal psychology attempts to intigrate Western psychology to translate spiritual principles into empirical based scientife language.

Transpersonal psychology is a field inquiry which includes theory, research and practices for evaluating and confirming or disconfirming it's finding.

A core practice for transpersonal psychology includes meditation, mindfulness and contemplation. While rituals has hobben indentified a core practice in transpersonal psychology, though it is central in many cultural and religious traditions that promote spiritual values.

Cognitive Theory

Many psychologist laid emphasis on the cognitive aspect to be influential in development of personality. *Model dealing with cognitive theory is discussed below.*

Mischel's Cognitive - Affective Model

Walter Mischel is a personality researcher whose work has helped to shape the social-cognitive theory of personality. Mischel's experiments suggested that an individual's behaviour is not simply the result of his or her traits, but fundamentally dependent on situational cues-the needs of a given situation. Mischel's ideas led him to develop the cognitive-affective model of personality .

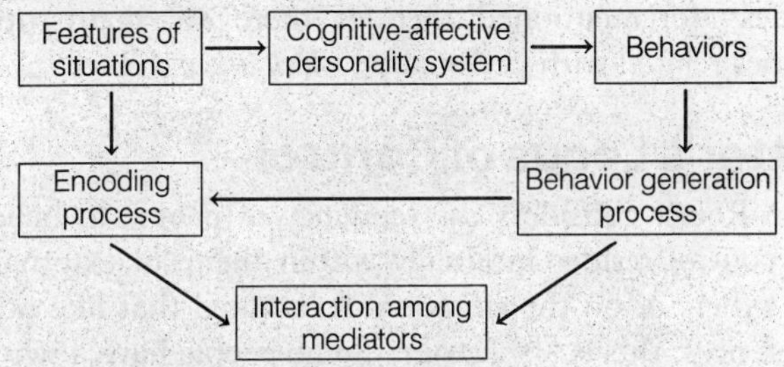

Basic Aspect of Mischel's Cognitive-Affective Model are

The Person-Situation Debate

The conflict of ideas between trait theories and Mischel's cognitive-affective model became known as the *person-situation debate,* or 'trait v/s state.' If someone is considered 'nice,' are they nice in every situation? Is the trait more important in predicting behaviour, or the situation? Some traits, like intellect, are stable across situations; however, people may change other aspects of their personality from situation to situation. Although his early research focused mostly on the importance of situation, this controversy was stimulated specifically by Mischel's later research showing that both trait and situation are important in predicting behaviour. This argument contradicted the fundamental tenet of trait theory that only internal traits, not external situations, should be taken into account.

Personality Signatures

Mischel suggested that consistency would be found in distinctive but stable patterns of 'if-then' situation-behaviour relations that form personality signatures. In other words, if x situation occurs, then y behaviour might result. Rather than defining people merely by their traits ("he is an irritable person"), he argued that personality research should factor in the importance of the context ("he is irritable when talked down to"). In this way, Mischel emphasised the importance of physical, social and environmental forces in shaping behaviour.

Self-Regulation

One of Mischel's most notable contributions to personality psychology is his work on self-regulation. Self-regulation refers to the ability to set and work toward goals; it is often described as willpower and often relates to the ability to delay gratification. Delayed gratification is the concept of denying oneself a reward in the present to get a better reward in the future.

Other Important Theories

Besides aforementioned theories there are many other theories related with personality, *which are as follows*

Rotter's Locus of Control

Julian Rotter considers the tendency of people to believe that control resides internally within them, or externally, with others or on the situation. It is noted that like other preferences, this is a spectrum. Some people have a wholly internal or external locus of control, but many will have views, perhaps varying with situation. *For example* Some will be more internal at home and more external at work.

'Locus of Control' For many people, their only exposure to the ideas of Julian B. Rotter in his concept of generalised expectancies for control of reinforcement, more commonly known as *locus of control.* Locus of control refers to people's very general, cross-situational beliefs about what determines whether or not they get reinforced in life. People can be classified along a continuum from very internal to very external.

People with a strong internal locus of control believe that the responsibility for whether or not they get reinforced ultimately lies with themselves. Internals believe that success or failure is due to their own efforts. In contrast, externals believe that the reinforcers in life are controlled by luck, chance, or powerful others. Therefore, they see little impact of their own efforts on the amount of reinforcement they receive.

Rotter has written extensively on problems with people's interpretations of the locus of control concept. *First,* he has warned people that locus of control is not a typology. It represents a continuum, not an either/or proposition. *Second,* because locus of control is a generalised expectancy it will predict people's behaviour across situations.

However, there may be some specific situations in which people who *e.g,* are generally external behave like internals. That is because their learning history has shown them that they have control over the reinforcement they receive in certain situations, although overall they perceive little control over what happens to them. Again, one can see the importance of conceiving of personality as the interaction of the person and the environment.

Seligmans Explanatory Style

Explanatory style is a psychological attribute that indicates how people explain to themselves why they experience a particular event, either positive or negative.

Dr. Martin Seligman is considered as a founding father of positive psychology, former head of the American Psychological Association (APA), Dr. Seligman is a leading authority in the field and had a hand in developing early attribution style theories based on the learned helplessness model which later evolved into a more robust explanatory style.

The modern theory of explanatory style plays a prominent role in mediation between positive and negative mental states stemmed originally from the work of Overmier and Seligman in which they formulated the learned helplessness model.

During the study, rats were given electric shocks over which they had no control. It was found that rats learned that the outcome was independent of their responses and became passive, thereby learning helplessness.

Based on the findings, Seligman proposed three dimensions of explanatory style, summarised by the three Ps

(i) **Pervasiveness** Global/Specific: Whether or not the factors influencing an outcome are seen to be event-specific or globally applicable.

(ii) **Permanence** Stable / Unstable: If the outcome is based on factors which are (changeable) unstable or perceived to be temporally fixed (stable).

(ii) **Personalisation** Internal/External: Relating to the level of personal control an individual feels they hold relating to an outcome.

Based on these dimensions, individuals can display an optimistic or pessimistic explanatory style.

Over the years, Seligman has refined and validated the theory as well as proposed several methods of measuring an individual's explanatory style, including the Attributional Style Questionnaire (Peterson, Semmel, Von Baeyer, Abramson, Metalsky, and Seligman, the Children's Attributional Style Questionnaire (Kaslow, Tannenbaum, and Seligman, and the Content Analysis of Verbatim Explanations Technique (Peterson, Schulman, Castellon, and Seligman.

Kohlberg's Theory of Moral Developments

Lawrence Kohlberg agreed with Piaget's theory of moral development in principle but wanted to develop his idea further. He used Piaget's technique to tell people stories involving moral dilemmas. In each case, he presented a choice to be considered *e.g.* between the rights of some authority and the needs of some deserving individuals who is being unfamily treated.

Kohlberg's Theory of Moral Development: An Overview

Level/Stage	Description
Preconventional Level	
Stage 1 Punishment and obedience orientation	Morality judged in terms of consequences
Stage 2 Naive hedonistic orientation	Morality judged in terms of what satisfies own needs or those or others
Conventional Level	
Stage 3 Good boy-good girl orientation	Morality judged in terms of adherence to social rules or norms with respect to personal acquaintances
Stage 4 Social order-maintaining orientation	Morality judged in terms of social rules or laws applied universally not just to acquaintances
Postconventional Level	
Stage 5 Legalistic orientation	Morality judged in terms of human rights, which may transcend laws
Stage 6 Universal ethical principle orientation	Morality judged in terms of self chosen ethical principles

The Preconventional Level

At the first level of moral development, the **preconventional level**, children judge morality largely in terms of consequences. Actions that lead to rewards are perceived as good or acceptable ones that lead to punishments are seen as bad or unacceptable.

For example A child at this stage might say, "The man should not steal the drug, because if he does, he'll be punished".

The Conventional Level

As children's cognitive abilities increases, Kohlberg suggests, they enter a second level of moral development, the conventional level. Now, they are aware of some of the complexities of the social order and judge morality in terms of what supports and preserves the laws and rules of their society.

Thus, a child at this stage might reason, " It's ok to steal the drug, because no one will think you are bad if you do. If you don't and let your wife die, you'll never be able to look in anyone's eye's again".

The Postconventional Level

Finally, in adolescence or early adulthood individuals enter a third level known as the *postconventional level*, or principled level. At this stage, people judge morality in terms of abstract principles and values rather than in terms of existing laws or rules of society. Persons who attain this stage often believe that certain obligations and values transcend the laws of society.

The rules follow are abstract and ethical, nor concrete like the ten commandments and are based on inner conscience rather than on external sources of authority.

For example a person at this stage of moral development might argue for stealing the drug as follows. "If the man doesn't steal the drug, he is putting property above human life; this makes no sense.

People could live togther without private property , but a respect for human life is essential." In contrast, if they argue for not stealing the drug, they might reason, "If the man stole the drug he would not be blamed by others, but he would probably blame himself, since he has violated his own standards of honesty and hurt another person for his own gain."

EXAM BASED QUESTIONS

1 A personality theory is a/an

(a) category used to describe personality.
(b) interrelated system of concepts used to explain personality.
(c) relatively permanent set of behaviour patterns.
(d) subjective evaluation of person.

2 The term personality refers to

(a) the hereditary aspects of one's emotional nature.
(b) unique and enduring behaviour patterns.
(c) favourable and unfavourable personal characteristics.
(d) charisma, character or temperament.

3 One problem psychologists have with personality type is they

(a) are hypothetical constructs
(b) oversimplify personality
(c) describe character, not personality
(d) are not observable or measurable

4 Theories and beliefs differ in that

(a) theories are more important than beliefs.
(b) beliefs are more important than theories.
(c) theories rely on systematic observations, but beliefs do not.
(d) beliefs can make predictions, but theories cannot.

5 Which of the following is not included in the definition of personality psychology?

(a) It deals with adaptations to the environment.
(b) It deals with how traits influence the environment.
(c) It deals with how the environment influences traits.
(d) All of the above

6 Which of the following could account for a major personality change in middle adulthood?

(a) Moving to a new city (b) Changing your looks
(c) Making new friends (d) A personal tragedy

7 Research on the consistency of personality across situations has shown that there is

(a) a lot of consistency
(b) no consistency
(c) consistency only with central traits
(d) consistency only in very similar situations

8 Definition of the nature of human personality is based on

(a) human behaviour is complex
(b) behaviour is not always what is appears to be
(c) we are not always in control of the factors determining our behaviour
(d) All of the above

9 Which one of the following statements about source trait is incorrect?

(a) They appear to be influenced by genetic endowment.
(b) They describe superficial attributes.
(c) They refer only to temperamental characteristics.
(d) They were discovered by Eysenck.

10 Trait approach to personality asserts that traits are

(a) adjectives describing behaviour.
(b) discrete and discontinuous categories of people.
(c) generalised systems which ensure consistency in behaviour of individuals.
(d) psychological categories of temperament associated with specified body physique.

11 According to Eysenck's theory, in which of the following traits, the genetic factors explain maximum variation?

(a) Extraversion
(b) Intelligence
(c) Neuroticism
(d) Psychoticism

12 Who believed that traits existed as part of the nervous systems?

(a) Costa and McCrae (b) Allport
(c) Cattell (d) Rogers

13 According to Cattell, traits that are numerous and can easily be seen by other people are called

(a) central traits
(b) cardinal traits
(c) surface traits
(d) source traits

14 Cattell's method of gathering data in the absence of any pre-existing hypothesis is called the

(a) intuitive method
(b) orthogonal technique
(c) hypothetico-deductive method
(d) inductive method

15 Allport suggested that each individual has a unique set of personality traits. He called these personal disposition, arrange them in order

(a) cardinal, central and secondary
(b) central, secondary, cardinal
(c) secondary, central, cardinal
(d) None of the above

16 Which of the following is correct order of hierarchical model of personality?

(a) Trait, Super trait, Specific response, Habitual
(b) Super trait, Specific response, Trait, Habitual
(c) Specific response, Habitual, Trait, Super trait
(d) Habitual, Trait, Super trait, Specific response

17 Which of the following is the proper x-y axis sequence of psychoticism dimension?

(a) Neurotic, Extrovert, Stable, Introvert
(b) Introvert, Stable, Neurotic, Extrovert
(c) Stable, Neurotic, Introvert, Extrovert
(d) None of the above

18 Which of the following correctly orders Eysenck's hierarchical structure?
(a) Habitual acts, Specific acts, Narrow traits, Super traits
(b) Specific acts, Habitual acts, Narrow traits, Super traits
(c) Super traits, Specific acts, Habitual acts, Narrow traits
(d) Narrow traits, Super traits, Specific acts, Habitual acts

19 The five factor model is based on
(a) the lexical approach
(b) the statistical approach
(c) factor analysis
(d) All of the above

20 A trait is best described as
(a) a cluster of surface factors.
(b) a temporary attitude toward a person or event.
(c) a relatively permanent disposition of a person.
(d) an environmentally determined hypothetical construct that shapes an individual's behaviour and thought.

21 Which of the following is false about shyness?
(a) Shyness is related to public self-consciousness and other psychological factors that can be altered, thereby helping some people overcome shyness.
(b) Shyness typically involves social anxiety, evaluation fears and a lack of social skills.
(c) Shyness is marked by heightened public self-consciousness and a tendency to regard one's shyness as a lasting trait.
(d) Shyness can be decreased by replacing supportive thoughts with self-defeating beliefs.

22 Which of the following is true about trait theory?
(a) The earliest theory of personality classified people into types according to their predominant humour or body fluid.
(b) Most psychologists conceive of personality differences as being represented by degree, not kind.
(c) Personality traits are the factors that underlie patterns of behaviour.
(d) All of the above.

23 Factor analysis identifies variables that tend to be correlated, to study personality, which of the following is false?
(a) Researchers must observe the behaviour of a large number of people.
(b) The observations are limited to responses to questions on telephonic conversation.
(c) Investigators observe people's behaviour in semi-natural situations.
(d) Statistical procedures then permit investigators to determine, which items a given person tends to answer in the same way.

24 The five factors model trait dimensions have been shown to have
(a) no relevance in other culture
(b) only 20% rate of heritability
(c) relevance only for Western cultures
(d) abut 50% rate of heritability across culture

25 Which one of the following factors is not included in the 'Big Five' dimensions of personality?
(a) Extraversion (b) Neuroticism
(c) Agreeableness (d) Intelligence

26 In the Big Five theory of personality 'C' stands for
(a) conscientiousness (b) consciousness
(c) contrariness (d) complexity

27 Elsie's daughter gave her a microwave oven for her birthday. Elsie has never used a microwave and is scared to use this one. Instead, she lets it sit in her kitchen and refuses to let her daughter teach her how to use it. Elide would probably score very low on
(a) agreeableness (b) neuroticism
(c) introversion (d) openness

28 Which of the following is not one of the traits found to have a genetic component in studies of identical twins?
(a) Intelligence (b) Leadership ability
(c) Antagonism (d) Aggressiveness

29 Which of the following lists corresponds to the five-factor theory of personality?
(a) Introversion, Neuroticism, Sociability, Openness and Psychoticism
(b) Openness, Introversion, Practicality, Punctuality and Conscientiousness
(c) Neuroticism, Extraversion, Conscientiousness, Agreeableness and Openness
(d) Extraversion, Emotionality, Impulsivity, Neuroticism and Agreeableness

30 Psychodynamic perspective emphasises the role of
(a) cognitive processes on decision making
(b) tendencies towards personal growth
(c) internal forces and conflicts in behaviour
(d) cultural factors on various aspects of behaviour

31 Which among the following are related with the persist worries in the five factor theory of personality?
(a) Introversion (b) Punctuality
(c) Neuroticism (d) Openess

32 Which of Freud's parts of the personality is most likely a dictator?
(a) Id (b) Super ego
(c) Ego (d) Ego ideal

33 In Freud's view of the personality, the devil would be seen as the
(a) conscience (b) Id
(c) ego (d) super ego

34 According to Freud, which part of the personality makes the person feel pride when doing the right thing?
(a) Ego (b) Super ego
(c) Ego ideal (d) Unconscious

35 **In which psychosexual stage might fixation result in a person, who is excessively neat and fussy?**
(a) Oral (b) Anal
(c) Phallic (d) Genital

36 **Freud outlined three major stages of development. Arrange them in chronological order.**
(a) Infancy, latency, genital period
(b) Latency, genital period, infancy
(c) Genital period, latency, infancy
(d) Genital period, infancy, latency

37 **Which of the following represents the proper order of personality development, according to Freud in infantile stage?**
(a) Oral, anal, phallic (b) Anal, oral, phallic
(c) Phallic, latency, genital (d) Latency, phallic, anal

38 **According to psychoanalytic theory , the basic elements of personality are id, ego and super ego. These three are respectively represented as**
(a) biological, psychological and social dimensions
(b) unconscious, conscious and self identity dimensions
(c) oral stage, latency period and genital stage
(d) pre-conscious, subconscious and unconscious

39 **Transpersonal psychology consist of**
(a) Qualitative method
(b) Quantitative method
(c) Both a and b
(d) None of the above

40 **Who is considered as founding father of positive psychology?**
(a) Carl Jung (b) Martin Seligman
(c) Alfred Adler (d) Karen Horney

41 **Which one of the following option is correct? A relative lack of effect in interpersonal relationships; lack of concern with conventional morality and low ideological commitment are some of the characteristics of persons, who are**
(a) high on need for achievement
(b) high on need for power
(c) low on need for affiliation
(d) high on machiavellism

42 **In general, Neo-Freudians such as Alfred, Adler and Karen Horney accepted many of Freud's views but placed more emphasise on**
(a) development throughout the life span
(b) the collective unconscious
(c) the role of id
(d) social interactions

43 **Adler recognised four modes of safeguarding through withdrawal. They are order in the following manner, which one?**
(a) Moving backward, standing still, hesitating, constructing obstacles
(b) Hesitating, constructing obstacles, moving forward, standing still
(c) Moving backward, the unhesitating, constructing obstacles, standing still
(d) None of the above

44 **In Jungian psychology, introversion and extroversion are regarded as**
(a) integral (b) function
(c) archetypes (d) complexes

45 **Which of these is not a substage of Jung's childhood period?**
(a) Monarchic (b) Oral
(c) Dualistic (d) Anarchic

46 **The process of becoming whole or complete *i.e.* actualising the various components of personality is called**
(a) active imagination (b) individuation
(c) introspection (d) maturation

47 **Roger believed that in order for people to become fully functioning, they must receive .... from the important people in their lives.**
(a) unconditional positive regard
(b) conditional positive regard
(c) positive reinforcement
(d) positive modeling

48 **In his theory of motivation, Maslow assumed that**
(a) people in different cultures have different basic needs
(b) motivation is nearly always conscious
(c) people are motivated by one need at a time
(d) people are continually motivated by one need or another

49 **Maslow's concept of hierarchy of needs assumes that**
(a) higher needs have prepotency over lower needs
(b) lower needs have prepotency over higher needs
(c) love needs are more basic than physiological needs
(d) cognitive needs must be satisfied before aesthetic needs become motivators

50 **Which one of the following is a major assessment method used by humanistic psychologists?**
(a) Q-sort (b) Self respect
(c) Projective (d) Case study

51 **In Rogerian theory, the actualising tendency**
(a) is synonymous with the formative tendency
(b) has the same or nearly the same meaning as self-actualisation
(c) refers to the person's organismic experiences
(d) refers to the tendency to actualise the perceived self

52 **Inner tension arises, Rogers said, when a conflict exists between the**
(a) actualising tendency and the organismic self
(b) emotion and cognition
(c) the values of others and one's own values
(d) the formative tendency and the actualisation tendency

53 Maslow argued that self-actualisation is achieved only after the satisfaction of several other important, but lesser needs, arrange the lesser needs in order.
(a) Physiological needs, Safety needs, Attachment needs, Esteem needs
(b) Esteem needs, Physiological needs, Safety needs, Attachment needs
(c) Attachment needs, Esteem needs, Physiological needs, Safety needs
(d) None of the above

54 Rogers therapy is the relational climate created by the therapist's attitude to their client, the process that is followed based on the success of the conditions are
(a) congruence : unconditional positive regard: empathy
(b) unconditional positive regard : empathy : congruence
(c) empathy : unconditional positive regard : congruence
(d) All of the above

55 With regards to needs, which of these statements would Maslow endorse?
(a) Safety needs must be satisfied more fully than physiological needs.
(b) People are usually conscious of their underlying needs.
(c) The order of needs may be reversed in certain cases.
(d) One need must be completely satisfied before another can become a motivator.

56 When a patient develops maladaptive habits and the key focus of psychotherapy is on changing specific observable response pattern identified as a problem, the therapy is known as
(a) psychoanalytic therapy (b) behaviour therapy
(c) humanistic therapy (d) family therapy

57 Which one of the following is the key concept in Bandura's theory?
(a) Self-defence and self -actualisation
(b) Self-reinforcement and self-defence
(c) Self-actualisation and self-efficiency
(d) Self-efficacy and self-reinforcement

58 A person is terribly afraid to dogs. To overcome his fear, he is first shown some slides of small friendly looking dogs and later, of bigger and bigger dogs. Finally he is exposed to slides of large and lunging dogs. This procedure is called
(a) cognitive therapy
(b) systematic desensitisation
(c) covert sensitisation
(d) aversion therapy

59 Learning sex-appropriate behaviour is greatly influenced by
(a) self-reinforcement and resolution of unconscious conflicts.
(b) identification and imitation.
(c) toilet training and early feeding contacts.
(d) valuing and self-regard.

60 Behavioural theories of personality are often criticised for their
(a) inability to test or verify concepts.
(b) limited recognition of temperament, emotion and subjective factors.
(c) ability to explain behaviour after the fact only.
(d) emphasis on the conditions under which behaviours occur.

61 Learning theorists
(a) have removed the person from personality
(b) emphasise situational determinants of behaviour
(c) stress the role of the unconscious
(d) would view a trait as stable in all situations

62 According to behaviourists,
(a) hostile, generous or destructive impulses arise in the unconscious.
(b) personality is acquired through conditioning and observational learning.
(c) personality is strongly influenced by one's self-image.
(d) personality develops from initial feelings of inferiority.

63 Behaviourists are to the external environment as humanists are to
(a) stress (b) personal growth
(c) humankind (d) internal conflicts

64 The social learning theorists potray
(a) learner as passive recipient of environmental influences.
(b) no individual difference with explaining behaviour.
(c) learner as having internal cognitive processes to explain imitation etc.
(d) Both a and c

65 Attribution of one's own motive to others is called
(a) identification (b) projection
(c) association (d) reacion formation

66 Frankl did not argue for a particular meaning to life or a particular set of values, he suggested three ways in which meaning can be created in life, arrange them in order.
1. Achievement
2. Transcendent experience
3. Attitude toward unavoidable suffering

Codes
(a) 2, 3 and 1 (b) 2, 1 and 3
(c) 1, 3 and 2 (d) 1, 2 and 3

67 Which statement is most consistent with Bandura's concept of humanity?
(a) People are most strongly motivated to increase self-efficacy.
(b) Human personality is formed mostly by the forces of biology.
(c) People must successfully navigate the stages of development in order to become psychologically healthy.
(d) Humans have the capacity to become many things within the limits set by biology.

68 Bandura first became interested in clinical psychology when he

(a) entered graduate school at Stanford University.
(b) worked on the Alaska highway after graduation from high school.
(c) met Skinner at the 1972 APA convention.
(d) entered graduate school at the University of Iowa.

69 The levels of cognition of interest to personality psychologists are

(a) Perception, Interpretation, Beliefs, Desires
(b) Perception, Beliefs, Desires, Interest
(c) Interpretation,Beliefs, Development, Perception
(d) None of the above

70 Which of the following correctly explains the process of learned helplessness?

(a) Uncontrollable bad events : Perceived lack of control : Generalised helpless behaviour
(b) Generalised helpless behaviour : Uncontrollable bad events : Perceived lack of control
(c) Uncontrollable bad events : Generalised helpless behaviour : Perceived lack of control
(d) None of the above

71 According to whom, we can discover life's meaning by doing a deed, experiencing a value and suffering?

(a) Victor Frankl (b) Rollo May
(c) Carl Rogers (d) Abraham Maslow

72 Who said that by expanding self awareness people can acquire freedom of action?

(a) Rogers (b) Maslow (c) May (d) Frankl

73 The psychological situation expectancy and reinforcement value are important concepts in

(a) social learning theory (b) Gestalt theories
(c) radical behaviourism
(d) instrumental conditioning

74 Classical conditioning is based on the work of which person?

(a) Freud (b) Pavlov
(c) Bandura (d) None of these

75 Skinner drew distinction between which among the following?

(a) Rats and humans
(b) Normal and abnormal conditioning
(c) Operant and respondent behaviour
(d) Cognition and emotion

76 What is a positive reinforcement?

(a) Any consequence where someone pleasure is needed
(b) A classical conditioning technique
(c) Both a and b
(d) Neither a nor b

77 The technique of shaping was used by which of the following?

(a) Watson (b) Skinner
(c) Pavlov (d) None of these

78 Which of the following is an example of disengagement of internal control?

(a) A student skips class, then tells the instructor that she had to attend her grandmother's funeral.
(b) A child is punished for playing with his genitals and consequently represses the experience.
(c) A conscientious doctor performs an illegal operation, but justifies her actions to herself by saying the surgery was necessary to save a life.
(d) A store clerk shoplifts merchandise, feels guilty and returns it before anyone notices.

79 Rotter's concept of humanity assumes that people

(a) are motivated by their view of events more than by the events themselves.
(b) are motivated by unconscious needs.
(c) react to events rather than interacting with their meaningful environments.
(d) are motivated primarily by past experiences.

80 Who among the following developed the theory of depression based on the idea of learned helplessness?

(a) Seligman (b) Rotter (c) Adler (d) Bandura

81 Who among the following developed interpersonal trust scale ?

(a) Bandura (b) Rotter (c) Roger (d) Kelly

82 Seligman proposed three dimension of explanatory style known by the three Ps. Correct the right option ?

(a) Pervasiveness, Prediction and Personalisation
(b) Pervasiveness, Permanence and Personalisation
(c) Permanence, Probability and Pervasiveness
(d) None of the above

83 Concept of person-situation debate is related with which approach of personality developments?

(a) Social learing (b) Humanistic
(c) Neo-freudian (d) Cognitive

84 Which of the following pairs is not correctly matched?

(a) Cognitive needs : Curiosity, exploration, understanding of world
(b) Esteem needs : To be competent and recognised
(c) Attachment needs : To love and to be loved, to have friend
(d) None of the above

85 Which of the statements of pairs is correctly explained in the self concept?

1. The Self-Concept: It includes all those aspects of one's identity that are perceived in awareness.
2. The Ideal Self: Our view of our self as we would like to be or aspire to be.

Codes

(a) Only 1 (b) Only 2
(c) Both 1 and 2 (d) Neither 1 or 2

86 Match the following

List I (Stage)		List II (Ego-Functioning)
A. Conscientious	1.	Reconciles inner conflicts renounce what can not be attained
B. Autonomous	2.	Cores with inner conflict tolerates differences
C. Integrated	3.	Follows internal rules, guilt
D. Presocial	4.	Unaware of distinction between self and non-self

Codes

	A	B	C	D		A	B	C	D
(a)	3	2	4	1	(b)	3	2	1	4
(c)	1	3	2	4	(d)	1	4	3	2

87 Match the following

List I (High Score Characteristic)	List II (Factor)
A. Creative, artistic, curious imaginative and non- conforming	1. Neuroticism
B. Organised, reliable neat and ambitious	2. Agreeableness (A)
C. Talkative, optimistic sociable and affectionate	3. Extraversion (E)
D. Good natured, trusting and helpful	4. Conscientiousness(c)
E. Working, insecure ancious and temperamental	5. Openness (o)

Codes

	A	B	C	D	E
(a)	1	4	3	5	2
(b)	4	1	2	3	5
(c)	5	4	3	2	1
(d)	5	3	4	2	1

88 Match the following

List I (Authors)		List II (Tests/Techniques)
A. HJ Eysenck	1.	Seven point rating scale to measure somato type
B. WH Sheldon	2.	Orthogonal method
C. GW Allport	3.	Repertory grid
D. DG Kelley	4.	Idiographic method

Codes

	A	B	C	D		A	B	C	D
(a)	1	2	4	3	(b)	2	1	3	4
(c)	1	2	3	4	(d)	2	1	4	3

89 Which of the following pairs is/are correctly matched?

(a) Cardinal Traits : A trait, so dominant a person's entire life revolves around it

(b) Central Traits : Characteristics that are exhibited in specific situations

(c) Secondary Traits : Qualities that characterise a person's daily interactions

(d) All of the above

90 Match the following

	List I (Theorists)		List II (Aspects of Human Nature)
A.	Hobbes	1.	Humans are selfish
B.	Rousseau	2.	Humans are good
C.	Freud	3.	Natural impulses are detrimental to society
D.	Rogers	4.	Natural impulses are noble and good

Codes

	A	B	C	D		A	B	C	D
(a)	3	1	4	2	(b)	1	3	4	2
(c)	1	2	3	4	(d)	3	1	2	4

91 Match the following

	List I (Low Scores Characteristic)		List II (Factor)
A.	Conventional and uncreative	1.	Conscientiousness
B.	Unreliable, lazy and careless negligent and spontaneous	2.	Openness
C.	Reserved and comfortable being alone	3.	Agreeableness
D.	Rude, uncooperative and irritable aggressive and competitive	4.	Extraversion

Codes

	A	B	C	D
(a)	2	3	4	1
(b)	2	1	4	3
(c)	1	4	2	3
(d)	1	2	4	3

92 Match the following

	List I(Socio-Cultural Processes)		List II(Labels)
A.	Similarities in behaviour between a child and model, child's motive to be like the model and the process of taking on the attributes of the model	1.	Cultural sanctions
B.	In an experiment, a man is found to be willing to deliver severe shocks to a male opponent, but not to female opponent	2.	Effect of moderator variables
C.	After a certain age, males are not rewarded for displaying, dependency, but similar dependent behaviour may be acceptable in females	3.	Vicarious reinforcement
D.	The child in an impoverished neighbourhood sees that tough looking gangsters have status, power and other nice things and appreciates them	4.	Identification

Codes

	A	B	C	D
(a)	4	2	3	1
(b)	4	2	1	3
(c)	2	4	1	3
(d)	2	4	3	1

93 Match the following

List I (Reactions)	List II (Defence Mechanism)
A. A man who is angry with his neighbour goes deer hunting	1. Denial
B. A smoker insists there is no convincing evidence that smoking impairs health	2. Displacement
C. Someone who secretly enjoys drug and works to outlaw it	3. Projection
D. A man who beats his wife writes a book arguing that people have an instinctive need for a aggressive behaviour	4. Reaction formation

Codes

	A	B	C	D		A	B	C	D
(a)	3	1	2	4	(b)	4	1	3	2
(c)	1	2	3	4	(d)	2	1	4	3

94 Match the following

List I (Attributes)	List II (Consequences)
A. Person's final goal	1. The striving for success or superiority
B. Force behind a person's activity	2. A creation of the creative power
C. Personality	3. No real existence yet influence individuals
D. Fictions	4. Subjective perceptions

Codes

	A	B	C	D		A	B	C	D
(a)	3	1	2	4	(b)	2	1	4	3
(c)	4	1	3	2	(d)	1	2	3	4

95 Match the following

List I (Psychological)	List II (Concepts)
A. Alfred Adler	1. Importance of childhood social tension
B. Karen Horney	2. Sought to balance Freud's masculine biases
C. Carl Jung	3. Emphasises collective unconscious

Codes

	A	B	C		A	B	C
(a)	3	1	2	(b)	2	1	3
(c)	3	2	1	(d)	1	2	3

96 Match the following

List I (Concepts)	List II (Theories)
A. Simply refers to the development history of energy	1. Ego psychology
B. Proceeds through different stages characterising conflicts between individual self and society	2. Psychosexual theory
C. Humans have one basic tendency to self actualise	3. Self-actualisation theory

Codes

	A	B	C
(a)	1	2	3
(b)	3	2	1
(c)	1	3	2
(d)	2	1	3

97 Match the following

List I (Individual Behaviour)	List II (Theories)
A. The process of imitating others apparently plays a part in the way children learn to be aggressive or altruistic	1. Self Actualisation Theory (Carl Rogers)
B. Human beings are powerful architects of themselves; and display actualising tendency	2. The Psychoanalytic Theory of Personality (Freud, S)
C. Emphasis on the conflict between inborn instincts and societal demands	3. The Social Learning Theory (Bandura, A)

Codes

	A	B	C		A	B	C
(a)	3	1	2	(b)	2	1	3
(c)	1	2	3	(d)	2	3	1

98 According to Kohlberg's model of the Development of Moral Judgement, which of the following pairs are correctly matched?

1. Social order orientation : In this behaviour the sort that makes society function in an orderly way
2. Legalistic orientation : People have a right to do this
3. Universal ethical principle orientation : Does this behaviour follow the rules that one personally believe in

Codes

(a) 1 and 2 (b) 1 and 3
(c) 2 and 3 (d) 1, 2 and 3

99 Which of the following pairs is/are correctly matched?

1. Loevinger sentence : Ego-development completion test
2. Personal orientation : Self-actualisation inventory
3. Strange situation : Infant attachment procedure

Codes

(a) Only 1 (b) 1 and 2 (c) 1, 2 and 3 (d) 2 and 3

100 Which of the following pairs are correctly matched?

1. Mesomorph : Least powerful
2. Endomorph : Round soft body build
3. Ectomorph : Tall & thin
4. Eurymorph : Somatotonia

Codes

(a) 1 and 2 (b) 3 and 4 (c) 2 and 3 (d) 1 and 4

101 Which of the following concepts had made major contributions to dynamic approach to personality?

1. Super ego
2. Social cognition
3. Psychosexual development
4. Unconscious impulses
5. Repression

Select the correct answer using the codes given below

(a) 1, 4 and 5 (b) 2, 3 and 4
(c) 1, 3, 4 and 5 (d) 1, 2, 3 and 5

102 Karen Henry proposed that the neurotic needs may be classified as moving towards, moving away from or moving against people. Which of the following underlying these three?

1. Love 2. Independence
3. Power 4. Inferiority

Select the correct answer using the codes given below

(a) 1, 2 and 4 (b) 1, 2 and 3
(c) 2, 3 and 4 (d) 1, 3 and 4

103 Which of the following statements is/are correct?

1. Bandura's theory does emphasis and detail the role of biology and inheritance in areas such as aggression.
2. In old age, high self-efficacy may cause a person to seek new challenges and the benefits of knowledge and experience over their life.

Codes

(a) Only 1
(b) Only 2
(c) Both 1 and 2
(d) Neither 1 nor 2

104 According to Kohlberg's model of the Development of Moral Judgement which of the

1. Punishment and obedience orientation	:	Would be punished
2. Naive hedonistic orientation	:	Would enjoy it
3. Good boy-good girl orientation	:	Is this what people expect

Codes

(a) Only 1 (b) 1 and 2
(c) 2 and 3 (d) 1, 2 and 3

105 Arrange the following effects of fixation of Freud's psychosexual development.

1. Orderliness or sloppiness.
2. Lasting concerns with dependence and independence.
3. Difficulty feeling closeness males.

Codes

(a) 2, 1 and 3 (b) 1, 2 and 3 (c) 3, 2 and 1 (d) 1, 3 and 2

106 Horney theorised that to deal with basic anxiety, the individual has the following options, arrange them in chronological order.

1. Accept the situation and become dependent on others.
2. Resist situation and become aggressive.
3. Withdraw from others and become isolated.

Codes

(a) 2, 1 and 3 (b) 3, 1 and 2
(c) 1, 2 and 3 (d) 1, 3 and 2

107 Which of the following statement is/are correct?

1. Rotter distinguished between learning a behaviour and performing the behaviour.
2. Bandura's social learning theory is more focused on performance rather than how we come to learn the behaviour in the first place.

Select the correct answer using the codes given below

(a) Only 1 (b) Only 2
(c) Both 1 and 2 (d) Neither 1 nor 2

108 Arrange the four stage of Bandura's observational learning.

1. Attentional process
2. Motor reproduction process
3. Motivational processes
4. Retention process

Codes

(a) 1, 4, 2 and 3 (b) 1, 2, 4 and 3
(c) 1, 3, 2 and 4 (d) 1, 3, 4 and 2

109 Consider the following statements

1. Behaviourists have traditionally discouraged scientifically minded psychologists from basing their work in unobservable process.
2. Behaviourists believe that behaviour is only the surface manifestations of personality.

Which of the statements given above is/are correct?

(a) Only 1 (b) Only 2
(c) Both 1 and 2 (d) None of these

110 Consider the following statements

1. By early adulthood, most people have moved far beyond this level and judge moral right and wrong on the basic of less immediate outcomes.
2. The implications of behaviour for relationships between people or the extent to which the behaviour is consistent with general principles of right and wrong.
3. They consider staling to be wrong because of the harm it does to other or the violation of their principles of ethics.

Which of the statements given above is/are correct?

(a) Only 1 (b) 1 and 2
(c) 2 and 3 (d) None of these

111 Consider the following statements
1. Eysenck classified countries by the personality scores of thousands of people.
2. He assessed the percentage of persons having different blood types.

Which of the statements given above is/are incorrect?
(a) Only 1 (b) Only 2
(c) 1 and 2 (d) None of these

112 Eysenck's trait-type theory posits the following four hierarchically organised levels of personality.
1. Traits 2. Habitual response
3. Types 4. Specific response

The correct order of their organisation starting from the lowest to the highest is
(a) 4, 2, 3, 1 (b) 2, 4, 1, 3 (c) 2, 4, 3, 1 (d) 4, 2, 1, 3

113 Consider the following statements

The 'individuality' and 'personality' of an individual are
1. different in that individuality stands out in a group while personality is group adaptive.
2. different in that individuality reflects more of the potentiality of the individual, while personality is the resultant effect of environmental factors.
3. individual-oriented and synonymous.

Which of the statements given above is/are correct?
(a) Only 2 (b) Only 1 (c) 1 and 2 (d) Only 3

114 Allport recognised levels of functional autonomy
1. Perseverative functional autonomy
2. Propriate functional autonomy
3. Extensive functional autonomy
4. Intervene autonomy

Select the correct answer using the codes given below
(a) 1 and 2 (b) 2 and 3
(c) All of these (d) None of these

115 Consider the following statements
1. Hans Eysenck added consideration of individual differences that result from some people's greater biological predisposition to anxiety.
2. Anxiety-prone individuals are more likely to avoid behaving in ways that they have learned would lead to arousal of their excessive anxiety.

Which of the statements given above is/are correct?
(a) Only 1 (b) Only 2
(c) Both 1 and 2 (d) None of these

116 Consider the following statements
1. In Eysenck's theory, super factors are also called source traits.
2. People who score high on the psychoticism(P) are egocentric, aggressive, hostile.
3. People who score high on the neuroticism (N) scale are emotionally over reactive.
4. According to research reported by Eysenck's sick people, who react to their illness with anger and aggression are most likely to die from heart disease.

Which of the statements given above is/are correct ?
(a) 2 and 4 (b) 1 and 2
(c) 2, 3 and 4 (d) 3 and 4

117 Consider the following statements
1. Factor C in the five-factor theory is conscientiousness.
2. People who score low on intelligence tend to be quiet and reserved.
3. According to Mc Crae and Costa, the ultimate contributor to personality is self-concept.
4. A person's view of what he or she like is called objective biology.

Which of the statements given above is/are correct?
(a) Only 1 (b) 2 and 4 (c) 2 and 3 (d) All of these

118 Consider the following statements
1. Eysenck proposed that personality can be explained by three major types.
2. Traits are more stable than states.
3. Eysenck would say that his relationship with his parents, as well as other childhood experiences, played a significant role in shaping his personality.
4. Eysenck's theory is based mainly on trait level factors.

Which of the statements given above is/are correct?
(a) 1 and 2 (b) 2 and 3
(c) 3 and 4 (d) 1, 2 and 4

119 Consider the following statements
1. Adler's safeguarding tendencies the ego from the pain of anxiety.
2. He believed that people's present behaviours are strongly influenced by their experiences of the past.

Which of the statements given above is/are incorrect?
(a) 1 and 2 (b) Only 2
(c) Only 1 (d) None of the above

120 Which of the following are true for self in Jungian psychology?
1. Self is the archetype of completion and wholeness.
2. Self is the center or essence of personality.
3. Self includes the other archetypes.

Select the correct answer using the codes given below
(a) Only 1 (b) 1 and 2
(c) 2 and 3 (d) All of these

Directions (Q. Nos 121-136) *In the question given below are two statements, labelled Assertion (A) and Reason (R). In the context of the two statements, which one of the following is correct?*

Codes

(a) Both A and R are true and R is the correct explanation of A

(b) Both A and R are true, but R is not the correct explanation of A

(c) A is true, but R is false

(d) A is false, but R is true

121 Assertion (A) In researching human behaviour, personality theorists often use various measuring procedures and these procedures must be both reliable and valid.

Reason (R) Reliability refers to a measuring instrument's consistency whereas validity refers to its accuracy or truthfulness.

122 Assertion (A) Most current personality research addresses ways, in which individuals and groups differ, not human universals.

Reason (R) Personality psychologists specialise in a particular domain, such as biological aspects of personality or how culture impacts personality.

123 Assertion (A) Personality research is often informed by personality theory.

Reason (R) Theory has several key purposes such as serves as a guide for researchers, organises known findings.

124 Assertion (A) Both trait and type theories do not explain personality in its totality.

Reason (R) There is some truth in the distinction between individuality and personality.

125 Assertion (A) Allport listed six criteria for psychological health.

Reason (R) Allport believed that people are motivated by both the need of environment and to grow towards psychological health.

126 Assertion (A) Trait theory describes personality in terms of characteristic behaviours or traits, such as agreeableness or extra version.

Reason (R) Trait theorists assess personality by developing a profile of a person's traits.

127 Assertion (A) Alfred Adler proposed that people's primary motivation is a striving for superiority.

Reason (R) Each person adopts his or her own method of striving.

128 Assertion (A) Allport has written eloquently about personality, but his views are based more on philosophical speculation and common sense than on scientific studies.

Reason (R) It rates low on its ability to organise psychological data and to be falsified.

129 Assertion (A) Person on many different occasions and is his attempt to measure individual or unique rather than common traits.

Reason (R) Cattell also used the dR (differential R) technique, which correlates the scores of a large number of people on many variables obtained at two different occasions.

130 Assertion (A) Raymond Cattell and Hans Eysenck have used factors analysis to identify traits (*i.e.* relatively permanent dispositions of people).

Reason (R) Cattell has identified a large number of personality traits, whereas Eysenck has extracted only three general factors.

131 Assertion (A) Psychoanalysis is rated high on its ability to generate research, very low on its openness to falsification.

Reason (R) It lacks operational definitions, it rates high on internal consistency.

132 Assertion (A) Defence mechanisms are unconscious strategies with which people reduce anxieties relating to impulses from the id.

Reason (R) Freud believes that people develop a range of defense mechanisms to deal with it.

133 Assertion (A) Rotter's interactionist position holds that human behaviour is based largely on the interaction of people with their meaningful environments.

Reason (R) Personality can change at any time, it has a basic unity that preserves it from changing as a result of minor experiences.

134 Assertion (A) Behaviour can be predicted by the basic prediction formula.

Reason (R) It states that the potential for a behaviour to occur in a particular situation in relation to a given reinforcement is a function of people's expectancy.

135 Assertion (A) Bandura does not suggest that the three factors in the reciprocal determinism model make equal contributions to behaviour.

Reason (R) The relative influence of behaviour, environment and person depends on which factor is strongest at any particular moment.

136 Assertion (A) The heart of observational learning is modeling, which is more than simple imitation.

Reason (R) It involves adding and subtracting from observed behaviour.

Directions (Q. Nos 137-141) *Read the passage given below and answer the questions that follow.*

According to Freud, defense mechanisms operate to protect the ego against the pain of anxiety. Repression involves forcing unwanted, anxiety-loaded experiences into the unconscious. It is the most basic of all defense mechanisms because it is an active process in each of the others. Undoing is the ego's attempt to do away with unpleasant experiences and their consequences, usually by means of repetitious ceremonial actions. Isolation, in contrast, is marked by obsessive thoughts and involves the ego's attempt to isolate an experience by surrounding it with a blacked-out region of insensibility.

A reaction formation is marked by the repression of one impulse and the ostentatious expression of its exact opposite. Displacement takes place when people redirect their unwanted urges onto other objects or people in order to disguise the original impulse.

Fixations develop when psychic energy is blocked at one stage of development, making psychological change difficult. Regressions occur whenever a person reverts to earlier, more infantile modes of behaviour. Projection is seeing in others those unacceptable feelings or behaviours that actually reside in one's own unconscious. When carried to extreme, projection can become paranoia, which is characterised by delusions of persecution.

Introjections take place when people incorporate positive qualities of another person into their own ego to reduce feelings of inferiority. Sublimations involve the elevation of the sexual instinct's aim to a higher level, which permits people to make contributions to society and culture.

137 Which of the following matches the defence mechanism DENIAL ?

(a) A man who is angry with his neighbour goes deer hunting.
(b) A smoker insists there is no convincing evidence that smoking impairs health.
(c) A man who beats his wife writes a book arguing that people have an instinctive need for aggressive behaviour.
(d) None of the above

138 Freud identified many defense mechanisms, including regression (coping with anxiety by retreating to an earlier developmental stage) and projection (disguising threatening impulses by attributing them to others). All defense mechanisms distort or disguise reality and all are

(a) conscious (b) unconscious
(c) preconscious (d) rationalisations

139 With this defense mechanism, a repressed desire finds an opposite and exaggerated expression

(a) displacement (b) denial
(c) reaction formation (d) projection

140 A completely weaned child goes back to the bottle after a younger sister is born. This return to a more infantile pattern of behaviour expresses a

(a) repression (b) regression
(c) rationalisation (d) sublimation

141 Chand has great admiration for his history teacher. He attempts to imitate his teacher's lifestyle and mannerisms. This is an example of

(a) introjection (b) denial
(c) sublimation (d) reaction formation

Directions *(Q. Nos. 142-146) Read the passage given below and answer the questions that follow*

We can conceive of personality characteristics as types or traits. The earliest theory of personality classified people into types according to their predominant humour or body fluid. Today, most psychologists conceive of personality differences as being represented by degree, not kind. Personality traits are the factors that underlie patterns of behaviour. Presumably, these factors are biological in nature, although they may be the products of learning as well as heredity. The search for core personality traits began with Allport, who studied how everyday words are used to describe personality characteristics. Although, he never isolated a core set of traits, his work inspired others to continue the search for such traits.

Several researchers developed their theories of personality through factor analysis, a statistical method of reducing a large amount of data to two or three themes or ideas (called factors). Cattell's analysis indicated the existence of 16 personality factors; Eysenck's research suggested that personality is determined by three dimensions: extraversion (versus introversion), neuroticism (versus emotional stability) and psychoticism (versus self-control). Mc Crae and Costa's five-factor model, based on an analysis of words used to describe people's behavioural traits, includes extraversion, neuroticism, agreeableness, openness and conscientiousness. There is strong cross-cultural agreement on the first three factors, but not on the fifth.

142 Which of the following researchers proposed biological substrates for his traits?
(a) Cattell (b) Wiggins
(c) Eysenck (d) Leary

143 Which of the following of Cattell's traits is most similar to extraversion?
(a) Interpersonal warmth (b) Intelligence
(c) Emotional stability (d) Conformity

144 The five factor model is based on
(a) the lexical approach (b) the statistical approach
(c) factor analysis (d) All of these

145 According to Eysenck, introverts and extroverts are different in many respects. The most important difference is
(a) psychological health *vs* psychological disturbance
(b) subjectivity *vs* objectivity
(c) their way of viewing the world
(d) level of cortical arousal

146 The theories of Cattell and Eysenck rate
(a) high on biological determinants of personality
(b) high on teleology
(c) low on their ability to generate research
(d) high on free will *vs* determinism conformity

PREVIOUS YEARS' QUESTIONS

July 2018

1 Match List I with List II and select the correct answer by choosing from the codes given below.

List I (Psychologists)	List II (Concepts)
A. Bruner	1. Conservation
B. Vygotsky	2. Iconic mode of representation
C. Sternberg	3. Scaffolding
D. Piaget	4. Componential analysis

Codes

	A	B	C	D		A	B	C	D
(a)	2	3	4	1	(b)	4	2	3	1
(c)	2	3	1	4	(d)	3	2	4	1

2 Read each of the following statements Assertion (A) and Reason (R) and indicate your answer using codes given below

Assertion (A) Personality factors such as D, J, K and P are not incorporated in Cattell's 16 PF test.

Reason (R) Some personality factors appeared only in Life-data (L-data) measures.

Codes
(a) Both A and R are true and R is the correct explanation of A
(b) Both A and R are true, but R is not the correct explanation of A
(c) A is true, but R is false
(d) A is false, but R is true

3 Which of the following concepts is/are not found in Freudian Psychoanalysis?
1. Unconscious motivation
2. Collective unconscious
3. Striving for superiority
4. Instincts

Codes
(a) 1 and 2 (b) 2 and 3 (c) 3 and 4 (d) 1, 2 and 4

4 In Erikson's theory, which psycho-social crises preceed and succeed Autonomy *v/s* Shame?
(a) Basic trust *vs* mistrust and industry *vs* inferiority
(b) Initiative *vs* guilt and industry *vs* inferiority
(c) Industry *vs* inferiority and identity *vs* role confusion
(d) Basic trust *vs* mistrust and initiative *vs* guilt

5 Which one of the trait theories/models is/are not based on factor analytic methodology?
1. Allport's Theory
2. Costa and McCrae's Model
3. Goldberg's Model
4. Eysenck's Theory

Codes
(a) Only 1 (b) 1 and 3
(c) 2 and 3 (d) 2 and 4

6 Which of the following personality questionnaires have a lie scale?
1. Edward Personality Preference Schedule
2. Eysenck Personality Questionnaire
3. Minnesota Multiphasic Personality Questionnaire-2
4. Rotter's Locus of Control Scale

Codes
(a) 1 and 2 (b) 1 and 3
(c) 2 and 3 (d) 1, 2 and 3

7 Which of the following terms explains the reinforcement which is given only if a specific response is made?
(a) Concurrent reinforcement
(b) Incremental reinforcement
(c) Contingency contract
(d) Contingent reinforcement

November 2017

8 Match List I with List II and select the correct answer by choosing from the codes given below.

List I (Concepts)		List II (Descriptions)
A. Type	1.	Consistent style of behaviour or emotions, a person display across the situations
B. Trait	2.	A cluster of many dispositions
C. System	3.	Enduring qualities that define the individual and distinguish individuals from one another
D. Structure	4.	A collection of highly interconnected parts of personality whose overall behaviour reflects them being organised

Codes

	A	B	C	D		A	B	C	D
(a)	1	2	3	4	(b)	2	1	4	3
(c)	3	2	1	4	(d)	4	3	2	1

9 Read each of the following two statements - Assertion (A) and Reason (R) and indicate your answer using codes given below.

Assertion (A) Conditioning done using partial reinforcement schedule decreases resistance to change.

Reason (R) Partial reinforcement schedules influence rate of responding.

Codes

(a) Both A and R are true and R is the correct explanation of A
(b) Both A and R are true, but R is not the correct explanation of A
(c) A is true, but R is false
(d) A is false, but R is true

10 "Development is the result of individual's active participation in the development process in interaction with important environmental influences." This is the assumption of which of the following approaches?

(a) Maturational/Biological (b) Psychodynamic
(c) Behavioural (d) Cognitive

11 Read each of the following two statements - Assertion (A) and Reason (R) and indicate your answer using codes given below

Assertion (A) Cattell incorporated factors Q1, Q2, Q3 and Q4 in 16 PF.

Reason (R) Some factors appeared only in L-data, not in Q-data.

Codes

(a) Both A and R are true and R is the correct explanation of A
(b) Both A and R are true, but R is not the correct explanation of A
(c) A is true, but R is false
(d) A is false, but R is true

12 Rollo May's description of personality development can be explained in which of following sequences?

(a) Innocence → Dependence → Rebellion → Ordinary Consciousness of self → Creative consciousness of self
(b) Dependence → Innocence → Rebellion → Ordinary Consciousness of self → Creative consciousness of self
(c) Innocence → Rebellion → Dependence → Ordinary Consciousness of self → Creative consciousness of self
(d) Dependence → Innocence → Rebellion → creative consciousness of self → Ordinary consciousness of self

13 Humanistic theories of personality are characterised as

1. having optimistic ideas about human nature
2. emphasise personal responsibility
3. focus on present than on past
4. believe that fate is an important determinant of human behaviour

Codes

(a) 1 and 2 (b) 2 and 4
(c) 1, 2 and 3 (d) 2, 3 and 4

14 Read each of the following two statements - Assertion (A) and Reason (R) and indicate your answer using codes given below :

Assertion (A) Some persons engage in activities such as collecting thing, being good listeners, or being gullible persons.

Reason (R) In Freudian psychoanalysis, it is assumed that fixation at oral stage results in the development of oral incorporative character.

Codes

(a) Both A and R are true and R is the correct explanation of A
(b) Both A and R are true, but R is not the correct explanation of A
(c) A is true, but R is false
(d) A is false, but R is true

15 According to Skinner, which of the following are the characteristics of 'Respondent Behaviour'?

1. It is elicited
2. It is emitted
3. It is conditioned
4. It is unconditioned

Codes

(a) 1 and 3 (b) 2 and 3
(c) 1, 3 and 4 (d) 2, 3 and 4

16 Allport defined personality as

(a) response style
(b) social stimulus value
(c) intervening variable
(d) thinking style

January 2017

17 **Read each of the following two statements - Assertion (A) and Reason (R) and indicate your answer using codes given below.**

Assertion (A) According to Adler, a child's birth order is important in shaping his/her personality.

Reason (R) There are unique experiences associated with birth order of every child.

Codes

(a) Both A and R are true and R is the correct explanation of A
(b) Both A and R are true, but R is not the correct explanation of A
(c) A is true, but R is false
(d) A is false, but R is true

18 **Match List I with List II and select the correct answer by choosing from the codes given below.**

List I (Learning)	List II (Ways)
A. Observational learning	1. Learning where an object is located
B. Place learning	2. A response that can be observed by others
C. Overt responding	3. The process whereby information is acquired by attending to events in the environment
D. Latent learning	4. Learning that takes place independent of reinforcement

Codes

	A	B	C	D		A	B	C	D
(a)	2	4	3	1	(b)	3	1	2	4
(c)	2	1	3	4	(d)	3	4	2	1

19 **Match List I with List II and select the correct answer by choosing from the codes given below.**

List I (Therapies)	List II (Therapists)
A. Systematic desensitisation	1. Albert Bandura
B. Social-Learning Therapy	2. Meichenbaum
C. Cognitive Therapy	3. Joseph Wolpe
D. Cognitive Behaviour Modification	4. Aaron Beck

Codes

	A	B	C	D		A	B	C	D
(a)	1	2	3	4	(b)	3	1	4	2
(c)	2	3	4	1	(d)	4	3	2	1

20 Read each of the following two statements - Assertion (A) and Reason (R) and indicate your answer using codes given below

Assertion (A) According to Rollo May, to grow psychologically, our values must be constantly challenged.

Reason (R) Rollo May proposed that neurotic anxiety occurs when our values are challenged.

Codes

(a) Both A and R are true and R is the correct explanation of A
(b) Both A and R are true, but R is not the correct explanation of A
(c) A is true, but R is false
(d) A is false, but R is true

21 **According to Jung, which of the following is the deepest and darkest part of collective unconscious and contains all of the animal instincts?**

(a) Anima (b) Animus (c) Shadow (d) Persona

22 **In classical conditioning, progress of conditioning can be examined by indexing Conditioned Response (CR) in terms of**

1. Quantity
2. Latency
3. Rate
4. Density

Codes

(a) 1, 2 and 4 (b) 2, 3 and 4
(c) 1, 2 and 3 (d) 1, 3 and 4

23 **According to Bandura, which of the following cognitive mechanisms are adopted by a person to act contrary to his or her moral principles without experiencing self-contempt?**

1. Moral justification
2. Dehumanisation
3. Displacement of responsibility
4. Diffusion of responsibility

Codes

(a) 1, 2 and 3 (b) 1, 2 and 4
(c) 2, 3 and 4 (d) All of these

24 **Rogers use Q-sort technique to identify**

(a) Internal and external frame of reference
(b) Real self and ideal self
(c) Conditional and unconditional positive regards
(d) Conditions of worth and worthtlessness

25 **In Pavolian conditioning paradigm the strongest and most rapid conditioning occurs in**

(a) Simultaneous conditioning
(b) Trace conditioning
(c) Short-delay conditioning
(d) Long-delay conditioning

July 2016

26 **Which of the following statement is/are true, when the Eysenck Personality Questionnaire (EPQ or EPQ-R) and Costa and McCrae's NEO-PI-3 are compared?**

1. EPQ-R Psychoticism (P) scale is uncorrelated with Five-Factor Agreeableness (A) and Consentiousness (C) scale.
2. P scale is positively correlated with A and C scales.

3. P scale is negatively correlated with A and C scales.
4. EPQ-R has Lie scale, NEO-PI-3 has no lie scale.
5. Both EPQ-R and NEO-PI-3 have lie scale.

Codes
(a) 1 and 4 (b) 2 and 5 (c) 3 and 4 (d) 1 and 5

27 Which of the following are the correct explanations of discrimination and stimulus generalisations?
1. Learning to respond to one stimulus but not to the other similar stimuli.
2. Learning to respond to one stimulus but not to the other different stimuli.
3. Stimuli similar to the one used during conditioning also elicit the conditioned response.
4. Stimuli different to the one used during conditioning also elicit the conditioned response.

Codes
(a) 1 and 3 (b) 1 and 4 (c) 2 and 3 (d) 2 and 4

28 Read each of the following two statements - Assertion (A) and Reason (R) and indicate your answer using codes given below.

Assertion (A) According to Rogers, ideal condition for the development of a healthy self concept and movement toward becoming fully functioning is unconditional positive regard.

Reason (R) With unconditional positive regard there is incongruence between true self and experience.

Codes
(a) Both A and R are true and R is the correct explanation of A
(b) Both A and R are true, but R is not the correct explanation of A
(c) A is true, but R is false
(d) A is false, but R is true

29 Match List I with List II and select the correct answer by choosing from the codes given below.

List I (Concepts)	List II (Explanations)
A. Trait	1. Specific emotional and behavioural qualities of personality that are thought to be biologically based
B. Type	2. A collection of highly interconnected traits or dispositions which determine personality integration
C. System	3. Clustering of many stable and enduring dispositions or qualities.
D. Temperament	4. Consistent pattern of emotional and behavioural reactions a person displays across variety of situations

Codes

	A	B	C	D		A	B	C	D
(a)	1	2	3	4	(b)	2	1	3	4
(c)	3	2	4	1	(d)	4	3	2	1

30 According to Freud following are the characteristics of instinct.
1. A source in some bodily deficit.
2. An aim that focuses on gratification of need.
3. An impetus that propels the person to act.
4. An object through which instinct achieves its aim.

Codes
(a) 1 and 4 (b) 1, 2 and 4
(c) 2, 3 and 4 (d) All of these

31 Read each of the following two statements - Assertion (A) and Reason (R) and indicate your answer using codes given below.

Assertion (A) Classical conditioning is quick when UCS is presented immediately after CS rather than before.

Reason (R) According to cognitive perspective, classical conditioning occurs because CS provides expectancy about the coming of UCS.

Codes
(a) Both A and R are true and R is the correct explanation of A
(b) Both A and R are true, but R is not the correct explanation of A
(c) A is true, but R is false
(d) A is false, but R is true

32 Which of the following have been explained by Freud in his psycho-analytic theory of motivation?
1. Homeostasis 2. Drives
3. Hedonism 4. Instincts

Codes
(a) 1, 2 and 4 (b) 1, 3 and 4
(c) 2, 3 and 4 (d) 1, 2 and 3

33 Match List I with List II and select the correct answer by choosing from the codes given below.

List I (Books)	List II (Authors)
A. Toward a Psychology of Being	1. May
B. A Way of Being	2. Maslow
C. Man's Search for Meaning	3. Rogers
D. Love and Will	4. Frankl

Codes

	A	B	C	D
(a)	1	2	3	4
(b)	2	3	4	1
(c)	3	2	1	4
(d)	4	1	2	3

34 Match List I with List II and select the correct answer by choosing from the codes given below.

List I (Terms in factor analysis)	List II (Examples/Brief explanations)
A. Factor extraction method	1. Correlations among varimax rotated factors
B. Cattell's scree	2. Promax
C. Factor rotation method	3. Principle axes
D. Inter-factor correlation matrix	4. Correlation among oblique-rotated factors
	5. Method to decide number of factors for rotation

Codes

	A	B	C	D		A	B	C	D
(a)	3	5	2	4	(b)	3	5	2	1
(c)	5	3	2	4	(d)	2	3	5	4

35 Who first attempted to describe personality traits in terms of Lexican descriptors?

(a) Ross Stagner (b) Allport and Odbert
(c) RB Cattell (d) Coasta and McCrae

36 Match List I with List II and select the correct answer by choosing from the codes given below.

List I (Types of Conditioning)	List II (Explanations)
A. Delayed conditioning	1. The onset of UCS precedes the onset of the CS and the UCS goes off before CS comes on
B. Trace conditioning	2. The CS and UCS come one and go off at the same time
C. Simultaneous conditioning	3. The onset of CS precedes the onset of the UCS and the CS goes off before the onset of UCS
D. Backward conditioning	4. The onset of the CS precedes the onset of the UCS and the CS remains on for the initial part of UCS

Codes

	A	B	C	D		A	B	C	D
(a)	1	2	4	3	(b)	4	2	3	1
(c)	4	3	1	2	(d)	4	3	2	1

37 Arrange in sequence the stage of personality development according to Rollo May.

(a) Innocence → Ordinary consciousness of self → Rebellion → Creative consciousness of self
(b) Innocence → Rebellion → Ordinary consciousness of self → Creative consciousness of self
(c) Ordinary consciousness of self → Innocence → Rebellion → Creative consciousness of self
(d) Rebellion → Innocence → Ordinary consciousness of self → Creative consciousness of self

December 2015

38 According to Piaget, the children are able to grasp the concept of object permanence and conservation in

(a) sensory motor stage (b) pre-operational stage
(c) concrete operational stage (d) formal operational stage

39 Which of the following is the correct sequence of reinforcement schedules in terms of their effectiveness in response rate and resistance to extinction during learning experiments?

(a) Variable Ratio → Fixed Ratio → Variable Interval → Fixed Interval → Continuous Reinforcement Schedule
(b) Fixed Ratio → Variable Ratio → Fixed Interval → Variable Interval → Continuous Reinforcement Schedule
(c) Continuous Reinforcement schedule → Variable Ratio → Fixed Ratio → Variable Interval → Fixed Interval
(d) Variable Ratio → Variable Interval → Fixed Ratio → Fixed Interval → Continuous Reinforcement Schedule

40 Which one of the following statements is true?

(a) The 'Global Five' factors in personality refer to the second order factors of 16 PF, latest edition
(b) The 'Global Five' factors refer to the factors assessed by the NEO-Five Factor Inventory, latest edition
(c) The 'Global Five' factors refer to the factors assessed by Goldberg's bipolar adjectives
(d) The 'Global Five' factors are derived from Eysenck Personality Profiler, latest edition

41 Cattell propounded gf-gc Theory of Intelligence mainly based on

(a) first order factors of abilities
(b) second order factors of abilities
(c) third order factors of abilities
(d) higher order factors of abilities

42 Which of the following are elements in Carl Rogers' person centered Theory of Personality and Psychotherapy?

1. Ideal self 2. Congruence
3. Positive regards 4. Dissonance

Codes

(a) 1, 2 and 3 (b) 2, 3 and 4
(c) 1, 3 and 4 (d) 1, 2 and 4

43 Read each of the following two statements - Assertion (A) and Reason (R) and indicate your answer using the codes given below.

Assertion (A) In pre-conventional stage, children understand morality on the basis of social customs and values.

Reason (R) In pre-conventional stage, children make decisions based on whether they will be rewarded or punished.

Codes

(a) Both A and R are true and R is the correct explanation of A

(b) Both A and R are true, but R is not the correct explanation of A

(c) A is true, but R is false

(d) A is false, but R is true

44 **Match the items of List I with List II and select the correct answer from the answers given below.**

List I (Scholars)		List II (Concepts)
A. Cattell	1.	Assortative mating
B. Jensen	2.	Investment hypothesis
C. Sternberg	3.	Wisdom
D. Spearman	4.	Positive manifold

Codes

	A	B	C	D		A	B	C	D
(a)	1	2	3	4	(b)	2	1	4	3
(c)	3	4	2	1	(d)	2	1	3	4

45 **Which of the following is correct while comparing classical and operant conditioning?**

(a) Operant conditioning takes place before reinforcement while classical conditioning takes place after reinforcement.

(b) Operant conditioning takes place as a result of some voluntary action while classical conditioning takes place without choice.

(c) In operant conditioning, response is elicited while in classical conditioning it is emitted.

(d) In operant conditioning magnitude of the response is the index of conditioning while in classical conditioning it is the rate of response.

46 **Backward conditioning occurs when**

(a) CS and US are presented simultaneously.

(b) CS is presented first and US is presented before the termination of CS.

(c) CS is presented first and US is presented after the termination of CS.

(d) US is presented first and CS is presented after the termination of US.

47 **Biologically based emotional and behavioural tendencies that are evident in early childhood represent**

(a) trait (b) type

(c) temperament (d) style

48 **In Jungian Theory, the idea that energy is automatically redistributed in the psyche in order to achieve equilibrium or balance depicts**

(a) principle of equivalence

(b) principle of synchronicity

(c) principle of entrophy

(d) principle of opposites

49 **Match the items of List I with the items of List II. Select the correct answer from the answer codes given below.**

List I (Concepts)		List II (Theorists)
A. Rational functions	1.	Freud
B. Impetus	2.	Jung
C. Masculine protest	3.	Adler
D. Hyper competitiveness	4.	Horney

Codes

	A	B	C	D		A	B	C	D
(a)	1	2	3	4	(b)	2	1	3	4
(c)	3	2	4	1	(d)	4	3	1	2

50 **What is the role of positive and negative reinforcement?**

(a) To increase the likelihood that responses preceding both will be repeated.

(b) To decrease the likelihood that responses preceding negative reinforcement will be repeated.

(c) To increase the likelihood that responses preceding only positive reinforcement will be repeated.

(d) To ensure that there are no negative consequences following the behaviour.

51 **An accused is harassed and tortured until he confesses to the crime is an example of**

(a) negative reinforcement (b) punishment

(c) primary reinforcement (d) secondary reinforcement

52 **Which of the following sequence is correct?**

(a) Oral → Anal → Latency → Phallic → Genital

(b) Anal → Oral → Phallic → Latency → Genital

(c) Oral → Anal → Phallic → Latency → Genital

(d) Oral → Phallic → Anal → Genital → Latency

June 2015

53 **Which of the following is not correct for the Piaget's theory?**

(a) Disequilibrium terminates in structural change.

(b) Individual stages of development cannot be skipped or omitted from the sequence.

(c) Stages of equilibrium do not last as long as stages of disequilibrium.

(d) Later stages are independent of the elements and experiences of early stages.

54 **According to Erikson, adequate training, sufficient education and good models during the age range six to eleven years will lead to**

(a) initiative (b) identity

(c) industriousness (d) autonomy

55 **Read each of the following two statements Assertion (A) and Reason (R) and indicate your answer using the codes given below.**

Assertion **(A) Ego-involved learners are driven by performance goals.**

Reason (R) Ego-involved learners are pre-occupied with them serves and are concerned with their evaluation by others.

Codes

(a) Both A and R are true and R is the correct explanation of A
(b) Both A and R are true, but R is not the correct explanation of A
(c) A is true, but R is false
(d) A is false, but R is true

56 According to Piaget, which is the primary motivating force behind development?

(a) Accommodation (b) Assimilation
(c) Equilibration (d) Adaptation

57 According to cognitive approach, the role of a teacher is to

1. correct wrong answers.
2. correct misconceptions.
3. facilitate and supervise.
4. teach effective strategies.

Codes

(a) 1 and 3 (b) 1 and 4 (c) 2 and 3 (d) 2 and 4

58 Match List I with List II and indicate your correct choice by using codes given below.

List I (Theories of Motivation)		List II (Characteristics)
A. Drive theories	1.	Pulling by goal
B. Incentive theories	2.	Information
C. Opponent process theories	3.	Hedonic
D. Cognitive (social)	4.	Pushing toward goal

Codes

	A	B	C	D		A	B	C	D
(a)	1	2	3	4	(b)	4	1	3	2
(c)	2	1	3	4	(d)	4	3	2	1

59 Match List I with List II and select the correct answer by choosing from the codes given below.

List I		List II
A. Libido	1.	Human beings strive to return to an inorganic state of balance that preceded life, in which there is no painful struggle to satisfy biological needs
B. Thantos	2.	Psychic and pleasurable feelings associated with gratification of life instincts
C. Suppression	3.	A person's refusal to perceive an unpleasant environment in external reality
D. Denial	4.	Individual's active and conscious attempt to stop anxiety provoking thoughts by simply not thinking about them

Codes

	A	B	C	D		A	B	C	D
(a)	1	2	3	4	(b)	3	1	2	4
(c)	2	1	4	3	(d)	4	3	2	1

60 Rollo May's views on personality development can be described in following sequence.

(a) Physical dependence - Psychological dependence - Rebellion - Ordinary consciousness of self - Creative consciousness of self
(b) Physical dependence - Rebellion - Ordinary consciousness of self, Self actualisation
(c) Psychological dependence - Physical dependence - Ordinary consciousness of self - Creative consciousness of self
(d) Physical dependence Psychological dependence - Ordinary consciousness of self - Rebellion - Creative consciousness of self

61 Which of the following are the sources of error in social cognition?

1. Counterfactuals thinking
2. Thought suppression
3. Magical thinking
4. Judging by resemblance

Codes

(a) 1 and 2 (b) 1, 2 and 3
(c) 1, 3 and 4 (d) 3 and 4

62 According to Kohlberg .... and .... are the major reasons of moral behaviour during the stage of conventional morality.

(a) gaining acceptance; getting rewards
(b) avoiding censure by others; achieving justice
(c) gaining acceptance; avoiding censure by others
(d) avoiding censure by others; achieving justice

63 Which of the following is an application of operant conditioning?

(a) Aversive conditioning
(b) Behaviour modification
(c) Systematic desensitisation
(d) Transfer of learning

December 2014

64 Match List I with List II and select the correct answer by choosing from the codes given below.

List I (Authours)		List II (Concepts)
A. Cattell	1.	General and specific factors
B. Spearman	2.	Fluid and crystallised intelligence
C. Gardner	3.	Triarchic theory of intelligence
D. Sternberg	4.	Multiple Intelligence theory

Codes

	A	B	C	D		A	B	C	D
(a)	1	3	4	2	(b)	2	1	4	3
(c)	3	4	2	1	(d)	4	3	2	1

65 Which is the one that is not a 'Big Five' factor of personality?

(a) Extraversion (b) Psychoticism
(c) Conscientiousness (d) Agreeableness

66 A form of conditioning in which the onset of the Conditioned Stimulus (CS)precedes the onset of the Unconditioned Stimulus (UCS)and the presentation of CS and UCS do not overlap is termed as

(a) backward conditioning
(b) delayed conditioning
(c) trace conditioning
(d) simultaneous conditioning

67 Match the items of List I (Concepts) with List II (Originators) and indicate your answer with the help of the codes given below

List I (Concepts)	List II (Originatiors)
A. Locus of Control	1. CG Jung
B. Learned helplessness	2. Abraham Maslow
C. Deficiency needs	3. Martin Seligman
D. Archetypes	4. Julian Rotter

Codes

	A	B	C	D		A	B	C	D
(a)	1	2	3	4	(b)	3	2	1	4
(c)	4	3	2	1	(d)	3	1	4	2

68 Among the following concepts which are related to Alfred Adler's theory of personality?

1. Organ inferiority 2. Psychoticism
3. Archetypes 4. Masculine protects

Codes

(a) 1 and 4 (b) 2 and 3 (c) 1 and 2 (d) 4 and 3

69 Rogers in his person centred counselling approach emphasises ...... and ....

(a) empathy; sympathy
(b) experiential focussing; unconditional positive regard
(c) congruence; sympathy
(d) unconditional positive regard; empathy

June 2014

70 Read each of the following two statements Assertion (A) and Reason (R) and indicate your answer using the codes given below.

Assertion (A) Conditioning fails to occur when unconditioned stimulus and conditioned stimulus are paired in a random order.

Reason (R) Cognitive processes involving expectation play an important role in classical conditioning.

Codes

(a) Both A and R are true and R is the correct explanation of A
(b) Both A and R are true, but R is not the correct explanation of A
(c) A is true, but R is false
(d) A is false, but R is true

71 In which of Piaget's stages of development would a child be when he has just developed object permanence?

(a) Sensorimotor
(b) pre-operational
(c) Concrete operational
(d) Formal operational

72 Match the items of List I (Theories) with List II (Theorists) and indicate your answer with the help of the codes given below.

List I (Theories)	List II (Theorists)
A. Dialectical humanism	1. JB Watson
B. Avoidance-Avoidance conflict	2. Gordon Allport
C. Behaviourism	3. Erich Fromm
D. Functional autonomy	4. Dollar and Miller

Codes

	A	B	C	D
(a)	1	2	4	3
(b)	4	3	1	2
(c)	3	4	1	2
(d)	4	3	2	1

73 According to Albert Bandura, any behaviour produces two sets of consequences. They are

1. inhibition
2. self-evaluation
3. external outcomes
4. habit

Codes

(a) 1 and 2 (b) 3 and 4
(c) 2 and 3 (d) 1 and 4

ANSWERS

Exam Based Questions

1 (b)	2 (b)	3 (b)	4 (c)	5 (d)	6 (d)	7 (c)	8 (d)	9 (a)	10 (c)
11 (d)	12 (b)	13 (c)	14 (d)	15 (a)	16 (c)	17 (a)	18 (b)	19 (d)	20 (c)
21 (d)	22 (d)	23 (b)	24 (d)	25 (d)	26 (a)	27 (d)	28 (c)	29 (c)	30 (c)
31 (c)	32 (c)	33 (b)	34 (b)	35 (b)	36 (a)	37 (a)	38 (a)	39 (c)	40 (b)
41 (d)	42 (d)	43 (a)	44 (b)	45 (b)	46 (b)	47 (a)	48 (d)	49 (c)	50 (c)
51 (c)	52 (b)	53 (a)	54 (a)	55 (b)	56 (b)	57 (d)	58 (b)	59 (b)	60 (b)
61 (b)	62 (b)	63 (b)	64 (b)	65 (a)	66 (d)	67 (d)	68 (b)	69 (a)	70 (a)
71 (a)	72 (c)	73 (a)	74 (b)	75 (c)	76 (a)	77 (b)	78 (c)	79 (a)	80 (a)
81 (b)	82 (b)	83 (d)	84 (d)	85 (c)	86 (b)	87 (c)	88 (d)	89 (a)	90 (c)
91 (b)	92 (b)	93 (d)	94 (d)	95 (d)	96 (d)	97 (a)	98 (b)	99 (c)	100 (c)
101 (c)	102 (b)	103 (b)	104 (d)	105 (a)	106 (c)	107 (d)	108 (a)	109 (a)	110 (d)
111 (d)	112 (d)	113 (c)	114 (a)	115 (c)	116 (c)	117 (a)	118 (a)	119 (b)	120 (d)
121 (a)	122 (a)	123 (a)	124 (b)	125 (a)	126 (a)	127 (a)	128 (b)	129 (a)	130 (b)
131 (c)	132 (a)	133 (b)	134 (b)	135 (a)	136 (a)	137 (b)	138 (b)	139 (b)	140 (b)
141 (a)	142 (c)	143 (a)	144 (d)	145 (d)	146 (a)				

Previous Years' Questions

1 (d)	2 (a)	3 (c)	4 (c)	5 (d)	6 (b)	7 (c)	8 (b)	9 (d)	10 (d)
11 (b)	12 (b)	13 (c)	14 (a)	15 (c)	16 (c)	17 (a)	18 (b)	19 (b)	20 (c)
21 (c)	22 (c)	23 (d)	24 (b)	25 (c)	26 (c)	27 (a)	28 (c)	29 (d)	30 (d)
31 (a)	32 (b)	33 (b)	34 (a)	35 (b)	36 (d)	37 (b)	38 (b)	39 (a)	40 (a)
41 (b)	42 (a)	43 (d)	44 (d)	45 (b)	46 (d)	47 (c)	48 (c)	49 (b)	50 (a)
51 (d)	52 (c)	53 (d)	54 (c)	55 (a)	56 (c)	57 (d)	58 (b)	59 (c)	60 (a)
61 (b)	62 (c)	63 (b)	64 (b)	65 (b)	66 (c)	67 (c)	68 (a)	69 (d)	70 (a)
71 (a)	72 (c)	73 (c)							

Motivation and Emotion

Motivation refers to the dynamics of behaviour, the ways in which our actions are initiated, sustained, directed and terminated. Many motivated activities begin with a need or internal deficiency. Motivation is derived from the word motive which is defind as a need that requires satisfaction.

Motivation

Motivation is defined as the inner state of individual that activates him or make him move to achieve. It is a combination of forces which initially direct and sustain the behaviour towards goal, the arousal of motivation to form some act is attributed to an interaction between motives of an individual and the factors in the situation that confront it. When we study motivation, *we are primarily concerned with*

- What energies human behaviour?
- What directs and channel human behaviour?
- How is the behaviour maintained or sustained?

Motivation include both the push and pull factor that drive the organism. The mechanism of motivation begins in need and ends with need satisfaction. Motivation can be both conscious and unconscious.

Motivation is the activation or energisation of goal oriented behaviour. It is reason, incentive, enthusiasm or interest that causes a specific action or certain behaviour. Motivation is present in every moment of life. Simple acts such as eating are motivated by hunger. Education is motivated by desire for knowledge. Motivators can be anything from reward to coercion.

According to various theories, motivation may be rooted in the basic need to minimise physical pain and maximise pleasure or it may include specific needs such as eating and resting or a desired object, hobby, goal, state of being ideal or it may be attributed to less apparent reasons such as altruism, selfishness, morality or avoiding morality.

In this Chapter

Characteristics of Motivation

Basic characteristic of motivation are as follows

- Motives can only be inferes through behaviour, they are never be directly seen.
- A single act may express several motives.
- A single motive may give rise to several behaviour.
- Cultural and personal variation may significantly moderate the mode of expression of certain motive.
- Motives are dynamic in nature, any individual at any one time usually have a multiple needs and desires, not only the motives change but also conflict with each other.
- Considerable individual difference occur in a manner, in which they select certain motive over other and the intensity with which they persue the motive.
- The intensity of certain motives gets considerably reduced upon gratification and when this happen, other motives come to the forefront.
- Disruption in person's functioning occur, when motivated behaviour doesn't lead to goal accomplishment.
- Drives and motives vary in their strength, not only between individual, but within the same individual.
- Motivation is characterised by energy concentration. This energy concentration makes the individual restless, forcing it to perform vigorous activity.
- Motivation is goal directed. In the absence of goal, there can be no motivation. Higher is the motivation, greater is the persistent in goal directed behaviour.
- Many motives generally interact to produce behaviour and motives help us to predict behaviour.

Types of Motivation

Motivation is a dynamic in nature, therefore motivation can be categorised into two types, *which are as follows*

Intrinsic Motivation

Intrinsic motivation refer to motivation which has originated due to internal factors. It occurs when people are compelled to do something out of pleasure, importance or desire. This form of motivation has been studied by social and educational psychologists since the early 1970s. Intrinsic motivation has been explained by Fritz Heider's attribution theory, Bandura's work on self-efficacy and Ryan and Deci's Cognitive Evaluation theory.

Students are likely to be intrinsically motivated if they

- attribute their educational results to internal factors that they can control.
- believe that they can be effective agents in accomplishing desired goals.
- are interested in mastering a topic, rather than just rote learning to get good grades.

Extrinsic Motivation

Extrinsic motivation occurs when external factors compel the person to do something. It comes from outside of the individual. Money is one of the obvious example, but coercion and threat of punishment are also common extrinsic motivation. While competing, the crowd may cheer for the performer, which may motivate him or her to do well. Trophies are also extrinsic incentives. Competition in general are extrinsic because it encourages the performer to win and beat others, not to enjoy the intrinsic rewards of the activity.

Social psychological research has indicated that extrinsic rewards can led to over justification and a subsequent reduction in intrinsic motivation. In one study demonstrating their effect, children who expected to be rewarded with a ribbon and a glad star for drawing pictures spent less time playing with the drawing materials in subsequent observations than children who were assigned to an unexpected reward condition received no extrinsic reward.

Categories of Motives

Motivation deals with the question as to why we do, what we do. The answer to this is that what we do because of our instincts, drives, arousal or excitement, achievement of power, affiliation or friendship and for self fullfilment.

Psychologists define motivation as the internal and external factors that cause and direct behaviour. As a psychological concept, 'motive' is proposed as a unifying link between stimuli and behaviour. *Motives can be divided into four categories i.e. biological, emotional, cognitive and social.*

(i) **Biological Motives** Biological motives include hunger, thirst, the pursuit of pleasure and the avoidance of pain. An early attempt to specify how these motives affect animal behaviour was the ambitious theory of Clark Hull. Hull tried to explain all human and animal motivation using mathematical formulas. Hull borrowed from the concept of homeostasis or biological regulation. He assume that biological motives followed the pattern of homeostasis, which is reflected in modern concepts such as the set-point which for fat regulation.

(ii) **Emotional Motives** Things like having the desire to know that you can always have someone to talk to and share things with. To be able to open up to others and communicate. Emotional motives imply the selection of goals according to personal and subjective criteria.

(iii) **Cognitive Motives** Influence of implicit motivation on both basic and complex cognitive processes in the stages of attention and encoding as well as experimentally controlled studies demonstrate that individual differences in implicit motives have an influence on each step of learning and memory process.

(iv) **Social Motives** Social motives are when people do or give things because they feel they have a sense of responsibility to their community. People with social motives may have endured racial discrimination, poverty or may want to live in a selfless way. *The five social motives are*

- **Belonging** People are motivated to affiliate and bond with each other.
- **Understanding** To belong, people are motivated to create an accurate enough shared social understanding.
- **Controlling** People are motivated to feel competitive and effective in their dealings with the animate and inanimate environment.
- **Enhancing Self** Hoping that other will see you as socially worth, fits the core social motive of enhancing self.
- **Trusting** Viewing the world as benevolent enables people to participate in many groups without under suspicion or vigilance.

Theories of Motivation

To have a proper understanding of the different dimension of motivation, many theories were propounded, *which are as follows*

Instinct Theory

In Instinct theory of motivation, all organisms are born with innate biological tendencies that help them to survive. This theory suggests that instincts drive all behaviours.

Instincts are basically goal directed and innate patterns of behaviour that are not the result of learning or experience. *For example* Infants have an inborn rooting reflex that helps them seek out a nipple and obtain nourishment, while birds have an innate need to build a nest or migrate during the winter. Both of these behaviours occurs naturally and automatically.

They do not need to be learned in order to be displayed. Various psychologists carry different views regarding the instinct motivation concept. **Darwin** suggests that we are born with instincts, which push us towards certain forms of behaviour. The most basic of these behaviour is the instinct to survive.

According to **Freud**, "an instinct is an inborn biological need or bodily demand on psychological life". *For example* The state of thirst may be described in physiological terms as a condition of water deficit in the tissue of the body.

Whereas psychologically it is represented as a wish for water. The wish acts as a motive for behaviour and therefore instincts are considered as the propelling factors of behaviour.

Freud differentiated two basic instincts- the Life instinct or Eros and the Death instinct or Thantos. The first includes all those impulses, which are involved in the survival of the individual and the species. The second involves the fear of death from this life.

Drive Reduction Theory

According to drive reduction theory, humans are motivated to satisfy physiological needs in order to maintain homeostasis. The word 'drive' stands for an act of motivation like thirst or hunger that have primarily biological purposes. Whereas, the world 'homeostasis' stands for an ability to adjust its internal environment to maintain stable equilibrium, such as the ability of warm blooded animals to maintain a constant temperature.

Motivation describes the wants or needs that direct behaviour towards a goal. Motivations are commonly divided into two types: drives are acts of motivation like thirst or hunger that have primarily biological purposes, while motives are fueled primarily by social and psychological mechanisms.

Drive reduction theory was developed by **Clark Hull.** According to this theory, deviations from homeostasis create physiological needs. These needs result in psychological drive states that direct behaviour to meet the need and ultimately bring the system back to homeostasis. When a physiological need is not satisfied , a negative state of tension is created; when the need is satisfied, the drive to satisfy that need is reduced and organism returns to homeostasis. In this way, a drive can be thought as an instinctual need that has the power to motivate behaviour.

Need Hierarchy Theory (Maslow)

Humanist psychologist Abraham Maslow synthesised a number of different theories into a hierarchy of needs. If and only if our needs at a lower level are met, then we can be motivated by higher level needs. Maslow characterised that there are some needs that are basic to all human beings. Once we satisfy basic needs we can move on to higher needs. In other words, once a lower level is satisfied, it no longer serve as a motivator.

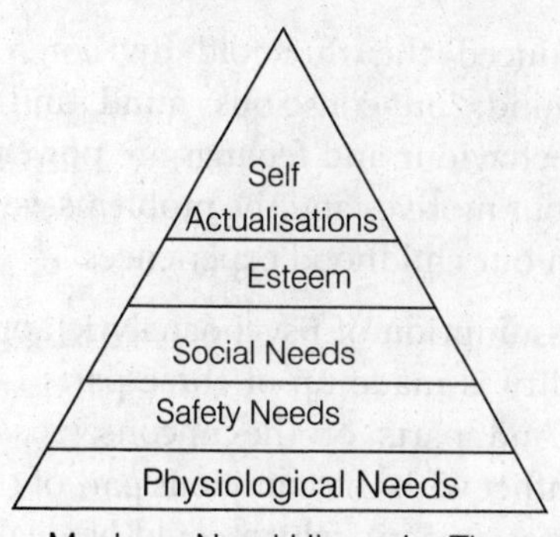

Maslow : Need Hierarchy Theory

The most basic of Maslow's needs are physiological needs. Physiological needs refer to the need for food, water and other biological needs. These needs are basic because when they are lacking, the search for them may overpower all other urges. Imagine being very hungry. At that point, all your behaviour may be directed at finding food. Once you eat, though, the search for food ceases and the promise of food no longer serves as a motivator.

Once physiological needs are satisfied, people tend to become concerned about safety needs. Are they free from the threat of danger, pain, or an uncertain future? On the next level up, social needs refer to the need to bond with other human beings, be loved and form lasting attachments with others. Infact, attachments, or lack of them, are associated with our health and well-being. The need to belong: Desire for interpersonal attachments as a fundamental human motivation. The satisfaction of social needs makes esteem needs more salient.

Esteem need refers to the desire to be respected by one's peers, feel important and be appreciated. Finally, at the highest level of the hierarchy, the need for self-actualisation refers to 'becoming all you are capable of becoming.' This need manifests itself by the desire to acquire new skills, take on new challenges and behave in a way that will lead to the attainment of one's life goals.

Arousal Theory

According to arousal theory of motivation, each person has a unique arousal level that is right for them. When our arousal levels drop below these personalised optimal levels, we seek some sort of stimulation to elevate them.

The major reason by people are driven to perform any action is to maintain the optimal level of physiological arousal. The optimal level of arousal varies from one person to another. Arousal is one of the fundamental aspects required for attention and information process. So, maintaining the optimal arousal level is vital for a person's task performance.

Arousal Levels are Highly Individual

Optimal arousal levels vary from one individual to the another. There are many factors that might influence each person's optimal arousal levels, including genetics, experience and current mood. Your arousal preferences in general may be specified by your genetic makeup, but environmental factors can also play a role in how you are feeling at any given moment.

One person may have very low arousal needs while another individual might require very high levels. The person with low arousal needs might be motivated to pursue simple activities such as crocheting or watching a movie in order to maintain their arousal levels. The individual with high arousal needs, on the other hand, might be motivated to seek risky or thrilling activities such as motorcycle racing or skydiving in order to maintain his or her ideal levels.

No matter what your arousal needs are, you will be motivated to act in order to maintain these levels. If you need more arousal, you will pursue actions designed to raise those levels. If you need less, you will seek out ways to calm down and relax.

In general we perform best at moderate levels of arousal. This concept is called the *Yerkes- Dodson law*. Think about getting ready for the Scholastic Assessment Test (SATs.) If you are too pumped up, your sympathetic nervous system kicks in and it is hard to concentrate. If you are not aroused at all, you just won't put your all in and still will not perform well. The Yerkes-Dodson law basically states that their is a middle, or moderate, level or arousal in which we all perform best.

Incentive Theory

An incentive is either a promise or an act that is provided for the sake of greater action. As arousal theory focuses on internal stimuli. Incentive theory holds that certain external stimuli act as incentives, pulling us towards some behaviour. Incentives are pleasing external stimuli that can serve as goals towards which our behaviour is directed. Incentive is a motivational variable discussed at length by **Kenneth Spence**.

Incentive refers to the activation and energisation of behaviour that takes place before and in apparent anticipation of goal and symbols. Incentives, like drive, multiplies with habit strength, so that a more complete statement of excitary potential for a response would have to include drive, habit and incentive components.

Incentives are the product of other reinforcement variables like amount, quality and attractiveness of reinforcement. The greater the amount of reward and higher the quality, the more incentive one has to work for it. Hull and Spence defined incentive without referring to any of the terms like values, purpose and will.

Motivational Cycle

Motivational cycle is a transition of states within an organism that propels the organisms towards the satisfaction of a particular need, where motivation itself is considered a hypothesised state. Psychologists use the concept of need to describe the motivational properties of behaviour.

The cycle of motivation is comprised of four different states, which takes place in an organism to drive him towards each action. Each action is first initiated because of particular **need**. The need **drives** the person into taking actions. Positive results, caused due to the actions, further acts as an **incentive** motivating a person towards the goal. But, the individual can never stop after achieving a certain **goal** and this phenomena continuous on and on. This phenomena is called *motivational cycle*.

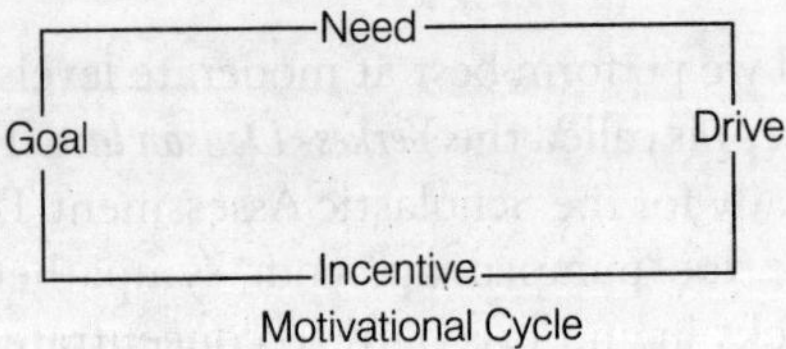

Motivational Cycle

Approaches to Study Motivation

To understand all dimension of motivation, we need to study following approaches

Psychoanalytical

Psychoanalytical theory was derived from Freud's clinical experience in treating neurotic patients. Freud recognised two fundamental motivating forces. The first one is the constructive one called the *Eros* of life urges and the others is the destructive one called *Thanator* or death urges. Eros finds its output through drives known as *self preservation* drive or ego drive or ego drive and sex drive which play a significant role in Freudian psychoanalysis.

Self destructive behaviour, he believed was one expression of the death drive. However, he believed that these death instincts were largely tempered by the life instincts. The motivating principle in life is the pleasure principle, which according to psychoanalysis is the tendency to avoid pain and seek pleasure. This dominates sex drive. As one attains maturity, this is supplemented by the reality principle.

Freud introduced the threefold division of mind into conscious mind, pre-conscious mind and unconscious mind. Our behaviour and feelings are powerfully affected by unconscious motives and the problems we face as adults are rooted in our childhood experiences.

One basic assumption of psychoanalytic approach is that our personality is made up of three parts *i.e.* id, ego and super ego. And parts of the unconscious mind are in constant conflict with the conscious part of the mind. This conflict creates anxiety, which could be dealt with by the ego's use of defence mechanisms and the personality is shaped as the drives are modified by different conflicts at different times in childhood.

Ethological Approach

Human ethology can be defined as the biology of human behaviour. Human ethology focuses on the evolutionary and adaptive significance of human behaviour. The fixed action pattern (inherited movement coordination) is a fundamental ethological concept.

An important aspect for the survival of organisms is behaviour actualisation on the basis innate mechanisms, called as 'key stimuli'. In the majority of cases, behaviour of the organism results from certain kinds of motivational states and its intensity and a specific external stimulus. The searching of organisms with a high inner motivational state for such an adequate stimulus situation is called *appetitive behaviour.*

Pulliam and Dunford describe social learning as a shortcut for obtaining adaptive behaviour, since it need not to rely on individual trial and error learning. They propose primary reinforces which have resulted from natural selection which facilitate this process. The cognitive development theory of **Kohlberg**, which postulates that imitation is intrinsically motivated, is compatible with this point of view. Imitation and identification since long has been given importance in behavioural development in humans and also been found to have an important effect on human adaptiveness.

The observable result of modelled action can influence imitation is well established. With regards to this, **Gewirtz** proposes that all imitation is performed ultimately because of external reinforcement and Bandura states that identificatory responses are greatly influenced by reinforcing the consequences of the behaviour. **Lumsden and Wilson** also describe imitation and vicarious learning as one of the primary means of 'culturgen' transmission, with people assessing the costs and benefits of an action before deciding to adopt a particular culture choice.

Self-Regulation Approach

According to **Zimmerman** and **Schunk**, "self-regulation is the control of one's present conduct based on motives related to a subsequent goal or ideal that an individual has set for him or herself". In other words self-regulation involves controlling one's behaviour in order to achieve a goal.

Behavioural self-regulation, also known as *executive functioning,* has three central components: attention, control, working memory and inhibition control.

(i) **Attention Control** It is a central component because it allows children to carry out behaviours, focus on a task or problem, access working memory and complete tasks. It is also important for learning correct behaviour from models.

(ii) **Working Memory** It allows children to remember and follow directions and helps them plan solutions to problems and it may be involved as the child compares the behaviour he produced with that modelled earlier.

(iii) **Inhibitory Control** It develops rapidly during early childhood and helps children control behaviour by stopping incorrect solutions to a problem or incorrect behaviours and carrying out more adaptive responses or behaviours.

Another term in self regulation *i.e. effortful control,* on the other hand is defined as "the ability to suppress a dominant response to perform a subdominant response".

According to **Bandura's** Social-Cognitive theory, "self-evaluation plays a central role in the development of self-regulation. Children learn about which behaviours are rewarded and punished in the environment through action and observing the actions of others and evaluating the effects of these actions".

These evaluations lead to the development of expectations for the outcomes of future behaviours and the establishment of internal criteria for judging the adequacy of the behaviours. Children then use these criteria to evaluate and regulate their own behaviour and evaluate their effectiveness.

Bronson argues that motivation and self regulation are interwined in two ways: first, people are innately rewarded by competence and control and second, people need self regulated control to reach other goals. Children take pleasure in controlling their own activities and producing effects in the environment and this can lead to feelings of competence. People are also motivated to reach specific goals and earn rewards such as social approval or material gain and self-regulation is usually required to achieve these goals and rewards. Whether the activity is intrinsically or extrinsically motivated, it is self-regulation that enables goal attainment and motivation that facilitates self- regulation. Simply put, we are motivated to self-regulate.

Cognitive Theory

The cognitive theories of motivation include the Expectancy-value theory, Goal Setting theory and the Attribution theory. The **Expectancy-value theory**, stresses that the probability to occurrence of behaviour depends upon individuals' perception of the value of a goal as well as their expectaion of reaching it. Expectancy-value theories hold that people are goal oriented beings. The behaviours they perform in response to their beliefs and values are undertaken to achieve some end.

Utilising this approach, behaviour, behavioural intentions or attitudes are seen as an function of

(i) expectancy (or belief)-the perceived probability that an object possesses a particular attribute or that a behaviour will have a particular consequence.

(ii) evaluation-the degree of affect, positive or negative, toward an attribute or behavioural outcome.

The **Goal-setting theory** was proposed by Edwin Locke in the 1960s. This theory proposes that the goal setting has an influence on task performance. Specific and challenging goals are more likely to motivate a person and lead to a better execution of tasks, whereas vague and easy goals may result to poor task performance.

According to **Attribution theory**, "humans naturally seek to understand why events have occurred, especially when the outcome is important or unexpected".

We all try to explain our performance through causal attributions, interpretations of events based on past performance and social norms. Attribution theory rests on three basic assumptions. First, it assumes that we do attempt to determine the causes of both our own behaviour and that of others. Secondly, the assignment of causes to behaviour is not done randomly *i.e.* rules exist that can explain how we come to the conclusions we do about the cause of behaviour. Lastly, the causes attributed particular behaviours will influence subsequent emotional and non-emotional behaviours. The attributions we make, then, may activate other motives.

Humanistic Approach

Humanistic approach of motivation is based on the idea that people have a strong cognitive reason to perform various action. It derives its views from the behaviour of artists, poets, novelists and philosophers. Towards that second and third decade of this century, there emerged a group of psychologists, who were dissatisfied with behaviourism on the one hand and psychoanalysts on the other. Leading among the humanistic psychologists were Rogers, Maslow, Goldstein, Allport. They argued that psychoanalysis and behaviouralism, though apparently differing from each other, however, they have certain common limitations.

Humanistic Model

The humanistic model while not denying the importance of organic and physiological motives, nevertheless, makes a positive assertion about the independence and primacy of psychological motives in and by themselves. Among the humànistic theories Maslow's theory of motivation is the most popular due to its theoretical and practical value.

According to **Maslow**, "humans are innately good and have an innate capacity for constructive growth, honesty, generosity and love". He believed that our actions are motivated in order to achieve certain hierarchy of needs which is a combination of *deficiency needs* (need for survival, need for safety) and *growth needs* (need for love and belonging, need for esteem, need for self-actualisation). This hierarchy suggests that people are motivated to fulfill basic needs before moving on to other, more advanced needs.

The five different levels in Maslow's hierarchy of needs include the physiological need, such as the need for water, air, food and sleep. These needs are the most basic and instinctive needs in the hierarchy because all needs become secondary until these physiological needs are met. Second, is the *security need*, which are important for survival. But they are not as demanding as the physiological needs. Third, is the *social needs*, which include needs for belonging, love and affection.

Fourth, is the *esteem needs*, which includes the need for things that reflect on self-esteem, personal worth, social recognition and accomplishment. Lastly, is the highest level need termed as *self-actualising needs*. According to **Maslow**, "self-actualisation can be described in the following way: A musician must make music, an artist must paint, a poet must write, if he is to be ultimately at peace with himself. What a man be, he must be".

Self actualised people are characterised by an acceptance of themselves, spontaneity, the need for privacy, resistance to cultural influences, empathy, profound interpersonal relations, a democratic character structure, creativeness and a philosophical sense of humour.

Curiosity Approach

A novel situation may or may not produce fear. With many animals a novel object or situation induces observant, manipulative and exploartory behaviour. Curiosity is also referred to as 'exploratory motive.' When an organism is placed in a novel or strange situation, the organism automatically tends to explore surrounding thoroughly. Infact, our ignorance about a number of things in the surrounding becomes a powerful motivator and prompts us to be curious and explorative. This motive has been observed in a variety of experiments done on animals and humans. Humans if allowed to explore, get internal satisfaction reflected in their smiles and babbling.

Butter and Harlow, the visual curiosity and exploratory behaviours starts from the very beginning of life gradually increases with gradual maturity owing to such increase, ability to located objects in the surrounding and learning to discriminate develops, which finally leads to building up of strong need to explore the world visually.

Berlyne reviewed theories of curiosity and proposed a view that agrees with common observation. He postulated that, when a novel stimulus affects the receptors of an organism, a curiosity drive is aroused. When the stimulus that arouses curiosity continues to affect the receptors, the curiosity diminishes Berlyne related these postulates to the Hullian system and made several predictions that confirmed experimentally.

In one experiment, Berlyne demonstrated that rats spent more time exploring a novel object than an object they had previously explored. Furthermore, they spent less time exploring an object the second time they encountered it. In others words, curiosity was reduced, when familiarity replaced novelty, Berlyne has developed and extended his work on exploratory behaviour.

This works agrees with the experience of laboratory workers generally. Novelty does excite observant, manipulative and exploratory behaviour. Repetition of the situation leads to reduction in the amount of such behaviour.

Exploratory Behaviour Approach

It is common knowledge among laboratory workers that, when a rat is placed in new piece of apparatus his first response is to run about, looking, sniffing, touching objects. If a rat is hungry when placed in a novel apparatus, he will explore before eating; if thirsty, he will explore before drinking . In other words, exploratory behaviour dominates the animal's activities in a novel environment.

Montgomery described the exploratory drive as a primary drive, aroused by external stimuli, which undergoes a decrement in strength when another primary drive, such as hunger or thirst, is present. The conditions, which determine the strength of the exploratory drive are different from, but related to the conditions that determine hunger or thirst.

Dember and **Earl** argue that organism are motivated to seek a level of complexity slightly above their current level. According to **Dember and Earl**, "only a certain range of stimuli will be acceptable". **Berlyne** has suggested that the mechanism underlying exploratory and play attention to an object is sufficient to produce information processing. Once all the information has been processed, the individual will be inclined to seek out new stimuli.

The tendency to explore is reduced by high levels of arousal, such as those produced by drugs and also by fear. Because individuals often differ in terms of arousal levels and fear, it is not surprising that there is also great difference in their tendency to explore. Teachers and parents may be able to increase children's tendency to explore by creating an environment that is relaxed.

Zuckerman's Sensation Seeking

Sensation seeking is a personality trait defined by the degree to which an individual seeks novel and highly stimulating activities and experiences. People who are highly stimulating in sensation seeking are attracted to the unknown and as a result consistently seek the new, varied and unpredictable things.

Examples of such behaviours are varied, but sensation seekers may be attracted to extreme sports, frequent travel, diverse foods and music, new sexual partners and experiences and challenges existing viewpoints. Often, sensation seekers are likely to be impulsive and engage in behaviours that others would find too risky. The risks may be physical (*e.g.* skydiving), social (*e.g.* risking embarrassment by dressing unusually), financial (*e.g.* gambling) or legal (*e.g.* vandalism). Because sensation seekers are easily bored, they actively avoid situations and activities likely to be overly repetitive and predictable.

Sensation Seeking Theory

Marvin Zuckerman originally developed the concept of sensation seeking and has contributed the most important research and relevant theory. Zuckerman's work is especially noteworthy because of his firm and long-standing emphasis on the biological and evolutionary bases of sensation seeking (and personality more generally). Specifically, Zuckerman's basic proposition is that sensation seeking is based on individual differences in the optimal level of sensation caused by biological nervous system differences.

People who are high in sensation seeking are individuals who have relatively low level nervous system activation and therefore seek arousal from their external environment by looking for novel stimuli and engaging in varied experiences. In contrast, individuals who are low in sensation seeking have a naturally higher level of internal activation and thus do not tend to seek sensation from external sources.

Sensation Seeking Measurement

Zuckerman first created the sensation seeking scale in 1964. He aims to measure an individual's overall level of susceptibility to excitement or boredom in the content of sensory deprivation experiments.

Current version of measure include

(i) **Thrill and Adventure Seeking** The extent to which individuals engage in or are interested in participating in risky activities such as parachuting or skiing.

(ii) **Experience Seeking** The degree to which one seeks excitement through the mind, such as from music, art and travel.

(iii) **Disinhibition** Seeking sensations through social stimulation and disinhibitory behaviours such as drinking and sex.

(iv) **Boredom Susceptibility** Avoiding monotonous, repetitive and boring situations, people and activities.

Types of need

David Mcclelland and his research team developed a theory to explain how different people are motivated, known as Mcclelland's Needs theory. It consist of three needs-*Achievement, Affilication and Power, which are explained below.*

Achievement

The need to achieve is basically defined as a need to be successful "in competition with some standard of excellence," wherein "doing as well as or better than someone is a primary concern". Behavioural manifestations of achievement occur as an effective response "in connection with evaluated performance." Thus, the elements of success, standard of excellence, competition and evaluated performance are all elements related to the conception of the achievement motive.

Researches on achievement had found that achievement is developed in early childhood within the dynamics of the mother child interaction. Besides that other researchers has found that individuals who have high need to achieve and low anxiety scores, show preference for tasks with intermediate probability to success. Such individuals also maintain a generally high performance level and are persistent in problem solving tasks. Whereas, individuals who are low in achievement and high in anxiety scores tends to choose tasks with probabilities for success at either extreme *i.e.* they tend to select unrealistic levels of aspiration. Such individuals are also less effective in their performance and less persistent in problem solving situations.

Murray saw achievement as a generalised need. Like others, he believed that the pleasure of achievement is not in attending the goal, but rather in developing and exercising skills. In other words it is the process that provides the motivation for achievement.

David McClelland research related to the achievement motives. This extensive contributions are summarised in his book 'Human Motivation'. In order to measure the achievement motive with more precision, McClelland and his colleagues adapted the Thematic Appreciation Test (TAT) and developed a precise method for scoring the achievement motive.

A number of studies to assess the validity of the TAT measure that they devised show that a generalised motive or disposition does exist and that it can predict behaviour in a wide variety of situation.

Affiliation

Affiliation is type of psychological need for friendly social interactions and relationship with others. This is called as need for affiliation. People who have high in this need seek to be liked by others and to be held in high regard by those around them. This makes high affiliation people good team players, whereas a person high in achievement just might run over a few team members on the way to the top.

Measurement of Need for Affiliation

Boyatzis has reviewed the literature on measurement of affiliation. Like need for achievement, need for affiliation has been measured in terms of stories told about pictures. The first step was to show that certain conditions could arouse the need for affiliation, as measured by TAT scoring. The second step was to conduct research to determine the construct validity of an affiliation by showing differential performance of high and low affiliation people in other situations.

Boyatzis considers a major theoretical issue to be whether there are indeed two different kinds of affiliation namely hope of affiliation and fear of rejection.

The theoretical similarity to the distinction between hope of success and fear of failure is obvious. Boyatzis' conclusion is that the TAT scoring procedures do not distinguish between the two dimensions, although the distinction make intuitive sense. Another projective test French test of insight may distinguish between them in better way but the issue is unsettled.

Determinants of Affiliation

There is considerable evidence that, when people are fearful, they prefer to be with others. Presumably, other people have less anxiety. Even with rats, it is found that in an apparatus where they have previously been shocked the animals are less fearful if there is another animal present. Furthermore, they are more active yet if the other animal itself has not previously been shocked suggests three ways, by which the presence of other person may reduce response to aversive stimuli. *First*, the other person may serve as a 'calm' model for the anxious person to imitate. *Second*, the companion may do something to distract the subject. *Third*, the mere physical presence of another might be fear reducing, even though the other person does nothing.

Some of the best-known human research on this topic is by Schachter. Schachter's subjects were threatened with either strong or week electric shock and than were given the choice of waiting alone or with other subjects. This strong-shock subjects had a greater preference for waiting with other. It was not demonstrated, however, that being with others are actually anxiety reducing other investigators (wrightsman) have found self-reports of lower anxiety from subjects waiting with other subjects in a threatening situation.

Power Similar to Achivement

Power represents your ability to get things done through other people. The more power you have, the more things you can do. But remember: with great power comes great responsibility. There's nothing morally wrong with wanting more power.

According to **Josh Kaufman's**, "all human relationships are based on *power*, the ability to influence the actions of other people. We can never control people because we don't have direct access over the inner processes that make people do the things they do. All we can really do is to act in ways that encourage people to do what we suggest".

The use of power typically takes on one of two fundamental forms; influence or compulsion.

(i) **Influence** in the ability to encourage someone else to want what you suggest.

(ii) **Compulsion** is the ability to force someone else to do what you command.

Encouraging an employee to 'go the extra mile' out of a sense of loyalty or craftsmanship is influence. Forcing the employee to work over the weekend by threatening to fire them if they refuse is compulsion. The actions that employee takes may be exactly the same, but how they feel about taking those actions will be quite different.

Motivational Competence

Motivational competence theory is a conceptual framework designed to explain individual's motivation to participate, persist and work hard in any particular achievement. The central thesis of the theory is that individuals are attracted to participate in activities at which they feel competent or capable. The theory can be used by researchers and practitioners in sport and exercise psychology fields to identify why and how children, adolescents and adults can be encouraged to participate and to exert effort in these achievement contexts.

The first psychologist to produce a theory of motivation that was widely accepted was propounded by **Clark Hull** . He said that people are motivated by biology and called his theory **Drive theory.** He said that people were motivated to reduce the tension caused by such things, such as hunger and thirst. In other words, people want to satisfy their urges. But many psychologists came to see this explanation as incomplete.

In 1959, **Robert White** wrote an article for the psychological review about his new thinking on the subject of motivation. In the article, he outlined his idea, which he called *effectance motivation*. He said that people wanted to have an effect (usually positive) on their environment. This motivated a desire to be competent. By competent he meant that the individual was motivated to show that they were qualified to perform a task. This idea was later expanded on by **Susan Harter**, who devised a scale to determine an individual's motivations.

White's Theory of Competence

One of the most influential articles on the nature of mastery and competence was published by Robert White. Drawing heavily on the work concluded in the early 1950s. which showed that curiosity and exploratory behaviour are not tied to primary drive such as hunger, thirst and sex, he suggested that the tendency to explore is based on more general motive, which he called *Effectance Motivation*. This motive, white suggested is directed towards understanding the nature of the environment and the order inherent in it. Feeling of efficacy occur, when the individual comes to understand or know that he or she is able to affect the environment. Such feelings, White argues can act as a reward.

Piaget's Theory of Competence

Piaget believed that the need to interact with the environment, forces the child to engage in the process of mastery. Piaget conceptualised this in terms of two complementary processes. First, the child has to develop cognitive structures, a process called *accommodation*. Equipped with certain cognitive structures, the child then integrates information contained in his or her environment through a process called *assimilation*, which most psychologists now simply call information processing.

Dweck's Theory of Competence Developement

Dweck and her colleagues have suggested that we can understand difference in achievement and competency by understanding the implicit theories that people have about the origins of achievement and competency. She argues that some people views competency in term of skill and knowledge they possess.

According to **Dweck's model**, "people who believe in the entity theory are motivated to select goals that will indicate that they do have ability and to avoid goals that might provide evidence that they lack ability". People, who believe in the incremental theory tend to select goals that will enable them to increase their competence. If ability can be acquired, it is important to select goals that can maximise learning. Motivation is one of the core components of self regulation, let us study in detail:

Self Regulation

Self regulation is the ability to monitor and manage your energy states, emotions, thoughts and behaviour in ways that are acceptable and produce positive results such as well-being, loving relationships and learning, It is how we deal with stressors and as such, lays the foundation for all other activity. Developing this ability requires self-awareness, emotional intelligence, efficient filtering of sensory stimulation, coping effectively with stress, relating well to others and sustaining focus.

You can think of self-regulation in terms of how a thermostat works. A thermostat is set to kick on or off to keep a room at a certain desired temperature–a 'set point'. To do that, it needs to keep track of temperature changes, compare them to the set point and 'know' whether to heat or cool the room to get back to the desired temperature.

Flow

Think of a runner competing in a marathon. His goal is clear. He needs to reach the finish line faster than his competitors. He has trained long and hard for this. He knows he can do it and he is focused on winning the race. There is nothing else in his mind but crossing the finish line. He sees it as a challenge to his skills and he is ready to take it on. His heart is beating fast in anticipation. The race starts and he bursts into a run. His legs are pounding the ground in time with his heartbeat. He's not conscious of himself or his environment. He is single-mindedly focused on crossing the finish line. Nothing else exists. He is in what positive psychology calls the 'Flow State'.

Mihaly Csikszentmihalyi, a distinguished professor of Psychology and Management at Claremont Graduate University, first coined the term. He is known for his work in the realms of happiness and creativity. According to him, people are at their happiest when they're in a state of flow. They forget about all concerns, fully motivated and focused on the present moment. There is no time, no ego and no other need. They are totally immersed in the task at hand; mind, body and soul and their skills are being utilised to the fullest.

Conclusion

For the above understanding of motivation; it's concept and theories it is evident that it is self-regulatory which refers through the process by which individual learner attempts to monitor and control their own learning. But it should always go in a flow in which the motivation cycle works *i.e.* Need→Drive→Incentive→Goal. Thus , in order to work in motivational cycle one must be self-regulatory and flow the cycle so that the desired goal can be achieved.

Emotion

Most theories either explicitly or implicitly acknowledge that an emotion is not a simple phenomena. It cannot be described completely by a person who describe his emotional experience. It cannot be described completely by the expressive or motor behaviour that occurs in emotion. Emotion is a reaction consisting of subjective cognitive states, physiological reactions and expressive behaviours.

They involve three major components

(i) Physiological changes within our bodies *i.e.* shifts in heart rate, blood pressure and so on.

(ii) Subjective cognitive states *i.e.* the personal experience we label as emotions and

(iii) Expressive behaviours *i.e.* outward signs of these internal reactions.

Emotion is associated with mood, temperament, personality, disposition and motivation. Emotions can be considered as thoughts that you can't identify. *For instance*, when you feel something , it must be that you are thinking about something unconsciously.

We feel them in our bodies as tingles, hotspots and muscular tension. They are cognitive aspects, but the physical sensation is what makes them really different. Emotions are partly derived from feelings. A model of consciousness can be used to explain this derivation. Consciousness has three modes or parts *i.e.* will, mind and feeling.

Consciousness is the totality of the person, whilst mind is only one feature of it. However, this model has an innovative feature-the three modes are separate, but they interlock by the production of desires and emotions. Like, so many psychological phenomena, emotion is easily recognised but hard to define. Most theories hold that emotion is a syndrome, a complex entity with many components.

Elements of Emotions

Emotions have these elements

- Physiological response
- Cognitive events
- Sensory inputs
- Behavioural correlates *e.g.* expression of emotion

Characteristics of Emotion

Emotions have certain characteristics

- Temporary or transitory in nature.
- Valence or quality: We feel good or bad.
- To some degree passive: We don't directly choose how we feel.
- Experience: We know what emotions feel like.
- Learning.
- Prepare us for action (*e.g.* fear preps us to run)
- Shape behaviour of an individual
- Regulate social interaction and facilitate communication

Physiological Correlates of Emotion

There in an arousal individual expresses emotion. This obviously means that some changes in whole body mechanisms occurs that distinguish emotional state from non-emotional state.

Prominent among such changes are

(i) Internal changes in emotion *i.e.* visceral changes.

(ii) External changes in emotion *i.e.* facial, vocal pastural etc.

Internal changes of body has not voluntary control, but in external changes, these are subject to voluntary control. Therefore, measurement of physiological changes is considered most sensitive and objective indicators of emotion.

Internal Changes in Emotion

Due to development of emotion, several changes are witnessed in body. *They are*

- **Heart Rate and Blood Pressure** In case of intense emotion such as anger, there is an increase in the heart beat *i.e.* increase in the heart rate. This increase is accompanied by more rigorous contraction of body. This is caused by hyper functioning of the sympathetic nervous system.
  This hyper functioning of sympathetic nervous system also brings changes in blood pressure. But these changes in blood pressure cannot predict clearly in the state of emotion.
- **Changes in Breathing** In some state of emotion, there is changes in respiratory system, these respiratory changes in emotion are very complex.
- **Changes in Temperature** Sometimes, It has been been reported that there is up and down of temperature of body during emotion. *For example* In stress results in drop of the body temperature.
- **Changes in Glandular Responses** When there is intense emotion, adrenal glands secrets adrenalin as well as non-adrenalin hormones into blood. Under influence of adrenalin the liver releases stoned sugar into blood. This causes chemical changes in blood resulting in quick clotting of blood, rise in blood pressure, changes in the eye pupil *i.e.* enlargement, rise in the skin temperature etc.
  Grandular responses help in emotionally charged individuals to cope physically with the emergency situation during emotion. However, if there sudden provoking situation to emotion, if not met by direct action, the hyper grandular functioning has been found harmful to individual.
- **The Galvanic Skin Responses** (GSR) In a state of emotion, certain changes in electrical properties of skin takes place.

  There are two important changes take place

  (i) The tissues generate electromotive force.

  (ii) The electrical resistance of skin is changed.

  These changes are measured by a very sensitive electrical appartus called Galvanic Skin Response (GSR). This response is named as psychogalvanic response. GSR in combination with blood pressure and respiration is highly sensitive indicator of emotion. In lie detection, this is most' ' used. In lie detection, both critical and normal question are put and a comparison of degree of emotion to different question is made by measuring the rate of respiration, blood pressure and GSR.
- **Pupilometrics** It has been stated that during emotion, certain changes in pupils of the eye take place. To measure their changes in pupils, **Eckhard Hess** discovered a new device in the year 1960, which is known as *pupilometrics*. Hess demonstrated his device for measuring the changes of pupil size. The image of the eyes, greatly magnified, is shown on the television monitor. This apparatus is used in a variety of tests. This apparatus is also expected to be great use in lie detection and psychotherapy.
- **Some other Changes** Some other changes are visualised in various state of emotion. Such as dryness of mouth, disruption in digestive system, **secretary** functions of salivary gland, sweating and dryness of skin, hyper excretion etc.

External Changes in Emotion

Facial expression, vocal expressions, gestures are external changes in different state of emotion. They have direct manipulation from the environment. These external expression serve as important indicators of emotional experiences.

Some of these external signs are described here

Facial Expression

One of the first attempts to categorise emotions came from **Wundt**, who used introspection to identify emotional experience in relation to three dimensions: pleasantness/unpleasantness; relaxation/tension and calm/excitement.

In recent times, emotions have been studied by references to facial expressions, in an attempt to establish 'universal' human emotions. **Ekman and Friesen**, were able to identify six such universal emotion in this way.

According to **Ekman** and **Friesen**, these are six primary or basic emotions from which all other emotions sprout.

(i) Fear (ii) Sadness (iii) Anger
(iv) Happiness (v) Disgust (vi) Surprise

They would regard these are the only states that could be regarded as pure emotions and nothing else. However, it is difficult to accept this classical approach to emotions, as it is almost impossible to say how each of these states would be experienced in different situations, *e.g.* you may be surprised to find friends and relatives in your house on your birthday and you may also be surprised to see two cars crash into one another in the street.

Behaviour Pattern

Each emotion is accompanied by a definite behaviour pattern. *It may be classified into four broad categories namely.*

(i) **Destruction** Destruction is typical of anger. The individual who is angry may indulge directly in distroying or injuring the person who aroused anger in him.

(ii) **Approach Reaction** Approach reactions seek to prolong and facilitate further stimulation. They may be overt as in the case of physical approach such as shaking hands, huggings or symbolic approach as writing letters, using favourable language in speech.

(iii) **Retreat** Retreat response involves flight or withdrawal.

(iv) **Arrest of Response** Arrest of response is a reaction which is more psychological than fear. In grief or sorrow, the usual responses are with held. In more extreme cases the individual refuses to respond even to the most strong stimulus such is called depression.

Verbal Expression

Just like facial expressions we also have the verbal expressions. These include voice and speech. It a person is very angry thee will be a rise in the pitch of the voice.

Posture and Gesture

Emotions are also expressed by posture and gesture. In fear, a person flies or is "rooted to the sport". In anger he usually makes agreessive gestures and may even clench his first move to attack. In sorrow a person tends to slump with face downwards but these expression differ widely from society to society.

Other Changes

The skin reacts externally to the emotions. It goes pale when an individual is frightened or shocked. If a person is very angry or surprised the hair on the skin stand erect. These are called goose lashes or goose pimples.

Theories of Emotion

Psychologist have proposed a number of theories about the origins and function of emotions. The theorists agree on one thing that emotions has a biological basis, which is evidenced by the fact that the *amygdala* (part of the limbic system of brain), which plays a large role in emotion, is activated before any direct involvement of the *cerebral cortex* (where memory, awareness and conscious 'thinking' take place). There are the following theories which explain the complex mental and physical experiences that take place in humans called as *feelings*. *These are as follows*

James-Lange Theory

William James and Carl Lange independently came to the conclusion that the commonsense view of emotion was not only wrong, it was infact a reversal of reality. Commonsense might suggest that emotions begin with the subjective feeling, which is than transmitted to the rest of the body through the Autonomic Nervous System (ANS).

James and Lange suggest that it is the ANS that responds to the stimulus, either through specific physiological changes or through muscle activity, which then sends messages to the cortex to produce the emotional feelings.

In some ways, it is possible to regard this theory as 'common sensical', as it could be associated with the notion of 'gut feeling', which are supposed to be the way we respond to some of the more basic emotions. There are numerous situations where our bodies display automatic responses that are later interpreted as a particular emotional state *e.g.* when you hear a loud noise your reaction will be to jump.

James-Lange view is that different physical reactions are associated with different emotions. Therefore, the emotional experience depends, on which aspect of the ANS has been activated, rather than just suggesting that emotions will be judged from a general level of arousal.

The sound of a baby crying will make the hairs on the back of our neck stand on end; the sound of an ambulance siren will probably make the heart beat faster, but it won't make us jump. Therefore, there seems to be some support for the view that different physical reactions lead to different emotional states. According to **James**, "we don't run because we are scared, we are scared because we run".

This phenomenon is summarised in the following table

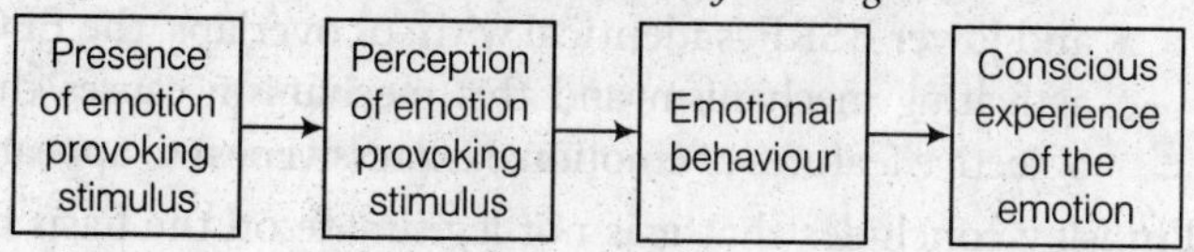

Cannon-Bard Theory

Cannon performed a number of animal experiments to test the basis of the James-Lange theory and to consider possible alternatives. Cannon viewed that the feeling of emotion and the peripheral arousal that accompanied it, were completely independent and although they occur simultaneously, it was not possible to suggest that the one caused the other.

Many of the arguments behind Cannon's view have already been outlined as part of the evaluation of James-Lange. The emotional sequence of Cannon-Bard is summarised in figure given below.

Cannon-Bard make three important points

(i) The thalamus plays a centrally important role in passing messages to the cortex concerning the feeling of emotion.

(ii) The hypothalamus receives messages simultaneously from the thalamus, which are then transmitted through to the body leading to arousal.

(iii) All emotional stimuli produce the same pattern of ANS activity.

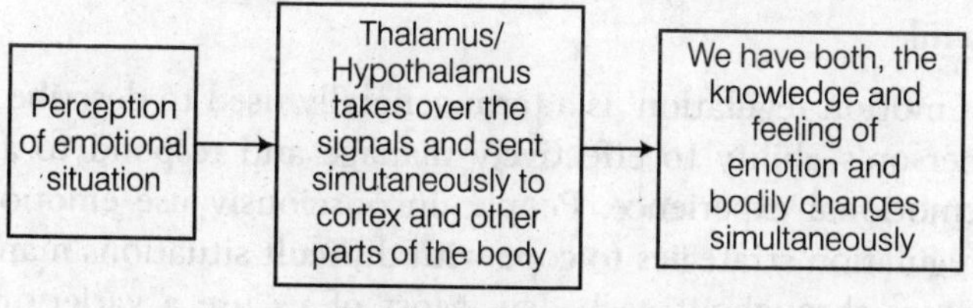

Emotional Sequence

Although, autonomic reactions are crucial in the process of general arousal, the experience and expression of a specific emotion is independently triggered elsewhere, in the cortex. It is this combination of general arousal and the simultaneous registering of the emotional experience in the cortex that allows us to distinguish between arousal in the presence of a bear from arousal in the presence of a member of the opposite sex. The theory is useful as it successfully anticipated later explanations of the role of the limbic system in emotion.

Schachter and Singer Theory

Schachter and Singer theory, sometimes known as *two factor theory* in which emotion provoking events produce increased arousal. Due to these feelings, we look for external environment in order to identify the cause behind them. The factors we then select play a key role in determining the label we place on our arousal and so in determining. The emotion we experience. In short, we perceive ourselves to be experiencing the emotion that external cues tell us we should be feeling.

This theory by Schachter and Singer is called *Cognitive Labelling theory* as it relies on appropriate labels being applied to the situation in order to experience the emotion correctly. Of course, there is no right or wrong way of experiencing an emotion, but if you are going to behave in appropriate ways then it is important that you apply the right label and therefore come up with the appropriate behaviour for the situation.

The James-Lange theory showed the need for a certain level of arousal, but failed to identify different forms of arousal for each and every emotion. The Cannon-Bard theory was able to provide a role for complex brain structures in the process based around a view of general arousal, which is useful for distinguishing between arousal in the presence of a bear and arousal in the presence of a member of the opposite sex, but still failed to include complex attributional factors in the process.

Schachter and Singer observed the effect of a general level of arousal, combined with a cognitive labelling process employed by the participants to explain their feeling of arousal. According to them, it is this combination that will produce an emotional experience.

Lazarus's Cognitive Theory

The importance of cognitive interpretation of circumstances in determining the arousal levels is central to Lazarus theory. In this theory he suggests that some degree of cognitive processing is essential before an emotional reaction, either over or internal, can occur.

Lazarus proposed a theory suggesting that emotion is a cognitive function, arising as result of appraisal of a situation. A situation may be appraisal as non-threatening leading to positive emotional stress.

The actual emotion experienced depends upon other characteristics or circumstances. A stimulus appraised as threatening leads to direct action, such as attack, retreat or freezing, together with physiological responses such as these which accompany negative states, including fear, anger or depression.

If direct action is impossible, coping strategies may be employed to reappraise the situation benignly, in order to live with the threat. These coping strategies may be simply to redefine the threat as 'not' as bad as it was first perceived.

For example Why does a wife continue to live with her husband who is violent towards her? The husband who is the stimulus is appraised as threatening, but for various reasons the wife cannot take direct action. Probably she cannot fight back, as her husband is stronger, she cannot run away, as she has no one and nowhere to go.

In such cases, the situation is to be reappraised and a different solution is to be found such as staying on with the husband and losing the extreme fear and doing things that may prevent violence etc.

A different thinking pattern may also perhaps help. In other words, the woman may start thinking that the husband may not perhaps hit her again and that he is very considerable the next day and so on. Living with this reappraised threat is less problematic than fear of the outside of that situation. This theory is primarily descriptive, but the underlying mechanisms involved in emotion such as the relationship between cognitions, feelings and expressions of emotion are undefined to a great extent.

Lindsley's Activation Theory

The American psychologist and neuroscientist Donald Benjamin Lindsley's germinal work on activation in the general area of emotion shows the importance of the brain-stem portion of the brain called the *reticular substance*. Lindsley's activation theory is based, in particular, on research involving thc Electroencephalogram (EEG) and its relevance toward understanding the interaction of the cerebral cortex and the subcortical structures.

The activation theory was advanced not only as an explanatory concept for emotional behaviour, but it was related also to the phenomenon of sleep-wakefulness, to EEG recordings of cortical activity and to different types of abnormal behaviour involving various psychiatric symptomatologies. *The activation theory states.*

(i) The EEG in emotion shows an activation pattern with reduction in alpha (synchronised) rhythms and induction of low-amplitude, fast activity.

(ii) The EEG activation pattern is reproducible by electrical stimulation of the brain-stem reticular formation (BSRF).

(iii) Destruction of the rostral end of the BSRF abolishes EEG activation and allows restoration of rhythmic discharges in the thalamus/cortex.

(iv) The behaviour associated with destruction of the rostral end of the BSRF is the opposite of emotional excitement, namely, apathy, somnolence, lethargy and catalepsy.

(v) The combined mechanism of the basal diencephalon and lower BSRF is identical with, or overlaps, the EEG activating mechanism and this mechanism causes the objective features of emotional expressiveness to appear.

Lindsley concludes that it is not legitimate on the basis of the existing experimental evidence to attempt to account for all the varieties of emotional expression and further research is advised on the influences of learning, habituation and memory on emotional expression. The activation theory is able to account for the extremes of emotional behaviour but is not able to explain completely the intermediate and mixed states of emotional expressiveness.

Emotion Regulation

All of us fell and experience both negative and positive emotion each and every day. Emotions are a normal part of our everyday lives. Everyone experiences them. For some, feeling these emotions can seem overwhelming, like an out-of-control roller coaster. It is common for one or more strong emotions to occur before an individual engages in self-injury. These often include: guilt, sadness, feeling overwhelmed or frustrated, anger, self-blame and low self-worth. This feeling of being overwhelmed emotionally can lead to a deep need to do something that will stop the intensity. Self-injury can serve as a short-term fix to stop the overwhelmingness of the feeling at least for a little while.

'Emotion regulation' is a term generally used to describe a person's ability to effectively manage and respond to an emotional experience. People unconsciously use emotion regulation strategies to cope with difficult situations many times throughout each day. Most of us use a variety of emotion regulation strategies and are able to apply them to different situations in order to adapt to the demands of our environment. Some of these are healthy, some are not.

Healthy Way of Emotion Regulation

- Talking with friends
- Writing a Journal
- Therapy
- Exercising
- Meditation
- Getting adequate sleep

Unhealthy Way of Emotion Regulation

- Self injury
- Abusing alcohol or other substance
- Physical or verbal aggression
- Excessive social media use
- Avoiding or withdrawing from difficult situation

EXAM BASED QUESTIONS

1 In psychology, the term 'motivation' refers to the
(a) cognitive interpretation of events
(b) activation of behaviour
(c) development of self esteem
(d) body arousal associated with feelings

2 Which is the following is true of motivation?
(a) It activates and directs behaviour.
(b) It is accompanied by physiological arousal of the autonomic nervous system produced in response to a stimulus.
(c) It involves the cognitive interpretation of body arousal.
(d) It involves a positive or negative conscious experience.

3 Among the given statements select the most suitable explanation of 'motivation'?
(a) It activates one's behaviour.
(b) It effects the selection of one's behaviour over others.
(c) It is associated with one's reaction to stimuli.
(d) It is accompanied by psychological arousal of the autonomic nervous system produce in response to stimuli.

4 Stimulus motives are
(a) needs that are learned, such as the needs for achievement.
(b) innate, but not necessary for survival.
(c) not innate, but necessary for survival.
(d) innate and necessary for survival.

5 Unlearned biological motives necessary for survival are termed
(a) primary motives
(b) secondary motives
(c) drive motives
(d) stimulus motives

6 Stimulus motives differ from primary motives in that they
(a) are unlearned and necessary for survival.
(b) appear to be innate, but are not necessary for survival.
(c) are acquired through various forms of conditioning and learning.
(d) include needs for security, status, approval and achievement.

7 Which of the following is primary motive ?
(a) Curiosity
(b) Money
(c) Physical contact
(d) Thirst

8 Secondary motives are
(a) needs that are learned, such as the needs for power or for achievement.
(b) innate, but not necessary for survival.
(c) not innate, but necessary for survival.
(d) innate and necessary for survival.

9 Psychological motives that are
(a) universal
(b) not influenced by learning
(c) not directly related to survival needs
(d) regulated by the hypothalamus

10 Motives are activated by
(a) thoughts
(b) internal physiological states
(c) external cues
(d) All of the above

11 Homeostasis is a term used to describe
(a) lateral inhibition in neural networks
(b) the opponent-process theory of motivation
(c) autonomic nervous system arousal
(d) physiological balance

12 Which of the following is an example of a behaviour regulated by homeostasis?
(a) Going skydiving for the sheer thrill of it
(b) Arranging food on a plate for aesthetic appeal
(c) Standing in the shade on a hot day
(d) Calling a friend to cheer you up

13 Which of the following behaviours is most likely motivated by homeostasis need?
(a) Feeling full but eating a slice of pie because it looks so good.
(b) Drinking four glasses of water on a hot summer day.
(c) Placing scented candles around your house because the smells make you happy.
(d) Taking a hot bubble to relax.

14 What is a homeostatic mechanism?
(a) A process that regulates the essential, internal biological states.
(b) The regulation of behaviour in response to external stimuli.
(c) The tendency to seek out stimulation and novel environments.
(d) The tendency to increaser stimulation to create pleasurable feelings.

15 Motivational levels affect learning by way of
(a) strengthening the stimulus-response associations
(b) increasing the frequency of the response
(c) providing greater energy for the response
(d) giving direction to the response

16 Which one the following is the most eclectic classification of the motive?
(a) Innate and acquired motives
(b) Physiological, psychological and mixed motives
(c) Primary, secondary and personal motives
(d) Physiological, personal and social motives

17 **Which one of the following statements regarding the sensation seeking motives is correct?**

(a) The optimum level of arousal for peak performance will depend upon the nature of the task.

(b) The need to explore the environment and the need for sensory stimulation both include sensation seeking motives.

(c) Relationships between physiological process such as hormone production and psychosocial processes such as early socialisation explain sensation seeking behaviour.

(d) The sensation seeking behaviour recorded in the first persons's accounts reflects both a general state of negativity and the specific feeling of intense anger.

18 **Motive arousal is a function of**

(a) motivational disposition X incentive X expectation

(b) curiosity X drive X achievement

(c) hunger X thirst X need

(d) need X valence X achievement

19 **Psychological response to pain stimuli is largely determined by**

(a) cutaneous receptors (b) efferent nerves

(c) afferent nerves (d) brain processes

20 **Which is true regarding the influence of cultural values on eating behaviours?**

(a) They are the primary cause of innate taste aversion.

(b) They greatly affect the incentive value of various food.

(c) They determine a person's set point for various food.

(d) They have a homeostatic influence on amount of food consumed.

21 **What does one mean by intrinsic motivation?**

(a) It occurs when obligations on approval are factors.

(b) There is no obvious external reward for one's behaviour.

(c) There are obvious external factors controlling behaviour.

(d) Extrinsic motivation is also high.

22 **From where does extrinsic motivation stems?**

(a) Obvious external factors (b) Intrinsic motivation

(c) Primary drives (d) Self-actualisation

23 **Painting portraits because one is being paid to paint portraits is an example of engaging in an activity as a result of**

(a) primary motive

(b) intrinsic motivation

(c) the opponent process theory

(d) extrinsic motivation

24 **Being a model employee because one enjoys the admiration of one's co-workers is an example of**

(a) intrinsic motivation (b) self-actualisation

(c) homeostatic (d) extrinsic motivation

25 **A toddler goes to great length to open a box. She knows there is nothing in the box. This is an example of**

(a) homeostasis (b) extrinsic motivation

(c) intrinsic motivation (d) secondary motivation

26 **In terms of the value of extrinsic rewards, which of the following is true?**

(a) Providing extrinsic rewards will strengthen existing intrinsic motivation.

(b) Extrinsic rewards should only be given, when intrinsic motivation is evident.

(c) providing extrinsic rewards will weaken existing intrinsic motivation.

(d) Extrinsic rewards should be avoided because they prevent the development of intrinsic motivation.

27 **Among the following, which is the best example of intrinsic motivation?**

(a) Scuba diving as part of a rescue mission.

(b) Scuba diving to find sunken treasure.

(c) Scuba diving because your husband wants you to learn to scuba dive.

(d) Scuba diving with delight in underwater scenery.

28 **According to Maslow's hierarchy theory**

(a) people are more influenced by psychological than biological needs.

(b) feeling loved is a need that must be met before any other needs.

(c) the order of needs is less important than meeting all five needs.

(d) People won't be motivated to fulfill higher needs, if lower needs remain unmet.

29 **According to Maslow's theory, the basic needs include**

(a) physiological, safety and security needs

(b) safety, love and belonging needs

(c) physiological and belonging needs

(d) security and esteem

30 **Which of the following is the content theory of motivation?**

(a) Equity theory (b) Goal setting theory

(c) Needs hierarchy theory (d) Valence-expectancy theory

31 **What is the correct order of needs in Maslow's hierarchy?**

(a) Physiological; Esteem; Safety; Self-actualisation; Love and belonging

(b) Self-actualisation; Physiological; Safety; Love and belonging; Esteem

(c) Physiological; Safely; Love and belonging; Esteem; Self-actualisation

(d) Self-actualisation; Safety; Love and belonging; Esteem; Physiological

32 **Which of the following observation appears not to support Maslow's hierarchy of needs?**

(a) You are stuffed full of lobster and steak, but you still order dessert.

(b) You live in a homeless shelter, but make sure you take the bus to school everyday and study every night.

(c) You work as a photographer because it puts bread on the table.

(d) After watching your friend's house burn down, you install smoke detectors in your home.

33 Maslow's theory of need hierarchy suggests a certain sequence for the fulfilment of needs. Which of the sequence is the one suggested by him?
(a) Physiological, Belongingness, Safety, Self esteem, Self-actualisation
(b) Physiological, Safety, Belongingness, Self esteem, Self-actualisation
(c) Physiological, Safety, Self esteem, Belongingness, Self-actualisation
(d) Physiological Belongingness, Self esteem, Safety, Self-actualisation

34 The demise of instinct theory left a conceptual vacuum which is filled by
(a) drive concept (b) biological appraises
(c) achievement concept (d) cognitive motive

35 Which of the following motivation is contrasting to the drive reduction goal theories?
(a) Sensation seeking
(b) Sexual motivation
(c) Hunger
(d) Homeostasis

36 The aroused condition of an organism that results from some bodily or tissue deficit is called
(a) Drive (b) Motive
(c) Goal (d) Incentive

37 Which of the following statements about the sex drive is correct?
(a) Most psychologists believe that sex is a primary motive because it is necessary for individual survival.
(b) Normal male animals are always ready to mate.
(c) Normal female animals are always ready to mate.
(d) The sex drive is considered a primary motive because it is primarily homeostasis in nature.

38 The optimal arousal theory states that individuals are motivated to
(a) increase stimulation in order to increase arousal.
(b) decrease stimulation in order to decrease arousal.
(c) maintain neither too much nor too little stimulation and arousal.
(d) maintain whatever is the current level of stimulation and arousal.

39 Which of the following is the correct sequence for the motivational process?
(a) Drive, Need, Behavioural response
(b) Need, Drive, Behavioural response
(c) Drive, Behavioural response, Need
(d) Behavioural response, Drive, Need

40 Which of the following is an assumption of arousal theory?
(a) Zero level of arousal is the most desirable
(b) High level of arousal are the most desirable
(c) Optimal level of arousal exist for each person
(d) Optimal level of arousal exist for various activities

41 At the highest levels of arousal
(a) the individual becomes emotional, frenzied disorganised.
(b) only biological needs can be met.
(c) performance on the most complex tasks improves.
(d) intellectual products exhibit great creativity.

42 In motivational cycle, first stage refers to
(a) Need (b) Goal (c) Incentive (d) Drive

43 There are how many components in the motivational cycle?
(a) One (b) Two
(c) Three (d) Four

44 To whom credit goes for propounding Psychoanalytic theory?
(a) Bruner (b) Sternberg
(c) Freud (d) Piaget

45 The biology of human behaviour is known as
(a) Zoology (b) Ethology
(c) Etiology (d) Cosmology

46 ...... described social learning as a shortcut for obtaining behaviour.
(a) Kohlberg (b) Gewirtz
(c) Pullian and Dunford (d) Lumsden and Wilson

47 Which among the following is not central component of Behavioural self-regulation?
(a) Attention control (b) Inhibitory control
(c) Working memory (d) Fast control

48 Expectancy-value theory falls under which of the following approach?
(a) Ethological (b) Cognitive
(c) Self-regulation (d) Humanistic

49 According to which of the following theory humans naturally seek to understand why events have occurred?
(a) Goal- setting theory
(b) Attribution theory
(c) Expectancy-value theory
(d) None of the above

50 In reaction to behaviourism and psychoanalysis approach, which approach emerged?
(a) Cognitive (b) Zuckerman
(c) Ethological (d) Humanistic

51 What are major benefits of curiosity?
(a) Act as motivator (b) Allow us to explore
(c) Remove our ignorance (d) All of these

52 Who described the exploratory drive as a primary drive, aroused by external stimuli?
(a) Montgomery (b) Berlyne
(c) Gewirtz (d) Murray

53 Sensation seeking theory has been given by
(a) David McClelland (b) Freud
(c) Marvin Zuckerman (d) Boyatzis

54 In which year Zuckerman had created the sensation seeking scale?
(a) 1962 (b) 1964 (c) 1966 (d) 1968

55 Who is known for the development of the drive theory?
(a) Clark Hull (b) Dweck
(c) Susan Harter (d) Piaget

56 What is cardinal feature of the motivational competence?
(a) Competition gives motivation.
(b) Motivation helps in enhancing competence.
(c) People attract towards activities in which they feel competent.
(d) None of the above

57 ...... is a ability to monitor your energy states, emotions, thoughts and behaviours in ways that are acceptable and produce positive result.
(a) Management (b) Self-regulation
(c) Controlling (d) Self-assessment

58 Who is distinguished psycologist known for coining word flow?
(a) Broca
(b) Binet
(c) Galton
(d) Mihaly Csikszentmihalyi

59 Positive emotional reactions are associated with
(a) greater activation of the left cerebral hemisphere
(b) the activation of hypothalamus
(c) the activation of autonomic nervous system only
(d) the activation of hindbrain

60 Which theory of emotion holds the view that bodily changes precede emotion and that we experience an emotion after our body react?
(a) Commonsense Theory (b) The Cannon-Bard Theory
(c) Attribution Theory (d) The James-Lange Theory

61 Emotion is the perception of bodily changes that have already occurred in response to an event is related to the theory of
(a) James-Lange (b) Cannon-Bard
(c) Schachter and Singer (d) Lindsey

62 In Schachter and Singer's classic study, participants were physically aroused by
(a) exposure to a happy man (b) exposure to an angry man
(c) receiving phrine (d) watching an excited film

63 What is the suitable definition of 'Emotion'?
(a) An individual responses to situation.
(b) Reaction to emotional stimulus.
(c) An excited state arising in response to stimuli for which the individual doesn't have adequate readymade reactions.
(d) Display of excessive or irrational behaviour as a result of unexpected or intense stimuli.

64 Which one of the following statements is not correct for the primary emotions?
(a) They have innate neural basis.
(b They are universally expressed.
(c) They are culturally specific.
(d) They are linked functionally to the temporal limbic regions.

65 Emotional thoughts and actions are controlled by
(a) autonomic nervous system (b) limbic system
(c) digestive system (d) temperament

66 The motivation, emotion and other internal forces which underlie behaviour is known as
(a) Personality dynamics (b) Personality traits
(c) Personality types (d) Multiple personality

67 Which one of the following reactions cannot be considered as an expression of emotions?
(a) Electrical conductance of the skin as measured through galvanic skin response.
(b) Heart rate is measured through electrocardiogram.
(c) Knee jerk response.
(d) Pupil dilation.

68 An emotional reaction showing a deceleration of the heart and an increase in the skin conductance, is known as
(a) directional fractionation (b) counter deceleration
(c) counter reaction (d) directional reaction

69 Which of the following are considered as a component of emotions?
(a) Physiological response (b) Cognitive events
(c) Sensory inputs (d) All of these

70 Emotions are quite dynamic in nature, among the following which is not characterstic of emotion?
(a) Regulate social interaction (b) Shape behaviour
(c) Permanent (d) Prepare us for action

71 Due to emotion which of the following internal changes are witnessed in body?
(a) Changes in breathing
(b) Heart rate and blood pressure
(c) Both a and b
(d) None of the above

72 Who discovered a new device pupilometrics?
(a) Wundt (b) Eckhard Hess
(c) Friensen (d) Engen

73 How many universal emotion have been identified by Ekman and Friensen?
(a) Three (b) Six
(c) Nine (d) Twelve

74 In how many categories behaviour pattern may be classified
(a) two (b) three
(c) four (d) five

75 **Which of the following statements about the relationship between motivation and emotion is incorrect?**
(a) Motives are often accompanied by emotions.
(b) Emotions can have motivational properties of their own.
(c) The arousal of emotions activates behaviour similar to motives.
(d) Emotions and motives always bring changes in behaviour.

76 **According to James-Lange theory of emotions, felt emotions depend upon the**
(a) activity of lower brain areas
(b) perception of bodily changes
(c) activity of higher brain processes
(d) interpretation of bodily arousal

77 **Which theory of emotion would predict that people with spinal cord injuries that prevent them from experiencing sympathetic arousal would show decrease emotion?**
(a) James-Lange theory (b) Schatcher-Singer theory
(c) Cannon-Bard theory
(d) Facial Feedback hypothesis

78 **Major outcomes of cannon-Bard theory were**
(a) The thalamus plays a central role.
(b) The hypothalamus receives messages simultaneously.
(c) All emotional stimuli produce the same pattern of ANS activity.
(d) All of the above

79 **Which theory of emotion implies that people can change their emotions simply by changing the way they label their arousal?**
(a) The James-Lange theory
(b) The Cannon-Bard theory
(c) Schachter's Two-Factor theory
(d) Opponent-Process theory

80 **Rahul is alone in night at hostel. Rahul think he heard someone downstairs breaking into the house. According to the James Lange theory of emotions**
(a) Rahul feel afraid and then you tremble because you are afraid.
(b) Rahul tremble and feel afraid because he is trembling.
(c) Rahul tremble and feel afraid at the same time.
(d) Rahul cognitively assess the situation and then realise that he should be afraid.

81 **In a nutshelt, the James Lange theory claims that**
(a) physiological arousal precedes conscious emotional experience.
(b) conscious emotional experience can either precede or follow physiological arousal.
(c) conscious emotional experience and physiological arousal occur at the same time.
(d) you cognitively assess the situation and then realise you should be afraid.

82 **According to James Lange theory of emotions, you feel**
(a) your heart pounding and that feel afraid.
(b) your heart pounding see that a car is coming at you and then feel afraid.
(c) our heart pounding at the same time you feel afraid.
(d) you are afraid and then notice your heart is pounding.

83 **According to Cannon-Bard theory**
(a) the thalamus plays a central role in producing emotions.
(b) the cerebellum must give go head for emotion.
(c) activity in the occipital and parental lobes happens simultaneously to produce emotion.
(d) The sympathetic and parasympathetic nervous systems work in context.

84 **Activity in the thalamus causes emotional feelings and bodily arousal simultaneously, is according to**
(a) Cannon-Bard theory
(b) James-Lange theory
(c) Schatcher's Cognitive theory
(d) None of the above

85 **Which theory claims that emotions are organised in the brain and the emotional feelings and bodily expressions occures simultaneously?**
(a) The Commonsense theory (b) The Cannon-Bard theory
(c) Attribution theory (d) Facial feedback

86 **The theory of emotion which is based upon the law of physics *i.e.* every action produces a reaction.**
(a) Cannon-Bard theory (b) Schatcher-Singer theory
(c) Opponent process theory (d) None of these

87 **The theory of emotion proposed by Schatcher and Singer is a**
(a) social theory of emotions
(b) neurobiological theory of emotions
(c) cognitive theory of emotions
(d) psychoanalytic theory of emotions

88 **According to Schatcher and Singer emotional experience involves the interaction of**
(a) cognitive social and affective factors
(b) physiological and affective factors
(c) cognitive social and physiological factors
(d) cognitive and environment factors

89 **Maslow describes .... as a person's need to be and do that which the person was 'born to do'.**
(a) Safety needs (b) Self actualisation
(c) Esteem needs (d) Physiological needs

90 **........... is something outside the person that energises behaviour.**
(a) Extrinsic motivation (b) Intrinsic motivation
(c) Inborn motive (d) Need achievement motive

91 **Maslow refers self-actualisation need as**
(a) deficiency needs (b) basic needs
(c) specific needs (d) growth needs

92 Maslow refers physiological need as
(a) deficiency needs (b) basic needs
(c) specific needs (d) growth needs

93 Which amongst the following is motivational tension or arousal that energises behaviour in order to fulfil some need?
(a) Incentive (b) Drive
(c) Motive (d) Instincts

94 Which amongst the following is a complex psychological state that involves three distinct components: a subjective experience, a physiological response and a behavioural or expressive response?
(a) An emotion (b) A motive
(c) An instinct (d) A desire

95 .... is the process by which the body regulates its internal conditions to achieve equilibrium and maintain proper bodily functions.
(a) Instinct (b) Homeostasis
(c) Balancing (d) Heterostasis

96 In emotional response .... shall occur.
(a) increase in sweet gland activity
(b) lowering of skin resistance
(c) rise in skin conductance
(d) All of the above

97 An ability of a person to effectively manage and respond to an emotional experience is known as
(a) Emotion-regulation (b) Self- regulation
(c) Self- analysis (d) Self- control

98 Among the following given elements which is not part of healthy way emotion regulation
(a) Therapy
(b) Talking with friends
(c) Meditation
(d) Excessive social media use

99 What is the correct sequence of events for hunger motivation ? Indicate your answer using codes given below
1. Energy level to its set point
2. A bowl of eating
3. Presence of an energy deficit
4. Satiation
5. Hunger

Codes
(a) 1, 2, 3, 4, 5 (b) 2, 1, 3, 5, 4
(c) 3, 5, 2, 1, 4 (d) 5, 4, 3, 1, 2

100 As per Schatcher and Singer's theory of emotions, one shall experience emotions based on situational clues when
1. there is a physiological arousal.
2. there are cognitive/explanations available for arousal.
3. there is no physiological arousal.
4. there is no proper explanation available for one's arousal.

Codes
(a) Both 1 and 2 (b) Both 1 and 4
(c) Both 2 and 3 (d) Both 3 and 4

101 According to ethological theory, species specific behaviour has following characteristics.
1. Fixed action pattern 2. Instinctive
3. Unlearned 4. Innate

Codes
(a) 1, 3 and 4 (b) 2, 3 and 4
(c) 1, 2 and 3 (d) 1, 2, 3 and 4

102 Choose the correct sequence of emergence of the following theories of emotion.
1. Jamer-Lange 2. Cannon-Bard
3. Schatcher and Singer
4. Darwin

Codes
(a) 1, 3, 2, 4 (b) 4, 3, 2, 1
(c) 4, 1, 2, 3 (d) 1, 2, 3, 4

103 What is true about drives ?
1. Internal states
2. Arousal by tension
3. Underlying need
4. Guided by external stimuli

Codes
(a) 1, 2 and 4 (b) 1, 2 and 3
(c) 2, 3 and 4 (d) 1, 2, 3 and 4

104 Consider the following statements
1. Drive concept came along just instinct theories had been discredited.
2. Drive concept denied the fact that central brain structure monitor the state of body.

Which of the statements given above is/are correct?
(a) Only 1
(b) Only 2
(c) Both 1 and 2
(d) None of the above

105 Arrange the following theories of functions appeared in the chronological order
1. James-Lange 2. Cannon-Bard
3. Lindsley 4. Schatcher-Singer

Codes
(a) 1, 2, 3, 4 (b) 1, 3, 4, 2
(c) 2, 3, 4, 1 (d) 4, 3, 1, 2

106 Lazarus suggests different components of emotions. Arrange them in sequence.
1. Cognitive appraisal
2. Person-environment relationship
3. Emotional responses

Codes
(a) 2, 3 and 1 (b) 1, 3 and 2
(c) 1, 2 and 3 (d) 2, 1 and 3

107 Which of the following pairs is/are correctly matched?

1. Primary motive Curiosity motive
2. General motive Maternal drive
3. Personal motive Cognitive motive

Codes

(a) Only 1 (b) Only 2
(c) Only 3 (d) None of these

108 Which of the following pairs is/are correctly matched?

1. Biological motive Long lasting
2. Social motive Cyclic
3. Psychological motive Innate

Codes

(a) 1 and 2 (b) 2 and 3
(c) 1 and 3 (d) None of these

109 Which among the following statements is/are correct?

1. In James-Lange theory, body arousal precedes the experience of emotion.
2. Lazarus incorporated the facial feedback hypothesis into the Cannon-Bard theory of emotion.

Select the correct answer using the codes given below

(a) Only 1 (b) Both 1 and 2
(c) Only 2 (d) Neither 1 nor 2

110 Which of the following pairs is/are correctly matched?

1. Complex process involving cognitions, subjective feeling, physical arousal and behavioural reaction: James -Lange theory
2. Feedback from facial expressions, helps determine ones's emotional experiences: Sylran-Tomkins theory
3. Our emotions depend upon a kind of double cognitive interpretation: Singer-Schachter theory

Codes

(a) Both 2 and 3 (b) Both 1 and 3
(c) Both 1 and 2 (d) All of these

111 Arrange the following appear in Schachter-Singer theories of emotion in the chronological order.

1. Cognitive appraisal of stimulus
2. Stimulus
3. Subjective experience of emotions
4. General physiological arousal

Codes

(a) 1, 2, 3, 4
(b) 2, 1, 3, 4
(c) 3, 2, 1, 4
(d) 2, 4, 1, 3

112 Arrange the following stages in the expression of emotions as described by Cannon-Bard theory in correct sequence

1. Eliciting stimulus
2. Instrumental response
3. Subjective expression of emotions
4. Physiological arousal

Codes

(a) 1,3, 2, 4 (b) 1, 3, 4, 2 (c) 3, 1, 4, 2 (d) 3, 1, 2, 4

113 Which of the following pairs is/are correctly matched?

1. Motivation is an expression of unconscious wish: Psychoanalytic approach
2. Motivation is a search for self-realisation: Cognitive approach
3. Motivation comes into process because of perceptual defences: Humanistic approach
4. Motivation arises from internal physiological imbalance: Homeostatic approach

Codes

(a) 1 and 4 (b) 2 and 3 (c) 1 and 3 (d) 2 and 4

114 Match the following

	List I (Theories)		List II (Descriptions)
A.	James-Lange	1.	Triggering the feeling of pleasure and pain simultaneously
B.	Cannon-Bard	2.	Emotional experience comprise of the physiological arousal and its cognitive labelling
C.	Opponent Process	3.	Emotion arising stimulus simultaneously triggers physiological responses and the subjective experience of emotions
D.	Two Factor	4.	Emotional experience refers to our awareness of our physiological responses to emotion arousing stimuli

Codes

	A	B	C	A		A	B	C	A
(a)	4	3	2	1	(b)	4	2	3	1
(c)	3	2	4	1	(d)	3	4	1	2

115 Match the following

	List I (Psychologists)		List II (Descriptions)
A.	Rogers	1.	Self-actualisation
B.	Maslow	2.	Full functioning
C.	Robert White	3.	Extended the concept of control
D.	De Charms	4.	Competence motivation

Codes

	A	B	C	D		A	B	C	D
(a)	2	1	4	3	(b)	4	3	2	1
(c)	1	2	3	4	(d)	3	4	2	1

116 Match the following

List I (Motives)	List II (Concepts)
A. Kinesics	1. Body language
B. Stimulus motives	2. Innate, but not necessary for survival
C. Polugraph measure	3. Attribution
D. Secondary motive	4. The desire for money

Codes

	A	B	C	D		A	B	C	D
(a)	1	2	3	4	(b)	2	1	4	3
(c)	3	4	1	2	(d)	4	3	2	1

117 Match the following

List I (Motivations)	List II (Works)
A. Extrinsic	1. Feeling of competence when complete a task
B. Intrinsic	2. External object satisfy some object that satisfy some expectation
C. Affective	3. Positive emotional experience

Codes

	A	B	C		A	B	C
(a)	1	2	3	(b)	1	3	2
(c)	2	3	1	(d)	2	1	3

118 Match the following

List I (Theories)	List II (Explanations)
A. Arousal theory of Schatcher and Singer	1. Emotion-provoking stimuli simultaneously evoke physiological arousal and subjective states, which are labelled as emotions
B. Solomon's Opponent -Process theory	2. Emotion-provoking events produce physiological reactions and their awareness is labelled as emotions
C. James-Lange theory	3. Emotion-provoking events produce increased arousal and their cognitive appraisal determines the emotion
D. Cannon-Bard theory	4. Emotional reactions are followed automatically by opposite reactions

Codes

	A	B	C	D		A	B	C	D
(a)	1	2	3	4	(b)	4	3	1	2
(c)	2	1	4	3	(d)	3	4	2	1

119 Match the following

List I (Concepts)	List II (Psychologists)
A. Instinct	1. Maslow
B. Achievement	2. James
C. Emotions	3. Freud
D. Self-actualisation	4. McClleland

Codes

	A	B	C	D		A	B	C	D
(a)	3	4	2	1	(b)	4	2	3	1
(c)	2	4	1	3	(d)	1	3	2	4

120 Match the following

List I (Concepts)	List II (Theorists associated)
A. Aggressive instinct	1. Miller and Dollard
B. Needs hierarchy	2. Freud
C. Achievement motivation	3. Maslow
D. Frustration-aggressive hypothesis	4. McClelland

Codes

	A	B	C	D
(a)	2	3	1	4
(b)	3	2	1	4
(c)	3	2	4	1
(d)	2	3	4	1

121 Match the following

List I (Psychologists)	List II (Concepts)
A. Cannon-Bard theory	1. Physical reactions come before experiencing emotions
B. Schatcher-Singer theory	2. Emotions and bodily responses occur simultaneously
C. James-Lange theory	3. Emotional experience depends on perception of a given situation
D. Tomkins theory	4. The feedback from facial expressions cause or intensity the experience of emotions

Codes

	A	B	C	D
(a)	1	2	4	3
(b)	2	3	1	4
(c)	3	4	2	1
(d)	4	1	3	2

122 Match the following

List I (Theories)	List II (Explanations)
A. Arousal theory	1. Motivation is strongly influenced by setting specific and allowable goals
B. Expectancy theory	2. Motivation is a matter of being pushed from within by urges
C. Goal setting theory	3. Motivation is being pulled from without by desired outcomes
D. Drive theory	4. Motivation is increasing the general level of activation to an optimal level

Codes

	A	B	C	D
(a)	1	2	3	4
(b)	2	3	4	1
(c)	3	4	2	1
(d)	4	3	1	2

123 Match the following

	List I (Idea)		List II (Scholars)
A.	Felt emotion is based on the interpretation of the reasons for bodily arousal	1.	Cannon-Bard theory
B.	Felt emotions of a person are due to his/her perception of bodily reaction to stimuli	2.	Richard-Lazarus theory
C.	Felt emotions result from appraisal about the environmental situation arising out of memories, dispositions, thought and states of body	3.	James-Lange theory
D.	Felt emotions and bodily reactions emotions are independent of each other and triggered simultaneously by activity of lower brain area	4.	Schatcher-Singer theory

Codes

	A	B	C	D		A	B	C	D
(a)	3	1	4	2	(b)	1	2	3	4
(c)	4	3	2	1	(d)	2	4	1	3

124 Match the following

	List I (Idea)		List II (Scholar)
A.	Felt emotions occur after bodily changes	1.	Plutchik theory
B.	Bodily reactions and felt emotions are independent	2.	Schachter-Singer theory
C.	Emotions result due to interpretation of arousal	3.	James-Lange theory
D.	Primary emotions can be arranged to bring out relationships among emotions	4.	Cannon-Bard theory

Codes

	A	B	C	D
(a)	4	3	1	2
(b)	3	4	1	2
(c)	3	4	2	1
(d)	4	3	2	1

125 Match the following

	List I (Scholars)		List II (Concepts)
A.	Plutchik theory	1.	Felt emotions and bodily changes are independent
B.	Lazarus theory	2.	Certain primary emotions derived from evolutionary process can be arranged in orderly way to bring out realities
C.	Cannon-Bard theory	3.	Emotion we felt results from appraisals of information coming from environment situation and from with in the body
D.	Schatcher-Singer theory	4.	Emotion we feel is due to our interpretation of aroused bodily state

Codes

	A	B	C	D		A	B	C	D
(a)	1	4	3	2	(b)	2	3	1	4
(c)	4	1	2	3	(d)	3	4	1	2

Directions (Q. Nos. 126-138) *In the questions given below are two statements labelled as Assertion (A) and Reason (R). In the context of the two statements, which one of the following is correct?*

Codes

(a) Both A and R are true and R is the correct explanation of A

(b) Both A and R are true, but R is not the correct explanation of A

(c) A is true, but R is false

(d) A is false, but R is true

126 **Assertion** (A) According to Maslow, after gratification of basic needs we move in positive direction, but it is not automatic.

Reason (R) We often fear our best side, our talents, our finest impulses, our creativeness.

127 **Assertion** (A) The high achievement motivation displayed by children has emotional roots.

Reason (R) Highly motivated children often have parents who encourage their independence from an early age and praise and reward them for their successes.

128 **Assertion** (A) If the cognitions about an event are present, but arousal is absent, then emotion will still be experienced.

Reason (R) Perceived emotion is a joint function of arousal, appraisal and labelling cognition.

129 **Assertion** (A) Rare people can achieve self actualisation need.

Reason (R) It comes at top of the hierarchical model of Maslow.

130 **Assertion** (A) The physiology of learning is an important problem in its own right.

Reason (R) Physiology data influence our thinking about the concept of learning.

131 **Assertion** (A) Motives are always active, but the manifestation of a specific motive is a function of its intensity at a particular time.

Reason (R) Motivation is a continuous process, through motives come to play only in successive hierarchical order.

132 **Assertion** (A) Human beings are motivated by needs beyond basic biological survival.

Reason (R) Individuals strive to achieve self improvement.

133 **Assertion** (A) If the emotional counterpart is blocked, the motivated behaviour is inhibited.

Reason (R) Motivation is a goal directed action based on prior affective experiences.

134 Assertion (A) Emotion can develop through learning.

Reason (R) A child can be conditioned to show a particular emotion to particular stimuli.

135 Assertion (A) Emotion is a form of energy mobilisation.

Reason (R) It help the individual to overcome an obstacle.

136 Assertion (A) In James-Lange theory of emotions, body arousal precedes the experience of emotions.

Reason (R) Carrol developed the facial feedback hypothesis in support of Cannon Bard theory.

137 Assertion (A) The Cannon-Bard theory and the cognitive theory or emotion both state that body arousal precedes the experience of emotion.

Reason (R) In the cognitive theory of emotion, interpretation of arousal are critical to the conscious experience of emotion.

138 Assertion (A) Whether emotions have evolved out of physiological motives or have originated in some other, way, it is clear that they have a motivational significance.

Reason (R) Motivational theory suggest that motives may be characterised as anticipatory goal reactions based upon prior associations of pleasure or pain.

Direction (Q. Nos. 139-143) *Read the passage given below and answer the following questions.*

Lazarus and Folkman differentiate two types of appraisal: primary and secondary. Primary appraisal is the individual's evaluation of an event in terms of his goals, values and beliefs. Primary appraisal addresses the question of whether anything is at stake for the individual in the context of the event. Secondary appraisal indicated what, if anything can be done in response to the event. It involves the assessment of available coping resources had the likelihood that those coping resources will be effective in the particular situation.

Lazarus and Folkman further differentiate five types of primary appraisal : irrelevant, harm, threat and challenge. Event appraised as irrelevant are not associated with any particular emotion because the event has no bearing on the individual values, beliefs or goals. Events appraised as positive are likely to give rise to positive emotions such as happiness or satisfaction and are unlikely to call for any type of coping response.

Events appraised as loss are usually associated with negative emotions such as sadness or anger and those appraised as threat are usually associated with negative emotions such as anxiety. A challenge appraisal, the evaluation of a situation as having the potential for gain, is usually associated with both positive and negative emotions. Whereas appraisal of challenge is likely to prompt feelings such as excitement and enthusiasm, there is also the potential for anxiety and fear because the outcome is uncertain.

139 Who differentiated between types of appraisal?

(a) Lazarus
(b) Folkman
(c) Miller
(d) Lazarus and Folkman

140 What is primary appraisal?

(a) It is the individual's evaluation of an event in terms of his goal, value and belief.
(b) It is the individual's evaluation of any situation.
(c) It is the individual's perception of others feelings.
(d) It is the individual's evaluation of his emotion.

141 Which of the following is not a type of appraisal defined by Lazarus and Folkman?

(a) Irrelevant (b) Benign
(c) Love (d) Threat

142 What type of feeling promoted by appraisal of challenge?

(a) Excitement (b) Happiness
(c) Sorrow (d) Fear

143 Current appraised as loss are usually associated with what type of negative erosion ?

(a) Frustration (b) Fear
(c) Anger (d) Sorrow

PREVIOUS YEARS' QUESTIONS

November 2017

1 Emotions can be characterised as

1. Giving rise to affective experiences
2. Stimulating generation of cognitive explanations
3. Triggering a variety of internal neurobiological changes
4. Always eliciting rewarding behaviour

Codes

(a) 1, 2 and 3 (b) 1, 3 and 4
(c) 2, 3 and 4 (d) 1, 2, 3 and 4

2 Read each of the following two statements - Assertion (A) and Reason (R) and indicate your answer using codes given below.

Assertion (A) Every cigarette packet has a verbal and pictorial warning about negative consequences of smoking.

Reason (R) Inconsistent cognitions have the motivational properties.

Codes

(a) Both A and R are true and R is the correct explanation of A
(b) Both A and R are true, but R is not the correct explanation of A
(c) A is true, but R is false
(d) A is false, but R is true

3 When students study and practice hard with interest and enjoyment, it is called

(a) Emotional engagement (b) Cognitive engagement
(c) Behavioural engagement (d) Healthy adjustment

4 If the teacher presents the extrinsic motivator in a controlled way, then

(a) it will enhance competence of students
(b) it will interfere with autonomy of students
(c) it will enhance their overall learning
(d) it will enhance the autonomy of students

January 2017

5 Match List I with List II and select the correct answer by choosing from the codes given below

List I (Concepts)	List II (Explanations)
A. Drive	1. A state of deficiency or excess of something in the organism, the fulfilment or elimination of which is essential for survival and balance
B. Yerkes-Dodsan Law	2. A state of psychological readiness that motivates the organism to act for the fulfilment of need and reduction of tension
C. Power Motive	3. The level of arousal beyond which performance begins to decline
D. Need	4. Tendency or capacity to produce intended effects on the behaviour or emotions of other persons

Codes

	A	B	C	D		A	B	C	D
(a)	1	2	3	4	(b)	2	3	4	1
(c)	3	4	1	2	(d)	4	3	2	1

June 2015

6 As per Schatcher and Singer's Theory of Emotions, one shall experience emotions based on situational clues when

1. there is a physiological arousal.
2. there are cognitions/explanations available for arousal.
3. there is no physiological arousal.
4. there are no proper explanations available for one's arousal.

Choose the correct codes

(a) 1 and 2 (b) 1 and 4
(c) 2 and 3 (d) 3 and 4

7 What is not true of facial feedback hypothesis of emotions?

(a) Acting as another acts does not help us to feel what another feels.
(b) Facial expressions influence our emotional experience.
(c) To be empathic mimic other's emotional expressions.
(d) Professional actors exhibit expression specific autonomic nervous system changes .

8 Read each of the following two statements Assertion (A) and Reason (R) and indicate your answer using the codes given below

Assertion (A) According to Maslow, after the gratification of basic needs, we move in positive direction, but it is not automatic.

Reason (R) We often fear our best side, our talents, our finest impulses, our creativeness.

Codes

(a) Both A and R are true and R is the correct explanation of A
(b) Both A and R are true, but R is not the correct explanation of A
(c) A is true, but R is false
(d) A is false, but R is true

December 2014

9 **Match List I (Studying Motivations) with that of List II (Explanations) and mark your answer with the help of the codes given below**

List I (Approach)	List II (Explanations)
A. Behaviouristic approach	1. Interpersonal relations with community
B. Humanistic approach	2. Incentives rewards and punishment
C. Cognitive approach	3. Actualising needs
D. Socio-cultural approach	4. Behaviour is determined by our thinking and attribution

Codes

	A	B	C	D
(a)	2	3	4	1
(b)	3	2	4	1
(c)	1	2	4	3
(d)	1	3	2	4

ANSWERS

Exam Based Questions

1 (b)	2 (a)	3 (d)	4 (b)	5 (a)	6 (b)	7 (d)	8 (a)	9 (c)	10 (d)
11 (d)	12 (c)	13 (b)	14 (a)	15 (c)	16 (a)	17 (b)	18 (a)	19 (d)	20 (c)
21 (b)	22 (a)	23 (d)	24 (d)	25 (c)	26 (c)	27 (d)	28 (d)	29 (a)	30 (c)
31 (c)	32 (b)	33 (b)	34 (a)	35 (b)	36 (a)	37 (b)	38 (d)	39 (b)	40 (d)
41 (a)	42 (a)	43 (d)	44 (c)	45 (b)	46 (c)	47 (d)	48 (b)	49 (b)	50 (d)
51 (d)	52 (a)	53 (c)	54 (b)	55 (a)	56 (c)	57 (b)	58 (d)	59 (c)	60 (d)
61 (a)	62 (c)	63 (c)	64 (c)	65 (b)	66 (b)	67 (c)	68 (b)	69 (d)	70 (c)
71 (c)	72 (b)	73 (b)	74 (c)	75 (d)	76 (c)	77 (a)	78 (d)	79 (a)	80 (b)
81 (b)	82 (a)	83 (a)	84 (a)	85 (b)	86 (c)	87 (b)	88 (c)	89 (b)	90 (a)
91 (d)	92 (a)	93 (b)	94 (a)	95 (b)	96 (d)	97 (a)	98 (d)	99 (b)	100 (b)
101 (d)	102 (c)	103 (b)	104 (a)	105 (a)	106 (d)	107 (c)	108 (a)	109 (a)	110 (a)
111 (b)	112 (b)	113 (a)	114 (a)	115 (a)	116 (a)	117 (d)	118 (d)	119 (a)	120 (c)
121 (b)	122 (d)	123 (c)	124 (c)	125 (b)	126 (a)	127 (a)	128 (a)	129 (a)	130 (d)
131 (b)	132 (b)	133 (b)	134 (a)	135 (b)	136 (c)	137 (d)	138 (a)	139 (d)	140 (a)
141 (c)	142 (a)	143 (c)							

Previous Years' Questions

1 (a)	2 (a)	3 (a)	4 (b)	5 (b)	6 (b)	7 (a)	8 (d)	9 (a)

CHAPTER 24

Conflict, Stress and Coping

Conflict and stress are part and parcel of our life. They both are negative and positive in nature. Stress is frequent cause of conflict, and conflict can increases stress. Conflict arises because individual have different needs, interest and goals. Coping is a means to come out of stress.

Conflict

Conflict occurs between people in all kinds of human relationships and in all social settings, because of the wide range of differences among people, the absence of conflict usually signals the absence of meaningful interaction. Conflict by itself is neither good or bad. However, the manner in which conflict is handled determines whether it is constructive or destructive.

Conflict is defined as an incompatibility of goals or values between two or more parties in a relationship, combined with an attempt to control each other and antagonistic feelings towards each other. The incompatibility or difference may exist in reality or may only be perceived by the parties involved. Nonetheless, the opposing actions and the hostile emotions are very real hallmarks of human conflict. Conflict has the potential for either a great deal of destruction or creativity and positive social change. Therefore, it is essential to understand the basic processes of conflict so that we can work to maximise productive outcomes and minimise destructive ones.

Characteristics of Conflict

Following are some common characteristic of conflict

- Conflict is a Process Conflict occurs in 'stages'. First stage is always misunderstanding. The other stages are differences of values, differences of view point , differences of interest and interpersonal differences. It is also called a process because it begins with one party perceiving the other to oppose or negatively affect its interests and ends with competing, collaborating, compromising or avoiding.

In this Chapter

- **Conflict is Inevitable** Conflict exists everywhere and the two persons are not same. Hence, they may have individual differences and the differences may be because of values or otherwise, lead to conflict. Although inevitable conflict can be minimised, diverted or resolved. Conflict develops because we are dealing with people's lives, jobs, children, pride, self concept and ego.
- **Conflict is a Normal Part of Life** Individuals, groups and organisations have unlimited needs and different values, but limited resources. Thus, this incompatibility is bound to lead to conflicts. The conflicts is not a problem, but if it is poorly misplaced priorities that leads to conflict.
- **Perception** It must be perceived by the parties, otherwise it doesn't exist. In interpersonal interaction, perception is more important than reality. What we perceive and think affects our behaviour, attitudes and communication.
- **Opposition** One party in the conflict must be perceiving or doing something the other party doesn't like or want.
- **Interdependence and Interaction** There must be some kinds of real or perceived interdependence. Without interdependence there can be no interaction. Conflict occurs when some kinds of interaction take place.
- **Everyone is Inflicted with Conflict** Conflict may occur within an individual, between two or more individuals, groups or between organisations.
- **Conflict is not Unidimensional** It comes into different ways in accordance with degree of seriousness and capacity.

Sources of Conflict

Conflicts may be caused by any one or more of the following reasons

- **Economic Conflict** Economic conflict involves competing motives to attain scarce resources. Each party wants to get the most it can and the behaviour and emotions of each party are directed towards maximising it gain. Union and management conflict often is one of its sources.
- **Value Conflict** Value conflict involves incompatibility in ways of life, ideologies; the preferences, principles and practices that people believe in. International conflict often has a strong value component, wherein each side asserts the rightness and superiority of its ways of life.
- **Power Conflict** Power conflict occurs when each party wishes to maintain or maximise the amount of influence that it exerts in the relationship and the social setting. It is impossible for one party to be stronger without the other beings weaker, atleast in terms of direct influence with each other. Thus, a power struggle answers which usually ends in a victory and defeat, or in a 'stand-off' with a continuing state of tension. Power conflicts can occur between individuals, between groups or between nations, whenever one or both parties choose to take a power approach.

Another important source of conflict is **ineffective communication**. Miscommunication and misunderstanding can create conflict even where there are no basic incompatibilities. In addition, parties may have different perceptions as to what are the facts in a situation and until they share information and clarify their perceptions, resolution are impossible. Self centeredness, selective perception, emotional bias, prejudices, etc. are all forces that lead us to perceive situations very differently from the other party.

Stages of Conflict

There are various stages of conflict. *These are*

(i) People recognise lack of resources, diversity of language or culture. Sensitiveness may possibly result in conflict.

(ii) If there are serious differences between two or among more than two groups, the latent conflict in a competitive situation may turn out into violent conflict.

(iii) An incident may trigger a latent conflict into war.

(iv) Once a problem has been solved, the potential for conflict still remains in the aftermath. In fact, the potential is bigger than before, if one party perceives that the resolution has resulted into win-loss situation.

Types of Conflict

Conflict can occur at a number of levels of human functioning. Conflict in your head between opposing, motives or ideas is shown by your 'internal conscience' and is at the interpersonal level. Beyond that, the primary concern here is with social conflict *i.e.* conflict between people whether they are acting as individuals, as members of groups, or as representatives of organisations or nations. *Types of conflict are as follows*

Interpersonal Conflict

Interpersonal conflict occurs when two people have incompatible needs, goals, or approaches in their relationship. Communication breakdown is often an important source of interpersonal conflict and learning communication skills are valuable in preventing and resolving such difficulties. At the same time, very real differences occur between people that cannot be resolved by any amount of improved communication.

'Personality conflict' refers to very strong differences in motives, values or styles in dealing with people that are not resolvable. Common tactics used in interpersonal power struggle include the exaggerated use of rewards and punishments, deception and evasion, threats and emotional blackmail, flattery and integeration. Unresolved conflict usually repeat and escalates to the point of relationship breakdown and termination.

Role Conflict

Role conflict involves differences in role definitions, expectations or responsibilites between individuals who are interdependent in a social system. If there are ambiguities in role definitions in an organisation or unclear boundaries of responsibilities, then the stage is set for interpersonal friction between the person involved.

Unfortunately, the conflict is often misdiagnosed as interpersonal conflict rather than role conflict and resolution is then complicated and misdirected. The emotional intensity is often quite high in role conflict since people are directly involved as individuals and there is a strong tendency to personalise the conflict.

Intergroup Conflict

Intergroup conflicts occur between group of people such as ethnic or racial groups, departments or levels of decision making in the same organisation, union and management. Competition for scarce resources is a common source of intergroup conflict and societies have developed numerous regulatory mechanisms, such as collective bargaining and meditation for dealing with intergroup conflict in less discruptive ways. Intergroup conflict is especially tense and prone to escalation and intractability when group identifies are threatened. The costs of destructive intergroup conflict can be extremely high for a society in both economic and social terms.

Multi-Party Conflict

Multi party conflict occurs in societies when different interest groups and organisations have varying priorities over resource management and policy development. These complex conflicts typically involve a combination of economics, values and power sources. This complexity is often beyond the reach of traditional authoritative or adversarial procedures and more collaborative approaches to building consensus are required for resolution.

International Conflict

Occurs between states at the global level. Competition for resources certainly plays critical role, but value and power conflict are often intertwined and sometimes predominate. The differences are articulated through the channels of diplomacy in a constant game of give and take, or threat and counter-threat.

Stress

Stress can be defined either as a reaction or as a stimulus. In terms of reaction, the meaning of stress is change that human biological system is experiencing. As stimulus, the definition of stress is related to environmental events that causes those changes. The stressful events can be acute, chronic, remitting and continuous chronic form.

Stress can be dangerous if it is prolonged or severe, but it is not always bad. As Canadian stress research pioneer Hans Selye observed, 'To be totally without stress is to be dead'. That's why because stress in the mental and physical condition that occurs when we adjust or adapt to the environment.

A stress reaction begins with the same automatic nervous system arousal that occurs during emotion. Imagine you are standing at the top of a wind-whipped ski jump for the first time. Internally, you would experience a rapid surge in your heart rate, blood pressure, respiration muscle tension and other ANS response. Short-term stresses of this kind can be uncomfortable, but they rarely do any damage. Long-term stresses are another matter entirely.

Now days it can be said, that stress is a global phenomenon and it is the result of positive or negative life's experiences. The concept of stress is significant because it provides a way of understanding the person as a whole in life's various changes.

Signs of Stress

During the stage of resistance, body comes under to stress. As the body's defences comes into action symptoms of the stress disappear with time, everything seems normal. However, this appearance of normality comes at a high cost. The body is better able to cope with the original stressor, but its resistance to other stress is lowered. *For example* Animals placed in extreme cold become more resistance to the cold but more susceptible to infection. It is during the stage of resistance that the first signs of psychosomatic disorders begin to appear.

Continue stress leads to the stage of exhaustion, in which the body's resource are drained and stress hormones are depleted.

Some of the typical signs or symptoms of impending exhaustion include the following

- **Emotional Signs** Anxiety, apathy and mental fatigue.
- **Behavioural Signs** Avoidance of responsibility and relationships, extreme or self destructive behaviour, self-neglect poor judgement.
- **Physical Signs** Excessive worry about illness, frequent illness, exhaustion, over use of medicines, physical ailments.

Factors of Stress

There are multiple factor of stress, which are as follows

Personal

- Injury or illness, especially if they are non-curable or longterm.
- Pregnancy and ultimately becoming parents (it is also cause of happiness as well stress).
- Situation of bereavement brings intense stress on people.
- Whenever people organise event such as marriage, birthday parties. Then there is stress of managing all thing in efficient manner.
- Responsibility of household chores and traveling for different purposes brings stress on body.

Friends and Family Managing friends and family is also stressful work, *it includes*

- Getting married with someone.
- Going through a break-up or getting divorced.
- Instability in family-quarrel with parents, siblings, friends or children.
- Dependence of family members and friends one can be hugely stressful.

Study and Work

- To be good in study and scoring high grades causes stress among student.
- Starting a new job is also cause of stress. Even who don't get job according to their wish causes more stress to them.
- As age of retirement comes nears, stress level of a person goes up.

Housing

- Housing problem such as poor living condition, lack of security or homelessness.
- Sometime neighbours also become cause of stress.

Models of Stress

The theoretical models that have been formulated for interpreting stress are helping to identify stressors in a particular situation and predicting the possibility of an individual's adaptation to stressful situation. There are main theoretical models for stress, each one interprets stress differently either as a stimulus, as a response or as transaction, *which are as follows*.

Stimulus Based Models

In this models, the stress is interpreted as a stimulus, a life event or a circumstances which may awaken normal or psychological reactions, which may increase the vulnerability of the individual to disease. According to Holmes, there are 43 life events or lifestyle changes, which can cause stress. According to this theory, both positive and negative life events are considered stressful. The scale of stressful events is used to record the recent stress experiences of the individual, such as divorce, pregnancy and retirement.

Since similar scales have been developed, however, they should be used with caution, since the extent of stress, which is embodied to life events depends on the way in which is interpreted by the individual. Moreover, those scales must have been validated in the age and in the socio-economic status, in addition they must have been culturaly adapted.

Response Based Model

In those theoretical models, stress is interpreted as a response. The definition of stress as a response was developed and described by **Hans Selye**, who defined stress as a non-specific response of the body to any kind of demands applied on it.

Selye's model is called General Adaptation Syndrome (GAS). Selye in order to differenciate the cause of stress from the response to this introduced the term 'stressor', naming so any factor can cause stress and affect the balance of the individual. Selye mentions, the fact that stress is a state of the body, it can only observed by the changes occurring in it. This fully body response general adaptation syndrome, is manifested by releasing certain hormones, which resulted in the change in the structure and chemical composition of the body. Apart from the adaptation of whole body, it is possible a that reaction may take in any part of body. This response to stress is called Local Adaptation Syndrome (LAS).

Transaction Based Models

All theoretical models that interpreted stress as a transaction are based on the theory of Lazarus, who focused on the fact that there are differences among people in interpretation of stress as a stimulus or as a response.

None of the previous theories, according to Lazarus, could exactly explain, which factors may lead some people to manage stress properly, while others are not, he stated that there is a lack in theories into the interpretation of the factors that help some people to adjust for a longer period than others into a stressful stimuli.

Personality Types

On the basis of stress, personality can be categorised into different type

Type A

People having their personality traits that are hard driving and competitive. They are always in constant pressure. They strive for recognition and advancement. They undertake multiple activity with a deadline for completion. These people are active, completent and efficient. But they are likely to become hostile, impatient, anxious and disorganised, when put under stress conditions.

Some characteristics of Type A personality are

- Always in hurry, eats fast, walks and talks fast
- Restless when waiting
- Highly competitive
- Very precise
- Ambitious, sets own goal, take work very seriously
- Tries to do more than one thing at a time
- Aggressive

Type B

These people are quiet and just opposite to type 'A'. Type B people are easy going, non-competitive, placed, unflappable. They manage easily. They are comparable to the tortoise in the famous story of Tortoise and Hare. Type 'B' may be little dull, but are likely to live longer than type 'A'. Thus, type 'B' may be defined as absence of Type 'A' traits.

People who have Type B personality tend to be more relaxed. They don't take stressful situations personally.They can be highly competitive, but they don't have the same urgency to see a successful outcome happen. You will find that this personality trait tends to procastinate a lot, waiting until the last possible second to submit work and if there isn't a deadline in place, they will just submit the work on their own time. If given the choice between working or chilling with their friends, they will likely choose the later.

Type C

People who have a Type 'C' personality like to focus on the fine details of any given situation. They like to get lost in whatever information is available to them to glean out new opinion from the data. Instead of being assertive about what they want to do, this personality type tends follow path created by other's and set their desires aside for a later time. This tends to cause higher levels of stress in their folks and often regret "If I had only been a little more assertive..... ".

Type D

People who have a Type 'D' personality tend to see the world in a very negative way. Although there may be situations that most people would to be optimistic, this personality type will always be pessimistic about any potential outcome. Their outlook towards life itself can be severely negative as well. There is a constant fear of rejection in some way, which often causes this personality type to live a fairly isolated life. This is the personality types that has the highest risk of suffering from depression at some point during their lifetime.

Stress Management Strategies

Stress management is a set of techniques for helping people who are seldom labelled as patients (*e.g.* hospital personnel, factory workers and students) to cope with the challenges that life poses for all of us. Stress management has also been used successfully for several specific diseases, including tension, headaches, cancer, hypertension, AIDS, chronic pain etc. Stress management encompasses a variety of techniques.

The major aim of stress management resources is to control person's level of stress, whether chronic, acute and unique. Stressors are constantly present throughout life, there is no major keys to overall wellness and happiness for the effective management of stress. The symptoms of stress can affect both the body and the mind. They range in severity depending on the person and the circumstances.

Stress management techniques provide a way to cope with stress and to promote and maintain general well-being. There are several different approaches to the management of stress including conventional medicine, alternative medicine and self-help therapies. The effectiveness of each of these strategies remains difficult to fully assess as the field still requires additional research in their area.

Various stress management strategies are as follows

Biofeedback Therapy

Biofeedback is a non-invasive process that helps you and your clinician to better understand how stress, emotions are difficult to manage and situational factors impact on your body. These bodily changes are measured through sensors and are displayed on a computer monitor that both you and your clinician can see. It provides immediate feedback regarding the level of physical reactivity to stress. Learning to be aware of and to manage these reactions can help you to improve your health and resilience to stress.

By learning biofeedback strategies, you can learn how to

- Lower your blood pressure
- Improve GI Symptoms
- Increase your energy level
- Improve your quality of sleep
- Manage chronic pain conditions
- Manage anxiety and depression
- Face phobias
- Dampen the impact of migraine and tension headaches
- Address factors contributing to neck and back pain
- Loosen jaw pain (TMJ) and muscle tension
- Increase peak performance in life activities and sports

Music Therapy

Listening to music can have a tremendously relaxing effect on our minds and bodies, especially slow, quiet classical music. This type of music can have a beneficial effect on our physiological functions, slowing the pulse and heart rate, lowering blood pressure and decreasing the levels of stress hormones. Music, in short, can act as a powerful stress management tool in our lives.

As music can absorb our attention, it acts as a distraction at the same time, it helps to explore emotions. This means it can be a great aid to meditation and helping to prevent the mind wandering.

Musical preference varies widely between individuals, so only individual can decide what they like and what is suitable for each individual. But even, if you don't usually listen to classical music, it may be worth giving it a try while selecting the most soothing music.

When people are very stressed, there is a tendency to avoid actively listening to music. Perhaps it feels like a waste of time, not helping to achieved anything. But as we know, productivity increases when stress is reduced, so this is another area where you can gain vast rewards. It just takes a small effort to begin with.

A person with clinical depression or bipolar disorder might listen to music to help with their worst and lowest moods.

Breathing Exercises

Breathing exercises offer an extremely simple, effective and convenient way to relieve stress and reverse your stress response, reducing the negative effects of chronic stress. There are definite benefits of breathing exercises. While simple diaphragmic breathing can provide relaxation and stress relief, there are several different types of breathing exercises to try, each with its own twist. Hence, the several breathing exercises are commonly recommended, some of which are unique and all of which can better help in managing stress.

Progressive Muscular Relaxation

Progressive Muscle Relaxation (PMR) is a deep relaxation technique that has been effectively used to control stress and anxiety, relieve insomnia and reduce symptoms of certain types of chronic pain. Progressive muscle relaxation is based upon the simple practice of tensing, or tightening, one muscle group at a time followed by a relaxation phase with release of the tension. Doctors have used progressive muscle relaxation in combination with standard treatments for symptom relief in a number of conditions including headaches, cancer pain, high blood pressure and digestive disturbances.

Most practitioners recommend tensing and relaxing the muscle group one at a time in a specific order, generally beginning with the lower extremities and ending with the face, abdomen and chest. You can practice this technique seated or lying down and you should try to practice with comfortable clothing on and in a quiet place free from all distractions.

Guided Imagery

Guided imagery is an effective stress management technique and has remained popular for several reasons. It can quickly calm your body and simultaneously relax your mind. It's pleasant to practice and not overly difficult or intimidating to learn. And it can help you to de-stress in minutes, but can also be a useful strategy for maintaining resilience toward stress during difficult times. If this sounds like something you can use in your life, read more about when guided imagery is used and how it may be a useful in stress reliever for you.

Guided imagery has been found to provide significant stress reduction benefits, including physically relaxing the body, quickly and efficiently and even helping participants get in touch with deeper levels of wisdom (held on a sub-conscious level) that would help them better manage their lives in ways that would reduce stress. The studies demonstrating the health benefits of imagery are so numerous that many hospitals are incorporating imagery as an option to help with treatment. Fortunately, its a simple enough technique that it can be used at home as well, with positive results.

Mindfulness

Mindfulness is mind body based training that uses different exercises and techniques to help you to live in the present. The different methods will teach you to manage your feelings and thoughts, which can be particularly useful when you feel stressed. Your physical wellbeing is affected by the way you think and feel. So tuning into them and becoming more aware will help you to manage them and cope with situation.

Nine ways of mindfulness that helps in coping with stress are

(i) **You become more aware of your thoughts** You can then step back from them and not take them so literally. That way, your stress response is not initiated in the first place.

(ii) **You don't immediately react to a situation** Instead, you should pause and then use your 'wise mind' to come up with the best solution. Mindfulness helps you do this through the mindful exercises.

(iii) **Mindfulness switches on your 'being' mode** of mind, which is associated with relaxation. Your 'doing' mode of mind is associated with action and the stress response.

(iv) **You are more aware and sensitive to the needs of your body** You may notice pains earlier and then take appropriate action.

(v) **You are more aware of the emotions of others** As your emotional intelligence rises, you will rarely get into conflict.

(vi) **Your level of care and compassion for yourself and others rises** The compassionate mind soothes you and inhibits your stress responses.

(vii) **Mindfulness practice reduces activity in the part of your brain called the amygdala** The amygdala is central to switching on your stress responses so effectively, your background level of stress is reduced.

(viii) **You are better able to focus** So you complete your work more efficiently, you have greater sense of well-being and this reduces the stress responses. You are more likely to get into 'the zone' or 'flow,' as it's termed in psychology by Mihaly Csikszentmihalyi.

(ix) **You can switch your attitude about the stress** Rather than just seeing the negative consequences of feeling stressed , mindfulness offers you the space to think differently about the stress itself. Observing how the increased pressure helps energise you has a positive effect on your body and mind.

Meditation (Yogasana)

Standard management prescriptions cannot bring about mental relaxation, primarily because individuals have worries at the back of their minds even when they attempt to relax physically. In order to solve this problem, Indian yogis have recommended a few dynamic and strategic techniques for reducing stress.

Yoganidra or 'meditation' is a yogic tool for mind management; it takes case of both internal and external relaxations because it aims to reach the inner self by going beyond the physical and mental planes. Yoganidra is an approach that links up an individual's conscious awareness with the transcendental body.

Infact, Yoga means unison and 'nidra' means the purest form of relaxation. Yoganidra, in this sense, a total relaxation with complete awarences about one's spiritual origin. This complete self-awareness empowers the mind to face the odds of any type and reduces tensions and stresses of the employees.

Stress Inoculation Training

Stress Inoculation Training (SIT) is a form of cognitive behavioural therapy for post-traumatic stress disorder. This therapy is commonly used form of therapy that can help you to recognise and change incorrect or negative thoughts that have been influencing your behaviour. Exposure therapy and cognitive processing therapy are other examples of such therapy. *Stress inoculation has three phases*

(i) **Initial Conceptualisation** In this phase, the therapist educates the patient about the general nature of stress and explains important concepts such as appraisal and cognitive distortion that plays a key role in shaping stress reactions.

(ii) **Skill Acquisition and Rehearsal** The particular choice of skills taught is important and must be individually tailored to the needs of individual patients and their particular strengths and vulnerabilities if the procedure is to be effective.

(iii) **Application and Follow Through** The therapist provides the patient with opportunities to practice coping skills. The patient may be encouraged to use a variety of simulation methods to help increase the realism of coping practise.

Coping

Dewe, Guest and Williams consider coping as an attempt to remove the feeling of discomfort. Defined coping as the process which involves efforts towards solution of a problem. It occurs when a person faces a threatening or dynamic change or problem that defines known or usual ways of behaviour and might give rise to anxiety, guilt, grief and shame and again form the necessity of adaptation.

Pearlin and Schooler have suggested that coping responses are the behaviours, cognitions and perception, in which people engage when actually contending with their life problems. Coping responses represent some of the thing that people do to deal with the life strains they counter in their different roles.

Psychological and environmental factor of coping makes a distinction between the trait oriented and process-oriented approaches.The trait approaches assume that coping is mainly a property of the person and variation in stressful situation is of not much significance. In contrast, process oriented approach assumes that coping is a response to the psychological and the environmental demand of specific stressful encounters.

Categorisation of Coping

Coping responses can be categorised one of the three general categories of problem-focused coping, social coping and avoidance coping.

(i) **Problem focused coping** responses include any behavioural or cognitive efforts to directly address the source of the stress.

(ii) **Social coping responses** involve turning to others for information, advice or support.

(iii) **Avoidance coping** responses are aimed at putting the stress out of mind, at least temporarily and include responses such as use of alcohol or drugs or engaging in a distracting activity to avoid thinking about the stressor, versions of these three factors have emerged in a number of studies.

Components of Stress and Coping

There are three major components in the stress and coping process; appraisal, emotion and coping. In the context of a given stressful event, appraisal produces emotion and prompts coping which, in turn, influences emotion and subsequent reappraisal of the situation. This appraisal-emotion-coping-emotion-reappraisal process continues until the situation is resolved or the appraisal are such that the event is no longer viewed as stressful. Empirically, it is difficult to capture a causal direction among appraisal, coping and emotion because they influence each other, often in a very short period of time. There is, however, some emerging evidence that coping may be more likely to predict subsequent emotion that emotion is likely to predict subsequent coping. The strength of the causal link is likely to depend on a variety of factors including the particular coping response, the nature of the stressful event and time between measurements.

Appraisal

Lazarus and **Folkman** differentiate two types of appraisal primary and secondary. Primary appraisal is the individuals evaluation of an event in terms of his goals, values and beliefs. **Primary appraisal** adresses the question of whether anything is at stake for the individual in the context of the event. **Secondary appraisal** indicates anything can be done in response to the event. It involves the assessment of available coping resources and the to those coping resources will be effective in the particular situation.

Lazarus and Folkman gave five types of primary appraisal irrelevant, benign, harm, threat and challenge. Event appraised as irrelevant are not associated with any particular emotion because the event has no bearing on the individual values, beliefs or goals. Events appraised as positive are likely to give rise to positive emotions such as happiness or satisfaction and are unlikely to call for any type of coping response.

Events appraised as loss are usually associated with negative emotions such as sadness or anger and those appraised as threat are usually associated with negative emotions such as anxiety. A challenge appraisal, the evaluation of a situation as having the potential for gain, is usually associated with both positive and negative emotions. Whereas appraisal of challenge is likely to prompt feelings such as excitement and enthusiasm, there is also the potential for anxiety and fear because the outcome is uncertain.

Coping and Emotion

Problem focused strategies are associated with lower levels of negative emotion and higher levels of positive emotions. It is likely that there is an adaptive cyclical association, in which problem-focused coping leads to increased positive affect and decreased negative affect, which, in turns, promotes further problem-focused coping. Avoidance coping strategies are usually associated with increased negative emotion and decreased positive emotion.

The exact conditions, under which positive and negative emotions have different coping antecedents and consequences have yet to be fully explicated, but possibilities include differential time frames of effectiveness for different coping responses, situational factor such as controllability of the stressor and personality characteristic that the individual brings to the stressful situation.

EXAM BASED QUESTIONS

1 What do you mean by conflict?
(a) Different views of two people
(b) Working with an organisation harmonously
(c) When we don't accept two different viewpoints
(d) None of the above

2 Why it is said that conflict is important in any kind of setting?
(a) Conflict is the result of meaningful interaction
(b) Conflict is violent
(c) Conflict always lead to positive result
(d) Conflict is the part of successful process

3 What are the two most important determinents of conflict?
(a) Constructive (b) Destructive
(c) Both a and b (d) Neither a nor b

4 What is the basic process of conflict?
(a) To maximise productivity and minimise destruction
(b) To spread peace
(c) To establish the violent social environment
(d) To maximise productivity

5 What is true with respect to conflict?
(a) Conflict is positive force (b) Conflict is violent
(c) Conflict is a process (d) Conflict is evitable

6 What is said to be the position of conflict?
(a) Conflict exists everywhere
(b) Conflict is a ego concept
(c) Conflict is a new social concept
(d) Conflict resides in the mentality of a person

7 What is the basic reason of conflict?
(a) It is the result of globalisation
(b) It is because of the individual differences
(c) It is the part of development
(d) It is the by- product of socialisation

8 In what type of interaction, perception is important?
(a) Group activities (b) Mass communication
(c) Intrapersonal (d) Interpersonal

9 What is the role of perception?
(a) Perception is the sense object contact
(b) Perception is prior knowledge
(c) Perception is based on our pre-conceived notion
(d) All of the above

10 What one means by 'opposition' in the conflicts?
(a) Opposition is major part of conflict
(b) Opposition is always negative
(c) Opposition is not important
(d) Opposition is one who always works in disagreement with other party

11 Which among the following is the part of conflict?
(a) Interdependence (b) Interaction
(c) Only b (d) Both a and b

12 Is it true to say that conflict is unidimentional?
(a) Yes (b) No
(c) Can't say (d) May be

13 What one means by economic conflict?
(a) How to gain money?
(b) How to remove the deficit in the society?
(c) How everyone will slice up the 'economic pie'?
(d) All of the above

14 What type of conflict are incure if we face incompatibility in the ideologies?
(a) Power conflict
(b) Value conflict
(c) Economic conflict
(d) Social conflict

15 In a power conflict, one party need to be strong and other party need to weak. Is this statement correct?
(a) Yes (b) No
(c) Can't say (d) May be

16 What is the main cause of conflict in the case of power?
(a) When one party tries to control other
(b) When one party is economically powerful
(c) When parties carries different ideologies
(d) None of the above

17 Which of the following is a major source of frustration between two opposing motives?
(a) Approach (b) Avoidance
(c) Conflict (d) Repression

18 The conflict can be affected by
(a) Religious scripture
(b) Loss of self-control
(c) Search for companionship
(d) All of the above

19 What is marked as the first stage of conflict?
(a) Lack of resources
(b) Uneven distribution of resources
(c) Diversity of language and culture
(d) All of the above

20 If any violent conflict occurs then what will happen?
(a) It will divert from the main cause
(b) It may trigger a latent conflict into open conflict
(c) It is irrelevant to look for a cause
(d) None of the above

21 What is interpersonal conflict?
(a) When a person in not satisfied with the own idea.
(b) When there is two or many people involved.
(c) When two people have incompatible needs, goals and approaches.
(d) When there is no common ground.

22 What can be best way to remove interpersonal conflict?
(a) Improved communication
(b) Written communication
(c) Believing in one's ideas
(d) Formulating representative government

23 What does one mean by role conflict?
(a) Uneven economic distribution
(b) Real differences in role definitions
(c) Individual need to gain more
(d) Conflict with collective people

24 Which among the following intensity is high in role conflict?
(a) Mutual (b) Economic
(c) Emotional (d) Developmental

25 What is the reason for multi layed conflict?
(a) Resource management (b) Policy development
(c) Only b (d) Both a and b

26 What is the international conflict deals with?
(a) Global level
(b) Countries boundaries
(c) Political issues conflict
(d) Mechanical propaganda

27 Which of the following are the basic sources of stress?
(a) Environment
(b) Social stressors
(c) Physiological thoughts
(d) All of these

28 Which one of the following statements is not correct?
(a) Persons who have good sleep habits are able to resolve stress better.
(b) The state to health includes only physical and mental well being.
(c) Scheier and his colleagues have developed a measure to assess optimism.
(d) Social psychological and spiritual well being is also included in the state of health.

29 Studies have shown that people who are not outcome oriented, experience
(a) less strain
(b) less mental health problem
(c) less physical health problem
(d) All of the above

30 Stress mainly arises from three important sources which include
(a) physical (b) social
(c) psychological (d) All of these

31 Which amongst the following are the characteristics of positive stress?
(a) It improves performance (b) It feels exciting
(c) It motivates (d) All of these

32 Which amongst the following are the characteristics of negative stress?
(a) It causes anxiety (b) If feels unpleasant
(c) It decreases performance (d) All of these

33 The physical, environmental and social causes of the stress state are termed
(a) Stress (b) Stressors
(c) Distress (d) None of these

34 According to whom, "An individual would not experience stress unless the individual perceives a situation as threatening"?
(a) Lazarus (b) Erikson (c) Adler (d) Harney

35 Examples of social stressors are
(a) financial problems (b) divorce
(c) loss of a loved one (d) All of these

36 Examples of physiological stressors are
(a) menopause (b) giving birth
(c) sleep disturbances (d) All of these

37 Which amongst the following are true about the behaviorual symptoms of stress?
(a) The subject starts eating more of less
(b) The subject starts sleeping more or less
(c) The subject isolates himself/herself from others
(d) All of the above

38 The general adaptation syndrome consists of three stages which include
(a) The alarm reaction (b) The stage of resistance
(c) The stage of exhaustion (d) All of these

39 What is concept behind the stress?
(a) It is a normal event
(b) It makes person feel upset in some way
(c) Person is hopeless
(d) Person is excited

40 What will happen with the continuous stress?
(a) Stage of exhaustion
(b) Body resources drained
(c) Stress hormones depleted
(d) All of the above

41 Stress management is about learning
(a) how to avoid the pressures of life
(b) how to develop skills that would enhance our body's adjustment when we are subjected to the pressures of life
(c) Both a and b
(d) None of the above

42 Which of the following statements is true about stress management?
(a) Stress management is learning about the connection between mind and body.
(b) Stress management helps us to control our health in a positive sense.
(c) Stress management teaches us to avoid all kinds of stress.
(d) Both a and b

43 According to Holmes, there are how many life event which can cause stress
(a) 41 (b) 42 (c) 43 (d) 44

44 General Adaptation syndrome has been propounded by
(a) Lazarus (b) Parkinson
(c) Zajonc (d) Selye

45 Transaction based models are based on the theory of which psychologist?
(a) Cattell (b) Lazarus
(c) Spearman (d) Sternberg

46 Technique of Guided imagery is related with
(a) Regulation of emotion (b) Self regulation
(c) Stress management (d) Motivation

47 Which amongst the following methods are used for coping with stress?
(a) Relaxation training
(b) Meditation
(c) Biofeedback and systematic desensitisation
(d) All of the above

48 In Lazarus early transactional model of stress, what follows primary appraisal?
(a) A coping effort
(b) An emotional response
(c) Assessment of one coping potential
(d) A behavioural response

49 According to Lazaurs, which appraisal types are the emotions of sadness and depression associated with?
(a) Loss/harm (b) Challenge
(c) Threat (d) None of these

50 According to Lazarus appraisal process, "May be I can manage this if I revise really hard" is an example of.
(a) Threat + no resource = stress
(b) Challenge + possible intend resource= less stress
(c) Threat + limited internal resources= stress
(d) Challenge + external resources= less stress

51 Which hormone is released by the adrenal cortex at the time of stress?
(a) Acetylcholine (b) Noradrenaline
(c) Adrenaline (d) Cortisol

52 Stress as a response can be measured using physical and physiological indices, such as
(a) salivary secretory immunoglobulins
(b) blood pressure
(c) galvanic skin response
(d) All of the above

53 Which one of the following statements about type A individuals is not correct ?
(a) They are aggressive
(b) They are impatient
(c) They are very sociable
(d) The worry about dealiness

54 Which one of the following is not the characteristic of type 'A' personality?
(a) Excessive compulsion for time keeping
(b) Always in hurry
(c) Meticulous analysis of problems
(d) Sleeplessness

Directions (Q. Nos. 55-59) *In the questions given below are two statements labelled as Assertion (A) and Reason (R). In the context of the statements, which one of the following is correct?*

Codes
(a) Both A and R are true and R is the correct explanation of A
(b) Both A and R are true, but R is not the correct explanation of A
(c) A is true, but R is false
(d) A is false, but R is true

55 **Assertion** (A) Stress is useful for personality enrichment.

Reason (R) To be totally without stress is to be dead.

56 **Assertion** (A) Parachutling elicit fear in people.

Reason (R) End or phin response can be triggered not only by physical stressor, but by fear.

57 **Assertion** (A) Conflicts are integral part of life.

Reason (R) There are different stages of conflict.

58 **Assertion** (A) Stress management is set of techniques for helping people who are under going through stress.

Reason (R) Music therapy is not part of the stress management.

59 **Assertion** (A) Stress can be viewed as a response to a stimulus or as the stimulus itself.

Reason (R) Teaching people to relax deeply and to apply these skills to real life stressors can be helpful in lowering stress.

60 Which among the following are the source of conflict?
1. Economic 2. Value
3. Power 4. Religion

Codes
(a) 1, 2 and 4 (b) 1, 2 and 3 (c) 1 and 3 (d) 2 and 4

61 Consider the following statements
1. Stretching exercises increase the arousal level of the body.
2. Aerobic exercises have a calming effect.
3. Yogic asanas provide systematic stretching to all the muscles and joints of the body.
4. Yogic asanas massage the glands and other body organs.

Which of the above statements is/are correct?

(a) 1, 2, 3 and 4 (b) 1 and 2
(c) 3 and 4 (d) 1, 3 and 4

62 Consider the following statem nt about stress Inoculation Training?

1. Skill acquisition and rehearsal
2. Initial conceptualisation
3. Application and follow through

Arrange the following phases in correct sequence

(a) 3, 1 and 2 (b) 1, 2 and 3
(c) 2, 1 and 3 (d) None of these

63 Component of the stress and coping includes.

1. Appraisal
2. Emotion
3. Coping

Codes

(a) Only 1 (b) 1 and 2
(c) 1 and 3 (d) All of these

64 Match the following

	List I (Stress Management Technique)		List II (Benefit)
A.	Biofeedback Therapy	1.	Prevent the mind wandering
B.	Music Therapy	2.	Increase energy level
C.	Breathing Exercise	3.	Control digestive disturbances
D.	Progressive Muscular Relaxation	4.	Manages stress

Codes

	A	B	C	D		A	B	C	D
(a)	3	4	2	1	(b)	2	1	3	4
(c)	1	2	4	3	(d)	4	1	3	2

65 Match the following

	List I (Personality Type)		List II (Reflection)
A.	A	1.	Highly competitive
B.	B	2.	Follow other's
C.	C	3.	Hostile
D.	D	4.	Pessimistic

Codes

	A	B	C	D		A	B	C	D
(a)	3	1	2	4	(b)	4	2	1	3
(c)	2	4	3	1	(d)	1	2	4	3

Directions *(Q. Nos. 66-68) Read the passage given below and answer the following questions.*

A 'dual burden' of serious maternal complications and premature birth occurs in about one in 270 births, a new study finds.

But hospital staffs are often blind to the stress caused by this double whammy, researchers say.

"The situation of combined maternal and newborn complications is likely to be extremely stressful for families concerned for both the mother's and the infant's heath. However, health care providers may not fully recognise this, especially when maternal and newborn care are delivered by different specialists", said study lead author Audrey Lyndon, of New York University College of Nursing.

"There's not enough attention to the combined effect on the family," Lyndon, the assistant dean for clinical research, said in a university news release.

For the study, researchers examined data on all 3.1 million births in California from 2007 through 2012. The investigators found that rates of preterm birth were 876 per 10,000 births and rates of serious maternal complications during childbirth were 140 per 10,000 births.

One-quarter of women with serious maternal complications also had their babies prematurely. The majority of these dual burden births occurred in cases of preterm labor (61%) rather than births that needed to occur early for medical reasons (23%).

Serious maternal complications during childbirth include severe bleeding that requires a blood transfusion, blood clots, heart failure and emergency hysterectomies. Premature infants those born before 37 weeks' gestation have a number of health challenges. These may include breathing, digestive and developmental problems.

Black mothers were twice as likely as white mothers to have dual burden births. Other factors associated with higher risk were cesarean-section delivery, having more than one baby, smoking during pregnancy, being underweight, high blood pressure and diabetes.

The study was published online in July 17 in the Journal of Maternal-Fetal and Neonatal Medicine.

Previous studies have found associations between premature birth and serious maternal complications, but this is the first to examine rates of dual burden births, according to the researchers. Dual burden births have immediate and long-term physical, mental, social and financial consequences for women and their families. These include the risk of post-traumatic stress disorder for mothers and their partners, the study authors said.

66 What do you mean by dual burden?

(a) Maternal complication and postmature birth
(b) Maternal complication and premature birth
(c) On doctors and hospital staff
(c) Birth of Twins

67 Most of the dual burden birth occured in case of

1. Preterm Labour 2. Medical reason
3. Health of parents 4. Drugs

Codes
(a) 1 and 2 (b) 1, 2 and 4
(c) 1, 2 and 3 (d) All of the above

68 According to the passage who among the following is more likely to have dual burden birth.
(a) White mothers (b) Black mothers
(c) Equal ratio (d) None of these

Directions (Q. Nos. 69-73) *Read the passage given below and answer the following questions.*

Lazarus and Folkman differentiate two types of appraisal: primary and secondary. Primary appraisal is the individuals evaluation of an event in terms of his goals, values and beliefs. Primary appraisal addresses the question of whether anything is at stake for the individual in the context of the event. Secondary appraisal indicated what, if anything can be done in response to the event. It involves the assessment of available coping resources had the likelihood that those coping resources will be effective in the particular situation.

Lazarus and Folkman further differentiate five types of primary appraisal : irrelevant, benign, harm, threat and challenge. Event appraised as irrelevant are not associated with any particular emotion because the event has no bearing on the individual values, beliefs or goals. Events appraised as positive are likely to give rise to positive emotions such as happiness or satisfaction and are unlikely to call for any type of coping response. Events appraised as loss are usually associated with negative emotions such as sadness or anger and those appraised as threat are usually associated with negative emotions such as anxiety. A challenge appraisal, the evaluation of a situation as having the potential for gain, is usually associated with both positive and negative emotions. Whereas appraisal of challenge is likely to prompt feelings such as excitement and enthusiasm, there is also the potential for anxiety and fear because the outcome is uncertain.

69 Who differentiated between types of appraisal?
(a) Lazarus (b) Folkman
(c) Miller (d) Lazarus and Folkman

70 What is primary appraisal?
(a) It is individual's evaluation of an event in terms of his goal, value and belief
(b) It is the individual's evaluation of any situation
(e) It is the individual's perception of others feeling
(d) It is the individual's evaluation of his emotion

71 Which of the following is not a type of appraisal defined by Lazarus and Folkman?
(a) Irrelevant (b) Benign (c) Love (d) Threat

72 What type of feeling promote by appraisal of challenge?
(a) Excitement (b) Happiness
(c) Sorrow (d) Fear

73 Events appraised as loss are usually associated with what type of negative erosion?
(a) Frustration (b) Angser (c) Fear (d) Sorrow

ANSWERS

1	(c)	2	(a)	3	(c)	4	(a)	5	(c)	6	(a)	7	(b)	8	(d)	9	(a)	10	(d)
11	(d)	12	(b)	13	(c)	14	(b)	15	(b)	16	(a)	17	(c)	18	(d)	19	(d)	20	(b)
21	(c)	22	(a)	23	(b)	24	(c)	25	(d)	26	(a)	27	(d)	28	(a)	29	(d)	30	(d)
31	(d)	32	(d)	33	(b)	34	(a)	35	(d)	36	(d)	37	(d)	38	(d)	39	(b)	40	(d)
41	(b)	42	(d)	43	(c)	44	(d)	45	(b)	46	(c)	47	(d)	48	(c)	49	(a)	50	(b)
51	(d)	52	(d)	53	(b)	54	(c)	55	(d)	56	(a)	57	(b)	58	(d)	59	(b)	60	(b)
61	(c)	62	(c)	63	(d)	64	(c)	65	(b)	66	(b)	67	(a)	68	(b)	69	(d)	70	(a)
71	(c)	72	(a)	73	(b)														

CHAPTER 25

Social Psychology

Social Psychology deals with the way feelings, thoughts, beliefs, intention and goals are constructed and how such psychological factor, in turn influence our interaction with others. Social psychology includes social perception, attitude, pro social behaviours etc.

Introduction to Social Psychology

Social Psychology is the scientific study of how people's thoughts, feelings and behaviours are influenced by the actual, imagined or implied presence of others. Here 'scientific' refers to the empirical method of investigation. The terms, thoughts and behaviours include all of the psychological variables that are measurable in a human being.

Social psychology emerged at the interface of psychology and sociology in the early 20th century. While psychology analysis the nature of humans, sociology analysis the nature of society. The sphere of social psychology is social and its focus is individual. It is basically the study of individual in social situation. This social situation can vary from person to person interaction, person to group interaction and a group related to another. A social psychologist uses scientific methods to study how we perceive peoples and social events, how we influence others and get influenced, social relation and communication and group dynamics. A relatively recent field, social psychology has none-the-less significant impact not only on the academic worlds of psychology, sociology and social sciences in general, but has also influenced public understanding and expectation of human social behaviour.

Definitions of Social Psychology

Social psychology is the study of the manner in which personality, attitudes, motivations and behaviour of the individual influence and are influenced by social groups.

According to **Encyclopedia Britanica**, "Social psychology is the study of the behaviour of individuals in their social and cultural setting. Although the term may be taken to include the social activity of laboratory animals or those in the wild, the emphasis here is on social behaviour."

In this Chapter

According to **Merriam-Webster** "The social psychology is a study of the manner in which the personality, attitudes, motivations and behaviour of the individual influence and are influenced by social groups".

According to **Baron, Byrne** and **Suls** social psychology is "the scientific field that seeks to understand the nature and causes of individual behaviour in social situations."

According to **Karf Lewin**, social psychology is "the scientific study of individual behaviour in social situation".

According to **Kimble Young**, social psychology is "the study of individual behaviour in groups and how individual behaviour, feeling and thought are influenced by other."

Nature of Social Psychology

Social psychology can mainly be categorised as analytical and scientific in nature.

Analytical Nature of Social Psychology

The last century witnessed the creation of new sciences and specialised branches for specific needs together with the technological developments that have changed the scenario of education and knowledge. New social realities created new problems, as a result of which social psychology came into existence. So in nature, social psychology has to be analytical and at the same time, capable of providing solutions to the problems arising out of the analysis of the upheavel created in the human world.

Scientific Nature of Social Psychology

Scientists involve themselves in the activities of people through communication and interaction and in turn shape the behaviour of individuals. The study of social psychology enables us to understand the dynamics of human behaviour in social situations and what effects do these situations exert on individuals and in what ways do these situations get changed by the behaviour of the individuals.

Social psychology intrudes social life by providing practical recommendations in various areas. The practical needs of the discipline have arisen out of increased demand for efficient management in the areas of industry, education, health , mass communication system, struggle against anti-social behaviour, public services and sports etc. Social psychology is thus scientific in nature and its approach to the range of topics it deals with.

One may find many common explanations and literary works that tell us about interpersonal relations, love, jealousy, aggression, altruism and the roles of individuals in groups. The difference lies in the approach that a social psychologist adopts. He or she adopts scientific methods using a three step basic process. *These steps are as follows*

(i) The collection of carefully made observations, careful observation requires gathering of information about issues and processes of interest and attitude of scepticism.

(ii) The ordered integration of these observations and the statement of general principles.

(iii) The utilisation of these general principles to predict futures observations.

Scope of Social Psychology

Social psychology has great scope when it comes to understand the relationship between minds, groups and behaviours. Actually, social psychology employs three general ways to study and analyse various inter relationships to expand its scope. *They are as follow*

(i) Social psychology tries to see how the thoughts, feelings and behaviours of individuals are influenced by the actual, imagined or implied presence of others.

This includes social perception,social interaction and many kinds of social influences like trust, power and persuation. *It deals with questions like*

- How do small group dynamics impact cognition and emotional states?
- How does the group impact the individual?
- How does the individual operate within the social group?
- It tries to understand the influence, that individual perceptions and behaviours have upon the behaviour of groups. How does persuasion work to change group behaviour, emotion or attitudes?

(ii) Social psychology also tries to understand the influence of things like group productivity in the work place and group decision-making. *It looks at questions like*

- What are the reasons behind conformity, diversity and deviance?

(iii) Finally social psychology tries to understand groups themselves as behavioural entities and the relationships and influences, that one group has upon another group. *It asks questions like*

- What makes some groups hostile to one another and others neutral or civil?
- Do groups behave in a different way than an individual outside the group?

A new way called the *ideological method* is also emerging gradually under the scope of social psychology. It studies the societal forces that influence the human psyche.

Historical Development of Social Psychology

Social psychology came into being at the dawn of twentieth century, when scientists first started to systematically and formally measure the thoughts, feelings and behaviours of human beings. The first published study in this area was an experiment by **Norman Triplett** in 1898 on the phenomenon of social facilitation. The first social psychology textbook was published in 1908 by **McDougall** and **Ross**. During the 1930s, many Gestalt psychologists, particularly, **Kurt Lewin** along with **Leon Festinger** refined the experimental approach to study behaviour and established social psychology as a rigorous scientific discipline.

Kurt Lewin is sometimes known as *The father of Social Psychology*, because he initially developed many of the important ideas related to social psychology including a focus on dynamic interactions among people.

Social Psychology During 1930

Social psychology was energised by psychologists who tried to understand how the German dictator, Adolf Hitler, could have produced such extreme obedience and frightful behaviours in his followers. The studies on conformity conducted by **Muzafer Sherif** and **Solomon** as well as the studies on obedience by **Stanley Milgram** exhibited the importance of conformity pressures in social groups and how people in authority could create obedience, even to the extent of leading people to cause severe harm to others.

Social Psychology During World War Second

During World War Second, social psychologists studied persuasion and propaganda for the US Military. After the war, researchers became interested in variety of social problems including gender issues and racial prejudice. **Leonard Berkowitz** pioneered the *Study of Human Aggression*. Social psychologists like **Irving Janis** focused on group behaviour, studying why intelligent people sometimes made decisions that led to disastrous results when they worked together.

Social psychology expanded to study other topics. **John Darley** and **Bibb Latane** developed a model that helped explain, when people do and don't help others in need. Other social psychologists like **Gordon Allport** and **Muzafer Sherif** focused on inter-group relations with the motive of under standing and potentially reducing the occurrence of stereotyping, prejudice and discrimination.

Social Psychology During the 2nd Half of 20th Century

The later part of the 20th century saw an expansion of social psychology into the field of attitudes with a particular emphasis on cognitive processes. The social psychologists developed the first formal models of persuasion with the aim of understanding how advertisers and other people could present their messages to make them most effective.

These approaches to attitudes focused on cognitive processes that people use while evaluating messages and on the relationship between attitudes and behaviour. In the 1970s and 1980s, social psychology became even more cognitive in orientation as social psychologists used advances in cognitive psychology, which were themselves based largely on advances in computer technology to inform the field.

Social Psychology During 21st Century

The focus of these researchers including Alice, Eagly, Susan Fiske, E Torry Higgins, Richard Nisbett, Lee Ross, Shelly Taylor and many others was on social cognition, which implies an understanding of how our knowledge about our social worlds develops through experiences and the influences of these knowledge structures on memory, information processing, attitudes and judgement.

In the 21st century, the field of social psychology has been expanding further into unknown or new realms of life.

For example An interest in how social situations influence our health and happiness, the important roles of evolutionary experiences and cultures on our behaviour and the fields of social neuroscience have been the topics of study in today's world. Social psychologists continue to seek new ways to measure and understand social behaviour and field continues to evolve.

Traditional Theoretical Perspectives

There are many different ways of thinking about human behaviour. Psychologists adopt a variety of perspectives while studying how people think, feel and behave. Some researchers focus on one specific school of thought, such as the biological perspective, while others take a more comprehensive approach that incorporates multiple points of view. There is no single perspective that is better than the others, each simply emphasises different aspects of human behaviour.

The major traditional theoretical perspectives are as follow

- The Behavioural Perspective
- The Cognitive Perspective
- The Biological Perspective
- The Cross Cultural Perspective
- The Evolutionary Perspective
- The Humanistic Perspective

Brief description of these perspectives is given below

- **The Behavioural Perspective** It focuses on learnt behaviours. Instead of emphasising on internal states, it is totally centred on observable behaviours.

This school of thought dominated in the early years of twentieth century, but it began to lose its hold during 1950s. Today the behavioural perspective is concerned with how behaviours are learned or reinforced. Behavioural principles are often applied in mental health settings, where therapists and counsellors use these techniques to explain and treat a variety of illnesses.

- **The Cognitive Perspective** A new perspective emerged during 1960s, which was termed as cognitive perspective. It focuses on mental processes such as memory, thinking problem solving, language and decision-making. Influenced by psychologists such as **Jean Piaget** and **Albert Bandura**, this perspective has grown notably in recent years.

  Cognitive psychologists often utilise an information processing model, comparing the human mind to a computer, to conceptualise how information is acquired, stored and utilised.

- **The Biological Perspective** The study of physiology a major role in the development of psychology as a separate science. This perspective is known as *biological perspective* today. It emphasises on the physical and biological basis of behaviour.

Researchers of this perspective look at how genetics influence different behaviours or how damage to specific areas of the brain influences behaviour or personality. Things like nervous system, genetics, the brain, the immune system and the endocrine system are just a few of the subjects that interest biological psychologists.

This perspective has grown significantly over the last few decades, especially with advances in our ability to explore and understand the human brain and nervous system. Tools such as Magnetic Resonance Imaging (MRI) scans and Positron Emission Tomography (PET) scans allows researchers to look at the brain under a variety of conditions. Scientists can now look at the effects of brain damage, drugs and diseases in ways that were simply not possible in the past.

- **The Cross Cultural Perspective** It is a fairly new perspective that has grown significantly over the last twenty years. Psychologists and researchers in this school of thought look at human behaviour across different cultures. By looking at these differences, one can learn more about how culture influences our thinking and behaviour.

For Example Researchers have looked at how social behaviours differ in individualistic and combined cultures. In individualistic cultures, such as the USA, people tend to exert less effort when they are part of a group, a phenomenon known as *social loafing*. In combined cultures, such as China, however, people tend to work harder when they are part of a group.

- **The Evolutionary Perspective** It is focussed on the study how evolution explains physiological processes . Psychologists and researchers take the basic principles of evolution and apply them to psychological phenomena. This perspective suggests that these mental processes exist because an evolutionary purpose *i.e.* they aid in survival and evolution.

- **The Humanistic Perspective** The humanistic perspective is a school of thought that emerged during 1950s. It emphasises on the role of motivation in thought and behaviour as it is greatly influenced by the work of prominent humanists like **Carl Rogers** and **Abraham Maslow**.

Self actualisation is an essential component of this perspective. Researchers working on humanist perspective on the ways that human beings are driven to grow, change and develop their personal potential. Positive psychology also has its roots in the humanistic perspective. It focuses on helping people live happier and healthier lives.

Field Theory

Kurt Lewin is known as the *founder of field theory*. In the quest to examine human behaviour, he looked for inspiration in theories about relativity and quantum physics. Fields theory of physics drew his attention. To make that theory part of psychology, he decided to study behaviour, but without separating it from its natural context. Accordingly, he focussed on studying groups. It is experiments revolved around group psychology, the dynamics of organisational change and leadership.

He established two basic conditions for his field theory *i.e.*

(i) A behaviour comes through a totality of co-existing facts.

(ii) These co-existing facts have the characteristics of a dynamic field implying that the state of each one of the field's parts depends on all the others.

In physics, a fields as an areas of space where there are properties that show up as physical quantities like temperature, energy etc. Lewin used the concept of an 'energy field' from physics in his field theory to explain the environmental factors that play a part in human behaviour.

According to him, behaviour doesn't depend on the past or the future. It actually depends on all current facts and events and how a subject sees them. The facts are interconnected and they make up a *dynamic energy field* which he termed as the *life space.*

The Life Space

The life space in the psychological energy fields are the surroundings that encompass a person and his or her perception of his or her immediate reality.
Actually, it is a subjective, personal space.
It is like a concised view of the way one looks at the world with one's objectives, possibilities, fears, experiences and expectations.
Field theory studies one's behaviour with a sense of total perspective.
The psychological field's influences on one's behaviour is so huge that Lewin even said that if there are no changes in the field, there won't be any changes in the behaviour.

Variables Affecting Behaviour

In energy field, each part impacts every other part. The variables, that play a part in understanding our behaviour, also require our attention Lewin came up with three key variables to explain this idea. *They are as follows*

(i) **Energy** Energy is what causes actions and what motivates them. When there is a need, an energy or energy field will appear which will lead to an action. All these actions have a change, either positive or negative. The positive charge of these actions leads to other actions and negative charge pushes the action back.

(ii) **Tension** It is the difference between a person's goal and his or her current state. The tension is internal and pushes one to go through one's intentions.

(iii) **Need** It is what gives the motivating tension a start. When a person has a physical or psychological need, an internal state of tension will take place inside them. This state of tension makes the system or the person change to try to get back to its initial state and satisfy its need.

Cognitive Dissonance

The term 'cognitive dissonance' is used to describe the feelings of discomfort that arises when one's beliefs are against one's behaviour or new information that is presented to one. It refers to a situation involving conflicting attitudes, beliefs or behaviours.

It produces a feeling of mental discomfort leading to an disagreement in one of the beliefs, attitudes or behaviours to restore the balance.

Psychologist **Leon Festinger** first proposed a theory of cognitive dissonance centred on how people try to reach internal consistency. He suggested that people have inner need to ensure that their beliefs and behaviours are consistent. Inconsistent or conflicting beliefs lead to disharmony, which people strive to avoid.

In his book 'A Theory of Cognitive Dissonance' written in 1957, Festinger explained, "Cognitive dissonance can be seen as an antecedent condition which leads to an activity oriented towards dissonance reduction just as hunger leads towards an activity oriented towards hunger reduction."

Influencial Factors Behind Cognitive Dissonance

The degree of dissonance, people experience, can depend on a few different factors, including how highly they value a particular belief and the degree to which their beliefs are consistent. *The over all strength of the dissonance can also be influenced by factors mentioned below*

- Cognitions that are more personal, such as beliefs about the self, tend to result in greater dissonance.
- The ratio between dissonant thoughts and constant thoughts.
- The greater the strength of the dissonance the more pressure, there is to relieve the feelings of discomfort.

Sociobiology

The concept of sociobiology first gained major recognition with **Edward O Wilson's** 1975 publication 'Sociobiology: The New Synthesis'. He introduced the concept of sociobiology as the application of evolutionary theory to social behaviour. Sociobiology is based on the premise that some behaviours are atleast partly inherited and can be affected by natural selection. It begins with the idea that behaviours have evolved over time, similar to the way that physical traits are thought to have evolved. Animals will, therefore, act in ways that have proven to be evolutionary successful over time, which can result in the formation of complex social processes among other things.

Sociobiology is Investigative in Nature

According to sociobiologists, many social behaviours have been shaped by natural selection. Sociobiology investigates social behaviours such as making patterns, territorial fights and pack hunting. It argues that just as selection pressure led to animals evolving useful ways of interacting with the natural environment, it also led to the genetic evolution of advantageous social behaviour. Behaviour is therefore seen as an effort to preserve one's genes in the population and certain genes or gene combinations are thought to influence particular behavioural traits from generation to generation.

Sociobiology and Human Behaviour

Like Charles Darwin's theory of Evolution by natural selection, in the same way sociobiologists modelled the evolution of human behaviours using various behaviours as the relevant traits.

Sociobiologists believe that evolution does not only include just genes but also psychological, social and cultural features. When humans reproduce, their offsprings inherit their genes. When parents and children share genetic, developmental, physical and social environments, the children inherit the gene-effects of their parents. Sociobiologists also believe that the different rates of reproduction are related to different levels of wealth, social status and power within that culture.

Psychodynamic Approaches

The psychodynamic approaches originated with the work of **Sigmund Freud**. This view of psychology and human behaviour emphasises the role of unconscious mind, early childhood experiences and interpersonal relationships to explain human behaviour and to treat people suffering from mental illnesses.

Freud conceived of the mind as being composed of three key elements, *which are as follows*

(i) **The ID** (meaning 'it' in Latin) It represents our most impulsive, untamed desires and pays no regard for what is acceptable or reasonable. Innate instincts such as the need for food, water, warmth and sexual desires originate in id. The id abides by the pleasure principle which asserts that we seek to maximise pleasure and avoid pain wherever possible. The death drive, a self destructive impulsiveness which drives one to the end of one's life, is also contained within the id.

(ii) **The Ego** The ego acts as an intermediary between the unreasonable demands of the id and outside reality. It tries to satisfy the needs of the id as much as is practically possible without necessarily understanding why some demands might be unreasonable.

It remains self centred and does not give consideration to other people's needs or wishes. It acts based on the reality principles, which in contrast to the pleasure principle of id, accepts the limits of what can be obtained from the outside world.

(iii) **The Superego** The superego feels compassion for others again tries to satisfy the needs of the id, but understands that some of those needs may adversely affect others. It acts as a filter for our behaviour and maintains our conscience, leading to an understanding of other people's emotions and to emotional guilt.

Social Cognition

Social cognition is a sub-topic of various branches of psychology that focuses on how people process, store and apply information about the other people and social situations. It focuses on the role that cognitive process play is social interaction.

Psychologists have always been interested in the hidden link between external stimuli and overt behavioural responses. Behaviourists (*e.g.* Skinner) in particular, have argued that behaviour can be explained better in terms of reinforcement contingencies (reward and punishment) than of mediating cognitive processes. In contrast, Gestalt theorists (*e.g.* Koffka, Wertheimer) have always emphasised that it is not the stimulus that influences our behaviours, but how we see it in other words, how we mentally construct and represent reality.

The cognitive link between stimulus and response allows social behaviour to be far more context-sensitive than rigid biological routines. Excluding this link from social-psychological research would result in a severely impoverished picture of human conduct. To quote from one of the most prominent European social psychologists, Henri Tajfel : The greatest adaptive advantage of social cognition is its capacity to modify his behaviour as a function of the way in which he perceives and understands a situation.

If social behaviour is not directly determined by the external stimulus situation, but is mediated by the internal mental representation of a given situation, we need to understand how individual construct their subjective reality in order to understand social behaviour and its mediating factors. Concerned with the study of social knowledge and the cognitive processes that are involved when individuals construct their subjective reality.

The aim of social cognition is to investigate how information is encoded, stored and retrieved from memory, how social knowledge is structured and represented and what processes are involved when individuals compute judgements and make decisions.

Assumption Related to Social Cognition

Following are assumption related with social cognition.

One basic assumption holds that social judgements are only partly determined by the stimuli of given situation, our judgements will also heavily depend on the prior knowledge we bring to that situation.

A second basic assumption holds that our thinking is strongly influenced by the limitations of processing capacity.

Third, cognitive processes can differ with respect to their automaticity and controllability (Shiffrin and Schneider) some processes can be controlled more easily than others. *For example* When required, individuals can actively call to mind some particular content from their memory, such as the applicant's performance in an assessment centre. However, information may also come to mind automatically.

Social Cognition and Information Processing

The social aspect is not confined to the nature of the stimulus as such, just as a young child could hardly learn her first language from a radio and just as social interaction in peer groups is a necessary condition in Piaget's theory of cognitive development, the most important message guiding the present chapter is that (social) cognition is a genuinely social process.

The importance of the social component of human intelligence can be illustrated by Cosmiders' evolutionary approach to logical reasoning. The persistent failure of even highly intelligent people in logical reasoning tasks is due to the fact that reasoning experiments are often detached from the social context, in which the reasoning ability has evolved.

Social Perception

Social perception refers to the ability to make accurate interpretations and inferences about other people from their general physical appearance, verbal and non-verbal patterns of communication. Things like facial expressions, tone of voice, hand gestures and body position or movement are all questions people with higher levels of social perception pick up on to work out what other people are thinking, feeling or are likely to do next.

Components of Social Perception

Social perception encompasses three main components, Non-verbal communication, Attribution, and Impression formation and management, which are discussed below.

Non-verbal Communication

Non-verbal communication occurs without using any oral or written word. Instead of written or oral words, it relies on various non-verbal cuses like physical movements, tasks, colours, signs, symbols, signals charts etc. to express feelings, attitudes or information.

Major types of non-verbal communication are as follows

(i) **Body Language** Body language is a type of a non-verbal communication in which physical behaviours, as opposed to words, are used to express or convey the information. Such behaviour includes facial expressions, body posture, gestures, eye movement, touch and the use of space. Body language exists in both animals and humans, but this focuses on interpretations of human body language. It is also known *as kinesics*.

(ii) **Facial Expression** Facial expressions are most important form of non-verbal communication.A facial expression is one or more motions or positions of the muscles beneath the skin of the face. It conveys the emotional state of an individual to observers.

They are a primary means of conveying social information between humans, but they also occur in most other mammals and some other animal species.

(iii) **Eye Contact** The eyes play on important role in non-verbal communication and such things as looking, starting and blinking are important non-verbal behaviours. When people encounter people or things that they like, the rate of blinking increases and pupils and dilate. Looking at another person can indicate a range of emotions including hostility, interest and attraction.

(iv) **Touch or Haptic** Haptic communication is a branch of non-verbal communication that refers to the ways in which people and animals communicate and interact through the sense of touch. The sense of touch allows one to experience different sensations such as : pleasure, pain, heat or cold. One of the most significant aspects of touch is the ability to convey and enhance physical intimacy.

The sense of touch is the fundamental component of haptic communication for interpersonal relationships. Touch can be categorised in many terms such as positive, playful, control, ritualistic, task-related or unintentional. It can be both sexual (kissing is one example that some perceived as sexual) and platonic (such as hugging or a handshake).

Attribution

In social psychology, attribution is the process of inferring the causes of events or behaviours in real life, attribution is something we all do every day, usually without any awareness of the underlying processes and biases that lead to our inferences.

For example Over the course of a typical day, you probably make numerous attributions about your own behaviour as well as that of the people around you.

Theory of Correspondent Inference

Theory of Correspondent inference is a psychological theory proposed by Edward E Jones and Keith E Davis that "systematically accounts for a perceiver's inferences about what an actor was trying to achieve by a particular action".

The purpose of this theory is to explain why people make internal or external attributions. People compare their actions with alternative actions to evaluate the choices that they have made and by looking at various factors they can decide if their behaviour was caused by an internal disposition.

Kelly's Theory of Casual Attribution

Harold Kelley's theory of casual attribution is also known as *covariation* model is an attribution theory in which people make causal inferences to explain why other people and ourselves behave in a certain way. It is concerned with both social perception and self-perception.

The covariation principle states that, "an effect is attributed to the one of its possible causes with which, over time, it covaries". That is, a certain behaviour is attributed to potential causes that appear at the same time. This principle is useful when the individual has the opportunity to observe the behaviour over several occasions. Causes of an outcome can be attributed to the person (internal), the stimulus (external), the circumstance or some combination of these factors. Attributions are made based on the three criteria: Consensus, Distinctiveness and Consistency.

Impression Formation

It is a part of human nature that we tend to form impressions of people, things and objects. We tend to classify people as good, bad, strong, weak, helpful, unhelpful and infact into so many other categories. Similarly, we form impressions about things and objects. An excellent example of this is what is called *brand loyalty*.

Some tend to form their impression on the basis of their own experiences and others tend to accept impressions from others. *For example* If I tell my close friend that a particular individual is good and competent he is most likely to accept it.

While on the one hand all of us tend to form impressions of people and things, there are people who, by the same logic stand to gain by creating impressions in the minds of others who matter. A young man appearing for an interview tries to be at his best when facing the interview board.

Impression Management

Impression management is a conscious or subconscious process in which people attempt to influence the perceptions of other people about a person, object or event by regulating and controlling information in social interaction. It was first conceptualised by Erving Goffman in 1959 in 'The Presentation of Self in Everyday Life' and then was expanded upon in.

An example of impression management theory in play is in sports such as soccer. At an important game, a player would want to showcase themselves in the best light possible, because there are college recruiters watching. This person would have the flashiest pair of cleats and try and perform their best to show off their skills. Their main-goal may be to impress the college recruiters in a way that maximizes their chances of being chosen for a college team rather than winning the game. Impression management is usually used synonymously with self-presentation, in which a person tries to influence the perception of their image.

The notion of impression management was first applied to face-to-face communication, but then was expanded to apply to computer-mediated communication. The concept of impression management is applicable to academic fields of study such as psychology and sociology as well as practical fields such as corporate communication and media.

Attitude

According to psychologists, attitude is a learnt tendency to evaluate things in a certain way. This can include evaluations of people, issues, objects or events. Such evaluations can be positive or negative, but they can also be uncertain at times. *For example* One might have mixed feelings about a particular a person or issue. Different components that make up attitudes are usually referred as CAB or ABCs of the attitude. *These components are as follows*

- **Cognitive Component** These are one's thoughts and beliefs about the subject.
- **Affective Component** How an object, person, issue or event makes one feel, is termed as affective component.
- **Behavioural Component** How the attitude influences one's behaviour, is categorised as behavioural component.

Attitude can also be explicit or implicit. **Explicit attitudes** are those that we are consciously aware of and that clearly influence our behaviours and beliefs.

Implicit attitudes are unconscious but still have an effect on one's beliefs and behaviours.

Factors like experience, social roles, norms and learning play a major role in the formation of attitudes.

Change of Attitude within Cultural Context

Attitudes are general evaluations of objects, ideas and people, one encounters throughout one's life. Attitudes are important because they can guide thought, behaviour and feelings. Attitude change can occurs at any time, an attitude is modified *i.e.* change occurs when a person goes from being positive to negative, from slightly positive to very positive or from having no attitude to notable one.

Changes in attitude can be occurred through low and high effort process *which are as follows*

Low-Effort Processes

Low-effort processes are those that occur when one puts forth relatively little cognitive effort. These include associative processes and inferential processes.

(i) **Associative Processes** Associative processes are mainly influenced and caused by factors like classical conditioning, affective priming and mere exposure. *For example*.

- **Classical Conditioning** It is one way to produce attitude change in the absence of effortful thought where an initially neutral attitude object is repeatedly associated with another stimulus that already possesses a positive or negative meaning.
- **Affective Priming** It is a process that involves the association of two stimuli. Here, a positive or negative stimulus is encountered just prior to a novel attitude object. When this happens, one's reaction to the positive or negative stimulus will come to modify the evaluation of the new object, producing attitude change.
- **Mere Exposure** According to mere exposure effect, the repeated exposure to an object in the absence of association can also change attitudes. It requires only that one is repeatedly exposed to an attitude object.

(ii) **Inferential Processes** Factors like balance, attribution and heuristics influence and cause inferential processes. *For example*

- **Balance** Inferential process of attitude change involves cognitive balance. Balance is achieved when people agree with those they like and disagree with those they dislike.
- **Attribution** Attribution concerns the inferences that people make about themselves and others after witnessing a behaviour and the situation in which it Occurred. These inferences cause attitude change.
- **Heuristics** Low-effort attitude change can also occur through the use of heuristics or simple decision rules based on prior experiences or observations. Although there are countless heuristics, some common examples are 'Experts are usually correct' and 'bigger is better'.

High-Effort Processes

High effort processes are those that occur with relatively high cognitive effort.These attitude change processes requires a greater use of mental resources.

They are further sub-divided into cognitive processes, expectancy-value processes and dissonance processes. *Brief description of these processes is given below*

(i) **Cognitive Processes** When people's attitudes change through the use of the high cognitive effort, some of the most important aspects to consider are their actual thought *i.e.* cognitive responses towards the attitude object and any persuasive message that is received on the topic. Three components of thought have proved very important in producing change. They are favourable or unfavourable thoughts about the attitude object or message, degree of thinking about an attitude object and level of confidence about the attitude object.

(ii) **Expectancy Value Processes** According to the Reasoned Action theory, attitudes are created through an individuals' assessment of how likely it is that a given attitude object will be associated with positive or negative consequences or values.

(iii) **Dissonance Processes** According to Cognitive Dissonance theory, People are motivated to hold consistent attitudes. Due to this motivation for consistency, people experience unpleasant physiological arousal when they willingly engage in a behaviour that is counter to their beliefs. When people make a choice out of the given alternatives, dissonance processes will often produce attitude change.

Prosocial Behaviour

Prosocial behaviour refers to "voluntary actions that are intended to help or benefit another individual or group of individuals". This definition refers to consequences of a doer's actions rather than the motivations behind those actions. These behaviours include a broad range of activities, sharing, comforting, rescuing and helping. The term prosocial behaviour originated during the 1970s and was introduced by social scientists as an antonym for the term antisocial behaviour.

A general, prosocial behaviour may result either from the ultimate goal to benefit oneself (egoistically motivated behaviour) or from the ultimate goal to benefit another person (altruistically motivated behaviour). The middle-level term 'prosocial behaviour', which includes egoistically and altruistically motivated helping behaviour is generally used because it refers to the central issues.

The term 'altruistic behaviour' is used only to emphasise the fact that a particular behaviour is altruistically motivated. 'Prosocial behaviour' is that in which an actor tries to help another person the actor is not motivated by the fulfilment of professional obligations and recipient is a person and not an organisation. Related terms which have a slightly different meaning are 'helping behaviour' and 'altruism.' Biological individualistic, interpersonal and social system theory are taken into account. Two of the most important explanatory concepts are empathy and social responsibility. Prosocial behaviour also varies with respect to the effort that is involved.

On one hand, people give small amounts of money to beggars sitting on the pavement or at the entrance to an underground station. They pick up fallen groceries or return an overpayment. On the other hand, they jump into a river to save a child's life or rush into a burning building to rescue the occupants. These examples illustrate the constrast between non-serious (low-cost) and serious (high-cost) helping (Smithson, Amato and Pearce, 1983). Serious and non-serious helping may be distinct forms of prosocial behaviour, but they share common characteristics that are included in the major explanations of prosocial behaviour.

Approaches of Prosocial Behaviour

Some of the important approaches of Prosocial Behaviour are as follows

Biological Approach

The biological approach explains prosocial behaviour in terms of inborn or genetic tendencies. This raises the interesting question of how the process of natural selection could favour a genes that increases the tendency of an individual to help others. Prosocial behaviour can be understood as the result of natural selection, if it increased rather than decreased an individual's (or her relatives) chance of reproducing. Two general processes may have contributed to the development of prosocial behaviour: *kin selection* and *reciprocity*.

Individualistic Approach

Like the biological approach, the individualistic approach accounts for altruism in terms of individual tendencies to be helpful however, these tendencies are not necessarily assumed to be genetically determined (although they can be), but acquired by social learning. There are basically two types of individualistic theories of altruism, one explains altruistic behaviour in terms of *mood states,* while the other assumes that altruism is determined by *enduring personality characteristics*.

Prosocial Personality and Model

Elements of the prosocial personality include **social responsibility, empathy** and **internal locus of control**, whereas social responsibility and internal locus of control facilitate bystanders feelings of obligation to help in emergency situations, high empathy contributes to a better understanding of the needs of other persons.

Another characteristic of the prosocial personality is the just-world belief, which refers to the generalised expectancy that people get what they deserve. Undeserved suffering of others is a strong threat to the belief in a just world.

Therefore, behavioural and cognitive strategies are employed to restore the belief in a just world, these include either reducing the victims suffering by helping them or devaluing the victims. Both strategies are efficient, when they reaffirm the belief in a just world by eliminating the impression of undeserved suffering.

From a theoretical viewpoint, the relation between belief in a just world and prosocial behaviour depends on the expected effectiveness of prosocial behaviour.

A summary of empirical research indicates that dispositional empathy and prosocial behaviour are positively correlated. Dispositional empathy is understood as a vicarious emotion, which is elicited by perceiving another in need. In the studies of Bierhoff et al and Oliner and Oliner, showed that helpers expressed higher empathy than non-helpers.

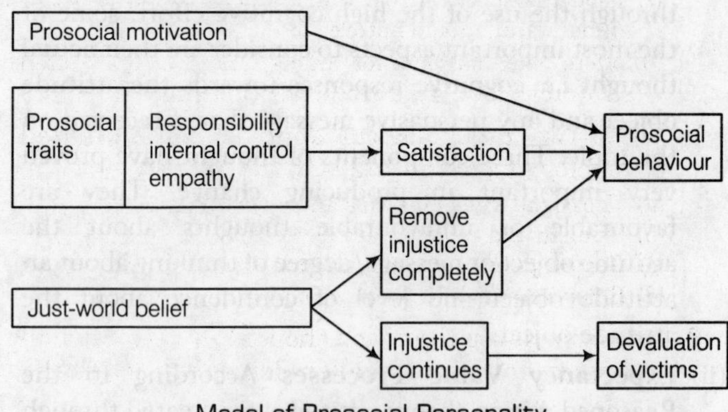

Model of Prosocial Personality

The model of the prosocial personality is illustrated in the figure. It includes three components prosocial motivation, prosocial traits and just world belief. While it is assumed that prosocial motivation and prosocial traits exert a positive influence on prosocial behaviour in a variety of situations, the effect of the just world belief depends on whether people expect that the injustice will be removed completely by helping.

EXAM BASED QUESTIONS

1 What is the focus of social psychology?
(a) Individual
(b) Society
(c) Behaviour
(d) Mentality

2 Social psychology has significant impact on
(a) the academic world of psychology, sociology and social sciences.
(b) public understanding.
(c) expectation of human social behaviour.
(d) All of the above

3 Social psychology began to emerge as the vibrant field it is today during
(a) The depression of the early 1930s when researchers examined the effects of deprivation on aggression and altruism.
(b) World War First when psychologists conducted studies of social conflict and cooperation.
(c) World War Second when researchers performed studies of persuasion and soldier morale.
(d) The Korean War when psychologists examined the effects of brainwashing on prisoners of war.

4 In comparison to the sociologist, the social psychologist
(a) is more likely to study the social causes of behaviour
(b) is more likely to study individuals than groups
(c) gives less attention to our internal functioning
(d) relies more heavily on correlational research

5 In comparison to personality psychology, social psychology
(a) has a shorter history.
(b) is more concerned with the biological causes of behaviour.
(c) is more likely to use case studies in theory development.
(d) has greater concern for differences between individuals.

6 The text states that as a scientific discipline, social psychology
(a) is superior to those disciplines which assume a more subjective approach to the study of human nature.
(b) can assist in explaining the meaning of life.
(c) is one perspective from which we can view and better understand human nature.
(d) offers explanations for human nature that often contradict the claims of other disciplines.

7 What two psychological approaches dominated psychology from the 1920s to the 1950s?
(a) The cognitive perspective and structuralism
(b) Monism and evolutionary psychology
(c) Gestalt psychology and functionalism
(d) Behaviourism and the psychodynamic approach

8 Amber believes that each thought or memory can be broken down into smaller elements, such as the emotions and concepts behind them.
In which historical approach to psychology would she find people who believe the same thing?
(a) Psychoanalysis (b) Structuralism
(c) Gestalt (d) Functionalism

9 Which of the following options was not a field that contributed to early understandings of psychological thought?
(a) Biology (b) Physiology
(c) Astronomy (d) Philosophy

10 What is a similarity between early physiologists and modern biological psychologists?
(a) Both focus on the question, 'Do we have a soul'?
(b) Both believe that the environment is the most important factor in determining behaviour.
(c) Both use evolution to explain behaviour.
(d) Both believe that physical traits and changes in the body can affect behaviour.

11 Which event best marks the beginning of the modern study of psychology?
(a) When Rene Descartes published his viewpoint that the mind and body are separate in the 1640s.
(b) When Charles Darwin proposed his theory of evolution in 1859.
(c) When Sigmund Freud travelled to America and introduced his theories in 1909.
(d) When William James published the first psychology textbook in English in 1890.

12 What was philosophy's major contribution to early understandings of human psychology?
(a) Philosophy's focus on empirical data led to a scientific focus for psychology.
(b) The debate on the relationship between the mind/soul and the body led people to consider how the mind worked.
(c) Philosophy's idea that we have four humours that affect our behaviours led early psychologists to look for other ways the body impacted behaviour.
(d) Philosophy's idea that we have four humours that affect our behaviours led early psychologists to look for other ways the body impacted behaviour.

13 Which of the following approaches to psychology did not exist at the same time with the others?
(a) Sociocultural (b) Structuralism
(c) Functionalism (d) Psychoanalysis

14 "The most important thing a psychologist can study is how a behaviour or thought helps a person navigate the world, rather than how that thought comes to be or what it is made of."
This viewpoint probably comes from somebody who believes in what historical theoretical approach?
(a) Structuralism (b) Functionalism
(c) Gestalt (d) Psychoanalysis

15 Marnie is handed a teddy bear and begins to describe what she is experiencing: "This is brown it is soft, it is wearing a red bow." What historic research technique is she using?
(a) Introspection (b) Psychoanalysis
(c) Dualism (d) Structuralism

16 Charles Darwin proposed that natural selection leads to the development of characteristics most suited to the survival and reproduction of a species.
His theory has most influenced which branch of psychology?
(a) Humanism (b) Evolutionary psychology
(c) Cognitive psychology (d) Behaviourism

17 How do cognitive approaches to learning differ from traditional behaviourist explanations?
(a) Cognitive psychologists focus on the changes in neural networks that result from learning.
(b) Cognitive psychologists try to explain learning from an evolutionary perspective.
(c) Cognitive psychologists believe that learning involves some sort of thinking.
(d) Cognitive psychologists believe that researchers should only focus on observable behaviours.

18 Which of these serves as the best evidence that there are cognitive factors in learning?
(a) Several behaviours can be chained together through operant or classical conditioning.
(b) If somebody wants to artificially create a taste aversion by poisoning an undesired food, it is less effective if the subject knows there is medicine in his food that is making him or her ill.
(c) Reinforcement or punishment can include other activities as well as tangible objects.
(d) Some behaviours simply cannot be conditioned because they are not physically possible for the subject.

19 Which theory of personality least believes in personality change?

(a) Psychoanalytic (b) Humanist
(c) Social cognitive (d) Trait

20 Functionalism was a school of psychology that focused attention on the

(a) struggles with unconscious drives and conflicts
(b) adaptive value of conscious thoughts and emotions
(c) treatment of psychological disorders
(d) adaptive value of unconscious thoughts and emotions

21 After Mr Jones suffered a stroke, a section on the left side of his brain was severely damaged. Now, Mr Jones lost the ability to speak fluently.
This change in his verbal skills can be best be explained using which approach?

(a) Behaviourist (b) Evolutionary
(c) Cognitive (d) Biological

22 Which of the following approaches seems to lack the most scientific support, since it seems to rely on after the fact explanations about correlations about childhood experiences and adult personality?

(a) Behavioural (b) Psychoanalysis
(c) Evolutionary (d) Cognitive

23 Calvin displays aggressive behaviours because he witnessed his father acting aggressively when in similar situations
This behaviour can best be explained through which approach to psychology?

(a) Humanistic (b) Behavioural
(c) Cognitive (d) Evolutionary

24 Which of the following would be of least interest to an evolutionary psychologist?

(a) Increasing rates of childhood obesity
(b) Classroom discipline procedures
(c) Patterns of sexual behaviours
(d) Aggressive behaviours

25 Many humans across cultures share similar taboos, ideas or behaviours that are unacceptable. The perspective of evolutionary psychology would most likely explain this by saying

(a) taboos develop because of behaviours that have caused harm or diminished reproductive success across past generations.
(b) taboos develop because of social norms created by institutions.
(c) children learn from a young age what is and is not acceptable from parents and other adults.
(d) humans share a common morality that creates an aversion to certain behaviours.

26 According to the evolutionary psychologists, human behaviour is

(a) a result of learned behaviours an organism has acquired over the lifespan.
(b) a result of repressed thoughts and urges of which we're largely unaware.
(c) an attempt to reach full human potential through actualisation.
(d) the result of psychological adaptations to changing human environments across generations.

27 Which of the following explanations of obesity best fits with an evolutionary perspective of psychology?

(a) Higher body fat indicates material wealth, thus attractiveness.
(b) The ability to gain weight and difficulty in losing weight carries a survival advantage.
(c) Modern processing of food leads to higher fat content.
(d) Cultural influences greatly affect the likelihood of obesity.

28 Roger is a freshman in college and is having trouble adjusting to the changes in his life. What type of psychologist should he be referred to?

(a) Developmental (b) Psychiatrist
(c) Clinical (d) Counselling

29 As the owner of a company, you want to make as much profit as possible. Happy employees will be better producers, hence, more money to be made.
What type of psychologist would you use to ensure your employees were happy on the job and producing to the best of their ability?

(a) Counselling (b) Industrial organisational
(c) Psychiatrist (d) Clinical

30 Which of the following was a significant factor in determining the degree of obedience in Milgram's series of experiments?

(a) The tone of voice used by the experimenter.
(b) Whether the experimenter was male or female.
(c) Amount of complaining, shouting and crying by the learner.
(d) The setting in which the experiment was conducted.

31 What were the conclusions drawn about ordinary people based on Milgram's famous study of obedience?

(a) People will engage in high levels of destructive obedience, when faced with strong situational pressures.
(b) People will engage in low levels of destructive obedience, when faced with strong situational pressures.
(c) People's personality is the strongest determinant of obedient behaviour.
(d) People will challenge authority figures, when they become distressed by their commands.

32 The concern for how others are evaluating us is

(a) self-protection evaluation (b) ego evaluation
(c) apprehension evaluation (d) social evaluation

33 Which of the following is true of Milgram's (1963) study of obedience? The study found that

(a) quite ordinary people taking part in a laboratory experiment were not prepared to administer electric shocks just because an experimenter told them to do so.

(b) participants believed that the shocks they administered would not harm anyone.
(c) apparently pathological behaviour may not be due to individual pathology, but to particular social circumstances.
(d) None of the above

34 Subjects in Milgram's experiment, who gave large shocks rationalised that they were not personally responsible for their actions. This raises questions about our willingness to commit inhumane acts as a result of
(a) coercive power
(b) obedience to a legitimate authority
(c) expert power
(d) conformity to group pressure

35 When subjects in Milgram's obedience experiments received their orders over the phone, they
(a) conformed more completely due to the formality of the telephoned instructions.
(b) completely refused to participate.
(c) were only slightly more obedient than they were in face-to-face conditions.
(d) were far less obedient.

36 According to evolutionary psychologists,
(a) women tend to be concerned with whether mates will devote time and resources to a relationship.
(b) men place less emphasis on physical attractiveness.
(c) women place more emphasis on sexual fidelity.
(d) men are biologically driven to have multiple partners.

37 Research suggests that we seek out the company of others because of which motives?
(a) To obtain information (b) To reduce anxiety
(c) To compare ourselves with similar others
(d) All of the above

38 Which of the following is not one of the three basic processes of social cognition?
(a) Encoding (b) Categorisation
(c) Attention (d) Retrieval

39 Our current mood and feelings are best described by the term
(a) effect (b) feeling (c) emotion (d) affect

40 Counterfactual thinking is closely related to the experience of
(a) joy (b) relief (c) anger (d) regret

41 We tend to use much social information efficiently
(a) without many errors in social thought.
(b) on very select occasions.
(c) despite the enormous amount of information we regularly receive.
(d) even though others regularly encourage us to not do so.

42 Ruby tastes her food, then salts it. Naroj assume that the food needed salt, therefore Naroj attribute Ruby's actions to a/an
(a) internal cause (b) external cause
(c) setting (d) situational demand

43 The degree of attraction among group members relates to the dimension of
(a) compatibility (b) structure
(c) cohesiveness (d) conformity

44 A reference group is
(a) one with, which a person has face-to-face contact.
(b) any group, in which one plays an active role or has membership.
(c) any group, outside one's social distance boundaries.
(d) any group, whose values and attitudes are seen as relevant to one's own.

45 Physical proximity increases attraction because it
(a) increases frequency of contact
(b) enhances social comparisons
(c) establishes common norms
(d) reduces development of incompatible roles

46 Solomon Asch's classic experiment was arranged to test the limits of
(a) social perception (b) indoctrination
(c) coercive power (d) conformity

47 Social position in a group determines one's
(a) competence (b) autokinetic norms
(c) role (d) usefulness

48 Social facilitation refers to an increase in dominant responses in the presence of others of the same species, leading to
(a) improved performance on both well- learned/easy tasks and poorly learned/ difficult tasks.
(b) improved performance on well-learned/easy tasks and deterioration in performance on poorly learned/difficult tasks.
(c) deterioration in performance on well-learned/easy tasks and improved performance on poorly learned/difficult tasks.
(d) deterioration in performance on both well-learned/easy and poorly learned/difficult tasks.

49 The study of unspoken rules for the use of interpersonal space is called
(a) Kinesics (b) Psychoecology
(c) Proxemics (d) Tterritoriality

50 Interpersonal attraction is encouraged by which one of the following?
(a) Personal space (b) Proxemics
(c) Competition (d) Similarity

51 Cognitive dissonance theory is based on human need for
(a) self-actualisation (b) gain-loss
(c) cognitive dissonance (d) consistency

52 A student who is unprepared for a final exam complains that he has a stomach ache and cannot take the exam. If the student's roommate ignores this complaint, he or she has probably attributed the student's symptoms to the
(a) object (b) actor
(c) situation (d) need for affiliation

53 Who among the following has written the book, 'A Theory of Cognitive Dissonance' in 1957?

(a) Festinger (b) Davis
(c) Kurt Lewin (d) Wilson

54 Who among the following is known as the 'Rounder of Field Thoery'?

(a) Kurt Lewin (b) Carl Rogers
(c) Abrahm Maslow (d) Jean Piaget

55 According the Kurt Lewin, which among the following is/are to the basic conditions for his field theory?

(a) A behaviour comes through a totality of co-existing facts.
(b) The co-existing facts have the characteristics of a dynamic field implying that the state of each one of the Field's parts depends on all the others.
(c) Both b and c
(d) None of the above

56 Who among the following defined empathy as a set of separate, but overlapping constructs?

(a) Davis (b) Eisenberg
(c) Oliver (d) None of these

57 Sociobilogy : The New Synthesis' of Edward O Wilson was published in

(a) 1975 (b) 1980
(c) 1985 (d) 2000

58 The ability to make accurate interpretation and inference about other people from their general physical perception is known as

(a) Attitude (b) Social cognition
(c) Social perception (d) Pro social behaviour

59 Social perception does not include which of the following component.

(a) Verbal communication
(b) Attribution
(c) Impression formation
(d) Non-verbal communication

60 The term kinesis refer to

(a) Spoken words
(b) Kind of exercise
(c) Interpretation of body language
(d) None of the above

61 The process of inferring the causes of events or behaviours is called

(a) Prosocial behaviour (b) Attribution
(c) Communication (d) Attitude

62 Theory of casual attribution has been propounded by

(a) Harold Kelley
(b) Keith E Davis
(c) Edward E Jones
(d) Kurf Lewin

63 Attitude is made up of three component CAB or ABC here CAB or ABC refer to

(a) Behavioural, Affection, Cognitive
(b) Cognitive, Affective, Behavioural
(c) Cognitive, Affective, Biological
(d) All of the above

64 Voluntary action that are intended to help or benefit another individual is known by term

(a) Prosocial behaviour
(b) Anti-social behaviour
(c) Attitude
(d) Social cognition

65 Which of the following statement is/are correct?

1. Social psychology is the scientific study of human behaviour.
2. Social psychology emerged as interface of psychology and biology.
3. The first social psychology text was published in 1908 by McDougall.

Select the correct answer using the codes given below

(a) 1 and 2 (b) 2 and3 (c) Only 1 (d) 1 and 3

66 Which of the following is true regarding field theory?

1. Kurf Lewin founded field theory.
2. He established two basic condition in his theory.
3. According to his theory behaviour does not depend on past experiences.

Codes

(a) Only 1 (b) Only 2
(c) Both 1 and 2 (d) All of these

67 Sigmund Freud concept of psycho dynamics concept, mind is composed of

1. ID 2. Ego
3. Super Ego 4. High ID

Codes

(a) 1, 2 and 3 (b) 1, 2 and 4 (c) 3 and 4 (d) 1 and 2

68 Social perception consist of which of the following component.

1. Non-verbal communication
2. Attitude
3. Attribution
4. Prosocial behaviour

Codes

(a) 1 and 2 (b) 1, 2 and 3 (c) 1 and 3 (d) All of these

69 Attitude is made up of different component, which includes

1. Cognitive 2. Affective
3. Behaviourial 4. Attribution

Codes

(a) 1 and 2 (b) 1, 2 and 3
(c) 2 and 4 (d) All of these

70 Match the following

List I (Social Psychologists)		List II (Years of Study)
A. Norman Triplett	1.	1798
B. Muzafir Sherif	2.	1936
C. Solomon	3.	1952
D. Stanley Milgram	4.	1974

Codes

	A	B	C	D		A	B	C	D
(a)	1	2	3	4	(b)	4	3	2	1
(c)	2	4	1	3	(d)	3	1	4	2

71 Match the following

List I (Theories)		List II (Scholars)
A. Field Theory	1.	Sigmund Freud
B Cognitive Dissonance	2.	Edward D'Wilson
C. Sociobiology	3.	Leon Festinger
D. Psychodynamic Approaches	4.	Kurt Lewin

Codes

	A	B	C	D		A	B	C	D
(a)	1	2	3	4	(b)	4	3	2	1
(c)	2	4	1	3	(d)	3	1	4	2

72 Match the following

List I (Theories)	List II (Scholars)
A. Behaviourist	1. Henri Tajfel
B. Gesalt Theorist	2. Skinner
C. European Social Psychologist	3. Shiffrin and Schneider
D. Automaticity and Controllability	4. Koffka

Codes

	A	B	C	D		A	B	C	D
(a)	1	2	3	4	(b)	4	3	2	1
(c)	2	4	1	3	(d)	3	1	4	2

73 Match the following

List I (Theories)		List II (Scholars)
A. Theory of Cognitive Development	1.	Cosmiders
B. Evolutionary Approach to Logical Reasoning	2.	Trivers
C. Casual Attribution	3.	Piaget
D. The Theory of Reciprocal Altruism	4.	Fritz Heider

Codes

	A	B	C	D		A	B	C	D
(a)	1	2	3	4	(b)	4	3	2	1
(c)	2	4	1	3	(d)	3	1	4	2

74 Match the following

List I (Concept)	List II (Scholars)
A. Serious (High Cost) Helping	1. Smithson, Amato and Pearce
B. Indirect Fitness	2. Hamilton
C. Meta Analysis	3. Carlson, Charlin and Miller
D. Affect-as-Information Model	4. Schwarz

Codes

	A	B	C	D		A	B	C	D
(a)	1	2	3	4	(b)	4	3	2	1
(c)	2	4	1	3	(d)	3	1	4	2

75 Match the following

List I (Concept)		List II (Scholars)
A Empathy	1.	Ieisen, Horn and Rosenhan
B. Just-World Belief	2.	Estrada Hollenbeck and Heatherton
C. Interpersonal Guilt	3.	Lerner
D. Happy Mood and Charity	4.	Davis

Codes

	A	B	C	D		A	B	C	D
(a)	1	2	3	4	(b)	4	3	2	1
(c)	2	4	1	3	(d)	3	1	4	2

76 Match the following

List I (Models)	List II (Scholars)
A. Covariation Model	1. Weiner
B. Emotional Liability	2. Kelly
C. Attributional Theory	3. Schachter
D. Social Representation Theory	4. Moscovici

Codes

	A	B	C	D		A	B	C	D
(a)	2	3	1	4	(b)	3	1	2	4
(c)	2	4	1	3	(d)	3	4	2	1

77 Match the following

List I	List II
A. Black-sheep effect	1. Highly rated in group member
B. Bystander effect	2. Less likely occurrence of helping behaviour
C. Physical proximity effect	3. Affects interpersonal attraction in couple
D. Primacy effect	4. Information plays a powerful role

Codes

	A	B	C	D
(a)	1	2	3	4
(b)	2	1	3	4
(c)	4	2	3	1
(d)	3	1	2	4

78 Match the following

List I (Scholars)	List II (Theories)
A. Abraham Tesser	1. Cognitive dissonance theory
B. Festinger	2. Self-evaluation maintenance theory
C. Baron	3. Distraction conflict theory
D. Steele	4. Self-affirmation theory

Codes

	A	B	C	D		A	B	C	D
(a)	1	2	3	4	(b)	2	1	3	4
(c)	4	2	3	1	(d)	3	1	2	4

79 Match the following

List I (Scholars)	List II (Theories)
A. Solomon Asch	1. Confirm to authority
B. Morton Deutsch	2. Conflict resolution
C. Festinger	3. Cognitive dissonance
D. Milgram	4. Line experiment

Codes

	A	B	C	D
(a)	4	2	3	1
(b)	4	3	2	1
(c)	3	4	1	2
(d)	3	1	4	2

Directions (Q. Nos. 80-94) *In the questions given below are two statements labelled as Assertion (A) and Reason (R). In the context of the two statements, which one of the following is correct?*

Codes

(a) Both A and R are true and R is the correct explanation of A
(b) Both A and R are true, but R is not the correct explanation of A
(c) A is true, but R is false
(c) A is false, but R is true

80 **Assertion** (A) An individual's construal of the social situation is important.

Reason (R) Different subjective construals of the situation may lead individuals to respond differently in the same situation.

81 **Assertion** (A) Social psychologist prefer scientific experiment over folk wisdom.

Reason (R) Folk wisdom doesn't provide mechanisms allowing one to choose between competing explanations for social behaviours.

82 **Assertion** (A) Social psychologist consider individual's subjective construal of the situation.

Reason (R) Kurt Lewin applied Gestalt principles to social perception.

83 **Assertion** (A) Choosing to go through an unpleasant will lead us to value the outcome of the experience.

Reason (R) We will protect our self-esteem by attempting to justify past behaviour.

84 **Assertion** (A) Research on obedience found that the proximity of the victim to the patient plays a significant role.

Reason (R) The victim was seen as a patient.

85 **Assertion** (A) The loss of self-awareness and evaluation apprehension is called deindividuation.

Reason (R) Deindividuation shows that a group experience that diminishes self-conscious also tend to disconnect their behaviour from their attitudes.

86 **Assertion** (A) People should help those, who have helped them.

Reason (R) Positive responses to favourable treatment, but negative responses to unfavourable treatment.

87 **Assertion** (A) Undeserved suffering of others threatens belief in a just world and motivates attempts.

Reason (R) Generalised expectancy that people get what they deserve.

88 **Assertion** (A) A heuristic is a well-used no-optimal rule of thumb used to arrive at a judgement that is effective in many, but not all cases.

Reason (R) Stereotypes are often said to function as heuristics.

89 **Assertion** (A) The social situation comprises all influences on behaviour that are external to the individual.

Reason (R) A situational factor might be the presence of other people, real or imagined that influences behaviour.

90 **Assertion** (A) The self is concerned with maintaining positive self-feelings, thoughts and evaluations.

Reason (R) The self demands that we preserve what we have, especially that, which makes us feel good about ourselves.

91 **Assertion** (A) A change in one component of an attitude structure might very well lead to changes in the others.

Reason (R) An attitude structure is dynamic with each component influencing the others.

92 **Assertion** (A) The phenomenon of a message having more impact on attitude change after a long delay than, when it is first heard is known as the sleeper effect.

Reason (R) There is no enough time that the counting cue and the message become associated and people remember, which source said what during sleeping effect.

93 **Assertion** (A) Behaviour motivated by the desire to relieve a victim's suffering is called altruism. Other times we help because we hope to gain something from it for ourselves.

Reason (R) The distinction between altruism and helping behaviour lies in the motivation for performing the behaviour, not the outcome.

94 Assertion (A) In classical conditioning, the individual's behaviour is strengthened or weakened by means of reward or punishment.

Reason (R) Classical conditioning occurs by repeatedly pairing the stimulus with a stimulus that does have the power to evoke the response.

Directions (Q. Nos. 95-99) *Read the passage given below and answer the following questions.*

Elements of the prosocial personality include social responsibility, empathy and internal locus of control, whereas social responsibility and internal locus of control facilitate bystanders feelings of obligation to help in emergency situations, high empathy contributes to a better understanding of the needs of other persons (Davis, 1994).

With respect to social responsibility as an element of the prosocial personality, the evidence is quite strong. Oliner and Oliner (1988) interviewed rescuers of Jews in Nazi Europe and found that, compared to a control group of people who did not help Jews,the rescuers were characterised by a higher degree of social responsibility.This result was replicated in a study of first aiders, who intervened on behalf of injured traffic-accident victims.

Another characteristic of the prosocial personality is the just-world belief (Lerner, 1980), which refers to the generalised expectancy that people get what they deserve. Undeserved suffering of others is a strong threat to the belief in a just world.

Therefore, behavioural and cognitive strategies are employed to restore the belief in a just world, these include either reducing the victims suffering by helping them or devaluing the victims. Both strategies are efficient, when they reaffirm the belief in a just world by eliminating the impression of undeserved suffering.

From a theoretical viewpoint, the relation between belief in a just world and prosocial behaviour depends on the expected effectiveness of prosocial behaviour.

A summary of empirical research indicates that dispositional empathy and prosocial behaviour are positively correlated (Davis, 1994, Eisenberg and Fabes, 1991). Dispositional empathy is understood as a vicarious emotion, which is elicited by perceiving another in need. In the studies of Bierhoff et al. (1991) and Oliner and Oliner (1988) helpers expressed higher empathy than non-helpers.

Davis (1983) defined empathy as a set of separate, but overlapping constructs. He developed the interpersonal reactivity index as a multidimensional empathy questionnaire.

95 Elements of the prosocial personality include

(a) social responsibility
(b) empathy
(c) internal lower of control
(d) All of these

96 In which of the following year Oliner and Oliner interviewed rescuers of Jews?

(a)1989 (b)1988
(c) 1998 (d) 2000

97 The relation between belief in a just world depends on

(a) effectiveness of prosocial behaviour
(b) social responsibility
(c) Both a and b
(d) None of the above

98 The behavioural and cognitive strategies are employed to

(a) restore the belief in a just world
(b) reducing the victims suffering
(c) Both a and b
(d) None of the above

99 Who among the following defined empathy as set of separate, but overlapping construct?

(a) Davis (b) Oliver
(c) lerner (d) Oliner

PREVIOUS YEARS' QUESTIONS

July 2018

1 Match List I with List II and select the correct answer by choosing from codes given below

List I (Term)	List II (Description)
A. Conformity	1. Rules indicating how individuals are expected to behave in a specific situation
B. Compliance	2. Social influence involving direct request from other
C. Social norms	3. Social influence wherein individuals change their attitude to go along with existing norms
D. Intense indoctorinisation	4. Process in which members of extreme group accept the beliefs and rules in unquestioning way

Codes

	A	B	C	D		A	B	C	D
(a)	1	2	3	4	(b)	2	3	4	1
(c)	3	4	1	2	(d)	3	4	2	1

November 2017

2 Today social psychology studies

1. Social Cognition
2. Ethnic Diversity
3. Multiculturalism

Codes

(a) 1 and 2 (b) 1 and 3
(c) 2 and 3 (d) All of these

3 Read each of the following two statements Assertion (A) and Reason (R) and indicate your answer using codes given below

Assertion (A) People perform in accordance to the social positions they hold.

Reason (R) People select relevant information from tremendous amount of social information.

Codes

(a) Both A and R are true and R is the correct explanation of A
(b) Both A and R are true , but R is not the correct explanation of A
(c) A is true, but R is false
(d) A is false, but R is true

January 2017

4 Besides psychology which behavioural science contributed in the development of organisational psychology as a field of study?

1. Sociology
2. Anthropology
3. Political Science
4. Social work

Codes

(a) 1 and 2 (b) 1, 2 and 4 (c) 2, 3 and 4 (d) 1, 2 and 3

5 The different schemas had an impact on social cognitive which refer to

1. Persons 2. Groups 3. Roles 4. Events

Codes

(a) 1, 2 and 3 (b) 2, 3 and 4
(c) 1, 2 and 4 (d) 1, 3 and 4

6 Match List I with List II and select the correct answer by choosing from the codes given below.

List I (Concept)	List II (Process)
A. Cohesiveness and conformity	1. Social influence based on individual's desire to be liked by others
B. Norms and social influence	2. Social influence based on individual's desire to be correct to possess the accurate perceptions of the social world
C. Individuation	3. The need to be distinguishable from others in some respect
D. Information and social influence	4. Accepting influence of those we like

Codes

	A	B	C	D		A	B	C	D
(a)	4	3	2	1	(b)	3	4	2	1
(c)	2	3	1	4	(d)	4	1	3	2

7 Read each of the following two statements Assertion (A) and Reason (R) and indicate your answer using codes given below

Assertion (A) According to Vygotsky, human thinking and reasoning are products of social activity.

Reason (R) Every cognitive process appears first on social plane and then on psychological plane after internalisation.

Codes

(a) Both A and R are true and R is the correct explanation of A
(b) Both A and R are true, but R is not the correct explanation of A
(c) A is true, but R is false
(d) A is false, but R is true

July 2016

8 Evolutionary social psychology research seeks to investigate

(a) changes in human behaviour.
(b) seeks to investigate the potential role of genetic factors on social behaviour.

(c) interrelationships between people of two groups of different social environment.
(d) focuses on individual's behaviour.

December 2014

9 Social psychology focuses on......and their........ .
(a) individuals; feelings
(b) groups; experiences
(c) people, feelings
(d) people; thoughts

June 2014

10 Children of affluent and educated parents tend to score higher on tests of ability than children of parents living in poverty and who are not well educated. This relationship between socio-economic status and scores on ability tests is because of

1. genetic differences in ability between different social classes.
2. differences in the adequacy of the biological and environmental factors in nutrition and healthcasre.
3. differences in the cultural and learning experiences provided for children from different social classes.

Codes
(a) 1 and 3 (b) 2 and 3
(c) 1 and ? (d) All of these

ANSWERS

Exam Based Questions

1	(c)	2	(d)	3	(c)	4	(b)	5	(a)	6	(a)	7	(d)	8	(b)	9	(c)	10	(d)
11	(d)	12	(b)	13	(a)	14	(b)	15	(a)	16	(b)	17	(c)	18	(b)	19	(d)	20	(b)
21	(d)	22	(b)	23	(b)	24	(b)	25	(d)	26	(c)	27	(b)	28	(d)	29	(b)	30	(a)
31	(a)	32	(c)	33	(c)	34	(b)	35	(d)	36	(a)	37	(a)	38	(b)	39	(d)	40	(d)
41	(c)	42	(b)	43	(c)	44	(d)	45	(a)	46	(d)	47	(c)	48	(b)	49	(c)	50	(d)
51	(a)	52	(c)	53	(a)	54	(a)	55	(c)	56	(a)	57	(a)	58	(c)	59	(a)	60	(c)
61	(b)	62	(a)	63	(b)	64	(a)	65	(d)	66	(c)	67	(a)	68	(c)	69	(b)	70	(a)
71	(b)	72	(c)	73	(d)	74	(a)	75	(b)	76	(a)	77	(a)	78	(b)	79	(a)	80	(a)
81	(a)	82	(a)	83	(a)	84	(c)	85	(b)	86	(b)	87	(a)	88	(b)	89	(a)	90	(b)
91	(a)	92	(c)	93	(a)	94	(d)	95	(d)	96	(a)	97	(a)	98	(c)	99	(a)		

Previous Years' Questions

1	(c)	2	(d)	3	(b)	4	(d)	5	(d)	6	(d)	7	(a)	8	(b)	9	(d)	10	(d)

Group and Social Influence

Group and Social influence affects the emotions, opinions and behaviours of an individual. Social influence is incredibly broad and covers conformity, peer pressure, persuasion, compliance, obedience, reactance etc. aggression, group dynamics and leadership style are prominent aspect of social influence.

Social Influence

Social influence can be defined as a process by which individuals make real changes to their feelings and behaviours as a result of interaction with others who are perceived to be similar, desirable or expert. People adjust their beliefs with respect to others to whom they feel similar in accordance with psychological principles such as balance. Individuals are also influenced by the majority when a large portion of an individual's referent social group holds a particular attitude, it is likely that the individual will also adopt it. Individuals may also change an opinion under the influence of another who is perceived be an expert in the matter at hand.

Theories Related with Social Influence

There are two main theories associated with social influence, which are as follows

Social Facilitation Theory

It is a theory which states that a person's performance depends a lot on the presence of somebody else. Depending on this situation, the task he or she is given whether simple or complex, will decide if this performance becomes better or worse in the presence of people. In other words it can be understood as the tendency of people to perform better when they are being watched or when they are competing with others doing the same task.

For example In a class when a student is asked to solve an easy problem on the board in front of other students and teacher, the student stays confident about himself and it doesn't require much of attention, focus or time to solve the problem easily and perform better. And when the same student is asked a complex problem to solve on

In this Chapter

- *Social Influence*
- *Aggression*
- *Group Dynamics*
- *Leadership Style and Effectiveness*
- *Theories of Intergroup Relations*

the board in front of all, he probably gets scared to get up and go towards the board , thinking he might make a mistake. However, when he reaches the board two things would bother him.

(i) How to solve this complex question?
(ii) What will happen if I am unable to solve it? What impression would it make on the teachers and the students? What if they laugh at my stupidity?

This makes him nervous, giving less attention to the main area of concern the problem. Thus, he performs poorly and social facilitation theory applies here.

Social Loafing Theory

It states that a person in a group of people working on the same project, may not strive to achieve the expected goal. His contributions might be lesser than the others resulting in less effective output. This can be one big reason behind 'not a very good performance' from a group as compared to their individual capabilities. Now the question arises why would people not give in their 100% in a group?

There may be following reasons behind it like

- People think that their contributions might not really matter in a group of brilliantly working people, so they either pretend to do work or just don't get into anything, quietly taking credits for group performances . But they forget that a group was made to give better performances with a joint effort of every one.
- People just take advantage of others in a group, not helping them out with work, instead leisurely spend their time on works of their interest.

For example Working on a project or an assignment in a group of four or five in school, a student may very well remember that there were one or two such people who would not work at all. They would just sit and watch while the others exhausted their brains on the project.

Similarly, in case of rope pulling that was conducted to test social loafing, it was found out that few exerted less effort along with people as compared to that when they pulled individually. Social loafing follows the 'free rider theory', resulting in the sucker effect. It mainly happens due to people not being able to evaluate and calculate their contributions towards a given work and hence they don't contribute.

Social influence is caused by various factors like conformity, compliance, obedience, peer pressure, persuasion, social power and reactance etc. *The same have been described in brief below*

Conformity

Conformity is a kind of social influence, which involves a change in belief or behaviour in order to fit in or within a group. This change is in response to real or imagined group pressure. Conformity is also known as majority influence or group pressure. Conformity may take different forms *e.g.* bullying, persuasion, leasing, criticism etc. *To understand conformity in detail, solomon Asch-Conformity is explained below*

Solomon Aschs-Conformity Experiment

Solomon Asch conducted an experiment to investigate the extent to which social pressure from a majority group could affect a person to conform. In 1951, Solomon Asch conducted his first conformity laboratory experiments at Swarthmore College, laying the foundation for his remaining conformity studies.

The experimental procedur and its findings are discuss below

Experiment

Group of eight male college students participated in a simple 'perceptual' task.

In reality, all but one of the participants was confederate and the true focus of the study was about how the remaining participant would react to the confederate's behaviour.
The confederate knew the true aim of the experiment, but was introduced to the subject as other participants. Each student viewed a card with a line on it, followed by another with three lines labelled A, B, and C (see accompanying figure). One of these lines was the same as that on the first card and the other two lines were clearly longer or shorter (*i.e.* a near 100% rate of correct responding was expected). Each participant was then asked to say aloud which line matched the length of that on the first card. Before the experiment, all actors were given detailed instructions on how they should respond to each trial (card presentation). They would always unanimously nominate one comparator, but on certain trials they would give the correct response and on others, an incorrect response. The group was seated such that the real participant always responded last.

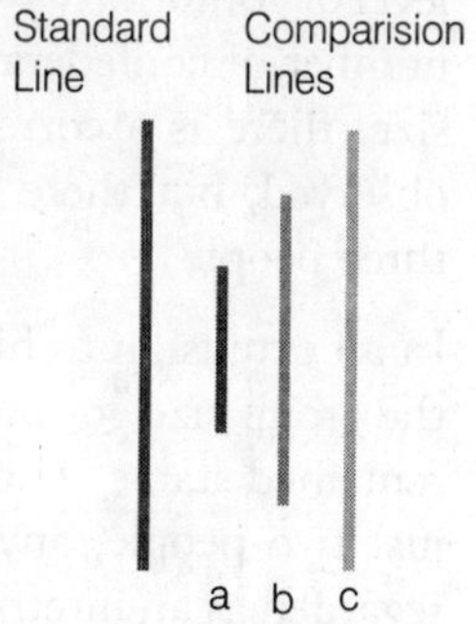

Standard Line
Comparision Lines
a b c

Results

Asch found that one-third of real participants gave the same wrong answer as the confederates at least half the time. Forty per cent gave some wrong answer and only one-fourth gave correct answers in defiance of the pressure to conform to the wrong answers provided by the group.

Asch found that those that answered incorrectly, in conformance with the group, believed that the answers given by the confederates was correct, some thought that they were suffering a lapse in perception for originally thinking an answer that differed from the group, while others admitted that they knew that they had the correct answer, but conformed to the incorrect answer because they did't want to break from the majority.

The Asch experiments have been repeated many times over the years with students and non-students, old and young and in groups of different sizes and different settings. The results are consistently the same with one-third to one-half of the participants making a judgement contrary to fact, yet in conformity with the group, demonstrating the strong power of social influences.

Factors that Affect Conformity

Two main factors that affect the conformity are as follow

Moderators of Normative Influence

There has been numerous replications and extensions of the classic experiments by Sherif and Asch. These studies have confirmed the robust nature of informational and normative social influences, but also identified a number of different factors that either increase or decrease the level of social influence in any given situation. The *first* of these is group cohesiveness, which is the degree to which a group is perceived to have a strong sense of inter connectedness.

A *second* factor that affects the level of conformity is group size. The level of conformity that is observed appear to be proportional to the number of confederates; but only up to a point. As groups grow in size, there is a corresponding increase in the level of conformity observed, but there is a levelling off once the group size reaches three people.

In an extension to his classic study, Asch (1952) found that when the group size got progressively bigger than three, then conformity remained stable at about 35%. The idea here is that when there are just two people, any disagreement between participants could be regarded as an interpersonal issue (*i.e.* their group status would not be noticeable).

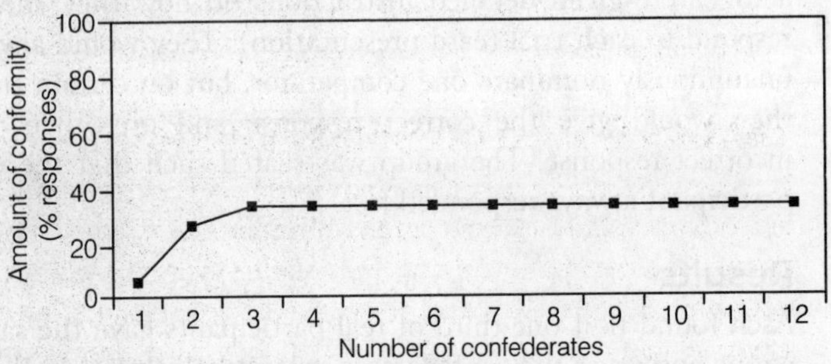

Illustration of the relationship between group size and conformity

A third factor that affects conformity is social **support**. This is different from group cohesiveness and group size because instead of increasing the level of conformity, social support decreases the level of conformity. In a further extension to Asch's original study, if just one confederate agreed with the participant (*i.e.* gave the correct answer rather than the scripted incorrect answer given by the confederate majority), then conformity dropped dramatically.

Moderators of Informational Influence

There are two factors that can affect informational influence. The *first* is located within the person, perceived self-confidence. The less self-confident participants are the more likely it is that they will be susceptible to informational influence. This of course, make sense. If you are generally unsure about your own attitudes and abilities, then it is more likely that you will look to others to guide your judgements in general (*i.e.* informational influence).

The *second* factor affecting informational influence is located with in the situation. As task difficulty increases, the extent of informational influence will also increase, again, this makes sense.

Finally, another important situational factor influencing the level of observed conformity is cultural norms. Although, it was surprising that Asch's studies led to such a high level of conformity in individualist cultures like the United States, when replicated in more collectivist cultures (like Japan), the level of conformity was substantially higher.

Compliance

Compliance can be defined as "behaviour in accordance with group pressures without the values and norms of group as our own". In a two persons group, it ensures that availability of reward, but at the same time it strengthens the power of the dominant person and reaffirms the dependence of the weaker one.

Robert Cialdini has concluded that although techniques for gaining compliance may have different forms, they all rest on six basic principles *i.e.* friendship/liking, commitment/ consistency, scarcity, reciprocity, social validation and authority.

Tactics Based on Friendship/Liking

In general, we are more willing to comply with requests from friends or from people than from strangers or people whom we don't like. Therefore, several techniques are used for increasing compliance through liking for making impression on others. **Integration** is such a technique for gaining compliance, in which requests include target person to like them, then attempt to change their behaviour in some desired manner.

Integration includes a number manoeuvers, through which lower status (dependent/weaker) person makes himself more attractive in the eyes of higher status (powerful) person.

Integration is a set of behaviours for obtaining the support or approval of others. Such techniques include giving compliments, behaving in a pleasing manner and agreeing with or conforming to the expressed opinions of others.

Tactics Based on Commitment/Consistency

When, we are committed to ourselves to a position/action, we are not willing to comply with requests for behaviours that are consistent with that position.

- **Foot-in-the Door Technique** This is the principle, where the small requests are granted then to move on to the requests of higher level. It is a procedure for gaining compliance in which requesters begin with a small request and then, when this is granted, escalate to a larger one (the one, they actually desired all along). Once, the target person says yes to the small request, because doing so would be some what inconsistent with the first response.

  The result of many studies indicate the foot in the door technique really works and that its effectiveness stems, at least in part from the operation of consistency principle. The first of these conclusion that the foot in the door really works in supported in a fairly dramatic way by a famous study conducted by Freedman and Fraser.
- **Low Ball Procedure** This is a technique for gaining compliance in which an offer or deal is changed to make it less attractive to the target person after this person has accepted it.
- **Bait and Switch Tactic** This is a technique for gaining compliance in which items offered for sale are available or of very low quality. This leads customers to buy a more expensive item that is available.

Tactics Based on Reciprocity

One of the most powerful variables influencing your attraction towards other person is the way that person feels about you. Friendship are strengthened by signs of mutual respect, interest and attraction. A one way relationship involving lack of reciprocal attraction is not likely to continue.

- **Door-in-Face Technique** It is a procedure for gaining compliance in which requesters begin with a larger request and then when this is refused, retreat to a smaller one (the one they actually desired all along).

  Several studies indicate that it can be quite effective. *For example* In an initial study, Cialdini and his collegues stopped college students on the street and represented them with a gigantic request, would they agree to serving as non-paid counsellors for juvenile delinquents two hours a week for two years period?
- **That is not all Technique** It is a technique for gaining compliance in which a requester offers additional benefits to target persons before they have decided whether to comply with or reject specific requests.

  Here, an initial request is followed before the target person can make up her or his mind to say yes or no, by something that sweetens the deal a small extra incentive from the person using the tactic is offered.
- **Reciprocity Principle** When people feel that they are in a relationship with another person no matter how trivial, they often feel that they owl this person some consideration simply because the relationship exists. *For example* Friends help friends when they need assistance and person who perceive themselves as similar in some manner may feel that they should help one another when the need arises.
- **Foot-in-the-Mouth Tactic** This is a procedure for gaining compliance in which the requester establishes some kind of relationship, no matter how trivial, with the target person, thereby increasing this person's feeling of obligation to comply. Briefly, this involves a requesters establishing some kind of relationship, no matter how trivial, with the target person and so increasing the target's feelings of an obligation to comply with reasonable requests.

Tactics Based on Social Validation

It is a psychological phenomenon where one or more passive individuals follow or conform to the actions of others within a group. In a psychological context, one or more people set an example of behaviour and their experience leads a second group of one or more people to follow suit. We often comply with requests that we view as being consistent with what people similar to ourselves are doing (or thinking). This technique is closely related to conformity and especially to informational social influence.

Tactics Based on Authority Individuals are more likelier to comply if an authority endorses the product. The authority can be an actual authority figure such as a medical doctor endorsing a vitamin supplement or simply a celebrity.

Tactics Based on Scarcity

It's a general rule of life that things that are scarce, rare or difficult to possess are viewed as being more valuable than those that are easy to obtain. Thus, we are often willing to expend more comfort or go to greater expense to obtain items or outcomes that are scarce than to obtain ones that are common. This principle too serves as the basis for several techniques for gaining compliance. One of the most intriguing of these is playing hard to get.

Playing hard to get is an effort to increase compliance by suggesting that a person or object is scarce and hard to obtain.

Other Tactics for Gaining Compliance

While many techniques for inducting compliance seem to rest on the basic principles described by Cialdini, other seems to involve other mechanisms. One of the most interesting of these involves an action in which most of us engage everyday complaining, it involves expressions of discontent or dissatisfaction with oneself or some aspect of the external world and often such statements are simple expressions of personal states or comments on the external world sometimes, however, complaining is used as a tactic of social influence.

If our tendency to ignore many requests from strangers is indeed due to such mindlessness, then anything that shocks people out of this mindless state and gets them to think about a request might increase compliance with it. This reasoning is the basis for the pique technique, a procedure for increasing compliance based on piquing target person's interest.

Obedience

Obedience is a form of social influence where an individual acts in response to a direct order another individual, who is usually an authoritative figure. It is assumed that without such an order the person would not have action this way.

It differ's from compliance (which involves changing your behaviour at the request of another person) and conformity (which involves altering your behaviour in order to go along with rest of group).

Milgram's Study of Obedience

Work on obedience was inspired by the atrocities observed in the World War Second. Stanley Milgram was interested in what made Nazi guards go along with orders to commit atrocities against the Jews.

Milgram did not think that a whole nation of people could be inherently evil, but rather that there might be conditions under which anyone might abandon their own sense of his classic studies on obedience. These studies are today considered unethical, but nonetheless are highly informative and were highly influential is subsequent theoretical and empirical work on social influence.

Explaining Obedience

Milgram argued that three factors are at work in contexts where obedience is hight *First*, there is a general cultural norm to obey authority. People are generally rewarded for obeying authority operant conditioning explanations for attitude formation. People expect authority figures to be trustworthy and legitimate. *Second*, in his experiment the requests to obey increasingly immoral act were gradual. People were led into shocking at potentially lethal levels over a relatively long time, so that before they knew it, they were administering apparently lethal schocks. *Third*, Milgram argued that there is a shift in agency, so that people no longer regard themselves as personally responsible, but attribute responsibility (agency) to others.

Peer Pressure

Peers are people who are part of the same social group, so the term 'peer pressure' means the influence that peers can have on each other. Although peer pressure is not always necessarily negative, yet pressure implies that the process influences people to do things that may be resistant to do *i.e.* applying restriction one's choice of action. The term 'pressure peer' is used when people are talking about behaviours that are not considered socially acceptable or desirable such as experimentation with alcohol or drug use.

Adolescents Main Target of Peer Pressure

Peer pressure is usually applied to younger people, specially teenagers. Adolescents are particularly vulnerable to peer pressure because they are at a stage of development when they just begin to differentiate themselves from their parent's influence, but have yet not established their own values or understanding about human relationships or the consequences of their behaviour. They are also typically striving for social acceptance at this stage and may be willing to engage in activities that are against their welfare such as smoking etc. However, adults can also be vulnerable to peer pressure. Many adults drink too much because according to them, it is the only way they can have a social life. So being aware of and carefully choosing the influence of peers that will lead to healthy and happy experiences in a lifelong process.

Role of Peers

Peers play a prominent role in the social and emotional development of children and adolescents. Their influence begins at an early age and increases through the teenage years. It is natural, healthy and important for children to have and rely on friends as they grow up and mature. Peers can be positive and supportive. They can help each other develop new skills or stimulate interest in books, music or extracurricular activities. However, peers can also have a negative influence. They can encourage each other to skip classes, steal, cheat, use drugs or alcohol, share inappropriate material online or become involved in other risky behaviours. The peer pressure can take place in person or on social media.

Persuasion

An element of social influence, persuasion can be defined as "a symbolic process in which communicators try to convince other people to change their attitudes or behaviours regarding an issue through the transmission of a message in an atmosphere of free choice" **Perloff**.

Persuasion is a powerful force and has a major influence on society as a whole. Politics, legal decisions, mass media, news and advertising are all influenced by the power of persuasion which influence people in turn.

Key Elements of Persuasion

The key elements of persuasion are as follows

- Persuasion is symbolic, utilising words, images and sound etc.
- It involves a deliberate attempt to influence others.
- Self persuasion is a key, people are not coerced, they are instead free to choose.
- Methods of transmitting persuasive messages can occur in a variety of ways including verbally and non-verbally through television, radio, internet or face to face communication.

Principles of Persuasion

Robert Cialdini, Professor Emeritus at Arizona State University, he has formulated different principles in the area of persuasion. *His six principles have been used in business schools as well as in boardrooms.*

(i) The first principle is **reciprocity**, where one gives and gets back. This feeling, that something is owed, can be very powerful.

(ii) The second principle of **commitment** and **consistency** is about having consistency in beliefs and behaviours.

(iii) The third principle is **social proof**, when people tend to make choices that appear popular.

(iv) The fourth principle is about **authority** where having a credible expert is considered to be useful.

(v) The fifth principle is **liability**, it occurs when a person is regarded as a trusted friend.

(vi) The sixth and last principle is **scarcity**, it is important because people fear that an item may be in short supply.

Social Power

Social power is the potential for social influence. The available tools one has to exert influence over another can lead to a change in that person. Social power is the ability of one person or group to get others to do his or her will. It has long been of interest to social psychologists. Perhaps this is because so much of human interaction involves the change or attempt to change the beliefs, attitudes or behaviours of another.

The person or group *i.e.* the source of influence is commonly known as the influencing agent whereas object of the attempted or successful influence attempt is commonly known as the target of the influence. Thus, influencing agents have social power which acts as the means to influence the targets.

Types of Social Power

Social power can be categorised into following types

- **Informational Social Power** Informational social power is the ability to rationally persuade someone.
- **Social Power of Expertise** Social power of expertise is similar to informational power except that in expertise, arguments are not necessary because the target trusts the influencing agent.
- **Referent Social Power** The referent type of social power is based on the target's identifying and liking the influencing agent and because of this, the target wants to comply with his or her requests.
- **Coercive Social Power** Coercive social power involves threat of punishment. These can be things such as monetary fines (impersonal) or simply personal disapproval.

- **Social Power of Reward** Social power of reward stems from the ability of the influencing agent to grant some kind of reward, either impersonal or personal.
- **Legitimate Social Power** Based on what general society typically expects of us, legitimate social power includes. First, the formal legitimate (or position) norm, which is the right to ask for something based simply on position or job title.

Secondly, the reciprocity norm, whereby someone does something for you, you owe him or her the favour in return.

Thirdly, the equity form , the idea that one is expected to help others receive what they deserve.

And **fourthly**, the social responsibility (or dependence), whereby people are obligated to help those who depend on them.

The type of social power used in an influence attempt, often depends on a person's motivations. Sometimes people are consciously aware of their motivations and sometimes they are not. The clever influencing agents often choose the kind of influence they use based on considerations of potential effectiveness and other factors.

Reactance

American psychologist **Jack Brehm** first introduced Reactance theory in 1966. This theory states that when people are restricted in some way, they feel a strong need to resist and fight back to gain their freedom. It is a very common notion that people who are told not to do something often feel an urge to do the very thing they are denied.

Freedom and Reactance Theory The basis of Jack Brehm's Reactance theory is founded on the removal of freedom from choices. The more important the person's freedom is perceived to be, the larger is the reaction to the removal of it. In other words, if the freedom being threatened, is perceived very important to the individual, they will react on a larger scale than if the freedom is seen as not so important. It implies that the stronger is the feeling of freedom, the larger will be the resistance to the limitations. When several freedoms are threatened, the reaction is even greater.

Aggression

In psychology, the term aggression refers to a range of behaviours that can result in both physical and psychological harm to yourself, others or objects in the environment. This type of behaviour centers on harming another person either physically or mentally. It can be a sign of an underlying mental health disorder, a substance use disorder or a medical disorder.

Social psychologists define aggression as behaviour *i.e.* intended to harm another individual who does not wish to be harmed **(Baron and Richardson)**.

Because it involves the perception of intent, what looks like aggression from one point of view may not look that way from another and the same harmful behaviour may or may not be considered aggressive depending on its intent. Intentional harm is, however, perceived as worse than unintentional harm, even when the harms are identical.

Forms of Aggression

Aggression can take a variety of forms, including

- Physical
- Emotional
- Verbal
- Mental

While we often think of aggression as purely in physical forms such as hitting or pushing, psychological aggression can also be very dangerous, intimidating or verbally berating another person *e.g.* are examples of verbal, mental and emotional aggression.

Purposes of Aggression

Aggression can serve a number of different purposes, including

- To express anger or hostility
- To intimidate or threaten
- To express possession
- A reaction to pain
- To assert dominance
- To achieve a goal
- A response to fear
- To compete with others

Types of Aggression

Psychologists distinguish between two different types of aggression

(i) **Impulsive Aggression** Also known as affective aggression, impulsive aggression is characterised by strong emotions, usually anger. This form of aggression is not planned and often takes place in the heat of the moment.

When another car cuts you off in traffic and you begin yelling and berating the other driver, you're experiencing impulsive aggression. Research suggests that impulsive aggression, especially when it's caused by anger, triggers the acute threat response system in the brain involving the amygdala, hypothalamus and Periaqueductal Gray.

(ii) **Instrumental Aggression** Also known as *predatory aggression*, instrumental aggression is marked by behaviours that are intended to achieve a larger goal. Instrumental aggression is often carefully planned and usually exists as a means to an end. Hurting another person in a robbery or car-jacking is an example of this type of aggression. The aggressor's goal is to obtain money or a vehicle and harming another individual is the means to achieve that aim.

Factors that can Influence Aggression

A number of different factors can influence the expression of aggression, including

- **Biological Factors** Men are more likely than women to engage in physical aggression. While researchers have found that women are less likely to engage in physical aggression, they also suggest that women do use non-physical forms, such as verbal aggression, relational aggression and social rejection.
- **Environmental Factors** How you were raised may play a role. People who grow up witnessing more forms of aggression are more likely to believe that such violence and hostility are socially acceptable. Bandura's famous Bobo doll experiment demonstrated that observation can also play a role in how aggression is learned. Children who watched a video clip where an adult model behaved aggressively toward a Bobo doll were more likely to imitate those actions when given the opportunity.
- **Other Factors** Epilepsy, dementia, psychosis, alcohol abuse, drug use and brain injuries or abnormalities can also influence aggression.

Theories of Aggression

There are various theories related to aggression. *Following are the main theories of aggression*

- **Psychodynamic Theory of Aggression** Freud argued that all human beings possess two important instincts, the life **instinct (Eros)** and the death **instinct (Thanatos)**.

  The conflict between life and death instincts results in self destructive tendencies which led to aggressive behaviour.

  The struggle between life and death instincts creates a build up of tension in our unconscious mind. This tension needs to be released either through suitable outlets such as sport (sublimation) or onto others (displacement). Failure to relieve these aggressive impulses may result in an out burst of uncontrollable aggression. This theory of Freud is also known as the *hydraulic model* of aggression.
- **Frustration-Aggression Theory** It is essentially a behaviourist approach that suggests aggression is a learnt response to frustration. Frustration occurs when an individual is exposed to external situations (stimulus) that cause discomfort or anger. *For example* Prolonged queing, overcrowding, failure to achieve a goal etc. Frustration is cumulative. It builds up aggression and violence in an individual until it is discharged through an aggressive act (response). The frustration-aggression hypothesis is sometimes known as *drive reduction theory*. **Dollard** is considered to have propounded this theory.
- **Cognitive Neo-association Theory of Aggression Berkowitz** has proposed that aversive events such as frustrations, provocations, loud noises, uncomfortable temperatures and odours produce negative affect. This negative affect stimulates various thoughts, memories, expressive motor reactions and physiological responses associated with both fight and flight tendencies. In cognitive neo-association theory, aggressive thoughts, emotions and behavioural tendencies are linked together in memory. This theory not only subsumes the earlier frustration-aggression hypothesis but also provides a casual mechanism for explaining why aversive events increase aggressive inclinations. This model is particularly suited to explain hostile aggression.
- **Social Learning Theory of Aggression** According to social learning theories of **Bandura** and **Mischel** , people responses the same way, as they learned from other complex forms of social behaviour either by direct experience or by observing others. Social learning theory explains the acquision of aggressive behaviours through observational learning processes and provides a useful set of concepts for understating and describing the beliefs and expectations that guide social behaviour.
- **Script Theory of Learning Aggression Huesmann** proposed that when children observe violence in the mass media, they learn aggressive scripts. Scripts define situations and guide behaviour. The person first selects a script to represent the situation and then assumes a role in the script. Once a script has been learnt, it may be retrieved at some later time used as a guide for behaviour.
- **Excitation Transfer Theory of Aggression** Zillman proposed the excitation transfer theory of Aggression. According to him, physiological arousal dissipates slowly. If two arousing events are separated by a short amount of time, arousal from the first event may be misattributed to the second event. If the second event is related to anger, then the additional arousal should make the person even angrier.

- **Social Interaction Theory of Aggression Tedeschi** and **Felson** proposed Social Interaction theory. This theory interprets aggressive behaviour as social influence behaviour *i.e.* an actor uses coercive actions to produce some change in the target's behaviour. Coercive actions can be used by an actor to obtain something of value like information, money, goods, sex, services, safety to exact retributive justice for perceived wrongs or to bring about desired social and self identities like toughness and competence. This theory provides an excellent way to understand recent findings that aggression is often the result of threats to high self-esteem, specially to unwarranted high self-esteem *i.e.* narcissim.
- **General Aggression Model Anderson** and **Bushman** proposed the General Aggression Model (GAM). This model tries to integrate existing mini-theories of aggression into a unified whole. The model is based on the concept of knowledge structures and how they operate to produce behaviour. Knowledge structures, arising out of experience, influence and perception, can become more or less automatic in some cases and are linked to affective states, beliefs and behaviour. In essence, they are used to guide responses to the environment.

  Knowledge structures include perceptual schemata, person schemata and behavioural scripts which define the kinds of behaviours that are appropriate in various situations. The model focuses on characteristics of the person and the situation as they relate to a person's present internal state (affect, arousal and cognition) and ultimately appraisal and decision-making processes lead to either impulsive or thoughtful actions, which in turn cycle back to the next social encounter.

Group Dynamics

Group dynamics is the scientific approach to understand dynamics of groups. It implies an interactive psychological relationship in which members of a group develop a common perception based on feelings and emotions. Group dynamics refer to the changes that take place within the group. It also refers to forces operating within the groups.

Group dynamics is related to the field theory of **Kurt Lewin,** which assumes man's behaviour to be a function of the field existing at the time of the occurrence of behaviour. We can further say that it is the study of group processes, their objective analysis, measurement and the effect of group membership on individual members. Our behaviour is not static. It means that the change of behaviour is through interaction in the group.

Segal proposed the *Theory of Group Dynamics*. According to him, it is a process by which one considers other individuals and a problem in the group at the same time. It not only tends to increase understanding of the problem, but also creates a solution which the individual practises in bringing about emotional balance. It can also be said that group dynamics is influenced by sympathy, suggestion and imitation.

Sympathy enables the members of a group to perceive the psychological state of other members. Suggestion plays a big role in influencing group behaviour. The suggestions put forward by leader of a group are implemented by the members of the group.

The behaviour of the leader of the group is imitated by the members of the group . Thus, the concept of group dynamics is helpful in understanding social changes which involve not only the introduction of an innovation but also in overcoming of resistance.

The Roles of Group Dynamics in Psychology

The roles of group dynamics in psychology are as follows

- The group can influence the thinking of its members. The members are always influenced by the interactions of other members in the group.
- The group can affect the synergy *i.e.*if the group consists of positive thinkers then its output is more.
- Group dynamism can give job satisfaction to the members.
- The group dynamism can bring team spirit among the members.
- The attitudes, perceptions and ideas of members depend on group dynamism.
- If the group works as a cohesive group, the cooperation and convergence can result in maximisation of productivity.

Leadership Style and Effectiveness

A leadership style refers to a leader's characteristic behaviours while directing, motivating, guiding and managing groups of people. Great leaders can inspire political movements and social changes. They can also motivate others to perform, create and innovate. **Kurt Lewin** proposed various leadership styles in 1939.

The brief description of his leadership styles is given below

- **Authoritarian Leadership (Autocratic)** Authoritarian leaders also known as *autocratic leaders*, provide clear picture of what needs to be done, when it should be done and how it should be done. This style of leadership is strongly focussed on both command by the leader and control of the followers. There is also clear division between the leader and the members. Authoritarian leaders make decisions independently with little or no input from the rest of the group. It is best applied to situations where there is little time for group decision-making or where the leader is the most knowledgeable member of the group.
- **Participative Leadership (Democratic)** Participative leaders, also known as *democratic leaders*, offer guidance to a group members and allow input from other group members. They encourage group members to participate but retain the final say in the decision-making process. Group members feel engaged in the process and are more motivated and creative. Democratic leaders tend to make followers feel like they are an important part of the team, which helps foster commitment to the goals of the group. According to **Kurt Lewin's study**, "democratic leadership is the most effective leadership style."
- **Delegative Leadership** Delegative leaders offer little or no guidance to group members and delegate decision-making process in the hand of group members. While this style can be useful in situations involving highly qualified experts, it often leads to poorly defined roles and lack of motivation. Delegative leadership is also termed as Laissez-faire leadership. According to **Kurt Lewin, Laissez-Faire** "leadership tended to result in groups that lacked direction where members blamed each other for mistakes, refused to accept personal responsibility and produced a lack of progress and work."

New Styles of Leadership

In addition to the three main styles identified by Kurt Lewin and his colleages, a few other characteristic patterns have also emerged. *They are as follow*

(i) **The Transformational Leadership Style** It is often identified as the single most effective style. Researcher **Bernard M Bass** elaborated this form of style which was first described during late 1970s. Some of the key characteristics of this style of leadership are the abilities to motivate and inspire followers and to direct positive changes in groups. Transformational leaders tend to be emotionally intelligent, energetic and passionate. They are not only committed to helping the organisation to achieve its goals but also to helping group members to fulfill their potential.

(ii) **The Transactional Leadership Style** This style views the leader-follower relationship as a transaction. By accepting a position as a member of the group, the individual has agreed to obey the leader. In most situations, it involves the employer-employee relationship and the transaction focusses on the follower completing required tasks in exchange for monetary compensation.

One of the main advantages of this leadership style is that it creates clearly defined roles. People know what they are required to do and what they will be receiving in exchange for completing these tasks.

It also allows leaders to offer a great deal of supervision and direction if it is needed. Group members may also be motivated to perform well to receive rewards. One of the biggest drawbacks of this style is that it tends to stifle creativity and out of the box thinking.

(iii) **Situational Leadership Style** It stresses the significant influence of the environment and the situation on leadership. **Hersey and Blanchard's model** is one of the best known situation theories published in 1969. *They sub-divided situational leadership styles into various forms.*

- **The Telling Style** It is characterised by telling people what to do.
- **The Selling Style** It involves leaders convincing followers to buy into their ideas and messages.
- **The Participating Style** It is marked by allowing group members to take a more active role in the decision-making process.
- **The Delegating Style** It involves taking a hands-off approach to leadership allowing group members to make the majority of decisions. It is low both in direction and support.
- **The Directing Style** It involves giving orders and expecting obedience, but offers little in the way of guidance and assistance.
- **The Coaching Style** It means giving lots of orders, but leaders also give lots of support.
- **The Supporting Style** It is an approach that offers plenty of help, but very little direction.

Theories of Intergroup Relations

Social psychology aims to study human experiences and behaviours in social situations within the socio-historical contexts, ways to improve inter-group harmony and prevent inter-group conflicts have had social psychologists interested in intergroup relations whether it is multi-ethnic society, migration, international relations, war or ethnic conflicts, social psychological studies of intergroup relations becomes a socially relevant topic of study. The theories of inter-group relations help understand various explanations for the ways people of one group relate to the other group members. These also tend to explain the reasons for frequently observed conflicts between two groups of people.

These theories have been described in brief below

Minimal Group Experiment

The minimal group experiment is a procedure that researchers use to create new social groups in the laboratory. The goal is to categorise individuals into groups based on minimal criteria that are relatively trivial or arbitrary. The minimal group experiment creates a situation in which individuals are separated into novel ingroups and outgroups and these individuals have no previous experience with these groups. It was first used in the 1960s to examine whether social prejudice and discriminatory behaviour result from the mere categorisation of people into ingroups and outgroups.

Henri Tajfel and his colleagues demonstrated that participants assigned to groups using the minimal group experiment behaved in ways that favoured their new ingroup and disapproved the outgroup. Thus, conflict between groups does not appear to be necessary to produce ingroup favouritism.

Social Identity Theory

Henri Tajfel through his experiments, brought to the fore 'achieving and maintaining a positive social identity' as an important process influencing inter-group relations. Apart of a person's self concept is related to the value and emotions that he/she attaches to being a member of a group or a set of groups. Through the experiments conducted by him and his associates, he could notice that the mere perception or awareness of being categorised into a group (ingroup) and not the other (outgroup) creates a favourable attitude towards members of the ingroup and a negative attitude towards the outgroup members. Recent research has shown that such an intergroup discrimination is more associated with situations where people perceive that the social order or the sociopolitical hierarchy in which their groups are placed is unstable or illegitimate.

Relative Deprivation Theory

Relative deprivation theory proposes that a group's satisfaction about its position in the society is not related to any objective situation. It is rather associated with comparison with other group's position. The group's dissatisfaction is rooted in the its comparison with a 'better off' group especially when the group members feel that they are capable of achieving a better position and that they deserve to do so. **Samuel Stouffer** proposed this theory during World War Second.

Realistic Conflict Theory

Muzafer Sherif, a social psychologist who did some classic experiments to understand intergroup relations, provided some important insights into the phenomenon. According to his research findings, inter-group conflicts occur due to a competition over scarce resources.

The scarce resources that become a ground for competion could be either material (*e.g.* money, physical space) or social (*e.g.* status or power). These conflicts resolved through a super-ordinate goal *i.e.* a goal for which the groups at conflict have to work towards a common or mutually acceptable goal by combining their existing resources.

Balance Theory

Fritz Heider, a social psychologist who developed a theory about situations involving psychological inequality. He named it 'balance theory'. His idea was that everyone wants to maintain psychological stability and therefore, they form relationships : that balance their likes and dislikes.

The P D X Triangle Fritz Heider developed the PDX triangle to examine relationships in a group. Each corner of the triangle represents a different element. P, D and X. P is the person who has to make a decision or choice between two other persons D and X, who are at cross-roads against each other. In this triangular relationship, two types of relationship dynamics take place. The *first* is the unit relationship or how much the different elements of the triangle belong together. Here psychological balance will be directly proportional to the similarities between each element.

The *second* type of relationships are sentiment relationships or how one feels about something. Heider categorises all feelings in one of the two areas; liking or disliking. In most situations, if a positive relationship exists, a positive sentiment relationship will exist as well. Likewise, negative unit relationships and negative sentiment relationships tend to go together.

Similarly, in case of the PDX triangle as a maths equation: On multiplying the three positives, the result will also be positive. If there are two negative relationships with one positive relationship, balanced state of positive relationship will apply here also, as in maths, two negatives on being multiplied make positive.

However, in case of two positive relationship with one negative relationship, there will arise an unbalanced state or a situation that causes psychological discomfort.

Equity Theory

Equity theory is based on the assumption that a person or group desires that justice prevails in the relationship with other person or group. People feel distressed once they perceive injustice in the relationship.

The justice or injustice is based on the comparison of the ratio of outcomes and inputs of one group with the other. Equity theory consists of four propositions. *They are as follow*

(i) **Self-inside** Individuals seek to maximise their outcomes (where outcomes are defined as rewards minus costs).

(ii) **Self-outside** Groups can maximise collective rewards by developing accepted systems for equitably apportioning rewards and costs among members. Systems of equity will evolve within groups and members will attempt to induce other members to accept and adhere to these systems. The only way groups can induce members to equitably behave is by making it more profitable to behave equitably than inequitably. Thus, groups will generally reward members who treat others equitably and generally punish (increase the cost for) members who treat others inequitably.

(iii) **Others inside** When individuals find themselves participating in inequitable relationships, they become distressed. The more inequitable the relationship, the more distress individuals feel. According to equity theory, both the person who gets 'too much' and the person who gets 'too little' feel distressed. The person who gets too much may feel guilt or shame. The person who gets too little may feel angry or humiliated.

(iv) **Other-outside** Individuals who perceive that they are in an inequitable relationship attempt to eliminate their distress by restoring equity. The greater the inequity, the more distress people feel and the more they try to restore equity.

Social Exchange theory

The genesis of social exchange theory goes back to 1958, when American sociologist **George Homans** published an article entitled 'Social Behaviour as Exchange.' Homans devised a framework built on a combination of behaviourism and basic economics. In the immediate years that followed, other studies expanded the parameters of Homans' fundamental concepts.

Social exchange theory is a concept based on the notion that a relationship between two people is created through a process of cost-benefit analysis. In other words, it's a metric designed to determine the effort poured in by an individual in a person-to-person relationship. The measurement of the pluses and minuses of a relationship may produce data that can determine if someone is putting too much effort into a relationship.

The theory is unique in the sense that it doesn't necessarily measure relationships on emotional metrics. Rather, its systematic processes rely on mathematics and logic to determine balance within a relationship. While the theory can be used to measure romantic relationships, it can also be applied to determine the balance within a friendship.

The foundation of social exchange theory rests on several core assumptions regarding human nature and the nature of relationships. The first assumption is that humans tend to seek out rewards and avoid punishments. Another tenet is the assumption that a person begins an interaction to gain maximum profit with minimal cost. A third assumption is that individuals tend to calculate the profit and cost before engaging. Finally, the theory assumes that people know that this 'payoff' will vary from person to person, as well as with the same person over time.

EXAM BASED QUESTIONS

1 Social influence is
(a) being influenced by others.
(b) the influence of society on us.
(c) influencing how society operates and determining how it will operate in the future.
(d) the efforts on the part of one person to alter the behaviour or attitudes of one or more others.

2 If a stranger asks you for money to make a phone call and you give him money. This is considered
(a) conformity
(b) obedience
(c) compliance
(b) obligation

3 The researcher, most closely associated with conformity studies and the line judgement task was
(a) Heider
(b) Newcomb
(c) Sherif
(d) Asch

4 Standing up while hearing our National Anthem at a sporting event is an example of
(a) obedience
(b) compliance
(c) a social norm
(d) an obligation

5 Which of the following is a reason that individuals do not conform?
(a) A desire for personal control
(b) A desire to be liked
(c) A desire for social acceptance
(d) A desire to have many friends

6 Which of the following is a form of social influence?
(a) Conformity
(b) Compliance
(c) Obedience
(d) All of these

7 Politicians rarely shift their positions on major foreign policy matters. This may be an example of how
(a) a 'we-they' feeling has emerged between the major political parties.
(b) public commitment reduces susceptibility to social influence.
(c) high self-esteem is strongly related to non-conformity.
(d) emotional distance from victims leads to disregard for their welfare.

8 Studies of risky shift eventually led to the formulation of
(a) social facilitation theory
(b) group polarisation hypothesis
(c) the reactance effect
(d) the diffusion of responsibility effect

9 According to Zajonc's social facilitation model, what factor facilitates the expression or inhibition of dominant responses?
(a) The task performed
(b) Prior experience
(c) Presence of other
(d) Group identity

10 Studies of conformity indicate that people are more apt to be influenced by others, if they
(a) are concerned about the approval of others
(b) have low needs for certainty and structure
(c) are in temporary rather than established groups
(d) are in very large groups

11 What term is assigned to changing ones behaviour due to the imagined or actual presence of others?
(a) Conformity
(b) Obedience
(c) Minority influence
(b) Social impact

12 Who are more likely to conform according to Hodges and Geyer?
(a) Young people
(b) Individualistic cultures
(c) Older people
(d) Collectivist cultures

13 Conformity occurs when
(a) individuals change their behaviour in order to fit that of other persons in their group
(b) individuals adhere to conventions of a society, such as wearing clothes
(c) individuals influence each other
(d) individuals mimic each other

14 Why is conformity somtimes not a good thing?
(a) It isn't; we should always do it.
(b) It may threaten individuation on our part.
(c) Deviating from the behaviour of the majority is productive.
(d) It is best that people all behave differently.

15 Strength, immediacy and the number of people in the group are determinants of conformity in which theory?
(a) Schema-congruence
(b) Cognitive appraisal theory
(c) Social impact theory
(d) Informational theory

16 According to the early studies of conformity, who seemed to conform more than their counterparts?
(a) Males compared to females
(b) Blacks compared to whites
(c) Females compared to males
(d) Whites compared to blacks

17 Cohesiveness influences conformity in that
(a) we are more likely to yield to influence from larger groups.
(b) we are more likely to yield to influence from people we like.
(c) we are more likely to yield to influence in the absence of social support.
(d) we are more likely to yield to influence in the face of threats.

18 The size of the group that applies pressure to conform is
(a) irrelevant
(b) important through an indefinite group size
(c) unimportant
(d) important through group size 3-4

19 Which of the following social-psychological principles is not illustrated by the conformity literature?
(a) Behaviour shapes attitudes
(b) The fundamental attribution error
(c) The inoculation effect
(d) The power of the situation

20 People who observed alone individual in a group of four misjudge blue stimuli as green were subsequently
(a) more likely to conform to a group's erroneous judgements.
(b) less likely to conform to a group's erroneous judgements.
(c) less likely to value individualism.
(d) more likely to value wisdom.

21 In conducting a study of conformity, the experimenters decide to tape-record the instructions that are to be presented to all subjects. Their decision is most likely an attempt to minimise the effect of
(a) hindsight bias (b) mundane realism
(c) naturalistic fallacy (d) demand characteristics

22 Which of the following is true regarding individual differences in conformity?
(a) Females conform slightly more than males.
(b) French participants conform slightly more than Norwegian participants.
(c) People's self-esteem test scores are excellent predictors of conformity.
(d) American participants conform slightly more than German participants.

23 When a person with little or no authority makes a direct request to another person, the situation involves
(a) Compliance (b) Obedience (c) Coercion (d) Conformity

24 The person who agree to a small request initially is more likely later to comply with a larger demand. This describes the
(a) door-in- the-face-technique
(b) foot-in-the-door-technique
(c) low-ball technique
(d) high-ball technique

25 Someone asks you to bring dip to a party and you agree. Later, the person asks you to also bring popcorn, chips and sodas.The person has used which compliance strategy?
(a) The low-ball technique
(b) The over-commitment strategy
(c) The whole-part technique
(d) The passive obedience method

26 The compliance technique of suggesting that a person or object is scarce is called
(a) low-balling
(b) door- in-the-face
(c) playing hard to get
(d) deadline

27 According to Robert Cialdini, there are how many principle of compliance?
(a) Four (b) Six
(c) Eight (d) Ten

28 'That is not all technique" is related with which principle of compliance?
(a) scarcity
(b) Authority
(c) Reciprocity
(d) Commitment

29 Publicly acting in accord with social pressure while privately disagreeing is called
(a) acceptance (b) compliance
(c) reactance (d) interaction

30 Both acting and believing in accord with social pressure is called
(a) acceptance (b) reactance
(c) compliance (d) interaction

31 Philip hates to attend concerts but goes because his wife wants to. After three years Philip comes to genuinely enjoy concerts. This is an example of
(a) how acceptance can lead to compliance
(b) how compliance can lead to acceptance
(c) the 'boomerang effect'
(d) how psychological reactance can lead to acceptance

32 Which of the following is true regarding the original experiments an obedience by Stanley Milgram?
(a) The experimenter pressured participants to continue the experiment when the 'victim' signalled distress.
(b) The participants were always told that since they were the ones delivering the shocks, they were responsible for the victim's welfare.
(c) Strong shocks were actually given to the participant.
(d) When the experiment was moved from Yale to a rundown office building in a nearby city, the level of obedience was sharply reduced.

33 Which of these factors may have led to obedience in Milgram's experiment?
(a) Conflicting norms and gradual commitment
(b) Normative social influence
(c) Informative social influence
(d) All of the above

34 Which of the following reduced obedience in the Milgram studies to 30%?
(a) Learner complained of pain.
(b) Conducting the experiment away from Yale University.
(c) Pounding on a wall by the victim.
(d) Having to actually place the victim's hand on a shock plate.

35 What percentage of participants fully obeyed the experimenter's command to deliver a 450-volt shock to the learner in the experiment detailed in the text?
(a) 5% (b) 20% (c) 35% (d) 65%

36 How social pressure may lead us to perform immoral acts is best illustrated by studies of
(a) psychological reactance (b) spontaneous self-concept
(c) obedience to authority (d) informational influence

37 Most psychologists believe that aggression is
(a) an innate biological responses to frustration
(b) linked to sexual drive
(c) a learned response
(d) a drive that builds up over time and must be released

38 The frustration-aggression hypothesis
(a) assume that aggression is basic instinct
(b) claims that frustration and aggression are both instinctive
(c) assumes that frustration produces aggression
(d) was developed by social learning theorist

39 We are more likely to experience which of the following during adolescence than at any other time in our lives?
(a) Moodiness (b) Parent-child conflicts
(c) Risky behaviour (d) All of these

40 Which of the following is not a part of group influence?
(a) Social class (b) Social group
(c) Reference group (d) Personality

41 The one common characteristic of all social norms is
(a) they are obeyed more by adults than children
(b) they all work through voluntary compliance
(c) they are obeyed more by children than adults
(d) most people obey them most of the time

42 Widespread disobeying of social norms would lead to
(a) social chaos.
(b) teaching children not to be slavish conformists.
(c) lowering the authoritarianism of the population.
(d) more questioning of the government than other institutions.

43 According to Alicke et al , what is the most frequent reason people give for complaining?
(a) Seeking sympathy (b) Seeking information
(c) Seeking advice (d) Expressing frustration

44 Milgram reported that a participant's tendency to obey the experimenter decreased dramatically
(a) when two other participants defied the experimenter.
(b) when the participant could not hear the responses of the learner.
(c) when the experimenter was a female.
(d) when the experimenter was younger than the participant.

45 A social norm is a
(a) written rule
(b) law that has legal status in court
(c) spoken and unspoken rules concerning how we ought to behave
(d) the same as a taboo

46 Ancient astronomers who observed the stars occasionally saw a star that seemed to move very abruptly. This is probably an example of
(a) the autokinetic effect
(b) the inoculation effect
(c) astronomical impact theory
(d) normative social influence

47 The 'that's not all' technique
(a) is untested
(b) really does work, according to the research
(c) has been shown to be ineffective by research
(d) has generated mixed results in research

48 When an auto dealer offers you an extra option as a 'closer' for a deal, the dealer is using the
(a) doubled compliance technique
(b) covert request technique
(c) integration technique
(d) 'that's not all' technique

49 The training of torturers by the military junta in Greece in the early 1970s illustrates
(a) psychological reactance
(b) the inoculation effect
(c) the foot-in-the-door phenomenon
(d) the role of personality in conformity

50 'Bait and switch' refers to
(a) getting customers to buy a product on sale and then switch it for another product after the sale.
(b) presenting customers with a small request followed by a large request.
(c) presenting customers with a large request followed by a small request.
(d) advertising a good deal, but having only an inferior product available when the customer comes to buy.

51 Psychological reactance theory provides an explanation for
(a) resistance to authority.
(b) obedience to authority.
(c) why compliance is more common than acceptance.
(d) why people are most likely to conform when the group is unanimous.

52 Milly generally likes to go home to visit her family during vacation. How, after her father tells her she must be home during spring vacation, Milly decides to remain at college. We can probably best understand Milly's behaviour in terms of
(a) reaction formation
(b) regression
(c) psychological reactance
(d) self-serving bias

53 The process, by which certain group members motivate and guide the group is called
(a) leadership (b) group dynamics
(c) social control (d) social facilitation

54 A compulsion by decision makers to maintain each others approval even at the cost of critical thinking and good judgement is called
(a) the halo effect (b) expert power
(c) groupthink (d) social conformity

55 The real danger of 'groupthink' is that it
(a) is contagious
(b) occurs in cohesive groups
(c) disrupts coordinated efforts at group problem solving
(d) leads to a suspension of critical thinking

56 Groupthink is happening when member desire to
(a) control (b) freedom
(c) harmony (d) power

57 Group discussion
(a) weakness the initial dominant point of view
(b) enhances pluralistic ignorance
(c) weakness informational influence
(d) enhances risk taking

58 Which of the following is not a symptom of groupthink?
(a) An illusion of invulnerability
(b) Free rider
(c) Self-censorship
(d) Rationalisation

59 According to social identity theory, from what do we derive a large part of our identity and feelings about ourselves?
(a) Where we were born
(b) The amount of prejudice experienced
(c) The groups we belong to
(d) Competition between groups

60 According to the social identity theory, what determines conformity?
(a) Whether the individual internalises group membership as part of their self-concept
(b) Informational influence
(c) Identification with the out-group
(d) Normative influence

61 Creation of superordinate goals has been shown to be effective in reducing
(a) intergroup conflict (b) authoritarianism
(c) cognitive dissonance (d) social posturing

62 Which theory holds that a relationship must be profitable to endure?
(a) Complementary need theory
(b) Social exchange theory
(c) Gain loss theory
(d) Social comparison theory

63 .... is a change in behaviour or belief as a result of group pressure.
(a) Cohesiveness (b) Conformity
(c) Compliance (d) Obedience

64 Conformity is highest when the response is ...... and ....
(a) private; made without prior commitment
(b) public, made without prior commitment
(c) nonverbal; made in response to inanimate objects
(d) insignificant; made with prior commitment

65 Increasing the size of the group from .... is likely to produce the greatest increase in conformity.
(a) 1000 to 2000 (b) 50 to 100
(c) 2 to 5 (d) 5 to 10

66 The effect of group size on conformity has been explained by .... theory.
(a) cognitive dissonance (b) social norm
(c) psychological reactance (d) social impact

67 In Asch's study of perceptual judgement involving the length of lines, naive participants conformed .... of the time to the false judgements of the confederates.
(a) 10 percent (b) 37 percent
(c) 68 percent (d) 92 percent

68 Group size affects perceived conformity pressure in that, the .... the group, the ...... pressure is exerted.
(a) larger, more (b) more compliant, less
(c) smaller, more (d) more cohesive, less

69 Moe was stopped by a person asking for donations. The requester first asked if he was a student. Moe replied that he was and the requester said that he was also a student. The requester then asked for a donation. Because of the .... , Moe will probably donate.
(a) foot-in-the-door technique
(b) door-in-the-face technique
(c) low-ball-technique
(d) foot-in-the-mouth technique

70 Normative influence is to informational influence as .... is to ....
(a) autokinetic effect; cohesiveness
(b) compliance; acceptance
(c) conformity; reactance
(d) acceptance; reactance

71 Participants' tendencies to obey the experimenter's commands to shock a victim were highest when the experimenter was .... and the victim was ....
(a) close; distant. (b) close; close
(c) distant; distant (d) distant; close

72 To determine whether changing one variable (like education) will produce changes in another (like income), we need to conduct .... research.

(a) survey (b) correlational
(c) experimental (d) statistical

73 Peer Pressure influence the people in

(a) Positive way (b) Negative way
(c) Both a and b (d) None of these

74 Milgram's study is famous for

(a) Obedience (b) Peer pressure
(c) Both a and b (d) None of these

75 Who among the following stated that "the leadership tended to result in groups that lacks direction where members blamed each other for mistakes etc"?

(a) Kurt Lewin (b) Abraham Maslow
(c) Adam Smith (d) Fredrikson

76 Which of the following statements is/are correct?

1. A focused group is a group based on social comparison.
2. A frustration aggression hypothesis states that frustration tends to lead to aggression.
3. Categories are small groups of well-defined instances that belong together.
4. The process of categorisation produces clear demarcations between categories.

Select the correct answer using the codes given below

(a) 1 and 2 (b) 2 and 3
(c) 2 and 4 (d) 3 and 4

77 Which of the following statements is/are correct?

1. Group members work less hard on additive tasks.
2. Group members perceive themselves as working just as hard in the group or individually.
3. Group leadership is directly related to power and *vice versa*.
4. People obey blindly only in ambiguous situations or when disobedience will lead to serious punishment.

Select the correct answer using the codes given below

(a) 1 and 2 (b) 2 and 3
(c) 3 and 4 (d) Only 1

78 Which of the following statements is/are correct?

1. Compliance and conversion are technically the identical process.
2. A reference group is a group of which one is a member.
3. Normative pressure is a very effective method to bring about change in peoples behaviour.
4. The extent, to which people conform depends very much on their personalities.

Select the correct answer using the codes given below

(a) Both 1 and 2 (b) Both 2 and 3
(c) Both 3 and 4 (d) Only 3

79 Which of the following statements is/are correct?

1. Lewin found that letting a group norm become established was very in getting them to comply.
2. The opportunity for a minority to successfully change the majority view can be increased by consistency.
3. It would be difficult to account for social change, if we ignore influence of minority groups.
4. The success of a minority depends predominantly on its size.

Select the correct answer using the codes given below

(a) 1 and 2 (b) 2 and 3
(c) 3 and 4 (d) 1 and 3

80 Which of the following statements is/are correct?

1. Women are easier to convince.
2. Referent informational influence is a concept derived of social identity theory.
3. Social identity theory does not give rise to inter-group discrimination.
4. Henri Tajfel proposed social identity theory.

Select the correct answer using the codes given below

(a) 1 and 2
(b) 2 and 3
(c) 3 and 4
(d) 2 and 4

81 Match the following

	List I (Concept)		List II (Scholars)
A.	Conformity	1.	Solomon Asch
B.	Compliance	2.	Cialdini
C.	Obedience	3.	Milgram
D.	Autokinetic experiment	4.	Sherif

Codes

	A	B	C	D		A	B	C	D
(a)	1	2	3	4	(b)	4	3	2	1
(c)	2	4	1	3	(d)	3	1	4	2

82 Match the following

	List I (Theories)		List II (Scholars)
A.	Reactance Theory	1.	Berkowitz
B.	Psychodynamic Theory of Aggression	2.	Dollard
C.	Frustration Theory of Aggression	3.	Freud
D.	Cognitive Neo-association Theory of Aggression	4.	Jack Brehm

Codes

	A	B	C	D		A	B	C	D
(a)	1	2	3	4	(b)	4	3	2	1
(c)	2	4	1	3	(d)	3	1	4	2

83 Match the following

List I (Theories)	List II (Scholars)
A. Script Theory of Learning Aggression	1. Tedeschi and Felson
B. Excitation Transfer Theory of Aggression	2. Huesmann
C. Social Interaction Theory of Aggression	3. Anderson and Bushman
D. General Aggression Model	4. Zillman

Codes

	A	B	C	D		A	B	C	D
(a)	1	2	3	4	(b)	4	3	2	1
(c)	2	4	1	3	(d)	3	1	4	2

84 Match the following

List I (Theories)	List II (Scholars)
A. Group Dynamics	1. Kurt Lewin
B. Leadership Style	2. Samuel Stouffer
C. Social Identity Theory	3. Segal
D. Relative Deprivation Theory	4. Henri Tajfel

Codes

	A	B	C	D
(a)	1	2	3	4
(b)	4	3	2	1
(c)	2	4	1	3
(d)	3	1	4	2

85 Match the following

List I (Theories)	List II (Scholars)
A. Realistic Conflict Theory	1. Muzafer Sherif
B. Balance Theory	2. Fritz Heider
C. Minimal Group Paradigm	3. Henri Tajfel
D. Social Exchange Theory	4. George Homans

Codes

	A	B	C	D
(a)	1	2	3	4
(b)	4	3	2	1
(c)	2	4	1	3
(d)	3	1	4	2

Directions (Q. Nos 86-95) *In the questions given below are two statements labelled as Assertion (A) and Reason (R). In the context of two statements which one of the following is correct?*

Codes

(a) Both A and R are true and R is the correct explanation of A
(b) Both A and R are true, but R is not the correct explanation of A
(c) A is true, but R is false
(d) A is false, but R is true

86 **Assertion** (A) Social influence refers to the change in behaviour that one person causes in another.

Reason (R) The changed person does not perceive himself in relationship to the influencer, other people and society in general.

87 **Assertion** (A) Social loafing theory states that a person in a group of people, working on the same project, may not strive to achieve the expected goal.

Reason (R) He/she might think that his/her contribution may not matter in a group of brilliantly working people.

88 **Assertion** (A) According to Solomon Asch, error rate of the participants rises in the presence of people.

Reason (R) Participants conform to majority's view point.

89 **Assertion** (A) Informational influence involves changes in both public and private attitudes.

Reason (R) The perceives is using other people's opinions as guide to form their own attitude.

90 **Assertion** (A) Compliance can be defined as behaviour in accordance with group pressures without the values and norms of group as our own.

Reason (R) In general, we are more willing to comply with requests from friends or known people than strangers.

91 **Assertion** (A) Fit in the door technique is a principle where the small requests are granted then to move on the requests of higher level.

Reason (R) It is a procedure for gaining compliance.

92 **Assertion** (A) Under Bait Switch tactic, items offered for sale are at low quality.

Reason (R) It leads customers to buy a more expensive available item.

93 **Assertion** (A) Door-in-face technique is a procedure for gaining conformity.

Reason (R) Under door-in-the-face technique, requests are made in descending order.

94 **Assertion** (A) That is not all technique offers additional benefits to target persons for compliance.

Reason (R) The people cannot reject the offer cum request.

95 Assertion (A) Foot-in-the-mouth tactic is a procedure for gaining compliance.

Reason (R) The requester establishes some kind of relationship to increase the feeling of obligation to comply.

Directions (Q. Nos. 96-00) *Read the passage given below and answer the following questions.*

Jerome S Bruner is a cognitive psychologist, with primary interest in the development of mental abilities. He had a major impact on the education profession with the publication of his book 'The Process of Education (1960)'. He later proposed some theorems regarding instruction illustrated by the teaching of mathematics and moved further toward a theory of instruction in a subsequent collection of essays (Bruner, 1966).

He goes on to specify four features that a theory of instruction must encompass.

(i) **Predisposition to Learn** A theory of instruction must be concerned with the experiences and contexts that will tend to make the child willing and able to learn when he or she enters school.

(ii) **Structure of Knowledge** It must specify the ways in which a body of knowledge should be structured so that it can be most readily grasped by the learner.

(iii) **Sequence** It should specify the most effective sequences in which to present the materials.

(iv) **Reinforcement** It should specify the nature and pacing of rewards, moving from extrinsic rewards to intrinsic ones.

Bruner has taken the position that, with sufficient understanding of the structure of a field of knowledge, something anticipating the later, more advanced concepts can be taught appropriately at much earlier ages. His aphorism has been widely quoted : "Any subject can be taught effectively in some intellectually honest form to any child at any stage of development."

The developmental aspect of Bruner's theory lies in his interest in cognitive development, originally stimulated by Piaget. This has led him to emphasise three modes of representation in a developmental sequence: the enactive , the iconic and the symbolic. The inactive mode is learning through action, an essentially wordless learning, such as learning to ride a bicycle. The iconic mode is based on representation through perceptual means (hence the 'icon' or image standing for something). A mental map that permits us to follow a route from where we are to where we are going constitutes such an iconic representation. Finally, the symbolic mode enables the translation of experience into words and these permit eventually the kinds of transformations that at the later stages become of so much interest to Piaget.

96 This passage shows that Bruner is primarily concerned with

(a) application of learning theory
(b) application of principles of development to education
(c) role of language in human development
(d) teaching of mathematics

97 Prescriptive theory is one which

(a) suggests practical applications
(b) sets objectives or goals
(c) has educational relevance
(d) specifies learning outcomes

98 According to Bruner

(a) concepts can be taught only in appropriate stages
(b) concepts should only be taught after emergence of words
(c) concepts can be appropriately taught at any stage of development
(d) children should learn concepts only though action

99 A theory of instruction must deal with predisposition to learn which refers to

(a) sequencing of development stages
(b) individual differences among children
(c) cognitive development
(d) the conditions of child's environment before entering school

100 In Bruner's theory, structure of knowledge refers to

(a) existing organisation of knowledge in learner's mind
(b) organisation of knowledge to facilitate understanding
(c) iconic, enactive and symbolic modes of knowledge
(d) images associated with a system of knowledge

PREVIOUS YEARS' QUESTIONS

November 2017

1 Match List I with List II and select the correct answer by choosing from the codes given below

List I (Phenomena)		List II (Explanations)
A. Just world phenomenon	1.	Tendency to have first agreed to a small request and to comply with a larger request
B. Foot-in-door phenomenon	2.	A situation where conflicting parties are being caught for protecting self interest
C. Social trap	3.	The phenomenon where repeatedly facing novel stimuli increase their liking
D. Mere exposure phenomenon	4.	The belief that world is just and the people get what they deserve to get and *vice-versa*

Codes

	A	B	C	D		A	B	C	D
(a)	1	2	3	4	(b)	2	3	4	1
(c)	3	2	4	1	(d)	4	1	2	3

July 2016

2 Read each of the following two statements Assertion (A) and Reason (R) and indicate your answer using codes given below

Assertion (A) Individuals high in self-esteem have a relatively weak desire for social rewards.

Reason (R) Social anxiety and loneliness are both associated with unrewarding social interactions.

Codes

(a) Both A and R are true and R is the correct explanation of A
(b) Both A and R are true, but R is not the correct explanation of A
(c) A is true, but R is false
(d) A is false, but R is true

December 2015

3 The following social factors play a role in educational settings

1. Cooperation
2. Competition
3. Peer influence
4. Role modelling

Codes

(a) 1 and 2 (b) 2 and 3
(c) 3 and 4 (d) All of the above

ANSWERS

Exam Based Questions

1	(d)	2	(c)	3	(d)	4	(a)	5	(a)	6	(d)	7	(b)	8	(a)	9	(c)	10	(a)
11	(a)	12	(d)	13	(a)	14	(b)	15	(c)	16	(c)	17	(b)	18	(d)	19	(c)	20	(b)
21	(d)	22	(a)	23	(a)	24	(b)	25	(a)	26	(c)	27	(b)	28	(c)	29	(b)	30	(a)
31	(b)	32	(a)	33	(d)	34	(d)	35	(d)	36	(c)	37	(a)	38	(c)	39	(d)	40	(c)
41	(d)	42	(a)	43	(d)	44	(a)	45	(c)	46	(a)	47	(b)	48	(d)	49	(c)	50	(d)
51	(a)	52	(c)	53	(a)	54	(c)	55	(d)	56	(c)	57	(d)	58	(a)	59	(c)	60	(a)
61	(a)	62	(b)	63	(b)	64	(b)	65	(c)	66	(d)	67	(b)	68	(a)	69	(d)	70	(b)
71	(a)	72	(c)	73	(c)	74	(a)	75	(a)	76	(c)	77	(a)	78	(b)	79	(d)	80	(d)
81	(a)	82	(b)	83	(c)	84	(d)	85	(a)	86	(c)	87	(a)	88	(a)	89	(a)	90	(b)
91	(b)	92	(a)	93	(d)	94	(a)	95	(b)	96	(b)	97	(b)	98	(c)	99	(d)	100	(b)

Previous Years' Questions

1	(d)	2	(b)	3	(d)

Applied Social Psychology

Social psychology can be defined as the science that seek to understand how people think, feel about, relate to and influence one another. Social psychology can be applied to different field for better understanding of them. These field include health, environment, personal space, crowding territoriality.

Introduction of Applied Social Psychology

Applied social psychology can be defined as using social psychological theories, principles, research, findings and experimental methods to understand social issues and to offer real world solutions for a variety of social problems.

As a discipline, applied social psychology functions on the basis that problems are, at their heart, caused by human behaviour. To understand and change these problem behaviours, applied social psychologists conduct a scientific examination of individual's thoughts, feelings and behaviours as they pertain to a variety of social influences. Through their research, applied social psychologists hope to offer practical suggestions for improving human social behaviour in areas ranging from work place productivity to safer sexual activity. Applied social psychology also focuses on health, environment and the related laws.

Evolution of Applied Social Psychology

While an earlier generation of psychologists had been predominantly interested in the structure and measurement of mental tasks in the laboratory, the 20th century saw a paradigm shift in which psychologist started showing their interest in application of social psychology in different such as health, environment and low personal space etc.

In 1903, experimental psychologist **Walter Dill Scott** wrote 'The Theory and Practice of Advertising', suggesting that consumer habits could be influenced by emotional suggestions. In 1908, psychologist **Hugo Munsterberg** defined applied psychology as "research adjusted to fit the problems encountered in everyday life".

In works on industrial psychology, advertising, and education, **Munsterberg, Scotti** and others began exploring the possibilities of an applied psychology. In 1917, psychologist **GS Hall** founded the 'Journal of Applied Psychology' to further explore the potential of this new field.

By the 1920s, there was an undeniable enthusiasm for applied research in the psychological community, despite its reputation as an 'undignified' pursuit. In addition to the new challenges it presented, applied research was also attractive because private corporations often provided better salaries than academic institutions.

The work of **Kurt Lewin** marks the beginning of modern applied social psychology. Lewin, best known for his field theory suggesting that behaviour is a function of an individual's personality and his or her environment, proposed that social psychologists should engage in what he called action research. A social activist himself, Lewin believed that social issues should inspire social psychological research. Applied social psychology has been growing in prestige since the 1980s.

Applied social psychological research continues within academic institutions, private and government grants, as well as full-time research positions within large corporations, have allowed researchers the flexibility and opportunity to study a diverse array of social phenomena.

By understanding psychological factors that influence health, and constructively applying that knowledge, health psychologists can improve health by working directly with individual patients or indirectly in large-scale public health programs. In addition, health psychologists can help train other healthcare professionals (*e.g.* physicians and nurses) to take advantage of the knowledge the discipline has generated, when treating patients. Health psychologists can work with people on a one-to-one basis, in groups, as a family, or at a larger population level.

Applying Social Psychology to Health

Social psychology play a prominent role in various dimensions of health. It is concerned with understanding how psychological, behavioural and cultural factors' contribute to physical health and illness. Psychological factor can affect health directly. *For example* Chronically occurring environment stressors affecting the hypothalamic pituitary adrenal axis, comulatively can harm health.

Social health psychologists apply their expertise in many settings, including private practices, hospitals and primary care programs, universities, corporations, government agencies and specialty practices, such as oncology, pain management, rehabilitation and smoking cessation.

Helping people make choices that have a positive impact on their health and the well-being of their families, the workforce and their communities is at the heart of this dynamic field.

Social psychology in health can be easily understood by below given components

Clinical Health Social Psychology

Clinical health Social psychology is the application of scientific knowledge, derived from the field of health psychology, to clinical questions that may arise across the spectrum of healthcare. Clinical health social psychology is one of many specialty practice areas for clinical psychologists. It is also a major contributor to the prevention focused field of behavioural health and the treatment-oriented field of behavioural medicine. Clinical practice includes education, the techniques of behaviour change, and psychotherapy. In some countries, a clinical health psychologist, with additional training, can become a medical psychologist and thereby, obtain prescription privileges.

Public Health Social Psychology

Public health social psychology is population-oriented. A major aim of PHS is to investigate potential causal links between psychosocial factors and health at the population level. Public health psychologists present research results to educators, policy makers, and healthcare providers in order to promote better public health. PHS is allied to other public health disciplines including epidemiology, nutrition, genetics and biostatistics. Some public health social psychology interventions are targeted toward at risk population groups. (*For example* Undereducated, single pregnant women who smoke) and not the population as a whole (*e.g.* all pregnant women).

Community Health Social Psychology

Community health social psychology investigates community factors that contribute to the health and well-being of individuals who live in communities. Community health social psychology also develops community level interventions that are designed to combat disease and promote physical and mental health. The community often serves as the level of analysis, and is frequently sought as a partner in health related interventions.

Critical Health Social Psychology

Critical health social psychology is concerned with the distribution of power and the impact of power differentials on health experience and behaviour, healthcare systems and health policy. Critical health social psychology prioritises social justice and the universal right to health for people of all races, genders, ages, and socio-economic positions. A major concern is health inequalities. The critical health psychologist is an agent of change, not simply an analyst or cataloger. A leading organisation in this area is the International Society of Critical Health Psychology.

Role of Social Health Psychologist

Social health psychologist play following prominent roles

- Identify behaviours that may damage your patient's health, *e.g.* smoking, physical inactivity and poor diet.
- Encourage positive healthcare behaviours such as healthy eating, attending health checks and regular exercise.
- Explore patient behaviour to identify appropriate psychological interventions that can be used to support your patient.
- Develop interventions to address your patient's health beliefs in empowering them to develop their own sense of control over their health issues.
- Look at the psychological impact of illness on patients, families and careers.
- Provide information and advice to a range of organisations involved in public health, such as the NHS and local authorities.
- Advise doctors on how to improve their communication with their patients.

Applying Social Psychology to the Environment

Environmental psychology is the study of transactions between individuals and their physical settings. In these transactions, individuals change the environment, and their behaviour and experiences are changed by the environment. Environmental psychology includes theory, research, and practice aimed at improving our relationship with the natural environment and making buildings more humane.

The task of psychologists, interested in the environment, is to examine a great variety of topics besides the issues involved in extreme actions aimed at defending the natural environment. Environmental psychologists study not only how the physical environment affects our behaviour, thinking and well-being but also how our behaviour affects the environment.

There are social psychological aspects to many topics examined by environmental psychologists such as violence in jails, weather and altruism, crime, privacy, crowding and territoriality, the effects of noise and lighting on interpersonal relations: spatial arrangements in offices, schools and social aspects of managing natural resources.

However, good social scientists also want to understand why people act the way they do. Therefore, psychologists who focus on the physical environment have developed interesting theories to help, explain things such as who will cooperate, who will not when resources are scarce, how cultures vary in seeking privacy, the cultural meanings conveyed by building illusions, the strategies residents use for dealing with spatial conflicts within their homes, how children learn to find their way around their neighbourhoods and which furniture arrangements encourage social interaction.

As environmental problems and concerns grow, social scientists must learn more about individual and small group contributions to ecological degradation. As humans who dwell in societies, we extract, refine, use and dispose of many natural resources. However, societies are composed of individuals and ultimately people make these choices as individuals and small groups in their homes, at work and during their leisure hours.

Component of Applied Social Psychology in Environment

Applied social psychology in environment has several component, which are as follows

Place Identity

Place identity has been described as the individual's incorporation of place into the larger concept of self; a "potpourri of memories, conceptions, interpretations, ideas, and related feelings about specific physical settings, as well as types of settings". As a person interacts with various places and spaces, he/she is able to evaluate which properties in different environments fulfill his/her various needs.

When a place contain components that satisfy a person biologically, socially, psychologically and/or culturally, it creates the environmental past of a person. Through 'good' or 'bad' experiences with a place, a person is then able to reflect and define their personal values, attitudes, feelings and beliefs about the physical world.

Place Attachment

Many different perceptions of the bond between people and places have been hypothesised and studied. The most widespread terms include place attachment and sense of place. One consistent thread woven throughout most recent research on place attachment deals with the importance of the amount of time spent at a certain place (the length of association with a place). While both researchers and writers have made the case that time and experience in a place are important for deepening the meanings and emotional ties central to the person-place relationship, little in-depth research has studied these factors and their role in forging this connection.

Environmental Consciousness

Leanne Rivlin theorised that one way to examine an individual's environmental consciousness is to recognise how the physical place is significant, and look at the people/place relationship.

Environmental cognition (involved in human cognition) plays a crucial role in environmental perception. All different areas of the brain engage with environmentally relevant information. Some believe that the orbitofrontal cortex integrates environmentally relevant information from many distributed areas of the brain. Due to its anterior location within the frontal cortex, the orbitofrontal cortex may make judgements about the environment, and refine the organism's 'understanding' through error analysis, and other processes specific to prefrontal cortex.

Behaviour Settings

In his book 'Ecological Psychology'

Barker stresses the importance of the town's behaviour and environment as the residents' most ordinary instrument of describing their environment. "The hybrid, eco-behavioural character of behaviour settings appear to present midwest's inhabitants with no difficulty; nouns that combine milieu and standing behaviour are common, *e.g.* oyster supper, basketball game, turkey dinner, golden gavel ceremony, cake walk, back surgery, gift exchange, livestock auction, auto repair."

Scope of Applied Social Psychology in Environment

Major areas in environment where social psychology plays a critical role

- Perception and evaluation of buildings and natural landscapes.
- Cognitive mapping, spatial cognition, and way finding.
- Ecological consequences of human actions.
- Evaluation of building and natural landscapes.
- Design of, and experiences related to, the physical aspects of workplaces, schools, residences, public buildings, and public spaces.
- Leisure and tourism behaviour in relation to their physical settings.
- Psychological and behavioural aspects of people and nature.
- Theories of place, place attachment, and place identity.
- Psychological aspects of resource management and crises.
- Environmental risks and hazards; perception, behaviour, and management.
- Stress related tu physical setting.

Strategies for Inducing Pro-Environmental Behaviour

Psychologists who are interested in environmental issues also study other uses and abuses of resources such as pollution, the rate of energy, used in households and work organisations, recycling and transportation. Usually, they consider the potential power of a few factors that, they think, might influence people to engage in a more pro-environment behaviour such as to reduce their use of some resource to pollute less or to recycle more.

Some of the main factors include the following appeals from authorities, improvements in educational campaigns, goal setting and public commitment by individuals to change their behaviour, feedback, modeling and norm activation. The first two of these have not been found to be particularly effective in changing behaviour. This might be surprising in he case of educational campaigns given that they represent a widely used strategy and cost considerable sums to implement. The value of educational campaigns lies in their priming ability *i.e.* they get people ready to make a change rather than actually get them to change.

The goal-setting and public commitment strategies work better. If a person decides, to reduce household energy use by a specified and reasonable amount and also announces this goal to family and friends, actual behaviour change is more likely.

The use of role models has proven to be effective in facilitating the increase in pro-environment behaviour. We learn from watching others. This basic principle of social learning theory has been shown to increase conservation behaviours in studies of university students showering practices and to improve home energy conservation.

Modeling can be used to encourage other environmentally conscious behaviours as well. **Kahle** and **Beatty** demonstrated that recycling will increase, when significant number of others are depicted as recycling. A similar strategy, combining role models and persuasion, is to identify individuals in a neighbourhood, who can encourage their neighbours to recycle.

Applying Social Psychology to Law

Law and policing has become a remarkably diverse field of applied psychology and covers almost all major areas of psychology.

For example Organisational psychology, personal selection, clinical psychology and counselling, psychological assessment, social and personality psychology.

Direct Operational Assistance

Apart from an indirect impact of psychology on the police mission by optimising personal skills and situational variables, psychology can directly support criminal investigations by providing empirically based guidelines for such things as conducting interviews or prepairing eyewitness identification procedures.

Interviewing Witnesses

Kebbell and **Milne** report that police officer acts on the opinion that witnesses usually play central role in criminal investigations. A report by the Rand Corporation also noted that a major factor that determines whether or not a crime is solved the completeness and accuracy of the witness account. Indeed law enforcement personnel were found to spend as much as 85% of their total working time talking to people.

One approach to increase the information, a witness provides is forensic **hypnosis**. However, the empirical evidence for the memory enhancing potential of hypnosis is equivocal. Whereas, some anecdotal reports claim that hypnosis may enhance memory in criminal cases, controlled laboratory studies have produced mixed results.

A less controversial technique for improving memory retrieval is the cognitive interview, which was developed by **Geiselman** and **Fisher**. In its original form, it comprises four basic retrieval aids or mnemonic strategies together with some ways of helping witnesses to recall specific bits of information. *First*, interviewees are instructed to mentally reconstruct the context of the witnessed event, to form an image or an impression of the environmental aspects of the scene and to remember their emotional feelings and thoughts.

The *second* strategy is to encourage witnesses to report everything they remember, even if they think the details are not important. The *third* component is to ask witnesses to recall the event in a variety of temporal orders or to make retrieval attempts from different starting points *e.g.* from the most memorable element. *Finally*, witnesses are encouraged to recall the event from different physical locations, just as if they were viewing it with another person's eyes.

Fisher and **Geiselman** later refined the technique considerably, particularly by addressing the social dynamics and communication between the interviewer and the eyewitness and called this refined version, the enhanced cognitive interview.

Eyewitness Identification

Whereas courts and juries often view the identification of a defendant by an eyewitness as a particularly convincing piece of evidence, analysis of proven wrongful convictions have consistently shown that mistaken eyewitness identification is responsible for more miscarriages of justice than all other potential causes combined. To be an accurate eyewitness, a person must successfully complete three stages of memory processing.

Eyewitnesses can be inaccurate because of problems at any of these three stages.

(i) **Acquisition**
- People notice and pay attention to information in the environment.
- They cannot perceive everything that is happening around them.
- They acquire only a sub-set of the information available.

(ii) **Storage** The process by which people store the information, they have acquired from the environment in memory.

(iii) **Retrieval** People recall information, stored in their memories.

Different variables affecting eyewitness identification are discussed below.

Estimator Variables

Shapiro and **Penrod** conducted a mega-analysis in order to assess the effects of various estimator variables on identification accuracy. The result of the meta-analysis suggests that stable characteristics of eye witnesses such as intelligence , gender and personality traits are only weakly, if at all, related to identification accuracy. In particular, self-reported facial recognition skill is not reliably associated with actual performance.

The most important variable of the stable target characteristic seems to be facial distinctiveness. Faces that are highly attractive or highly unattractive are substantially better recognised than non-distinct faces.

Whereas neither the race of the perpetrator nor the race of the witness alone are strongly associated with recognition performance, these variables interact such that cross-race identifications are less accurate than own-race identifications known as cross race effect *i.e.* the tendency of the people of one race to have difficulty recognising and processing faces are facial expressions of members of a race or ethnic group other than their own. The majority of experiments on estimator variables have looked at the effects of environmental conditions at the time of the crime.

System Variables

Factors that are under the control of the criminal justice system are called *system variables*. With regard to recognition tests, false identifications can have two causes.

First, random error can occur. In this case, the witness chooses the suspect purely by chance. Any other member of the lineup was just as likely to be selected as the alleged offender.

Second, a false identification may result from systematic error. A systematic error when certain properties of the lineup procedure or the composition of the lineup leads the witness to choose the suspect even, if he or she is not the criminal.

Identification errors from lineups are the most common cause of wrongful convictions. Witnesses often choose the person in a lineup who most resembles the criminal, even if the resemblance is not very strong.

To avoid the guess work and other problems related to lineups, *psychologists gave the following steps to be followed*

- Make sure everyone in the lineup resembles the witness's description of the suspect.
- Do not always include the suspect in an initial lineup.
- Present witnesses with both photographs of people and sound recordings of their voices.

Random Errors

Witnesses may want to present themselves as 'good' and constructive persons, who can help the police catch the offender and thereby solve the crime. Further, witnesses tend to see the whole lineup procedure as a technique to convict an already sufficiently well known criminal. In the erroneous belief that the police are best served by a positive identification of one of the individuals in the lineup, they may choose the individual who must resemble the fuzzy pictures of the offender in their memory.

Systematic Errors

A lineup is conducted in order to test the hypothesis that

(i) the suspect is the guilty part and

(ii) the suspect is not the criminal. The lineup recognition test thus, resembles an experiment and the general methodological principles for experimental research and hypothesis testing apply.

From this point of view, two types of systematic errors can be distinguished

(i) The composition of the lineup or the arrangement of the photographs can lead to the suspect standing out from the other individuals. Malpass and Devine referred to this as a structured error.

(ii) Errors can occur during the procedure of the recognition test that would lead the witness to select the suspect. This type of error is referred to as a procedural error.

Evaluating Witness Statements: Assessment and Attribution of Credibility

Witness statements, whether they may be descriptions of events or person identifications, can rarely be taken at face value. Numerous factors have been found to be able to cause discrepancies between statements and the actual facts. These factors can be separated into two different classes.

On the one hand, witness, although trying to give a correct and complete report of an event or an accurate description of a person, may be subject to unintended errors and distortions, caused by forgetting sub-optimal perception conditions, misleading post event information etc.

Assessment of Credibility

Objective indicators of truth and deception have been examined four behavioural areas

(i) The content of the statement.

(ii) The way of the statement is verbally presented *i.e.* speech behaviour and stylostatistic characteristic.

(iii) The accompanying non-verbal behaviour of the witness.

(iv) Psychophysical phenomena.

Burgeon and **Buller** have proposed an 'Interpersonal deception theory.' They are critical of most investigations of deception for having used a unidirectional view, such that a liar actively transmits signals, which a receiver passively observes. However, this paradigm lacks the process of interpersonal communication that involves feedback and mutual influence.

In an ongoing conversation, the character of deceit may change when the deceived continually monitor their performance, while adapting to the receiver's feedback. As a consequence, behavioural patterns evidenced at the outset of an exchange may differ radically from the one, manifested later. According to his position, averaging behaviour frequencies across a lengthy interaction may produce weak effects, although clues to deception may indeed exist.

SVA consists of three major components. The *first* component is an open ended investigative interview. The *second* component of SVA is a criteria based content analysis. In this phase, the transcript of the statement is analysed with regard to certain content characteristics like, quantity of detail or the description of unexpected complications during the incident.

The *third*, all obtained case information including the witness's cognitive and verbal abilities and information about the origin of the statement, is integrated into a final judgement as to whether or not the statement is likely to be an account of what actually happened.

Attribution of Credibility

Research on the attribution of credibility has examined how successful people are, in discriminating truthful and deceptive statements, which behavioural cues they utilise for their judgements and how access to different communication channels influences this attribution. Interestingly, people with experience in credibility judgements achieve no better results than inexperienced subjects.

Experienced subjects are, however, more confident in the correctness of their judgements than by people. Apparently, the more frequency of credibility judgements does not help to improve judgement accuracy because subjects don't receive any detailed feedback.

Applying Social Psychology to the Criminal Justice System

Crimes are committed directly including both violent offences (*e.g.* murder, robbery, uttering a death threat) and non-violent offences (*e.g.* fraud, voyeurism, exhibitionism). Commiting rape, an example of criminal behaviour, is a **Social** Act, where it involves violations of socially defined laws.

The work of social psychologists is to bring to these issues, some theories and methodologies that take into account, the role of both person and situation to account for behaviour. This approach provides a more integrative and multilevel framework for addressing the issues of crime than does focussing only on the person or only on the environment.

To illustrate, criminal acts may be viewed from a social ecological perspective *i.e.* as the result of an interaction between the person and the environment. This notion is derived from **Kurt Lewin's** famous theorem B = f (P, E), which states that behaviour is a function of the person (P), the environment (E) and the interaction between the two.

In practice, social psychology has been of the value to the police in developing techniques for interviewing suspects, to defence attorneys in demonstrating how a person can come to be wrongfully accused of a crime, to a lawyer in selecting possible jurors for a trail and to forensic psychologists conducting risk assessment of offenders to predict the probability of future criminal behaviour.

The Origin of Criminal Behaviour

Existing theories of criminal behaviour implicate a wide range of variables that reside within a person, the person's immediate environment and the broader sociological context which are responsible for origin of criminal behaviour. Which follows some of the major theoritical paradigm from biology, sociology and social psychology that have been put forth to explain criminal behaviour.

It is important to always remember that the perspectives of other disciplines contribute to a more complete understanding of psychological phenomenon, including the etiology of criminal behaviour.

Biological Theories

Biologically based theories view criminal behaviour as the result of genetics, psychophysiology, neurological functioning and biochemistry. The well documented findings that males have a greater propensity for physical aggression than do females, have been attributed to higher levels of testosterone and the presence of extra Y chromosome (XYY), although the latter observation has been disputed.

Even the acquired biological deficit may influence criminal behaviour. Even before birth, factors may conspire against the developing fetus, predisposing it to impulsive, hyperactive or aggressive behaviour.

Sociological Theories

Some of the most enduring theories of crime are those that are based on sociological principles. These traditional theories (*e.g.* anomie, strain, control, sub-culture) although widely diverse, attempt to explain crime in relation to various factors in society such as social class, poverty and social inequality.

Thus, a person's socio-economic status, determined by education, occupation, income and neighbourhood characteristics explains substantial variability in criminal behaviour.

Sub-Culture Theory

It states that individuals, who engage in criminal activity are merely conforming to imitating the criminal behaviour of others, receiving positive consequences for engaging in criminal behaviour (*e.g.* peer approval), realising that such behaviour can effectively lead to desired outcomes (*i.e.* have instrumental value) and developing a high sense of self efficacy in using anti social means to achieve one's aim.

Thus, subsequently focuses on the general personality and social psychological model of criminal behaviour that has been developed by Andrews and Bonta.

According to **Andrews** and **Bonta's model**, "the likelihood that a person will develop a tendency to engage in criminal behaviour is increased by the presence of risk factors in his on her life". The categories of risk factors, some personal and some environmental are: the hedonistic, hostile and destructive values of lower class culture. Indeed, in the deviant sub-culture the non-conformists who don't engage in theft, drug use and gang affiliation are said to be the true deviants.

Social Psychological Theories

Theories of criminal behaviour from a social psychological perspective tend to consider the influence of both dispositional and situational factors, as **Hoge** noted, social ecological models explain crime as a function of the interaction among multiple forces operating at the level of the individual, their immediate social environment and other factors within the larger social environment.

According to **Bandura**'s "social learning theory, criminal activity represents learned behaviours that developed through a person's interactions and experiences with the social environment."

This learning takes place as a result of various processes, including observation and

- An early age of onset for antisocial behaviour.
- Negative parenting and family experiences (*e.g.* harsh and abusive discipline, low family cohesion and parental criminality).
- Temperamental and personal characteristics that are conducive to criminal activity.
- Low levels of school or vocational achievement.
- Association with pro-criminal peers and isolation from non-criminal associates.
- Anti-social attitudes, values and beliefs.

Andrew and **Bonte** *identified five elements which contribute to an antisocial pattern of attitude (includes belief and values)*

(i) High tolerance for deviance in general.

(ii) Rejection of validity of legal authority and institution.

(iii) Use of cognitive distortions (*e.g.* rationalisation, denial) to make some body's antisocial behaviour acceptable.

(iv) Interpretation of a wide range of environmental stimuli as a reason for anger.

(v) A style of thinking *i.e.* generally antisocial.

For the life-course persistent group, the influence of the deliquent peer group follows a more lengthy and complex developmental pathway. These individuals tend to engage in a wide variety of antisocial acts (*e.g.* violence, drug use, vandalism) referred to as versatility.

They are also at particular risk for becoming chronic and serious offenders with lengthy criminal careers the antisocial behaviour of life course persistent adolescents is further reinforced within their deliquent peer group, where it becomes more serious and diverse in nature often including violence. This process, by which this peer group reinforcement takes place is referred to as deviancy training.

Treatment Implication

In keeping with the general personality and social psychological approach, the effective treatment of antisocial behaviour involves targeting factors such as antisocial attitudes, beliefs and peer association as well as family factors. One successful intervention strategy, the Multisystematic Treatment Programme for Seriously Violent Youths attempts to influence the multiple social system, in which young people are embedded (*e.g.* family, school, peer, neighbourhood, justice system) to bring about a decrease in criminal behaviour.

Thus, programme staff members intervene in several ways and areas, including working with the family to modify parenting practices and dysfunctional dynamics within the youth's homes, linking the families to community support, diverting the youth from negative peer associations, providing individual counselling and providing support at schools.

Applying Social Psychology to Personal Space

Personal space refers to the physical area surrounding an individual that is considered personal or private. When another person intrudes in this area, the individual experiences discomfort. Interpersonal space is a related concept which refers to the area that people keep between themselves and the interaction partner. As in individual's personal space increases, interpersonal distances will also increase.

The size of personal space depends on individual and situational differences. The shape of personal space does not completely follow the lines of a circle or bubble, as the preferred distances at the front of a person are generally found to be larger compared with the rear.

Functions of Personal Space

Physical interpersonal spacing behaviour serves important functions

- Distancing oneself from others promotes, controls and maintains autonomy. In such a case, influence of others is reduced.
- Conversely, proximity fosters interpersonal communication and cooperative behaviour, smooth interactions and increases inter personal liking.

Determinants of Inter-personal Space

Personal space should not be considered as static construct because it varies across individuals and situations. Inter personal distance is basically influenced by the nature of relationship between the interacting individuals.

Types of Interaction in Personal Space

Edward Hall distinguished four types of interaction distances observed in Western societies

(i) **Intimate Distance** It ranges from o to 18 inches. *For example* Two individuals making love.

(ii) **Personal Distance** It ranges from 18 to 48 inches. *For example* The distance between two close friends.

(iii) **Social Distance** It rangers from 4 to 12 feet. *For example* Business interactions.

(iv) **Public Distance** It ranges from 12 feet to infinite length. *For example* Formal interactions like teaching or public meetings.

Origin of Personal Space

We all know that infants do not mind being touched, kissed or taken into arms. It is because they have not formed their own personal space bubbles at that point of time.

Actually, one's personal space bubbles start forming around the age of three to four years. During the phase of adolescence, these personal space bubbles attain a fixed size scientists have researched to confirm that these bubbles are socially and culturally constructed.

They are also formed with the help of a part of our brain, called the *amygdala*. The amygdala is the part of our brain that feels fear and is activated when there is a perceived threat to our safety. Daniel Kennedy and his colleagues, after deep research, concluded that personal space bubbles are constructed by the amygdala. They observed that a woman, with damage to her amygdala, had no personal space.

They also explained that autistic individuals, with defects in amygdala of the brain, face difficulties in understanding appropriate personal limits.

Measurement of Personal Space

Personal space or interpersonal spacing behaviour has been studied using two different kinds of distance measures. *These are*

(i) **Projective Measures** Some researchers used projective measures in which individuals are asked to indicate the preferred distance to an imagined other person. These projective measures may be contrasted with real life measures including unobtrusive observations of actual spacing and placements or selections of chair's.

As interpersonal spacing behaviours is mostly regulated in an automatic fashion, individuals are generally unaware of the distance that they keep from others. As a result, people may find it difficult to clearly indicate their preferred interpersonal spaces. Indeed, projective measures show low correspondence with actual interpersonal behavioural measures and are considered to be less useful in studying personal space.

(ii) **Immersive Virtual Environment Technology** Benefitting from technical progress, several researchers have recently studied interpersonal spacing behaviour using immersive virtual environment technology in which participants approach virtual other people. People seem to keep distance from these virtual persons quite naturally, as if they approach real individuals. Virtual reality is a potentially useful tool to enlarge researchers' understanding of personal space.

Applying Social Psychology to Crowding

Crowding refers to a psychological construct wherein the amount of space available is less than desired. The immediate presence of others, particularly in living working spaces, gives rise to the term 'crowding'.

Crowding has varying psychological and physical perspectives, for example

- A high density social event like birthday party or a marriage ceremony brings a lot of fun and positivity.
- A high density living or work space usually results in chaos and negativity.

In both the above examples, physical perspective more or less remains the same, yet psychological perspective has contrastingly varied. This variation in psychological perspective brings to light that crowding illustrates how the physical environment can affect human behaviour.

One experiences crowding when one needs more space and yet can't have it. The most common reaction to 'crowding' is stress, particularly over time and in an important space like home or office. Crowding can also lead to feelings of helplessness wherein one starts to question one's own ability to effectively manage the environment.

Impact of Crowding on Individuals

Studies in India and USA have found that children and adolescents who live in more crowded homes, independent of socio-economic status, are less likely to persist on challenging puzzles, giving up sooner than those living under uncrowded conditions.

Crowding also changes the social interaction of the people. Such people may withdraw from others, create more psychological space when physical space is limited and may become more irritable and potentially aggressive.

Crowding may also lead to increased blood pressure or stress hormones over a long period of time.

Applying Social Psychology to Territoriality

Territoriality is a pattern of attitudes and behaviour held by a person or group that is based on perceived, attempted or actual control of a physical space, object or idea, which may involve habitual occupation, defence, personalisation and making of the territory. Here, personalisation implies marking something in a manner that indicates one's identity and marking means placing an object or substance in a space to indicate one's territorial intentions.

Types of Territories

Territoriality is extremely widespread. The signs of human territoriality are everywhere. *For example* Name plates, fences, locks, no-trespassing signs and even copyright notices etc.

There are billions of territories in that world, some are large, some are small, some are nested within others are some are shared. *Broadly, territoriality can be categorised into the following*

(i) **Primary Territory** Primary territories are spaces owned by individuals or primary groups, controlled on a relatively permanent basis by them and central to their daily lives. Examples include one's bedroom or family's dwelling. The psychological importance of primary territories to their owners is always high.

(ii) **Secondary Territory** Secondary territories are less important to their occupiers than primary territories. But they do possess moderate significance to their occupants. A person's desk at work, favourite restaurant, locker in the gym and home playing field are a few examples of secondary territory.

(iii) **Public Territory** Public territories are areas open to anyone in good standing with the community. Beaches, sidewalks and hotel lobbies are public territories. Occasionally, public territories are closed to some individuals because of discrimination or unacceptable behaviour. *For example* Retail stores are public territories, open to everyone. However, it may be out of reach for someone who causes trouble.

(iv) **Body Territory** The physical self may be considered as a body territory. Skin is perceived as a boundary of body territory. Bodies may be touched or entered with permission in case of a surgery or without permission in case of knife attack etc. Some people mark and personalise their own bodies with make-up, jewellery, tatoos, piercings and clothing. Owners of body territory certainly defend and try to control access to their bodies by other people.

Objects and ideas under one's possession are also sometimes categorised as types of territories, although they are not universally considered territories. Such types of territories are often defended through patents and copyrights. Plagiarism is also not legally valid.

Types of Territoriality Infringement

Even though territories usually work to keep society hassle-free, *yet sometimes they are infringed upon in following three ways.*

(i) **Invasion** The most obvious form of infringement is invasion, in which an outsider physically enters someone else's territory, usually with the intention of taking it from its current owner. *For example* One country trying to take territory of another.

(ii) **Violation** The second from of infringement is violation. It is a temporary infringement of someone's territory. Usually, the goal is not ownership but annoyance or harm. *For example* Vandalism, hit and run attacks and burglary, sometimes a violation occurs out of ignorance.

(iii) **Contamination** The third form of infringement is contamination, in which the infringer fouls someone else' territory by putting something awful over there. *For example* A chemical company leaving poisonous waste for later residents to deal with, a house leaving the kitchen filthy or pesticide spray drifting into other's yard.

Types of Territoriality Defences

There are there different types of defences just like territoriality infringements. *These defences are as follows*

(i) **Prevention Defence** Prevention defence takes place when someone uses a coat, sign or fence to defend a territory. Here, one anticipates infringement and acts to stop it before it occurs.

(ii) **Reaction Defence** Reaction defences are the responses to an infringement after it happens. *For example* Physically striking the infringer or court actions for copyright violations.

(iii) **Social Boundary Defence** The social boundary defence consists of a ritual engaged in by hosts and visitors. *For example* Need of a password to enter many websites or customs office at the national border. Social Boundary defenses serve to separate wanted visitors from unwanted ones.

EXAM BASED QUESTIONS

1 Which of the following does applied social psychology use to understand social issues and to offer real world solutions for a variety of social problems?

(a) Social psychological theories
(b) Research
(c) Experimental methods
(d) All of the above

2 On which of the following does applied social psychology focus?

(a) Health (b) Environment
(c) Law (d) All of these

3 Who has propounded 'Field theory'?

(a) Kurt Lewin (b) Kugo Munsterberg
(c) Walter Dill Scott (d) G S Hall

4 According to field theory of kurt Lewin behaviour of an individual, is function of

(a) consciousness
(b) personality and environment
(c) parents
(d) None of the above

5 Social psychology can help in understanding which of the following factor of health and illness?

(a) Psychological factor (b) Behavioural factor
(c) Both a and b (d) Physiological factor

6 Social health psychologist apply their expertise in many setting. It includes

(a) private practices (b) hospitals and primary care
(c) universities (d) All of these

7 Social psychology consists of how many components?

(a) Two (b) Three (c) Four (d) Five

8 Which statement is true regarding clinical health social psychology?

(a) It is population-oriented.
(b) Clinical practice includes education and the techniques of behaviour change.

(c) It involves community level intervention.
(d) Distribution of power and the impact of power differential on health.

9 Which among the following are associated with the risk population group?
(a) Clinical health social psychology
(b) Community health social psychology
(c) Public health social psychology
(d) Critical health social psychology

10 Universal right to health and social justice is theme of which of the following component?
(a) Critical health social psychology
(b) Moderate health social psychology
(c) Individual health social psychology
(d) Clinical health social psychology

11 Major role of social health psychologist are
(a) encourage positive healthcare
(b) look at psychological impact of illness on patient
(c) provide advices to improve their communication
(d) All of the above

12 Which of the following is not part of encouraging healthcare behaviours?
(a) Healthy eatings
(b) Drinking beverages
(c) Regular exercises
(d) Attending health checkup

13 The study of transaction between individuals and physical setting is called
(a) Social psychology (b) Individual psychology
(c) Group psychology (d) Environment psychology

14 The main role of psychologist in the content of environment is
(a) conserving natural resources
(b) how our behaviour are affected by the environment
(c) study types of flora and fauna
(d) None of the above

15 What has been described as the individuals incorporation of place into larger concept of self
(a) place attachment
(b) place identity
(c) environment consciousness
(d) behaviour setting

16 Who theorised that one way to examine an individual's environmental consciousness is it recognise how the physical place is significant, and look at the place/people relationship?
(a) Scott (b) Leanne Rivlin
(c) Hugo Munsterberg (d) Kurt Lewin

17 Which of the following are scope of applied social psychology in environment?
(a) Ecological consequences of human action
(b) Stress related to physical setting
(c) Evaluation of natural landscape
(d) All of the above

18 Which theory states that in order for people to make a change in their health behaviour, they must have an intention to do so, a positive attitude about the behaviour and a view that their social network will be supportive?
(a) Stages of change model
(b) Social cognitive model
(c) Self-determination theory
(d) Theory of reasoned action

19 Which of the following does not boost an eyewitness confidence?
(a) Getting no feedback from the lineup interviewer.
(b) Learning that another witness had fingered the same person.
(c) Being asked the same question repeatedly.
(d) Preparing for cross examination.

20 The original protection motivation theory claimed that health related behaviours are a product of and therefore predicted by, five components. Which of the following is not one of these?
(a) Fear (b) Severity (c) Benefits (d) Self efficacy

21 According to Lazarus, the degree to which a potential stressor will produce stress depends on the role of which psychological process?
(a) Coping
(b) Appraisal of the stressor and how to cope with it
(c) Sympathetic activation
(d) Degree of fear

22 Researchers had participants working in a room either by themselves or with two strangers. When smoke was pumped into the room through a vent, the solitary participant
(a) noticed the smoke quicker than those in groups
(b) was less likely to act
(c) thought the smoke was a fire
(d) finished the task quickly

23 What would be the best approach to help Marcus quit smoking, if he is in the precontemplation stage?
(a) Providing him with information about nicotine patches.
(b) Helping him evaluate the pros and cons of quitting smoking.
(c) Giving him a reward for cutting down on smoking.
(d) Taking him to a hospital to visit patients with smoking related emphysema.

24 Which of the following is not true about eyewitness testimony?
(a) Confidence is a good predictor of accuracy.
(b) A person's memory of an event may be affected by his attitude.
(c) Testimony about an event often reflects information obtained after the event.
(d) Instructions can affect an eyewitness's willingness to make an identification.

25 The negative emotional experience resulting from a mismatch between the individual's appraisal of a stressor and the individual's ability to cope with the stressor is a common definition for which psychological phenomenon?

(a) Fear (b) Susceptibility
(c) Stress (d) Symptom perception

26 Discrimination refers to behaviours that

(a) allow us to tell one ethnic group from another.
(b) occur, when members of a racial group threaten an individual's security.
(c) prevent individuals from doing things they should be able to do.
(d) are directed toward a particular group.

27 Which of the following is/are the goal (s) of social design?

(a) Create physical setting
(b) Change in Behaviour
(c) Occupant satisfaction
(d) All of these

28 Who among the following report that police officer acts on the opinion that witnesses usually provide?

(a) Geiselman and Fisher (b) Kebbell and Milne
(c) Malpass and Devine (d) None of these

29 Psychology has an important role to play at all stages of chronic illnesses such as Coronary Heart Disease (CHD). But, which one of the following is usually not the case in terms of the psychology behind such an illness?

(a) Someone who believes that "lots of people recover from heart attacks" may lead an inactive and sedentary lifestyle.
(b) If someone has a history of heart attacks in their family and is resigned to that fate, that person is more likely to develop the illness either by affecting behaviour or by having an impact of the immune system.
(c) A person who copes with their illness by tasking definite action and making plans about how to prevent it from deteriorating is in a state of denial and may make the situation worse.
(d) Believing that a heart attack is due to genetic weakness rather than a product of lifestyle may mean that a person is less likely to attend a rehabilitation class and be less likely to try and change the way they behave.

30 Research has indicated that the beliefs of health professionals can affect the initial diagnosis that they make. Which beliefs have been identified as affecting the practice of health professionals?

(a) Stereotypes of the illness or people with the illness.
(b) Perspective or philosophy of the professional.
(c) Seriousness of the disease potentially represented by symptoms.
(d) All of the above

31 Which of the following would be considered an acute stressor?

(a) Colon cancer (b) A pop quiz
(c) Marital discord (d) HIV disease

32 The link between extreme stress and cardiovascular problems can be explained by all of the following except

(a) increased adrenaline
(b) increased negative coping strategies
(c) increased hostility
(d) increased physical activity

33 In order, starting from the first stage, what are the stages of the general adaptation syndrome?

(a) Resistance, alarm, exhaustion
(b) Alarm, exhaustion, illness
(c) Resistance, illness, alarm
(d) Alarm, resistance, exhaustion

34 Sub-Culture theory was propounded by

(a) Wolfgeng and Ferracutti
(b) Bandera and Bandura
(c) Malpass and Devine
(d) Geiselman and Fisher

35 People who drink alcohol because it is fun for them are motivated by

(a) social motives (b) coping motives
(c) enhancement motives (d) extrinsic motives

36 How is body mass index calculated?

(a) By comparing a person's weight to his or her age
(b) By measuring waist circumference
(c) By a treadmill test
(d) By comparing a person's height to his or her weight

37 According to Selye, the General adaptation syndrome include

(a) Alarm stage (b) Resistance stage
(c) Exhaustation stage (d) All of the above

38 During which stage of the stages of change model does relapse occur?

(a) Maintenance
(b) Contemplation
(c) Preparation/determination
(d) Action/willpower

39 The organisation of roles patterns of communication and power in a group defines the groups

(a) status (b) structure
(c) cohesiveness (d) norms

40 The rules which one attains voluntarily are called

(a) Ascribed roles (b) Achieved roles
(c) Positions (d) Social selves

41 The fact that physically attractive people also tend to be rated more highly on traits such as intelligence and honesty is an example of

(a) social magnetism (b) role modeling
(c) social comparison (d) the halo effect

42 A person leaves smoking at once after visiting Sai Baba temple, he is hearing

(a) high self efficacy (b) high faith in God
(c) good company of friends (d) can't be determined

43 Who coined the term 'Resource Dilemma'?

(a) Wades (b) Dawes (c) Stefen (d) None of these

44 The loss of identify and feelings of responsibility which arises due to group membership is known as what?

(a) Dehumanisation (b) Deindividuation
(c) Obedience (d) Conformity

45 Which of the following is false regarding psychological research.?

(a) Experimenters standardise their instructions to subjects to minimise demand characteristics.
(b) Major psychological organisations have developed a number of ethical principles to guide investigators.
(c) Informed consent is an important ethical principle to be followed in conducting research.
(d) deception should never be used in conducting research.

46 What is influenced by the nature of relationship between the interacting individuals?

(a) Crowding (b) Territoriality
(c) Personal space (d) Social design

47 Formal interactions like teaching or meetings of large gathering are examples of which types of distance?

(a) Public distance (b) Social distance
(c) Personal distance (d) Intimate distance

48 Which of the following may be caused by persistent crowding?

(a) Increased blood pressure
(b) Rise in stress hormones
(c) Tendency to give up sooner
(d) All of the above

49 Which kind of territory is the space owned by individuals or primary groups, controlled relatively on a permanent basis by them?

(a) Primary territory
(b) Secondary territory
(c) Public territory
(d) Body territory

50 Which of the following is/are a type of territoriality defence?

(a) Prevention defence
(b) Reaction defence
(c) Social boundary defence
(d) All of these

51 ...... and .... offer challenging opportunity for health psychology.

(a) Health behaviour, psychological stress
(b) Mental fitness, sports
(c) Marriage, divorce
(d) Money, wealth

52 The most common response to traumas is .... which is mild transient reaction to .... events.

(a) irritation, painful (b) resilience, stressfull
(c) power, joyous (d) querrel, unhealthy

53 The health belief model has been developed to explain why people fail to perform .... behaviours such as .... or screening tests.

(a) reflective, orientations (b) casual, dance
(c) healthy, diet oriented (d) preventive, vaccinations

54 .... and .... are two important cognitive variable omissions is the health belief model.

(a) Health, exercise
(b) Motivation, exposure
(c) Self efficacy, behavioural intention
(d) Excitements, plausibility

55 According to the text, ... tends to make people overconfident about the validity of their judgements and predictions.

(a) the fundamental attribution error
(b) illusory correlation
(c) the naturalistic fallacy (d) the hindsight bias

56 Which of the following sets of stage models of health behaviour is in correct chronological order?

1. People are unaware of health issues.
2. People are aware of the issue but never thought about adopting the precaution.
3. People decide against adopting the.
4. People act on their decision.

Codes

(a) 1, 2, 3, 4 (b) 1 , 2, 4, 3 (c) 2, 1, 3, 4 (d) 2, 1, 4, 3

57 Which of the following sets of interaction distances is in correct chronological order distance wise?

1. Personal Distance 2. Public Distance
3. Intimate Distance 4. Social Distance

Codes

(a) 1, 2, 3, 4 (b) 4, 3, 2, 1 (c) 2, 4, 1, 3 (d) 3, 1, 4, 2

58 Consider the following statement regarding evolution of applied psychology.

1. The work of Kurt Lewin marks the beginning of modern applied psychology.
2. In the recent year, use of applied psychology follow.

Codes

(a) Only 1 (b) Only 2
(c) Both 1 and 2 (d) Neither 1 nor 2

59 To be an accurate eyewitness, a person must pass the following stages. Arrange the following in chronological order.

1. Acquisition 2. Retrieval 3. Storage

Codes

(a) 1, 2, 3 (b) 2, 1, 3
(c) 1, 3, 2 (d) 3, 1, 2

60 Which of the following statement is correct regarding public health social psychology?

1. In it social psychology intervention are targeted toward of risk population groups
2. It investigate causal link between psychological factor
3. It include technique of behaviour change.

Codes

(a) 1 and 2 (b) 2 and 3
(c) 1 and 3 (d) All of these

61 Which of the following is true for applied social psychology?

1. Applied social psychology functions on the basis that problems are caused by human behaviour.
2. Applied social psychologists work to improve human social behaviour in various areas.
3. Applied social psychology does not focus on environment.
4. Applied social psychology is not scientific in nature.

Codes

(a) 1 and 2 (b) 2 and 3 (c) 3 and 4 (d) Only 2

62 Which of the following is true for goals of social psychology in health?

1. Creates mental setting
2. Enhances building user's personal control
3. Facilitates social support
4. Promotes prosperity

Codes

(a) 1 and 2 (b) 2 and 3 (c) 3 and 4 (d) All of these

63 Which of the following is true for health psychology?

1. Health behaviours seem to be important in predicting mortality.
2. Health behaviour cannot help us to predict longevity.
3. Health psychologists have turned to the study of health beliefs as potential predictors of behaviour.
4. A person who has been treated for cancer is more likely to donate money to cancer charity.

Codes

(a) 1 and 2 (b) 2 and 3 (c) Only 4 (d) 1 and 3

64 Which one of the following statements about social support is true?

1. Social support in a broad social network impacts positively on health and stress.
2. Social support in small groups helps one resist pressures to comply with an outside majority or to obey an immoral authority.
3. People who don't have an alarm system fitted to their house deserve to get burgled.
4. Helping others is the same as being unselfish and acting like a saint.

Codes

(a) 1 and 2 (b) 2 and 3 (c) 3 and 4 (d) Only 4

65 Which of the following are not necessarily characteristic of an authoritarian personality?

People With authoritarian personalities tend to

1. have experienced harsh family rearing strategies.
2. hate their parents.
3. idolise power figure.
4. strive for a changing world order.

Codes

(a) 1 and 2 (b) 2 and 3 (c) 2 and 4 (d) 1 and 3

66 Using interviews with patients suffering from a variety of illnesses, Leventhal et al identified several type of illness beliefs.

1. Susceptibility 2. Perceived cause
3. Consequences 4. Antecedents

Codes

(a) 1 and 2 (b) 3 and 4 (c) 2 and 3 (d) 1 and 4

67 Which of the following pairs is/are not correct?

1. Social psychologist advice doctor to improve their communication.
2. Psychologist does not help in improving health care behaviour.
3. Critical health social psychologist is concerned with control of power.
4. Psychologist are not able to bring much change.

Codes

(a) 1 and 2 (b) 2 and 3 (c) 1 and 4 (d) Only 1

68 According to applied social psychology in environment, which of the following are function of psychologist?

1. Removing stress related to physical setting.
2. Assesing ecological consequences of human action.
3. Cognitive mapping and spatial cognition.
4. Perception and evaluation of building and natural landscape.

Codes

(a) 1 and 2 (b) 2 and 3
(c) 3 and 4 (d) All of these

69 Which of the following statements is/are correct?

1. Heider's work demonstrated that we respond ask per our experience.
2. The case of Kitty Genovese in New York is classical example of bystander effect.

Codes

(a) Only 1 (b) Only 2
(c) 1 and 2 (d) None of these

70 'Environmental psychologists study not only our affect on environment, but also how environment affect us

Which of the following affects of the environment?

1. Territoriality
2. Crowding
3. Interpersonal relation

Codes

(a) 1 and 2 (b) 2 and 3
(c) 1 and 3 (d) 1, 2 and 4

71 Match the following

List I (Model)		List II (Scholars)
A. Concept of Stress	1.	Leanne Rivlin
B. Stage Models of Health Behaviour	2.	Van Brukelene
C. Environmental Consciousness	3.	Kahle and Beatty
D. Common Dilemma	4.	Robyn Dawes

Codes

	A	B	C	D
(a)	1	2	3	4
(b)	4	3	2	1
(c)	2	4	1	3
(d)	3	1	4	2

72 Match the following

List I (Model)		List II (Scholars)
A. Social Design	1.	Kurt Lewin
B. Cognitive Interview	2.	Shapiro and Penrod
C. Estimator Variables	3.	Fisher and Geiselman
D. Field theory	4.	Robert Sommer

Codes

	A	B	C	D
(a)	1	2	3	4
(b)	4	3	2	1
(c)	2	4	1	3
(d)	3	1	4	2

73 Match the following

List I (Theory)		List II (Scholars)
A. Interpersonal Deception Theory	1.	Zajonc
B. Bystander Intervention	2.	Burgeon and Buller
C. The Notion of Social Facilitation	3.	Berkowitz
D. Frustration-Aggression Hypothesis	4.	Darley and Latane

Codes

	A	B	C	D
(a)	1	2	3	4
(b)	4	3	2	1
(c)	2	4	1	3
(d)	3	1	4	2

74 Match the following

List I (Thoery)		List II (Scholars)
A. Sub-Culture Theory	1.	Andrews and Bonta
B. Social Psychological Model of Criminal Behaviour	2.	Henggeler
C. Social Learning Theory	3.	Wolfgang and Ferracuti
D. Multi-systematic Treatment Programme to Violent Youths	4.	Bandura

Codes

	A	B	C	D
(a)	1	2	3	4
(b)	4	3	2	1
(c)	2	4	1	3
(d)	3	1	4	2

75 Match the following

List I (Theory)		List II (Scholars)
A. Types of interaction	1.	Edward Hall
B. Construction of personal space bubbles by amygdala	2.	Daniel Kennedy
C. Applied social psychology	3.	Kurt Lewin
D. The theory of planned behaviour	4.	Ajzen

Codes

	A	B	C	D
(a)	1	2	3	4
(b)	4	3	2	1
(c)	2	4	1	3
(d)	3	1	4	2

76 Match the following

List I (Distance)		List II (Length)
A. Public Distance	1.	0 to 18 inches
B. Social Distance	2.	18 to 48 inches
C. Personal Distance	3.	4 to 12 feet
D. Intimate Distance	4.	12 feet to infinite length

Codes

	A	B	C	D
(a)	1	2	3	4
(b)	4	3	2	1
(c)	2	4	1	3
(d)	3	1	4	2

77 Match the following

List I (Theory)		List II (Scholars)
A. Frustration aggression hypothesis	1.	Cohen
B. Strain theory	2.	Berkowitz
C. Sub-culture theory	3.	Wolfgang
D. Social ecological perspective	4.	Kurt Lewin

Codes

	A	B	C	D
(a)	2	1	4	3
(b)	2	1	3	4
(c)	3	4	1	2
(d)	4	3	2	1

78 Match the following

List I (Study)		List II (Explanation)
A. Stanford prison study	1.	On prejudice
B. Robbers cave study	2.	Guards readily assumed their roles seriously
C. Bystander effect	3.	Measure attributional style
D. Locus of control	4.	Most likely to be helped by solitary stranger than several strangers

Codes

	A	B	C	D
(a)	2	1	4	3
(b)	3	4	2	1
(c)	2	1	3	4
(d)	4	3	1	2

79 Match the following

List I (Function)		List II (Definition)
A. Object appraisal	1.	Help identify with people whom we like and dissociate from people whom we dislike
B. Social adjustment	2.	Summarise the positive and negative attributes of objects in our environment
C. Ego-defence	3.	Protect the self from internal conflict
D. Value expression	4.	Express self-concept and personal values

Codes

	A	B	C	D		A	B	C	D
(a)	1	2	3	4	(b)	2	1	3	4
(c)	4	2	3	1	(d)	3	1	2	4

80 Match the following

List I (Scholar)		List II (Model)
A. Rober Sommer	1.	Interpersonal deception
B. Kohnken	2.	Social design
C. Kurt Lewin	3.	B=F (P,E)
D. Burgeon and Buller	4.	Statement validity assesment

Codes

	A	B	C	D
(a)	1	2	3	4
(b)	2	4	3	1
(c)	2	3	4	1
(d)	1	3	4	2

Directions (Q. Nos. 81-95) *In the following questions given below are two statements as Assertion (A) and Reason (R). In the context of the two statements, which one of the following is correct?*

Codes

(a) Both A and R are true and R is the correct explanation of A
(b) Both A and R are true, but R is not the correct explanation of A
(c) A is true, but R is false
(d) A is false, but R is true

81 **Assertion** (A) Empathy refers to an unpleasant feeling that we usually experience, when we encounter a person in distress.

Reason (R) Empathy is more likely response, when we see a distressed person, who is similar to ourselves.

82 **Assertion** (A) The bystander-calculus model of helping behaviour incorporates both cognitive as well as physiological processes.

Reason (R) Someone is distress is more likely to be helped by a solitary stranger.

83 **Assertion** (A) Lewin's theorem gave importance to person and environment relationship.

Reason (R) Interaction between person and environment leads to behaviour.

84 **Assertion** (A) Schema helps in understanding social situation and other's behaviour in such situations.

Reason (R) Schema is a mental framework.

85 **Assertion** (A) Contact with friends and acquaintances provide us with emotional support, attention and the opportunity to evaluate our opinions and behaviour through the process of social comparison.

Reason (R) Most theorists agree that intimacy is an essential component of many different interpersonal relationships.

86 **Assertion** (A) Females report more guilt over using aggression than do males and are more concerned about the harm their aggression may inflict on others.

Reason (R) There is also evidence that there is a gender difference in brain neurochemistry related to aggression.

87 **Assertion** (A) We rely on cues from other bystanders more and more as the ambiguity of the situation increases.

Reason (R) In highly ambiguous emergency situations, we might expect the presence of the other who are passive to suppress helping.

88 **Assertion** (A) The older people changed their attitudes following a positive or negative experience as much as, if not more than the younger people.

Reason (R) This finding supports for the impressionable years model and argues against the lifelong openness model, which emphasises that people can form new attitudes throughout their life.

89 **Assertion** (A) The size of the personal space depends on individual and situational difference.

Reason (R) Distancing oneself from others promotes control and maintains autonomy.

90 **Assertion** (A) Personal space should not be considered a static construct.

Reason (R) Personal space varies across individuals and situations.

91 **Assertion** (A) Infants do not mind being touched, kissed or being taken into arms.

Reason (R) Infants do not form their own personal space bubbles before three years of age.

92 **Assertion** (A) The amygdala is the part of our brain that feels fear and is activated when there is a perceived threat to our society.

Reason (R) Personal space bubbles are constructed by the amygdala.

93 **Assertion** (A) Crowding is a social construct where in the amount of space available is less than desired.

Reason (R) Crowding can lead to feelings of aloofness.

94 **Assertion** (A) Territoriality is a pattern of attitudes and behaviour held by a person or group.

Reason (R) Control of secondary territories is less essential to the occupant and is more likely to change, rotate or be shared with strangers.

95 **Assertion** (A) Violation is a permanent infringement of someone's territory.

Reason (R) Sometimes, a violation occurs out of ignorance. For example when a boy, who can not yet real, walks into a women's washroom.

Directions (Q. Nos 96-100) *Read the following given below and answer the following questions.*

In social learning theory, Albert Bandura (1977), states behaviour is learned from the environment through the process of observational learning. Children observe the people around them behaving in various ways. This is illustrated during the famousbobo doll experiment (Bandura, 1961). Individuals that are observed are called models. In society, children are surrounded by many influential models, such as parents within the family, characters on children's TV, friends within their peer group and teachers at school.

They pay attention to some of these people (models) and encode their behaviour. At a later time they may imitate (*i.e.* copy) the behaviour they have observed. They may do this regardless of whether the behaviour is 'gender appropriate' or not but there are a number of processes that make it more likely that a child will reproduce the behaviour that its society deems appropriate for its sex.

First, the child is more likely to attend to and imitate those people it perceives as similar to itself. Consequently, it is more likely to imitate behaviour modelled by people the same sex as it is. Second, the people around the child will respond to the behaviour it imitates with either reinforcement or punishment. If parent sees a little girl consoling her teddy bear and says "What a kind girl you are", this is rewarding for the child and makes it more likely that she will repeat the behaviour. Her behaviour has been reinforced *i.e.* strengthened.

Answer the following question based on the experiment mentioned above.

96 Children learn many social behaviours by imitating parents and other models. This type of learning is called

(a) Observational learning (b) Reinforced learning
(c) Operant conditioning (d) Classical conditioning

97 Bandura believes that modeling is not automatic. Whether a child willimitate a model depends in part on the

(a) child's family connections to the model.
(b) chid's ability to distinguish right from wrong.
(c) reward's and punishments received by the model.
(d) child's age in relation to that of the model.

98 There is considerable controversy about the effects of heavy exposure to television programs showing violence. However, most experts agree that repeated viewing of TV violence

(a) makes all viewers significantly more aggressive
(b) has little effect on viewers
(c) dules the viewer's sensitivity to violence
(d) makes viewers angry and frustrated

99 Parents are powerful models of behaviour. They are most effective in getting their children to imitate them if

(a) thier words and actions are consistent.
(b) they have outgoing personalities.
(c) one parent works and the other stays home to care for the children.
(d) they carefully explain why behaviour is acceptable in adults, but not in children.

100 Consider the following statements

1. Children tend to imitate what a model both does and says, whether the behaviour is prosocialor antisocial.
2. If a model's actions and words are inconsistent, children may imitate that hypocrisy.

Which of the statements given above is/are correctly matched?

(a) Only 1
(b) Only 2
(c) Both 1 and 2
(d) Neither 1 nor 2

PREVIOUS YEARS' QUESTIONS

July 2018

1 Read each of the following statements - Assertion (A) and Reason (R) and indicate your answer using codes given below.

Assertion (A) Perceived fairness of the interpersonal treatment is used to determine organisational outcomes.

Reason (R) People expect informational transparency and respect in organisations.

Codes

(a) Both A and R are true and R is the correct explanation of A
(b) Both A and R are true, but R is not the correct explanation of A
(c) A is true, but R is false
(d) A is false, but R is true

2 Read each of the following statements - Assertion (A) and Reason (R) and indicate your answer using codes given below.

Assertion (A) Rational persuation refers to the use of logical arguments and facts to persuade others for achieving a desired result.

Reason (R) Managers use several techniques to influence others in organisations.

Codes

(a) Both A and R are true and R is the correct explanation of A
(b) Both A and R are true, but R is not the correct explanation of A
(c) A is true, but R is false
(d) A is false, but R is true

November 2017

3 Read each of the following two statements - Assertion (A) and Reason(R) and indicate your answer using codes given below.

Assertion (A) According to Dollard and Miller, observational learning will occur only if organism's overt behaviour is followed by reinforcement.

Reason (R) Copying behaviour involves guiding of one person's behaviour by another person.

Codes

(a) Both A and R are true and R is the correct explanation of A
(b) Both A and R are true, but R is not the correct explanation of A
(c) A is true, but R is false
(d) A is false,but R is true

January 2017

4 The degree to which variations in environment can affect the development of individuals with the particular genotype is

(a) Canalisation (b) Co-dominance
(c) Reaction range (d) Ritualisation

5 Read each of the following two statements Assertion (A) and Reason (R) and indicate your answer using codes given below.

Assertion (A) Minor frustrations will add upto produce considerable frustration but not to aggression.

Reason (R) Disruption of goal-directed behaviour usually leads to frustration.

Codes

(a) Both A and R are true and R is the correct explanation of A
(b) Both A and R are true, but R is not the correct explanation of A
(c) A is true, but R is false
(d) A is false, but R is true

6 Read each of the following two statements Assertion (A) and Reason (R) and indicate your answer using codes given below.

Assertion (A) In general, members of joint family read to be low on stress than those of mucleus family.

Reason (R) Social support increases the stress responses.

(a) Both A and R are true and R is the correct explanation of A
(b) Both A and R are true, but R is not the correct explanation of A
(c) A is true, but R is false
(d) A is false, but R is true

July 2016

7 Perceived fairness of the amount and rewards among individuals refers towhile perceived fairness of the ways used for rewards and pays refers to

(a) organisational justice, distributive justice
(b) equity organisational justice
(c) distributive justice; procedural justice
(d) procedural justice; distributive justice

8 The need for .... produces active, controlling social behaviour while need for .... produces more passive, less controlling social behaviour.

(a) affiliation; self-esteem (b) confidence; intimacy
(c) affiliation; intimacy (d) intimacy; affiliation

9 Read each of the following two statements- Assertion (A) and Reason (R) and indicate your answer using the codes given below

Assertion (A) Projective techniques are difficult to standardise and norm.

Reason (R) Projective techniques are not timed tests.

Codes

(a) Both A and R are true and R is the correct explanation of A
(b) Both A and R are true, but R is not the correct explanation of A
(c) A is true, but R is false
(d) A is false, but R is true

December 2014

10 Among the following descriptions of major defence mechanisms, which one describes 'projection'?

(a) Assigning logical of socially desirable motives to that , we do.
(b) Directing a motive that cannot be gratified in one form into another channel.
(c) Denying that an unpleasant reality exists.
(d) Assigning our own undesirable qualities to others.

11 The degree to which one can control an event ....the stress and inability to predict the occurrence of an event usually ...... the stress.

(a) increases, increases
(b) increases, decreases
(c) decreases, increases
(d) decreases, decreases

12 Which of the following are the physiological reactions to stress?

1. Decrease in metabolic rate.
2. Dilation of pupils
3. Lower blood pressure 4. Increased heart rate

Codes

(a) 2 and 4 (b) 1, 2 and 4
(b) 1,3 and 4 (d) 2, 3 and 4

June 2014

13 Defence attorneys often protest prosecutor's use of eyewitness testimony because

(a) eyewitnesses are more prone to forgetting.
(b) a confident witness is usually right.
(c) source errors may cause an eyewitness to make a false identification.
(d) poor eyesight of eyewitnesses tends to invalidate their testimony.

14 Match the following

List I (Concept)	List II (Theorist)
A. Shaping and chaining	1. Tolman
B. Law of effect	2. Skinner
C. Cognitive map	3. Bandura
D. Modeling	4. Thorndike

Codes

	A	B	C	D
(a)	1	3	4	2
(b)	2	3	1	4
(c)	2	4	1	3
(d)	3	4	2	1

ANSWERS

Exam Based Questions

1 (d)	2 (d)	3 (a)	4 (b)	5 (c)	6 (d)	7 (c)	8 (b)	9 (c)	10 (a)
11 (d)	12 (b)	13 (d)	14 (b)	15 (b)	16 (b)	17 (d)	18 (d)	19 (a)	20 (c)
21 (b)	22 (a)	23 (d)	24 (a)	25 (c)	26 (c)	27 (d)	28 (b)	29 (c)	30 (d)
31 (b)	32 (d)	33 (d)	34 (a)	35 (a)	36 (d)	37 (d)	38 (b)	39 (b)	40 (b)
41 (d)	42 (a)	43 (b)	44 ()	45 (a)	46 (c)	47 (d)	48 (d)	49 (a)	50 (d)
51 (a)	52 (b)	53 (d)	54 (c)	55 (d)	56 (a)	57 (c)	58 (a)	59 (c)	60 (a)
61 (a)	62 (d)	63 (d)	64 (a)	65 (c)	66 (c)	67 (d)	68 (d)	69 (b)	70 (a)
71 (a)	72 (b)	73 (c)	74 (d)	75 (a)	76 (b)	77 (b)	78 (a)	79 (b)	80 (b)
81 (b)	82 (b)	83 (a)	84 (a)	85 (b)	86 (a)	87 (a)	88 (c)	89 (b)	90 (a)
91 (a)	92 (a)	93 (c)	94 (b)	95 (d)	96 (a)	97 (c)	98 (c)	99 (a)	100 (c)

Previous Years' Questions

1 (d)	2 (d)	3 (b)	4 (c)	5 (d)	6 (c)	7 (c)	8 (c)	9 (b)	10 (d)
11 (c)	12 (b)	13 (c)	14 (c)						

CHAPTER 28

Developmental Processes

When we think of development, we naturally think of children growing up into adults. But even as adults, we never really stop changing. Developmental psychology, the study of progressive changes in behaviour and abilities involves every stage of life from conception to death.

Development

The term growth, development, maturation and learning all refer to the physical, mental, social, emotional, aesthetic, moral and spiritual changes, which the human being experiences as he advances through life. Some psychologists use the terms growth and development interchangeably. Others reserve growth for changes of a quantitative nature and development for those which are qualitative. This distinction serves a useful purpose on the theoretical level, but in practical situations, one cannot be separated from the other. Children do not grow without developing nor do qualitative changes occur unaccompanied by some quantitative changes.

Maturation refers to the changes either quantitative or qualitative, which result from the natural unfolding of inherited tendencies or the actualisation of innate potentialities. Learning pertains to the changes which result from the modification or direction of these tendencies through individual effort and environmental influence. Here again, maturation and learning are not mutually exclusive process, but are intrinsically connected and dependent upon one another. Lacking a sufficient degree of maturity, a person cannot learn. Learning affects the manner in which maturation takes place.

Nature of Development

There are two concepts associated with human changes *i.e.* growth and development. Generally, both the words are used interchangeably. But they differ from each other with respect to the nature of changes they brought in the individuals. Growth basically refers to quantitative changes in the body proportion like change in weight, height, internal organs etc. Development on the other hand, reflects the qualitative changes in the individual. It may be defined as a progressive series of orderly, coherent changes. The term progressive denotes the changes that lead forward.

In this Chapter

Orderly and coherent changes assume that there is a definite relationship between the changes occurring and those that precede or will follow them. These changes bring functional maturity in an individual.

So, development is a qualitative change in the person which is reflected in the improvement in working or functioning of the person. *For example* If we measure the height and weight of the child then we are dealing with the concept of growth, but when we talk in terms of improvement in functioning like writing with pen or keeping object on high place, then these changes in the child denotes the developmental process.

Comparison of Growth and Development

Development	Growth
Development refers to overall changes in the individual in an orderly and coherent manner towards goal of maturity.	Growth refers to physiological changes.
Development changes in quality along with quantitative aspect.	Changes is quantitative respect is termed as growth.
Development is progressive and continues throughout life.	Growth does not continue throughout life and stops after maturation.
Development is organisational.	Growth is cellular.
Development is a wider and comprehensive term.	Growth is one of the part of the development process.
Development is possible without growth.	Growth may or may not bring development.

Principles of Development

A principle is a judgement from which other judgements flow. A principle in short, is the beginning or source of knowledge about a subject. The principles of development, which follow are sources of knowledge about human behaviour, *are as follows*

Development is Continuous

For the purpose of convenience in discussing human development, psychologists divide the developmental continuum into stages or phases. *The life span is divided into the following periods by Piteumas.*

- **Prenatal Period** The time during, which major bodily structures and functions are established to form a biological basis for psychological development. This period includes the stage of the **zygote**, from conception until 2 weeks afterward, the stage of the embroyo, from about 2 weeks to 2 months and the stage of the **fetus,** from 2 to 9 months.
- **Neonatal Period** The first 3 or 4 weeks after birth, when the new born infant must make radical adjustments to the demands of the outside world.
- **Early Infancy** The period from 1 or 2 until about mont'ıs, wherein the individual develops from passively receptive person into one who is capable of seeking new experiences and relationships in his environment.
- **Late Infancy** The period from about 15 to 30 months, when the individual enlarges his world still further by the acquisition of verbal language.
- **Early Childhood** The period from about $2\frac{1}{2}$ to 5 years. During these pre-school years, the child develops skills, abilities and self-concept, but remains largely restricted to his family environment.
- **Middle Childhood** (From 5 to 9 years), During these first school years, many social and intellectual changes take place in the individual as a result of his interaction with persons outside the family.
- **Late Childhood** (From ages 9 to 12), During these years, the child rapidly develops a strong sense of personal identity and a firm relationship with his peer society. This stage is also referred to as preadolescence.
- **Adolescence** The years, during which the individual matures and somewhat establishes his system of values and interests, preparing for the responsibilities, his system of values and interests, preparing for the responsibilities and privileges of adult life.
- **Adulthood** The years, during which the individual enters adult society, acquires an occupation, usually establishes a family and continues to consolidate and evaluate his previous achievements and aspirations.
- **Senescence** The years past 70, which employs the term infancy childhood and adolescence do not always agree with one another as to the chronological ages, which an individual enters or leaves these stages. The names of the stages and the corresponding age levels,then, are quite arbitrary.

Development is Cumulative

In the developmental sequence, certain changes impress the individual himself or the interested observer with their dramatic suddenness and the prospects of their far-reaching consequences. The child's first spoken word, his first step and the appearance of his first tooth etc. are considered by many parents as matters worthy of recording in the family archives.

His first hair cut, his first day at school, his confirmation, graduation, first date and first shave are properly regarded as turning points of his life. But each of these milestones is an event towards, which the child has been advancing and for which he has been preparing consciously or unconsciously, all his life. Each is the culmination of his prior growth and experience. The manner in which he takes his first step, what he does in school on that memorable first day and how he behaves on his first date are all dependent upon things he did or things that were done to him earlier in life, he himself might not even remember.

Development is Orderly

The direction of human development is from undifferentiated, mass responses to more refined, localised or goal-directed. The first bodily movements of the infant are random and undirected. Gradually, they become differentiated enough for grasping, pushing, walking and climbing.

During the first year of life, the typical child begins to walk unaided, but he does so in an awkward manner. Eventually, his leg muscles are brought under sufficient control to enable him to walk backwards, skip, hop and dance. Then, with an increase in maturity and experience, his movements are made even more specific, so that he performs several different kinds of dance steps. This same process of differentiation is true of other aspects of his development.

Development is Complex

A human being is a complex of many interrelated dynamic factors, which do not keep pace with one another in their rates of development. *For example* At a given period in the child's life, he may be growing faster mentally than he is emotionally or he may be more mature physically than he is socially.

One year, he may make comparatively small intellectual gains than social, while in the next year, the opposite may be true. So, we see that there is nothing specific, development can be possible in any sphere, anyway.

Development is Unified

The statement that a child is a certain number of years of age old leaves out of account the fact that he has ages other than the chronological age, that the several aspects of his development do not adhere strictly to a time table and that they do not always keep pace with one another. To take into account the various ways in which individuals develop and the differing rates of the process, **Olson** and **Hughes** have submitted the concept of organismic age. *Organismic age* is the average of all available growth ages, usually including height, weight, mental, reading, carpal, grip and dental ages.

Olson and Hughes maintain that when all of these ages are averaged up, they yield a more significant indication of the child's overall maturity level than does his chronological age.

Factor Influencing Developmental Process

Several factors influence human development. *These factors are as follows*

- **Hereditary Factors** Heredity exerts an influence on human development. The physical characteristics like height, weight, eye colour etc. and psychological characteristics such as intelligence, personality, creativity etc. are hereditary and innately determined. The genetic code provides the base on which brain and body grow and manifest in observable appearance and behaviour.
- **Environmental Factors** The environment where an individual lives influences human development. Environment consists of wide range of stimuli and it provides necessary input and experiential base for development. Enrichment or impoverishment of environment produces differences in abilities of an individual.

  The home environment plays a major role in development as it builds self-concept. Supportive, warm and harmonious environment leads to normal development of an individual while unsupportive and stressful home environment leads to poor development.
- **Cultural Factors** Culture refers to a system of beliefs, attitudes and values that are transmitted from one generation to next . This system of culture, customs and traditions influence the socialisation process through which an individual learns the habits, beliefs, attitude, skills etc. Thus, culture influences development of an individual.
- **Socio-Economic Status** Socio-economic status plays an important role in the development of an individual. An individual having low socio-economic status develops as malnourished illiterate, hence, his normal development gets hampered. High socio-economic status exposes an individual to better social opportunities, better nutrition, good medical treatment and intellectual stimulation.
- **Normative Influences** The influences that occur in a similar way for majority of people in a particular group are called *normative influences* while non-normative influences are the unusual life events in an individual's life. Normative influences may be

biological or environmental. Biological influences include deterioration in old age and environmental influences include entering school at about 6 yrs of age. These all factors influence development of an individual.

- **Education and Training** Education and training influence human development. Every individual is equipped with certain abilities which need to be nurtured through proper education and training. These abilities need to be identified and recognised and adequate opportunities should be provided to develop the same. If the abilities are not identified properly and adequate facilities are not provided, innate abilities of an individual may not develop.

Stages of Development

The development across the entire life span was described by Erikson. He suggested that all human beings passes through specific stages or phases of development. He believed that each stage of life is marked by a specific crisis or conflict between competing tendencies. Only if individuals negotiate each of these hurdles successfully, they can continue to develop in a normal, healthy manner.

The stages of development are as follows

- **Trust v/s Mistrust** This is the initial stage of development which occurs during infant stage of life (age 0-1.5 years). This stage focuses on the crisis of trust versus mistrust. Infants learn to trust others to satisfy their needs. However, if the needs are not met, infants fail to develop feeling of trust in others and remain forever suspicious and wary.
- **Autonomy v/s Shame and Doubt** This is the second stage of development which centres on the crisis of autonomy versus shame and doubt. It occurs during toddler years of life (age 1.5-3 years).

  Toddlers learn to regulate their own bodies and act in independent ways. If they are successful in these tasks, they develop a sense of autonomy.

  However, if they fail or it they are labelled as inadequate by the persons who care for them, they may experience shame and may doubt their abilities to interact effectively with the external world.
- **Initiative v/s Guilt** This is the third stage of development which occurs during pre-school years (age 3-5 years) and involves crisis of initiative versus guilt. During these years, children acquire many new physical and mental skills and develop capacity to control their impulses. Thus, for proper development, there should be right balance between feelings of initiative and guilt. However, if initiative overpowers guilt, children may become too unruly and if guilt overpowers initiative, children may become inhibited.
- **Industry v/s Inferiority** This is the fourth stage of development which occurs during early school years (age 6-11 years) and involves crisis of industry versus inferiority. During these years, children learn to make things, use tools and acquire many of skills necessary for adult life. Children who successfully acquire these skills form a sense of competence and those who do not acquire may compare themselves unfavourably with others and suffer from low self-esteem.
- **Identity v/s Role Confusion** This is the fifth stage of development which occurs during adolescence (age 12-18 years) and involves crisis of identity verus role confusion. Adolescents integrate various roles into a consistent self identify. For this, they consider many possible social selves *i.e.* different kind of persons they might potentially become. Out of these experiences, they develop a self schema *i.e.* a cognitive framework for understanding themselves. If they fail so do so, they may experience confusion over who they are.
- **Intimacy v/s Isolation** this is the sixth stage of development which occurs during late adolescence and early adulthood (age 19-40 years). It involves crisis of intimacy versus isolation. During this individuals develop ability to form deep and intimate relationships with others and form strong emotional attachments to others. People who fail to resolve it successfully live is isolation, unable to form truly intimate and lasting relationship.
- **Generativity v/s Self-Absorption** This is the seventh stage of development which occurs during 41-65 years of age and involves crisis of generativity versus self-absorption. During this stage, adult take active interest in helping and guiding younger person and overcome their selfish and self-centered concerns. People who do not help or guide others become absorbed in their own lives and cut themselves off from an important source of growth and satisfaction.
- **Integrity v/s Despair** This is eighth stage of development which occurs at age of 65+ years. During this stage, individual ask themselves whether their lives had any meaning. It they can answer yes, they attain a sense of integrity and if they answer no, they experience despair.

Eriknson's Stages of Development

Stage of Development/Crisis	Age	Basic Virtue Learnt
Trust v/s Mistrust	Infant (0-1.5 Yrs)	Hope
Autonomy v/s Shame and Doubt	Toddler (1.5-3 Yrs)	Will
Initiative v/s Guilt	Pre-school (3-5 yrs)	Purpose
Industry v/s Inferiority	School child (6-11 yrs)	Competency
Identity v/s Role confusion	Adolescent (12-18 yrs)	Fidelity
Intimacy v/s Isolation	Young adult (19-40 yrs)	Love
Generativity v/s Self-absorption	Middle adult (41-65 yrs)	Care
Integrity v/s Despair	Older person (65+yrs)	Wisdom

Successful Ageing

The concept of successful ageing can be traced back to 1950s and was popularised in 1980s. Traditional definitions of successful ageing have emphasised absence of physical and cognitive disabilities. Successful ageing has been equated with life satisfaction. happiness, good health and longevity.

Rowe and **kahn** have developed a distinction between usual and successful ageing within the category of normal or non-pathological ageing. Usual ageing is defined as ageing in which extrinsic factors heighten the effects of intrinsic ageing processes whereas successful ageing refers to ageing in which extrinsic factors counteract intrinsic ageing, so that there is little or no functional loss.

Components of Successful Ageing

The components of characterisitics of successful ageing are as follows

Freedom from Disease and Disability

The disease and disability can be prevented by

- Early detection of disease
- Proper nutrition
- Vigorous exercise
- Vaccinations
- Avoiding sugary food, alcohol abuse and drug abuse
- Social support

High Cognitive and Physical Functioning

High cognitive and physical functioning can be achieved by

- Continuing education and mental challenges through reading, skill games, puzzles, learning new subjects etc.
- Maintaining cardiovascular fitness through daily aerobic exercise.
- Engaging in useful, satisfying work or voluntary activities.
- Memory training.
- Maintaining appropriate social support.

Social and Productive Engagement with Life

Social support involves giving and receiving positive information, trust, care, love, esteem, network membership and mutual obligation. Socio-emotional support and instrumental support are necessary for successful ageing.

Productive activity is promoted through health, social support and self-efficacy.

Theories of Development

There are few major theories that influence and help in doing research in human development. *These are*

Psychoanalytical Theory

The psychoanalytical theory asserts that development is shaped by unconscious forces that motivate human behaviour. **Sigmud Freud** (1856-1939), a Viennese physician developed psychoanalysis as a therapeutic approach aimed at giving patient insight into unconscious emotional conflict and other theorist and practitioners including Erik H Erikson have expanded and modified the psychoanalytic theory.

Sigmund Freud Psychosexual Development

Freud believed that people are born with biological drives that must be redirected to live in society. He proposed that personality is formed in childhood as children deal with unconscious conflicts between these inborn urges and the requirements of civilised life.

These conflicts occur in an unvarying sequence of five maturational based stages of psychosexual development, in which sexual or sensual pleasure shifts from one body zone to another from the mouth to the arms and then to the genitals. At each stage, the behaviour that is the chief source of gratification (or frustration), changes from feeding to sexual activity.

According to **Freud**, "a key event in psychosexual development occurs in the phallic stage of early childhood." Freud based his theories about normal development, not on a population of average children, but on a clientele of upper-middle class adults, mostly women, in therapy. His concentration on the importance of sexual feelings and of early experience does not take into account other influences on personality including the influences of society and culture.

Behaviouristic Theory

Behaviourism is a mechanistic theory, which describes observed behaviour as a predictable response to experience. Although, biology sets limits on what people do, behaviourists view the environment, as much more influential.

They hold that human beings at all ages learn about the world, the same way other organisms do by reaching to conditions or aspects of their environment, that they find pleasing, painful or threatening. Behaviourists look for events that determine whether or not a particular behaviour will be repeated.

Behavioural research focuses on associative learning which are classified as classical conditioning and operant conditioning.

Classical Conditioning

The Russian physiologist Luan Pavlov (1849-1936) devised experiments, in which dogs learned to salivate at the sound of a bell that rang at feeding time. These experiments were the foundation for classical conditioning, in which a response (salivation) to a stimulus (the bell) is evoked after repeated association with a stimulus that automatically elicits it (food).

One of the earliest and most famous demonstrations of classical conditioning in human being was given by Watson and Rayner, 1920. Watson set out to teach 11 months old baby known as *little Albert* to fear furry white objects.

Classical conditioning is a natural form of learning that occurs even without intervention. By learning what events go together, children can anticipate what is going to happen and this knowledge makes their world a more orderly, predictable place.

Operant Conditioning

Operant conditioning is a process through which organisms learn to repeat behaviours that yield positive outcomes or permit them to avoid or escape from negative consequences is known as *operant conditioning*. In situations involving operant conditioning, probability that a given behaviour will occur changes depending on consequences that follow it. These probabilities are determined by reinforcement (procedures that strengthen behaviour) and punishment (procedures that suppress behaviour).

Cognitive Theory

The cognitive perspective focuses on thought processes and the behaviour that reflects those processes. This perspective encompasses both organismic and mechanistically influenced theories. It includes the cognitive stage theory of Piaget, the newer information processing approach and neo piagetian theories, which combine elements of both. It also include contemporary findings of brain research to the understanding of cognitive process.

Jean Piaget's Cognitive Stage Theory

Piaget's clinical method combined observation with flexible questioning. To find out how children think, Piaget followed-up their answers with more questions. In this, he discovered that a typically year-old believed that bennies or flowers were more numerous, when arranged in a line than when heaped or piled up from his observation of his own and other children. Piaget created a comprehensive theory of cognitive development.

Piaget believed that cognitive development begins with an inborn's ability to adapt to the environment. By rooting for a nipple, feeling a pebble or exploring the bound aris of a room, young children develop a more accurate picture of their surroundings and greater competence in dealing with them.

Adaption is Piaget's term for how children handle new information in light of what they already know.

Adaption involves two steps

(i) Assimilation, taking in new information and incorporating it into existing cognitive structures.

(ii) Accommodation, changing one's cognitive structures to include the new information.

Equilibration, a constant striving for a stable balance or equilibrium dictates the shift from assimilation to accommodation. Thus, assimilation and accommodation work together to produce equilibrium and cognitive growth.

The major stages in Piaget's theory are as follows

Stage	Age	Characteristic
Sensorimotor	0-2 years	This is the earliest stage of cognitive development in Piaget's theory. The child develops basic ideas of cause and effect (idea that they can manipulate objects and produce effects) and object permanence (idea that objects continue to exist even when hidden continue to exist even when hidden from view).
Preoperational	2-6 years	The child begins to represent the world symbolically. In this stage of cognitive development, children become capable of mental representations of external world.
Concrete Operations	7-11years	The child gains understanding of relational terms (lighter, larger, softer); seriation (ability to arrange objects in order along some dimension); reversibility (many physical changes can be undone by a reversal of original action) and logical thought.
Formal Operations	12-adult	In this stage, individual acquires the capacity for hypothetico-deductive reasoning (ability to generate hypothesis and think logically about symbols, ideas and propositions) and interpropositional thinking (thinking in which a child seeks to test validity of several propositions).

Various Aspects of Development

There are numerous aspects of development which include language development, motor development, sensory development, emotional development, moral development etc. *Details about these aspects are as follows*

Language Development

Language development is the process by which children understand and communicate language during early childhood. Language development begins before birth. Towards the end of pregnancy, a fetus begins to hear sounds and speech coming from outside the mother's body.

Language development is enriched by verbal interactions with other children and adults. Parents and care givers can have a significant impact on early language development.

Children Develop Language Skills is Following Phases

Phase (Average Age)	Language Behaviour Demonstrated by Child
12 weeks	Smiles when talked to; makes cooing sounds
16 weeks	Turns head in response to human voice
20 weeks	Makes vowel and consonant sounds while cooing
6 months	Progresses from cooing to babbling that contains all sounds of human speech
8 months	Repeats certain syllables (e.g. 'ma-ma')
12 months	Understands some words; may say a few
18 months	Can produce up to fifty words
24 months	Has vocabulary of more than fifty words; uses some two-word phrases
30 months	Has vocabulary of several hundred words; uses phrases of three to five words
36 months	Has vocabulary of about a thousand words
48 month	Has mastered most basic elements of language

Components of Language

Language consists of several subsystem that deal with sound, meaning, overall structure and everyday use. Language development involves knowing language entails, mastering each of these aspects and combining them into a flexible communication system.

The components of language are as follows

- **Phonology**, the *first* component, refers to the rules governing the structure and sequence of speech sounds. In English, you easily apply an intricate set of rules to comprehend and produce complicated sound patterns.
- **Semantics**, the *second* component, involves vocabulary, the way underlying concepts are expressed in words and word combinations. Once mastery of vocabulary is under way, children combine words and modify them in meaningful ways.
- **Grammar**, the *third* component of language, consists of two main part: **Syntax**, the rules by which words are arranged into sentences and **morphology**, the use of grammatical markers indicating number, tense, case, person, gender, active or passive voice and other meanings (the endings-s and -ed are examples in English). Finally, pragmatics refers to the rules for engaging in appropriate and effective communication. To converse successfully,children must take turns, stay on the same topic and state their meaning clearly.

Theories of Language Development

Language development is a complex process involving several aspects to learning, many cognitive processes and various genetically determined mechanisms. *The following theories tend to explain mechanism for acquistion of language*

(i) **Social Learning Theory** According to this theory, speech is acquired through a combination of operant conditioning and imitation. Children are praised or rewarded by their parents for making sounds close to their native language or parents model sounds, words or sentences for them. Together these both forms of learning contribute to acquistion of language.

(ii) **Noam Chomsky Language Acquisition Theory** According to Noam Chomsky, language acquisition is atleast partly innate. He contends that human beings have a Language Acquisition Device (LAD). LAD is a built-in neural system that provides them with an intuitive grasp of grammar. Thus, humans are prepared to acquire language rapidly.

(iii) **Cognitive Theory** This theory was given by Slobin who recognised the importance of both innate mechanisms and learning. According to this theory, children possess certain information processing abilities or strategies that they use in acquiring language. These are known as *operating principles* and seen to be present or develop early in life. *The operating principles includes*

- 'Pay attention to the ends of words' principle-children pay more attention to ends than to beginning or middle of words.
- 'Pay attention to order or words's principle-children pay more attention to word order.

Sensory-Motor Development

Sensory-motor development refers to the learning of relationship between actions and external world by an infant. Virtually all parents eagerly await their infants mastry of new motor skills. Baby books are filled with proud notations as soon as children hold up their heads, reach for objects, sit by themselves, crawl and walk alone. Parent's enthusiasm for these achievement makes perfect sense. They are indeed, milestones of development. With each new motor skill, babies master their bodies and the environment in a new way. Voluntary reaching permits babies to find out about objects by acting on them and own their opportunities for exploration and multiplied.

Babies motor achievement have a powerful effect on their social relationship. *For example* Parents start to restrict the activities of a beginning crawler in ways that were unnecessary when the baby placed on a blanket, would stay there! New motor skills, such as pointing to and showing toys, permit infants to communicate more effectively. In response, parent devote less time to physical care and more to game playing and verbal request. Babies' expression of delight, laughing, smiling and babbling as they work on new motor competencies trigger pleasurable reactions in other, which encourage infant's efforts further. In this way, motor skills, social competencies, cognition and language develop together and support one another.

The Organisation and Sequence of Motor Development

Gross motor development refers to control over actions that help infants get around in the environment, such as crawling, standing and walking. In contrast, fine motor development has to do with smaller movements, such as reaching and grasping. There is organisation and direction to the infant's motor achievements. *First,* motor control of the head comes before control of the arms and trunk and control of the arms and trunk is achieved before control of the legs. This head-to-tail sequence is called the *cephaslocaudal trend. Second,* motor development proceeds from the center of the body outward, in that head, trunk and arm control is mastered before coordination of the hands and fingers. This is the *proximodistal trend*. Physical growth during the prenatal period as well as during infancy and childhood, follows these same trends. Because physical and motor development conform to the same general sequence; the cephalocaudal and proximodistal trends are believed to be generally determined in, maturational pattern.

Motor Skills are Complex System of Action

Motor skills are not a series of isolated, unrelated accomplishments. Earlier in this century, researchers made this mistake; but today we know that motor development is a matter of acquiring increasingly complex systems of action. When motor skills work as a system separate abilities blend together each cooperating with others to produce more advanced ways of exploring and controlling the environment.

During infancy, new systems of action emerge constantly. *For example* Control of the head and upper chest are combined into sitting with support. Kicking, rocking on all fours and reaching are gradually put together into crawling. Then crawling, standing and stepping are united into walking alone.

The way simple motor acts are reorganised into more effective motor systems is most obvious in the area of fine motor skills. As babies become increasingly aware of a world of tantalising things to be explored, they perfect these skills and combine them into successful reaching for objects.

Once reaching is accomplished, infants can coordinate it with other actions to produce even more complex skill, such as stacking blocks, putting objects into containers and eating with a spoon.

Emotional Development

Emotional development refers to the ability to recognise, express and manage feelings at different stages of life and to have empathy for the feeling of others. The development of these emotions are largely influenced by relationship with parents, siblings and peers. *Some of the theory related to emotional development are as follows*

Behaviourism and Social Learning Theory

From this beginning of this century, behaviourists accorded emotional reactions an important role in children's development.

According to **John Watson**, "three innate emotions are present at birth: fear, induced by loud noises or loss of support rage, prompted by restriction of body movements and love, evoked by touching and caressing." One of Watson's major findings was that emotional reaction to new stimuli, such as 9 months old Albert's fearful reaction to a furry white rat, could be learned through classical conditioning.

Social learning theory emphasises on modeling of other's emotional reactions as another important means, through which children associate feelings with particular situations. In recent years, Albert Bandura has expanded this view, adding a cognitive component to traditional social learning theory.

Cognitive-Developmental Discrepancy Theory

According to **Hebb**, "when children encounter a new stimulus, they compare it to a scheme or internal representation of a familiar object."

The similarity between the novel stimulus and the child's scheme determines the emotional response. Little discrepancy produces very mild distress, but as the discrepancy increases, the child's distress reaction intensifies. When the discrepancy is very great, the stimulation can no longer be assimilated and the distress reaction declines.

Emotions as Determinants of Cognitive Processing

Emotional reactions can lead to learning that is crucial for survival. *For example* The newly waking toddler does not need to receive a shock from an electric outlet or fall down a staircase to learn to avoid these dangerous situations. Instead, the care giver's highly charged command is enough to get the child to acquire these self protection behaviours.

Unlike proponents of discrepancy theory, most functionalist theorists believe the relationship between emotion and cognition is bidirectional. Michael Lewis and his colleagues found evidence for this first half-year of life.

Two to eight months olds were trained to pull a string attached to their wrists, which produces a slide of a smiling baby and a recording of a children's song. By tracking facial expressions, the researchers found that interest, happiness and surprise increased as the infants learned the task-reactions that reflected pleasure at mastery of a new contingency.

Next, a short non-reinforcement period followed, in which pulling the string no longer activated stimuli. Emotions were intimately interwoven with cognitive processing, serving both as outcomes of mastery and as the foundation for infant's approach to the next learning phase.

Emotion as Determinants of Social Behaviour

Children's emotional signals, such as smiling, crying and attentive interest affect the behaviour of other people in powerful ways. Similarly, emotional reactions of others regulate children's social behaviour. *For example* Careful analysis of mother-infant face-to-face interaction reveal that by 3 months a complex communication system is in place, in which each partner responds in an appropriate and carefully timed fashion to the cues of the other.

In several studies, this exchange of emotional signals was disrupted by having mothers assume either a still-faced, unreactive pose or a depressed emotional state. Infants tried facial expressions, vocalisation and body movements to get their mothers to respond again. When these efforts failed, they reacted to their mother's sad, vacant gaze by turning away, frowning and crying.

Moral Development

The study of moral development in children involves tracing the process by which the child internalises a set of culturally defined norms of social conduct. Traditionally,the end product of this development was described as a conscience or superego.

Aspects in Moral Development

Moral development can be conveniently divided into three parts-behavioural, affective and cognitive aspects of morality. The behavioural aspect has generally referred to the child's ability to resist temptation in the absence of external surveillance. The affective aspect focuses on the emotional reaction of the child to transgression, the existence of internalised norms as inferred from emotional reaction such as guilt which may follow violation of these standards. Much of the research in this area has been influenced by psychoanalytic theory.

The third approach to moral development has been judgemental or cognitive. The aim of the approach is to delineate the changes occuring with age in the child's understanding and interpretation of moral rules.

Theories of Moral Development

The various theorists who have made contributions to the field of moral development are as follows

Piaget

Piaget's The Moral Judgement of the Child (1948), has primarily been responsible for the recent research on the cognitive aspects of morality. According to **Piaget**, "two clearcut stages of moral development-the hetermonous and autonomous stages can be distinguished and 7 years is the approximate dividing age."

In the *first* or heteronomous stages, two defects in cognitive functioning limit the young child's understanding of moral rules. Because of the first limitation realism the child is unable to distinguish subjective and objective phenomena and hence views adult rules as fixed external entities. The *second* defect- egocentrism- lends the child to confuse his own and other person's perspectives; the result is a failure to regard moral rules a relative to various individuals and purposes.

Children at each of the two moral stages differ in their definition of right and wrong and in their conception of justice. In the heteronomous stages *e.g.* children judge the severity of an act in terms of the amount of physical damage and disregard the internationality of the action, only in the autonomous stages does intent replace consequences as the basis for judgement. Similarly, the younger child believes in intrinsic justice rather than in naturalistic causality and favours explative over restrictive justice.

Kohlberg

This theorist differs from Piaget in numorous ways. **Firstly**, it views moral development as an extended and complex process rather than a single step from heteronomous to autonomous morality. Instead of merely two stages of moral judgement, kohelberg's investigations have revealed six distinct stages, which are assumed to form an invariant sequence.

"In contrast to the 'superego strength' view of moral learning as a matter of increased strength of conscience response to the developmental approach views moral learning in terms of age-related sequences of changes by which moral attitudes emerge from qualitatively different pre-moral attitudes and concepts" (Kohlberg, 1963).

Secondly, Kohelberg analysis assumes that the passage from one stage to the next involves an integration and displacement of modes of though associated with earlier stages, support for these assumptions has been provided by the recent experimental work of **Turiel** (1966), in which subjects of a known stage of moral development were exposed to examples of moral reasoning either one stage below, one stage above or two stages above their present stage of moral development.

The finding that subjects assimilated moral reasoning associated with one stage higher than their own more readily than two stage higher lends support to Kohlberg's fixed sequence notion. Moreover subject accepted moral judgement one stage higher more readily than moral judgements one stage lower than their own; this finding support Kohlberg's second assumption concerning the integration of lower stages into higher stages of thought.

The major levels of moral reasoning described by kohlberg are

(i) **Preconventional Level or Morality** At this level, children think in ways that fall short of customary moral concerns of society. Their reasoning is ego-centric and focuses on personal consequences of individual's behaviour. It includes two stages

- **Punishment and Obedience Orientation** In this stage, morality is judged in terms of consequences. Actions that lead to rewards are perceived as acceptable and that leads to punishment are seen as unacceptable.
- **Naive Hedonistic Orientation** In this stage, morality is judged in terms of what satisfies own needs or those of others.

(ii) **Conventional Level or Morality** At this level, children think in ways that are considered to be acceptable moral rules by societies. It includes two stages.

- **Good-Boy-Good Girl Orientation** In this stage, morality is judged in terms of adherence to social rules or norns with respect to personal acquaintances.
- **Social Order-Maintaining Orientation** In this stage morality is judged in terms of social rules or laws applied universally, not just to acquaintances.

(iii) **Post-Conventional Level of Morality** A person enters this level in adolescence. At this level, an individual rely on abstract principles that go beyond commonplace views of ethics and morality. It includes two stages.

- **Legalistic Orientation** In this stage, morality is judged in terms of human rights which may be stronger than existing laws.
- **Universal Ethical Principle Orientation** In this stage, morality is judged in terms of self-chosen ethical principles.

For example A person who is in dilemma to steal a drug for his chid may take following decision.

- He might focus on punishment and will not steal the drug because he might get caught and put in jail. This is the preconventional level of morality.
- He might not steal because it is against the law. This is the conventional level of morality.
- The might not steal the drug because if everyone takes such actions, social order could break down. This is post-conventional levels of morality.

Social Development

The first 'Social' relationship most infants form is with a parent and in most cultures that parent is the mother. Various theorists have offered various ideas about the psychological significance of the relationship.

Piaget emphasised the cognitive aspects of infancy. In the infant's ways of 'relating' to parents and others Piaget saw signs of sensorimotor intelligence.

Sigmund Freud's view was quite different. He saw infancy, the oral stage, as a time, when issue of dependency were being dealt with and when physical satisfaction was derived from stimulation in the oral region of the body. Freud saw at least some parts of the infant-mother relationship as sensual in nature.

Another theorist, Erik Erikson argued that mother interaction is a context for the baby's basic conflict between trust and distrusts of the world.

Despite their differences, all three theorists would have agreed that infants typically form intimate attachments to their mothers. If we are to understand social development infancy, we must understand how these attachment develop.

Attachment

Attachment is an early, stable, affectional relationship between a child and another person, usually a parent. Early efforts to study this relationship were clinical and somewhat informal. Bowlby went on to make clinical observations of the normal course of attachment in early life, other researchers studied attachment in a more structured way. Their work yielded a surprisingly consistent picture.

- Initially, the infant develops an attraction to social objects in general and to humans in particular; the baby shows proximity maintaining behaviours (crying and other behaviours that serve to keep humans nearby).
- Next the baby distinguished familiar from unfamiliar people and the primary caretaker (usually the mother) from other familiar people; then proximity-maintaining behaviours begin to be aimed more directly at familiar persons, particularly at the primary care taker.
- By the second half of their 1st year, most infants develop a true attachment to the primary caretaker; they recognise that person and direct proximity, maintaining behaviours towards that person and not towards others.
- By the first birthday, the attachment is so strong that children react negatively to as separation from the primary caretaker; they grow fearful and tearful *e.g.* when their parent leaves them with a sitter.

The picture of attachment presented by Bowlby and others raises some difficult questions for the times we live in. Men who would like to join their wives as equal partners in child care may wonder whether infants will grow as equal attached to their fathers as to their mothers.

EXAM BASED QUESTIONS

1 Maturation involves within it
(a) quantitative changes (b) qualitative changes
(c) Both a and b (d) None of these

2 Which among the following is right about 'Development'?
(a) It reflects the qualitative changes
(b) Progressive series of orderly changes
(c) Coherent changes
(d) All of the above

3 Which among the following brings functional maturity in an individual?
(a) Development (b) Growth
(c) Both a and b (d) None of these

4 Who among the following divided the human life span into 10 periods?
(a) Baumrind (b) Bee and Mitchell
(c) Piteumas (d) Sigmund Freud

5 Neonatal period of human development is
(a) period from 1 or until about months
(b) period from 15 to 30 months
(c) first three or four weeks after birth
(d) None of the above

6 Senescence is know as the period
(a) years past 70
(b) years during which individual matures
(c) when individual enters adult society
(d) None of the above

7 Which among the following is not a principle of development?
(a) Development is unified
(b) Development is cumulative
(c) Development is irresistible
(d) Development is complex

8 'Development can be possible in any sphere, anyway'. This statement represents the principle of
(a) Development is unified
(b) Development is complex
(c) Development is orderly
(d) Development is cumulative

9 The genes that are more active in influencing the traits are called
(a) Dominant genes (b) Recessive genes
(c) Both a and b (d) None of these

10 According to a majority of developmental psychologists, basic elements in development would comprise
(a) equilibration, maturation and experience
(b) maturation, experience and social transmission
(c) experience, social transmission and equilibration
(d) reciprocation, maturation and utilisation

11 The stage of intellectual development at which one begins to reason hypothetically, work at the consequence of imaginary courses of action, distinguish the form of an argument from its content and deduce principles from abstract data is known as
(a) Pre-operational stage
(b) Formal operational stage
(c) Operational stage
(d) Cognitive stage

12 In the case of human development, the strongest evidence for the critical-period hypothesis is found in
(a) imprinting
(b) language acquisition
(c) embryonic development
(d) development of vocational interests

13 Which one set of the following psychologists developed a theory that early experiences affect adult behaviour?
(a) Freud, Watson and Harlow
(b) Freud and Harlow
(c) Watson and Freud
(d) Harlow and Watson

14 Adult development is less predictable than childhood development because the former is more closely related to
(a) language and imitation factors
(b) maturational and health factors
(c) social and environmental factors
(d) physiological factors

15 Ability is transmitted in humans by
(a) zygote (b) gene
(c) chromosome (d) hormone

16 Which of the following factors favour normal development of an individual?
(a) Stressful environment
(b) Harmonious environment
(c) Low socio-economic status
(d) Lack of education

17 Which of the following is correct with respect to normative influences?
(a) These are unusual life events is an individual's life.
(b) The influences that occur in similar way for majority of people in particular group.
(c) Both b and d
(d) They may be biological or environmental influences.

18 Which of the following factors influence developmental process?
(a) Normative influences (b) Education and Training
(c) Hereditary factors (d) All of the above

19 Research has shown that an infant's memory for specific word sounds
(a) may predispose infants to respond to different situations in the same way.
(b) develops by the age of 2.
(c) is genetically controlled for specific languages.
(d) develops in the uterus.

20 The concept of stages is not needed if development
(a) is strictly qualitative
(b) involves reorganisation
(c) is made up of new strategies
(d) consists only of additions

21 Which of the following the best example of a maturational change is
(a) the increase in aerobic fitness from exercise between ages 20 and 30.
(b) the gradual acquisition of underarm hair during puberty.
(c) weight gain following improved diet in a deprived child.
(d) improved job performance following disciplinary action.

22 All of the following are characteristic of maturation except
(a) it is universal
(b) it is sequential
(c) it cannot occur without practice
(d) it appears across cultural boundaries

23 The ecological perspective in developmental psychology
(a) uses evolutionary theory to explain inborn pattern of behaviour.
(b) emphasises teaching children about protection of the natural environment.
(c) looks at the context in which the child grows up.
(d) was first suggested by Hall.

24 As children begin their elementary school years, they enter Erikson's stage of
(a) initiative versus independence
(b) industry versus inferiority
(c) education versus indolence
(d) autonomy versus conformity

25 According to Erikson, a major conflict in the first year of life is that between
(a) trust versus mistrust
(b) initiative versus guilt
(c) autonomy versus shame and doubt
(d) relatedness versus isolation

26 A child who is just starting school, trying to learn good habits and to do well, is in Erikson's stage of development called
(a) initiative versus guilt
(b) industry versus inferiority
(c) generativity versus stagnation
(d) integrity versus despair

27 Freud believed that the norms and moral structures of the family and society are incorporated in the
(a) ego
(b) id
(c) libido
(d) super ego

28 A Freudian psychoanalyst would say that one-year-old zachary's personality is made up of
(a) only the ego
(b) only the id
(c) the id and the ego
(d) only the super ego

29 The name most associated with the ecological perspective in the study of human development is
(a) John Bowlby (b) Sigmund Freud
(c) Urie Bronfenbrenner (d) John Watson

30 Freud's term for the unconscious instinctual sexual drive is
(a) instinct (b) ego (c) libido (d) super ego

31 Freud proposed that the structure of personality has three parts which he called
(a) assimilation, accommodation, equilibration
(b) physiological needs, lone and belongingness need and self actualisation
(c) id, ego and superego
(d) anal, oral and phallic

32 How does Erickson's psychoanalytic theory differ from that of Freud?
(a) It is described as psychosexual.
(b) It focuses on psychosocial stages influenced by common cultural demands.
(c) It includes both a phallic and genital stage.
(d) It states that a child's success depends in interaction with people and objects.

33 A comparison of the theory of Freud and Erikson indicate that
(a) Freud's theory was much more a psychosocial theory.
(b) Erickson failed to consider adult stages.
(c) Both placed strong emphasis on libido.
(d) Both emphasised the importance of interactions with other people.

34 The central figure in cognitive development theory is
(a) Erik Erikson
(b) Jean Piaget
(c) Sigmund Freud
(d) Albert Bandura

35 Piaget believed that cognitive development is
(a) characterised by great irregularities.
(b) shaped by the environment.
(c) an active process of exploration, manipulation and examination.
(d) random and unpredictable.

36 **In Piaget's theory, adaptation includes**
(a) accommodation, assimilation and libido
(b) trust, identity, integrity
(c) assimilation, sexuality and ego
(d) accommodation, assimilation and equilibration

37 **According to Piagetian theory, the most essential component of constructivism is when students**
(a) actively build meaningful understandings through experience and interactions.
(b) are given assistance to create physical constructs through experiences and interactions.
(c) are given guidance to build positive social interactions through learning.
(d) actively experience emotional uplifts through learning.

38 **Piaget found that children did not conscientiously use and follow rules until**
(a) age 15
(b) the age of concrete operations
(c) they were in the zone of proximal development
(d) age 10-12

39 **When it came to asking children questions pertaining to moral development, Kohlberg like Piaget**
(a was mainly concerned with the direction of the child's answer.
(b) was concerned not so much with the direction of the child's answer as with the reasoning behind it.
(c) disagreed with Erickson on the stage theory of development.
(d) believe that cognitive structures were largely inherited.

40 **Piaget's theory of cognitive development has been criticised for**
(a) underestimating the abilities of young children.
(b) incorrectly predicting the order of the stages.
(c) its overemphasis on the socio-cultural influence of cognitive development.
(d) its lack of appreciation for individual in progression through the stages of cognitive development.

41 **According to Piaget, children's thinking is**
(a) qualitatively different at different stages.
(b) quantitatively different at different stages.
(c) not affected by their experiences.
(d) the result of observation and imitation of developmentally more advanced children.

42 **According to Piaget's theory, if you can form a complete mental representation of the route to the grocery store, you have displayed**
(a) Concrete operational thought
(b) Reversibility
(c) Preoperational thought
(d) Conservation of area

43 **Which one set of the following is the correct order for Piaget stages of cognitive development?**
(a) Preoperational, sensorimotor, concrete operational, formal operational
(b) Preoperational, sensorimotor, formal operational, concrete operational
(c) Sensorimotor, preoperational, formal operational, concrete operational
(d) Sensorimotor, preoperational, concrete operational, formal operational

44 **According to Piaget, the middle childhood years bring a new set of skills, concrete operations, that**
(a) build on and expand development in fine and gross motor capabilities.
(b) facilitate emotional development as the child resolves common cultural demands and tasks.
(c) reduce anxiety in children at this stage by distorting reality to assist them in understanding.
(d) provide general, abstract rules and strategies for examining and interacting.

45 **Piaget referred to a child's belief that rules are permanent and handed down from some higher authority, who will exact a punishment for any transgression as**
(a) concrete morality
(b) moral relativism
(c) moral realism
(d) concrete operational thinking

46 **Which of the following advancements would be new to a child reaching the preoperational stage?**
(a) The ability to consider multiple aspects of a problem.
(b) The ability to consider past and present activities.
(c) The ability to experiment with circular reactions.
(d) The ability to calculate probabilities.

47 **Using a story such as 'The Porcupine and the Moles,' Gilligan was able to demonstrate that**
(a) Kohlberg's system is concerned mainly with the ethics of justice.
(b) boys tend to use an ethic involving care and responsibility.
(c) girls tend to choose a solution based on justice.
(d) Kohlberg's morality system is true for both boys and girls.

48 **Recent research involving Kohlberg's and Piaget's theories of moral reasoning suggest that**
(a) there is no relationship between level of cognitive development and moral reasoning.
(b) they underestimated children's moral reasoning capabilities.
(c) they overestimated children's moral reasoning capabilities.
(d) they focused too much attention on children's actions in a moral situation.

49 **Kohlberg studied moral development by**
(a) having subjects keep a daily journal of their actions.
(b) evaluating criminal and delinquent person's court records.
(c) posing moral dilemmas to children of different ages.
(d) having subjects perform various legal or illegal behaviours.

50 Which one of the following statements is correct? For Kohlberg, the development of morality primarily involves

(a) cognitive development
(b) affective development
(c) neurolinguistic development
(d) development of coordination

51 Which one of the following is the correct sequence according to Kohlberg's theory of moral development?

(a) Amoral, premoral and moral.
(b) Premoral, morality of convention and morality of individual principles.
(c) Premoral, parental injunctions of morality and individuality of moral principles.
(d) Amoral, morality of individual principles and morality of socio-cultural conventions.

52 According to Kohlberg's theory concrete individualistic perspective is followed by the child in which stage?

(a) Stage 1
(b) Stage 2
(c) Stage 3
(d) Stage 4

53 Which research design followed by Kohlberg?

(a) Cross sectional
(b) Longitudinal
(c) Sequential
(d) Counter balance

Directions (Q. Nos. 54-79) *In the questions given below are two statements labelled as Assertion (A) and Reason (R). In the context of two statements, which one of the following is correct?*

Codes

(a) Both A and R are true and R is the correct explanation of A
(b) Both A and R are true, but R is not the correct explanation of A
(c) A is true, but R is false
(d) A is false, but R is true

54 **Assertion** (A) Infant utter more words than they comprehend.
Reason (R) Comprehension develops earlier than production.

55 **Assertion** (A) A learning theorist stress on the role of nurture in the development of language.
Reason (R) Language is attained through unlearned response pattern.

56 **Assertion** (A) New born infants enter the world equipped with the rooting reflex, sucking reflex and grasping reflex.
Reason (R) The infants sensory capabilities promote the development of relationship with care givers.

57 **Assertion** (A) All children born with a biological predisposition to learn language.
Reason (R) Children possess a 'universal grammar.'

58 **Assertion** (A) According to Erikson, the psycho-social conflict of late adulthood is ego integrity versus despair.
Reason (R) Life satisfaction in late adulthood in highest when you maintain your previous level of activity.

59 **Assertion** (A) The development of object permanence is characteristic of the sensorimotor stage.
Reason (R) In this stage, the infant explores the environment and acquires knowledge through sensing and manipulating objects.

60 **Assertion** (A) In concrete operational stage, child develops the ability to think logically, about concrete objects and situations.
Reason (R) Child become less egocentric in their thinking.

61 **Assertion** (A) Piaget's theory has been criticised.
Reason (R) Piaget underestimated the impact of social and cultural factors on cognitive development.

62 **Assertion** (A) The cone of proximal development refers to the gap between what children can accomplish on their own and what they can accomplish with the help of others, who are more competent.
Reason (R) Vygotsky believed that cognitive development is strongly influenced by social and cultural factors.

63 **Assertion** (A) The role of heredity in development is limited.
Reason (R) Heredity determines the range of reaction of individuals.

64 **Assertion** (A) A child who understands that stealing is bad will not steal in real life.
Reason (R) Kohlberg's theory says that stages of moral development require that certain cognitive development has already taken place.

65 **Assertion** (A) Mastery of developmental tasks is important for effective and normal development.
Reason (R) Failure in developmental tasks results in deviant behaviour.

66 **Assertion** (A) Many children develop the habit of nail-biting.
Reason (R) Maternal deprivation affects child's personality development.

67 Assertion (A) Language development is encouraged by the use of infant directed speech.

Reason (R) There are three stages of language development.

68 Assertion (A) Gender roles consist of the behaviours, attitudes and personality traits.

Reason (R) Gender identity refers to a given person's psychological sense of being either male or female.

69 Assertion (A) Toddler girls play more with soft toys.

Reason (R) Girls tend to be less rigid than boys.

70 Assertion (A) Mental representations influence gender-role development.

Reason (R) Children actively develop mental categories or schemes for masculinity and feminity.

71 Assertion (A) A critical period during development is a time during, which the child is a maximally sensitive to environmental influences.

Reason (R) The fetal period is the second period' of prenatal development, extending from the third week through the eight week.

72 Assertion (A) Development psychology is the study of how people change physically, mentally and socially over the life span.

Reason (R) The major themes in developmental psychology are the common patterns of growth and development people share.

73 Assertion (A) Education and training influence human development.

Reason (R) Education and training helps to nurture innate abilities of an individual.

74 Assertion (A) Growth is cellular.

Reason (R) Development is organisational.

75 Assertion (A) In stage 1 of Erikson's stages of development, infants learn to trust others to satisfy theiry needs.

Reason (R) In stage 4 of Erikson's stages of development, children learn to make things, use tools and acquire skills necessary for adult life..

76 Assertion (A) The 6th stage of Erikson's stage of development involves crisis of generativity versus self absorption.

Reason (R) The stage 5 of Erikson's stages of development involves crisis of identity versus role confusion.

77 Assertion (A) Gene expression is flexible

Reason (R) Characteristic of an organism is determined by the interaction of genetic and environmental factor.

78 Assertion (A) The concept of successful ageing was popularised in 1980s.

Reason (R) The components of successful ageing include freedom from disease and disability, engagement with life and high cognitive and physical functioning.

79 Assertion (A) Temperament refers to the inborn predispositions to consistently behave and react in a certain way.

Reason (R) Attachment is the emotional bond that forms between the infant and his or her care givers.

Directions (Q. Nos 80-84) *Read the passage given below and answer the following questions.*

Hurlock cites several studies which indicate that childhood is the foundational period of life for various physical and psychological traits. Habits and attitudes formed in the early years determine, to a considerable degree, the behaviour of the individual in later years. Over-weight adults *e.g.* have been found to be products of eating habits established in early life and of over-protection during childhood. The limited interests of middle-aged and retired people are attributed to their failure to develop a wide interest range when they were children. Studies of people admitted to mental hospitals show that, as children, they displayed symptoms withdrawal, shyness, listlessness and excessive of day-dreaming.

Delinquent behaviour in adolescence has been found to result from methods of meeting frustrations that were established early in life. Attitudes toward the opposite sex and marital adjustment are profoundly influenced by early interpersonal experiences in the home and in the peer group. In order to understand, predict and control the behaviour of an individual at his current stage of development, it is therefore necessary to have some knowledge of his past experience. And in dealing with him, it must be remembered that his present experiences are preparing the way for his future development.

80 In order to understand, predict and control the behaviour of an individual at his current age, what is necessary?

(a) Knowledge about his parent
(b) Knowledge about his past experience
(c) Knowledge about his peer group
(d) Knowledge about his society

81 Name the psychologist who perform several studies which indicate that childhood is the foundational period of life for various physical and psychological traits?

(a) Hurlock (b) Mickel
(c) Tyles (d) Aerghes

82 Why middle age and retired people have limited interest?
(a) They have like their age
(b) They have ample experience
(c) They fail to develop a wide interest range when they were children
(d) They have to look after the children

83 What results in delinquent behaviour in adolescence?
(a) Method of meeting frustration in early life
(b) Method of meeting stress in childhood
(c) Method of meeting some challenging task
(d) Method of meeting stress results from demice of pasent in childhood

84 What influence attitude toward opposite sex and marital adjustment?
(a) Interpersonal experiences in home and peer group
(b) Study with opposite sex
(c) Movie, TV programme (d) Magazines

85 Consider the following statements
1. Damage to a single chromosome can have disastrous effect.
2. The concept of stages of development suggests that behaviour occur voluntarily.

Which of the statements given above is/are correct?
(a) Only 1 (b) Only 2
(c) Both 1 and 2 (d) Neither 1 nor 2

86 Consider the following statements
1. Developmental psychologists are least likely to disagree about the sequence of stage.
2. Freud believed that development took place in a series of stages.

Which of the statements given above is/are correct?
(a) Only 1 (b) Only 2
(c) Both 1 and 2 (d) Neither 1 nor 2

87 Consider the following statements
1. Erikson believed significant personality developed continued through life.
2. According to Erikson, individuals develop a sense of trust during the oral-sensory stage.

Which of the statements given above is/are correct?
(a) Only 1 (b) Only 2
(c) Both 1 and 2 (d) Neither 1 nor 2

88 Consider the following statements
1. During the latency period, Erikson claims that children learn to master tasks and attain goals.
2. Coping with identity crises is the problem Erikson feels is crucial to the psychological development of mature adult.

Which of the statements given above is/are correct?
(a) Only 1 (b) Only 2
(c) Both 1 and 2 (d) Neither 1 nor 2

89 Consider the following statements
1. Erikson's theories are particularly difficult to investigate with retrospective interviews.
2. Kohlberg focused on cognitive development.

Which of the statements given above is/are correct?
(a) Only 1 (b) Only 2
(c) Both 1 and 2 (d) Neither 1 nor 2

90 Consider the following statements
1. Jean Piaget focused on derivation.
2. Piaget revised the theory of stages of cognitive development.

Which of the statements given above is/are correct?
(a) Only 1 (b) Only 2
(c) Both 1 and 2 (d) Neither 1 nor 2

91 Which of the following are the developmental tasks of late childhood?
1. Getting ready to read.
2. Developing a conscience.
3. Learning to get alongwith age-mates.

Select the correct answer using the codes given below
(a) 1, 2 and 3 (b) 1 and 2 (c) 2 and 3 (d) 1 and 3

92 Consider the following statements
1. Piaget's initial phase of cognitive development sub-divided into five stages.
2. The first two years after birth are critical to self concept formation.

Which of the statements given above is/are correct?
(a) Only 1 (b) Only 2
(c) Both 1 and 2 (d) Neither 1 nor 2

93 Consider the following statements
1. During 12 month's of a child, friends become differentiated from strangers.
2. The most mature view of sex would be evident in genital stage.

Which of the statements given above is/are correct?
(a) Only 1 (b) Only 2
(c) Both 1 and 2 (d) Neither 1 nor 2

94 Which of the following is correct sequence of Erikson's stage of development?
1. Trust v/s Mistrust 2. Integrity v/s Despair
3. Industry v/s Inferiority
4. Autonomy v/s Shame and Doubt

Codes
(a) 4, 1, 3, 8 (b) 1, 4, 3, 8
(c) 3, 1, 4, 8 (d) 8, 4, 1, 3

95 Arrange the following stages of development in correct sequence?
1. Generativity v/s Self-absorption
2. Initiative v/s Guilt
3. Intimacy v/s Isolation

Codes
(a) 2, 3, 1 (b) 1, 2, 3 (c) 3, 2, 1 (d) 1, 3, 2

96 Consider the following statements

1. Erikson's trust versus mistrust stage occur during infancy.
2. Watson identify three distinct emotional responses in human infants.

Which of the statements given above is/are correct?

(a) Only 1 (b) Only 2
(c) Both 1 and 2 (d) Neither 1 nor 2

97 Consider the following statements

1. The new born engages in babbling.
2. In comparative growth curve, females develops more rapidly than male.

Which of the statements given above is/are correct?

(a) Only 1 (b) Only 2
(c) Both 1 and 2 (d) Neither1 nor 2

98 Consider the following statements

1. According to Piaget, the process through which a young child relates something, he sees to something he already know is called assimilation.
2. Developmentally speaking, the earliest group in which a person participate is monadic.

Which of the statements given above is/are correct?

(a) Only 1 (b) Only 2
(c) Both 1 and 2 (d) Neither 1 nor 2

99 Consider the following statements

1. A child who says it is wrong to steal because she might get caught would be in Kohlberg's instrumental hedonism stage.
2. A teenager who took alcohol because all of this friends taking it probably in Kohlberg's authority stage.

Which of the statements given above is/are correct?

(a) Only 1 (b) Only 2
(c) Both 1 and 2 (d) Neither 1 nor 2

100 Consider the following statements

1. Critics of Kohlberg claim that his theory reflects a culture bias.
2. Pragmatics is learning a new word.

Which of the statements given above is/are correct?

(a) Only 1 (b) Only 2
(c) Both 1 and 2 (d) Neither 1 nor 2

101 Consider the following statements

1. Infants utter their first word around 10 months age.
2. After 18 months infants acquire approximately nine new words a day.

Which of the statements given above is/are correct?

(a) Only 1
(b) Only 2
(c) Both 1 and 2
(d) Neither 1 nor 2

102 Consider the following statements

1. Piaget propose the perceptual assimilation made.
2. Statistical learning refers to using regularities in speech to isolate words.

Which of the statements given above is are correct?

(a) Only 1 (b) Only 2
(c) Both 1 and 2 (d) Neither 1 nor 2

103 The mechanism that allow the child to progress from one stage to the other are

1. assimilation 2. concept formation
3. schemes 4. accommodation
5. equilibration

Select the correct answer by using the codes given below

(a) 1, 2 and 3 (b) 2, 3 and 4
(c) 1, 4 and 5 (d) 1, 3, 4 and 5

104 Consider the following statements

1. According to Piagetian theory, cognitive development is influenced by perception.
2. According to Erikson, trust is the ability to fuse one's identity with some one else's without fear.

Which of the statements given above is/are correct?

(a) Only 1 (b) Only 2
(c) Both 1 and 2 (d) Neither 1 nor 2

105 Match the following

List I		List II
A. Freud's developmental theory	1.	Psychodynamic
B. Fixed at the oral stage	2.	Chronic nail biter
C. Self oriented love	3.	Phallic stage
D. Altruistic love	4.	Genital stage

Codes

	A	B	C	D		A	B	C	D
(a)	1	2	3	4	(b)	2	1	4	3
(c)	3	4	2	1	(d)	4	3	2	1

106 Match the following

List I (Period)		List II (Development)
A. Foetal period	1.	Onset of initial heartbeat
B. Germinal period	2.	Second week until eight week
C. Embryonic period	3.	First two weeks
D. Germinal period	4.	Eight weeks until birth

Codes

	A	B	C	D		A	B	C	D
(a)	2	1	3	4	(b)	4	3	2	1
(c)	1	3	4	2	(d)	3	2	1	4

107 Match the following

List (Concepts)		List II (Explanations)
A. Assimilation	1.	Building mental representation through direct interaction
B. Adaptation	2.	Fitting new information into existing cognitive frameworks

List (Concepts)		List II (Explanations)
C. Conservation	3.	Alteration of existing concepts following encounter with new information
D. Accommodation	4.	Understanding that certain attributes of object remain unchanged despite apparent changes

Codes

	A	B	C	D		A	B	C	D
(a)	1	3	4	2	(b)	2	1	3	4
(c)	1	4	2	3	(d)	2	1	4	3

108 Match the following

List I (Scholars)		List II (Styles)
A. Baumrind	1.	Nativistic thinker
B. Skinner	2.	Identification
C. Freud	3.	Moral development
D. Kohlberg	4.	Parenting style

Codes

	A	B	C	D		A	B	C	D
(a)	1	4	3	2	(b)	1	4	2	3
(c)	4	1	3	2	(d)	4	1	2	3

109 Match the following

List I (Period)		List II (Development)
A. Prenatal Period	1.	First 3 or 4 weeks
B. Neonatal Period	2.	Zygote
C. Early Infancy	3.	15 to 30 months
D. Late Infancy	4.	1 to 2 months

Codes

	A	B	C	D		A	B	C	D
(a)	1	2	3	4	(b)	2	1	4	3
(c)	1	4	3	2	(d)	2	3	4	1

110 Match the following

List I (Development)		List II (Age)
A. Middle Childhood	1.	Year past 70
B. Late Childhood	2.	12-19 years
C. Adolescence	3.	9 to 12 years
D. Senscence	4.	5 to 9 years

Codes

	A	B	C	D		A	B	C	D
(a)	1	2	3	4	(b)	2	3	4	1
(c)	4	3	2	1	(d)	3	4	1	2

PREVIOUS YEARS' QUESTIONS

July 2018

1 Read each of the following statements - Assertion (A) and Reason (R) and indicate your answer using codes given below

Assertion (A) Pre-operational child is incapable of performing operations.

Reason (R) Pre-operational child cannot mentally re-arrange a sequence of events into reverse order.

Codes

(a) Both A and R are true and R is the correct explanation of A
(b) Both A and R are true, but R is not the correct explanation of A
(c) A is true, but R is false
(d) A is false, but R is true

November 2017

2 Which of the following concept, according to which each mental event has a unique time of ascendency, the plan for which is contained in the organism's gene?

(a) Epigenesis
(b) Maturation
(d) Genotype
(d) Phenotype

January 2017

3 Match List I with list II and select the correct answer by choosing from the codes given below

List I (Theorist)		Lis II (Explanation)
A. Piaget	1.	Children construct knowledge through social interaction with others
B. Kohlberg	2.	Children are embedded in a number of environmental systems and influences
C. Bronfenbrenner	3.	Children construct knowledge by transforming, organising and reorganising previous knowledge
D. Vygotsky	4.	Children's moral thoughts are advanced through discussions with others

Codes

	A	B	C	D		A	B	C	D
(a)	1	2	3	4	(b)	2	4	3	1
(c)	3	2	1	4	(d)	3	4	2	1

December 2015

4 Which of the following statements best defines maturation?

(a) It is directly based on social-cognitive learning
(b) It is an automatic biological development of the body that naturally unfolds over time
(c) It does not take place in human beings
(d) It is the basis of all physical and psychological developments

5 Trace the sequence of events turning default female sex of the fetus into male.

1. SRY gene produces sry protein.
2. Presence of Y chromosome.
3. Testosterone masculanise Wolffian duct into seminal vesicles.
4. Primitive gonad develop into testes.
5. Mullerian inhibiting hormone dehumanises the fetus.

Codes

(a) 2 1 4 5 3
(b) 2 4 5 1 3
(c) 2 4 1 5 3
(d) 4 2 1 3 5

December 2014

6 Temporary support that parents provide to a child to do a task until the child can do it alone, is termed as

(a) ageism (b) induction
(c) scaffolding (d) power assertion

June 2014

7 A parent deliberately ignores a child's temper tantrums in an attempt to discourage them. The parent's strategy is in accordance with

(a) negative reinforcement (b) extinction
(c) operant escape (d) operant avoidance

ANSWERS

Exam Based Questions

1 (c)	2 (d)	3 (a)	4 (c)	5 (c)	6 (a)	7 (c)	8 (b)	9 (a)	10 (b)
11 (b)	12 (b)	13 (b)	14 (c)	15 (b)	16 (b)	17 (c)	18 (d)	19 (d)	20 (d)
21 (b)	22 (c)	23 (c)	24 (b)	25 (a)	26 (b)	27 (d)	28 (b)	29 (c)	30 (c)
31 (c)	32 (b)	33 (d)	34 (b)	35 (c)	36 (d)	37 (a)	38 (d)	39 (b)	40 (a)
41 (a)	42 (a)	43 (d)	44 (d)	45 (c)	46 (b)	47 (a)	48 (b)	49 (c)	50 (a)
51 (b)	52 (b)	53 (b)	54 (a)	55 (d)	56 (a)	57 (a)	58 (b)	59 (a)	60 (b)
61 (a)	62 (b)	63 (a)	64 (a)	65 (d)	66 (d)	67 (b)	68 (b)	69 (a)	70 (a)
71 (b)	72 (b)	73 (a)	74 (b)	75 (b)	76 (d)	77 (a)	78 (b)	79 (b)	80 (b)
81 (a)	82 (c)	83 (a)	84 (a)	85 (c)	86 (c)	87 (b)	88 (a)	89 (d)	90 (c)
91 (d)	92 (b)	93 (d)	94 (b)	95 (a)	96 (c)	97 (c)	98 (a)	99 (d)	100 (a)
101 (b)	102 (b)	103 (c)	104 (a)	105 (a)	106 (b)	107 (d)	108 (d)	109 (b)	110 (c)

Previous Years' Questions

1 (a)	2 (a)	3 (c)	4 (b)	5 (a)	6 (c)	7 (b)

CHAPTER

29

Psychopathology and Psychotherapies

A conception of Psychopathology attempts to define the term to delineate, human experiences that are considered psychopathological. Psychotherapy and be short term, dealing with immediate issues or long term issues dealing with complex issues.

Psychopathology

Psychopathology is the scientific study of mental, emotional and behavioural disorders. The term also refers to mental disorders themselves, such as schizophrenia or depression and to behaviour patterns that make people unhappy and impair their personal growth. Defining any kind of abnormality can be tricky. We might begin by saying that psychopathology is characterised by subjective discomfort.

Psychopathology does not always cause personal anguish. A person suffering from mania might feel elated and 'on top of the world.' Also, a lack of discomfort may reveal a problem *e.g.* if a person showed no signs of grief after the death of a close friend, one might suspect psychopathology. In practice, subjective discomfort explains most instances, in which people voluntarily seek professional help.

Other than this, statistical abnormality tells us nothing about the meaning of deviations from the norm. Only the lower score is regarded as abnormal or undesirable. In the same sense, it is unusual for a person to speak four languages or to win an event at the olympics, but these are desirable, if rare, accomplishments.

Statistical definitions fail to draw a line between normality and abnormality. *For example* Obesity is statistically normal but not associated with good health. To take another example, left handedness has no bearing on normality or abnormality but statistically left handedness is considered abnormal.

In this Chapter

Causes of Psychopathology

There are various causes that contribute to the development of psychopathology and medical problems. Knowing why the disorder occurs, what its origins are and how it affects thought and emotional and behavioural process may lead to new ways of treating and ideally preventing it. An analysis of causality will be an important part of our discussion of each individual disorder. *Here, we introduced two general categories of causal factors i.e. biological and psychological.*

Biological Causes

The brain is a complex organ, whose interrelated elements are held in delicate balance. Subtle alterations in its chemical messengers, the neurotransmitters or its tissue can have significant effects

Genetic factors, brain injury and inflation are a few of the causes of these alternations that technological advances in brain imaging techniques allow mental health professionals to view the structure of the brain and specific biochemical processes in living individuals without surgery. Using these techniques, biologically oriented researchers are discovering new links between psychological disorder and specific abnormalities in the brain. Continuing advances in the field of behavioural genetics have improved researcher's abilities to identify the links between specific genes and the presence of psychological disorders.

Psychological Causes

Psychological approaches focus on the causal role of psychological or social factors in the development of psychopathology. These approaches perceive personal experiences, traumas, conflict and environmental factors as the root causes of psychological disorders. *We will outline three dominant psychological causes of abnormality the psychodynamic, the behavioural and the cognitive.*

Psychodynamic Causes

According to the psychodynamic view, early childhood experiences shape both normal and abnormal behaviour. In psychodynamic theory, behaviour is motivated by drives and wishes of which people are often unaware. Symptoms of psychopathology have their roots in unconscious conflict and thoughts. If the unconscious is conflicted and tension-filled, a person will be plagued by anxiety and other disorders. Much of this psychic conflict arises from struggles between the irrational, pleasure seeking impulses of the Id and the internalised social constraints imposed by the Super Ego.

The ego is normally the mediator of this struggle, however, its ability to perform its function can be weakened by abnormal development in childhood. Individuals attempt to avoid the pain caused by conflicting motives and anxiety with defence mechanisms, such as repression or denial. Defences can become overused, distorting reality or leading to self-defeating behaviours. The individual may then spend so much psychic energy in defences against anxiety and conflict that there is little energy left to provide a productive and satisfying life.

Behavioural Causes

Because of their emphasis on observable responses, behavioural theorist have little use for hypothetical psychodynamic processes. These theorists argue that abnormal behaviours are acquired in the same fashion as healthy behaviours through learning and reinforcement. They do not focus on internal psychological phenomena or early childhood experiences.

Instead, they focus on the current behaviour and the current conditions or reinforcements that sustain the behaviour. The symptoms of psychological disorders arise because an individual has learned self-defeating or ineffective ways of behaving. By discovering the environmental contingencies that maintain any undesirable, abnormal behaviour, an investigator or clinician can then recommend treatment to change those contingencies and extinguish the unwanted behaviour. Behaviourists rely on both classical and operant conditioning models to understand the processes that can result in maladaptive behaviour.

Cognitive Causes

Cognitive perspectives on psychopathology are often used to supplement behavioural views. The cognitive perspective suggests that the origins of psychological disorders cannot always be found in the objective reality of stimulus environments, reinforcers and overt responses. What matters as well is the way people perceive or think about themselves and about their relations with other people and the environment.

Among the cognitive variables that can guide or misguide-adaptive responses are a Person's perceived degree of control over important reinforcer, a person's beliefs in his or her ability to cope with threatening events and interpretations of events in terms of situational or personal factors. The cognitive approach suggests that psychological problems are the result of distortions in perceptions of the reality of a situation, faulty reasoning or poor problem solving.

Classification of Psychopathology

Mental illness is classified today according to the Diagnostic and Statistical Manual of Mental Disorder, Fourth Edition (DSM IV), published by the American Psychiatric Association (1994). The DSM uses a multiaxial or multidimensional approach to diagnosing. *It assesses five dimensions as described below*

(i) **Axis I Clinical Syndromes** This typically includes the clinical disorders that may be a focus of clinical attention. *For example* Major depressive episode, schizophrenic episode, panic attack, social phobia, schizophrenia.

(ii) **Axis II Development Disorder and Personality Disorders** Developmental disorder includes the five Pervasive Developmental Disorder (PDD), also known as Autism Spectrum Disorder (ASD), as defined by the Diagnostic and Statistical Manual of Mental Disorders (DSM-IV). These include the Autistic disorder, Pervasive developmental disorder, Asperger's disorder, Rett's disorder and Childhood disintegrative disorder.

- Personality disorder are clinical syndromes which have a more long lasting symptoms and affects the individual's way of interacting with the world. They include paronoid disorders, antisocial personality disorder, avoidant personality disorder, borderline personality disorder, narcissistic personality disorder, obsessive compulsive personality disorder and Schizotypal personality disorder.

(iii) **Axis III Physical Conditions** It plays a role in the development, continuance of Axis I and II disorders.

Physical conditions such as brain injury or HIV/AIDS that can result in symptoms of mental illness are included here.

(iv) **Axis IV Severity of Psychosocial Stressors** Events in a person's life, such as death of a loved one, starting a new job, college, unemployment and even marriage can impact the disorders listed in Axis I and II. These events are both listed and rated for Axis IV.

(v) **Axis V Highest Level of Functioning** It contains the global assessment of functioning, which is a numerical scale that measures the level of functioning of the clients. The scale ranges from 0 (inadequate information) to 100 (high functioning with no symptoms of mental illness present).

Mental Status Examination

The mental status examination is the psychological coequivalent test of a physical examination that describes the mental states and behaviour of the persons being tested. It includes both the objective observations of the clinician and the subjective descriptions given by patients.

The examination provides information for diagnosis and assessment of disorder and the response to treatment. It provides a clear snap shot of the mental health of a person at a particular time.

To assess the mental status information gathered from the patient, their history, education, culture and social factors are taken into account. It is important to ascertain what is normal to the patient. *For example* speaking fast may be abnormal but some people always speak fast. *The mental status examination contains the following components*

Appearance

Appearance is tested on the following parameters

- Build, posture, dress, grooming
- Physical abnormalities
- Level of alertness
- Emotional facial expressions
- Attitude towards the examiner: whether cooperative or non-cooperative.

The behaviour of a person is tested on the following parameters

- Eye contact
- Psychomotor activity such as retardation or agitation
- Movements such as hand wringling, tremors, abnormal movements

Speech

The speech can be tested by

- Rate of speaking-increased, decreased, monosyllabic, latency.

Mood and Affect

The mood and affect are tested on the basis of

(i) Prevalent emotional state of the patient.

(ii) Mood states such as elated, depressed, anxious, sad, angry, irritable etc.

(iii) The emotional state we observe, such as
  - Euthymic (normal wood)
  - Dysphoric mood (depressed, irritable, angry)
  - Euphoric (elevated, elated mood)

Thought Process

The thought process describes the rate of thoughts, now they flow and their connection. *Thoughts can be*

- Normal-tight, logical and linear, coherent and goal directed.
- Abnormal-associations are not clear, organised and coherent. *For example* Loose ideas, flight of ideas, clanging and thought blocking.

Thought Content

It refers to the themes that occupy the patient's thoughts and perceptual disturbances. The examples include preoccupations, illusions, ideas of reference, hallucinations, delusions etc.

The patient may be preoccupied with suicidal thoughts, obssession or compulsions. They may have sensory, auditory of any other type of hallucinations. Delusions include false beliefs firmly held by the patient.

Cognition

Cognitive abilities are tested on the basis of

- Level of consciousness
- Attention and concentration the ability to focus, sustain and appropriately shift mental attention.
- Memory-immediate, short term and long term memory
- Abstraction-dealing with ideas rather than events.

Psychotherapy

Psychotherapy refers to any psychological technique that can bring about positive changes in personality, behaviour or personal adjustment. In most cases, psychotherapy is based on a dialogue between therapists and their clients. Some therapists also use learning principles to directly alter troublesome behaviours. Therapists have many approaches to choose from psychoanalysis, desensitisation, Gestalt therapy, client-centered therapy, cognitive therapy and behaviour therapy etc. As we will see, each therapy emphasises different concepts and methods. For this reason, the best approach for a particular person or problem may vary from person to person.

Dimensions of Therapy

The terms listed here describes basic aspects of various therapies. Notice that more than one term may apply to a particular therapy *e.g.* it is possible to have a directive, action-oriented group therapy or a non-directive, individual insight-oriented therapy.

- **Individual Therapy** A therapy involving only one client and one therapist.
- **Group Therapy** A therapy session in which several clients participate at the same time.
- **Insight Therapy** Any psychotherapy whose goal is to lead clients to a deeper understanding of their thoughts, emotions and behaviour.
- **Action Therapy** Any therapy designed to bring about direct changes in troublesome thoughts, habits, feelings or behaviour, without seeking insight into their origins or meanings.
- **Directive Therapy** An approach in which the therapist provides strong guidance to the patient.
- **Non-directive Therapy** A style of therapy in which clients assume responsibility for solving their own problems, the therapist assists, but does not guide or give advise.
- **Time-limited Therapy** This therapy begins with the expectation that it will last only a limited number of sessions.
- **Supportive Therapy** An approach in which the therapist's goal is to offer support, rather than to promote personal change. A person trying to get through an emotional crisis or one who wants to solve the day-to-day problems may benefit from supportive therapy.
- **Positive Therapy** Techniques designed to enhance personal strength, rather than 'fix' weaknesses.

Types of Psychotherapies

There are various kind of Psychotherapies, which are explained below

Behavioural Therapy

The focus of behavioural therapies is on the 'here and now'. Overt behavioury are taken to be indicative of the patient's problem and they are to be corrected by therapy. The client's actual behaviour is taken to be the essence of his or her problem.

Such therapies are criticised on the grounds that they only change overt behaviour and do not root out underlying causes. Therefore, the patient's problem may still exist and symptom substitution may occur.

Biofeedback has its applications in behavioural medicine, but its usefulness and applications are more limited than were originally thought. Again, biofeedback could be 'curing' the overt behaviour, but not the underlying cause. In a hospital situation, it has been suggested that improved interaction with staff, due to the introduction of behavioural programmes is the real reinforcer that has brought about improvement in behaviour patterns. Behaviour modification appears to offer a technology, by which we can help people, but we cannot dominate them.

Behavioural therapies have been criticised on ethical grounds, in that they aim to remove unacceptable behaviours and substitute acceptable behaviours. Decisions on acceptability rest with the therapist. Do therapists have the right to make decisions, which affect other people's lives? In the real-world situation, the therapist should discuss with adult patients what their goals are and work towards those. In the case of a child, consultation would be with the child or the parent or guardian.

Psychoanalysis Therapy

Psychoanalysis therapy was developed by Sigmund Freud. Freud's patients usually reclined on a couch during therapy, while Freud sat out of sight taking notes and offering interpretations. This procedure was supposed to encourage a free flow of thoughts and images from the unconscious. However, it is the least important element of psychoanalysis and many modern analysis have abandoned it.

Freud developed four basic techniques to uncover the unconscious roots of neurosis

(i) **Free Association** Saying whatever comes to mind is the basis for free association. Patients must speak without worrying whether ideas are painful, embarrassing or illogical. Thoughts are simply allowed to move freely from one idea to the next, without self-censorship. The purpose of free association is to lower defences, so that unconscious thought and feeling can emerge.

(ii) **Dream Analysis** Freud believed that dreams provide a 'royal road' to the unconscious because they freely express forbidden desired and unconscious feelings. Such feelings are found in the latent content of dreams. Normally, we only remember a dream's manifest content, which tend to cover information from the unconscious.

Freud was especially interested in unconscious messages revealed by dream symbols. Lets say a young man reports a dream, in which he pulls a pistol from his waist band and aims at a target while his wife watches. The pistol repeatedly fails to discharge and the man's wife laughs at him.

Freud might have seen this as an indication of repressed feelings of sexual importance, with the gun serving as a disguised image of the penis.

(iii) **Analysis of Resistance** When freely associating or describing dreams, patients may resist talking about or thinking about certain topics. Such resistance reveal particularly important unconscious conflicts. As analysts become aware of resistances, they bring them to the patient's awareness, so the patient can deal with them realistically. Rather than being read blocks in therapy, resistances can be challenges and guided.

(iv) **Analysis of Transference** Transference is the tendency to transfer feelings to a therapist that match those the patient had for important persons in his or her past. At times, the patient may act as if the analyst is a rejecting father, an unloving or overprotective mother or a former lover e.g. as the patient re-experiences repressed emotions the therapist can help the patient recognise and understand them.

Troubled persons often provoke anger, rejection, boredom, criticism and other negative reactions from others. Effective therapists learn to avoid reacting as others do and playing the patient's habitual resistance and transference games. This, too contributes to therapeutic changes.

Rational Emotive Behaviour Therapy (REBT)

This therapy was originally called *Rational Emotive therapy*, but in 1993, Ellis changed its name to Rational Emotive Behaviour Therapy. He did this to express the three major dimensions of the therapy *i.e.* tackle problems at the rational level, at the emotive level and also at the behaviour level.

Rational Emotive Behaviour Therapy or REBT, is concerned with the irrational ideas, which neurotic people often hold and which seem to be instrumental in their unhappiness and problems. Ellis in 1977, argued that these ideas tend to fall into three major groups. The *first* of these is the idea that the person absolutely must do well and win other people's approval, the *second* is the idea that other people absolutely must act considerately and fairly towards that person at all times. And the *third* is the idea that the world, in which they live should always be an absolutely fair and unfrustrating place. These ideas, Ellis maintained are totally unrealistic. They are also illogical and self-defeating, but they are nonetheless very common as the key to psychological problems.

Ellis's rational emotive behaviour therapy aims to challenge these irrational beliefs and to put the patient in touch with a more realistic, sensible and constructive way of evaluating their day-to-day experiences. Since, these ideas tend to be very rigidly held, though, Ellis believes that they need a powerful form of therapy to redirect them.

Strategies that are useful to understand Rational Emotive Behaviour Therapy are discussed below:

Awfulising

Ellis argues that clients tend to get into cycles of self-destructive arguments, which are self-sustaining and which prevent them from making a rational appraisal of their situation. He argued that they tend to 'awfulise' events-imaging an event to be an 'awful' thing, so serious as to be unthinkable. Instead of 'awfulising', Ellis argued, people need to be encouraged to think through what would really happen-recognising that even though things might be bad, that does not necessarily make them 'awful'. So, much of the job of the rational emotive behaviour therapist consists of helping the client to see that their world is not going to collapse, if one person does not like them or if they fail to be absolutely perfect in some way.

Another part of the work of a rational emotive behaviour therapist might include behaviour therapy exercises, which will allow clients to explore and try out new behaviours for themselves, so they can see their tendency to 'awfulise' as being the unrealistic cognitive process that it really is *e.g.* a client might be asked to be deliberately late for something or not turn up on a date, so that they can learn how to deal with negative outcomes constructively.

Homework Assignments

Rational emotive therapists often negotiate 'homework assignments' for their clients to work on it between visits. These are exercises directed at helping the client to feel able to deal with things that they have been 'awfulising' in a way, which is more psychologically healthy like encouraging them to feel sad rather than depressed or concerned rather than anxious.

For example A man might be asked to work on a persistent impression that being turned down after asking a girl for a date would be 'awful'. By visualising the situation and thinking it through, he would try to accept it in a rational manner, realising that, although it would not exactly be a pleasant experience, it wouldn't be a complete personal rejection, which made him utterly worthless either.

The homework exercises can sometimes be accompanied by a kind of operant conditioning, encouraging a more rational approach. Rational emotive behaviour therapy encourages clients to accept themselves fully as human beings and to realise that they are too complex for any simplistic judgement about their self-worth.

Family Therapy

RD Laing's work in the 1960s focused attention on the way that some families as a whole are seriously disturbed. Part of this involved identifying how much families often create a climate, in which one individual becomes the 'scapegoat' for this disturbance, by being deemed to be mentally ill. Clinical psychology was receptive to this idea.

Bowen, in 1960, had observed how many schizophrenic patients seemed to improve while they were in hospital, but then relapsed when they got home and suggested that some families might be schizophrenogenic, actually liable to induce schizophrenia in certain family members. One of the central concepts in the relationship between family and schizophrenia was the idea of the double-bind, which Bateson described as an unresolvable sequence of experience. Bateson listed five necessary ingredients for a double-bind. Family therapy draws much of its idea from psychoanalysis, behaviour therapy and personal construct therapy. Historically, four major schools of thought emerged in the development of family therapy, *which are as follow*

Psychodynamic Family Therapy

It is based on psychoanalytic ideas, which emphasise the importance of early experience for a child. The early psychodynamic family therapist focused particularly on the Object Relations Theory developed by **Melanie Klein**. Klein emphasised the importance of early experiences, which were seen as being passed on from other relationships with the earlier family. So disturbances in early experience resulted from disturbance, which the parents experienced as children in their earlier families. The therapy therefore focused on coming to terms with the past, using psychoanalytic techniques in order to enable members of the family to develop more satisfying relationship with each other.

Structural Family Therapy

It concentrates mainly on the boundaries and divisions, which occur between subsystems within the family. A subsystem in this framework might consist of paired relationships, such as mother-son, sister-sister or wife-husband or of triangles.

The subsystems are not confused with other systems, but they can also influence and be influenced from outside. But in some families, subsystems become disturbed or out weighted by others, so that some come to dominate the family interaction at the expense of other family members. Therapeutic intervention in such cases is directly at balancing the subsystems, often by strengthening alliances between individuals. Structural family therapy also maintains a strong emphasis on age appropriate behaviour within the family, insisting that it is unrealistic to expect, say, adult behaviour and attitude from a child.

Systemic Family Therapy

It focuses on seeing the family as a working system, not just as a collection of individuals. It therefore included recognising the influences of other family members, like grandparents, in the nature of the interactions going on within the current family. In one metaphor, a family system is visualised as a mobile, with each member being separate, yet attached by strings and rods to the others.

The aim of family systems therapy is to teach members of the family to respond actively and sensitively to one another, rather than simply reacting to each other as a source of irritation or discomfort.

Modern Approaches to Family Therapy

In modern family therapy, the tendency of therapists is to focus more on the positive coping aspects of family behaviour and less on their dysfunctioning aspects. There are a couple of relatively new approaches, which have emerged, although in these too, the therapists will also adopt techniques developed through other forms of family therapy. In solution focused therapy, the therapist helps the family to identify the symptom, which is causing them most distress and helps them to work out when it is least distressing. The emphasis is on solutions rather than on talking about problems as such. In narrative therapy, the focus is on the unhelpful 'narratives' or accounts, which people can develop about their own lives.

Gestalt Therapy

Gestalt therapy is based on the idea that perception or awareness is disjointed and incomplete in maladjusted persons. The German word Gestalt means 'whole' or 'complete'. Gestalt therapy helps people rebuild thinking, feeling and acting into connected wholes. This is achieved by expanding personal awareness, by accepting responsibility for one's thoughts, feelings and actions and by filling in gaps in experience.

The Gestalt approach is more directive than client-centered or existential therapy and it emphasises immediate experience. Working either one-to-one or in a group setting, the Gestalt therapist encourages clients to become more aware of their moment-to-moment thoughts, perceptions and emotions. Gestalt therapists believe that expressing such feelings allow people to take care of unfinished business and break through emotional impasses. Gestalt therapy is often associated with the work of Frederick Perls. In all his writings, Perls' basic message comes through clearly. "Emotional health comes from knowing what you want to do, not dwelling on what you should do."

Transactional Analysis (Therapy)

Transactional analysis, is a therapy, which does not restrict itself to those individuals considered to be 'neurotic' or 'in need of help'. Instead, it maintains that it has something to offer everyone, as a way of understanding their everyday interaction better. In contrast to the Freudian or other psychoanalytic approaches, transactional analysis assumes that our behaviour is conscious and deliberate or atleast can become so once we know how to recognise our behaviour for what it is. Transactional analysis aims to provide the tool for recognising it.

Various concepts of transactional analysis are as follows

The Ego State

The main concept of transactional analysis is that of the ego state. According to this system, every person has three different ego states within them and these states are triggered by different situations. The three states are parent, child and adult. The parent state is controlling and authoritarian, although it may be well meaning as well as critical. The child state occurs when the person is thinking and feeling like a child being helpless, rebellious or conforming. And the adult state is the realistic, balanced and logical way of interacting with other people, which most people consider desirable.

Transactions

A second important concept in transactional analysis is the idea of the transaction. A transaction is a unit of human communication, between one person's ego state and that of someone else with two people. There are six ego states in total and a transaction may take place between any of them. A transaction may be as brief as an exchange of greeting as two people pass in the street or it might be a whole episode, such as a manager reprimanding an employee for lateness.

Games

The concept of game is the third important concept in transactional analysis. Games are orderly series of transactions, which are played on two levels and which results in bad feelings as the payoff. Berne described a number of these in the book game people play. In games, people act in stereotyped ways, which leads to the payoff.

The concept of the game may sound trivial, but it provides people with a conceptual framework, which allow them to understand the patterned nature of many types of interactions. Moreover, by coming to see it as a game, a client is encouraged to perceive that there are other way of playing and so they are more likely to identify practical ways of changing their behaviour.

Strokes

Another concept in transactional analysis is that of the stroke. Strokes are positive units of human recognition, like telling someone that they have done something well or that you like them. Berne argued that strokes are essential to people's psychological well-being. They also help to dissipate the bad feelings produce by a series of games, to allow someone to escape from a cycle.

Transactional analysis, then sees the individual as autonomous, responsible and able to make their own decisions. The therapeutic process is a service, provided by the therapist, which will not affect a medical cure. Rather, it assumes that the client is willing and competent to achieve the goals of the contract between the two of them, client and therapist. Responsibility for the client's progress rests squarely on the shoulders of the client, but what the therapist does is to provide the client with the conceptual tools for achieving that progress.

Existential Therapy

Existential therapy presented by Viktor Frankl and Rollo May, differ widely in the particular techniques as they both tried to make their clients aware that they always have choices and thus some control over their fate. This idea extends to the problems or symptoms, that bring people in therapy. *For example* An overweight person who complains that he cannot control his eating is probably wrong.

The techniques of encouraging clients to exercise and even exaggerate their problem behaviour is called *Paradoxical intention*. Its objective is to emphasise that the client can have control over the problem and he is responsible for overcoming it. Through techniques of this sort, existential therapists try to pursue people into taking control of their lives. Clients will come to see their problems as resulting from their own free choices of how to behave.

They will thus learn that they are free even obligated to choose better ways of coping. For the existentialist, an important part of healthy coping is a well developed system of values, a clear sense of what one is living for. This emphasis reveals the close link between existential therapy and the philosophical perspective known as *existentialism*. In fact, existential therapy is not so much a specific set of techniques as it is an intriguing blend of philosophy and psychology.

Person Centered Therapy

A person centered therapy is a state of incongruence. The role of the therapists in this situation is to reverse the whole condition. Rogers (1959) called his therapeutic approach as client centered or person centered therapy because of the focus on the person's subjective view of the world.

One major difference between humanistic counsellors and other therapists is that they refers to those in therapy as clients not patients. This is because they see the therapist and client as equal partners rather than as an expert treating a patient.

Unlike other therapies the client is responsible for improving his or her life, not the therapist. This is a delibrate change from both psychoanalysis and behavioural therapies where the patient is diagonses and treated by a doctor. Instead, the client consciously and rationally decides for themselves what is wrong and what should be done about it.

The therapist is more of a friend or counsellor who listens and encourages on an equal level. One reason why Rogers rejected interpretation was that he believed that, although symptoms did arise from past experience, it was more useful for the client to focus on the present and future than on the past. Rather than just liberating clients from their past, as psychodynamic therapists aim to do, Rogerians hope to help their clients to achieve personal growth and eventually to self actualise.

There is an almost total absence of techniques in Rogerian psychotherapy due to the unique character of each counselling relationship of utmost importance, however, is the quality of the relationship between client and therapist. Rogers regarded everyone as a 'potentially competent individual' who could benefit greatly from his form of therapy. The purpose of Rogers' humanistic therapy is to increase a person's feelings of self-worth, reduce the level of incongruence between the ideal and actual self and help a person become more of a fully functioning person.

Acceptance Commitment Therapy (ACT)

Acceptance commitment therapy is a type of psychotherapy that helps you accept the difficulties that come with life. Acceptance Commitment Therapy (ACT) has been around for a long time, but seems to be gaining media attention lately.

Categorically speaking, ACT is a form of mindfulness based therapy, theorising that greater well-being can be attained by overcoming negative thoughts and feelings. Essentially, ACT looks at your character traits and behaviours to assist you in reducing avoidant coping styles. ACT also addresses your commitment to making changes and what to do about it when you cannot stick to your goals.

Acceptance commitment therapy focuses on three areas

(i) Accept your reactions and be present
(ii) Choose a valued direction
(iii) Take action

Acceptance

Whether it be a situation you cannot control, a personality trait that is hard to change or an emotion that overwhelms, accepting it can allow you to move forward. Obsessing, worrying and playing things over and over keeps you stuck. In this sense, asking to leave you helpless, ACT invites you to accept the reality and work with what you have.

Defusion

Another aspect of ACT is the skill set of learning how to cognitively defuse psychologically heightened experiences.

Defusion involves realising thoughts and feelings for what they really are, like passing sensations or irrational things that we tell ourselves instead of what we think. They are like feelings that will never end or factual truths. The goal of defusion is not to help you avoid the experience, but to make it more manageable for you.

The Principles of ACT Theory

ACT theory commonly employs six core principles to help clients to develop psychological flexibility; *These are*

(i) **Cognitive Defusion** It is the learning methods to reduce the tendency to maladaptive thoughts, images, emotions and memories.
(ii) **Acceptance** It allows unwanted thoughts, fellings and urges to come and go without struggling with them.
(iii) **Contact with Present Moment** It is the awareness of the here and now, experienced with openness, interest and receptiveness.
(iv) **The Observing Self** It is accessing a transcendent senses of self, a continuity of consciousness which is unchanging.
(v) **Values** It is discovering what is important to one oneself.
(vi) **Committed Action** It is setting up of goals according to values and carrying them out responsibly in the service of a meaningful life.

Cognitive Behavioural Therapy (CBT)

Cognitive behavioural therapy is a short-term, goal oriented psychotherapy treatment that takes a hands on practical approach to problem solving. Its goal is to change the patterns of thinking or behaviour that are behind people's difficulties and so change the way they feel . It is used to help treat a wide range of issues in a person's life from sleeping difficulties or relationship problems, to drug and alcohol abuse or anxiety and depression.

CBT works by changing people's attitudes and their behaviour by focusing on the thoughts, images, beliefs and attitudes that are held and how these processes related to the way a person behaves, as a way of dealing with emotional problems.

Cognitive behavioural therapy can be thought of as a combination of psychotherapy and behavioural therapy. Psychotherapy emphasises the importance of the personal meaning we place on things and how thinking patterns begin in childhood. Behavioural therapy pays close attention to the relationship between our problems, our behaviour and our thoughts. Most psychotherapists who practice CBT personalise and customise the therapy to the specific needs and personality of each patient.

Dialectic Behaviour Therapy (DBT)

It is an evidence based psychotherapy that began with efforts to treat borderline personality disorder. DBT has been proven useful in treating mood disorders, suicidal ideation etc.

DBT evolved into process in which the therapist and client work with acceptance and change-oriented strategies and ultimately balance and synthesise them, in a manner comparable to the philosophical dialectical process of hypothesis and antithesis, followed by synthesis.

This approach is designed to help people increase their emotional and cognitive regulation by learning about the triggers that lead to reactive states and helping to assess which coping skills to apply in the sequence of events, thoughts, feelings and behaviours to help avoid undesired reactions. A modified form of Cognitive Behavioral Therapy (CBT), DBT was developed in the late 1980s by Marsha M Linehan, a psychology researcher at the University of Washington, to treat people with borderline personality disorder and chronically suicidal individuals.

Research on its effectiveness in treating other conditions has been fruitful; DBT has been used to treat people with depression, drug and alcohol problems, Post-Traumatic Stress Disorder (PTSD), Traumatic Brain Injuries (TBI), Binge-eating disorder and Mood disorders. Research indicates DBT might help patients with symptoms and behaviours associated with spectrum mood disorders, including self-injury. Recent work also suggests its effectiveness with sexual abuse survivors and chemical dependency.

Mindfulness Based Cognitive Therapy (MBCT)

Mindfulness based cognitive therapy is a type of psychotherapy that involves a combination of cognitive therapy, meditation and the cultivation of a present-oriented, non-judgemental attitude called *mindfulness*.

In this therapy, people can learn how to use cognitive methods and mindfulness meditation to interrupt the automatic process often triggering depression. Low mood, negative thoughts and certain body sensations such as weariness and sluggishness often occur together during an episode of depression.

Even after the episode passes, connections may still exist between the different symptoms and it is possible for a small negative stimulus to trigger a large downward spiral. Researchers have found when people with a history of depression experience a low mood, they may also experience negative memories and thoughts from the past, which may, in turn lead to worry about the future and physical sensations such as fatigue.

MBCT helps participants learn how to recognise their sense of being and see themselves as separate from their thoughts and moods. This disconnect can allow people to become liberated from thought patterns in which the same negative messages may be replayed over and over.

After developing an awareness of the separation between thoughts, emotions and the self, people in treatment may find that while the self and the emotions may exist simultaneously, they do not have to exist within the same dimension. This insight can contribute to healing by helping individuals learn to interject positive thoughts into negative moods in order to disarm those negative moods.

Play Therapy

Play therapy is a form of therapy primarily geared towards children. In this form of therapy, a therapist encourages a child to explore life events that may have an effect on current circumstances, in a manner and pace of the child's choosing, primarily through play but also through language.

Play therapy can help individuals to communicate, explore repressed thoughts and emotions, address unresolved trauma and experience personal growth and is widely viewed as an important, effective and developmentally appropriate mental health treatment. Children are referred for play therapy to resolve their problems. Often, children have used up their own problem solving tools and they misbehave, may act out at home with friends and at school.

Play therapy allows trained mental health practitioners who specialise in play therapy to assess and understand children's play. Further, play therapy is utilised to help children cope with difficult emotions and find solutions to problems. By confronting problems in play therapy, we can discover the lasting resolutions and lifelong strategies.

Although, everyone is benefited from play therapy but children age 3-12 years are most benefited. We have seen that teenagers and adults have also benefited from play techniques and recreational processes. To that end, use of play therapy with adults within mental health agency and other healthcare contents is increasing.

Positive Psychotheraphy

Positive psychology is relatively a new form of psychology. It emphasises the positive influences in a person's life. These might include character strengths, optimistic emotions and constructive institutions. This theory is based on the belief that happiness is derived from both emotional and mental factors. Positive psychology aims to help people identify happiness from moment to moment. It emphasises this over only appreciating happy moments when looking back on them.

People seeking therapy who desire to experience greater sense of joy and liberation from their current circumstances may find this approach helpful. Many find it easier to focus on positive emotions they experience in the present after treatment has ended.

Positive psychotherapy is the application of positive psychology principles in a professional therapeutic setting. It is based on the concept that happiness may be broken down into three more manageable components *which are*

(i) Positive Emotion (ii) Engagement
(iii) Meaning

Art Therapy

Art therapy is a hybrid field largely influenced by the disciplines of art and psychology, uses the creative process, piece of art created in therapy and third party artwork to help people in treatment develop self awareness, explore emotions, address unresolved emotional conflicts, improve social skills and raise self-esteem.

Art therapy primarily aims to help individuals experiencing emotional and psychological challenges, achieve personal well-being and improve levels of function. Neither previous artistic experience nor natural artistic ability is necessary for successful treatment and any individuals seeking the help of a mental health professional may benefit from art therapy.

Art therapy is founded on the belief that self expression through artistic creation has therapeutic value for those who are healing or seeking deeper understanding of themselves and their personalities.

According to the **American Art Therapy Association**, "art therapists are trained to understand the roles that colour, texture and various art media can play in the therapeutic process and how these tools can help to reveal one's thoughts, feelings and psychological disposition". Art therapy integrates psychotherapy and some form of visual arts as a specific, stand alone form of therapy, but it is also used in combination with other types of therapy.

Performing Arts Therapy

Art is something that stimulates an individual's thoughts, emotions, beliefs or ideas through the senses. Art therapy is a form of expressive therapy that uses are materials such as paints, chalks, art materials etc.

Art therapy combines traditional psychotherapeutic theories and techniques with an understanding of the psychological aspect of the creative process such as the affective properties of the art materials.

Art making is seen as an opportunity to express one's self imaginatively and spontaneously. This leads to personal fulfilment, emotional reparation and recovery. At therapy emphasises upon drawings, paintings, dance etc. as helpful in communicating issues, emotions and conflicts. The art image becomes significant in enhancing verbal exchanges between the person and the therapist for achieving insights into the patients and resolving conflicts. This leads to problem solving, formulating new perceptions and positive growth and healing.

The purpose of Art therapy is same as any other therapy. It ensures well-being and improves mental health and emotional happiness. Art therapy is used in many settings with different forms.

It generally includes music therapy, drama therapy and dance therapy. These therapies are generally non-verbal and emphasises upon professional ways of treating a patient the Art therapists use materials and interventions appropriate to their client's needs to achieve goals such as insights into the client, cope with stress, work through traumatise experience, increases cognitive abilities and have better relations with family and friends.

EXAM BASED QUESTIONS

1 Psychopathology is the scientific study of

(a) mental state (b) emotions
(c) behaviour (d) All of these

2 What is considered statistically 'abnormal' for a person to score in an IQ Test?

(a) Below 55 (b) Above 145
(c) Both a and b (d) None of these

3 In which of the following approach brain imaging is used?

(a) Psychological approach (b) Biological approach
(c) Behavioural approach
(d) Psychodynamic approach

4 Which among the following is correct about behavioural approach?

(a) It focuses on internal psychological phenomena
(b) It focuses on early childhood experiences
(c) It focuses on the current behaviour
(d) None of the above

5 Mental illness is classified according to

(a) diagnostic manual (b) statistical manual
(c) Both a and b (d) None of these

6 Which among the following is/are included under Pervasive Development Disorder?

(a) Autistic disorder (b) Asperger's disorder
(c) Rett's disorder (d) All of these

7 The DSM-IV-TR definition of mental disorder is perhaps the best current definition because

(a) it includes information about both violation of social norms and dysfunction.
(b) it includes many components none of which can alone account for mental disorder.
(c) it is part of the current diagnostic system.
(d) it recognises the limits of our current understanding.

8 Which among the following is not a major psychological problem listed in the DSM-IV-TR?

(a) Mood disorder (b) Personality disorder
(c) Insanity disorder (d) Anxiety disorder

9 Which is not a key feature of DSM-IV-TR?

(a) Separate dimension
(b) Axes
(c) Discrete diagnostic categories
(d) Mental issue

10 **Which model of abnormality explains abnormal behaviour as caused by illogical thinking?**
(a) Psychoanalytic (b) Cognitive
(c) Behavioural (d) Biological

11 **Which axis of the DSM-IV-TR would a therapist use to classify the loss of a person's job?**
(a) I (b) II
(c) III (d) IV

12 **Which model of abnormality talks about rewards, shaping and imitation as ways of developing abnormal behaviour?**
(a) Psychoanalytic (b) Behaviour
(c) Behavioural (d) Cognitive

13 **Which of the following pairs is not correctly match?**
(a) Axis V : Global assessment of functioning
(b) Axis I : Personality disorders
(c) Axis III : General medical conditions
(d) Axis IV : Psychosocial and environmental problems

14 **An irrational fear of blood would be a**
(a) social phobia (b) specific phobia
(c) type of agoraphobia (d) type of acrophobia

15 **Sandhya has the tendency to make everything seem so much worse than it usually is. Bicky would say that Sandhya has a tendency to**
(a) overgeneralise (b) minimise
(c) do all-or-nothing thinking (d) magnify

16 **Which one is not a real physical disorder?**
(a) Psychosomatic disorder
(b) Psychophysiological disorder
(c) Somatoform disorder
(d) Disease of adaptation

17 **Lina has started having feelings of fearfulness about going to school. She has begun to suffer from headaches and stomachaches and has missed several days of school already. Lina's illness are probably a form of**
(a) phobic disorder
(b) somatisation disorder
(c) generalised anxiety disorder
(d) dissociative disorder

18 **When anxiety is unrelated to any known, realistic factor, it is called**
(a) Free-floating anxiety (b) Panic
(c) Phobia (d) Acute

19 **A therapy whose goal is to lead clients to a deeper understanding of their thoughts, emotions and behaviour is**
(a) Insight therapy (b) Directive therapy
(c) Group therapy (d) Individual therapy

20 **Techniques designed to enhance personal strength, rather than 'fix' weaknesses is known as**
(a) Supportive therapy (b) Positive therapy
(c) Time-limited therapy (d) Action therapy

21 **Psychoanalysis by Freud is developed by which of the following basic techniques?**
(a) Free association (b) Dream analysis
(c) Analysis of resistance (d) All of these

22 **For psychotherapy to be effective**
(a) the therapist must provide a protected setting to clients to reveal their feelings.
(b) the therapist should maintain emotional distance from the client.
(c) clients and therapists should avoid warmth in their relationship.
(d) therapist should choose one style of therapy for all of his clients.

23 **Among the following, all are potential barriers to effective theory listed by Sue and Sue when culture or ethnic backgrounds of therapist and clients are different except which of these**
(a) language (b) cultural values
(c) social class (d) gender

24 **The newest drugs being developed to treat psychotic symptoms are the**
(a) typical neuroleptics
(b) atypical neuroleptics
(c) anticonvulsants
(d) partial dopamine agonists

25 **For which of the following disorders have anti-depressants not been used?**
(a) Panic disorder
(b) Dissociative amnesia
(c) Obsessive- compulsive disorder
(d) Post-traumatic stress disorder

26 **Electroconvulsive shock therapy is useful in preventing suicide attempts because it**
(a) is more effective than drug therapies
(b) has few negative side effects
(c) works more quickly than anti-depressants
(d) makes people happy

27 **The reality television shows that deliberately force people to face their 'worst fear' are similar to which therapy technique?**
(a) Systematic desensitisation
(b) Oversion therapy
(c) Flooding (d) Extinction

28 **At Skinner elementary school, teachers pass out 'Skinner bucks' to students, who turn in papers on time, obey the teacher and finish their homework. The paper 'bucks' can be used at the end of the week to trade for special treats or game-playing time of the classroom computers. This system most resembles a**
(a) participant modeling technique
(b) contingency contract
(c) group extinction procedure
(d) token economy

29 Which of the following would be and unlikely strategy for a rational emotive behaviour therapist to use in treating a client?

(a) Arguing with the client's statements.
(b) Repeating what the client has just said without interpreting it.
(c) Giving the client homework.
(d) Pointing out irrational beliefs to the client.

30 The Rational emotive therapy was renamed as Rational emotive and behaviour therapy by

(a) Sigmund Freud (b) Albert Ellis
(c) AT Beck (d) Erik Frikson

31 Which person might benefit the least from a group therapy environment?

(a) Sarita, who has a phobia of cats
(b) Rohan, who has a drinking problem
(c) Janbi, who is painfully shy
(d) Ela, who suffers from depression

32 The psychoanalyst knows that repressed information is just 'below the surface' of the conversation, when the patient begins to experience

(a) free association (b) dream interpretations
(c) resistance (d) transference

33 Compared to traditional psychoanalysis, modern psychoanalysis and modern psychodynamic therapy are

(a) more directive (b) less directive
(c) more active (d) more focused on the id

34 Humanistic therapies are different from psychoanalysis because the humanistic therapies are

(a) more directive
(b) action oriented
(c) focused only on conscious thought and behaviour
(d) insight therapies

35 Which of the following is not one of the four basic elements of Rogers' person-centered therapy?

(a) Conditional positive regard
(b) Empathy
(c) Reflection
(d) Authenticity

36 Which of the following types of therapy makes the greatest use of body language?

(a) Psychoanalysis (b) Person-centered therapy
(c) Gestalt therapy (d) Rogerian therapy

37 Who among the following focused attention that some families as a whole are seriously disturbed?

(a) Laing (b) Davis
(c) Ellis (d) All of these

38 Art therapy uses which of the following techniques to improve well-being of clients?

(a) Music therapy (b) Dance therapy
(c) Drama therapy (d) All of these

39 Which of the following techniques mainly uses the body language for therapy?

(a) Rogerian therapy (b) REBT
(c) Art therapy (d) Play therapy

40 Irrational fear of blood is known as

(a) Hemophobia (b) Acrophobia
(c) Hydrophobia (d) Hemophobia

41 The Dialectic Behaviour therapy was developed in the late 1980 by

(a) Sigmund Freud (b) Anna Freud
(c) M Linehan (d) Jean Piaget

42 The dialectic behaviour therapy can be used to treat which of the following disorders?

(a) Post Traumatic stress disorders
(b) Traumatic brain injuries
(c) Mood disorders
(d) All of the above

43 In existential therapy, technique of encouraging clients to exaggerate their problem behavirour is known as

(a) Dereflection (b) Desensitiation
(c) Paradoxical intention (d) None of these

44 Which of the following is not a component of the mental status examination?

(a) Mood and Affect (b) Behaviour
(c) Thought content (d) Sleep

45 The Euthymic emotional state describes which of the following types of mood?

(a) Depressed (b) Elated (c) Normal (d) Disturbed

46 Which of the following correctly describes the abnormal thought process of a patient?

(a) Tight and coherent thinking
(b) Coal oriented thoughts
(c) Loose ideas and clanging
(d) None of the above

47 Delusions can be deseribed as

(a) Auditory sensations (b) false beliefs
(c) Sensory hallucinations (d) All of these

Directions (Q. Nos. 48-52) *Read the passage given below and answer the questions that follow.*

Several explanation for eating disorders have drawn on psychoanalytic modes of thought. In classic Freudian theory, eating is seen as a substitute for sex and one explanation is that anorexia is a way of repressing or rejecting sex. This is closely linked to the idea proposed by Bruch, that girls, who become anorexic are unconsciously trying to hold back the onset of maturity, because they do not want to face up to their full social role as women in modern society. Another view, which Bruch also discussed, is that it is unconsciously seen as a way of avoiding pregnancy, because fatness and pregnancy are unconsciously perceived as the same thing.

Although, these symbolic interpretation of anorexia may not seem particularly realistic, there does appear to be some evidence that childhood trauma makes people more vulnerable to anorexia later in life. It is not uncommon for both anorexics and bulimics to have suffered sexual abuse during childhood. The trauma and self-disgust, which children feel as a result of this invasion of their bodies lingers on, if the child does not receive appropriated psychotherapy. In adolescence or even later, the individual express their self-disgust punitively, by ignoring the demands of the body and taking satisfaction out of the deprivation of their bodily needs.

48 How the individual express their self-digust punitively?
(a) By ignoring the demand of the body and taking satisfaction out of deprivation of their bodily needs.
(b) By fulfiling the demand of their body.
(c) By enjoying themself.
(d) By giving others pain .

49 In Classical Freudian theory, eating is seen as a substitute for what?
(a) Drink (b) Sleep (c) Sex (d) Dream

50 Who proposed that girls, who become anorexic are unconsciously trying to hold back the onset of maturity?
(a) Bruch (b) Freud
(c) Kazadin (d) Murphy

51 Why anorexia is seen as a way of avoiding pregnancy?
(a) Sex is avoided.
(b) Fear of opposite sex member.
(c) Fatness and pregnancy are unconsciouly perceived as the some thing.
(d) Pregnancy is believed as a curse.

52 Anorexia is a way of repressing which of the following?
(a) Thirst (b) Hunger
(c) Sex (d) Urge to play

53 Consider the following statements
1. The Axis I of DSM-IV-TR include all diagnostic categories except the personality disorders and mental retardation.
2. People don't consult a mental health professional for depression or anxiety disorder.

Which of the statements given above is/are correct?
(a) Only 1 (b) Only 2
(c) Neither 1 nor 2 (d) None of these

54 Consider the following statements
1. Mental illness is not universal.
2. Cultere have an influence on mental illness.

Which of the statements given above is/are correct?
(a) Only 1 (b) Only 2
(c) Both 1 and 2 (d) Neither 1 nor 2

55 Consider the following statements
1. DSM-IV-TR attempts to enhance cultural sensitivity by providing a general framework for evaluating the role of culture.
2. Caffeine withdrawal syndromes associated with headache, fatigue.

Which of the statements given above is/are correct?
(a) Only 1 (b) Only 2
(c) Both 1 and 2 (d) Neither 1 nor 2

56 Consider the following statements
1. Premenstrual dysphoric disorder is marked by anxiety and depression.
2. This category is similar to premenstrual syndrome.

Which of the statements given above is/are correct?
(a) Only 1 (b) Only 2
(c) Both 1 and 2 (d) Neither 1 nor 2

57 Consider the following statements
1. Clinical disorder contains the disorder that bring most people to the attention of a psychological professional.
2. Personality disorder seem to exist from birth and are relatively stable and enduring.

Which of the statements given above is/are correct?
(a) Only 1 (b) Only 2
(c) Both 1 and 2 (d) Neither 1 nor 2

58 Consider the following statements
1. The main symptom in anxiety disorder is excessive or unrealistic anxiety and fearfulness.
2. Conduct disturbance is an example of dissociative disorder.

Which of the statements given above is/are correct?
(a) Only 1
(b) Only 2
(c) Both 1 and 2
(b) Neither 1 nor 2

59 Consider the following statements
1. Free-floating anxiety is an anxiety *i.e.* related to any realistic known source.
2. Phobia is an irrational, persistent fear of an object, situation or social activity.

Which of the statements given above is/are correct?
(a) Only 1 (b) Only 2
(c) Both 1 and 2 (d) Neither 1 nor 2

60 Consider the following statements
1. Specific phobia is a fear of objects.
2. Claustrophobia is fear of being in a small place.

Which of the statements given above is/are correct?
(a) Only 1 (b) Only 2
(c) Both 1 and 2 (d) Neither 1 nor 2

61 Consider the following statements
1. Acrophobia is the fear of being in a place or situation from which escape is difficult.
2. Agoraphobia is fear of heights.

Which of the statements given above is/are correct?
(a) Only 1 (b) Only 2
(c) Both 1 and 2 (d) Neither 1 nor 2

62 Consider the following statements
1. In obsessive-compulsive disorder intruding, recurring thoughts or obsessions create anxiety that are relieved by performing a repetitive, ritualistic behaviour.
2. Panic attack is sudden onset of intense panic in which multiple physical symptoms of stress occur, often with feelings that one is dying.

Which of the statements given above is/are correct?
(a) Only 1 (b) Only 2
(c) Both 1 and 2 (d) Neither 1 nor 2

63 Consider the following statements
1. Generalised anxiety disorder is a disorder in which a person has feelings of dread and impending doom along with physical symptom of stress.
2. Magnification is the tendency to interpret situations as more easy and beautiful.

Which of the statements given above is/are correct?
(a) Only 1 (b) Only 2
(c) Both 1 and 2 (d) Neither 1 nor 2

64 Consider the following statements
1. Psychosomatic disorder is disorder, in which psychological stress causes a real physical disorder or illness.
2. Psychophysiological disorder is the modern term for psychosomatic disorder.

Which of the statements given above is/are correct?
(a) Only 1
(b) Only 2
(c) Both 1 and 2
(d) Neither 1 nor 2

65 Consider the following statements
1. In somatisation disorder person dramatically complains of a specific symptom such as nausea.
2. In conversion disorder person experience a specific symptom in the somatic nervous system functioning.

Which of the statements given above is/are correct?
(a) Only 1 (b) Only 2
(c) Both 1 and 2 (d) Neither 1 nor 2

66 Consider the following statements
1. In dissociative disorder, loss of memory for personal information occur.
2. In dissociative amnesia disorders occurs in which there is a break in conscious awareness.

Which of the statements given above is/are correct?
(a) Only 1 (b) Only 2
(c) Both 1 and 2 (d) Neither 1 nor 2

67 Consider the following statements
1. In psychoanalysis, Freud emphasise the revealing of unconscious conflicts.
2. Manifest content is the symbolic or hidden meaning of dream.

Which of the statements given above is/are correct?
(a) Only 1 (b) Only 2
(c) Both 1 and 2 (d) Neither 1 nor 2

68 Consider the following statements
1. Latent content is the actual content of one's dream.
2. In Freudian technique of free association, patents are encouraged to talk about anything that comes to mind.

Which of the statements given above is/are true?
(a) Only 1 (b) Only 2
(c) Both 1 and 2 (d) Neither 1 nor 2

69 Consider the following statements
1. In reflection therapy technique the therapist restates what the client says rather than interpreting those statement.
2. Unconditional positive regard refers to the warmth, respect and accepting atmosphere created by the therapist for the client.

Which of the statements given above is/are correct?
(a) Only 1 (b) Only 2
(c) Both 1 and 2 (d) Neither 1 nor 2

70 Consider the following statements
1. Empathy is the ability of the therapist to understand the feelings of the client.
2. Gestalt therapy is a form of indirective insight therapy.

Which of the statements given above is/are correct?
(a) Only 1 (b) Only 2
(c) Both 1 and 2 (d) Neither 1 nor 2

71 Consider the following statements
1. Humanistic therapies are different from psychoanalysis as it is focussed only on conscious thoughts and behaviour.
2. Empathy is not one of the four basic elements of Rogers' person-centered therapy.

Which of the statements given above is/are correct?
(a) Only 1 (b) Only 2
(c) Both 1 and 2 (d) Neither 1 nor 2

72 Consider the following statements

1. Applied behaviour analysis is the use of learning technique to change undesirable behaviour and increase desirable behaviour.
2. Systematic desensitisation is the behaviour technique used to treat mental disorder.

Which of the statements given above is/are correct?

(a) Only 1 (b) Only 2
(c) Both 1 and 2 (d) Neither 1 nor 2

73 Consider the following statements

1. Counter conditioning is replacing an old conditional response with a new one by changing the unconditioned stimulus.
2. Aversion therapy is a form of behavioural therapy, in which a desirable behaviour is paired with an aversive stimulus.

Which of the statements given above is/are correct?

(a) Only 1 (b) Only 2
(c) Both 1 and 2 (d) Neither 1 nor 2

74 Consider the following statements

1. Flooding is a technique to use treat stress disorders in which a person is exposed to fear provoking situation.
2. Modeling is learning through observation.

Which of the statements given above is/are correct?

(a) Only 1 (b) Only 2
(c) Both 1 and 2 (d) Neither 1 nor 2

75 Consider the following statements

1. Reinforcement is the strengthening of a response by following it with a pleasurable consequence.
2. Token economy is the use of objects called tokens to reinforce behaviour.

Which of the statements given above is/are correct?

(a) Only 1 (b) Only 2
(c) Both 1 and 2 (d) Neither 1 nor 2

76 Consider the following statements

1. Extinction is a process in which a person is removed from the situation that provides reinforcement for undesirable behaviour.
2. Time-out is the removal of a reinforcer to reduce the frequency of a behaviour.

Which of the statements given above is/are correct?

(a) Only 1 (b) Only 2
(c) Both 1 and 2 (b) Neither 1 nor 2

77 Consider the following statements

1. In cognitive therapy, focus is given on helping the client recognise distortions in their thinking and replace distorted unrealistic beliefs.
2. Arbitrary inference is distortion of thinking in which a person draws a conclusion that is not based on any evidence.

Which of the statements given above is/are correct?

(a) Only 1 (b) Only 2
(c) Both 1 and 2 (d) Neither 1 nor 2

78 Consider the following statements

1. In arbitrary inference and distortion of thinking, in which a person cannot draw a conclusion based on any evidence.
2. In selective thinking, person focus on only one aspect of a situation while ignoring all other relevant position.

Which of the statements given above is/are correct?

(a) Only 1 (b) Only 2
(c) Both 1 and 2 (d) Neither 1 nor 2

79 Consider the following statements

1. In magnification therapy, a person blows a negative event out of proportion to its importance, while ignoring relevant positive events.
2. In personalisation, a person takes responsibility or blame for events that are unconnected to the person.

Which of the statements given above is/are correct?

(a) Only 1 (b) Only 2
(c) Both 1 and 2 (d) Neither 1 nor 2

80 Arrange the following in chronological order.

1. Medical Model
2. Psychological Model
3. Salem Witch Hunt

Codes

(a) 1, 2, 3 (b) 3, 2, 1 (c) 3, 1, 2 (d) 2, 1, 3

81 Arrange the following in chronological order.

1. Jean Charcot 2. Franz Mesmer
3. Emil Kraepelin

Codes

(a) 1, 2, 3 (b) 3, 2, 1 (c) 2, 1, 3 (d) 1, 3, 2

82 Arrange the following in chronological order.

1. Personality disorder
2. Clinical disorder
3. Paranoid Personality disorder

Codes

(a) 1, 2, 3 (b) 2, 1, 3 (c) 3, 1, 2 (d) 2, 3, 1

83 Arrange the following in chronological order.

1. Anorexia nervosa
2. Restriction of food intake
3. Severely distorted body image

Codes

(a) 1, 2, 3 (b) 2, 1, 3
(c) 3, 2, 1 (d) 1, 3, 2

84 Arrange the following in chronological order.

1. Kazdin 2. Terry 3. Silverman

Codes

(a) 1, 2, 3 (b) 3, 2, 1 (c) 2, 1, 3 (d) 3, 1, 2

Directions (Q. Nos 85-102) *In the questions given below are two statements labelled as Assertion (A) and Reason (R). In the context of the two statements, which one of the following is correct?*

Codes

(a) Both A and R are true and R is the correct explanation of A

(b) Both A and R are true, but R is not the correct explanation of A

(c) A is true, but R is false

(d) A is false, but R is true

85 **Assertion** (A) Psychopathology is characterised by subjective discomfort.

Reason (R) Psychopathology refers to mental disorder themselves.

86 **Assertion** (A) A person suffering from mania might feel elated and 'on top of the world'.

Reason (R) Psychopathology always cause personal anguish.

87 **Assertion** (A) Many eccentric characters are charming and emotionally stable.

Reason (R) Strictly following social norm is guarantee of mental health.

88 **Assertion** (A) In panic disorder, panic attack occurs frequently.

Reason (R) Person has difficulty in adjusting to daily life.

89 **Assertion** (A) In panic disorder with agoraphobia, person fears of leaving his familiar surrounding.

Reason (R) The person fears of a panic attack in public.

90 **Assertion** (A) Somatoform disorders take the form of bodily illness and symptoms.

Reason (R) In this, there is no real physical disorder.

91 **Assertion** (A) In somatoform disorder, the person is pre-occupied with every sensation of the body.

Reason (R) The person is terrified of being sick and worries constantly, going to the doctor frequently.

92 **Assertion** (A) Globe anesthesia is actually a sign of a conversion disorder.

Reason (R) Globe anesthesia is anatomically impossible.

93 **Assertion** (A) In anti-social personality disorder, person behaves in an impulsive manner.

Reason (R) The person has no morals or conscience.

94 **Assertion** (A) A person is moody, unstable, lacks a clear sense of identity and often clings to others.

Reason (R) Person is suffering from borderline personality disorder.

95 **Assertion** (A) A person always overreacts, use excessive emotions to draw attention from others.

Reason (R) The person is suffering from histonic personality disorder.

96 **Assertion** (A) Symptoms are caused and maintained by interpersonal problem.

Reason (R) Interpersonal therapy is a psycho dynamic therapy that focuses on current relationship.

97 **Assertion** (A) Aversive conditioning is a behaviour based on classical conditioning.

Reason (R) It involves modifying behaviour by conditioning a new response that is incompatible with a previously learned response.

98 **Assertion** (A) In systematic desensitisation, phobic responses are reduced by pairing relaxation with a series of mental images.

Reason (R) It is based on the principle of counter conditioning.

99 **Assertion** (A) Motivational interviewing is designed to help clients overcome the mixed feelings or reluctance they might have about committing a change.

Reason (R) The main goal of motivational interviewing is to encourage or strengthen the client's self-motivated statements.

100 **Assertion** (A) Shaping used with extremely impaired patients in whom the desired responses do not normally occur.

Reason (R) Shaping involves reinforcing successive approximation of a desired behaviour.

101 **Assertion** (A) Psychological problems are due to maladaptive pattern of thinking.

Reason (R) Cognitive therapy is based on the assumption that depression caused by biased perception.

102 **Assertion** (A) Cognitive therapy focuses on changing the clients unrealistic beliefs.

Reason (R) The treatment technique focuses on recognising and altering unhealthy thinking pattern.

103 Match the following

List I (Disorders)	List II (Examples)
A. Schizophrenia	1. Depression
B. Mood disorder	2. Delusional disorder
C. Anxiety disorder	3. Phobia
D. Somatoform disorder	4 Hypochondria

Codes

	A	B	C	D
(a)	3	4	2	1
(b)	1	2	4	3
(c)	2	1	3	4
(d)	4	3	1	2

104 Match the following

List I (Disorders)	List II (Examples)
A. Factitious disorder	1. Anorexia
B. Dissociative disorder	2. Multiple personality
C. Sexual disorder	3. Paraphilias
D. Eating disorder	4. Pathological lying

Codes

	A	B	C	D
(a)	2	4	1	3
(b)	4	2	3	1
(c)	1	3	2	4
(d)	3	1	4	2

105 Match the following

List I (Disorders)	List II (Examples)
A. Sleep disorder	1. Conduct disturbances
B. Impulse-control disorder	2. Pyromania
C. Adjustment disorder	3. Narcolepsy
D. Amnesia	4. Parkinson's

Codes

	A	B	C	D
(a)	1	2	3	4
(b)	3	2	1	4
(c)	2	1	4	3
(d)	4	3	2	1

106 Match the following

List I (Phobias)	List II (Scientific Names)
A. Washing	1. Ablutophobia
B. Spiders	2. Arachnophobia
C. Lightning	3. Ceraunophobia
D. Dirt, germs	4. Mysophobia

Codes

	A	B	C	D
(a)	4	3	2	1
(b)	3	4	1	2
(c)	1	2	3	4
(d)	2	1	4	3

107 Match the following

List I (Phobias)	List II (Scientific Names)
A. Snakes	1. Ophidiophobia
B. Darkness	2. Nyctophobia
C. Fire	3. Pyrophobia
D. Foreigners	4. Xenophobia

Codes

	A	B	C	D
(a)	2	1	3	4
(b)	1	2	4	3
(c)	3	4	1	2
(d)	4	3	2	1

108 Match the following

List I (Axis)	List II (Examples)
A. Axis I	1. Personality
B. Axis II	2. Clinical disorders
C. Axis III	3. General medical conditions
D. Axis IV	4. Psycho social and environmental problems

Codes

	A	B	C	D
(a)	2	1	3	4
(b)	4	1	2	3
(c)	3	2	1	4
(d)	1	3	2	4

109 Match the following

List I (Problems)	List II (Primary Symptoms)
A. Psychotic disorder	1. Loss of contact with reality
B. Mood disorder	2. Mania
C. Anxiety disorder	3. Bodily complaints without an organic basis
D. Somatoform disorder	4. High anxiety

Codes

	A	B	C	D
(a)	2	1	3	4
(b)	1	2	4	3
(c)	3	4	1	2
(d)	4	3	2	1

110 Match the following

List I (Problems)	List II (Primary Symptoms)
A. Dissociative disorder	1. Drug abuse
B. Personality disorder	2. Unhealthy personality pattern
C. Sexual disorder	3. Deviant sexual behaviour
D. Substance disorder	4. Amnesia

Codes

	A	B	C	D
(a)	2	4	3	1
(b)	3	1	2	4
(c)	4	2	3	1
(d)	1	3	4	2

PREVIOUS YEARS' QUESTIONS

July 2018

1 Read each of the following statements - Assertion (A) and Reason (R) and indicate your answer using codes given below

Assertion (A) Behaviour therapy helps people to respond to life situations in the way they would like to respond.

Reason (R) Positive therapeutic relationship is a necessary but not sufficient condition for effective behaviour therapy.

Codes

(a) Both A and R are true and R is the correct explanation of A
(b) Both A and R are true, but R is not the correct explanation of A
(c) A is true, but R is false
(d) A is false, but R is true

2 Which of the following significant changes have been incorporated in DSM-5 ?

1. The title of the manual is not DSM-V, but DSM-5, a deliberate shift from traditional Roman numerals used in previous editions toward Arabic numerals.
2. Multiaxial Assessment System - a central feature of DSM since its introduction in DSM-III in 1980, has been dropped altogether from DSM-5.
3. DSM-5 authors have overhauled the manual to emphasise neuropsychological or biological roots of mental disorders.
4. DSM-5 authors have removed 5 of 10 personality disorders previously included in that section. Dropped disorders are paranoid, schizoid, histrionic, dependent and narcissistic personality disorders.

Codes

(a) 1, 2, 3 are correct; 4 is incorrect
(b) 2, 3 and 4 are correct; 1 is incorrect
(c) 1 and 2 are correct; 3 and 4 are incorrect
(d) 3 and 4 are correct; 1 and 2 are incorrect

November 2017

3 Match List I with List II and select the correct answer by choosing from the codes given below

List I (Tests)	List II (Authors)
A Cognitive Assessment Battery	1. Cattell, RB
B Deviation IQ	2. Terman
C Cognitive Assessment System	3. Wechsler
D Stanford-Binet Scales	4. Naglieri and Das

Codes

	A	B	C	D
(a)	1	2	3	4
(b)	2	3	4	1
(c)	4	3	1	2
(d)	1	3	4	2

4 DSM-III is considered qualitatively different and superior to its predecessors, because

1. it is multi-axial
2. it deleted misnomer words
3. it introduced coding system
4. it used experimental data

Codes

(a) 1, 2 and 3
(b) 1, 3 and 4
(c) 2, 3 and 4
(d) All of these

July 2016

5 Match List I with List II and select the correct answer by choosing from the codes give below

List I (Concepts)	List II (Explanations)
A Personality Structure	1 Psychological reactions and motives that change dynamically over relatively brief periods
B Personality Process	2 Stable and enduring qualities that define the individual and distinguish individuals from one another
C Personality Development	3 People sometimes change and sometimes resists change or are unable to change accordingly
D Psychopathology and Change	4 Everybody comes up to be an unique individual by adulthood

Codes

	A	B	C	D
(a)	1	2	3	4
(b)	2	3	4	1
(c)	2	1	4	3
(d)	4	1	2	3

6 Sleep disorders can be categorised as

(a) Parahilias and Dysfunctions
(b) Insomnia and Hypersomnia
(c) Parasomnias and Dyssomnias
(d) Serotonergic and Dopaminergic

December 2015

7 Motion sickness can occur when

1. one loses his vestibular sense.
2. one relies only on visual information.
3. one's visual information and vestibular system's information are congruent.
4. one's visual system and vestibular system are in conflict.

Codes

(a) Only 1
(b) 1 and 2
(c) Only 4
(d) 1 and 4

8 The following disorders are coded on Axis I of a five axis diagnosis

1. V codes 2. Personality disorders
3. Clinical conditions 4. Intellectual deficit

Codes

(a) 1 and 3 (b) 2 and 4 (c) 1 and 4 (d) 2 and 3

June 2015

9 Arrange the four basic characteristics of instincts as per Freud's psychoanalytic theory in terms of sequence.

1. An impetus 2. A source
3. An object 4. An aim

Choose the correct code for sequence of events

(a) 2 1 4 3 (b) 3 2 14
(c) 2 4 1 3 (d) 1 2 3 4

10 Match List I with List II and indicate your answer using the codes given below

List I (Tests)		List II (Dimensions/Traits assessed)
A. EPPS	1.	State anxiety
B. EPQ-R	2.	Psychoticism
C. NEO-PI-R	3.	Achievement motivation
D. STAI	4.	Openness to experience

Codes

	A	B	C	D
(a)	3	2	4	1
(b)	1	2	4	3
(c)	3	4	2	1
(d)	1	4	2	3

11 The evidence that sleep is a biological motive comes from .... in lengthy sleep deprived subjects.

(a) rebound effect of slow wave sleep
(b) rebound effect of REM sleep
(c) insomnia
(d) enhanced stage I and stage II sleep

December 2014

12 Mental grouping of similar objects, events or people is called

(a) cognition (b) concept
(c) prototype (d) thinking

13 Match the items in List I with list II and mark your answer using the given codes

List I (Therapies)	List II (Clinical Conditions)
A. Cognitive Behaviour Therapy	1. Anxiety disorder
B. Exposure techniques	2. Post-traumatic stress disorder
C. Dialectic Behaviour Therapy	3. Depression
D. Eye-movement desensitisation and reprocessing	4. Borderline personality disorder

Codes

	A	B	C	D
(a)	3	1	4	2
(b)	4	2	3	1
(c)	2	4	1	3
(d)	1	3	2	4

ANSWERS

Exam Based Questions

1 (d)	2 (c)	3 (b)	4 (c)	5 (c)	6 (d)	7 (b)	8 (b)	9 (a)	10 (b)
11 (d)	12 (b)	13 (b)	14 (b)	15 (d)	16 (c)	17 (b)	18 (a)	19 (a)	20 (b)
21 (d)	22 (a)	23 (d)	24 (d)	25 (b)	26 (c)	27 (c)	28 (d)	29 (b)	30 (b)
31 (c)	32 (c)	33 (a)	34 (c)	35 (a)	36 (c)	37 (a)	38 (d)	39 (a)	40 (a)
41 (c)	42 (d)	43 (c)	44 (d)	45 (c)	46 (c)	47 (b)	48 (a)	49 (c)	50 (a)
51 (c)	52 (c)	53 (a)	54 (b)	55 (c)	56 (a)	57 (c)	58 (b)	59 (b)	60 (c)
61 (d)	62 (c)	63 (a)	64 (c)	65 (c)	66 (d)	67 (a)	68 (b)	69 (c)	70 (a)
71 (a)	72 (a)	73 (a)	74 (c)	75 (c)	76 (b)	77 (c)	78 (b)	79 (c)	80 (c)
81 (b)	82 (b)	83 (b)	84 (a)	85 (c)	86 (c)	87 (c)	88 (b)	89 (a)	90 (b)
91 (b)	92 (a)	93 (a)	94 (a)	95 (a)	96 (b)	97 (a)	98 (b)	99 (b)	100 (a)
101 (c)	102 (a)	103 (c)	104 (b)	105 (b)	106 (c)	107 (a)	108 (a)	109 (b)	110 (c)

Previous Years' Questions

1 (c)	2 (d)	3 (d)	4 (a)	5 (c)	6 (b)	7 (c)	8 (a)	9 (c)	10 (a)
11 (a)	12 (b)	13 (a)							

Psychological Innovations

Psychological research finds that people who are intrinsically motivated are often more productive and innovative than those motivated by extrinsic factors. Psychological counselling maintains focus upon facilitating personal and interpersonal functioning across the lifespan of an individual.

Introduction

We have read about the multiple theories and models within psychology which helps us to understand the day to day behaviour of people around us. This study helps us to understand the theoretical aspect of concepts like motivation, learning, guidance and counselling etc. But, here we will focus on the application of the theoretical knowledge about these topics.

Motivation in Education

Education must transfer from generation to generation, the core of our culture's accumulated body of knowledge. Humans have an intrinsic desire to learn and this desire is fueled by the basic psychological needs for autonomy, competence and relatedness. For students to be motivated in their studies, they need to know that what they are studying is indeed of real significance.

Learning is self-initiated, but it must be aided by motives so that the learner will persist in the learning activity. A definite motive is valuable in all work, as motives make for readiness. The greater the readiness, the greater will be the attention given to the work and the sooner will the desire result be achieved.

In this Chapter

Theories of Motivation in Education

Motivation is a force used within the educational system to encourage student's learning and understanding. In the educational setting, motivation is either an internal force or external force. There are different theories of motivation in the educational setting, which those state that student's behaviour is dictated either due to external or internal factors. This discussion concerns the effects of intrinsic and extrinsic motivations and their effect on student's learning and success within an educational setting.

The locus of control greatly affects motivation. The idea that people control their own decisions and actions determines their destinies indicates an internal locus. Individuals who are operating using an external locus believe that outside forces are responsible for the events that occur in their lives and feel that they have little control over situations. Those with an internal locus will often use intrinsic motivation, which is person centered and comes from within an individual, whereras those with an external locus may need extrinsic rewards or consequences as an effective motivational tool.

Two types of motivations are as follows

Intrinsic Motivation

According to humanistic theories set forth by Carl Rogers, motivation might come from within an individual without any thought to the external reward. Students receive their own internal reward through an increase in self-esteem and sense of achievement when they reach their desired goals. They may just feel the desire to succeed based on factors such as their own interest in an activity or the feeling of satisfaction that is achieved when they complete the necessary steps to achieve the desired accomplishment. This drive is called internal or intrinsic motivation, which means there are no outside forces that dictate whether individuals will ultimately achieve their goals. The individual does not attempt to achieve an external reward, but instead works toward the intrinsic value associated with the success of the project.

Consequences of Intrinsic Motivation

A cognitive approach of motivation is an intrinsic form that requires students to think through the consequences of their actions and base their decisions on the expected outcome of those decisions. If students are able to think through the situation at hand and determine the value of success, regardless of whether they gain a reward, they are operating under the internal locus of control. Students who are successful in the classroom usually operate under the internal locus of control. They do not put too much weight on mistakes or bad grades and are still able to maintain a level of esteem regardless of failures of successes. They do not blame external factors such as the teacher or classmates. They take responsibility for their own actions.

Extrinsic Motivation

Students who need reinforcement to succeed are operating under the behaviourist theories set forth by BF Skinner, who suggests a punishment and reward system as a motivational tool. In external motivation *i.e.* required to drive the individual's positive behaviour is offered in the form of a system that reinforces the desired behaviour or negates undesirable actions.

Students might receive a physical reward in terms of a pat on the back or a stricker on a completed paper. They might also receive negative consequences such as detention or a call home to parents. Through the administration of negative consequences for unwanted behaviours and positive reinforcement for the desired actions, students who respond to extrinsic motivation are more likely to succeed in their endeavours.

Consequences of Extrinsic Motivation

Students who are externally motivated are more likely to see the teacher, classroom, book or other external force as a reason for their failure.

These students have an external locus of control and will tend to see their failure as all encompassing rather than a one time mistake. Their self esteem may suffer greatly due to this lack of cognitive focus and internal awareness. They tend to believe that their failure is related to their lack of ability and they are more likely to give up if they do not achieve success continually.

Maslow's Motivational Theory

According to Maslow, Man's motives become hierarchically arranged in the following order

- Physiological drives.
- Needs for safety, security and freedom from anxiety.
- Love and acceptance in interpersonal relations.
- Self and social esteem.
- Self-actualisation.

In this hierarchy from lower to higher level motives, man's greatest satisfaction is in self-actualisation which is his most 'profound joy'.

The lower order needs however, are more demanding and until they are reasonably well satisfied, higher motives have little effect on behaviour. Lower order needs include physical, Biological and safety needs include friendship, affection, love, trust, dignity, self esteam etc. The final stage in the Theory of maslow includes self actualisation.

Many individuals are denied self-actualisation and intrinsic joy in learning and work. Maladjusted children and youth, frustrated in their needs for security, love and esteem, are often ineffectual and unhappy in school. A study by Schoeppe, Haggard and Havighurst indicates that when adolescents are deprived of these basic satisfaction, they become retarded in social maturing.

Implications of Maslow's Teaching

According to **Maslow's theory**, "When a child's lower level needs are reasonably satisfied, he does not have to be pressed into constructive and creating study and work. The opportunity for self-actualisation offers its own intrinsic reward".

When a child is uninterested in school, rebels against or otherwise resists study and school work, the teacher should assume that his energies are all bound up in frustrating attempt to satisfy lower order needs or that he is not being given suitable learning opportunities. In either case, the teacher should not attempt to drive or press the pupil into constructive effort. He should try to adapt the curriculum to the child's interests, abilities and needs. By helping the child in every possible way to satisfy amply the lower-level need for safety, love and esteem he would release the child's energies for constructive work.

This theory of motivation is consistent with the assumption that children need security, praise and success. It recognises the importance of developing children's interests, of providing children knowledge of their progress and opportunities for self-enhancement and of promoting a healthy, but not overanxious need to achieve.

Role of Motivation in Learning

According to the definition of motivation, learning behaviour is aroused, sustained, directed and selectively reinforced by the individual's motives and incentives. This concept implies that efficient learning and performance are dependent upon efficient motivation.

Classroom experience and many other life experiences support this implication. Several experiments indicate that individual differences in school achievement are related to corresponding differences in the intensity of achievement.

The Need to Achieve School Accomplishment

Probably as a combination of several motives, which vary from person to person, children and youth develop different degrees of intensity to achieve upto a general age, which significantly affects their school accomplishment.

The high achievers give answers, which indicate self-confidence, focused application, seriousness of purpose, conformity and reasonableness in interpersonal relations and a sense of accomplishment.

Another approach to the problem confirms the significant relationship between the strength of the need to achieve and the effectiveness of learning since success and doing one's best in school, at work, in social affairs and in competitive play activities are often rewarded, which may lead an individual to become preoccupied with achievement.

Although, everyone in our culture has some desire to achieve, the diverse factors which determine individual development also cause variations their due consideraction for achievement. Students, who are relatively high in need to achieve make sustained and continuous progress learning task. Students with little desire to achieve make no appreciable progress and they may drop in level of performance. High school and college students, highly motivated by the need to achieve often require no extrinsic motivation for effective learning.

School Motives and Incentives

Due to learning, we associate basic motive satisfactions with numerous incentives, goal objects and events. Combinations of motive satisfaction vary in different individuals. It constitutes the general need to achieve. An inventory of motive-incentive appeals will suggest more specific ways of motivating children and youth in the schools.

Such an inventory includes the following

- Curiosity and desire to understand one's world and oneself through science, social studies, literature and many other observational and problem-solving experiences.
- Intrinsic satisfaction in creative constructive activity stimulated by rich, varied learning environments.
- Individual or group pursuit of interest-satisfying knowledge, understanding and skills as in self-selected reading, uniquely suitable roles in projects or creative self-expression in art.

- Mastery achieved by adjusting learning task in every curriculum area to the individual's level of maturity and pattern of abilities.
- Knowledge of progress-revealed by a progress-curve graph of vocabulary by checking the correctness of combinations in arithmetic or by comparing compositions written in early and later periods of an English course.
- A sense of self-enhancement of one's potentialities or talents for constructive self-expression and social contributions. Self-enhancement is, of course, dependent on knowledge of progress in specific activities.

The following are motives and incentives that are applied in the school setting to motivate the children

Security v/s Threat and Punishment

Early in the history of education, teachers resorted to scolding, criticising, threats and other kinds of punishment to motivate children's learning effort and conformity to strict standards of discipline. But these appeals to negative motives have been almost completely abandoned with developing emphasis on such aims as democratic, self-reliant citizenship, emotional health, happy and cooperative interpersonal relationships among children, adults and with growing scientific understanding of motivation. There has been a shift in teacher's attitudes towards the positive incentivisation.

The changed attitude of teachers is implied in the result of a study by Briggs, who asked high school principals and teachers whether children's various positive and negative incentive had 'made them work better, the same or worse'. These principals and teachers believe that "Commendation, praise and encouragement are superior to censure, ridicule, threats and punishment".

Competition and Cooperation

Competition has been used as a motivating influence during the entire history of pedagogy. Competitive conditions of one sort or another generally increase efficiency of work and facilitate learning.

In some cases, however, 'the competitive spirit' is aroused in situations, where failure is anticipated, it may 'disrupt the individual or result in a change in the direction of competive effort'.

The role of competition in emerging school learning (or performance) is illustrated in the following experiment. **Chapman** and **Feder** directed two equated groups of 5th grade children in daily 10 minutes practice sessions. The non-competitive group was motivated only by interest and conditions of serious school work.

The competitive group in addition to having these incentives, was competing for status on the list of daily scores and for stars for being in the upper 50% of their class. The average performances under these two conditions of motivation were graphed. The children competing for individual rewards surpassed those in the non-competing group in similar experiments with other age groups. **Hurlock** has confirmed the effect of individual competition as a simple learning task.

Praise and Reproof

In their day-to-day experiences in the classroom, some children and youth are often commended for superior achievement, for constructive contributions to class discussions and projects for courteous, friendly and cooperative social behaviour, for leadership or for attractive appearance.

In contrast others are scolded and otherwise disapproved for inferior achievement, misconduct and failure to complete assignments or to cooperate in group projects. Although, both praise and reproof sometimes motivate children to better achievement and conduct, some research suggests that the relative effectiveness of these techniques depends on individual differences in personality. When motivation is already high because of intrinsic interest and other incentives, neither praise nor reproof is likely to enhance performance.

However, on the basis of incentives for learning and discipline, praise is much more effective and beneficial to the healthy development of personality than reproof.

Success and Failure

Many teachers have observed that successful learning experiences tend to motivate further learning. Mastery of worthwhile concepts and skills leads the individual, by conditioning, to feel confident, worthy and eager for new ventures in learning. On the other hand, frequent failures produces anxiety, feelings of inferiority, disinterest and self-defensive avoidance of learning activities, all of which impair learning.

Gebhard found that college students who manipulated success and failure experiences with 9 intellectual tasks, such as verbal arithmetic, code learning, sentence completing, symbol transposing and algebraic reasoning tends to prefer the particular activities on which they have been successful and may expect further success.

Knowledge of Progress

In many school activities reading, language, spelling, handwriting, arithmetic, shorthand, typewriting, athletic performances and other skill requiring long-continued practice, it is possible by repeating comparable tests and ratings to give the learner specific knowledge of his progress at each stage of mastery.

In each step, the child's self-esteem is enhanced. School curriculum in music, art, science, mathematics, athletics and perhaps in every other area provide opportunities for increasingly valued individual and social expression of talents. These self-enhancing opportunities continue through adulthood in increasingly responsible occupational, family, social and political roles.

As **Cantril** suggests, we value more highly those experiences, which we share with others, which employ our talents in socially constructive ways and which give some order and direction to our lives. Such motivation explains the thrill in creative effort. It explains the eagerness of children and youth for increased responsibilities and for opportunities to make greater contributions to their social groups. Such motivation is effective in long-range learning projects because long-range goals can be symbolised and well justified anticipations of attaining them make the striving itself internally satisfying.

Factors in Educational Achievement

Educational achievement has been recognised as one of the important goals of education in the world. It is general observation that learners placed in an identical set of academic situations vary in their scholastic achievement. Various researches have been conducted to prove the academic achievement phenomenon.

The psychology of higher secondary student who is no longer a child and not yet an adult too is an important area in the study of human behaviour. The study of emotional phenomenon of the adolescent students is equally important as the study of their behaviour, the cognitive, affective and motivational states. The psychologists have divided anxieties: anxieties as state of the adolescent pupils and anxieties as a trait. In the educational setting anxiety as a state is of crucial significance.

There are several factors responsible for educational achievement. *These are*

Sources of the Variation in School Achievement

- Some students are more knowledgeable than others despite spending the same amount of time in the schools . Endless research and discussions have been carried out to study these variations. Despite making all efforts, only partial answers have been derived. Moreover, the predictions of individual's probable achievements can be done with limited accuracies. But, certain factors have certainly been derived that can be attributed to the variations in school achievements in students. These factors include.

1. There is a consistent dependable relationship between school achievement and intelligence. Thus, school success depends upon the intelligence levels of an individual.
2. Intelligence is corelated with specifically designed achievement tests rather than teacher given grades. Thus, grades provided by teachers do not determine intelligence levels and achievement outcomes of students. A student performing good in exams can not be considered a high achiever and vice-versa.
3. Achievement is also dependent upon the subject matter that a student sutdies. Learning outcomes generally tend to be high for Engslish language, some what lower for science, lower for social studies and very low for mathematics.

The evidence summarised by **PE Vernon** (1950), indicates that a considerable part of the differences between individuals in school achievement can be accounted for in terms of differences in 'g'(neogenetic reasoning ability) .

Another part of the variation arises from differences in the 'vied' factor, which could be characterised as aptitude in 'book learning' and which can be measured by test of vocabulary, arithmetic, spelling or general information. There is also a third non-intellectual factor, which Vernon labels 'x' which is a complex of personality traits, interest and background characteristics.

Vernon feels that it is hardly worthwhile to look for special aptitudes that many have something to do with scholarship in one area alone. The idea of basing our judgements of students on the best evaluations we can get value of 'g', vied and the X-factor which is appealing in its simplicity and it is in accord with the correlational data obtained.

Sources of Under Achievement

With the resurgence of public interest in education that occurred during the 1950s, research on the problem of achievement differences took on a somewhat different character.

The emphasis shifted from questions related to prediction and selection to questions related to diagnosis and treatment. Why do many students often those, who score at the upper levels of our intelligence scales fail in school? Why do other accumulate distinguished scholastic records even though they appear to have only average scholastic aptitudes?

The most thorough studies have been made on groups of college graduates. Here, there does seems to be a fairly high relationship between academic achievement and intelligence. Success, particularly at the upper academic achievement and later success particularly at the upper intelligence levels studies do not of course separate intelligence from grade getting.

It is quite possible that the success of honour student is a reflection primarily of their high ability and has little to do with what they learned in college or with non-intellectual qualities contributing to their high scholarship.

This study does point out the fact that even among persons of outstanding intellectual ability there are wide variations in life success and that some of the sources of the variation are identifiable in the school record.

Probably, the most extensive and thorough study of factors related to different criteria of success in a professional group is to be found in one investigation of physicians. Great care was taken in formulating meaningful criteria of success for each of the four main types of medical career-urban general practice, rural general practice, speciality practice, teaching and research.

When medical school course grades and other criteria of success in training were correlated with these measures of career success only a small number of significant correlations emerged to fall easily within the range of what would be expected by chance. The conclusion appears inescapable that these two variables-success in medical school and success in medical careers are essentially uncorrelated.

The problem that needs to be addressed, then, is incompatibility between the claim that social psychology is in principle uniquely suited to contribute to educational practice and the conclusion that dubious message and jammed channels reduce to insignificant social psychology's contribution to educational practice.

The problem is an incompatibility between possibility and actuality. *Solutions to such problems always take one of three forms*

(i) Verification that the possibility is non-existent and that the actual already approximates the desirable.

(ii) Modification of the actual so that it realises the possible.

(iii) Joint modification: diminishing conceptions of the possible and augmenting actual achievement.

Teacher's Effectiveness

This section examines in more detail the different sources of professional knowledge that teacher draw from and the specific skills that make up effective teachers. The professional knowledge that must be possesed by a teacher involves various sections of knowledge and skills to deal with those conditions.

Professional Knowledge

According to research, effective teachers use five following types of knowledge

(i) **Content Knowledge** *First*, teacher must know the subject matter they intend to teach, also known as *content knowledge*. Effective teachers know their subject matter extremely well. Some studies suggest that strong subject matter knowledge, typically measured as having a major *i.e.* relevant to the field to be taught, is associated with teacher effectiveness and having a master's degree in the field contributes more to teacher effectiveness than having a master's degree in a different field. In most institutions, teachers learn content knowledge through courses in the disciplinary field.

(ii) **Pedagogical Knowledge** Although necessary, well-developed content knowledge is not sufficient to make someone a good teacher. Otherwise, all experts in any domain would be good teacher by definition and that is not the case.

Infact, many experts lack the ability to verbalise the knowledge and skills that they have developed over time.

Thus, in addition to content knowledge, it is necessary to have general pedagogical knowledge, an understanding of principles of learning, development, classroom management, motivation and assessment that can be used across content domains. General pedagogical knowledge is typically learned in educational psychology course such as this one. *For instance* you will soon learn that effective teachers are aware that students make rather than take new information.

(iii) **Knowledge About Learners** Effective teaching requires significant knowledge about the numerous way, in which learners think and behave depending on their unique characteristics.

Teacher should know how to plan instruction which are appropriate for development of student of different ages and they should be sensitive to the needs of student's from diverse backgrounds. The valuable gain of knowledge about learner will describe a role that a student's developmental age, gender, language and cultural background and abilities play in learning; it will also provide useful strategies to help all students learn effectively.

(iv) **Knowledge About Curriculum** Even when teachers are provided with instructional material such as text book for their classrooms, they need to know what to teach based on the guidelines developed by national, state and local standards, knowledge about curriculum, including standards and benchmarks for content area, will allow the teacher to make important instructional decisions including the selection of materials, the design and sequencing of tasks based on student's learning needs and how to assess student's learning.

(v) **Professional Skills** Professional knowledge is all the information that one learns about teaching and learning and professional skill is the ability to use the knowledge effectively and readily in the classroom. A teacher might have read many books and journal articles about classroom management, but, if he is very disorganised or has not developed effective classroom routines, than he won't be a very effective teacher for his students. *It includes planning, communication, motivation, classroom management, assessment and technology skills.*

- **Planning Skills** Teacher need to set a variety of learning goals and organise plans for reaching these goals. As teacher plan instruction, they consider when and how instruction should be given, what activities students should do and the types of assessment that can be used to evaluate student's learning.
- **Communication Skills** Teachers need to be good verbal and non-verbal communicators. Effective teacher speak clearly, actively listen to students and parents, interpret student's body language and constructively resolve conflicts in the classroom. They also have assertive rather than passive or hostile communication styles and will to improve student's communication skills.
- **Motivation Skills** Effective teachers give students the opportunity to think about their personal interests and goals and use strategies to help them become self-motivated and responsible for their own learning.

  In addition, teachers with good motivation skills set high standards for all students yet adjust the level of challenge and give support to different ability levels to ensure that every child becomes motivated to succeed. *For example* A third-grade reading teacher might expect a gifted student to understand stories at the fifth-grade level, an average student to understand stories at the third-grade level and a student with a learning disability in reading to understand stories at the second-grade level.
- **Classroom Management Skill** Teachers need to manage their classroom to create a successful, orderly environment *i.e.* conducive to learning. To this end, effective teachers use a set of skills for developing classroom rules and given procedures, monitoring and preventing misbehaviour and intervening, when discipline problem arise.
- **Assessment Skills** Effective teachers regularly assess the knowledge and skills of their students with a variety of formal and informal method. Formal assessments include students presentations, quizzes project assignments and mandatory test.

  Teachers also use informal assessments, such as portfolios of student work, student journals and examination of student's questions, comments and behaviours during classroom and group activities. This set of skills includes the planning, development, administration, evaluation and revision of classroom assessment and the administration and evaluation of commercially made tests.
- **Technology Skills** Effective teachers also have well developed technological skills and critically evaluate the potential of technology before integrating computer into their classrooms for technology-based instruction to improve learning.

Guidance in School

The need for guidance had existed all times. **Traxler** considered guidance as a help which enables each individual to understand his abilities and interests, to develop himself, to relate life goals and to reach a state of complete and mature self guidance as a desirable member of social order.

The following problems create need for guidance from educational point of view

Problems of Mass Education

Mass education, as exemplified by modern educational systems, has produced immense benefits for all mankind. For one thing, it makes available to virtually everyone within reach of a school a common body of the skills and information that are essential for functioning in a civilised world. Further more, it put within everyone's grasp the means for finding a place in the social order and for realising his potentialities.

On the other hand, mass education has undeniable shortcomings. It does lend itself to the control of a few people at the top, particularly in those countries or communities, where political power is the monopoly of an elite group. In such societies, well-organised school systems became the convenient channels for political propaganda and provide only limited opportunities for mental growth.

Even in the more democratic societies systems of mass education tend to produce a kind of educational bureaucracy that acts to prevent educational change and restricts the freedom of the class teacher. Such weaknesses are not due so much to any basic flow in the idea of organised mass education as they are due to apathy, inaptitude or a lack of understanding of educational goals and processes on the part of the citizenery.

Personal Problems

The second kind of need likely to be overlooked in a system geared entirely to provide mass education is what we might call the 'personal need' *i.e.* the need steming from personal problems. But the difference here lies in the severity of the problem and extent to which it dominates the life of the child. The learning capacity of a child in the emotionally disturbed. Category is continually threatened or impaired by the problems he must face in his every day life. Only a few children in the average classroom will need continuing psychological help over a long period of time.

On the other hand, virtually all children have to deal with psychological problems at some time or other. The very unpredictability of life is bound to cause some anxiety. However, every child must occasionally deal with problems when a new brother or sister is born, the family decides to move, mother has to go to work, father is called for military service and forth. These are the crises of everyday living.

Meeting the individualised needs of students for instruction, is chiefly a function of the classroom teachers. Teachers are limited in this respect only by their ability to diagnose special needs and the time they can devote to the giving of this help.

'Dropout

Some of the inadequacies of a system of mass education are reflected in what is called the *dropout rate i.e.* the proportion of students, who leave school before graduation. At first glance, it seems a rather strange paradox that in a land where education is the key to opportunity and where education is more or less free for the first grade graduate from high school, one of the first explanations that comes to mind is that those, who drop out are the ones, who cannot benefit from education. Yet an uncomfortably high proportion of the students, who drop out have above average to superior aptitude furthermore, we really do not know at what point or at what level young people really bacame uneducable.

Although, it is impossible to measure the direct social cost of an incomplete high school education, statistical studies show that the 'holding power' of high schools is related to a number of indices of economic, social and political viability.

The Need for Individualised Education

Children need special help because they have special problems. These problems cannot be handled easily because they have special problems. These problems cannot be handled easily and successfully on a mass basis. To be sure, we can organise special programs for groups of children, who are socially disadvantaged, hard of hearing or mentally retarded, but such group treatment is only a partial solution to the problem. At some point, we must intervene as individuals and work with students as individuals.

Most culturally deprived children must be given individual attention, because they, unlike middle-class children, are relatively unable to respond to social reinforcement and ego rewards. Hard of hearing and mentally retarded children not only need a great deal of personal care on the part of teachers, but specialised professional people, such as physicians and psychologist, must give them individual diagnostic attention as used. And sometimes what is needed is merely some kind of personal attention, which should remind us that the need for attention is a basic psychological need that must be satisfied, if the human organism is to operate efficiently. Whatever learning the individual student accomplishes under ordinary classroom conditions can be increased by giving him a little personal attention.

Meeting the individualised needs of students for instruction is chiefly a function of the classrom teachers. Teachers are limited in this respect only by their ability to diagnose special needs and the time they can devote to the giving of this help.

Some of the special help and attention can be given by teachers in the classroom during the instructional period, some of it can be given by teachers during free periods, after school or at other odd times, but much of it can provided more efficiently and effectively by persons, who are specialists, persons who are referred to as student personal workers or guidance workers.

Organisational Setup

The organisational setup to provide guidance in school is as follows

The School Counsellor

The school counsellor is perphaps the least specialised of the several kinds of guidance workers. Most counsellors are teachers or former teachers, who have a strong interest in working with students on a person-to-person basis and who have developed some special skills in interviewing and testing. There is a growing trend to require teachers to take professional training in counselling and guidance before being appointed to counsellor positions. Some states prescribe special credentials for counsellors. A generation or so age counsellors were inclined to specialise in problems of vocational choice-helping adolescent select their life work and advising select them about appropriate courses.

Hence, there is and has been a tendency for counsellors to render services that cover a widening sector of the students, whom they counseled in many schools, they are people in helping the individual student to adjust to the school program and in adapting the school program to the needs of the individual student.

The School Psychologist

The role of the school psychologist is closely related to that of the counsellor, in that both the counsellor and the psychologist help individual students with their problems. However, there are some important differences and distinctions, most counsellors are educators with some additional training in psychology, whereas a great many (although by no means all) school psychologists are primarily psychologists, who have some additional training in dealing with school problem.

School counsellors are member of the teaching or the administrative staff of the school, where they work, most of them teach some classes in the school, psychologists very seldom teach classes. This is partly because they need special equipment and facilities that are best kept separate from the hustle and bustle of school buildings and partly because elementary school have smaller enrollments than secondary school are unable to afford or may not require the services of a full time psychologist.

Medical Specialists

Another role that is growing in importance is that of the psychiatrists *i.e.* medical doctors, who have received specialised training in the diagnosis and treatment of psychopathology. They are usually included in the guidance programs as part time members of the psychological clinic staff, where they serve as consultants or as key members of psychiatric teams consisting of psychologists and social workers.

A small portion of the children referred to school psychologists and social workers involves problems of mental and physical health, the presence of a medical doctor on the staff of a clinic is highly desirable.

In actually, there is a considerable overlap in the roles of counsellor, school psychologist, school social worker and psychiatrist. They all may deal with emotional problems, they may all make referrals and they may all serve as consultants to teachers and administrative personal. The need for special instruction is perphaps the first that comes to the mind of most teachers.

The Guidance Worker

Guidance worker helps to solve the problem of the drop out. There are several ways, in which he can help. He can help, first of all, by listening sympathetically to the complaints and problems that students bring to him. Attending school, like any other kind of group activity, is an experience likely to be characterised by frustrations and injustices which, in turn, arouse hostility and/or anxiety. Many students are able to get over these feelings or at least to push them into the background, keeping in mind their main objective of finishing high school.

Techniques of Guidance in School

The techniques to provide guidance in school are

The Case Conference

One of the most effective approaches to pupil personnel problems, is the case conference, in which the guidance worker, who has been working closely with a certain students sits down with teachers, administrators and other staff members to discuss the problems encountered by the students. Usually, the guidance worker has the results of his interviews with the student as well as psychological test data, interviews with parents and cumulative records.

In the second place, case conferences help teachers, who have a child in a classroom to gain some new insights and understanding into his behaviour. In the third place, a case conference is a cooperative venture in communication.

The fourth advantage to the case conference is that it gives the guidance worker a chance to share some of his findings about students in general. This is quite different from having the guidance worker get up in faculty meetings and say what is wrong with the programme and what needs changing his arguments are for more eloquent, when he tells the teachers participating in a case conference about the problems faced by a child in trouble.

Over a period of time, case conferences are bound to highlight the inadequacies of the school program. The guidance worker may not even have to point them out as inadequacies. It is as a consulting participant in a case conference that the guidance worker can do some of his most effective work in helping the school adjust to the needs of the individual student.

Life-Space or Crisis Interviewing

One approach that **William C Morse** (1963) has found to be useful in helping teachers gain a better understanding of the world, in which children and young people's live consists of a technique of interviewing, which he had used to good effect in a camp for disturbed hostile aggressive boys.

The steps used in life-space interviewing are as follows

- The teacher begins his conversation with the student in an interested, accepting, non-judgemental way, allowing him to describes the situation or problem in his own terms, just as he sees it, even though it may be distorted or incorrect.
- The teacher explores the possibility that there may be other, related problems. Perhaps, the problem of the moment is merely a side issue.
- The teacher then raises the question. 'What do you think ought to be done about it?' The pupil's system of values comes into play at this point and he is likely to reveal any anxiety he has about committing himself to any course of behaviour that might change things. Sometimes, the problem 'solves itself' at this stage.
- The teacher becomes some what more active in the interview at the next stage, in that he indicates any features of the real world that the student may have overlooked and that might have implications for the problem at hand. This is done in factual manners, without any change from the accepting attitudes the teacher has expressed from the beginning. At this point, pupil motivation for change is explored.

It should be kept in mind that life interviewing has two aims

(i) To improve the understanding and empathy of the teacher.

(ii) To help the student with an emotional or social problem that is causing difficulties.

Morse is optimistic about the attainment of both objectives. He believes that many teachers have empathic and intutive resources that will enable them to develop skill at using the method and that children generally will respond to it.

Counselling

The earliest known healers were the shaman or the religion men and doctors of primitive societies. Gradually, following the growth of modern medicine, beginning with the work of Hippocrates, the medical profession emerged as the foremost among the helping profession. Correspondingly, the diverse psychotherapeutic techniques employed by healers differed from culture to culture and one society to another. The work of Freud gave the psychotherapeutic movements a great impetus. Freud's depth psychology tried to explain the cause of several psychoneurotic disorders.

Counselling Process

The term 'counselling process' implies continuous change or changes that take place or rather, which should take place in the client in promoting personality changes in a desired direction.

The kind of change that the counselling process aims at is

- Awareness on the part of the client.
- Behavioural change in a desired direction, through which the cilent can achieve his goals.
- Understanding his potentialities, limitations and how best to utilise them in achieving his goals.

The counselling process, by and large is the same for all problems and for all individuals. However, certain important difference need to be clarified. In vocational and educational counselling, the major emphasis is on collecting factual information and helping the client understand this information in a proper perspective. In such situations, the emotional problem, though present, are not the main concern of the counsellor. In educational and vocational counselling the decision-making and planning model occupies the counsellor's attention such that he tries to help rational problem-solving processes, clarify self-concepts values etc.

Steps in the Counselling Process

Stage 1 The first stage is the awareness of a need for help. Most individuals go about their day-to-day lives without much awareness of their situation and they appear to be unharmed for it.

Stage 2 The second important stage in cousellling consists of the development of relationship. This can be viewed as a bridge connecting the counsellee's personality with that of the counsellor's penetrating through the outer defences.

Usually, the defence strategies fall under two basic kinds of manipulative devices

(i) The client may take a helpless attitude and get the counsellor to do what he wants him to do.

(ii) The counsellee may arouse sympathy and attention and avoid unpleasant.

Stage 3 The third step in counselling is to aid the expression of feelings and clarification of problems. In psychoanalytic terminology, this is similar to 'catharsis'. In sense, it is a ventilation of feelings and the client experiences a feeling or relief consequent to the release of tension.

Stage 4 The next stage comprises the exploration of deeper feelings. We have said in the preceeding section that the client may mistake ventilation of feelings for resolution of feelings. It is necessary that the counsellor should not be content with a superficial view of the client's feelings. This step, therefore involves analysis.

Stage 5 The preceeding stage logically leads to the next stage, comprising the integration process. This stage, therefore, consists of working in close harmony with the client with due understanding, regard and sympathy for the client's innermost feelings. In the course of such a process, the counsellor is able to synthesise and integrate counsellee potentialities, needs and aspirations and direct them towards appropriate goals.

Stage 6 The next stage, though not spelt out very clearly, is concerned with the time perspective. Clients usually are confused about their time perspective. Naturally, they appear saffled as they are unable to explain to themselves the 'how' and 'why' of things and usually come to grief.

Stage 7 This stage is one of developing the awareness of the counsellee. A number of counsellors and psychotherapists stress the importance of helping the client gain insight into himself as well as insight into the world around him. This term, **insight**, is usually used synonymously with awareness. Psychoanalytic therapy, for instance, aims at providing insight into one's conflicts, repressions and inhibitions and when once these are seen in their true perspective, they cease to be painful.

In the **psychotherapeutic process**, the importance of awareness can not be over emphasised. There is another sense, in which awareness is used. It can refer to the awareness of goals, the direction, in which the self is to reach out or move forward.

Stage 8 The last stage in counselling is generally the most crucial one, in which the client is encouraged to make use of the psychotherapeutic or counselling benefits he many have gained to adjust himself to the world of realities, therefore this stage is the actual test to determine the success of counselling.

Variables Affecting the Counselling Process

The variables affecting the counselling process include general characteristics of counsellors and personality characteristics of counsellors.

General Characteristics of Counsellors

The importance of the counsellor's attitudes to counselling outcomes cannot be overemphasised. *In order to identify the counsellor characteristics, which are of concern, investigators employed three approaches.*

(i) **Speculation** The question as to what the characteristics of an effective counsellor are led to much speculation. The National Vocational Guidance

Association (NVGA), listed such characteristics as interest in people, patience, sensitiveness, emotional stability and objectivity as being important for good counselling.

According to the Association for Counsellor Education and Supervision, the counsellor should possess six basic qualities: belief in each individual, commitment to individual, alertness to the world, open-mindedness, understanding of self and professional commitment.

(ii) **Hypothesised Characteristic** This approach is used to find out whether certain characteristic that have been hypothesised as necessary for counselling are present and functioning.

Bandura tested the hypothesis that competent psychotherapist are

- Less anxious than those judged to be less competent.
- Possess greater insight into the nature of their own anxiety than do less competent therapist. He concluded that "the presence of anxiety in the therapist, whether recognised or not, affects his ability to do successful psychotherapy and insight into his anxiety alone is not sufficient.

(iii) **Correlational Analysis** This approach consists of exploring the relationship between counsellor variables and some criterion to measure the effectiveness derived from correlational analysis. Studies conducted by Johnson and her associates indicated the following conclusion. Effective male counsellor trainees were confident, friendly, affable, likeable and generally were satisfied with themselves and were more like each other than their counterparts from the less effective group.

The characteristics of counsellors are assessed, employing the self-report and rating techniques. Four types of criteria are frequently employed, namely supervisor ratings, counsellors peer rating, client rating and Q-techniques, to measure the effectiveness of the counsellors. In short, the effective counsellor was found to exhibit qualities such as tolerance, maturity, understanding and an ability to maintain an appropriate emotional distance from the counsellee. Variables, such as age, experience and sex also, to a certain extent, affect the counselling process.

Personality Characteristics of the Counsellors

Several studies have attempted to determine the personality characteristics of counsellors, which are basic to effective counselling. *Weitz, Snyder and Taylor have suggested the following traits of successful counsellors.*

- **Interested in Helping People** Some investigators have reported that a 'social service need' is necessary for success and satisfaction with a counselling job. Other investigators like Steffle, King and Leafqren, Mills, Chestnut and Hartzell that Demos and Zuwaylif found that counsellors liked people and are interested in helping. This attitude makes the client feel comfortable in their presence.
- **Perceptual Sensitivity** The counsellor should perceive and understand the thoughts and feelings of the client and should be sensitive to the clues given by him/her.
- **Personal Adjustment** It is natural for counsellors, as any other individuals, to have problems of adjustment. The counsellor should be able to cope with his problem in a constructive manner and should not attempt to try and solve the problems of clients, when he himself is facing difficulties.
- **Personal Security** Weitz suggested that feelings of personal security is another important factor. The counsellor may feel secure in his counselling role and feel insecure in certain areas outside counselling.
- **Genuineness** The counsellor should establish a genuine relationship with his clients, by which they can achieve their counselling goals. Rogers suggests that the counsellor should be a real person to his clients.

Counselling Areas

The areas where counselling act as an aid are as follows

Educational Counselling

Counselling in the educational context comprises a very important and vital part of educational activities. Many students at different levels of education have been found to function at levels for below their capacities. Counselling assistance would certainly help to brighten the lives many young people.

Counselling is indeed an important dimension of education. It promotes emotional maturity, personality development, self-responsibility, creativity and ability to solve problem. In the complex contemporary world, counselling is rapidly becoming an important part of the educational structure. The administration has to take a positive attitude towards counselling and provide the required facilities to the counsellors to function optimally.

Home and community resources should be meaningfully harnessed for the counselling needs of pupils/students. The main bulk of counselling responsibility will fall on the teachers, at least in the school. They need the necessary training for acquiring the necessary skills. They have to cultivate a healthy attitude towards counselling. Counselling programmes need to be evaluated from time to time. The specialist skills for making objective evaluations are generally not available with the teachers or even with some trained counsellors. However, the importance and need for evaluation cannot be underestimated.

Family Group Consultation

The counsellor would do well to leave these sensitive issues alone. It is the job of the counsellors to actively promote this intercourse. There is likely to be initial resistance and the families should be allowed to overcome the resistance and learn to narrate their stories naturally. Usually, the family group consultation method needs as many as 8 to 12 sessions.

Counselling with Families Counselling Children

The family is the primary group of society. Its characteristic feature is the effective bonds among the members in the family and a concern for each other. Counselling cannot afford to ignore such an important aspect of human life. Family relations are broadly of two types.

The parents-child relations and the husband-wife relations. When the members of the family are discented, tension, distress and misery are the natural out comes. The family counsellor should help to find ways and means of reducing, if not eliminating, the strife, mutual dirtrust and ill-will among the members of the family. Most problems in family relations have been identified to result from misunderstandings, which is the Laymans's term for lack of communication.

The parents-child relationship comes under stress and strain for very simple reason. Growth is a natural process and a normal phenomenon. Children grow and consequently become progressively less dependent on their parents. Each family has its own ethics and provides to its members a philosophy of life, which is communicated through non-verbal and informal means.

Counselling with Parents

Most probably children are products of problem homes. The disturbing feature in a home affect the harmonious development of the children. The incalculable harm, which parents do to their children is usually not grasped by most parents.

Parents counselling is aimed at helping parents, become sensitive to the possible adverse effect of their behaviour on their children. By helping the parents gain a better understanding of themselves and their own personalities much harmony could be established.

Parent counselling deals with the area of parent-child relationships concerning the dimension of dependence-independence. Most parents are deeply concerned about the well-being of their children and are afraid that, if left to themselves the children may harm themselves. Hence, they become overprotective, which is resented by the children.

Another area of parent-child conflict concern vocational choice. Most parents begin with the presumption that they know what is best for their children. Children have their own ideas and this usually results in a clash of ideas, interests and personalities. Parent counselling thus is one of the important service that can help foster a healthy home atmosphere.

Counselling the Delinquent

Delinquency is a symptom of emotional immaturity leading to socially unacceptable or reprehensible behaviour of the youth. Delinquency is one of the most common problems reported among the post-puberty or early adolescent children. One of the common symptoms of delinquency is truancy. Delinquents are emotionally immature and their behaviour is a compensatory reaction. Sometimes it becomes an act of gangsterism. The emotional upheaval and brittleness resulting from rapid physical growth and accelerated endocrinal functioning result in extra energy seeking expression in suitable outlets.

There is also a greater need for recognition. Horror, crime and other movies as well as story books provide the adolescent with a convenient material for day-dreaming and self-identification. Most adolescents limit themselves to day-dreams. But a few also resort to socially unacceptable means of expressing their energies to seek recognition. They fail to adapt and adjust to social norms. Counselling of such people is not easy.

Counselling Reluctant Clients

Counselling, we have observed earlier, is help voluntarily sought by the client. But this not always the case. Occasionally, counsellors have to work with clients, who are reluctant to discuss matters with the school, home and work situations. Reluctant clients are usually those, who are the referral cases. They do not take any responsibility and exhibit an unwillingness to communicate. The counsellors find that they exhibit non-facilitative emotion.

Counselling Skills

The counselling process is influenced by counsellor's personnel as well as professional skills. The professional skills that are required to be an effective counsellor are known as *counselling skills. The counselling skills are as follows*

(i) **Active Listening** Counsellors not only listen to spoken words but also to feelings, facial expression, emotion, gestures and unspoken thoughts of clients. Active listening helps the counsellor to derive objective assessment of client's problem.

(ii) **Attending** Counsellors should give total attention to the client. Total attention includes body language, facial expression, eye contact, head nod and such other non-verbal expressions. Egan has summarised the useful non-verbal behaviour in counselling as **SOLER**.

- **S** Facing the client **squarely** indicates total attention to the client.
- **O Open** posture, crossed arms/legs may indicate less involvement of counsellor.
- **L Leaning** towards client shows counsellor's interest.
- **E Eye** contact with client.
- **R Relaxed** state of counsellor which acts as social modeling for client to achieve relaxation.

(iii) **Paraphrasing** This refers to restating the content back to the client to assure the client that counsellor has understood the problem as narrated by the client.

(iv) **Empathy** Empathic skill involves use of attending, listening and interpersonal sensitivity of the counsellor. It is the counsellor's ability to sense what the client is feeling, experiencing and thinking.

(v) **Asking Questions** Counsellors ask questions for finding fault and engaging with the client. Open-ended questions help counsellor in engaging and establishing a relationship with the client and elicit a response from client.

(vi) **Immediacy** It refers to disclosure of feelings about the client or the therapeutic interaction at that moment as it happens by the counsellor.

(vii) **Self Disclosure** It refers to the counsellor stating feelings about a similar situation as client is presently in.

(viii) **Summarising** It refers to condensing the essence of what the client is saying or feeling. It helps to understand the frame of reference of client and helps client to place his/her problem in perspective.

(ix) **Goal Setting** After assessing the problem, counsellor works with the client to set realistic goals or behavioural changes the client wants to accomplish.

Counselling Techniques

The counselling techniques include behavioural counselling techniques and cognitive behavioural therapy techniques.

Behavioural Counselling Techniques

These techniques are based on the classical and operant conditioning theories. *It includes exposure therapies; stimulus control by using reinforcement and punishment; role play and token economy.*

(i) **Exposure Therapies** Exposure therapies are used to reduce the disabling feelings and emotions of anxiety, fear, anger, phobia etc. The client is gradually exposed to problem situations or in imagination under the supervision of the counsellor. The behavioural assessment indicates that problem behaviour is not because of inadequacy of skills.

(ii) **Stimulus Control By Using Reinforcement and Punishment** The systematic use of reinforcement and punishment for stimulus control is governed by the principles of operant conditioning. In the technique of stimulus control, the focus is on the antecedent to the occurrence of a behaviour.

(iii) **Role Play** Role play refers to imitating the behaviour of others. This technique is used by counsellors to modify behaviours or make the client learn a new behaviour. In this, the counsellor and client assume specified roles and enact a problem situation.

Initially, the counsellor plays role of client and client does role of other actor in problem situation. In the following session, they exchange the roles. Thus, the client in the session, play his/her original role in problem situation and attempts to model his/her behaviour on behaviour demonstated by counsellor in first session. Thus, client learns new behaviour or modifies the existing behaviour so that situation is no more problematic.

(iv) **Token Economy** In this technique the behaviour is modified using positive reinforcement. The rules are established prior to the start of the treatment. These rules specify the behaviour to be modified and the reward to be given. Each time the client exhibits the desired behaviour, it results in the reward of a token and undesirable behaviour results in removal of a token. The token rewarding is gradually withdrawn as client starts displaying the desired behaviour without a reward.

Cognitive Behavioural Therapy Techniques

Cognitive Behavioural therapy technique are based upon the understanding that human behaviour is influenced by cognition or thought process. *The following techniques are used by cognitive behavioural therapists*

(i) **Cognitive Rehearsal** In this technique, the counsellor asks the patient to rehearse the same event in which he/she feels uncomfortable. *For example* A person gets nervous by travelling in the metro train. The counsellor will tell him that he/she needs to explore some other things to reduce the anxiety during the travelling in train. One of the things could be to do a breathing exercise or listening to music.

(ii) **Validity Testing** The counsellor helps the client in confronting and testing the validity of the beliefs of the client to expose these thoughts as baseless.

For example Mother of Rohan started thinking that she is a bad mother as she could not spend more time teaching Rohan. She feels depressed and approaches a therapist for help.

The therapist asks her to note down points regarding the behaviours that proves that she is a bad mother. As she did so, the therapist helped her to confront and test validity of her beliefs.

(iii) **Guided Discovery** The counsellor asks a series of specific questions about the client's thoughts, feelings and emotions regarding the maladaptive behaviours. The counsellor helps the client link the distorted thought pattern and maladaptive behaviour.

(iv) **Writing and Journal** The client is asked to note down her everyday anxiety behaviour and the thoughts and emotions surrounding such behaviour for about 2-3 weeks.

The journal is reviewed by the counsellor and client to discover the unhelpful thought patterns and emotions that causes the anxiety behaviour in the client.

EXAM BASED QUESTIONS

1 According to theories of motivation, behaviour of student is determined by

(a) external factor (b) internal factor
(c) Both a and b (d) None of these

2 Individuals who are operating using an external locus believe that

(a) outside forces are responsible for the events in their life
(b) inside forces are responsible for the events in their life
(c) Both a and b
(d) None of the above

3 Intrinsic motivation is

(a) person centered
(b) comes from within an individual
(c) Both a and b
(d) None of the above

4 Humanistic theory of motivation was propagated by

(a) Skinner (b) Chapman
(c) Feder (d) Carl Rogers

5 Students receive their own internal reward through

(a) an increase in self-esteem
(b) sense of achievement
(c) when they reach their desired goal
(d) All of the above

6 Behaviourist theory of motivation was propagated by

(a) Feder (b) BF Skinner
(c) Carl Rogers (d) Chapman

7 Which among the following are motivational tools according to Skinner?

(a) Reward system (b) Punishment
(c) Both a and b (d) None of the above

8 Students who are successful in the classroom usually operate under

(a) the internal locus of control
(b) external force as a reason
(c) Both a and b
(d) None of the above

9 Cognitive approach of motivation is an

(a) intrinsic form (b) extrinsic form
(c) Both a and b (d) None of these

10 The student who have an external locus of control tends to see their failure as

(a) all encompassing (b) as one-time mistakes
(c) Both a and b (d) None of these

11 Concepts are generally learned in one of two ways, most of what we know is learned from

(a) observation (b) classical conditioning
(c) paired-associate learning (d) one-trial learning

12 The research approach in which the teaching practices of effective teachers are recorded through classroom observation is called
(a) observational learning
(b) direct instruction
(c) a process-product study
(d) a time-motion study

13 Given the well-documented differences in learning styles and preferences, what are the effects of different teaching styles on student learning?
(a) The effects of teaching style on different learners has been difficult to demonstrate conclusively.
(b) A non-directive teaching style works best with children, who are inductive learners.
(c) A formal lecture style works best with about half the students in most classes.
(d) A relaxed, humourous teaching style works best with children, who learn best by listening.

14 According to teachers, what teaching strategy might be considered to be least effective ?
(a) Short independent practice assignments
(b) No independent seatwork
(c) Independent seatwork with too much feedback
(d) Independent seatwork without feedback

15 In planning instruction, what three components are essentially incorporated?
(a) Ways to integrate music, art and as many of the other disciplines as possible.
(b) Computer assisted learning alongwith handson learning.
(c) Learning theory, subject matter and particular student development levels .
(d) Technology theories, graphics and seatwork.

16 Perhaps the most important thing that a teacher should know about transfer of learning is
(a) it needs a minimum of three students to be effective.
(b) how to accomplish this with students whose first language is not English.
(c) that a student must be prepared for it by having the teacher present the appropriate mnemonics before-hand.
(d) that it cannot be assumed.

17 When presenting a lesson, effective teachers
(a) will give clear indications about the most important elements of the lesson by saying, *e.g.* "It is particularly important to note that.....".
(b) will use a wide variety of visual aids and graphics to drive important points.
(c) will wander off the topic frequently to give humourous, but largely irrelevant examples.
(d) will talk slower at the points in the lesson that are particularly important.

18 Research has shown that teachers tend to give up too rapidly on students whom they perceive to be low achievers. How long should a teacher wait for the answer?
(a) Teachers who wait approximately 5 seconds after asking a student a question obtain better learning results than do those who give up more rapidly.
(b) Teachers who wait approximately 2 seconds after asking a student a question obtain better learning results than do those who give up more rapidly.
(c) Teachers who wait approximately 8 seconds after asking a student a question obtain better learning results than do those who give up more rapidly.
(d) Teachers who wait approximately 3 seconds after asking a student a question obtain better learning results than do those who give up more rapidly.

19 Teachers can check for understanding by
(a) using 'learning probes' during the lesson.
(b) stopping the lesson and administering a pop quiz.
(c) testing them the next school day on the lesson material.
(d) having students write what they recall from the lesson at the end of the school day.

20 Research in between class ability grouping has been shown
(a) most effective in the elementary grades.
(b) that students assigned to low-track classes gain the most and augment the benefits gained by students in the college prep classes.
(c) that students assigned to low-track classes lose the most and balance out the benefits derived by students in the college prep classes.
(d) to boost student achievement across the board.

21 The amount of time a teacher has for teaching depends largely on two factors. Which of the following is one of them?
(a) The amount of preparation a given lesson will require.
(b) The amount of materials required by a given lesson.
(c) The amount of time the teacher schedules for instruction.
(d) The rate at which a small group of students learn a given lesson.

22 When setting learning objectives for a lesson, it suits the teacher
(a) to use a standard formula for all their lessons, this makes learning easier for students and gives them a sense of security.
(b) to use objectives couched in theoretically based terms.
(c) to make the list as short as possible.
(d) not to give the students too narrow a set of objectives, which may lead them to devalue or ignore other meaningful aspects of a lesson.

23 **The concept of motivation is closely tied to the concept of**
(a) classical conditioning
(b) operant conditioning
(c) the zone of proximal development
(d) one trial learning

24 **One concept that is central to attribution theory is**
(a) operant conditioning (b) self-actualisation
(c) locus of control (d) discrimination learning

25 **When students are motivated by the desire to gain recognition from others, their goals are**
(a) performance goals (b) learning goals
(c) self-actualised goals (d) primary goals

26 **A reward that is external to the activity, such as recognition or a good grade is called**
(a) an intrinsic incentive (b) an internal drive state
(c) an extrinsic incentive (d) a primary reinforcer

27 **Having students in mixed ability groups and holding them to high standards, but providing many ways for them to reach these standards is called**
(a) achievement based grouping
(b) fixed ability correlations
(c) untracking
(d) between class ability grouping

28 **What is the name of a system of instruction that seeks to enable all students to achieve instructional objectives by allowing learning time to vary**
(a) corrective instruction (b) insight learning
(c) mastery criterion (d) mastery learning

29 **A teacher's praise can be an effective motivator if**
(a) praise is delivered contingently.
(b) praise focuses students attention on their neighbour's task-relevant behaviour.
(c) praise is delivered just for showing up for class
(d) praise is delivered the same day the praised behaviour happens.

30 **Teachers can apply many strategies to reduce the negative impact of anxiety on learning and performance such as**
(a) creating a classroom climate that is accepting.
(b) giving students a chance to correct errors or improve their work.
(c) providing clear, unambiguous directions.
(d) All of the above

31 **Among these which is the specific responsibilities and roles of school counsellor?**
(a) Individual counselling and advisement
(b) Student appraisal
(c) Career development
(d) All of the above

32 **Career counselling was originally called**
(a) counselling (b) job counselling
(c) vocational guidance (d) None of the above

33 **Reinforcement theory of motivation is given by**
(a) Skinner (b) Pavlov (c) Jung (d) Maslow

34 **................ is driven by an interest or enjoyment in the task itself and exists within the individual rather than relying on external pressures or a desire for reward**
(a) Intrinsic motivation (b) Extrinsic motivation
(c) Push motivation (d) Pull motivation

35 **According to which theory, needs are arranged in order of importance to human life, from the basic to the complex?**
(a) Flow theory
(b) Herzberg two factor theory
(c) Maslow's need hierarchy theory
(d) None of the above

36 **According to .... theory, there is a tendency of individuals to seek consistency among their cognitions (*i.e.* beliefs, opinions).**
(a) evolutionary theory (b) cognitive dissonance
(c) transformative learning (d) operant conditioning

37 **Person-centered counselling is a form of**
(a) cognitive behavioural psychotherapy
(b) humanistic psychotherapy
(c) psychoanalytic psychotherapy
(d) None of the above

38 **A person-centered counsellor's role would best be described as a**
(a) Expert (b) Facilitator
(c) Counsellor (d) Therapist

39 **Among the options given below, which is the goal of counselling?**
(a) Make people intelligent and smart
(b) Given correct medication
(c) Diagnose correctly the issue
(d) Promote personal growth and productivity

40 **Who developed the Rational Emotive Behaviour Therapy (REBT)?**
(a) Albert Ellis (b) Truman Kelley
(c) Carl Rogers (d) John Dollard

41 **What is the ultimate aim of counselling for the individuals to attain?**
(a) Self-knowledge (b) Self-understanding
(c) Self-discovery (d) Self-motivation

42 **Which of the following is true about the ways of learning for students?**
(a) Speed of learning is same for all students
(b) Each child has a unique learning style
(c) Children follow the way other students learn
(d) All children immediately follow teacher's instruction

43 Cognitive dissonance occurs when
(a) the attitude to an object and the behaviour towards it are inconsistent
(b) the attitude to an object and the behaviour towards it are consistent
(c) the attitude is negatively inclined
(d) the attitude is positively reinforced

44 Among the given options which should be based upon understanding the needs and problems of the students, competence and interest of the guidance personnel?
(a) Guidance principles (b) Guidance techniques
(c) Guidance services (d) None of these

45 A practitioner counsellor should
(a) develop theories of his kind to treat clients
(b) not be only proficient in existing therapies of counselling and psychotherapy, but also be aware of its relevance and effectiveness with diverse clients
(c) make his/her clients aware of all counselling theories
(d) ignore theories and just focus on practice by developing instant theories by own experiences

46 Abraham Maslow developed a theory in which he postulated that the healthiest people were 'self-actualising transcenders'. What is the name of this theory?
(a) Self-actualising theory (b) Transcending theory
(c) Theory Z (d) None of these

47 What is the highest level of Maslow's Hierarchy of need model?
(a) Self-actualisation (b) Esteem
(c) Love (c) Safety

48 The need for recognition from others is on which level of Maslow's Hierarchy of needs model?
(a) Self-actualisation needs
(b) Esteem needs
(c) Belonging and love needs
(d) Safety needs

49 Maslow believed human beings have an inborn nature that is essentially
(a) Good or atleast neutral
(b) Inherently evil and must be tamed
(c) Clever
(d) Spiritual

Directions (Q. Nos. 50-54) *Read the passage given below and answer the following.*

The family is the primary group of society. Its characteristic feature is the effective bonds among the members in the family and a concern for each other. Counselling cannot afford to ignore such an important aspect of human life. Family relations are broadly of two types. The parents-child relations and the husband-wife relations. When the members of the family are disunited, tension, distress and misery are the natural outcomes. The family counsellor should help find ways and means of reducing, if not eliminating, the confllict, mutual disrespect and ill-will among the members of the family. Most problems in family relations have been identified to result from misunderstandings which is the Layman's term for lack of communication.

The parents-child relationship comes under stresses and strains for very simple reason. Growth is a natural process and a normal phenomenon. Children grow and consequently become progressively less dependent on their parents. Each family has its own ethics and provides to its members a philosophy of life, which is communicated through non-verbal and informal means. Many a time parents forget that children cannot be judged from their own standards of morality or decency or culture. Quite often parents try to compensate for their failures by wanting their children to achieve what they could not. They tend to become unrealistic in their demands and this cause frustration on both sides.

50 What is the main cause of frustration in both parent and children?
(a) Parents want their child to be obedient
(b) Parents put unrealistic demands before the child
(c) Children often behave in rude manner with parents
(d) Children put extravegant demand before parents

51 In what way parents try to compensate for their failure?
(a) Try again to achieve success
(b) Want their children to success
(c) Want their children to achieve what they could not
(d) Force their children to study

52 What is the characteristic feature of a family?
(a) Effective bonds among the members of the family
(b) It is a primitive group
(c) All live under same roof
(d) All work for the happiness of the family

53 What is the outcome of a disunited family?
(a) All have their independent life
(b) Members talk closely with each other
(c) Tension, distress
(d) Members live happily

54 What is the cause of most problems in a family relation?
(a) Lack of communication
(b) Jealousy
(c) Alcoholic father
(d) Irresponsible mother

Direction (Q.Nos. 55-66) *In the questions given below are two statements labelled as Assertion (A) and Reason (R). In the context of the two statements, which one of the following is correct?*

Codes

(a) Both A and R are true and R is the correct explanation of A
(b) Both A and R true, but R is not the correct explanation of A
(c) A is true, but R is false
(d) A is false, but R is true

55 Assertion (A) Vocational adjustment is the most crucial adjustment of life.

Reason (R) It is closely indentified with the self concept of the individual.

56 Assertion (A) Emotional problem that disturb the functioning of individual students are not the kind of problem that can be treated by change in the curriculum.

Reason (R) They cannot interfere with the capacity to learn.

57 Assertion (A) Guidance worker is useful in school.

Reason (R) They can handle vocational counselling more efficiently and effectively than a class teacher.

58 Assertion (A) Pre-marital counselling is important.

Reason (R) It makes marriage happy.

59 Assertion (A) Intelligence tests are more highly correlated with the scores on achievement tests than they are graded by teachers.

Reason (R) Teachers are not very good judges of school accomplishment.

60 Assertion (A) Developmental psychologist uses descriptive research extensively.

Reason (R) A survey is an example of descriptive research.

61 Assertion (A) Action research is criticised as it lacks the objectivity sought in other form of research.

Reason (R) The people involved in the experiment are the educator themselves.

62 Assertion (A) We can retrieve information from long term memory.

Reason (R) We can make multiple connection with existing knowledge, using knowledge frequently.

63 Assertion (A) Rohit scores high in Science and Math.

Reason (R) His logical Mathematical intelligence is high.

64 Assertion (A) Children realise that an object continue to exist even when removed from their view.

Reason (R) In sensorimotor stage, children exhibit object permanence.

65 Assertion (A) At expertise stage, learner have extensive knowledge of a topic.

Reason (R) Study and practice for many year contribute to new knowledge to learner.

66 Assertion (A) Student learn effective reading to learn strategies by observing and imitating.

Reason (R) Reciprocal teaching is an effective mode of teaching.

67 Consider the following statements

1. Rehearsal is defined as repeating information verbatim, either mentally or aloud.
2. Students are more likely to be intrinsically motivated when they have a sense of self-esteem.

Which of the statements given above is/are correct?

(a) Only 1 (b) Only 2
(c) Both 1 and 2 (d) Neither 1 nor 2

68 Consider the following statements

1. Students may find that acquiring more knowledge and skill in a particular area enhance their sense of commitment.
2. Students become increasingly able to distinguish among various attributes.

Which of the statements given above is/are correct?

(a) Only 1 (b) Only 2
(c) Both 1 and 2 (d) Neither 1 nor 2

69 Consider the following statements

1. Students attributions are totally the result of their previous success and failure experience.
2. Teacher must be careful when they attribute either success or failure to effort.

Which of the statements given above is/are true?

(a) Only 1 (b) Only 2
(c) Both 1 and 2 (d) Neither 1 nor 2

70 Consider the following statements

1. The school accountability movement in the United States has made ample use of standardised tests in their campaign to hold schools accountable for students learning outcome.

2. Consider by some educators be the most useful and flexible of all test forms, verbal analogies and matching items can be used in tests for most school subjects.

Which of the statements given above is/are correct?

(a) Only 1 (b) Only 2
(c) Both 1 and 2 (d) Neither 1 nor 2

71 Consider the following statements

1. Considered by some educators to be the most useful and flexible of all tests forms, multiple choice items can be used in tests for most school subjects.
2. As children develop, they advance from associative play to cooperative play.

Which of the statements given above is/are correct?

(a) Only 1 (b) Only 2
(c) Both 1 and 2 (d) Neither 1 nor 2

72 Arrange the following in correct chronological order.

1. Rendering guidance
2. Follow-up programme
3. Collecting data

Codes

(a) 1, 2 and 3 (b) 3, 2 and 1
(c) 2, 1 and 3 (d) 3, 1 and 2

73 Consider the following statements

1. A key concep to pre-school education is readiness training.
2. Research on kindergarten indicates that kindergarten promotes readiness and achievement in the first and second grade, but these effects disappear by the third or fourth grade.

Which of the statements given above is/are correct?

(a) Only 1 (b) Only 2
(c) Both 1 and 2 (d) Neither 1 nor 2

74 Consider the following statements

1. In terms of cognitive development, middle childhood is characterised by the child's attainment of the stage of concrete operations.
2. During middle childhood, self concept and academic performance are negatively correlated.

Which of the statements given above is/are correct?

(a) Only 1 (b) Only 2
(c) Both 1 and 2 (d) Neither 1 nor 2

75 Consider the following statements

1. During middle childhood, children begin to use social comparison to evaluate themselves.
2. Children who are well accepted by their peers tend to be cooperative, helpful and caring.

Which of the statements given above is/are correct?

(a) Only 1 (b) Only 2
(c) Both 1 and 2 (d) Neither 1 nor 2

76 Consider the following statements

1. During adolescence, self-esteem is at its lowest, when the child enters middle school or junior high school.
2. Using flash cards for review is developmentally appropriate for adolescents.

Which of the statements given above is/are correct?

(a) Only 1 (b) Only 2
(c) Both 1 and 2 (d) Neither 1 nor 2

77 Match the following

List I (Scholars)		**List II** (Theory)
A. Carl Rogers	1.	Extrinsic motivation
B. Skinner	2.	Competition
C. Chapman	3.	Intrinsic motivation
D. Hurlock	4.	Cooperation

Codes

	A	B	C	D		A	B	C	D
(a)	1	2	3	4	(b)	1	2	4	3
(c)	3	1	2	4	(d)	2	4	3	1

78 Match the following

List I (Scholars)		**List II** (Concept)
A. Fritz Heider	1.	Social conformity
B. ER Guthrie	2.	Operant behaviour is much more representative of the real life human learning
C. BF Skinner	3.	All learning depend on the contiguity of stimulus and response

Codes

	A	B	C
(a)	2	1	3
(b)	1	2	3
(c)	3	1	2
(d)	1	3	2

79 Match the following

List I (Theories)		**List II** (Characteristics)
A. Motive	1.	Association between a stimulus and response
B. Instrumental behaviour	2.	Sensory motor learning
C. Habit strength	3.	Inner dynamics
D. Learning cycle	4.	The second stage of motivational cycle

Codes

	A	B	C	D
(a)	2	1	4	3
(b)	2	1	3	4
(c)	1	2	3	4
(d)	3	4	1	2

80 Match the following

List I (Theories)		List II (Scholars)
A. Child Psychoanalysis	1.	Sigmund Freud
B. Interpretation of dreams	2.	Anna Freud
C. Element of reality	3.	GW Leibniz
D. Deficiency need	4.	A Maslow

Codes

	A	B	C	D
(a)	2	1	3	4
(b)	1	2	3	4
(c)	3	4	1	2
(d)	4	3	1	2

81 Match the following

List I (Effect)		List II (Behaviour)
A. Lateral hypothalamus	1.	Activates sustained eating
B. Hawthrone effect	2.	Motivation
C. TAT	3.	Aggressive behaviour
D. Limbic system	4.	Measure achievement motivation

Code

	A	B	C	D
(a)	1	2	4	3
(b)	2	1	4	3
(c)	4	3	1	2
(d)	4	3	2	1

ANSWERS

1 (c)	2 (a)	3 (c)	4 (d)	5 (d)	6 (b)	7 (c)	8 (a)	9 (a)	10 (a)
11 (a)	12 (c)	13 (c)	14 (d)	15 (c)	16 (d)	17 (a)	18 (d)	19 (a)	20 (c)
21 (c)	22 (d)	23 (b)	24 (c)	25 (a)	26 (c)	27 (c)	28 (d)	29 (a)	30 (d)
31 (d)	32 (c)	33 (a)	34 (a)	35 (c)	36 (b)	37 (b)	38 (b)	39 (d)	40 (a)
41 (b)	42 (b)	43 (a)	44 (b)	45 (b)	46 (c)	47 (a)	48 (b)	49 (a)	50 (b)
51 (c)	52 (a)	53 (c)	54 (a)	55 (a)	56 (c)	57 (b)	58 (b)	59 (a)	60 (b)
61 (a)	62 (a)	63 (a)	64 (a)	65 (a)	66 (b)	67 (a)	68 (b)	69 (c)	70 (a)
71 (b)	72 (d)	73 (c)	74 (a)	75 (b)	76 (a)	77 (b)	78 (d)	79 (b)	80 (a)
81 (a)									

CHAPTER 31

Psychology and Social Issues

Our society is facing lots of social issues such as gender discrimination, poverty, marginalisation etc. Psychology can help us in many ways in understanding causes and consequences of various social issues and can help in sorting out these issues.

Social Issues

Being the world's largest democracy, India's dream of becoming an egalitarian nation is still unaccomplished. India has made remarkable achievements in the field of science, technology, literature, medicines, space, infact in each an every field which is known to mankind, yet there are numerous social issues which our country is still facing. These social issues are creating obstacles for India in accomplishing the goal of inclusive development.

Few of the major social problems are gender discrimination, poverty, disability and migration. Such social issues affect a large portion of population in our country and resolving these issues have become the need of the hour.

Understanding, analysis and finding solutions of these issues have become a major concern for psychologists too. They try to resolve these issues by acting as consultants, advocates and agents of change. It has become very important to make general masses aware and sensitise them regarding these social problems, so that these social evils can be curbed completely from our society, and young generation get motivated to eradicate these social stigmas from our country.

Meaning of Social Issues

A problem that affects a large segment of population in a negative manner is called a *social problem*. It is dynamic in nature *i.e* it changes with time and change in the society. Social problems can be latent *i.e.* unrecognised or can clearly manifest themselves as a threat.

In this Chapter

Social problems if remain unresolved proves to be an impairment to country's development. *Some of the major social issues which our country is facing are discused below*

Issue of Gender Discrimination

Modern India has made huge progress towards inclusion of women in diverse fields ranging from Indian Navy to Indian Space Research Programmes, but still a lot more remains to be done for the better acceptance and fair position which females deserve. Discrimination or bias is the differential treatment made/done towards a person based on the group, class or category the person belongs to. Gender discrimination is the differential treatment made towards a person based on his/her gender.

Gender Discrimination/Bias

Discrimination is done between male and female child in all areas of life from providing education to a child to making a child financially stable. Being a developing country *Women empowerment* and *Women equality* is a much talked issue but headlines in newspaper every day about domestic violence, rape, acid attacks on females put a full stop behind these two words.

Since ages the role of male and female members in our society are predefined. Males are the earners and females are home makers. Males being earners always enjoy a more powerful role and has no hesitation is dominating women physically and emotionally.

Today the scenario has changed a lot and women are actively participating in professional jobs, particularly those job areas which were initially restricted for women only. It includes fields like army, navy, judiciary etc. Women have not only made themselves strong but have also proved their mettle in each and every field of Science and Technology.

But it's a pity, that still in major parts of India and the world, females are denied their basic rights like education, they are considered to be financial burdens by parents and are married off at an early age.

Female Foeticide

A girl child is killed in her mother's womb, which leads to inbalance in sex-ratio and enhanced crimes against women. In developed countries though women are allowed to work but discrimination is prevalent at all levels of work place, like low pay to women for the same jobs, for which males are earning a lot more. Incidents of sexual abuse and harassment are also common.

A pioneering work was done by Anand Lakshmi, who showed the gender discrimination present in our society. The status of girl child was studied in Andhra Pradesh, Bihar, Delhi, Gujarat, Karnataka, Kerala, Madhya Pradesh, Maharashtra, Odisha, Punjab, Rajasthan, Tamil Nadu, Uttar Pradesh, and West Bengal with a sample of 13, 200 girls. Their age ranged from 7 to 18 yrs. *The findings are as follows*

- The girl child in India is discriminated even before birth. Studies on aminocentesis a procedure to monitor a developing foetus have shown that female foeticide is widespread. Figures on female infanticide were also high.
- Even after girl is born, she has to cope with deep rooted gender stereotypes and prejudices. For instance the birth of a girl is generally not celebrated.
- At mealtimes, the girl waits until the men of the family have eaten.
- Girls usually stay at home to help with the household chores and look after younger siblings, while boys are sent to school.
- At puberty, the girl finds her movements highly restricted, her marriage becomes the priority for a family rather than her all round development.
- Once she is married, the girl is often harassed for bringing inadequate dowry or for producing a girl child.
- In order of time spent a girl child is engaged in activities like: sweeping (72%), cooking (65%), fetching water (43%), cleaning (42%) and child care (33%).

The findings of the above studies brings forefront our social reality which is a growing evil if not resolved timely will take a demon shape.

Factors Affecting Gender Discrimination

Some of the main factors of gender discrimination in India are

(i) **Decision-Making Power within Family** In patriarchy men are given the privilege of being the authority, occupying roles of controlling property and power over women and children. Most of Indians follow a patriarchal customs. There is rampant discrimination against women. *For example* Marriage includes the custom of dowry. Married females cannot support their parents in old age even if she is earning as husband has a control over her money too.

(ii) **Preference for a Male Child** Boys are preferred more in comparison to girls, as girls are considered to be a financial liability because of dowry system. Sons have a right to inherit the property whereas girls don't inherit property of their parents. Sons are seen as an asset as they can work outside their homes. These factors leads to the preference of a male child over female child.

(iii) **Dowry** Dowry is the cash or some kind of valuable gift which the bride's family gifts to the groom during marriage. It is widespread and is followed in most of the religions. But this has created a perception that girl child is a burden on her parents. Though dowry has been prohibited under the 1961 Dowry Prohibition Act, in Indian Civil Law and by Sections 304 B and 498 A of the Indian Penal Code.

(iv) **Lack of Education** Education enhances a person's wisdom and make him/her stand for their rights. Lack of education is the key cause behind the existence of gender descrimination.

(v) **Lack of Exposure** Due to the lack of exposure women are confined only to the roles within the house. They lack skills to face the fast changing world.

(vi) **Dependence on Males** Females are always dependent on their male counterparts during each stage of their life. May it be a daughter, a sister, a wife or a mother, males dominate over them. Thus, they consider themselves always subordinate to male members.

But, today due to industrialisation and urbanisation role of women in Indian society has been changing. Women today are more aware of their rights and resist any sort of harassment openly.

There are numerous legal provisions, welfare schemes and programmes to empower women and make them self sufficient. Indian women too are no longer silent or apologetic about claiming a share and visibility in all spheres of life, be it family, in public place or political front women are everywhere.

We all must realise that without removing this social stigma, development of the country can never be achieved. The role of government and NGOs in accomplishing this mission by making people aware of negative consequences of this social stigma very important.

Issue of Poverty

Poverty is also another social problem which is widespread in India. Though pockets of poverty are found across the country but states having the highest numbers of poor include Bihar, Jharkhand, Uttar Pradesh and Madhya Pradesh. These states account for almost 196 million multi-dimensionally poor people in India. Across nearly every state, poor nutrition is the largest contributor to multi-dimensional poverty. Lack of education is the second largest contributor to poverty.

Poverty can be defined as the scarcity or the lack of basic resoures or material possession to afford a decent standard of living. It is a condition that falls at the lower end of the socio-economic scale. Poverty can be approached from either an absolute or relative perspective. The threshold at which absolute poverty is defined is considered to be about the same, independent of the persons, location or time period. Whereas, Relative poverty is when a person living in a particular country does not enjoy a certain minimum level of 'living standard' as compared to rest of the population of that country. That's why threshold of relative poverty varies from one country to another.

If a group of people lacks the resources to meet the essential needs like accommodation, nutrition, clothing, education and health, then that group is termed as poor.

Poverty line separates population in two categories

(i) Those who have an adequate standard of living.
(ii) Those who live without adequate means.

The factors that contribute to poverty line are – calorie intake, per capita income and per capita consumption.

The concept of poverty is socially driven and is influenced by the demography of a country. Thus, two people with same expenditure may experience different levels of well-being and different levels of poverty.

Human Development Index

It considers poverty more as denial of opportunities and choices which is most basic to human development. Poverty has been studied differently by researchers from different disciplines. In psychology poverty is studied as a socio-psychological phenomena and its consequences on individual and society. Poor people feel deprived as their interests are in disadvantaged position in comparison to other members of the society. So, deprivation and disadvantage are the result of poverty.

- **Deprivation** It is an individual's experience where he/or /she feels sense of loss or suffering. It is related to poverty, but, it's a subjective notion of feeling deprived of basic needs. *For example* Basic resources like water and sanitation.
- **Disadvantage** It is a group or community phenomenon in which people suffer from increased chances of failure because they belong to or are member of a particular group or community. It is related to the socio-economic hardships that are determined by social structure.

Poverty from a psychological point of view is an individuals perception of his/her own condition in comparison to others in a given society. Thus, we can say that poverty is rooted in the notion of inequality, which one feels in comparison to other members of society.

Causes of Poverty

The factors related to poverty are

(i) **Individual** Individual doesnot take initiative towards his/her own upliftment, unwillingness to work hard, practices like gambling or drinking are the main causes of being poor.

(ii) **Demographic** Overpopulation of our country is one of the main cause of poverty. Overpopulation leads to massive unemployment that results in poverty.

(iii) **Economic Causes**

Following are the main economic causes of poverty

- **Poor Agricultural Infrastructure** Outdated farming practices, lack of proper irrigation infrastructure, and lack of formal training in crop handling has led to the downfall of the productivity in this sector.
- **Unemployment** Unemployment rates are high in India and according to 2015 survey, 77% of families do not have a regular source of income.
- **Inflation and Price Hike** Increase in prices of commodities and fall in purchasing value of money are also contributors to poverty as salaries and wages do not rise at the same pace.
- **Faulty Economic Policies** Economic reforms initiated by government in 1991 were suited to international firms and foreign investments, making rich more richer and poor more poorer.

(iv) **Social Issues** Social issues which contribute towards poverty *are as follows*

- **Education and Illiteracy** Education and poverty form a vicious cycle as both of them individually leads to the other.
- **Outdated Social Customs** Social customs like the caste system and marginalisation of certain sections of the society, leaves very limited and low paying jobs for these people. This leads to poverty among marginalised sections.
- **Lack of Skilled Labour** Lack of adequate vocational training makes India a poorly skilled country. Lack of skills leads to low paying jobs for majority of the population.
- **Gender Inequality** Discrimination against women by not letting them work outside homes results in 50% of the population being dependent on others for the fulfillment of their basic needs. They are left unemployed and do not contribute to family income.

Consequences of Poverty

The consequences of poverty are numerous and disastrous. *Few of these are as follows*

- Children coming from poor families show cognitive impairment and low academic achievement.
- Educational Gap, which is the performance of children coming from disadvantaged group as compared to the children coming from prosperous group tend to increase with age. This is the reason behind high rate of dropout up to 80% from schools class 5.
- Lack of nutritious meals and basic amenities affect the physical and psychological development of children. They are slow , show apathy and are undernourished.
- The individuals growing up under adverse socio-economic conditions are more prone to mental illness and they show low level of motivation towards any task assigned to them. They are more prone to indulge in socially maladaptive behaviour like truancy, theft, robbery etc.

Psychological Analysis of Poverty

Pareek proposed a Psychological Model of Poverty. He proposed that behaviour is a product of the social system in which an individual lives. Behaviour produced by motivation and motivational patterns are influenced by various factors . They strengthen or weaken human behaviour by producing expectation of reward or punishment. The expectancy framework built on the basis of reinforcing mechanism influences the feedback to the social system. From this perspective poverty is both a structure and a product of a system.

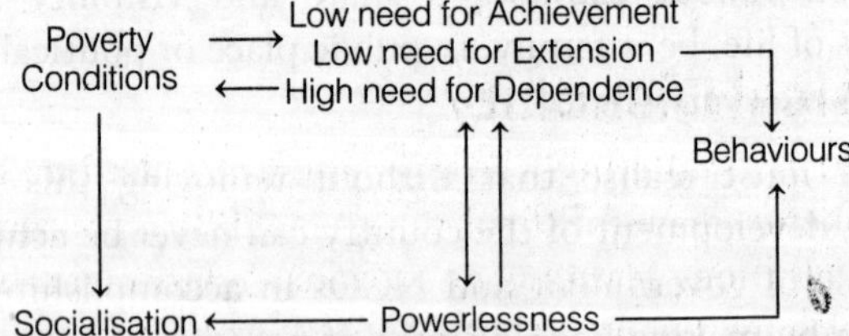

The model shows how poverty as a structure produces a three fold motivational pattern characterised by low need for achievement, low need for extension and high need for dependence.

Poverty Alleviation Programmes in India

It is quite evident that poverty acts as a great blockage to the development of our country. Thus, government has taken the initiatives and started numerous programmes and schemes for the upliftment of poor people.

Programmes such as TRYSEM (Training Youth for Self Employment), IRDP (Intergated Rural Development Programme), DWCRA (Development of Women and Children in Rural Areas) under SGSY (Swarnjayanti Gram Swarozgar Yojana), MGNREGA, Antodaya Plan, Self Employment Program, Housing Schemes etc. have been started in recents years.

The Anti Poverty Programmes are of three kinds: land reforms, asset provision, and income and consumption support. Though there have been success in these efforts but still our country has along way to go in order to eradicate the evil of poverty from our country. Psychological interventions and support from home and schools must be provided to poor children for betterment of their performance. For the successful results of these interventions the focus must be on all levels *i.e.* individuals, groups and community.

Issue of Disability

Disability is basically an umbrella term that covers impairments, which means limitations as well as restricted participation of an individual in various areas. Impairment is considered as a problem in body due to disability. Difficulties are encountered by an individual in executing a task or action, while a restriction in participation is a problem experienced by an individual in involvement in common life situations. According to **WHO** "Disability is thus not just an health problem. It is a complex phenomenon, reflecting the interaction between features of a person's body and features of the society in which he or she lives."

Types of disabilities can be categorised under two broad categories i.e. Physical and Mental Disability

Physical Disability

Individuals suffering from physical disabilities or impairments have difficulty in mobility, coordination, communication, learning or personal adjustment because physical impairment act as a barrier to the normal growth and development of an individual be it physiological, social, emotional or mental.

Physical disabilities can be of various types

Orthopedic Impairment

These are the disorders of locomotion that are caused by defect in bone or muscle joint. As a result of the mobility of the limbs the extremities become restricted which causes difficulty in movement. Orthopedic impairment can be classified in terms of ambulation disability.

+

Ambulation Disability refers to an individual's inability to move. It affects the vitality of the individual *i.e.* his ability to sustain life. A person with such disability have difficulty to access a building, moving from one place to another, use toilet facilities etc.

Ambulation disabilities are further classified into two types

(i) **Cerebral in Origin** Cerebral palsy, it is caused by damage to brain before birth and is characterised by impaired motor coordination. Individual suffering from the above show signs of rigidity of limbs, spasticity, tremors.

The child is lump and sloppy, have difficulty in speaking, controlling and balancing body etc. They need physical and occupational therapy for the improvement in their condition.

(ii) **Non-Cerebral in Origin**

- **Muscular Dystrophy** It is progressively weakening and degeneration of the voluntary muscles.
- **Spinal Muscular Atrophy** It affects the spinal cord and results in progressive degeneration of the motor nerve cells.
- **Poliomyetitis** (Infantile paralysis) It is a viral infection that affects or destroys the cells in the spinal cord. The destroyed cells make the muscles connected to them to die or become paralysed.
- **Clubfoot** A disorder in which a child's one or both feet are turned down and inwards from birth.
- **Amputation** This is missing limbs. It can be the result of an accident or early foetal developmental disorder.

Convulsive Disorders

These are characterised by uncontrolled electrical discharges in the brain which results in fits or seizures. It is called *epilepsy* and it affects the vitality, alertness and mental health of an individual. It affect the child in a manner and to a degree that he/she may show severe loss in his/her ability to function in a normal setting.

Speech Disorders

These are the disorders of language and communication exhibited by an individual. It can be an articulation of speech disorder, voice disorder or fluency disorder. There can be visible deformity of speech organs, natural breaks while speaking words and phrases and frequent mispronouncing of speech sounds.

Hearing Impairments

Hearing is one of the most important sensory function as it further influences learning and other aspects of maturation. Hearing impairment means different levels of hearing loss in an individual.

Hearing impairment can be grouped at four levels as proposed by Webster. Mild, moderate, severe or profound individual with hearing impairments face many difficulties in learning and understanding language, which lead to reading difficulties and make them under achievers.

Visual Impairments

Visual impairments is defined as the reduction in the ability to see. The terms partially sighted, legally blind, low vision and totally blind are commonly used to describe visual impairments. Visuals impairment further leads to inefficiency of a person at social front as 90% of the inputs from outside world we get is through the medium of vision.

Visual impairment can be divided into two categories

(i) **Blindness** The national programme for control of Blindness in India has given a simple definition of blindness describing it as the inability of a person to count fingers from a distance of six meters or 20 fts.

(ii) **Low Vision** It describes individuals who can generally read. Although they may depend on optical aids, such as magnifying lenses or other means to enlarge the size of the print.

Mental Disabilities or Intellectual Disabilities

Mentally challenged or intellectually disabled is a term used to describe people whose IQ (Intelligence Quotient) is below the normal intelligence.

Intellectual Disability is a more humane term used to describe people, who were previously referred as 'Mentally Retarded'. It is a way to give positive regard to such individuals, who have limited intelligence. This would make better impact on the life of people.

According to **American Psychiatric Association**, 1994, "Intellectual disability is defined as a significant sub-average intellectual functioning existing concurrently with deficits in adaptive behaviour". Sub average intellectual functioning refers to the intelligence quotient which remains at or below 70 as per the standardised intelligence test.

Individuals with intellectual disability/mentally challenged exhibits certain characteristics like

- Delayed speech and language development.
- Self destructive traits.
- Short attention span.
- Deficient ability in skills required for normal and daily functioning like perceptual motor skills, self care, social skills, self direction, health and safety, sensory and motor coordination etc.
- Low academic achievement.
- Impaired learning process, memory, attention and reduced ability to generalise and conceptualise.
- Low motivation for work.
- Poor self image.

Thus, we observe that disability whether physical or mental in nature, it makes the individual go through a lot of suffering. But if provided proper guidance and timely rehabilitation, individuals suffering from disability can adapt to a great extent to the normal ways of life.

Challenges Faced by People with Disabilities

(i) **Social Isolation /Social Suffering** One of the major challenges faced by people with disabilities are that family and friends may not understand their special needs and try to compare them with other normal individuals.

They do not give attention to the special needs of people with disabilities. They are often neglected and isolated from social gatherings. They face lack of acceptance from family, friends and society. This makes them emotionally weak and it leads to lack of confidence amongst them.

(ii) **Lack of Infrastructure and Civic Amenities** Individuals with disabilities have their special needs in reference to their particular disability, but due to the lack of infrastructure like provision of ramps in buildings, assistive devices in schools, lack of supporting staff in schools, creating a disabled friendly environment is not an easy task.

Because of absence of all these facilities these individuals do not get access to even basic education and to various vocational educational programmes. Thus, they could not pursue jobs because of lack of qualification. This makes them economically dependent on others for their basic needs.

Even the basic amenity of using public toilet at times becomes difficulty for such individuals because of their physical constraints and lack of modification in public toilets.

(iii) **Social Segregation** People with disability are segregated from the normal population as they differ in their needs and physical appearance.

(iv) **Education** The disabled persons lack equal opportunities to attain education. This is due to the discrimination against disabled people in comparison to able bodied children.

(v) **Health** Access to health facilities is also quite challenging for disabled as most of the times health facilities are inaccessible and unaffordable. As they lack knowledge in reproductive and general health, this leads to lack of family planning. As a result they have many children which consequently increase their financial burden.

(vi) **Stigma** Parents of children with disability and the individual himself/herself are subject to stigma. Most members of community lacks knowledge about disability and have low tolerance for behaviour outside the norm. Disabled people are often sensitive to drawing negative attention to their families in public areas.

(viii) **Socio/Psychological Challenges** Our society view disabled individuals as incompetent, failure and non-human. They pass remarks and comments that are insensitive. People often use derogatory words and look down upon people with disability. These attitudes of neglect are common at government and international level too. *For example* 2016 Para Olympics had difficulties in finding sponsors while normal Olympics never faced such issues.

Its not easy for a disabled person to get married to an able bodied individual because of the stigma attached to being disable. There are a lot a of superstitions present in our society which considers disabled person responsible for his/her condition.

(viii) **Economic Challenges** Disabled person faces lot of financial issues as due to the disability status they cannot compete with able-bodied persons in the income generating activities.

They could not even get half of the education which their counterparts have received. The society always look down an individual with disability. Discrimination against disabled is also prevalent in all areas of work.

Government Interventions for People with Disability

(i) A nationwide flagship Accessible Indian Campaign (Sugamya Bharat Abhiyan) was started to achieve universal accessibility for persons with disabilities and to create an enabling and barrier free environment.

(ii) The number of categories of disability have also be increased from 7 to 21 so that more number of disabled could be brought into the ambit of government's new initiatives.

(iii) Ministry of Social Justice and Empowerment is working to make public areas more accessible by considering more over in
- Built environment
- Public transportation and information
- Communication technologies

(iv) National Trust for the welfare of Persons with Autism, Cerebral Palsy, Mental Retardation and Multiple Disabilities, New Delhi launched several schemes like
- Disha (Early Intervention and School Readiness Scheme)
- Badhte Kadam (Awareness and Community Interaction)
- GHARAUNDA (Group home for adults)
- NIRAMAYA (Hearth insurance scheme)
- SAMBHAV (Aids and assisted devices)
- SAHYOGI (Caregiver training scheme)
- GYAN PRABHA (Educational support)
- PRERNA (Marketing assistance)
- SAMARTH (Respite care)
- VIKAAS (Day care)

Now, we are well aware of the challenges faced by the people with disability in different spheres of life. They live a life of isolation, neglect, stigma and social suffering. The role of society is very crucial in providing better facilities and convey hope to these individuals.

People with disability have their own strength areas too, and if these areas are recognised and are refined, they too can lead a good life. Because of this reason only Prime Minister Narendra Modi suggested use of word 'divyang' for person with disability. Government shall seek to provide as much opportunities to such individuals as possible.

They must initiate community based rehabilitation centres and make sure that these centres are run efficiently by worthy people. Training programmes must be organised regularly for the parents of such individuals, so that they are well equipped to cater to the distinct needs of such individuals.

Migration

Migration is the movement of people to a new area or country in order to find work or better living conditions. Mainly migration occurs from villages to cities, where people come in search of jobs, greater or attractive income sources. It is a shift from agrarian occupation to industrial and service oriented occupation. The concentration of people in urban cities pose various challenges for the inhabitats and governance.

Historically, there is a reference to two types of habitations by *Panini* in India which is the grama and the nagar.

A city was the dwelling place for the trades and industrial workers with modern amenities of life whereas villages were home to agricultural workers and craftsman, leading a simple life. But, presently the scenario has changed, due to industrialisation and development in and around cities, people tend to migrate from villages to cities in order to live a better life and increase their earnings.

'City life' now has become synonymous to modernisation, and commercial activities. Life in cities is fast and cities are growing in size. People from nearby rural areas are attracted towards cities because of better development and living conditions in cities.

Challenges Faced Due to Migration

Due to the explosion of population in cities of India, various problems have arised that are creating a lot of menace in the life of people. *Given below are problems that results in continued migration of population towards cities*

(i) **Maintainence of City** The overburden of population in the cities has led to the deterioration of basic infrastructure. Basic facilities like public utilities, clean drinking water, proper drainage and sewage, maintaining cleanliness in cities have taken a down turn. All this is posing a negative impact on the health and well being of individuals living in cities.

(ii) **Law and Order** As the population is increasing in cities, this has lead to mass unemployment. Unemployment and other factors have given rise to crimes like murder, human trafficking, drugs peddling which in turn has created a situation of apathy for the police and it has become difficult to maintain law and order in cities.

(iii) **Transportation and Traffic** As cities are large, people travel long distances from their home to work places. They either use public transport or private transport, both of these create lot of traffic on roads and in turn leads to air and noise pollution.

Increased level of pollution is causing lot of health issues for inhabitants of cities as respiratory and lung disorders are on a rise in people living in cities. Pollution creates stress and affects adversely the mental health of people too.

(iv) **Growth of Slums** Slums are an area developed around the big city which is overcrowded, have lack of sanitation facilities, lack of safety and Cleanliness. *For example* Slums around Mumbai and Delhi. Crime and spread of diseases are quite common in slum areas because of the adverse living conditions.

(v) **Crowding and Depersonalisation** Crowding or over population creates other problems like high rate of crimes, murder, robbery and social apathy. Bystander apathy is very common in cities where people do not help victims, who seriously need help. People see and ignore those who are in need and move ahead with their own work.

(vi) **Housing Problems** As cities have limited space, housing is a major problem of city life. Multistoried buildings have come up with dense houses. Living in small spaces creates more problems for its residents.

Thus, we can conclude that migration of people from villages to cities has created a lot of pressure on major cities and given rise to numerous problems. Long term planning, people's participation, huge investment and political initiatives are required to tackle these menaces of migration. Cities require proper planning to incorporate both the needs of its residents and ecological balance.

Measures to Control Migration

Uncontrolled migration has created multiple problem in cities therefore it has become inevitable to take effective step to control migration. *Some of the measures are as follows*

- **Inter-State Migrant Workmen** (Regulation of Employment and Conditions of Service) **Act of 1979** It seeks to address the unjust working conditions of migrant workers, including the necessity of gaining employment through middlemen, contractors or agents who promise a monthly settlement of wages but do not pay when the times comes. The government from time-to-time has taken various initiatives to combat farmers distress and enhance livelihood opportunities in rural areas. *For example* Deendayal Antyodaya Yojana-National Rural Livelihoods Mission (DAY-NRLM),Mahatma Gandhi National Rural Employment Guarantee Act, Attracting and Retaining of Youth in Agriculture (ARYA), Infrastructure development in rural areas etc.

- **Rurban Mission** It seeks to stimulate local economic development, enhance basic services and create well planned Rurban clusters (cluster villages). One of the main objective is to reduce the rural-urban divide *i.e.* economic, technological and those related to facilities and service.
- **PURA** (Providing Urban Amenities to Rural Areas) It seeks to tackle the problem of migration of people from rural to urban areas for employment. It seeks to develop technology in villages, provide better connectivity, enhance livelihood opportunities etc.
- **Smart Villages** It is a concept adopted by national, state and local governments in India, as an initiative focused on holistic rural development. The Eco Needs foundation has initiated the concept of 'Smart Village'. Under this project the foundation is created by adopting villages and putting efforts for sustainable development by providing basic amenities like sanitation, safe drinking water, internal roads, tree plantation, water conservation.

Stigma

Stigma is an attribute or characteristic that makes a person different from others and extensively discredits his or her identity. It is a greek term, which meant a mark or a cut buried into the body of a person who is considered to be morally defective such as a slave, criminal etc.

Stigmatisation always have negative effects on those who bear stigmatising marks. *Effects can be studied into two categories direct and indirect.*

Direct Effects

Following are the direct effects of stigmatisation

- **Social Rejection** Poor treatment is given to people at work places, educational settings, healthcare system etc.
- **Exclusion** People who are stigmatised are mostly avoided and excluded from society.
- **Discrimination** Differential negative treatment is given to people who are stigmatised. It can be at institutional or interpersonal level. *For example* Women are denied a job as a pilot because of her physical characteristics.
- **Expectancy Confirmation Processes** When people holds certain beliefs about a person having a particular characteristic like mental illness, they treat people according to their pre-conceived beliefs like avoiding or rejecting people with mental illness.

Such behaviour can result in anger and hostility among stigmatised person. This happens without the stigmatised person even being aware that the other person holds negative stereotypes.

Indirect Effects

Following are the indirect effects of stigmatisation

- **Interpretation of the Social World Being Negative by the Stigmatised** They anticipate rejection and devaluation and also interpret their social world negatively. These negative devaluations become a collective representation of the people attached to that stigma.
- **Identity Threat** A psychological state in which the stigmatised person thinks that he/she will be evaluated negatively because of their stigma. It is situational and whenever identity threat is experienced it creates anxiety and stress on the bearer.
- **Attributional Ambiguity** It stems from the bearer awareness, that they will be targets of prejudice and discrimination because of their stigma. Most of the times they are unsure whether the reason behind their rejection is their stigma or their lack of performance.
- **Faulty Social Relationships** Bearer of stigma are often exposed to inconsistent treatment, so they are unable to make accurate self assessment thus resulting in impaired social relationships.

Types of Stigma

Sociologist Erving Goffnan described stigma "as an attribute that spoils a person's identity, reducing him or her in other's minds from a whole and usual person to a tainted and discounted one".

Stigma is the negative evaluation or devaluing a person who have certain characteristics. It becomes the basis of excluding, discriminating and avoiding people who posses these stigmatising marks.

Goffman, described three types of stigma

(i) **Tribal Stigma** This stigma is passed from generation to generation and includes people belonging to devalued ethnic, racial and religious groups.

(ii) **Abominations of the Body** Physical characteristics that are devalued comes under it. It includes birth disorder, muscular dystrophy, leprosy etc.

(iii) **Known Deviations in Personal Traits** Behavioural or individual personality characteristics that are devalued such as homosexuality, mental disorders, addiction etc.

Thus, stigma is not an individual phenomena. It is determined by the society and are socially constructed by the people living in a social setting.

We can conclude that stigma influence the perception, interpretation and interaction of the social world of the bearer. At times it is common that even in the absence of any discriminatory behaviour the bearer of stigma perceive discrimination, even when others are unknown to that behaviour.

Marginalisation

In marginalisation people are blocked from or denied full access to various resources, opportunities and rights that are normally available to other members of different group. Marginalisation at the individual level results in individual's exclusion from meaningful participation in society. It is a form of social exclusion, whereby something or someone is pushed to the edge of the group and accorded lesser importance. The basic facilities like housing, employment healthcare, civic engagement are denied to members of marginalised community. The **Encyclopedia of Public Health** defines marginalised group as. "To be marginalised is to be placed in the margins and thus exclude from the privilege and power found at the the center."

Various Marginalised Groups

Most vulnerable marginalised groups are

- **Women** Marginalisation is one of the manifestation of gender inequality. Exclusion of women from certain jobs and fields is a form of marginalisation. Women are always marginalised in comparison to men in all cultures and countries.
- **People with disabilities** These people have to face discrimination and stigmatisation everywhere. It has left people with disabilities in a severe state of impoverishment for centuries. Proportion of the disabled population in India is about 21.9 million.
- **Scheduled Caste and Scheduled Tribes** Marginalisation of people belonging to a particular caste or tribes. This leads to violation of their basic human rights and results in their socio-economic deterioration.
  Caste and tribe based marginalisation is one of the most serious human right issue across the world. Today, approx 260 million people reside in India, who are discriminated on the basis of caste and 84.3 million people who belong to Scheduled Tribe. They all are considered to be socially and economically backwards.
- **Children** Manifestation of marginalisation among children are visible in cases of child labour, child trafficking, commercial sexual exploitation and other forms of violence and abuse. India has the largest number of child labours under the age of 14 in the world. Trafficking of children also continues to be a serious problem in India.
- **Sexual Minorities** Another group that faces stigma and discrimination are sexual minorities like those identified as gays, lesbians, transgenders, bisexual etc. These people face major discrimination in society and are not allowed to access basic medical and health facilities. They are ridiculed and isolated from their families.

Consequences of Marginalisation

Following are the various consequences of marginalisation

- Negative psychological and emotional responses like sadness, disappointment, jealousy, anger and shame.
- Negative impact on health as marginalised group faces discrimination in accessibility to health centres and facilities.
- Behavioural response like aggression and anti social activities are commonly practiced by people of marginalised group as they try to establish their identity by posing a threat to others.

Social Suffering

Marginilisation often leads to social suffering to individuals, as it creates stress and pain from social exclusion. Social suffering is the experience of pain, damage, deprivation for an individual or a community in the social setting. The social conditions and prevailing form of mindset leads to aggravation of social suffering of the marginalised group. It in an unpleasent experience that is associated with actual or potential damage to one's sense of social connection because of social rejection, exclusion, negative social evaluation or loss.

Social suffering is the result of the social conditions in which a person is living. Rampant discrimination, inequality and marginilisation are some of the causes of social suffering. Feelings of humiliation, fear and guilt affects the experience of an individual and their social environment. According to famous sociologist **Klienman** "social suffering is the result of a the devastating injury that social force can inflict on human experience".

Domestic Violence

Domestic Violence and Child Abuse, both these evils are affecting a major portion of people in our society by causing them physical, emotional, and psychological trauma. Inspite of so many efforts done in our country to eradicate violence against women and child abuse, both of these are on a rise. Lets discuss main issues regarding these two social evits.

Domestic violence is defined by United Nations in its declaration of the eliminations of violence against women as, "physical, sexual, and psychological violence occuring in the family, including battering, sexual abuse of female children in the household, dowry related violence, marital rape, female genital mutilation and other traditional practices harmful to women, non spousal violence and violence related to exploitation."

Domestic violence is a form of violence which happens inside a house, and abusive behaviour of one partner against other. But it is commonly practiced by male partners against their female counter parts. It is a way of males to maintain power and control over women.

Women constitute 50% of the country's population and are crucial to the growth and development of any nation. The importance of women as a mother, teacher, at times breadwinners and guardians cannot be neglected. If they are subjected to any form of violence by the males, then the situation is critical and requires immediate handling of the issue. Various forms of expression of domestic violence are exploitation, childhood marriage, violence by in-laws, female child labour, denial of self expression, female infanticide, negative cultural attitudes, dowry deaths etc.

Types of Domestic Violence

There are five major types of domestic violence.

Type of Domestic Violence	Way of Expressing
Physical	Assault, pinching, pushing, hitting, slapping, choking, shooting, stabbing, murder etc. which causes any physical harms to another person.
Sexual Abuse	Forced sexual participation, unwanted and unsafe sexual activity, forced sex even by spouse.
Verbal	Abusing some one verbally, to criticise , demean the other person, decrease their confidence, making the other person guilty, fearful, shameful etc.
Emotional or Psychological Abuse	Decrease self worth and independence, shaming, blaming, leading to anxiety, depression and making other feel helpless.
Economic or Financial Abuse	Limiting or curbing the financial freedom and security of the victim.

Causes of Domestic Violence

There are different ways to explain the major causes which lead to domestic violence. From psychological point of view, mental characteristics and personality traits of the perpetrator are considered. Factors such as prepetrator's family structure, stress and social learning area also considered. But no single approach explains the causes behind domestic violence completely.

Psychologically this approach considers the personality traits and mental characteristics of the offender. It is considered that psychopathology and other personality disorders, abuse observed by an individual during childhood make them more violent.

Dutton and Golant argued that offenders in domestic violence are mostly individual with borderline personality which is developed early in life.

Following are the various causes of domestic violence

- **Jealousy** Goetz gave an evolutionary explanation stating that it is male attempt to control female reproduction and sexual exclusivity for himself through violence. Males with jealousy suspect that females are either unfaithful or will leave them.
- **Social Stress** Stress is another factor causing domestic violence. stress can be high in families with more dependable members and few earning members.
- **Voilence** Seltzer and Kalmuss, found that violence is a form of expression of stress by certain people. Jewkes, concluded that poverty also affects the violence between couples. It is because of the limited financial resources there are more quarrels among spouses.
- **Social Leaning** This theory explains violence in terms of social learning. If an individual observes violence in the family and among near relatives it is quite obvious that he too will act in the same manner or imitate it.

  If there is no resistence from the victim then it tends to aggravate the behaviour of the perpetrator . Often, violence is transmitted from generation to generation in a cyclical manner.
- **Power and Control** Abusers abuse in order to exercise power and control over the victim. Through violence he tries to prove his power and control over victim. Causes of violence can be psychological, social or cultural but it's a way to feel adequate and powerful by the abuser.

Consequences of Domestic Violence

The consequence of domestic violences engulfs not only the victim but the family as a whole. Victims face physical impacts, psychological and financial impacts, but children in the family too suffer a lot. They have a traumatic childhood which leaves scars throughout their lives.

Consequences of Domestic Violence on Victim and Family

Impact	Symptoms
Children	• Development and psychological problems. • Behavioural problems like increased aggressiveness, anxiety, socialisation in family etc. attitudnal and cognitive problems in schools. • Chances of being a perpetrator in adulthood. • Exhibit post traumatic stress disorder.
Physical Effect	• Broken bones, internal bleeding etc. • Arthiritis, irritable bowel syndrome . • Miscarriage, Preterm Labour in case of pregnant victim.
Psychological Effect	• High in stress, fear, anxiety, depression, increased risk of suicide, high risk of suffering from post traumatic stress disorder.
Financial Effect	• Lack of financial resources, victims of domestic violence often lacks education and specialised skills thus they are stuck in vicious cycle of not leaving their habits and sustain domestic violence.
Long term Effect	• Mental health and psychological issues. • Chronic physical health problems. • Homelessness. • Poverty.

Child Abuse

According to **UNICEF** Child Abuse is "Physical, and mental abuse, injury and neglect, negligent treatment, exploitation and sexual abuse. Abuse can take place in homes, schools, orphanages, residential care facilities, on the streets, at the workplace, in prisons and at places of detention."

A child who faces abuse have impaired development in physical, social and psychological domain. If abuse is prolonged and is extreme in nature, it can even result in death of a child.

Child abuse in India is often a hidden phenomenon and it is occurs within the four walls of a house. Children lives with their families and at times are abused by the so called caretaker. Caretaker can be their parents, close relatives or others. Children are supposed to be submissive and are highly dependent on elders of the family, thus most of the time the abuse which happens inside the house goes unreported. Maltreatment by caregiver's is quite common these days.

Other form of abuse that are publically visible are child labour, prostitution, child marriage, societal abuses includes poverty and its impact on children like malnutrition, lack of education, poor health, neglect etc.

Child Abuse Statistics in India

As per UN Bihar has the highest percentage of child marriages in India *i.e.* 60% whereas in Goa, Kerala and Manipur its 11%, 15% and 13% respectively.

Children under the age of 18 contribute to 44.4% of India's current population, half of which are not provided with basic education, nutrition and health. Current estimates shows that 18% to 50% of the country's children have experienced some form of child sexual abuse. Girls reports higher incidence of child sexual abuse whereas boys report more of physical and psychological abuse.

A research conducted in major cities of Indian concluded that 68% of children never report physical abuse though they have faced it.

A report by Ministry of Women and Child Development, Government of India shows that 53.22% children reported having faced one or more forms of sexual abuse. Andhra Pradesh, Delhi, Assam, Bihar reported the highest percentage of sexual abuse cases among both boys and girls.

The figures are quite disturbing and the gravity of the situation demands that the issue of child abuse is handled efficiently at the society, community, state and national level. Though there are various programs and schemes started by the national government like National and State Commissions for protection of rights of the child, the integrated child protection scheme etc. but a lot still need to be done.

It will be an endeavour from all sections that includes government, civil society, community, family and parents to provide a protective environment for children, so that they can enjoy a loving and blissful childhood.

Psychological-Social Model to Understand Sexual Abuse

To bridge the gap between psychological and sociological interpretations of sexual abuse, David Finkelhor proposed a multi factor model which explained both the factors. Finkelhor developed a hierarchial model which included individual factors related to the victims, abuser and the family. It covered social and cultural factors as well.

All the factors that contribute to child sexual abuse are grouped into four pre-conditions

(i) **Motivation** The potential abuser needs to have some motivation to abuse. It could be emotional congruence or blockage when alternative sources of gratification are not present.

(ii) **Internal Inhibitions** The potential abuser must overcome internal inhibitions that may act against his motivation to abuse.

(iii) **External Inhibitors** The potential abuser must overcome external obstacles and inhibitions prior to sexual abuse. External inhibitors that may restrain the abuser's actions include family, neighbours, peers and social sanctions.

(iv) **Resistence** Finally, the potential abuser has to overcome the child's possible resistence to being sexually abused. It is to be noted that the first two are psychological factors and last two are social factors influencing child abuse.

Theories of Child Abuse

The explanatory theories for child abuse can be classified into two groups: Unitary and Interactive.

Unitary Theories

- **Psycho Analytic Theory** This approach propounds that unconscious parental drives and conflicts determine abusive behaviour. The primary cause of child abuse is seen to be in the parents psychological troubles. Kempe described the abuser as the 'Psychological member of the family'.
- **Social Learning Theory** This theory suggests that child abuse is learned behaviour. Violence in one's family of orientation is seen as predictive of violence in one's family of procreation. Another important finding by Parke and Collmer is that individual who have experienced violent and abusive childhoods are more likely to grow up to become child abusers.
- **Environment Theory** This theory explains that child abuse is a result of social and environmental stress. Stressful life events and conditions like poverty, unemployment, inadequate housing and a violent social environment are prominent factors contributing to Child Abuse. Child abuse can be viewed as a symptom of distress in family that comprises its ability to protect and nurture children.
- **Cognitive–Developmental Theory** This theory states that Child abuse reflects an underlying ego centricity of the parent's understanding of the child and parental role.

Each of the above theories are described as "Unitary theories in other words, each offers an explanation of child abuse from a single point of view."

Interactive Theories

These theories are based on the fact that different aspects of culture, family, parent and stress interact and result in child abuse. Child abuse in this theoretical context is understood as a symptom of dysfunction in a complex ecosystem with many interacting variables. Under this approach a well known model was proposed by Garbarino, 1975 known as *'Human Ecologic Model'*. This model suggests that parents, the abused child and other children in family interact in such a way that abuse is the result of the stress, that occurs in this period.

Types of Child Abuse

Child abuse can be categorised into following types

Physical Child Abuse

Physical child abuse is an injury resulting from physical aggression. Even if the injury was not intended, the act is considered physical abuse. The injury from physical child abuse may be the result of Beating, slapping or hitting, pushing, shaking, kicking or throwing, pinching, biting, choking or hair-pulling, burning with cigarettes, very hot water or other hot objects.

Sexual Child Abuse

Sexual abuse of a child is any sexual act between an adult and a child, including penetration, intercourse, incest, rape, oral sex and sodomy. *Other examples include*

- **Fondling** Touching or kissing a child's genitals, making a child fondle an adult's genitals.
- **Violations of Bodily Privacy** Forcing a child to undress, spying on a child in the bathroom or bedroom.
- **Exposing Children to Adult Sexuality** Performing sexual acts in front of a child, exposing genitals, telling 'dirty' stories, showing pornography to a child.
- **Commercial Exploitation** Sexual exploitation through child prostitution or child pornography.

Emotional Abuse

Emotional abuse happens when people consistently say things and behave in a way that conveys to the child that they are inadequate, unloved, worthless or only valued as far as the other person's needs are concerned. This can have a profound, long-term impact on the child. *Such as*

- Not allowing children to express their opinions, ridicule and silencing them.
- Frequently shouting at or threatening them.
- Telling them they are 'no good' or 'a mistake'.
- Preventing normal social interaction with peers and others.
- Ill-treating another person in front of the child and emotionally blackmailing them.

Neglecting Child

Child neglect is when a parent or caregiver persistently fails to meet the basic physical and psychological needs of a child, resulting in impairment of the child's health and development. *It involves*

- Not providing appropriate food, clothing or medical care.
- Leaving a child alone for a longtime.

EXAM BASED QUESTIONS

1 What is the main characteristic of a social issue?
(a) It affects an individual.
(b) It affects considerable number of individuals in a society.
(c) It affects a particular group of people.
(d) It affects people of a particular religion.

2 Gender of a person differentiates between
(a) a boy and a girl
(b) a male and female
(c) masculinity and femininity
(d) man and woman

3 Which of the following factors affect gender discrimination among women?
(a) Preference to male child (b) Dowry
(c) Education (d) All of the above

4 Who gave basic explanation to the concept of gender?
(a) John Money (b) Henry Watson Fowler
(c) Tania Ehrhardt (d) Antonin Scalia

5 What is gender identity?
(a) Personal identification with a particular gender.
(b) Categorisation as male or female.
(c) Biological difference of male or female.
(d) Sense of self.

6 Who coined the term gender roles?
(a) Kate Bornstein (b) Antonin Scalia
(c) John Money (d) Henry Watson Fowler

7 What is Androcentrism?
(a) Keeping male view point in the center.
(b) Avoiding females viewpoint.
(c) Sharing personal information about one's preference.
(d) The nature of other's gender.

8 What is the main principle behind Biological Determinism?
(a) Human behaviour is controlled by an individual's genes.
(b) Causal roles of genes.
(c) Gender is defined by the social structure.
(d) Biological characteristics defines one's gender.

9 Discrimination is the differential treatment done towards
(a) an individual (b) a society
(c) a country (d) a state

10 Who has done a famous research on gender discrimination in Indian context?
(a) Ved Prakash (b) Anand Lakshmi
(c) Heerabai (d) Girishwar Mishra

11 Which of the following is a discriminatory practice towards females even before birth?
(a) Child marriages
(b) Female infanticide
(c) Selective sex killing
(d) Female foeticide

12 What is a 'Stereotype'?
(a) Ideology
(b) Widely adopted thought about specific type of individuals
(c) Original thought
(d) Unimaginative

13 What Section of IPC considers Dowry as a crime?
(a) 304B and 498A
(b) 403B and 498A
(c) 203B and 498A
(d) 304B and 488A

14 What is a 'Patriarchial Society'?
(a) Where power rests in the hand of male head of community.
(b) Where male holds the supreme position in a country.
(c) Males have the power to vote.
(d) Power is held by and transferred through men.

15 What is Feminism?
(a) An ideology to study women related issues.
(b) A women related power.
(c) A concept concerning a role and position of female in society.
(d) Philosophy that holds that men and women are equal.

16 According to 2012 survey, what percentage of population lives below poverty line in India?
(a) 14% (b) 15%
(c) 12% (d) 10%

17 What is the estimated number of poor people according to World Bank?
(a) 296 millions (b) 300 millions
(c) 292 millions (d) 276 millions

18 Poverty is defined in terms of
(a) lack of money and standard of living
(b) lack of house and education
(c) lack of food and shelter
(d) lack of money to afford basic needs

19 What are the two main types of poverty?
(a) Social and economic (b) Absolute and relative
(c) Social and individual (d) Material and relative

20 Which type of poverty is not affected by the person's location?
(a) Absolute (b) Relative
(c) Social (d) Economic

21 How does relative poverty change?
(a) It varies from individual to individual.
(b) It varies with the change in governance or system.
(c) It varies from the country to country or society to society.
(d) It varies according to your expenses.

22 What strategies government can use to decrease poverty?
(a) Tax avoidence (b) Debt
(c) Loan (d) Wages

23 What are the secondary problems related to poverty?
(a) Slums and malnutrition
(b) Crime and drug addiction
(c) Illness and apathy
(d) Urbanisation and population explosion

24 What are the tertiary problems related to poverty?
(a) Hunger
(b) Lack of education
(c) Mental retardation
(d) Malnutrition

25 What is depriviation?
(a) Notion of inequality.
(b) Discrimination on the basis of social standing or membership to a group.
(c) Sense of loss or suffering, it's a subjective feeling.
(d) Socio-economic hardship determined by social structure.

26 Who proposed a psychological analysis of poverty in Indian context?
(a) Pareek (b) Ajit K Dalal
(c) Anand Lakshmi (d) Dr Girishwar Mishra

27 What is Protective Discrimination Policy?
(a) Providing social privelege to children of marginalised class.
(b) Discrimination is done between two equally capable individuals.
(c) Reservation of seats in educational institutions and jobs for members of disadvantaged group.
(d) Discrimination is practised but recipient is unknown to it.

28 What are three kinds of anti poverty programmes?
(a) Social, cultural and economic reform schemes.
(b) Nutrition, housing, job schemes.
(c) Land reform, asset provision and income and consumption support.
(d) Community, state and national schemes.

29 What is the full form of 'IRDP'?
(a) Integrated Rural Development Program
(b) Integrative by Rural in Development
(c) Initiative by Government for Development of Poor
(d) Integrated Rural Development Policy

30 What is the basic principle behind psychological interventions for poverty?
(a) People must be provided vocational training at school.
(b) Community participation is important for the upliftment of poor.
(c) Mental health of poor people must be taken care for.
(d) Human development is shaped by the experiential base of the child.

31 What does 'Ambulation' in disability means?
(a) Child's ability to move
(b) Child's health and ability of sustain life
(c) Child's progressive disorder
(d) Child's restless behaviour

32 What are two major types of ambulation disabilities?
(a) Origin in cerebral, origin in upper body
(b) Birth defect, physical defect
(c) Origin from brain, origin from birth
(d) Origin in cerebral, non-cerebral origin

33 What is the main characteristic of cerebral palsy?
(a) Difficulty in motor movement
(b) Social deficits
(c) Motor deficits, rigidity, spasticity, tremors
(d) Sensory deficits

34 **What is 'Amputation'?**
(a) Missing speech (b) Missing limbs
(c) Missing sense of touch (d) Missing sense of taste

35 **What is Spinal Muscular Atrophy?**
(a) Affects spinal cord and brain.
(b) Affects spinal cord and body balance.
(c) Affects spinal cord and progressive degeneration of motor cells.
(d) Affects spinal cord and body temperature.

36 **What are the three types of speech disorder?**
(a) Observable, natural, frequent
(b) Articulation, voice, frequency
(c) Pitch, loudness, resonance
(d) Mild, moderate and profound

37 **What are the two different types of habitations mentioned by Panini?**
(a) Village and city (b) Rural and urban
(c) Grama and nagar (d) Grama and urban

38 **What is the major occupation of city dwellers?**
(a) Technocrats and service
(b) Industrial and service sector
(c) Traders and businessman
(d) Industrial and traders

39 **What type of population is mainly found in cities?**
(a) Socially active (b) Socially heterogenous
(c) Socially homogenous (d) Socially inclusive

40 **What of the following is required for maintenance of big cities?**
(a) National integration (b) Long term planning
(c) Construction of metro trains
(d) Construction of roads

41 **Not helping or ignoring someone who need urgent help and just watching someone die. What is this behaviour called?**
(a) Depersonalisation
(b) Bystandar rigidity
(c) Bystandar apathy
(d) Bystandar inhumanity

42 **What are the ill effects of crowding in cities?**
(a) Pollution and population
(b) High infant mortality and competition
(c) Hunger and poverty
(d) Malnutrition and crimes

43 **What are the major community facilities required for day to day life of an individual?**
(a) Street light and clean surroundings
(b) Clothing and housing
(c) Sewage and drinking water
(d) All of the above

44 **What do you mean by migration?**
(a) Movement of people new area
(b) Move after marriage
(c) A social ritual
(d) Type of folk dance

45 **Most dominating type of migration among the following is**
(a) village to village (b) cities to villages
(c) village to cities (d) cities to cites

46 **Inter-state Migrant Workmen Act was enacted in which year?**
(a) 1978 (b) 1979 (c) 1980 (d) 1981

47 **Concept of smart of village has been initiated by**
(a) Government of India
(b) Patanjali
(c) Gram Panchayat Development Association
(d) Eco Need Foundation

48 **What are three types of stigma?**
(a) Tribal, abominations of body, known deviation in personal traits
(b) Tribal, personal, bodily
(c) Physical, social, tribal
(d) Stereotype, tribal, personal

49 **What is expectancy-confirmation process in stigma?**
(a) Prejudice on the basis of any physical disability.
(b) Discrimination on the basis of gender.
(c) Acting in consistency to the belief one possess for the other person.
(d) Expectation of positive treatment from people.

50 **Which of these is not the direct effect of stigma?**
(a) Attributional ambiguity (b) Social rejection
(c) Exclusion (d) Identity threat

51 **Marginalised group is denied from**
(a) Participation (b) Privilege
(c) Both a and b (d) None of these

52 **Which of the following group fall in the category of marginalised group?**
(a) Scheduled caste and scheduled tribe
(b) Womens
(c) Minorities
(d) All of the above

53 **Long term prevalence of marginalisation lead to**
(a) inclusive society (b) social suffering
(c) harmony (d) development

54 **What are the long term effects of Domestic Violence?**
(a) Homelessness (b) Physical bruises
(c) Fear (d) Anxiety

55 **What are the psychological effects of domestic violence?**
(a) PTSD (b) Poverty
(c) Irritable bowel syndrome (d) Lack of education

56 **What is Emotional Child Abuse?**
(a) Abusing a child by pushing
(b) Abusing a child by discriminating
(c) Abusing a child by neglect
(d) Abusing a child by making him/her work

57 Who proposed Human Ecological Model of child abuse?

(a) Skinner (b) Bandura
(c) Finkelhor (d) Garbarino

58 What are the four components of Psycho-Sociological model for child sexual abuse?

(a) Victim, child, activity, external inhibitor
(b) External inhibitor, internal inhibitor, resitance by child, victim
(c) Perpetrator, internal inhibitor, external inhibitor, resistance by child
(d) Resistance, child, activity, internal inhibitor

59 Who developed psycho-sociological model for child sexual abuse?

(a) Garbarino (b) Finkelhor
(c) Kalra (d) Kempe and Helfer

60 What are the three main variables in socio-psychological model of child abuse?

(a) Stress, aggressive parent, a special child
(b) A special parent, stress, a special child
(c) Parent, stress, child
(d) Realistic parent, physical disabled child, stress

61 Which of the following is not an environmental characteristic that can lead to child abuse?

(a) Poor housing (b) Alcoholism
(c) Chronic stress (d) Child's temperament

62 Which of the following is a behavioural manifestation of child abuse by the victim?

(a) Cuts, bruises (b) Sores
(c) Anxiety (d) Fracture

63 What is the main characteristic of a society?

1. People have shared customs
2. An orgainsation
3. People have different cultures
4. Company of other people

Codes

(a) 1 and 2 (b) 3 and 4 (c) 1 and 4 (d) 1, 2 and 4

64 What are the elements surrounding gender roles?

1. Clothing 2. Speech Patterns
3. Occupations
4. Physiology

Codes

(a) 1 and 2 (b) 2 and 3 (c) 3 and 4 (d) 1,2 and 3

65 What are the social consequences of gender discrimination?

1. Impact sex ratio
2. Impact health of over their lifetimes (mostly women)
3. Impacts social status of women
4. Impacts women participation at work

Codes

(a) 1 and 2 (b) 2 and 3 (c) 3 and 4 (d) All of these

66 What among the following is the dimension of poverty?

1. Low income
2. Family income cannot support housing facilities for its family members
3. Inability to acquire basic goods and services necessary for survival with dignity
4. No job for family members

Codes

(a) 1 and 2 (b) 2 and 3
(c) 1 and 3 (d) 1, 2 and 4

67 Match the following

List I (Disorder)	List II (Units)
A. Fluency disorder	1. Mental schema
B. Moderate category of hearing loss	2. Limited and distorted speech sounds
C. Figurative language	3. 41-55 db
D. Syntax	4. Combined units of meaning

Codes

	A	B	C	D		A	B	C	D
(a)	3	2	1	4	(b)	2	3	1	4
(c)	4	3	1	2	(d)	2	3	4	1

68 Match the following

List I (Child Abuse)	List II (Way)
A. Physical	1. Fondling
B. Sexual	2. Silencing them
C. Emotional	3. Burning
D. Neglect	4. Leaving alone

Codes

	A	B	C	D
(a)	4	2	1	3
(b)	3	1	2	4
(c)	2	4	1	3
(d)	1	3	4	2

69 Match the following

List I (Factor)	List II (Component)
A. Individual	1. Customs
B. Demographic	2. Inflation
C. Economic	3. Overpopulation
D. Social	4. Gambling

Codes

	A	B	C	D		A	B	C	D
(a)	1	2	3	4	(b)	2	1	4	3
(c)	3	4	1	2	(d)	4	3	2	1

70 Match the following

List I (Scheme)	List II (Purpose)
A. NIRMAYA	1. Aid and assisted devices
B. GHARAUNDA	2. Health Insurance scheme
C. SAMBHAV	3. Group home for adults
D. SAHYOGI	4. Caregiver training scheme

Codes

	A	B	C	D		A	B	C	D
(a)	2	3	1	4	(b)	4	1	3	2
(c)	1	4	2	3	(d)	3	4	1	2

Directions (Q. Nos. 71-86) *In the questions given below are two statements labelled as Assertion (A) and Reason (R). In the context of two statements, which one of the following is correct?*

(a) A and R are true and R is the correct explanation of A
(b) A and R are true, but R is not the correct explanation of A
(c) A is true, but R is false
(d) A is false, but R it true

71 **Assertion** (A) Social problems involve situations in which norms of the mainstream society are violated.

Reason (R) Social problems have an objective perspective.

72 **Assertion** (A) There are different perceptions of social issues by each individual.

Reason (R) Social problems have a subjective approach.

73 **Assertion** (A) Individual is also responsible for his poor condition, not always social structure can be blamed.

Reason (R) Bad habits like alcoholism, drug addiction, large family members etc. are causes of poverty.

74 **Assertion** (A) Cultural system prevailing in the community of the poor is also responsible for existence of poverty in its inhabitants.

Reason (R) Cultural system streamlines the attempts of society to change the values, norms and upgrade life style of poor.

75 **Assertion** (A) Poverty and social disadvantage is both a social and psychological reality.

Reason (R) Various socio-cultural conditions create inequality of opportunities that make poor people poorer.

76 **Assertion** (A) Social system produces motivational patterns and reinforcing mechanisms for behaviour.

Reason (R) Schooling and family are main components of our social systems.

77 **Assertion** (A) Poverty is both a structure and product of a system.

Reason (R) Expectancy of powerlessness defines poverty as a structural component.

78 **Assertion** (A) Low need for achievement is also one of the cause of poverty.

Reason (R) Low need for achievement directs one's behaviour towards control, not towards chance.

79 **Assertion** (A) Fear of failure is an individual characterstic resulting in poverty driven behaviour.

Reason (R) People who are high in dependency needs have a constant fear of failure and lacks a initiative taking ability.

80 **Assertion** (A) The motivational patterns and behaviour towards poverty can be changed.

Reason (R) It can be changed through reservation policies.

81 **Assertion** (A) Cumulative deficit data is high as the age increases.

Reason (R) Difference in performance between prosperous and disadvantaged group increase with age.

82 **Assertion** (A) women finds it difficult to adjust with the demands of the other world when they go for jobs.

Reason (R) Lack of exposure and confinement to family roles, makes women alien to outside world.

83 **Assertion** (A) Women must have awareness about their legal rights.

Reason (R) Women Empowerment is the need of an hour.

84 **Assertion** (A) Sadness and shame in an individual is the result of social exclusion.

Reason (R) Marginalisation puts a community or group of individual in the centre of the society.

85 **Assertion** (A) Domestic violence is violence against someone inside a house.

Reason (R) Abusing someone verbally is not a form of violence as it has no negative impact.

86 **Assertion** (A) Poverty and stress prevailing in families are interrelated.

Reason (R) When income is limited, stress arises from the conflict on expenditure.

Directions (Q. Nos. 87-91) *Read the passage given below and answer the following questions that follow.*

The historical nature of gender based violence confirms that it is not an unfortunate aberration, but systematically entrenched in culture and society, reinforced and powered by patriarchy. Violence against women maintains the structures of gender oppression; be it carried out by individuals in private or by institutional forces in the public sphere. Families, communities and social, legal and civic institutions may covertly and overtly endorse it. Whilst violence commands greater attention and fear; sexism and misogyny do their share to shape inequality, by defining and upholding restrictive gender norms.

Patriarchy is about the social relations of power between men and women, women and women and men and men. It is a system for maintaining class, gender, racial and heterosexual privilege and the status quo of power relying both on crude forms of oppression, like violence and subtle ones, like laws; to perpetuate inequality. Patriarchal beliefs of male, heterosexual dominance lie at the root of gender based violence.

Patriarchy is a structural force that influences power relations, whether they are abusive or not. Power sets the agenda for patriarchy. But, conflating it with abuse or masculinity is problematic and we need a more complex analysis of the typical power and control explanations. Feminism, which is about women claiming their rights to self-determination and equality, confronts gender conformity and aims to replace relationships of power with relationships of meaning. Culture is used to justify gender inequality and violence by evoking traditional cultural beliefs about how women should be treated. The defence of the culture of a place, country, religion etc. is in fact a defence of the culture of patriarchy in that country, religion, identity and the culture of violence everywhere. The culture of patriarchy is not static: its manifestation on an army base differs from that in a rural town; just as the culture of patriarchy in US differs from that of Gulf or India.

87 The historical nature of gender based violence confirms it as

1. an unfortunate aberration.
2. systematically entrenched culture of patriarchy.
3. reinforce inequalities.

Codes

(a) 1 and 2 (b) 2 and 3 (c) 1 and 3 (d) Only 3

88 Patriarchy is about social relations of power between

1. Men and women
2. Women and women
3. Men and men

Codes

(a) 1 and 2 (b) 2 and 3 (c) 3 and 1 (d) 1, 2 and 3

89 Complex analysis of the typical power and control helps us to understand

(a) patriarchy (b) feminism
(c) Both a and b (d) None of these

90 ...... is used to justify gender inequality and violence.

(a) Sexism (b) Culture
(c) Religion (d) Region

91 Feminism refers to

(a) superior status of women
(b) replacing relationships of power with relationships of meaning
(c) status quo of power
(d) fighting against patriarchy

Directions (Q. Nos. 92-96) *Read the passage given below and answer the following questions that follow.*

The Right of Children to Free and Compulsory Education Act, 2009 guarantees to all children within the age group 6-14 years the right to education in proper schools with trained teachers. It was a long, long time coming, but this historic legislation, despite the many loopholes, has the power to transform the lives of millions of poor Indian children who have so far been deprived of the opportunity to make their lives better than those of their parents.

Since Independence, elementary education has grown into a multi-headed monster of sorts, with its own caste system of service-providers - government ordinary, government elite, private elite, private-run but government-funded and so on. It has provided children of the privileged classes a springboard to greater privilege, while doing nothing to eradicate child labour or provide poor children with even basic literacy, let alone the broader gains of education.

Broadly, the vast majority of the population, both rural and urban, send their children to government-run schools as these are free, that is, they do not charge fees. However, given that the quality of education in these schools is usually quite poor, the fast increasing middle class prefer to send their children to privately-run schools.

The new act addresses some of these issues, but not the more important concern - teacher absenteeism. Various studies have shown that at any given time, 30% of teachers at government schools are absent from their classrooms. While the Act mandates the number of teaching hours per year, it does not address the lack of accountability on the part of the teacher or the system if the mandated number of hours is not actually provided.

Other problems include discrimination on a caste basis, violence and abuse of children and discrimination against girls. The latter is not often overt but a result of certain existing situations: e.g. 27% of schools do not have even one female teacher, resulting in a lack of confidence on the part of parents, especially of older girls. 50% of schools do not have separate toilets for girls.

As a result, it is estimated that for every 100 girls who enrol in school in rural India, 40 will reach Class IV, 18 will reach Class VIII, 9 will reach Class IX and only 1 will make it to Class XII. And finally and more significantly, what are children learning?

The stated aim of elementary education is to provide the child with the knowledge, skills and qualities to become an independent, thinking, creative human being. But a report shows that on the ground we are far from even providing them the basic literacy skills.

92 The Right of children to free and compulsory Education Act, 2009 guarantees to all children the right to

(a) education in proper schools with trained teachers.
(b) education to all children within the age group of 3-14 years in proper schools with trained teachers.
(c) education to all children within the age group of 6-14 years in proper schools with trained teachers.
(d) education to all children of all age groups in proper schools with trained teachers.

93 Since independence, elementary education has grown into a multi-headed monster of sorts, with its own caste system of service providers. Which of the following are these 'monsters'?

(a) Government ordinary, government elite, private elite, private-run but not government funded
(b) Government elite, government ordinary, private elite, private-run but not government funded
(c) Government ordinary, government elite, private elite, private-run, but government funded
(d) Government elite, non-government ordinary, private elite, private run, but government funded

94 The fast-increasing middle class prefer to send their children to privately-run schools because

(a) they charge less fee.
(b) they provide less quality education.
(c) they provide education on par with government run schools.
(d) they provide more quality education.

95 The stated aim of elementary education is to provide the child with

(a) the knowledge, skills and qualities to become a dependent, thinking, creative human being.
(b) the knowledge, skills and qualities to become an independent, thinking creative human being.
(c) the knowledge, skill and qualities to become an independent, thinking destructive human being.
(d) All of the above

96 The Right of Children to Free and Compulsory Education Act, 2009 mandates

1. specified number of teaching hours per year.
2. accountability of teachers.
3. discrimination on caste basis.

Codes

(a) Only 1 (b) 1 and 2 (c) 2 and 3 (d) 1, 2 and 3

ANSWERS

1 (b)	2 (c)	3 (d)	4 (c)	5 (a)	6 (c)	7 (a)	8 (a)	9 (a)	10 (b)
11 (d)	12 (b)	13 (a)	14 (d)	15 (d)	16 (c)	17 (d)	18 (d)	19 (b)	20 (a)
21 (c)	22 (c)	23 (a)	24 (c)	25 (c)	26 (a)	27 (c)	28 (c)	29 (a)	30 (d)
31 (d)	32 (d)	33 (c)	34 (b)	35 (c)	36 (b)	37 (c)	38 (b)	39 (b)	40 (b)
41 (c)	42 (a)	43 (d)	44 (a)	45 (c)	46 (b)	47 (d)	48 (a)	49 (c)	50 (d)
51 (c)	52 (d)	53 (b)	54 (a)	55 (a)	56 (b)	57 (d)	58 (c)	59 (b)	60 (b)
61 (d)	62 (c)	63 (d)	64 (d)	65 (d)	66 (c)	67 (c)	68 (b)	69 (d)	70 (b)
71 (b)	72 (a)	73 (a)	74 (b)	75 (a)	76 (a)	77 (a)	78 (c)	79 (a)	80 (c)
81 (a)	82 (a)	83 (a)	84 (c)	85 (c)	86 (a)	87 (b)	88 (d)	89 (a)	90 (b)
91 (b)	92 (c)	93 (c)	94 (d)	95 (b)	96 (a)				

Peace Psychology

Peace psychology is important dimension of psychology. Its major objective is to promote prevention and mitigation of conflicts. Peace psychology helps in broad understanding of various aspects of conflict and violence and help in their resolution.

Introduction of Peace Psychology

Peace psychology seeks to develop theories and practices aimed at the prevention and mitigation of direct and structural violence. Framed positively, peace psychology promotes the non-violent management of conflict and the pursuit of social justice, which is known as peace making and peace building respectively.

Peace psychology is study of mental processes and behaviour that lead to violence, prevent violence and facilitate non-violence. It involves promoting fairness, respect and dignity for all, for the purpose of making violence a less likely occurrence and helping to heal its psychological effect.

The above definition by **MacNair** clearly specifies the need of studying peace psychology for promoting non-violence and equality for all human beings.

Scope of Peace Psychology

- Peace psychology promotes the non-violent management of conflict and the pursuit of social justice, what we refer to as peace making and peace building, respectively.
- The psychological causes and consequences of war and other forms of violence are studied by peace psychologist.
- Peace psychology provides the remedies to violent behaviour including conflict resolution and peace education.
- Along with the causes of war and other forms of violence the psychological consequences of violence to both victims and perpetrators has received attention from peace psychologists.
- In 1982, Psychologists for Social Responsibility was founded and focused on preventing nuclear war.

In this Chapter

- *Introduction of Peace Psychology*
- *Violence*
- *Non-Violence*
- *Conflict*

- Albert Bandura and colleagues identified and investigated many of the cognitive processes behind various forms of violence. They argued that the most inhumane behaviour comes from psychological processes which leads to disengagement of original ideas of moral conduct.
- Throughout decades various forms of peace education have developed. For the various approaches of peace education, there has been an upsurge of publications practices and studies of effectiveness.

Emergence of Peace Psychology

Peace psychology has its deep roots in the philosophy but it gained the interest of researchers in 1950's and after. The study of peace psychology deals with psychological aspects of peace, conflict, violence and war. It analyses the violent and non-violent behaviours as well as the structural mechanisms attending conflicts and understanding of processes which lead to more desirable human condition.

The peace psychology brings in light the realities of the Post Cold War era, where the major concern was not just to end the nuclear war between two superpowers USA and USSR, but the focal area of concern was to improve the condition of the people who are dying slowly because of prevalent structural violence which leads to the depriviation of human needs. It was at this time when the need arose for the study of 'Peace' in psychology and many psychologists came together to fight for the human cause.

William James is considered to be the first peace psychologist as he challenged the over simplistic and misguided view that war is an inevitable part of human behaviour. He introduced the phrase 'Moral Equivalent of War' in his speech at Stanford University, 1906. Though he recognised war as the means to express spiritual inclination by human beings, he also argued that there are other alternatives than war for the expression of such human values.

In **1960's**, several well known psychologist published numerous articles which supported the work of peace psychology like the articles by Osgood (1962), Brofen Brenner (1961) and Moeton Deutsch (1961). These articles guided much of the superpowers' foreign policies during Cold War and many of the concepts were further developed in books published during the Vietnam War in 1966. *All these publications differ from the earlier work done in the area of war and peace in several ways like*

- Analysis has shifted from behaviour of an individual to that of nations.
- Emphasis was laid not on preparation for war rather on its prevention.
- New work was critical of US foreign policies.

In **1980s**, 'Peace' again caught attention of psychologists, as there was a constant hostility between the leaders of the two superpowers. At that time it was almost understood that nuclear war is the result of human behaviour and hence psychology has a major role to play in it.

White's 1986 work in his book 'Psychology and the Prevention of Nuclear War', has been quite instrumental in forming the basic principles and ideologies of the early peace psychology.

In **1988**, the 'Journal of Social Issues' focused on 'Psychology and the Promotion of Peace'. It defined peace in more active terms *i.e.* building cooperative relations between people and nations is a long term process dependent on the satisfaction of human needs.

In **1991**, American Psychological Association Division 48, the society for study of peace, conflict and violence, peace psychology was established by some psychologists who began to identify themselves as 'peace psychologists.'

Today three main themes are emerging in Post Cold War peace psychology, *which are as follows*

(i) Greater sensitivity to geo historical context.
(ii) A more differentiated perspective on the meanings and types of violence and peace.
(iii) A systematic or multilevel view of the determinant of violence and peace.

Sensitivity to Geo Historical Context

The geographical location of a country and its historical background plays an important role in determining how countries focal point of peace and war differs from each other. *For instance*, countries aligned with global South tend to associate peace building efforts with social justice due to political instability and scarce and unequal distribution of the resources.

Whereas in South-East Asia the major concern of peace building is to reduce political and economic forms of oppression because they have authoritarian regimes.

In North Ireland, the focal point is the prevention of violent episodes through promotion of positive inter group relations between Catholics and Protestants.

Similarly, in the US peace psychologists are concerned with the violence that is prevalent at all levels like the recent incidents of gun-shooting by young students etc. and also at interpersonal forms of violence.

Violence

Violence is defined as the intentional use of physical force or power, thereatened or actual, against oneself, another person or against a group or community that either results in or has a high likelihood of resulting in injury or death, psychological harm, maldevelopment or deprivation.

The above words means that a person or a group must have an intention to use physical force or their power, against another person or group, which will eventually cause them harm either physically or psychologically in order to be called an *act of violence*.

Thus, we can say that unintentional injury or harm towards someone else does not categorise into a violent act. The above definition also takes into account not only the physical force but also the use of threatening or actual power.

Types of Violence

Johan Galtung made distinction between direct and structural violence. It was in contrast to the relationship between social justice and peace that was evident during the Cold War.

Post Cold War Peace psychology has adopted a more differentiated perspective on nature of violence and peace in consonance with the field of peace studies.

(i) **Direct Violence** It is episodic and manifests as an acute insult to well-being that typically harms or kills people quickly and dramatically. Interpersonal aggression, such as bullying, war etc. comes under the direct violence.

(ii) **Structural Violence** Violence which is inbuilt in political and economic systems forms the basis of structural violence. It harms or kills people, slowly through permanent social arrangements that deprive people of the basic needs for survival.

It is prevalent both at the level of within and between the nations. *For example* Afghanistan and Sudan are the countries where every year thousands of people die from starvation while there is sufficient food in the world. This is a form of structural violence. In words of Gandhiji structural violence can be summarised as, "the Earth provides enough to satisfy every man's need, but not enough to satisfy every man's greed". Structural violence is versatile in nature and is more rampant where people do not have a voice or political representation.

People who always feel alienated and are unable to fulfill the basic needs of their families and themselves, often indulge in direct violence.

The process of violence from structural to direct is often circular in nature. *For example* If a political party which aims to suppress the needs and demands of people and it tries to curb the voice raised by common people who are protesting sub-standard living it will results in a conflict situation which will lead to direct violence like lathicharge, rally etc.

Direct Violence	Structural Violence
• Aggression	• Belief in a just world
• Armed Conflict	• Ideologies that normalise social exclusion
• Genocide	• Patriarchy
• Identity based violence	• Protestant work ethic
• Inter group violence	• Sexism
• Media violence	• Sexual harassment
• Militaristic attitude	• Social dominance theory
• Terrorism	• Social injustice
• Traumatic stress	• System justification theory
• War	

Methods of Resolving Violence

Violence can be resolved by adopting peace approach. Galtung also differentiated between three kinds of peace activities *which are as follows*

(i) **Peace Keeping** It is a response to an acute situation and typically involves the containment and de-escalation of violence and the enforced separation of would be combatants.

(ii) **Peace Making** It is focused on arising at settlements or agreements within a conflict situation.

(iii) **Peace Building** It is a more proactive attempt aimed at healing a post conflict society and reducing structural violence in an effort to prevent conflict and violence from erupting in future.

Peace making, peace keeping and peace building has a major utility in moving a relationship from violence to non-violence (peace keeping), to conflict resolution (peace making) or to social equity or transformation (peace building). These dimensions of peace are not mutually exclusive.

Thus, we can say that peace psychology is an endeavour defined by theory and practice to develop various patterns of behaviour and cognitions to prevent both structural and episodic form of violence.

Perspectives on Nature of Violence and Peace

Peace psychology overlaps with social psychology as it includes the cognitive analysis of decision-making and psychodynamic perspective of peace and conflict. Due to this overlap, it focuses on the area of conflict management and that too on the constructive processes of conflict management *i.e.* process that promote cooperative relationships .

Peace psychology stands out from other branches of psychology as it focuses on the cultures and systems in case of violent episodes. Thus, violent episodes are mere manifestations of interactions among host of destructive factors embedded in one's political, social and historical factors. Thus, we can say that peace psychologists are actively engaged in practice that attend to psychological level of analysis and macro level phenomena, most notably political and cultural levels. The major issues that have received a good amount of interest by peace psychologists are peace keeping *i.e.* moving a relationship from violent (peace keeping) to non-violent, peace making conflict resolution, trauma reduction etc.

Another important feature of violence is that it is prevalent in variety of settings and levels from the interpersonal to the international level.

Levinger and Rubin provide a helpful typology and set of principles that can guide us through the process of generalisation of violence. They suggest that all conflicts have some features in common *i.e.* their derivation from perceived divergence of interests and mixture of motives. However, generalisation is dependent on the number of parties involved and their issues.

If the conflict is between two people than finding interest is simple, whereas, if conflict is between nations then interest involved are complex and thus, the model developed for domestic disputes would be inappropriate to apply.

The origins of many forms of **collective violence**, such as terrorism can be found in structure based inequalities *e.g.* Pakistan produces maximum number of terrorists in world, because the difficult life condition of certain segment of people, gives rise to psychological processes including destructive intergroup ideologies.

Interpersonal violence can be in the form of bullying. It happens among young people and can take form of physical, psychological or verbal aggression. It can be direct if we are hurting someone directly or indirect if we are spreading rumours or false news about anyone. Though in today's world most of us are aware of the ill effects of bullying still it is prevalent and is on rise.

Non-Violence

Violence is always considered to be a force by people to gain power and spread their fame. Numerous wars have been fought by human beings in order to conquer other countries and make themselves more powerful and omnipotent. But it's not always violence which has enabled humans to gain power, non-violence also has its importance as it spreads happiness and peace among and within all nations and people.

Non-violence is a moral philosophy that forbids the use of violent means in order to attain social or political goal and promote the use of other means like disobedience and persuasion (convincing) *e.g.* **Mahatma Gandhi** in his struggle for India's freedom has used non-violent means of disobedience and boycotted the Britishers by calling off the use of British made goods. Similary the movement was propagated by **Martin Luther King** for the attainment of civil rights for African Americans etc.

Non-violence is a way of bringing changes at a larger level without the use of physical violence against others.

The activists of non-violence use diverse methods for bringing about social and political changes like civil disobedience, mass non-cooperation etc.

Non-violence at times is considered to be passive, but this notion is outrightly rejected by its advocates as non-violence refers to absence of violent behaviour and passivity is the choice to do nothing at all.

The origins of non-violence can be traced back to its roots in the religions like Jainism, Buddhism and Hinduism. It is closely linked to the concept of 'Ahimsa', advocated and preached widely by the famous Tirthankara of Jainism, Lord 'Parsvnatha' around eight century BC. Also, Lord Mahavira strengthened the idea of 'Ahimsa'.

Types of Non-Violence

The common people of a country bestow power on the government by giving them their cooperation and consent. The roots of civil or political power in all regimes depends on the compliance it gets from its citizens. Thus, a non-violent way to show their disagreement to those in power is to withdraw their consent and cooperation from those in power .

This ideology was adopted by Mahatma Gandhi in his fight for India's struggle for freedom. There are two major dimensions of non-violent action. The first one is ethical or principled approach where emphasis is on human harmony and a moral rejection of violence and coercion and the other is pragmatic where conflict is seen as normal and the rejection of violence as an effective way of challenging power. The leading figures acknowledging these approaches are **Gene Sharp** and **Mahatma Gandhi**.

Ethical or Principled Non-Violence

It is a view which promotes that violence can be unlearned by practicing love and compassion. It is to reject the impulse which results in hatred towards anyone. This view promotes love for everyone even those with whom one strongly disagrees.

The practitioners of this view explicitly state their intention to conduct and resolve conflict without violence. They are ready to sacrifice their lives. They strongly oppose practices like slavery, racial or gender discrimination, war etc. They fairly distinguish between the culprit and the evil, seeking to draw out the moral capacity of each person. This approach was followed by Mahatma Gandhi and Martin Luther King.

Pragmatic Non-Violence

It is majorly concerned with the results non-violence can achieve. It is to achieve practical advantages through non-violent means. The practitioners of this approach believe that non-violence is a more powerful weapon than violence. **Gene Sharp** is the key scholar of pragmatic non-violent action. Pragmatic non-violence is effective measure which is used against a specific war, oppression etc. *For example* Use of apartheid in Africa is the example of pragmatic non-violence.

Gene Sharp outlines three methods of non-violent actions, *which are as follows*

(i) **Non-Violent Protest and Persuasion** These are used to show dissent towards a particular policy or specific issue. These are also used to gain publicity. *For example* Parades, visits, posters etc.

(ii) **Non-Cooperation** To remove oneself from cooperation or obeying the activity or institution one disagress with. Methods used are boycotts, acts of civil-disobedience etc.

(iii) **Non-Violent Intervention** It is an endeavour to disrupt or deconstruct established institutions, behaviours or policies that are viewed as undesirable by the non-violent actor. Non-violent interventions may also strive to create new patterns and institutions to take their place. Methods of disruption are blockades, fasting etc.

Conflict

Conflict is basically a situation of disagreement, clash or argument between two or more groups of people or countries. Conflict can occur at both the micro level and the macro level.

At micro level it focuses on individuals and their interactions like the relationship between young children and their parents. The study of conflicts at micro level is restricted to just small scale. It basically deals with the study of individuals and their social interactions.

At the macro level the focus changes to social structure, social processes and problems and their inter relationships. *For example* The effect of employment policies on youth, education system, relevance etc.

In conflict resolution we study the methods and processes involved in facilitating the peaceful ending of a conflict.

Conflict Resolution at Macro Level

Conflict at the macro level is the result of the grievances, deprivation, injustice etc. which were till now suffered silently by a group or individuals. When suddenly they decide to aggressively or openly express their dissatisfaction by eliminating the other party, it leads to conflict at the macro level as the situation escalates to an entire group, ethnic, state or even national and international level.

At times it becomes difficult for the parties to resolve conflict without the aid of external party. Then the help is taken from external parties, but at times these parties complicate the conflict situation and is difficult to identify because their involvement is through war and weapons; financial support etc. These are known as *Shadow Parties* in conflict. Macro conflict focuses on an entire society of countries, social class etc. and the change of macro conflict is also widespread for a nation.

There are several causes of conflicts at the macro level like

- **Rigid Social Order** Certain social norms are harsh and oppressive in nature, which puts one section of society in advantageous position and other at disadvantaged position. Those who are benefitted by these norms, they use this freedom to do wrong with other section. Thus, the exploitation which the disadvantaged section suffer can at times gives rise to conflict eruption *e.g.* violence against women.
- **Values** At times the ideologies, philosophy, religions etc. of two groups may differ. Different parties have their different viewpoint regarding rightness and goodness. All these differences in their view points give rise to incompatible goals and lead to conflict. They tend to have fix mindsets and considers the values and policies of others as discrimination and thinks that others are creating blockage in their way to progress.
- **Resources** When two or more groups aspire to get the same scarce resource and the resource is not enough to fulfill the needs of both parties, it leads to conflict. Mostly the fight starts over the natural resources which are scarce like oil or water . The privileged group wants to control the resources while the other group feels oppressed and this leads to conflict.
- **Mismanagement of Information** Any mismanagement of information can create fatal conflict as information is vital at human and organisational interactions and relationships.

Thus, proper and tactful management of information is required to maintain a peaceful environment at both individual and organisational level.

Major Theories of Conflict Resolutions

The theories that govern conflict resolution are as follows

(i) **The Basic Human Need Theory** John Buston one of the pioneers of the human needs theory, opines that "conflict is likely to be caused by the need for identity, recognition, security of the identity and other such human, societal values" and so 'facilitated' conflict resolution must aim at determining such human needs and values and then assisting parties to deduce what alterations in structures, institutions and policies are required to enable the fulfilment of needs. **Abraham Maslow**'s Hierarchy of Needs also influenced the Basic need theory, which states the different kinds of human needs and their endeavour to fulfill these needs.

(ii) **The Marxist Theory** Conflict theory developed by Karl Marx states that due to the never ending competition in society for the ownership of limited or finite resources there will be always a state of conflict. It implies that those in possession of wealth and resources will hoard them and poor people will struggle constantly to gain them. He says that conflict is a social phenomena embedded in the social structure. The basic point this theory makes is that if government is unable to reduce the degree of inequality in a society conflict will be there.

(iii) **Feminist Model** The feminist model of conflict resolution approaches conflict through the focus on the violence, oppression and inequality towards woman.

It aims to resolve inequality towards women at multiple level of existence : Intrapersonal and Interpersonal community, society and international level. The violence against women must be avoided to control the conflictual situations.

(iv) **Environmental Perspective** Due to urbanisation and rapid increase in population, human being have exploited their environment knowingly or unknowingly. *Environment is degrading in two forms*

- Overuse of resources leading to its depletion.
- Degradation of resources because of increase in pollution. Global warming, ozone layer depletion, acid rain etc. are causes of environmental degradation. Increasingly the impact of environmental degradation is global and affecting not only individuals or communities but nations and continents.

Conflict Resolution Mechanisms

Following mechanisms help in resolving conflicts

(i) **Mediation** In this style third party play role of mediator. The role of mediating party is to create the favourable environment for both parties in conflict. The mediator helps both parties to arrive at a common ground and have trust of both parties. Mediator only manages negotiation between two parties but does not impose solution on the parties.

(ii) **Arbitration** It is a way to resolve disputes alternatively *i.e.* a neutral third party hears the dispute and gives an award or decision which is binding for both parties in conflict. It is a third party intervention where parties in conflict choose a non-violent way to settle conflict.

(iii) **Adjudication** The use of courts and litigation process for conflict resolution is called *adjudication*. It is a legal process by which an arbiter or judge review's evidence and argument including legal reasoning set fourth by opposing parties or litigants.

It is a non-violent way of resolving conflicts and disputes. Although it's an expensive and a long process, where the winner takes all and loser is left with nothing. The judgement given by court is binding to both parties in conflict.

(iv) **Conciliation** It's an Alternative Dispute Resolution (ADR) process whereby the parties in dispute use a conciliator who meets with the both parties separately and together in order to resolve their differences. It involves facilitation. The aim of conciliation is to reduce tension between both parties. It tries to improve communication between parties by interpreting issues and exploring potential solutions which leads to mutually acceptable outcomes.

(v) **Collaboration** It is a process in which parties work together on their own to resolve problem. It helps to build trust, respect and confidence between groups or nations. It aims at increasing the activities and dialogues between two parties. This method does not involve the interference of third party. The parties in conflict tries to build friendly relations of their own by doing joint projects and shared utilities.

(vi) **Negotiation** It is a kind of dialouge between two or more people or parties intended to reach a beneficial outcome. The parties involved in negotiation are aware of the prevalent conflict between them and try to sort it out through dialogue or communication. Negotiations can be positional or collaborative. Positional negotiation are adversarial and competitive in nature, parties in this try to win over other rather than coming to mutual beneficial outcome while in collaborative negotiation, parties educate each other on their needs and concerns and each group seeks for the best ways to solve their problems in ways that the interest and fears of both or all parties are met. The emphasis is on mutual understanding and feeling.

Thus, we conclude that stated above are the Alternative Dispute Resolution (ADR) methods for conflict resolution. These are all non-violent methods which can be used in the effective conflict resolution.

Multi Track Approach

Diamond and McDonald in 1996, also introduced multi track approach to peace or conflict resolution. According to them, there are nine tracks of conceptual and practical framework that assist and work in peace building sector.

These are

(i) **Government** Government is involved in maintaining law and order and also making policies for peace building at official level.

(ii) **Non Government/Professional Conflict Resolution** It includes the activities of NGO's and professional in the area of conflict resolution and peace building.

(iii) **Business or Commerce** Economic and commercial activities provided by business leads to enormous contribution in peace building.

(iv) **Private Citizens and Personal Involvement** Individuals can be involved in peace building through voluntary organisations, NGO's etc.

(v) **Research, Training or Education** It covers three areas of research as it connects to educational institutions, think tanks and special research centres including training program in conflict resolution and peace building.

(vi) **Activism or Advocacy** It deals with the campaigns and practices for the promotion of peace, non-violence and human rights.

(vii) **Religion** It deals with the beliefs and value system of dominant religious followers.

(viii) **Funding** Funding which the peace building organisations receive from the developed countries is crucial for their functioning.

(ix) **Communication and Media** Media in all forms print, electronic, video, films all plays a vital role in conflict resolution if it chooses to spread peace, otherwise result can be *vice versa*.

Role of Media in Conflict Resolution

In a situation of conflict , media plays a major role in its resolution, as media has the power of changing and framing the perceptions of human beings. By providing intelligent and reliable information regarding the present conflict, media can allow citizens to form their own views. Media often promotes the political and social participation of people as it gives voice and power to citizens to express themselves. The role of media in reporting conflicts is in terms of framing, constructing and distributing the news.

Arno said that "media can and do operate as effective third parties, in conflict resolution."

Wolsfeld suggested the "Media serves as the public forums in which disputing parties can be engaged in dialogue."

Spencer argues that "Media inherently can play a role in peace by attracting public attention and pressurising politicians to facilitate diplomacy and engage in peace negotiations."

Botes suggests that "Media can facilitate when the communication among conflicted parties is limited or strained."

Scholars **Helene Deutsch** have noted the media's potential to detect initial signs of violence in society thus enabling an early intervention in inter-state conflicts.

Thus, the above researches show how media plays a very important role in conflict resolution. *The role of media in conflict resolution can be summarised as follows*

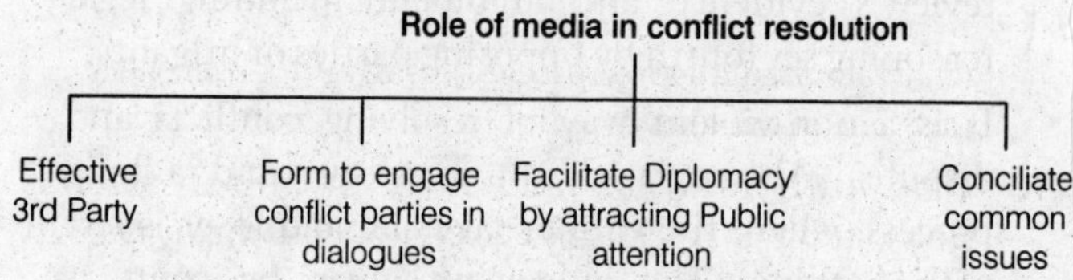

One more important theoretical framework for the role of media in conflict resolution is given by **Johan Galtung**, who proposed peace journalism for journalists to show how value bias towards violence can be avoided while covering war and conflict. At times it is also known as *conflict solution journalism*, or *conflict sensitive journalism*.

EXAM BASED QUESTIONS

1 **Peace Psychology works towards the idea of sustainable peace. The means used to reach 'peace' are**

(a) education based (b) non -violent
(c) research based (d) theory based

2 **Peace as defined in Peace Psychology is not merely an absence of war but it's the absence of**

(a) direct violence (b) structural violence
(c) cultural violence (d) All of these

3 **Which model of Conflict Resolution was proposed by Charles E Osgood?**

(a) Mediation model (b) Affiliation Model
(c) GRIT Model (d) No-Arms Model

4 **Who is known as the father of Peace Psychology?**

(a) William James (b) Michael Wessells
(c) James Russell (d) Christie

5 **When was the Journal of Conflict Resolution initiated?**

(a) 1948 (b) 1957 (c) 1962 (d) 1961

6 **Who made the distinction between the direct and structural form of violence?**

(a) Johan Galtung (b) Christine
(c) Winger (d) AR Wagner

7 **Which one of the following is not an example of direct violence?**

(a) Aggression (b) Bullying
(c) Interstate war (d) Starvation

8 **How Peace Psychology differs from the neighbouring specialities?**

(a) Its focus on violence and non-violence.
(b) Its focus on peace making and peace building.
(c) Frequent reference to systematic and cultural origins of violent episodes.
(d) None of the above

9 **What are the major issues of concern for peace psychologists?**

(a) Peace making (b) Peace building
(c) Maintaining peace (d) Both a and b

10 **What are the basis of collective violence?**

(a) Historical background (b) Cultural setup
(c) Oppression prevalence (d) Structural setup

11 **How many well known psychologists came together by close of World War Second for manifesto human nature and peace?**

(a) 11 (b) 15 (c) 13 (d) 17

12 **Who coined the phrase "The Moral Equivalent of War" in his famous speech at Stanford University?**

(a) William James (b) Christie
(c) Helene Deutsch (d) Thompson

13 **What does 'moral equivalents' means in famous phrase moral equivalents of war?**

(a) Peace and non-violence
(b) Inclination towards self sacrifice and personal honour
(c) Deep rooted inclination for war
(d) Both b and c

14 What does 'GRIT' (Osgood) stands for?
(a) Graduated and Reciprocal Initiatives in Tension reduction
(b) Graduated and Reciprocal Inclination in Trauma reduction
(c) Graduated and Reciprocal Initiative in Total peace
(d) None of the above

15 Who authored the famous book "International Behaviour : A Social-Psychological Analysis in 1965"?
(a) Kelman (b) Rivera (c) White (d) Thompson

16 What according to realistic group conflict theory is the main cause of conflict?
(a) Scarce resources (b) Clean water
(c) Arable land (d) All of these

17 What is/are causes of conflict at the macro level?
(a) Changes in social structure
(b) Changes in social processes
(c) Problems and their interrelationships
(d) All of the above

18 What is the most important aim of Conflict Resolution?
(a) To find a unique solution
(b) To appoint a strong third party
(c) Negotiation
(d) To search solutions

19 What are the positive ways to maintain peace and cordial relations between two parties?
(a) Helpfulness (b) Coordination
(c) Cooperation (d) All of these

20 Name two broad categories on which Conflict Resolution techniques are based?
(a) Interest based and needs based
(b) Peace making and peace building
(c) Coordination and effective communication
(d) None of the above

21 Who are the pioneers of interest based approach of Conflict Resolution?
(a) Fisher and Ury (b) Staub
(c) Kelman and Fisher (d) Ashmore

22 Who is known as the pioneer in non-violence work in Peace Psychology?
(a) Fisher (b) Gene Sharp
(c) Wagner (d) Wilde

23 What are the two major types of non-violence?
(a) Ethical approach and pragmatic approach
(b) Social approach and cultural approach
(c) National approach and international approach
(d) Religious approach and cultural approach

24 In which approach of Conflict Resolution, 'an award' is given by the neutral third party who hears the dispute?
(a) Mediation (b) Arbitration
(c) Adjudication (d) Conciliation

25 Who authored the famous book on Conflict Resolution 'Getting to Yes'?
(a) Holsti (b) Flare
(c) Fisher and Ury (d) Deutsch

26 In which approach of Conflict Resolution participants are not government representatives?
(a) Need based approach (b) Integrative approach
(c) Interest based approach (d) Both a and c

27 " Peace is its own reward." Who said this?
(a) Mahatma Gandhi (b) Martin Luther King
(c) Jimi Hendrix (d) Buddha

28 "An eye for an eye only ends up making the whole world blind". Who said this?
(a) Jimi Hendrix (b) Martin Luther King
(c) Eleanor Roosevelt (d) Mahatma Gandhi

29 "Peace is the only battle worth waging". Who said this?
(a) Mahatma Gandhi (b) Buddha
(c) Albert Camus (d) Dalai Lama

30 Theories and practices in Peace Psychology aims at
(a) peace and non-violence
(b) positive and negative peace
(c) prevention and mitigation of direct and structural violence
(d) None of the above

31 Which style of Conflict Resolution deals with having dialogue between parties in conflict?
(a) Negotiation (b) Collaboration
(c) Communication (d) Interaction

32 What are two different types of 'Negotiation'?
(a) Positional and comparative
(b) Comparative and interactive
(c) Positional and collaborative
(d) Interactive and descriptive

33 Who proposed the famous Multi Track Approach in Conflict Resolution?
(a) Wilde and Wagner
(b) Christie and Sharp
(c) Marx and Staub
(d) Diamond and McDonald

34 Which among the following is not the part of Multi Track Approach by Diamond and McDonald?
(a) Government (b) Religion
(c) Funding (d) Constitution

35 "Non violence is the weapon of strong". Who said this?
(a) Mahatma Gandhi (b) Dalai Lama
(c) Sigmund Freud (d) Albert Einestein

36 What is 'negative peace'?
(a) Freedom from conflict (b) A state of security
(c) Absence of war
(d) Calmness of mind and heart

37 "If we being with the need to survive, we immediately see that peace is a primary requirement of the human condition itself." Who said this?

(a) Johan Galtung (b) Wilhelm Reich
(c) Dalai Lama (d) MK Gandhi

38 Which approach of Conflict Resolution is applicable in domestic and international conflicts?

(a) Need based approach (b) Interest based approach
(c) Both a and b (d) Incentive based approach

39 'Positional flexibility' is the result of which Conflict Resolution Approach?

(a) Interest based approach
(b) Need based approach
(c) Both a and b
(d) None of the above

40 In which approach of Conflict Resolution agreements are non binding?

(a) Incentive based approach
(b) Conciliation based approach
(c) Need based approach
(d) Negotiation based approach

41 Direct violence is .... it occurs physically or verbally.

(a) visible (b) directive
(c) invisible (d) non-directive

42 Cultural violence .... direct and structural form of violence.

(a) justifies (b) neglect
(c) promotes (d) disapprove

43 Non-violence is moral philosophy to attain social or political proclaims, by means such as disobedience or the power of ....

(a) pacifism (b) attainment
(c) social change (d) persuasion

44 In ethical non-violence, violence is .... by practicising love and compassion for all .

(a) unbiased (b) observed
(c) withdrawn (d) unlearned

45 .... is an ethical concept evolved in vedic texts of Hindus.

(a) Non-violence (b) Satya
(c) Renaissance (d) Ahimsa

46 Conflict is an opposition among .... directed against each other.

(a) social entities (b) political entities
(c) socio-political entities (d) individual entities

47 In conflict at macro level .... is important.

(a) coherence
(b) external-aid assistance
(c) pacification
(d) withdrawl of power

48 At times the presence of secondary parties in a conflict situation, further .... the situation.

(a) complicate (b) ease (c) necessary (d) resolution

49 Social norms are at times .... in nature that leads to conflicts.

(a) oppressive (b) conventional
(c) traumatising (d) equalitarian

50 The involvement of third party is important in conflict management as it provides .... ground that are safe.

(a) friendly (b) peaceful talks
(c) neutral (d) contentment

51 A .... is an extreme situation in conflict which has reached a point where critical decisions have to be taken to avoid escalation of conflict to extreme violence.

(a) international conflict (b) micro conflict
(c) degenerative conflict (d) crisis

52 Conflict is

(a) unavoidable (b) a result of value clashes
(c) stressful (d) All of the above

53 Conflict Resolution is

(a) an agreement
(b) an attempt to resolve a conflict
(c) a proposal (d) a treaty

54 Individualistic cultures tend to resolve conflict by

(a) ensuring that each individual's needs are met
(b) ensuring interpersonal harmony
(c) avoid direct communication
(d) All of the above

55 Collective cultures tend to resolve conflict by

(a) Ensuring interpersonal harmony
(b) Avoid direct communication
(c) Maintaining the relationship
(d) All of the above

56 The Conflict Resolution approach that corresponds with a high level of assertiveness and a low level of cooperativeness is referred as

(a) compromising (b) avoiding
(c) collaborating (d) accommodating

57 Social identity theory particularly emphasises that inter group conflict can be understood in forms of

(a) the loss of identity
(b) people acting in terms of their group identity
(c) intergroup conflict
(d) situations that involve a material conflict of interest

58 Digital media technologies have increased .... and .... dissemination in conflict settings.

(a) communication and technology
(b) war and peace
(c) communication and information
(d) violence and peace

59 The role of media in a conflict situation must be
(a) conveyance of factual information
(b) conveyance of factual views
(c) being neutral
(d) All of the above

60 .... and .... reporting of conflicts is largely encouraged during the emergence of conflicts and disagreement.
(a) Sensitive and careful (b) Neutral and positive
(c) Truthful and objective (d) Real and objective

61 The function of media in ending a conflict is
(a) passing awareness to citizens and educate them.
(b) in establishing a platform where individuals can convey their expressions of dissent and dissatisfaction.
(c) give political parties ethnic outlooks and influence ethnic communities of people.
(d) Both a and b

62 The watchdog role of journalism is
(a) setting up a channel for the enhancement of divergent political ideologies.
(b) capacity of holding all the leaders and statesman to account.
(c) initiating conflict transformation through variety of activities.
(d) None of the above

63 How can media transform conflicts between disagreeing parties?
(a) Acting as a watchdog
(b) Swift flow of constructive and accurate content
(c) Enhancing confidence and negotiation
(d) Parliamentary democracy and a free election

64 In a conflict situation media content should endeavour to promote .... other than negative ethnicity that is the enemy of cohesive society.
(a) identities (b) ideologies
(c) communication (d) disagreements

65 Conflict is a situation of .... both large and small.
(a) agreement (b) collaboration
(c) difference (d) understanding

66 We respond to conflicts based on our
(a) perceptions (b) emotions (c) thinking (d) objectivity

67 The unhealthy responses to a conflict are
(a) explosive (b) calm
(c) seek compromise (d) Both a and b

68 The healthy response to a conflict situation is
(a) non-defensive (b) seek compromise
(c) readiness to forgive (d) All of these

69 The ability to resolve conflict depends on
(a) being aware and respecting differences of others
(b) controlling the situation
(c) communication of needs
(d) All of the above

70 Choose the correct sequence
(a) Peace keeping - Peace building-Peace making
(b) Peace keeping - Peace making-Peace building
(c) Peace making - Peace keeping- Peace building
(d) Peace building- Peace keeping-Peace making

71 Match the following

List I (Psychologists)	List II (Area of Interest)
A. William James	1. Non-violence
B. Gene Sharp	2. Peace Psychology
C. Galtung	3. Violence
D. Pythagoras	4. Structural violence

Codes

	A	B	C	D		A	B	C	D
(a)	1	2	3	4	(b)	2	1	3	4
(c)	3	4	2	1	(d)	4	3	1	2

72 'Conflict' can be characterised as
1. potentiality or a situation
2. as a structure or a manifestation
3. as an event or a process

Codes
(a) 1 and 2 (b) 2 and 3
(c) 1 and 3 (d) 1, 2 and 3

73 Peace making, a method of conflict resolution include
1. Diplomacy 2. Mediation
3. Reparation 4. Conscientization

Codes
(a) Only 1 (b) Both 1 and 2
(c) 1, 2 and 4 (d) All of these

74 Consider the following statements
1. Peace psychology promotes the non-violent management.
2. Peace psychologist study impact of wars
3. Peace psychologist helps in conflict resolution.

Work of peace psychologist includes

Codes
(a) 1 and 2 (b) 2 and 3
(c) 1 and 3 (d) All of these

75 Direct violence consists of
1. Armed conflict 2. Sexual harassment
3. Genocide 4. Patriarchy

Codes
(a) 1 and 2 (b) 1, 2 and 3
(c) 1 and 3 (d) All of these

76 According to Gene Sharp, methods of non-violent resolution are
1. Non-cooperation
2. Civil-disobedience
3. Non-violent Protest and persuation
4. Non-violent resolutions

Codes

(a) 1, 2 and 3 (b) 1, 3 and 4
(c) 1, 2 and 4 (d) All of these

77 Various causes of conflict at macro level are
1. Rigid social order
2. Values
3. Resources
4. Mismanagement of information

Codes

(a) 1 and 2 (b) 1, 2 and 3
(c) 1, 2 and 3 (d) All of these

Directions (Q. Nos. 78-88*) In the questions given below are two statements labelled as Assertion (A) and Reason (R). In the context of the two statements, which one of the following is coreect?*

(a) Both A and R are true and R is correct explanation of A
(b) Both A and R are true, but R is not the correct explanation of A
(c) A is true, but R is false
(d) A is false, but R is true

78 **Assertion** (A) Role of media is quite critical in Conflict Resolution.

Reason (R) Media can help to bring together different groups to discuss conflict issues .

79 **Assertion** (A) Peace Journalism helps in Conflict Resolution and promote harmony among all.

Reason (R) It is reactive in nature.

80 **Assertion** (A) Social injustice is a form of structural violence.

Reason (R) Structural violence is indirect form of violence.

81 **Assertion** (A) Structural violence kills people slowly.

Reason (R) Structural violence leads to acute insult to the wellbeing of an individual.

82 **Assertion** (A) Media can help to improve Governor of a country.

Reason (R) Media should be secretive and politically framed.

83 **Assertion** (A) Mediation is one of the most important style in Conflict Resolution.

Reason (R) Media can act as a mediator between two conflicting parties.

84 **Assertion** (A) Ownership of resources is one of the major cause of conflict.

Reason (R) Resources are sufficient and ample in nature.

85 **Assertion** (A) Human beings try to fulfill their needs in a hierarchial manner.

Reason (R) Self actualisation is the highest level of human need.

86 **Assertion** (A) Aparthied is a form of direct violence as it lead to killing of people.

Reason (R) Direct violence is episodic and quick in nature.

87 **Assertion** (A) Peace psychology emerged as a distinct area of research during cold war era.

Reason (R) At that time the main focus was to prevent the nuclear war between two super powers.

88 **Assertion** (A) Structural violence is more inhumane than direct violence.

Reason (R) Structural violence is widespread and kills more people.

ANSWERS

1	(b)	2	(d)	3	(c)	4	(a)	5	(b)	6	(a)	7	(d)	8	(c)	9	(d)	10	(d)
11	(c)	12	(a)	13	(d)	14	(a)	15	(a)	16	(d)	17	(d)	18	(d)	19	(d)	20	(a)
21	(a)	22	(b)	23	(a)	24	(b)	25	(c)	26	(a)	27	(a)	28	(d)	29	()	30	(c)
31	(a)	32	(c)	33	(d)	34	(d)	35	(a)	36	(c)	37	(a)	38	(b)	39	(a)	40	(c)
41	(a)	42	(a)	43	(d)	44	(d)	45	(d)	46	(a)	47	(c)	48	(a)	49	(a)	50	(b)
51	(d)	52	(d)	53	(b)	54	(a)	55	(d)	56	(b)	57	)	58	(c)	59	(d)	60	(a)
61	(d)	62	(b)	63	(b)	64	(a)	65	(c)	66	(a)	67	(a)	68	(d)	69	(d)	70	(b)
71	(b)	72	(d)	73	(b)	74	(d)	75	(c)	76	(d)	77	(d)	78	(a)	79	(b)	80	(a)
81	(b)	82	(b)	83	(a)	84	(b)	85	(a)	86	(a)	87	(a)	88	(b)				

Well-Being and Self-Growth

Well-being and self-growth play very important role in psychology. Future of person depends on the efforts he/she has made toward well-being and self-growth.

Well-Being

Well-being is synonymous to happiness or positive mental state. It is the feeling of satisfaction or contention one has with his/her own life. It encompasses dimension of physical, mental and social well-being and moves far ahead of the traditional view of being healthy which was only limited to the physical health of a person.

According to **Naci and Loannidis**, "Well-being includes the choices and activities aimed at achieving physical vitality, mental alacrity, social satisfaction, a sense of accomplishment and personal fulfillment."

Well-being is an important concept of positive psychology. It is mainly characterised by the presence of positivity as compared to frequent negativity in life. Positive psychologists agree that a person must live an engaging, happy and a meaningful life.

Martin Seligman, the pioneer who worked extensively in the area of positive psychology gave an important model of well-being, called the *flourish model*. He believed that these five elements can help people to reach a life of fulfillment, happiness and meaning. *The five main achivements of his theory are*

(i) **Positive Emotions** This includes a wide array of emotions which makes us feel good like happiness, satisfaction, excitement, pride etc. The people who experience such emotions lives a fulfilling and a long healthy life.

(ii) **Engagement** This is basically when a person is fully absorbed in a task and the person is in 'flow' (a concept given by Mihaly Csikszentmihalyi). It is a feeling of intensity which leads to sense of ecstasy and clarity. Though, the task may demand a higher skills or looks challenging, but the person is passionate enough to accomplish it. The person is fully absorbed losing self consciousness while completing the task. *For example* When you work on something you are passionate about; like painting, dance, travelling, writing or anything you love to do and enjoy it doing.

In this Chapter

- Well-being
- Self-Growth
- Character Strengths
- Resilience
- Post-Traumatic Growth

(iii) **Relationships** All the family, social, romantic or work related relationships plays an important role in the overall well-being of a person. If the relationships a person shares with others is healthy and fulfilling enough to promote his/her self-growth then it leads to positiveness in outlook and complete happiness. Whereas, negative or abusive relationships leads to distress and unhappiness in one's life. It becomes a road block of his/her growth and finally ruins life.

(iv) **Meaning** A sense of meaning and purpose can be derived from belonging to and serving something bigger than the self. There are various societal institutions that enable a sense of meaning such as religion, family, science, politics, the community etc.

(v) **Accomplishments** Each and everyone of us has a goal in life. We endeavour to achieve our goal and put genuine efforts to accomplish our goal. *For example* You are reading a book to clear an exam, once you pass through the exam, you accomplish your goal and that achievement gives you a sense of accomplishment resulting in feeling of happiness and satisfaction.

The main application of the Flourish Model is that, it can be applied to institutions to develop programs to help people develop new cognitive and emotional tools. The acronym used to remember the main points of the model is '*PERMA*' (Positive, Emotion, Engagement Relationships, Meaning and Accomplishment).

Types of Well-being

The two main conceptions around which the concept of well-being revolves are hedonic and eudemonic well-being

Hedonic well-being

This view is based on the principle of pleasure and pain. It equates well-being with pleasure and happiness. It is basically the felling of excess pleasure, over pain.

It defines happiness as merely excess of positive emotions over the negative ones. This approach originated with the perspective given by Greek philosopher **Aristippus**, which says that each one of us tries to experience high level of pleasure and avoid painful experience from our life.

For example Imagine a friend or any of your acquaintance who is always busy in shopping, partying or socialising with friends. These type of people are associating happiness to all the fun and excitement, they get from buying new clothes, meeting people and going to parties. They ignore the tasks which are tedious and require hard work like studies or working *i.e.* pain avoidance. In short, the objective of people following this principle is to spend maximum time and energy, having fun and minimum time in doing tedious task. *The main component to this approach are*

(i) **Positive Emotions** comes from the positive appraisal or evaluation of a situation by a person. These are the emotions of joy, gratitude, calmness, interest, hope, pride, inspiration, amusement, aim and love.

(ii) **Negative Evaluation** of a situation gives way to negative emotions like anger, shame, embarrassment, contempt, disgust, guilt, hate etc.

Human beings are always eager to increase their degree of positive emotions, whereas decreasing negative emotions.

(iii) **Life Satisfaction** It's the way one looks at his/her own life. It's the evaluation of one's own life. Human beings evaluate their life being good or bad, the baseline standards for comparison are individually different and self-created. Some one finds satisfaction in company of his/her loved ones or family while another person is satisfied living alone and being not attached to any one.

Eudemonic Well-being

The another type of well-being is eudemonic well-being. While Aristippus has contributed majorly towards **Hedonic view**. Aristotle gave an alternative that is referred as the 'Eudemonic view.' He considered hedonic happiness to be incompetent and pointed that true happiness is found in the expression of virtue. This well-being refers to effectiveness of an individual's psychological functioning in which individual realise their true potential.

Professor **Carol Ryff** gave the most important model for the study of psychological well-being under Eudemonic approach. Her model is inspired from the work of several psychologists done earlier like Erikson's Psychosocial Stages, Buhler's Basic Life Tendencies and Neugarten's Personality Changes, Maslow's Conception of Self Actualisation; Allport's conception of Maturity; Roger's Theory of Fully Functioning Person and Jung's Nation of Individuation.

All these proves to be the groundwork on which Ryff's model is based. Ryff's model is multidimensional and included six distinct components of psychological well-being. *The six main components of well-being described in this model are*

(i) **Autonomy** The people who possess this characteristic have internal locus of appraisal, high sense of self determination, evaluates self by personal standards and have personal authority. They are able to resist social pressures.

(ii) **Environmental Mastery** These people actively change, manage and shape environment according to personal needs and values. They can control complex array of external activities.

(iii) **Personal Growth** It includes the process of personal development realising one's own potential and aiming towards self actualisation. It is like working towards self improvement to enhance one's own capabilities. It is a sense of continued growth.

(iv) **Positive Relations** It comprises of having warm, loving, satisfying and trustful relationship with others. It is an ability to love and empathise with others.

For example Helping those who are in need, poor and destitute. Positive relationships of a person includes loving parents, caring spouse and colleague.

(v) **Purpose in Life** Psychologically happy individuals have goal in life, they work to find meaning and purpose of their life. They work towards their ultimate goal in life. Leaders like Mahatma Gandhi, Abraham Lincoln devoted their whole life for a purpose, which defines their existence.

(vi) **Self Acceptance** If you possess a positive attitude yourself, then you will acknowledge and accept multiple aspects of yourself including both good and bad qualities and feel positive about your past life.

The above model is one of the major model that describes the basic principles of eudemonic view of well-being. Although both views try to explain the well-being in humans happiness, yet none of it can define happiness completely. It would be wise to consider happiness as a multi dimensional phenomena which has traits from both the approaches.

Models of Well-being

Following are the models of well-being

Diener Model of Subjective Well-being

As per Diener's model which is based on the concept of **Subjective Well-being**, (SWB) subjective well-being is defined as "a persons's cognitive and affective evaluations of his or her life". SWB is a self reported measure obtained by questionnaire. This model is also called a tripartite model of subjective well-being in 1984. It has three main components which are distinct but often related to each other. *These are*

(i) **Frequent Positive Affect** An affect is called positive when the feelings, moods and emotions are pleasent (*i.e.* love, care, elation etc) and if the feelings, moods and emotions are unpleasent in nature then the affect is called *negative affect* (*e.g.* guilt, anger, disappointment etc).

(ii) **Absence of Negative Affect** Absence of negative affect means absence of feelings and moods which makes a person sad, feel low and unpleasent. Feelings of less self worth and failure are negative emotions. Absence of this leads to a happy person.

(iii) **Life Satisfaction** It is also called the global judgement of one's life and satisfaction with the specific and major life domains like work satisfaction etc. Happiness is also commonly used in regard to life satisfaction. It is also the excess of positive affect over negative. Though affective states are momentary in nature, satisfaction is almost stable over time.

Measurement of the Components of SWB

The componets of subjective well-being are measured as

- **Self Report Measures** They are the most commonly used measure to evaluate a person's SWB. In this measure effectivity can be measured by the **PANAS** (Positive Affect and Negative Affect Schedule).
- **Life Satisfaction** It is the way in which people show their emotions, feelings (moods) and how they feel about their future. It is assessed in terms of mood, satisfaction with relationships, achieved goals, self concepts and ability to cope with one's daily hassles of life. In simple terms, life satisfaction is the global judgement of one's life satisfaction and satisfaction of a person with specific life domains like job, work etc are considered to be important components of subjective well-being.

  'Happiness' when described as the satisfaction of desires and goals in one's life is also an important component of life satisfaction. Both happiness and life satisfaction are considered to be the stable factors of subjective well-being as these are consistent and remains up to one's lifetime.
- **Experience Sampling Method** In this method the respondent is beaded through a pager randomly at different point of time and the respondent has to record his feelings at that point of time when they are paged. These measurements are evaluated over a period of time such as a month or 6 weeks and then average is taken out to assess the level of positive and negative affect.

Factors Affecting Subjective Well-being

Following factors affect subjective well-being

(i) SWB is strongly associated with the personality factors described in Big Five Model given by **Costa and McCrae** 1980. Neuroticism predict poorer subjective well-being while extroversion, agreeableness, conscienti ousness and openness to experience predict higher SWB.

(ii) Genetics has a strong effect on the SWB of an individual.

(iii) Traits like trust, affiliation, optimism, emotion stability facilitates subjective well-being.

(iv) Friends, wealth, health and other social influence subjective well-being of person.

(v) Leisure satisfaction (*like exercise*) is also directly correlated with the SWB of an individual.

(vi) People who are spiritual and those who find meaning and purpose of their lives are more happier.

Apart from the above factors contributing to the SWB, Diener also differentiated between top-down and bottom- up factors important to SWB.

- **Bottom up Factors** External events, situations and demographics like marriage , race, health, wealth etc all contribute to SWB.
- **Top-down Factors** It represents individual factors such as goals and values. These factors in return also influence the external factors that influence the well-being of an individual.

Thus, it can be concluded that the integration of both top down-and-bottom up approaches leads to the better and firm understanding of well-being. None of the above approach can individually explain the concept fully.

According to **Kohn and Juster**, "The psychological debate between defining well-being according to either objective or subjective definitions continues." Perhaps suggesting the holistic impact of culture and the unfathomable attempt to develop a universal or homogeneous notion of well-being applied cross culturally.

Corey Keyes Contribution to Well-being

Keyes important work in which he emphasised the importance of complete mental health *i.e.* a psychological well-being or an absence of mental illness-the state of someone who is functioning at a satisfactory level of emotional and behavioural adjustment is notable. *Keyes is known for introducing the following concepts*

- **Flourishing** It describes mentally healthy adults. Flourishing of an individual depends on the positive emotions, engagement and interest. He/she has to find a meaning and purpose of his life and accomplish other important factors such as self-esteem, optimism, resilience, vitality, self determination and positive relationships.
- **Languishing** These are individuals those who are not mentally ill, but they show few signs of mental health.

His model for well-being is known as *The Two Continuum Model* as it holds that mental illness and mental health are related but distinct in nature.

Self-Growth

Self-growth is also known as *self development or personal growth*. It involves physical, mental, social, emotional and spiritual growth that allows a person to live a prosperous and a satisfying life within the regulations of the society. The best way to enhance self-growth is through the development of life skills.

Life skills are that skills necessary for living a harmonious and productive life. It includes feeling about self, intimacy, family, friends, community, job, leisure and spirituality. This also includes a person's awareness about his feelings, setting realistic and attainable goals for self and employing problem solving strategies.

Abraham Maslow and Carl Rogers also intertwined the concept of self-growth, in their prespective concept of Self-actualisation and Theory of Growth Potential (by Carl Rogers). Self-actualisation represents a concept of growth of an individual toward fulfillment of the highest needs.

Carl Rogers in his theory of growth potential proposed that congruent integration of the 'real self' and the 'ideal self' leads to the self-actualisation. Thus, self-growth is an important aspect of an individual well-being.

Character Strengths

Character strengths are the, "Positive traits reflected in thoughts, feelings and behaviours". Character strengths are the distinct qualities that are best in a person. As we all know that our strengths help us to improve in everything we do.

If we apply our strengths in right direction and at right places, we are able to improve our well-being and life satisfaction. Character strengths help us to bring out the best from us and enhance our level of inspiration and engagement with the work in hand.

Thus, we can say that character strengths plays an important role in the overall well-being of a person. The famous work done in the area of character strength was undertaken by Martin Seligman and his colleagues park, Peterson in 2004. They proposed the scientific classification of human strengths, while setting up of VIA (Values in Action) Institute. In 2004 there was the publication of preliminary classification of character strengths and virtues.

Seligman believed that "We will learn how to build qualities that help individuals and communities not just endure and survive but also flourish". This work of classification of human strengths and virtues can be used to assist in developing practical applications of Positive Psychology in the same manner as DSM (Diagnostic and Statistical Manual) is used to assess and facilitate research on mental disorders.

Character strengths and virtues identify six classes of virtue (*i.e.* core virtues), made up of twenty six measurable character strengths, *which are as follows*

Classification of Strengths and Virtues

Wisdom and Know-ledge	Courage	Humanity	Justice	Temperance	Transcendence
Creativity	Bravery	Love	Citizenship	Forgiveness	Hope
Curiosity	Persistance	Kindness	Fairness	Mercy	Humor
Open-minde dness	Integrity	Social Intelligence	Leadership	Humility	Excellence
Learning	Vitality			Prudence	Gratitude
Perspective	Zest			Self-control	Spirituality
Innovation					Appreciation of beauty

Criteria of Character Strength

There are multifold criterion for deciding character strength

(i) It should be manifested in range of human behaviour like thoughts, feelings or actions, so that it can be assessed.

(ii) It must be fulfilling for an individual *i.e.* it allows individual to achieve more than just absence of disease and disorder.

(iii) Each strength is morally valuable in its own, even in the absence of obvious beneficial outcomes.

(iv) The display of the strength by one, should not diminish other people nearby but elevates them.

(v) It is nurtured in larger societies as they have institutions and associated rituals for cultivating strengths and virtues.

(vi) It is absent in some individuals.

(vii) Present in famous people.

(viii) Existence on consensually recognised paragons of virtue.

(ix) Observable in child prodigies .

(x) A final criterion is that the strength is arguably undimensional and not able to be decomposed into other strengths in the classification.

Apart from the development of above taxonomy VIA project also developed assessment tools for the study of character strengths like VIA-IS, (Value in Action Inventory Strength) VIA-RTO (Value in Action Rising to the Occasion Inventory), Value in Action Inventory of Strength for Youth (VIA-youth). Notably, the VIA-IS is the tool by which people can identify and capitalise on their own strength.

The classification of character strength and virtues has a major application in the field of therapy and in promoting well-being among humans. This classification helps people to recognise their own strength and build upon them. It is in alignment with the Positive Psychology movement which aims at making people life more fulfilling rather than just treating mental disorders.

Resilience

Resilience is described as an ability to recover or return to the level of function present before adversity occurred with only minimal reactions following that exposure.

The present world is full of distress and miseries like war, poverty, aggression etc. None of us will ever choose to have a trauma or distress in our life, but at times when one has to face a trauma many hidden virtues of our personality comes into action. One has no clue till that, he/she ever possessed these skills or strengths to face such a crisis and emerge as a survivor.

The 'phenomenon' where a person develops psychological and behavioural capabilities that allows him/her to remain calm during chaos, and move ahead in life without sustaining long term negative impact of this trauma is called *'Resilience'*.

It is the ability to bounce back from an adversity and a way to fight back. It takes a lot of courage, creativity and strength to be resilient in life. It's a way one survives tragic and traumatic life event, indeed its a way of survival. The way one survived his/her trauma is nothing to feel ashamed for, yet it is something to be celebrated.

Resilience often gives birth to a positive approach in one's life like, people appreciate life after a horrendous car crash, or surviving any life threatening disease like cancer or tumor. It results in greater optimism, positive affect and satisfaction. The personal qualities of becoming more stronger, wiser and accepter is also strengthened in human persona.

Post-Traumatic Growth

A person becomes positively more stronger, wiser, loving, compassionate accepting and more capable after a traumatic life event is called *Post-Traumatic Growth* (PTG). It is just opposite to Post-Traumatic Stress Disorder (PTSD), where traumatic life events leads to stress, anxiety and other negative effects in life.

The term PTG was coined by Richard G. Tedeschi and Lawrence G Calhoun. They explained that growth does not occur as a result of trauma, rather it is the result of the struggle with the new reality after any traumatic life event. It also does not happen in all people facing trauma. It requires an individual's abilities to adapt to highly negative sets of circumstances that can put high levels of distress which typically has unpleasant psychological reactions. It is an individual struggle with the new reality in the aftermath of trauma that is crucial in determining the extent to which post traumatic growth occurs.

Few prediction of post-traumatic growth are

(i) **Spirituality** High correlation with post-traumatic growth.
(ii) **Social Support** It also changes our pathological response to stress in the brain.
(iii) **Acceptance Coping** An ability to accept situations that cannot be changed is crucial for PTG.
(iv) **Emotional Disclosure** Still under investigation that it leads to PTG or not.
(v) **Extroversion and Openness to Experience**

Accorting to Richard Tedeschi and Lawrence Calhoun their clients have found growth in five main areas

(i) Personal strength
(ii) Deeper relationship with others
(iii) New perspectives in life
(vi) Appreciation of life
(v) Spirituality.

They gave a model for Post-Traumatic Growth in individuals and families.

They estimated at least 90% of trauma survivors experience at least one aspect of PTG. This also shows a positive side of human psyche which has a natural inclination towards growth rather than stress.

But one important aspect is that growth always comes from an individual's own actions and will to fight with challenges in life. The vital point is, "It is how we work with suffering, so that it leads to awakening of the heart and going beyond the habitual views and actions that perpetuate suffering".

EXAM BASED QUESTIONS

1 Well-being implies
(a) the absence of illness
(b) emotional, psychological and mental health
(c) an external locus of control
(d) Both b and c

2 Well-being is a condition of an affect or ....
(a) group
(b) personality
(c) self acceptance
(d) happiness

3 Well-being of a person is diverse and inter connected between his physical, mental and
(a) social well-being
(b) vitality
(c) environmental well-being
(d) pleasure

4 Who gave the concept of 'flow' in Positive Psychology?
(a) Martin Seligman
(b) Mihaly Csikszentmihalyi
(c) Aristotle
(d) Carol Ryff

5 Which one of the following is not an element of well-being model proposed by Martin Seligman?
(a) Positive well-being (b) Engagement
(c) Relationship (d) Meaning

6 The following is a factor in psychological well-being as opposed to social well-being
(a) Mastering environmental challenges
(b) Self control and wellness
(c) Manageability and control
(d) All of the above

7 When did Martin Seligman gave his famous theory of well-being?
(a) 2011 (b) 2009 (c) 2012 (d) 2008

8 What did Martin Seligman considered most important to attain a happy and satisfied life?
(a) Engagement with work
(b) Purpose
(c) Using of signature strengths
(d) Accomplishments

9 Emotions like pride and awe constitute which element of PERMA theory by Seligman?
(a) Engagement (b) Meaning
(c) Accomplishments (d) Positive emotions

10 'A' in PERMA theory by Seligman stands for
(a) attitude (b) affect
(c) accomplishments (d) autonomy

11 Seligman believed that to find meaning of one's life one must be attached to something .... than just one's life.
(a) larger (b) outside
(c) wide (d) internal

12 PERMA stands for
(a) Positive Emotion, Engagement, Relationship, Meaning, Accomplishment
(b) Positive Emotion, Engagement, Resilience, Meaning, Accomplishment
(c) Permanent Engagement, Resilience, Meaning, Accomplishment
(d) Positive Emotion, Exitement, Resilience, Meaning, Accomplishment

13 Which of the following are types of well-being
(a) Hedonic (b) Eudemonic
(c) Both a and b (d) None of these

14 Component of Hedonic well-being consists of
(a) Positive emotion
(b) Negative evaluation
(c) Life satisfaction
(d) All of these

15 To whom credits goes for originating concept of Eudemonic well-being?
(a) Socrates (b) Aristotle (c) Plato (d) Aristippus

16 Two main approaches taken to understand well-being are based on the principal of
(a) balance between positive and negative affect, self acceptance.
(b) distinguishing positive and negative affects, life satisfaction.
(c) optimal occurance of emotions, positive growth.
(d) mental peace, positive relationships.

17 Which of the following is not one of Ryff's fundamental elements of psychological well-being?
(a) Life purpose (b) Social growth
(c) Positive relatedness (d) Self acceptance

18 The part of my behavioural facilitation system that determines how I react to a good class grade, a raise at work or my confidence is called
(a) Positive affectivity (b) Social affectivity
(c) Emotions (d) Over reaction

19 According to Ryff (1989), which of the following statements best describes individuals who have a strong sense of environmental mastery?
(a) They see self as improving.
(b) They see self as developing.
(c) They see self as controlling an array of external activities.
(d) They see self as independent and self determining.

20 Which of the following best describes an individuals who is in a low positive affect state?
(a) By feelings and emotions of calm, relaxed and at rest.
(b) By feelings and emotions of enthusiastic and excited.
(c) By feelings and emotions of being distressed, fearful.
(d) By feelings and emotions of being dull, sleepy and sluggish.

21 Who gave the concept of good life?
(a) Martin Seligman (b) Carol Ryff
(c) Diener (d) Easterlin

22 According to Ryff, the striving for perfection that represents the realisation of one's true potential is
(a) Eudemonic well-being (b) Subjective well-being
(c) Hedonic well-being (d) Psychological well-being

23 Carol Ryff's model of Psychological Well-being consist of how many components?
(a) 4 (b) 5 (c) 6 (d) 7

24 Which among the following is not included in the component of the psychological well-being?
(a) Anatomy (b) Purpose in life
(c) Personal growth (d) Self-actualisation

25 Who gave Tripartite model of well-being?
(a) Diener (b) Carol Ryff
(c) Martin Seligman (d) Guttman

26 In top down perspective of SWB, ... personality traits influence a person's perception of events in a positive or negative manner.
(a) internal (b) external
(c) stable (d) dynamic

27 Bottom up approaches of SWB are based on the idea that happiness results from the fulfillment of
(a) secondary needs (b) basic human needs
(c) safety needs (d) higher order needs

28 Optimism is a feeling where a person feels that more .... things will happen in future than ....
(a) bad, good
(b) negative, positive
(c) good, bad
(d) failure, success

29 Diener Model is associated with which of the following?
(a) Well-being (b) Growth
(c) Resilience (d) Trauma

30 Diener Model of subjective well-being consist of how many component?
(a) One (b) Two (c) Three (d) Four

31 Income and personality traits both have an equivalent role to play in the SWB of an individual. Whose work is emphasised in above philosophy?
(a) Diener (b) Kaufman
(c) Seligman (d) Frankl

32 Subjective well-being is described as the person's ...... and ..... evaluations of his/her life.
(a) cognitive and affective (b) individual and group
(c) social and cultural (d) ethnic and religious

33 The concept of subjective well-being is influenced by ...... perspective of well-being.
(a) hedonic (b) eudemonic
(c) positive affect (d) Both a and c

34 Affectivity in subjective well-being can be measured by
(a) ESM (b) Projective test
(c) Self Report Measure (d) PANAS

35 Empirical investigations consider subjective well-being to be
(a) frequency of positive mood
(b) an experience of overall life satisfaction
(c) satisfaction with particular domains of life
(d) All of the above

36 The 'Big five' personality traits are strongly correlated with subjective well-being measures
(a) Extraversion (positively) and Neuroticism (negatively)
(b) Openness (positively) and Neuroticism (negatively)
(c) Agreeableness (positively) and Openness (negatively)
(d) None of the above

37 The theory of Growth Potential was propounded by
(a) Diener (b) Martin Seligman
(c) Carl Rogers (d) Richard Tedeschi

38 Who wrote the book 'Character Strengths and Virtues (CSV)'?
(a) Ryff, Seligman
(b) Chirstopher Peterson, Seligman
(c) Seligman, Guttman
(d) Seligman, Keyes

39 What was the main aim behind the development of CSV model?
(a) The organisation of virtue and strengths
(b) Provide a theoretical framework for practical application of positive psychology
(c) Scientific study of strength and virtues
(d) All of the above

40 Forgiveness character strength comes under which core virtue?
(a) Justice (b) Humanity
(c) Wisdom and knowledge (d) Temperance

41 Social Intelligence character strength comes under which core virtue?
(a) Humanity (b) Temperance
(c) Courage (d) Transcendence

42 What is the impact of the character strength of an individual on the character strength of others?
(a) Positive Impact (b) Negative Impact
(c) Neutral (d) Mixed Impact

43 .... means to remain calm during chaos and move ahead in life without sustaining long term negative effort.
(a) Trauma (b) Escape
(c) Management (d) Resilience

44 Tedeschi and Calhoun provided evidence for a phenomena they described as a positive psychological change experience as a result of the struggle with highly challenging life circumstances. What is the name of the phenomena?
(a) Negative Stress Positive Outcome
(b) Kindling-Behavioural Sensitisation
(c) The Healing Effect
(d) Post Traumatic Growth

45 Growth post trauma would be associated to a person's well-being and .... psychological distress.
(a) increased (b) decreased
(c) no effect (d) global

46 Who is responsible for coining term Post-Traumatic Growth?
(a) Richard G Tedeshi (b) Lawrence G Calhoun
(c) Both a and b (d) Martin Seligmen

47 Where does the difference comes between thriving and resilience?
(a) Level of functioning before trauma
(b) Fighting the trauma
(c) Recovery point
(d) Suffering caused by trauma

48 Pick the condition that do not constitute the well-being of an individual.
1. Physical vitality
2. Pleasure
3. Sense of accomplishment
4. Egoistic

Codes
(a) 1 and 2 (b) 1 and 3
(c) Only 4 (d) 2 and 3

49 Well-being of a person can refer to a series of possible states. Which of the following do not describe well-being effectively?

1. Virtue 2. Cognitive structure
3. Objectivity 4. Emotional judgement

Codes

(a) Only 1 (b) Only 2
(c) Only 3 (d) All define well-being

50 Which disciplines of psychology are critical in study of well-being?

1. Developmental Psychology
2. Personality Psychology
3. Clinical Psychology
4. Cognitive Psychology

Codes

(a) Only 1 (b) Only 2 (c) 1 and 3 (d) 1, 2 and 3

51 Which factors are taken into account by Eudemonic approach to well-being ?

1. Psychological well-being
2. Social well-being
3. Emotional well-being
4. Physical well-being

Codes

(a) and 2 (b) 1, 2 and 3
(c) 2 and 3 (d) None of these

52 What is the main principle behind the hedonic view of happiness?

1. Increase in positive emotions over negative ones
2. Increase in pleasure over pain
3. Life satisfaction
4. Psycho-social happiness is very important

Codes

(a) Only 1 (b) Both 1 and 2
(c) 1, 2 and 3 (d) None of these

53 Which Psychologist's work has not inspired Carol Ryff model of Happiness?

1. Erikson 2. Buhler
3. New garten 4. Freud

Codes

(a) 1 and 2 (b) 2 and 3
(c) Only 4 (d) 1 and 4

54 Personal growth as described in the model by Carol Ryff is synonymous to

1. personal happiness
2. personal well-being
3. self actualisation
4. personal satisfaction

Codes

(a) 1 and 2 (b) 1 and 3 (c) 3 and 4 (d) Only 3

55 Post traumatic growth occurs only in

1. individual facing trauma
2. whole society
3. near ones of those facing trauma
4. friends and collegues

Codes

(a) Only 1 (b) Only 2
(c) 1 and 3 (d) 1, 3 and 4

56 Which personality trait have as positive impact on post traumatic growth?

1. Openness to experience
2. Consciousness
3. Extraversion
4. Agree ableness

Codes

(a) 1 and 2 (b) 1, 2 and 3
(c) 3 and 4 (d) All of these

57 Post-Traumatic Growth (PTG) is a result of which factors?

1. Adversity 2. Trauma
3. Adaptation to circumstances
4. Struggle of an individual

Codes

(a) 1 and 2 (b) 1 and 3
(c) 3 and 4 (d) 2 and 3

58 Personal well-being can be defined in terms of

1. how satisfied we are with our lives
2. our day to day emotional experiences
3. happiness and anxiety
4. personal finance

Codes

(a) 1 and 2 (b) 2 and 3
(c) 1 and 4 (d) All of these

59 Match the following

List I (Perspective of Well-being)		List II (Basic Concept)
A. Bottom up	1.	Global judgement
B. Top down	2.	Accumulation, happy experiences
C. Life satisfaction	3.	Emotions, moods
D. Affective balance	4.	Personality factors

Codes

	A	B	C	D
(a)	4	1	2	3
(b)	1	4	2	3
(c)	2	4	1	3
(d)	2	1	4	3

60 Match the following

List I (Psychologists)		List II (Main Contributions)
A. Richard Tedeschi	1.	Character and values strengths
B. Diener	2.	Big five personality traits
C. Martin Seligman	3.	SWB model
D. Costa and McCare	4.	PTG model

Codes

	A	B	C	D
(a)	4	3	1	2
(b)	1	3	4	2
(c)	4	2	1	3
(d)	2	4	1	3

61 Match the following

List I (Components of Post Trauma Growth)	List II (Individual Model)
A. Stressor event	1. Family
B. Challenges	2. Writing /talking
C. Rumination	3. Threat
D. Social content	4. High magnitude that disturbs status quo

Codes

	A	B	C	D
(a)	1	2	3	4
(b)	4	2	3	1
(c)	2	3	1	4
(d)	4	3	2	1

Directions (Q. Nos. 62-74) *In the question given below are two statements labelled as Assertion (A) and Reason (R). In the context of the two statements, which one of the following is correct?*

Codes

(a) Both A and R are true and R is the correct explanation of A
(b) Both A and R are true, but R is not the correct explanation of A
(c) A is true, but R is false
(d) A is false, but R is true

62 **Assertion** (A) Subjective well-being is an individual's experience of affective reactions and cognitive judgements.

Reason (R) Well-being has a more wide-ranging description than happiness.

63 **Assertion** (A) Well-being is defined on the basis emotions one feels about self and others.

Reason (R) Emotional component refers to what individual feels about her life satisfaction in terms of family life, work, life as a whole etc.

64 **Assertion** (A) A person exhibiting high sense of well-being will have a positive affect.

Reason (R) The affective components is associated with emotions, feelings and moods.

65 **Assertion** (A) While measuring SWB, affective balance and life satisfaction must be calculated individually.

Reason (R) Self report is not considered an efficient measure of well-being.

66 **Assertion** (A) Self report method to measure well-being is considered efficient enough for estimating the correct measure of well-being.

Reason (R) Self report measures have an issue over validity thus cannot be trusted fully.

67 **Assertion** (A) All human beings seeks happiness, it is an universal factor.

Reason (R) There exist cultural differences on the perception of happiness.

68 **Assertion** (A) Happiness is also an act of giving.

Reason (R) Happiness was never considered to be an passive act of joy.

69 **Assertion** (A) Personality traits of a person also plays a very important role in the subjective well-being component.

Reason (R) People who are introvert have high SWB as they are concerned about self and do not get much involved in other's distress.

70 **Assertion** (A) SWB is not a single entity, it comprise of various factors like personality traits, emotions, cognitions of an individual.

Reason (R) All factors of SWB are dependent on each other.

71 **Assertion** (A) Well-being of an individual have an impact on his/her psychosomatic functions.

Reason (R) It does not affect their immunity but makes their brain strong.

72 **Assertion** (A) Happy people have high sense of self acceptance.

Reason (R) They try to work more consistently on their weakness and flaws.

73 **Assertion** (A) Happy parents give birth to happy children.

Reason (R) SWB is influenced by genetic disposition of an individual.

74 **Assertion** (A) Seeking happiness is a universal phenomena, but have cultural differences.

Reason (R) Cultural differences arise because of the education and economic infrastructure of a country.

Direction (Q. Nos. 75-78) *Read the passage given below and answer the following questions.*

Have you ever wondered why some people seeem to remain calm in the face of disaster while others appear to come undone? People that can keep their cool have what psychologists call resilience or an ability to cope with problems and setbacks.

Resilient people are able to utilise their skills and strengths to cope and recover from problems and challenges. These problems may include job loss, financial problems, illness, natural disasters, medical emergencies, divorce or the death of a loved one. Instead of falling into despair or hiding from problems with unhealthy coping strategies, resilient people face life's difficulties head-on. This does not mean that they experience less distress , grief or anxiety than other people do. It means that they handle such difficulties in ways that foster strength and growht. In many cases, they may emerge even stronger than they were before.

Those who lack this resilience may instead become over whelmed by such experiences. They may dwell on problems and use unhealthy coping mechanisms to deal with life's challenge. Disappointment or failure might drive them to unhealthy, destructive or even dangerous behaviours. These individuals are slower to recover from setbacks and may experience more psychological distress as a result.

Resilience does not eliminate stress or erase life's difficulties. People who possess this resilience don't see life through rose-coloured lenses. They understand that setbacks happen and that sometimes life is hard and painful. They still experience the emotional pain, grief and sense of loss that comes after a tragedy, but their mental outlook allows them to work through such feelings and recover.

75 How people react to any disaster?

(a) Some people remain calm
(b) Some people come under stress
(c) Both a and b
(d) None of the above

76 How resilient people are able to stand in front of disaster and recover quickly?

(a) Utilise their skills and strength
(b) Resilient people are stronger than distaster
(c) They are financially stable
(d) None of the above

77 *In the questions given below are two statements labelled as Assertion (A) and reason (R). In the context of the two statements, which one of the following is correct?*

Assertion (A) Resilient people are able to cope and recover from problem.

Reason (R) Resilient people utilise unhealthy mechanism to deal with life challenges.

Codes

(a) Both A and R are true and R is the correct explanation of A
(b) Both A and R are true, but R is not the correct explanation of A
(c) A is true, but R is false
(d) A is false, but R is true

78 Which of the following statements is true about life from the point view of Resilient person?

(a) There are no setbacks in life
(b) Sometime life is hard and painful
(c) Life is full of happiness
(d) There is no sorrow in life

ANSWERS

1 (c)	2 (d)	3 (a)	4 (b)	5 (a)	6 (d)	7 (b)	8 (c)	9 (d)	10 (c)
11 (a)	12 (a)	13 (c)	14 (d)	15 (b)	16 (b)	17 (b)	18 (a)	19 (c)	20 (c)
21 (c)	22 (b)	23 (c)	24 (d)	25 (a)	26 (c)	27 (b)	28 (b)	29 (a)	30 (d)
31 (a)	32 (a)	33 (a)	34 (d)	35 (d)	36 (a)	37 (c)	38 (b)	39 (d)	40 (d)
41 (a)	42 (c)	43 (d)	44 (d)	45 (b)	46 (c)	47 (a)	48 (c)	49 (c)	50 (a)
51 (a)	52 (b)	53 (c)	54 (a)	55 (a)	56 (c)	57 (c)	58 (d)	59 (c)	60 (c)
61 (d)	62 (a)	63 (a)	64 (a)	65 (c)	66 (a)	67 (a)	68 (b)	69 (c)	70 (c)
71 (a)	72 (a)	73 (a)	74 (a)	75 (c)	76 (a)	77 (c)	78 (b)		

Health

Health is a state of physical, mental and social well-being in which disease and infirmity are absent. People view it from only physiological point of view but it has psychological aspect also. Psychology plays a prominent role in understanding different aspects of health.

Concept of Health

The term *Health* is frequently used by most of us in our day-to-day life. We all wish to live a long, healthy and a prosperous life. Indeed to remain healthy and physically active is one of the major goal in a person's life. Today, the general masses have become quite aware of the benefit of a good health, thus, they keep a track on their eating habits, exercising etc.

In modern times enormous information regarding the benefits of regular exercising and maintaining a health promoting routine is available on internet and is accessible to all. This has created a realisation that indeed 'Health is wealth'.

Majority of us believe that health is merely absence of any disease or illness in our body. But this is a very narrow viewpoint of health. Health is defined by **World Health Organisation** (WHO), as "A state of complete physical, mental and social well-being and not merely absence of disease or infirmity". The above definition of health gives a wider perspective to the concept of 'Health'. It includes the mental and social well-being of an individual in determining the health of a person.

Advent of Health in the Field of Psychology

Since the evolution of mankind, the issue of health has always remained a major concern for survival. Societies and cultures all over the world have their own traditional and modern practices to improve human health. In India too practices like Ayurveda, Unani, Yoga and Naturopathy, Siddha and Homeopathy have been practiced since ages.

But until 19th century most model in health were bio-medical in nature, which believed that disease either come from outside the body and causes physical changes in the body or are present because of genetic factors.

In this Chapter

The causes of disease were chemical imbalances, bacteria and viruses. According to this model individuals are not seen responsible for disease rather they were regarded as **victims**. Medical professionals treat the disease through surgery, chemotherapy etc.

Bio-medical model follows an all or none principle in which one is either healthy or ill, there is no continuum in between. Body was regarded as being distinct from mind and mind just act as a harbour to feelings and emotions, where as body is a physical matter. Any change happening in either of the two is independent of the other. This model never gave weightage to psychological cause of illness, although it considered psychological consequences to illness like heart attack can cause trauma, but stress was never considered to be the cause of heart diseases.

But with the advent of 20th century and emergence of psychosomatic medicines in response to **Freud** analysis of connection between mind and physical illness and secondly the rise of behavioural health, challenged the notion that claims mind and body being different. Latest development is that of behavioural medicine which is an amalgam of elements from the behavioural science disciplines psychology, sociology, health education and focuses on health, treatment and illness prevention, as described by Schwartz and Weiss.

This field publicised the use of **behaviour therapy** and **behaviour modification** for the treatment and prevention of various disease like high stress, addictive and compulsive behaviour, phobias, depression etc. It also became clear that illness like psychosis and neurosis are not treatable alone by medicines, it needs the intervention of behaviour and cognitive therapies. Hence, inclusion of psychology in the area of health studies became important with the change from just treating the illness to prevention and intervention of illness.

Health Psychology

Health psychology emerged in the 1970s as a result of urbanisation and industrialisation. There was a drastic change in the life style and the nature of disease affecting people like people were engaging more in smoking, drinking, overeating and focusing less on exercises. Stress was more and coping skills depleted rapidly. All this had led to the more frequent cases of heart disease, cancer etc. which were taking human lives.

At this time health psychology which studies the maintenance and promotion of health and prevention of dysfunctional behaviour leading to illness became quite important. It also challenged the notion of mind-body split and emphasised, that mind has an important role in both causing and treating human illness.

Health psychology has a multidimensional view which takes into account all factors like biological, environmental, psychological and socio-cultural, which influence human health and prevents illness. It also studies factors of social and psychological human structure which helps in better coping with illness and factor causing it.

Recently health psychologists have recognised that many deadly disease like coronory heart disease, cancer etc. have social and psychological factors contributing to it. Thus, we can hereby say that this field is wide and has lot of practical application in improving human health and assisting in reducing stress.

Perspective of Health Psychology

Health psychology claims that illness is caused by a combination of biological, psychological and social factors. An important model to elaborate on this approach was developed by **Engel**, called *Bio-Psychosocial Model of Health.* Health psychology approves this model and also believes that mind and body cannot be separated while studying health related processes. This model includes 'bio' contributing factors like genetics, viruses, bacteria and structural defects.

The psychological aspects of health and illness were described in terms of cognitions, emotions and behaviours. Some of the major researches in the area of health psychology focus on the health promoting and health compromising behaviour, identification of such behaviour helps in the better planning of intervention plan for various illness.

Health Promoting and Health Compromising Behaviours

Behaviour of an individual in influenced by several personal, psychological, environmental and socio-cultural factors.

Health Promoting Behaviours

Health Promoting behaviours are those adaptive behaviours that an individual exhibit in an effort to improve or maintain positive health. These behaviours if followed leads to the promotion and maintenance of good health and prevention of disease.

Few health promoting behaviours are listed below
- Improving sleep habits
- Having balanced and nutritious diet
- Regular physical exercise
- Managing stress
- Less or no smoking
- Minimise sugar consumption
- Avoid processed food and red meat
- Avoid excess calorie intake
- No substance abuse

Health Compromising Behaviours

These are those behaviours which if followed leads to negative impact on the psychological, social and physical functioning of an individual. Peer pressure is seen as one of the major reasons why one indulges in such negative behaviours.

List of Health Compromising behaviours are
- Smoking
- Drinking excess alcohol
- Substance abuse
- Practicing unsafe sex
- Unhealthy life Style
- Inability to cope with stress
- Lack of sleep, sleep disturbances

Theories and Models Describing Health Behaviour

There are several theories which illustrates the causes behind a particular behaviour and also shows how behaviour changes happens in a person. *The theories and models describing health behaviour are as follows*

Health Promoting Model

This model believes that each individual has unique personal characteristics and experiences that affect subsequent actions. The set of variables for behavioural specific knowledge and affect have important motivational significance. Basically its a concept that focus on complex bio-psychosocial processes which leads to the engagement of a person in health promoting behaviours.

Assumptions of the Health Promotion Model

The assumptions of health promotion model are
- Individuals seek to actively regulate their behaviours.
- Individuals interact with their environment, progressively transform the environment and get transformed over time.
- Health professionals constitute a part of the interpersonal environment, which exerts influence on person throughout their life span.
- Self initiated reconfiguration of person-environment interactive pattern is essential to change behaviour.

Major Concepts of Health Promotion Model

The major concepts of health promotion model are
- **Personal Factors** It includes **biological factors** like age, gender, Body Mass Index (BMI), pubertal status, aerobic capacity, strength, agility or balance etc.
- **Personal Psychological Factors** self esteem, self motivation, personal competence etc.
- **Personal Socio-Cultural Factors** are race, ethnicity, acculturation, education and socio-economic status.

Other concepts which are included in the model are
- **Perceived Benefits of Action** Anticipated outcome of health behaviour.
- **Perceived Barriers to Action** Perceptions of the blocks, hurdles and personal costs of undertaking health behaviour.
- **Perceived Self Efficacy** Personal capability to organise and execute a particular health behaviour with self confidence.
- **Activity Related Affect** Subjective feeling occurring prior to, during and following a specific health behaviour.
- **Interpersonal Influences** Family, peers, norms, social support, role models, perceptions concerning the behaviours, beliefs or attitudes of others in regard to engaging in a specific health behaviour.
- **Situational Influences** Options, demand characteristics, aesthetics, perceptions of the compatibility of life or the environment with engaging in specific health behaviour.
- **Commitment to a Plan of Action** Intention to carry out a particular health behaviour and identification of strategies to do so successfully.
- **Immediate Competing Demands and Preferences** Alternative behaviour that intrude into consciousness as possible courses of action just prior to the intended occurrence of a planned health behaviour.

Theoretical Prepostion of Health Promotion Model

The major theoretical proposition of Health Promotion Model are

(i) Prior behaviour and inherited acquired characteristic influence beliefs and enactment of health promoting behaviour.

(ii) Engaging in behaviour that derive personal valued benefit is always of interest.

(iii) Perceived barriers can constrain commitment to action.

(iv) Perceived competence or self efficacy to execute a given behaviour increases the likelihood of commitment to actual and actual performance of the behaviour.

(v) Greater perceived self efficacy results in perceived barrier to a specific health behaviour.

(vi) When any behaviour is associated with a positive feeling or emotion, the probability that the behaviour will re-occur and increased will be more.

(vii) Individual is more likely to engage in a health promoting behaviour if he/she observes others, mainly people whom he/she likes or follows, engage in the same behaviour. Also the expectations by the 'significant' others regarding health behaviour and their perceived support too leads to increase in the chances of engaging in health promoting behaviour.

(viii) Families, peers and health care providers are important sources of interpersonal influence that can increase or decrease commitment to and engagement in health promoting behaviour.

(ix) Situational influences in the external environment can increase or decrease commitment to or participation in health promoting behaviour.

(x) The greater the commitment to a specific plan of action the more likely health promoting behaviours are maintained over time.

(xi) Commitment to a plan of action is less likely to result in the desired behaviour when competing demands over which persons have little control require immediate action.

(xii) Commitment to a plan of action is less likely to result is the desired behaviour when other actions are more attractive and thus preferred over the target behaviour.

(xiii) Persons can modify cognitions, affect , interpersonal influences and situational influences to create incentives for health promoting behaviour.

This model defines person as a bio-psychosocial organism who works actively on his environment and transform it accordingly. This model also give due importance to social cognitive theory, as HPM strongly suggest that for people to alter their behaviour, it is important to alter their thinking. This model identifies factors that influence health behaviour. It helps in understanding the major determinants of health behaviours and assist professionals in behavioural counselling to promote healthy lifestyles.

Transtheoretical Model (Stages of Change)

The stages of change model also called the *Trans theoretical model of behaviour* was developed by Prochaska and DiClemente. This model describes the process involved in behavioural change by synthesising 18 therapies. This model describes behaviour change as dynamic in nature, rather than all or none process. *It has six stages of behaviour change which may or may not occur in linear fashion.*

(i) **Pre Contemplation** Thinking prior to and during the course of indulging in unhealthy behaviour like over eating. I love food so I shall eat as much as I want.

(ii) **Contemplation** Thought process which comes after realising negative outcomes of unhealthy behaviour. *For example*. I am getting fat. I shall eat in limit.

(iii) **Preparation** What a person tries to do to control his/her unhealthy behaviour? *For example*. I will eat only homemade food and avoid fatty food and drinks.

(iv) **Action** In the stage, people who have recently changed their behaviour and intended to keep forward with that behaviour. *For example* I have stopped eating junk food.

(v) **Maintenance** In this stage, people intend to maintain the behaviour change forward. *For example* I regularly take nutritious food.

(vi) **Termination** In the stage, people have no desise to return to their unhealthy behaviour.

This model also examines how we ascertain the costs and benefits of a particular behaviour and also at different stages a person focus either on the costs of a behaviour (Eating less will make me feel hungry) or the benefits (Reducing weight will make me look more fit and good).

Health Belief Model

The Health Belief Model breaks down health decisions into a series of stages and offers a catalogue of variables that influences health action, it does not provide a model of how exactly these operate. In the Health Belief Model the likelihood that a person will follow a preventive behaviour is influenced by their subjective weighing of the costs and benefits of the action.

Health Belief Model (Rosenstock 1950)	
Perceived Suspectibility	What percentage of individuals believe that they have a chance of getting a specific health condition
Perceived Barriers	The road blocks or threats individual to address the health condition
Perceived Benefits	The individuals believe taking action to address the health condition
Cue to action (Trigger for prompting engagement in health promoting behaviours)	External or internal factors that stimulate individuals to act (based on their perceptions) *e.g.* mass media, newspaper articles
Self Efficacy	The level of confidence individuals have their ability to act.
Perceived seriousness	How seriously individuals believe that certain condition will affect their life situation

The Protection Motivation Theory

It was developed by Rogers. It added additional factors to health belief model. It added response effectiveness (changing my eating habits would improve my health), Self efficacy (I am sure I can follow a nutritious diet plan) as related to coping appraisal (apprising individual themselves) and added fear, severity and suspectibility as threat appraisal (apprising an outside threat). The two types of information sources *i.e.* environmental (*e.g.* verbal persuasion, observational learning etc.) and intrapersonal (*e.g.* prior experience) influences the five components of the theory.

Theory of Reasoned Action

It is proposed by Martin Fishbein and Icek Ajzen According to this theory behavioural intention is the predictor of behaviour. This theory states intention is determined jointly by attitudes toward the behaviour and perceived social pressures to engage in a behaviour.

The three major elements or factors of behavioural intention are

(i) **Individual's Attitude** or personal opinion, on whether a specific behaviour is goods or bad, positive or negative, favourable or otherwise.

(ii) **Subjective Norms** These are the ways in which the perceptions of relevant groups or individuals such as family members, friends and peers may affect one's performance of the behaviour.

Azjen defines subjective norms as the " Perceived social pressure to perform or not perform the behaviour".

(iii) **Important Norms** Beside the attitude and subjects norm, important norm is social group is also an important indicator towards measurable behaviour.It is the social norm that is believed by society or social environment where the person lives.

This theory claims the intentions comes before behaviour and are the main predictor of a behaviour. Intentions are formulated by attitudes the person have toward a behaviour and subjective norms. Application of the theory can be used for promoting positive behaviours like quitting tobacco, having safe sex etc.

Theory of Planned Behaviour

This theory is an extension of the Theory of Reasoned Action proposed in 1980. As we know that Theory of Reasoned Action (TRA) explain all behaviour over which one can exert self control. The key component of TRA is that behaviour is the result of behavioural intentions, which are influenced largely by attitude a person holds, about the expected outcome of a behaviour and subjective norms about the behaviour.

The Theory of planned behaviour states that behaviour is the outcome of several factors like

- **Behavioural Beliefs** Beliefs about the likely consequences of the behaviour.
- **Normative Beliefs** Beliefs about the normative expectations of others.
- **Control Beliefs** Beliefs about the presence of factors that may facilitate or impede performance of the behaviour.

Consequently, **Behavioural beliefs** produce a favourable or unfavourable attitude toward behaviour, normative belief result in perceived social pressure of subjective norms and control belief give rise to behavioural control.

In short the more favourable the attitude and subjective norm and greater the perceived control, the stronger is the person's intention to perform the behaviour. This theory can be applied to change health compromising behaviour into health promoting behaviour.

These were the important models and theories of behaviour change. Though it needs a lot of efforts by an individual for a behaviour change but shifting from health compromising to health promoting behaviour is an essential step which one must undertake in order to live a health, long, life free from disease.

Lifestyle And Chronic Disease

Lifestyle as described in psychology dictionary, means "the way in which a group or an individual prefers to live, which then becomes characteristic of that group or person". The term lifestyle was coined by the famous psychologist **Alfred Adler** with the meaning of "a person's basic character as established early in childhood".

The lifestyle of an individual is related to both his/her demographic variables like age, gender, race, community in which he/she lives and also psychological variables like personal values, preferences and out looks.

With the recent urbanisation and technological advancement the lifestyle of humans have changed drastically since last few years. Busy work schedules and the drift from family environment has made people more vulnerable to poor lifestyle choices, such as smoking, over use of alcohol, lack of nutritious diet, increase in the amount of fatty and sugary food in our meals, eating more of processed food, overeating and under exercising, are all making the present generation more prone to chronic disease like diabetes, hypertension and coronary heart disease.

Diabetes

Diabetes is a condition that impairs the body's ability to process blood glucose, known as *blood sugar*. Glucose is important for our body as it provides energy to the cells and aid in the making of muscles and tissues. Glucose is the main source of fuel for brain.

There are two types of diabetes Type 1 and Type 2. The causes behind both types are different, but in both types, there is an excess sugar in blood. The excess amount of blood sugar leads to serious health problems.

Some of the common signs and symptoms of type 1 and Type 2 diabetes are

- Increased thirst
- Extreme hunger
- Presence of Ketones in the urine
- Irritability
- Show healing sores
- Frequent urination
- Unexplained weight loss
- Fatigue
- Blurred vision
- Frequent infections

When a person is diagnosed with diabetes, he/she visit a specialist doctor who prescribe him/her medicines to control diabetes. But, in addition to medications, healthy lifestyle choices remain essential for the efficient management of diabetes.

These changes include the adoption of a healthy and active lifestyle like

- **Physical Activity** Engaging in $2\frac{1}{2}$ hrs each week of moderate intensity physical activity or 1 hour 15 minutes of high intensity workout is must.
- **Weight Loss** A person who is over weight has difficulty is controlling diabetes, thus losing weight is very important for diabetes management.
- **Nutritious Diet** A healthy and nutritious diet helps in the management of diabetes. Inclusion of food which are rich in proteins, seeds like fenugreek, flax seeds, nuts like almonds, walnuts etc. and avoiding food which have high cholestrol and drinks like coca-cola etc. will help in the better management of diabetes.
- **Stress Management** As its a known fact that stress can greatly affect insulin resistance and blood sugar levels. Thus, stress management is very important to control diabetes. It can be done through yoga, pranayam, mediatton etc. Regular exercise also acts as an efficient stress buster.

Thus, we conclude that several lifestyle changes like managing weight, following healthy lifestyle, staying alert, regular health checkups and regular monitoring by having regular blood test, lipid profile etc. management of diabetes is not tough.

Hypertension

It is a condition of high blood pressure in which force of the blood against the artery walls is high enough to cause health problems such as heart disease, kidney disease, strokes etc.

The goal of doctors dealing with hypertension patients is to lower the blood pressure, so that they can be protected from damage. In combination with medicines, some lifestyle changes also aids in the treatment of hypertension *are*

- **Eating a Healthier Diet** Eating a diet rich in whole grains, vitamin D, omega 3, fruits and vegetables like beets, kale, celery, almond etc. helps in reducing hypertension. Also limiting the intake of junk food, high sodium food, carbohydrates, refined sugar etc. is must.
- **Maintaining Sodium to Potassium Ratio** Maintaining sodium to potassium ratio is also very important as imbalance between the two can lead to hypertension. Decreasing the use of sodium in diet through less salt intake and increase in the amount of potassium can help in managing hypertension.

- **Eating Fermented Foods** Eating yogurt, cheese and fermented food improves the gut microbe and helps in management of hypertension.
- **Intake of Vitamin D** Optimising vitamin D is also important as deficiency of Vitamin D causes inappropriate activation of renin-angiotension system that leads to hypertension. Vitamin D can be obtained through exposure to Sun and taking supplement of vitamin D.
- **Regular Exercises** Indulging in regular exercise for 30-60 minutes everyday can help in lowering hypertension.
- **Weight Loss** Maintaining optimum body weight with BMI (Body Mass Index 18.5-24.9 Kg/m^2) is recommended with health waist circumference *i.e.* men 102cm and women below 88cm.
- **Stress Management** Stress remains the main culprit in elevating the blood pressure thus, managing stress is very important for maintaining the blood pressure and also overall health especially heart health. Yoga, prayanam, meditation are techniques for stress management.
- **Limiting the Consumption of Alcohol and Tobacco** Consuming more than moderate amount of alcohol and consuming tobacco or smoking can increase blood pressure many times. Restricting drinking and smoking can be quite beneficial in treating hypertension.

The above are the few important lifestyle changes which helps one in effective management of hypertension together with medication and regularly monitoring of blood pressure at home.

Coronary Heart Disease

Coronary heart disease develops when the major blood arteries that supply heart with blood, oxygen and nutrient become narrow, damaged or diseased. *For example* Heart attack, heart blockage etc. If immediate medical aid is not provided to the patient then heart disease can be fatal.

In combination with medicines as prescribed by doctors certain lifestyle change is required for the better management of CHD. Lifestyle changes that are considered to be beneficial is case of Coronary Heart Disease (CHD) *are*

- **Diet** Diets which is high in cholesterol, fatty acids, transfat and saturated fats are linked directly to the development of heart problems. A healthy diet includes fruits, vegetables, whole grains, low-fat dairy, lean protein, nuts , legumes and vegetables- based oils. A healthy and nutritions diet helps in preventing and controlling coronary heart disease. A caution must be taken by the person regarding his/her diet in order to control coronary heart disease.
- **Physical Inactivity** Lack of physical exercises is the major cause of numerous health related problems. Lack of physical exercise leads to obesity, high blood pressure and diabetes which also aggravates the condition for CHD (Coronary Heart Disease). Thus, regular exercise is a must to prevent CHD.
- **Smoking and Excess Consuption of Tobacco and Alcohol** It has been researched in various studies that excess drinking alcohol and tobacco usage can prove to be detrimental to the health of an individual and especially to heart disease as alcohol increases the level of triglycerides (a form of cholesterol), which can harden arteries and lead to several heart problems. Nicotine present in cigarettes raises blood pressure of an individual and carbon monoxide reduces the amount of oxygen that the blood carries, thus increasing the risk of heart problems.

Role of Psychology in CHD

Psychology has a role to plays at all stages of CHD

(i) Our beliefs about both health and illness leads to the onset of disease. Like those who believe that Heart attack has nothing to do with physical inactiveness, or high cholesterol food etc. will lead to inactive and sedentary lifestyle. Such unhealthy behaviour would lead to onset of CHD.

(ii) Secondly in the progress of disease also a person's belief plays an important role, like if someone believe that "I got Heart attack due to my genetic makeup" he/she will not understand the importance of healthy behaviour as they think that they can do nothing about their health.

Finally, we know that major chronic disease are accelerated by the unhealthy lifestyle choices made by mankind in recent years. Moving toward the positive changes like taking care of diet, more physical activity, less intake of alcohol, quitting smoking etc. can help us either in prevention or effective management of diabetes, hyper, tension and coronary heat disease.

Psychoneuroimmunology

Psychoneuroimmunology, also referred as psychoendoneuro immunology or psychoneuroen- docrinoimmunology is the study of the interaction between psychological processes and the nervous and the immune systems of the human body. It studies the influence of emotional states like stress on the nervous system and on the immune function, especially in the onset and development of disease.

Its's an interdisciplinary approach which is based on the researches done by psychologists, psychiatrists and biologists. It studies the effect of psychological states on our physical system and immune system. Basically it studies the complex bidirectional interactions between the nervous and immune systems. It does not consider mind and the body to be distinct entities. It is based on the growing recognition that mental and physical events are so intricably inter-related that nothing can happen to one without affecting the other.

Origin of Psychoneuroimmunology

In 1975, Robert Ader and Nicholas Cohen coined the term *Psychoneuroimmunology* with their series of scientific experiments done on lab rats, through classical conditioning, to prove that a signal through nervous system (taste, in case of Alder's and Cohen experiment on rats) was affecting the immune system (*i.e.* leading to death of rats).

Another series of researchers in Switzerland Hugo Besedovsky, Adriana del Ray and Anna Sorokin too reported multidirectional immune-neuro endocrine interactions, which proves that not only brain influences immune system but vice-a-versa is also true *i.e.* responses in immune system too affect brain and neuro endocrine systems.

In 1981, David L Felten too discovered a network of nerves leading to blood vessels as well as cells of immune system. He also found nerves in the thymus and speech ending near clusters of lymphocytes, macro phages and mast cells, all of which help to control immune system. This discovery helps to related how neuro-immune interaction occurs.

These above researches and many recent studies done in the area of psychoneuroimmunology aids in understanding that now stress, negative reactions, anger, violence etc. have an impact on our immune system. Many conditions such as heart disease, cancer, HIV/AIDS are related to the negative emotions and stress in the life of an individual. Psychoreuroimmunology strengthens the age old beliefs that there is a concrete effect of mind on healing as well as in development of disease.

Doctors have often reported the cases where a terminally ill patients live longer than their expected life time because of their desire to live and their positive attitude towards life.

Placebo effect in healing also shows that how a sugar pill can cure a patient from his pains and aches just because there in a belief that pill will work and has medicinal values.

Thus, we can conclude that psychoneuroimmunology provides a scientific framework for researchers to investigate an aspect of healing in which a physical link between the immune system and psychological factors are formed. It shows how negative mental states like stress, depression can signal immune system and bodily defences are lowered.

Initially scientists and medical practitioners were not convinced about psychoneuroimmunology but by the advent of 21st century the scenario is chaning and this field is gaining wider acceptance.

Psychoneuroimmunology (PNI) and HIV/AIDS

HIV is a virus that targets and alters the immune system increasing the risk and impact of other infections and diseases. If it is left without any treatment, then the infection progresses to another level, an advanced diseased stage known as AIDS (Auto Immuno Deficiency Syndrome).

In AIDS, the immune system of a person weakens and the person is at risk of life threatening infections and cancers. Once a person is infected by this HIV (Human Immunodeficiency Virus), it stays inside the body for life time.

The virus is spread through blood, semen, rectal fluids, vaginal fluids and breast milk. It cannot spread through saliva, sweat or urine. It is mainly carried from infected person to another by exchange of fluids.

As AIDS weakens the immune system of the patient the symptoms are not clearly visible. It affects the nervous system, lungs, eyes, brain, skin etc.

Several studies done since 2000 have supported the view that psychosocial distress and negative life events leads to the faster progression from HIV to AIDS in an infected person.

Thus, we can conclude that psychoneuroimmunology has a crucial role to play in the study of HIV/AIDS as AIDS is a virus which weaken the human immune system and psychoneuroimmundogy studies the impact of psychological states on nervous system and immune system. Thus, PNI contributes to establish the associations between psychological stress and disease, hence aids in the better management of disease.

Psychoneuroimmunology and Cancer

Cancer is a disease caused by an uncontrolled division of abnormal cells in a part of the body, which can even spread to other body parts. Numerous researches have been done to show the effect of stress on the onset and progression of cancer. A major study was done by S Mukherjee which clearly states the role of psychological factors in the onset of stress. Immune system helps body to combat with different kinds of infections and disease. Psychoneuroimmunology studies the impact of psychological states on immune system. As discussed before stress disregulates the immune system thus leads to the progression of cancer in human body.

Similarly, research done by K Rose suggested that psychological factors play an important role in cancer progression and mortality. A recent study done by JR Satin W linden and MJ philips concludes that mortality rates are 39% higher among breast cancer patients diagnosed with major or minor depression compared to those not depressed.

Norepinephrine, epinephrine, catecholamines released by sympathetic nervous system during stress can lead to promote tumor cell proliferation.

NK (Natural Killer) cells which are an important anti-tumor defense stress alters their activity too leading to progression of cancer. Thus, it can be concluded that stress leads to the weakening of our immune system and have a major impact in making human beings more prone to various illnesses and disease.

Thus, it has become important to manage stress effectively in which the field of psychoneuroimmunology is very crucial, also the traditional view that immune system is an autonomous mechanism stands false, now we know it is a regular interactionss with brain cells.

EXAM BASED QUESTIONS

1 'Health' in psychology is used to refer
(a) mental health
(b) physical health
(c) social health
(d) All of these

2 Health psychology originated from which field of psychology?
(a) Social psychology
(b) Cultural psychology
(c) Clinical psychology
(d) Organisational psychology

3 Health psychologists study behaviour and experiences that promote health and factors like
(a) Influence and effectiveness of healthcare
(b) Improving healthcare facilities
(c) Personality characteristics and its impact on health
(d) All of the above

4 The two major therapies used by health psychologists in treatment are
(a) CBT and behaviour modification
(b) Behaviour therapy and cognitive therapy
(c) Classical conditioning and chaining
(d) Shaping and instrumental conditioning

5 In 1900, most deaths in the US were caused by ...., whereas today, most are due to ......
(a) pneumonia, cancer
(b) chromic disease, cancer
(c) infectious disease, chromic disease
(d) cancer, alcohol related causes

6 The bio-psycho-social model of health was proposed by
(a) Sigmund Freud (b) Carl Rogers
(c) Fishbein (d) George L Engel

7 The biological factors included in bio-psychosocial model are
(a) genetics (b) personality
(c) behaviour (d) All of these

8 The psychological factors included in bio-psychosocial model of health are
(a) bio chemical factors (b) demographics
(c) mood (d) Both a and b

9 The social factors included in bio-psycho-social model are
(a) socio-economic status (b) medical
(c) cultural factors (d) All of these

10 What is the basic principle behind bio-psycho-social model of health?

(a) Biological, psychological and social factors are dependent on each other.
(b) All three factors are independent.
(c) All issues relating to health are products of the interplay of three factors.
(d) None of the above

11 According to bio-psycho-social model of health, the psychological influences contributing to illness are

(a) depression
(b) negative thought process
(c) lack of self control
(d) All of these

12 "Health is the mere absence of illness". What other factor has been added in the recent definition of heath?

(a) Wellness/ wellbeing
(b) Mental wellbeing
(c) Social wellbeing
(d) All of these

13 What paradigm shift has taken place in social sciences in understanding health?

(a) Health is a result of biological factors.
(b) Health is a result of biological and social factors.
(c) Health is a result of interaction between biological, social and psychological factor.
(d) Health is an independent notion.

14 According to new Bio Model of Health, health is

(a) an active mechanism
(b) a passive mechanism
(c) a neutral entity
(d) a complex structure

15 When was health psychology identified as an independent field of study?

(a) 1972 (b) 1978
(c) 1976 (d) 1982

16 What is the main characteristic of health promoting behaviour?

(a) It aims to maintain an optimal weight of body
(b) It aims to maintain perfect BMI
(c) It aims to maintain positive health
(d) All of the above

17 What are health related behaviours?

(a) Health promoting behaviours
(b) Health compromising behaviours
(c) Both a and b
(d) None of the above

18 What are the examples of health compromising behaviour?

(a) No smoking
(b) No drinking
(c) Substance use
(d) Minimise sugar consumption

19 Does indulging in health compromising behaviour always leads to negative impact on body?

(a) Yes, it always has negative impact.
(b) No, it have negative impact but slowly.
(c) It results in pleasure initially when a person indulge in it.ss
(d) None of the above

20 Health compromising behaviour to a large extent is a result of

(a) family influence (b) peer pressure
(c) self presentation (d) All of these

21 Why does health compromising behaviour cannot be altered easily?

(a) It is rewarding (b) Poor self control
(c) Body increasingly adapt to it and demands higher doses
(d) Weak coping strategies

22 Strong desire to engage in health compromising behaviour is which form of learning?

(a) Classical conditions (b) Operant conditional
(c) Observation learning (d) Cognitive learning

23 Why it is difficult to withdraw from addiction of substance use?

(a) Unpleasant physical symptoms experienced
(b) Unpleasant psychological symptoms experienced
(c) Physical dependence on the substance
(d) Both a and b

24 .... has been shown to interact with cholestrol to increase rates of hypertension and CHD.

(a) Depression (b) Stress
(c) Obesity (d) Smoking

25 Smoking is more likely among individuals with ..... together both are linked to increase risk for cancer.

(a) depression (b) stress
(c) obesity (d) None of these

26 Materials that can be used by an individual to assist in the modification of a personal habit is called

(a) Pamphlets (b) News paper
(c) Flyers (d) Self help aids

27 An excessive accumulation of body fat in which BMI is greater than 30 is called

(a) Obesity (b) Binge eating
(c) Bulmia (d) Fat

28 Theory of .... targets autonomy and self control.

(a) Perceived self control (b) Self determination
(c) Self assessment (d) Self control

29 .... cause of obesity focus on having the infrastructure necessary to exercise, healthy foods available.

(a) Social (b) Environmental
(c) Psychological (d) Contextual

30 Who proposed the Health Promoting Model ?
(a) Nola J Pender (b) Cohen
`(c) James Lange (d) Hans Seliye

31 The major assumption of HPM is
(a) person actively regulate his/her environment
(b) interaction between individual and environment is progressive
(c) health professionals has an important role play in a person health maintenance
(d) All of the above

32 The major concepts of HPM included in personal factors are
(a) biological factors, psychological factors, socio-cultural factors
(b) cultural factor, environmental factors, social factors
(c) perceived benefit of action, perceived barrier to action perceived self efficacy
(d) Both a and c

33 According to HPM, which statement given below is correct?
(a) The greater the commitment to a specific plan of action the more likely is health promoting behaviour.
(b) People cannot modify their conditions, affect, interpersonal and situational influences.
(c) Lesser perceived self efficacy results in perceived barrier to a specific health behaviour.
(d) Both a and b

34 Theory of Reasoned Action was proposed by
(a) Alfred Adler
(b) Roger
(c) Martin Fishbein and Icek Ajzen
(d) Rosenstock

35 Which of the following is extension of Theory of Reasoned Action?
(a) Theory of Planned Behaviour
(b) Health Belief Model
(c) Protection Motivation Theory
(d) Health Promoting Model

36 Which of these is not an element of the Health Belief model?
(a) Threat (b) Expectations
(c) Cure (d) Socio-demographic factors

37 Which of these is a stage in stages of change mode?
(a) Study (b) Contemplation
(c) Deliberation (d) Mediation

38 What does the term mortality refer to
(a) death (b) illness (c) health (d) morbidity

39 Which one is not the components of Protection Motivation theory in health?
(a) Fear (b) Self efficacy
(c) Severity (d) Benefits

40 What is the sequence of stages in model of illness by Leventhal?
(a) Coping, Interpretation, Appraisal
(b) Appraisal, Coping, Interpretation
(c) Interpretation, Appraisal, Coping
(d) Interpretation, Coping, Appraisal

41 Which of the following is not a principle behind the study of psycho-neuro-immunology?
(a) Mind over matter
(b) Thinking well
(c) Good thought
(d) Positive thinking and positive health

42 Factor in coronary heart disease which can be modified are
(a) educational status (b) social morbidity
(c) social class (d) smoking

43 Name the Psychologist who used the term lifestyle?
(a) Levanthal
(b) Freidman and Rosenman
(c) Karasek
(d) Alfred Adler

44 Stress is seen as an interaction between
(a) a person and his social class
(b) a person and his expectations
(c) a person and his environment
(d) a person and his religion

45 What influence a person's illness, his medical treatment and their adjustment to disease?
(a) Beliefs and behaviours
(b) Social and personal environment
(c) Beliefs and class
(d) Family stress

46 Which of the following are symptom of diabetes?
(a) Increased thirst (b) Extreme hunger
(c) Fatigue (d) All of these

47 Which nutrient of food aids in reducing coronary heart disease?
(a) Fibre (b) Vitamin
(c) Calcium (d) Carbohydrates

48 What is the characteristics of people with Hypertension?
(a) Alertness (b) Tense clipped speech
(c) LP (d) High BP

49 After chronic heart disorder, which among the following is not suitable?
(a) Vegetable (b) High fatty food
(c) Whole grain (d) Lean protein

50 Which of the following is not a method of qualitative research?
(a) Focus groups (b) Open ended interviews
(c) Observation (d) Questionnaires

51 Which hormone is released in response to sympathetic-adrenal-medullary axis in our body?
(a) Cortisol
(b) Catecholamines
(c) Thyroxin
(d) Estrogen

52 **What do you understand by health beliefs?**
(a) Perception of healthy behaviour
(b) Perception of healthy and unhealthy behaviours
(c) Perception of risk or beliefs about the severity of an illness
(d) Perception or beliefs about persons own health

53 **In psychoneuroimmunology which psychological factors are identified that can modify immune functioning of an individual?**
(a) Mood (b) Thought suppression
(c) Stress (d) All of these

54 **........... and .... can influence whether a person becomes ill in the first place, and their coping with illness.**
(a) Behaviour and modelling
(b) Beliefs and behaviours
(c) Thoughts and perceptions
(d) Beliefs and cognitions

55 **Most people think smoking is bad, but still continue smoking, why?**
(a) Attitude towards a behaviour
(b) Faulty perception
(c) Faulty health belief
(d) Perceived behavioural control

56 **During periods of prolonged stress the hypothalamus triggers the**
(a) Endorphins (b) Pituitary gland
(c) ACTH hormone (d) Adrenal gland

57 **.............. personalities are at a greater risk for CHD.**
(a) Type D (b) Optimistic
(c) Type B (d) Type A

58 **During acute stress the adrenal medulla releases .... that increase heart rate and respiration.**
(a) endorphins (b) dopamine
(c) catecholemines (d) acetycholine

59 **The release of .... reduces the effectiveness of the immune system in response to prolonged stress.**
(a) Corticosteroids (b) Dopamine
(c) Endorphins (d) Section

60 **Acute stress involves activation of the .... system; and prolonged stress involves activation of the ....system.**
(a) sympathetic, endocrine
(b) parasympathetic nervous, endocrine
(c) sympathetic and parasympathetic
(d) endocrine, parasympathetic

61 **What health behaviours was the HBM (Health Belief Model) developed from?**
(a) HIV/AIDS (b) Heart desease
(c) TB screening (d) Kidney

62 **Rosenstock proposed which theory?**
(a) PHM (b) TRA
(c) HBM (d) None of these

63 **Which of the following is belief relevant to the HBM?**
(a) Self efficacy (b) Percieved benefit
(c) Percieved barrier (d) All of the above

64 **............ is the theory of planned behaviour is often found to be the weakest predictor of intention to perform a behaviour?**
(a) Objective Norm (b) Subjective Norm
(c) Both a and b (d) None of these

65 **Which theory was developed by Rogers?**
(a) Theory of Reasoned Action
(b) Healthy Belief Model
(c) Protection Motivation Theory
(d) Change Model

66 **Which of the following is not a cognition, which is relevant to the HBM?**
(a) Likelihood of recovery (b) Suspectibility to illness
(c) Severity of illness (d) Cost v/s benefit involved

67 **What did Becker and Maiman (1975) add to the HBM?**
(a) Socio-Psychological (b) Demographics
(c) Quest to action (d) Health nominations

68 **Which of the following systems is responsible for producing the stress response associated with fight or flight?**
(a) The control nervous system
(b) The endocrine system
(c) The digestive system
(d) The sympathetic nervous system

69 **The third stage in the stages of change model is**
(a) determination (b) action
(c) contemplation (d) maintenance

70 **Stress is seen as an interaction between the .... and their ....**
(a) social, behaviour. (b) person, family
(c) person, life events
(d) person, environment

71 **Match the following**

	List I (Model)		List II (Context)
A.	Health Belief Model	1.	Social network engaging
B.	Theory of Planned Action	2.	Influenced by media
C.	Direct Modeling	3.	Perceived severity
D.	Symbolic Modeling	4.	Attitudes

Codes

	A	B	C	D
(a)	3	4	1	2
(b)	4	3	2	1
(c)	1	3	4	2
(d)	3	4	2	1

72 Match the following

List I (Model)	List II (Psychologist)
A. Unrealistic optimism	1. Diclemented
B. Theory of Reasoned Action	2. Weinstein
C. Model of illness behaviour	3. Fishbein and Ajzen
D. Stages of change model	4. Leventhal

Codes

	A	B	C	D		A	B	C	D
(a)	1	2	3	4	(b)	4	3	2	1
(c)	2	3	4	1	(d)	3	2	1	4

73 Match the following

List I (Models of Stress)	List II (Main Concepts)
A. Cannon Bard	1. Appraisal
B. Holmes and Rake	2. Exhaustion
C. Hazardus	3. Schedule of Recent Experience
D. Hans Selye	4. Fight or Flight

Codes

	A	B	C	D		A	B	C	D
(a)	1	4	2	3	(b)	3	4	1	2
(c)	4	3	1	2	(d)	4	1	3	2

74 Match the following

List I (Models of Health)	List II (Name of Psychologists)
A. Health Belief Model	1. Rosenstock
B. Theory of Reasoned Action	2. Martin Fishbein
C. Trans Theoretical Model	3. Prochaska and Diclemente

Codes

	A	B	C		A	B	C
(a)	3	1	2	(b)	2	4	1
(c)	1	2	3	(d)	1	2	4

75 Match the following

List II (Stages of Trans-Theoretical Model)	List II (Descriplion)
A. Precontemplation	1. Ready
B. Contemplation	2. Not ready
C. Preparation	3. Modification Behaviour
D. Action	4. Getting Ready

Codes

	A	B	C	D		A	B	C	D
(a)	2	4	1	3	(b)	4	3	2	1
(c)	2	1	3	4	(d)	1	2	4	3

76 Match the following

List I (Stages of Change Model)	List II (Sequence of Stages)
A. Contemplation	1. I
B. Action	2. II
C. Preparation	3. III
D. Precontemplation	4. IV

Codes

	A	B	C	D		A	B	C	D
(a)	3	4	2	1	(b)	1	2	3	4
(c)	4	3	2	1	(d)	1	2	4	3

77 Match the following

List I (Health Belief)	List II (Description)
A. Attitude towards others	1. Beliefs of significant
B. Subjective norms	2. Related to past behaviour
C. Cue to action	3. Trigger
D. Behavioural control	4. Evaluation

Codes

	A	B	C	D		A	B	C	D
(a)	1	2	3	4	(b)	4	1	3	2
(c)	4	3	1	2	(d)	2	3	1	4

78 Put in sequence the stage of Hans Selye GAS model of stress?

1. Body adapts to stressor
2. Body breaks down
3. Changes in immune system
4. Body is initial response

Codes

(a) 4, 1, 2, 3 (b) 3, 1, 2, 4 (c) 3, 2,1, 4 (d) 4, 2, 1, 3

79 What are the characteristies of people with type a behaviour?

1. Hostility 2. Relaxed
3. Loudspeaking 4. Energy

Codes

(a) 1, 2 and 3 (b) 2, 3 and 4 (c) 1, 3 and 4 (d) 1 and 4

80 Common sign and symptom of diabetes are

1. fatigue 2. frequent urination
3. decreased thirst 4. weight loss

Codes

(a) 1 and 3 (b) 1, 2 and 3
(c) 1, 2 and 4 (d) All of these

81 Arrange the following in sequence.

1. Pre-Contemplation 2. Preparation
3. Action 4. Maintenance

Codes

(a) 4, 3, 2 and 1 (b) 1, 2, 3 and 4
(c) 3, 2, 1 and 4 (d) 2, 1, 3 and 4

82 Major concept of Health Promoting Model are

1. Personal factor 2. Real Barrier
3. Activity Related affect 4. Situational affect

Codes

(a) 1 and 2 (b) 1, 2 and 3 (c) 1, 2 and 4 (d) 1, 3 and 4

Directions (Q. Nos. 83-88) *In the questions given below are two statements labelled as Assertion (A) and Reason (R). In the context of two statements, which one of the following is correct?*

(a) Both A and R are true and R is correct explanation of A
(b) Both A and R are true, but R is not correct explanation of A

(c) A is true, but R is false
(d) A is false, but R is true

83 **Assertion** (A) Stressful events leads to increased heart rate.

Reason (R) During stress the activity in SNS increases.

84 **Assertion** (A) Stress triggers changes in HPA (Hypothalamic-Pituitary-Adreno Cortical) system.

Reason (R) HPA system is activated due to the production of catecholamines.

85 **Assertion** (A) Stress can result in decreasd immune function.

Reason (R) Stress leads to production of cortisol.

86 **Assertion** (A) Cancer is caused by increase in number of T Cell.

Reason (R) Stress leads to decrease in number of T Cell.

87 **Assertion** (A) Secondary appraisal of an event is important to develop a coping style.

Reason (R) In primary appraisal an individual initially appraises the event.

88 **Assertion** (A) The stage of resistance in Selye's GAS model, involves coping and attempts to reverse the effects of alarm stage.

Reason (R) Increase in activity occurs immediately a person is exposed to a stressful event.

Directions *(Q. Nos. 89-92) Read the passage given below and answer the following questions.*

There are an estimated 650000 people living with HIV/AIDS (PLHA) in China. HIV infection impacts not only PLHA but also their whole family. Given the family-oriented structure of Chinese society, HIV can have a devastating effect on Chinese families. Many PLHA are parents and caregivers who are supposed to attend to the needs of their child; they have to cope with their own physical health symptoms, complex medication regimens, stigma and fear of AIDS-related death and must also care for their families.

The psychological burden and stress affect their overall mental health and depression is common among parents and caregivers as they struggle with financial limitations. Many caregivers find that they can no longer work as the disease progresses and their health deteriorates and unemployment lead to extreme economic hardships.

HIV can also have an effect on relationship between family members. Chronic illness in the parent can change family roles causing anger or guilt. Family members can become isolated. The ability of HIV positive parents and caregivers to care for their children is also impaired, as poverty induced by HIV/AIDS increases the risk of illness and death among children.

89 **Who are mainly impacted by the HIV/AIDS?**
(a) Whole family
(b) Person living with HIV/AIDS
(c) Parents
(d) Neighbours

90 **What challenges are faced by PLHA and their families?**
(a) Physical health symptoms
(b) Stigma
(c) Complex medication regimens
(d) All of the above

91 **In the questions given below are two statement labelled as Assertion (A) and Reason (R). In the context of two statements, which one of the following is correct?**

Assertion (A) Chronic illness in the family causes stress.

Reason (R) HIV/AIDS can often lead to emotional and behavioural change in children.

Codes
(a) Both A and R are true and R is correct explanation of A
(b) Both A and R are true, but R is not correct explanation of A
(c) A is true, but R is false
(d) A is false, but R is true

ANSWERS

1	(d)	2	(c)	3	(d)	4	(a)	5	(a)	6	(d)	7	(a)	8	(c)	9	(d)	10	(c)
11	(d)	12	(d)	13	(c)	14	(a)	15	(b)	16	(c)	17	(c)	18	(c)	19	(c)	20	(d)
21	(c)	22	(a)	23	(d)	24	(d)	25	(a)	26	(d)	27	(a)	28	(c)	29	(c)	30	(a)
31	(d)	32	(a)	33	(a)	34	(c)	35	(a)	36	(a)	37	(b)	38	(a)	39	(d)	40	(d)
41	(c)	42	(d)	43	(c)	44	(c)	45	(a)	46	(d)	47	(a)	48	(d)	49	(b)	50	(d)
51	(b)	52	(c)	53	(a)	54	(b)	55	(d)	56	(c)	57	(d)	58	(c)	59	(a)	60	(a)
61	(c)	62	(c)	63	(d)	64	(b)	65	(c)	66	(a)	67	(b)	68	(d)	69	(d)	70	(d)
71	(a)	72	(c)	73	(c)	74	(c)	75	(a)	76	(c)	77	(b)	78	(a)	79	(c)	80	(c)
81	(b)	82	(d)	83	(a)	84	(c)	85	(a)	86	(d)	87	(a)	88	(a)	89	(a)	90	(d)
91	(b)																		

Psychology and Technology Interface

In last few decades technology has gradually dominated every aspect of our life. Even it has also impacted psychological aspect. Interface of technology yielded both positive and negative consequences such as digital learning, cyber bullying and pornography.

Technology

We are living in a modern world and technology has become an indispensable part of human existence. Technology is everywhere in form of different gadgets we are using from TV to washing machine, fridge, AC, mobile phones, computers oven, etc. We are dependent on gadgets for our major to micro needs. Now with so much advancement in science and technology, life of a human being has become quite comfortable, as he/she can do shopping from all over the world while sitting at his/her home through e-shopping and improve their knowledge through e-learning platforms.

Technology has shrinked the world into a global village and things which seemed to be impossible few years back, are easily achievable today. The influence of technology on human lives is tremendous. Digitalisation is a major change which has affected humans in numerous ways. Digital media also a form of tech advancement. We are able to visualise a lot of information on our phones, TV, computers etc. It is not only presenting realities to us, but in different way's shaping our thought process too.

As we all are aware that visual information has a major impact on human brain, so what we see on media creates thoughts and influence our behaviour. Thus, media shows us what it wants to show. Technology has been both empowering and over powering for humans. It has a major impact on the children and youth of today. The time which child should spend playing active games with his friends outside the house, is spent sitting passively infront of video games or on screen virtual games. Today kids have a passive childhood because of TV and internet. This is the main reason why children or youngsters are facing lots of social emotional issues, as they

In this Chapter

- *Technology*
- *Digital Learning*
- *Digital Etiquette*
- *Cyber Bullying*
- *Cyber Pornography*
- *Parental Mediation of Digital Usage*

don't know how to adjust themselves into a society. They have become socially and emotionally disabled. They are missing on sports field, social interactions and hangout activities, which could teach them numerous social skills during childhood and make them a better and well adjusted individual in life.

Though, it cannot be denied that technology has made our lives very comfortable and smooth, but its negative impacts cannot be overlooked. The only point is how smartly and intelligently we can use technology to make our lives much better and knowledgeable.

Digital Learning

As human behaviour is largely influenced by its thinking, intentions and cognition, technology is playing a major part in constructing and redefining our thought process. Thus, it has become quite important for a psychology student to study about Psychology and Technology Interface.

Learning is a relatively permanent change in behaviour as a result of experience. The psychology of learning focuses on how people learn and interact with their environment. Today in the era of digitalisation when everything is digital in nature, human can also enhance their learning through information available on digital devices like computers, mobile phones, i-pad etc.

Digital Learning therefore can be defined as any type of learning that is accompanied by technology or by instructional practice that makes effective use of technology. It encompasses the application of a wide spectrum of practices, including virtual learning. *It's a form of learning which combine technology with content and instruction.*

Digital Content

Digital Content is any content that exists in the form of digital data. It is also known as digital media and is stored on digital or analog storage in specific formats. Digital content has increased in the past decade due to the high accessibility of internet in more and more households.

Digital content in digital learning is the content which is academic in nature and is related to the topic of interest. It is formulated and designed by the experts of the field. It is engaging, interactive and highly informative.

It is visual, audio and in the form of games too. Digital content makes the learning interesting as it's presentation is attractive and creative. Students get the benefit of learning from the experts in the field, even if they are in different countries. Students can attend their lectures and even ask them their queries. Digital content has made learning an interesting and an engaging experience.

Instruction

Though digital learning has changed the concept of traditional learning where the teacher used to write on a black board and students just copied. It has changed the role of a teacher, but not eliminated the need of a teacher. With the help of digital learning teachers are also able to give more attention and assistance to their students. They are able to provide personalised attention to children through interaction and group discussion to ensure that students are learning and stay on track. Teacher plays the role of a guide, not a person who just comes to a class, dictate and go.

Elements of Digital Learning

Digital learning is also characterised by element of control *which are as follows*

- **Time** Learning can be initiated anytime whenever it suits the user, just an access to internet is required. Thus, there is no restriction of time in digital learning.
- **Place** Student can learn the concepts anywhere and everywhere. There is no requirement of coming to a particular school, college or place for it. With the proliferation of internet, learning can be done at anywhere.
- **Path** Student can learn concepts in his/her own unique way and style. Learning is no longer restricted to the pedagogy used by teacher. Interactive videos allows students to realise how much they have learnt.
- **Pace** The speed at which an individual learn is no more a problem. A student can learn fast or slow, spending more or less time on a concept as per his/her speed.

Thus, digital learning has created many improvements in the methods of traditional learning.

Advantages of Digital Learning

Digital learning has been used extensively in contemporary times as it has four fold advantages over traditional form of learning. *These can be summarised as follow.*

(i) **Flexibility** It provides complete flexibility to user regarding time, place etc.

(ii) **Convenience** Digital learning is quite convenient as the content can be accessed from any place, it can be a park, office or home, just an access to internet is required.

(iii) **Cost Effective** With proliferation of internet the cost of digital learning has become quite low and also it saves person's travelling cost for going to any institution.

(iv) **Interactivity** Digital learning encourages interactivity through the medium of audio-visual communication between teacher and students and also with other students.

Thus, we can conclude that digital learning has made learning quite convenient and easy going.

Disadvantages of Digital Learning

There are few downsides too of digital learning *which are as follows*

- **Lack of Social and Cultural Interaction** The more time we spent in front of screen, more distance we are making from social interactions. In digital learning peer interaction is minimal, thus it results in lack of social and cultural interactions which individuals used to enjoy in a classroom. This is one of the biggest challenge of digital learning.
- **Feeling of Isolation** Digital learning often creates feeling of isolation among learners as it's an individual way of learning and as learners are away from group and classroom, it creates a sense of loneliness.
- **Lack of Focus** Learners who lack focus and motivation lag behind in digital learning as there is no teacher to monitor their progress, and also there is no deadline. Learners often neglect the time duration they take to learn a concept and there by become lazy and keep on procrastinating things.

Current Trends in Digital Learning

Though there are few cons of digital learning, many digital learning platforms have come into existence with the huge demand for learning through digital medium. Platforms like Udemy, Udacity, Teachable etc. are quite common these days.

The current trends in digital learning include

- **Mobile Learning** With the rise in the usage of mobile phones, mobile learning has become quite valuable and even it can run on desktop, laptop and tablets.
- **Micro Learning** It's a short term learning activity, and the course can even last for 60 minutes. It is easier and affordable to produce and run such courses.
- **Gamification** It's a way to convert learning into games and make it more interactive and engaging for the users.
- **Social Learning** It's emphasis is on bringing the concept of social learning into digital learning. It is done through building student network, discussions with fellow classmates through collaboration and exchange of knowledge and problem solving.
- **Interactive Videos** Interactive videos enhance active engagement and the performance of the learners. Thus, interactive videos are quite accepted trend these days.

Thus, we see how digital learning has changed the trend of learning from last decade. It's more engaging, informative and progressive in nature as compared to traditional methods of learning.

Digital Etiquette

According to the dictionary, "Etiquette is the customary code of polite behaviour in society or among members of a particular profession or group".

In simple words it is the code of conduct or the acceptable behaviour within the norms of society, class or group in which an individual resides.

Digital Etiquette as defined by **Ribble & Bailey**, refers to "the standards of conduct expected by other digital technology users".

As it is expected from a person who lives in a society to be fair and polite towards other members of the society, similarly in the digital world most of people expect digital etiquette.

It is expected from all the users to be fair, polite, treat others with respect and avoid embarassing others. Though these points seems to be commonsense, but things do change while people interact with others online.

As they are not doing face-to-face communication, people don't have any personal feelings about the person they are interacting with. They criticise, develop negative opinions, bully and disrespect others they don't like through digital communication. The consequences of such behaviour whether it's online or personal is quite hazardous.

Simply, digital etiquettes are referred as internet manners. It should not be forgotten that though no one watches who is posting a picture or a video on net, but the impact of what is posted online is widespread. So one has to be really careful while posting any video, photo or opinion on social media. In-appropriate pictures and messages have become quite common these days and its impact is really harmful as at times these messages and pictures are viewed by children or people who are still ineligible to view such content. It creates a negative impact on their development.

Similarly posting pictures of someone in an embarrassing situation is also incorrect as it creates problem in the life of the concerned individual. Calling someone by names or insulting others publicly are all examples of disgracing digital etiquette.

Digital etiquette is about using manners in cyber space and using technology in a responsible way. The golden rule of using technology responsibly is by treating others the way you want to be treated yourself by others.

Few Digital Etiquette

Few Digital Etiquette one must remember while being digitally active are

- Hate messages and criticising anyone online. saying bad words, cursing, or calling names to others online is an uncultured behaviour. If you don't like any message or any form then tell in a polite manner rather than using demeaning and degrading language.
- Never share or put objectionable pictures like that of drug-use, naked pictures, unedited home videos etc. of someone or yourself or any one related to you.
- Don't repost the messages which are not checked for facts or hoax messages which can create a lot of problem for someone who follows it. Messages related to cure of some aliments if followed without consultation with doctor or an expert, can have major negative impact on one's health.
- When you borrow something from some source on net, always give the credit to the writer.
- Always use good and acceptable language when online. Don't use abusive language.
- Don't share each and every detail about what's going on in your life online, as many may not be interested to what you ate in lunch and at what time you woke up in the morning. Try to enjoy your private life rather than making everything public.
- Learn to differentiate between what matter shall go for public viewing and what shall go to the personal e-mail of the concerned person. Exaggerating public opinion, political view etc is not a good point.
- Use of proper language and precision is always required while posting information online. Use of slangs must be avoided and using all capital letters is regarded as shouting so it should be kept in mind. Messages and content must be precise and clear.
- Respect diversity of opinions and avoid being racist, sexist, ageist. Try to be liberal in your approach and never criticise or have radical opinions regarding others religion, culture or country. Don't be a hate spreader.
- Like real world situations, controlling anger is very important while using digital media too, as using bad language or aggressive tone can lead to negative image. Rather try to be rational and easy going, even if you feel angry about something posted on internet. A bit of thinking and time will help in sorting the condition fairly.

But few of us do not understand these simple rules and indulge in behaviour which are negative and harm others. The harm may not be physical in nature as the communication is not face-to-face, but the negativity which one indulges in has an impact on the social, emotional and mental well-being of others.

Cyber Bullying

Bullying as defined by APA, (American Psychological Association) is a form of aggressive behaviour in which someone intentionally and repeatedly causes injury or discomfort to another person. Bullying can be physical, verbal or more subtly actions. Most definitions of bullying also emphasise a power difference between the two parties involved such that the target is less in social, physical or psychological resources than the one who is bullying.

Cyber bullying is a type of bullying that takes place over digital devices like mobile phones, computers, tablets etc. It can be done through text messages, comments etc which can be veined and shared by people. With the increase in the usage of digital devices and social media, the incidents or cyber bullying is on a rise.

Unlike bullying, in cyber bullying target is not face-to-face to the person who bullies him/her, but it doesn't mean that the impact of cyber bullying is less as compared to that of face to face bullying. In fact cyber bullying can be done at any time of the day, any day of the week and throughout the year. In real time bullying the bully can be identified but in cyber bullying bully is mostly anonymous. Real time bullying is limited to the onlookers, but cyber bullying can go viral in a matter of seconds.

As cyber bullying is widespread its consequences are also hazardous especially on the psychological well-being of the victim.

Factors Affecting Cyber Bullying

The major factors contributing to an individual engaging in cyber bullying can be summarised as follows

Personality Factors

Individuals involved in cyber bullying are those who

- Experience high levels of hostility
- Have Low level of self confidence
- Try to boost their ego by down grading others
- Think bullying others is a source of entertainment
- They think it will improve their social status like other's
- They feel powerful after bullying others
- Drug and alcohol abuse can also make a person irrational and influence him to be a bully

Family Characteristics

Individuals who are involved in Cyber bullying others have disruptive family ties. There is

- Lack of parental supervision over children's media activities
- Frequent family conflicts make children more prone to become a bully, as they become aggressive by observing frequent sights in the family
- Lack of family cohesion too plays an important role in making a person bully

Types of Cyber Bullying

Bullies use various ways to bully others. Few ways of Cyber Bullying as reported by ''Stop a Bully Report' are

- Showing/hitting
- Spreading rumours
- Fighting
- Exclusion/leaving out
- Racist comments
- Threats/intimidation
- Homophobic comments
- Sexual comments
- Cell phone messages

Major types of cyber bullying, adopts the following ways

- **Exclusion** Deliberately excluding someone from an online group.
- **Gossip** Posting or sending cruel gossip to damage a person's reputation and relationships with friends and family.
- **Harassment** Repeatedly sending offensive, rude and insulting messages to someone.
- **Outing and Tricking** Tricking someone to reveal secrets or embarrassing information which is then publicised online.
- **Cyber Stalking** Sending unwanted, messages to some one.
- **Cyber Threats** Remarks on the internet threatening or implying violent behaviour, displaying suicidal tendencies.

Models of Cyber Bullying

The two major theories/models which clearly gives the explanation of the factors leading to cyber bullying are

General Aggression Model (GAM)

GAM model is the integrative framework for domain specific theories of aggression. The model was proposed by Anderson, Bushman, Lindsay and Dill. This model of 'aggression' helps us to understand the causes behind an individual engaging in the act of cyber bullying. Initially it was used to understand the negative impact of video games on players, but now it is clear that this model can be used to explain the factors leading to a person involvement in cyber bullying.

The model is centralised around 'knowledge structures'. The other three main areas which affect a person's behaviour are inputs (personal, situational), Routes (cognitive, affective and arousal routes through which input variables have their impact) and outcomes (outcomes of the underlying appraisal and decision making processes).

According to this model, aggression (cyberbullying is a form of aggression) is largely based on the activation and application of aggression related knowledge structures (*e.g.* scripts schemes).

It also holds that repeated exposure to violence whether in real life or virtual (media) can accumulate overtime in real life or virtual (media) can accumulate overtime solidifying aggression related knowledge structures in an individual, potentially creating an aggressive personality. Thus, knowledge structures have an important part to play in cyber bullying.

Thus, we can see that GAM attempts to explain not only an episodic aggressive behaviour, but also personality development So GAM tries to explain the development of aggressive and anti-social personalities (A person who is involved in cyber bullying is an anti-social personality).

Two main areas which affects a person's behaviour are

(i) **Inputs** are built on the foundation of knowledge structures and describe personal and situational factors which are linked to aggressive behaviour.
   - **Personal Factors** include age, gender, motives, personality, psychological states, socionomic status, technology use, values, perceptions and other maladaptive disorders.
   - **Situational Factors include** Provocation and perceived support, parental involvement, school climate and perceived anonymity.

(ii) **Routes** are different path like cognition, affect and arousal. These routes are derived from the social, cognitive, emotional and behavioural outomes determined by person and situational inputs.

General Strain Theory

This theory was developed by Robert Agrew. It is a theory of criminology but can be used to understand the causes behind a person's involvement in cyber bullying. Agrew described four characteristics of strain or stress that can result in negative experiences and makes a person more prone to involve in crimes (cyber bullying).

(i) Strains are seen as unjust
(ii) Strains are seen as high in magnitude
(iii) Strains are associated with low social control
(iv) Strains create some pressure or incentive to engage in criminal coping

He also categorised strains in four categories

(i) Failure to achieve positively valued goal
(ii) Dis-junction between expectations and achievements
(iii) Removal of positive stimuli
(iv) Introduction of negative stimuli

These forms of strains often elicit or produce feelings of anger, frustration, or depression which can surface as negative behavioural outcomes. Agrew maintains that the individual who faces strains are at risk of indulging in deviant or delinquent behaviours. Thus the victim of cyber bullying is more prone to indulge in deviant coping strategies.

Emotional and Psychological Consequences of Cyber Bullying

Cyber bullying has harmful impact on the emotional and psychological well being of an individual

The major impact of cyber bullying on youth as concluded by Stop Bullying report is depression and anxiety. Other negative consequences include

- Indulgence in drugs and alcohol
- Skipping school, not regular at studies
- Lowered self esteem and frustration
- Health complication like recurrent headaches etc due to prolonged stress
- Changes in sleep and eating patterns

It has also been found in several researches that the youth who have been bullied retaliate by indulging in extreme violent behaviours like incidents of school shooting is US etc.

Thus it can be concluded that cyber bullying is a severe crime and it has long and short term impact on the victims and perpetrator both. The usage of social media and internet is increasing day by day. It is the responsibility of parents or any other responsible adult to have a check over the online activities of their children. Adults must be vigilant to identify any signs of 'being bullied' or 'being a bully' in the youngsters.

Children must be assured frequently that if they are ever caught in an act of cyber bullying, they must reveal about it to guardian and try to resolve it rationally. Children must be counselled time to time and must be encouraged to understand that they are not alone, they shall not bully back, they shall not hurt other's if they are bullied and above all its not their fault if they are bullied.

Above all, children today need, 'Smart Parents' instead of getting only 'Smart Phones', parents must realise this truth.

Cyber Pornography

Pornography is the depiction of erotic behaviours through pictures or writings intended to cause sexual excitement. It can be presented through media, books, magazines, photographs, postcard, drawing, sculpture, film, video etc.

Cyber Pornography is similar to pornography, but it is the usage of cyberspace to create, display, import or publish pornography or obscene materials.

Cyber Pornography consumption is on a rise in recent years as use of internet has increased rapidly, thus the viewership of online content has also taken an exponential pace. But it is also quite common that some individuals especially children may seek out sexually explicit content online out of curiosity, but many encounter it accidently.

Thus, it is important for the parents to keep a watch and filter out the unwanted pornographic material from their gadgets. There are many type of 'filters' which can be installed in phones or on screen devices to keep out this unwanted material from access of children *e.g.* 'Family Shield'.

Consumption of Cyber Pornography

Dr. Victor Cline, an expert on Sexual Addiction found that there is a four step progression among many who consume pornography, *which are as follows*

(i) **Addiction** Pornography provides sexual stimulant or aphrodisiac effect, followed by sexual release most often through masturbation.

(ii) **Escalation** Over addicts require more explicit and deviant material to meet their sexual needs.

(iii) **Desensitisation** What was perceived as gross, shocking and disturbing in mean times becomes common and acceptable.

(iv) **Acting Out Sexually** There is an increasing tendency to act out behaviour viewed in pornography.

Statistics shown that there are more than 420 million individual pornographic webpages today.

Implications of Cyber Pornography

- **Shaping and Encouraging Distorted Behaviour** By viewing sexually explicit material the individual and family both suffer. The person starts to create a distorted picture of the environment around him and creates disturbance for his family too.
- **Brain Function** Several researches have shown that pornography users have more difficulty with attention, working, memory. These difference become a part of the user's behaviour.
- **Violence** It has also been found that males who watch pornography are physically violent towards their female counterpart. Males also feel less attracted towards their spouse and chances of infidelity also rises among males who watches pornography.
- **Promiscuous Behaviour** Pornography may lead to addiction, escalation, desensitisation and acting out sexually by one person. Addiction to pornography leads to adultery, prostitution and many unreal expectations that can result in promiscuous behaviour.
- **Child Pornography** Another grave issue which arise from cyber pornography is that of child pornography. Child pornography is a mean of depicting or promoting sexual abuse of a child, including print or audio. It's an inhumane and unlawful activity which is a punishable offence.

Thus, it can be concluded that addiction to pornography material give rise to distorted human behaviour and it also changes an individual's attitudes towards his spouse and family. However due to the internet's increased access for the common citizen, the pornographic material has slowly entered the public discourse. However. the impact of 'cyber pornography' on human mind and behaviour is irreparable, especially if it is consumed by youth, then it leads to grave consequences as children at young age are naive and unable to discriminate between what is good for them and what would disturb their mind.

Thus, it is important to make general masses aware of the disadvantage of the publication and extreme consumption of porn material on internet. Also the laws must be strict for the offenders who publish the obscene pictures or material of someone without the consent of other person. It should be understood that viewers of porn material are also equally responsible for encouraging cyber pornography as the one who uploads such material. So in order to curb this crime, the viewers shall have to restrict themselves and not support such websites financially.

Parental Mediation of Digital Usage

Livingstone and Helsper defined parental mediation as "a form of parental socialisation in which parents acts as a primary socialisation agents to influence their children's behaviour and attitudes to become more competent technology users".

Digital learning and media usage form an important aspect of contemporary life and have a prominent impact on the social and psychological development of an individual. Today a modern home has numerous ultra-tech devices which are used to make human lives more comfortable and easy going.

Most of these devices are internet operated. Few devices which can easily be used by children too are laptops, gaming boards, computers etc. Providing access to the internet and computers for children are considered must for their development and enhancing knowledge. But the question that arises, how to control or mediate the digital usage by children? We all are well aware that mobile phones, laptops and other devices that provide entertainment like films, games and music have changed the landscape of family media use. Though all these gadgets and media offer unlimited access to knowledge, information and feedback, they both potentially solve and potentially intensify many dilemmas of family life. It has became a task for parents to intelligently mediate the digital usage by their children.

The Role of Parents in Regulating Digital Use by children

Parents, being "the most influential people in the development and socialisation of children" also have primary responsibility of guiding their children's media behaviour. First studies on children television viewing and parental mediation identified. *three general approaches of parental mediation which are as follows*

(i) **Instructive/Active Mediation** It refers to parents explaining and discussing media with their child.

(ii) **Restrictive Mediation** It is when parents set rules regarding the period of time and the kind of content with which their child is allowed to engage.

(iii) **Co-Viewing** It refers to shared usage of media between parents and children in which there is no parental intruction and discussion.

It has been found that active mediation is more effective than other two forms of mediation because active mediation is based on parent child conversation and discussion is more likely to cultivate critical thinking in children and to lead children to be more responsive to parents' initiatives.

But with the advent of digital technology and addressing to changes in media environment some studies identified additional types of parental mediation strategies.

Like Livingston and Helsper identified strategies, which are as follows

- **Monitoring** It refers to parents checking of children's email, messages, or sites that a child has visited. This can be done overtly or covertly after child's internet usage.
- **Supervision** It refers to parents keeping an eye on the child and the device and allowing children to surf the web only when parents are present.
- **Active Co-use** This category suggests that sharing the media is more active when the child uses internet than when they watch television. During co-use parents guide children regarding the restrictions associated with communication of personal information online. This was proposed by Livingstone and Helsper.
- **Interaction Restrictions** This strategy involves prohibition of contacting others (e.g. using e-mail, chat, game playing).
- **Technical Restrictios** It represent the installation or use of software that, for example, filter content and prevent access to some websites.

Factors Associated with Parental Mediation

Several researches indicate numerous factors that are related to parental mediation of technology use. These factors are

- The demographic variables like age and gender of the parents, parental education, age and gender of the child.
- Household socio-economic status and family size.
- Parents perception of child's digital skills, level of child and parents' media literacy, the level of parents' digital skills, child's motivation to use media, the frequency of media use in family and the parents views on the various effects of media's content on their children.
- The culture of a country and the country's level of welfare also have an impact on mediation by parents on digital usage of their children.

With the increasing number of incident of cybercrimes (cyber bullying, cyber pornography, etc) it has become quite necessary that parents must mediate the digital usage of their children as it will help them to balance the risks and opportunities of the content their children encounter online.

EXAM BASED QUESTIONS

1 How is social media increasing the feeling of social rejection among its users?
(a) Chatting online with strangers
(b) Lots of friends online but no real friend
(c) Out costing someone from social group which is online
(d) Not fulfilling social needs of an individual

2 How is increased usage of media affecting child development?
(a) Kids playing online games process information differently than kids who play physical games and online kids become hyperactive.
(b) They have very few interactions with their same age group children.
(c) They feel neglected.
(d) They feel novice while interacting with their friends.

3 What is the technology in digital learning?
(a) It's a hardware
(b) It's a software
(c) It's a type of programming
(d) It's a medium for the delivery of the content

4 What are the constituents of the digital content in digital learning?
(a) It's from the books by expert
(b) It's academic and related to the topic of interest
(c) It's in the form of lectures
(d) It's only visual material

5 What is the unique characteristic of digital learning that make it different from general learning?
(a) Time (b) Place (c) Path (d) All of these

6 What does the element of 'Path' in digital learning indicate?
(a) The way of learning by the student
(b) Pedagogy used by the teacher
(c) The method of learning taught to students
(d) Learning terms used by the instructor

7 What does the element of 'Pace' indicate in digital learning?
(a) The method of learning adopted by student.
(b) The speed of learning is not dependent on other classmates.
(c) The speed of the instructor at which concepts are taught.
(d) The speed of the whole class.

8 What is digital content?
(a) It's a hardware in computer for delivery of lessons
(b) It's a software in device for the lectures
(c) It's what a student learns
(d) It includes internet access and hardware

9 What are the unique features of digital content?
(a) Engaging (b) Interactive
(c) Video games (d) All of these

10 How does digital learning affect one's social well being?
(a) Lack of knowledge and expertise
(b) Lack of human touch
(c) Less peer interaction
(d) Lack of competitiveness

11 What is the main feature of current trend in digital learning that has fostered its mass growth?
(a) Micro learning (b) Gamification
(c) Interactive videos (d) Mobile learning

12 What is 'Gamification' in digital world?
(a) Learning through digital games.
(b) Playing games as a break activity during learning.
(c) Playing games with your peers.
(d) Convert digital content into games and making it interactive.

13 How the concept of social learning be included in digital learning?
(a) Lectures
(b) Concept formation
(c) Intelligence
(d) Collaboration and exchange of ideas

14 'Digital Etiquette' are based on what major principle?
(a) Treat others politely
(b) Trust others
(c) Treat others equally
(d) Treat others the way you want yourself to be Reated

15 Why one must be careful while writing anything on digital forum?
(a) Words chosen speaks about your education background
(b) Your messages shows your true feelings
(c) People can just read your words as tone is absent
(d) Words chosen are a way to portray one's own thinking style

16 What are the disadvantages of the absence of tone in a communication?
(a) It does not show what the speaker intends to say
(b) Communication is incomplete without tone
(c) Ambiguity clouds the entire conversation
(d) It is a form of sarcasm

17 What are the examples of misinterpretation in a communication?
(a) Sarcasm (b) Unclear speech
(c) Irony (d) All of these

18 Why behaving inappropriately while using technology is a common practice?
(a) People don't know what is Digital Etiquette
(b) People can hide their identity
(c) People are unaware how to use technology
(d) People are unaware of their rights

19 What can be done if you don't agree with some one's idea on online forum?

(a) Tell the person openly.
(b) Ignore the comment.
(c) Suggest ways to improve it.
(d) Post your disagreement and hope people will understand.

20 If someone insults someone online, then the person must

(a) assume they want to start a flame war and immediately insults back.
(b) report them so they can be banned.
(c) ignore the insult by not responding to it.
(d) None of the above.

21 E-mails, text messages, blog comments and conversations in chat rooms should

(a) always be written in capital letters.
(b) never contain emotions.
(c) not contain any information that one wouldn't say out loud in public.
(d) None of the above.

22 Bullies are often people who have unresolved

(a) needs (b) wants
(c) ego (d) conflicts

23 What are the family characteristics that make a person bully?

(a) Lack of family cohesion
(b) Family conflict
(c) Lack of parental supervision
(d) All of the above

24 Cyber bullying occurrence is often

(a) circadian (b) frequent
(c) once in few days (d) daily

25 The one who bullies at times do it for

(a) time pass (b) entertainment
(c) self-actualisation (d) to fulfill their unsaid wants

26 What are the situational factors in cyber bullying as described by GAM?

(a) Arousal
(b) Interaction of internal states
(c) Provocation
(d) Socio-economic states

27 Who proposed the General Strain theory of Cyber Bullying?

(a) Agrew (b) Kowalski
(c) Anderson (d) Bushman

28 What are the behavioural outcomes of strains as per GST?

(a) Frustration
(b) Social isolation
(c) Lack of confidence
(d) Lack of self efficacy

29 What is 'cyber pornography'?

(a) Watching adult material online
(b) Watching porn movies online
(c) Create or display porn material online
(d) None

30 What are devices called which are used to keep unwanted materials out of reach from children?

(a) Filters (b) Shield (c) Gaure (d) Netting

31 Who discovered four steps in cyber pornography addiction?

(a) Carl Rogers (b) Bushman
(c) Victory Cline (d) Anderson

32 What is the meaning of 'Escalation' in Clive's four steps progression in cyber pornography?

(a) Requirement of more gross and explicit material
(b) Sexual stimulation increases
(c) Perception of sexual material changes in intensity
(d) There is a tendency for sexual act out

33 What is not a stage from Clive's four step progression in cyber pornography?

(a) Addiction (b) Escalation
(c) Hierarchial upgrade (d) Desensitisation

34 What is 'Desensitisation' in cyber pornography progression?

(a) Requirement of more gross material.
(b) Sexual liberty.
(c) Non sensitivity towards sexual partner.
(d) What was considered gross, shocking before has now become more acceptable.

35 Who are the primary socialisation agents of a child?

(a) Peers (b) Schools (c) Neighbours (d) Parents

36 What is the literal meaning of parental mediation?

(a) Parental control (b) Parental intervention
(c) Parental influence (d) Parental interaction

37 What are the three main type of media intervention strategies used by parents?

(a) Interactive/Restrictive/Co-use
(b) Active/Restrictive/Co-use
(c) Active/Restrictive/Co-viewing
(d) Active/Restrictive/Super vision

38 What is a cybercrime?

(a) Crime in which a person is using digital media to disturb others
(b) Computer based cyber bullying
(c) Cyber pornography
(d) Child abuse

39 What is active mediation?

(a) Discussion between parents and children regarding media use.
(b) Parents set rules regarding media usage.

(c) Parents are using media with their kids.
(d) Parents are actively supervising what children are watching online.

40 What is the major benefit of adopting active mediation strategy by parents?
(a) Kids are open regarding their views
(b) Parents can influence kids decision
(c) Kids develop critical thinking while discussion with parents
(d) None of the above

41 Who invented the strategy of 'monitoring' by parents?
(a) Austin
(b) Livingston and Helsper
(c) Nikken and Jansz
(d) Fujioka

42 What is 'Monitoring' in parental mediation?
(a) Parents checking what their child is seeing online.
(b) Parents checking of children e-mail, messages etc.
(c) Parents tracking their children online activity.
(d) Parents keeping a check on the time their children spend online

43 Who proposed the strategy of 'Supervision' in parental mediation?
(a) Austin
(b) Livingston and Helsper
(c) Nikken and Jansz
(d) Fujioka

44 Which of the following strategy of parental mediation was not proposed by Livingston and Helsper?
(a) Active co-use
(b) Super vision
(c) Monitoring
(d) Technical restriction

45 What are the technical restrictions in digital use?
(a) Prohibition by parents to children regarding talking to strangers.
(b) Parents restriction on the use of Facebook or other social media platform.
(c) Installation of software to filter content on the digital device.
(d) Not allowing access to game playing.

46 What are the socio-economic factors that contribute to parental mediation in digital use?
(a) Family's educational background
(b) Family usage of media
(c) Family neighbourhood
(d) Family financial status

47 .... is the shared usage of media between parent and children without parental instruction.
(a) Active Mediation
(b) Restrictive Mediation
(c) Co-viewing
(d) None of these

48 It has been found in several researches that pornography users have more difficulty in .... and ....
(a) attention and working memory
(b) cognition and affect
(c) LTM and retentich
(d) episodic and declarative memory

Directions (Q. Nos. 49-67) *In the questions given below are two statements labelled as Assertion (A) and Reason (R). In the context of two statements. which one of the following is correct?*
(a) Both A and R are true and R is the correct explanation of A
(b) Both A and R are true, but R is not the correct explanation of A
(c) A is true, but R is false
(d) A is false, but R is true

49 **Assertion** (A) The learning is based on technology.

Reason (R) Educators are not essential to digital learning.

50 **Assertion** Digital content is interactive and adaptive software like video lectures, games, etc.

Reason Digital content is not a simple PDF of text.

51 **Assertion** (A) Digital learning has eliminated the role of a teacher.

Reason (R) Digital learning has changed the role of a teacher.

52 **Assertion** (A) Cyber pornography leads to high rate of infidelity among its users.

Reason (R) Pornography leads to desensitisation and distorted sexual orientation.

53 **Assertion** (A) Mediation by parents is a must in child's digital usage of media.

Reason (R) Parents are the primary agents of socialisation for kids.

54 **Assertion** (A) Parents can use active mediation for controlling child's digital usage.

Reason (R) In active mediation parents can set rules regarding the amount of time a child can spend online.

55 **Assertion** (A) Literate people use more media devices.

Reason (R) Media usage in a country is an indrator of country's welfare.

56 **Assertion** (A) Addicted person has a need to Act out sexually.

Reason (R) Cyber pornography increases the case of violence against women.

57 **Assertion** (A) Emotions are instigated when encountering emotion provoking situation.

Reason (R) People do not get emotionally hurt while communicating online.

58 **Assertion** (A) Stress created from cyber bullying makes the victim feel lack of self efficacy.

Reason (R) Depression is a negative cognitive state.

59 **Assertion** (A) Cyber bullying has a major impact on the emotional well being of the victim.

Reason (R) Absenteeism from school is common among the victims of cyber bullying.

60 **Assertion** (A) Psychological well being is an important component of sound physical health too.

Reason (R) Psycho somatic ailments are resultant of constant stress.

61 **Assertion** (A) Victimisation by a bully at times makes a person 'bully'.

Reason (R) Constant bullying by someone makes a person hostile.

62 **Assertion** (A) Addiction to pornography leads to desensitisation issues.

Reason (R) Pornography addicts are hyperactive.

63 **Assertion** (A) Males feel more attracted towards their spouse and wants to act out.

Reason (R) Infidelity rises in people who are addict to pornography.

64 **Assertion** (A) Pornography viewing is always international.

Reason (R) Digital users watching pornography is increasing day-by-day.

65 **Assertion** (A) In digital learning peer interaction is minimal.

Reason (R) Digital learning creates a feeling of vacuum in a person's life.

66 **Assertion** (A) Children who are doing digital learning are highly motivated and future oriented.

Reason (R) Digital learning provides lot of audio visual material for content.

67 **Assertion** (A) Person with low level of confidence are mostly bullies.

Reason (R) Personal factors also plays an important role in shaping a person into a bully.

68 How are 'routes' derived in GAM?

1. Personal factors
2. Situational factors
3. Emotional outcomes
4. Behavioural outcomes

Codes

(a) 1 and 3 (b) 2 and 3 (c) 1 and 2 (d) 1 and 4

69 What are the 'Proximal Processes' in GAM?

1. Primary appraisal
2. Thoughtful action
3. Interaction of internal states
4. Impulsive action

Codes

(a) 1 and 2 (b) 2 and 3 (c) 1, 2 and 4 (d) 1 and 4

70 What is/are not a feature of digital learning?

1. Adaptive learning
2. Learning objects
3. Real teacher
4. Textbooks

Codes

(a) 1 and 2 (b) 2 and 3 (c) 1 and 3 (d) 3 and 4

71 'Cyber bullying' is a form of aggressive behaviour which is characterised by

1. International
2. Physical
3. Causing discomfort
4. Digital medium

Codes

(a) Only 1 (b) 1, 2 and 3
(c) 1, 3 and 4 (d) 1 and 2

72 What are the type/types of strain in GST?

1. Anticipated presentation of negative value stimuli
2. Anticipated presentation of positive value stimuli
3. Anticipated removal of positive value stimuli
4. Anticipated failure to achieve positive value stimuli

Codes

(a) 1, 2 and 3 (b) 2, 3 and 4
(c) 1, 3 and 4 (d) 1 and 4

73 Arrange the steps of progression on sexual addiction by Dr. Victor Clive.

1. Desensitisation
2. Addiction
3. Acting out
4. Escalation

Codes

(a) 3, 2, 4, 1 (b) 1, 4, 3, 2
(c) 2, 4, 1, 3 (d) 3, 4, 2, 1

74 Cyber pornography consumption is mostly

1. International
2. Accidental
3. Out of curiosity
4. To enhance one's knowledge

Codes

(a) 1 and 2 (b) 2 and 3
(c) 1, 2 and 3 (d) 1, 2, 3 and 4

75 What are the behavioural consequences of increased social media usage on an individual's behaviour?

1. Comparison
2. Negative relationships
3. Digital literacy
4. Social favouritism

Codes

(a) 1 and 2 (b) 2 and 3 (c) 1 and 4 (d) 1, 2 and 3

76 What are the ways which are used by cyber bullies to bully others?

1. Stealing
2. Exclusion
3. Fake news
4. Accidents

Codes

(a) 1 and 2 (b) 2 and 3 (c) 1, 2 and 3 (d) 4 and 3

77 What are the 'inputs' according to 'GAM' model of bullying in commintting cyber-bullying ?

1. Personal factors
2. Situational factors
3. Present internal states
4. Arousal

Codes

(a) 1 and 2 (b) 2 and 3 (c) 3 and 4 (d) 1 and 4

78 What are the important constituents of digital learning?

1. Technology
2. Instruction
3. Media devices
4. Content

Codes

(a) 1, 2 and 3 (b) 2, 3 and 4
(c) 4, 2 and 1 (d) 1 and 2

79 Match the following

List I (Concepts)	List II (Specifics)
A. Digital Content	1. Robert Angrew
B. Digital Etiquette	2. High Speed
C. GAM Model	3. Cursing
D. GST Theory	4. Bushman, Anderson

Codes

	A	B	C	D
(a)	4	1	3	2
(b)	1	2	3	4
(c)	1	3	2	4
(d)	2	3	4	1

80 Match the following

List I (Concepts)	List II (Specifics)
A. GST Theory	1. Micro learning
B. GAM Model	2. Threat
C. Digital Learning	3. Inputs
D. Cyber Bullying	4. Srtrain

Codes

	A	B	C	D
(a)	4	3	1	2
(b)	1	2	3	4
(c)	4	1	2	3
(d)	3	1	2	4

81 Match the following

List I (Types of Cyber Bullying)	List II (Description)
A. Exclusion	1. Sending threatening message to someone
B. Gossip	2. Posting message to damage reputation
C. Outing	3. Tricking
D. Cyber Stalking	4. Removing

Codes

	A	B	C	D
(a)	2	4	1	3
(b)	4	2	3	1
(c)	1	2	3	4
(d)	4	1	3	2

82 Match the following

List I (GAM Model)	List II (Description)
A. Personal factors	1. Cognition
B. Routes	2. Thoughtful action
C. Decision-making	3. Gender
D. Outcomes	4. Psychological health

Codes

	A	B	C	D
(a)	4	2	3	2
(b)	2	3	1	4
(c)	3	1	2	4
(d)	3	2	1	4

Direction (Q. Nos. 83-84) *Read the passage given below and answer the following questions.*

Cyber bullying is the use of technology to harass, threaten, embarrass or target another person. By definition, it occurs among young people. When an adult is involved, it may meet the definition of cyber harassment or cyber stalking, a crime that can have legal consequences and involve jail.

Sometimes cyber bullying can be easy to spot for example, if your child shows you a text, tweet or response to a status update on Facebook that is harsh, mean or cruel. Other acts are less obvious, like impersonating a victim online or posting personal information, photos or videos designed to hurt or embarrass another person. Some kids report that a fake account, webpage or online persona has been created with the sole intention to harass and bully.

Cyber bullying also can happen accidentally. The impersonal nature of text messages and e-mails make it very hard to detect the sender's tone, thus, one person's joke could be another's hurtful insult. Nevertheless, a repeated pattern of e-mails, texts and online posts is rarely accidental. Because many kids are reluctant to report being bullied, even to their parents, it's impossible to know just how many are affected, But recent studies about cyber bullying rates, have found that about 1 in 4 teens have been the victims of cyber bullying and about 1 in 6 admit to having cyber bullied someone. In some studies, more than half of the teens surveyed said that they' ve experienced abuse through social and digital media.

83 What do you mean by cyber bullying?
(a) Bullying any one physically
(b) Harass anyone with the use of technology
(c) Both a and b
(d) None of these

84 Different means of cyber bullying can be
(a) text message (b) tweet
(c) comment on status (d) All of these

85 In the question given below are two statements labelled as Assertion (A) and Reason (R). In the context of two statements. Which one of the following is correct?

Assertion (A) Cyber bullying does not have any legal consequences.

Reason (R) Cyber bullying also can happen accidentally.

(a) Both A and R are true and R is correct explanation of A
(b) Both A and R are true, but R is not correct explanation of A
(c) A is true, but R is false
(d) A is false but R is true

86 Consider the following statement
1. Kids are frank in reporting cyber bullying to their parent.
2. Through research cyber bullying rates have been found to be 1:4.
3. Sometime one person's joke could be insult for others.

Choose the correct codes regarding cyber bullying

Codes
(a) 1 and 2 (b) 1 and 3
(c) 2 and 3 (d) All of these

ANSWERS

1	(c)	2	(a)	3	(d)	4	(b)	5	(d)	6	(b)	7	(b)	8	(c)	9	(d)	10	(c)
11	(d)	12	(d)	13	(d)	14	(d)	15	(c)	16	(c)	17	(d)	18	(b)	19	(c)	20	(c)
21	(c)	22	(d)	23	(d)	24	(a)	25	(b)	26	(c)	27	(a)	28	(a)	29	(c)	30	(a)
31	(c)	32	(a)	33	(c)	34	(d)	35	(d)	36	(c)	37	(b)	38	(a)	39	(a)	40	(c)
41	(b)	42	(b)	43	(c)	44	(b)	45	(c)	46	(b)	47	(b)	48	(a)	49	(c)	50	(a)
51	(d)	52	(a)	53	(b)	54	(c)	55	(c)	56	(a)	57	(c)	58	(a)	59	(a)	60	(a)
61	(a)	62	(d)	63	(d)	64	(c)	65	(c)	66	(b)	67	(a)	68	(c)	69	(c)	70	(d)
71	(c)	72	(c)	73	(c)	74	(c)	75	(d)	76	(a)	77	(a)	78	(c)	79	(d)	80	(a)
81	(b)	82	(c)	83	(c)	84	(d)	85	(d)	86	(c)								

PSYCHOLOGY

Model Paper-1

General Instructions

1. There are total one hundred questions in this paper. Each question carries 2 marks.
2. All questions are compulsory.

1 When participants take benefit from the first test the phenomena is known as

(a) Beginner Luck (b) Practice effect
(c) Experience (d) None of these

2. A trait is best described as

(a) a cluster of surface factors
(b) a temporary attitude toward a person or event
(c) a relatively permanent disposition of a person
(d) an environmentally determined hypothetical construct that shapes an individual's behaviour and thought

3 Which of the following is incorrect about Signal Detection Theory?

(a) It is a framework for interpreting data.
(b) Two or more stimulus classes are sampled repeatedly.
(c) Performance in task is limited by observer's sensitivity.
(d) SDT restricts performance to be predicted across paradigms.

4 Which among the following is not a principle of development?

(a) Development is unified
(b) Development is cumulative
(c) Development is irresistible
(d Development is complex

5 Match the following

	List I (Theories)		List II (Scholars)
A.	Field Theory	1.	Sigmund Freud
B.	Cognitive Dissonance	2.	Edward D'Wilson
C.	Sociobiology	3.	Leon Festinger
D.	Psychodynamic Approaches	4.	Kurt Lewin

Codes

	A	B	C	D		A	B	C	D
(a)	1	2	3	4	(b)	4	3	2	1
(c)	2	4	1	3	(d)	3	1	4	2

Directions (Q. Nos. 6 and 7) *In the questions given below are two statements labelled as Assertion (A) and Reason (R). In the context of the two statements, which one of the following is correct?*

Codes

(a) Both A and R are true and R is the correct explanation of A
(b) Both A and R are true, but R is not the correct explanation of A
(c) A is true, but R is false
(d) A is false, but R is true

6. Assertion (A) An individual's construal of the social situation is important.
Reason (R) Different subjective construals of the situation may lead individuals to respond differently in the same situation.

7 Assertion (A) According to Maslow, after gratification of basic needs we move in positive direction, but it is not automatic.
Reason (R) We often fear our best side, our talents, our finest impulses, our creativeness.

8 Match the following

	List I (Methods)		List II (Procedures)
A.	Experimental method	1.	Time sampling
B.	Survey method	2.	Correlations
C.	Observation method	3.	Personal Interview
D.	Non-experimental method	4.	Case histories
		5.	Casual relations

Codes

	A	B	C	D		A	B	C	D
(a)	1	3	4	2	(b)	5	2	4	3
(c)	1	2	4	3	(d)	5	3	1	2

9 What are the socio-economic factors that contribute to parental mediation in digital use?
(a) Family's educational background
(b) Family usage of media
(c) Family neighbourhood (d) Family financial status

10 Who was the early ancient physician who laid the foundation of psychology proposing that "mental life is a function of brain"?
(a) Hippocrates (b) Kant (c) Alcmeon (d) Sheldon

11 Arrange the steps in order in Pavlov's experiment
1. Selecting stimulus and response
2. Establishing classical conditioning
3. Testing for conditioning

Codes
(a) 1, 2, 3 (b) 3, 1, 2 (c) 2, 1, 3 (d) 1, 3, 2

12 Lesion studies on non-primate have given information about
(a) vision and memory (b) vision and taste
(c) vision and hearing (d) taste and memory

13 Match the following

	List (Tests)		List II (Functions)
A.	Maslach-Burnout Inventory	1.	Measure burnout
B.	Individualised Education Program	2.	For disabled student
C.	Least Restrictive Environment	3.	Enable placement decisions
D.	Curriculam-Based Measurement	4.	Monitoring progress

Codes

	A	B	C	D		A	B	C	D
(a)	1	2	3	4	(b)	4	3	2	1
(c)	3	2	1	4	(d)	4	1	2	3

14 Consider the following statements
1. Students may find that acquiring more knowledge and skill in a particular area enhance their sense commitment.
2. Students become increasingly able to distinguish among various attributes.

Which of the statements given above is/are correct?
(a) Only 1 (b) Only 2
(c) Both 1 and 2 (d) Neither 1 nor 2

15 Match the follwing

	List (Brain Imagings/Recordings)		List II (Functioning Principles)
A.	Electroencepholography	1.	Increased delivery of radioactive water
B.	Magneto-encephalography	2.	Venous oxygen Concentration
C.	Position Emission Tomography	3.	Magnetic Fields with in the brain
D.	Magnetic Resonance Imaging (MRI)	4.	Electrical activity from the scalp.

Codes

	A	B	C	D		A	B	C	D
(a)	1	2	4	3	(b)	1	3	4	2
(c)	4	3	1	2	(d)	4	2	1	3

16 Consider the following statements
1. Visual information from the retina is carreied by ganglion cell axons to the thallamic dorsal lateral geniculate nucleus.
2. The retino-spinal pathways are important for the synchronisation of behavioural activity to that of the light-dark cycle.

Which of the statements given above is/are correct
(a) Only 1 (b) Only 2
(c) Both 1 and 2 (d) None of these

17 Match the following

	List I (Test)		List II (Characteristics of Variance)
A.	Levene's test	1.	Equality of covariance
B.	Box's m test	2.	Homogeneity of variance
C.	Post hoc test	3.	Significant difference in variable
D.	Partial eta square	4.	Explaining independent variable

Codes

	A	B	C	D		A	B	C	D
(a)	2	1	4	3	(b)	4	3	1	2
(c)	1	2	3	4	(d)	4	2	3	1

Directions (Q. Nos. 18-22) *Read the following passage carefully and answer the questions that follow.*

Early research on the brain's control of hunger and satiety suggested that the Lateral Hypothalamus (LH) controlled the initiation of eating and the Ventromedical Hypothalamus (VHM) controlled the inhibition of eating or resulted satiety. Lesion studies on rats found that damage to the LH produced an animal that would not eat, whereas damage to the VMH caused a rat to over eat. Stimulation of the two areas produced the complementry effect; : LH stimulation in eating and VMH stimulation resulted cause an animal to stop eating.

Thus, the LH became known as the *hunger center* and the VMH as the *satiety centre*. This view is now known to be an over simplification. More recent studies show that two fiber tracts, rather than two fiber tracts, rather than two localised structures, are involved in the initiation and lessation of feeding, but first let us examine the information that was accumulated on the role of the LH and VHM.

18 Which structure is involved in the initiation and cessation of feeding?
(a) Two fiber tracts (b) Two localised structure
(c) Hypothalamus (d) Ventricles

19 Which of the following, control the initiation of eating?
(a) Ventro medical hypothalamus
(b) Ateral hypothalamus
(c) Hyperphagia
(d) Aphagia

20 What control the inhibition satiety?

(a) Lateral hypothalamus
(b) Ventro medical hypothalamus
(c) Adipsia (d) Aphassia

21 Which is known as hunger centre?

(a) LH (b) VMH (c) MH (d) VSH

22 What is known as satiety centre?

(a) LH (b) VMH
(c) MH (d) VSH

23 Match the following

List I (Koshas as per Indian Context)	List II (Description of Sheaths)
A. Atman	1. Food
B. Manomaya	2. Life
C. Annamaya	3. Mental sheath
D. Pranamaya	4. Joyous sheath

Codes

	A	B	C	D		A	B	C	D
(a)	1	2	3	4	(b)	1	3	2	4
(c)	4	3	1	2	(d)	2	3	1	4

24 Likert scale is a type of

(a) Intelligence test (b) Aptitude test
(c) Attitude scale (d) None of these

25 Match the following

List I (Neurotransmitter)	List II (Effect)
A. Acetylcholine	1. Regulation of mood
B. Nor-epinephrine	2. Learning and memory
C. Serotonin	3. Control of alertness

Codes

	A	B	C		A	B	C
(a)	2	3	1	(b)	2	1	3
(c)	3	1	2	(d)	3	2	1

26 Consider the following statements

1. During the latency period, Erikson claims that children learn to master tasks and attain goals.
2. Coping with identity crises is the problem Erikson feels is crucial to the psychological development of mature adult.

Which of the statements given above is/are correct?

(a) Only 1 (b) Only 2
(c) Both 1 and 2 (d) Neither 1 nor 2

Direction (Q. No. 27) *In the questions given below are two statements labelled as Assertion (A) and Reason (R). In the context of the two statements, which one of the following is correct?*

Codes

(a) Both A and R are true and R is the correct explanation of A
(b) Both A and R are true, but R is not the correct explanation of A
(c) A is true, but R is false
(d) A is false, but R is true

27 **Assertion** (A) Stressful events leads to increased heart rate.

Reason (R) During stress the activity in SNS increases.

28 What serves as pressure sense in hairless regions of the body?

(a) Meissner corpuscles (b) Merkel's corpuscles
(c) Both a and b (d) None of these

29 Consider the following statements

1. Counselling is non-cyclic and periodic model.
2. Counselling helps to make informed choices in field of education, career and social relations.

Which of the above statement is/are correct?

(a) Only 1 (b) Both 1 and 2
(b) Only 2 (d) None of these

30 Match the following

List I (Laws)	List II (Descriptions)
A. Weber's Law	1. Sensory on subjective magnitude grows in proportion to the physical intensity of the stimulus.
B. Steven's Power Law	2. To amount of change, increases/decreases in a stimulus necessary to detect it as different is proportional to magnitude of stimulus
C. Fechner's Law	3. The magnitude of a sensation is a logarithmic function of the stimulus

Codes

	A	B	C		A	B	C
(a)	2	1	3	(b)	3	2	1
(c)	1	2	3	(d)	3	1	2

31 What are the characteristics of people with type a behaviour?

1. Hostility 2. Relaxed 3. Loudspeaking 4. Energy

Codes

(a) 1, 2 and 3 (b) 2, 3 and 4
(c) 1, 3 and 4 (d) 1 and 4

32 'Positional flexibility' is the result of which Conflict Resolution Approach?

(a) Interest based approach (b) Need based approach
(c) Both a and b (d) None of the above

Directions (Q. Nos. 33 and 34) *In the questions given below are two statements labelled as Assertion (A) and Reason (R). In the context of the two statements, which one of the following is correct?*

Codes

(a) Both A and R are true and R is the correct explanation of A
(b) Both A and R are true, but R is not the correct explanation of A
(c) A is true, but R is false
(d) A is false, but R is true

33 Assertion (A) Social problems involve situations in which norms of the mainstream society are violated.

Reason (R) Social problems have an objective perspective.

34 Assertion (A) In researching human behaviour, personality theorists often use various measuring procedures and these procedures must t be both reliable and valid.

Reason (R) Reliability refers to a measuring instrument's consistency whereas validity refers to its accuracy or truthfulness.

35 What are the social consequences of gender discrimination?

1. Impact sex ratio
2. Impact health of over their lifetimes (mostly women)
3. Impacts social status of women
4. Impacts women participation at work

Codes

(a) 1 and 2 (b) 2 and 3 (c) 3 and 4 (d) All of these

36 The DSM-IV-TR definition of mental disorder is perhaps the best current definition because

(a) it includes information about both violation of social norms and dysfunction.
(b) it includes many components none of which can alone account for mental disorder.
(c) it is part of the current diagnostic system.
(d) it recognises the limits of our current understanding.

37 Match the following

List I (Psychologists)	List II (Main Contributions)
A. Richard Tedeshi	1. Character and values strengths
B. Diener	2. Big five personality traits
C. Martin Seligman	3. SWB model
D. Costa and MC Care	4. PTG model

Codes

	A	B	C	D		A	B	C	D
(a)	4	3	1	2	(b)	1	3	4	2
(c)	4	2	1	3	(d)	2	4	1	3

Direction (Q. No. 38) *In the questions given below are two statements labelled as Assertion (A) and Reason (R). In the context of the two statements, which one of the following is correct?*

Codes

(a) Both A and R are true and R is the correct explanation of A
(b) Both A and R are true, but R is not the correct explanation of A
(c) A is true, but R is false
(d) A is false, but R is true

38 Assertion (A) Empathy refers to an unpleasant feeling that we usually experience, when we encounter a person in distress.

Reason (R) Empathy is more likely response, when we see a distressed person, who is similar to ourselves.

39 A problem solving heuristic is

(a) guaranteed to find a solution, if one exists.
(b) a strategy that guides a search through the problem space.
(c) likely to be less effective than a strategy such as means-end analysis.
(d) needed for unfamiliar problems, but not for familiar problems.

40 Match the following

List I (Propounders)	List II (Concepts)
A. Herman Ebbinghaus	1. Primacy effect
B. Luchin's	2. Information processing view of memory
C. Glanzer	3. Recency effect result from STM
D. Atkinson	4. Keyword system for remembering information

Codes

	A	B	C	D		A	B	C	D
(a)	2	1	3	4	(b)		2	4	3
(c)	3	4	1	2	(d)	4	3	2	1

41 Match the following

List I (Research Paradigms)	List II (Eminent Personalites)
A. Epistemology	1. F Bacon
B. Methodology	2. Parmenides
C. Ontology	3. Plato
D. Theory of Knowledge	4. Socrates

Codes

	A	B	C	D
(a)	2	1	4	3
(b)	2	1	3	4
(c)	3	1	2	4
(d)	3	1	2	4

Directions (Q. Nos. 42 to 46) *In the questions given below are two statements labelled as Assertion (A) and Reason (R). In the context of the two statements, which one of the is following is correct?*

Codes

(a) Both A and R are true and R is the correct explanation of A
(b) Both A and R are true, but R is not the correct explanation of A
(c) A is true, but R is false
(d) A is false, but R is true

42 Assertion (A) Social injustice is a form of structural violence.

Reason (R) Structural violence is indirect form violence.

43 Assertion (A) Observation is a primary method of any scientific enquiry.
Reason (R) Empirical studies are based on experience and experimentalist.

44 Assertion (A) Intelligent people are more creative.
Reason (R) Intelligence and creativity are positively related.

45 Assertion (A) Emotional problem that disturb the functioning of individual students are not the kind of problem that can be treated by change in the curriculum.
Reason (R) They cannot interfere with the capacity to learn.

46 Assertion (A) All creative children are children with exceptional intelligence.
Reason (R) Creativity generally involves an incubation period.

47 Which of the following is true about experimental designs?
(a) Internal validity is controlled
(b) Are the weaker designs
(c) Easier to conduct
(d) Control groups are not used

48 Match the following

List I (Types of Cyber Bullying)	List II (Descriptions)
A. Exclusion	1. Sending threatening message to someone
B. Gossip	2. Posting message to damage reputation
C. Outing	3. Tricking
D. Cyber Stalking	4. Removing

Codes

	A	B	C	D		A	B	C	D
(a)	2	4	1	3	(b)	4	2	3	1
(c)	1	2	3	4	(d)	4	1	3	2

49 Which of the following statements is/are correct?
1. Group members work less hard on additive tasks.
2. Group members perceive themselves as working just as hard in the group or individually.
3. Group leadership is directly related to power and vice versa.
4. People obey blindly only in ambiguous situations or when disobedience will lead to serious punishment.

Select the correct answer using the codes given below
(a) 1 and 2 (b) 2 and 3 (c) 3 and 4 (d) Only 1

50 Consider the following statements
1. Atkinson was the first to recognise a distinction between short-term and long-term memory.
2. William James developed a model that capture the distinction between LTM and STM.
3. Rehearsal is a method of storing information in long-term memory.
4. Maintenance rehearsal is sufficient to keep the information in short-term memory, but insufficient to move it into long-term memory.

Which of the statements given above is/are correct?
(a) 1 and 2 (b) 2 and 3 (c) 3 and 4 (d) 1 and 4

51. 'Cyber bullying' is a form of aggressive behaviour which is characterised by
1. International 2. Physical
3. Causing discomfort 4. Digital medium

Codes
(a) Only 1 (b) 1, 2 and 3 (c) 1, 3 and 4 (d) 1 and 2

52 What are the 'Proximal Processes' in GAM?
1. Primary appraisal 2. Thoughtful action
3. Interaction of internal states
4. Impulsive action

Codes
(a) 1 and 2 (b) 2 and 3 (c) 1, 2 and 4 (d) 1 and 4

Direction (Q. No. 53) *In the questions given below are two statements labelled as Assertion (A) and Reason (R). In the context of the two statements, which one of the following is correct?*

Codes
(a) Both A and R are true and R is the correct explanation of A l
(b) Both A and R are true, but R is not the correct explanation of A
(c) A is true, but R is false (d) A is false, but R is true

53 Assertion (A) Most current personality research addresses ways, in which individuals and groups differ, not human universals.
Reason (R) Personality psychologists specialise in a particular domain, such as biological aspects of personality or how culture impacts personality.

54 Arrange the following processes involved in information processing model of memory in correct chronological order.
1. Sensory input 2. Long-term storage
3. Retrieval 4. Rehearsal buffer

Codes
(a) 1, 3, 2, 4 (b) 1, 2, 3, 4
(c) 1, 3, 4, 2 (d) 1, 4, 2, 3

55 The term 'Constructivism' is related to which famous theory is Psychology?
(a) Piaget's theory (b) Kohlberg's theory
(c) Adler's theory (d) Erik Ericson theory

56 Which one of the following is the correct chronological order of theorists, who proposed their theories of intelligence ?
(a) Spearman, Jensen, Piaget, Guilford
(b) Spearman, Piaget, Guilford, Jensen
(c) Piaget, Spearman, Guilford, Jensen
(d) Guilford, Jensen, Spearman, Piaget

57 Discrimination refers to behaviours that
(a) allow us to tell one ethnic group from another.
(b) occur, when members of a racial group threaten an individual's security.
(c) prevent individuals from doing things they should be able to do.
(d) are directed toward a particular group.

58 Which among the following things should be considered while formulating a hypothesis?
(a) Expected relationship between the variables
(b) Operational definition of variables
(c) Hypothesis should be formulated after reviewing the literature
(d) All of the above

59 Two main approaches taken to understand well-being are based on the principal of
(a) balance between positive and negative affect, self acceptance.
(b) distinguishing positive and negative affects, life satisfaction.
(c) optimal occurance of emotions, positive growth.
(d) mental peace, positive relationships.

60 Match the following

List I (Stages of Trans-Theoretical Model)	List II (Description)
A. Precontemplation	1. Ready
B. Contemplation	2. Not ready
C. Preparation	3. Modification Behaviour
D. Action	4. Getting Ready

Codes

	A	B	C	D		A	B	C	D
(a)	2	4	1	3	(b)	4	3	2	1
(c)	2	1	3	4	(d)	1	2	4	3

61 Match the following

List I (Factors)	List II (Components)
A. Individual	1. Customs
B. Demographic	2. Inflation
C. Economic	3. Overpopulation
D. Social	4. Gambling

Codes

	A	B	C	D		A	B	C	D
(a)	1	2	3	4	(b)	2	1	4	3
(c)	3	4	1	2	(d)	4	3	2	1

62 Consider the following statements
1. Highly creative boys exhibit more uniqueness and originality in their drawing than highly creative girls.
2. Highly creative boys have more internal tension than girls.

Which of the statements given above is/are correct?
(a) Only 1 (b) Only 2
(c) Both 1 and 2 (d) None of these

63 James (1890) differentiated between which types of attention?
(a) Various forms of top-down attention
(b) Auditory (top-down) and visual (bottom-up)
(c) Various forms of bottom-up attention
(d) Active (top-down) and passive (bottom-up)

64 Consider the following statements
1. Specific phobia is a fear of objects.
2. Claustrophobia is fear of being in a small place.

Which of the statements given above is/are correct?
(a) Only 1 (b) Only 2
(c) Both 1 and 2 (d) Neither 1 nor 2

65 Match the following

List I (Scholars)	List II (Theories)
A. Carl Rogers	1. Extrinsic motivation
B. Skinner	2. Competition
C. Chapman	3. Intrinsic motivation
D. Hurlock	4. Cooperation

Codes

	A	B	C	D		A	B	C	D
(a)	1	2	3	4	(b)	1	2	4	3
(c)	3	1	2	4	(d)	2	4	3	1

Directions (Q. Nos. 66-70) *Read the passage given below and answer the following questions.*

Rank-order correlation procedure is developed by Charles Spearman. It is also known as *Spearman's rho* (r_s). It was developed to compute correlation, when the data is presented on two variables for 'n' subjects.

In can also be calculated for data of 'n' subjects evaluated by two judges for inter-judge agreement. It is suitable for the rank-order data. If the data on 'x' or 'y' or not both the variables are in rank-order then Spearman's rho (*rs*) is applicable. It is used to assess a monotonic relationship. The range of Spearman's rho (r_s) is also from −1.00 to +1.00. Like Pearson's correlation, the interpretation of Spearman's rho is based on sign of the coefficient and the value of the coefficient.

If the sign of r_s is positive then relationship is positive, if the sign of r_s is negative then the relationship is negative. If the value of r_s is close to zero then relationship is weak and as the value of r_s approaches to ±1.00, the strength of relationship increases. When the value of r_s is zero then there is no relationship between X and Y. If r_s is ±1.00, then the relationship between X and Y is perfect.

66 Rank order correlation procedure is developed by
(a) Pearson (b) Guilford
(c) Spearman (d) None of the above

67 Spearman's rho is symbolised as
(a) r_b (b) r_r (c) r_p (d) r_s

68 Spearman's rho is used to assess
(a) monotonic relationship (b) eliatonic relationship
(c) tritonic relationship (d) None of these

69 If the value of r_s is close to zero the relationship is
(a) strong (b) weak (c) moderate (d) stable

70 The range of spearman's rho is from
(a) +1.00 to −1.00 (b) −1.00 to +1.00
(c) 0 to +1.00 (d) −1.00 to 0

Direction (Q. No. 71) *In the questions given below are two statements labelled as Assertion (A) and Reason (R). In the context of the two statements, which one of the following is correct?*

Codes
(a) Both A and R are true and R is the correct explanation of A
(b) Both A and R are true, but R is not the correct explanation of A
(c) A is true, but R is false
(d) A is false, but R is true

71 **Assertion** (A) One may do his research in a laboratory or a hospital or natural habitat or any other setting and may still be an experimental psychologist.
Reason (R) In psychological experiments, causal relationships between variables are studied under controlled conditions.

72 According to Holmes, there are how many life event which can cause stress?
(a) 41 (b) 42 (c) 43 (d) 44

73 Which of the following psychotherapy was developed by Fritz Perls?
(a) Existential psychotherapy (b) Transpersonal therapy
(c) Gestalt therapy (d) Humanistic therapy

74 Depending upon the task characteristics, there is a gradual transition from simpler forms of learning to the level of higher complex ones. These different forms are
1. Establishment of simple S-R relationship
2. Acquiring motor and verbal skills
3. Concept formation 4. Problem-solving
The correct order of learning sequence is
(a) 1, 4, 2, 3 (b) 1, 2, 3, 4 (c) 2, 4, 1, 3 (d) 2, 3, 4, 1

75 The bio-psycho-social model of health was proposed by
(a) Sigmund Freud (b) Carl Rogers
(c) Fishbein (d) George L Engel

76 Arrange the following research methods in order of their increasing potential to find casual relationship.
1. Experiments 2. Field studies
3. Surveys 4. Quasi-experiments
Codes
(a) 1, 2, 3, 4 (b) 3, 2, 4, 1
(c) 3, 4, 2, 1 (d) 1, 3, 2, 4

Directions (Q. Nos. 77 and 78) *In the questions given below are two statements labelled as Assertion (A) and Reason (R). In the context of the two statements, which one of the following is correct?*

Codes
(a) Both A and R are true and R is the correct explanation of A
(b) Both A and R are true, but R is not the correct explanation of A
(c) A is true, but R is false
(d) A is false, but R is true

77 **Assertion** (A) A learning theorist stress on the role of nurture in the development of language.
Reason (R) Language is attained through unlearned response pattern.

78 **Assertion** (A) Elements which has same shape are grouped together while perceiving.
Reason (R) Law of proximity states that when an individual perceives an assertment of objects, they perceive objects which are close to each other as forming a group.

79 Consider the following statements
1. Item difficulty index is measured using $\frac{U_P - L_P}{U}$.
2. Item discrimination index is measured using $\frac{U_P + L_P}{U + L}$
Which of the above statements is/are correct?
(a) Only 2 (b) None (c) Both 1 and 2 (d) Only 1

80 According to Gene Sharp, methods of non-violent resolution are
1. Non-cooperation 2. Civil-disobedience
3. Non-violent protest and persuation
4. Non-violent resolutions
Codes
(a) 1, 2 and 3 (b) 1, 3 and 4 (c) 1, 2 and 4 (d) All of these

81 Match the following

List I (Psychologists)	List II (Known for)
A. Roberto Assagioli	1. Autogenic training
B. JH Schultz	2. Buddhist psychology
C. Caroline Davids Rhys	3. Zen meditation
D. Friedrich Heiler	4. Psychosynthesis

Codes

	A	B	C	D		A	B	C	D
(a)	1	2	3	4	(b)	4	3	2	1
(c)	2	1	4	3	(d)	3	4	1	2

Direction (Q. No. 82) *In the questions given below are two statements labelled as Assertion (A) and Reason (R). In the context of the two statements, which one of the following is correct?*

Codes
(a) Both A and R are true and R is the correct explanation of A

(b) Both A and R are true, but R is not the correct explanation of A
(c) A is true, but R is false
(d) A is false, but R is true

82 Assertion (A) A researcher with subjective ontological assumption believes in awareness of social conditions which can be achieved through interaction with environment and experience.
Reason (R) Researcher with subjective ontological view gather qualitative data.

83 Consider the following statements
1. Indian perspective of psychology takes a qualitative and spiritual position and warrants inner development the may enable direct experience.
2. Indian perspective of psychology is more rigorous and inclusive than Western empirical approach.

Which among the above is/are correct?
(a) Only 1 (b) Only 2
(c) Both 1 and 2 (d) None of these

84 Which of the following tests is/are classified as non-parametric?
1. F-test 2. Signed-rank test
3. T-test 4. U-test

Which of the statements given above is/are correct?
(a) 1 and 3 (b) 2 and 4 (c) 2 and 3 (d) 3 and 4

Direction (Q. No. 85) *In the questions given below are two statements labelled as Assertion (A) and Reason (R). In the context of the two statements, which one of the following is correct?*

Codes
(a) Both A and R are true and R is the correct explanation of A l
(b) Both A and R are true, but R is not the correct explanation of A
(c) A is true, but R is false
(d) A is false, but R is true

85 Assertion (A) Psychological tests of specific attitudes and skills are now at a reasonably advanced stage of development.
Reason (R) They have been in the process of evolution and improvement for many years.

86 Consider the following statements
1. Abhidhamma Pitaka of Buddhism, articulates philosophy, psychology and ethics as well.
2. Psychoanalysts like karen Thomey and Fritz Peals studied Zen-Buddhism.

Which among the above is / are correct?
(a) Only 1 (b) Only 2
(c) Both 1 and 2 (d) None of these

Directions (Q. Nos. 87-89) *In the questions given below are two statements labelled as Assertion (A) and Reason (R). In the context of the two statements, which one of the following is correct?*

Codes
(a) Both A and R are true and R is the correct explanation of A
(b) Both A and R are true, but R is not the correct explanation of A
(c) A is true, but R is false
(d) A is false, but R is true

87 Assertion (A) A person exhibiting high sense of well-being will have a positive affect.
Reason (R) The affective components is associated with emotions, feelings and moods.

88 Assertion (A) According to Thorndike's law of effect, behaviours that result in unpleasantness are more likely to occur again.
Reason (R) He drew on Gestalt psychology to argue that animals could learn the connections between stimuli and did not need any explicit biologically significant event to make learning occur.

89 Assertion (A) Laboratory methods employed in the experimental analysis of behaviour are based upon BF Skinner's philosophy of radical behaviourism.
Reason (R) Everything that organisms do is behaviour (including thinking) and all behaviour is lawful which allows itself to be experimentally studied.

90 Identify the correct concepts related with Cattell's theory of personality.
1. Dynamic Lattice 2. Specification Equation
3. Orthogonal Rotation 4. Ergs

Codes
(a) 2, 3 and 4 (b) 1, 2 and 4 (c) 2 and 4 (d) 1, 2, 3 and 4

91 Consider the following statements
1. Stretching exercises increase the arousal level of the body.
2. Aerobic exercises have a calming effect.
3. Yogic asanas provide systematic stretching to all the muscles and joints of the body.
4. Yogic asanas massage the glands and other body organs.

Which of the above statements is/are correct?
(a) 1, 2, 3 and 4 (b) 1 and 2
(c) 3 and 4 (d) 1, 3 and 4

92 Which of the following statements is/are correct?
1. Bandura's theory does emphasis and detail the role of biology and inheritance in areas such as aggression.
2. In old age, high self-efficacy may cause a person to seek new challenges and the benefits of knowledge and experience over their life.

Codes
(a) Only 1 (b) Only 2
(c) Both 1 and 2 (d) Neither 1 nor 2

Direction (Q. No. 93) *In the questions given below are two statements labelled as Assertion (A) and Reason (R). In the context of the two statements, which one of the following is correct?*

Codes

(a) Both A and R are true and R is the correct explanation of A
(b) Both A and R are true, but R is not the correct explanation of A
(c) A is true, but R is false
(d) A is false, but R is true

93 Assertion (A) Auditory neurons are sensitive to the differences in the arrival times of an auditory stimulus.
Reason (R) Sound that occurs directly in front will arrive at the right and left ears at same time.

94 Ruby was listening to a tape recording of a famous speech that was played backward. She just heard gibberish until a classmate said the phrase 'meet me in St Louis' was clearly spoken, The tape was rewound and as Ashlynn listened this time, she also clearly heard the same phase. Ruby's ability to detect the phrase the second time through the tape illustrates

(a) the opponent-process model of perception
(b) top-down processing model of perception
(c) the bottom-up processing model of perception
(d) the electric model of perception

95 Match the following

List I (High Score Characteristics)	List II (Factors)
A. Creative, artistic, curious imaginative and non-conforming	1. Neuroticism
B. Organised. reliable neat and ambitious	2. Agreeableness (A)
C. Talkative, optimistic sociable and affectionate	3. Extraversion (E)
D. Good natured, trusting and helpful	4. Conscientiousness(c)
E. Working, insecure ancious and temperamental	5. Openness(o)

Codes

	A	B	C	D	E
(a)	1	4	3	5	2
(b)	4	1	2	3	5
(c)	5	4	3	2	1
(d)	5	3	4	2	1

96 Which is the highest state in human consciousness?

(a) Self efficacy
(b) Self understanding
(c) Self actualisation
(d) Truth or bliss or pure consciousness

97 A teacher's praise can be an effective motivator if

(a) praise is delivered contingently
(b) praise focuses students attention on their neighbour's task-relevant behaviour
(c) praise is delivered just for showing up for class
(d) praise is delivered the same day the praised behaviour happens

98 What are the secondary problems related to poverty?

(a) Slums and malnutrition
(b) Crime and drug addiction
(c) Illness and apathy
(d) Urbanisation and population explosion

99 Which of the following is correct statement?

1. Lesion is a probe to test specific hypothesis.
2. Lesion is created by researcher on healthy human brain.

Codes

(a) Only 1
(b) Only 2
(c) Both 1 and 2
(d) None of the above

100 Sigmund Freud's psychodynamics concept of mind is composed of

1. ID 2. EGO
3. Super Ego 3. High ID

Codes

(a) 1, 2 and 3 (b) 1, 2 and 4
(c) Only 3 and 4 (d) Only 1 and 2

ANSWERS

1 (b)	2 (c)	3 (d)	4 (c)	5 (b)	6 (a)	7 (a)	8 (d)	9 (b)	10 (c)
11 (a)	12 (a)	13 (a)	14 (b)	15 (a)	16 (a)	17 (d)	18 (a)	19 (b)	20 (b)
21 (a)	22 (b)	23 (c)	24 (c)	25 (a)	26 (a)	27 (a)	28 (a)	29 (b)	30 (a)
31 (c)	32 (a)	33 (b)	34 (a)	35 (d)	36 (b)	37 (c)	38 (b)	39 (b)	40 (a)
41 (c)	42 (a)	43 (a)	44 (d)	45 (c)	46 (d)	47 (a)	48 (b)	49 (a)	50 (c)
51 (c)	52 (c)	53 (a)	54 (d)	55 (a)	56 (b)	57 (c)	58 (d)	59 (b)	60 (a)
61 (d)	62 (c)	63 (d)	64 (c)	65 (b)	66 (c)	67 (d)	68 (a)	69 (b)	70 (b)
71 (b)	72 (c)	73 (c)	74 (b)	75 (d)	76 (c)	77 (d)	78 (b)	79 (b)	80 (d)
81 (a)	82 (a)	83 (c)	84 (d)	85 (a)	86 (c)	87 (a)	88 (c)	89 (a)	90 (b)
91 (c)	92 (b)	93 (b)	94 (b)	95 (c)	96 (d)	97 (a)	98 (a)	99 (a)	100 (a)

PSYCHOLOGY

Model Paper-2

General Instructions

1. There are total one hundred questions in this paper. Each question carries 2 marks.
2. All questions are compulsory.

---

1 Which of the following concepts had made major contributions to dynamic approach to personality?

1. Super ego
2. Social cognition
3. Psychosexual development
4. Unconscious impulses
5. Repression

Select the correct answer using the codes given below

(a) 1, 4 and 5 (b) 2, 3 and 4
(c) 1, 3, 4 and 5 (d) 1, 2, 3 and 5

2 Which of the following pair is/are correctly matched?

1. Primary motive – Curiosity motive
2. General motive – Maternal drive
3. Personal motive – Cognitive motive

Codes

(a) Only 1 (b) Only 2
(c) Only 3 (d) None of these

3 Which of the following statements is/are correct?

1. Women are easier to convince.
2. Referent informational influence is a concept derived of social identity theory.
3. Social identity theory does not give rise to inter-group discrimination.
4. Henri Tajfel proposed social identity theory.

Select the correct answer using the codes given below

(a) 1 and 2 (b) 2 and 3
(c) 3 and 4 (d) 2 and 4

4 Consider the following statements

1. Jnana Yoga talks about the spiritual knowledge.
2. Sankhya Yoga talks about the role of action of 'Karma'.

Which among the about is/are correct?

(a) Only 1 (b) Only 2
(c) Both 1 and 2 (d) None of these

5 According to whom, "An individual would not experience stress unless the individual perceives a situation as threatening"?

(a) Lazarus (b) Erikson
(c) Adler (d) Harney

6 Consider the following statements

1. The 'g' factor depend's on the general cortical or neural energy at the disposal of the individual.
2. The 'g' factor doesn't play in activities called neogenetic.

Which of the statements given above is /are correct?

(a) Only 1
(b) Only 2
(c) Both 1 and 2
(d) Neither 1 nor 2

7 Match the following

List I (Types of Reliability)	List II (Measures the Consistency of)
A. Test-retest	1. Individual items of a test
B. Inter-rater	2. Same test over time
C. Parallel form	3. Same test conducted by different people
D. Internal consistency	4. Different versions of a test which are designed to be equivalent

Codes

	A	B	C	D		A	B	C	D
(a)	2	3	1	4	(b)	1	4	3	2
(c)	2	4	3	1	(d)	2	3	4	1

8 Calvin displays aggressive behaviours because he witnessed his father acting aggressively when in similar situations

This behaviour can best be explained through which approach to psychology?

(a) Humanistic (b) Behavioural
(c) Cognitive (d) Evolutionary

9 Which of the following statements is/are not correct about a research problem or subject?

1. Subject which is overdone should not be normally chosen.
2. Subject selection should be familiar.
3. Controversial subject should be avoided.

Select the correct answer using the codes given below

(a) 2 and 3 (b) Only 3
(c) 1 and 2 (d) None of these

10 Decay theory of memory loss seems to be most appropriate for

(a) memory based on visual images
(b) long-term memory
(c) short-term memory and sensory memory
(d) muscular memory

11 Major concept of Health Promoting Model are

1. Personal factor
2. Real Barrier
3. Activity Related affect
4. Situational affect

Codes

(a) 1 and 2 (b) 1, 2 and 3
(c) 1, 2 and 4 (d) 1, 3 and 4

12 Which of the following statements regarding quasi-experiments are correct?

1. There is no random assignment of subjects in quasi-experiments.
2. There are no independent and dependent variables in quasi-experiments.
3. Quasi-experiments are ex-post facto studies.
4. Casual inferences cannot be made from quasi-experiments.

Select the correct answer using the codes given below

(a) 1 and 3 (b) 2 and 4
(c) 1, 3 and 4 (d) 1, 2 and 3

13 Match the following

	List I (Scheme)		List II (Purpose)
A.	NIRMAYA	1.	Aid and assisted devices
B.	GHARAUNDA	2.	Health Insurance scheme
C.	SAMBHAV	3.	Group home for adults
D.	SAHYOGI	4.	Caregiver training scheme

Codes

	A	B	C	D		A	B	C	D
(a)	2	3	1	4	(b)	4	1	3	2
(c)	1	4	2	3	(d)	3	4	1	2

Direction (Q. No. 14) *In the question given below are two statements labelled as Assertion (A) and Reason (R). In the context of the two statements, which one of the following is correct?*

Codes

(a) Both A and R are true and R is the correct explanation of A
(b) Both A and R are true, but R is not the correct explanation of A
(c) A is true, but R is false
(d) A is false, but R is true

14 **Assertion** (A) While carrying out surveys, if possible, random samples are preferred to non-random samples.

Reason (R) Random samples usually permit less accurate generalisation from samples to populations.

15 Materials that can be used by an individual to assist in the modification of a personal habit is called

(a) Pamphlets (b) News paper
(c) Flyers
(d) Self help aids

Directions (Q.Nos. 16 to 18) *In the question given below are two statements labelled as Assertion (A) and Reason (R). In the content of the two statements, which one of the following is correct?*

Codes

(a) Both A and R are true and R is the correct explanation of A
(b) Both A and R are true, but R is not the correct explanation of A
(c) A is true, but R is false
(d) A is false, but R is true

16 **Assertion** (A) Neurons in the arcuate nucleus of the hypothalamus produce neuropeptide 4.

Reason (R) Energy defecit is produced due to food deprivation.

17 **Assertion** (A) Psychopathology is characterised by subjective discomfort.

Reason (R) Psychopathology refers to mental disorder themselves.

18 **Assertion** (A) The learning is based on technology.

Reason (R) Educators are not essential to digital learning.

19 Match the following

	List I (Scholars)		List II (Theories)
A.	Abraham Tesser	1.	Cognitive dissonance theory
B.	Festinger	2.	Self-evaluation maintenance theory
C.	Baron	3.	Distraction conflict theory
D.	Steele	4.	Self-affirmation theory

Codes

	A	B	C	D		A	B	C	D
(a)	1	2	3	4	(b)	2	1	3	4
(c)	4	2	3	1	(d)	3	1	2	4

20 **Which neurotransmitters are synthesised from a single amino acid?**

(a) Amino acid (b) Monoamine
(c) Soluble gas (d) Acetylcholine

21 **Which of the following are needed for creativity?**

1. Focused recall
2. Identification of problem
3. Contrary recognition
4. Observing specific rules

Codes

(a) 1, 3 and 4 (b) 1, 2 and 4 (c) 1, 2 and 3 (d) 2, 3 and 4

22 **Well-being of a person can refer to a series of possible states. Which of the following do not describe well-being effectively?**

1. Virtue **2. Cognitive structure**
3. Objectivity **4. Emotional judgement**

Codes

(a) Only 1 (b) Only 2
(c) Only 3 (d) All define well-being

23 **What among the following is the dimension of poverty?**

1. Low income
2. Family income cannot support housing facilities for its family members
3. Inability to acquire basic goods and services necessary for survival with dignity
4. No job for family members

Codes

(a) 1 and 2 (b) 2 and 3 (c) 1 and 3 (d) 1, 2 and 4

24 **Consider the following statements about focus of behavioural theories of learning**

1. stimulus and response units.
2. principle of contiguity.
3. comprehension of underlying principle.
4. organisation of stimuli.

Which of the statements given above is/are correct?

(a) 1 and 2 (b) 2 and 3
(c) 1 and 4 (d) 3 and 4

25 **Which of the following pairs is/are correctly matched?**

1. J von Kries : Duplicity theory of vision
2. Max schultze : Colour deficiency
3. J Mueller : Doctrine of specific energy nerve

Codes

(a) 1 and 2 (b) 2 and 3
(c) 1 and 3 (d) 1, 2 and 3

26 **Consider the following statements**

1. A key concept of pre-school education is readiness training.
2. Research on kindergarten indicates that kindergarten promotes readiness and achievement in the first and second grade, but these effects disappear by the third or fourth grade.

Which of the statements given above is/are correct?

(a) Only 1 (b) Only 2
(c) Both 1 and 2 (d) Neither 1 nor 2

27 **Match the following**

List I (Terms used in Sufism)	List II (Physical Aspect)
A. Nafs	1. Heart
B. Ghalb	2. Soul
C. Ruh	3. Self
D. Jihad	4. Inner battle

Codes

	A	B	C	D		A	B	C	D
(a)	1	2	4	3	(b)	4	3	1	2
(c)	1	2	3	4	(d)	3	1	2	4

28 **Which of the following are the conditions necessary for a Short-Term Memory (STM) process to produce a Long-Term Memory (LTM)?**

1. STM runs its own course without disruption.
2. There is rehearsal of information.
3. STM undergoes consolidation.
4. There is interruption of learning.

Select the correct answer using the codes given below

(a) 1 and 2 (b) 1, 2 and 3
(c) 2 and 3 (d) 1, 3 and 4

29 **Match the following**

List I (Types of Variable)	List II (Examples)
A. Continuous variable	1. Voice pitch
B. Artificially discrete variable	2. Caste
C. Real discrete variable	3. Intelligence
D. Qualitative variable	4. Examination results in terms of pass and fail

Codes

	A	B	C	D		A	B	C	D
(a)	2	1	3	4	(b)	3	4	2	1
(c)	2	4	3	1	(d)	3	1	2	4

30 **Match the following**

List I (Organs)	List II (Functions)
A. Oral cavity	1. Bile secretion
B. Liver	2. Storage of bile
C. Gall bladder	3. Moistanong
D. Duodenum	4. Secretion of CCK

Codes

	A	B	C	D		A	B	C	D
(a)	4	2	3	1	(b)	1	3	2	4
(c)	3	1	2	4	(d)	1	3	4	2

31 Which of the following is true for applied social psychology?
1. Applied social psychology functions on the basis that problems are caused by human behaviour.
2. Applied social psychologists work to improve human social behaviour in various areas.
3. Applied social psychology does not focus on environment.
4. Applied social psychology is not scientific in nature.

Codes
(a) 1 and 2 (b) 2 and 3 (c) 3 and 4 (d) Only 2

32 Which of the following statements fall within the scope of physiological psychology.
1. Effects of the stimulation of limbic system on approach and avoidance.
2. Effect of lesions in frontal lobe on manipulation of symbols and numbers.
3. Effect of excessive smoking on blood pressure and functioning of heart.
4. Effect of hyperthyroidism on development of general mental ability.

Which of the statements given above are correct?
(a) 1, 2 and 3 (b) 1, 3 and 4 (c) 1, 2 and 4 (d) 2, 3 and 4

Direction (Q. No. 33) *In the question given below are two statements labelled as Assertion (A) and Reason (R). In the context of the two statements, which one of the following is correct?*

Codes
(a) Both A and R are true and R is the correct explanation of A
(b) Both A and R are true, but R is not the correct explanation of A
(c) A is true, but R is false
(d) A is false, but R is true

33 **Assertion** (A) While measuring SWB, affective balance and life satisfaction must be calculated individually.
Reason (R) Self report is not considered an efficient measure of well-being.

34 Which of the following are included in the Gestalt principles of perceptual organisation?
1. Figure-ground proximity, continuity
2. Proximity, continuity, good form
3. Continuity, good form, closure
4. Good form, closure, facilitation

Select the correct answer using the codes given below
(a) 1 and 2 (b) 3 and 4 (c) 1, 2 and 3 (d) 2 and 3

35 Most psychologists believe that aggression is
(a) an innate biological responses to frustration
(b) linked to sexual drive
(c) a learned response
(d) a drive that builds up over time and must be released

36 Direct violence consists of
1. Armed conflict 2. Sexual harassment
3. Genocide 4. Patriarchy

Codes
(a) 1 and 2 (b) 1, 2 and 3 (c) 1 and 3 (d) All of these

37 Match the following

List I (Intelligence)	List II (Propounders)
A. Emotional intelligence	1. Ian Marshall
B. Spiritual intelligence	2. Goleman
C. Multiple intelligence	3. Howard Gardner
D. Practical intelligence	4. Sternberg

Codes

	A	B	C	D		A	B	C	D
(a)	2	1	3	4	(b)	2	3	1	4
(c)	3	2	1	4	(d)	1	4	2	3

38 Match the following

List I (Correlation methods)	List II (Symbols)
A. Biserial	1. r_{pb}
B. Point biserial	2. r_b
C. Tetrachoric	3. r_t
D. Phi	4. ϕ

Codes

	A	B	C	D		A	B	C	D
(a)	1	2	3	4	(b)	2	1	3	4
(c)	1	3	4	2	(d)	2	4	3	1

39 Match the following

List I (GAM Model)	List II (Description)
A. Personal factors	1. Cognition
B. Routes	2. Thoughtful action
C. Decision-making	3. Gender
D. Outcomes	4. Psychological health

Codes

	A	B	C	D		A	B	C	D
(a)	4	2	3	1	(b)	2	3	1	4
(c)	3	1	2	4	(d)	3	2	1	4

40 Match the following

List I (Psychologists)	List II (Theory)
A. Peterson and Birdsall	1. General recognition theory
B. Neyman and Pearson	2. Engineering theory
C. Ashby and Townsend	3. Energy detection model
D. Davegreen et all	4. Statistical inference

Codes

	A	B	C	D		A	B	C	D
(a)	1	3	2	4	(b)	1	2	3	4
(c)	3	2	1	4	(d)	4	3	1	2

41 Match the following

List I (Models of Stress)	List II (Main Concepts)
A. Cannon Bard	1. Appraisal
B. Holmes and Rake	2. Exhaustion
C. Hazardus	3. Schedule of Recent Experience
D. Hans Selye	4. Fight or Flight

Codes

	A	B	C	D		A	B	C	D
(a)	1	4	2	3	(b)	3	4	1	2
(c)	4	3	1	2	(d)	4	1	3	2

42 The tendency to perceive a quarter as being round even when it is viewed at an angle is called

(a) Size constancy (b) Shape constancy
(c) Brightness constancy (d) Colour constancy

43 Who made the distinction between the direct and structural form of violence?

(a) Johan Galtung (b) Christine
(c) Winger (d) AR Wagner

44 Match the following

List I (Types of Knowledge)	List II (Main Characteristics)
A. Propositional knowing	1. Artistic rehearsal process
B. Practical knowing	2. Feedback in real time
C. Experiential knowledge	3. Contemporary science
D. Presentational knowledge	4. Doing what is proposed

Codes

	A	B	C	D		A	B	C	D
(a)	4	3	2	1	(b)	2	1	3	4
(c)	1	3	4	2	(d)	3	4	2	1

45 According to Maslow's hierarchy theory

(a) people are more influenced by psychological than biological needs
(b) feeling loved is a need that must be met before any other needs
(c) the order of needs is less important than meeting all five needs
(d) People won't be motivated to fulfill higher needs, if lower needs remain unmet

Directions (Q. Nos. 46 and 47) *In the question given below are two statements labelled as Assertion (A) and Reason (R). In the context of the two statements, which one of the following is correct?*

Codes

(a) Both A and R are true and R is the correct explanation of A
(b) Both A and R are true, but R is not the correct explanation of A
(c) A is true, but R is false
(d) A is false, but R is true

46 **Assertion** (A) If the cognitions about an event are present, but arousal is absent, then emotion will still be experienced.

Reason (R) Perceived emotion is a joint function of arousal, appraisal and labelling cognition.

47 **Assertion** (A) Under Bait Switch tactic, items offered for sale are at low quality.

Reason (R) It leads customers to buy a more expensive available item.

48 Existential psychotherapy deals with

(a) family relations
(b) issues of life such as death, loneliness and freedom
(c) way of thinking of an individual
(d) None of the above

49 What is a cybercrime?

(a) Crime in which a person is using digital media to disturb others
(b) Computer based cyber bullying
(c) Cyber pornography
(d) Child abuse

50 Which of the following pairs is/are incorrectly matched?

1. Fernald — Emotional Intelligence
2. Bhatia — Giftedness
3. Polarisation — Decision-making in groups tend to show regular shift

Codes

(a) Only 1 (b) Only 2
(c) Only 3 (d) None of these

51 Arrange the following in correct sequence related to research process.

1. Identifying the problem
2. Literature search
3. Collection of data
4. Formulating hypothesis
5. Formulating research design
6. Analysis data

Codes

(a) 1, 2, 3, 4, 5, 6
(b) 1, 2, 5, 4, 3, 6
(c) 1, 2, 4, 5, 3, 6
(d) 1, 4, 2, 5, 3, 6

52 Match the following

List I (Scholars)	List II (Concept)
A. Fixt Allport	1. Social conformity
B. Fritz Heider	2. Interpersonal relationships
C. ER Guthrie	3. Operant behaviour is much more representative of the real life human learning
D. BF Skinner	4. All learning depend on the contiguity of stimulus and response

Codes

	A	B	C	D		A	B	C	D
(a)	2	1	3	4	(b)	1	2	3	4
(c)	3	4	2	1	(d)	3	4	1	2

53 What is 'Jiva' in Indian Psychology?

(a) Witness (b) Non-Participant
(c) Experiential self (d) Objective

54 Which of the following neurotransmitter is known as 'master' wakefulness promoting neurotransmitter?

(a) Histamine (b) Dopamine (c) Serotonin (d) Orexin

Directions (Q. Nos. 55 to 59) *Read the passage given below and answer the questions that follows.*

Kasparov's unique brain, together with his years of experience, allowed him to play chess using heuristics. Heuristics are rules of thumb or clever and creative mental shortcuts, that reduce the number of operations and allow one to solve problems easily and quickly. In the late 1990s, Kasparov's clever and creative shortcuts or heuristics, had given him the advantage over the fixed and not so creative algorithms of computer programs. However, computers now have been programmed with new algorithms that increase their speed of 'thinking' from analysing 100000 chess moves per second to 2.5 million.

As a result of this increased speed, human chess grand masters, whose thinking focuses on using clever heuristics, no longer have a clear advantage over a computer's 'thinking' ability (Boyce, 2002). Besides being used to solve chess problems, heuristics are often used in daily life to make decisions or draw conclusions (Bailensonet al, 2000).

A commonly used heuristic is called the availability heuristic. The availability heuristic says that we rely on information that is more prominent or easily recalled and overlook other information that is available, but less prominent or notable. *e.g.* the murder rate in the United States actually decreased in the late 1990s.

However, during this time, network cover age of homicides increased 473%, which made news of murders more available and according to the availability heuristic, led people to conclude that murder rates had become epidemic (Comarow, 2001).

Using the availability heuristic to make a decision means taking a mental shortcut. Although heuristics allow us to make quick decisions, they may result in bad decisions, since we make them using shortcuts, which limits the amount of information we use (F Bower, 1997).

55 Which of the following most likely makes use of heuristics?

(a) A chemical equation for the synthesis of sulphuric acid
(b) A recipe for making cookies on the back of a box of cornflakes
(c) An article by a Nobel Prize winner titled 'How to Succeed in Science'
(d) A computer program for keeping track of inventory at a department store

56 Frank lost a contact lens in the kitchen, he is searching for it by examining each linoleum tile in turn to see, if the lens is contained within the square. Gemma similarly lost a lens in the kitchen; she is looking for it near the base of the fridge and around the stove, the two appliances she remembers using when she was last in the kitchen. Which statement best describes the problem-solving strategies of these two individuals?

(a) Both Frank and Gemma are using algorithms
(b) Both Frank and Gemma are using heuristics
(c) Frank is using a heuristic, whereas Gemma is using an algorithm
(d) Frank is using an algorithm, whereas Gemma is using a heuristic

57 Each of the following is a reason to use a heuristic rather than an algorithm, except

(a) sometimes no algorithm is available to solve a particular problem
(b) heuristics often require less time and effort to apply than do algorithms
(c) heuristics produce successful problem solutions with sufficient frequency to justify their use
(d) heuristics yield the single best solution to a problem

58 Consider the following statements

1. The use of heuristics is a 'best guess' that does not guarantee a solution.
2. Using the availability heuristic to make a decision means taking a mental shortcut.

Which of the above statements is/are correct about heuristics?

(a) Only 1 (b) Only 2
(c) Both 1 and 2 (d) Neither 1 nor 2

59 A rule that guarantees the solution to a problem when it is correctly applied is termed a(n)

(a) heuristic (b) mental set
(c) algorithm (d) schema

60 Arrange the following tests with respect to their ability to elicit projective responses from low to high.

1. Sentence Completion Test
2. Rorschach Inkblot Test
3. Resenzweig Picture Frustration Study
4. Thematic Apperception Test

Codes

(a) 2, 4, 3, 1 (b) 1, 3, 4, 2
(c) 4, 2, 1, 3 (d) 2, 1, 4, 3

61 Which of the following should be considered in item writing?

1. Adaptable difficulty level
2. Clarity
3. Avoid inter-locking items
4. use of stereotyped words
5. use of irrelevant clues

Codes

(a) 4 and 5 (b) 1, 2 and 3 (c) 1, 4 and 5 (d) 2, 3 and 4

Directions (Q. Nos. 62 and 63) *In the question given below are two statements labelled as Assertion (A) and Reason (R). In the context of the two statements, which one of the following is correct?*

Codes

(a) Both A and R are true and R is the correct explanation of A
(b) Both A and R are true, but R is not the correct explanation of A
(c) A is true, but R is false
(d) A is false, but R is true

62 **Assertion** (A) The sign test is a non-parametric test that is used to test whether two groups are equally sized or not.
Reason (R) The sign test is used when dependent samples are ordered in pairs, where the bivariate random variables are mutually independent.

63 **Assertion** (A) Vocational adjustment is the most crucial adjustment of life.
Reason (R) It is closely Indentified with the self concept of the individual.

64 Psychodynamic perspective emphasises the role of
(a) cognitive processes on decision-making
(b) tendencies towards personal growth
(c) internal forces and conflicts in behaviour
(d) cultural factors on various aspects of behaviour

65 Which one of the following problem solving strategies, though time consuming guarantees solution?
(a) Trial and error
(b) Use of algorithm
(c) Use of heuristics
(d) Study of the problem in parts

66 Integral yoga is also called the.
(a) Higher Conscious yoga (b) Higher level yoga
(c) Supramental yoga (d) Subliminal yoga

67 Who wrote 'Buddhist Manual of Psychlogical Ethics'?
(a) Rhys Dovids (b) Carl Rogers
(c) Eric Fromm (d) DT Suzuki

68 In which a person begins with multiple ideas and reaches one solution?
(a) Vertical thinking (b) Brainstorming
(c) Divergent thinking (d) Convergent thinking

69 The concept of Inspection Time (IT) in relation to intellion to intelligence was provided by
(a) AR Jensen (b) CR Brand
(c) HJ Eyesenck (d) S Sternberg

70 The word 'Samkhya' in Indian philosophical practice means
(a) union of mind and body
(b) knowledge of reality
(c) knowledge of self.
(d) knowledge of self and universe

71 What is Protective Discrimination Policy?
(a) Providing social privelege to children of marginalised class.
(b) Discrimination is done between two equally capable individuals.
(c) Reservation of seats in educational institutions and jobs for members of disadvantaged group.
(d) Discrimination is practised but recipient is unknown to it.

Directions (Q. No. 72) *In the question given below are two statements labelled as Assertion (A) and Reason (R). In the context of the two statements, which one of the following is correct?*

Codes

(a) Both A and R are true and R is the correct explanation of A
(b) Both A and R are true, but R is not the correct explanation of A
(c) A is true, but R is false
(d) A is false, but R is true

72 **Assertion** (A) Psychological tests help in development of career of a person.
Reason (R) Psychological tests are designed to discover skills, aptitudes and talents of an individual.

73 Which of the following strategies facilitate problem solving?

1. Algorithms
2. Mental set
3. Planning fallacy
4. Heuristics
5. Analogy

Codes

(a) 1, 2 and 4 (b) 2, 3 and 4 (c) 1 and 5 (d) 1, 4 and 5

74. Match the following

List I (Tools)	List II (Types)
A. Experiment	1. Structured v/s unstructured
B. Interview	2. Participant v/s non-participant
C. Observation	3. Etic v/s emic
D. Cross-cultural studies	4. True v/s Quasi

Codes

	A	B	C	D		A	B	C	D
(a)	1	4	3	2	(b)	1	3	4	2
(c)	4	1	2	3	(d)	4	1	3	2

Directions (Q. Nos. 75 to 77) *In the question given below are two statements labelled as Assertion (A) and Reason (R). In the context of the two statements, which one of the following is correct?*

Codes

(a) Both A and R are true and R is the correct explanation of A
(b) Both A and R are true, but R is not the correct explanation of A
(c) A is true, but R is false
(d) A is false, but R is true

75 Assertion (A) The size of the personal space depends on individual and situational difference.
Reason (R) Distancing oneself from others promotes control and maintains autonomy.

76 Assertion (A) Dedective reasoning involves creativity.
Reason (R) It doesn't allow us to learn new things.

77 Assertion (A) Social psychologist consider individual's subjective construal of the situation.
Reason (R) Kurt Lewin applied Gestalt principles to social perception.

78 Which of the following pairs is correctly matched?

(a) Artificial Intelligence : Roger Schank
(b) Influential theory : Goleman
(c) Semantic differential : Piaget
(d) Linguistic relativity : Vygotsky

79 Match the following

List I (Types of Thinking)	List II (Characteristics)
A. Autistic thinking	1. Reasoning
B. Realistic thinking	2. Drawing facts
C. Convergent thinking	3. Unusual uses
D. Creative thinking	4. Fantasy

Codes

	A	B	C	D		A	B	C	D
(a)	1	3	4	2	(b)	3	1	2	4
(c)	2	1	3	4	(d)	4	3	2	1

80 Rorschach test, Thematic apperception test and MMPI are used to measure?

(a) Intelligence (b) Attitude
(c) Personality (d) Achievement

81 Arrange the following in a sequence of stage of remembering.

1. Learning
2. Defining
3. Recalling
4. Recognising pairs

Codes

(a) 1, 2, 3, 4 (b) 2, 1, 4, 3
(c) 1, 2, 4, 3 (d) 1, 4, 2, 3

Directions (Q. No. 82) *In the question given below are two statements labelled as Assertion (A) and Reason (R). In the context of the two statements, which one of the following is correct?*

Codes

(a) Both A and R are true and R is the correct explanation of A
(b) Both A and R are true, but R is not the correct explanation of A
(c) A is true, but R is false
(d) A is false, but R is true

82 Assertion (A) According to Wallach and Kogan, creativity and intelligence are considered two distinct modes or thinking.
Reason (R) There are sub stantial correlation among intelligence tests as well as among creativity tasks while there are not substantial correlations between intelligence tests and creativity tasks.

83 Which of the statement given above is/are correct?

1. A concept referring to a objective having atleast one of a number of feature is a conjunctive.
2. Going from general principles to specific situations is called deductive thought.

Select the correct answer using the codes given below

(a) Only 1 (b) Only 2
(c) Both 1 and 2 (d) None of these

84 Match the following

List I (Theorist)	List II (Theory)
A. Thorndike	1. S-R theory without reinforcement
B. Tolman	2. S-R reinforcement theory
C. Guthrie	3. Sign-Gestalt theory
D. Lewin	4. Field theory

Codes

	A	B	C	D		A	B	C	D
(a)	2	3	4	1	(b)	3	2	4	1
(c)	3	2	1	4	(d)	2	3	1	4

85 In the case of human development, the strongest evidence for the critical-period hypothesis is found in

(a) imprinting
(b) language acquisition
(c) embryonic development
(d) development of vocational interests

Directions (Q. No. 86) *In the question given below are two statements labelled as Assertion (A) and Reason (R). In the context of the two statements, which one of the following is correct?*

Codes

(a) Both A and R are true and R is the correct explanation of A
(b) Both A and R are true, but R is not the correct explanation of A

(c) A is true, but R is false
(d) A is false, but R is true

86 Assertion (A) Cancer is caused by increase in number of T Cell.
Reason (R) Stress leads to decrease in number of T Cell.

87 According to teachers, what teaching strategy might be considered to be least effective?
(a) Short independent practice assignments
(b) No independent seatwork
(c) Independent seatwork with too much feedback
(d) Independent seatwork without feedback

88 According to Lazarus, the degree to which a potential stressor will produce stress depends on the role of which psychological process?
(a) Coping
(b) Appraisal of the stressor and how to cope with it
(c) Sympathetic activation
(d) Degree of fear

89 "More the practise, better the performance" the statements represents
(a) Regression (b) Correlation
(c) Factor analysis (d) Ethnography

90 The word 'Paradigm' was first used by
(a) Robert Owen
(b) Thomas Cock
(c) Kuhn
(d) None of these

Directions (Q. Nos. 91 and 92) *In the question given below are two statements labelled as Assertion (A) and Reason (R). In the context of the two statements, which one of the following is correct?*

Codes
(a) Both A and R are true and R is the correct explanation of A
(b) Both A and R are true, but R is not the correct explanation of A
(c) A is true, but R is false
(d) A is false, but R is true

91 Assertion (A) Objective tests of personality have more validity than projective tests.
Reason (R) They are relatively free from the influence of the examiner's own beliefs or rater bias.

92 Assertion (A) Individual is also responsible for his poor condition, not always social structure can be blamed.
Reason (R) Bad habits like alcoholism, drug addiction, large family members etc. are causes of poverty.

93 Parkinson's disease affect
(a) basal ganglia (b) substantia nigra
(c) Both a and b (d) None of these

94 When was the first time the work 'psychology was used in texts?
(a) 16th Century (b) 17th Century
(c) 15th Century (d) 18th Century

95 Arrange the following steps involved in test construction in chronological order
1. Specifying construct of interest
2. Evaluating reliability and validity of test
3. Choosing a method
4. Deciding test's function
5. Designing item content

Codes
(a) 1, 4, 3, 5, 2 (b) 1, 3, 4, 5, 2
(c) 1, 4, 3, 2, 5 (d) 1, 3, 4, 2, 5

96 Psychology shares borders with various other fields like
(a) Physiology (b) Anthropology
(c) Sociology (d) Both a and b

97 The main motive of Basic research is
(a) to increase data (b) to reduce hypothesis
(c) to understand situation (d) to enhance knowledge

98 The term 'Design of Experiments' is used by
(a) Medical Science (b) Social science
(c) engineering (d) None of these

99 Which among the following is also known as longitudinal study?
(a) Retrospective short study (b) Prospective cohort study
(c) Time series (d) None of these

100 Cherry (1953) investigated which phenonenon?
(a) Focused auditory attention
(b) Cocktail Party phenomenon
(c) Visual Disparity
(d) Focused visual attention

ANSWERS

1 (c)	2 (c)	3 (d)	4 (a)	5 (a)	6 (a)	7 (d)	8 (b)	9 (d)	10 (c)
11 (d)	12 (c)	13 (a)	14 (c)	15 (d)	16 (b)	17 (c)	18 (c)	19 (b)	20 (b)
21 (c)	22 (c)	23 (c)	24 (a)	25 (c)	26 (c)	27 (d)	28 (a)	29 (b)	30 (c)
31 (a)	32 (c)	33 (c)	34 (c)	35 (a)	36 (c)	37 (a)	38 (b)	39 (c)	40 (c)
41 (c)	42 (b)	43 (a)	44 (d)	45 (d)	46 (a)	47 (a)	48 (b)	49 (a)	50 (c)
51 (c)	52 (d)	53 (c)	54 (a)	55 (c)	56 (d)	57 (d)	58 (c)	59 (a)	60 (b)
61 (b)	62 (b)	63 (a)	64 (c)	65 (b)	66 (a)	67 (a)	68 (d)	69 (a)	70 (b)
71 (c)	72 (a)	73 (d)	74 (b)	75 (b)	76 (d)	77 (a)	78 (a)	79 (c)	80 (c)
81 (d)	82 (c)	83 (b)	84 (d)	85 (b)	86 (d)	87 (d)	88 (b)	89 (b)	90 (c)
91 (a)	92 (a)	93 (c)	94 (a)	95 (a)	96 (d)	97 (d)	98 (c)	99 (b)	100 (b)

PSYCHOLOGY

Model Paper-3

General Instructions

1. There are total one hundred questions in this paper. Each question carries 2 marks.
2. All questions are compulsory.

1 **Match the following**

	List I (Attributes)		**List II** (Consequences)
A.	Person's final goal	1.	The striving for success or superiority
B.	Force behind a person's activity	2.	A creation of the creative power
C.	Personality	3.	No real existence yet influence individuals
D.	Fictions	4.	Subjective perceptions

Codes

	A	B	C	D		A	B	C	D
(a)	3	1	2	4	(b)	2	1	4	3
(c)	4	1	3	2	(d)	1	2	3	4

2 **Match the following**

	List I (Researcher)		**List II** (Contribution)
A.	Bouillau and Broca	1.	Stain that turn dying axon brown
B.	Miskhkin and colleague	2.	Neural basic of vision and memory
C.	Walle Nauta	3.	correlation between speech and frontal lobe

Codes

	A	B	C		A	B	C
(a)	3	2	1	(b)	3	1	2
(c)	2	1	3	(d)	3	2	1

3 **The most important thing a psychologist can study is how a behaviour or thought helps a person navigate the world, rather than how that thought comes to be or what it is made of."**

This viewpoint probably comes from somebody who believes in what historical theoretical approach?

(a) Structuralism (b) Functionalism
(c) Gestalt (d) Psychoanalysis

4 **What is the most important aim of Conflict Resolution?**

(a) To find a unique solution
(b) To appoint a strong third party
(c) Negotiation
(d) To search solutions

5 **The concept of mental age in calculating IQ was given by**

(a) Cattell (b) Galton (c) Spearman (d) Binet

6 **What is the main characteristic of health promoting behaviour?**

(a) It aims to maintain an optimal weight of body
(b) It aims to maintain perfect BMI
(c) It aims to maintain positive health
(d) All of the above

7 **Consider the following statements**

1. **Factor C in the five-factor theory is conscientiousness.**
2. **People who score low on intelligence tend to be quiet and reserved**
3. **According to Mc Crae and Costa, the ultimate contributor to personality is self-concept**
4. **A person's view of what he or she like is called objective biology**

Which of the statements given above is/are correct?

(a) Only 1 (b) 2 and 4 (c) 2 and 3 (d) All of these

Directions (Q. No. 8) *In the question given below are two statements labelled as Assertion (A) and Reason (R). In context of the two statements, which one of the following is correct?*

Codes

(a) Both A and R are true and R is the correct explanation of A
(b) Both A and R are true, but R is not the correct explanation of A
(c) A is true, but R is false
(d) A is false, but R is true

8 Assertion (A) Mann-Whitney 'U' test is a non-parametric test that can be used to analyse data from two group independent groups design when measurement is atleast ordinal.

Reason (R) Each sample has been randomly selected from the population it represent.

9 Which of the following regulates homoeostatic pressure to sleep?

(a) Orexin
(b) Melatonin
(c) Adenosine
(d) All of the above

10 For psychotherapy to be effective

(a) the therapist must provide a protected setting to clients to reveal their feelings
(b) the therapist should maintain emotional distance from the client
(c) clients and therapists should avoid warmth in their relationship
(d) therapist should choose one style of therapy for all of his clients

11 What is the main principle behind Biological Determinism?

(a) Human behaviour is controlled by an individual's genes
(b) Causal roles of genes.
(c) Gender is defined by the social structure.
(d) Biological characteristics defines one's gender.

Directions (Q. No. 12) *In the question given below are two statements labelled as Assertion (A) and Reason (R). In context of the two statements, which one of the following is correct?*

Codes

(a) Both A and R are true and R is the correct explanation of A
(b) Both A and R are true, but R is not the correct explanation of A
(c) A is true, but R is false
(d) A is false, but R is true

12 Assertion (A) Indian psychology is spiritual.

Reason (R) It studies levels of consciousness and works to help a person to attain higher level of consciousness.

13 Match the following

	List I (Components of Post Trauma Growth)	List II (Individual Model)
A.	Stressor event	1. Family
B.	Challenges	2. Writing/talking
C.	Rumination	3. Threat
D.	Social Content	4. High magnitude that disturbs status quo

Codes

	A	B	C	D		A	B	C	D
(a)	1	2	3	4	(b)	4	2	3	1
(c)	2	3	1	4	(d)	4	3	2	1

14 Consider the following statements

1. **A correlation exists, when two different measures of the sample people, events or things vary together.**
2. **A scatterplot that appears to have no shape or reveals no trend whatsoever is associated with a correlation coefficient of 0.50.**

Which one of the statements given above is/are correct?

(a) Only 1 (b) Only 2
(c) Both 1 and 2 (d) None of these

Directions (Q. No. 15) *In the question given below are two statements labelled as Assertion (A) and Reason (R). In context of the two statements, which one of the following is correct?*

Codes

(a) Both A and R are true and R is the correct explanation of A
(b) Both A and R are true, but R is not the correct explanation of A
(c) A is true, but R is false
(d) A is false, but R is true

15 Assertion (A) A case study is an unavoidable technique in the clinical setting.

Reason (R) If provides a complete picture of the subject for diagnosis and prognosis.

16 Which of the following is not a major reason for information loss in long-term memory?

(a) Faculty organisation
(b) Displacement of old information by coming information
(c) Interference
(d) Inappropriate retrieval strategy

17 Who invented the strategy of 'monitoring' by parents?

(a) Austin (b) Livingston and Helsper
(c) Nikken and Jansz (d) Fujioka

18 With whom is 'Contiguity theory of learning' associated?

(a) Thorndike (b) Guthrie (c) Hull (d) Pavlov

19 Consider the following statements

1. Bipolar neurons are the most common type in the central nervous system.
2. The cell membrane is formed by a dual layer of lipid molecule.

Which of the statements given above is/are correct?

(a) Only 1 (b) Only 2
(c) Both 1 and 2 (d) Neither 1 nor 2

20 Which of the following are benefits of psychological tests in the field of military?

1. Assigning duty status
2. Preserve biological health of fighting force
3. Interrogation of prisoners

Codes

(a) 2 and 3 (b) 1, 2 and 3 (c) 1 and 3 (d) 1 and 2

21 Match the following

List I (Theories)	List II (Explanations)
A. Arousal theory	1. Motivation is strongly influenced by setting specific and allowable goals.
B. Expectancy theory	2. Motivation is a matter of being pushed from within by urges
C. Goal setting theory	3. Motivation is being pulled from without by desired outcomes
D. Drive theory	4. Motivation is increasing the general level of activation to an optimal level

Codes

	A	B	C	D		A	B	C	D
(a)	1	2	3	4	(b)	2	3	4	1
(c)	3	4	2	1	(d)	4	3	1	2

22 Consider the following statement

1. Range is a measure of central tendency.
2. The smaller the range of values defining a confidence interval, the greater the error in estimation.

Which one of the statements given above is/are correct?

(a) Only 1 (b) Only 2
(c) Both 1 and 2 (d) None of these

23 Students who are successful in the classroom usually operate under

(a) the internal locus of control
(b) external force as a reason
(c) Both a and b
(d) None of the above

24 In formula, $r = \frac{Cov_{xy}}{S_X S_Y}$, 'S' stands for

(a) Covariance
(b) Standard deviation
(c) Product moment
(d) None of the above

Directions (Q. Nos. 25-29) *Read the passage given below and answer the following questions.*

Within the yogic and Indian psychology traditions the means of 'Knowing' have been described with precision.

Three aspects of knowing are the refinement of knowing within the training system of the Patanjali Yoga-Sutras, Sri Aurobindo's views of the four types of knowledge and Sri Aurobindo's views of the process of intuition.

The eight limbs described in the Patanjali Yoga-Sutras provide ways of readying and purifying the body, emotions and mind for a form of knowing through being or identifying with what is to be known, achieved through 'Samyama,' the intensive and conjoint practice of the last three limbs of dharana (concentration), dhyana (contemplation or meditation) and samadhi (absorption).

The several limbs of Patanjali Rajayoga i.e. yama, niyama, asana, pranayama, pratyahara, dharana, dhyana, samadhi-providc methods for systematically reducing the possible environmental social, bodily, sensory, emotional and cognitive sources of noise or distraction that might serve as impediments to or distortions of accurate and sensitive knowing.

25 In which traditions 'knowing' have been described with precision?

(a) Oriental psychology (b) Indian psychology
(c) Western psychology (d) None of these

26 Patanjali yoga-sutras consist of

(a) 5 limbs (b) 6 limbs (c) 7 limbs (d) 8 limbs

27 Patanjali yoga-sutras provide ways of readying and purifying the

(a) body (b) emotions (c) mind (d) All of these

28 'Samyama', the intensive and conjoint practice includes

(a) dharana (concentration) (b) Dhyana (meditation)
(c) Samadhi (absorption) (d) All of these

29 Which among the following are part of Patanjali Raja yoga?

1. Yama 2. Niyama 3. Samyama 4. Pratyahara

Codes

(a) 1 and 2 (b) Only 3
(c) 1, 2 and 4 (d) All of the above

30 Which of the following psychotherapy involves emphasis on family relations in promoting psychological health?

(a) Transpersonal therapy (b) System therapy
(c) Existential therapy (d) Psychodynamic therapy

31 According to Maslow's theory, the basic needs include

(a) physiological, safety and security needs
(b) safety, love and belonging needs
(c) physiological and belonging needs
(d) Security and esteem

32 Match the following

List I (Psychologist)	List II (Concept)
A. MC Kellar	1. Assimilation and accommodation
B. Freud	2. Rational thinking
C. Piaget	3. Pre-conscious, conscious and unconscious
D. Guilford	4. Divergent thinking

Codes

	A	B	C	D		A	B	C	D
(a)	1	2	3	4	(b)	2	3	1	4
(c)	3	4	2	1	(d)	4	1	3	2

33 Match the following

List I (Concepts)	List II (Researchers)
A. Flashbulb memory	1. Broadbent
B. Organisation as in library	2. Brown and Kulik
C. VLTM	3. Bahrick and Bahrick
D. STM	4. Wickens

Codes

	A	B	C	D		A	B	C	D
(a)	2	1	4	3	(b)	2	1	3	4
(c)	1	2	3	4	(d)	4	1	3	2

34 Write in correct sequence.

1. End of cannula to be inserted is cut at an angle.
2. Cannula is inserted in right angle.
3. Other end of cannula is sealed.
4. A small hole is drilled into skull.

Codes

(a) 1 2 3 4 (b) 2 3 1 4 (c) 3 1 2 4 (d) 1 3 4 2

Directions (Q. Nos. 35-36) *In the question given below are two statements labelled as Assertion (A) and Reason (R). In context of the two statements, which one of the following is correct?*

Codes

(a) Both A and R are true and R is the correct explanation of A
(b) Both A and R are true, but R is not the correct explanation of A
(c) A is true, but R is false
(d) A is false, but R is true

35 Assertion (A) Recall is the verbal reproduction of previously learnt material.

Reason (R) Recognition in the identification of learnt material from a combination of learned and unlearned materials.

36 Assertion (A) Unconscious perception will be used to lower all cases when responses are governed by stimuli of which the recipient is unaware.

Reason (R) Subliminal perception will be reserved for those cases where the stimulus is, in fact, below some independently determined limen.

37 Match the following

List I (Psychologist)	List II (Theory)
A. BF Skinner	1. Statistical learning theory
B. EL Thorndike	2. Systematic desensitisation
C. Estes	3. Transfer through common elements
D. Wolpe	4. Operate conditioning

Codes

	A	B	C	D		A	B	C	D
(a)	3	4	2	1	(b)	4	3	1	2
(c)	4	3	2	1	(d)	3	4	1	2

38 Match the following

List I (Methods)	List II (Data Suited for)
A. Kruskal Wallis	1. Independent samples
B. Friedman	2. Independent samples
C. Mann Whitney	3. Related samples
D. Wilcoxon	4. Related samples

Codes

	A	B	C	D
(a)	1	3	2	4
(b)	4	3	2	1
(c)	3	4	2	1
(d)	3	1	2	4

39 What does one mean by role conflict?

(a) Uneven economic distribution
(b) Real differences in role definitions
(c) Individual need to gain more
(d) Conflict with collective people

40 Consider the following statements

1. Freud opened the 'Institute for Experiment Psychology' in Germany.
2. Wilhelm Wundt's School of Psychology was called voluntarism.

Which among the above is/are correct?

(a) Only 1 (b) Only 2
(c) Both 1 and 2 (d) None of these

Directions (Q. No. 41) *In the question given below are two statements labelled as Assertion (A) and Reason (R). In context of the two statements, which one of the following is correct?*

Codes

(a) Both A and R are true and R is the correct explanation of A
(b) Both A and R are true, but R is not the correct explanation of A
(c) A is true, but R is false
(d) A is false, but R is true

41 Assertion (A) Insulin promotes use of glucose.

Reason (R) Glucose is the primary source of energy by the body.

42 A Cardinal assumption of stimulus generalisation theory of Pavlov is that

(a) locus of generalisation gradients is in the testing rather then in the training phase
(b) generalisation gradients might be the result of variations in discriminative thresholds
(c) a process that develops automatically during conditioning along with the spread of associative strength
(d) stimulus generalisation occurs due to 'failure of association'

Directions (Q. Nos. 43) *In the question given below are two statements labelled as Assertion (A) and Reason (R). In context of the two statements, which one of the following is correct?*

Codes

(a) Both A and R are true and R is the correct explanation of A.
(b) Both A and R are true, but R is not the correct explanation of A.
(c) A is true, but R is false.
(d) A is false, but R is true.

43 Assertion (A) Role of media is quite critical in Conflict Resolution.

Reason (R) Media can help to bring together different groups to discuss conflict issues.

44 Consider the following statements regarding Thorndike's 'Law of Effect'

1. It is only a case of law of exercise.
2. It emphasises only on situational reinforcers but does not refer to cognitive aspects of learning.
3. It cannot be applied in achievement-oriented learning.
4. It ignores the functional effect of persons-environment interaction in learning.

Which of the statements given above is /are correct?

(a) Only 1 (b) 2, 3 and 4
(c) 2 and 3 (d) 3 and 4

45 Ontology is the nature of our beliefs about

(a) research (b) subjects (c) reality (d) world

46 Consider the following statements.

1. Rollo May introduced existential perspective in USA
2. Viktor Frankl developed Logo therapy

Which among the above is/are correct?

(a) Only 1
(b) Only 2
(c) Both 1 and 2
(d) None of the above

Directions (Q. No. 47) *In the question given below are two statements labelled as Assertion (A) and Reason (R). In context of the two statements, which one of the following is correct?*

Codes

(a) Both A and R are true and R is the correct explanation of A
(b) Both A and R are true, but R is not the correct explanation of A
(c) A is true, but R is false
(d) A is false, but R is true

47 Assertion (A) Semantic memory is the sum total of our general abstract knowledge.

Reason (R) Procedural memory is declarative memory, stores information regarding how things are done.

48 Epistemology is also known as the

(a) Theory of reality
(b) Theory of knowledge
(c) Analysis of reality
(d) Justification of knowledge

49 Which among the following is the least used in meassures of central tendency?

(a) Mean (b) Median
(c) Mode (d) None of these

50 Memory is the function of the contact of these samskara with

(a) self (b) atman
(c) mind (d) None of these

51 With whom is 'Contiguity theory of learning' associated?

(a) Thorndike (b) Guttrie
(c) Hull (d) Pavlov

52 Which of the following is not an element involved in observational learning.

(a) attention (b) retention
(c) reproduction (d) perception

53 Consider the following statements about

1. Experimental method has introduced the quantitative measurement in psychology.
2. It is low on replicability.

Which of the statements given above is/are correct?

(a) Both 1 and 2 (b) Only 2
(c) Only 1 (d) Neither 1 nor 2

54 Which of the following is not correct about the hypothesis?

1. It is a suggested testable answer to a problem
2. It is an interrogative statement
3. It is based on operationally defined concepts
4. It involves higher monetary expenses
5. It should always be in accord with other hypothesis of the same field

Select the correct answer using the codes given below
(a) Only 1 (b) Only 2 (c) 2, 4 and 5 (d) 2, 4 and 3

55 Which one of the following hypothesis emphasises the role of language in thinking?
(a) Thinking is active imagination carried on in words
(b) Process of thinking is sun-vocal talking or implicit speech when the larynx is in a state of low tonus
(c) Linguistic relativity determines the nature of thinking
(d) Thinking can occur without words as we can thinking about things, for which we do not have name

Directions (Q. Nos. 56) *In the question given below are two statements labelled as Assertion (A) and Reason (R). In context of the two statements, which one of the following is correct?*

Codes
(a) Both A and R are true and R is the correct explanation of A.
(b) Both A and R are true, but R is not the correct explanation of A.
(c) A is true, but R is false.
(d) A is false, but R is true.

56 Assertion (A) Stress is useful for personality enrichment.

Reason (R) To be totally without stress is to be dead.

57 Match the following

	List I (Theory)		**List II** (Scholars)
A.	Sub-Culture Theory	1.	Andrews and Bonta
B.	Social Psychological Model of Criminal Behaviour	2.	Henggeler
C.	Social Learning Theory	3.	Wolfgang and Ferracuti
D.	Multi-systematic Treatment Programme to Violent Youths	4.	Bandura

Codes

	A	B	C	D		A	B	C	D
(a)	1	2	3	4	(b)	4	3	2	1
(c)	2	4	1	3	(d)	3	1	4	2

58 Arrange the following processes in order in which they occur in test construction.
1. Item analysis 2. Validity
3. Reliability 4. Norms

Codes
(a) 1 2 3 4 (b) 2 1 3 4 (c) 1 3 2 4 (d) 4 3 1 2

59 Consider the following statements
1. In pscyhoanalysis, Freud emphasise the revealing of unconscious conflicts.
2. Manifest content is the symbolic or hidden meaning of dream.

Which of the statements given above is/are correct?
(a) Only 1 (b) Only 2
(c) Both 1 and 2 (d) Neither 1 nor 2

60 Which famous text book of psychology was authored by Wilhelm Wundt?
(a) Fundamentals of Psychology
(b) Foundation of Psychology
(c) The Principles of Psychology
(d) Psychology an Emerging Science

61 Match the following

	List I (Variances)		**List II** (Features)
A.	Systematic variance	1.	Randomisation
B.	Extraneous variance	2.	Methodology artifacts
C.	Control of variables	3.	Effect of independent variables

Codes

	A	B	C		A	B	C
(a)	1	2	3	(b)	3	2	1
(c)	3	1	2	(d)	1	3	2

62 Consider the following statements about Noam Chomsky
1. He called himself a Cartesian linguist.
2. He analysed syntax.
3. He wrote about transformational grammar.
4. He developed an artificial language called Yerkish.

Which of the statements given above are correct?
(a) 1 and 2 (b) 1 and 4 (c) 1, 2 and 3 (d) 2, 3 and 4

Directions (Q. Nos. 63 and 64) *In the question given below are two statements labelled as Assertion (A) and Reason (R). In context of the two statements, which one of the following is correct?*

Codes
(a) Both A and R are true and R is the correct explanation of A.
(b) Both A and R are true, but R is not the correct explanation of A.
(c) A is true, but R is false.
(d) A is false, but R is true.

63 Assertion (A) Hue is detectable at relatively low intensities, if the surrounding is coloured.

Reason (R) Colour detectability is higher in the figure sector than in the ground portion of the visual field.

64 Assertion (A) Infant utter more words than they comprehend.

Reason (R) Comprehension develops earlier than production.

65 Match the following

	List I (Test Name)		**List II** (Inventor)
A.	TAT	1.	Cattel
B.	PF Test	2.	Rosenzweig
C.	Draw a man	3.	Murray
D.	16PF	4.	Bender

Codes

	A	B	C	D		A	B	C	D
(a)	4	1	2	3	(b)	3	2	4	1
(c)	1	4	3	2	(d)	2	3	1	4

66 Which is true regarding the influence of cultural values on eating behaviours?

(a) They are the primary cause of innate taste aversion
(b) They greatly affect the incentive value of various food
(c) They determine a person's set point for various food
(d) They have a homeostatic influence on amount of food consumed

67 Match the following

List I (Sense receptor)	List II (Function)
A. Exteroceptor	1. Info about skeletal muscle and joints
B. Interoceptor	2. Info about visceral organs
C. Proprioceptor	3. Info about external environment

Codes

	A	B	C		A	B	C
(a)	3	2	1	(b)	3	1	2
(c)	2	3	1	(d)	2	1	3

68 Arrange the following theories in order of proposal

1. Classical Conditioning (Pavlov)
2. Social Development Theory (Vygotsky)
3. Stage Theory of Cognitive Development (Piaget)
4. Erikson's Stages of Development (Erikson)

Codes

(a) 2 1 3 4 (b) 1 2 3 4 (c) 4 3 2 1 (d) 3 2 4 1

Directions (Q. Nos. 69 to 71) *In the question given below are two statements labelled as Assertion (A) and Reason (R). In context of the two statements, which one of the following is correct?*

Codes

(a) Both A and R are true and R is the correct explanation of A
(b) Both A and R are true, but R is not the correct explanation of A
(c) A is true, but R is false
(d) A is false, but R is true

69 **Assertion** (A) Digital learning has eliminated the role of a teacher.

Reason (R) Digital learning has changed the role of a teacher.

70 **Assertion** (A) Researcher's position regarding Ontology will determine how questions and answers about the nature of both social and political reality are to be investigated.

Reason (R) Researcher's Ontological view determines the focus, chosen methods and how data is gathered, interpreted or analysed.

71 **Assertion** (A) Research on subliminal perception has been sporadic.

Reason (R) Initially the scientists considered the idea as non sense.

72 Match the following

List I (Theories)	List II (Scholars)
A. Script Theory of Learning Aggression	1. Tedeschi and Felson
B. Excitation Transfer Theory of Aggression	2. Huesmann
C. Social Interaction Theory of Aggression	3. Anderson and Bushman
D. General Aggression Model	4. Zillman

Codes

	A	B	C	D		A	B	C	D
(a)	1	2	3	4	(b)	4	3	2	1
(c)	2	4	1	3	(d)	3	1	4	2

73 Statistics is a branch of mathematics devoted to

(a) collection (b) completion
(c) interpretation (d) All of these

74 Which of the following aspects of physical environment influences human behaviour?

(a) Light (b) Noise
(c) Temperature (d) All of these

Directions (Q. No. 75) *In the question given below are two statements labelled as Assertion (A) and Reason (R). In context of the two statements, which one of the following is correct?*

Codes

(a) Both A and R are true and R is the correct explanation of A
(b) Both A and R are true, but R is not the correct explanation of A
(c) A is true, but R is false
(d) A is false, but R is true

75 **Assertion** (A) In general, the reliability of a test increases with the number of items on the test.

Reason (R) Obtaining a correlation coefficient (R) of 1.42 indicates an error in calculation.

76 Match the following

List I	List II
A. Neuropsychological Test	1. Inkblot Test
B. Achievement Test	2. Wisconsin Card sorting test
C. Personality Test	3. Peabody Individual Test

Codes

	A	B	C		A	B	C
(a)	2	3	1	(b)	3	2	1
(c)	1	2	3	(d)	2	1	3

77 Widespread disobeying of social norms would lead to
(a) social chaos
(b) teaching children not to be slavish conformists
(c) lowering the authoritaritarianism of the population
(d) more questioning of the government than other institutions

78 Broadbent's model suggests that early selection of items to be attended is done on the basis of
(a) Physical characteristics (b) semantic characteristics
(c) interest (d) need

79 Various causes of conflict at macro level are
1. Rigid social order
2. Values
3. Resources
4. Mismanagement of information
(a) 1 and 2 (b) 1, 2 and 3
(c) 1, 2 and 3 (d) All of these

80 Which of the following is not a kind of independent variable?
(a) Task variable (b) Environmental variable
(c) Subject variable (d) Experimental variable

81 Which of the following is the correct chronological order of given Gestalt psychologists?
(a) Wertheimer, Koffka, Kohler, Lewin
(b) Kohler, Wertheimer, Koffka, Lewin
(c) Lewin, Kohler, Koffka, Wertheimer
(d) Koffka, Lewin, Wertheimer, Kohler

82 Which Psychologist's work has not inspired Carol Ryff model of Happiness?
1. Erikson 2. Buhler
3. New garten 4. Freud
Codes
(a) 1 and 2 (b) 2 and 3 (c) Only 4 (d) 1 and 4

83 Consider the following statements
1. Developmental psychologists are least likely to disagree about the sequence of stage.
2. Freud believed that development took place in a series of stages.
Which of the statements given above is/are correct?
(a) Only 1
(b) Only 2
(c) Both 1 and 2
(d) Neither 1 nor 2

84 Who invented Transcendental Meditation?
(a) Sri Aurobindo (b) Swami Rama
(c) Mahesh Yogi (d) Swami Vivekananda

85 Consider the following statements
1. Perception is not directly observable
2. Perception is followed by sensation
3. Perception can be modified
4. Perception is inherited
Which of the following statements given above is/are correct?
(a) Only 2 (b) Only 1 (c) 2 and 3 (d) 1 and 3

86 Consider the following statements
1. Conventional statistical procedures are called Parametric tests.
2. Parametric test are trustworthy of the computed sample statistics.
Which among the above is are correct?
(a) Only 1 (b) Only 2
(c) Both 1 and 2 (d) None of these

87 Consider the following statement.
In the experimental method, the psychologist attempts to
1. systematically vary the independent variable
2. make a detailed case study of the individual
3. observe whether the experimental manipulation has of these statements
Which of the statements given above is/are correct?
(a) 1 and 3 (b) 1 and 2
(c) 2 and 3 (d) All of these

88 Match the following

List I (Tests)	List II (Function)
A. Intelligence Tests	1. Measures functioning of brain
B. Personality Tests	2. Clinical interview
C. Neuropsychological Tests	3. Measures cognitive functioning
D. Clinical Observation	4. Analysis of personality disorder

Codes

	A	B	C	D
(a)	4	3	2	1
(b)	4	3	1	2
(c)	3	4	1	2
(d)	3	4	2	1

89 Match the following

List I (Variable)	List II (Features)
A. Independent variable	1. Randomisation
B. Dependent variable	2. Counter-balancing
C. Carry over effect	3. Measurement
D. Control of variables	4. Active manipulation

Codes

	A	B	C	D
(a)	4	3	1	2
(b)	3	4	2	1
(c)	3	4	1	2
(d)	4	3	2	1

90 Match the following

List I (Psychologists)	List II (Area of Interest)
A. William James	1. Non-violence
B. Gene Sharp	2. Peace Psychology
C. Galtung	3. Violence
D. Pythagoras	4. Structural violence

Codes

	A	B	C	D		A	B	C	D
(a)	1	2	3	4	(b)	2	1	3	4
(c)	3	4	2	1	(d)	4	3	1	2

91 Consider the following statements

1. The eight limbs described in the Patanjali Yoga-Sutras provide ways of purifying the body, emotions and mind.
2. Within the yogic and Indian psychology tradition the means of 'knowing' have been described with precision.

Which among the above is/are correct?

(a) Only 1
(b) Only 2
(c) Both 1 and 2
(d) None of the above

92 Which of the following sets of interaction distances is in correct chronological order distance wise?

1. Personal Distance
2. Public Distance
3. Intimate Distance
4. Social Distance

Codes

(a) 1 2 3 4 (b) 4 3 2 1 (c) 2 4 1 3 (d) 3 1 4 2

Directions (Q. Nos. 93) *In the question given below are two statements labelled as Assertion (A) and Reason (R). In context of the two statements, which one of the following is correct?*

Codes

(a) Both A and R are true and R is the correct explanation of A
(b) Both A and R are true, but R is not the correct explanation of A
(c) A is true, but R is false
(d) A is false, but R is true

93 **Assertion** (A) A reliable test is one that measure what it is supposed to measure.

Reason (R) A correlation coefficient of +0.46 indicates a stronger relationship that a coefficient 0.56.

94 Match the following

List I (Component of Personality)	List II (behavioural Manifestation)
A. Id	1. Reality principle
B. Ego	2. Moral principle
C. Super ego	3. Aggressiveness, sea, hunger

Codes

	A	B	C		A	B	C
(a)	3	2	1	(b)	1	2	3
(c)	3	1	2	(d)	2	1	3

95 Consider the following statements

1. Creative disposition depends upon many components.
2. Creative individual think with greater fluency, with more flexibility.

Which of the statements given above is/are correct?

(a) Only 1 (b) Only 2
(c) Both 1 and 2 (d) None of these

96 According to whom, "Thinking is an implicit problem-solving behaviour"?

(a) Ross (b) Glimer
(c) Garrett (d) Mohsin

97 What is the fundamental principle of Gestalt perception?

(a) Law of effect (b) Law of pragnanz
(c) Law of similarity (d) Law of pattern

98 Which one of the following is a control process of short-term memory?

(a) Retrieval (b) Attention
(c) Recognition (d) Recall

99 'A' in PERMA theory by Seligman stands for

(a) attitude (b) affect
(c) accomplishments (d) autonomy

100 According to Kohler learning is a

(a) behavioural change process
(b) trial and error process
(c) perceptually organising process
(d) conditsssssioning process

ANSWERS

1 (d)	2 (a)	3 (b)	4 (d)	5 (d)	6 (c)	7 (a)	8 (b)	9 (c)	10 (a)
11 (a)	12 (a)	13 (d)	14 (a)	15 (a)	16 (b)	17 (b)	18 (b)	19 (b)	20 (b)
21 (d)	22 (d)	23 (a)	24 (b)	25 (b)	26 (d)	27 (d)	28 (d)	29 (c)	30 (b)
31 (a)	32 (b)	33 (b)	34 (b)	35 (b)	36 (b)	37 (c)	38 (a)	39 (b)	40 (b)
41 (b)	42 (c)	43 (a)	44 (b)	45 (c)	46 (c)	47 (c)	48 (b)	49 (c)	50 (c)
51 (b)	52 (d)	53 (c)	54 (c)	55 (c)	56 (d)	57 (d)	58 (a)	59 (a)	60 (c)
61 (b)	62 (c)	63 (a)	64 (a)	65 (b)	66 (c)	67 (a)	68 (b)	69 (d)	70 (a)
71 (a)	72 (c)	73 (d)	74 (d)	75 (b)	76 (a)	77 (a)	78 (b)	79 (d)	80 (d)
81 (a)	82 (c)	83 (c)	84 (c)	85 (c)	86 (c)	87 (a)	88 (c)	89 (d)	90 (b)
91 (c)	92 (c)	93 (a)	94 (a)	95 (c)	96 (d)	97 (b)	98 (b)	99 (c)	100 (a)